The First Reconstruction

The John Hope Franklin Series in African American History and Culture

Waldo E. Martin Jr. and Patricia Sullivan, editors

The First Reconstruction

Black Politics in America from the Revolution to the Civil War

VAN GOSSE

The University of North Carolina Press
Chapel Hill

Set in Adobe Text Pro by Westchester Publishing Services
Manufactured in the United States of America

The University of North Carolina Press has been a member of the
Green Press Initiative since 2003.

Library of Congress Cataloging-in-Publication Data
Names: Gosse, Van, author.
Title: The first Reconstruction : black politics in America from the Revolution
    to the Civil War / Van Gosse.
Other titles: John Hope Franklin series in African American history and culture.
Description: Chapel Hill : University of North Carolina Press, [2021] |
    Series: The John Hope Franklin series in African American history and culture |
    Includes bibliographical references and index.
Identifiers: LCCN 2020018437 | ISBN 9781469660103 (cloth : alk. paper) |
    ISBN 9781469660110 (ebook)
Subjects: LCSH: African Americans—Politics and government—18th century. |
    African Americans—Politics and government—19th century. | African
    Americans—History—To 1863.
Classification: LCC E185.18 .G67 2021 | DDC 973/.0496073—dc23
LC record available at https://lccn.loc.gov/2020018437

Jacket illustration: Text excerpt, "Lincoln Is Sure to Be Defeated," *The New York Herald*, November 6, 1860. Courtesy of Chronicling America, a joint project by the National Endowment for the Humanities and the Library of Congress.

This book is dedicated to the black people who have sought since the Revolution to save American democracy—"the land that never has been yet." Their tenacity astounds.

And to my beloved warrior, Deborah.

Contents

Figures, Maps, and Tables

Tables

The First Reconstruction

Introduction

At present the slaves and non-freeholders amount to nearly ¾ of the State. The power is therefore in about ¼. . . . Were slaves freed and the right of suffrage extended to all, the operation of government might be very different.

—James Madison, in a note to himself, 1791

There is one black man in Dover who is no more an abolitionist than . . . [various white politicians]. Such a one, in Portland, is as hard-shelled a Whig as Henry Clay himself. Some of these two genera are to be found among black men, all over New England. Indeed, there are about 7000 black voters in the nation. That is, there are about 4000 in New York State, about 2,700 in New England, and possibly 300 in Wisconsin. Of that number, at least nine-tenths vote pro-slavery [Whig] tickets. . . . [In 1849, New York's Liberty Party] showed its contempt for negro-hate by nominating one black man on its State ticket, and three others for local offices, and another still for the State Senate. With a golden bribe in his hand, a New York City black man hired some and coaxed others to vote the Whig ticket, and he was aided by some of the most influential of the same class, in the Empire city, and what is still worse, they found the most part of our people hirable and coaxable enough to do the dirty deed of meanness.

—Samuel Ringgold Ward, in *The Impartial Citizen*, May 8, 1850

The Dred Scott decision was . . . based on assumed historical facts which were not really true. . . . Chief Justice Taney . . . insists at great length that negroes were no part of the people who made, or for whom was made, the Declaration of Independence, or the Constitution of the United States. On the contrary, Judge Curtis, in his dissenting opinion, shows that in five of the then thirteen states, to wit, New Hampshire, Massachusetts, New York, New Jersey and North Carolina, free negroes were voters, and, in proportion to their numbers, had the same part in making the Constitution that the white people had. He shows this with so much particularity as to leave no doubt of its truth.

—Abraham Lincoln, speaking in Springfield, Illinois, June 26, 1857

German Voter—I wish to deposit my vote, sir.

Inspector—How long have you been in the State?

German—Almost seven years.

Inspector—You can't vote.

Negro—Hello, Sam, is you gwine for to vote to day?

Sam—I dosn't know, chile, I'se ony been here free days.

Negro—Dat dosen't make a diff-a-bitterance heah: jist go right up and vote.

—Bellefonte (Pa.) *Democratic Watchman*, August 11, 1859

Black Marxists in the mold of W. E. B. Du Bois and the unreconstructed partisans of Jefferson Davis can agree on one thing: our history pivoted with the Reconstruction of 1865–77. The military subjugation of the Southern Confederacy, followed by the uncompensated emancipation of four million human chattels, then making those formerly-enslaved people into citizens and declaring the men among them voters, marked a watershed with few equals in modern history. Even during the subsequent eighty years, when the federal government left the white South alone and Reconstruction was derided by all but African Americans and a few white radicals, it remained "America's unfinished revolution."

This book does not argue with Reconstruction's centrality; rather, it proposes a different narrative for how the United States arrived at such a revolutionary moment. What if the postbellum Reconstruction was not so completely new? What if it had been foreshadowed since the republic's earliest days? What if a nonviolent, slow-moving Reconstruction—defined by emancipation, the birthright citizenship of any man born on the soil, and the enforcement of juridical equality—began as early as 1778, when the town meetings of revolutionary Massachusetts rejected the whites-only franchise stipulated in their new state's constitution? Indeed, what if a Black Reconstruction was always a possibility in America's politics, constantly evoked by its enemies and consistently advanced by a fraction of white jurists, statesmen, and party leaders?

Historians are beginning to consider the history of slavery and emancipation in this fashion. Steven Hahn has argued that, rather than "two discrete emancipations," a postrevolutionary North separated temporally and spatially

---

A Note on Political Slang: Certain epithets recur so often in this narrative that the reader should know what they mean. Long after the demise of the Federalist Party, Jacksonian Democrats called their Whig opponents "federalists" (or used the adjective "federal") because of the defunct party's association with aristocracy if not treason. Whigs, on the other hand, routinely called all Democrats "locofocos" (or "loco-focos" or just "locos") or derided their policies as "locofocoism," because that was the name adopted by a particularly militant group of New York Democrats.

from a post–Civil War South, the extinction of chattel slavery was "a connected and remarkably protracted process," which requires that we envision "the social and political history of the nineteenth century in very different ways" than heretofore. He further posits that "either Reconstruction must be seen as a similarly extended phenomenon initiated in the northern states well before the southern (and thus almost coincidental with American nation building more generally), or we have to acknowledge a great many more 'rehearsals' for the large-scale Reconstruction of the Civil War era."[1]

This book argues for a First Reconstruction beginning in the North during the Revolution and continuing, in fits and starts, into the 1850s. It has three initial premises: first, the cumulative evidence demonstrating that free black men participated in politics as citizens, voters, and party activists since the Founding; second, the commitment to nonracial politics among some whites since the Founding, especially in the "Greater New England" diaspora from Maine to Iowa; last but best-known, the opposing tradition of frank Negrophobia, which grew steadily in power after 1800, and especially after 1821. I will examine these in reverse order.

Some white politicians have always found it useful to bait their opponents by evoking the specter of black citizenship. As early as 1796, the South Carolina congressman William Loughton Smith denounced Jefferson's presidential candidacy because the Virginian corresponded with the black scientist Benjamin Banneker: "What shall we think of a *secretary of state* thus fraternizing with negroes, writing them complimentary epistles, stiling [*sic*] them *his black brethren*, congratulating them on the evidence of their *genius*, assuring them of his good wishes for their speedy emancipation?" Smith was a Federalist, but after Jefferson's 1800 victory, such attacks became associated with his Republicans, as in their 1808 campaign ditty, "Federalists with blacks unite," based on that party seeking black voters in New Jersey, New York, Massachusetts, and even North Carolina; those charges accelerated during the Federalist resurgence prompted by Jefferson's Embargo, with Massachusetts Republicans alleging Governor Caleb Strong won reelection in 1812 with "negro votes." As editor of Tammany Hall's *National Advocate* after 1816, Mordecai Noah introduced a harsher racialism into northern politics, consistently baiting old Federalists and Clintonian Republicans as favoring black over white. In February 1820, during the Missouri Crisis, Kentucky's Republican senator, Richard M. Johnson, mocked Yankees who defended black citizenship in their states, asking them, "If your humanity has conquered your prejudice, till you know no color, where are your *magistrates,* your governors, your representatives, of the black population? You proclaim them equal, but you are still their lawgivers."[2]

Racial invective was episodic prior to the late 1810s, however. Jeffersonians used it mostly when they lost, and sometimes competed for black votes. The

Missouri Crisis, and the events surrounding it in 1818–22, changed the nature of political debate, not just because for the first time a sectional (what we call "regional") rather than partisan alignment showed itself in Congress, but also because in three Lower North states (Rhode Island, Connecticut, and New York) Republicans moved to limit voting to white men. The result was the emergence over the following decade of a national party, Andrew Jackson and Martin Van Buren's "Democracy," committed to the defense of the South and slaveholding. In that context, white racialism, as a modern ideology of absolute hierarchy, swept through northern politics. By the 1850s, conjuring up the black bogeyman was how Democrats summoned the faithful. On any given day, some Democratic editor—often a chorus, reprinting each other—attacked "Black Republicans" for granting black men political rights over white men, especially Irishmen. It is impossible to capture the volume of this "brutish negrophobia," Pavlovian in its regurgitative quality, like the crowds chanting "White Men! White Men!" to support Stephen A. Douglas in his 1858 debates with Lincoln. The 1860 election climaxed with a vast Democratic parade through Manhattan, featuring a float containing an actor got up as "a large and good-looking nigger wench" embracing Horace Greeley, the Republican editor, standing next to Lincoln, with a banner proclaiming "Free love and free niggers will certainly elect Old Abe if he pilots us safe."[3]

Many historians will say there is nothing new here, since it is well established that the "Democracy" inaugurated by Jefferson and consolidated by Van Buren and Jackson was built upon whiteness and slavery. But assuming that the Democrats' racialist discourse was hegemonic, as many historians do, skews the early republic's politics. Certainly, these "democrats" were popular, but they were never dominant in the long term, simply because, as James Oakes has argued, no party ever achieved that control before the Civil War. Putting Negrophobic partisanship in context as sharply contested and often derided shines a new light on the politics of whiteness. Paralleling the development of racialized politics, a lineage of notable white men (including some northern Jeffersonians) insisted on the legitimacy of black citizenship and denounced the ideology of racial difference.

During the Missouri Crisis's final stage, a different Republican senator, New Hampshire's David Morril, delivered an emphatic version of this anti-racialism in response to Missouri's submission of a constitution excluding black citizens of other states:

> Take from the inhabitants slaves and aliens, and the remainder are citizens. Colour, does not come into consideration, and it has no share in characterizing an inhabitant or a citizen. . . . If you can proscribe one class of citizens, you may another. . . . You may as well say a tall citizen

shall not settle in Missouri, as a yellow [mulatto] citizen may not. If one state can do this, all may; the consequence will be, that size, profession, age, shape, colour, or any disgusting quality in a citizen, will be a sufficient reason, why he should be precluded settling in any state.

Morril did not avow an abstract concept; he then listed by name black Yankees known as men of probity, one of whom had held offices in his state since before the Revolution. Nor was he an outlier, since a bipartisan group from neighboring states joined in, all powerful figures in their respective parties. Together, these white men represented the antiracial republicanism long practiced in the Upper New England of Massachusetts, Vermont, New Hampshire, and the Maine District, and shared by others like John Jay and his allies and sons in New York. This politics found a new tribune in John Quincy Adams during his postpresidential career in Congress, beginning with his 1836 fight against the "Gag" on antislavery petitions, and lasting until his death in 1848. It reached high tide in the radical wing of the second Republican Party founded in 1854–56, including New York's William Seward, Pennsylvania's Thaddeus Stevens, Massachusetts's Charles Sumner and Henry Wilson, and Ohio's Salmon Chase. Collectively, they promulgated a worldview radically different from the white nationalism of southern and western Republicans like John C. Calhoun and R. M. Johnson, and then the Democracy personified in Jackson.[4]

It is one thing to show that some leading politicians affirmed black citizenship before the Civil War, and another to argue that a significant number of African Americans acted as voters throughout this period. The discovery of black men's extensive participation in partisan electioneering in the postrevolutionary era precipitated this study. That evidence contradicted what most historians had written about antebellum politics. No general account of this formative stage in U.S. history, even those paying attention to the problems of slavery and race, acknowledges any such thing as black electoral politics. Slave rescues, the Underground Railroad, and intensive agitating, orating, and pamphleteering against slavery by black men and women have received ample attention, as have the "slave politics" of southern farm and plantation households. But the politics of seeking electoral influence over or within the state, involving caucuses, conventions, and nominations, the mobilization of voters by party apparatuses, the rituals of campaigns and election days, capped by the act of voting itself followed by postelection maneuvering for patronage—all these are presumed to have been off-limits to black men. With the exception of works by William and Aimee Lee Cheek on Ohio, Robert Cottrol on Providence, Phyllis Field on New York, Kathryn Grover on New Bedford, and, most recently, Stephen Kantrowitz on Boston, most accounts have asserted that black men were effectively barred from electoral politics prior to 1865, based on two premises: first, that 88 percent of African Americans were enslaved in 1860, and thus self-evidently outside the body politic; second, that so few free men of color lived in states with a nonracial suffrage that their electoral presence was too small to see or measure. Nearly sixty years ago, Leon Litwack's foundational *North of Slavery: The Negro in the Free States, 1790–1860* asserted that "By 1840, some 93 per cent of the northern free Negro population lived in states which completely or practically excluded them from the right to vote," leaving only a few thousand in Massachusetts, Maine, New Hampshire, and Vermont eligible to vote, at a time when the national electorate numbered in the millions.[5]

As Samuel Ringgold Ward's above polemic suggests, contemporary observers knew a considerably larger number cast ballots. Ward claimed 7,000 in 1850, and he omitted Ohio, where many of the 5,822 black men twenty-one and over in 1850 voted regularly; by 1860, a careful observer would have noted a larger number, given the rapid expansion of New York and Ohio's black electorates. Yet the conventional view is that the nominal voting rights conferred on free men of color at the Founding were rapidly whited-out by a rolling disfranchisement that began in Maryland and Delaware in 1783 and 1787, and culminated in Tennessee, North Carolina, and Pennsylvania in 1834–38. Certainly, black suffrage was eliminated or made conditional in many states over these decades. This narrative of declension does not acknowledge, however, how black men's electoral weight expanded in those states where they maintained the franchise: all of New England except Connecticut after Rhode Island reenfranchised them in 1842; New York, where the property qualification set at the 1821 constitutional convention was met or circumvented after 1845; Ohio, following an 1831 state supreme court decision defining anyone with less than half "African blood" as white.[6]

The importance of black suffrage as a political fact rather than a lost opportunity or future possibility does not rest solely on whether individual African Americans could go to the polls next to whites. It mattered even more as a collective practice, acknowledged by white political operatives in specific locales. Thus, this book documents not just black voting, but black-and-white partisanship via the participation of free men of color in the successive Party Systems of the early republic. This is what I mean by "black politics," acknowledging that later uses of the term focus on the election or appointment of black men and later women to public and party office (which happened only occasionally before 1860) and that a broader-based citizenship politics encompassed considerably more than electoralism. Over time, this biracial political praxis influenced most of the parties: the Federalists and Jeffersonian Republicans through 1820; the National Republicans, Antimasons, and Whigs of the 1830s and 1840s (though rarely their Democratic opponents); the radical Whigs who split off to found the Liberty Party in 1840, and its successor, the Free Soil Party of 1848–54; even the American or "Know-Nothing" Party of the mid-1850s. All of these fed into the sprawling coalition of Whigs, Free Soilers, old Liberty men, renegade Democrats, and Know-Nothings that reclaimed the name "Republican" after 1854. The latter was the one revolutionary political party in U.S. history, and, as recent scholarship by James Oakes and Eric Foner demonstrates, it was far more committed to the destruction of slavery and, among its radical wing, the forging of a nonracial republic on the New England model, than heretofore acknowledged.[7]

Here some historical perspective is vital. To understand why black citizenship seemed neither impossible nor absurd to men like Adams, Seward, Wilson, Stevens, and Chase, we need to see the early republic the way they did. They knew that in most of the original states, black men had participated in elections to ratify the Constitution; in his denunciation of *Dred Scott*, Lincoln cited New Hampshire, Massachusetts, New York, New Jersey, and North Carolina, but a more accurate number was ten, given that Rhode Island, Connecticut, Pennsylvania, Maryland, and Delaware also authorized some form of black suffrage as of 1789. These radical Republicans decried disfranchisement as a form of political corruption, with Wilson, Seward, and Chase all working to empower black electorates in their states; when Democrats raged at "Black Republicans" for putting black over white, it was not merely calculated racial hysteria. The last epigraph above, from a Pennsylvania Democratic newspaper, pitting a "German Voter" against a newly-arrived black man in Massachusetts, could have appeared anywhere, given the period's ubiquitous reprinting. There are hundreds of similar squibs littering that party's press, all evoking widely known facts, such as that Rhode Island Whigs enfranchised men of color but disfranchised the foreign-born in 1842. In another example, Massachusetts Know-Nothings in 1855 sought to extend to twenty-one years the bar on naturalized citizens voting, while at the same time mobilizing every native-born black man to vote. We remember *Dred Scott*'s abrogating the Missouri Compromise by nationalizing slaveholders' ability to carry their chattels anywhere, but Northern Democrats also hoped Chief Justice Taney's declaration that African Americans had never been U.S. citizens would curtail "Negro Votes."

In fact, *Dred Scott* was startlingly ineffective. It stimulated the renewed defense of black rights, as a wave of nullification rolled across "Greater New England" in 1857–58. This frightened the South as much as the mass mourning in the North that followed John Brown's December 1859 execution. Republican legislatures and state supreme courts affirmed the absolute equality of their states' citizens of color; Massachusetts's secretary of state began issuing passports to African Americans; New Hampshire authorized a black militia company in defiance of federal exclusion; and a new crop of "personal liberty" laws guaranteed legal aid to those claimed as fugitive slaves and severely penalized any law officer aiding their capture. A Vermont General Assembly resolution indicates this nullification's force, that "all laws of Congress which recognize the right of property in man, or deprive any person of liberty without due process of law and a jury trial . . . are unconstitutional, void, and of no effect," and further, "no ingenious sophistry," meaning Taney's syllogisms, "can make it appear that the citizens of each State are not citizens of the United States, and . . . entitled, as such, to all rights and privileges of citizens of the several States." The Green Mountain legislators concluded with a fire-breathing threat worthy of South Carolina: "whenever the government or judiciary of the United States refuses or neglects to protect the citizens of each State in their lives and liberty . . . it becomes the duty of the sovereign and independent States of this Union to protect their own citizens, at whatever hazard or cost."[8]

Republicans were hardly united, however. In Illinois and Pennsylvania, claiming they sought to protect only white men's rights, party members tried to distinguish between containing slavery and recognizing black citizenship, while Ohio's governor Salmon Chase addressed mass meetings next to the black lawyer John Mercer Langston and New York Republicans deployed a statewide black campaign apparatus. If the First Reconstruction began haltingly in the postrevolutionary decades, by the late 1850s it burgeoned in those northern states where black men voted. The possible consequences were clear, if it spread to the entire North. White southerners could see the pending reorganization of the nation along nonracial lines, with "Negro voters" an electoral fact, and "Negro magistrates," their long-threatened bugaboo, on the horizon. In Maine and Massachusetts, black men began winning local offices, even serving as jury men. The cornerstones of sectional comity, reinforced since 1800 to protect slavery, were cracking on all fronts, and southerners declared the counterrevolution of secession to bring the republic back to what they insisted it had once been.

Narratives of American Politics: The Problem of Whiteness

By this point, readers may wonder why, if a cadre of white leaders affirmed black citizenship and black voting was so long-lasting, this history has remained invisible. The convergence of several trends in late twentieth-century historiography explains the obscurity into which antebellum black politics fell postbellum, and their continuing effacement, despite black history's renaissance since the 1960s.

The first trend is how historians have allowed the power of "whiteness" to white-out what actually transpired. We have all been Taneyites, in effect, reading the *Dred Scott* decision back into the prior seventy years as an affirmation of what was always-already there. Rather than letting facts speak, scholars have insisted a priori that black citizenship barely, rarely, or never existed. As often the case with those whom Eric Wolf famously called "the people without history," black political agency has been hidden in plain sight, such as when twenty-year-old Frederick Bailey arrived in New Bedford in 1838 and Nathan Johnson, a local black leader, told him "that there was nothing in the constitution of Massachusetts to prevent a colored man from holding any office in the state."[9]

That scholars have explored so many other expressions of black agency complicates this history of elision. Since the 1950s, a sea change has revolutionized American history. Bringing African Americans back into the national narrative is at the center of that change. Why, then, have black electoral politics before the Civil War received so little attention? The explanation here is contemporary. Since the 1970s and for good reason, old-style *political* history, focusing narrowly on the evolution of parties, elections, voting, and what the state does, has been pushed aside in favor of *social* history, the narratives of families, communities, races, ethnicities, classes, and genders, and the social movements stemming from those identities and locations. The meaning of "politics" has expanded in every direction. Regarding antebellum black people, it now encompasses clothing and hair, dance and music, commerce between the enslaved and masters, sexuality, preaching, techniques of religious worship, and the implications of holiday celebrations. By including everything, however, "politics" becomes just another word for the struggles of daily life. The result is a dense social history that ignores the organized political activism of free black people, as if their votes, their efforts to vote, and their relationship to parties and politicians amounted to little. While this turn to "the social" away from "the political" has deservedly broadened the definition of who or what constitutes a historical subject, it also relegates the actual arrangements of power—elections and the control of institutions, parties, offices, and legislatures—to the sidelines, obscuring black men's fervent political engagements. Our students know something about Nat Turner, an armed rebel for a few weeks, but nothing at all about J. M. Langston, the black Ohioan who held office from the 1850s to the 1890s, ending as a Virginia congressman. We hold up Douglass as the apotheosis of the "heroic slave," tracing his speaking tours and polemics, but prior to David Blight, Douglass's biographers scanted his long efforts to position himself for office. Truly, we have missed the forest for the trees, if we want to take antebellum free black people seriously on their own terms, in which "politics" in the traditional sense figured centrally.[10]

Inserting black politics into the existing history has unsettling implications for how we understand postrevolutionary American politics. There are two diametrically opposed narratives of U.S. politics before the Civil War: one Whiggish and liberal, celebrating America's progress; the other dystopian and radical, damning the U.S. as a herrenvolk democracy. The older, still entrenched account was powerfully articulated by Arthur M. Schlesinger, Jr., in *The Age of Jackson*, and updated by Sean Wilentz in *The Rise of American Democracy: Jefferson to Lincoln*. They see the early American republic as the world's vanguard of freedom, led by Jefferson's Republicans, who "vindicated the political equality of the mass of American citizens," and even more by their successors, the Jacksonian Democrats, a party committed to universal white manhood suffrage and a culture of rude egalitarianism. Wilentz states the irrelevance of black citizenship in this history: "to impose current categories of democracy on the past is to block any understanding of how our own, more elevated standards originated. It is to distort the lives of Americans who could barely have anticipated political and social changes that we take for granted. It is to substitute our experiences and prejudices for theirs." In this version of America's democratic promise, black people, however real their oppression, remained on the outer margins through no fault of their own, and the unhindered ability of white men to vote continues to be the measure of history's progress, as it was for Schlesinger. Other than Wilentz, whose canvas does encompass the tension between slavery and freedom, the most influential contemporary expositor of this perspective is Gordon Wood, a preeminent historian of the Revolution whose major works almost entirely elide race and the institution of slavery. Wood's perspective on the United States' political evolution is summed up in his ebullient paean to republican triumph circa 1810, which describes how "these insignificant borderland provinces had become a giant, almost continent-wide republic of nearly ten million egalitarian-minded bustling citizens who not only had thrust themselves into the vanguard of history but had fundamentally altered their society and their social relationships. Far from remaining monarchical, hierarchy-ridden subjects on the margin of civilization, Americans had become, almost overnight, the most liberal, the most democratic, the most commercially minded, and the most modern people in the world." In Wood's history, black people truly are what Gary Nash has called "the forgotten fifth."[11]

Alexander Saxton's *The Rise and Fall of the White Republic*, David Roediger's *The Wages of Whiteness*, and Don E. Fehrenbacher's *The Slaveholding Republic* counter this national-patriotic narrative. Collectively, they underline that postrevolutionary America began as an imperial White Republic organized around slavery, monolithic racism, and genocidal dispossession of native peoples. Their clear-eyed refusal of a progressive teleology premised on American exceptionalism constitutes a devastating indictment, but one containing a basic weakness: they treat the White Republic as an accomplished fact rather than the program of a powerful but fragile coalition. This premise refuses the possibility that there was more than one republic, let alone a reconstructed Yankee Republic emerging from the Revolution to compete with the "slaveholding republic." Ironically, this newer narrative has deeper cultural roots than the accounts of Schlesinger, Wilentz, and Wood. It evokes the Puritan jeremiad of declension and corruption, a "mood of almost implacable destiny and inevitability," in Robert Forbes's pungent description, with the Calvinistic implication that slavery was an original sin, making "American democracy itself in some occult fashion contaminated by racism at its very essence."[12]

These two historical schools, otherwise completely opposed, thus agree on a central fact: there never could have been any black voters worth counting, or any such thing as black participation within the American party systems, or any large number of white men who believed in nonracial citizenship. The unintended convergence of these historiographies, the Jeffersonian-Jacksonian tradition focusing on white men's democracy and its opposite, the radical history of whiteness, leaves a remarkable gap, which this book seeks to fill. I do not want to intimate, however, that its arguments are entirely original. Rather, it builds upon those accounts of antebellum politics that take race (or rather racialism) seriously as an animating impulse in U.S. political development, but do not insist that that development was all-white, all the time. In his *The Political Culture of the American Whigs*, Daniel Walker Howe, drawing upon Lee Benson, took as normal the existence of black voters in the North, and sought to explain their affinity for the Whig sensibility, "a vision of national progress . . . both moral and material. Society would become more prosperous and at the same time cleansed of its sins" via the Protestant spirit of self-improvement and Christian universalism. More recently, in his sweeping *What Hath God Wrought: The Transformation of America, 1815–1848*, Howe notes that "Black abolitionists had an agenda of their own, and it included getting involved in politics whenever possible"; he also deftly deflated remaining romanticism about Old Hickory ("The Jacksonian movement . . . although it took the name of the Democratic Party, fought so hard in favor of slavery and white supremacy, and opposed the inclusion of non-whites and women within the American civil polity so resolutely, that it makes the term 'Jacksonian Democracy' all the more inappropriate"). The Whig America within which the black political class of the 1830s and 1840s emerged is very much the world Howe has shown us, reviving the history of a progressive nationalism that abjured Jacksonian militarism and populist demagogy in favor of planned development and market-oriented egalitarianism.[13]

Like many other scholars, I am also indebted to James Brewer Stewart's thesis that only in the "sudden conjuncture" of the late 1820s and early 1830s did racial difference come to define the "modernizing political culture of the free states," following a generation during which the North "fostered a surprisingly open premodern struggle over claims of 'respectability' and citizenship put forward by many social groups, and in particular by free African Americans." In Stewart's analysis, Jacksonian political hegemony "solidified into an unmovable political consensus of highly ordered white supremacy . . . buttressed by a system of democratic white politics premised on the modern assumption that 'nature' had always divided 'black' and 'white' as inferior and superior, and always must." Although I differ on the strength of that consensus, Stewart's analysis is key to understanding the impulses that drove white opposition to racialism, from High Federalist conservatives and stray northern Republicans in 1790–1820 to Whig nationalists in the 1840s and 1850s. Taking advantage of this partisan terrain, black men framed their own vernacular ideology in opposition to the new racial modernity, invoking a "pure republican" tradition and the Protestant orthodoxy that "God hath made of one blood all the nations of the world." Their discourse of "black republicanism" combined natural rights ideology and the commonsense authority of birthright. This authorized them to address northern whites first as potential allies against southern "nabobs," and later positioned them against the foreign Catholics whom Democrats avidly recruited.[14]

Finally, this book would not exist without Rogers Smith's *Civic Ideals: Conflicting Visions of Citizenship in U.S. History.* Smith points out that from the Founding, two traditions have competed regarding what made an "American," one rooted in English common law and simple birthright, and the other more ascriptive, insisting on some mix of Protestantism, ethnicity, and "race." It was from Smith that I derived the centrality of black citizenship, and why that possibility fretted even James Madison, who as early as 1791 contemplated the political implications if "slaves [were] freed and the right of suffrage extended to all." Smith forces one to remember that, for every provisional affirmation of African American citizenship—whether Congress granting certificates to black mariners as "citizens" to protect them from British impressment; Congress pensioning black Revolutionary veterans; or individual states enacting nonracial suffrage laws—just as often state supreme courts, the federal legislature, and U.S. attorneys general denied black citizenship was anything more than a privilege an individual state might grant or withdraw.[15]

Of States and Their Rights

Besides seeing whiteness as a contingent practice rather than a settled premise and insisting social movements and conventional politics must be studied in tandem, this book rests on a final proviso. We should cease framing antebellum American politics in terms of North and South, or free versus slave. That traditional division, with the Civil War as telos, obscures rather than clarifies. It ignores the devotedly national, antisectional functioning of the parties until the 1854–56 rupture that birthed the Republicans, and how the Age of Jackson saw "the only truly nationwide party system in America prior to the rebirth of the southern Republicans" in the late twentieth century. It effaces how long slavery persisted in the North. It ignores where black citizenship actually operated, in parts of both North and South until the 1830s. Finally, it substitutes two notional regions for the political spaces where most politics actually took place. It is not only that, as Hahn puts it, "freedom for African Americans was highly contingent and to be found in discrete geopolitical zones"; more precisely, freedom and political rights were to be found in discrete *states*.[16]

As a fixed political category, the demarcation into "North" and "South" arrived in fits and starts between 1790 and 1860. Well after 1800 it was common to pose not that binary, but a four-part division between the "eastern" or New England states, the "middle" ground of Pennsylvania, New York, and New Jersey, the "southern" as in seaboard slaveholding states, and the emerging "West" encompassing new states north and south of the Ohio, some of which permitted enslavement and some not. Sectional polarization surfaced only periodically in the Northern Federalists' wartime revival circa 1812, the Missouri Crisis of 1819–21, the Gag Rule fights in Congress of 1836–44, and the Wilmot Proviso votes in the late 1840s. Otherwise, a partisan division along sectional lines was repressed for practical reasons—the seeming impossibility of a sectional organization winning a national election.

This fluid national politics slowly hardening around a sectional fissure points to how most antebellum politicking took place within "the States," as they were called: "Most Whigs and Democrats in this period considered control of state governments to be as important as control of the national government," since patronage and economic decisions emanated largely from the state capitals. Certainly, federal power led national development in dramatic and ruthless ways, killing Native Americans and clearing land via military conquests across the Mississippi Valley, defeating sundry rivals from Tecumseh's confederated tribes to the British at New Orleans, and forcing the Spanish out of Florida. National politics had limited resonance in ordinary life, however. In Congress, representatives bargained for their states in ways hard to imagine today, and many top leaders functioned exclusively at the state level, or returned there after brief congressional sojourns. The national arena possessed great ideological authority, as in the Nullification Crisis of 1831–32, but less practical effect than the workings of state governments. It was DeWitt Clinton's New York that built the Erie Canal, the nineteenth century's most impressive effort at economic development, and Jackson's actions as president were mostly negative, for example, the Bank War and the Maysville Road veto. Long after the Civil War, the entire federal apparatus would have fit into a small office building, and individual members of Congress had no staff.[17]

In studying antebellum politics, therefore, we should focus on individual states, rather than generalizing across them. Each was its own partisan world, and adjoining states often had dramatically differing political cultures, as demonstrated by the antislavery Free Soil Party's showing in 1848: over a quarter of voters in Vermont, Massachusetts, Wisconsin, and New York versus hardly any in Pennsylvania and New Jersey. Black men's exclusion from national politics gives added force to putting the states first. African Americans had no direct access to Congress, and the District of Columbia's location made any activism there dangerous, versus Boston, Albany, Columbus, and other capitals where they convened, lobbied, and testified with increasing frequency. This narrative therefore prioritizes four polities: Pennsylvania, Upper New England, New York, and Ohio, each making up a section of the book. Before engaging with "the States," however, it commences with the ideological arena within which black politics operated. Chapter 1 examines how black men utilized the vernacular republicanism that was America's political lingua franca to fashion their own black republicanism, modeled on the original but uttered by voices different from the farmer-soldiers and city mechanics who led the Revolution from below, or the northern merchants and lawyers and southern planters who organized its armies and legislatures.[18]

I begin with Pennsylvania because its 1780 act for gradual emancipation was a decisive turn in American and world history, and on that basis, Philadelphia developed the North's largest free black community. Chapter 2 traces the consolidation of that city's black civil society from the 1790s, its intense "shadow politics," and finally its peculiar stasis in the late 1830s. This is emphatically not another city study, however, as chapter 3 documents black electoral politics in rural Pennsylvania versus the electoral abstentionism practiced by Philadelphia leaders. Local studies of Bucks, Lancaster, and Franklin Counties underline how black men kept going to the polls into the 1830s. Pennsylvania's 1838 disfranchisement via a constitutional convention and a state supreme court decision was the high-water mark of a long effort to drive black men out of politics. By that time, however, black Philadelphians had retreated into anti-politics, and after 1840 the Keystone State was seen as a reactionary backwater by most black people.

From Pennsylvania, I proceed to the radically different environment of Upper New England (Massachusetts, Vermont, and New Hampshire, plus Maine in 1820). By the 1790s, New England was the first *society without slaves* in the former British North America. Following that emancipatory process, the evolution of a nonracial Yankee Republic shaped the nation's politics in pointed contrast to the Lower North states, which moved to end black political participation. After 1800, all parties consistently pointed to this region, with 18 percent of the republic's free population in 1820, as the place where black men voted without hindrance, organized as partisans, and operated as race-less subjects within the law, however degraded socially. With increasing frequency, Upper New England's men of color gained political standing, testifying to legislatures, occupying minor offices, trading votes for advantage. By the final prewar years, Massachusetts and its adjoining states had become the trope for where black men might gain higher standing than some whites, or at least the reviled Irish. Chapter 4 surveys New England as a whole circa 1770–1830, and chapters 5 through 7 examine specific locations for black political mobilization in the following decades: Portland, Maine, the world's lumber capital, where a concentrated electorate achieved considerable traction as Whigs and Republicans; New Bedford, Massachusetts, an even more prosperous port whose large African American constituency maneuvered between all parties (Whig, Democratic, Liberty, then Free Soil) before becoming Republicans; and Providence, Rhode Island, whose black community regained political standing in the 1840s as a counter posed by "Law and Order" Whigs against a Democratic-cum-Irish insurgency.

Next comes New York. The scale, sophistication, and geographic scope of electoral organizing by the Empire State's black political class surpassed all rivals, producing a host of leaders, including Samuel E. Cornish, Henry Highland Garnet, James McCune Smith, and Samuel R. Ward. Their fortunes repeatedly ebbed and then advanced, conditioned by a gradual emancipation process beginning in 1799, with the 4,000 remaining enslaved people only freed in 1827. Chapter 8 documents the period circa 1800–21, when black votes were sufficient to change the composition of local and state governments and affect national politics. In 1821, a state constitutional convention managed by Martin Van Buren hobbled black voters with a "freehold" property requirement, cutting their electorate to almost nothing. Despite that restriction, black men reentered partisan politics in the 1830s. New York was at the center of northern politics, producing modern electoral machines and consistently brokering national elections, and this dynamism helped its black leadership position itself; nowhere else do we find black men allied over decades with party chiefs like Thurlow Weed, who managed the state's Whig and Republican apparatuses. Chapter 9 traces their campaign for equal suffrage in 1837–46, when it was overwhelmingly rebuffed in a referendum. In these years, black leaders aligned either with the Whigs, from traditional affinities spurred by William Seward's exemplary record as governor in 1839–42, or with the Liberty Party, founded in upstate New York in 1840, and led by the powerful philanthropist Gerrit Smith. Chapter 10 covers 1847–60, during which New York's black electorate rapidly expanded, and some of those men moved into state politics as part of the Sewardite Republicans. Finally, during 1855–60, led by the pragmatic insider Stephen Myers, a former slave who had known Seward and Weed for decades, black men lobbied for another suffrage referendum, securing that vote in 1860. Although they again lost, black Yorkers entered the war as a cohesive cohort near to the centers of power.

Ohio ends these studies. Never a colony, entirely Indian lands when eastern Pennsylvania, the Hudson Valley, and southern New England were urbanizing, it experienced neither slavery nor emancipation. Its politics began just before statehood in 1802, versus the seaboard, where politics had been practiced for generations. Equally new was its statutory subordination of free people of color (mostly recently manumitted people from Virginia), an explicit denization unlike in any of the original thirteen. From the state's founding, they were guaranteed the barest negative freedom and stripped of most citizenship rights via Black Laws regulating their entrance and barring them from voting, the courts, eventually the public schools. This panoply of oppressions marked black Ohioans as lesser; paradoxically, a series of state supreme court decisions from 1823 on made thousands of mixed-race men "white" under the law, raising them higher than in any neighboring state. Ohio also included one of the nation's most antiracialist terrains, the Western Reserve counties along Lake Erie settled entirely by Yankees, where black men entered fully into politics by the 1850s and achieved their greatest visibility within a Republican Party led by Salmon P. Chase.

The reader will note how much of the nation is left out, including states where black men played minor political roles, as in the rest of the Midwest, or were excluded from politics early, as in New Jersey, Connecticut, Maryland, and Delaware, or because I address their role elsewhere, as in Tennessee and North Carolina. Much as race functioned across a legal and cultural patchwork of exclusions and openings, so too did black politics—sometimes agency was exerted strictly locally in places like New Bedford, Oberlin, Hudson (New York), or Columbia (Pennsylvania). Sometimes white men recognized black men as a constituency or threat on a statewide basis, as in New York or Ohio. Always, they cycled in and out of the various British imperial havens encircling the young United States, escaping or waiting to come home. Their politics was contained within enclaves of limited power and contingent forms of state citizenship, but if their influence was exaggerated by Negrophobes, it was also real and consequential. The First Reconstruction was hardly revolutionary. It resembled, rather, many small wars of position, a "long march through the institutions," in the phrase attributed to Antonio Gramsci. In antebellum America, the relevant "institutions" were preeminently the parties, the world's first mass electoral formations, to which we now turn.[19]

Parties and Party Systems: A New Periodization

A long-standing thesis traces the history of American electoral politics as a series of "party systems," beginning with a First Party System of Federalists and Jeffersonian Republicans in 1790–1824, followed by a Second pitting National Republicans and Whigs against Democrats in 1828–54 (with John Quincy Adams's presidency in 1825–29 merely a pause), and then a Third, from 1854 to 1896, during which yet another Republican Party was more or less evenly matched by old-guard Democrats. This book does not seek to overturn the argument for party systems. Instead, I qualify it by putting the politics of race at the center of each. I stress race over slavery because it is a grave mistake to think so-called antislavery politics revolved entirely around whether racially bound labor would be tolerated or extended. As Donald Robinson pointed out long ago, we should not "focus on slavery as the basic issue, which it was not. The basic issue was relations between the races, and it is because of reluctance to confront this issue squarely that American democracy has been unable to solve its greatest and continuing crisis by political means." All politically sentient persons then knew that slavery could never be separated from the political status of free persons of color. As emancipation via legislation, court decisions, and individual manumissions proceeded across the North in 1780–1827, more and more enslaved people became free. Would they be citizens, in full or in part? Would they be deported, or paid to leave? Would they be relegated to a permanently inferior "caste" (a word constantly invoked), meaning subject to white men's summary rules? These questions made black suffrage a "practical and symbolic focus of amelioration" and a "lightning rod for fears and hopes tied to the whole racial question in the North," as Ronald Formisano pointed out, also long ago. In many ways, this book is about that debate playing out in the states where enough white men decided that black men were citizens with political rights, which shaped the rest of the nation.[20]

Analyzing American politics from the perspective of race clarifies the fragility of the party systems, and the work of maintaining them, given the powerfully destabilizing effects of "the Negro Question." Attitudes toward race operated on a zero-sum reckoning. White southerners insisted that the color line should be observed everywhere in the Republic, whereas free people of color in states like Massachusetts saw it in exactly opposite ways—that the Constitution's "privileges and immunities" clause gave them national citizenship rights—and pressed this perspective on their white allies. Recognition of black citizenship, especially black suffrage and participation in politics, was understood as directly inimical to slavery. When northern whites defended black suffrage, their best argument was that disfranchising black men was "bending the knee" to the Slave Power. The epithet for white men who bent in that fashion was "doughfaces," and surprisingly often, that charge worked. The driving logic of the antebellum party systems was to maintain national unity despite these centrifugal pressures. Men like Daniel Webster hailed the sacral Union, but the real purpose of "unionist" politics was more prosaic. Everyone engaged in electoral politics wanted to win, which meant carrying most or all of one section, usually the South, and just enough of the other, usually the North; even in 1860, a unified Democratic Party would have overwhelmed the Republicans.

Here we see two opposing dynamics. Until the Whigs' collapse in 1854, the need for a candidate who could appeal to both sections drove party leaders seeking control of Congress and the ability to implement their program, whether the Whigs' "American System" or the Democrats' "Manifest Destiny." But the requirements of unionism spun off fractions in both sections. In the North, first Federalists, later National Republicans and Whigs, finally even some Democrats rejected the South's demands, meaning racialism as a guiding principle. In the South, first "Old Republicans" in the 1810s, then South Carolina Nullifiers circa 1831, and finally Deep South "fire-eaters" in the late 1840s and 1850s challenged the national parties, charging that sectional compromises in Congress and federal authority were mortal threats to their way of life.

How should one re-periodize these seventy years, on the basis of an inherently racialized sectional politics in dialectical tension with the requirements of national unity? Rather than two grand party systems circa 1790–1854, I break the early republic into four periods: 1790–1815, when the southern-dominated Republicans crushed the predominantly northern Federalists; 1816–28, during which this first Republican Party broke down along sectional lines; 1829–47, when the new Jacksonian Democratic Party dominated national politics; and 1848–60, when the most decisive realignment in U.S. history birthed a second Republican Party committed to eroding slavery by all constitutional means.

1790–1815

Even now, the years 1790–1815 are divided neatly into an Era of Federalism, the presidencies of Washington and Adams, followed by the Jeffersonian Revolution, comprising the four terms of Jefferson and his successor, Madison. Taken together, they suggest steady progress in nation-building. If one foregrounds the politics of race, however, this period takes on a less triumphal coloration. The emergence of self-identified parties in 1795 sprang from southern objections to the treaty John Jay had negotiated with Britain, because it ignored claims against the British for their liberating thousands of Americans' chattels in 1775–83. The first Republican Party came together out of proslavery Anglophobia combined with revolutionary Francophilia and hostility to Federalist "aristocrats" among northern farmers and artisans. If chattel slavery had been confined to those of the original thirteen states that continued sanctioning it, as many hoped in the 1780s, a permanent sectional compromise was possible. Instead, it metastasized post-1800, spreading across lands formerly under Spanish, French, and Native American dominion. These years describe the triumph of Jefferson's party, an unbroken Virginian dynasty, while the enslaved population nearly doubled, from 893,602 in 1800 to 1,538,022 in 1820. Acceptance of the peculiar institution was the true "revolutionary settlement," however unstable. The politics of race always obtruded, despite efforts to suppress debate. The absence of southern allies after 1800 freed northern Federalists to find moral clarity, and they became notorious for their connections to emancipation and accepting black voters as "good federalists," as New York's *Evening Post* described a black leader in 1809. The second war with England prompted a brief Federalist renascence, but that conflict's end terminated their hopes. Northern Republicans were never a solid proslavery phalanx, however. If unlikely to join Federalists' mockery of Jefferson's election by "Negro Votes," meaning enslaved persons counted toward representation in the Electoral College, some avowed antiracialist sentiments.

1816–1828

The 1816–28 period has long perplexed U.S. political historians. It does not fit into the traditional narrative of First and Second Party Systems, and is usually treated as in-between time, an interregnum of no-parties. After 1816, Rufus King, the last Federalist presidential candidate in that year, was the only remaining leader of that party. The period's transitional status was signaled in 1824, when four Republicans vied for the presidency in a "struggle for sectional command": Georgia's William Crawford; Kentucky's Henry

Clay; Tennessee's Andrew Jackson; Massachusetts's John Quincy Adams—the sole northerner, implicitly opposed to slavery's prerogatives. Jackson won the popular vote based on dominating the South, and a plurality in the Electoral College, but the election was decided in the House, where each state cast one vote, and Adams won. For most historians, however, 1824 was merely a chaotic prelude to the arrival of representative democracy with Jackson's election in 1828, powered by the Old Hero's claim to represent ordinary white men against the aristocratic Adams.[21]

Certainly, 1828 was a far more decisive election than the prior three contests, whether the barely competitive 1816 race, when King carried only Massachusetts, Connecticut, and Delaware against James Monroe, the latter's uncontested reelection in 1820, or 1824's intra-Republican brawl. Seen through the lens of race, however, those twelve years look rather different. Rather than formless flux, this period saw two major developments: the first clear alignment along sectional lines in Congress, during the Missouri Crisis of 1819–21; in response, the formation of a new national party, "the Democracy," as it called itself, for the purpose of protecting the South. The architect of this realignment was Martin Van Buren. He began by making his Bucktail Republican faction New York's dominant force in 1817–21. Then, in the 1820s, he consolidated his position until ready to cement the partnership of "the planters of the South and the plain Republicans of the north." In his famous 1827 letter to the Virginia editor Thomas Ritchie, he added, "Geographical divisions founded on local interests or, what is worse prejudices between free & slave holding states will inevitably take their place" in the absence of a coherent party, whereas "party attachment in former times furnished a complete antidote for sectional prejudices by producing counteracting feelings. It was not until that defense had been broken down that the clamor against Southern Influence and African Slavery could be made effectual in the North," a sage prediction of the next realignment, along sectional lines, after 1854.

1829–1847

The years 1829–47 remain "the Age of Jackson," however we judge them. Democrats won the presidency in 1828 and 1832 with Jackson himself, in 1836 with Van Buren, and again in 1844 with "Young Hickory," James K. Polk. These leaders combined an imperial nationalism with a minimalist state—an odd fusion surviving ever since as rightist populism. Always, they sought external "monsters to destroy," in John Quincy Adams's prophetic warning, whether Mexicans, Indians, or Englishmen. As early as 1818, Tammany Hall hailed the General as "the Scourge of British insolence, Spanish perfidy and Indian cruelty." Internally, the Democracy's task was to protect the insertion of a vast slave proletariat into newly conquered lands while uplifting plebeian whites of every sort. It was fiercely "democratic" in its opposition to class, cultural, and ethnic hierarchies while utterly antidemocratic in guarding racial caste. Jackson's Bank War epitomized a class struggle between white men, with the president using control over federal deposits to rein in an emerging commercial bourgeoisie attached to the opposition Whigs. The latter was a grab-bag of northern reformers from the Antimasonic Party and Adams's National Republicans plus southerners like Henry Clay, a pro-business slaveowner who acknowledged the institution itself was morally wrong. The glue knitting Whigs together was opposition to Jackson's militaristic "Caesarism" and their support for an active federal state pursuing systematic economic development. Because of whom they opposed (and perhaps whom they represented), the Whigs were the natural home for antislavery men.[22]

Although 1828–47 saw the triumph of the Slaveholders' Republic, with the benefit of hindsight, these years dug its grave. In 1829, no one could have foreseen the catastrophic internal war that would smash slavery to pieces. Discussion of slavery was effectively banned in Congress, and, since "sectional ideologies and issues were consciously kept out of politics . . . the party system had a certain artificial quality." An agrarian capitalism based on the superexploitation of human capacities spread unabated into eastern Texas and Arkansas, with the enslaved population growing from 1,983,860 in 1830 to 3,200,364 in 1850. This imperial expansion was profoundly destabilizing, however, and by 1848–50, "ultras" in both sections mooted the possibility of disunion. The Free Soil Party's attempt to realign the North against slavery in 1848 failed, but it proved a reliable augury of Lincoln's sweep twelve years later. In assessing the causes of the Civil War, therefore, a major impetus was the Jacksonians' arrogance of power, from "gagging" antislavery petitions to Congress in 1836–44 to forcing a Fugitive Slave Act on the North in 1850. The other central factor was the sudden arrival after 1830 of a powerful social movement, the vast swirl of biracial abolitionism invading the churches and firesides of northerners with "moral suasion" that made it impossible to ignore slavery and dealt mortal blows to the parties holding the Union together.[23]

1848–1860

Malcolm X's comment following President Kennedy's assassination, that "the chickens have come home to roost," is an appropriate way to understand the political implosion of the years 1848–60. Finally, the bills came due for the compromises that had allowed slavery to grow at a pace no Founder could have imagined, and the accumulated grievances of North versus South. Accounts were settled, first in the breakdown of the party system, and then, after Lincoln's election, by physical force.

Party politics after 1848 saw repeated failures to reinstate partisan arrangements that would mute the problems of race and slavery. The multiple disintegrations that generated a civil war can be traced via the two main parties, neither of which survived the decade. In 1848, most northern Whigs stuck with their party rather than voting "Free Soil" because of assurances that its nominee, the Louisiana slaveholder Zachary Scott, was committed to slavery's nonextension. That may have been true, but "Old Zack" died prematurely and was succeeded by the conservative New Yorker Millard Fillmore. In 1850, Fillmore and a majority of northern Whigs assented to another great Compromise, including a Fugitive Slave Act which abrogated habeas corpus, turning "the average citizen into a slave catcher" with "a national police enforcement mechanism." Heedless, in 1852 the Whigs nominated Winfield Scott on a platform upholding the Compromise of 1850, and a proslavery Democrat, New Hampshire's Franklin Pierce, won big. As of 1853, the evidence suggested that proslavery Unionism would always triumph, and 1856 confirmed that common sense when Pennsylvania's James Buchanan, the ultimate doughface, won in a three-way contest against California senator John C. Frémont, nominee of the newly minted Republicans, and Fillmore, who ran as the "American" or Know-Nothing candidate, a last futile effort to rebuild cross-sectional unity by attacking immigrants and Catholics.[24]

But Buchanan's victory was illusory, as normal partisan competition had already collapsed. The leader of the Northern Democracy, Illinois senator Stephen A. Douglas, effectively wrecked his party in spring 1854 by pushing through Congress the "Nebraska Act," which allowed settlers in new territories to decide if they wanted slavery. Repealing the Missouri Compromise, the only real barrier to slavery's expansion, upended northern politics. That fall, the Whigs were replaced in many states by all-party "Anti-Nebraska" tickets, and Democrats were crushed, losing nearly all their northern House seats. By 1856, a sectional and antislavery Republican Party had emerged, and Frémont's carrying eleven northern states forecast its Electoral College win in 1860. Crisis followed crisis over the next four years, splitting Democrats into not just southern and northern but "Administration" and "Douglas" wings, while the Republicans (absorbing most of the American Party) consolidated their dominance of the North. The result was a four-way race along sectional lines, for or against slavery's long-term existence: Lincoln, of course; the Northern Democrat Douglas, running to keep the Union-as-it-is against

"Black Republican" fanatics; Vice President John C. Breckinridge, the Southern Democrat committed to slavery's prerogatives; finally, Tennessee senator John Bell representing the Constitutional Union Party, ex-Whigs wishing for Henry Clay. This was Lincoln's "House Divided," which had destroyed the successive party systems designed to suppress racial and sectional imperatives. He had it right.

Political History as Men's History

This book's version of political history contains a paradox that must be confronted directly. The conventions of American political history have always implied a dismissal of those who are left out because they were unable to vote. The rejection of that dismissal led to social history's emphasis on enslaved people, Native Americans, the poor, immigrants, and women, all "the people formerly without history," to demonstrate that they were never passive or irrelevant. The process of establishing that free African American men were not automatically excluded from the politics of voting and partisanship, and therefore should not be excluded from "political history," reinforces the exclusion of others, especially black women. One can dig out episodic evidence of black men supporting women's rights before 1860, and instances where black women forced their way into the political arena, but these are few and far between. Historians have excavated an intensive *social politics* inside antebellum black communities, amounting to a separate movement for women's rights, but otherwise black politics was black men's politics, and they embraced that fact. The central claim of their version of republicanism, "We are Americans," meant, in fact, "We are American men and should not be treated as you treat your women," and it would be sentimental and anachronistic to insist that black women were fully included in that assertion.[25]

To be clear, black women were militant in their use of physical force against slavery, but that kind of politics—of the street, the mob, breaking into courtrooms to seize a fugitive—is not the subject of this book. Even there, we can see a politics of gendered exclusion at work: while all the evidence suggests black women remained just as "unruly" on the eve of war in the late 1850s as they had been five years earlier, the famous "rescues" of the 1850s, in Christiana, Boston, Syracuse, and Oberlin, were organized mainly by black and white men acting in unison, and the dockets at subsequent trials were filled entirely by men. In that sense, the politics of black republicanism involved more than birthright citizenship. They also revolved around the right of a man to participate in the public sphere like other men, and not be pushed out, as women were. The justifications offered by white men for what we today call "second-class citizenship" rested on feminizing black men—that they should be accorded the state's protection but only civil rather than political rights, the position occupied by white women. In the antebellum context, free black men could have chosen to avoid politics, and embrace their feminized status as a safe harbor. The latter was the road taken by Philadelphia's prosperous black elite. As chapter 2 explores, their most prominent leaders publicly renounced all forms of electoral participation, attempting to hold off Jim Crow by declaring themselves no more than "citizens for protection," the status held by women. Outside of Philadelphia, black men rejected that option, and insisted their manhood trumped their suspect complexion or enslaved antecedents.

There are two qualifications to acknowledging that, for black as much as white, "political history was men's history" in this period. The first is that defining the "political" as primarily electoral was a new development. Only after the Revolution did voting, participation in electoral rituals, and self-conscious partisanship become the essence of popular politics and the marker of civic equality among men. As Barbara Clark Smith has shown, elections were considerably less central in British North America's public sphere, when a majority of white men could not vote, but all men (and sometimes women) participated in a plebeian "out-of-doors" politics of militia musters, crowd actions, executions, mass meetings, and, eventually, society-wide economic boycotts. The arrival of much larger electorates and formal parties organized over vast spaces of state and nation narrowed the definition of politics, making it more unequivocally men's business.[26]

The second qualification is a truism, but had special force regarding the North's free people of color. Women's labor has always enabled men to go "politick" with other men. Somebody had to keep house (and therefore stay at home, even if working for money). The gendered division of labor into separate spheres had a distinct meaning for black families, however, because their ordinary lives put the northern black community outside prevailing norms. In principle, antebellum American society rested on male authority over the household economy. Republican fathers worked to make themselves financially independent and able to support their families. Republican mothers kept Christian homes, raising chaste, meek daughters and equally chaste, dutiful sons. Black households rarely approximated that ideal. Because of the abject poverty imposed on most free people of color, their lack of capital and familial resources, and deep social exclusion, all only worsening between 1800 and 1860, only a minority ever met the expectations of gendered respectability. Most gained freedom after the Revolution, often gradually, and were locked out of the common history shared by northern whites as aspiring landowners, cash-poor but self-sufficient. By 1800, generations of rural development informed those whites' self-understanding. A vast network of diversified family farms stretching to the Canadian border provided economic security and a shared identity into the nineteenth and even twentieth centuries. Although pockets of black farmers did fan out across New England, New York, Pennsylvania, and Ohio after the Revolution, they were a small fraction of the North's black population. The great majority lacked access to this core material and cultural heritage. They had no places to which they could return, no rooted rural bases of mutual support and communal subsistence, surviving instead in back-alley cellars and shanties in the cities and on the fringe of country life as day laborers and cottagers on stray pieces of land.[27]

These facts point to the fundamental difference marking black women's history. In slavery, most labored in the fields throughout their lives, doing the same work as men. In freedom, black women's life experience also set them apart. Since only a fraction of free black men could support a family, most free women of color earned money to survive and feed their children. This historically exceptional category of wage-earning women included many claiming respectable status. Entrepreneurialism was common among the wives, mothers, and daughters of the black elite, the political class who are this book's protagonists. There were few African American families more eminent than Salem's Remonds; the patriarch, John, born in Curacao, was a merchant-caterer tied to that city's political leaders and his son, Charles Lenox Remond, became a famous lecturer on abolitionism's trans-Atlantic circuit. This family was quite different from the prominent white abolitionist clans, however. John Remond's wife, Nancy Lenox Remond, did not stay at home, nor did her daughters. She was a cakemaker, and her three daughters ran a hair salon, founded the state's largest wigmaking business, and marketed Mrs. Putnam's Medicated Hair Tonic. Further examples abound: Freelove Slocum was a major investor in her brother Paul Cuffe's maritime enterprises; in the 1840s, Grace Bustill Douglass, a leading Philadelphia abolitionist and daughter of a baker, was a successful milliner and the Female Trading Association, a "cooperative grocery store with one hundred members," operated in New York City, selling everything from chocolate to candles. Nor was the practice of economic autonomy restricted to the free states. In her study of Petersburg, Virginia, Suzanne Lebsock showed that women of color "constituted almost half of the paid free black labor force," and 40 to 50 percent of free black property-owners.[28]

There is no simple explanation for why middle-class women of color broke so sharply with white society's domestic ideology. Their tendency toward commerce perhaps stemmed from combinations of familial and personal ambition, a protofeminist quest for independence, and an acute awareness of economic insecurity. Having noted all of the above, as well as black women's exceptional agency in the practical work of abolition, it is difficult to measure their influence on black men's partisan activism other than the typical resolution voted at the 1844 New York State convention of black men: "We need and earnestly solicit the aid and approbation of our noble-hearted women, who have never been backward in any measure of general good."[29]

Sources and Style

Anyone sampling this book will notice its focus on the minutiae of political intercourse between black and black, white and white, and black and white. Its narrative largely avoids any panoptic overview or synthetic history, choosing instead to show the reader what was happening year-by-year, sometimes month-by-month or week-by-week, in a particular place. How do I justify such a detailed history of partisan activism? The goal here is to *re*-write the history of antebellum American politics by putting back in what has been left out—black men's constant, low-level participation in elections and parties in large parts of the early republic. If convincing, this revision proves that the politics of racial exclusion came considerably later and was far more contingent than heretofore asserted. To insist on such a rewriting requires precise explications set in place and time. It will not do to make general assertions backed by anecdotes and a mass of footnotes. The reader must enter into the milieus of quotidian partisanship to see and hear how different they were from the received accounts that do not see or hear black men. I seek to re-create the back-and-forth in locales that were among the most economically dynamic sites in antebellum America: Pennsylvania's most prosperous counties, several of New England's thriving port cities, and two of the regions where agrarian capitalism took off—upstate New York and northern Ohio.

A second point is that, however effaced postbellum, this politics was always in plain sight. It was told then, and is recovered now, through the era's thousands of newspapers, which Jeffrey Pasley accurately describes as "the political system's central institution, not simply a forum or atmosphere in which politics took place," and one remarkably useful in recording ordinary political lives. As Richard John has brilliantly documented, newspapers played an outsized role in the early republic, first as the principal medium for organizing local politics, and second, as the transmission belt connecting the local to the national. The 1792 Postal Act fostered a "highly decentralized informational environment" by authorizing a powerful government subsidy to local publishers, overturning the public arena formerly dominated by coastal elites. The proliferation of newspapers in the new republic's interior created "a new kind of public sphere . . . disembodied . . . not in a particular place but rather in the imaginations of millions of people, most of whom would never meet face-to-face," in turn facilitating "a national community that extended to every citizen living within its boundaries an invitation to participate in public affairs." It is of enormous significance that white editors across the nation, from the Deep South of Mississippi to the Far North of Maine, consistently noticed black men's political efforts; indeed, it is the best measure of their presence.[30]

An abundance of journalistic comment regarding black men in politics, from every corner of the republic and always colored by partisanship, must be balanced against the thinness of archival materials, especially the absence of the dense correspondence between networks of leaders upon which political historians have usually relied. The lack of that sort of archive evidently drove the presumption that if black men were absent from the private records of white men they were a priori absent from politics. To reconstruct their political history has required relying instead on the public record, not just newspapers, but debates in Congress, state legislatures, and constitutional conventions. Needless to say, black men did not speak in those various assemblies, but they were remarkably present, invoked as constituents and sometimes as individuals by allies and enemies. Finally, there are court cases and election challenges, producing testimony and depositions, which document as nowhere else the actual places and times and means whereby men of color voted, sometimes despite legal bars.

I note here that the private record of politicians' correspondence as well as diaries and other personal documents is not as silent as has been assumed. Scattered through the papers of prominent white men are references to and correspondence with black men. Some are unremarkable requests for congressional documents, minor patronage, or just encomia, like letters received from obscure white men. The exception, noted in the *Journal of Negro History* in 1942, is the voluminous correspondence between Gerrit Smith and dozens of black men over decades. In some ways, the Smith papers are the archive of black politics, still not mined fully, but they must be used carefully. Smith was one of the nation's richest men, dedicated to giving his money away for "Bible politics," but, then as now, everyone relating to such a powerful donor was aware of the consequences of his disfavor. Smith was their friend and comrade, intimately involved in biracial campaigns for justice starting in the 1830s, but nearly every black man who figures in this narrative needed his money, usually badly. His wealth colored every collaboration. Further, Smith could be ruthless. He was a soft touch, derided by southerners because of his affection for "darkeys," but his perspective on right and wrong was fixed and dogmatic. He constantly chided black men about their perverse fondness for major party politics and applied sanctions, as in his 1839 attempt to suppress the first truly political black newspaper, the *Colored American,* because it published editorials by the Reverend Samuel E. Cornish, an unrepentant Whig.[31]

A final, crucial source is the manuscript U.S. census (and for New York, the state censuses), which allowed me to construct collective profiles of the black political class for many of the locales examined here. Taken collectively, these prosopographies suggest new conclusions regarding the economic standing and social characteristics of that class.[32]

———

Historians, including those committed to an inclusive history of who is American, have omitted this history. Why? To ignore the extent to which free black men focused their attention on electoral and party politics may be an unfortunate version of "radical history," as if these men's efforts to vote, caucus, lobby, and maneuver for nominations and offices were mired in forms of false consciousness and their history should be narrated selectively. Or it may simply reflect the discipline's methodological conservatism, wherein scholars operate mainly within a given subfield—political, social, cultural, or some other specialization. It suggests, at the least, how much more investigation needs to be done as we move past the recuperative phase.

For myself, the origins of black politics lie in the unresolved character of the American Revolution, not simply in 1800, 1865, or even 1965, but in the present we inhabit. For that reason, I believe this history is fundamentally timely. James Oakes has suggested that a "new version of early American history is still being constructed. . . . The outlines are becoming clear and they look something like this: the American Revolution set in motion a long and bitterly divisive struggle over slavery and race in the new nation." This book intends to fill in a significant ellipsis within that long struggle.[33]

Chapter 1

Our Appeal for a Republican Birthright

The Ideology of Black Republicanism before the Civil War

We are Americans. We were born in no foreign clime. . . .

    We have not been brought up under the influence of other, strange, aristocratic, and uncongenial political relations. In this respect, we profess to be American and republican. With the nature, features and operations of our government, we have been familiarized from youth; and its democratic character is accordant with the flow of our feelings, and the current of our thoughts. . . .

    We call upon you to return to the pure faith of your republican fathers. We lift up our voices for the restored spirit of the first days of the republic— for the great principles then maintained, and that regard for man which revered the characteristic features of his nature, as of more honor and worth than the form and color of the body in which they dwell. For no vested rights, for no peculiar privileges, for no extraordinary prerogatives, do we ask. *We merely put forth our appeal for a republican birthright.*

—*Convention of the Colored Inhabitants of the State of New York, To Consider Their Political Disabilities,* "Address to the People of the State of New York," August 1840

One hundred thirty-four men representing thirty-three of New York's fifty-seven counties issued this manifesto, which became the exemplary black political text of the antebellum era. Their unprecedented gathering built on a statewide drive for "equal suffrage" in the nation's premier electoral arena. Probably authored by the Reverend Henry Highland Garnet, a twenty-four-year-old fugitive and now a well-educated Presbyterian minister, their "Address" set the terms for the next generation. Aimed at white Whigs and ex-Federalists for whom Jacksonian Democracy meant mob rule, it mixed familiar patriotic tropes with nativist disdain for those "born in foreign climes" who had brought with them "strange, aristocratic" habits. The "appeal for a republican birthright" reminded New Yorkers that black men voted in the Empire State from 1777 until 1821, when most were disfranchised by a "freehold" property qualification, meaning real estate worth $250. Above all else, however, Garnet evoked a declension from "the pure faith of your republican fathers." With supreme audacity, he claimed for black men the Revolution itself, "the first days of the republic" and "the great principles then maintained," before modern corruption set in.[1]

Yet this first statewide black convention, the dozens of conclaves it inspired over the next twenty years (statewide meetings from Maine to California, including ten in New York), and the movement represented at those conventions, are now largely unknown, eclipsed by stories of slave resistance and the Underground Railroad. Consider the best-known speech by a black American in this period, Frederick Douglass's 1852 "What to the Slave is the Fourth of July?": "What have I, or those I represent, to do with your national independence? . . . I am not included within the pale of this glorious anniversary! Your high independence only reveals the immeasurable distance between us. . . . The rich inheritance of justice, liberty, prosperity and independence, bequeathed by your fathers, is shared by you, not by me. . . . This Fourth of July is *yours*, not *mine*." Douglass's antipatriotic excoriation has been quoted dozens of times as the authentic voice of black alienation. How could it be otherwise? How could black people declare *"We are Americans"* as long as slavery drove the nation's economy, laws, and politics? From that perspective, Garnet's 1840 address seems irrelevant or deluded. What kind of "republican birthright" could a slave hope to share?[2]

In defiance of the notion that slavery defined African Americans, northern free men of color, led by self-emancipated slaves like Garnet and Douglass, made the claim "We are Americans" over and over. Douglass's 1852 oration was a provocation, one of the things he did best. By then, he was an international celebrity whom even Negrophobes flocked to see. Speaking to whites in Rochester, he pressed upon them the republic's inevitable damnation while slavery persisted. They wanted Douglass's lash, and they got it, in high style. But his views speaking to his peers one year later conformed exactly to the terms Garnet set out in 1840. In July 1853, Douglass presided at the Colored National Convention in Syracuse, and chaired the committee that drafted its address "to the People of the United States." This document repeated the 1840 language almost verbatim, with a dollop of aggressive Protestantism for good measure: "We are Americans, and as Americans, we would speak to Americans. We address you not as aliens or exiles . . . [but] as American citizens asserting their rights on their own native soil. . . . We ask that, speaking the same language and being of the same religion, worshipping the same God, owing our redemption to the same Savior, and learning our duties from the same Bible, we shall not be treated as barbarians."[3]

To make sense of these addresses, we must stop thinking of men like Douglass as simply defiant fugitives and firebrand agitators—the way they portrayed themselves for popular consumption, on the lecture circuit in countless towns and dozens of "slave narratives." We should see them instead as they knew themselves: as leaders of an embryonic political class several thousand strong, ambitious for office, practical men focused on issues of organization, program, alliances, and advancement—on politics, in sum.

Usually, politics consists of two interlocking activities: *speaking*, in person and via printed texts, and *assembling*, to act together through voting, rallying, canvassing, and lobbying. This chapter focuses on the former, on antebellum African Americans' political speech, for two reasons. First, because the study of discourse (what people say to or about their political friends and enemies) is the quickest way to get at the premises of their practice. Second, because a common discourse was the only truly national component of black political culture before Reconstruction, when black men first entered Congress. I call this discourse "black republicanism," meaning a version of American republicanism, the lingua franca of all who operated within the public sphere. As Daniel Walker Howe underlines, "Republicanism was a paradigm for understanding political life and a vocabulary for explaining it." Everyone "spoke the language of republicanism. Every group interpreted it in a distinctive way and claimed to be its rightful heir." To position themselves within the national family, African Americans needed to prove that they were, save a few details of phenotype, identical to other Americans. They could not afford the separateness of the Quakers or the Jews, the nation's two recognized ethnoreligious minorities. The only vehicle for their claim was a republicanism incorporating the distinctly American notion of birthright, meaning citizenship defined entirely by nativity and thus common ownership in a country. But birthright alone was not enough, so black men added their own ascriptive Americanism, a quasi-ethnicity made up of Protestant evangelicalism, speaking English, and military service, all the attributes marking them off from recent Irish and German immigrants. Together, these assertions of inclusion based on native birth, nativism, and "colored patriotism" constituted the positive ideology of black republicanism. This chapter examines how over time these tropes forged a reliable synthesis available to black men and their white allies as a vernacular politics focused on voting and electoral participation.[4]

There is one more piece to the argument, hard to comprehend in retrospect. Antebellum persons of color did not share today's overriding focus on race. When they declared "We are Americans," they meant it without qualification, as an unremitting assault on assertions of difference between them and other native-born citizens. Backed by an elite cohort of whites, and sometimes even by ordinary white men, African Americans confronted the new scientific racism by deriding the notion of race as no more than a foolish obsession with "complexion." Their republicanism was emphatically nonracial, in ways that confound our contemporary understanding of blackness and whiteness. And as we shall see, noting the possible permutations of any man's complexion, whether "yellow," "black," "tawny," or "dark," was a key weapon in black republicanism's arsenal.[5]

"Of Aliens and Natives"

Black republicanism germinated in the distinctly American assertion of birthright citizenship, and the special authority the new republic conferred on the native-born. Birthright citizenship has a complex history in Anglo-America. Its roots are feudal, in the equal status assigned to all His or Her Britannic Majesty's subjects, as famously defined by William Blackstone in 1765: "The first and most obvious division of the people is into aliens and natural-born subjects. Natural-born subjects are such as are born within the dominions of the crown of England, that is, within the ligeance, or as it is generally called, the allegiance of the king; and aliens, such as are born out of it." Even more well-known was his assertion that the "spirit of liberty is so deeply implanted in our constitution, and rooted even in our very soil, that a slave or a negro, the moment he lands in England, falls under the protection of the laws; and so far becomes a freeman." This passage is commonly cited for its antislavery content, but its key affirmation is the civil equality of subjects.[6]

The free people of color gained distinct advantages from subjectship's basis in English common law, how that legal category evolved in British North America, and the emergence of a historically unprecedented conception of citizenship during and after the Revolution. At each stage in this process, juridically recognized and widely accepted precedents ignored race, emphasizing either religious affiliation, as in the transnational categories of Protestant, Catholic, and Jew, or the centrality of jus soli, the birthright of the native-born. Taken together, these precedents pointed toward citizenship for free black men as "Christians" (meaning Protestants) born in America, regardless of how that logic offended many whites' social, cultural, and political sensitivities.[7]

The original law of subjectship, as codified in *Calvin's Case* (1608), asserted an irrevocable relationship between the monarch and all born under the king's authority, mandating both obedience ("ligeance") and an entitlement to protection. In England, however, the native-born were privileged over everyone else. Well into the nineteenth century, English law recognized a hierarchy of legal rights and privileges "between natural-born subjects, naturalized subjects, and 'denizens,' all of whom were members of the community in some sense" (a denizen being "a sort of halfway member who ranked above the alien yet somewhat below the native-born or naturalized subject").[8]

In this legal order, free black men born in British North America could only have been subjects at the time of the revolutionary separation. They had no other possible identity, however much slave-state (and sometimes free-state) jurists and legislators strained to create one out of nothing after 1820. Therefore—and this was the crucial leap of republican faith—they became citizens with all the other "inhabitants" who had heretofore been British subjects. At least that was how Garnet, Douglass, and dozens of other black men asserted their citizenship after 1790, the earliest form of "originalism" in American political discourse.[9]

Their argument gained force through how subjectship itself was radically simplified in the thirteen settler colonies strung along the Atlantic. Their legislatures and courts "moved toward a new understanding of the ties that bind individuals to the community," reversing the English focus on an alien's existing allegiance by birth, privileging instead his choice of a new allegiance that was "volitional and contractual." Through a squatter's rights revision of the common law, colonial assemblies promulgated much looser definitions of subjectship, enacting "generous naturalization policies that promised aliens virtually the same rights as Englishmen." Desperate to attract new members, especially young men, these precarious statelets voided the three-part distinction between the native-born, denizens, and naturalized persons which remained central in British law, and regularly granted political rights to foreigners, sometimes even Catholics and Jews, so that "the distinctions between the various categories of subjects—still quite real in the mother country—began to soften and blur." In British North America, immigrants made an easy transition from aliens with full property rights to naturalized subjects with full political rights. Periodically, particular colonies enfranchised whole groups of Protestant foreigners (Huguenots or German Moravians), and men of foreign birth held high offices out of reach in England. British authorities tolerated these colonial aberrations, just as they accepted that a much higher proportion of men voted than at home. To regulate the promiscuous granting of equal rights to immigrants, a 1740 Act of Parliament declared that seven years of continuous inhabitance "in any of His Majesty's colonies in America," accompanied by the usual oaths to prove Protestantism (Jews and Quakers exempted), would guarantee subjectship, with "the certificates of naturalization issued under this statute . . . recognized in all courts throughout the British Empire." Almost 7,000 persons gained subjectship in this fashion, with lists sent to the Board of Trade each year, mainly from Pennsylvania. By midcentury, therefore, "England's hierarchical ranking of natives, naturalized aliens, and denizens [had] collapsed in America"—they were subjects all, including those of a darker hue.[10]

The second instance of black men benefiting from white men's politics came during the Revolution. As the provisional American governments separated from Great Britain, they necessarily avoided distinguishing between different groups of subjects. The Founders could not afford to permit anyone under their fragile dominion to opt out of the new category of "Americans." All Americans were required to transfer their "ligeance" as subjects; thus all Americans (other than slaves) became citizens, whether born in England, or creoles born of English parentage, or people who had arrived freely (or not so freely, as indentured servants) from somewhere other than England. A single, inclusive nationality was asserted on June 24, 1776, when Congress created American citizenship by revoking allegiance to the king, declaring "that all persons residing within any of the United Colonies, and deriving protection from the laws of the same, owe allegiance to the said laws, and are members of such colony." Underlining the capaciousness of this new citizenship, in 1781 Congress welcomed "all such foreigners" deserting from the British forces, and specified in Article Four of the Articles of Confederation that "the free inhabitants of each of these states (paupers, vagabonds, and fugitives from justice excepted) shall be entitled to all privileges and immunities of free citizens in the several states."[11]

It is impossible to read these stipulations covering "*all* persons" and "*the* free inhabitants" as implicitly excluding one complexion or phenotype. Nonetheless, many scholars have presumed or implied that the refusal to exclude people of color by inserting the word "white" was an accident or oversight. That argument was easily disposed of at the time of *Dred Scott*. Republicans from Supreme Court Justice Benjamin Curtis to Abraham Lincoln pointed to incontrovertible evidence that during the 1770s and 1780s (but not the 1790s) the Founders rejected attempts to racialize American citizenship. In February 1859, during a House debate over admitting Oregon as a state, the Ohio Republican John A. Bingham asked the rhetorical question "Who, sir, are citizens of the United States?" and answered, "First, all free persons born and domiciled within the United States—not all free white persons, but all free persons," adding that it would be useless to look "in the Constitution of the United States, for that word white; it is not there." He then made the central point, that "the omission of this word—this phrase of caste—from our national charter, was not accidental, but intentional," and sent his colleagues to the appropriate page in the *Journal of the Continental Congress*, documenting how "on the 25th June, 1778, the Articles of Confederation being under consideration, it was moved by delegates of South Carolina to amend the fourth article, by inserting after the word 'free,' and before the word 'inhabitants,' the word 'white,'" so as to limit "the privileges and immunities of citizens in the several States . . . exclusively to white inhabitants." South Carolina's motion was defeated, with eight states opposed and only one agreeing. As he stated, "this action of the Congress of 1778 was a clear and direct avowal that all free inhabitants, white and black, except 'paupers, vagabonds, and fugitives from justice,' (which were expressly accepted,) were 'entitled to all the privileges and immunities of free citizens in the several States.'"[12]

Bingham was hardly the first to cite this precedent. William Jay described it in his influential 1834 pamphlet, *An Inquiry Into the Character and Tendency of the American Colonization and American Anti-Slavery Societies*, William Yates noted it in his 1838 treatise *Rights of Colored Men to Suffrage, Citizenship, and Trial by Jury*, and in 1845, New York's annual black suffrage convention also cited and quoted the 1778 decision. Over many decades, Federalists like John Jay and his sons, Whigs like Thaddeus Stevens and William Seward, and finally Republicans like Salmon P. Chase, Seward, and Stevens referred to nonracial citizenship as established fact. The most authoritative assertion came from the nineteenth century's leading legal theorist, James Kent (known as Chancellor Kent because he held New York State's highest judicial office from 1814 until Van Burenites abolished it in 1822). In the fourth edition of his *Commentaries on American Law*, published in 1840, Kent explicated the status of persons of African descent, asserting, "Citizens, under our Constitution and laws, mean free inhabitants, born within the United States, or naturalized under the laws of Congress. If a slave born in the United States be manumitted, or otherwise lawfully discharged from bondage, or if a black man be born within the United States and born free, he becomes thenceforward a citizen." Kent's reasoning was similar to that of North Carolina's chief justice, William Gaston, who declared in 1838 that since free persons prior to the Revolution were British subjects, they all became citizens of North Carolina during the Revolution, and further, since the laws recognized only "two classes; free men or aliens" other than slaves, "slaves manumitted in the state became freemen, and, therefore, if born within North Carolina were citizens of North Carolina and all free persons born within the state were citizens of the state."[13]

However eminent, these jurists were also in the minority; Kent in 1821, and Gaston in 1835, protested in vain their states' decision to abolish or severely limit black suffrage. Legislators and judges subscribing to the Jacksonian creed vehemently disagreed with these old Federalists attached to the English common law. A parallel, racialist legal tradition steadily accumulated precedents, culminating in Taney's insistence that persons of African descent had always been outside of American nationality, alienated by racial antecedents which made their place of birth irrelevant. The record was rife with pronouncements like that of the 1838 Pennsylvania supreme court decision disfranchising black men, which asserted that the state's founders had "settled the province as a community of white men," and it necessarily remained so. Anyone who chose to could find ample precedents for denying black citizenship: that the first Congress in 1790 had limited naturalization to "white" immigrants, and the Militia Act in 1792 excluded men of color from military service, followed by repeated denials of passports by secretaries of state of all parties. The exclusion of black men from juries was automatic, even where they voted, and in defiance of common-law definitions of Anglo-American subjectship, state judges either resurrected "denizenship" or invented new categories of lesser citizenship, asserting that the fact of prejudice against people of African descent exempted them from birthright citizenship. Most damningly, after 1800 every new state but Maine reserved the vote to white men, and the majority of those founded earlier took it away from black men.[14]

Antebellum Americans thus lived with unresolvable contradictions. The Constitution avoided the word "white" and only obliquely referenced slavery, while fundamentally guaranteeing the peculiar institution. It never defined citizenship other than its "implicit assumption that birth within the United States conferred citizenship," since the qualifications for the presidency did "encompass all persons born within the states and territories of the new nation." The deepest contradiction derived from Article Four's specifying "The citizens of each state shall be entitled to all privileges and immunities of citizens in the several states," suggesting each state could decide citizenship within its borders, and confer some kind of national citizenship "in the several states" by doing so. If one state refused to recognize citizens of others as citizens of the United States, that was an act of nullification, which is why "the question of black citizenship took on tremendous political and ideological significance." By their very existence, free black people forced the ambiguity of American citizenship into the open, compelling the white South to make new law and break with existing precedents. By 1859, southerners had gone far down that road, with a Mississippi judge snorting that while Ohio might confer "citizenship on the chimpanzee or the ourang-outang," his state had no obligation to honor it. It was a short step from Taney's repudiation of the common law to the Confederacy's vice president, Alexander Stephens, repudiating the Declaration of Independence in his "Cornerstone" speech of March 21, 1861.[15]

The Constitution's "privileges and immunities" could never be adequately defined because the Founders had collectively punted. Instead of a clear juridical definition of national citizenship, Americans improvised from a radically simplified version of English subjectship eliminating the category of "denizen," so the colonies-turned-states of the 1780s had no lower rung to which they could assign free blacks. Attempts to define "citizens" as "white" were defeated during the Revolutionary era, including Massachusetts in 1778,

Pennsylvania in 1780, and New York in 1785. The new nation's subsequent political evolution in 1790–1800 ensured that this deliberately decentered understanding of citizenship was fixed in place. As Douglas Bradburn has explained, attempts by Federalists like Chief Justice John Jay to assert that "the nation came before the states" and, as Jay put it, sovereignty resided "in the people of the nation" with all "equal as fellow citizens," were decisively defeated by the Jeffersonian ascendance. Citizenship after 1800 remained "a largely local affair, not because of any inevitability but because the Federalist vision was defeated, rejected, and overthrown. The Federalists looked toward uniformity of national citizenship and the eventual disappearance of all regional and ethnic differences," which Jeffersonians of all persuasions rejected.[16]

Expatriating Free People

How do we get from 1790, when the free black population was not quite 60,000, with little public identity other than petitioning in New England and Phillis Wheatley's politicized celebrity, to 1840, when the self-named "Colored Americans" numbered 386,000, led by men like Garnet insisting on his Americanness? By the early 1800s free men of color had jumped into electoral politics in port cities from Boston and Portland to New Bern, North Carolina. We have little access to these men's thoughts, however, other than a few petitions to Congress and occasional pamphlets or sermons. There is no substantive documentation of black men defining themselves as native-born Americans until 1817; the evidence suggests they found it unnecessary to make that claim before the advent of the Society for the Colonization of Free People of Color of America (usually known as the American Colonization Society, or ACS). The evolution of black politics took place in counterpoint to this formidable enemy.

In December 1816, a cross-section of eminent whites held a meeting in the Capitol chaired by George Washington's nephew, Supreme Court Justice Bushrod Washington, to publicly launch the ACS, one of the most powerful philanthropies in U.S. history. Its stated purpose was to solve the problem of slavery and the larger problem of African Americans as a disruptive, alien body by organizing their return to Africa. Through the Civil War, colonization remained the respectable alternative to emancipation, endorsed repeatedly by state legislatures and presidents, consuming vast amounts of time and money. Yet colonization was never more than a nostrum, given that the slave population grew to almost four million by 1860, while the ACS sent approximately 13,000, mainly southern freedpeople, to its various settlements (including the Republic of Liberia, founded in 1847), where many died of disease and the survivors created a racial dictatorship over indigenous Africans.[17]

The creation of the ACS defined the direction of black politics. If whites agreed that white and black were irredeemably antagonistic, birthright citizenship became irrelevant, and a mix of complexion and custom overruled law, auguring *Plessy v. Ferguson*'s dictum that "legislation is powerless to eradicate racial instincts or to abolish distinctions based upon physical differences." Yet black opposition to colonization was neither immediate nor foregone. The ACS's respectful approaches, offering to share leadership in redeeming Africa, drew in much of the North's tiny black elite. In January 1817, Philadelphia's people of color met to consider large-scale emigration, a plan drafted by their leaders, including the wealthy sailmaker James Forten and Bishop Richard Allen, founder of the African Methodist Episcopal (AME) Church, in conjunction with the famous New England seafarer Paul Cuffe. To Forten and Allen's shock, their proposal was vehemently repudiated by a crowd of 3,000 gathered at Allen's church. As elaborated in chapter 2, the meeting voted unanimously to denounce the ACS's plan "to exile us from the land of our nativity," declaring that "WHEREAS our ancestors (not of choice) were the first cultivators of the wilds of America, we their descendents [*sic*] feel ourselves entitled to participate in the blessings of her luxuriant soil, which their blood and sweat manured; and that any measure, or system of measures, having a tendency to banish us from her bosom, whould [*sic*] not only be cruel but in direct violations of those principles, which have been the boast of the republic." The collective memory of that decision generated a politics that was unambivalent about whether the people of color were "Americans." After 1817, black men confronted the ACS's intended denaturalization by insisting on their birthright and a loyalty grounded in the soil. When Bishop Allen convened the first black convention in 1830, its official "Address" assailed the ACS in nearly identical language, that "we who have been born and nurtured on this soil, we, whose habits, manners, and customs are the same in common with other Americans, can never consent to take our lives in our hands" by accepting voluntary deportation.[18]

The Road to *Dred Scott*

Between black Philadelphia's 1817 rejection of colonization and Justice Taney's 1857 denial of any citizenship for African Americans, blacks' status as native-born citizens intruded repeatedly upon conventional politics. The next major instance came during the Missouri Crisis's second stage in 1820–21, revolving around a provision in Missouri's constitution barring "free Negroes and mulattoes from coming to and settling in this State, under any pretext whatsoever," which excluded at least 92,273 citizens of the northern states, in clear violation of Article Four. Northern politicians made this provision a rallying cry for their states' authority to confer national citizenship. Pennsylvania Representative Joseph Hemphill, one of the few remaining Federalists, stated plainly: "If being a native, and free born, and of parents belonging to no other nation or tribe, does not constitute a citizen of this country, I am at a loss to know in which manner citizenship is acquired by birth." His declaration was amplified by a coordinated bipartisan front from Upper New England, speaking in both houses in December 1820.[19]

The Missouri Crisis had barely ended before New York's Constitutional Convention in fall 1821, at which Martin Van Buren's Bucktail Republicans disfranchised most black voters via an onerous property requirement. Prominent Federalists and Clintonian Republicans dissented, asserting the inviolable linkage of nativity and suffrage, with John Jay's son Peter declaring, "No man, no body of men, however powerful, have the right to do wrong" by barring "free born natives of its soil" from New York's polls because of their "complexion." Senator Rufus King, the sole signer of the Constitution present, stated plainly, "As certainly as the children of any white man are citizens, so certainly the children of the black men are citizens." Their arguments were quoted for decades, as was the ardent racial populism of the Van Burenites claiming that black voters were the former slaves and present tools of Federalist aristocrats, "whose shoes and boots they had so often blacked."[20]

Like the proverbial tar baby, the "privileges and immunities" clause kept exposing a fundamental tension between "the States." It was key to guaranteeing equality within the confederation but at odds with the slave states' ever-intensifying need to police all people of color. The South faced a political impasse. To recognize free black men as juridically equal was unthinkable, yet to deny the rights of men recognized by their own states as citizens was a standing insult to "Northern rights," equal to assigning legal disabilities to Jews or Catholics who otherwise voted, traded, contracted, and held office in their home states.[21]

In 1826, Gilbert Horton of Westchester County, New York, was imprisoned as a fugitive slave in the District of Columbia, and Judge William Jay, another son of the Founder and a pillar of the Protestant philanthropic establishment, led a successful campaign lobbying Governor DeWitt Clinton "to demand from the proper authorities the instant liberation of Horton, as a free citizen of the State of New York." This effort was a prelude to decades of interstate battles. As antislavery became a force in northern politics, governors with abolitionist sympathies defied the "Slave Power" by defending the rights of their black citizens, including refusing requests for extradition and overruling warrants granted slave-catchers.[22]

Equating native birth with citizenship helped a new generation of black and white abolitionists define African Americans, whether free or enslaved, as citizens unjustly deprived of their rights. In 1827, "Africanus" in the *Genius of Universal Emancipation* rebutted the ACS's insistence that free people of color were "natives, and not yet citizens" by avowing his patriotism, that "born in the United States it would be very unnatural for me to have no love for my country." In that same year, a petition to Congress from Pennsylvania, using a model drafted by Benjamin Lundy, the *Genius*'s editor, and endorsed by the American Convention for the Abolition of Slavery, "argued that every African American born in America, slave or free, was a 'natural born' U.S. citizen," via the Constitution's bar on any "attainder of blood." In 1828, the Reverend Hosea Easton told black citizens in Providence that "they are Americans, and perhaps distantly related to some of the white members [of churches], by reason of the brutal conduct of their fathers," and examples abound of black ministers and leaders echoing this claim. The discourse of birthright citizenship clearly influenced William Lloyd Garrison. In his first speech as an abolitionist at Boston's Park Street Church in 1829, he insisted that almost all of "our colored population were born on our soil and are therefore entitled to all the privileges of American citizens." In his 1832 *Thoughts on African Colonization*, he announced that the "sacred duty of the nation" included not merely emancipation but "to recognize the people of color as *brethren and countrymen*" and the 1832 constitution of the New England Anti-Slavery Society called for "instant recognition of EVERY American-born citizen, as a countryman and brother!" By mid-decade, the discourse of fellow-Americanism was second nature to Garrisonians; in 1835, Theodore Weld drafted a petition for Ohio's female abolitionists, asking for emancipation in the District of Columbia, which had them "plead . . . on behalf of a long oppressed and deeply injured class of native Americans."[23]

By the late 1830s, therefore, a united front encompassing Garrisonians, increasingly assertive black leaders, and some northern politicians, usually Whigs with New England roots, affirmed that black people possessed equal rights with other Americans, and certainly more rights than immigrants possessed. Some of the rhetoric affirming jus soli shocks even today. Scholars who claim that only a few radical whites advocated interracial equality should examine the scorn for racialism expressed by John Quincy Adams as a Massachusetts representative in Congress. He provoked southern congressmen in 1837 by presenting a petition purportedly from Virginia slaves, reinforcing the determination of slave-state members to "gag" Whigs like him. Adams's response to the Gag, a widely reprinted letter "To the Inhabitants of the Twelfth Congressional District of Massachusetts," asserted that anyone born in America was a "countryman." It is worth quoting: "The sentiment in the bosom of any free American that one sixth part of its country-men, are by accident of their birth deprived even of the natural right of prayer [e.g., to petition] is degrading enough to human nature, but because in one portion of this Union the Native American, becomes by descent from African Ancestry an outcast of human nature, classed with the brute cre-ation, within the boundaries of the State in which he was born, therefore it is beneath the *dignity* of the general Legislative Assembly of a Nation founding its existence upon the natural and inalienable rights of man to listen to his prayer or even receive his petitions is an opinion to which I trust your judg-ments will never assent."[24]

Adams drew upon the arguments made by his friend, Judge William Jay. In 1834, Jay agreed to lend legal expertise to the new American Anti-Slavery Society (as Washington's nephew Bushrod had done for the American Colo-nization Society), publishing a comprehensive *Inquiry Into the Character and Tendency of the American Colonization and American Anti-Slavery Societies* to vindicate the latter. For the first time, a credentialed expert sur-veyed the evidence for or against black citizenship. Much of Jay's reasoning was inductive, citing occasions when attempts to exclude free persons of Afri-can descent from citizenship were defeated in Congress. His conclusion was unequivocal: that if white Americans "admit free negroes to be *men*, and to be *born* free in the United States . . . it is impossible to frame even a plausible ar-gument against their citizenship," quoting his father, the future Chief Justice, from 1785: "I wish to see all unjust and unnecessary discriminations every where abolished, and that time may soon come, when all our inhabitants, of every COLOR and denomination, shall be free and EQUAL PARTAKERS OF OUR POLITICAL LIBERTY."[25]

"Drunken Irishmen and Ignorant Dutchmen"

It would be foolish to deny, however, that many whites scoffed at the cultural authority of the Jays, Adams, and Kent, or constitutional precedents. The no-tion that legal opinions and judicial rulings could guarantee black people's citizenship ignores the populistic, Anglophobic, often savage tenor of the Age of Jackson. Outside of New England and regions populated by Yankees like western New York, Ohio's Western Reserve, and the Upper Midwest, the majority of northern whites found the idea of "black freemen" repugnant or absurd. Rougher medicine was needed to overcome this disposition, and black rhetoric turned steadily harsher. The assertion of a superior status as natives became the drumbeat against immigrants, especially the Irish. One example is a Newark speech by John S. Rock in February 1850, supporting a campaign for black suffrage in New Jersey that was briefly successful with

Whig legislators: "If we, who have always been with you, do not understand something of the regulations of this country, how miserably ignorant are the thousands of voters who arrive in the country annually, who know nothing of this government, and but little of any government!" He derided the entire notion of white "nationality," mocking how "Africa is urged upon us as the country of our forefathers! . . . This sophistry is not designed to aggrandize any but the descendants of European nations: Africa is the country for the Africans, their descendants and mongrels of various colors; Asia is the country of the Asiatics; the East Indies the place for Malays; Patagonia the country for the Indian; and *any place the white man chooses to go*. HIS country!" The dentist, physician, and lawyer Rock was a new type—a flagrantly insolent, well-educated black man, one of a crew of polemicists, including the historian William Cooper Nell, the professional lecturer William Wells Brown, the lawyer and judge Robert Morris, the traveling organizer William J. Watkins, the Glasgow-trained physician James McCune Smith, and the ministers Henry Highland Garnet, Samuel Ringgold Ward, Charles B. Ray, Samuel E. Cornish, and James W. C. Pennington. Together, they gave as good as they got, baiting "ruffians," "Democrats," and "Irishmen," often the same person, as less "American" than they were.[26]

There is no point in listing black men's denunciations of how "miserably ignorant" immigrants were privileged over natives because they did so all the time and everywhere. This routine but effective juxtaposition is illustrated by Wells Brown telling Philadelphians in 1854 about his return from an English tour. He encountered two "foreigners" on the boat home, who "when they landed in this country . . . were boasting that they had arrived at a land of liberty where they could enjoy religious and political freedom." They walked into Philadelphia together and "hailed an omnibus; the two foreigners got in; I was told that 'niggers' were not allowed to ride. Foreigners, mere adventurers, perhaps, in this country, are treated as equals, while I, an American born, *whose grandfather fought in the revolution*, am not permitted to ride in one of your fourth-rate omnibuses."[27]

But black nativism was qualitatively different in its relative restraint. African Americans refused the Know-Nothings' hysterical conspiracy-mania about Catholics and the sneering, class-ridden Hibernophobia of their Yankee allies. Nor was their disdain for immigrants rooted mainly in competition between fractions of the working class, a "race to the bottom" between unskilled laborers. Focusing on black anger at being pushed off the docks by Irish gangs, or their disgust with the proslavery sympathies of figures like New York's Catholic bishop John Hughes, misses their main complaint—that foreigners immediately gained the rights of citizenship denied to "native-born Americans" with dark complexions.[28]

Nativism thus had specific political uses through which black men cemented their alliances with white men. Well before the Famine drove over a million Irish to America in 1845–52, eminent figures in the American establishment compared the welcome accorded to whites just off the boat with the ill treatment of black Americans. In 1837, New York's newly elected Whig mayor, Aaron Clark, gratified the *Colored American*'s editors by telling the Common Council, "Several thousands of colored people . . . remain among us, entitled to the protection of our laws," but "the increasing influx of needy emigrants has deprived them, from time to time of patronage, until, in many cases, they are thereby turned into the foulest conditions in life—driven into corners, cellars, and dens, where virtue cannot breathe." He painted a picture of "idle male pauper emigrants . . . furnished with food and fuel" by the prior Democratic administration, "whilst both have been denied to sober colored widows, with small children, in extreme necessity."[29]

After 1840, the invidious contrast between immigrant voters and disfranchised Americans became a staple. Anticipating the defeat of a referendum on restoring equal suffrage in 1846, New York's *Albany Evening Journal*, edited by Thurlow Weed, asked, "Is it just, is it democratic, to admit the *drunken* white *bondman*, fresh from every foreign *lordling* on the globe, to the right of ruling us, through the ballot box, if we at the same time deny that right to those born free among us and reared in the same cradle of liberty with ourselves?" That Election Day, after watching the referendum's defeat, Horace Greeley, editor of the Whiggery's other flagship, the *New York Tribune*, linked native birthright, black patriotism, and Democratic thuggery, describing how "the polls were given up almost wholly to the Adopted Citizens of German or Irish birth . . . called out by skillful appeals to their hatred of the unfortunate African race." Greeley played the veteran's card, the last item in the antiracialist argument, how "hundreds who have not been six years in the country earnestly and abusively" demanded "the disfranchisement of men whose fathers' fathers were born here, and many of them shed their blood for our liberties in the war of the Revolution." As the immigrant vote mushroomed, the invective grew nastier. In November 1860, just before a second New York referendum on black suffrage, *The Independent*, a leading Protestant magazine, put the choice "to be submitted to the Christian people of this State next Tuesday" was "whether this State shall continue to exact of its native colored citizens a money qualification for voting, which it does not demand of the ignorant, foul, priest-ridden Paddy just landed upon the dock at Castle Garden. We say, away with a restriction so senseless, so mean, so unjust." The state went for Lincoln, but black suffrage lost again, and Frederick Douglass knew who was responsible: "drunken Irishmen and ignorant Dutchmen, controlled by sham Democrats."[30]

As these slurs indicate, the equation of native birth and citizenship led to positing a true Americanism shared by all "natives," black and white together. The assertion of an ethnocultural fraternity transcending race sprang from long-term efforts to align the free black community with sectors of northern white society. Beginning in the 1790s, black leaders worked with great resolve to create their own institutions comparable to those run by whites, and comport themselves as self-respecting and respectable, "Americans" rather than "Africans," citizens rather than servants. By the 1830s, they had built a rooted civil society in northern cities and towns, visible in an array of voluntary associations and the bricks and mortar of their churches, with funds banked for mutual assistance. As Garrison reported to an English audience in 1833, "They have flourishing churches . . . public and private libraries. . . . They have their temperance societies, their debating societies, their moral societies, their literary societies, their benevolent societies, their savings societies, and a multitude of kindred associations."[31]

The partisan divisions of the early republic, separating white Americans along ethnic and sectional lines, further stimulated free black people's efforts to blend into the new America. The decades after Jefferson's victory over Adams in 1800 saw the rise of a regional nationalism in the Greater New England extending across upstate New York and the Midwest. Open anti-Southernism was first asserted by Federalists, like the Massachusetts congressman Josiah Quincy's describing "Democracy" as "a great tobacco planter, who had herds of black slaves," but northern Republicans picked it up too during the Missouri Crisis. It resurfaced in the 1830s among antislavery Whigs and abolitionists, the political descendants of New England Federalism. Finally, in the 1840s and 1850s, as Irish votes boosted the Democracy, the black and New Englandish versions of Americanism became explicitly biracial. As eastern cities filled up with strange-sounding Europeans, black men found an audience for their claim to be "Americans" among Whigs and the ultra-republicans in the Liberty Party, founded in 1840.[32]

Readers conscious of the gross racial parodies in the minstrel shows dominating antebellum popular culture are likely unaware of the parallel stream of amused contempt aimed at Hibernians. On stage and in print, Irish-baiting featured "Paddys" whose detestation of black people was portrayed as humorously ludicrous. Josephus Erin O'Riley "loved his country because it was oppressed . . . loved America because it was free, and . . . hated negroes because they were black," as a tale in a New Orleans paper put it. It was commonplace to insert "Dinah," the stock black woman, as in the story of a Paddy tricked into kissing a "a great strong negro wench" and his farcical horror: "Do me eyes desaive me? Am I in me sinsis? Be the rock of Cashel! You're not me *collen baan*—me own Nancy Clancy; but a naygur, as black as the ace of spades, and as ugly as an ourang-o'tang!" Indeed, this word—"naygur," "negur," or "nagur"—was the payoff in many Paddy tales. Even in Ireland, Americans were told, bitter Catholics referred to Oliver Cromwell or the local taxman as a "bloody nagur." Sometimes this became an ironic comment on abolitionism, as in "Paddy in Africa," recounting "a negro celebration" in Ohio at which the speaker impressed an Irishman: "Bedad, he speaks well for a nagur; didn't he, now?" When told the man was "only a half negro," he replied, "Only a half nagur, is it? Well, if half a nagur can talk in that style, I'm thinking a whole nagur might bate the prophet Jeremiah."[33]

This was white man's fun, however. Black editors and orators avoided this crude vernacular; one searches their newspapers in vain for the anti-Irish slurs common to the mainstream press. In print or on the stump, men of color abjured "Paddy" stories, even the word itself, and if they assailed Irish violence, they had a point, as the Irish reputation for brawling was well earned, with organized clan battles ingrained in the island's stubbornly collectivist peasant culture. The closest black men got to the casual bigotry of white nativists was *Frederick Douglass' Paper* reprinting a story on an August First celebration in Ohio where the people of color were "all very well dressed, and well behaved and all perfectly sober. The only absolutely drunken man we saw was an Irishman, who had been led out, and who was very confident that he could whip '*anny Nagur* on the ground.'" African Americans participated enthusiastically in Anglo-America's Protestant culture, with its axiomatic opposition to the ritualistic hierarchy of Roman Catholicism, but they rarely joined in the contemptuous dismissal of "papists."[34]

The furthest extent of black hostility was the outrage felt by the "gentleman of color" Robert Purvis, son of a wealthy Scottish-born merchant in Charleston and his common-law wife, herself the daughter of a Jewish immigrant and a woman reputed to be a Moor. In the 1840s and 1850s, Purvis was Pennsylvania's best-known black leader, living on an estate outside Philadelphia. Phenotypically white but proud of his African heritage, he vented his disgust with "this modern Democratic, Christian Republic" at the Annual Meeting of the American Anti-Slavery Society in 1860, asking, "Who makes your mobs on your canal lines, and in the construction of your railroads? Who swells your mob in your beer gardens, and in your Sunday excursions? Who make your Native and Anti-Native American mobs?" He was "sure, not the colored people! Not the native-born Americans who have tilled your soil in times of war, and whose reward has been disfranchisement and threatened annihilation, but your foreign-born European immigrants of yesterday—men who can't speak your language, and don't respect your laws." Now they were "invested with all the franchise of the country, including that of trampling on the black men," even if they were "the most turbulent and most insolent class of the whole American population." Purvis believed "in the equal natural rights of all men; and hence it is that I protest against the anti-republican and unjust distinctions in favor of a stranger and foreigner against a native-born American, against whom no charge can be made except that of the complexion which the Almighty God has given him." He asserted that men like him were not only Americans, but the best kind of Americans, those who refused to join mobs of any kind. By implication, those others, "the most turbulent and most insolent class," were the worst sort, the dregs—perhaps not "American" at all.[35]

"Brave and Hardy Troops"

After 1815, fewer and fewer black people identified as "African" in other than a nominal sense. Instead, "the *native*-born Colored AMERICAN," as the editors of the newspaper of that name framed it in 1837, became "a 'respectable' alternative to 'African'" and a way of underlining one's birthright against the colonizationists. To be from somewhere, black people inside the United States had to assert they were ethnically "American" by virtue of their habits, tastes, faith, and attitudes. This task their leaders grasped, to forge from a motley collection of peoples a single identity, a "nation within the nation." As James Brewer Stewart explains, the first generation of African American leaders "succeeded magnificently in shaping ethnically diverse groups of urban transients into enduring communities," but this process often required "drastic alterations of identity and allegiance" among "families with bloodlines that had mixed African, Indian, and Euro-American ancestors." They had some advantages: the notion that someone born in West Cork or Dusseldorf, speaking heavily-accented or no English and practicing a heterodox religion, was more "American" than an English-speaking, native-born Protestant did not come so easily then.[36]

To claim birthright over phenotype, black men consciously emulated northern Anglo-America, the "Universal Yankee Nation" spreading westward below Canada. Henry Highland Garnet's 1840 "Address to the People of the State of New York" embodies this reframing, at a time when ubiquitous minstrel shows depicted slaves cavorting and free people of color dressing up like infants on parade. Against these degrading stereotypes, Garnet insisted, "Cut off from the sympathies of our fellow citizens, almost abject in poverty . . . we have nevertheless, by the practical operation of common sense, by habits of industry, and the cultivation of the religious sentiments, been enabled to elevate ourselves above abasement, and possess ourselves of many of the advantages of RELIGION, INTELLIGENCE and PROPERTY." He made sweeping assertions of respectability, that "there are but few families in which books are not a common and necessary commodity. In all parts of the state, from Montauk to Buffalo, literary and debating societies and clubs exist among our people." To this, he added a verifiable fact: "Throughout the State, we have upwards of forty independent religious congregations . . . each with a temple erected to the worship of the Almighty; most with settled pastors under a regular yearly stipend."

No matter how often repeated, however, these litanies of familial probity, Protestant orthodoxy, and self-improvement were hardly sufficient to convince whites that blacks were "fellow Americans." Whether in 1840 or 1940, African Americans remained deeply exotic. Lacking the access to cheap land that enabled the majority of whites to gain economic autonomy, most existed on society's margins. Black men needed a trump card to prove their citizenship. To gain a quasi-ethnic advantage, they invoked the same history as white men after 1775—that they had served their country in wartime, and were thus superior to latecomers.

Black men's references to heroic combat were not easily discounted. Enough whites had seen them in action in 1775–83 and 1812–15 so that even in 1841 an aged "veteran of the revolution" remembered a crucial battle where he witnessed "a regiment of negroes fighting for our liberty and independence—not a white man among them but the officers. . . . Had they been unfaithful, or given way before the enemy, all would have been lost. Three times in succession were they attacked with a most desperate fury, by well disciplined and veteran troops, and three times did they successfully repel the assault, and thus preserve an army. . . . They were brave and hardy troops." By the 1830s, black leaders could list decades of exemplary military service, as well as volunteering en masse during Philadelphia's 1794 yellow fever epidemic, and again during the War of 1812, when 2,500 men of color marched out to build fortifications along the Delaware. A typical instance was *The Appeal of Forty Thousand Citizens, Threatened with Disfranchisement, to the People of Pennsylvania*, issued in 1838 to protest the insertion of the word "white" into the state constitution's suffrage clause. Written by Purvis, its main thrust was revolutionary filiopiety, beginning with an attack on the recent Constitutional Convention: "Was it made the business of the Convention to deny that all men are born equally free, by making political rights depend upon the skin in which a man is born? Or to divide what our fathers bled to unite, to wit, TAXATION and REPRESENTATION?" Following the usual claims for colorblindness at the Founding and the achievements of black Pennsylvanians ("22 churches, 48 clergymen, 26 day schools, 20 Sabbath schools, 125 Sabbath school teachers, 4 literary societies, 2 public libraries, consisting of about 800 volumes, besides 8,333 volumes in private libraries,

2 tract societies, 2 Bible societies, and 7 temperance societies"), Purvis focused on black veterans. He began with Philadelphia congressman Charles Miner's 1828 statement in the House ("The African race make excellent soldiers") and cited delegate Robert Clarke at the 1821 New York convention ("In the war of the revolution these people helped to fight your battles by land and by sea"). Then came the coup, quoting Andrew Jackson's official communiqué hailing his black troops' role in the republic's greatest triumph, the defeat of British regulars outside New Orleans in 1815. Pennsylvania's Negrophobe Democrats must have snorted at reading their hero quoted by a man of color:

> SOLDIERS! When, on the banks of the Mobile, I called you to take up
> arms, inviting you to partake in the perils and glory of your white fellow
> citizens, I expected much from you. . . . I knew with what fortitude you
> could endure hunger and thirst, and all the fatigues of a campaign. I
> knew well how you loved your native country, and that you had, as well
> as ourselves, to defend what man holds most dear, his parents, relations,
> wife, children, and property. You have done more than I expected. . . . I
> find, moreover, among you a noble enthusiasm, which leads you to the
> performance of great things. SOLDIERS—the President of the United
> States shall hear how praiseworthy was your conduct in the hour of
> danger, and the representatives of the American people will, I doubt not,
> give you the praise which your deeds deserve.

Here we see colored Americanism's elasticity, skating over the irregularities in America's racial patchwork, using white men's obsession with "color" to black people's advantage. For decades, men like Purvis made Jackson's paean a staple of their oratory, and "no single historical event outside the Revolution received greater attention from black pamphleteers." In fact, the "Free Men of Color" whom Jackson praised had little in common with the North's "colored Americans." They were either the sons of men who founded militia companies under the Spanish in the 1780s to suppress slave insurrections, or the mulattoes of the "Battalion of St. Domingue Volunteers," exiled from the island's civil wars. As professional soldiers, they spared no effort to prove their loyalty, patrolling New Orleans during the 1811 Pointe Coupée slave rebellion. In 1862, their descendants offered themselves to the Confederacy as "Native Guards." In antebellum America, however, what mattered was the uses to which they could be put in the pageantry of "Colored Americanism."[37]

William Cooper Nell's *Colored Patriots of the American Revolution* in 1855 completed this martial narrative. In over 300 pages, Nell told of black men's unrequited commitment to the republic, cataloguing every instance of military service and raising Crispus Attucks to a position he has never lost as the Revolution's first martyr. For a skilled propagandist like Nell, the Battle of

New Orleans was one piece in a tapestry stretching from Attucks's death under British muskets to the present. He did not fabricate anything out of whole cloth, and backed up his account with copious quotations from respectable sources. Given the public silence over black collaboration with British forces in 1775–83 and 1812–14, Nell was able to present a remarkably one-sided account of the "colored patriots," providing lecture notes and debating points to dozens of white and black men.[38]

Here the realities of American politics aided the black freedom struggle. Southern leaders were acutely alert to how the British could summon a potential reserve army off their plantations. They referred to this danger constantly in private communications between state and federal officials, ordering the disposition of troops and equipment to guard armories, and watching for "British agents" stirring up slaves. In public, however, they maintained a discreet silence. Any discussion of a permanent fifth column might encourage insurrectionary hopes, as confirmed by the testimony of witnesses and informers in the trials of the leaders like Gabriel Prosser and Denmark Vesey.[39]

Who Did Not Enter

As already noted, black women rarely appear in the narrative of black politics prior to 1861 because, like all women (other than in New Jersey before 1807), they were excluded from the public sphere associated with voting, elections, and parties. Certainly, free black women demonstrated social and political agency in the antebellum decades. Inside the separate institutions of black "shadow politics," its churches and benevolent societies, they may even have exerted more power than white women. Martha Jones has documented that black women developed their own movement for rights in the 1830s and 1840s, separate from that pioneered by white women in defining "its objectives relative to the parameters of African American society rather than American society writ large." They sought the authority to participate and the right to preach, with limited success, before retreating into more traditional support for men's organizing, and relief of the suffering, in the 1850s. Attempts to enter the spaces where black men's politics were debated were generally rebuffed. Briefly, at the 1848 National Colored Convention in Cleveland, Frederick Douglass (who had just participated in the Seneca Falls convention) and his associate Martin Delany convinced the assembled men to vote that "we fully believe in the equality of the sexes" followed by "three cheers for women's rights," but that support was short-lived, and conventions in the 1850s repeatedly denied black women the right to attend, speak, and vote. On the streets, black working women were unquestionably militant, raucous, and unladylike, in ways that upset black Whigs like Samuel E. Cornish, but that is a different kind of politics, more akin to what the woman whom John Brown called "General Tubman" implemented—direct action against slavery. A study focused on the partisan and electoral arenas, and entrance into the state via parties and offices, therefore pays little attention to women.[40]

"This Line of Distinction Is So Nice That You Cannot Tell Who Is White or Black"

We have seen how black men asserted their birthright against the spurious citizenship awarded to "foreigners," backing that claim through a narrative of military service. To these arguments for citizenship, they and their allies added the dismissal of race itself as no more than a difference in "complexion."

Most scholarship on antiracialism in the early republic locates its origins in Protestantism's commitment to the absolute brother- and sisterhood of all Christians, if not all human beings. How Protestantism of a certain sort led toward antiracialism is a well-told story, relying on pronouncements by eminent Puritans like Cotton Mather and Samuel Sewall (later chief justice of Massachusetts) expressing their disdain for notions of immutable racial difference. From there historians trace a line to Garrison, Gerrit Smith, and John Brown, for whom the requirements of Christianity necessitated action against slavery by any means necessary—even the dissolution of the Union or armed struggle.[41]

It is a mistake, however, to see antiracialism as proceeding entirely from Protestant universalism, as if only an immersion in austere faith could soak the racism out of white Americans. One did not need to be an evangelical Yankee to find the newfangled ideology of "whiteness" a humbug, a bad and dangerous joke. The modernizing racialism of the Jeffersonian and Jacksonian ascendancies overturned an established social order based on class, defined as a combination of property, education, and perceived status. It also undermined logic, by leveling all white men up or down into a single mass. For that reason alone, as the new race "science" asserting inherent biological characteristics spread in 1830–60, some prominent whites dissented in an earthy vernacular, scorning the notion that "complexion" signified anything more than vagaries of climate, health, or individual heritage.[42]

In his still-invaluable study of "American Attitudes towards the Negro, 1550–1812," Winthrop Jordan traced how pretentions to "whiteness" were mocked by commenting on the "dark" or "swarthy" visages of factional opponents, hinting at the glass houses inhabited by many southern white families. This counterdiscourse extended into the nineteenth century, with black men joining in. Consider again Robert Clarke at the 1821 New York convention, expostulating against inserting "white" into the constitution's suffrage clause, since it was "repugnant to all the principles and notions of liberty . . . and to our Declaration of Independence." He then ceased to speak of "principles" and focused on persons, saying a color bar would be "impractical" given the "many shades of complexion," as some "men descended from African ancestors" were "pretty well white-washed by their commingling," and other whites had a "swarthy complexion." During the same debate, Chancellor Kent spoke in an equally dismissive fashion: "What shall be the criterion in deciding upon the different shades of colour? The Hindoo and Chinese are called yellow—the Indian *red*!" The stenographer underlined his comments, adding an exclamation mark, since Kent had pointed out what perplexes every school child at some point—that Indians were hardly as red as a British lobsterback's uniform, any more than Jefferson or Washington were truly white like rice.[43]

Clarke's use of "complexion" was more than a synonym for "color." Complexion is variable and personal. It can be affected by personality (think of the words "apoplectic" or "splenetic" applied to ill-tempered white men), season, health, tastes in food or drink, and more. Men and women are sallow and pale, rather than white; ruddy or olive-skinned, rather than black. Throughout the seventeenth and eighteenth centuries whites in Anglo-America consistently employed "complexion" rather than "color" or "race" as the best way to describe non-European (sometimes simply non-English) others. The Pennsylvania Emancipation Act of 1780 asserted, "It is not for us to enquire, why, in the Creation of Mankind, the Inhabitants of the several parts of the Earth, were distinguished by a difference *in Feature or Complexion*. . . . We find in the distribution of the human Species, that the most fertile, as well as the most barren parts of the Earth are inhabited by Men of Complexions different from ours and from each other, from whence we may reasonably as well as religiously infer, that he, who placed them in their various Situations, hath extended equally his Care and Protection to all, and that it becometh not us to counteract his Mercies." In 1791, North Carolina's slaveholding legislators agreed, writing into their laws a guarantee of slaves receiving equal treatment in their courts, since a slave was "equally a human creature, but merely of a different complexion."[44]

After 1800, however, the language of difference began to harden, in Europe through the increasing demarcation of "races" rather than nations and peoples, and at home via the wide influence of Jefferson's *Notes on the State of Virginia*, wherein he speculated on the separate, lower humanity of people from Africa. In that context, the trope of "complexion" asserted an alternative understanding of phenotypical difference, authorizing a very republican disdain for it as no more significant than hair color or height. The dismissal of complexional difference was a special feature of William Jay's writings. In his 1834 *Inquiry Into the Character and Tendency of the American Coloniza-tion and American Anti-Slavery Societies*, he observed mordantly, "So far as we are aware, men with red hair are not styled citizens in the laws of Congress, or any of the States," which hardly prevented them voting, adding that "in no country in Europe is any man excluded from refined society, or deprived of literary, religious, or political privileges on account of the tincture of his skin," and "only two" of the original thirteen states "were so recreant to the principles of the Revolution, as to make a white skin a qualification for suffrage."[45]

Judge Jay steadily moved left. On the final page of his 1839 *On the Condition of the Free People of Color*, he asked readers to think of "HE that hath made us, and not we ourselves," and how even the lowliest soul possessed "an imperishable jewel—a SOUL, susceptible of the highest spiritual beauty, destined, perhaps, to adorn the celestial abodes, and to shine forever in the mediatorial diadem of the Son of God. Take heed that ye despise not one of these little ones!" There was something ecstatic in this language, common to white people born again to the realization of human brother- and sisterhood. And as with Gerrit Smith and John Brown, "Bible politics" led inexorably to physical force. In 1845, Jay suggested to a fellow abolitionist that "Whenever any of our colored citizens are imprisoned at the South, on account of their complexion, to seize an adequate number of the citizens of the state committing the outrage, who may be found on our soil, and to hold them as hostages for the liberation and full compensation of said colored citizens." By the 1850s, he was regularly forwarding fugitives to the Albany black leader Stephen Myers, for the latter's very aboveground "railroad." Before dying in 1858, he denounced the *Dred Scott* decision by noting the absurdity of allowing birthright to be overridden by complexion, how "the Laplander, Esquimaux, or Chinese may seek for redress of injuries in the Supreme Court of the United States, but if a native born citizen of the State of New York, an elector, and eligible to the highest offices presumes to seek for justice in the same court, the Judges examine his complexion, and if it reaches within a certain shade of black, he is ignominiously turned out of court, with the intimation that the founders of the Republic regarded people to whom God had given such a skin as void of *all rights*."[46]

The scorn with which Jay referred to "Esquimaux" and "Laplanders" to mock distinctions based on "race" took on a sharper edge in other hands. Needling southern white men about their hidden-in-plain-sight black relations was John Quincy Adams's specialty. In his diary, Adams speculated with relish on the suspect antecedents of southern members of Congress. Publicly he turned that prurience into politics, gleefully proposing in 1842 a "Committee on Color" to investigate all members of Congress "for the examination of their respective pedigrees . . . and in all cases where the parties shall be found to have the least drop of colored blood in their veins, they shall be expelled from office and their places filled by persons of pure Anglo Saxon blood." This sally seems quaint now, when we accept the inviolability of whiteness—that a person really is what he or she claims to be. The possibility of passing back and forth or getting stuck in-between was more immediate then.[47]

Mocking "complexion" was especially useful for African Americans. In one of the first appearances by a black person before a U.S. legislative body, Charles Lenox Remond, son of a prosperous immigrant from Curacao, testified in 1842 against railroad segregation before a committee of the Massachusetts House of Representatives. On returning from the World's Anti-Slavery Convention in London and touring Great Britain, he was Jim Crowed on the Boston-Salem railroad, an opportunity abolitionists' legislative allies used to advantage. Remond's testimony began by declaring he could foresee when in "this city, the Athens of America, the rights, privileges and immunities of its citizens" would no longer be "measured by complexion, or any other physical peculiarity or conformation. . . . Complexion can in no sense be construed into crime, much less be rightfully made the criterion of rights. . . . It is JUSTICE I stand here to claim, and not FAVOR for either complexion." Remond pointed to his traveling in England "without any regard to my complexion," and how he asked the Salem railroad's superintendent "if, in the event of his having a brother with red hair, he should find himself separated while travelling because of this difference, he should deem it just." What if "West or East India planters and merchants should visit our liberty loving country, with their colored wives," or "R. M. Johnson, the gentleman who has been elevated to the second office in the gift of the people?"—was the superintendent "prepared to separate him from his wife or daughters?" The reference to President Van Buren's vice president, who lived openly with his black mistress (whom he called his "wife") and their two daughters, provoked an "involuntary burst of applause, instantly restrained." Remond pressed his advantage: "Sir, it happens to be my lot to have a sister a few shades lighter than myself, and who knows, if this state of things is encouraged, whether I may not on some future occasion be mobbed in Washington street, on the supposition of walking with a white young lady!," leading to "suppressed indications of sympathy and applause."[48]

Seventeen years later, Remond's sister Sarah used "complexion" to batter George Mifflin Dallas, minister to the Court of St. James (another former vice president), for refusing her a passport to go from London to Paris. After the legation's secretary threatened to physically eject her and her sister from his office because Sarah commented, "Thank God we are in a country where our rights are respected," she got the *Philadelphia Inquirer* to publish her letter to Dallas, that "being a citizen of the United States, I respectfully demand, as my right, that my passport be *vised* by the Minister of my country." He refused, and on January 25, 1860 the *National Principia* of New York printed her rejoinder: "You now lay down the rule that persons free-born in the United States, and who have been subjected all their lives to the taxation and other burdens imposed upon American citizens, are to be deprived of their rights as such, merely because their complexion happens to be dark."[49]

Disparaging "complexion" as an all-purpose denial of racialism had specific partisan uses. In a celebrated 1848 speech in Cleveland, William Seward, leader of northern antislavery Whigs, used it to signal his abolitionism. In Seward's words, the United States' "democratic system . . . is founded on the natural equality of all men—not alone all American men, nor alone all white men, but all MEN of every country, clime, and complexion, are equal—not made equal by human laws, but born equal." These claims were intended to reassure Clevelanders they could be antiracial and still vote for Zachary Taylor, the slaveholding Whig presidential candidate, against the Free Soil candidate, Van Buren.[50]

The attack on "complexion" reached its apogee before the Civil War. In 1849, the Massachusetts Whig Horace Mann denounced slavery in the District of Columbia on the House floor by insisting that linking "complexion" to racial subordination posed an imminent danger to "fellow-members," since he had "frequently seen some . . . with a jaundiced skin more sallow and yellow than that of many of a slave . . . in this city." He was "disposed to give a friendly caution to keep their 'free papers' about their persons, lest suddenly, on the presumption of color, they should be seized and sold for runaway slaves. A yellow complexion here is so common a badge of slavery, that one whose skin is colored by disease is by no means out of danger." Sometimes, however, it was merely a joke, as when the eminent Ohio Whig Thomas Corwin, known as "Black Tom" because of his saturnine complexion (he was Hungarian and Armenian), liked to pretend he had been mistaken for a man of color in federal offices. Similarly, when the Republicans in New York's Assembly approved an equal suffrage amendment to their Constitution in 1860, a Buffalo assemblyman, "whose complexion is very dark," explained he "would vote for the measure in self-defense. He was not sure he might not be driven from the polls some time, or possibly be captured by a United States Marshal in pursuit of an escaped chattel."[51]

The leitmotif here was complexion's chimerical quality, how it might depend on diet, season, a propensity for spirits, or the ultimate trickery of sex, who jumped into whose bed. Like Mann, both whites and blacks regularly referred to enslaved people who looked "white" and the whites who appeared yellow, brown, red, swarthy, dark, or even, amazingly, "black." Nor were these necessarily poor whites of uncertain provenance. The nation's most admired statesman was known as "Black Dan" Webster, a sobriquet persisting via Stephen Vincent Benét's story, later a movie, *The Devil and Daniel Webster*. In theory, it referred to his coal-black hair and dark countenance, but by the late 1840s, abolitionists derided Webster's coloring, already further darkened by his propensity for alcohol. At a packed "Anti-Webster Meeting of the Colored Citizens of Boston" to denounce the Fugitive Slave Act in March 1850, the Reverend Samuel R. Ward, a brilliant, coal-black orator, made rich use of this trope.

> There is a man who sometimes lives in Marshfield [site of Webster's estate], and who has the reputation of having an honorable dark skin. Who knows but that some postmaster may have to sit upon [hold as a fugitive] the very gentleman whose character you have been discussing to-night? (Hear, hear.) "What is sauce for the geese, is sauce for the gander." (Laughter.) If this bill is to relieve grievances, why not make an application to the immortal Daniel of Marshfield? (Applause.) There is no such thing as complexion mentioned. It is not only true that the colored men of Massachusetts—it is not only true that the fifty thousand colored men of New York may be taken . . . but any one else also can be captured. My friend Theodore Parker alluded to Ellen Craft [a phenotypically white slave who escaped by dressing up as a Southern aristocrat with her husband William playing the part of a servant]. I had the pleasure of taking tea with her, and accompanied her here tonight. She is far whiter than many who come here slave-catching. This line of distinction is so nice that you cannot tell who is white or black. As Alexander Pope used to say, "White and black soften and blend in so many thousand ways, that it is neither white nor black." (Loud plaudits.)

By then, New York's Liberty Party had already run Ward for the Assembly and secretary of state, and soon he would receive his party's nomination for vice president.[52]

———

Black republicanism was successful to the extent it was commonsensical, whether in a legislative chamber or a local assembly, voiced by a Whig politician or a former slave. Even in small towns, black men hammered home the core points of the 1840 "Address to the People of the State of New York." A November 1848 "Meeting of Colored Citizens" in Columbia, Pennsylvania, decried the "obliteration of rights and privileges, in our persons, that have, from the foundation of the government, been regarded as the birth-right claim of the native-born citizen." This was hardly different from a Connecticut Whig in 1855, backing re-enfranchisement of black men. Speaking in its House, he dismissed a Democrat who pontificated on the "feeling of aversion to the colored race, implanted by nature in man," declaring there was "no reason why the elective franchise should not be extended to native-born Americans, who came here with our forefathers, and assisted us in achieving our liberties, and were acquainted with our institutions. . . . The gentleman . . . was in favor of admitting foreigners of every color except African, though their sentiments were as entirely repugnant to our institutions as light to darkness." These were the terms upon which black men fought for their rights as Americans, to convince fellow Americans of a different complexion that those rights were inalienable. Over seven decades, as the Gordian knot of race and slavery gutted national unity, black men found a niche inside some northern states' politics by insisting on a republicanism that was purer, older, and more authentic than the corrupt contemporary version. They convinced some whites but rarely "won" in conventional terms. Many state courts ruled against black citizenship rights, and when "Equal Suffrage for Colored Men" was tested in state referenda, in state legislatures, and at state constitutional conventions, it went down to defeat year after year. In 1857, the Supreme Court mandated black people's permanent exclusion from the body politic in *Dred Scott v. Sandford*. Thus, this account of how black men used vernacular republicanism to insist on their place in the republic, whether via birthright, antiracialist folk humor, or waving the bloody shirt of military service, has no evident conclusion other than "And the war came."[53]

PART I

Caste versus Citizenship in Pennsylvania

As the first polity in world history to legally abolish slavery, at the Revolution's high tide in 1780, Pennsylvania was an ideal location for developing a robust black citizenship politics. After the Revolution, Philadelphia, the hemisphere's most dynamic entrepôt, became a mecca for the Chesapeake's freed and runaway slaves, and soon boasted the new nation's leading community of free black people. Further, under the 1780 Act of Emancipation and the state's 1790 constitution, African Americans in Pennsylvania were "freemen," citizens with the same legal rights as whites, including the suffrage if they paid the nominal tax required of men twenty-one years old and older.

Citizenship is not a passive or purely ascriptive status, however. The citizenship politics examined in this book manifested itself via continuing assertions, especially voting but also lobbying, petitioning, and protesting. A different black politics matured in Philadelphia (although not statewide), the "shadow politics" of a separate caste, disavowing the rights, responsibilities, and perceived dangers of political citizenship. Instead, black men and women created their own institutional world, which they defended using the courts and inside which they fought for control.

Why did black Philadelphians accept the status of second-class "citizens for protection," in the words of an 1833 *Memorial* to the General Assembly? Philadelphia anchored a vast borderland. Every year for decades hundreds of formerly enslaved people flooded into the city from Maryland, Delaware, Virginia, and rural Pennsylvania. Beginning in 1805, whites proposed measures to ban this immigration and enact a "Black Code" making free people of color a stigmatized caste, as in the South and the new state of Ohio. Black leaders met this threat by focusing on self-improvement and self-control via church, school, and home, while avoiding any hint that black men would engage politically at the polls or in the streets. These leaders feared that the assertion of their political rights would wreck the delicate balance that allowed some to prosper and the rest to survive. They were, indeed, protected by the Quaker elite which governed the colony before the Revolution, and still exerted great weight in legal, business, and political circles, including the Federalist Party and the Pennsylvania Abolition Society, a very effective lobby. The interracial politics of caste thus enforced a class politics within Philadelphia's black folk of middle-class amelioration in the face of lower-class intemperance and indiscipline. Over time these habits of separate development, self-policing, and deference to white protectors developed into a formal antipolitics called "Moral Reform," based on renouncing any explicitly "complexional" political efforts.

The narrative of black Philadelphia takes up chapter 2. It concludes in the 1830s, when the rising prosperity and sheer numbers of black Pennsylvanians provoked a storm of partisan abuse from Negrophobic Democrats eager to cement their southern alliance. In 1837–38, a constitutional convention and the state's supreme court stripped black men of citizenship's central attribute, the vote, even though they had never claimed that right in Philadelphia. By common agreement then and since there is little to say about black Philadelphia after 1838 since their shadow life became self-centered and petty.

There is a problem with this narrative, however: its omission of the significant black communities outside of Philadelphia, who after 1800 constituted the majority of black Pennsylvanians. The extensive scholarship on Philadelphia's "elite of our people" treats that majority as adjuncts, just as the Philadelphians saw them. To challenge that metropolitan perspective, chapter 3 offers a second, less-familiar narrative organized around the mundane politics of voting.

Nearly all scholarship to date has assumed that 1838's disfranchisement was essentially ritualistic, formalizing long-established practices. This assumption is fundamentally inaccurate. A closer examination of the state's history reveals a long history of electoral participation outside of Philadelphia, not as black men but as Pennsylvanians, with a juridical and even cultural identity little different from other native-born "freemen." Black men in some of the state's largest counties voted alongside whites for decades, while in others they were excluded as "illegal voters" on the same dubious grounds as other suspect groups—poor men ("paupers"), immigrants and their sons, and transients whose residency was in doubt. Further, the counties where they voted had a distinctly partisan cast, first as the Federalist rump in a Jeffersonian state and later as bastions of Whiggery or Anti-Masonry. Looking at that history underscores the mistake of presuming black politics originated in antislavery mobilizations. In Pennsylvania like much of the early republic, black electoral participation developed organically as part of the ordinary politics of partisan organizing. Put simply, men of color were present, they were free, and they were native-born, and the opportunity costs of bringing in this group of additional voters were low, until the partisan exigencies of a particular state or county (and the example of others) suggested the viability of driving them out.

The histories traced in chapters 2 and 3 paralleled each other over half a century, rarely intersecting, a dynamic reflecting Pennsylvania's localist, de-centered political culture and the character of its black population, living next to three slave states. A side-by-side narrative is thus appropriate for beginning this book's series of state or regional histories.

Chapter 2

Citizens for Protection

The Shadow Politics of Greater Philadelphia, 1780–1842

We wish not to legislate, for our means of information and the acquisition of knowledge are, in the nature of things, so circumscribed, that we must consider ourselves incompetent to the task, but let us, in legislation, be considered as men.

—James Forten, *Letters From a Man of Colour*, 1813

We ask not for a participation in the councils of the nation, we do not wish to alter any of its laws.

—John B. Vashon, 1828

Your Memorialists . . . appear here in an attitude strictly defensive. . . . They are not here asking for a declaratory law, to secure to them the right of being assessed or voting. . . . The coloured population merely ask to be left as they are. They believe they have constitutional rights, and are sure whatever may be the state of other questions connected with them, that they are at least citizens for protection.

—*TO THE HONOURABLE THE SENATE AND HOUSE OF REPRESENTATIVES OF THE Commonwealth of Pennsylvania, IN GENERAL ASSEMBLY MET: The Memorial of the Subscribers, free people of colour, residing in the City of Philadelphia*, 1833

These epigraphs suggest that the deliberate abstention from active citizenship politics by Philadelphia's black elite reflected a profound caution, perhaps even a deeply held conviction that their people *were* "incompetent to the task" and should be content with being "citizens for protection" under white guardianship. Rather than leading, the Philadelphians lagged far behind smaller communities throughout New England, New York, and even North Carolina that used their votes to acquire power and guarantee protection.

Early on, the top tier of black Philadelphia developed a defensive, sideways style of political action, operating along two axes. First, far away from whites, they practiced "shadow politics," meaning "the mimicry of formal political activity in black-controlled institutions." The results (notably, black churches pastored by black-elected ministers) were visibly impressive. However, these accomplishments depended on a second axis of "deference politics" attaching those men and the institutions they led to white leaders in the Pennsylvania Abolition Society (PAS), who provided legal cover, access to fundraising, expert advice, and protection via interventions in Pennsylvania's legislature and courts. The interaction of these two practices from the 1780s to the 1830s enforced strict limits on black autonomy, until the shadow world of black Philadelphia declined into feuding cliques, as their former protectors died off.[1]

In the Shadow of "The Best Poor Man's Country"

Pennsylvania's free black community developed from the emancipation process that began before 1780, and the ensuing demographic boom of free people of color along the Maryland border, the fabled "best poor man's country" drawing European peasants to its rich farmlands. By itself, the 1780 Act for the Gradual Abolition of Slavery did not generate a large free community. It declared that children born of slave mothers after March 1, 1780 would reach freedom after twenty-eight years of indentured servitude to their owners. Slaves entering the state could not be kept in bondage, their children could not be enslaved, and "no Man or Woman of any Nation or Colour," other than those already enslaved, "shall at any time hereafter be deemed, adjudged or holden, within the Territories of this Commonwealth, as Slaves or Servants for Life, but as freemen and Freewomen." These provisions presumed a generation growing slowly into a bounded freedom, as their indentures matured, while their parents remained chattels for life.[2]

Formal emancipation was one part of an accelerating process of freedom through both social and legal processes. Before the Revolution, heavy taxes made importing slaves unprofitable, and self-purchase became widespread through contracts between master and slave; Richard Allen, the founder of the African Methodist Episcopal church, freed himself by agreeing to pay his owner $2,000 over five years. Some masters felt pressure from the Quakers, who manumitted in large numbers, but many simply wanted to get out with a profit, given how easy running away had become. Many slaves found freedom by simply disappearing into the city, or moving to another county. In densely populated alleys of suburbs like Southwark and Moyamensing, the fugitives built communities congenial to the stranger, as freedpeople did in hundreds of Quaker homesteads to the city's south and west where they constituted a cheap, loyal labor force. In prosperous Chester County, slavery peaked in 1765, when the county held 552 enslaved Africans and thirty-six free people of color, 2 percent of the population. By 1820, only eight slaves were left, but the free community had mushroomed to 2,734, one in sixteen residents.[3]

Although the state had a substantial black population across its entire southern tier, scholarly attention has focused on Philadelphia. Within the city, historians have traced the activities of the literate, socially active, propertied minority, the roughly 20 percent who left some record and are the subjects of this study. Who made up this quintile, and how did they organize themselves? Notably, they were never stratified along strictly class lines. In the words of their principal historian, "Free black leaders were influential because they were skilled and committed" rather than wealthy, and ordinary tradesmen featured prominently, while some well-off men led entirely private lives. Neither skin color nor free origins conveyed special status. Many leading men were former slaves and black, rather than "brown" and freeborn, and a notable fraction came from outside the United States, including a Francophone group, part of the influx of Saint-Dominguan refugees in the early 1790s. Like the emerging black petty bourgeoisie in other states, they performed personal services in businesses connected to hair-grooming, as perfumers, cake makers, caterers, and "sweeps" directing teams of boys up chimneys. These occupations relied on expertise rather than capital, and depended on individual patronage rather than a mass consumer base; unlike small-scale shoe or textile production, the classic locations for early capitalist ventures into manufacturing, none were available for industrialization. It is easy to caricature this master-servant ethos—curling the hair of genteel families, cooking for their banquets, driving their carriages; the banker Nicholas Biddle even composed an "Ode to [Robert] Bogle," celebrating his caterer. At best, this species of employment fostered an intimate personal politics, useful for passing information, rumors, and hints. At worst, patron-client relationships underline the black elite's profound dependence on friendly whites.[4]

Above these small entrepreneurs, some of whom amassed modest fortunes by real estate speculation and "note-shaving" short-term loans, was an individual embodying black men's highest aspirations. James Forten operated one of the largest sail-making workshops in this key port, employing dozens of black and white journeymen and training the region's "best class of colored youth." By the early 1800s, he was a recognized participant in Philadelphia's mercantile bourgeoisie, associated with the firm of Willing and Francis (whose principal, Thomas Willing, was among the nation's main bankers), and foreign visitors noted his success. Forten stood alone in the nation, however, his only equal Paul Cuffe, the famed Afro-Indian sea captain of New Bedford. These two were singular figures, rather than a bourgeoisie in embryo.[5]

Black Philadelphia's social hierarchy was reproduced across the state, from Lancaster and West Chester out to York, Gettysburg, Harrisburg, and Pittsburgh, each led by a cohort of barbers, caterers, restaurateurs, and the like, with a few ministers at their apex. The class and occupational structure of this upper fifth stayed frozen through 1860, but the condition of the lower 80 percent steadily worsened, with the bottom quarter declining into a lumpen proletariat stigmatized by color—transient, drifting through county poorhouses, sometimes criminal, dying early. In Lancaster or York in the 1850s, as in Philadelphia earlier, black social mobility was limited to those day laborers or carters who set up as small tradesmen. The northern United States was transforming, led by market-oriented farmers and a new manufacturing sector, but men of color were excluded from these forms of capital accumulation. In 1820, the white and black middle classes were relatively similar in property and occupations, but by 1860 a significant fraction of whites had built large-scale businesses employing dozens, even hundreds of white men and women as wage laborers. Everywhere, however, in the shops and early trade unions, this working class drew a color line; a national survey for the 1855 National Colored Convention documented hundreds of skilled black men and women who could not find work, including 186 in Pennsylvania alone.[6]

Given these constraints, the self-organization of Philadelphia's black leadership was impressive. In 1787, they founded the Free African Society (FAS) with "the two-fold objects of a beneficial and moral reform society," based in "a love of the people of their complexion whom they beheld with sorrow, because of their irreligious and uncivilized state." Over the next seven years, Richard Allen and Absalom Jones initiated a tradition of community mobilization alternating with deferential negotiation, public service mixed with defiance. Sometime between 1787 and 1792, elders at St. George's Methodist Church relegated worshippers of color to a "negro gallery." In response, Jones and others knelt to pray, resisting physical duress and verbal abuse, until the black Methodists "all went out of the church in a body, and they were no more plagued with us." Allen and Jones then focused on organizing black congregations, resulting in Allen's founding Bethel Church in 1794 and Jones's establishment of St. Thomas's Episcopal in 1795, inaugurating the practice of black-run institutions subordinate to white control. St. Thomas's specified the right to hire its own ministers and that "none . . . but men of colour, who are Africans . . . can elect, or be elected into any office . . . save that of minister," but the Episcopal convention ordained Jones as a deacon on condition that his church was excluded from future conventions. Similarly, the Methodists stipulated that their bishops retained the right to preach in Bethel and to name its minister. It took Allen twenty years to wrest his church away from whites, and black Episcopalians remained vassals within their diocese through the Civil War. These two leaders also organized a massive volunteer effort during the city's yellow fever epidemic of 1793, recruiting black Philadelphians to act as nurses and caretakers. When the editor Mathew Carey attacked them for profiteering, Allen and Jones published the first text copyrighted by Americans of color, *A Narrative of the Proceedings of the Coloured People during the Late Awful Calamity in Philadelphia, in the Year 1793.* By erecting churches and getting them chartered by the state, leading civic campaigns, and publishing pamphlets, the Philadelphians made themselves leaders of the nation's free people of color, then emerging as a self-conscious group united across distance. Their next steps between 1797 and 1801 suggested a move into citizenship politics, but the response was so repressive that such hopes were shelved.[7]

Until the late nineteenth century, other than voting, petitioning was the essential political act—a right enshrined in the Constitution and taken seriously by legislative bodies, which allocated much time to receiving and referring petitions to committees. In January 1797, every member of Congress understood the significance when Philadelphia Republican John Swanwick presented a petition from four former North Carolina slaves, now in his city. They asked Congress to facilitate manumission and prevent kidnapping of free people, asserting, "We cannot claim the privilege of representation in your councils, yet we trust we may address you as fellow-men, who, under God, the sovereign Ruler of the Universe, are intrusted with the distribution of justice." They denounced slavery, declaring "the unconstitutional bondage in which multitudes of our fellows in complexion are held, is to us a subject sorrowfully affecting; for we cannot conceive their condition . . . to be less affecting and deplorable than the situation of citizens of the United States, captured and enslaved through the unrighteous policy prevalent in Algiers." To compare slaveholders to the "Algerine" states of North Africa, then holding hundreds of white Americans as slaves, was deeply insulting. In debate, Swanwick told the southerners his black constituents had "an undoubted right to petition the House," but their petition was refused 50–33, although a majority of the North's sixty congressmen voted across party lines that black men had free men's rights.[8]

In retrospect, the 1797 petition was a singular instance of militancy. Its successor, the January 1800 "Petition of the People of Colour, free men, within the City and Suburbs of Philadelphia," signaled a retreat. The Quaker Federalist Robert Waln presented this plea, organized by Absalom Jones and signed by seventy-three men. It disavowed any "immediate emancipation of the whole, knowing that their degraded state and want of education would render that measure improper," seeking only "an amelioration of their hard situation," a ban on kidnapping, and "adoption of such measures as shall in due course emancipate the whole of their brethren from their present situation." The one assertion of rights was that "[we] conceive ourselves authorized to address and petition you on their [the slaves] behalf, believing them to be objects of your representation in your public councils, in common with ourselves and every other class of citizens within the jurisdiction of the United States."[9]

There was no more space for debating black citizenship in Congress. After two days of derision by the assembled House, Waln renounced his action and Jones's petition was refused 85–1, anticipating the antiblack racialism of the Jeffersonian era. Afterward, James Forten thanked the arch-Federalist Maine representative, George Thatcher, who had insisted on recording his lone support for black men's rights. Forten's letter evoked a deep resignation:

> WHEN . . . the generality of mankind turn unpitying from our complaints, if one . . . commiserates our situation, endeavours all in his power to alleviate our condition, our bosoms swell with gratitude. . . . We, therefore, sir, Africans and descendants of that unhappy race, respectfully beg leave to thank you for the philanthropic zeal with which you defended our cause. . . . We derive some comfort from the thought that we are not quite destitute of friends; that there is one who will use all his endeavours to free the slave from captivity, at least render his state more sufferable, and preserve the free black in the full enjoyment of his rights.

In New England's ports where black men voted in some numbers (Boston, New Bedford, Salem, and Portland), Forten's letter was disseminated by Federalist editors. Especially striking is its last reprinting in January 1802 in Baltimore, where black men had been disfranchised: "Will any one shew us a composition of Mr. Jefferson, equal in correctness and elegance to the address of C. J. Forten [*sic*], in this day's Anti-Democrat?" As with Richard Allen's 1799 eulogy to Washington (see below), Federalists enjoyed baiting southern "nabobs" through a black man's voice.[10]

Scholars describe the 1797 and 1800 petitions as indicating waning antislavery sentiment in Congress, but most political action took place in the states. Here black Philadelphians also attempted citizenship politics, but the rebuff came from their supposed allies. In January 1800, Pennsylvania's men of color petitioned their legislature to be assessed a special tax "for the purpose of emancipating the slaves within this commonwealth," still numbering 1,706 mostly in the border counties of Adams, Cumberland, Franklin, Westmoreland, and Lancaster. This was a canny notion, absolving the state of slavery at no cost. No debate between pro- and antislavery factions was necessary, allowing the free people to lead in emancipating their enslaved brethren, a powerful precedent. A bill implementing this request passed overwhelmingly in the House, but lost in the Senate because the Pennsylvania Abolition Society objected to its legitimizing slavery, hoping for a judicial decision declaring it unconstitutional, as in Massachusetts. PAS members also wanted to keep black men in their place; as a jealous rival later put it, they thought "that every measure concerning the blacks which did not originate from them was mistaken."[11]

These 1800 petitions were the last time for many years that Pennsylvania's men of color directly advanced their interests. Between 1801 and 1812, Philadelphia's black leaders cultivated their congregations, their businesses, and a charitable network of benevolent societies. This retreat was a response to mounting white fears of southern black migrants. The year 1805 saw the first of many attempts to legislate formal restrictions, accompanied by a "gradual tendency to a state of apathy" among the members of the PAS because of "the success, rather than the misconduct of the Society." Increasingly, white men claimed that former slaves, "freed from the shackles, but not from the vices of slavery" naturally became criminals and paupers. Philadelphia newspaper coverage suggests how black people operated in the public sphere, very cautiously: the July 1804 advertisement for an "African Free School" announced that a committee headed by Allen would establish one "for such as may be unable to pay for their own education"; a February 1807 notice of "a meeting . . . at the house of the Rev. Absalom Jones, to take into consideration the distressed situation of those who have suffered by the late fire" by raising money from whites; on January 1, 1808, the day the slave trade became illegal, resolutions from a May 1807 meeting to "tender to the mild government under which we live, and the friends of humanity in general our grateful acknowledgements"; in August 1810, the announcement of a Union Society "For the Establishment and Support of a School or Schools, and for improving the condition of the Coloured People," with Jones as treasurer, giving "the public an opportunity to subscribe such sums as their humanity and ability may induce." Against this were a few, scattered reports of aggressive self-assertion by plebeian black men, as in 1808 when a group "violently assaulted and abused the Mulatto, who on Monday last, performed the office of hangman to the negroes who had been convicted of the murder of Mrs. Crofts." A more notable instance was July 4 and 5, 1804, when up to 200 men formed companies, and marched through the city with cudgels to celebrate Haitian independence, "damning the whites and saying they would shew them St. Domingo." Unlike in New York and New England, however, Philadelphia developed no tradition of black parading, in part because local Federalists avoided recruiting black men. There were no meetings of "colored electors," or public black opposition to legislation curbing immigration and curtailing their rights—the PAS took care of all of that.[12]

The only formal protest came late, in a plaintive tone. The War of 1812 spurred intense concern about increased black immigration. Philadelphia's city council and mayor petitioned the legislature that "the number of negroes in the city was 9672 on record, and 4000 runaways not on record, who were becoming nuisances. The petitioners prayed for a law that all people of color should be registered; that authority should be given to sell for a term of years the services of those of them who were convicted for crimes, and that a tax be levied on them for the support of their own poor." Before the PAS blocked this move, with a memorial advocating for "our African fellow citizens . . . a large portion of them are entitled to the reputation of respectable, industrious, and useful members of society," Forten published a series of anonymous *Letters From a Man of Colour*, first as a pamphlet and then in the Federalist *Poulson's American Advertiser*. Ever since, they have been lauded as assertions of black humanity: "The dog is protected and pampered at the board of his master, while the poor African and his descendant, whether a Saint or a felon, is branded with infamy, registered as a slave, and we may expect shortly to find a law to prevent their increase, by taxing them according to numbers, and authorizing the Constables to seize and confine every one who dare to walk the streets without a collar on his neck!" They were also deeply circumspect. At no point did Forten describe his achievements as a Revolutionary veteran and businessman, or that men like him were not "poor Africans" but native-born Americans; his anonymity underlines their restraint, whether because Forten foresaw retaliation or through an excess of gentility. Most fundamentally, they were politically abstentionist. Thirty-three years after emancipation, Pennsylvania's principal black leader forswore participation in elections and any "wish to legislate" since "we must consider ourselves incompetent to the task," while avowing, "There are men among us of reputation and property, as good citizens as any men can be, and who, for their property, pay as heavy taxes as any citizens are compelled to pay." The best explanation for this reticence is fear. In the sentences following the word-picture above, Forten imagined himself compelled to register and then chased down the street by thugs and constables, shouting, *"Hoa, Negro, where is your Certificate?"* If that was how this celebrated "gentleman of color" envisioned his future, his reserve is understandable.[13]

Having barely evaded proscription, black Philadelphians were eager to again prove their worth. After the British burned the nation's capital on August 24, 1814, Philadelphia's official Vigilance Committee invited every civic, religious, and ethnic group to spend a day building earthworks on the Delaware. Forten's associate Russell Parrott published a notice in *Poulson's* notifying "The Men of Colour of the City and County, that have volunteered their service for one days labour on the fortifications . . . that the committee of defence have appointed Wednesday, the 21st" as their day, asking "Those Gentleman that have men of colour in their employment . . . to suffer them to join their brethren in this laudable undertaking." Four hundred marched out, one of the larger contingents. Certainly, this was a small victory, allowing Forten and his allies to proclaim their patriotism as they had in 1793. But it also marked them as separate and inferior—despite proposals from whites, including a Frenchman's offer to raise a "Black Legion," men of color were excluded from the militia musters whose notices crowded the papers.[14]

Shadow politics did produce lasting gains. The social activism of black traders, artisans, and skilled workers forged a civil society boasting dozens of institutional nodes, all visible in the buildings they erected, their dignified presence on the streets, and constant fundraising campaigns. Without this base, the state's free people of color would have remained a caste of pauperized menials, like their Deep South counterparts. Shadow politics constituted an implicit challenge to the rising racialism, a mirror to mock its pretensions.

Displays of Mutual Deference

When black leaders did engage with whites, it was usually via a racialized version of "deference politics," the traditional patronage rituals of gentlemen and ordinary men in colonial America. Deference brought alliances demonstrating that the people of color were not disposable, warding off legislative, physical, and juridical attacks. But deference also brought severe restraints, not just avoiding electoral politics, but the ceding of control over black life. Habits of deference shaped the world of shadow politics, which often proved less autonomous than hoped for then or claimed later.

The forms of deference are defined by those who extend guarantees of safety and succor: in this case, a group of patrician merchants and lawyers who set the boundaries within which black people lived postemancipation. These men traced their roots to the Pennsylvania Society for Promoting the Abolition of Slavery, the Relief of Free Negroes Unlawfully Held in Bondage, and for Improving the Condition of the African Race, founded in 1775. Usually known as the Pennsylvania Abolition Society (PAS), this was the early republic's preeminent abolitionist organization, leading a national network across the Upper South and North, the American Convention for Promoting the Abolition of Slavery and Improving the Condition of the African Race. "A virtual who's who of prominent citizens," the PAS structured black-white relations in Pennsylvania through vigilant defense of the black populace, acting as "a legal aid system" throughout the Chesapeake by "using loopholes, technicalities, and narrow legal opinions to liberate African Americans on a case-by-case base." In the half-century after 1780, people of color had every reason to accept the PAS's embrace, even if it insisted upon their abstention from political agitation. Indeed, the poorest black people had the most reason to follow the society's direction.[15]

This is the conundrum of antislavery in early national Pennsylvania: it centered the nation's abolitionist movement, but relegated black people to the sidelines. The thousands of formerly enslaved people in Pennsylvania were wards to be cared for and supervised. Their views were not solicited; their opinions were not published; they were not invited to attend, let alone speak at, PAS meetings. Relations with Pennsylvania's black community were the province of a Committee of Inspection designed to "superintend the morals, general conduct, and ordinary situations of the Free Blacks, and afford them advice and instruction, protection from wrongs, and other friendly offices." Over decades, these gentlemen convened meetings in black churches and walked into hundreds of black homes to hand out pamphlets and give counsel on learning rectitude, given black people's "natural propensity to thoughtlessness and amusements."[16]

Pennsylvania's African Americans thus operated in a social space defined by highly effective patronage and explicit segregation. Whether this system reflected what we call racism or the Friends' separatist imperative combined with "Quaker patriarchalism," a "worldview . . . in which the morally enlightened and educated hoped to control the lower order, regardless of color," is difficult to say. What is clear is that the politics of deference functioned very well. Black men regularly appealed to the public for funds, founding churches and societies with white support, and the PAS secured state charters for those institutions with the attendant legal protections from the General Assembly. Indeed, in 1810, with the state overtaken by a bank frenzy, a parody in *The Tickler*, America's first satirical newspaper, named prominent whites and blacks as directors of the "Angola Bank," with "Richard Allen, Esq." as "cashier, bakause he is so good a hand at collecting and taking care of de money."[17]

Beyond what the PAS delivered materially, public association with these bourgeois gentlemen had subversive implications, suggesting that class-based markers of status might efface "complexion." Forten, Allen, Jones, and the several dozen other leaders demonstrated in their persons the ideological rewards of a politics of deference. For workingmen of any race to see a man of color accepted as a gentleman by white gentlemen, as when "a number of the most respectable merchants" called "to congratulate and drink punch with" Forten on his 1809 marriage, was a powerful statement of possibility. All black men, regardless of their wealth and culture (the two standards for a gentleman, his propertied independence and good manners) were beneath the white gentry. But whether a sufficiently well-off, couth, literate black man was beneath all white men was still undecided. This fragile bridge of cross-racial gentility would not survive—even in the early 1800s it wore thin on Phila-delphia's streets, where urchins felt free to harass men like Forten. When a deferential politics of class operated, however, it gave deference a certain sweetness, the hope of social mobility, if a man could acquire the right bear-ing, clothes, and speech, ultimately the furniture, books, silver, and polite children that bespoke a gentleman; one thinks of Garrison writing in 1832 (while staying with Forten's aristocratic son-in-law, Robert Purvis), "There are colored men and women, young men and young ladies, in that city, who have few superiors in refinement, in moral worth, and in all that makes the human character worthy of admiration and praise." Long after Andrew Jack-son's Democracy swept away the politics of gentility, a white man remem-bered he had "scarcely ever seen . . . a more interesting gentleman, in elegance of person, ease and agreeableness of manners, together with fluency and per-tinence in conversation," as Forten.[18]

While Philadelphia's black elite avoided the polls and the raucous pro-cessions, dinners, and ceremonies characteristic of the Jeffersonian era's party battles, deference occasionally provided opportunities for partisanship. Like most propertied black men, their sympathies were Federalist. In early 1800, that party's editors noted with satisfaction the Reverend Richard Al-len's solemn eulogy to Washington, "the sympathising friend and tender father," who had "watched over us and watched our degraded and afflicted state with compassion and pity." Allen made the politics of his praise explicit by hailing the Founding Father's posthumous manumission of his bondspeo-ple: "He dared to do his duty, and wipe off the only stain with which man could ever reproach him. . . . The bread of oppression was not sweet to his taste, and he 'let the oppressed go free'—he 'undid every burden'—he pro-vided lands and comfortable accommodations for them." Widely excoriated as "Tories" due to the Alien and Sedition Acts, Federalists appreciated Al-len's calling the general a friend of equal rights, but white "democrats" were unlikely to be impressed by his suggestion that black people understood "the propriety and necessity of wise and good rulers . . . and of submission to the laws and government of the land," the Federalist virtues.[19]

This chimera of biracial Federalism had serious costs. There was a basic difference between the postrevolutionary deference politics of white and black in Philadelphia and traditional practices. Scholars argue over how much colonial politics depended on voluntary deference, but all agree it revolved around Election Days. In the 1760s, when Washington first ran for office, he lined up endorsements by his county's grandees, asking them to cast the first votes on his behalf, while paying for enormous quantities of alcohol to "treat" the few hundred electors. After the Revolution, in New England, New York, New Jersey, and North Carolina, interracial politics included going to vote with white "friends" and marching in Federalist parades. For reasons peculiar to Philadelphia, black men were excluded from electoral bargaining there. This norm was apparently established early on, other than isolated instances of "Negro voting" in the 1790s and early 1800s. Influential Federalists used every means to free slaves in transit and protect fugitives, but the assessors they elected left black men off the city's tax rolls, thus ensuring they could not vote, and PAS leaders, all Federalists, counseled avoiding the polls (the mechanics of disfranchisement are examined in chapter 3).[20]

What did black Philadelphians achieve by their strategies of separation and supplication? The 1833 *Memorial* quoted at this chapter's opening declared, "The coloured population merely ask to be left as they are," and, regarding voting rights, "We will let this sleeping question lie, we seek no more." These statements and many like them suggest the black elite believed the protections they gained far outweighed the uncertain possibilities of full citizenship. They could anticipate some measure of fairness in the courts, and when Federalists ran the city (most of the time through the 1820s), they were assured of police protection, despite the many poorer whites who liked roughing up black people and kidnappers ready to abduct black children. Most importantly, when Republicans proposed legislation making their caste status de jure, restricting the right of free movement and selling people of color convicted of crimes, they could rely on Federalists in the PAS to bottle up those bills.[21]

Out of the Shadows: A Brief Efflorescence

Why were men like Forten so careful for so long, given that obscurer, poorer black men in other states organized as voters, spoke out against their oppressors, and paraded with banners and swords? Certainly, the numbers, visibility, and location of the Philadelphians made them a larger target, which, combined with the constant influx of black countrypeople from the greater Chesapeake, excited a level of white animus not felt in New England or New York. Only briefly in 1816–17 did the mask of deference fall away, with the elite shaking off old habits under massive plebeian pressure, briefly assuming a defiant stance. That this assertion of forceful autonomy was short-lived does not vitiate it as a watershed acknowledged by whites and other free people of color.

By 1816, black Philadelphia was the capital of free people of color in the North and Upper South: in religious terms, through Richard Allen's African Methodist Episcopal (AME) Church; economically, through the prominence of Forten and other entrepreneurs; culturally, via the regular issuing of sermons and addresses matched only by New Yorkers. Allen, Forten, and Absalom Jones were the nation's best-known black men other than Paul Cuffe, poised to extend their model of institutional base-building regionally, with black men in eastern Pennsylvania, New Jersey, Delaware, and Maryland consciously emulating Philadelphia. The AME's expansion marks this spread of influence. By 1822 the denomination had grown to over forty churches in the middle Atlantic states and southward, and by the 1850s, it included hundreds of congregations as far as California and Canada.

Black Philadelphia was indeed impressive—larger and richer than other communities, an entire civil society built upon deep connections to eminent whites. The best historian of black life in rural Pennsylvania reports every southeastern town replicated Philadelphia's class structure—a tiny group of prosperous families, followed by a larger stratum of property-owning artisans, below them farm and day laborers (renters but also church members), and finally a bottom layer, perhaps 15 to 20 percent, of indigent paupers. In the smaller towns, ties to whites were often familial—the same Quakers who manumitted a black family continued to exercise care over them.[22]

Two victories marked this period of open defiance in 1815–17, with black Philadelphians rejecting white authority in fundamental ways. After years of striving for independence, in January 1816 Bishop Allen used the courts to wrest his Bethel Church (its property and the right to direct its affairs) away from white Methodists. This was unequivocally political, to claim an autonomous space, even if it did not translate into ongoing citizenship politics. Even more dramatically, the intended fruit of biracial deference politics, a transatlantic settlement project directed by white and black elites, was stopped cold in January 1817. Soon after the American Colonization Society was founded in the nation's capital, thousands of black Philadelphians, summoned by Forten and Allen to Bethel to approve its program, shouted down their leaders in favor of staying put and claiming their birthright. Again, this was emphatically political, pushing the existing leadership into a much more resolute position; again, no citizenship politics followed in its train.

Allen's triumph over the Methodist hierarchy demonstrated how an all-black association might claim power in the larger world. Before and long after 1816, "Mother Bethel" was Philadelphia's preeminent black institution, built brick by brick by Allen. Its history documents the purposeful dance between deference and defiance, separation and inclusion. Like other African American churchmen of the founding generation, "the still largely unappreciated black founding fathers . . . a group of mostly young men who became the rootstock of postwar black society," Allen could not have initiated his spiritual empire via complete independence. He needed a regular Protestant ordination; no black minister wanted to be derided as an ex-slave exhorter, untutored and countrified. Ordination as a deacon by a white denomination was a political negotiation, resting on their supervision over church property and preaching. Allen conceded all this in 1796, when Bethel was named a Methodist congregation with Articles of Association specifying white control, including naming its minister. In 1799, he publicly affirmed this subordination by publishing those articles. But in 1807, Allen "unequivocally repealed white economic and clerical authority" by promulgating an "African Supplement" to the articles. From here on, a war of attrition simmered, escalating to physical confrontation. In 1812, white Methodists began legal moves to reassert authority over what was now one of the city's largest churches—Bethel's tithes were a valuable asset. Allen was a redoubtable opponent, having built community support, political capital among whites, and financial resources. The contest came to a head in 1815 with suits and countersuits. In January, after he expelled a founding trustee, Pennsylvania's Supreme Court ruled against Allen in *Green v. The African Methodist Episcopal Society*, but in doing so the court recognized Bethel's independent legal standing. Allen then enlisted leading lawyers (David Paul Brown, Israel Ingersoll, Horace Binney), preparing a showdown. For years, Methodist leaders had tried to claim their right to preach at Bethel. When they made another push in spring 1815, worshippers blocked the aisles, and the Methodists put the building up for sale. Allen was the first bidder on June 22, paying the sheriff $9,600 accrued from his decades as a successful businessman. After another legal battle, including charges that Bethel's parishioners were "armed with deadly weapons to prevent me from officiating there," a Methodist official returned on December 31, 1815; preaching from the aisle, he was drowned out with "a violent shout or ecstasy." The next day, the Methodists applied to the state supreme court for a writ of mandamus, but the court affirmed Allen's authority, accepting Binney's argument that white Methodists had no "right to the pulpit of Bethel, contrary to the wish of the society. This was the decided opinion of the judges. The judge further asked, what profit might be expected by forcing himself upon them contrary to their wishes; and that they held too high a hand over the colored people." Soon after, Allen called together four congregations from Philadelphia's hinterlands to found the AME (the second black denomination, as the small, Delaware-based African Union Church was founded two years earlier).[23]

Clearly, the AME did constitute a new "bastion of black power," in Richard Newman's words, and the mass repudiation of colonization at Bethel in January 1817 further shifted the political trajectory. Black Philadelphians earned a permanent place in history by a "rigid defense of their rights" and the solid front against the ACS they maintained thereafter. Colonization posed a seductive threat. Its stated purpose was to redeem America's people of color by encouraging them, if free, or requiring them, prior to manumission, to populate the society's coastal settlements. Once in Africa, supplied with farming and trading implements, they would erect a colored America-in-Africa. Certainly, many northerners imagined that steadily reducing the slave population would cut the Gordian knot of slavery. But southern colonizationists like Henry Clay declared from the outset that the society's purpose was to rid the nation of a dangerous element, the free people of color.[24]

Throughout the antebellum period, colonizationism functioned as "a kind of national therapy" for the problem of black people in America. Endorsed by Congress, state legislatures, eminent ministers, judges, and philanthropists, it claimed to further emancipation while promulgating a discourse of black criminality and vice, asserting free people of color were responsible for their own plight. In retrospect, its claims were patently ridiculous: first, that money would be found to buy and settle millions of impoverished former slaves on a hostile shore; second, that a mass of supposedly shiftless people shipped nearly 5,000 miles to a "native" land they had never seen would build a Christian republic like Vermont. The colonizationists' self-deception was always evident, but their cause functioned as a grand diversion. Exposed to "relentless and withering opposition" by almost all African Americans, some whites broke with the ACS, but that realization came late. In its first fifteen years, the ACS drew in the North's benevolent elite, including future abolitionists like Lewis and Arthur Tappan, Gerrit Smith, James Birney, and the young editor William Lloyd Garrison.[25]

For black Americans, the ACS marked both crisis and opportunity. Many northern colonizationists were sober men, ministers who viewed colonization as a responsibility akin to rescuing prostitutes or drunkards. They recognized the value of black support and approached Captain Paul Cuffe of New Bedford, who had long traded with Britain's Sierra Leone colony. Cuffe believed in redeeming Africa through commercial exchange and selective emigration, ideas he had floated with British abolitionists in 1811. In 1813–14, he founded auxiliaries of the British-based African Institution in New York, Boston, and Philadelphia. The ACS hoped to forge a coalition with Cuffe's project, while leveraging federal support. Cuffe recruited Forten and Allen. Evidently, the ACS's offers were quite substantial. At Forten's 1842 funeral, his son-in-law Robert Purvis declared that "this society of innate wickedness" declared "he would become the Lord Mansfield of their 'Heaven-born republic,'" a powerful incentive, given that "Lord Mansfield" was a trope for both imperial authority and a sweeping emancipation.[26]

At first, the prospects for an interracial colonization movement seemed excellent, but press reports on the ACS's December 1816 meeting in Washington generated suspicion because of the slaveholders present, and Henry Clay's address stressing the society's intent to "rid our own country of a useless and pernicious, if not dangerous portion of its population," while avoiding "any question of emancipation." Washington's black community published a defiant "Counter-Memorial," challenging the ACS on the grounds of birthright citizenship, and Forten wrote Cuffe that "the People of Colour" in Philadelphia "were very much fritened."[27]

Here Forten's public and private stances diverged. For the next half-century, black politics' founding narrative recounted how in January 1817 Forten and others convened a meeting at Bethel to consider "the propriety of remonstrating against the contemplated measure . . . to exile us from the land of our nativity." As Forten eloquently remembered in 1835, the crowd of 3,000 unanimously shouted their opposition with "one *long*, loud, aye, TRE-MENDOUS NO" shaking the rafters. There is no doubt the meeting vehemently rejected the ACS. Unknown until scholars unearthed the Forten-Cuffe letters was Forten's proposing an alliance with it. Writing Cuffe, Forten recounted his chagrin at the response, with "not one sole . . . in favour of going to Africa," and his resolve to keep his head down: "they will never become a people untell they com out from amongst the white people, but as the majority is decidedly against me I am determined to remain silent."[28]

With Cuffe dead by September 1817, and the ACS's increasingly apparent Negrophobia, Forten turned wholeheartedly against it. The "Spirit of '17" became part of abolitionist folklore, recounted over and over. In subsequent years, colonizationists recorded many polite but scathing rebuffs by Forten. How do we square this legend with Forten and Allen assenting to a scheme of denaturalization and emigration? What matters most is how the event was understood contemporaneously. The Bethel meeting was universally recognized as African Americans' collective insistence that they *were* "Americans," disdaining any permanent "African" identity. As traced in chapter 1, the claim that since their "ancestors (not of choice) were the first cultivators of the wilds of America, we their descendents feel ourselves entitled to participate in the blessings of her luxuriant soil, which their blood and sweat manured" became the basis for a nationwide citizenship politics. The attempted accommodation with whites, tacitly renouncing American citizenship, also matters, however, as an indication of why Philadelphia's elite never forged a viable stance other than deference. Over the next forty years, emigration's siren song—to Haiti, Canada, some unsettled western territory, Trinidad, once again West Africa—exerted a special fascination in Pennsylvania, suggesting a deep-seated ambivalence. Never participating in ordinary politics, unlike black men in New York, New England, Ohio, and the rest of Pennsylvania, the Philadelphians never saw themselves as part of the nation. Many scholars have detected the seed of a separatist nationalism in Forten writing Cuffe, "they will never become a people untell they come out from amongst the white people," but the more appropriate word here is pessimism, a dystopian perspective informing both will and intellect. If Forten's group were nationalists, their nationhood was conservative and quietist, resembling their orthodox Quaker patrons' resolve to being "in but not of" the world. Out of solidarity or prudence Forten assented to the January 1817 declaration, "We never will separate ourselves voluntarily from the slave population in this country; they are our brethren by the ties of consanguinity, of suffering, and of wrongs," but there is no evidence he or other Philadelphians anticipated any emancipation in the foreseeable future. Ultimately, the inability to move beyond affirming the "Spirit of '17" was disastrous. Masses of working and poor people need leaders. Either they produce those leaders themselves, or they accept leaders from another class. In the absence of either, those masses are left defenseless, as was the case in Pennsylvania for forty years, while younger elite members followed in Forten's footsteps, from austere self-respect into isolation and decline.[29]

The 1820s: "Citizens for Protection"

For the moment, however, Philadelphia's leaders continued to decisively repudiate deference. In August 1817, Forten and his younger colleague, Russell Parrott, convened a second meeting against colonization, issuing *An Address to the Humane and Benevolent Inhabitants of the City and County of Philadelphia*. In 1818, Forten lobbied the PAS-led American Convention of Abolition Societies' annual meeting, which agreed to refuse endorsement of the ACS. In 1819, the *Resolutions and Remonstrances of the People of Colour Against Colonization on the Coast of Africa* reiterated the "unanimous and decided disapprobation" of "the respectable inhabitants of colour in this city and county." The ACS's founder, Rev. Robert Finley of New Jersey, deemed their opposition so significant that in mid-1818 he pseudonymously published a series of heavenly "Dialogues, Between William Penn, Paul Cuffee [*sic*], and Absalom Jones" in the *Franklin Gazette*, imagining a scenario wherein the revered Quaker founder, aided by the black Quaker mariner, persuaded the just-deceased Reverend Jones to reverse his opposition to colonization.[30]

Outspoken denunciations of colonization had no equivalent locally, however, where caution remained the norm. Presumably inspired by the new spirit of self-determination, a few well-born young black men initiated a politically consequential organization—the African Fire Association (AFA), a volunteer fire company. In an era when fire companies competed with militia musters as forms of masculine public display, this was an audacious assertion of equality. White Philadelphians' outrage at the prospect of uniformed men of color pulling painted wagons through the streets, fighting for access to the pumps, and standing around drinking grog while their engines doused the blaze, just like white men, was instantaneous. It would not be tolerated.[31]

The response to this disastrous gambit began with a notice in a Republican newspaper: "Those Committes [*sic*] that have been appointed by the ENGINE AND HOSE COMPANIES, to devise the most suitable means of preventing the NEGRO Fire and Hose Companies, from going into operation, will please meet at Stell's . . . this evening," followed by a report on the meeting of twenty-one companies resolving that "the formation of Fire Engine and Hose Companies, by persons of color, will be productive of serious injury to the peace and safety of the city in times of Fire. . . . It is earnestly recommended to the citizens of Philadelphia, to give them no support, aid or encouragement." White patrons of black people responded anxiously, with "Justice" reporting (in the Federalist *Poulson's*) a "great deal of agitation in the public mind." He would "allow due credit to the Men of Colour for their motives, many of them are respectable men and good citizens," but was sure "they will be the first to relinquish . . . when they know that their services are not wanted." Then the shoe dropped: "The young men of the Hose and Engine Companies . . . will not associate with them as companions—their feelings, their education, and their habits, revolt at it, they therefore declare with one voice, that they will resign their post as Firemen, render their Carriages useless, and shut up their engine houses, leaving the whole business to the Men of Colour, and those who chose to support them."[32]

Partisan implications surfaced. The white firemen called on the veteran Federalist mayor, Robert Wharton, already targeted as a proponent of black voting, saying there was "a report in circulation, that he had encouraged the blacks in their undertaking, and assisted them by a subscription." Wharton assured them it was "totally unfounded, and requested them to do him justice in their report." Whether Republicans spread the rumor to discredit Wharton, or he had contributed to the AFA, cannot be discerned. The committee "also waited upon the Chairman of the Watering Committee," who stated that he "had no discretion on the subject, the Ordinance directing them to grant a license to any fire association applying for the use of the plugs," and recommended "a direct application to the [city] councils on the subject."[33]

It ended there. The black firemen published their "deep regret," hoping "to vindicate and relieve ourselves from unjust imputations, and assure [the public] of the rectitude of our intentions, inasmuch as we were influenced solely by a wish to make ourselves useful," adding, "Had we conceived that such dissatisfaction would have resulted, we should not have progressed this far. We are, however, willing to *relinquish our objects*, and hope so in doing, to again merit that confidence heretofore placed in us." The second signer, as secretary, was James Allen, the bishop's son. Perhaps he assumed his social position was at least equal to the white apprentices flocking into the white companies. He had been corrected.[34]

The leadership's role in this episode was abject. Rather than defend their juniors' right to serve, Forten and Parrott called a meeting which noted that "the few young men of color" in the AFA were motivated by "a pure and laudable desire to be of effective service," but "we cannot but thus publicly enter our protest against the proposed measure, which we conceive would be hostile to the happiness of the people of color, and which, as soon as known to us, we made every effort to repress." The visible disjuncture between protests directed to the external world (a pamphlet, a request to editors to publish an address) versus submission in the here and now, set a pattern. Fears of mob attacks may explain a practice of retreat, but it does not explain why no alternative was proposed. The contrast between these two faces of black Philadelphia's politics was reproduced many times. One face was proudly self-respecting. Refusing the ACS meant forgoing the rewards of collaboration: money, financial and personal sponsorships, ultimately even office, as a magistrate, customs officer, or governor of an African settler colony. That Philadelphia's black leaders scorned these sinecures, driving out anyone who succumbed, gained them great credit abroad. New Englanders, New Yorkers, Jerseyans, Marylanders, and Ohioans looked to them for leadership, until the scales finally fell away in the late 1830s. Over time it became clear that the Philadelphians' show of defiance was only one face. The one turned to the white men ruling at home was different: conciliatory, supplicatory, averse to any conflict. Repeatedly, they avowed "an attitude strictly defensive," disclaiming any "slumbering privileges" of citizenship, asking *merely . . . to be left as they are*" as "citizens for protection."[35]

––––––––

The 1820s saw the regularization of shadow politics, as a new generation formed societies, held meetings, and issued addresses. This was the heyday of American voluntarism and Philadelphia's black middle-class joined in with gusto, associating in greater numbers than any equivalent group in the North. Religious and benevolent societies flourished, from five churches in 1813 to sixteen by 1837, and the eleven mutual aid groups quadrupling to forty-four by 1831 and almost 100 by 1837, "a privately supported substitute for the public poor relief system" which "enrolled about 80 percent of the city's black adults." Nor did they avoid political declarations; on the face of it, the Philadelphians were immensely active. As an astute insider put it in 1841, "They never let a subject of peculiar importance to them, that may be agitated in the community, pass without a public expression of their view," while demonstrating an acute "inability to act with efficiency," which "makes but little difference with most of the leading men. A meeting they must have." What mattered was that the Philadelphia elite looked like leaders, rather than actually mobilizing, marching, petitioning, or lobbying, let alone casting the ballots to which they were legally entitled.[36]

How did the black elite engage with the white hierarchy? Two incidents in 1822 exemplify their mix of separatist pride and subaltern cooperation. Both centered on Forten. Soon after that fall's Election Day, the victorious Federalist congressman, Samuel Breck, noted in his diary

> rather a singular circumstance, considering the abject state in which the blacks are held in these United States. A Negro man named Fortune or Forton accosted me in the street by offering his hand to me, which (knowing his respectability) I accepted, when he told me that at my late election to Congress, he had taken 15 white men to vote for me. [He said] In my sail-loft (he is a sailmaker), I have 30 persons at work, 15 of whom are white, the rest coloured. All the white men went to the poles, and voted for you.

Certainly, this incident suggests an assertion of power both personal and political. Forten's biographer argues, "As an employer of white men in an era when secret ballots were unknown, he took part in the political process, albeit indirectly. He paid his workers and considered himself justified in telling them how to vote and accompanying them to the polling-place to make sure they obeyed his orders." What struck Breck was Forten's singularity. He alone among black men could boss white men; if Forten had brought to the polls the hundreds of black men he might have influenced, he would have had real weight. That prospect was impossible, as Breck clarified: "Notwithstanding the laws of Pennsylvania do not forbid it, no blacks vote at elections, at least in the eastern part of the state" as "owing to custom, prejudice or design, they never presume to approach the hustings, neither are they taxed or summoned upon juries or at militia musters." Forten's performance of Federalism was a play of gentility obscuring caste, much like when the lone black pharmacist or teacher in some southern town was permitted to vote during Jim Crow.[37]

This chance encounter initiated an ongoing relationship. A more public event demonstrated again how Philadelphia's shadow politics often translated into enforcing subordination. Earlier in 1822, renewed white hysteria over black criminality led to Forten and his allies meeting at Bethel to set up a thirty-man Committee of Vigilance. The irony here is heavy: in the 1840s and 1850s, black Committees of Vigilance were visible expressions of solidarity with slaves, feeding and clothing runaways, sending them to Canada, defending them with violence and guile. This committee was entirely different. Its mission was to aid the mayor in suppressing black vice, "burdened with shame that [crimes] should have been traced to that unfortunate portion of society to which we belong," promising that, although white-owned "tippling-houses, gaming-houses, petty pawnbrokers" were to blame, as "lovers of order, friends of morality and religion," respectable people of color would cooperate by informing on their own.[38]

The 1820s and 1830s saw more admissions by black leaders that poor black folk were as criminal as whites alleged, a practice of deference with clear returns—protection from the gangs who roamed southeastern Pennsylvania hunting black bodies for sale. In a sense, the political abstentionism of Pennsylvania's elite was justified by how kidnapping trumped disfranchisement. They understood themselves as "citizens for protection" because they desperately needed protection, and black Pennsylvanians did secure impressive juridical and legislative safeguards during this decade in advance of other northern African Americans.

Since the early 1810s, kidnapping of free black people had become a cause célèbre in the Mid-Atlantic states, a chance to assert those states' right to protect their citizens, regardless of complexion. In Pennsylvania, this campaign peaked in 1825–26. Mayor Joseph Watson, like his predecessor Wharton a staunch Federalist, acted forcefully against Delaware's Cannon Gang, which abducted up to sixty minors annually through black and white agents running safe houses and using forged documents. In 1826, Mississippi's attorney general and two planters in that state wrote Watson exposing the gang and hoping that "the coloured people of your City and other places [could be] guarded against similar outrages." Watson pressed for indictments, offered large rewards, and sent the city's high constable to Mississippi, but his city lacked professional police, and the kidnapped children could not legally testify against white men. Eventually ten were recovered, but many more were never found, and the only kidnappers jailed were two black men. The terror felt by thousands of Philadelphia parents underlines why the state's African Americans practiced deference, as the only way to invoke the state's shield.[39]

Well before Watson, the PAS lobbied to bolster the basic rights of black Pennsylvanians, whatever their former status. In early 1820, facing reelection, Governor William Findlay responded by supporting a new "Act to prevent kidnapping," imposing heavy penalties and fines on law officers enforcing the 1793 federal fugitive recovery law—the nation's first "personal liberty" bill. Maryland's legislature was further outraged when a Chester County resident, John Read, killed two Marylanders trying to recapture him in December 1820 and was twice acquitted of murder (he was finally convicted of manslaughter). In 1821–22, Maryland petitioned Congress to act against the "ready protection given to escaping slaves in Pennsylvania" but got nowhere, and two of its legislators were treated roughly while trying to recover chattels in Pennsylvania. Furious lobbying by Maryland led to an 1826 bill in Pennsylvania's General Assembly, based on Delaware legislation mandating a $500–$1,000 fine and up to a year in jail for interfering with recapture, and that "any Negro found without a properly executed pass or unable to give a good account of himself . . . [be] jailed immediately and dealt with as a runaway," while punishing kidnappers with up to sixty lashes, three to seven years in solitary confinement, and hanging for a second offense. Then the Cannon Gang's crimes became known, and the PAS sent Quakers onto the assembly floor to buttonhole legislators. The bill was amended in ways that made it impossible to reclaim fugitives, since "the oath of the owner or owners, or any other person interested, shall in no case be received in evidence," and owners invoking the 1793 statute faced indictment for kidnapping.[40]

Abhorrence of "negro stealers," as even Mississippi's attorney general called them, was akin to deploring murder, rape, or the slave trade—these were clear moral abominations, with no relation to political rights. Indeed, the most influential eyewitness testimony against kidnapping, by the Philadelphia physician Jesse Torrey, endorsed African colonization and treated claims of black citizenship as patently false—they had only "the common privileges of aliens and strangers, or at least of prisoners of war." While the PAS was highly effective against kidnappers, it did nothing to counter Jim Crow's steady growth inside their state. Outside of Philadelphia, people of color faced relentless attacks on their status. Exclusion from inns, restaurants, and public facilities was pervasive by the 1820s, and eastern Pennsylvania's major towns all enacted racial controls unknown in states to their north. York led the way in 1803. Following an arson panic, it expelled nonresident black people and instituted a pass law, requiring people of color to register with the justices of the peace, while keeping in force a 1725 law allowing "counties the right of binding out illegitimate black children, black adults who had committed felonies, and blacks with no visible means of support." In 1820, Harrisburg authorized a white citizens' committee to oversee black neighborhoods, with "an ordinance directing every black arriving in town to register within twenty-four hours in a book kept by the mayor." That year, Lancaster passed a similar "ordinance prescribing regulations concerning free persons of colour," with the mayor issuing certificates and keeping a *Negro Entry Book*. This ordinance remained in force until at least 1849, and was copied by Doylestown, Reading, and Germantown.[41]

In the midst of this repression, Philadelphia's leaders acted, but not against their oppressors; they left politics to the PAS. While abjuring the ACS, Allen and Forten's response to Pennsylvania's tightening vise was to sponsor mass

expatriation to Haiti. This renewed emigrationism underlines their deep ambivalence about American citizenship. Certainly the most anomalous black
project prior to 1860, it was long hushed-up. In the mid-1820s, Haiti was in
desperate economic straits, but enjoying a respite from constant civil wars.
President Jean Boyer wanted skilled Americans to revive the island's economy. His Philadelphia-based emissary, Captain Jonathan Granville, gained
the support of ACS leaders and the powerful Philadelphia financiers Stephen
Girard and Nicholas Biddle. The main impetus came from Allen and Forten,
who formed the Haytien Emigration Society in August 1824, proclaiming
their "peculiar delight to assist a brother to leave a country, where it is but
too certain the coloured man can never enjoy his rights." In early 1825, twenty-
two ships left Philadelphia, bringing thousands of settlers, but the project
quickly collapsed, and by 1826 most of the Americans had returned. The Haytien Emigration Society was ignored in subsequent black debates other than
a cryptic reference by the 1832 National Colored Convention, which "discoun-
tenanced . . . any emigration to Liberia or Hayti, believing them only calculated to distract and divide the whole colored family." Other than this brief
mobilization, Philadelphia's elite were stuck in a time-warp during the 1820s,
oblivious or simply inured to the Negrophobia engulfing them. There were
no recorded calls to action, even as Bostonians and New Yorkers turned
toward aggressive agitation. Were the Philadelphians cautious because they
always had been? Or did their inaction reflect confidence in the PAS's pro-
tective embrace? An examination of three perspectives from the pivotal
election year of 1828, all from New York's *Freedom's Journal*, the first black
newspaper, suggests other explanations.[42]

The first is a letter from John B. Vashon of Carlisle, in the state's south-
center 120 miles from Philadelphia. The son of a prominent Virginian who
fought the Seminoles under Andrew Jackson, Vashon owned a saloon and liv-
ery stable. In the 1830s, he moved to Pittsburgh and became one of Garrison's closest supporters, earning his reputation as a militant abolitionist. In
February 1828, however, he was neither militant nor an abolitionist, and his
letter suggested men like him viewed most African Americans as ill-prepared
for freedom, and, if free, as yet incapable of citizenship.[43]

Vashon began by accepting slavery as a fait accompli: "True it is, that our
race has been doomed to ignominious servitude in this happy land; that
America has been stained by this foul blot on her character; but of this, we
say nothing. The thing is done: all our remarks will not correct it." All he desired for free black men was "to claim some of our rights . . . to have the liberty of expressing our thoughts publicly . . . to be the means of enlightening
some of our unhappy race." Like Forten in 1813, he renounced political engagement: "We ask not for a participation in the councils of the nation, we

do not wish to alter any of its laws." All men of color wanted was "a right and title to use the talent we have received from our Creator." Vashon praised *Freedom's Journal* for counseling the slaves to self-improvement rather than defiance, and what he incorrectly inferred was its disavowal of emancipation, that rather than "endeavoring to sow the seeds of rebellion" and "ripening into revolt those already disaffected . . . you have held out the only means of consolation, viz. the enlightening of the mind." He suggested slaves had "ample opportunities of spending time; which otherwise might be devoted to the most lawless design," and hailed the editors precisely because they did "not propose to alter the relation which exists between master and servant, but to stimulate to higher exertion the latter; to afford materials for amusement as well as instruction, and thus render life more tolerable." "*And thus render life more tolerable*" was bad enough, but he made a worse concession, reiterating the slur that freedpeople were habitually criminal: "The frequency of petty crimes committed by coloured persons proves my position, that unless their minds are enlightened, and made to see the end and consequences of guilt, all attempts at reformation will be useless."[44]

Other public commitments to internal policing could have been excused as necessary face-saving, but Vashon spoke here as a free man addressing other free people of color: he had no need to dissemble. Soon enough, like many he was radicalized by the events of 1829–31—mass expulsion from Cincinnati, the clandestine southern distribution of David Walker's *Appeal to the Colored Citizens of the World*, *The Liberator*'s debut, and Nat Turner's Rebellion. In 1828, however, his acquiescence was published without demur, and there is good reason to think Pennsylvania's leaders shared its gradualism, with no hint of resenting the self-imposed bar on participation "in the councils of the nation."

Clearly, some black Pennsylvanians accepted racial caste, but here an anomalous fact intrudes. In parts of the Keystone State, black men ignored the counsel of nonresistance and marched to the polls alongside their neighbors. In July 1828, a committee of young Philadelphians led by William Whipper, later the leader of antipolitical "moral reform," sent to *Freedom's Journal* their denunciation of a prominent "literary and critical gazette," *The Ariel*. Their tone was sharper than Vashon's, assailing the editor's dereliction from basic republican principles. In passing, they quoted his claim "that the policy adopted by Pennsylvania . . . of encouraging blacks to emigrate into our state, is of most lamentable character. Her laws have offered the fullest protection to the negroes. In some places they are allowed to vote—and in a single township in Bucks county, no less than about fifty votes of negroes are polled." Remarkably, representing a large community a mere day's ride from Bucks County in which thousands of black men did *not* vote, these youth could only add a haughty throwaway—"We would be happy if it were so in this city, until we would have power of keeping such fellows as [the *Ariel*'s editor] from rising to the dignity of a house mercenary." Whipper and his confreres spent their energies during this presidential year founding a "Reading Room Society, for Men of Colour" to aid "our rising generation. . . . We are well acquainted from experience with their present limited opportunities of improvement, and we feel bound to open an Institution, to which they may repair and qualify themselves, for future usefulness."[45]

In 1828, the *Freedom's Journal* cofounder, Reverend Samuel E. Cornish, published a critical assessment of Philadelphia's shadow politics. It began with his oft-quoted observation that "to see the elite of our people" one "must visit Philadelphia, which contains a larger number of them than any other city," praising how they are "more industrious and economical than we [New Yorkers] are . . . generally better off, are more respectable, and . . . more of them owners of real estate." But then Cornish, who grew up in Philadelphia (his brother James worked for Forten and co-signed the *Ariel* letter), made a barbed comment on this prosperity leading to the pettiest form of politics:

> They are proprietors of no less than six brick churches and one frame one in different parts of the city. This is a free country for enquiry and electioneering, and our Philadelphia brethren have been nothing backward in enjoying to the full extent their rights in this respect as regards ecclesiastical matters—in truth, this mauvais spirit has been carried too far, and been the cause of much hard feeling between persons who ought to join hand in hand in every thing which tends to the advancement of religion, and the respectability of our people.[46]

Indeed, by the 1820s the "elite of our people" had a national reputation for infighting within their church-affiliated networks, the dozens of vestries, death-and-benefit societies, sewing groups, lyceums, and literary forums, each with a disciplinary body ready to censure or expel. The wars inside Philadelphia's black churches dominated how African Americans viewed the city in the antebellum decades, with their "mauvais spirit" blamed for the failure to generate political action. Although personal and group rivalries are common to many communities, black Philadelphia was markedly factionalized. Division bred impotence was the verdict of their own leaders, as in 1831, when the Reverend John Gloucester, Jr., decried "the spirit of party prejudice . . . [which] generally forms a dislike of our most promising men." By the 1840s, this "spirit of party prejudice" was notorious among black people outside Philadelphia, who had witnessed these rivalries in the 1830–35 convention movement and the dead end of the American Moral Reform Society in 1836–41.[47]

The factional impulse cannot be separated from those leaders' entrepreneurialism. As early as 1789, the Free African Society expelled Richard Allen because he was "attempting to sow division among us" by proselytizing for Methodism. Allen figures often in the internal fights. Famous for his obduracy toward whites, his will-to-power had few limits and drew no color line, as memoirs by other black clergymen testified. In 1857, the Reverend William Catto of the First African Presbyterian Church described Allen's efforts to undermine Catto's revered predecessor, the Reverend John Gloucester, Sr. Without naming Allen, he catalogued the former's "sectarian bigotry . . . [a] bitter, malignant enemy to all that is not of its cast," as a form of "spiritual wickedness in high places." Allen had "intended to crush in the bud the least appearance of establishing a Presbyterian church." Worst of all, he was a hypocrite, "professedly . . . friendly, and seemingly much interested in his [Gloucester's] welfare," Allen's "real designs were selfish and mean," and he tried to counsel Gloucester that "it was a waste of time for him to attempt, in Philadelphia, to raise a Presbyterian church, that the people in heart were Methodist, and would finally all be received into Methodist churches." By the time Cornish indicted their infighting in 1828, battles over control had split each of Philadelphia's leading churches, including St. Thomas's in 1809–10 and again in 1821–22; Bethel in 1820 and 1822; and First African Presbyterian in 1824, spawning Second African Presbyterian.[48]

The larger context of 1828 underlines how small-bore shadow politics could be. Nowhere did Vashon, Whipper, or Cornish acknowledge that year's election, the triumph of Andrew Jackson's Democracy against John Quincy Adams's National Republicanism, a watershed of unprecedented partisan mobilization. To these black leaders the presidency was apparently irrelevant: Jackson's name never appeared in *Freedom's Journal*. Given this quiescence, it was a considerable surprise when the Philadelphians, led by Allen, abruptly left their shadows, convening black men from eleven states to debate their prospects in view of whites via a series of national conventions in 1830–35. Ultimately, however, these meetings failed at enacting any programs for political or social improvement; a profound antipolitical conservatism combined with deep-rooted factionalism to generate entropy. By the late 1830s, Philadelphia's elite were objects of derision by the North's emerging black political class, fighting over trivialities inside their fine brick churches amid disfranchisement and annual antiblack riots.

The 1830s: Conventioneering

In 1830, the shadow politics of building separate institutions took the national stage, as the Philadelphians discovered the satisfactions of hosting "conventions of the people of color." Those meetings lasted until 1835, when disputes between New York and Philadelphia shut them down. From 1836 to 1841, the Philadelphians and a few allies continued to meet as the American Moral Reform Society (AMRS), but this formation was an afterthought, since the New Englanders and New Yorkers voted with their feet to boycott. This decade of conventioneering climaxed Philadelphia's national leadership via an antipolitics of benevolent associationism rather than political action.

From the first, the colored conventions replicated the Philadelphia style, with factional rivalries over who had the right to call them, set the agendas, credential delegates, issue addresses, and preside over the year-round Conventional Boards, with vice presidents and secretaries assigned to every state from Maine to Virginia. "Rule or ruin" was the rule, as demonstrated in 1834, the one time the convention met in New York. That city's eminent William Hamilton opened the assemblage by calling for a "moral reformation . . . [to] begin here. By managing this conference in a spirit of good will and true politeness . . . [and] peace, order and harmony, rather than satire, wit and eloquence . . . charging each other with improper motives." He was ignored, as rival Philadelphia delegations immediately tried to unseat each other.[49]

The first meeting in 1830 was in response to reports of hundreds of black families being driven out of Cincinnati through a sudden enforcement of Ohio's long-dormant Black Code. In April 1830, Hezekiah Grice, a young Baltimore ice-dealer, sent letters proposing a meeting "for the purpose of comparing views and of adopting a harmonious movement either of emigration, or of determination to remain in the United States." As remembered thirty years later, he was visiting Bishop Allen when the latter heard that New Yorkers were organizing a convention. "My dear child, we must take some action immediately, or else these New Yorkers will get ahead of us," the bishop declared. Allen trumped his rivals, as forty men from nine states attended a September 20–24, 1830 meeting in Philadelphia. That meeting's stated goal was "purchasing land, and locating a settlement in the Province of Upper Canada," while expressing a commitment to "pursue all legal means for the speedy elevation of ourselves and brethren to the scale and standing of men." The second assemblage in 1831, confusingly titled "the First Annual Convention," was smaller, with only sixteen delegates from New York, Pennsylvania, Maryland, Delaware and Virginia, but included key New Yorkers like Hamilton, Thomas Jennings, and J. W. C. Pennington. It authorized provisional committees of forty-six men in seven states to raise money for a "manual labor college" in New Haven, with Samuel Cornish appointed general agent. The one concrete plan adopted during these six conventions, the college was blocked by intense white opposition. Following this debacle, no new sites were investigated or proposals made to the white philanthropists who had endorsed the college. The 1832 convention was little different, although the presence of twenty-nine delegates led to claims that they would soon "present a body, not inferior in numbers to our state legislatures." In 1833, twenty-five towns and cities sent representatives, a high-water mark.[50]

What significance did these meetings have? In the 1960s and since, scholars have described "the Negro Convention Movement" as proto-nationalist. More likely, they were expressing allegiance to the American creed of voluntarism, famously eulogized by Tocqueville, that associating for benevolent purposes was itself a good. Only in a nominal sense were the colored conventions political. Their main purpose was performative, to provide an arena where black men could show themselves officiating, voting, debating, recording, resolving, addressing, and publishing official proceedings; it is rarely noted that many whites attended as visitors, and the convention's debates were widely reported in newspapers. At points, the spectacle took on a real edge, and some participants' fondest memories were of ACS leaders given the floor and then humiliated by displays of black oratory.[51]

The conventions' unstated purpose was the same as white men's gatherings: fellowship away from wives, families, and everyday cares. An 1838 encomium to William Whipper at the 1834 meeting offers a glimpse: "His reflections on his way had made him sad. . . . When he met the Convention, finding the members in a very different mood—light of heart—enjoying life—jovial and feasting—his own soul, instead of catching the spirit of the scene before him, but assumed a shade of deeper sadness. Invitations to join his brethren at their dinners and parties he declined, and shut himself in his room." Being "in convention" was a social rather than political breakthrough, the highest expression of mimetic politics (except that the white Protestants who met in solemn philanthropic conclaves were also voters tied to partisan leaders). Reading through 152 pages of proceedings for 1830–35, each typically covering a ten-day meeting, is like holding sand. Setting specific policies, let alone organizing action campaigns, was deemed impossible because of "a very considerable diversity of sentiment as to the best means. . . . Our local situations operate to produce a great difference of feeling, as well as of judgment." The printed record is all procedure—listing committees, prayers offered, mentions of obscure fights over unrecorded resolutions. Typical is this 1832 passage: the Reverend J. W. C. Pennington proposed "a list of resolutions," which led to "very tedious debates," and it was finally "deemed inexpedient" to consider them at all. That the delegates accomplished little other than opposing colonization hardly seemed to matter.[52]

The only real ideological debate regarded whether to champion emigration to Canada's Wilberforce settlement. It was won by those insisting, "Ours is a defensive warfare; on our domicil [sic] we meet the aggressor, and if we move, or give our consent to move, and bid them to follow before we are driven, forcibly driven, from our lodgements . . . their denunciations would be just." In the commitment to stay in their "lodgements," the majority affirmed that they were, indeed, Americans, but it remained unclear what that meant politically. Only briefly in 1831 and 1834 were there references to citizenship rights. In 1832, with Jackson up for reelection, the "Conventional Address to the Free Coloured People of These United States" was vigorously antipolitical. Expressing the hope to impress whites by "devising plans and measures, for their personal and mental elevation, by *moral suasion alone*," it concluded by denouncing the "bewitching evil, that bane of society, that curse of the world . . . INTEMPERANCE," followed by a paean to uplift: "Be righteous, be honest, be just, be economical, be prudent, offend not the laws of your country." Black Americans need only "live in the constant pursuit of that moral and intellectual strength, which will invigorate your understandings, and render you illustrious in the eyes of civilized nations." The Philadelphians' electoral abstentionism was nationalized, with no recorded protest. Rather than campaign for political rights or against slavery, free black men were told to listen to the "host of benevolent individuals" seeking to raise them "from the degradation that we are now in, to the exalted situation of American freemen. . . . With a strong desire for our improvement in morality, religion, and learning, they have advised us strictly to practice the virtues of temperance and economy." In retrospect, it was a fool's errand to imagine that if people of color emulated upright whites, their rights would come, but utopian wish-fulfillment was not so evident during the Second Great Awakening, when people of all stations sought salvation through self-improvement.[53]

As these quotations indicate, calls for "moral reform" increasingly came to the fore as an explicit anti-politics. The 1834 convention published a "Declaration of Sentiment" calling for a National Moral Reform Society, almost certainly written by Whipper, which formally disclaimed any kind of citizenship politics: "Let us not lament, that . . . we are disfranchised; better far than to be partakers of its guilt. Let us refuse to be allured by the glittering endowments of official stations, or enchanted with the robe of American citizenship. But let us choose like true patriots, rather to be the victims of oppression." These were the years when black rights reached their nadir. Following Turner's bloody revolt, slave states banned manumission and harshly repressed free people, while violence spread across the North during 1834–35 targeting both prominent abolitionists and black people. The conventions ignored these developments, other than a few oblique references, and were similarly passive regarding the new "immediatist" abolitionism; although Philadelphia's leadership mustered crucial financial support for Garrison's *Liberator*, they evidently regarded that work as separate from what black men did in public. Politics was again displaced onto white patrons. The 1840s and 1850s saw the rise of black abolitionism led by men like Frederick Douglass and Henry Highland Garnet. In the 1830s, however, in their conventions, black men defined antislavery as white men's business. In their published proceedings, the word "abolitionist" was invariably denoted as white; in 1835, for instance, they voted "that this convention . . . shall have the power to elect any *abolitionist* as an honorary member . . . being from any city or place where there are no delegates to represent the *colored people*" (emphasis added). This stance of approval from the sidelines reproduced the worldview of Philadelphia's black elite.[54]

Substituting "Moral Reform" for political action expressed the ambition to direct tutelary self-improvement among Philadelphia's younger cohort. As early as 1831, the convention criticized the "dissolute, intemperate, and ignorant condition of a large portion of the colored population." Whether whites drove the impulse to cultivate their own gardens or advocates of respectability politics invoked whites to bolster their case is unclear. Whipper clearly viewed the Moral Reform of free black people as analogous to the Moral Suasion Garrisonians applied to slave-owners. The latter appealed to "the emerging black middle-class," as "an integrative and optimistic ideology, informed by faith in the potency of universal values. . . . America was, many believed, an open society, with abundant opportunities for those who imbibed the ideals of moral suasion." The Pennsylvania leaders "shared a consensus on the potency of the economically self-made man" because of their own material success, and hoped "that whites would welcome and embrace a morally upright, industrious, intelligent and economically elevated black man." Ex-slaves proving themselves worthy, they believed, would convince slave-owners to emancipate.[55]

These premises are retrospectively fantastical. Only someone who took Garrison literally instead of understanding his fundamentally coercive approach of shaming and threatening slaveholders could imagine that turning men and women barely subsisting at the bottom of the labor market into abstemious, thrifty bootstrappers was a realistic program. Pennsylvania's black leaders believed exactly that, however, and led their colleagues down a blind alley in the quest for respectability. The politics of deference remained in place, enforced by those who believed that any abolitionist agitation by black Americans invited physical assault, and convinced that the mass of free people of color lacked republican virtues.

The final 1835 convention in Philadelphia was an afterthought. The crucial decision had already been taken to found a National (later "American") Moral Reform Society. In 1833, Whipper pushed through an agreement to rotate conventions between New York and Philadelphia, but in 1835, the Philadelphians dispensed with any pretense of shared control. A Conventional Board of New Yorkers was named, but the new society's officers, all based in southeast Pennsylvania, asserted their annual meetings had replaced the conventions.

The Anti-Politics of "Moral Reform"

Examining the American Moral Reform Society (AMRS) is like looking through glass—lacking any program, it simply met, and, over time, bemoaned its own ephemerality. The 1830–35 conventions were at least representative, but the decade's latter half saw a decline into pure formality, with gatherings limited to one faction in Philadelphia's black middle class (including female delegates from benevolent associations). The first in 1836 continued the tradition of gaudy jeremiads, bemoaning the "unnecessary expense" of "mourning apparel" which demonstrated the "tyranny of fashion" over "the poor of the people." It urged "servants" to display "an obliging disposition" and "scrupulous punctuality" toward their white employers. Three years later, little had changed: "licentiousness" was "a great and crying evil" afflicting black society, and the society "deprecate[d] . . . feasting on 'holidays,'" and "the ruinous and wicked practice of purchasing lottery tickets." The AMRS mimicked the white politics of social control of this era, during which asylums and penitentiaries proliferated, with the obvious difference that it exerted no control beyond feeble warnings that drunks would be named in its *National Reformer* as "enemies of god and man," although much effective temperance organizing of black folk took place outside the AMRS. The late 1830s thus had a surreal character, with rising racial violence and disfranchisement counterposed to this leadership's unctuous detachment.[56]

James Forten's presence alone gave weight to this project. He was colonizationism's greatest foe but boycotted the 1830–35 conventions, presumably because, as a firm Garrisonian, he disdained separate "complexional" organizing; the AMRS claimed to be nonracial, campaigning vociferously against any "African" or "colored" identification. There was also a question of filial succession. One imagines Forten sitting proudly at the AMRS's August 1837 meeting as his nineteen-year-old namesake delivered an address calling for "the elevation of our people from ignorance and superstition, to light and knowledge," so as to "palsy the Herculean arm of prejudice," and "change the scornful look, the invidious frown, into an approving smile." The younger Forten warned his fellow "young men" against their "disposition to appear conspicuous in the eyes of the world . . . striving their best to imitate the fashionable follies of the day." He urged giving up "frivolous and unprofitable amusements" and hailed his people's pacifism, that "we have clothed our-selves in the panoply of non-resistance, and submitted patiently to Moboc-racy and Lynch Law." This oration ended with remarkable optimism, that when "moral reform . . . becomes general, the whole north will become aboli-tionists. They will perceive that we are an industrious people, equal to them in all that is moral and elevating, equally capable of self-government. Their finer feelings will be touched, and they will cry out, with one voice to the south, 'undo the heavy burden, break every yoke, and let the oppressed go free.'"[57]

Ultimately, the AMRS's main historical import was how it inspired a wave of angry criticism. This opposition was led by the first explicitly political black publication, New York's *Colored American*, a name intended to challenge the AMRS's anti-"complexional" phobia. In June 1837, the *American* highlighted the AMRS's local rival, the unapologetically all-black Philadelphia Associa-tion for the Mental and Moral Improvement of the People of Color (AMMI), which focused on practical "assistance to the children of such persons of color . . . unable to provide suitable clothing for them to appear decently at the free schools" while arguing for emigration to a U.S. territory or Canada where blacks could govern themselves. Two months later, Samuel Cornish, the paper's veteran editor, issued a systematic critique while attending the society's annual meeting where young Forten spoke. Confessing "many mis-givings . . . that all who had right hearts, had not straight heads," Cornish cut into "the colored citizens of Philadelphia, many of them wealthy and intel-lectual" but nonetheless "visionary in the extreme. (I cannot call them fanatical—they are not sufficiently self-sacrificing, to merit this appellation.)" Acknowledging their accomplishments, he still found them "more inefficient, and less prominent in the cause of human rights, than others who possess less means, and who are more obscurely located."[58]

Whipper, the AMRS's main ideologue, replied with "AN ADDRESS ON NON-RESISTANCE TO OFFENSIVE AGGRESSION," hailing "the great law of Love," since "the war principle, which is the production of human passions, has never been, nor can ever be, conquered by its own elements." Cornish re-fused to take this grandiose utopianism seriously, demanding that the soci-ety adopt "definite OBJECTS, as well as definite actions." Rather than puffery, it "should spend its means and strength in efforts to improve and elevate, the poor, proscribed, down trodden and helpless COLORED PEOPLE of our country." Above all, they should stop indulging themselves "in BOMBAS-TIC, HUMBUG EFFORTS, to improve the WHOLE NATION!"[59]

Liberated by Cornish's plain talk, well-known Pennsylvanians weighed in, including Philadelphia's F. A. Hinton mocking Whipper's "ridiculous non-sense," Harrisburg's Junius C. Morel announcing he had "opposed the for-mation of the 'National Moral Reform Society'" in 1834, the eminent John B.

Vashon, who made a large donation to the *Colored American* (now prescribed in Philadelphia), and the first of many essays by "Augustine" (the Pittsburgh leader Lewis Woodson), criticizing those "who think it impolitic and improper for us to acknowledge and speak of ourselves as a distinct class, in the community in which we live."[60] Commitments to political action and the *Colored American* proliferated—Hinton and John G. G. Bias, who had formed the AMMI, also founded a Philadelphia committee to back the paper, while Morel sounded the alarm about disfranchisement at the state constitutional convention that began meeting in May 1837.[61]

These debates foretold a deadlock not broken until another national convention finally met in 1843. Minus the Philadelphia leadership, no multistate meeting could be called, given their authority. This open confrontation was, in retrospect, a necessary birthing process. By 1840, antipolitical "moral reform" had been sidelined and leadership passed decisively to New Yorkers advocating engagement with party and legislative politics. In Pennsylvania, black men outside Philadelphia met to discuss suffrage, although with little success. The notion that black Americans' oppression stemmed from their self-imposed "degradation" had lost all legitimacy, and in late 1839 Whipper admitted he, too, had "been allured by false idioms." He acknowledged advocating "the doctrine that we must be '*elevated*' before we can expect to enjoy the privileges of American citizenship. We now utterly discard it, and ask pardon for our former errors." By that point, it no longer mattered in Pennsylvania. Violence and disfranchisement had done their work, after battles led by obscurer black men, the subject of chapter 3.[62]

Chapter 3

A Large Body of Negro Votes Have Controlled the Late Election

Black Politics in Pennsylvania, 1790–1838

> In the city of Pittsburgh, in Dauphin, where is the seat of government, in Bucks, Lancaster, Allegheny and perhaps other counties, every citizen being a freeman, without regards to his complexion, of the age of 21 or more . . . is permitted to vote. . . . In Philadelphia, and in some of the counties, all except white men, are excluded.

—"Address from Thomas Morgan, To His Constituents," 1816

> Resolved, That a large body of negro votes have controlled the late election in Bucks, and that Aaron Ivins has been returned to the assembly; Abraham Fretz, as commissioner; and Richard Moore, auditor of accounts, by the votes of negroes, illegally received in Middletown, and other election districts in the lower session of the County of Bucks, and that we will take the necessary measures to contest their respective elections. . . . Resolved, That individuals who lead negroes to the polls, PAY THEIR TAXES, INFLUENCE THEIR VOTES, and thus abuse and corrupt the elective franchise, are governed by feelings and principles, hostile to the perpetuation of our happy form of independence.

—From a meeting at Harris's White Bear Tavern in Northampton Township, Bucks County, October 21, 1837

Pennsylvania's black politics has been told entirely as a history of exclusion and "shadow politics." Almost no scholars have looked at how, when, and where black men entered into ordinary partisan politics. In fact, the state had a long history of black electoral participation prior to 1838. In many of the counties with substantial black populations, they began voting early in the nineteenth century in numbers large enough to roil the Commonwealth's politics. In at least eleven counties, many among the state's largest, including Franklin, Adams, and York along the Maryland line, Washington along the western Virginia border, Allegheny (including Pittsburgh), Bucks on the Delaware, and Lancaster and Dauphin along the Susquehanna, men of color regularly came to the polls as Federalists and Jeffersonian Republicans, and later Democrats, Whigs, and Antimasons, with their ballots exciting little notice (see map. 3.1).[1]

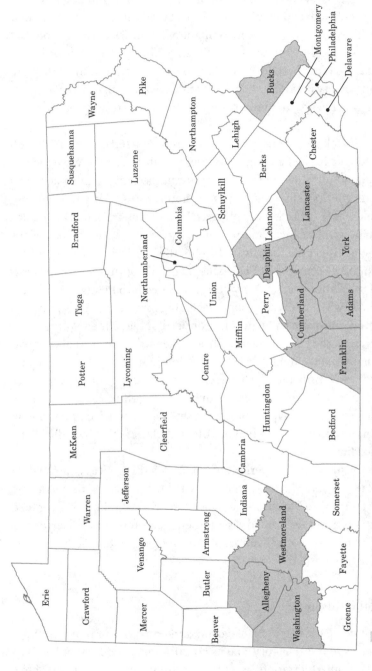

■ Counties where black men voted in 1820 (Juniata County was created from Mifflin County in 1831).

Map 3.1 Pennsylvania counties, 1820

This chapter offers an alternative periodization of Pennsylvania's black history. Before examining where Pennsylvanians of color did vote, it clarifies how their largest concentration of potential electors in Philadelphia was illegally disfranchised, and why those men accepted the deprivation of their political rights as the necessary concomitant of a politics of protection. But it was not always so. Efforts to mobilize the state's black electorate on behalf of the Federalist Party paralleled the famous repudiation of the American Colonization Society in 1817. Together, these discoveries suggest that citizenship politics was never a road not taken, but rather a strategy periodically attempted.

To be sure, black voters rarely functioned as organized groups. Although more likely to vote in the Federalist counties (or where conservative Republicans, so-called Quids, allied with Federalists), the only detailed accounts of their voting (in Franklin County in 1816, and Bucks County in 1837) contain many references to black men voting as Republicans and later Democrats. Their participation was local and personal, subject to the dynamics of the village or township where they lived. In 1816, the possibility of a larger bloc vote came to the fore amid factional jockeying. That option remained an issue through 1820, after which black suffrage subsided into Pennsylvania's customary morass, wherein many groups (including foreigners, transients, and paupers) voted "illegally." The promise or peril of black men voting reappeared in 1834, as the state's usual rivalries degenerated into an all-out war of partisan maneuver, threatening the long dominance of Jeffersonian and then Jacksonian "Democracy." The election in 1835 of an openly pro-black administration, headed by the Antimasonic governor Simon Ritner, set the frame for battles over nonracial suffrage in several counties, culminating in the exclusion of thousands of actual or potential black voters by judicial and constitutional fiat.

Before examining the two periods when black suffrage was contested, in 1816–20 and 1834–37, however, we must situate both active partisanship and electoral abstentionism by Pennsylvanians of color within the larger context. Their voting was never an isolated case; rather, their presence or absence was one facet of a chaotic political culture shaped by geographic, demographic, and ethnic fragmentation.

Unpacking the Keystone

The unexpected relevance of black voting in Pennsylvania requires explicating the state's political history, and its constitutional and legal order. Anything else risks romanticization, as if black partisanship was a quixotic hope rather than a hard fact. In the Old America, politicians survived through

Table 3.1 Pennsylvania's black and white electorate in 1820

County	Population County Rank	White Males	Black Males	Percentage of Total Electorate	1820 Turnout
Lancaster	68,336/no. 2	13,960	503	3.5	8,249
Washington	40,038/no. 5	8,395	171	2.0	4,851
York	38,759/no. 6	8,025	184	2.2	4,752
Bucks	37,842/no. 7	8,018	386	4.6	4,921
Allegheny	34,921/no. 9	7,662	154	2.0	3,731
Franklin	31,892/no. 10	6,428	346	5.1	4,630
Westmoreland	30,540/no. 12	6,287	57	0.9	4,470
Cumberland	23,606/no. 14	4,639	155	3.2	3,714
Dauphin	21,653/no. 15	4,286	141	3.2	3,304
Adams	19,370/no. 19	4,073	121	3.0	2,731

Note: The counties listed here are those historically identified as permitting black men to vote.

guaranteeing the number of voters they could get to the polls. Voting was the visible act of putting a ballot in a box or through a window, and operatives in a town or a rural township knew their own and their opponents' supporters by name and face. In this zero-sum game, when black men voted, their numbers mattered, just as it mattered when they did not, as in Philadelphia. As shown by public attacks on who sought black votes, county party leaders knew not only *which* black men voted, but *for whom*. Such detailed knowledge may seem impossible in a state whose electorate exceeded 100,000 by 1808, but the basis of representation in the General Assembly's lower House of Representatives remained remarkably small—1,500 "ratables" or taxpayers until 1814, and 1,750 until 1821. In the 1816 presidential election, for instance, the turnout was under 1,000 in many of the larger counties, including some accepting votes "without regard to complexion": 637 in Allegheny, 653 in Adams, and 819 in Delaware; see table 3.1 for an estimate of the black electorate in 1820, using the federal census.[2]

There are profound continuities to Pennsylvania's political culture. Extreme parochialism, "a whirlwind of clashing localities and interest groups" with "local self-control [as] the fundamental issue" have long characterized its politics, originally because of impassable physical barriers, including Appalachian ridges running southwest to northeast, and the east and west branches of the Susquehanna cutting north to south, one mile wide in places. Broken up by nature, its various regions oriented outward like spokes. The ambit of Philadelphia's densely populated hinterlands did not stretch even the seventy miles to Lancaster, whose economy was, like York across the

Susquehanna, linked more to Baltimore. The vast, thinly populated northern tier was settled from New England and culturally affiliated with New York. The state's western edge around Pittsburgh was part of the Ohio Valley, and well into the nineteenth century, accessible only by mountain roads so dangerous that "wagons and stages . . . overturned daily" and "stage drivers pointed out scenes of tragedy in tour-guide fashion."[3]

Pennsylvania's pattern of ethnic settlement was accentuated by geographic divides. English, Scottish, and Welsh settlers dominated the twelve southeastern counties, which in 1830 still held half of the state's population. The "German belt" spread out to the northwest, divided between "church people" (Lutherans and German Reform) and pacifist sectarians (Mennonites, Amish, Moravians, Schwenkfelders, and German Baptists); Lancaster County, with its German majority, was the republic's major non-English-speaking enclave. Besides the German vote, the other major fact was migration into the western counties by Presbyterian "Scots Irish" (then just "Irish") from Ulster beginning well before the Revolution. While putting up a string of Germans for governor, the Ulstermen's unrivaled political skills gave them dominance over the Republican Party, the judiciary, and the legislature after 1800. Pennsylvania politics, therefore, had a distinctly ethnic character via the "union of German and Irish interests," much celebrated after their 1799 victory over Federalists, seen as odious for their Alien acts, extension of naturalization to fourteen years, and repression of the antitax Fries's Rebellion by German farmers. Year after year, popular German governors brought in their *landsmen* on behalf of Irish county machines, to the exclusion of Anglo-Federalists based in Philadelphia and the pacifist counties, where Quakers and sectarian Germans remained staunchly anti-Republican because of that party's promotion of militia laws that fined pacifist "exempts."[4]

This ethnoreligious alignment was permanently skewed, however, with Federalists out of power after 1799 except via temporary coalitions with dissident Republicans. The state's traditional political history focuses on its "overwhelming and undeviating Republicanism," with that party carrying every gubernatorial race in 1799–1835, and every presidential contest until 1840, by which time they called themselves Democrats. But describing Pennsylvania as controlled by one party is deceptive. As early as 1805 the Republicans divided into durable factions competing at every level. Sharing contempt for "Tory" Federalists, they unified only during presidential years— and not always then. Meanwhile, Federalists maintained sufficient strength in Philadelphia and Luzerne, Chester, Delaware, Lancaster, and Adams Counties to ally with a particular Republican slate and carry the state. In 1805, for instance, Constitutional Republicans ("Quids") cooperated with Federalists to reelect an unpopular governor and win a large majority in the lower

House. Rather than single-party dominance, therefore, a two-and-a-half- (and sometimes three-) party system operated in Pennsylvania.[5]

Accounts of statewide partisan rivalries obscure local differences. In the early 1800s, feuding Republicans in Philadelphia created parallel ward-based structures which prefigured modern urban politics. A few landholders still dominated many rural counties, however, especially in the west where Ulster emigrants had claimed large tracts before the Revolution, and functioned as Republican agents. Their networks of relatives, tenants, and former slaves exerted considerable electoral weight. An 1817 "letter to the editor" from Franklin County detailed how these networks functioned. The writer boasted that his side had beaten (gubernatorial candidate William) "Findlay's whole connexion," even though the latter counted "twenty-three families, amounting from thirty-seven to forty voters, amongst whom are from ten to fifteen judges, generals, magistrates, militia captains, &c., who, with from thirty to thirty-five negroes, voted in solid column for Findlay."[6]

Besides innovations in party organization, Pennsylvania anticipated the performative mass partisanship of the Age of Jackson. The franchise was nearly universal; adult men qualified by paying a tax as little as twenty-five cents. The electoral calendar was nearly continuous, with annual elections for state representatives and county officers. Every fall included two Election Days in October, with the general election preceded by voting for inspectors and judges of election, crucial since control of those offices meant one could apply a strict standard to exclude an opponents' backers and a looser one to admit one's own. Presidential elections doubled the number of Election Days to four, since congressional and state balloting was held weeks before the presidential vote.[7]

From late summer, each party deployed committees of vigilance to publicize its local tickets, bring voters to the polls, and serve as "broad political bases for disseminating ideas among the people of the townships." The poll itself was very different from today's. Each county's "high sheriff" published a "public notice, to the electors of the said county," typically that "a general election will be held on the second Tuesday of October next, at the several election districts to wit—The electors of Washington district, to meet at the court house. . . . The electors of Somerset district to meet at the house of George McIlvaine." In rural areas, private homes usually served as polling places. Men assessed six months previously and therefore entitled to vote handed in ballots for each office (handwritten or printed by a party), at a window. Sometimes access was fought over, as in an 1837 Bucks County case between rival newspaper publishers. A Democrat charged that "the political party to which [the Whig] Hodgson belonged, were purposely obstructing the window at which the votes were taken in, in order to prevent the Democratic voters, who generally voted late, from getting in their votes," and that Hodgson had "fixed himself at the window, with his face in the window" to block ballots being deposited.[8]

Besides informal voter suppression, inspectors barred men from voting for many reasons: no proof of naturalization, no residency in the district for two years, or as a pauper receiving municipal charity. Unlike complexion, the last was a legal disqualification. On Election Day, different standards were applied depending on where one resided and who controlled the polls. As Representative Thomas Morgan pointed out in 1816, in usually Federalist Philadelphia City, "when the republicans are in the majority, a vote will be received, although the person tendering it, had not been included in an assessment at least six months before the election [but] when the federalists are in power, all are excluded, except those who were included in an assessment."[9]

Who permitted whom to vote was thus larger than whether men of darker complexions cast ballots. A 1785 "Act to regulate the General Elections of this Commonwealth" specified that "manifold frauds and abuses have arisen therein" so that "persons who had not the confidence nor suffrages of the major part of the legal electors have been returned." For the next half-century, most amendments focused on whether or when naturalized citizens (and their sons) might vote. In the late 1790s, Federalists made repeated efforts to adjust this law. In 1799, Governor Thomas Mifflin signed legislation specifying, "All who claimed the right of suffrage . . . had to prove they were citizens by birth, residence or naturalization. Anyone in the last category had to produce a court certificate in attestation." Complaints continued, such as after Republicans swept usually Federalist Lancaster in 1801: "We shall not at this time attempt to trace the causes of federal defection. . . . A number of illegal votes were received in the borough box; and at Elizabethtown Irishmen & others, paid a tax which was never assessed on them, and voted."[10]

Only after decades of wrangling did attention turn to allowing or barring men because of "complexion." The larger frame of this story is familiar: how the War of 1812 consolidated Republican dominance and then that party's sundering, from Monroe's overwhelming victory in 1816 through his uncontested reelection in 1820, and then a four-way race between nominal Republicans in 1824. In Pennsylvania, this disintegration was accelerated by established intraparty divisions, and Federalism's semi-covert network of well-connected men; as Philip S. Klein pointed out long ago, after 1816 Pennsylvania politics became "a game without rules." However, before documenting various attempts in this period to recruit Pennsylvania's black men, we should note the appearance of an ideological motive for such an attempt to broaden the electorate. In the late 1810s, it became politically expedient to demonstrate sympathy for the "poor African." Across the Lower North, politicians espoused a newly sectional antislavery, in part because of the large-scale kidnapping of free black people by gangs operating along the Mason-Dixon. Pennsylvania Republicans joined Federalists in bringing petitions to Congress demanding harsh penalties for this sordid business. An ostentatious anti-Southernism may have encouraged black men to see themselves as persons with rights, even if that was not what white men intended.[11]

Before turning to debates over black men voting, we need to understand why so many black Philadelphians never did. It was widely known that that city's black community avoided the polls in the half-century between 1790, when a new constitution enfranchised them, and 1838, when the state's supreme court and a second convention disfranchised them. Why they abstained has been obscured through scholars' persistent inattention to how voting actually worked in Pennsylvania, and that most black men had that right, whether or not they exercised it. Even after basic legal facts are clarified, however, the enigma remains of rights abjured, the worst type of voluntary subordination.

"Criminal Apathy and Idiot Coldness": The Mechanics of Disfranchisement

For decades, historians discussed black voting rights in Pennsylvania based on anecdotal evidence and untested assumptions. A few observations were repeated, such as the Philadelphia Quaker John Jay Smith telling Tocqueville in 1831 that "they can't present themselves at the polls" because "they would be maltreated. . . . The law with us is nothing if not supported by public opinion" or, nine years earlier, the Federalist Samuel Breck's diary entry quoted in chapter 2, that "notwithstanding the laws . . . do not forbid it, no blacks vote at elections, at least in the eastern part of the state. . . . They never presume to approach the hustings, neither are they taxed." Most note without elaboration that a few black men voted elsewhere, but no one has interrogated how many, where they voted, for how long, or their electoral impact, presuming that what mattered was Philadelphia, although at no point did Philadelphia County, let alone the city, contain a majority of the state's African Americans.[12]

With little attention to when and where black men voted, there is less clarity about Philadelphia itself. That black Philadelphians didn't vote because they couldn't vote has become a self-fulfilling syllogism, despite the fact that legally most could vote, given the nonracial provisions of the 1790 Constitution: "In elections by the citizens, every freeman of the age of twenty-one years, having resided in the State two years next before the election, and within that time paid a State or County tax, which shall have been assessed at least six months before the election, shall enjoy the rights of an elector." Neither can one presume that document's nonracialism was inadvertent. In 1780, during debates over emancipation, the minority's official protest stated that even if "slaves might be safely emancipated, we could not agree to their being made free citizens in so extensive a manner as this law proposes," insisting they should be paid for their labor and "protected in their lives and property, in the manner white persons are, without giving them the right of voting for, and being voted into offices, [and] inter-marrying with white persons," the clearest recognition that those rights were implied by emancipation. Further, in 1790, one of the state's most distinguished citizens, the Swiss immigrant Albert Gallatin, blocked the insertion of "white" into the suffrage clause by insisting that, as a dark-complected man, he might be disfranchised; while no contemporary accounts record this conflict, other delegates then present later certified its occurrence.[13]

Whether black men chose not to exercise the franchise ("they never presume to approach the hustings") or were kept from exercising that right ("they can't present themselves at the polls . . . they would be maltreated") is worth asking. The best-known argument is that black Philadelphians avoided the polls because they knew they would be mobbed. This was stated to many visitors, not just Tocqueville but the Englishman Andrew Bell a few years later: "I asked a Philadelphian why they did not come to the poll? His answer was significant, 'Just let them try!'" It was pronounced as fact by Negrophobic Democrats at the 1837–38 convention—that black men voting would spark a genocidal reaction. A black Philadelphian "could not, with safety, appear at the polls, and to bring him there would endanger the peace and safety of the whole black population. . . . The prejudice of the white is sufficiently strong against him now. . . . Injury, annihilation to the black, sir, would be the result of making him the equal at the ballot box." Luzerne County's George Woodward sketched a lurid scenario, insisting any hint of black voting would "be the signal for burning every negro dwelling in the city and county and would endanger the lives of the whole population."[14]

This explanation has the merits of consistency, with white men underscoring that other white men would riot, burn, and kill if black men voted: "Just let them try!" But black men's own explanation was less exculpatory, suggesting they were not frightened away by their enemies but counseled away by their friends. This note was sounded after the convention's January 20, 1838 vote to disfranchise: that they had been steered into a blind alley. Samuel Cornish, editor of New York's *Colored American* and born into the Philadelphia elite, bitterly charged, "The colored people of Pennsylvania have too long been advised, and badly advised, by timid friends. 'Keep from the Polls, and do not embroil yourselves in political strife,' has been religiously preached, and as religiously obeyed, for forty years." Cornish was quite clear that if the city's men of color had "exercised the elective franchise," as they could, "the voice of tyranny would never have been heard . . . but their own false timidity, and the mistaken, injudicious advice of their counselors, prevented this course, until their enemies, the designing demagogues . . . were emboldened to take measures to legalize their political non-entity." In Pennsylvania, references to "timid friends . . . religiously preaching" passivity had an obvious implication; Cornish meant the Quakers of the PAS. A decade later, James J. G. Bias, a black physician and minister, extended this reproof: "Who it was influenced the colored people of [Philadelphia] county to remain at home, when they had the right to exercise the Elective Franchise . . . [as] guaranteed by the Constitution of this State?" He suggested that this "influence acted upon them like some mighty power" and "lulled them to sleep until the Convention of 1833 [sic], when it was brought forward against them as a reason why it should be taken from them."[15] Note Bias's language—"lulling to sleep" suggests neither coercion nor fear. Cornish and Bias's anger, when too late to matter (Cornish insisted he had "always said, it was a bad and ruinous policy," but his newspapers were silent until after the fact) casts little light on why Quakers advised electoral abstentionism. Did "Friends" tell black Philadelphians to avoid the polls because they truly feared for black lives, or did they evoke that danger to keep black men in a state of vassalage?

A closer examination of the legal apparatus of voting suggests that the disfranchisement of black Philadelphians had little to do with intimidation and mobs: they did not vote because they were never assessed the minimal county tax required of men over twenty-one, and so their names were not listed on the tax rolls used as electoral registers. Instead of examining the taxpaying requirement, historians have assumed that only real property was taxed and thus only black property holders could have voted. In fact, the taxpaying requirement was so notional that Thaddeus Stevens, urging it be maintained at the 1837–38 convention, sneered, "It is well known that any man who chose to be assessed, could compel the assessor to tax him, if he has any taxable property, or any occupation. . . . If he laboured one day in the week, and begged all the rest of the time, he could compel the assessor to return him as a voter."[16]

That the connection between paying a modest poll tax and enfranchisement was well known to black Philadelphians is evidenced by an 1831 letter to *The Liberator* from "C. D. P.," who urged "for the consideration of my brethren in *Philadelphia* the propriety of a measure, which they well know has been too long neglected by them . . . an effort to gain their constitutional rights." He first pointed out that black men voted all over the state, "excepting in *Philadelphia*—where, by some illegal means, they have been cheated of their rights as freemen." Now was the moment: "Let them hold themselves in readiness for the ensuing election, to choose such men for representatives, as know of no distinction. Let them call upon the assessors of each ward for assessment, and in this manner they will find their way to the polls," a clear statement of what was missing, adding, "They have many friends yet untried by them, who are ready to be called to their assistance."[17]

Another window into how disfranchisement worked comes from reports by sympathetic whites seeking to demonstrate the bona fides of black Philadelphians. In 1826, the PAS commissioned a "census of the coloured people of the city and county," using 1820–22 documents showing "219 taxable estates reported, the value of which as returned by the assessors, amounted to $114,839; and two coloured men were assessed for a personal tax," at a time when the city held thousands eligible for such a "personal tax." At first glance, this would suggest that 219 black Philadelphians, presumably mostly men, were assessed and thus should have been able to vote. But an 1835 report in *The Friend* (using documents from Forten to show how few people of color claimed outdoor poor relief or entered the city's almshouses), noted, "For want of designating in the tax books the property of colored people, reference was made to receipts of tax-payers, to ascertain . . . the amount paid." In other words, the city taxed property-owners of color, but omitted their names from the assessment books to bar their voting. During the 1837–38 debates, Philadelphia Democrats affirmed the refusal to assess men of color. Charles Brown acknowledged that "every negro, by the Constitution of this State was entitled to a vote; but it was notorious, that very few of them were allowed to exercise that right, because, unless they were assessed, they could not vote," and the Negrophobe Benjamin Martin added, "In Philadelphia, we have hitherto escaped being associated with these persons at the polls, owing to a construction put on the Constitution, that the right to vote should not be exercised without a previous assessment." And this was a long-standing practice, since as far back as 1800, the city's roll of 6,625 "taxables" included only an estimated twenty-eight of the 243 most respectable black men.[18]

The sobering explanation for why black Philadelphians did not vote is the one repeatedly cited by their enemies—that they did not care enough to seek more rights and chose to abstain. In 1837, John M'Cahen, another Philadelphia Democrat, stated his certainty that "the negroes with perhaps a few exceptions, do not desire the right of voting," and were "opposed to any amendment to the constitution. . . . They knew, perfectly well, that the prejudices of the white people of Pennsylvania against them, were such, that they would not benefit by it." Woodward of Luzerne detailed how it worked—they were "exempted from the payment of such taxes as are assessed on the person, and from the performance of those duties which attend the right of suffrage."[19]

As self-justifying as such claims were, they had ample support in the published statements of Philadelphia's black leadership. Their preeminent figure, James Forten, declared in his 1813 *Letters From a Man of Colour,* "We wish not to legislate, for our means of information and the acquisition of knowledge are, in the nature of things, so circumscribed, that we must consider ourselves incompetent to the task." The January 1833 *Memorial of the Subscribers, free people of colour, residing in the City of Philadelphia* to the General Assembly (used as an epigraph to chapter 2) reiterated this disclaimer. Following Nat Turner's uprising, amid fears of Negro incendiaries fleeing North, Afro-Pennsylvanians were again threatened with an "Act to Prohibit the Migration of Negroes and Mulattoes Into This Commonwealth," requiring immigrants to post $500, carry a certificate of residency or be treated as a vagrant, fining those employing them without certificates, and directing local assessors to deposit "a census of all negro and mulatto persons" with county courts. The memorial stressed their disinterest in "abstractions or speculations, as to the absolute rights of the coloured man." It emphasized their acceptance of disfranchisement. Black men in Philadelphia were not

asking for a declaratory law, to secure to them the right of being assessed or voting. These slumbering privileges need not be awakened now: and your Memorialists have too clear a view of the elementary principles of the Constitution and laws, to believe that they ever ought to be urged here.... *The coloured population merely ask to be left as they are* [emphasis added]. They believe they have constitutional rights, and . . . are at least citizens for protection. It will be time enough to repel obtrusiveness, when they do ask for more than they enjoy; and when in asking it, they deserve the repulse. They do not ask it now.[20]

The phrase "at least citizens for protection" captures their acceptance of a status equivalent to that of women, minors, and paupers, the other groups with civil but not "political" rights.

Postdisfranchisement, this faintheartedness was denounced. In early 1838, John C. Bowers, who chaired the meeting that produced the 1833 *Memorial,* noted his contempt for "the modern Solomons who . . . have just discovered that we were not citizens nor freemen," admitting that "though we have never enjoyed the right of suffrage which justly belonged to us in the city of Philadelphia, yet our brethren in the country, many of them, did—and now to be deprived of it . . . has inflicted a wound upon our feelings, which words cannot express." The most telling verdict came from Junius Morel, a veteran Philadelphia activist. After describing most black people as "lookers on" ("Witness our criminal apathy and idiot coldness in the anti-slavery cause!"), he attacked his colleagues' passivity, and described an 1831 attempt (perhaps with

"C. D. P.") to overcome this "criminal apathy." If they had "years ago, claimed and properly exercised our Right of Suffrage, we should not at this late day find ourselves in the very doubtful position that we are in." Morel then gave a glimpse of his community's internal dynamics: "Many years ago, I was instrumental . . . in organizing in the city of Philadelphia, a Society known as the 'Political Association.' Funds were collected, eminent council [*sic*] consulted, and matters were made ready to assert our claim to the Elective Right. But a vain temerity on the part of some, and a suicidal apathy on the part of others, prostrated my designs." He alluded to the johnny-come-latelies like Bowers—"Many who are now alive to the importance of that subject, when, alas! it is too late, could not be induced at that time to act at all." "Apathy" was the leitmotif, accompanied by episodic rituals of defiance. The city's leadership finally bestirred itself in March 1838 to issue the often-quoted *Appeal of Forty Thousand Citizens of Pennsylvania, Threatened with Disfranchisement, to the People of Pennsylvania*. But the barn door had swung open, and this gestural politics revealed itself as impotence in the face of power.[21]

The "African Washington Benevolents" March

Once it was not always so, even in Philadelphia. Briefly, in 1815–17, the years when Richard Allen took control of his church and black Philadelphians repudiated colonization, the city's men of color paraded in public to signal their affiliation with the still-powerful local Federalists. Black Federalism was a well-established fact. From New England to North Carolina, black men shared that partisan identification, as noted derisively by a Philadelphia Republican paper in March 1816: "There is no class of the community in Philadelphia and New York so exclusively Federal as the Free Negroes, who like many of their betters think they become genteel when they turn Federalists." The local version was led by Forten, despite his ostentatious declarations about "not wishing to legislate." His main patron in business, Thomas Willing, was a close ally of Alexander Hamilton, the Federalists' founder, as were PAS figures like William Rawle. For many years, Willing chaired Federalist meetings, including the memorial dinner after Hamilton's death, and his high Federalist sympathies easily transferred to an aspiring member of the seaboard elite like Forten, equally tied to international trade and threatened by Republican embargoes.[22]

The first hint of black partisanship came via what one historian has called "cultural Federalism." In September 1812, Forten joined 200 other subscribers, including dozens of leading, mainly Federalist politicians, in pledging $10 to $20 to commission ornamental plates for Captain Isaac Hull and Lieutenant Charles Morris of the *Constitution*, which sank the British *Guerriere* at the outset of the War of 1812. In February 1813, a Philadelphia chapter of the party's Washington Benevolent Society (WBS) was founded, "to attract members and voters without regard to their social status," in particular "Foreigners," enrolling a spectacular 2,650 men. Whether this large fraction of the Philadelphia electorate included black men is unknown; none were among WBS ward leaders listed in newspaper notices. In May 1814, however, the Philadelphia WBS took out a public subscription of almost $120,000 for a grand Washington Hall to compete with the Republicans' Tammany "wigwam." The subscription lists eventually included 200 individuals pledging $20 to $5,000, including many tied to elite Federalism and antislavery (Willing, Robert Waln, William Rawle, John Sergeant, and Mayor Robert Wharton). Forten committed a whopping $500, and the black barber Joseph Cassey another $100. Soon after, the Federalists made their last big push with "a clean sweep of the city election" in 1814 and again in 1815, unofficially backed by the out-of-favor "Old School" Republicans; perhaps this coup authorized their plan to recruit black voters.[23]

Obviously, inclusion in private elite efforts offered compensations of recognition, but those did not extend into the public sphere until 1816, when Philadelphia Federalists, led by the redoubtable Robert Wharton, the city's longest-serving mayor, incorporated black men into the WBS. Here we encounter a basic problem: everything we know about this effort derives from Republican attacks on the "African Washington Benevolent Society." No records survive from inside the Federalist Party, and contemporary journalistic norms permitted any allegation, no matter how scurrilous. The following is clear. On Washington's birthday, February 22, 1816, the society's grand procession included a black contingent, like those Federalists of color who paraded in New York and Boston. Before they marched, however, invective rained down from John Binns's *Democratic Press*, the "Administration paper" linked to Governor Snyder and President Madison, asserting "a WASHINGTON BENEVOLENT SOCIETY OF COLOURED PEOPLE is organizing in this city; that arrangements are making for them to dine together on the 22nd instant." Supposedly, Wharton "promised to have the Constables, Etc., ordered out to keep the peace at the Long Room, where . . . the Colored Society shall, for the first time celebrate the Birth Day of General Washington" with the white men of the regular society.[24]

Following the march, Binns gleefully reported on the intraparty dissension he had stimulated, that "many people, particularly respectable federalists . . . could not believe that such an association, so patronized, was organizing." On the day itself, "a body of blacks, two and two, paraded the streets of this city, decorated with badges, adorned with ribbands," following the mayor and high constable. As this was "against [the] judgment of the more respectable federalists," the procession was "a mere shadow of the number and respectability [of prior Washington birthdays] . . . one to three to what it has been." Federalists elsewhere had incorporated black men decades earlier, but it had been too long avoided in Philadelphia to slip by unnoticed. Republican newspapers around the country happily reprinted stories of Federalist perfidy. Inserting up to 2,800 voters into an electorate under 13,000 as recently as 1808 was no minor plan. Enrolling black men would have produced gains equivalent to the Republicans naturalizing over a thousand Irish immigrants in the 1790s. Indeed, during an 1808 legislative debate over electoral reform, a Republican warned that several districts had grown so black that "without expressly excluding negroes from the elective franchise . . . if the district of Southwark should, at any future period, be erected into a separate election district . . . the people of colour would be able to return a black candidate." Federalists did not simply start assessing black men and quietly bringing them to the polls. They made a show of their inclusiveness by granting the recognition other groups had received so as to, in Binns's phrase, "entice all the black brethren to become members of their Society."[25]

Binns kept it going, claiming the black Washingtonians were horrified at being lured into a plot paid for by British gold. After that, his reportage descended into the satires typical for the period. Binns printed a letter from the African Benevolents to their would-be allies, saying, "If we follow the road you take . . . instead of finding ourselves as the best blood of the country . . . we shall find ourselves *noted* characters, and probably *noted* still more by becoming a *head shorter*." Federalist traitors should leave black men alone, as "in no way do we wish to be dishonored." He speculated lewdly about aristocratic Americans and Englishmen failing in their attempts to "mix" black and white dogs, printing toasts from black banquets, some quite pungent ("May de dimmicrats all be hanged, and none but our good frends de federalists allowed to lib in dis happy country. . . . Tom Jefferson—He be great rogue, cause he no own Black Sal—She be good for him, as we for our friends here. . . . De foreigners—de outcasts—May dey be all sent to Angola, or Goree—Day have no business here"). There was a subtext to this baiting, as one toast made clear: "Billy Duane—He begin to know which side his bread is butter'd— Spose he lately got acquainted with some of us." This item appeared just before a presidential election when Old School Republicans, led by William Duane of the *Aurora* (once the most powerful Republican paper in the nation; like Binns an Irishman), ran an unpledged ticket against the official Republican candidate, James Monroe, with the Federalists abstaining to back the Old Schoolers. All that year, Binns, as New School leader, had alleged Duane's faction was illicitly leagued with Federalists, to which a charge of Negrophilism was now added. Binns had solid grounds in fact, since a month before the black Federalists marched, Duane's son-in-law, Thomas Morgan, a representative from far western Washington County, proposed an election bill banning the use of "complexion" to disfranchise eligible voters.[26]

Thomas Morgan's Gambit

A novice like Morgan would not have made that proposal unaided. In late 1815, the Federalists and Old School Republicans evidently discussed how to enfranchise black men statewide, thereby reaping more than 4,000 new votes, in advance of the 1816 election (in which only 42,965 men voted). The Federalists had little capacity outside of Philadelphia and a few residual counties. In the dozens of solidly Republican counties, Federalists either abstained from nominations or made a token effort. In most of the state, the Old Schoolmen would be the beneficiaries of guaranteeing nonracial franchise.[27]

Concerns about inconsistent application of the election laws were a staple of Pennsylvania politics. In 1814, an amendment stipulated that Philadelphia's Inspectors of Election "shall choose and take to their assistance six reputable citizens *in addition* to those provided by law," presumably to scrutinize naturalized citizens and prevent fraud. On December 14, 1815, Governor Simon Snyder's annual message to the General Assembly suggested that "the qualifications necessary to exercise the right of suffrage . . . be more clearly defined and better secured"; otherwise it was left to "irresponsible officers, whose decisions on similar points are as dissimilar, as are the feelings, prejudices or opinions of the different individuals who constitute the various election tribunals." His request went to a committee of two Republicans (Morgan and another man) and one Federalist (a young James Buchanan), with Morgan the chair, suggesting an Old School–Federalist alliance. Notable here was Morgan's "family connection." In 1814, he had married Catherine Duane, the editor's daughter.[28]

On January 18, 1816, Morgan's committee submitted a comprehensive bill, and *Niles' Register*, that era's journal of record, pointed out that it contained "a provision to extend the right of suffrage to every freeman, '*without regard to complexion*,' being qualified in other respects." The electoral implications immediately reverberated. A Chester County Federalist paper accused Republicans of seeking "to white wash Black-a-moores," with legislation to "invite myriads of the sooty race from the southern States . . . designed without doubt to strengthen the Democratic ranks." The administration paper, Binns's *Democratic Press*, reprinted the phrase "WITHOUT REGARD TO HIS COMPLEXION" in a huge, ornate font, surrounded by pointing fingers, to inform New School Republicans of the looming danger. A consensus rapidly developed to expunge that section, and on February 25, 1816, when the House went into a committee of the whole (meaning no record was kept), the *Press* reported, "The words 'WITHOUT REGARD TO COMPLEXION' . . . were stricken out *by a very large majority*," adding, "There are those here who apprehend that the vote of this day will be the death of the African Washington Benevolent Society inasmuch as the object had in view at its formation cannot be attained." Binns insisted the bill "was an electioneering scheme; that Col. Duane's son-in-law aided by the federalists" had hoped to alter "the Constitution that the blacks were to vote at the next election, and that their masters had lent them their clothing for" the February 22 march "under an expectation, that their decent appearance might entice all the black brethren to become members of their Society." After that amendment, the bill's other sections passed on straight party-line votes, expanding the electorate by easing access for the naturalized. On March 9, the bill carried the House with fifty-seven in favor. As often happened, it then died in the Senate.[29]

So ended the "electioneering scheme" to add a few thousand votes to a temporary coalition of the outs. Morgan's gambit had a coda. In September 1816, his local faction nominated him for state senator against the incumbent Republican, Isaac Weaver, from neighboring Greene County. Another Washington County representative colluded with Weaver's men by distributing handbills accusing Morgan of "being an advocate for giving the negroes the right of suffrage" or even "*giving* the *slaves* a right to vote!" His response, "Address from Thomas Morgan, To His Constituents," was the most complete argument for why black men should vote in Pennsylvania until the 1837–38 convention.[30]

Morgan began by stressing that "under the same circumstances, a man would be permitted, or not permitted to vote, according as one, or another set of judges . . . or, according to the district, or county." From there, he pivoted to race: "In the city of Pittsburgh, in Dauphin, where is the seat of government, in Bucks, Lancaster, Allegheny and perhaps other counties, every citizen being a *freeman*, without regards to his complexion, of the age of 21 or more . . . is permitted to vote. . . . In Philadelphia, and in some of the counties, all except white men, are excluded." This localized discrimination was hardly unique, as in some counties, even "sons of aliens, born in this, or any other of the U. States . . . whose fathers shall not have been naturalized, shall not vote." Morgan emphasized why it was incumbent on him, as chair of the committee, "to get at the true meaning of the constitution," given "the contrariety of practice with respect to . . . complexion." As "one of the strongest cases embraced in the governor's message, it became my duty to ascertain whether our constitution makes any distinction on account of color." Self-evidently, it did not, given that the 1780 Act for the Gradual Abolition of Slavery had specified that other than the existing slaves, all other persons, "of any nation or colour" would be regarded as "free men and free women," and the 1790 Constitution's stipulation that "every freeman" of age who "paid a State or County tax" should enjoy "the rights of an elector." If Morgan had nonetheless claimed the constitution barred black voting, would he not have committed *"perjury?"* He concluded by pointing out how to disfranchise black men: "If then it be the will of the people . . . nothing more would be necessary than to pass a law exempting them from taxation." Still attempting to conciliate his constituents, he noted that a local dignitary, "Judge Addison," who had helped write the constitution, "under the obligation of an oath and as a judge of an election in Washington received the votes of men of color." Here lies the likely root of Morgan's advocacy—Washington County boasted one of the nation's oldest local antislavery societies, founded in 1793, and Judge Alexander Addison, president of the county court, was one of its leading members.[31]

"The King of the Ethiopians"

Pennsylvania's Federalists setting up a black auxiliary, or a law guaranteeing black men's votes, had major implications, but why pay close attention to voters in one rural county? In October 1817, the black vote in Mercersburg, county seat of Franklin, took on special weight as the home base of William Findlay, the controversial regular or New School Republican gubernatorial candidate, a longtime state treasurer charged with financial peculations by none other than Thomas Morgan. On Election Day, October 7, Findlay's closest associate, Judge Archibald Bard, brought to the polls forty to fifty black men, leading the opposition to award him a sardonic title of "King of the Ethiopians." This bloc vote drew the attention of leading jurists, including Pittsburgh's James Ross, U.S. senator in the 1790s and three-time Federalist gubernatorial candidate, and two others who had then just joined him on the state supreme court. Forty years later, following the *Dred Scott* ruling, one of them remembered "a conversation on the very subject of negro suffrage," and how "they all agreed, too, that the right had been occasionally exercised" and "in a few counties it was consistently exercised. Judge Gibson stated that he knew of an old colored man who had voted at the general election year after year, and . . . his right was unquestionable." Regarding Findlay's victory, "The vanquished party . . . was induced to question the fairness of the election . . . that in one election district in particular *fifty* votes had been given by *colored* persons. They were known to have been particularly friendly to the successful candidate. The fact of such persons having been in the practice of voting at that district for years before, was conceded."[32]

Franklin County offers a window into black rural voting across the North. It was one of twenty Pennsylvania counties along or near the Mason-Dixon, twelve of which contained more than 500 black people in 1820. This border-land was unique, however. In no other free state abutting slavery did men of color vote regularly prior to the 1840s, when men of color began voting in Ohio. Upper New England (Vermont, New Hampshire, Maine, Massachusetts), where they voted without disruption, was as far away from the slave states as one could get; New York's black men participated actively in elections before near-complete disfranchisement in 1821 and again later, but were also physically distant. New Jersey abutted slavery, but black suffrage ended abruptly there in 1807. The Keystone State alone shared a border with three slave states, a short carriage and later train ride from the slave marts of Baltimore, the District of Columbia, and Richmond, and its southern tier was prime territory for slavecatchers. That men of color in many of its border counties voted through 1838 poses a new paradigm.[33]

Franklin and the counties like it were a frontierish mix of eighteenth-century deference politicking and raffish post-1800 partisanship. Franklin featured a squirearchy of four major clans (a "kind of aristocracy . . . called family interest. . . . The county is divided into several connexions of this kind, instead of parties . . . the Reas, the Bards, the Maclays, the Findlays"), who typified the Scotch-Irish gentry dominating the state and competing for offices in the militia, the county, and the state and even national capitals. The Bards' connection to the Findlays (Archibald's brother's widow married William's brother John) was key because the latter family exerted considerable clout; in the 1820s, the Findlays sent to Congress a senator (William) and two representatives (his brothers John and James). On Election Day, local power-brokers faced off surrounded by their relatives and retainers, and some included black men among their "connexion"; the 1800 manuscript census shows the various Findlays and Bards (plus the former's in-laws, the Irwins) had thirty-one free people of color living in their households, as well as six slaves.[34]

The story was simply told by Findlay's enemies. Soon after his victory, a hostile Old School Republican editor in nearby Shippensburg reported Bard brought dozens of black men to vote as part of a push by "patent [meaning fake] Republicans." The latter were tarred as "office holders" controlling nominations and patronage via a closed caucus. The old trope of corruption was invoked with a racial spicing, that "flocks of blackbirds" appeared and "the negroes decided the day entirely." Notably, "a certain Judge got a *black ewe* and dressed it up with breeches and surtout, then sticking a ticket for Findlay in its fore foot led it up to the poll," declaring it was "an *African* that had *paid taxes*, however, upon the inspector's putting the question to the proposed voter, the animal unluckily cried *bah*." In following days, the editor added that the Colonization Society could use the judge "as a very suitable character to officiate in collecting and drilling the jetty gentlemen," with references to "black birds baked in a pie," and "Black spirits and white, Blue spirits and grey!" (a popular allusion to *Macbeth*); finally, "A patentee was heard to say, in Chambersburg, on the day of the election, that he had *lent his cow to a negro*, to make him *taxable*, in order to obtain his vote."[35]

The really high style came in a letter from a purported man of color in "Messabug" (Mercersburg):

> We had a tarnation fine dime of it on e day and bery plesurful meetun some days afore—at e meetun I vas chused chairman in Misser Baird secretary for e purpus iv gittin all e color man vote for Finlay, corden to reslushun we resolb las dime. . . . Misser Baird make a norashun . . . in wich he kount heep a black man hiv is gud a rite to vote is himself. Unkel Bob he tell e meetun as how he reed in Misser Binns baper dat all gud dimecrats are born equally free witout regardin e color. . . . We all agreed to vote for Misser Finlay cause he worin e gud cleber feller in bery kine to e color peple. Hullo! wat e debbel matter now! Cuzzin Jo, you crazzee— he run in e meetun like fule . . . tell e meetun as how eb Misser Heester wid be de gubernor all de negurs wid be hinged up. . . . Den Misser Baird maik a moshun dat we all support de demekratik kandedat, den we jurn till nix week sum tim for tak in considereshun de equill disbushun of lan, den I sen you a copy
>
> Jaco Jone
>
> P.S. Misser Baird say politiks is gud fur us all—mabe I rite sum again if key maik me justis of de peas.

Were there meetings chaired by a black man, with the judge acting as secretary, "for the purpose of getting all colored men to vote for Findlay," where Bard "made an oration" declaring "a black man has as good a right to vote as himself," after which "we all agreed to vote for Mr. Findlay?" Minus the racial humbuggery, this may be how citizenship politics operated, although references to the "equal distribution of land," the claim that if Joseph Hiester, Findlay's opponent, backed by Old Schoolers and Federalists, were governor, "all the negroes would be hanged," and the offer to make Mr. Jones a "justice of the peace" were obviously fakery.[36]

Who were these men? Were they all regular taxables ("The fact of such persons having been in the practice of voting at that district for years before, was conceded"), or were some lent property ("a cow") so they could be assessed for this election, a common practice? Unlike in Bucks County, another site of black voting, there was no link to friendly white abolitionists. Franklin's interracial politics were entirely practical, a "connection" based on the patron-client relations of family and neighborhood. Whether these men of color were born in Pennsylvania and grew up indentured to their parents' masters is unknowable; they were as likely manumitted in Maryland or Virginia and took themselves north; they could easily have been fugitives employed under new names. The racial slurs on Findlay's campaign persisted. Three petitions to the legislature asserted widespread illegal voting with no details. Subsequently, references recurred to Bard's and Findlay's affinity for black people, as in this aside: "It is said that Findlay has pardoned the negro lately sentenced to be hung at Harrisburg, in consequence of the mediation of Judge Bard in his favor."[37]

During Findlay's rematch with Hiester in 1820, race came up again. In July, pro-Hiester papers charged Findlay had owned slaves until recently, insisting voters would never "be induced to *make choice of a slaveholder for their chief magistrate*." Findlay's backers countered with affidavits indicating he had never really owned Hannah, the woman in question, just held her for his brother, and had freed his one slave in 1807, avowing that the "principles of slavery, are repugnant to those of justice," followed by evidence that Hiester had registered five slaves between 1780 and 1806. Repeatedly, each candidate's antislavery credentials were offered as a proof of his republicanism, clearly linked to the Missouri Crisis, which had "excited the public attention to the principles by which slavery has been introduced and defended into our country." The Findlayites further asserted Hiester had voted at the 1790 convention to limit voting by men under twenty-two to sons of "freeholders"; that and his supposed resistance to emancipation (both demonstrably false) proved he would "draw an aristocratical distinction between . . . the children of the *rich* and those of the *poor*" and desired, "by voting against our abolition law, to lord it forever over the wretched race of Africa. The two votes are consistent; the one . . . leading to the establishment, and the other to the perpetuation, of slavery." Conversely, a Philadelphia "Democratic Meeting" hailed Findlay "as the friend of enlightened freedom, without regard to the shade of color with which providence has marked his features," and the *Franklin Gazette*, his mouthpiece, called him an "undeviating advocate for equal rights and the abolition of slavery." The duel continued through Election Day. The Findlayites distributed a former slave's affidavit that "he was liberated by his master, William Findlay . . . in the year 1807; that it was a free and voluntary act on the part of his master; that he always understood he was opposed to slavery; nor was ONE CENT ever given by this deponent to his master for his freedom." Increasingly, they positioned their man as pro-black. When insults were directed at the governor's cook and fiddler, a pro-Findlay paper claimed the editor, John Binns, "pretends to despise the affidavit of *George Cuffee*, because he is *a negro*. Cuffee, although *black*, is a *freeman*; his character stands fair; and his affidavit will at any time or place outweigh . . . the '*perilous oath*' of John Binns." After Hiester's victory brought new charges of illegal voting, including by Negroes, a pro-Hiester Federalist paper reminded readers that "a Negro has the right of voting in this state."[38]

After 1820, disputes over black voting subsided, although the state's electoral muddle continued to trouble the executive.[39] In 1823, Hiester expressed concern about the "want of uniformity in the decisions of election officers respecting the admission of votes in different counties, in different districts of the same county, and sometimes in the same district at different times when the officers conducting the election happen to be different." He noted "the neglect or omission . . . to assess . . . at the appointed time," while "other districts, have received the votes of persons who have not been assessed at the usual period, permitting them . . . to pay their tax on the very day of election." In 1826, Governor John Andrew Shulze (Findlay's son-in-law) asked, "Do the same qualifications entitle similar persons to vote in all our different counties? Or do different constructions entitle whole classes of persons to vote in one district, whose votes would be rejected in the next? Is the term freeman, so construed in one district as totally to exclude, and in another freely to admit persons of colour to exercise the right of suffrage?" Pleas for rationalization fell on deaf ears. Where black men, paupers, the sons of immigrants, or recently naturalized men had voted, they continued without interruption. In counties where men of color were not assessed, they continued abstaining without protest. The "game without rules" was many local games, in which black men found their own places.[40]

Confrontations for Power, 1834–1838

Well into the Age of Jackson, enfranchisement and disfranchisement coexisted within Pennsylvania's decentralized polity. No one, white or black, was troubled by this incongruity, and no effort was made to swing the state either way, until a realignment threatened the Democratic (formerly Republican) Party that had controlled the state since 1799. Suddenly, a series of confrontations opened. These battles were public demonstrations of power—sometimes black men asserting rights, more often whites stripping whatever gains blacks had achieved. All ended in defeat for Pennsylvanians of color.

Elite-instigated violence defined the period, sanctioned by Democrats and coupled to their party's drive to disfranchise black men. A chorus of Negro-baiting in newspapers, in campaign rhetoric, and at party gatherings culminated in two judicial decisions and the state constitutional convention's vote to define suffrage as "white." This concerted campaign to erase even "citizenship for protection" turned Afro-Pennsylvanians into barely tolerated wards, and prefigured the 1890–1908 period in the former Confederacy, when disfranchisement also went hand in hand with mob violence. In both cases, the Democrats' vulnerability to biracial electoral coalitions was the spur to drive black men from the polls.[41]

The context for attacking black citizenship was the collapse of Democratic hegemony in the early 1830s. The decade's first half saw the rise of a durable Antimasonic Party led by the brilliant infighter Thaddeus Stevens, aided by pervasive Democratic factionalism. For the next quarter-century, this transplanted Yankee played a crucial role in Gettysburg and then Lancaster, consistently espousing his hatred of slavery. In 1835, Stevens's candidate, Simon Ritner, won the governorship in coalition with the Whigs, opposing two Democrats. Ritner and Stevens urged a new direction—the former's 1836 inaugural address urged Pennsylvanians to stop "bowing the knee to the dark spirit of slavery." This charge was potent since Pennsylvania's Democracy was the South's most reliable northern ally but provoked a counterattack using Ritner and Stevens's connections to abolitionism (the governor's son was a delegate to the Pennsylvania Anti-Slavery Society's 1837 founding; Stevens signed its call, and donated to the American Anti-Slavery Society). Whigs and Antimasons took the offensive first with an 1836 Registry Law requiring "an annual registration of voters" in Philadelphia County, "as a curb upon voting frauds in the populous Irish centers of Southwark and Moyamensing." This legislation targeted the gangs that controlled city and county polling places. It required that if "three electors thereof" requested assistance, the mayor, aldermen, or other officials must "clear any window, or avenue to any window . . . which shall be obstructed . . . to prevent voters from approaching . . . subject to a penalty of five hundred dollars." Results were immediate, and Whigs crowed that while "Jackson bullying and beating kept numbers from the polls" formerly, now "the election ground has ceased to be a scene of riot. Crowds do not block the polls and prevent the quiet, aged, and infirm citizens from voting."[42]

Democrats responded by assailing Ritner as "his Black Majesty," alleging the governor attended "a negro camp meeting" and fired Democratic state employees to "employ Negroes in their places." They charged that abolitionists and Ritner would literally put black men above "bogtrotters," as in the notorious cartoon *The Results of Abolitionism*, which showed a building site bossed by a black foreman ("White man, hurry up them bricks") under a white owner ("Sambo, hurry up the white laborers"), while Irishmen did the backbreaking labor, and black men enjoyed the skilled trades ("Bring up the mortar you white rascals"). These were the years when desperate Irishmen forced black men out of their traditional labor market niches, so this imagined reversal had special force. Eventually, the Democrats initiated a campaign of total disfranchisement to fire up their base. They excluded black voters in traditionally anti-Democratic counties such as Lancaster and Bucks, and trumpeted "negro domination" in counties where black men never voted. The threat of "Abolitionism and British Bankism" linked black rights to Jackson's campaign against the Whig-backed National Bank. Ritner was "an open and avowed abolitionist," one of the "set of misguided and designing men . . . plotting the dismemberment of our union and the destruction of the peace and liberty of its citizens, by inciting insurrections among the blacks of the south, and . . . placing the negro upon a footing of equality with the white man." If these plotters succeeded in importing "50,000 or 60,000 additional free negroes, to what a terrible state will the poorer classes of whites be reduced."[43]

Abolitionist Antipolitics

For all the noise about "Abolitionists," the latter's passivity predetermined the political eclipse of black Pennsylvanians. Here the historiography of Garrisonian abolitionism impedes understanding. Scholars assign Pennsylvania a major role, through Garrison's personal inspiration by James Forten, whom he met while working in Baltimore on Benjamin Lundy's *Genius of Universal Emancipation* in 1829–30, and Philadelphia's hosting the December 1833 founding of the American Anti-Slavery Society (AASS). This confuses the national and local. Pennsylvania's black elite did help build the new movement, furnishing most of *The Liberator*'s early subscribers, buying hundreds of copies of Garrison's *Thoughts on African Colonization*, and extending him financial aid. But Garrison was far away in Boston, and their radicalism was equally at a remove, as in their opposing the ACS. The AASS's coming to Philadelphia was a gesture to the PAS, as the new society's major leaders were from New England and New York. It did break with the PAS's racial exclusivity by admitting a few black delegates, electing eight (mainly Pennsylvanians) to its seventy-two-man Board of Managers, and declaring African Americans, "according to their intellectual and moral worth," should "share an equality with the whites, of civil and religious privileges." But biracial Garrisonianism remained stillborn in Pennsylvania, because of the PAS's steadfast moderation and the "Quietism" of even the antislavery Hicksite Quakers (the opposing Orthodox wing backed colonization and was so openly hostile that the acerbic black editor Samuel R. Ward later called Philadelphia "the head-quarters of Quaker negrophobia"). As late as May 1835, Pennsylvania contained only six of the AASS's 221 local auxiliaries, and they remained nearly all white: a search of their founders and officers shows minimal black participation.[44]

On occasion, the presumption of whiteness was explicit, as in August 1837, when the Junior Anti-Slavery Society of Philadelphia debated, "Is it *expedient for colored persons* to join Anti-Slavery Societies?" When the Pennsylvania

Anti-Slavery Society (PASS) finally organized in January 1837, quietism, racial separatism, and treating abolitionism as white people's business were givens. "Nearly one half of the members of the Convention" were "of the Society of Friends," while black men constituted only eight of 232 delegates, and none were among its thirty-four officers or appointed to any of the committees, even the group preparing "an address to the people of colour in this state." Although the outspoken Junius C. Morel denounced colonization as an "American Citizen" ("Here, Sir, were we born—here we drew our earliest breath—and here, repose in peace the bones and ashes of our fathers . . . here by their graves, are we determined to die"), he was "well aware that a part of this audience are not accustomed to colored persons speaking in their public assemblages," and his speech was omitted from the proceedings. The only man of color included in those was William Whipper, via a letter hailing the "influence of anti-slavery principles" on his people, "in checking their evil dispositions, and inculcating moral principles." The published "Address, to the Coloured People of the Commonwealth" emphatically instructed them to avoid offense. While affirming they were indeed Americans ("[Africa] is no more your native country than England, Ireland, or Germany is the native country of the whites"), it praised their passivity, akin to "the Lord's people when suffering under Egyptian bondage: and as it was with them, so will it be with you, if you can be preserved in patience, until the Lord's own time shall arrive." From here on, all was admonition: "The worst thing you can do is, to engage in broils and commotions." One senses a Quakerish fear about black people's propensity for armed self-defense—"avoid as far as possible all heats of passion, and all feelings of revenge," since "nothing . . . would please your enemies more than to be able to goad you on to some rash act." Mixed in with finger-wagging about the "inclination to collect together for frolicking, feasting, and sinful pursuits" by those who "live to gratify their animal propensities" was a fantastical optimism: "The child is now born who will live to see a perfect equality so far as the effects of colour are concerned. . . . LET EVERY ONE OF THE COLOURED PEOPLE, MALE OR FEMALE . . . FULFIL ALL THEIR MORAL, SOCIAL, AND RELIGIOUS DUTIES:—This is all you have to do to ensure your liberty and equality."[45]

Deep-seated quietism did not keep the men and women of the PASS from an unswerving dedication to aiding fugitives. They lived their witness, even when angry neighbors burned down their barns, and avowed the abolitionist ideal year-in and year-out. They also acted almost entirely separately from their fellow Pennsylvanians of color. The 1837 convention set the pattern of minimal black participation in the state's abolitionist movement, except when professional orators like Douglass, Charles Lenox Remond, or William Wells Brown were imported; indeed, a visitor of color was more likely to serve on a committee or speak at a PASS convention than any local black person. The exception was Purvis, who remained a prominent Garrisonian when most national black leaders defected to the American and Foreign Anti-Slavery Society and the Liberty Party. Why Pennsylvania's abolitionists made so little room for black people was clarified at the December 1849 PASS convention when the black New Yorker Thomas Van Rensselaer declared "abolitionists are censurable" for their failure to contribute to the "elevation of the free people of color." All present disagreed. J. Miller McKim, the society's chief lecturer, insisted their condition kept improving. Purvis called it "a preposterous idea that the abolitionists were to divert their energies from their great work, in order to benefit a few colored people. *We* are, he said, by the efforts of our anti-slavery friends, already in advance of public sentiment, and when slavery is abolished, we shall be able to take care of ourselves." A black Baltimorean, E. J. Williams, added her people had "too much love of display, and waste their means . . . on showy dress . . . consenting to their own degradation."[46]

In other states, biracial abolitionism facilitated black participation in the larger political world. Pennsylvania's pacifist, electorally abstentionist, and racially separatist version of antislavery had the opposite effect. Despite that roadblock, black electoral politics surged during the 1830s entirely outside of abolitionism's dead end. From 1834 through early 1838, black men mobilized to vote where they could and attempted to vote in new places, only to be decisively defeated. They were disfranchised juridically twice between late December 1837 and late February 1838, and Democrats used the specter of "negro voting" to disfranchise them constitutionally. In the most celebrated case, dozens of black men showed up at the polls in Bucks County, but their votes were invalidated and the men they elected tossed out of office. Their Antimasonic and Whig allies were overwhelmingly outvoted at the convention, and prominent black men were forcibly expelled from the galleries: can one imagine an eminent white merchant's son beaten in public, as James Forten, Jr., was? After 1838, it was clear that anything could be done to a black person in the Keystone State.

Rioting along the Susquehanna

The triumph of partisan Negrophobia began with carefully staged race riots in Columbia, a thriving river town on the Susquehanna whose wealthiest citizen was the black lumber dealer Stephen Smith. Founded and dominated by the Wright family, antislavery Quakers, Columbia embodied the convergence of white patronage and black demographic weight. The Wrights sponsored the immigration of whole plantations manumitted by Virginia and Maryland

Quakers, and settled them in plots on Tow Hill, "a conglomeration of tiny alleyways and side streets . . . the most congested area in town, its log and frame shanties sheltering hundreds of former slaves." By 1820, "the rate of black immigration . . . greatly exceeded the general rate of population growth," with 1800's black population of ten mushrooming to 288 free people of color and sixty-four remaining slaves in 1820, in a town of 1,092. Columbia was the state's blackest place outside of Philadelphia's Cedar Ward, but very different—as an entrepôt for lumber floated down the river and shipped to Philadelphia, it became a "black Eldorado" for entrepreneurs of color.[47]

These men were led by Stephen Smith; he was the riot's target, and the victory he achieved in alliance with Columbia's old-guard elites its most striking feature. Born in 1795 and originally a servant to a lumber merchant up the river in Dauphin County, he bought out of his indenture in 1816, and prospered. "Black Steve" began acquiring property and advertising his wares as a young man. By 1820 he owned two lots worth $300, and by 1829 he had five houses and five other lots worth $2,300. In 1833, he was worth $6,500. By 1849, his firm "had on hand several thousand bushels of coal, 2,250,000 feet of lumber, and twenty-two of the finest merchantmen cars running on the railroad from Columbia to Philadelphia and Baltimore," as well as "nine thousand dollars worth of stock in the Columbia bank," also owning fifty-two houses in Philadelphia and many more in Columbia. He routinely made the largest donation at state antislavery meetings and was remembered in legendary terms. In 1922, a local historian (who otherwise referred to the "hundreds of darkies, who, in earlier days, had worked in tobacco, cotton and corn fields down in Dixie") spoke respectfully of Smith as "the largest stockholder in his day in the Columbia bank," who "would have been president had it not been for his complexion," so he "was given the privilege of naming the white man who became president in his stead."[48]

In 1834, Columbia's black community embodied what many whites feared. It was well organized, well connected, and outspoken. As early as 1824, at a "Meeting of the Colored People . . . held in the African Methodist Episcopal church, for the purpose of taking into consideration the proposition of President Boyer" of Haiti, they "unanimously agreed—That the proposal of President Boyer is the most favorable of any we have yet received," appointing a committee to meet with his representative; Smith chaired the meeting. In 1831, they published a militant denunciation of colonizationism, and insisted they would "stay in the country for which some of our ancestors fought and bled." Worse yet, about one quarter of black families lived better than ordinary white laborers, as skilled workers, in services and trades, even as professionals and proprietors, like Smith and his wife, who kept an oyster house.

Their relationship with the town's Quaker founders was very visible, and they voted in large numbers for both parties.[49]

The Columbia riots were emphatically partisan. In 1834, a newer, less-wealthy group of Democratic businessmen tried to overturn the town's Quaker leaders, once Federalist, later National Republican, now founders of the local Whig Party. Taking a cue from New York and Philadelphia's recent antiabolitionist riots, these Jacksonians sought to arouse white workingmen against blacks and the latter's white protectors, charged with the "employing Negroes to do that labor which was formerly done entirely by whites." In Philadelphia, white and black men first fought around a popular carousel, the Flying Horses. Then, from August 12 to August 15, white apprentices went on a rampage, burning and looting black dwellings and churches, beating up residents, killing at least one. Reprints of Philadelphia news in Lancaster papers inspired copycat actions in response to Stephen Smith's rapid acquisition of rental properties and the black community's commitment to shielding fugitives.[50]

In Columbia, the mob focused on burning or tearing down houses and beatings, followed by orders of expulsion. White men first gathered on August 20 to complain about insufferable Negroes, and mob actions through early October spurred meetings to solve the crisis, for which black citizens were held entirely responsible. The first meeting expressed righteous grievance at the town's fathers and outrage at Negroes' outstripping whites in life's ordinary pleasures, so "poor honest citizens that so long have maintained their families by their labor" must "fly from their native place that a band of disorderly Negroes may revel with the money that ought to support the white man and his family." Evidently, some black people were living too well, and free to "commit the most lascivious and degrading actions with impunity, and wanton in riot and debauchery." The basic threat was economic, that "in course of time" they would be "engaged in every branch of mechanical business, and their known disposition to work for almost any price may well excite our fears that mechanics at no distant period will scarcely be able to procure a mere subsistence." After that, it was vintage Jacksonianism, the ersatz class struggle of the "white workingman" against aristocrats and negroes. Rich men wanted "the poor whites to amalgamate with the blacks." Their "diabolical design" was "to break down the distinctive barrier between the colors that the poor whites may gradually sink into the degraded condition of the Negroes—that, like them, they may be slaves and tools," as the aristos had "no intention . . . to marry their own daughters to the blacks." This pseudo-workingmen's address concluded on an electoral note: "We will not purchase any article (that can be procured elsewhere) or give our vote for any office whatever, to any one who employs Negroes to do that species of labor white men have been accustomed to perform."[51]

The Whigs quickly sought to head off further property destruction via a buyout of black property-holders, while warning them to cease harboring runaways. More meetings and more riots followed. At midnight on September 2, whites attacked Smith's house, "the porch and a part of the frame of which they tore down, the inmates leaving the building at the first alarm." The mob continued to his office, and "broke open the windows and doors, rifled the desk, and scattered the papers along the pavement" (perhaps records of his rental properties) while failing to "upset the building." A month later, two other prominent men of color, James Smith and James Richards, were attacked, with the latter beaten bloody in the street, his home, dental instruments, and schoolroom destroyed around him. Eight men, mainly laborers, were indicted for these mobbings, but were acquitted after prolonged delays and not made to pay court costs, a rare occurrence suggesting public approval.[52]

However, rather than a triumph for white workingmen and their self-appointed leaders, efforts to expel blacks and stigmatize their allies fizzled out. At first, the black middle class dissembled, telling a committee of respectables they were "decidedly favorable" to leaving ("Some of them are anxious, many willing, to sell at once provided a reasonable price were offered. . . . All to whom your committee spoke on the subject of harboring strange persons among them, seemed disposed to give the proper attention to the subject"). Playing a canny waiting game, Stephen Smith published weekly advertisements avowing his willingness to sell, until someone sent him a threatening letter, alleging he had again encouraged "the white people to bid up property, as you have been in the habit of doing for a number of years back," which would no longer be tolerated—"the less you appear in the assembly of the whites the better it will be for your black hide," since many whites "think your absence from it a benefit, as you are considered an injury to the real value of property in Columbia." Smith showed the letter to his business associates, James, William, and John L. Wright, and they published it with a $100 reward, adding, "We consider ourselves injured by threats made to prevent persons from attending and bidding on property advertised by the subscribers, at public auction." The Wrights' certification of Smith as a reputable businessman implied costs to attacking him. He was left alone and published more advertisements, that "desirous to avoid being associated with those heart-rending scenes, and unrighteous persecutions . . . directed against the colored population of this Borough," he had offered to sell "my entire stock of lumber" and "close my business in Columbia." He now felt a "renewed confidence" and would "continue to prosecute my business with my usual vigor." Making his connections to power explicit, he offered "hearty thanks . . . for the very liberal patronage I have always received, but more especially for their favors during that eventful period of excitement: for never before has there been a time, when I could place such a just estimate on the value of my friends."[53]

The Columbia riots have been well studied, but their partisan aspect remains obscure. At the time, it was well understood that dozens of house-owning black "Freeholders" (though not the ordinary "Freemen") were assessed and voted like other men for the party of their choice, although the majority seem to have been Whigs. In a remarkable evocation of a time before Negrophobia became his party's animating spirit, a "Jackson Democrat" insisted in 1868 that he did not share "the horror and dread" of his fellow Democrats "at the bare idea of voting with the negro."

> I went to the polls in this place and voted for Gen. Jackson (God bless his memory,) in 1832, a number of colored men also voted for him, one of whom is now living in Philadelphia, whose wealth is almost equal to the combined wealth of the entire Democracy of Columbia; I refer to Stephen Smith. James Burrell, a retired lumber merchant of Columbia, and Frank Knight, deceased, and formerly a pilot on the river, all voted the Democratic ticket. Perhaps two or three other colored men voted our ticket, their names I have forgotten. I remember quite a number who voted the Whig ticket, many of whom are yet living and will again vote. Thomas Waters, Jesse Burrell, Richard Rice, James Hollingsworth, Joshua P. B. Eddy, Harry Worthington, John Patterson, Jessee Mays and Alexander Smith.[54]

The above suggests that black men's electoral participation was ignored in the denunciations of Negro perfidy and white manipulation because both parties had sought their votes. What is the connection between their voting and the mobs of 1834? Black men's allies were prominent anti-Jackson men; John L. Wright was one of thirteen issuing the call for a "Lancaster County National Republican Meeting" in 1832. By 1834, those same men were confronting Jackson as Whigs, and Columbia Whigs briefly achieved national prominence when Daniel Webster presented their memorial to the Senate that June, supporting the Bank of the United States. Locally, Democrats excoriated these "Wigs of Columbia," linking them with efforts elsewhere to recruit "Colored Wigs." Equating the aristocratic, pro-Bank Whiggery with antislavery, the *Lancaster Journal* indicted the Columbians in June of that year as men "who have done more to create an unfriendly feeling between the people of this State and our brethren of Maryland and Virginia, than any other seventeen men in the Commonwealth." The Wrights and their allies were "practical abolitionists . . . who have ardently labored to set the slave against the master—encouraging runaways, and leaving nothing undone to protect them—legally and illegally." The Whigs' goal was to reduce "the *Peasantry*—the working people—the farming population of our free state to the same abject situation of their colored friends in Virginia!" The riots' partisan subtext emerged again in October, when that paper again attacked "De Wigs of Color!," outraged by efforts in Maine, Massachusetts, and even Delaware to recruit men of color into the pro-Bank campaign, "fraternizing with the blacks, Sambo, Cuffee and Caesar, to do the work of King Nicholas" (Biddle, the president of the Second Bank of the United States). The editor tied this recruitment to Columbia's mobs, insisting Whigs had "done the negroes real injury" by stirring up anger, which "led to the late disturbances." Black men had been "encouraged to take part in politics, and amalgamate with our tip-top gentry, the Wigs, in the formation of their ticket, and in memorializing Congress" and thus it was "no wonder that they should think of drawing the bonds of their alliance still closer." Had black Columbians like Smith participated in Whig nominations and drafting the memorial to Webster? The record is opaque, but this account is perfectly plausible, since the Whigs had done exactly that in Portland and Boston.[55]

William Fogg's Charge

Black Columbia and "Black Steve" Smith were famous or infamous in Pennsylvania's populous southeast, but the setting for Pennsylvania's next battle over black voting was a nearly-monochrome northeastern backwater. On October 13, 1835 a farmer named William Fogg tried to vote, and was refused by the inspector, Hiram Hobbs, and several judges of elections, because of his complexion. Fogg pressed a suit against Hobbs and others before Luzerne County's Court of Common Pleas, and won easily in early 1837. Almost all facts in the case derive from the state supreme court decision overturning that original ruling, which had stated simply, "The plaintiff . . . a colored man . . . brought this action for the purpose of establishing a right, which he claimed to have, of voting . . . as a citizen and a freeman of the state." He had obeyed the law by paying "a county tax, assessed at least six months before the said election; all which being made known to the plaintiffs in error, he offered to vote, but they . . . fraudulently and maliciously intending to injure and damnify him . . . absolutely refused to receive his vote."[56]

What bears noting is Fogg's identity as a "freeholder," one of hundreds of thousands of independent farmers from Maine to Michigan. He fit squarely into the upper tier of Luzerne's Greenfield Township, close to New York State. From a land dispute in the 1870s and online family trees, we know that Fogg had come with his mother Betsey from New London, Connecticut, where he was born in 1793 (he told census takers 1801 or 1803); she married a man named

Paddy Allen in 1807, and bore him three children. Allen absconded in 1832, after deeding his stepson William forty acres of 100 bought in 1808 and settled in 1811. In the 1850 census, 190 of 232 families in Scott (formerly Greenfield) Township were headed by farmers like Fogg, but only seventy-three owned land. Fogg's land, worth $1,000, put him among the middling sort, above the thirteen with holdings worth a few hundred dollars, but below the fifteen with farms valued above $2,000. In subsequent decades, Fogg kept accruing wealth, and was worth $2,500 by 1870.[57]

The politically relevant fact is that Luzerne's first settlers all came from New England, bringing a Yankee ethos akin to Ohio's Western Reserve. Since the Jeffersonian triumph of 1799, it had been Pennsylvania Federalism's strongest rural base. In Luzerne, as in New York and Ohio, sympathetic assessors and election inspectors likely permitted black voting; as a freeholder, Fogg would have voted since he came of age, as long as the right kind of transplanted Yankees controlled the polls.[58]

The case was heard by Judge David Scott, an eminent figure; he may have been Fogg's neighbor, since Greenfield Township was renamed Scott Township in 1846. Scott ruled that there "being no controversy between the parties as to the facts of the case," the verdict of the jury must be in his favor, since the defendant had suffered "a personal wrong, in being deprived of the right of suffrage by the defendants, who were officers of the election, they well knowing that he was a legal voter." Like other lawyers and judges, he could find no racial intent in the 1790 Constitution's language authorizing suffrage for "every freeman above the age of 21" who paid a tax and established residency. He endorsed Fogg's citizenship with enthusiasm. The defendants' final claim was "that the free negro or mulatto is not a citizen . . . and therefore is not entitled to the right of suffrage." Fogg as the plaintiff had brought the suit to settle that question, and Scott was happy to do so. There was "no expression in the constitution or laws of the United States, nor in the constitution or laws of the state of Pennsylvania, which can legally be construed to prohibit free negroes and mulattoes . . . from exercising the rights of an elector." He then went beyond the law, expressing his pride in how "The preamble to the act for the gradual abolition of slavery . . . breathes a spirit of piety and patriotism, and fully indicates an intention in the legislature to make the man of color a *freeman*."[59]

It is difficult to find a clearer statement of the old nonracial republicanism, but Scott's opinion was far from universal in Luzerne. The local account, reprinted in Philadelphia, Baltimore, and New York newspapers, reported, "No case for many years in this county . . . has excited more feeling than this," and the jury's apparent deadlock produced minimal damages of six cents, in response to the directed verdict. Beyond that, while Fogg may have "brought this action for the purpose of establishing a right, which he claimed to have, of voting," Hobbs clearly blocked his voting to assert the absence of any such right, given that his counsel, H. B. Wright, was a prominent Democrat whose case focused on denying any possibility of black citizenship.[60]

As detailed below, Fogg's case resulted in Pennsylvania's supreme court ignoring the 1790 state constitution as written, plus existing precedents, to make new law out of presumptions of caste. Fogg and his allies had made a strategic error. Until then, Pennsylvania's black voters had operated on Scott's premise, that there was no actual "expression in the constitution or laws of the United States, nor in the constitution or laws of . . . Pennsylvania" to bar black voting. By forcing the issue to establish an affirmative precedent, Fogg caused the opposite.

"Englishmen, Negroes, and Abolitionists": The Battle Joined in Bucks

Fogg's case remains obscure, but black voters were vividly on display in Bucks County, north of Philadelphia along the Delaware, a locale associated with Federalists and later Whigs. The fight over "negro voting" in Bucks, where African American men had voted for forty years, sparked statewide attention. A massive black turnout in October 1837 became the Democrats' demonstration case when the "Reform Convention" reconvened in late November. Their claims received crucial support when John Fox, head of the county's Democratic machine and president judge of the judicial district of Bucks and Montgomery, ruled that black voting was unconstitutional on historical grounds. Hailed by Democrats nationwide, his decision anticipated Taney's dictum by almost twenty years.[61]

The 1837 Bucks County election documents how black politics functioned and why they mattered. The *Doylestown Democrat*, a local party organ, documented exactly which men of color voted, followed by detailed rebuttals in the Whig *Bucks County Intelligencer*, further Whig assessments of black men to make them "taxables" so they could vote, and more names listed in the *Democrat*. These attacks furnish information on the black electorate: how they made their livings, where they came from, even their party affiliations—surprisingly, often Democratic, a clue to why black electoral participation was tolerated or encouraged for decades.[62]

In 1840, Bucks ranked sixth in population among Pennsylvania's fifty-four counties (with 48,107 of 1,724,033 inhabitants), full of the well-off farmers for which the state was known. It boasted a thriving local antislavery society, with seventy-one signers of the call to the PASS's founding. At the convention to reform the constitution, three of the county's four delegates, all Whigs, voted with the majority against the first attempt on June 23 to insert "white" into the suffrage clause. During these early debates, a Bucks County Whig, Phineas Jenks, ardently defended black men's voting rights, moving to amend "by striking out the word 'white' wherever it occurs," and stating with some pride that Bucks included "individuals of this description worth twenty and fifty, and . . . in one instance . . . a hundred thousand dollars." Men with "so deep a stake in society" should vote. Conversely, pitting class against race, Jenks supported the existing taxpayer qualification, otherwise "individuals who had no interest in society," residents of county poorhouses, might vote and determine "what amount other citizens should be taxed."[63]

The larger political frame matters here. In 1835, the Antimason Simon Ritner had won the governorship with a 47 percent plurality, and the divided Democrats had lost the General Assembly too. In 1836, the reunited Democrats won the lower House by carrying 72 of 103 seats. Bucks mirrored those results. In 1835, Ritner carried 52 percent of Bucks's voters. Although the Whigs won the county's November 1836 presidential vote, a month earlier they lost all four of its state House seats. This defeat set up a hard-fought local battle for the House in 1837 and the governorship in 1838.[64]

Following the convention's June 23, 1837 vote to maintain nonracial suffrage, Bucks Democrats made the Whigs' "pro-Negro Voting" a wedge issue. The focus became the Quaker township of Middletown, where men in historically black Attleborough Village voted in large numbers. Campaigning against "negro dominance" was a way to gin up the Jackson men, after the exhausting Bank War against Philadelphia financier Nicholas Biddle, personification of Whig "aristocracy." The specter of abolitionists importing "ruthless and drunken negroes" to subjugate white mechanics and farmers was an ideal bogeyman, added to the traditional threats, with the *Doylestown Democrat* announcing they were "contending for their ancient principles of Liberty and equal rights" versus "the old Federal party, fighting to regain their power, by means of a monied Aristocracy, the Bank Power." Now, however, "*Abolitionism* is in the field against us. The Negro Power is united with the Bank power, and he, who now votes for a federal candidate, gives two votes to *Sustain Negro Suffrage*."[65]

There was nothing subtle about the Democrats' habitual aura of paranoia. Mocking Judge Fox's "mono mania" and "political raving," Whigs claimed after their October 1837 victory that "Fox's madness defeated them," by repelling swing voters. But it wasn't all "raving." In 1837, local abolitionists and blacks disturbed the peace in alarming ways, and there were solid reasons to associate them with the Whiggery. Consider the sequence of events. In late June, Whig convention delegates from Bucks voted "to leave the constitution in reference to it [black suffrage] unaltered . . . convinced of the injustice of depriving the worthy and intelligent part of the community, whom God had blessed with a black skin, of this most invaluable right." Then came a celebrated slave rescue in August, whose actors clarified its relation to the electoral contest. Three recent fugitives, the Dorsey brothers, were employed on Robert Purvis's farm in Bensalem in lower Bucks. Purvis was a wealthy gentleman, phenotypically white, a staunch abolitionist, and the man "worth a hundred thousand dollars" whom the Whig Jenks had lauded at the convention; a few months later the Democrats warned that Whigs in power would put "the rich mulatto Purvis" onto juries to assess poor white men's guilt or innocence. Basil Dorsey's owner and slavecatchers grabbed him at the farm in July, but Purvis intervened to delay his extradition, with Dorsey's family and abolitionist whites filling the courtroom. Then, at an August 1 hearing before Judge Fox in Doylestown, Purvis brought in a leading Philadelphia lawyer (and Whig), David Paul Brown, who maneuvered to bar Dorsey's recapture, while black men gathered at the town's exits, ready for a rescue. When Fox freed Dorsey on a technicality, he was pushed into Purvis's carriage to be rushed out to New Jersey. This intervention, backed by a disciplined mob, provoked a frenzied Democratic response. In the words of their Whig opponents, Democrats charged that "negroes" were planning "to waylay the stages in the centre of Bucks County; for the purpose of committing murder: to shoot the judge on the bench, if circumstances rendered it necessary, or to create a general riot and massacre in order to defeat the operations of the laws of the Commonwealth." It was a fact, however, that leading Whigs, like Aaron Ivins, their successful House candidate, belonged to abolitionist families; five Ivinses from Bucks had signed the PASS's call that year.[66]

In early September, the *Democrat* alternated doom-and-gloom with wild optimism. Railing about black men imported to vote, it demanded "a law to punish severely any Judge of an election who should receive the vote of a negro or mulatto." Otherwise Bucks County would become "the negro paradise. Here they are encouraged to come by the abolitionists; and here they will come, unless we shut them out, and say to the south, keep your own paupers!" Yet the same paper boasted, "We shall scatter as by a whirlwind, the whole combined force of the federalists, composed of their Englishmen, Negroes, and Abolitionists." On the general election's eve, they warned of "Negro Ascendancy . . . the election of men, who are openly and avowedly the advocates of Negro Suffrage and Negro ascendancy over the White Man," since the Whigs had "dared to bring Negroes to the Polls on Friday last" to vote for election inspectors, and "In Middletown township, not less than *Seventeen Negro Votes* were received and recorded infavor [sic] of the Abolition Inspector and Assessors!," adding that many "*Negro Voters* are foreign bondsmen and runaway Slaves!" Outlandish claims were made, as if the American

Revolution had reignited in Bucks—"*British subjects*" [meaning *Intelligencer* editor James Kelly] were "uniting with *Negroes*" and "daily attacking the Government . . . forming an abolition party, which if successful, will overthrow the Government, and place the American citizens under the tyrannical yoke of the British Government." In reply, an anonymous abolitionist chortled over Judge Fox's furious efforts to control the "Inspectors' Election, in his own district." As men assembled to vote viva voce for "the judges for the general election, the voice of our *President Judge* was heard above the rest in stentorian tones,—'Come white men—come out here!'" and once the two groups had divided, "in their respective lines, he was heard to address his political opponents. . . . 'Nigger voter! stand in your ranks, or you'll not be counted.'"[67]

At the general election, Bucks's Whigs were aided by as many as 100 black votes in seven townships in the county's Quaker southeast (Middletown, Falls, Bristol, Upper and Lower Makefield, Newtown, and Buckingham). The day was tumultuous; a local historian later wrote, "At no time in the last sixty years were harder blows given and taken." The *Democrat*'s editor, John S. Bryan, assaulted Kelly's brother-in-law, foreman of the *Intelligencer* (another Englishman), for blocking the poll window, swearing "he hated negroes, but had rather see negroes on the [election] ground than Englishmen." The Whigs scored narrow victories in all but one contest, while statewide, Ritner's coalition narrowed the Democrats' House majority to 56–44, maintaining a 19–14 Senate majority. The assertion that "negro votes" turned the tide in Bucks was hardly implausible: the Whig Abraham Fretz was elected county commissioner by twenty-five votes (3,286 to 3,261), and Richard Moore won as auditor by only two (3,302 to 3,000).[68]

The Democrats immediately attacked the result. Their first report after the election evoked a little Haiti along the Delaware, with Quaker farmers and black laborers become a savage revolutionary force:

> A number of the negroes came to the polls with GUNS!—and one of them said HE HAD HIS GUN LOADED, AND WOULD HAVE SHOT IT HAD HE BEEN MOLESTED IN VOTING!!! . . . Tolerate such indulgence to the blacks for a few years longer,—hold out inducement and protection to runaways and harbor them in the lower end of Bucks, and they will make the very streets run with white man's blood. They are easily excited, will lend a ready ear, to oppose the laws of the land, and like Abolitionists and Englishmen are rife for revolution.

To overturn the Whigs, they began rallying "the Germans" in the county's northern townships. In late October, 600 met in Nockamixon, followed by a rally in Tinicum, and then at Northampton's White Bear tavern, each resolving that "a large body of negro votes have controlled the late election in

Bucks," and, after naming the victorious Whigs, that "we will take the necessary measures to contest their respective elections." In addition, "the conduct of any township or borough assessor, in assessing negroes, without any real or personal estate, and for the avowed purpose of securing their vote at any election, meets our decided reprehension." Shortly the *Democrat* published a list of black voters in Middletown, to which the Whigs replied that those men living in Doylestown had been stalwart Democrats, mocking how, after "fifty years . . . it has been discovered . . . that they are disfranchised, and not entitled to vote, notwithstanding they are assessed and *made to pay taxes*." The Whigs singled out a deceased next-door neighbor of Judge Fox, Bob Montgomery, who "was a freeholder, and during Bob's life, was brought to the polls by members of the Democratic party, and voted their ticket." They named various living men, such as "Norris Lee, the Barber, [who] while he lived in the town, voted . . . the same way," and Peter Jackson, who "is a freeholder to a considerable amount—has always voted, and generally the Democratic ticket," adding that he had bet on various Democrats winning (a favorite pastime then), and "was furnished by Democrats with tickets." Finally, they named "a voter for 40 years," Zachariah Cummings of Plumstead, noting, "He is greatly respected—is a freeholder, and uniformly solicited by and voted for Democrats. On all occasions that party has sought and got the negro vote *if they could*." Only then did the Whigs concede their bloc vote in the southeast: "Possibly in some of the lower townships our party got a majority [of black votes] . . . but if so it was because our opponents could not prevent it." The most sensational Whig charge was that a leading Presbyterian, the Reverend Nathaniel Irvin, "a power in the County and a strong Democrat," originally proposed black suffrage: "Their right to vote was a Democratic suggestion, emanating from the Rev. Mr. Irvine [*sic*], who for many years was the great apostle of Democracy in this County."[69]

In late November, the stakes got higher. The *Democrat* charged Whigs were using Bucks's 500 potential black voters (an estimate corresponding closely to 1840's census, a winning margin in a county with 6,500 voters) to gain "absolute control of the elections in the county," and would deploy 5,000 new "negro votes" elsewhere, to "govern the state. . . . The Negroes are tools fit for the aristocracy to work with, and they mean to use them." The consequences were clear, that "if they have the right to vote, it must be given to them, and if so, they clearly have all the other rights of citizens. They are therefore then entitled to be Prothonotaries, Registers, etc., and have an equal right with white citizens to be elected to any office, and be summoned to serve on Juries." "A Member of the Convention" suggested the Whigs and Antimasons would invite in hordes of runaway slaves, until the state was "overrun with a colored population . . . enjoying freedom and power. . . . Your executive chair, your magistracy, and your legislative halls would be filled, and your domestic rights endangered and perhaps violated in the most tender points, by your sable brothers."[70]

Minstrelsy made a ribald appearance. The Whigs' *Intelligencer* used a black man's voice to deride "de berry great meeting at de wite bear tabern," and then hit hard: "well dey tell us de color man make em lose de lection; tell berry big story, like dare printer, bout good old time, hang up color man—no judge, no jury;—well, when we vote Jackson ticket, berry well." The Democrats thundered about how "color man must no marry wid wite womans," to which the interlocutor responded, "what dey do den to Col. Johnson, *under president*, he hab a fine color family, what you say; I *cotch em* now; who chuse him, for that big place? He democrat, who vote him to office?" Targeting Vice President Johnson and his "colored family" was a favorite sport of Whigs, but this charge went further, hinting at the long-standing rumors Jefferson had sold his daughters—"old massa, and sons, make color womans hab children, sell em, mulatto sell high, from 1500 one sell, *pretty one*, do, for 4,500 dollar!"[71]

The *Democrat* then pretended to report on a Whig convention delegate, E. T. McDowell, buying a drink for the black freeholder Peter Jackson at the Doylestown Hotel ("Come Peter . . . step up—you are one of my constituents, what will you take with me?," followed by "Sanke, sanke massa—hope you may nebber die and some day be Govner of dis state—good luck—he knows I always votes for him"). The claim "the substance of the above is true" is reasonable, however, since treating one's constituents was the essence of politicking, and Jackson was a thirty-five-year-old freeholder in Doylestown.[72]

Blackface parodies told for political effect were old hat, but invoking a vast Negro-Abolitionist-English plot against the republic was new, as was "the Democracy" announcing itself as proslavery, unimaginable under Governors Snyder and Findlay. Before Christmas, the *Democrat* printed another meeting's address, attacking those fanatics who would "destroy the lives and property of an enlightened people, merely to relieve the half savage slave, from his civil obligation to labor." Forcing slaves "to labor for the necessaries and comforts of life" was a benevolent act, like those "most intelligent and prudent" parents, who "cause their children to be taught to labor, even by *compulsion*." As for abolishing slavery, "as well might a sect of emancipators be got up to abolish the relations of employer, and laborer, master and apprentice, of parent and child."[73]

Ignoring these attacks, the Whigs kept recruiting black voters even after Judge Fox on December 28 invalidated two of their victories. On January 17, a letter to the *Democrat* denounced Middletown's assessor, Aaron Tomlinson, for collecting taxes from men who had never voted. It waxed venomous about the "poisonous breath of a British emissary," and how "a crowd of Ethiopian blacks are to be thrust into their political counsils [sic], because an imbittered [sic] *foreign foe* says it," announcing that since the fall election "*thirty-seven Negroes have been assessed*." What, he demanded, if "the Whig assessors in each of the thirty townships" followed this pattern? The specter of a biracial party was again raised: "The Whigs are petitioning the Convention daily, to so alter the Constitution as to allow blacks the right of voting. . . . [Thirty] or 40 Negroes in each township" would be assessed and then "brought to the polls to vote for the reception of a new Constitution, giving them the right of suffrage forever!" The writer then listed the men newly assessed, and declared "Now, Aaron, were you an honest man, you would feel ashamed. . . . You are an officer, and took the oath. . . . Did you ever think of that oath after it was swallowed, Aaron? When you were hunting up houseless negroes, and runaway slaves to assess them . . . ?" Weeks later, the same man was still ranting on about how Tomlinson as an inspector had refused "a poor white man's vote . . . by the name of Brown, because he was lame with the rheumatism, your great legal knowledge told you he was a pauper, because he had received a little assistance from the township," while letting a black man vote—"Did you ever know whether James Sharp's family ever received any assistance from the township? By making the enquiry, you will find out he did. Get away white man Brown, you are a Democrat pauper, I contest your vote, come up black Sam, a whig pauper, we will take your vote."[74]

Notwithstanding local fears, in late January the *Democrat* crowed about the "Ascendency [sic] of the Whites Over the Blacks in Pennsylvania," following national acclamation of their leader Fox's judicial manifesto, and the convention's promulgating an exclusive racial suffrage. England had engineered an active subversion via "$100,000 . . . raised in London alone, to pay abolitionist preachers and lecturers, and to establish and maintain Abolitionist newspapers. . . . The English Government hopes to keep up in our very bosom, a hostile power in the negro race, which they can use to stab us to the heart in case of difficulty." But white men were now in the saddle, and the Democrats' state organ celebrated how Ritner would now "loose [sic] some thousands of votes . . . to secure which, his excellency has been for some time been adroitly catering."[75]

Whig vacillation suggests the thin reed on which Pennsylvania's black voters relied. While actively mobilizing black voters, Whigs avoided any defense of their right to vote. On Election Eve in early October, the *Intelligencer* "designedly abstained" from noticing the Democrats' "unprincipled falsehood and misrepresentation. . . . Every Democrat in the county . . . must be ashamed" of how they worked "to create unfounded excitements and improper prejudices." Soon after their victory, they insisted their convention delegates had never voted for any "enlarged privileges and rights" for Negroes, since the suffrage would stay "precisely the same as under the old Constitution." The Democratic assault was because of "some colored citizens having voted *the ticket to which the writer was opposed*. . . . In former times, many of these colored voters gave their suffrages to the party of which this political maniac is a member:—then, *all was right*:—but now, they must be disfranchised!" A week later, as the Democrats ginned up meetings, the *Intelligencer* retreated further: "Upon the subject of negro voting we have no particular predilections or prejudices. So long as we have known any thing in the county, a few colored people have been in the habit of voting." Neither Whig candidate, Fretz or Moore, contested Fox's ruling. At year's end, describing the furor over "Negro Voting" as "Negro Humbug," the Whigs' organ restated its neutrality: "If negroes are not legal voters, let them be denied the right of suffrage." A few weeks later, it repeated that "the present excitement against negroes voting, has been got up by men who have more than any other class, encouraged negro votes."[76] Otherwise, the *Intelligencer* kept silent until, following the convention's 77–45 vote on January 20, 1838 to insert "white" into the constitution's suffrage clause, it reprinted an article savaging Fox's assertion "that free born natives are not citizens, and that the true 'democratic' principle is founded on an 'aristocracy of color!' . . . Negroes, although native born, are not *citizens*. If so what are they? They certainly are not *aliens*."[77]

By that point, it was evident that black politics were effectively terminated in Pennsylvania; all that remained was the supreme court's ruling against William Fogg a few weeks later. There is no way to gauge when the tide shifted decisively toward disfranchisement. Whereas in June 1837 the delegates voted by a substantial margin to sustain nonracial suffrage, from John Fox's ruling on December 28, 1837 through the February 27, 1838 state supreme court decision, the Negrophobes swept the boards, forging new laws, new histories, and new ideologies with abandon. Pennsylvania was retroactively declared, in the language used by both courts, "a community of white men exclusively," in which any black citizenship was a priori impossible. Truly, this was Taneyism before Taney, but we should not treat that newfangled doctrine as a fact. White supremacy had to be made in Pennsylvania, and the "Reform Convention" of 1837–38 was the final act in its making, a precedent that James Buchanan must have had in mind nineteen years later, when he privately urged Chief Justice Taney toward his fateful ruling.

Race against Class: The Politics of Mutual Disfranchisement

Pennsylvania's trajectory of racial disfranchisement is well established. When the convention opened in May 1837, a Philadelphia Democrat, Benjamin

Martin, moved to insert "white" in the suffrage clause. After considerable debate, he was defeated 61–49 on June 23, 1837, with a Whig newspaper noting the "majority . . . are desirous to prevent the exciting subject from being agitated," happy to leave this local option alone. The Democrats had a covert strategy, however. Over summer and fall they stirred up outrage at the plot by Whigs and Antimasons to enfranchise the state's entire black population and import thousands of fugitive Negroes as "illegal voters." This outcry converted a significant number of Whigs and Antimasons, and influenced delegates from all parties who had not been present in June. On January 20, 1838, after bitter late-night debates, the convention voted 77–45 to add "white," denaturalizing the state's black men.[78]

There are competing explanations for this last major instance of racial disfranchisement. Most recently, Nicholas Wood has argued that Pennsylvania Democrats, true "northern men with southern sympathies," consolidated their sectional alliance by making black suffrage "a sacrifice on the altar of slavery." Their party's commitment to White Republicanism promised to raise whites up by pushing black men down. The stakes were considerable, as correspondence between Pennsylvania politicos and national figures like Senators James Buchanan and John C. Calhoun documents.[79]

Certainly, the exigencies of a national coalition based on a proslavery consensus provided reasons to disfranchise. Equally pressing, however, was internal partisan conflict and the gulf between the Whig-Antimasonic understanding of republican citizenship—an implicitly nativist vision grounded in Anglo-American birthright—and the reactionary racial modernism of the Jacksonians. Moreover, as the Whigs' aggressive recruitment of black voters in Bucks demonstrates, it is not true that Democrats attacked and Federalist-turned-Whig gentlemen retreated. In the convention, the "anti–Van Buren" delegates repeatedly invoked their fathers' nonracial republicanism, asking, "Is a human being—a part of the community—born upon your soil, anything but a citizen? What else can you make of him? . . . Who is a citizen, if he be not a citizen?" Those favoring a non-"complexional" suffrage named a different set of enemies, whom they lambasted as fiercely as Democrats derided men of color. Which whites should have no greater, perhaps even fewer, rights than black Pennsylvanians "born upon your soil?" This was an overlapping group within which class, condition, birth, and ethnicity cohered loosely. Lancaster's Emmanuel Reigart exemplified the antipathy some whites felt for other whites versus wealthy taxpayers like James Forten or Robert Purvis. He insisted on maintaining residency and taxpaying requirements to exclude paupers and transient laborers. Why would anyone, Reigart asked, "place the *vicious vagrant, the wandering Arabs, the Tartar hordes* of our large cities on a level with the virtuous and good man?" He posed "these Arabs, steeped in crime and vice" against "the industrious population who inhabit our hills and valleys, our towns and villages." If such "degraded, miserable, and infamous characters" voted, it would be because they had been marched to the polls by demagogues, and were "mere slaves of their keepers."[80]

Thaddeus Stevens, also of Lancaster, opposed enfranchising the white lumpen with exceptional ferocity. Early in the convention, he had derailed "resolutions prohibiting Negro immigration with every parliamentary trick he knew," and tried to guarantee a jury trial "to every human being, in all cases where his life or liberty is at question." Stevens pushed equally hard to preserve class-based suffrage limitations, sneering at a ten-day residency rule which would enfranchise a man even "if he had lodged in a barn in the district for ten days, and washed his cravat in a mud hole. That was sufficient to give him a participation in the Government. . . . The word 'freemen,' in this amendment, did not mean the honest farmer, the mechanic, or laborer, but the vile, the vagabond, the idle and dissipated." Moreover, within recent memory, Antimasons and Whigs like Reigart and Stevens had effectively disfranchised thousands of "vagabond, idle, and dissipated" whites in Philadelphia through their Registry Law. Not only was their fervor as visceral as that of the Negrophobes, they had struck the first blow.[81]

Their final trump was the nativist card. The "wandering Arabs," it was clear, derived from a particular "mudhole": Ireland's priest-ridden bogs, and given the thousands of transient Irishmen employed in digging Pennsylvania's canals, this was no idle claim. As the Pottstown *Anti-Abolitionist* acknowledged, the "prejudice of caste does not exist only with reference to the colored man—we have seen its manifestations also in reference to our Irish population; giving rise to riot and to bloodshed." What saved the Irish was their claim on phenotypical whiteness, the assumption that they would be "amalgamated with the great American mass." If instead they "were to continue amongst us (as will be the case with the blacks) a separate and distinct caste, increasing in strength and numbers," there would be dangers aplenty "to the peace and good order of society from the collisions even of this caste with the native citizens," an accurate prediction of the Know-Nothing agitations to come. The Irishmen among the delegates avoided overt national pride, other than a rare outburst about Pennsylvania's "noble and extensive improvements—her rail roads, canals and public works. . . . Whose labor was it effected these? The labor of the negroes? No. Of Americans? No. . . . It was the labour of the Irish that had done it." Similarly, Whigs and Antimasons usually denounced unspecified "foreigners," as when the Philadelphia Whig John Scott rued that "the Pennsylvania freeman, born on the soil, must contend, in personal conflict, with men, who are strangers to her institutions, and almost to her language."[82]

A clue that Hibernophobia competed sub rosa with Negrophobia was the enthusiastic response to the former, which sometimes crossed party lines. The openly racist Luzerne Democrat George Woodward also urged a committee to look into preventing any foreigners "who may arrive in this state after the fourth day of July, 1841, from acquiring the right to vote or to hold office in this commonwealth," since they were "frequently of the worst part of the population of those countries." At this, his fellow Democrat, the proud Irishman John Cummins, insisted "any naturalized citizen was a citizen of the United States, precisely as much so as if he had been born in the land," and that Woodward had uttered "a gross insult upon the Irish, and the other foreign population of this state."[83]

Here two notions of citizenship were perfectly opposed. The Democracy spoke up for the equality of *all men* who worked, regardless of whether they owned anything or were born in the United States, as long as they had white skins. Such a man might lack a fixed abode, he might become aged and infirm, thus a charge on the county, and a pauper. What mattered was he had labored in good faith, and perhaps served his country too. When Stevens attacked ten-day residency requirements as permitting "vagabonds" lodging in barns to vote wherever they found themselves, the Beaver County Democrat John Dickey declared, "He would not disqualify the pauper in the . . . poor house, who had been a revolutionary soldier. . . . Poverty was not to be regarded as a crime. . . . I would disqualify none but those guilty of infamous crimes." Cummins added, "Every white man that lived in Pennsylvania, who loved his country, and was willing to turn out and hazard his life in defense of its rights . . . ought to have, the right to vote." Any taxpaying or residency requirement subverted basic democratic principles. The Democrats largely succeeded, reducing residency to ten days, although a minimal taxpaying requirement was retained. Minus one word, Benjamin Martin's "white," these reforms would deserve the praise still accorded the Jacksonians by some historians. Nowhere in the world did election laws come so close to universal manhood suffrage. But the "Locofocos," as radical Democrats were labeled, invariably coupled their defense of "poor men" with attacks on "degraded negroes" as inferior, regardless of birth, heritage, military service, literacy, accomplishments, or property. Their language of class was always-already one of race in which "aristocrats," "Tories," and "Federalists" (the epithet Democrats applied to Whigs) encouraged lawless Negroes to undercut white men's wages, steal their jobs, and jostle them at the polls.[84]

The Negrophobes had the advantage in terms of the potential electoral calculus. In May 1837, Benjamin Martin pointed out what the state's black men and their white allies never acknowledged—that a nonracial suffrage enforced statewide would change the balance of power. In Martin's words, "If we admit the

7000 blacks to the polls of Philadelphia, they will be ready to go as they may be directed, influenced, and worked upon by some master of intrigue," likely an allusion to Stevens. He later painted a picture of black men "able, not only to carry the wards, but to distribute all the offices, independent of the wards." This prospect endangered the republic itself—"Supposing coloured men to be elected in this state as members to congress, who would sit by, or hold communion with them? Would it not be offering a gross insult to the southern states of the confederacy?" He pretended to be a disunionist at this prospect— "Pennsylvania had better withdraw from the Union at once, than venture upon an experiment of this kind. [It will] place coloured men in your jury boxes, where you, sir, [looking at the president] are sitting." The *Harrisburg Keystone*, a Democratic flagship, asked, "Which is the Abolition party, who wish to fill our country with negroes with the right to vote and hold office?" and warned, "If the slaves were set free, we should have at least 5,000 in Dauphin County, and our poor taxes would be five times as much as they now are." This became the statewide line of attack, as Democratic orators fanned out.[85]

When the convention moved to Philadelphia in late fall, its tone turned markedly antiblack. The language of birthright had no effect, and ten Antimasons, three Whigs, and five Democrats who had voted against Martin's June amendment defected in the final vote to disfranchise. Joined by eleven Democrats, four Antimasons, and three Whigs absent in June, the result was a lopsidedly racialist majority, 77–45. All that remained for the minority was the old standby of mocking "complexion." A Beaver County Whig insisted Martin's amendment would "exclude men from the right of voting, although their complexions might be as white, and their hair as straight, as that of any member of this body. . . . What chance would a white man, but of dark complexion, have at the polls in a time of great political and party excitement?"[86] After the vote, the Whiggish *Pennsylvania Telegraph* suggested there were "thousands of mixed blood as 'white' as many who come under that denomination," asking how should someone "prove that he is a 'white' man?" Harkening back to when Benjamin Franklin distinguished between "purely white people" and the "Spaniards, Italians, French, Russians and Swedes" with "a swarthy complexion; as are the Germans," it suggested that not only "the negro race, but Spaniards, Portuguese, Swabians, Polanders, and others" might be disfranchised. These assertions had no effect. The era of monolithic whiteness, the great blank page of Americanism, had arrived.[87]

"A Community of White Men"

Minus focus groups and rolling polls, we have no way of knowing (nor could the protagonists) when the tide shifted toward disfranchisement. In the two months between John Fox's December 28, 1837 ruling and the February 27, 1838 release of a concurring opinion by the state's supreme court, the Negrophobes swept the boards, forging new laws, new histories, and new ideologies with abandon. Both legal manifestoes ignored Pennsylvania's constitutional precedents to assert a newfangled theory of citizenship based on "caste."

Fox's decision, trolling the pre-1776 colonial code to document legal burdens imposed on people of color, was clever. Asking "what was the political condition of the negro in Pennsylvania, at the adoption of the present constitution" in 1790, he insisted the appropriate answer came from "the original charters from King Charles the second to Wm. Penn, and from Wm. Penn to the people. . . . It was under these charters that our ancestors settled this province" *as "a community of white men exclusively."* Since "the word *negro* manifestly implies a slave, and probably at that day, all negroes in Pennsylvania were slaves," even if persons of African descent "were free from the control of any private master, yet they were an inferior and degraded animal, and political slaves of the actual government." To him, it was "irresistible, that *negroes,* bound or free, were not considered by the framers of this constitution, as being *born free,* or as having any inalienable rights." Here was Fox's sleight-of-hand. Ignoring that the 1780 act of emancipation declared those born into freedom to be "freemen and Freewomen," the central term in the Anglo-American lexicon of subjectship, he asserted it "repealed the laws above cited for the government of negroes, *but it gave them no political rights,"* simply because it a priori could not: "The Legislature could not give the negro political power. They could not bring within the words of the constitution a class of men not contemplated by the convention which framed it," revising the legislative record fifty-seven years after the fact. Emancipation "left him [the black man] still in his inferior position. . . . Thus matters stood at the adoption of the present constitution in 1790. . . . The negro remained in his inferior and degraded condition," followed by a non sequitur much favored by proslavery orators, "the constitution of the United States had just been ratified by thirteen states, EIGHT of which were slave-holding states, and only five non slave-holding states, and even in these, slavery had been but very recently and partially abolished," ignoring that Congress had rejected inserting "white" into the Articles of Confederation's specification of citizenship. Fox then descended into the anxiety of whiteness ("What white man would not feel himself insulted by a serious imputation that he was a negro. . . . Into what depth of degradation would a white female . . . sink, who should dare to brave public feeling so far as to marry a negro?"), plus the durable red herring of black power ("If the word *citizen* gives the negro the right to vote, then also *it gives him the right to be voted for,* and exercise the office of governor, senator, or any other office"). Fox's ruling was popularized by Democratic organs in state and nation, useful grist for the convention's disfranchisers.[88]

The supreme court's ruling was terser, asserting simply that "our ancestors settled the province as a community of white men, and the blacks were introduced into it as a race of slaves," leading to "an unconquerable prejudice of caste, which has come down to our day, insomuch that a suspicion of taint still has the unjust effect of sinking the subject of it below the common level." The 1780 definition of ex-slaves as "freemen," the 1790 Constitution ignoring race as a condition of suffrage, and that black men voted for forty years in some counties were treated as either irrelevant or a mistake now rectified.[89]

That body's final deliberations on January 20 included sustained defenses of black citizenship. Attempting to shame the majority, several delegates, including Pittsburgh's Walter Forward, later secretary of the treasury in Tyler's administration but always an ally to people of color, denounced their opponents but were shouted down. ("Mr. Forward continued his remarks for some time amidst such noise and confusion. . . . In consequence of the weariness and impatience of the house . . . it was impossible to gather the argument.") The Negrophobes' camp-followers felt no need to respond logically and their speeches sound drink-addled, with one Whig vote-switcher declaring, "As a republican people, we are bound to respect every rank," citing a memorial from people of color as "proof that they have a knowledge of the rights of man, and of the laws of freedom," only to confess his "prejudices in common with the vast number of my fellow citizens. . . . They came fresh from my heart." He was "unwilling to tolerate an association with the blacks, or to exchange civilities with them. I, therefore, dare not vote, under these prejudices, for giving them the right of suffrage."[90]

Here black men appeared at last. Formerly, they had represented themselves via memorials which their allies sought to have printed. A few had been hailed as tributes to their race. Their attempted intervention in person proved utterly humiliating, however. On the day of the vote, four black men, including John P. Burr, Thomas Butler, and James Forten, Jr., claimed their right as citizens to sit on the spectators' benches. A "considerable disturbance took place," which "occasioned great excitement. . . . The assistant sergeant at arms denied admittance to the gallery to several negroes—and the officers . . . this morning removed one or two from the gallery." Later Forten, Jr., returned and "went into the gallery, against the order of the officers, and refused to leave," leading to "the doorkeeper forcibly removing him."[91]

After the crushing 77–45 vote, amendments were offered to maintain a residual black suffrage based on literacy or a freehold, as in New York, or to grandfather existing voters, but all lost overwhelmingly. The Democrats moved to take denaturalization to a higher plane. Just two days after the vote, presuming constitutional disfranchisement was delayed until ratification in October, Democratic legislators introduced measures to end black voting immediately. In the Senate, "General" William Rogers of Bucks proposed, "Whereas, in some election districts in the commonwealth, the inspectors and judges of the elections, have habitually received the votes of negroes, mulattoes, and other persons of the negro race . . . to prevent such proceedings hereafter, Be it enacted . . . that it is not lawful . . . to receive the vote any negro, mulatto, or other person of negro descent." Violators would be fined $100 and sent to prison for three months; a similar measure was introduced in the House.[92]

Disfranchisement was the entering wedge for vacating all black citizenship. Within weeks, colonizationists petitioned the convention for an annual appropriation of $20,000 to the Pennsylvania Colonization Society and "TO MAKE A CONSTITUTIONAL PROVISION, PROHIBITING COLORED PEOPLE FROM OWNING REAL ESTATE IN PENNSYLVANIA!!!," in the words of the PASS's *National Enquirer*. The supreme court's decision on February 27 was the final blow, making a constitutional amendment redundant. Even by contemporary standards, Chief Justice John Bannister Gibson's ruling was flimsy, resting on hearsay—"About the year 1795, as I have it from James Gibson, Esq., of the Philadelphia bar, the very point before us was ruled by the High Court of Errors and Appeals against the right of negro suffrage." Although no record could be found, "Mr. Gibson's remembrance of this decision is perfect, and entitled to full confidence. That the case was not reported is probably owing to the fact that the judges gave no reasons." As a legal expert pointed out twenty years later, "Here a great constitutional question is made to depend upon the precarious memory of an individual far advanced in life."[93]

It was open season on people of color, even in Philadelphia, where the authorities had long protected black lives and property. That protection was now withdrawn, and the results drew national attention equal to the 1834 burning of the Charlestown Convent, or the 1849 Astor Place riot, incidents of mass violence against the Irish. On May 14, 1838, the grand new Pennsylvania Hall opened, intended by the city's Quaker abolitionists as a forum for free discussion. Handbills immediately appeared, announcing that black and white had been seen mixing at the hall, where the Anti-Slavery Convention of American Women had opened its third national meeting. These notices raised a crowd that burned down the building the night of May 17, three days after its opening; grand jury testimony showed the "mob" was actually a few dozen men and boys, acting with the acquiescence of Whig mayor John Swift, a dereliction so egregious that a veteran watchman recalled his plea to dis-

perse the mob "as we had done in Mayor Wharton's time." Immediately afterward, the respected Quaker Joseph Parrish visited prominent black
families to secure their agreement to avoid interracial gatherings. More
evidence of nonracial republicanism's eclipse came in August, when Philadelphia Whigs solicited votes on an antiabolitionist platform: "Fellow
Citizen,—You have before you a Delegate Ticket, framed at a preparatory
meeting of the citizens of the ward, pledged to vote for no man's nomination
to office who countenances the fanatical proceedings of those disturbers of
society, called ABOLITIONISTS." Disfranchisement's implications kept
playing out. In 1840, petitioned by the Union Colonization Society of Chester County, the House authorized a select committee to consider "taxing
free people of color, for the purpose of raising a Colonization fund . . . the
purpose of defraying the expenses of colored persons wishing to emigrate to
Liberia." Although it never came to fruition, this proposal set the tone for
the coming decade.[94]

Coda

The Pennsylvania Default

Disfranchisement illuminates the make-believe world of black Philadelphia's "higher classes," battling against "complexional organization" while demanding "moral reform" by the poor. At best, they woke up belatedly, issuing their *Appeal of Forty Thousand Citizens, Threatened with Disfranchisement, to the People of Pennsylvania* months after disfranchisement was voted by the convention; at worst, they were indifferent to slavery, abolition, and citizenship—the verdict usually rendered by their contemporaries. Perhaps they expected to wait out the latest Negrophobic spasm, shielded by white men of conscience. Instead, a sequence of events in 1842 demonstrated that their blend of shadow and deference politics had run its course. Withdrawal, submission, and self-segregation were the new norm. The will to self-organization, politics, and power manifesting among black Americans in New York, New England, and Ohio collapsed in much of the Keystone State.

Formal closure came with James Forten's death on March 2, 1842, with a biracial funeral procession of 5,000 evincing respect for his probity. Forten's demise closed the era when Pennsylvania's black leaders had the ear of powerful whites. He was a gentleman, not merely a "gentleman of color," but gentility was no longer enough. Leadership passed to younger men less interested in conciliating whites, fugitives like Douglass, who made his spectacular debut at a Nantucket antislavery meeting a few months earlier.[1]

Sustained racial violence five months after Forten's passing clarified the past-ness of his past. Antiblack rioting had been annual summer's play for Philadelphia's apprentices and Irishmen, but 1842 set a new standard. Practical reform inside black Philadelphia stimulated a large-scale attack. In the late 1830s, separate from the AMRS, community policing took hold in Philadelphia. "Temperance principles suffused the black community," and clergymen began "systematically purging individuals from their congregations who persistently drank or who exhibited other signs of moral turpitude. . . . By the 1840s, virtually everyone except individuals at the lowest economic levels had adopted some form of the temperance pledge." This activism became political when agitators in vice-ridden Moyamensing, notorious for its Irish saloons, set up a hall called The Retreat and began "dragging in the drunks, persuading them to sign the pledge, and then sending them 'into the country to labor.'" By 1842 they had "reclaimed" 1,047 black people and 120 whites, infuriating the liquor sellers. On August 1, 1842 (the holiday celebrating West Indian Emancipation), black organizers led a march of 1,200 reformed tipplers.[2]

This assertion of community rights provoked an exceptionally brutal response, reportedly paid for by saloonkeepers, who started rumors that black men paraded with a banner depicting a burning Haitian town. When the march reached Fifth and Shippen in Philadelphia, it was attacked, neighboring black-owned homes were fired, and black men shot back. The ensuing riot, lasting several days, eventually required the militia's intercession. As violence spread unchecked, men like James Forten, Jr., ran from howling mobs, and an armed gang milled around Robert Purvis's home while he waited inside, gun in hand. After burning the Second African Presbyterian Church, the mob returned the next day, and the sheriff told Purvis that his family could not be protected. Deeply traumatized, the Purvises left the city forever. The Moyamensing commissioners tore down The Retreat as a danger to neighboring houses, and a grand jury assigned all blame to black people for provoking the riot.[3]

This was truly the end of black politics in Philadelphia. Purvis wrote to a white friend out of state that it confirmed "our utter and complete nothingness in public estimation. . . . I am sick, miserably sick. Every thing around me is as dark as the grave. . . . Despair black as Death hangs over us." Following those nights of fear, avoiding anything offensive to whites became the standing rule for nearly all of the city's nineteen black churches. Earlier, in 1838, the city's most prestigious, St. Thomas's Episcopal (whose vestry included Forten), barred discussion of controversial subjects, including slavery; William Whipper denounced this "spirit of selfishness. . . . They do not look upon their 'brethren in bonds, as being bound with them.' The *fear of mobs* is their fatal excuse, i.e. their governing principle. . . . The spirit of mobocracy has accomplished its purpose." In 1848, William Wells Brown invoked "shame upon the colored clergymen of Philadelphia and their churches! With but two exceptions, they were shut against me." Condemnations like his recurred regularly. The largest northern community of color turned its back upon agitation of any sort, making its role in national black politics "minimal . . . [the community's] activities . . . only reported on by individuals who were critical of them." Yet by virtue of its numbers, wealth, and a "network of schools, benevolent societies, and literary groups unmatched by blacks anywhere in the nation," Philadelphia's African American community dominated the state; they could afford to retreat into a comfortable isolation.[4]

Observers believed this retreat reflected a deep indifference. Mifflin Gibbs, later an Arkansas judge during Reconstruction and eventually U.S. consul in

Madagascar, remembered how in his youth those churches "under the auspices of white denominations" were "craven and fawning, content with the crumbs that fell from those peace-loving Christians," and "more interested in the physical excitement of a 'revival' than in listening to appeals in behalf of God's poor and lonely." The *Colored American*'s editor, Charles B. Ray, noted during an 1839 tour of southeast Pennsylvania that most black people were "really opposed to abolition," even if "most of their opposition grows out of not knowing what abolition is. . . . The question is often asked, what have abolitionists done, and especially for colored people." He contrasted these attitudes unfavorably with "the understanding our people of the East and North have and the interest they feel and take, in all those things which relate to the interest of our people" versus "the amount of interest (or want of it) . . . in the same class here."[5]

The anonymous 1841 *Sketches of the Higher Classes of Colored Society in Philadelphia* was scathing on the city's "numerous divisions . . . kept up with the most bitter and relentless rancor—arising . . . from ancient feuds or personal disagreements." The author listed the city's ills: "falsehood the most vile, slander, the most opprobrious, hypocrisy, violated faith, social traitorism," reserving special obloquy for how "too many men . . . desire to be considered the leaders and the chiefs in every matter of interest that is agitated," and "will not take part in forwarding any scheme, however well intended . . . unless they themselves were components of that original." The picture he painted of their "public meetings" was painful—"Blustering, loud speaking and unlimited denunciation . . . substituted for reason and common sense."[6]

The inability to sustain a Vigilance Committee to aid the tide of incoming fugitives marked their long-term failure. Repeatedly a group formed, briefly operated, and fell apart. Finally, in the 1850s, the outsider William Still made Philadelphia a central "depot" for the Underground Railroad. Another indication of political futility came when the 1855 Colored National Convention met in Philadelphia. The city's delegates avoided any political agitation at this moment of crisis over Kansas, focusing on a proposed "Mechanical Bureau" for "promotion of the Mechanical Arts amongst colored men," but their detailed proposal was derided and voted down.[7]

An Opening at the West

Pittsburgh activists posed a consistent challenge to Philadelphia's political sterility. As the industrial center of the Ohio Valley, that city's black and abolitionist communities drew strength from contiguity to Ohio's radical Western Reserve, while even in the 1840s connections to Philadelphia and points east required a difficult wagon passage through the mountains. In contrast to shadow politics, Pittsburghers like John Vashon, Lewis Woodson, and the latter's disciple, Martin R. Delany, aggressively engaged with power. Since the 1830s, they had built alliances with mayors of both parties and leaders like Walter Forward, who sponsored Vashon's son George for the bar in 1847, where a judge refused him because "Chief Justice Gibson, of Pennsylvania, had decided against colored people being citizens." In 1839, Delany convinced Pittsburgh's Democratic chief burgess (the mayoral title) to deputize black men to protect their neighborhood, Hayti, from mobs. The year before, in July 1838, Pittsburghers sent a "Memorial of the Free Citizens of Color in Pittsburg and its Vicinity Relative to the Right of Suffrage" to the convention, as "for the first time in state history, Pittsburghers organized and spoke for African Americans statewide, without the leadership of Philadelphia blacks." They denounced making voting depend on the "complexion, whether dark or fair, which it may have pleased God to confer on the good people of the Commonwealth." Their petition also pointedly listed "the amount of property and poll tax paid by the colored citizens of Pittsburgh [amounting] to four hundred and twenty two dollars," with the city collector specifying "there are at least one hundred men who pay a poll tax of $1.25 each" and thus voted, outraging the convention's Democratic majority.[8]

In January 1841, Pittsburghers challenged Pennsylvania's stasis by calling a state convention modeled on the August 1840 New York gathering. They failed. By June, Lewis Woodson expressed his shock at the "indifference as to the possession of the right of suffrage" which "prevails to an extent which we little dreamed of. The number who rightly appreciate its immense value, especially in the eastern part of the State, is comparatively small." Harrisburgers had "declared themselves opposed to the meeting of the Convention in that place, without condescending to give us a single reason," and Forten and Whipper had cast pocket vetoes, the former identified as a "citizen of Philadelphia, distinguished alike for his age, his wealth, and his private virtues" but "opposed to a Convention, on account of the 'expense,'" while the other, a "citizen of Columbia," insisted "he would rather forego the possession of the right of suffrage, than obtain it by holding a Convention distinguished by complexion!" Woodson concluded, "Our noble friends in Philadelphia have proposed our holding the Convention there . . . but we dread that city as the one most fatal to the very cause which we wish to advance," and "the seat of all that is discordant, visionary, and impracticable among us." When the convention met in Pittsburgh, its 150 delegates and officers were almost all local men. Philadelphia's fifteen representatives requested listing as "Honorary Delegates," since none bothered to attend. The convention issued a fiery address, appointing a state corresponding committee of twenty, nearly all Pittsburghers, to "call County Conventions, and form associations for raising money" to fund an agent, but these hopes were stillborn.[9]

The next nineteen years reprised the dynamic of Philadelphians stifling any action. Theirs was the defensive stance of a privileged fraction of the oppressed caste, to ensure *their* churches and homes would remain safe. They maintained a predilection for the formal semblance of politics, continuing to meet and issue addresses, with the content of their gatherings remarkably unchanging.[10] These rituals shared little with the constant agitation by black Yankees, Yorkers, and Ohioans. Rather than lobbying public officials, attending biracial political meetings, or pressuring party leaders, most colored Philadelphians practiced the politics of place—that is, keeping to their own place and not allowing anyone else in, reproducing the same fractious localism that produced mediocrities like James Buchanan in what Still labeled "notoriously the most pro-slavery State this side of Mason and Dixon's line."[11]

A more representative convention did assemble in Harrisburg in December 1848, including ten delegates from Philadelphia and fifty-five others. Preparations were made for a permanent suffrage organization, the Citizens' Union, with a central board in Philadelphia led by Stephen Smith, Dr. J. J. G. Bias, Robert Purvis, the young firebrand Mifflin Gibbs, and the veterans John C. Bowers and Abraham Shadd; a delegation was even welcomed by Governor William Johnson. At last, Pennsylvanians were poised to join the black political class. Because of the Philadelphians' endemic factionalism, however, those plans never matured. In June 1849, Charles Lenox Remond, the Massachusetts Garrisonian close to the Pennsylvanians, publicly rued their dysfunctionality, citing how the convention's plans ("a Campaign Paper . . . the circulation of petitions . . . sustaining of one or more Lecturing Agents; the raising of a fund of $5000") had "almost immediately die[d] on their birth." He described the failure of a Philadelphia meeting to "give effect to the deliberations of the one held in Harrisburg," revealing "their carelessness, indifference, and lack of appreciation of the Elective Franchise, and their envy, jealousy, estrangement, obstinacy and opposition to each other."[12]

After that, little came out of Pennsylvania other than periodic "Memorials" to the legislature and Delany's quixotic 1853 Emigration Convention in Pittsburgh. Here and there, light did break through. Even if black men could not vote, their violent response to the Fugitive Slave Act shaped how white men voted. In the state's capital, attempts to return longtime residents to slavery polarized the city against elected Democratic constables who jailed fugitives for substantial rewards. By 1853, two formerly antiblack Whig papers "opposed enforcement" of the act, and "the citizens of Harrisburg voted out three of the town's four elected constables for serving the federal commissioner as slave-runners," while the latter "resigned his office." The "local political hegemony of the Democratic party" was broken, and in 1855, one of the former constables went to jail for three years on a kidnapping charge.[13]

In Pittsburgh, the confrontation between pro- and antislavery voters was even more dramatic. Its black leaders shared platforms with politicians of all parties to denounce the Fugitive Slave Act. By 1854, Pittsburgh's Whigs were radicalized and endorsed complete abolition, with "no more slave states, no slave territory, no nationalized slavery, no national legislation for extradition of slaves." Any politician seen to favor southerners' property rights over Pittsburghers' human rights risked electoral eclipse, and black activists maintained a "secret and powerful organization of free negroes to promote escapes," as one hotel owner told southern guests. In 1855, a freshman state representative from Pittsburgh, D. L. Smith, introduced a measure in the General Assembly to authorize black suffrage, as a gesture to local sentiments.[14]

This narrative ends on a paradox. At the Civil War's outset, black Pennsylvanians were at most "citizens for protection," but many whites had woken up to the import of "bowing the knee to slavery." In the 1851 Christiana "riot" and dozens of other border fights, black people took up arms to fight their oppressors and in doing so, reclaimed their citizenship, as white judges and juries took their side, welcoming them back into the state. Pennsylvania had begun returning to its roots as a citadel of freedom, a place that black Americans might be proud to claim as their own.

———

Pennsylvania demonstrates myriad possibilities for black politics: established local organizing traditions in Bucks and Columbia; archaic practices of deferential electioneering in Franklin; Pittsburgh's leaders transcending disfranchisement to assert themselves in city politics. The downward trajectory of Philadelphia's elite demonstrates the dangers of equating community self-organization with opposition or resistance. As often as they face outward, communities turn in upon themselves via self-perpetuating hierarchies and rituals of affirmation. The capacity for conscious subordination (or internalized oppression) is inherent in the socialness of human life. Regardless of any community's capacity for agency, however, the larger frame of geography and culture was determinative, in that Pennsylvania remained "the keystone in the arch" of Jeffersonian-Jacksonian hegemony in national politics, the South's best friend.

The chapters in part I document how caution and self-interest prevailed in antebellum Philadelphia. That some electoral influence was not fantastical is shown by population centers like Bucks and Lancaster, which underline the fallacy of reducing a state or region to its metropole: Pennsylvania to Philadelphia; New England to Boston; New York to New York City. The failure of will by Philadelphia's elite does not deny the historical importance of James Forten and Bishop Allen. These were extraordinary men, self-made under adverse circumstances, who remained unfazed by white power, even if the evidence suggests that Allen was a calculating infighter. Forten was more ambiguous. A stubborn abolitionist, he lived a principled commitment against separate black organizing. Over time his personal resistance hindered efforts to mobilize statewide. He also believed, from the evidence, that insisting on the right to vote was not realistic.

PART II

The New England Redoubt

If there was a First Reconstruction, it began in the Upper New England states of Vermont, New Hampshire, Massachusetts, and Maine, the Yankee Republics constituting almost one-fifth of the nation in 1820, when Maine became a state rather than a "district" of Massachusetts. In 1780, Massachusetts affirmed nonracial suffrage, following popular rejection of a draft constitution in large part because it excluded men of color from the polls. Joined by its northern neighbors, the Bay State maintained this recognition of black citizenship for the next half-century, while states to its south and west enacted white suffrage. This regional tradition was consolidated in 1818–22, during a wave of disfranchisement in the lower North, when the states abutting Upper New England eliminated nearly all their black voters (Connecticut in 1818, New York in 1821, and Rhode Island in 1822), while Maine in 1819 became the one new state formally enfranchising black men after 1800, until Wisconsin in 1866. By the 1820s, juridically nonracial citizenship was part of Upper New England's identity, a way to claim moral superiority and a truer republicanism over the South. Its representatives affirmed this stance during the Missouri Crisis, when that state's draft constitution denied entrance to black citizens of other states. Beyond the ballot box, the northeastern states sometimes fostered nonracial citizenship socially as well as politically. Black Yankees, if they displayed the requisite Puritan virtues, could earn social standing as men of business, learning, or piety; a few participated in politics and held office. Like young white men from humble backgrounds, they drew upon traditional patronage networks within a society ordered by class. By the 1820s, black youths gained entrance to Bowdoin, Middlebury, and Amherst, with their academic degrees celebrated as proof of regional virtue.[1]

In the antebellum era, 1830–60, the central motif of the Yankee Republic's black politics was continuity rather than change. Black New Englanders coming of age before the Civil War inherited established practices of horse trading for votes and gaining minor patronage. No other section of the republic displayed this consistent nonracialism, which advanced in the 1830s with the advent of "immediatist" abolitionists berating slaveholders as moral monsters, and former president John Quincy Adams's congressional war upon the Slave Power. The hostility to slavery shared by the "Universal Yankee

Map II.1 New England

MAINE

VERMONT

● Portland

NEW
HAMPSHIRE

Salem ●
● Boston

MASSACHUSETTS

Providence ●
New Bedford

CONNECTICUT

RHODE ISLAND

Nation" that New Englanders carried into upstate New York and the upper Midwest is well documented; less familiar is how, as the Second Party System cohered, Afro-Yankees found a congenial home in the National Republicans and their successors, the Whigs. While the abolitionist Liberty Party spread across Upper New England in 1840–47, black men stayed away. Only as the Whigs slowly collapsed after 1848 did black Whigs seek a new electoral home, first in the Free Soil Party, then in the Know-Nothing American Party (which elevated them over their rivals, the Irish), and finally as Republicans.

Chapter 4 documents the evolution of New England's nonracial politics through the 1820s, in tandem with a surging sectional nationalism rooted in resentment of "slave representation" in Congress and the Electoral College via the Constitution's three-fifths ratio, which gave Virginia control of the federal government from 1800 to 1824. Beginning in the 1790s, Federalists (and sometimes Republicans too) sought black men's votes, especially in the rich port towns dotting the coast—New Bedford, Boston, Salem, Newburyport, and Portland. This chapter culminates with Jackson's 1828 victory over New England's second president, the younger Adams, signaling the ascendancy of white men's "Democracy."

Chapters 5, 6, and 7, covering 1830 to 1860, are case studies of three cities: Portland, Maine; New Bedford, Massachusetts; and Providence, Rhode Island. These chapters focus on voting behavior, partisan competition, electoral mobilization, and patronage—the elements of old-fashioned political history or political science, augmented by cultural analysis. In each of these cities, black men gained offices in various political parties and/or low-level municipal jobs, and, over time, their political participation became routinized.

Why go into such detail about electoral practices, if the point is simply to establish that black men voted freely in a particular region? There are two explanations. First, ever since Leon Litwack's 1961 *North of Slavery: The Negro in the Free States, 1790–1860*, it has been conceded that black men retained the suffrage in northern New England, and regained it in Rhode Island in 1842. But Litwack's assertion that those states contained so few black voters they hardly mattered has also survived. It is vitally important to demonstrate not only that their numbers were significantly greater than previously assumed but that black men's concentration in key cities gave them more influence than their percentage of a state's electorate would indicate. The outsize importance of small, geographically concentrated constituencies is hardly unique, whether the Cuban-American minority in south Florida, or the African Americans in key cities courted by President Truman in 1948. I make no such claim here. Black voters in Maine, Massachusetts, Vermont, or New Hampshire could not swing a statewide election (although they did provide that margin in Rhode Island after 1842), but there were certainly enough in the port towns to give them significant influence, which is why they were courted by Whigs and Republicans and attacked by Democrats. And when they divided their vote among competing antislavery parties, all paid attention. Always, there was the demonstration effect within a biracial electorate. White abolitionists could either follow black men out of, or accept their lead by staying in, the Whig Party, while that organization existed. Studying Portland, New Bedford, and Providence in depth illuminates these possibilities and demonstrates how men of color were incorporated into the larger partisan world in a region wielding much greater power than today.

These histories illustrate another central aspect about antebellum politics: that patterns of partisanship varied within the same region and the same party. Portland's fit between Whigs, abolitionists, and black men remained tight for decades. Men of color were recruited early as National Republicans, and became and stayed Whigs, holding party and city offices, until 1848. There was no separate black electoral mobilization in Portland, unlike in New Bedford, where black men organized autonomously from the major parties, which competed for their votes but avoided incorporating them into party organizations. In the 1840s, black Portlanders refused the Liberty Party's proffer, but in New Bedford some black businessmen joined it early and held major party offices, and black factionalism, unknown in Portland, was bitter in New Bedford. Providence resembled neither of these two cities, as its black men were excluded from its partisan arena until 1842. Rebuffed by the populistic Suffrage Association, which sought universal white manhood suffrage, Providence's black men turned to the forces of "Law and Order" during that year's quasi-revolutionary Dorr War. They joined biracial militia companies to put down the Suffragists, and were reenfranchised. For years to come, a black submachine helped keep the Whigs in power in city and state. Even in 1848, when black men throughout New England voted Free Soil, the Rhode Islanders remained Whigs.

Before moving on, however, the larger regional frame into which these local studies fit requires certain clarifications—how the avowedly antipolitical Garrisonians actually participated in party politics; why both white Garrisonians and black Yankees were comfortable within the Whig Party despite its slave-owning southern wing; how the arrival of John Quincy Adams as New England's champion authorized one to be a Whig-abolitionist.

Myth and Reality in Garrisonian Antipolitics

The tropes linking New England with William Lloyd Garrison are so powerful that it seems impossible to write about Afro-Yankees without focusing on their participation in his movement. Nonetheless, chapters 5, 6, and 7 focus on the large cohorts of black men who operated inside electoral politics at a considerable remove from Garrisonian agitation. Garrison drew passionate support from New England's colored citizens, but outside of Boston that relationship never defined their approach to parties and voting.

We also need to clarify the actual relationship of Garrisonianism to electoral politics. The notion that Garrison and his friends damned parties, elections, voting, and government in toto, maintaining their pure oppositionality, is vastly overstated. Their stance was, in fact, largely a pose of rectitude, taking the high ground for strategic advantage. Garrisonians insisted that they engaged with but not in the electoral process, and even there, the distinction was muddied in practice. In 1838, the Massachusetts Anti-Slavery Society instructed its members that candidates "should be reasonably interrogated" with their answers published. After that, "Your duties as voters are mainly negative. *Vote for no man, however estimable from general character and acquirements, who is not prepared to give a prompt, explicit, and satisfactory answer.*" In the absence of such answers, "do not stay away from the polls. Go, rather; and scatter your votes." "Scattering" was spoiling—writing in the names of prominent abolitionists to deny any candidate the majority necessary for election under Massachusetts law. The Garrisonians did turn to absolutism in the 1840s ("ultraism" it was called then), denouncing the Constitution as a "pact with the Devil" and advocating "disunion," meaning secession, with voting formally abjured. Many historians have thus described them as antipolitical, opposed to all forms of electoral politics. Such claims take their oratorical pyrotechnics too literally. In practice, such edicts had little force outside the "Boston clique" around Garrison and Wendell Phillips, since both men readily admitted that nearly all abolitionists identified as Whigs. Garrison and Phillips themselves often betrayed their Whiggish sympathies once the Liberty Party split off in 1840. Whig editors loved to quote *The Liberator* on the Liberty men as no better, if not worse, than Democrats. A typical example is from late 1844, when Garrison asserted that the "object of the miscalled 'Liberty party' journals [is] to do as much injury to the Whig, and as little to the Polk and Texas [Democratic] party, as possible." Rather than denouncing the Whigs, then running the slaveholder Henry Clay for president, he declared, "Just in proportion as [the Whig Party] resists southern encroachments, and [the Democratic Party] shows a disposition to go all lengths in support of slavery, do these *disinterested* and *impartial* journals anathematize Whiggism." Most readers understand this as an implied endorsement of the Whigs, whatever his protestations.[2]

The Black Whiggery, 1832–1848

To grasp why most Afro-Yankees were Whigs, consider that Democrats routinely tried to prove that Whigs and abolitionists were political bedfellows. In 1840, the Alabama Democratic Party quoted *The Emancipator* and *The Liberator* on William Henry Harrison's gaining the Whig nomination as "a great anti-slavery victory" and "a signal defeat of the slaveholding power," since "had it not been for Abolitionism, Henry Clay would undoubtedly have been nominated." Democrats across the South pilloried Harrison as the abolitionists' candidate, citing their slaves' enthusiasm for Harrison to demonstrate the Whigs' hidden agenda. In July, the leading Southern Democratic newspaper, the *Richmond Enquirer*, reported that "the late celebration at Tippecanoe" [site of Harrison's 1811 defeat of Tecumseh] included "at least 1,000 negroes in attendance, decorated with Harrison badges, and headed by five negro delegates from Tennessee, bearing appropriate Abolition devices," an allusion to how free men of color voted in Tennessee until 1834. By late September, with Harrison in the lead, it fulminated that "our negroes . . . are all for Harrison, or as some of them express it, 'tippitatoo men.'" Supposed "negro clubs . . . were accustomed to meet on Sabbaths, and at other times in the night, and spend the time in gambling, barbacuing meats, drinking whiskey, and talking politics."[3]

We should not assume this baiting was smoke with no fire. Garrison's ostentatious rejection of electoral politics never appealed to more than a few black men in his personal orbit plus allies in Philadelphia and New York. In this era of mass partisanship, black men—even slaves—jumped in enthusiastically wherever they could, mostly as Whigs. In 1835, an Englishman noted he "never knew a man of color that was not an anti-Jackson man."[4] Garrisonian ultraism gained them no advantages of recognition or material quid pro quos, aligning them with "fanatics" who smacked of irreligion and disunionism; they wanted to be in, not out.

New England Whigs generally accepted black men, as many in that newly minted party had personal experience recruiting them as Federalists. Black Whiggism was more than just enemy-of-my-enemy practicality, however. It expressed how black New Englanders understood themselves, as Americans of a certain sort, *Yankees*, which requires exploration of the Whiggery itself—a vanished political culture, but one of remarkable fervency. The Whigs embodied the "national republican" impulse, opposing the proslavery localism and antielitist libertarianism of the Democrats. Black men had learned very early to support the national state (and thus the Federalist Party) against "the States," so their adherence to the Whiggery was in some sense a given. Key elements of the Whig coalition also extended the Founding generation's nonracialism. Campaigning against Jackson's Indian removal policy in 1829–30 mobilized many who became both abolitionists and Whigs. Simultaneously, the short-lived Antimasonic Party bred a dynamic reform ethos, which the Whigs inherited. Former Antimasons became leading antislavery Whigs, including New York's Seward, Pennsylvania's Stevens, and Vermont's William Slade. Finally, the new party added a progressive evangelicalism—if the Church of England was long "the Tory Party at prayer," then the Whigs were the Second Great Awakening at the ballot box. They sought to make men good by helping them overcome their weaknesses through the new institutions of modern life (penitentiaries, libraries, common schools, asylums for the blind or insane), while banning barbaric customs such as "rum-selling," dueling, prostitution, and the human bondage that degraded slave and master. To the Whigs, these social ills represented not disorder but limitations on freedom. This ideological and cultural brew, the confluence of religion and patriotism, drew in black men, believing Protestants all, because it made space for them on their own terms, as redeemed slaves or reclaimed sinners.[5]

Evidence for New England's resolute black Whiggery came after 1840, when the Liberty Party appeared. Founded by Whigs sick of compromising with slavery, it steadily gained votes in Upper New England until merging into the Free Soilers in 1848.[6] But these were almost entirely white voters. New England Liberty leaders imported black orators like the Reverend Henry Highland Garnet with little effect, and Whigs gloated over how colored voters "regard the Liberty Party with distrust, dislike and contempt," as a spoiler for the Democrats. Why did colored men resist an antislavery party that was scoring real gains? The failure to attract black Yankees was summed up at an 1842 convention in Portland. Its goal was to align Maine's black electorate with the Liberty Party, but two of the conveners, Portland's Abraham W. Niles (who held a local office courtesy of the Whigs) and Bangor's John T. Carter, stated their "great objection . . . that there was no prospect of the Liberty Party being the dominant party." To belong to a ruling group was key, to gain patronage, and be in the state, not outside it. That the Whigs were hardly antislavery at the national level was secondary when "the States" mattered as much as the Union and local Whigs were firmly antislavery. Black Whiggism therefore made evident sense in Upper New England, no matter how black Liberty men elsewhere rued their obstinacy.[7]

New England's Vindicator

There was one more reason to remain a Whig, bound up in John Quincy Adams embodying an essential Yankeeism. Daniel Webster was the region's dominant Whig, espousing a rhetorical antislavery while defending "the Union, as it is," but Adams was the face of "Moral Whiggery," a line of radicalism stretching back to the English Revolution. After defeat by Jackson in 1828, Adams went back to Congress in 1831. From 1835 to his death in 1848, he waged an unrelenting campaign against the Slave Power, which kept many in the Whig Party.[8]

Leonard Richards and William Lee Miller have brilliantly narrated Adams's rebirth as a radical David facing down the southern Goliath. His attacks on the "Gag Rule" by which pro-southern majorities barred reception of the flood of abolitionist petitions (1,496 came in during just four months of 1838–39) forced northern Whigs to become Congress's first antislavery bloc, supporting Adams's roll call after roll call until the Gag collapsed in 1844. They had no choice. To expose themselves as "northern men with southern principles" like the Democrats undermined their party's rationale. As Seward later declared, "The Whigs . . . were chary . . . of committing their party to any positive support of the antislavery movement. Nevertheless, they were charged by the other side with sympathy in it; and the charge was measurably true."[9]

In the House, Adams fully earned Emerson's appraisal as "no literary old gentleman, but a bruiser" who "loves the melee." Rather than accruing moral capital, this "mischievous, bad old man," in John C. Calhoun's words, sought to morally expropriate the expropriators, asserting that slavery was "a wrong, and a crime, and a curse," calling House Speaker James K. Polk "an Anglo-Saxon, slave-holding exterminator of Indians" to his face. Not for nothing did Jackson label Adams a "traitor" in letters meant for public consumption. Adams also defended black people as Americans, and his transgressive audacity provided special pleasures for them. His 1841 Supreme Court plea for the *Amistad* prisoners was not exceptional magnanimity but the expression of a lifelong obligation to aid the vulnerable. After that defense, he was increasingly seen in public with delegations of grateful people of color, whom he addressed as "fellow citizens" in cities like Utica and Cincinnati. He also brought them into the House's conversation in unprecedented ways. In June 1842, during a debate over broadening suffrage in Alexandria (then part of the District of Columbia), Adams proposed to strike the word "white" from its elections law, citing the funeral of a well-known District resident, William Costin. Such a man, he insisted, "whose skin is not white—snow white—but who performs all the duties of a good citizen, a good husband, good father, and kind neighbor" should be able to vote. The new law would allow partisans to "ransack the prisons and bring in every convict—every idiot" to the polls, if he was white. "Why should such a man [as Costin] be excluded from the elective franchise, when you admit the vilest individuals of the white race to exercise it?" When opponents derided him, Adams returned the insult. "I ask gentleman to tell me what is a white man. (Laughter.). Is it the color of the skin that constitutes a white man? Then there are twenty members of this House that are not white men." He could easily find "a hundred respectable colored men of this city" who were whiter, and if one of the swarthier members tried to vote in Alexandria, that might require "going into the genealogy of the person," a threat he relished.[10]

In the 1840s, this blend of egalitarianism, noblesse oblige, and partisan venom became a regular feature of Adams's persona. When enslaved sailors mutinied, killed their white captors, and sailed their ships to British ports, Adams extolled their leader by name: "Are not the journals of our Senate disgraced by resolutions calling for war [with Great Britain], to indemnify the slave-pirates of the Enterprise and the Creole for the self-emancipation of their slaves; and to inflict vengeance, by a death of torture, upon the heroic self-deliverance of Madison Washington?" Against the new quack-science of polygenesis, claiming Africans were a different species, he sneered that "only the worshipper of mammon and the philosophical atheist" can avow the inferiority of Africans to "the white European man, that they are not of one blood, nor descendants of the same stock." The climax of his pro-black politics came in early 1844, during the final Gag Rule fight. The Alabama Whig, James Dellet, attacked Adams for a speech he made to "the colored people of Pittsburgh," quoting him: "We know that the day of your redemption must come. The time and manner of its coming we know not: It may come in peace, or it may come in blood; but *whether in peace or in blood*, LET IT COME." Dellet read this passage twice, to which Adams replied by uttering loudly, "I say now let it come." Dellet responded, "Yes, the gentleman now says let it come, though it *cost the blood of thousands of white men*." Adams was not intimidated, repeating slowly: "*Though it cost the blood of MILLIONS OF WHITE MEN, LET IT COME. Let justice be done, though the heavens fall*." Joshua Giddings, Ohio's great antislavery Whig, described the scene years later: "These words rose from the lips of the aged patriot like the prayer of faith from one of heaven's anointed prophets: A sensation of horror ran through the ranks of the slaveholders."[11]

Adams's outsize presence afforded Afro-Yankees the luxury of partisan choice. North of Providence, they were always more than clients, since enough white Whigs had left for the Liberty Party to make the latter viable. This was proven in 1848, when most black Whigs jumped to the Free Soilers, a road that would lead to the founding of Republican parties six years later, with black men cogs in the region's soon-to-be hegemonic machine. These local developments would be small potatoes, however, if they had not been joined to a new kind of partisan Americanism based in nativity and Protestantism. The prewar decades saw the rise of nativism and temperance linked to antislavery, pitting dirt-poor Irish against Yankee abolitionists and their Negro allies. Anti-Catholic nativism found its most profound expression in New England, and in zero-sum fashion, to be anti-Irish meant becoming pro-black. By the 1850s Democratic newspapers routinely juxtaposed the immigrants' disfranchisement in Maine and Massachusetts against the instant enfranchisement of fugitive slaves.[12]

From that perspective, a sunny vista loomed in the late 1850s for Yankee Republicans who happened to be black. A black militia company received state arms in Rhode Island, skirting the federal militia law, and "personal liberty" laws in Maine, New Hampshire, and Vermont effectively nullified the Fugitive Slave Act. Massachusetts began granting passports to its black citizens, and in New Bedford (the nation's richest city), an escaped slave ran for city council. Less visibly, across the region, black men obtained patronage positions. As of 1860, Upper New England was effectively reconstructed, poised to send black men into battle against the Slave Power, and to begin electing them to state office at war's end. Regional leaders like the Boston lawyer Robert Morris and the Newport restaurateur George T. Downing spoke confidently of running for office or withholding their votes from Republicans if not given tangible respect. In a sense, they had triumphed, although the limits to what their small electorate could demand were already apparent.

Separating Boston from New England

The reader will note this part omits Boston, focusing instead on three smaller cities. The reasons for this exclusion are evident to those familiar with the historiography. "Black Boston" has been extensively studied, with its history standing in for New England as a whole, another instance of the "metropole" versus "periphery." There is a more immediate reason as well, the two recent studies of Boston's interracial abolitionism by Bruce Laurie and Steven Kantrowitz. A chapter here would add little to these comprehensive explorations of how a powerful social movement engaged with politics in the Bay State's capital. Boston was also sui generis in how its people of color participated in (or abstained from) electoral politics. That specificity was rooted in the dominance of Garrison's "Boston Clique," a set of like-minded leaders like Phillips, Maria Weston Chapman, and Edmund Quincy. During the 1830s and 1840s, these deeply committed and deeply sectarian activists used persuasion, prestige, and patronage to bar black Bostonians from direct participation in partisanship. Their writ was essentially local, however—a minority viewpoint in New Bedford, ignored in Providence and Portland. As a consequence, for years Boston's black leaders were cut off from their region's (and the nation's) political contestation. Until Robert Morris led a contingent to embrace the Free Soilers in 1848, they remained trapped in a "nonresistant" time-warp. During the 1850s, however, the tide turned and Boston's men of color embraced party politics. Even Garrison's devoted acolyte, William Cooper Nell, permitted himself to be named as a state legislative candidate by the Free Soilers in 1850. Boston thus finally became part of the larger regional narrative.[13]

Chapter 4

All the Black Men Vote for Mr. Otis

Nonracial Politics in the Yankee Republic, 1778–1830

A property in slaves is founded in wrong, and never can be right. . . .
Government must of necessity put a stop to this evil, and the sooner they
entered upon the business the better. . . . It is proper enough to say
something about the rights of man, and to remind others, who are
frequently heard speaking of these rights, that by nature these enslaved men
are entitled to rights.

—Representative George Thatcher of the Maine District, in the House of
  Representatives, March 1798

He would strenuously and for ever oppose the extension of slavery, and
all measures which should subject a freeman, of whatever color, to the
degradation of a slave . . . divest him of his property and rights, and
interdict him from even passing into a country of which he was a legitimate
co-proprietor with himself.

—Senator Harrison Gray Otis of Massachusetts, speaking on Missouri's
  Constitution in the Senate, December 9, 1820

There are two narratives of New England's racial politics. The first dates from
the late nineteenth century and is still popular, honoring the region as abolitionism's heartland, where the first martyr of the Boston Massacre was a man
of color named Attucks, Garrison published his *Liberator*, and Douglass found
safety. Recently, however, that older history has been challenged by a less cel-
ebratory account. Joanne Pope Melish's *Disowning Slavery: Gradual Emancipation and "Race" in New England, 1780–1860* documents how white New
Englanders effaced their own participation in slave-owning and denied their
"visceral discomfort . . . with the actual, physical presence of individual persons of color in the landscape," posing their Free White Republic as "the an-
tithesis of an enslaved South." Drawing on Connecticut and Rhode Island,
the two Lower New England states with large slave populations, Melish argues that deep currents of racialized thinking and practice persisted into the
era of postrevolutionary emancipation.[1]

I pose a different history, focusing not on what white people chose to
remember or forget, but on what black people did, in conjunction with

often unlikely white allies like the notorious reactionary Harrison Gray Otis. *Disowning Slavery* is a salutary corrective to Yankee romanticism. But by focusing on Rhode Island and Connecticut, eliding Massachusetts and the northern frontier of Maine, New Hampshire, and Vermont, it misses a different "disowning": how other white New Englanders abjured race and quickly recognized basic citizenship rights for the newly freed. First in Massachusetts and then across the northern borderlands, white and black together constructed "a New England without races, at least as we have come to understand that term," a nonracial polity.[2]

Here, the divide between Upper and Lower New England is crucial: in the five years between 1818, when Connecticut disfranchised black men, and 1822, when Rhode Island followed suit, the new state of Maine affirmatively enfranchised its black men in 1819 and members of Congress from Massachusetts, Vermont, and New Hampshire vociferously defended black citizenship during the Missouri Crisis's second stage, in December 1820. This sequence of events separating New England's two subregions is not discussed in *Disowning Slavery*, nor are there any references to black men as political actors. This scanting of political history leads to the claim that, by the 1850s, Afro-Yankees had become "permanent strangers whose presence was unaccountable, and whose claims to citizenship were absurd," an assertion radically at odds with the facts.[3]

The evolution of Upper New England contrasts sharply with that of Pennsylvania, where formally nonracial citizenship was maintained from 1790 to 1838. The early republic's two most prominent black businessmen, James Forten and Paul Cuffe, demonstrate the widening gulf between the New England stretching northeast from Cuffe's base near New Bedford, and the Pennsylvania borderland running west from Forten's Philadelphia. Over time, these differing political cultures led to electoral mobilization in the former and abstentionism in the latter.

Forten and Cuffe are often linked as avatars of black advancement, but their political stances diverged sharply. Forten did not model any active citizenship politics. While developing a transatlantic reputation as a "gentleman of color," he never stepped out of his place, welcoming Federalist dignitaries to his home and contributing money to their building fund, but staying *at* home. In contrast, Cuffe became a transatlantic political actor. Even very young, in 1777–81, he and his brother John demanded "the same privileges . . . as the white people have," the right to vote, in their home town of Dartmouth, the first such assertion in American history and one never made in Philadelphia. Their campaign of tax resistance failed and the brothers paid up, but the challenge was noted by others. Thirty years later, as a prosperous ship captain, Cuffe repeatedly ventured to Sierra Leone to trade, while lobbying in various capitals on the colony's behalf. In 1811, he visited the House of Commons as William Wilberforce's guest, to secure British support for his mercantile ventures in Africa. Returning to the United States after war broke out, his ship was impounded for illegal trading with the enemy. He mounted a concerted push to get it released and gain congressional permission to continue commerce with Sierra Leone regardless of wartime, with the intercession of officials like Rhode Island's lieutenant governor. He visited Washington twice, meeting with President James Madison and Secretary of State Albert Gallatin. The latter assured him that "all of my property Was . . . to be Restored to me With out Reserve" and "any thing that the goverment Could do to Premote the Good Cause that I Was Presuing Consisting With the Constitution they Would Certenly be alwas Readey to Render me their help." The Senate passed Cuffe's bill but the House refused, despite Gallatin's support. By this time, he had become famous ("In traveling through the Country I Perceived that the People Seemed to have great knowledge of me"), an indicator of what black men might gain in New England, with a leading Federalist newspaper noting that its Baltimore counterpart called him "the celebrated African merchant and navigator," urging Congress to give him "that attention which his respectability and the important object of his mission so justly demand."[4]

Political Culture and Political Structure in the Yankee Republic

New England as a whole was defined by a shared political culture and similar political structures, which together facilitated the emergence of organized black politics even before 1800, and which (in Upper New England) encouraged black men in exercising their citizenship while every other northern state moved to curtail their rights.

Certainly, the region had a more formal identity than other state groupings. At its core was the religious heritage of Puritanism, represented by the hundreds of Congregational churches still anchoring town commons today, and the collective experience of persecution. This founding myth has long been reduced to cliché—images of Plymouth Rock and the First Thanksgiving; evocations of John Winthrop's providential "city on a hill." Well into the nineteenth century, however, the Puritan voyage into the wilderness did define the Yankee weltanschauung. The New England commonwealths cohered around what Perry Miller delineated as the "New England Mind," both a theological order and a plan of society: Puritans were the Elect, but any one church member's fate was preordained; one could but submit. Its institutional embodiment was an established church, the Congregational "Standing Order," dominating Massachusetts and Connecticut, the two major original colonies, under which each town's "orthodox" divine was paid from taxes collected from all inhabitants. Although persecution of Quakers, Baptists, and Catholics declined in the eighteenth century, the Congregational Church was only disestablished in Massachusetts in 1833, following Vermont in 1807, and Connecticut in 1818.[5]

Versus decentralized Pennsylvania, with its fractious ethnoreligious politics, New England circa 1790 presented a nearly uniform polity dominated by Anglo-American elites, including an established ministry educated at a single state-backed institution, Harvard College. Paradoxically, the Puritan *exilio* generated an intensely Anglophone culture based in attachments to home places in Old England and a "Puritan history" based in "the historical habits of mind common to eighteenth-century English Opposition agitators and American revolutionaries." In Kevin Phillips's description of this transatlantic connection, Old and New England were linked by the "guiding political culture of a Low Church, Calvinistic Protestantism, commercially adept, militantly expansionist, and highly convinced . . . that it represented a chosen people and a manifest destiny." This political culture reproduced itself in dozens of memoirs and biographies of nineteenth-century Yankees recording an ancestor's antecedents in a particular English town and the ship on which he came. On the Civil War's eve, William H. Seward reenacted this filiopiety in his biography of John Quincy Adams, describing his hero's father erecting a gravestone to the first American Adams, who had fled "the Dragon Persecution in Devonshire."[6]

The other key to New England's identity, surviving today in attenuated form, is the town meeting, a direct rather than representative democracy. Wealthy oligarchies dominated colonial politics, but at the local level, town meetings shaped region-wide habits of grassroots republicanism. During the Revolution, all of the newly formed New England states mandated a legislative body with representation for every town, even the smallest, meaning enormous and extremely responsive legislatures. Moreover, two annual rounds of legislative and gubernatorial elections (as in Pennsylvania) made politicking a constant activity. Finally, Massachusetts, New Hampshire, and later Maine required candidates for state and federal office to gain an absolute majority; otherwise the seat remained unfilled or was chosen by the legislature. These factors empowered determined minorities, as elections were often held repeatedly over days or weeks to see if one candidate could prevail. In the 1840s, abolitionists regularly "spoiled" the election of governors, congressional representatives, and state legislators all over New England. In that context, which party a particular town's black men supported—whether an antislavery Whig or Democrat, a Liberty man, or a Free Soiler—had a multiplier effect, with their electoral choices figuring more prominently than their tally of voters might suggest.[7]

Until the influx of Irish and French Canadians in the 1840s, there was a commonalty to white New Englanders' lives. For two centuries, Yankees felt and acted as a people, and in the early republic "a nation within the nation," as evidenced by New England leaders repeatedly considering secession in 1801–15. A shared religious culture, high levels of literacy, and an austere egalitarianism (in comparison with other British colonies or Great Britain itself) bred a moral earnestness that, however mocked as "Puritanical," was conducive to antislavery and antiracial sentiments.[8]

Our later understanding of New England is weighted down with myths, however. Both historiography and public memory are skewed toward greater Boston, with the larger region merely a periphery around the eastern Bay State. Historians reproduce the cultural imperialism of those nineteenth-century Brahmins who anointed Boston "the Athens of America." Studies of Connecticut and Rhode Island are rare, and the northern tier of Vermont, New Hampshire, and Maine are treated as Massachusetts's tributaries. This dismissal of particularity stems from historians' bias toward narratives of big states and large cities and presentist assumptions based on the small states' contemporary size. Today, Maine, New Hampshire, and Vermont are bywords for quaint and out-of-the-way; it is easy to presume they were always thus. Reading backward from the past century's demographic stasis effaces the surging populations and economic dynamism of Upper New England after the Revolution. Vermont and the Maine District were among the early republic's fastest-growing sections. In 1810, when New England controlled one-quarter of the House of Representatives (35 of 143 seats versus 21 of 435 in 2016), Vermont and the Maine District each sent four, and New Hampshire five, radically at odds with their later diminution (from 9 to 1 percent of the House). Despite its outsize historical reputation, Massachusetts was never dominant. Not including Maine, its share of the region's population peaked at three in eight inhabitants in 1790; by 1820, Massachusetts had less than one-third, while its three northern neighbors contained almost half (46.9 percent).[9]

Confusion over the relative weight of New England's various parts, reducing all except Connecticut to "Greater Massachusetts," leads to a facile identification of the region with ultra-Federalism and then the Whigs. While thoroughly "Yankee" culturally, New England was heterogeneous in partisan terms. Massachusetts and Connecticut remained Federalist long after the nation went Republican, and in the 1830s and 1840s, Massachusetts was thoroughly Whiggish. The Jeffersonians took over Connecticut in 1818, however, and were equally successful to Massachusetts's north, while their successors,

Jackson's Democrats, dominated New Hampshire and Maine from the 1830s to the 1850s; Vermont and Rhode Island never conformed to any pattern, with the former a center of Antimasonry and the latter dominated by a restricted rural electorate and a politics more personalist than ideological. The one political premise shared by most Yankees was a steadily growing antipathy to the South. Historians describe theirs as one of several "sectional nationalisms" inside the new nation. In the "Eastern States," as New Englanders described their region, anti-Southernism began with Jefferson's 1800 victory via "negro votes," the slaves counted as three-fifths of a person, giving him twelve additional electoral votes, sufficient to defeat Adams. Disgust with Jefferson's Francophilism further antagonized Yankees, who saw southern "nabobs" as hypocritical aristocrats leading the nation to perdition. It was hardened by Jefferson's embargo destroying the region's trade, and then "Mr. Madison's War." In David Waldstreicher's summation, by defining "New England as America," the region's leaders made "an attack upon southern distinctiveness," with "the southern planter the emblem of a national threat." New England became the site of "the true Revolution, and the real America, against the false patriots and the illegitimate state."[10]

Premature Abolitionists and Reactionary Radicals

From the Founding, Upper New England congressmen from both parties attacked the legitimacy of the "peculiar institution." Decades in advance of the antebellum antislavery debates, obscure Yankees sounded the same defiance against the Slave Power and avowals of black people's citizenship. The radical antislavery of the 1840s and 1850s and the Radical Republicanism of the 1860s and 1870s, both associated with New England, reasserted antiracialist convictions already in place before the Revolution, as suggested by this chapter's epigraph from Harrison Gray Otis. As a congressman in 1797–1801, state senator for most of 1805–11, U.S. senator in 1817–22, and Boston's mayor in 1829–32, he was known as an archconservative, but he was also the nephew of the revolutionary agitator James Otis, who had famously argued before the Supreme Court of Massachusetts in 1761, *"The colonists, black and white, born here, are free born British subjects, and entitled to all the essential civil rights of such."* The Otises were part of a larger troop of Yankees who, depending on political exigencies, periodically attacked slavery and avowed black citizenship. This alignment operated outside the partisan divide already emerging in the early 1790s, indicating how deeply held were these sentiments; antislavery and nonracialism may have been expressions of a sectional nationalism, but they cannot be reduced to High Federalist partisanship.

Within the larger group, one member stood out. As Mary Locke wrote in 1901, "for undaunted effort in season and out of season, for caustic language and refusal of compromise, the palm must be awarded to George Thatcher." This Maine Federalist was the forerunner of Giddings, Seward, Sumner, and, above all, John Quincy Adams and Thaddeus Stevens, with whom he shared a viper tongue. That he remains unknown underlines the inattention to the black presence inside American politics, since he spoke as their de facto representative. A brief instance of Thatcher and his allies baiting the slaveholders gives the flavor of the rancorous antislavery subtext that periodically erupted within the First Party System of the 1790s, sounding much like the savage polemics of the 1850s, although no one tried to beat Thatcher's head in, as Preston Brooks did to Charles Sumner in 1856.[11]

Thatcher had taunted southerners from the first Congress in 1789, but not until 1798 did he attempt to cut off the future Cotton Kingdom, and enact the Republican Party's program sixty years early. That March, Congress debated legislation creating the Mississippi Territory (present-day Mississippi and Alabama). Thatcher offered "a motion, touching on the rights of man," to delete the clause "excepting" the territory from the slavery exclusion in the 1787 Northwest Ordinance. Briefly, a sectional rather than partisan alignment surfaced. Two leading Republicans, Pennsylvania's Albert Gallatin and Massachusetts's Joseph Varnum, whose brother commanded Rhode Island's "Black Regiment" during the Revolution, supported Thatcher's motion. Varnum asked that "Congress would have so much respect for the rights of humanity as not to legalize the existence of slavery any farther," since "the practice of holding blacks in slavery in this country" was "equally criminal with that of the Algerines carrying our citizens into slavery." Gallatin stated the core issue frankly: "If this amendment is rejected, we establish slavery for the country not only during its temporary Government, but for all the time it is a State." Thatcher closed with the speech quoted at this chapter's head, that "government must of necessity put a stop to this evil, and sooner they entered upon the business the better," adding that "by nature these enslaved men are entitled to rights." Their bipartisan effort was doomed, however, by geopolitical realities and the thin hold of the federal government on those territories. As John Craig Hammond has pointed out, passage of Thatcher's amendment would have likely ensured "that the white inhabitants of the Natchez Country would rebel against American authority." It received only an unrecorded twelve votes. And, as we have seen in chapter 2, Thatcher finished his House career in 1800 speaking entirely alone for the rights of black men. On that last occasion, he was again deliberately obnoxious, suggesting that if his colleagues voted their "pointed disapprobation" of the Philadelphia petition, it would prove "that they hugged slavery as slavery, and loved it for its very odiousness."[12]

Outside of Congress, many Yankees expressed a similar disgust at the pretensions of southern republicans and fellowship with Americans of African descent as "of one blood" with themselves, "dark-complexioned citizens," as Thatcher called them. A short list of such men includes politicians and clerical intellectuals, the latter a powerful class fraction in New England. Consider the brothers Theodore and Timothy Dwight. The former was a main Federalist ideologue as a newspaper editor and member of Congress from Connecticut, later secretary of the Hartford Convention, and "one of the most eager and uncompromising advocates of immediate and total abolition to be found before the days of Garrison." In the 1790s, he declared, "It is impossible, in any situation, or under the authority of any laws, to acquire a property in a human being," and suggested that the Haitian Revolution was "a dispensation of Providence which Humanity must applaud." His brother Timothy, Yale president and a leading orthodox Congregationalist, was pilloried by Jeffersonians as Connecticut's "Federalist Pope." He also demonstrated over many decades a profound sympathy for his darker sisters and brothers in Christ. His epic poem, *Greenfield Hill*, lamented the fate of the enslaved child, in whom "slavery's blast bids sense and virtue die." By the 1810s, he foresaw a millennium "when all distinctions of party and sect, of name and nation, of civilization and savageness, of climate and colour, will finally vanish." First, however, would come the same fate that John Brown prophesied: "The land cannot be cleansed of the blood, which is shed therein, but by the blood of him that shed it."[13]

We should not mistake Federalists like the Dwights for radical democrats. Thatcher himself was a paradigmatic High Federalist, perhaps the most reactionary in all of Massachusetts. These Yankees found no contradiction in dismissing racialism while affirming the values of a society led by gentlemen of merit and virtue. But the New Englandish distaste for complexional hierarchy originally lay outside of partisan affiliations, and was shared by quite a few who did call themselves "democrats," men like Levi Lincoln, Jefferson's attorney general and lieutenant governor of Massachusetts in 1807–9. In 1783, he made the frankest avowal of racial equality in arguing for a man named Quock Walker in *Caldwell v. Jennison*, the case ending Bay State slavery: "This Quock is our brother, We all had one common origin, descended from the same kind of flesh, had the same breath of life. . . . Is it not a law of nature that all men are equal and free. Is not the laws of nature the laws of God. Is not the law of God, then, against slavery." Equally impressive is Joseph Varnum, who stood with Thatcher in 1798, and was Speaker of the House of Representatives in 1807–11 and a senator in 1811–17.[14]

Why did many New England leaders share a repugnance for both slavery and racialism, and why did this feeling grow over time? The mix of partisan and sectional motives was a constant: attacking slavery was a readily available stick with which to beat the South's local allies; for Federalists to attack Republicans, in other words. A Calvinist republicanism, in which neither god nor man should be "a respecter of persons," was important, but the politics of the time were just as central, via a comparison with the parent nation, Great Britain. Christopher Brown has shown how, following the American Revolution, British intellectual, political, and military leaders accrued a new fund of "moral capital" for their empire by extirpating the slave trade and showing the world how a great power could divest itself of an encumbrance like chattel slavery. Similarly, as New England found itself under attack by the southern Jeffersonians, it confirmed its purer republicanism by climbing up to a higher moral ground. Like the Old English, the New English insisted they were "unusually and distinctively free" because of "subjecting everyone, regardless of status, to the rule of law." From a mix of republican fervor and sectional resentments, leavened by opportunism, those whom Jefferson derided as "Anglomen" taught themselves to hate slavery and embrace black men as fellow-citizens, at least formally, in the public sphere and at the polls. For several decades, such a stance had few costs and many pleasures, and it is not surprising that the South's defenders routinely expressed contempt for the Yankees' sanctimonious "philanthropy." It is important, however, to remember the origins of this impulse. It was not, originally, an elite concern, but stirred during the revolutionary years among the middling sort who sat on juries and attended town meetings. Coming from the bottom up, ordinary Yankees forged a powerful consensus that drove their leaders.[15]

Revolution within the Revolution: Early Black Politics in Upper New England

Before delineating how nonracial citizenship germinated in Massachusetts and moved northward, the basic features of black life in New England from the eighteenth into the nineteenth century need outlining. There were three specific legacies of the Afro-Yankee society that developed before the Revolution. First, as Lorenzo Greene documented long ago, slavery operated differently in New England than in Britain's other mainland colonies. Colonial laws recognized slaves' "dual status . . . both as persons and as property before the law," including the right to marry, to be secure in their persons from grievous bodily harm, to sue and testify in court, to acquire and transfer property, and to make contracts. Further, Puritan patriarchalism made a householder responsible for the spiritual welfare of all under his roof, including servants and slaves. Combined with low population density, rarely more than one or two slaves per family (other than some plantations in Rhode Island's Narragansett County), these legal and spiritual stipulations rendered slavery less odious, a "slavish servitude" rather than the chattel principle.[16]

Besides laws granting slaves a semblance of legal personality, New England stood apart in that the farther north one moved, the fewer black people one found. In 1820, of 20,782 free persons of color in the six New England states (1.25 percent of the region's population of 1,659,854), only 2,618 lived in Maine, New Hampshire, and Vermont (with a population of 688,260); in that year Pennsylvania and New York alone held almost 60,000 free black Americans. Even if undercounted in the census, this was a minuscule fraction. There is a proviso, however, regarding the small numbers of African Americans in Upper New England. While colonial historians stress that New England's slaves were mainly servants of the wealthy in coastal towns, that geography changed rapidly postemancipation. Many of the newly freed moved north into the region's hinterlands, seeking the autonomy sought by all Yankees—a farm of their own. Another regionally specific feature was the pervasive presence of black Revolutionary veterans, often slaves who received freedom and land grants for serving. As local historians have recently uncovered, from the 1790s to the 1840s a distinctive black rural culture developed in a band stretching from the Berkshires in western Massachusetts through west-central Vermont and Rockingham County in New Hampshire, and up the Maine coast above Portland, with dozens of family clusters integrated into local economic, religious, and political life. To further complicate traditional notions of a monochromatic Upper New England, this frontier was a borderland with maritime Canada's large Black Loyalist community in Nova Scotia, part of an "Afro–New England diaspora" stretching north and east.[17]

More familiar is New England's casual triracialism. Rather than a clear binary dividing black and white, the region's racial customs reflected a fluid blur of colors and origins. Especially along the coast, Africans and Native Americans blended continuously because of the gender imbalances characterizing both groups (a dearth of Indian men; few black women) and Native Americans' willingness to accept foreigners who adopted Indian ways. Most narratives by or about Afro-Yankees refer to intermarriage with surviving tribal groups. The Cuffes are the best-known example. The patriarch, Kofi Slocum, married a Wampanoag, Paul's brother Jonathan joined the Gay Head community, and Paul himself wed a Pequot.[18] These clans were hardly the only version of racial mixing. While antiquarians have long noted coastal New England's Afro-Indian communities, the regular "amalgamation" of men of African descent and white women is equally significant. Many of New

England's black leaders, including Wentworth Cheswell, Lemuel Haynes, and Alexander Twilight, were the offspring of such unions, and their children often found white spouses. That intermarriage was more common in the early republic than later underlines how Upper New England remained "without races" for some time, in the modern understanding of racial difference.

Massachusetts

Massachusetts was the original site of black political mobilization in the 1770s and the first place that affirmed black citizenship, via disfranchisement's defeat in 1778. It offers the first evidence of a self-conscious black electorate and the United States's first black political leader, Prince Hall. Finally, along with New York, it saw the first attacks against those who facilitated black electoralism, usually Federalists.

This trajectory originated in a series of eighteen "freedom suits" from 1765 to 1783, in which slaves went to court to argue their bondage was invalid. These cases demonstrate Afro-Yankees' ability to make claims within the legal order, and are powerful indications of white sympathy since, as John Adams noted, "I never knew a jury by a verdict to determine a negro to be a slave. . . . They always found him free." A deliberate strategy was evident by the mid-1770s, when black Bostonians, likely inspired by the 1772 *Somerset v. Stuart* decision in England, petitioned the General Court to end slavery, invoking "naturel rights": "We are a freeborn Pepel and have never forfeited this Blessing by aney compact or agreement." Black men in New Hampshire and Connecticut followed, suggesting a regional committee of correspondence. Their lobbying skill is indicated by how, before their first petition in 1773, Boston's enslaved leaders asked James Swan, author of a pamphlet attacking the slave trade, to distribute a revised edition to every Massachusetts town, urging them to instruct their representatives to support a ban. A delegation also met with the royal governor, Thomas Hutchinson. These efforts imply a coordinated biracial campaign, since the Boston Town Meeting resolved as early as 1767 to seek emancipation; Mary Locke suspects Sam Adams was the chief organizer. Petitioning and suing climaxed in the early 1780s. According to Jeremy Belknap in 1795, the language that "All men are born free and equal, and have certain natural, essential, and unalienable rights" in Massachusetts's 1780 Declaration of Rights "was inserted not merely as a moral or political truth, but with a particular view to establish the liberation of the negroes as a general principle, and so it was understood by the people at large." Black people took advantage by suing for freedom and compensation for their unpaid labor. In every case they won, culminating in the 1783 *Jennison v. Caldwell* decision, declaring slavery unconstitutional.[19]

Emancipation in Massachusetts has been intensively studied. Less known is the decision five years earlier for a nonracial citizenship. In 1778, the state's leaders promulgated a draft constitution disfranchising all black, brown, and red men. Opponents charged this was a gesture to placate the South and discourage black emigration. The draft was emphatically rejected by the towns, with many decrying its racialized suffrage. It is difficult to overstate the significance of this event—the only instance of "white" suffrage overturned by popular revulsion prior to the Civil War. In 1778, none of the new American states had acted to exclude free black men from voting. If republican Massachusetts had gone another way, black citizenship everywhere else would have been crippled. Instead, a different precedent was established—that a statewide electorate (not a single town affirmed the complexional discrimination) believed republicanism and racialism mutually exclusive. On this basis, a Yankee Republicanism spread northward, forging over time the New England redoubt.

How was this precedent set? In 1777, to gain a broad mandate, the General Court asked all free male inhabitants over twenty-one to authorize the legislature to write a constitution. In February 1778, a draft text went to the towns for comment and approval. Article V stipulated who could become an elector: "Every male inhabitant . . . being free, and twenty-one years of age, excepting Negroes, Indians and Mulattoes . . . provided he has paid taxes in said town . . . and been resident therein one full year." This was clearly controversial, as the legislature's chaplain, Rev. William Gordon of Roxbury's Third Church, had already published a letter insisting "the inhabitants" of Massachusetts "are no respecters of persons and do *verily* believe that *God hath made of one blood all nations of man*, whether black, white, or otherwise coloured." Gordon ridiculed physical differentiations and suggested a more appropriate group to disfranchise were remaining Loyalists. Was it not "ridiculous, inconsistent and unjust, to exclude freemen from voting . . . though otherwise qualified, because their skins are black, tawny or reddish? Why not disqualified for being long-necked, short-faced, or higher or lower than five feet nine [sic]? A black, tawny or reddish skin is not so unfavorable an hue to the genuine son of liberty, as a tory complection."[20]

Once the constitution was published, Gordon (now removed as chaplain) published "Letters to the Freemen of Massachusetts-Bay," denouncing it. His second letter blasted the offending article as "an everlasting reproach upon the present inhabitants . . . evidence to the world, that they mean their own rights only, and not those of mankind, in their cry for liberty." Gordon's attacks stimulated popular outrage, and repudiation of complexional suffrage figured strongly in the towns' overwhelming rejection in May and June. Their resolutions used nearly identical language. Upton offered an elemental republicanism, that those "possessed of suitable property ought to enjoy full right of electing officers . . . without regard to Nation or Colour, seeing all Nations are made of one blood." Spencer and Westminster agreed that disfranchise-ment "for the Sole Cause of Colour" was "an Infringement upon the Rights of Mankind," depriving "a part of the humane Race of their Natural Rights, mearly on account of their Couler," which "no power on Earth has a Just Right to Doe." The constitution was withdrawn and, following another convention, a new charter was ratified in 1780, more conservative in some respects (it mandated a property requirement), but with nonracial suffrage and a bill of rights.[21]

In the early 1780s, who could vote was still left up to the towns. In Dart-mouth, for instance, the Cuffe brothers were barred from voting. "Within a few years," however, "the property qualifications were ignored, and every man who had a settled residence or paid a poll tax was allowed to vote," and as of 1786 "every common laborer" could vote, along with anyone "who could earn three pounds a year." Into this opening, some black men walked. By 1788, a Boston observer noted, "The negroes of sufficient property vote in town-meetings. . . . Prince Hall, Grand Master of the Black Lodge, constantly votes for Governour and Representatives; so do some others." Hall, born into slav-ery circa 1735 and manumitted in 1770, founded the first African American Masonic lodge in the United States in 1775. By the time of Shays's Rebellion, he had become an organizational leader, "*Primus Interparese* of the blacks in this town" in Jeremy Belknap's words, including writing Governor James Bowdoin to offer the African Lodge's support against the rebels, "as we have been protected for many years under this once happy constitution." Hall con-tinually petitioned the selectmen of Boston and the legislature, including a demand that black children be admitted to the common schools. The year 1788 saw further proof of his stature, when Governor John Hancock recov-ered three black Bostonians who had been kidnapped and sold as slaves: "The Congregational ministers, led by Dr. Belknap, and the negroes, led by Prince Hall, took advantage of the public sentiment aroused on this occasion, and the Act of 1788 [banning any further trade in slaves] was the result."[22]

For the next decade, evidence of black voting is scanty, although out-of-state newspapers made sport of Hancock's seeking the favor of those voters by hosting a 1793 ball for them, while refusing permission for theatrical per-formances. On this occasion, a black man supposedly "grasp[ed] his hand" and with "glistening in his eyes" declared, "Ah! Massa Gubbenur! . . . Me glad to see you, for de people say, You lubb de Neeger better dan de play." A black man's perspective on Massachusetts as a "garden of peace, liberty, and equal-ity," meaning political rights and a measure of social respect, can be found in what Hall told Belknap in 1795: "Harmony in a great measure prevails between us as citizens, for the good law of the land does oblige every one to live peaceably with all his fellow-citizens, let them be black or white. . . . As to our associating, there is here a great number of worthy, good men and good citizens, that are not ashamed to take an African by the hand." One notes the striking convergence here. In both cases, the Negrophobic parody and the proud black leader, the issue was the same, "taking the African by the hand." Evidently, there was also "a great number" not prepared to extend that courtesy.[23]

In purely juridical terms, black men had achieved a higher standing than the state's tiny Catholic population, who only gained the right to worship in public in 1780, and only in 1820 the right to be elected to office; long after, they could not be employed as schoolteachers in what remained a Protestant state for a Protestant people. Prince Hall's celebration of "the good law of the land" aside, however, former slaves in Massachusetts occupied a liminal status in the law. They might be citizens, but that category of belonging was far less comprehensive in the late eighteenth century. In New England, pauper laws disfranchised those with no means of subsistence and subjected them to state control, as wards. Historically, towns were responsible for supporting all their "inhabitants," whether aged, indigent, or infirm. Following emancipation, however, Massachusetts's towns sought to deny habitancy to ex-slaves and make the Commonwealth responsible for their maintenance. In a peculiar juxtaposition, those black men who had gained habitancy voted as "freemen," while others denominated "foreigners" were "warned out" or expelled on an explicitly racial basis, since the General Court had passed a bill in 1788 specifically naming "Africans and Negroes." As we shall see, this contradiction was on full display in 1800.[24]

Hancock's ball was a microcosm of a cross-class partisan alliance lasting for decades. What were the ideological or material bases for a long-term link between workingmen of color, led by a few entrepreneurs like Hall, and the propertied gentlemen of the Federalist Party (and their Whig descendants)? In 1917, the political scientist Dixon Ryan Fox asserted that black New Yorkers "had been reared in Federalist households; their cause had been advocated by distinguished Federalists, and it was under the auspices of that party, freedom was provided. When they reached the estate of citizens, their political attachments could be easily foretold." Similarly, in 1800, a Republican newspaper pictured Boston's ladies pinning the party's black cockade on "the hats of their coloured servants saying 'now George you must be a good federalist, it will soon be lawful for you to kill a Jacobin [a Jeffersonian] or burn his house.'" Ad hominem claims hardly suffice. The first basis for this pact was self-evident, rooted in racial solidarity. Free persons of color were naturally inclined to support the party that attacked slaveholders, and New England's Federalists ceaselessly execrated the South because its wealth and power rested upon enslaved black labor. Second, beyond enemy-of-my-enemy calculations, black men had sound reasons for distrusting the white plebeians whom Jefferson's party empowered. They found the Federalist vision of an ordered, law-respecting nationalism congenial, as a vehicle for general emancipation, a remarkably astute analysis. Finally, there was a political-economic logic to the connection between Federalists and black men. Yankee Federalists were deeply involved in Atlantic commerce. Theirs was a party that "flourished within sight of salt water," rooted in port towns like Portland, Portsmouth, Salem, Boston, New Bedford, Providence, and Newport. By the Revolution, Afro-Yankees were deeply embedded in those dockside economies. The Massachusetts and Connecticut state navies systematically recruited them, and Jeffrey Bolster has demonstrated how shipboard life provided the only egalitarian, interracial workplace where a black man could gain status, leading to "innumerable Yankee ships on which black men before the mast ranked higher and earned more than their white shipmates." About 20,000 of the 100,000 sailors annually employed in the U.S. merchant marine in the early nineteenth century were black, when the entire free black male population aged sixteen-plus (in 1820, the first year the census counted them by age cohort) was 64,455. Many more worked as stevedores, another black employment niche. Thus when an agrarian, westward-facing party hostile to commerce and led by slaveholders took over the government, later cutting off all trade through Jefferson's ill-advised 1807 Embargo and Madison's 1812–14 war with England, there were more than enough reasons for black Yankees to vote their pocketbooks by voting Federalist.[25]

Black electoralism began in Boston and spread along the Massachusetts coast, according to Republicans who found it intolerable that Federalists baited their "Negro Votes" from Virginia while recruiting actual Negro voters. Those Federalists likely spoke in black churches, visited homes, and distributed handbills, but little of that is documented; typical is an 1800 sneer about Boston's Federalists acting "so familiar on an Election day, with Citizen Cuffy, and politely accosting him with 'Adams and *liberty*,'" while handing him a printed ballot. Detailed coverage began with the 1798 anecdote, which produced this chapter's title. A New York paper reported that a poll-worker for General William Heath, Republican challenger to Representative Harrison Gray Otis, approached a black voter. The latter demurred, to which the Republican grumped, "All the black men vote for Mr. Otis," leading to the riposte that "and all the blackguards vote for General Heath!," an old comic standby, the punning jibe from a sly menial. Attention to Boston's black electorate surged in 1800, with Federalists divided and Republicans motivated. At first, Jeffersonians sounded a variety of notes. They mocked the Federalists' black cockade, asserting that only "a group of old men, swaggering through the streets, en militaires" and "a cluster of boys . . . interspersed with a few straggling negroes" bothered to wear it. The leading Federalist editor had "not been obeyed by any but a few weak females, boys, and some negroes." But Republicans also wanted African American ballots. Their newspapers exposed the hypocrisy of Federalists seeking black men's votes while their own selectmen published a "NOTICE TO BLACKS" listing 237 who had been "warned out" of the city pursuant to the 1788 act requiring people of color to gain official approval to enter Massachusetts. Denunciations by a writer named "Africanus" were fervent, that soon anyone with "a mended coat, or a greasy hat" would be expelled, and if "only the vagrants from abroad . . . are the objects of the law," why not include "emigrants from all other states in the Union, of whatever skin or color"?[26]

The Republican appeal awkwardly combined outrage at Federalists' winning elections via black men's votes with sympathy for how those voters were treated: "Is it because the *federalists* are losing their [majority] . . . in our town meetings . . . that they have . . . no further use for the *votes* of 'Blacks and people of colour' . . . ?" After reviewing how the latter were "driven in hundreds to Faneuil Hall . . . to vote for the *'Federal Ticket*,' and one of them by the name of Hawkins, now dead, paid for his services in obtaining votes," it stirred the partisan pot, that so many black men had voted "against Governor Adams and in favor of Cushing—against Doctor Jarvis and favor of Fisher Ames," and "The black and yellow votes thus obtained, decided the last election in favour of Mr. Otis and Mr. [Governor Caleb] Strong, for if their number, . . . or 300 had been neglected, neither of these gentlemen would have been chosen by the people." Its closing apostrophe was feeble: "Men of colour and black men! For all these services rendered to the Essex Junto [the Federalist central committee], you are to be rewarded by being driven out of the state!" Black men who had been "driven to Faneuil Hall" like cattle should now rally to Republicans who had never sought their votes.[27]

Nowhere did the writer suggest that Republicans would guarantee black rights. Only months earlier, Republicans had mocked the black Federalists who, at the funeral of the Hawkins referred to above (a professional cook and head of the African Masonic Lodge), had linked his name with Washington, and concluded by hailing his successor, Prince Hall, in the same company as Federalist grandees: "Friends and fellow citizens, we have this day lost a Hawkins and a Washington! But, thanks be to God, we have still left a Pickering, a Wolcott, and a Hall!" Further, in early 1801, the same Republicans who had claimed sympathy with blacks duped by Federalists asserted that their party had tried to pass a law "to check . . . the introduction of foreigners and negro-servants" in the port towns. Servants were seen trailing after their employers "and the vote of the former has always been the same with the latter. . . . The *Republicans* are desirous to have an act to give the *real Citizens* the right of Election, to the exclusion of *foreigners* and *straggling negroes*."[28]

Without question, Federalists were expert in "fagot voting" (nominal transfers of property to enfranchise poor men on Election Day). In 1805, Levi Lincoln told Jefferson, "Persons steeped in poverty were enabled by the federalist art and management, not charity, to claim property on the occasion, sufficient to qualify for voting." Lincoln avoided race, but his comrades repeatedly alleged that Governor Caleb Strong was elected with black men's ballots. As we have seen, this charge was first made in 1800. It waned until Strong, in office 1800–7, returned to power in 1812: "The *blacks* in this town are very numerous; and we are told, that almost to a man, they voted for Mr. Strong. . . . It is a fact that in 1812, had it not been for negro votes *Caleb Strong* would not have had a majority in Massachusetts." Republicans claimed that many offices depended on black votes: "In our elections the blacks vote, and commonly for the federal tickets. There is no doubt that the members of congress in the 2nd district, in this city, would have been republican, had no blacks voted. . . . Here, the vote of a negro is as powerful as that of a white man; and they have a direct representation both in Congress and the State Legislature." And these Federalists who denounced the South's "negro votes" were "the very men who have exulted in the election of Gov. Strong and a Congressional Representative, in Massachusetts, by negro votes" (although, one notes, the Jeffersonians never claimed black votes were actually *illegal* on account of race).[29]

How reasonable was the assertion that a bloc vote by black men constituted a balance of power? Not surprisingly, Republicans conflated the occasional with the general, to slur their opponents, as Strong won narrowly in 1800 and 1812, and by a mere 526 votes in 1806, but in most elections, his margins were considerably greater than the state's possible black electorate (1,684 in the 1810 census, when the total vote for governor was 90,813). The Jeffersonians also never stopped competing for those votes. In Boston, an 1813 pamphlet attacked the Federalists' Washington Benevolent Society and its leader, H. G. Otis, as "Beloved Harry" leading a group of "Tories" plotting sedition with "Albion." Among other misdeeds, the Federalists had bribed Prince Hall ("a teacher of the rising generation of his complexion") to come over to them, bringing his supporters, via a patronage job. After acknowledging "it hath been reported aforetime that he was of the tribe of the republicans," the Prince announced his switch:

> the chiefs of the tribe of tories, came unto me, and said,
>
> Verily, PRINCE, if thou will quit following the tribe of the republicans, and cleave unto us we will do that for thee which shall seem good in thine eyes.
>
> And we will exalt thee, inasmuch as thou shalt be placed in a comfortable situation, and shalt have no reason to take heed for the morrow.
>
> So I did adopt their counsel, and of a truth I did not find that they had deceived me.
>
> And when the people were called together, who reside in the town of BOSTON, the chief rulers did recommend that two hundred pieces of silver should be given unto me yearly.
>
> So those of the tribe of the tories who were present did say that they would, follow the *Select* rulers [Boston's selectmen] in this thing.

The Republican versifier had him conclude by admitting his abasement: "I will follow the tribe of the tories in all things. And though I be not suffered to walk with them when they go to the temple, because of my complexion, yet will I compass sea and land to gain them proselytes." All the evidence over several decades suggests that Hall was quite adept at "gaining proselytes" in Boston and points north, so this doggerel was no idle jest.[30]

The competition was heaviest in Salem, the state's second-largest city, ninth largest in the United States in 1810, and the nation's premier port in the eighteenth century. As early as 1802, Rev. William Bentley, an ardent Republican (a friend of Jefferson and later chaplain of Congress), recorded in his diary the "many dirty tricks practiced by the high [Federalist] party. . . . Such as, one alien Dutch man accepted, & another refused. . . . A Voucher for a man, whose family never lived in town. A Voucher for a Negro who had not one farthing of property." Via these devices, "The list of the high party obtained"—the Federalists won. Republicans fought back, and in 1810 Federalists denounced their "pitiful and contemptible means to obtain black votes," with "a meeting . . . near the mill pond" for "the ostensible purpose of instructing the black people of the neighborhood in the great concerns of religion." Hoping "to walk ankle-deep in federal blood," the Jeffersonians told the throng "they must all . . . vote for the democratic ticket; for should [Federalist governor Christopher] Gore and his associates be re-elected, the whole of them were to be purchased up, and transported to Jamaica or Cuba, and sold for slaves, for that was the object of the Federalists." In reply, Republicans jibed that if "the Republican majority was made up of negroes," that meant "they did not like the federal discipline . . . a proof that it was too bad even for negroes." Reverend Bentley's diary clarifies how Republicans got those black votes. Since the 1790s, a white Baptist, the Reverend Spaulding, a Republican like most Baptists, had been ministering to Salem's black community, and they apparently followed him in politics. In April 1811, Bentley recorded how partisanship and church affiliation were all mixed up. Spaulding told him "the high party [Federalists] . . . have a new plan to attach the Negroes to their interest in Salem." Spaulding had "induced the town to establish a school for small black children. He has fostered it with uncommon care & has brought many of the heads of families to discover some regard to instruction by his weekly meetings with them." The Federalists planned to one-up him and "bring these children & families into an opposite both political & religious interest by assigning the instructions of the Blacks to the young female communicants of the Tabernacle [Federalist-affiliated Congregational] Church."[31]

From here on, however, the calumniations went the other way. In March 1812, when Strong retook the governorship, a "Negro host . . . embodied in their phalanx" led to Federalist victory in Salem. Bentley recorded that "confidence in their numbers & success had made the Republicans overlook . . . that the rich must have greater influence on the ignorant & servile blacks than the body of industrious citizens could obtain. So we have lost every thing called Republican in Salem." A year later, the Republicans were still smarting. They brought a contingent of white sailors from a privateer in Salem's harbor, but were again outvoted, and fumed, "It ill becomes those who bring to the polls the *Negro* scrapings of the Great Pasture [in Salem], and other *Black holes* of the town, to abuse so valuable a class of citizens as our enterprizing Seamen." Boston's Republican organ chimed in. If "Salem has acquired a federal ascendancy, by what means was it effected? Did drunken negroes appear at the polls, instead of sober citizens?—Were unqualified voters admitted . . . well known to hold no property?" Republicans throughout the region were confounded by Federalist knavery conjoined with idiocy: "The greater part of federalists . . . actually believe that the Negroes are brought to the poll and vote in the southern states; as they do in the city of New York, in Boston, Salem, Newburyport, and Portland, in some of which places the majority is made out wholly by Negroes, and if it were not for their votes, the majority would be democratic." The final verdict was a plain truth—that "in Massachusetts the vote of any old stupid negro is equal in the selection of a Governor &c, to the vote of the man of the first talents." The old Bay State, seat of hierarchical elitism, had jumped over the hurdles to plebeian equality far ahead of any Jeffersonian heartland. Nor did Republican charges of dirty dealings in Salem go away, as in Reverend Bentley's asserting in 1816 that the "high party" brought a black woman in men's clothing to the polls.[32]

As Salem makes clear, this was never a one-sided competition, since Republicans also sought black votes. An anecdote from an 1890 Salem town history opens up this arena of black men trading votes on a par with whites through the 1850s, describing how, when "the colored population . . . was formerly very much larger," their votes were "sought by both political parties . . . Federalists and Republicans (Democrats), who had 'wire pullers' to influence them. The Federalists had . . . John Remond, the noted caterer, and York Morris (father of Robert Morris the colored lawyer of Boston). The Democrats, Prince Farmer and Mumford." Collectively, these four men indicate the presence of two "submachines," a term invented by a political scientist in the 1930s to mean apparatuses turning out voters defined by ethnicity, religion, or language. These bipartisan operations across the antebellum period indicate the special quality of Afro-Yankee politics: they had succeeded in becoming ordinary.[33]

John Remond and his family were the best known, and black Salem's progress can be traced through his life. He was born in Curacao, and at age ten in 1798 his mother sent him to Salem with a ship captain, where he became a baker's delivery boy. In 1808, he opened a perfumery and hairdressing shop, and the following year began operating a store on the ground floor of Hamilton Hall, just erected by the city's Federalist merchants as a gathering place. He catered his first dinner that same year for the Salem Light Infantry, with Governor Gore present, and was naturalized the following year by the County Court. By the 1810s, Remond ran a massive restaurant, catering, and food importation operation centered on the hall. He also gained a valuable piece of patronage in 1811, when the town's selectmen announced they "have appointed Mr. JOHN REMOND to superintend the sweeping of Chimneys in the town of Salem," via issuing licenses with fixed prices. Over decades, he organized annual dinners for Salem's militia companies and societies, the state's major politicians, and famous visitors, including General Lafayette in 1824, President Adams in 1825, and President Jackson in 1833, and was celebrated for his "uniform propriety of conduct, and an undeviating attention to business," which "has gained the respect of all classes of the citizens."[34]

About York Morris we know little more than that his May 1815 Seaman's Protection Paper certified he was "A Citizen of the United States of America," twenty-three years old, and born in Ipswich. He was later a waiter for Remond, and ran a shop for cleaning boots and shoes, dying in 1834, at age forty-eight. John "King" Mumford's career is more dramatic, as the boss of Salem's interracial underworld. Another antiquarian account described Salem's "Negro town" as under his control, "a colony of ten or twelve negro families, and on the left some four or five houses containing, probably, altogether some fifty or sixty inmates." Mumford was "chief of the tribe" on one side, and "on the left, the most noted was Prince Savage, an intelligent black man, highly respected." Eventually, this community became known as Roast Meat Hill. William Bentley noted in 1816 that it had been "a mere pasture" when he arrived but now there was "a Twine factory," around which congregated "about 100 huts and houses for Blacks from the most decent to the most humble appearance. . . . It is properly our black town, but too many marks of poverty in such a town not to indicate more the poverty of education, than of means." Trial records show that eventually Mumford owned several brothels. In 1825, "an affray" was reported at "Mumford's House" with "similar riots frequent in that neighborhood for the two years past. The house is said to be a nuisance, an eye-sore to the inhabitants and a stigma on the town." Two years later, the town convicted him "of letting houses for purposes for prostitution." All through, he remained a "wire puller" (a political operative), on behalf of "the Democrats," who presumably turned a blind eye to his businesses.[35]

The last of these men, Prince Farmer (whom the 1890 author perhaps mistakenly named "Savage"), was a high-end caterer like Remond and Prince Hall. An 1847 anecdote suggests his self-possession, and what was possible in the Yankee Republic. When President Polk visited Salem, Farmer, as a good Democrat, "marched up" to the empty presidential barouche "with great dignity," tipped the hostler, "ordered the steps to be thrown down, mounted them with his dog, folded his arms and seated himself with all the grace imaginable." The writer noted that Farmer departed "with a chuckle of gratification . . . exclaiming, with his well known pith and humor, 'There, do you just tell the President, when he takes his seat, that the *Prince* has been here before him.'"[36]

New Hampshire

Boston's Prince Hall was the first leader who mobilized voters, but a provincial backwater with a much smaller black electorate produced the first public official. The history of black politics in New Hampshire starts with Wentworth Cheswell (1746–1817), remarkable in terms of eminence and longevity in office. His career reveals either the relative absence or a very unfamiliar version of racialism. It was the centerpiece of Senator David Morril's impassioned denunciation of Missouri's 1820 attempt to deny black citizenship, which underlines that Cheswell's African heritage was a recognized fact: Morril named "a yellow man, by the name of Cheswell, who with his family were respectable in point of abilities, property, and character" and "held some of the first offices in the town in which he resided," including "justice of the peace for that county."[37]

Like Paul Cuffe, Cheswell (or Cheswill; he used both) was the son of a self-made man who made alliances across racial lines. His father, Hopestill, a master carpenter and son of a self-emancipated slave, built some of Portsmouth's most impressive mansions. He married a white woman, as had his father and as would the son. To underline his connection with the powerful, Hopestill named his heir for the province's dominant family, the Wentworths, who governed New Hampshire in 1741–75. In 1763, the younger Cheswell was enrolled in the first class at Dummer's Academy, a school for the provincial elite. By 1768, he was a married property owner, owner of a church pew, and active in town affairs in Newmarket, a coastal shipping center near Portsmouth. In April 1776, he was appointed to the school committee and elected town messenger for the Committee of Safety, earning renown as a local Paul Revere warning of British ships in the river. From then through his death, Cheswell held every possible office, including selectman on three occasions, town moderator for seven years, assessor for six, coroner for two, and from 1805 until his death, justice of the peace; he also ran for state senator in 1806. He was almost certainly Newmarket's wealthiest man, with an estate valued at $13,000. In this small state, with its closed elite, where most people of color were ex-slaves, Cheswell and his family stood alone. There is no record of any ties to the larger black community, although this does not mean they "passed" for white, a present-day anachronism. Morril's verdict is apt—he was of mixed race, a "mulatto" in the time's legal terminology, and calling him a "yellow man," however grating to modern ears, was the politest way to indicate that.[38]

Newmarket was not the center of New Hampshire's black life. The largest concentration was in Exeter, a few miles away in Rockingham County. By 1790, black families constituted almost 5 percent of its population, most living in their own households. In Exeter and inland settlements like Sutton and Warner, black veterans used land grants or money from former masters to become farmers, routinely going to court and otherwise entering civic life. Early on, some of these men were enfranchised (taxed on their "polls" and thus made "freemen") while others were excluded, or excluded themselves, as simply "Negroes," the word apparently a rough synonym for paupers nottaxed. Over time, the "Negro" status disappeared, and these endogamous, racially integrated communities survived into the mid-nineteenth century, with some black New Hampshiremen entering politics on church and school committees.[39]

New Hampshire offers one of the clearest examples of race and class interacting to reinforce the salience of the latter. As a family became more prosperous and respectable, typically by joining a white-led church, their race receded. We should, therefore, refuse the notion that Cheswell was a perfect exception—too light and rich to be considered black. The best evidence for him as an example rather than an exception comes from the next paragraph of Morril's 1820 speech, referring to another distinguished son of his state:

"a mulatto man, by the name of Thomas Paul, a regularly ordained baptist minister, pastor of a church of people of color [in Boston], at whose meeting many white people attend, and who preaches, by exchange or otherwise, with all the neighboring ministers of his denomination." Morril likely knew Thomas's father, Caesar, a prototypical Afro-Yankee: manumitted slave, former soldier, farmer, founder of a clan connected to Exeter's other propertied black families (Thomas's brothers, Nathaniel and Benjamin, also became leading ministers). The Pauls' "family connection" suggests how self-elevation, self-respect, and political citizenship ran together in the Yankee Republic. Men like Morril knew them and could not accept "complexion" as a binding measure of worth.

Vermont

Until the 1750s, Vermont was Indian land nominally claimed by New Hampshire and New York. During the Revolution its few settlers declared it an independent republic. Paradoxically, despite the "extreme youth of this northwestern sector" with "a remarkably vigorous and unmannered society" and "little respect for traditional ties and institutions," Vermont became the most Yankee regarding race, embracing nonracial citizenship while celebrating what individual men of color were able to achieve in their infant polity. Absolute opposition to slavery and unwavering egalitarianism was the Green Mountain mythos, proclaimed in 1804 by a state supreme court judge when a New York slave-owner sought his fugitive property, only to be told, "Nothing short of a bill of sale from the Almighty" would prove ownership. Fifty years later, the state's "very name in the South came to be a byword expressing, in the words of the Georgia Legislature of 1857, 'the maniac ravings of hell-born fanaticism.'" Vermont's leaders relished such vituperation, with a committee of its lower House describing slavery in 1849 as "a crime against humanity" against which their state's "voice has been, and is, and ever ought to be, in utter condemnation . . . her course one of determined and persevering opposition to it, by all allowable means."[40]

To a remarkable degree this oft-told story corresponds to reality. In one historian's words, Vermonters never "shrank from the revolution's radical faith in the equality of mankind," seeing themselves as "the symbolic fount of the young nation's truculent egalitarianism," stimulating "the strongest antislavery, Antimasonic, and free-soil sentiment in the nation." The 1777 Constitution declared all men free and equal, and a 1786 act barred any "sale and removal" from the state, declaring "all the subjects of the commonwealth, of whatever color, are equally entitled to the inestimable blessings of freedom." Vermont senator Stephen Bradley first proposed the legislation ending the slave trade and sought the death penalty for those violating it. Throughout the entire period, 1790–1860, its congressional representatives were "eternally opposed to any action, direct or indirect, which smacked of the interest of slaveholders," with the "Admission of Missouri, Texas, Arkansas . . . fought to the last ditch." In 1837, James Birney, later the Liberty Party's presidential candidate, remarked after visiting that he had "never seen our cause stand on such a high ground among political men as it does among those of the Vermont legislature."[41]

No party in Vermont had recourse to outright racialism. Even when Republicans attacked Federalists bringing to the polls "every worthless French emigrant from Canada; every unfortunate man who, with his helpless retinue of children, begs his daily bread . . . and every negro in the town," they still described black men as "an unfortunate race of beings who, in their places, deserve to be treated with humanity and civility, and to enjoy the right of suffrage" even if they were "not usually the most polite, genteel and well-informed part of the community." A "negro" may have been disreputable but he still had rights.[42]

Regarding its tiny black population, Vermont both differed from and resembled New Hampshire. In both, slavery had vanished by the 1790 census, but in the latter it faded away while Vermont voted it away. Vermont declared nonracial freemanship at the outset, versus New Hampshire's de facto black citizenship. Socially and demographically, they were alike. In both, as in Massachusetts and Maine, a visible sprinkling of black veterans emigrated seeking farmsteads, settling in "clusters . . . of one or two extended families" in towns east of Lake Champlain, including Ferrisburgh, Middlebury, Vergennes, Hinesburgh, and Charlotte, where well into the 1840s and 1850s, they constituted a surprisingly large share of the population. In these "family enclaves," they traded and went to church with whites, and often married white women without recorded public furor, sharing a "comfortable and natural interaction among neighbors, regardless of race." Fathers and sons "swore in" as freemen to vote, eventually gaining minor offices by the 1830s.[43]

As in New Hampshire and Maine, a few men of color became widely known, and their prominence was eminently political and partisan. The most famous was the Reverend Lemuel Haynes, far more controversial than Cheswell. A heroic figure to a generation of young white clerics, Haynes was a pillar of "orthodox" Calvinism, sought after for his Federalist politics and austere republicanism. His intimate relationship with white leaders led to the *Colored American* calling him in 1837 "the only man of known African descent, who has ever succeeded in overpowering the system of American caste." Inside the Yankee Republic, his fame endured; long after his death, he was cited in 1919 as "certainly one of the most remarkable ministers of his generation . . . one of the noblest of the New England Congregational ministers of a century ago."[44]

Born in 1753 in Connecticut to a white mother and a black father, Haynes was bound out to a pious white family in Granville, Massachusetts, who encouraged his Lincolnesque autodidacticism: "It became known that he possessed uncommon gifts in prayer and exhortation." He served in the Revolution under Col. Timothy Robinson, who sponsored his further education, leading to ordination in 1785 and an appointment in Torrington, Connecticut, with John Brown's parents among his parishioners. In 1787, Haynes took up a missionary pastorate in Rutland, in western Vermont's deistic wilderness, "a comparatively uncultivated field, where the peculiarity of his history would be least likely to awaken prejudice against his ministrations." He stayed for thirty years, steadily gaining fame, but losing his position in 1818 because of divisions resulting from his Federalism. In 1813, a deacon and local Republican politician had charged "the said Haynes hath been guilty of dishonesty in his talk—to the wounding of the feelings of some of the brethren," that he had declared "had it been in my power, I would have executed you, by hanging you right up" since he could not love "his republican brethren as well as he did his federal brethren."[45]

How do we assess Haynes's political role? Divines were then sought after by the powerful. Vermont's governor Richard Skinner and Chief Justice Royall Tyler admired Haynes for his oratory and intellectual authority, and befriended him. As Haynes's contemporary biographer put it, men like these kept "an eye out upon the humbler classes of society, with a view to cherish . . . every opening bud of piety and genius," knowing "how superior is the dignity . . . conferred by character" rather than birth. Patronage was credit given to worth, what worth was due. If an older man like Haynes was undermined by prejudices regarding his origins or complexion then his "friends" owed him continued support, and they gave it, ensuring new pastorates until death. Haynes's standing was publicly recognized by Middlebury College awarding him an honorary master of arts in 1804. Then came his encounter with the Unitarian Hosea Ballou (Unitarians were Congregationalists who rejected Calvinist theology, influential among Boston's upper classes). Their spontaneous debate in 1806 led to a pamphlet war earning Haynes "a transatlantic reputation as a ruthless polemicist in theological dispute." His *Universal Salvation, a Very Ancient Doctrine of the Devil* was reprinted over seventy times. To confirm his preeminence, he was elected moderator of the Vermont General Convention of Congregationalist ministers in 1813, and its delegate to a regional convocation of orthodox clergy in 1814.[46]

Haynes earned his sardonic ministerial celebrity, but he was also intensely partisan. Haynes's Federalism stemmed "from the experience of black people in day-to-day social interaction with ordinary white people." The latter's rise to equal citizenship "seemed a kind of nakedness to the black abolitionists, so the appeal to authority and patronage as means of securing freedom made clear sense." Like W. E. B. Du Bois, he was simultaneously a "traditionalist and radical . . . republican, not democratic." Haynes's partisanship was an avowal of his Yankee identity, authorizing a pungent critique of Jeffersonian populism. Given "the propensity of the human mind . . . to evil," he preached just after the Virginian's election, "our liberty" could easily "become a cloak of licentiousness. . . . A true republican is one who wishes well to the good constitution and laws of the commonwealth . . . respects magistrates . . . is peaceable and quiet under an wholesome administration." Using the standard Federalist tropes for Jeffersonian democracy, he assailed "anarchy and confusion" as "of all things most detestable," since a good citizen "grows better under the influence of a benign government."[47]

Haynes's New Englandism intensified as the Federalists assailed Virginia's plantocracy. As his first biographer recorded, "The spirit of party rapidly ripened into a spirit of deeply-rooted and unquenchable rancour," during which "the keenness of his satire often fell upon unprincipled parasites." The climax to his sermonizing came in 1814, when Federalists contemplated secession. While the ill-fated Hartford Convention met, Timothy Dwight invited Haynes to his New Haven pulpit. The black divine gave a sermon justifying separation from the ungodly—meaning the South—via the parable of the "treacherous sister Judah." The eminent Dwight was reduced to tears, and twenty years later, the president of Amherst remembered the sermon as "one of the most remarkable ever preached in New England."[48]

Other than Paul Cuffe, Haynes was New England's most prominent man of color, but Vermont produced a whole cohort of black ministers. Charles Bowles, another revolutionary veteran of mixed-race parentage, moved to Hinesburgh in 1816, and for the next twenty years was a roving Free Will Baptist preacher. Like Haynes, his complexion added to his fame, with Bowles declaring, "If people will be blessed by the water of life, they must be willing to drink it from a brown bowl," and "Hundreds have been led to Christ and converted just by my color." Another was Alexander Twilight, the "Iron-Willed Schoolmaster" of Brownington. Twilight represented the first generation born into Upper New England's rural black society. His father, Ichabod, was a freedman and veteran from Plattsburgh, New York, who moved to Corinth in 1792, and bought a farm in 1798. The 1790 and 1800 censuses recorded the six Twilights as persons of color, although later ones listed family members as white. Alexander was born in 1795 and grew up as a farmer's son until, sponsored by a local eminence, he entered Middlebury, graduating in 1823. Like most young collegians, he was ordained, in his case as a Congregational minister. His fame began in 1829, when he singlehandedly built a four-story granite schoolhouse, still standing today, in forbidding Orleans County, just below Canada. Over a quarter-century, Twilight educated many Vermonters who became important politicians, businessmen, and military officers. In 1836, to lobby against a division of his county's school fund, he was elected to the legislature, serving one term. By that point, his public identity as "black" was no longer mentioned, but the one photograph and later memories indicate his origins were never hidden.[49]

The common denominator of these early leaders was their visible connection to political power: certainly, they voted, and both Cheswell and Twilight held significant elected offices. More importantly, they made their way into the upper reaches of the region's political class, demonstrating in their persons the possibilities for interracial citizenship along the new nation's northeastern periphery.

The Yankee Republic Declares Itself, 1818–1822

For several generations, historians described the period after 1816 as a non-partisan "era of good feelings," when the Federalists effectively disappeared, President Monroe ran for reelection unopposed, and the Missouri Crisis only briefly hinted at a darker future. In this older history, slavery barely figured into politics. Recent scholarship has demolished that master narrative by documenting how the battle over Missouri's 1819 application for statehood was "the culmination of twenty years of Northern efforts to restrict slavery's Western expansion" led by "loyal Northern Republicans . . . fighting, as they had always done, against slavery and its expansion." As Padraig Riley has argued, "The quick passage from nationalist unity at the end of the war to the divisive Missouri Crisis of 1819–21 demonstrated the ongoing instability of the Jeffersonian political order," clarifying "there was no national consensus over the virtues of slavery."[50]

Regarding black politics, the years 1818–22 have a different symmetry, in which the national polity became clearly racialized, with Upper New England emerging as the sole nonracial bulwark. A contiguous bloc of the Lower North (New York, Rhode Island, and Connecticut) moved to disfranchise black men, while the Upper New England states, now including Maine, affirmed their color-blind citizenship, most dramatically in December 1820, during the congressional debates over Missouri's constitution.

The split between Upper and Lower New England appeared only gradually. Rhode Island and Connecticut had larger black populations than the states to their north. They both legislated gradual emancipations, maintaining white control over black bodies, versus the immediate freedom and freemanship granted or claimed in Massachusetts, New Hampshire, and Vermont. They both recruited large numbers of black soldiers during the Revolution, many of them slaves. Finally, both had extremely conservative political cultures, with minimal evidence of black voting, despite large potential electorates. This divergence between two parts of New England over slavery, emancipation, and citizenship reflected a basic political-economic divide. The Bay State and its northern neighbors bordering Canada formed a coherent bloc tied to British trading networks. Since the colonial era, however, Connecticut and Rhode Island had looked southward to New York and the Caribbean, in an economy centered around "the Long Island–Rhode Island Sound . . . a single integrated maritime region that could aptly be described as a Yankee Mediterranean . . . as closely integrated into Atlantic trading systems as Barbados and Anomabu."[51]

Connecticut

Every claim regarding the Federalist elite's defense of hierarchy and contempt for the mass was borne out in Connecticut. Its Federalist-Congregationalist establishment was committed to maintaining power, blocking any democratic reform. They had long enjoyed an impregnable majority, and never accepted partisan rotation in office. Town selectmen had the right to refuse admission as voters ("freemen") to those owning the requisite property but not "of good character." Unlike in Massachusetts, where nearly any man could meet the property requirement, Connecticut's excluded many white and most black men. In 1801, the legislature mandated viva voce voting, the "Stand Up Law," to further suppress Republicans. Dissenting Protestants, especially Baptists, found the authority of taxpayer-supported Congregational ministers oppressive, and Federalist domination provided ample grounds for an insurgency lasting from the late 1790s until 1817, when a "Tolerationist" coalition finally triumphed.[52]

Amid this partisan fray, black suffrage hardly mattered. Connecticut Federalists did not emulate their peers in Massachusetts and New York in recruiting black electors. The sole controversy over their voting was instigated by Federalists in 1803 charging that Wallingford Republicans had received an "illegal vote." After three years of admitting unqualified "young men . . . the democrats" had let a "negro ravisher" named Toby vote (he had once been whipped for climbing into a neighbor's bedroom). The year before a Republican legislator, John T. Peters, had proposed universal suffrage, and as late as 1816, Federalists exploited the convergence of these developments: "That J. T. Peters' plan of Universal Suffrage may yet be revived, and negro ravishers be admitted to the polls, as was once done in the case of Toby, by Democratic Justices in Wallingford."[53]

The successive disfranchisements by Federalists and Republicans have no evident cause. Federalists went first via a simple legislative act in 1814, changing the law to read "no person shall be admitted a freeman in any town . . . unless in addition to the qualifications already required . . . he be a free white male person." This amendment remained so obscure, however, that both later scholars and contemporaries missed it, and Republicans promulgated disfranchisement twice on gaining power. When the double blows of legislative and constitutional disfranchisement fell, however, certain Federalists objected, indicating they sometimes privileged respectable men of color over white paupers. At the September 1818 constitutional convention, Stephen Mitchell, former U.S. senator and chief justice of the state's highest court, moved to strike "white" from the suffrage clause. After an unrecorded debate, he lost by a large margin, although the new constitution grandfathered current black voters. Earlier that year, however, saw a brief but revealing polemic. A longtime Republican, Elisha Phelps, proposed an amendment "That every white male inhabitant of this State, of the age of twenty-one years" who met the property requirements, paid a tax, or served in the militia, be admitted to vote. The ensuing fight pitted a class-based nonracial hierarchy against white men's equality. Two arch-Federalists, Aaron Austin and Shubael Griswold, attacked Phelps's bill: "Mr. Austin, said . . . the expression in the bill 'all white male inhabitants' . . . appeared to him improper, there were some neither white nor black—and if in possession of other qualifications, he thought it improper to exclude them.—Nay, he would admit blacks to the polls, if they had property sufficient and a good moral character." Griswold also objected, snorting, "How much taxes must a man pay, how much military duty must he perform, how white must he be?," escalating the next day to a full-scale assault on universal suffrage, with race irrelevant: "Where will be the security of real property, when the poor and destitute can vote it away at pleasure[?] . . . Those who exercise the right of suffrage, ought to be independent freemen . . . not liable to be controuled by the wealthy. . . . If this was a natural right, every individual in society might vote. Even females would be entitled to the privilege."[54]

No matter; although the state's Whigs tried repeatedly to repeal disfranchisement in the 1840s and 1850s, Connecticut's black Yankees would not vote until passage of the Fifteenth Amendment.[55]

Rhode Island

Scholars have paid considerable attention to Rhode Island's black population before the Revolution, the North's largest. After that, the historiography thins out, and 1822's disfranchisement is as obscure in Rhode Island as it was in Connecticut. Why were black votes cut off without debate? Were Rhode Islanders following Connecticut's and New York's lead, or was it a response to Republican racial appeals, to appease those agitating against the archaic election law which disfranchised two-thirds of adult males? Did any of Rhode Island's black men vote prior to 1822? Here the evidence is anecdotal at best, as in the story told about Colonel William Richmond of Little Compton, who gave his former slaves land before the Revolution and insisted that one of them, Primus Collins ("who had been honored with election to the Negro governorship of Rhode Island"), be permitted to vote: "When he became a free voter, by the ownership of land, Colonel Richmond took him to the polls and told him to put in his vote. The moderator forbade it, and said he had no right. Colonel Richmond drew up his cane and with a loud voice declared, 'That man shall vote,' and Collins became a voter until his death."

The same local historian reported that another Little Compton eminence, Isaac Wilbour, as chief justice, "got the word white inserted in the statute respecting voting," but there is no evidence of that authorship. More concretely, in 1778, Anthony Kinnicutt, who ran "a victualing business, supplying food and liquor" to ships in Providence, petitioned the town's government to either "wholly forbear to tax him, or grant him the Privilege of being a Freeman of the Town like another man." The result was that he was exempted from taxation, and in 1800 the council removed propertied people of color from the tax rolls, to keep them out of schools, all of which suggests black voting was rare if not unknown in that city.[56]

The best explanation for Rhode Island's disfranchisement is Robert Cottrol's: "the deterioration of the free Negro's legal status . . . occurred as he became more of a potential threat to total white control." In Providence, their population grew from 48 slaves and 127 free persons in 1790 to 1,414 of the latter and only four slaves by 1825. These numbers, combined with increasing material success, encouraged whites to see them as either a danger or a convenient solvent of political ferment. In 1821, Providence's government embarked on a campaign to drive out transient black and Native persons, and the General Assembly passed a law "for breaking up disorderly houses kept by the negroes and mulattoes, and for putting such negroes and mulattoes to service." It may also be that Federalists had allowed some black men to vote, as alleged in 1811, when William Jones beat the incumbent Republican governor, James Fenner, by just 234 votes out of 7,546 cast, with "a remarkable increase of voters in the Federalist stronghold of Providence." A Republican newspaper charged "illegal votes . . . in Aristocratick Providence," where "every villain that could be bribed to receive a life lease, were obtained, qualified, and voted. His Excellency received a mark of homage never before conferred . . . the *vote of a negro*;—a vote unauthorized by the laws of this State." Soon after, Republicans proposed that "every white male citizen" of age "who is rated for a poll or property tax, or who is or has been enrolled in the militia" be allowed to vote. They continued pressing for suffrage reform, but often omitted complexion, asking merely for "the right of suffrage to citizens who are not freeholders, provided they pay taxes or do militia duty." In 1820, "the following bill was passed in the Senate, and postponed in the House . . . extending the right of suffrage to . . . every free able-bodied white male citizen . . . who shall have already equipped himself . . . and performed all the militia duty required by law." In late 1821 Republicans again proposed a "PROJECT OF A CONSTITUTION OR FORM OF GOVERNMENT" enfranchising "every free white male person" who "paid a state or town tax." Racial disfranchisement followed in January 1822, without explanation, as one of several token reforms: "The law was further amended so as to deny the privilege of voting to all persons except free *white* males."[57]

Maine

Maine's statehood usually receives mention as an addendum to the Missouri Crisis, because its application became the fulcrum for Henry Clay's "Compromise," whereby new admissions to the Union would balance slave and free, guaranteeing Senate parity. But Maine was also the only new state to enact and maintain nonracial citizenship after 1800 and before the Civil War. This was neither an afterthought nor uncontested. Its 1819 constitutional convention debated and dismissed restricting suffrage. On that basis Maine became, like Massachusetts, a center for black political mobilization.

Maine had a dual identity, as an extension of colonial Massachusetts but also part of the northeastern borderland, separated from Massachusetts by more than New Hampshire's narrow seacoast. Like the latter and Vermont, it was scarcely populated before the Revolution and grew vertiginously, from a mere 23,000 in 1763, to 56,000 in 1784, nearly doubling again to 96,540 by 1790, and more than 150,000 by 1800. Outside the southern coastal towns like Portland, its vast expanses remained a frontier, with little law or orthodox religion. Even more than Vermont, plebeian Mainers fostered a counterculture of evangelical libertinism. Maine's special feature was that most of its land had been claimed by "Great Proprietors," who sought the protection of the state government against thousands of squatters. Its statehood movement sputtered until the 1810s, but by then Massachusetts's Federalists wished to rid themselves of Maine's Republican electors, who threatened their statewide control.[58]

As in Vermont and New Hampshire, many black Mainers resided in clusters of veterans and the newly freed dispersed among whites. But the Pine

Tree State also had Portland, a booming seaport like Salem and later New Bedford. Its docks and wharves attracted a cosmopolitan working class, including many black men, who gained there a considerable degree of respect and prosperity. Politically, Maine was distinguished by its affirmative enfranchisement of black men in 1819, endorsed by leaders of both parties. Indeed, several years earlier, Republicans proposed the broadest suffrage for their future state, embracing all "citizens of the U.S. of age, not paupers, resident in the town or plantation where they vote." At the 1819 convention, black suffrage was briefly contested, but easily passed when a leading Republican, Representative (soon to be Senator) John Holmes, dismissed an attempt by an obscure member of his party, William Vance of Calais, to insert "Negroes" into the suffrage clause's exclusions, alongside "Indians not taxed." The latter, said Holmes, "were excluded not on account of their colour, but of their political condition. They are under the protection of the State, but they can make and execute their own laws." He knew "of no difference between the rights of the negro and the white man—God Almighty has made none—Our Declaration of Rights has made none." With little support, Vance's motion "did not obtain."[59] A few days earlier, a different debate suggested Mainers' disgust with southern-style racialism. This same Vance had his credentials challenged, since he lived outside Calais's limits. The venerable George Thatcher, overseeing the debate, discoursed on why Vance should be seated. Apparently, some of those opposed to seating Vance had asked "what the Convention would do, if a town should send a minor, or a black man?—would not the Convention have the right to turn them out?" Thatcher was emphatic that it would be "his duty to bail them, *black or white*, as *brother Conventioners*. If a town had a black man in it, or could find one out of it, whom they had rather confide their interests in than a white man, he did not think the Convention had any right to exclude him on account of the color of his skin." This was the last time black citizenship was challenged in Maine.[60]

Missouri and Its Crises

When historians refer to the Missouri Crisis, they usually mean the attempt to restrict slavery throughout the vast Louisiana Purchase. Otherwise, many northerners believed, slavery would extend beyond the Old Southwest where it was already exploding. The fights over slavery in Missouri in 1819–20 have been analyzed in great detail, but only at the end of 1820, after Missouri submitted its constitution, did the controversy become relevant to northern black politics. That document ordered the new state's legislature to bar entry by free black people, thereby abrogating the rights of thousands of citizens guaranteed by the Constitution's privileges and immunities clause. The ensuing congressional battle has received little attention, but it provided an arena for representatives of Upper New England to assert their region's nonracial citizenship and thereby beard the South. Briefly, in December 1820, the Yankee Republic made itself evident, with black citizenship emerging as a centrifugal force that might split the nation. Privately, Secretary of State John Quincy Adams told the Pennsylvania Republican Henry Baldwin that if Adams "were a member of the Legislature" he would denaturalize Missourians, and make them "aliens within the Commonwealth of Massachusetts." Further, until those "citizens of Massachusetts whose rights were violated . . . should be re-integrated in the full enjoyment and possession of those rights," he would "prohibit by law the delivery of any fugitive upon the claim of his master." Adams wrote in his diary that the South intended to rob "thousands of citizens of their rights," people he defined as "the poor, the unfortunate, the helpless, already cursed by the mere color of their skin; already doomed by their complexion to drudge in the lowest offices of society." Missouri's "barbarous article" would strip away "the little remnant of right yet left them—their rights as citizens and as men. . . . I would defend them, should the dissolution of the Union be the consequence." In public, however, Adams kept his mouth shut. Far more important were the Yankees who did avow black citizenship inside the Capitol.[61]

Before focusing on Upper New England's counterattack, the southern denial of "Negro or mulatto" citizenship requires examination. It was a compendium of true claims (that Congress had drawn a racial line by limiting naturalization and the militia to whites, and many northern states imposed racial restrictions); outright untruths (that the free people were all recently manumitted, which former status barred them from citizenship); syllogisms, creating new juridical categories out of thin air ("perpetual inhabitants," "non-descripts," "denizens"); deliberate evasions (citing laws penalizing paupers as if they were racially specific); finally, a "higher law" rationale anticipating Taney: "Every one . . . acquainted with the history of the first settlement of these States must know that the association was of white people—Europeans and their descendants . . . essentially a white community."[62]

In response, a bipartisan group from Pennsylvania, New York, and New England defended the free black people's citizenship in their states and thus equal protection under the Constitution. They argued from the well-founded presumption of "States' Rights"—an individual state's right to confer citizenship, which must be honored by others, even if the person emigrating fell short of the new state's regulations, such as racial, religious, or property tests for voting. The New Englanders, in particular, meant every word—theirs was sectional nationalism with a vengeance, the protection of men whom they knew, men who had voted for them, fellow Yankees.

Congress reconvened on November 13, 1820 for the Second Session of the Sixteenth Congress elected in 1818. Debate began on December 7. In the Senate, Rhode Island's aged Federalist James Burrill pointed out "that we have colored soldiers and sailors, and good ones, too, but under no pretext, whether of duty or any other motive, can they enter Missouri." He took a radically republican stance anticipating the Fourteenth Amendment, that it was not "difficult to define what constituted a citizen. If a person was not a slave or a foreigner—but born in the United States, and a free man—going into Missouri, he has the same rights as if born in Missouri." Then came the constitutional trump card, that "Missouri might, with the same right, go still further, and pass laws to exclude citizens born in certain portions or districts of the United States." South Carolina's William Smith, a Republican, replied with a barrage against Rhode Island's slave-trading past, naming James DeWolf, Speaker of the Rhode Island House, whose family imported thousands from Africa (and would shortly replace the deceased Burrill in the Senate). In the House, the Yankees held back, as Pennsylvania's John Sergeant and New York's Henry Storrs, both Federalists, provided detailed evidence of black "freemanship" in some states.[63]

December 9 was the red-letter day. From here through December 12, a bipartisan united front from Upper New England (minus one renegade) made the strongest defense of nonracial citizenship prior to the 1860s. Other northerners had asserted a theoretical equality, like the Philadelphia Federalist Joseph Hemphill admitting that, in Pennsylvania, "there have been instances of their voting, but they are seldom." The Yankees asserted black equality as a lived fact, a part of ordinary political life, and their speeches were covered in full.[64]

In the Senate, Vermont Federalist Isaac Tichenor reported his legislature's resolutions that "slavery . . . in any of the United States, is a moral and political evil" and any attempt "to prevent freemen of the United States from emigrating to . . . Missouri, on account of their origin, color, and features" was "anti-republican." Then matters heated up. Maine's newly elected Republican John Holmes, who had defended nonracial citizenship at home, tried to discredit his fellow New Englanders with standard tropes about free people of color as "ignorant and poor . . . infirm, decrepid, and vicious. Their vices and frailties render them an incumbrance, if not a nuisance, wherever they reside." He affirmed Missouri's right to exclude, since "to be forced, against our will, to receive free blacks from the slaveholding States, is a doctrine that I, as a northern man, do not so fully relish." Lauding South Carolina's Smith, he concluded, "In the broad and comprehensive definition of the citizen, lies the error. . . . The 'privileges and immunities' of citizens are nowhere extended to free blacks and mulattoes."[65]

If Holmes thought he would be allowed to defend his state's interests in this way, since delay in admitting Missouri imperiled Maine's admission, he miscalculated. Without a pause, the Federalist Harrison Gray Otis dismissed his "novel theory" that states could not make citizens, proceeding to "the circumstances which would give to a man the right of citizenship in Massachusetts; for if a man of color could be a citizen there, he would carry his privilege elsewhere." Like Republicans who spoke before and after him, he found no issue of construction. Inhabitants of Massachusetts "were either citizens or aliens"; indeed, "in all the States they were either citizens, aliens, or slaves." The logic of Blackstonean birthright was irrevocable: "All persons born within the realm of England were citizens. All persons born in Massachusetts, of free parents, were citizens; and all persons in that State, not aliens or slaves . . . were of consequence free citizens." Otis then insulted Holmes, whose "exposition of his ideas of the term citizen . . . Mr. O. said he was not able to comprehend, but which, if he did understand it, would enable a State to disfranchise all her citizens of all colors and complexions. He would not pause to consider that doctrine, nor, indeed to notice all the suggestions of that gentleman." He finished with a ringing peroration. He would "for ever oppose . . . all measures which would subject a freeman, of whatever color, to the degradation of a slave. . . . Every free citizen of color in the Union was joint tenant with himself in the public lands of Missouri . . . however humble and disadvantageous might be his sphere." Otis would never "consent to an act which would divest him of his property and rights, and interdict him from even passing into a country of which he was a legitimate co-proprietor with himself." This was pure republicanism seasoned with a happy vindictiveness, an old reactionary flaunting his one chance at radical showmanship, and it was long remembered by men like Garrison as exemplifying what their section represented.[66]

For the next two days, Holmes's southern allies must have thought this an ideal juxtaposition: a Maine Republican posed against Otis, the reviled Hartford Convention's emissary to Congress in 1815. The Missouri imbroglio could again be blamed on a cabal seeking to disrupt the Union. That hope lasted until the Senate reconvened on December 11, which began with a Tennessee senator offering a "proviso" to admit Missouri without "the assent of Congress to any provision in the constitution of Missouri" contravening the Constitution. His amendment was accepted and the resolution was on the floor. At this point, the New Hampshire Republican David Morril gave a remarkable speech. He called Holmes's remarks "novel and fallacious," and, as already described, named some prominent men of color in his home state (Cheswell, Haynes, Paul), stating plainly, "Blacks . . . are not degraded in New Hampshire. Custom has made a distinction between them and other men; but the Constitution and laws make none"; this was a nice "distinction," cele-brating the formal equality enjoyed by a few illustrious personages while black Yankees were routinely "degraded" in social intercourse. But Morril did not back down. When a southerner demanded what Yankees would do if a state elected to "send a mulatto man here," Morril replied crisply: "I would inquire . . . *what* rights are invaded? . . . I would seriously ask the Senate, if any State in the Union were duly to elect a yellow man Constitutionally qual-ified, commission and send him here with his credentials, you can exclude him a seat?" There was nothing in the Constitution about race, and "color is no more a qualification than height, profession, or nation." It took half a century before Morril's prediction was fulfilled, when Hiram Revels took Jef-ferson Davis's seat in 1870, but that possibility was foretold in the republi-canism averred by Morril, Otis, and their fellow Yankees.[67]

It was already clear a compromise would pass, and the Senate adjourned. The debate continued on December 12 in the House. The Delaware Federal-ist Lewis McLane denounced "the stale argument derived from the abstract doctrines announced in the Declaration" of Independence, asking, "Where is the wildest partisan who has stemmed the indignant sense of the commu-nity by enlisting electors from such ranks? . . . If usage and custom have con-ferred equal rights, where have these people held offices?," ignoring Morril's list of black Yankees, including Cheswell, elected many times. He invented a new constitutional category, deeming blacks "perpetual inhabitants," and challenging the elemental premise of states' rights constitutionalism: "States no longer have any power to create citizens in the sense of the Constitution. They may make denizens, and extend their local rights to aliens, to Indians, or to free negroes, but these give no claim to federal rights."[68]

McLane's heresy provided an opportunity for the Vermont Republican, Rollin C. Mallary. He declared Missouri's racial exclusion "a glaring and of-fending violation of the Constitution. . . . Those rights which have not been surrendered by the several States to the General Government still remain in their power. Among these, the right of a State to declare who of its own in-habitants may be its citizens still remains unimpaired," a principle that few would have challenged. To refute McLane's claim "that negroes or mulattoes, in every State . . . were deprived of all the essential rights of citizens," he quoted Vermont's constitution, whose "language is as broad and comprehen-sive as the race of man." Its suffrage clause embraced "all of every color, whether 'born in this country or brought from over sea.' . . . The light or shade of a countenance, which indicates an alliance with the great family of man, confers no exclusive privileges on the possessors, nor do they blot from a po-litical charter the immunities of citizens."[69]

Disclaiming Holmes, Upper New England's Republicans would cede no ground to Federalists in defending black citizenship. To underscore their sectional unity, William Eustis, who finished off Massachusetts Federalism by defeating Otis for the governorship in 1823, followed Mallary, evoking Rhode Island's Revolutionary "Black Regiment." "And who could have said to them, on their return to civil life after having shed their blood, in common with the whites . . . 'You are not to participate in the rights secured by the struggle, or in the liberty for which you have been fighting?' Certainly, no white man in Massachusetts." He defended the Constitution itself as nonracial, that to "justify the inference of gentlemen, the preamble ought to read, We the *white* people." The northern delegates in Philadelphia "could never have consented, knowing that there were . . . many thousands of people of color," who did "enjoy and did exercise the rights of free citizens, and have continued to exercise them." He reiterated Otis's thesis, that "black men and mulattoes, in Massachusetts at least, are citizens," adding practical proof: "They are also represented . . . directly, in this House. I very much doubt, sir, if there be a member on this floor from any one district in Massachusetts, whose election does not partake of the votes of these people." In his district, "their number . . . is not great; but, in an adjoining district, their number of qualified voters have been sufficient, and has actually turned the election of a member of this House." This was a remarkable closing, since Massachusetts Republicans had often bewailed black electoral clout. Facing the South, a principal leader celebrated it.[70]

What was the final result of the Missouri Crisis? Padraig Riley has argued against the assertion that it signaled "the emergence of a self-consciously white republic." Certainly, these battles did produce "a new era of white supremacy and the suppression of antislavery politics," but they also demonstrated "two of the main ways in which slavery would be contested," first by "attempting to limit its expansion and legal authority," and second, by "acknowledging the rights of free African Americans and, increasingly, fugitive slaves to basic legal protection." The Yankee Republic and like-minded expatriates across New York and the Midwest had not actually conceded to the South. In a guarded, half-conscious fashion, they had begun to fight.[71]

The 1820s: Boston's Political Class Announces Itself

A telling postscript came just months after the final compromise over Missouri. In June 1821, the Massachusetts legislature expressed alarm about new southern laws spurring an influx of "a great proportion of the free negroes of the South" to New England, where "persons of colour not only possess and exercise valuable rights and privileges, but where also from the habits of the people a greater regard and tenderness are manifested for them." The House appointed a committee to formulate a law barring "the burthen of an expensive and injurious population." Similar laws existed around the North, and Massachusetts again had an opportunity to align itself with racialism. Instead the committee, headed by Theodore Lyman, later Boston's mayor, reported in January 1822 that it could not prepare "a bill, the provisions of which they conscientiously vindicate to this House," without offending "the institutions, feelings, and practices of the people of this Commonwealth." Barring black immigrants "would entirely depart from that love of humanity, that respect for hospitality and for the just rights of all classes of men, in the constant and successful exercise and maintenance of which, the inhabitants of Massachusetts have been singularly conspicuous." The rest of the sixteen-page report consisted of unembarrassed boasting about their state's record of freedom. No more was heard of such moves in the four northeastern states, while they simultaneously led the nation in passing class-based laws to disfranchise "paupers" and, later, bar the in-migration of "foreign paupers."[72]

Massachusetts's larger political context clarifies the extent of Upper New England's antiracialism. From November 1820 to January 1821, suffrage extension and other democratic reforms were hotly debated in the first constitutional convention since 1780, but no delegate recurred to race as a means to elevate poor white men or denounced the suffrage's corruption by Negro paupers. Simultaneously, Boston experienced a peaceful political revolution by the "Middling Interest" coalition, overturning the Federalist oligarchy personified by H. G. Otis. Again, at no point did the insurgents play the race card, or accuse the Federalists of employing "negro voters." That shoe no longer dropped, confirming the evolution of a polity where race as a partisan lever was out of bounds; the figure who dominated the region's political imaginary for thirty years, Daniel Webster, was remembered for exiting a Massachusetts Colonization Society meeting in 1822, saying, "It is a scheme of the slaveholders to get rid of the free negroes. I will have nothing to do with it."[73]

The refusal to racialize citizenship cemented a distinctive regional stance, accompanied by Afro-Yankees' advance. To the south and east, the 1820s saw a steady tightening of restrictions on free black people. In Upper New England, they gained professional opportunities and economic status. Visible patronage broke down the color line, with conventional tracks to political advancement opened up. Most obvious was black men's matriculation in three of the region's colleges, displayed as evidence of New England's superiority. The first was Alexander Twilight, one of eighteen graduating from Middlebury in 1823 with his complexion unremarked, followed by the better-known cases of Edward Jones from Amherst in August 1826, and John Brown

Russwurm from Bowdoin a few weeks later. The latter gave the class address, praising "The Condition and Prospects of Haiti," something few white men would have dared, with his speech widely reported. Seen from Richmond or Savannah, this was the worst kind of social equality, hinting at future "Negro magistrates." Inside black America, it reinforced the sense that Massachusetts and its sister states treated black men fairly. Like many of his class and color, Russwurm was not "American." The son of a Jamaican planter and his common-law wife, he was sent to Maine for schooling; after his father died, he was adopted by a local merchant with abolitionist sympathies.[74]

White patronage was increasingly visible in business. Black men had been starting enterprises in New England's port towns for many years, and by the 1820s men like John Remond constituted a visible layer of hairdressers, perfumers, caterers, and restaurateurs, often branching out into real estate transactions. One grouping, the Massachusetts General Colored Association (GCA), declared itself a political organization, and is much cited because its leadership included David Walker, whose *Appeal to the Coloured Citizens of the World* in 1829 is inaccurately described as the beginning of New England's black politics. By the mid 1810s, certain whites continually derided black men's progress via broadsides under the general headline of "Bobalition," the word "abolition" pronounced in a vulgar patois (who produced those caricatures is unclear). Historians have focused on these sheets' grotesquerie—black men with blubbery lips, banners, pikes, swords, and Napoleonic hats marching like toy soldiers, giving orders and exchanging grandiose toasts. Less noticed is how these men spoke on their own behalf, touting their status as citizens in "De Tate of New-England—De son of Africa here set under de vine-tree and fig leaf, widout nobody to moless or make him scare." Often they acted as ventriloquists' dummies, as in an admiring 1823 sally about Boston's newly elected mayor Josiah Quincy: "De Mayor of Bosson—Ah! He debil of a hard *horse* for some folks to ride. 500 sober look—no grin—Song, '*Clear de way.*'" Occasionally, they insulted their enemies—"De Colonization Shocietee—What de debil's de reason dey cant let poor nigger die here as well as go to de spense of bury um five thousand mile tudder side beyond de water." The Bobalition series contributed to the enduring notion of "negroes" as both ridiculous and fascinating, about whom all white people know, but it also attested to black men's organizing—their parades and ceremonial dinners, full of pageantry like white men's affairs. Connecting Walker's *Appeal* to these parodies sold in Boston's bookshops since the 1810s leads to basic questions: who were these men of color, why did they get under white skins, and why did Walker go to Boston—what did he expect to find?[75]

The General Colored Association was led by fourteen men, the nucleus of a political class: C. A. De Randamie, L. M. Blancard, Domingo Williams,

George B. Holmes, Porter Tidd, Walker, William Keen, John T. Hilton, Thomas Dalton (its president), Coffin Pitts, Thomas Cole, Oliver Nash, John Eli, James Gould, and James G. Barbadoes. John Remond's accruing wealth and clout serving Salem's elite was not exceptional, it seems, but part of the emergence of a class fraction of expert providers to the carriage trade, often immigrants from elsewhere in the United States or the Atlantic littoral. Many had been developing their reputations for years, but in the 1820s they surfaced politically in Boston's orbit, including the major towns of Salem, New Bedford, and Portland. In each, black men were enfranchised, to some degree empowered, and militant when it came to enforcing their freedom. In each, they had ties to partisan whites. Here the focus is Boston, site of the most visible grouping. Rather than occupying black men's usual modest niche as barbers, always an entry point because of the minimal capital needed, these were substantial businessmen employing assistants and apprentices, with multiple side operations. De Randamie, from Surinam, sold "the Grease of the *celebrated white Bear, of Greenland*" at his hairdressing shop, while his rival Louis Blancard had "warranted English Razors," available in a "Perfumery," as well as "Haircutting, a la derniere mode." George Holmes and his successor John T. Hilton catered to Harvard men, their advertisements replete with treatises and verse paeans to silky locks. This class also included specialized waiters and musicians, who knew how to conduct a banquet or dance in ways that ensured propriety was observed. For several decades, Porter Tidd led a "cotillion band," enabling the latest dances to be learned. Best-known was Domingo Williams, eulogized on his death in 1832 as "of high respectability . . . for more than 20 years past, he has held the post of Attendant General to fashionable parties, assemblies and social entertainments." Another eulogy noted the "moral power exerted by him of great extent over his immediate acquaintance. . . . Who dare be guilty of excess when the reproving eye of a colored, uneducated waiter was over them?" Williams clearly possessed the Yankee virtues, as a "quiet, steady, and upright individual" who rose "above his humble lot in life by his integrity and good sense—moved onward in his constant occupation with propriety, civility and good will."[76]

These men were obviously not part of Boston's political and commercial elite; rather, they served it, but such relationships put them far above ordinary white workingmen, given that they never surrendered their political rights or willingness to speak out. That the Massachusetts gentry preferred black men arranging their social lives suggests a distinctive feature of New England culture; whites apparently liked the studied gentility men of color brought to their affairs, a republican version of noblesse oblige. Descriptions of a stratum engaged in catering and entertainment and defined by race usually presume the quiescence of the "house negro"—how could it be otherwise?

What wealthy white would tolerate that the black man setting his daughter's hair, pouring his port, and cooking his turtle soup was a ward boss at election time, given to what sound today like nationalist pronouncements? Yet that is how this group functioned, as a space for self-assertion and defiance of whomever got in their way, including slaveholders. In August 1825, they cheered the "Independence of Hayti" after its final treaty with France, with clear partisan overtones—one toast saluted "President Adams, and President Boyer. Both the choice of Freemen, and both the Friends of Civil Liberty, Equal Laws, and good Government," to which they added, "The *Government*, and *Army*, of Hayti. One has proved by black-and-white that it knows how to maintain Freedom, Equality, and Independence. The other, that they can always beat their enemies *black-and-blue*." Similarly, a January 1827 meeting convened to congratulate Aaron Ward, a New York congressman, "for his able and eloquent defence of the rights, and immunities of the people of color; and for the manly and just interest he was pleased to shew in the cause of Gilbert Horton," the black Yorker imprisoned in the District of Columbia. Praise of one white was followed weeks later by sneers at another, plus many Boston whites. An ACS agent, S. L. Knapp, had described black people as degraded and dirty in a State House speech. John T. Hilton issued a reproof: "On the day celebrated by the Africans, the majority of them are generally very handsomely clad," displaying "good sense, industry, and moral conduct." On that day, and "frequently at other times," they "are insulted by the lower class of the white population, 'for whom liberty has as yet done nothing.' . . . These are the people by whom Mr. Knapp was deceived; their faces being dirty, he supposed them to be black, but they were not so when washed."[77]

White anger at black men's visible defiance provoked expressions of disgust that Boston's authorities authorized annual "African Independence" celebrations of "five or six hundred negroes, with a band of music, pikes, swords, epaulettes, sashes, cocked hats, and standards . . . marching through our principal streets." Why, it was repeatedly demanded, did "the Selectmen . . . permit the town to be annually disturbed by a mob of negroes, whose parade and pageantry are as useless, unmeaning, and ridiculous, as their persons and the atmosphere which surrounds them in these days are offensive and disgusting?" That this remark was directed at Boston's town government, which did indeed offer "protection and countenance" to these parades, underlines that, like Bobalition, this was at root a complaint about black men's political legitimacy. A minor legal scrape involving David Walker and two other owners of used clothing stores on Brattle Street demonstrates their collective standing. In 1828, an "officer of the City Government" not "fully informed" of "the strict integrity of their characters" decided to prosecute these businessmen as fences who bought goods "far below their value." Instead, the case rebounded to their credit. The defendants' lawyers "clearly proved, that the sum paid by them to the seller, had been fully equal to the price usually paid to gentlemen of respectability, well known residents." Beyond that, Walker and others customarily gave "early information of suspicious persons to the Police." In a show of elite solidarity, "a crowd of witnesses of the first standing in society, testified to their integrity and fairness in their dealings, and moral characters, to be envied by some of a fairer complexion." It helped that Walker regularly placed advertisements for goods he had received, in case they might be stolen.[78]

A Portland court case demonstrates that Boston was not unique in providing a measure of juridical fairness. Maine produced no exemplary man of color like Cheswell or Haynes, but by the 1810s it had developed its own group of ambitious entrepreneurs. Most prominent was the Cape Verdean Christopher C. Manuel. After establishing a hairdressing business in Philadelphia, he opened a shop in Portland around 1800. Over time his establishment became "a sort of Merchants' exchange . . . for if anything new or startling happened in the city the customers congregated there"; he also organized the state's first brass band in 1825. He was joined by others, mainly barbers, butchers, and grocers. Another notable figure was Reuben Ruby, Portland agent for *Freedom's Journal* in 1827–29 and organizer of an 1826 appeal to "the kind attention of the benevolent, the pious, and the humane," requesting aid in "the erection . . . of a suitable house for public worship." It noted there was "accommodation" for only "a very few of our people" in the city's white churches, where it was "associated with such circumstances, as are calculated to repel rather than invite our attendance," meaning segregation. In 1835, Ruby was elected president of the Fifth Annual Convention for the Improvement of the Free People of Colour in Philadelphia. He was also Portland's leading black Whig, and eventually a Republican operative.[79]

An 1825 melee in Portland demonstrated that mob attacks on black property and lives would, in Upper New England if nowhere else, suffer legal repression. The target was Ira Gray, another entrepreneurial immigrant. He had partnered with Manuel in a barbershop in 1814, and by 1822 was selling "Wigs, Scalps, Braids, Etc.," with "Cash given for human hair." Early in 1825, Gray was fined ten dollars for "keeping a disorderly house," which could mean renting out a property used for prostitution; whether that or some other illicit side-business led to the attack is unclear. In August, he opened a "Boarding House For People of Color," and a few months later came the riot. It followed a common script. Late one evening, "a number of persons collected around" his house, "in a riotous and disorderly manner, and began an attack on it by throwing stones into the windows, and otherwise manifesting a disposition to assault the person of the occupant as well as of pulling down and destroying the building." Gray knew they were coming and fired several muskets "loaded with powder only," which angered the crowd so that "a musket was then fired into the house and some shot lodged in the side of Gray's neck." He "immediately discharged a gun loaded with shot" and "a man by the name of Fuller, a journeyman painter and foreigner was shot through the heart and expired immediately." Gray was not tried for manslaughter until May 1826, and received considerable public support: that April he opened a "New Barber's Shop," advertising he was "grateful for the encouragement he has heretofore received." At the trial, the prosecutor simply "proved . . . that *Thomas J. Fuller*, deceased, was killed by Gray, and . . . stopped," effectively conceding Gray's right of self-defense. Gray's counsel argued that "Fuller was one of the leaders in the riotous attack . . . that he . . . had sworn that he would kill Gray" and "discharged a gun at Gray's house." This foreigner, "instead of his being in the peace of the State . . . was proved to be at war with society, in the act of open and outrageous violation of law. . . . Gray was by law justified . . . for he acted only in defence of his house and his family." Acquitted, Gray opened an employment office for "SEAMEN and COOKS" on the same wharf where he kept his barbershop.[80]

The Maine cohort was organized, commercially successful, and active in low-level party activities, even gaining city jobs (see chapter 5), but only Boston developed a political organization, the General Colored Association and its predecessors. The GCA projected itself onto the national stage through a remarkable personage, Prince Ibrahima Abdulrahman of what is now Guinea, who was captured in Africa in 1788 and spent most of his life enslaved on a plantation near Natchez, Mississippi. In 1827, news of his identity filtered out, and the Sultan of Morocco, a state with which the United States enjoyed diplomatic relations, requested his freedom. The Adams administration arranged manumission with the stipulation that "he should only enjoy liberty in his native country." Ignoring that proviso, Secretary of State Henry Clay issued him a sort of passport: "The bearer hereof, Prince, is a Moor, reduced to captivity near a half century ago. The Executive of the United States, has obtained him from his master, with a view of restoring him to his friends and country. He and his wife, Isabella, intend visiting some of the Northern Capitals of the United States. I take pleasure in recommending him to the kind and friendly offices of all in whose company he may fall." The Prince campaigned across the North to free his large family still in captivity, attracting public fascination and support from the ACS, which agreed to send him to Liberia, near his ancestral birthplace of Timbo. After visiting Washington and New York he went to Boston, where the GCA gave him an elaborate dinner, replete with toasts (always the main item in newspaper reports). After tributes to "the Manumission Society" and abolitionists like Wilberforce and Lundy came the incitements. Domingo Williams, chairman of the Committee of Arrangements, hoped "the Slave holders of the world [would] be like the whales in the ocean, with the trasher [orca] at their heels, and the sword fish in their belly, until they rightly understand the difference between slavery and freedom." Chief Marshal George B. Holmes wanted the "spirit of Liberty which pervades our Northern Hemisphere today [to] be wafted . . . until it reaches that Southern Point where slavery abounds, and there diffuse its renovating influence till every Bondman's soul shall be filled with the knowledge of his Right." Oliver Nash saluted "The Island of Hayti, the only country on earth where the man of color walks in all the plentitude of his rights . . . the cradle of hope to future generations."[81]

Reports of this banquet put the Natchez publisher Andrew Marschalk, who had negotiated the Prince's freedom, in a quandary. As a Jackson partisan, he counterattacked under the headline "Mr. Adams and the Emancipation of Slaves and the violation of the faith of the Administration," describing how "a large party in what are called the FREE states, resolved to emancipate the slaves of the south at all hazards. This party has several presses under its command, which in the same sheet in which they advocate the re-election of Mr. Adams, are actually exciting the slaves to revolt, by the same species of arguments which produced the massacre of St. Domingo." Marschalk reprinted the negotiations with Clay, including that the freed slave "is not to enjoy the privileges of a free man within the United States of America," and told how the Prince had traveled widely until he arrived at the "dinner given him by the negroes of Boston." Reprinting from "a violent Adams paper," he put Domingo Williams's speech in capital letters, in particular the phrase "SWORD FISH IN THEIR BELLY," urging his subscribers to "Read again the toast of DOMINGO Williams, carrying with it the real DOMINGO [Haiti was then often called "Santo Domingo"] feeling, which deluged that ill-fated island with blood. . . . Does not this toast contain a most awful and bloody threat? Does it not in fact ask that 'the slave holders' should be put to the sword?" Marschalk underlined that "these toasts given by *Boston negroes*, at a public dinner to an emancipated slave, there under the protection of Messrs. Adams and Clay" were "printed by the . . . publisher of the *official* Adams paper at Boston." Mississippians would be putting "the torch" to their "own dwellings" and arming their "internal enemies" if they continued "in power, an administration that sends an emancipated slave to such dinners, and whose official journals, contain an invitation . . . to a general massacre." This scenario aroused derision in Natchez, but in nearby Louisiana, where the 1811 Pointe Coupee slave uprising was a recent memory, partisans erupted.

Recollect the iniquitous and profligate PLOT OF ADAMS AND CLAY to excite the prejudices of your Northern brethren against the SOUTH by employing an emancipated NEGRO TO ELECTIONEER FOR THEM. Yes! They thought they could not be withstood when they had AFRICA AT THEIR BACK!

But we WILL withstand them and their COADJUTORS OF THE HOUSE OF TIMBO, and conquer them too. TIMBO AND QUINCY! QUINCY AND TIMBO!

EBONY AND TOPAZ! TOPAZ AND EBONY![82]

This scandal, with its partisan overtones, puts a different light on the shocking discovery one year later that sailors from Boston were smuggling David Walker's *Appeal to the Coloured Citizens of the World* into southern ports for distribution to local slaves. In this light, Walker's gambit climaxed rather than began the practice of militant citizenship by Boston's black men. Walker vaulted to national infamy because he hoped to put a real "sword fish" into southern bellies by agitating their slaves to demand freedom. In the late twentieth century, his *Appeal* was rediscovered as a seminal text of black radicalism. Its contemporary significance, however, was registered by its reception, in particular the refusal of Boston's mayor, Harrison Gray Otis, to suppress Walker. The publicly nonracial politics of the Yankee Republic were again made plain: what kind of government within the federal Union would permit a "negro" to foment a servile war, given each state's constitutional obligation to aid in suppressing such uprisings? Savannah's mayor corresponded with Otis, seeking Walker's extradition. The latter deplored the *Appeal* as "extremely bad and inflammatory" but explained that its author had all the rights of a citizen. Otis had sent an emissary to talk with Walker, and reported "he openly avows the sentiments of the book and authorship" and intended "to circulate his pamphlets by mail, at his own expense." At this point, Otis, with what sound like crocodile tears, declared his "deep disapprobation and abhorrence." Nonetheless, "we have no power to control the purpose of the author, and without it, we think that any public notice of him or his book, would make matters worse." All Otis could do was "publish a general caution to captains and others, against exposing themselves to the consequences of transporting incendiary writings into your and the other southern states." This correspondence was not private. The eminent *New-York Journal of Commerce* reported that Walker "is said to be a coloured man, an old-clothes seller in Boston. The Mayor of that city, on being informed he was the author, took measures with a view to his prosecution. But on examination it was found that he had sinned against no law of the Commonwealth. He therefore has full sweep in the sale of his pamphlet." Walker's status as a Massachusetts freeman solidified Upper New England's identity as a free place, indelibly linked in southern white consciousness to *The Liberator*'s appearance in January 1831 and Nat Turner's Rebellion the following August. Following the latter, Virginia's governor John Floyd attributed Turner's settling of accounts to "the incendiary publications of Walker, Garrison and Knapp of Boston," although Walker had never actually called for insurrection.[83]

Boston's black political class was now part of the South's political discourse—as men speaking for themselves from one part of the republic where they had rights. New England *did* harbor white and black "fanatics" and politicians who succored them. Otis, the hard-shelled conservative, was no rebel. He expressed a sectional consensus that overt racialism was beneath a Yankee's dignity, much like Charles Sumner's father, a local judge, telling his son in the 1820s he would be "entirely willing to sit on the bench with a negro judge," and that, in public, "the color of the people one passed and spoke to" should have "no effect on a gentleman's demeanor." This regional culture composed of republican simplicity, amour propre, and contempt for southerners made the Yankee Republic a bastion from which black men could challenge the South. Their modest citizenship at home, at best a degree of symbolic power, acquired its force from being imagined at a distance; closer to home, it never erased the realities of social subordination and de facto Jim Crow, since not that many white Yankees had Judge Sumner's good manners.[84]

The expansion of black rights in Upper New England authorized a narrative of political equality—that there was a founding place where all lived on the same plane. In the 1840s and 1850s, African Americans appropriated this example as a stick with which to beat their opponents. The 1841 New York convention of black men asserted "there is a living and complete confutation of" the insistence that men could not "be *politically* equal and yet remain socially distinct. . . . The State of Massachusetts, which, rather than tax colored men without granting them votes, so long ago as 1792 [*sic*] enfranchised her colored population." Similarly, James McCune Smith told the 1855 Colored National Convention that free people of color occupied "various grades of social and political position, from equal citizenship in most of the New England States, to almost chattel slavery in Indiana and the Southern States." As William Cooper Nell proclaimed in 1855, Massachusetts had "a record . . . to be proud of," as "her colored citizens . . . stand, before the law, on an equality with the whites," an equality made tangible in Sumner and Nell's successful fight to desegregate Boston's schools. Afro-Yankees were the residual legatees of intense New England nationalism, which they made their own with political gains in the three decades preceding Fort Sumter, as chapters 5, 6, and 7 elucidate.[85]

Chapter 5

The Colored Men of Portland Have Always Enjoyed All Their Rights

The Politics of Respect

> When the negroes entered the hall, they were received by three cheers from the federalists. . . . After this a supper was prepared for them at a hotel . . . and Gen. Fessenden treated them at a grog shop. . . . The company of 58 blacks were prepared to march to the polls, and carried a majority of 21 votes over the free white population.
>
> —*Washington Globe*, reporting a National Republican victory in Portland, Maine, November 1832

> In this city, there are from fifty to a hundred or more colored voters. We understand that four of them, and no more, voted the Birney ticket. . . . This agrees with what we have heard of others of the same class throughout New England. They regard the Liberty Party with distrust, dislike and contempt, and especially, now that that party, by their insane obstinacy in New York have thrown the blacks of the whole country, free and enslaved, under the government of Polk and Calhoun.
>
> —*Portland Advertiser*, November 13, 1844

Chapter 4 proposed a sharp divergence in New England's political and cultural development between its upper and lower states. This chapter turns to the northernmost of those states, Maine, which long represented the essence of Yankee Republicanism. The chapter's brevity is not accidental. It points to the essential continuity, the routine quality of Portland's black politics, unlike in New Bedford's sharp partisan battles and multiparty environment, or Providence, where the vote was restored to black men amid a bitter class war among whites.

Portland's Yankee Republicanism was unswerving, and unchallenged on its home ground. As we have seen, at Maine's 1819 constitutional convention, the Old Federalist George Thatcher pilloried a Republican who proposed white suffrage. The contrast between Upper New England and the rest of the North was clear two years later, when other eminent Old Federalists were mocked at a New York convention by Bucktail Republicans bent on disenfranchising black men.

Portland was the biggest city north of Boston in a state with much greater electoral weight than today. Its black electorate of 100 to 200 voters, by virtue of their concentration, exerted statewide influence. There was a political-economic context for their electoral clout. They prospered politically where all men prospered materially. As in Bucks County, New York City, Albany, Boston, New Bedford, Providence, and other New England ports, black enfranchisement survived and sometimes flourished on a rising tide of mercantile expansion. Portland exemplifies this dynamic. In the early nineteenth century, it dominated the world's lumber trade, shipping millions of board-feet out of the Maine woods each year. Black men found their niche commanding Portland's waterfront, as stevedores, porters, laborers, and mariners.[1]

There was one other factor making Portland and Maine exemplary of Yankee Republicanism: the character of its Federalist-turned-Whig elite. While plenty of New England Federalists and some Republicans periodically endorsed the free people of color's formal equality, such men were an especially strong presence in Maine, starting with Thatcher as the District's congressman. His aggressive nonracialism was carried forward by General Samuel Fessenden, the North's most visibly pro-black Whig in the 1830s, and the premier Whig defector to the Liberty Party in 1840. His son William Pitt Fessenden vaulted to prominence that year as an antislavery Whig, taking Portland's seat in the House from a Democrat with the margin provided by Portland's black men (or so Democrats charged). That Thatcher and the Fessendens acted so openly on their beliefs reflected Maine's consensus. As a Democratic paper stated in 1870, reporting on Republican attempts to commandeer celebrations of the Fifteenth Amendment's passage, "The colored men of Portland have always enjoyed all their rights—have been permitted to vote as early and as often as anybody, and to pay their taxes regularly. They have had nothing to complain of in this latitude. They have been well behaved, orderly citizens, too, and to the best of our knowledge and belief nobody begrudged them their privileges. Certainly we never have." All of these influences—ideological, familial, and partisan; political-economic and geographic—defined Maine as "the best black man's place," an environ where Frederick Douglass could encounter a former Whig governor at an inn and be invited to share a dinner table.[2]

The narrative of black Whiggery begins in Maine since they came into the party earlier, and stayed loyal longer, than almost anywhere else; in that sense, Portland demonstrates how black and antislavery politics developed *inside* the party system. Black electoralism in Maine breaks down into three distinct periods. First, in the 1830s (and perhaps before), the Portland-based opposition in heavily Jacksonian Maine defied Democrats by welcoming black voters to help maintain their hold on the state's major city. General Fessenden, Maine's foremost lawyer and a former Hartford Convention Federalist, worked closely with the black businessman Reuben Ruby in this effort, which was denounced as far away as Georgia. Movement and politics cohered, as Fessenden and Ruby were first National Republicans and then Whigs together, and simultaneously founders of the Maine Anti-Slavery Society. This synergy of politics and movement culminated in 1840, when the Van Buren administration's national organ blamed Portland's black voters for a Democratic congressman losing his seat to the younger Fessenden, later Maine's most famous Republican.[3]

The next phase came with the advent of Maine's Liberty Party in 1841. General Fessenden was a principal leader of the new party, while the son remained a Whig. The older man brought Ruby and his sons into the new party, but they had little success in recruiting Portland's black electorate. An obdurate black Whiggism remained in force through 1844, when the Liberty Party candidate, James Birney, received hardly any of the city's votes. The final stage arrived with the party breakdown of 1848–56. The Whigs split apart, with many joining Liberty men and antislavery Democrats in Maine's Free Soil Party, and Portland's black voters switched over as well.

For those focused on Garrisonian abolitionism, this history began when the editor visited Portland in late October 1832. He was taken around the city by Ruby, who owned several hacks, the horse-drawn taxis that Ruby pioneered in Portland, and General Fessenden was "moved to tears" by his indictment of colonization, converting on the spot to immediatist abolitionism. By that time, Fessenden was already working with Ruby. On October 29, the same day the *Portland Advertiser* announced Garrison's talk, it published an "Address to the People of Maine," endorsing National Republican Henry Clay against Jackson. Ruby signed the address along with dozens of prominent political, social, and business leaders, heady company for a black man. The benefits of this partisan affiliation soon became manifest. Since Fessenden was president of Portland's Common Council, he presumably obtained Ruby his first city appointment in April 1833 as one of sixteen tythingmen, enforcers of the law barring travel or work on the "Lord's Day," authorizing interrogation of anyone found in public and entrance "into any of the rooms and other parts of an inn or public house of entertainment."[4]

This patronage was premised on electoral facts. On the first weekend in November 1832 Fessenden caucused with a group of black men, and then went with them to vote on November 6, when the National Republicans carried the city by twenty-one votes. The Jacksonians immediately denounced "the heartless and hypocritical attentions paid to *the black population* in this city, by such men as Samuel Fessenden." Supposedly, they were "frightened on the one hand, with the story that if Jackson should be re-elected they would be in actual danger of subjection to a state of slavery!" but "flattered, on the other . . . with the assurance that if they united in putting Jacksonism down, they would be aided in organizing . . . a religious society, and even stand a chance of being employed in some official stations!" The semiofficial *Washington Globe* picked up the story of "the Portland Nationals" forming "a coalition with a body of real Ebonies," whose votes were "obtained by the influence of an orthodox preacher." "Gen. Samuel Fessenden, a famous gentleman of blue-light [i.e., pro-British] memory . . . got up a caucus, and made a speech. . . . When the negroes entered the hall, they were received by three cheers from the federalists. . . . After this a supper was prepared for them at a hotel . . . and Gen. Fessenden treated them at a grog shop. . . . The company of 58 blacks were prepared to march to the polls, and carried a majority of 21 votes over the free white population." Portland's National Republicans hit back. The attack "in the government organ" was appropriate for "the region of negro slavery, and the White House of Andrew Jackson," the slaveholder, but was "illfitted for free, happy, and independent New-England, where the soul of a colored man is believed to be as white and as pure as that of a king on his throne, or the President. . . . By our constitution, the vote of a colored man is as good as that of a white man." It quoted Fessenden saying "he has done nothing, that he would not willingly do over again. . . . He never has been taught to set himself above one of his fellow citizens, nor to think a man of different complexion from himself beneath his attention. . . . The same God that made them, made him." It then clarified why "they were received with approbation in our caucus, on Saturday evening . . . chiefly because a few noisy obstreperous Heroites [acolytes of Old Hickory] who came there for a disturbance began to hiss upon their entering, which hisses were drowned by bursts of acclamation from every quarter."[5]

The partisan pattern was now set. Black men had helped carry Maine's National Republicans to victory in Portland. They would keep supporting it, sometimes as swing voters, and when that party reformed as the Whigs in 1834, Ruby attended their founding convention as a delegate. Once again, out-of-state Democrats trumpeted this proof of Whig perfidy: "The Bank Party in Portland, as one of the desperate means of carrying the election, deliberately called upon the *colored Wigs* to organize themselves, and choose three delegates to meet the *Bank Wigs without color* in convention, and make the *Wig* nominations." Post-election, they repeated the charge that Portland Whigs were recruiting black men as part of a regional strategy: "Negroes who had not been six weeks in *Portland*, and who were there only as sailors . . . were permitted to vote in that city, and did vote the Whig ticket."[6]

While black Portlanders' partisanship came to national attention in the 1830s, neither that nor Ruby's appointment as a tythingman was new. At least eight years earlier, another black man, Titus Skillings, had secured appointments, first as one of the city's measurers of corn and other grain in 1825–26 and then as one of fifteen tythingmen in 1830. Given the partisan character of these appointments, with the same men recurring over decades in city positions and party offices, Skillings must have got the job because he could marshal voters. Nor was black men's participation in party affairs restricted to Ruby's serving as a National Republican and then Whig founder. In 1834, James F. Bowes was a deputy marshal and speaker at the Portland Whigs' grand July 4 celebration, mocking "the tories of today" in his toast. He served on the Whigs' Ward 3 committee that year, and was elected, with Ruby, as a Whig convention delegate. The convergence of party and movement continued with the founding of the Maine Anti-Slavery Society later in 1834 in Augusta, where Ruby and Fessenden served as two of Portland's four delegates. Ruby's appointment as a tythingman was also regularly renewed. In these ways, Maine Whigs anticipated by a generation those postbellum Radicals who proclaimed their nonracialism via displays of black representation; the connection was clear in 1870, when the older Ruby, now a porter in the Republican-controlled Custom House, accompanied his son George, a newly elected Texas state senator, to a reception hosted by Portland's mayor and other grandees.[7]

Democratic outrage over Portland's black Whigs continued in 1836, although by then Portland's Whigs had joined in their party's national repudiation of "incendiary" abolitionism. In that year, southern Whigs mounted a campaign against Martin Van Buren for supporting "Negro Suffrage" at New York's 1821 constitutional convention. In fact, Van Buren had led the effort to severely restrict it, but this was twisted into a refusal to disfranchise. The Democrats' *Washington Globe* replied, charging the Whigs were "notoriously in favor of free negro suffrage," because "these lowest and most degraded voters . . . destitute of property, are always subject to the monied aristocracy. They hire them and command their votes." Portland drew special notice. "Gen. Fessenden . . . in the contested elections in his quarter, has attended the meetings of the negroes and led the black troops to the polls for federalism, precisely as the British led them to battle during the last war." The influential *Richmond Enquirer* explained that "the LEADING ABOLITIONISTS ARE LEADING WHIGS," with a roster of prominent figures, including Fessenden, accurately named as "the first Vice President" of "the National Abolition Society," as well as "a personal and political friend and fellow-student of Daniel Webster" (Webster was then the Whig presidential candidate in

New England; they fielded four, hoping to throw the presidential election into Congress). Fessenden was "the most virulent Whig" in Maine, and had, the *Enquirer* pointed out, "addressed a negro caucus, and persuaded the blacks of Portland to vote the entire Whig ticket."[8]

Up in New England, however, it was risky to truckle to the South, and antislavery crossed party lines. In 1837, the Whigs finally elected a governor, Edward Kent. In his first term, he refused a request from Georgia's governor to extradite a slave stowaway and the captain of the ship on which he escaped, and this refusal was continued by his Democratic successor, John Fairfield. As the *Colored American* reported approvingly, "Gov. Kent, in the dignity of a Freeman of course, made no such surrender of the men. . . . Gov. Fairfield coming into power in Maine . . . alike refused, and the Georgians are alike displeased." By then, Maine abolitionists had turned to questioning nominees, and responding positively as a candidate but voting differently in office could end a career, as Portland's Democratic congressman, Albert C. Smith, discovered in 1840. He had avowed opposition to the congressional "Gag" but then voted to renew it. His Whig challenger, William Pitt Fessenden, had a name calculated to arouse white abolitionists and black voters. When Fessenden won, Smith received national publicity for his charge he had been "beaten by only 70 votes out of 13,000; and this result was brought about by the aid of 100 negro votes. What a glorious victory for the Whigs of the South! A MEMBER OF CONGRESS ELECTED BY THE ABOLITIONISTS AND NEGROES. The latter held the balance of power at the late election!!" Portland's Whigs declared it "not true that he was beaten by the aid of 100 'negro votes.' There were not more than two thirds of this number of 'negro votes' thrown, and some of those were cast for Albert Smith himself." The controversy continued for weeks, with Smith insisting "I have always understood that there were about one hundred negro and mulatto voters in that district . . . and I have not the least suspicion that more than one voted for me." The last laugh came from the Reverend Amos Gerry Beman, an African American minister who had just taken a Portland pastorate. Noting "any man" who "has been here three months, paid his tax, is entitled to vote," he stipulated that this was "a right of which a very large majority of the colored people avail themselves. The most of them vote the Whig ticket, and through their influence and the abolitionists, the Hon. Wm. Pitt Fessenden, is elected in place of Albert Smith, who trampled upon the right of petition."[9]

The Emancipator, New York organ of the Liberty Party, sounded a cautionary note. It began by quoting the Maine *Advocate for Freedom*, on how Kent had defeated Fairfield to retake the governorship by winning *"abolition votes."* Had the Whigs "put up a candidate for whom abolitionists could not consistently have voted, *he could not have been elected.* . . . Had not

Mr. Fairfield abused abolitionists, and especially [like Smith], voted for the . . . gag in Congress, his popularity might have been sufficient to secure his re-election." *The Emancipator* then cited Smith's attack: "*One* remark to our colored friends in Maine or elsewhere, is that, if they do indeed hold the balance of power . . . they should never again give their votes for a man whose first public act after his election is to deny that colord [*sic*] Americans have equal rights," as both Democrats and Whigs in New England had repeatedly done.[10]

In 1841, Maine's Anti-Slavery Society left Garrisonianism and Whiggism behind, effectively becoming the state's Liberty Party. This new organization was led by General Fessenden, with his longtime connection to Portland's black community based in visiting homes and churches, providing legal and financial aid, and more. The older Fessenden carried a few with him, including Ruby's sons (their father had opened an oyster house in New York), and the new minister of the Abyssinian Church, the Reverend Amos N. Freeman, but even he could not move Portland's black voters away from the Whigs.[11]

In Maine, as elsewhere, Liberty men threatened the Whigs. The latter were already a minority and a third party to their left guaranteed that status—if it deadlocked state legislative elections or the governorship, the legislature's Democratic majority would decide. In 1842, the Democrats won back the governorship, with 41,000 votes to 27,000 for the Whigs, but the Liberty Party got close to 4,000, which the Whigs could hardly afford to lose. In 1843, the Liberty vote grew to 6,746, while the Democratic vote went down to 32,029 and the Whigs even further, to 20,973. Going into the presidential year of 1844, Maine's Liberty men were poised to act as spoilers. Keeping every possible antislavery voter, black or white, became a priority for the Whigs.[12]

Black Mainers' opposition to the Liberty Party surfaced in 1841–42, when their leadership called a New Hampshire and Maine convention. The September 1841 call in the *Colored American* was anodyne, with no political references. When the delegates assembled more than a year later at Freeman's church, however, the first address was on "the duty of colored voters sustaining the Liberty Party." The following day, the Committee on Anti-Slavery reported a "resolution on political action" declaring "we highly approve the nomination of Gen. James Appleton, as the Liberty party candidate for Governor of the State of Maine, and that it is the duty of every colored man to go to the polls . . . and support the Liberty party ticket." This "called forth a warm and animated discussion." A hardcore group defied the convention's organizers, which included the Reverend John W. Lewis, the major black Liberty leader in Upper New England, who provided "very interesting accounts of the advance of the Liberty party in N.H. and Vt." Reverend Freeman "urged the duty of coming on to the ground with this party," but was "warmly opposed by J. T. Carter and A. W. Niles." The resolution was laid on the table, and taken up again that evening, with Fessenden and the younger Rubys contending "that the Liberty party would do much, even in holding the balance of power, so as to control both the great political parties," against the plain fact that "there is no prospect of Liberty party being the dominant party." It was again laid on the table. Finally, on the convention's last day, after Appleton had spoken, the resolution passed, with twenty-one delegates voting to endorse and seven against, but "a large number not voting," suggesting a desire to avoid offending Fessenden. The endorsement had little effect, as attested by the near-total absence of black Mainers at the dozens of local, county, and state Liberty meetings in the next six years. By 1844, Niles, who strongly opposed the Liberty endorsement, had taken over Ruby's role as the Whigs' black committeeman and his city job as a tythingman.[13]

The city's 100-plus black votes hardly constituted the Whigs' margin of victory, even in Portland. But the sight of black men marching to the polls as Whigs was apparently effective, since the Liberty Party surged elsewhere but never gained much support in Portland. The rivalry for abolitionist voters culminated in 1844. The Whig nominee, Henry Clay, a slaveholder with a vaguely antislavery reputation, compromised his chances through indecision on Texas's annexation—unpopular in much of the North, much desired in the South. The Whigs' *Portland Advertiser* fired the initial salvo in July, asserting, "Our free colored friends have never failed to discriminate between the *true* and *false* friends of Abolition," the latter depicted as men who sought "a roving commission and a living . . . who organize a 'Liberty Party' to obtain,—if not office—the running for office." Here we see the Whig apparatus at work. New York was the center of antislavery Whiggism, and this article came from Thurlow Weed's *Albany Evening Journal*. The *Northern Star and Freedman's Advocate*, a black newspaper, had begun publishing in Albany in 1842, founded by Weed's longtime associate, Stephen Myers. In another editorial, the *Advertiser* relayed the damning verdict from this organ "published and edited by men of color," that a corrupt Liberty Party intended "not the abolition of slavery—but the possession of office, as its primary object; abolition is secondary, and is rapidly becoming a tertiary object with them." The *Northern Star* firmly backed the Whigs, asserting that because they "had the good fortune to do some anti-slavery work—therefore forestalling Liberty party work," they were the subject of unprincipled attacks. Its verdict was damning: "We believe that the Liberty men hate Whiggery—more than they hate slavery, and that they love office more than they love anti-slavery. We fear these office-seeking Liberty men," adding these were "the views of a very large proportion of the free colored people in the free states."[14]

While attacking Birney as a closet Democrat ("every vote stolen from the Whigs . . . will be counted for Polk and Texas"), the *Advertiser* kept reminding whites that African Americans "fear these office-seeking Liberty men." Their campaign succeeded. While Polk swept Maine, the Whigs lost Portland by a bare six votes (1,172 to 1,164), in large part because Birney got a mere fifty-six. The *Advertiser* gloated, "In this city, there are from fifty to a hundred or more colored voters. We understand that four of them, and no more, voted the Birney ticket." Afro-Yankees throughout the region "regard the Liberty Party with distrust, dislike and contempt," not an absurd claim since Polk's election was a southern victory, and by "their insane obstinacy in New York," the Liberty men had "thrown the blacks of the whole country, free and enslaved, under the government of Polk and *Calhoun*"; it was widely assumed that the 15,814 Birney votes in New York, three times Polk's margin of 5,016, had given him the presidency.[15]

In the 1840s, examples proliferated of black Mainers achieving exceptional political status. In 1844, nationwide attention focused on the first black lawyer, Macon B. Allen, an Indiana native who came to Portland to study law. With General Fessenden's backing, he was examined and admitted to the bar. The right to represent citizens in court, question witnesses, and address juries had obvious implications—black men were infiltrating those spaces where the authority of the state was displayed. Allen moved to Massachusetts and gained appointment to a judicial post from a Whig governor, another example of the openings in the Yankee Republic.[16]

Black Mainers gained respect in other ways. Upper New England remained notably receptive to black men as intellectuals. Two stand out. In 1844, the Reverend William E. Foy published *The Christian Experience together with the Two Visions he received in the months of Jan. and Feb. 1842*, even today a major text for Seventh Day Adventists. Earlier, Robert B. Lewis of Hallowell wrote an impassioned work of religio-history, *Light and Truth*, which led his local newspaper to comment that "Mr. Lewis . . . possesses 'a right smart sprinkling of Yankeeism.' Buy his book." Lewis was also an inventor and entrepreneur, gaining three patents, and marketing "Lewis' Arabian Hair Oil" and the "Robert Benjamin Lewis Oakum and Hair Mill" (oakum being the product used to make rope). These individual stories showed that, inhospitable as it was in other ways, Maine welcomed black people with the requisite "Yankeeism."[17]

In 1848–49, the Whig bulwark finally broke apart. Black Portlanders, like most of New England's antislavery voters, moved into the Free Soil Party, which offered a chance at power because of former president Van Buren's prestige and its recruitment of prominent Whigs and Democrats. In late September, a convention of Portland's men of color announced they were "approving of the Free Soil party, and recommending the nominations made at Buffalo to the support of colored people," and soon after the election, the Democratic *Eastern Argus* (which had backed the pro-southern Lewis Cass) exulted, "The 'colored population' of this city, mostly went in for Free Soil. To their honor be it said, Taylor with his 300 responsibilities [he owned 300 slaves], could'nt [*sic*] get their votes." It then got personal: "Deacon Niles could not whip them in. The Deacon's influence with the colored people is on the wane. The Deacon is not true to Free Soil, and can't prevail."[18]

This attack on Abraham Niles, one of Ward One's twenty-one Whig vote distributors, was answered by the *Advertiser*, in language admitting the loss: "Those who refused to vote for Taylor . . . have only served to help carry the State for Cass. . . . They can now see how anxious the Argus is that they should continue to thus throw away their votes. Deacon Niles can't be cheated by any such humbug—neither can Pierre" (Franklin G. Pier or Pierre was another black Whig). The Democratic *Argus* had also sneered, "Deacon Niles and Mr Pierre are complimented by the Advertiser. They are probably wanted for next time," to which the latter replied, "Of course they are, and if you want the 'Free Soilers,' why not say so—and not try to cheat them into supporting you by throwing their votes for a third ticket." The vote totals suggested defection, however: Van Buren received 206 votes in Portland, almost four times Birney's 1844 haul, including fifty-nine in Ward One. The following year, another "Colored Convention," with Niles as president, repudiated the Whigs explicitly: "That this Convention highly approve of the spirit of the Buffalo [Free Soil] platform, and so far as it goes for the overthrow of slavery and the rights of the free people of color, we go heartily with it, for we believe that neither of the great parties of the day have any aim at the abolition of American slavery."[19]

Portland's black electorate receded from public view in the 1850s. The Democratic *Argus* and Whig *Advertiser* ceased commenting on their presence, but the Free Soilers' (later Republican) *Portland Inquirer* almost never mentioned them either. Maine's politics in that decade were roiled by an issue with ethnic rather than racial connotations. Prohibition found its first national victory via the famous "Maine Law" passed in 1851 (repealed five years later), barring the production or sale of alcohol for other than medicinal or industrial purposes. The law's enforcers, led by "the Napoleon of Prohibition," Portland mayor Neal Dow, fought their opponents in the streets during the "Maine Law Riot" of 1855. Temperance so roiled normal partisanship that old-line Democrats fielded a state ticket with their "noble allies, the straight Whigs" in 1855. The year 1856 saw the advent of a powerful Know-Nothing Party opposed in equal measure to alcohol, Catholicism, and slavery. As in Massachusetts, that party was a way station for the Republicans, who took over the state for generations to come.[20]

Where were black men in this flux? The evidence suggests they joined white Free Soilers in various "fusion" efforts leading to Republicanism. In the early 1850s, Portland's Free Soil voters were concentrated in Ward One, where most black voters resided, which may be why Free Soil and Republican leaders ignored their black supporters, to avoid the taint of a "Negro party." Maine Democrats, like Democrats everywhere in the 1850s, became more explicitly proslavery as the antislavery men among them, notably Hannibal Hamlin, quit in disgust. Periodically, the *Argus* denounced "negrophilism" and alleged that "a considerable number of colored people— NON-RESIDENTS—have recently been imported for the express purpose of securing their fraudulent votes," and "Some corrupt Republicans are attempting to bribe voters. . . . They will learn, too, that Democrats are not to be bought and sold like niggers." By 1859, it insisted that "ere long men will be read out of the [Republican] party unless they are willing their sons and daughters shall marry negroes." Still, the old interracial affiliations continued in force. Meetings to denounce the Fugitive Slave Act in 1850 and form a vigilance committee to repel "kidnappers" were addressed by ex–Liberty men like General Fessenden and Reuben Ruby, returned from a profitable foray in California's goldfields. The state's reputation for nonracialism remained strong, with the 1848 edition of Chancellor Kent's *Commentaries on American Law* noting "in no part of the country, except Maine, did the African race, in point of fact, participate equally with whites in the exercise of civil and political rights." Frederick Douglass noted, "A man is a man in Maine" during an 1855 tour, that he was "treated at the Hotels with as much kindness as my paler fellow citizens," former Whig governor Edward Kent sharing "his potatoes with me at the Bangor Hotel," after which "he kindly invited me to attend Court, and to take a seat with him inside the bar."[21]

These encomia were grist for Democratic mills. Illinois senator Stephen Douglas, the "Little Giant" of northern proslaveryism, made Maine a whipping boy. In 1853, he called William Pitt Fessenden a "white man with a black man's heart" during Senate debate, supposedly quoting one of Fessenden's black constituents. The *Portland Advertiser* corrected him—that anecdote referred to his father, the general, who told it with pride. Later in the decade, in advance of his debates with Lincoln, Douglas made more political hay at Maine's expense. After his usual championing of race ("I believe that this Government was wisely founded upon the white basis. It was made by white men for the benefit of white men and their posterity"), he invoked "popular sovereignty" to mock how in Maine "they have decided that a negro shall have the rights of the elective franchise on an equality with the white man. I do not concur in the good sense or correct taste of that decision on the part of Maine," but if a white Mainer "think[s] the negro has the right to come and kill his vote by a negro vote, I have no disposition to interfere."[22]

Maine's black voters easily became Republicans, as in the "ardent colored supporter of Frémont," the 1856 Republican candidate, who was asked by a Democrat "what the Republicans would do in case they were beaten in the present contest. . . . 'Do!—we'll go up Salt River and *spawn*: and when we come down again, we shall be strong enough to eat you locos all up!'" Boston's huge "Wide Awake" march for Lincoln in late October 1860 included a black militia company from Portland, the Sumner Blues, led by Captain Henry Daniels. In the late 1850s, the old pattern continued, of low-level patronage for a black man to secure black votes. In this case, Jack Groves, a War of 1812 veteran and longtime ship's cook, was named tythingman in 1856 and kept that position through the war years. Once the Republicans gained the federal patronage, Reuben Ruby became a porter at the U.S. Custom House at $500 a year, a very respectable sum when Irishmen worked for fifty cents a day.[23]

As Douglas's comment hints, Maine's largest significance was not what black men did at the polls, but what white men did in its courts. Immediately after *Dred Scott*, Maine's legislature asked its Supreme Judicial Court to decide whether black men could still vote, as the Buchanan administration's appointees in Bath had immediately implemented the decision by stripping a black ship captain of his master's license. Led by Chief Justice John Appleton, the court nullified *Dred Scott* within the state's borders, using citations from state constitutions to demonstrate that at the Founding, free men of color had been citizens in many states, and were thus organically incorporated within the national compact. Further, they had always been citizens and voters in Massachusetts, which long included Maine. Appleton did more than that. In 1860, he published an influential treatise on *The Rules of Evidence*, dismissing as "absurd and illogical" the widespread use of racial exclusions in juridical processes, in particular barring black testimony against whites, which meant "any and all conceivable wrongs and injuries may be inflicted by any one of the dominant upon any one of the servient blood . . . without fear of punishment." By this point, Maine's political leadership had been thoroughly abolitionized—two of the other five justices on Appleton's court, Seth May and Woodbury Davis, "boasted long records of antislavery activism, including membership in the Liberty party."[24]

———

There is no endpoint to Maine as an exemplary site of black empowerment, affirmed in 1819 and enforced long after as a matter of Yankee pride, a marker of their higher civilization. Nonracial citizenship became unremarkable, as old-fashioned Yankee republicanism became a new, self-consciously Radical Republicanism in the war's aftermath. In Maine, that remaking culminated with a flourish in 1870 when state senator George T. Ruby returned from Texas to public acclaim (although he and his bride had been Jim Crowed in New York hotels). His brother William would go on to become deputy fire chief of Portland.[25] By then, there were signs of restiveness, that the only Custom House patronage for black men was the aged Reuben Ruby's sinecure; at the Fifteenth Amendment celebration noted above, the Democratic editor quoted a black man who "said he didn't seem to understand, if Mr. Kingsbury [the mayor] was so much their friend, why he didn't appoint a few colored police-men, and it struck him as odd that in all the Custom House crowd there was but one colored man, and he at the bottom of the lot." What was promising in the 1830s was no longer impressive. Black men had gained all that was pos-sible minus a large increment of new votes, but the immigrants changing Maine were white and Catholic, and its clusters of black voters receded into the prewar past. Their achievements were a triumph of the ordinary, easily forgotten.

Chapter 6

The Very Sebastopol of Niggerdom

Measuring Black Power in New Bedford

Threats and bribery were resorted to. One of the most prominent and leading whigs . . . remarked to some of the colored people, that he had been a good friend to them—that he had employed two or three in his house, and as many out and about it—but, for the future unless they voted the whig ticket, he would seek out some poor Irish to be the recipients of his favors. . . . If they were to be defeated by nigger votes, he would petition the Legislature to take from them the right of voting.

—Jeremiah Sanderson to William Lloyd Garrison, November 1841

When I take a retrospective view of my past life, and see how I have danced back and forth; first a Democrat, then a Whig, and lastly a Liberty party man, and seemingly could not reach the great object of my desire in either of those parties, to-day it seems to me, as Nathan said to David, "thou art the man." [Laughter and Cheers.] . . . I know, sir, that the two political parties of New Bedford will be somewhat alarmed when I return. I have one thing to tell them; some of them have told me, when they found I supported this free soil business, that it is all a humbug; I cannot argue with you upon politics, (the slaveholder has deprived me of that privilege,) but one thing I know—anything that John C. Calhoun is opposed to, I am in favor of. (Great and repeated applause.)

—Henry Johnson, at the Massachusetts Free Soil Party Convention,
    September 1848

New Bedford was the apex of antebellum black political power, cited by abolitionists and proslaveryites alike as a "Gibraltar" or "Sebastopol" (site of a famous siege during the Crimean War). No wonder David Ruggles, head of New York's powerful Committee of Vigilance, sent a young Frederick Bailey (later Douglass) to New Bedford in 1838, putting him under the care of Nathan Johnson. The latter was an emblematic black New Bedforder, another canny Afro-Yankee who did well by catering to wealthy whites, like John Remond. With his wife, Polly, he was celebrated for providing sweets; a typical advertisement listed "Ice cream, Lemonade, Soda, Cakes, Custards, Confections, &c. served in the best manner," to which they later added

"Strawberries, Cherries, and other rare and delicious fruits." Johnson was also a man of direct action. In 1827, he led a mob against a suspected informer, driving him from the town at the point of death. In the 1830s, he became a party activist as a Democrat, and Whigs tried to ruin his reputation; he also received votes in 1841 as an alternative "spoiler" candidate to the Massachusetts House, and was elected president of the 1847 National Colored Convention. The best hint to the worldview of men like him is recorded in Douglass's second autobiography in 1855, where on arrival, Johnson told him anything was possible in the Bay State, as "there was nothing in the constitution of Massachusetts to prevent a colored man from holding any office in the state."[1]

New Bedford also furnishes a cautionary tale about the limits on electoral influence minus a massive bloc vote like that mustered by the Irish. Independent biracial politics flourished in New Bedford during a period of intense inter- and intraparty competition. Signaling one's commitment to black freedom had electoral benefits when all factions sought the votes of white and black abolitionists. Putting men of color into party leadership and dispensing patronage appointments to them were two ways to broadcast that message. Once the new Republican Party achieved electoral dominance in 1856, however, there was no need to send that signal. Black New Bedforders continued to win minor city appointments and party positions, but no longer sat on the dais at rallies or held visible leadership roles, unlike in 1841–54.

New Bedford's politicians of color contrast with those in other New England cities, none of whom played party politics with quite their zest. After disdaining the Liberty Party for seven years, most of Portland's black Whigs became Free Soilers in 1848, and entered the Republican Party when it emerged. In Boston, most black abolitionists practiced Garrisonian abstentionism throughout the 1830s and 1840s, until some turned Free Soil in 1848, with more joining after 1850, and all becoming Republicans after 1855, following a brief Know-Nothing flirtation. Providence saw none of those shifts; its black Whigs remained Whigs as long as that party existed, as chapter 7 documents. New Bedford stands apart because its black men were never firmly Whiggish. If politics resembles a game, the New Bedforders played it hard, making tactical alliances and defying established structures of power. They policed their own, not at whites' behest but to enforce racial solidarity. In 1837, they entered politics as an independent group, circulating nonpartisan lists of candidates for whom the black electorate should vote. In 1841, biracial teams from the town's Liberty Party and its Garrisonian antislavery society united to "spoil" the election of any member of Congress. On this tripartisan terrain, clear distinctions between abolitionism and mere "antislavery" blurred. When convenient, a major-party politician might insist on his diehard abolitionism, while another who aided runaways was denounced for supporting his party's national ticket. In 1844's presidential election, this three-way competition generated vitriolic personal attacks. Douglass, on a regional tour to attack the Liberty Party, was maligned by its local leaders as a "tool" of the Whigs. In response, he portrayed the city's black Liberty men as childlike dupes in *The Liberator*. The next four years saw a hiatus, but in 1848 black men united with heterogeneous Whigs and Democrats in the Free Soil Party. By the early 1850s, local white moderates bewailed the radicalism of the city's electorate of color, who had aligned themselves with the firebrand ex-Democrat, mayor Rodney French, while Democrats elsewhere evoked the bogeyman of New Bedford's "eight hundred sixty negro voters." Although exaggerated, this specter of black power rested on a solid numerical foundation: proportionally, New Bedford had the North's largest urban black population, 8.8 percent of its population according to the 1853 state census, and likely considerably larger because of fugitives uncounted in any census.[2]

These were not obscure events in one of the dozens of poor, old, small cities dotting the Northeast, as New Bedford would be understood today. It was then a Mecca—fantastically prosperous, a site of dynamic modernity, and its electoral disruptions resonated nationally. Both wings of the deeply divided abolitionist movement had a base there, a further source of tension. Politics in New Bedford therefore became a theater for the nation at certain moments, like other thriving new cities with substantial black communities, including Syracuse and Rochester.

This chapter offers a granular, election-by-election narrative of New Bedford's partisan wars. For the Liberty Party, the city served as an example of how dishonest, dictatorial, and antirepublican most Whigs were in practice, despite their pretensions to "anti-slavery." They promised to meet abolitionists' demands on Election Day, and ignored them afterward. In return for nominal pledges, they expected complete obedience from antislavery men, especially if black, and took vengeance on anyone who defied them. But New Bedford also demonstrated how effectively the Whigs could control abolitionist and black votes: unlike in many other locations, the Liberty Party's vote barely increased between 1841 and 1844. This lack of progress suggests the effectiveness of Whig coercion combined with sufficient blandishments. Examining these four years demonstrates the messiness of mixing partisan and "movement" politics, the main result being disillusionment and defeat. In contests between morality and power, the latter usually wins, and New Bedford was no exception.

Rather than tropes of awesome power like "Gibraltar," it is more accurate to describe antebellum New Bedford as a laboratory—an example of what a substantial black electorate might command. Given leaders of sufficient audacity and a fluid electoral environment, they could avoid becoming a "captured vote," but this required room to maneuver and the commitment to engage. Colored men in Portland and Providence did not believe that they had other electoral options. In New Bedford, men of the same complexions and backgrounds were sought by all parties, Whigs, Democrats, Liberty men and later Free Soilers. If New Bedford had been the prototype for postbellum black politics, the United States would have taken a different direction; instead it documents a might-have-been.[3]

Quakers, Whales, and Money

New Bedford was the nation's most visible site of black political influence prior to 1860 because of a convergence of political, economic, and cultural factors. In the 1820s, it became the hub of the nation's whaling industry, pulling spermaceti, oil-filled blubber, and bone from the oceans for tremendous profits. By the 1840s, it was the United States' fourth-busiest harbor, after New York, Boston, and New Orleans, "a place of somewhat remarkable wealth," in the words of the local Free Soil newspaper. In ways that seemed inherent and logical at the time, moreover, New Bedford boasted both the nation's highest per capita wealth and its most ostentatious nonracialism.[4]

The relation between these apparently dissimilar facts is explained by the whaling industry's overwhelming need for labor, and the families who dominated that industry. The hundreds of ships pulling out of New Bedford's harbor every year generated an astonishing "congress of nations" along its wharves, where "Coal-black 'Bravas' from the Cape Verd islands [sic] jostle against the Americanized African negro" and "every tongue is heard . . . the typical Yankee's nasal twang, the Frenchman's jargon, the Irishman's brogue, the South Sea Islander's guttural tones, the Spaniard's oaths, mingled with the strange speech of the Portuguese, the Swede, the Norwegian, the German, the Italian, the Malay, and the Chinese." Amid this version of what Douglass later dubbed the "composite nation," English-speaking black Americans did very well, because of the industry's social origins in a tightly knit group of Quakers notable for their willingness to patronize and shelter African Americans, especially those fleeing the inherent violence of slavery. In 1787, New Bedford was carved out of Bristol County's Dartmouth township, and the families associated with its early development were all Friends: the Rotchs, Howlands, Tabers, Ricketsons, Congdons, and Rodmans, among others. In the antebellum years, these names recur so often in the town's Whig Party and its abolitionist movement that it is hard to tell where one begins and the other ends.[5] Under their influence, leaders of all parties and religious affiliations avowed their antislavery convictions.

New Bedford's nexus of multiracial labor and Quaker capitalism was exemplified in a local Friend warning a southerner trying to reclaim his slave in 1826: "We are not in Virginia now, but in Yankee town, and we want those colored people to man our whale ships and will not suffer them to be carried back to bondage." This anecdote reflected long-term habits of sanctuary. A remarkable number of "chattels personal" reached southeastern Massachusetts, in part through New Bedford's trade with Quaker merchants in the seaboard South. After the Civil War, the former slave George Teamoh's memoir evoked its status as a haven, that, as "most readers know . . . this locality has always been considered the fugitives' Gibraltar." As Teamoh's comment suggests, New Bedford's alliance of wealthy Quakers and black people became nationally known. It was highlighted in 1845's bestselling *Narrative of Frederick Douglass*, describing two prominent Quakers, William C. Taber and Joseph Ricketson (Jr.), encountering the author and his wife on the Providence stage: "They seemed at once to understand our circumstances, and gave us such assurance of their friendliness as put us fully at ease in their presence." As the Douglasses settled in, another wealthy Friend, George Howland, Jr. (whom black votes helped send to Massachusetts's House in 1839, and repeatedly elected mayor in the 1850s and 1860s), gave him valuable employment.[6]

The partisan nuances of this story document how mainstream Whiggery converged with radical Garrisonianism in the mid-1830s, and how they slowly broke apart. That the bourgeoisie of America's richest city were resolutely Whig and often just as abolitionist seems strange now—how could the self-described "conservative" party welcome onto its electoral tickets men who embraced the *dis*-order of Garrisonian immediatism? It did, and often. Two Whigs, James B. Congdon and Joseph Grinnell, both Quakers, document how fervent abolitionists coexisted in party leadership with men who disdained black people. Congdon was one of New Bedford's three selectmen every year but one between 1833 and 1845, often their chairman. He was also a pillar of the city's Anti-Slavery Society and stood on platforms with Garrisonians as they attacked the South, in 1844, offering city funds to hire a lawyer for a black constituent jailed in Virginia. Grinnell was a merchant and railroad executive, and U.S. representative in 1843–50. During those years, he enforced Jim Crow laws on his trains even as they were discarded throughout Massachusetts. Challenged in court, he acknowledged he found black people "offensive." In Congress he avoided antislavery positions, unlike most northern Whigs, and was pilloried by abolitionists. Yet these positions did not hurt his standing among local Whigs, including Congdon. New Bedford's Democrats repeatedly tried to remove Grinnell by appealing to abolitionists and black voters, but Whig unity always trumped abolitionism.[7]

Rather than face their contradictions, New Bedford Whigs looked backward to an origin tale fusing blackness and Quakerism, claiming their town as organically nonracial even when events like an 1842 antiabolitionist riot complicated that narrative. This mythohistory revolved around two men, both eminent Friends: Paul Cuffe (1759–1817), whose transatlantic fame brought the town distinction, and William Rotch, Sr. (1734–1828), patriarch of the Nantucket clan that began the town's whaling industry, who served as clerk of the New England Yearly Meeting in 1793. Rotch, Sr., was an admirer of the Haitian Revolution and an associate of Moses Brown, the Providence abolitionist. He was also Cuffe's friend, with stories told for decades about their association. In 1842, a Nantucket Quaker, Nathaniel Barney, attacked segregation on Joseph Grinnell's railroad by evoking the visit of "the venerable William Rotch, deceased" and "some friends . . . to the house of Paul Cuffe." At dinner, the latter, "in view of the popular prejudice, was proceeding to seat the strangers, when the patriarch discovered that Paul and his family intended either to take a separate table, or come after their white guests." Rotch declared, "Paul, I shall not take a place at thy table, unless thou and thy family seat yourselves with us." Barney hailed Rotch as an exemplary "true gentleman," and asked, "If Paul Cuffe and William Rotch were now with us . . . where would the regulations of the Railroad Company place the two individuals?"[8]

Rotch and Cuffe did have much in common. They were Friends, abolitionists, and businessmen engaged in commerce around the Atlantic littoral, yet their political legacies diverged sharply. Rotch's led toward the nexus of Whig partisanship and paternalistic reform, making space for African Americans as loyal workers and docile voters in a society organized by class. The Rotch legacy was on display at the founding of the Bristol County Anti-Slavery Society on July 4, 1834. William Rotch, Jr. (1759–1850), was elected its president, James B. Congdon was recording secretary, and other officers included Douglass's later benefactor, Joseph Ricketson, Andrew Robeson, an industrialist who funded *The Liberator*, and Treasurer John F. Emerson. These men were "New Light" Quakers disowned as too worldly by the town's Yearly Meeting in the 1820s. Their names would recur in town offices, Whig Party functions, and reform campaigns for decades; only a year later Congdon, Emerson, Ricketson, and Robeson founded the committee "to promote the suppression of the illegal traffic in ardent spirits" in 1835.[9]

Cuffe inspired a different tradition. His life evoked an unbending insistence on his own rights. Following him, black New Bedforders acted without a hint of deference, especially in comparison to Philadelphia, the nation's putative black capital. In the latter, public meetings typically saluted a white benefactor and issued an address, whereas New Bedford's assemblies rarely offered either racial deference or ritual pomp. Remonstrances, denunciations, boycotts, and threats of electoral reprisal were the norm, beginning with young Cuffe and other men of color petitioning the General Court about taxation without representation, which led to the legend, fostered by the town's first historian, Daniel Ricketson, attributing black men suffrage in Massachusetts to Cuffe's agency. Another story of defiance described Cuffe visiting President Madison prior to his 1812 trip to England. The Norfolk Customs Collector had confiscated his boat, declaring that as a man of color and thus not a citizen, Cuffe could not captain a U.S.-flagged ship. Supposedly, he remonstrated with the president, "James, I have been put to much trouble, and have been abused," and the latter ordered the ship's release.[10]

Regardless of exaggeration, the town's self-regarding narrative enabled black political autonomy, and black people participated happily in it. New Bedford's egalitarianism was noted well before immediatist abolitionism became a mass movement. In 1832, *The Liberator* described it as a "miniature republic" where "those unnatural distinctions, now so fashionable, are unknown." In 1837, the *Colored American* celebrated "the beautiful town of New Bedford," where, although it was "difficult to ascertain the exact number of colored citizens, it having never been the custom to discriminate between color, in taking the census," those people were "according to their number, better off than in any other place; nearly all of them, who are resident citizens, owning their own houses and lots, and many a number of houses, and are quite rich." New Bedford's exceptionalism was most obvious in its classrooms. In the North's blackest town, the public schools were integrated, whereas in neighboring cities with significant colored populations like Boston and Providence, fights for "equal school rights" were intensely divisive.[11]

Quaker patronage was necessary but hardly sufficient in fostering New Bedford's black political advancement. The town's maritime commerce allowed black families to prosper in myriad ways. Shipboard life's brutal egalitarianism found its fullest expression on whalers, with hundreds of black men serving as boatsteerers, harpoonists, cooks, stewards, mates, and occasionally captains. Above this self-respecting skilled proletariat were businessmen who specialized in meeting the consumption needs of wealthy whites, as in Boston and Salem—imported candies, fruits, and ice cream; bathhouses; hairdressing and perfumeries a la mode; restaurants and catering. Finally, New Bedford attracted an exceptional group of black artisans. As early as 1832 a visitor reported to *The Liberator* its many "first rate workmen," one of whom, the blacksmith Lewis Temple, revolutionized whale killing with his "Temple Toggle-Headed Harpoon."[12]

Five men named Johnson exemplified the city's black politics. Nathan Johnson, born in 1796 in Pennsylvania (and worth $15,500 in 1850, a princely sum in those days) was the first, and will figure again here. Another substantial merchant was an older man, Richard Johnson, also born in Pennsylvania (in 1780, the year of emancipation), who opened his store in 1806, selling all manner of goods; he was worth $31,000 at his death in 1853. By the 1820s, this Johnson was trading along the Atlantic Coast, and, in a notorious fracas, was almost jailed in Charleston under South Carolina's law quarantining black mariners, until proving he was the ship's "supercargo" in charge of goods. His sons, Richard Cummings Johnson (born 1808) and Ezra Rothschild Johnson (born 1814), were outstanding political operators as well as businessmen. In 1836, they garnered a measure of national renown by fitting out a whaler, the *Rising States*, like other New Bedford merchants. The following year, the Johnson brothers initiated the practice of a separate black-endorsed list of candidates for state legislative offices. The latter became a doctor, worth $150,000 at his death in 1872. The senior Johnson remained a Garrisonian, but in the 1840s and 1850s, his sons gained offices in the Liberty Party and its successor, the Free Soil Party.[13]

The 1830s: Into the Fray

Unlike in ports to its north, New Bedford's black voters did not attract jealous attention by Jeffersonians in the early 1800s, suggesting they never constituted a Federalist constituency. Their appearance on Election Day was long accepted: an 1831 article described the "hands . . . lifted up toward the box from a solid column on the floor mixed up masons and anti-masons, administration and opposition, black and white." This intimation of men of color freely entering into multiparty factional contestation was borne out over the following nine years, when "Jacksonmen" (Democrats), Antimasons, and the new Whig Party (formed by "Administration" National Republicans) all jostled for black men's ballots.[14]

The first appeal to colored voters came from the Democrats and Antimasons in 1835. William Lloyd Garrison had just been mobbed in Boston by a crowd instigated by wealthy Whigs, who wrecked his press, and the local "opposition" quickly tarred New Bedford's Whigs as racist colonizers, demanding rhetorically, "Who dragged a gentleman from his own house with a rope tied round his body through the streets?" and answering, "The same mild gentlemen who are opposed to the colored people treading their native soil . . . the WHIGS." This effort was maintained in 1836, when the Whigs' *Mercury* scoffed at the "Unwearied pains . . . taken by certain unprincipled partizans, to enlist the Abolitionists in the Van Buren ranks." To maintain the Whig claim to black votes, it reminded readers that Democratic gubernatorial candidate Marcus Morton had once represented a Virginia slaveholder trying to claim a fugitive who was, "for aught we see, a legal voter competent to all the rights of citizens."[15]

The competition for black votes continued. In October 1837, the Antimasonic *Gazette* attacked the Whigs' opportunism, that only when "anxious to obtain the votes of the colored men of this town, who generally poll anywhere from fifty to an hundred votes," were Whigs friendly to those electors. Fifty to 100 was a considerable bloc, given that in 1833 the top vote-getter among the town's nine state legislative representatives received 397 votes. Reportedly, a Whig "high in the counsel of his Excellency," Governor Edward Everett, visited "the house of a very respectable colored man" (one suspects Nathan Johnson) to convince him to support the governor's reelection. The Whig grandee told tall tales, that Democrats "had admitted Texas into the Union" and President Van Buren would "compel all the free colored men of that State to go into servitude again." "Is it so?" asked the black man, coyly; "Indeed it is," was the reply, suggesting "some of the principal men of our party" should attend "a meeting of your colored folks." The colored leader "went away, chuckling" at this "consummate impudence." The *Gazette* then saluted black electors: "If any party think that they can deceive the colored men of New Bedford, they are mistaken. . . . They can read as well, and understand as well, as any other men. . . . [T]hey are as much devoted to their principles of political action, are as well acquainted with the history and policy of the country as any other citizens in their walks of life . . . [and] are not to be duped, especially by the party whose organ considers the publishing of abolition sentiments sufficient cause for destroying a press and mobbing its owner."[16]

Evidently, all parties had taken notice of colored men's self-organization. Four days later, a paid "NOTICE" appeared in the Whigs' *Mercury*, announcing "a special meeting of the colored citizens of this town . . . THIS EVENING," to consider "what measures to adopt preparatory to the ensuing election." On November 3, five days before the election, the *Mercury* printed that meeting's "proceedings and resolutions," with a preamble praising them as "expressive of an open and honest determination of purpose," even though the assembled voters declared they had not "as yet discovered any sincerity in either party, therefore as Abolitionists we deem it our duty to stand aloof from all political parties." They had appointed a committee "to interrogate all candidates in this County" as to whether "Liberty [was] by the will of the Creator the birthright of all men," withheld only "by a wicked tyranny," whether Congress had the "power to abolish slavery in the district of Columbia; and the territories under the jurisdiction of the United States, and whether such power ought to be immediately exercised," and finally, did

Congress have the "power to put an end to the internal or domestic slave trade, and whether that trade ought to be immediately abolished." Another committee was tasked to prepare a "list of candidates to be supported as Representatives to the General Court."

This audacious act constituted a major breakthrough, the public mobilization of an independent electoral bloc, when New Yorkers had just begun petitioning for the restoration of equal suffrage, black voters in Boston and Portland were loyal Whigs, and Pennsylvania's black men were about to be disfranchised. Indeed, New Bedford's leadership, notably Richard C. Johnson as chairman and his brother Ezra on the endorsements committee, exacted a price—that their meeting's proceedings be published by all of the "insincere" parties; the Democratic *Gazette* carried this report, without comment on October 30, putting pressure on the *Mercury*.[17]

Inviting candidates to compete for black support was a prelude to the more calculated intervention in 1839. That October, a committee of black men published bipartisan endorsements for Bristol County's three state senators and New Bedford's nine state House seats. In the latter case, to maximize their influence, a "bullet" vote was suggested; in a multicandidate election, the individual voter's power is augmented by casting fewer than the permitted maximum. For the Senate, the Democrats had nominated well-known "Abolitionists" to gain an edge and two of those were endorsed, Seth Whitmarsh and Foster Hooper, plus the Whig abolitionist Nathaniel B. Borden. Only six House candidates received endorsements, and since a valid ballot required nine votes, black voters were instructed to write in the names of three additional prominent abolitionists.[18]

These endorsements exacerbated an already volatile atmosphere, as recorded in the correspondence of Deborah Weston with her sisters Maria Weston Chapman and Anne Warren Weston (all three were prominent members of the "Boston Clique" around Garrison, and Chapman was the most powerful woman in the abolitionist movement, elected to the Executive Committee of the American Anti-Slavery Society in 1839, editor of *The Liberator* in Garrison's absence). Deborah Weston had recently moved to New Bedford to teach in the abolitionist Whig John F. Emerson's high school. Her letters uncover both parties' conflation of ideology and partisanship, and the ruthless tactics used by Whigs to keep black votes: the artificial divide between "electoral politics" and "abolitionism" falls apart, revealing a scenario in which control of offices trumped all.[19]

The protagonist in this partisan dogfight was not on the ballot: the black confectioner Nathan Johnson. By that fall's election, his reputation was in tatters. Since 1834, Johnson had taken care of a black woman named Betsey and her three children at the request of a Georgia slave-owner and the children's father, Patrick Gibson. After Gibson died in March 1837, Johnson followed the executor's wishes that they be sent to Jamaica, but Betsey refused, uncertain of her future. Eventually she agreed, and a wary Johnson brought her and the children to Newport, Rhode Island, to embark for Jamaica via Georgia. A white busybody named Benjamin Rodman followed them and intervened, believing a rumor spread by Whigs that Johnson was consigning the Gibsons to renewed bondage. Rodman wrote the executor, who replied that Betsey Gibson and her children were still enslaved and could not be sent to Jamaica, with evidence showing they had never been legally freed (in 1801, Georgians lost the right to manumit). Well past the November 1839 balloting, the Whigs' *Mercury* reported this information to defame Johnson. Only in late February 1840 did it print a report by the Young Men's Anti-Slavery Society absolving him, and in March, *The Liberator* printed all the relevant correspondence. The consequences otherwise would have been catastrophic. Not only economic ruin and ostracization but violent retribution were likely outcomes, as Johnson himself had once led an assault on the house of such a traitor.[20]

Deborah Weston's first letter on the election's eve clarifies what was behind these attacks. She began by noting, "The whole town is up in arms about the elections, which are closely contested." Then came the key fact, that since "the col'd people hold the balance of power all the politicians are violent abolitionists," followed by an apparent non sequitur: "A most awful story has been got up about Nathan Johnson, in respect to the Gibson's." After summarizing the facts, that they were to go to Jamaica via Georgia, she explained that "Nathan is a democrat & the whigs took up the matter" and promoted the "most awful story" to discredit this prominent black Democrat, blocking his ability to marshal voters for his party's solidly abolitionist ticket. Weston's second letter underscored why the Whigs were running scared. She referred to her boss Emerson, a mainstay of the county antislavery society, "whom the whig party put up to get abolitionist votes." But he too was "warped by party notions. He was complaining of the col'd people, who he said passed very good resolutions, but yet were not going to act on them—They were going to vote the democratic ticket." Weston told him that she "did not wonder at" colored men voting for Democrats since that party's candidates, Rodney French and John Bailey, "were opposed to" Whigs who were not consistent abolitionists, and Emerson "assented to this." This tale implies that some white abolitionists, like Bailey and French, plus some black men like Johnson, took the Democrats' proclaimed egalitarianism seriously, despite that party's national reputation as the bulwark of slavery. Even if these alignments were local and tied to issues separate from slavery and race, they outline a biracial political arena hitherto unfamiliar.[21]

The results of the endorsement policy were self-evident—that a bloc vote of about fifty had tipped several elections. For the Senate, the endorsed Whig (Borden) won, running fifty-eight votes ahead of two other Whigs in New Bedford, while the endorsed Democrats, Hooper and Whitmarsh, ran fifty-six and fifty-three votes ahead of their losing ticket-mate. In the House races, bullet voting by colored men wrecked the Whigs: only four of nine seats were filled in the first round in a town Whigs normally swept. The black-endorsed Whigs John Emerson and George Howland, Jr., ran well ahead of their ticket, with 865 and 844 votes, respectively, as did an endorsed Democrat, the abolitionist Isaac C. Taber, with 824. The rest of the Democratic ticket, including two other endorsed candidates, the outspoken Garrisonians French and Bailey, came close to the 822 needed; another antislavery Whig, Charles W. Morgan, gained the fourth seat. The Whigs' *Mercury* reproduced the list carried by black voters with asterisks indicating those "voted for by the colored Abolitionists"; perhaps its editor, the Quaker Benjamin Lindsey, wanted more candidates like Emerson and Howland so as to beat men like Taber, French, and Bailey. He also printed the write-in or "scattering" votes. Nathaniel A. Borden, a black storekeeper, and Joseph Ricketson, Douglass's benefactor, received fifty-one votes, and another white activist gained thirty-three. It was clear that New Bedford was a town where black men played politics on their own terms, but Weston's third letter (following the second round of voting for House seats), also clarified that antislavery was not the only factor disturbing party loyalties. Strong feelings about temperance, pro and con, weighed heavily. She noted that Isaac Taber was "the sole representative of the democracy of N. B. for on the last trial all the whigs were chosen—I was very sorry for this as Rodney French and John Bailey were among the democratic candidates & all of them abolitionists." Apparently, "they lost their election . . . owing to about 25 of the democratic rum drinkers refusing to vote for temperance men [e.g., French and Bailey], at least so the story goes."[22]

These maneuvers did not go unnoticed. On Election Eve a year later, *The Emancipator*, national organ of the new Liberty Party, specified that in Massachusetts's Tenth Congressional District, "100 votes for the Liberty ticket will defeat the election. . . . Our colored friends in New Bedford alone, if they will be true to liberty and the slave, and vote the Liberty ticket, may ensure a defeat." The presidential election passed off uneventfully, however, as antislavery New Bedforders lined up behind the Whig Harrison versus Van Buren, with the Liberty candidate James Birney receiving only thirteen votes.[23]

Spoilers, 1840–1844

In parts of the North, the early 1840s foretold the 1850s and the coming of the Republican Party. Starting in 1841, explicitly abolitionist candidates contested elections for the Liberty Party, endangering the Whigs' margin of victory in their strongholds. As early as 1842, the Liberty men constituted either the balance of moral power, as they saw it, or a gang of deluded spoilers doing the Democrats' dirty work, as Whigs (and many Garrisonians) saw it. In Massachusetts, however, Garrisonians and Liberty men pursued the same strategy, to "spoil" elections to the U.S. House and the state legislature by preventing any nominee from gaining the absolute majority that state required. A mere 2 or 3 percent of voters could prevent anyone's victory where both major parties were competitive, as long as the spoilers kept showing up for repeated "trials." This was third-partyism with a vengeance, intended to ruin the normal electoral process.[24]

Whig and Liberty nominees usually competed for the antislavery voters whom Democrats ignored or mocked. Not so in New Bedford. In New Bedford, unlike in any other city of note, local Democrats sought abolitionist ballots, and the resulting three-way battle offered special opportunities for black men. No other location featured "Democratic Abolitionists" like Isaac Taber, Rodney French, and John Bailey repeatedly gaining nominations for office. The partisan battle in 1839 had almost blocked the election of New Bedford's traditional Whig slate to the state House, as black men discovered they could maneuver at will. After 1840, the Liberty Party complicated these operations, breeding vicious schisms, since Garrisonians regarded the Liberty men as traitors, and Whigs organized harsh retaliation against disloyal voters. The resulting free-for-all generated both biracial unity and intraracial factionalism.

In 1841, the assault on New Bedford's Whig oligarchy turned frontal, with the Democrats seeking every possible advantage. On July 6, David Ruggles, the notorious black abolitionist (in 1840, national Democrats had claimed Harrison sought "the support of the Arthur Tappans and David Ruggles of the North"), was expelled from a whites-only car on the Taunton and New Bedford Railroad, after which the Commonwealth brought suit for assault on his behalf. The railroad's president was Joseph Grinnell, an eminent Friend and leading Whig. Ruggles's suit was tried before police court justice Henry A. Crapo, the longtime Whig town clerk and treasurer. Grinnell testified that the regulation giving conductors authority to exclude "was made to render the passage pleasant and convenient to passengers and the public. It has operated very beneficially. The rule or regulation separates the drunken, dirty, ragged and colored people from the others." Under cross-examination, he admitted that he found "color alone offensive—that a colored man should be put in the cars with the dirty and intoxicated; and if I was going to Boston with my family, I would not go in the same car with a colored person." Ruggles lost his suit because Justice Crapo justified his violent removal on the grounds that the right to exclude colored people was "implied in the very nature of things and supported by common sense," to avoid "the loss of custom on the part of the Rail Road Companies, and . . . the annoyance and disturbance of all peaceable travellers."[25]

This incident is well known as one of a series that broke down Jim Crow on Massachusetts's railroads, but no account has considered its openly partisan resonances. Ruggles made these plain in *The Liberator*: "I trust that the friends of equal rights to New-Bedford will remember, that Justice Crapo holds his office of town clerk by the suffrages of treacherous colored men and spurious abolitionists." Democrats had already won the town's April elections through a Whig schism over temperance, running the abolitionist Rodney French for selectman, and they took further advantage of Whig racialism. French was prominent in the meeting to denounce Ruggles's treatment, and the Democratic *Register* mocked the Whigs' *Mercury* for its defense of Crapo, underlining that "this regulation . . . was intended to put all colored people, whether drunk or sober, clean or unclean, ragged and immoral, or otherwise, into the same car, and all the ragged, intoxicated, dirty and immoral whites in with them! Is this reasonable?" To cap it off, the whole affair was publicized nationally, embarrassing town leaders and providing more ammunition for French and the Democrats.[26]

The fall 1841 election also received national attention in the abolitionist press. Everywhere else, Garrisonians and Liberty Party members refused all cooperation. In New Bedford, both groups were notably biracial, which may have facilitated an alliance. *The Liberator*'s correspondent was the black leader Jeremiah Sanderson, while the brothers Johnson (Ezra and Richard) were prominent in the town's Liberty branch. Together, they spoiled the election of all nine New Bedford representatives to the state House of Representatives. After three days, Sanderson reported exuberantly on "the joy we feel for the victory obtained over the pro-slavery parties. . . . 'Thrice have we met the enemy, and thrice have they been beaten.' Nineteen hundred men, comprising all the 'gentlemen of property and standing,' and 'all the decency' of New-Bedford, defeated by about sixty poor despised abolitionists." He described how Whigs resorted to "threats and bribery," with one leader announcing he "had been a good friend to" black people, and "had employed two or three in his house . . . but, for the future unless they voted the whig ticket, he would seek out some poor Irish to be the recipients of his favors. . . . If they were to be defeated by nigger votes, he would petition the

Legislature to take from them the right of voting!" Ignoring Garrison's distaste for cooperation with Liberty men, Sanderson hailed their united front: "The liberty party stood their ground nobly. Not a man deserted their cause during the memorable three days. During the same time, the abolitionists [meaning Garrisonians] not only held their own, but added several to their number." *The Emancipator* also trumpeted the success of New Bedford's "heroic band of Liberty men, aided by some true-hearted men who are friends of the [Garrisonian]. . . . The Chairman of the Liberty Committee writes that there has been nothing heard of old and new organization, since the election commenced. The Liberty men and scattering work together like 'a band of brothers.'" ("Old organization" meant the Garrisonian American Anti-Slavery Society," and "new organization" indicated those who had split in 1840 to form the American and Foreign Anti-Slavery Society and the Liberty Party.)[27]

Evidence for this bloc's effectiveness appeared on the election's last day when the Whigs published a letter from their leading candidate, William H. Stowell, responding to two black men, William Berry and Thomas Jinnings, Jr. Stowell affirmed that he was "a decided Whig," but as abolition was "the cause of God," it would have "the pre-eminence in my mind over any and every measure of public policy." He went further: "I have long since made up my mind to make no distinction among my fellow men, on the ground of condition, complexion, or anything but character. I consider the colored citizens of this Commonwealth entitled to the same rights and privileges as the white citizens" and would never vote for any law declaring otherwise. This pledge was not enough. After the fourth day's trial yielded no majorities, the Democrats' *Register* explained that 978 votes were needed to win, but Stowell only gained 963, with the other Whigs declining to 939. The five Liberty candidates received 44–48 votes and the Garrisonian "Anti-Slavery" ticket 22–33, including twenty-two for the ex-Democrat Nathan Johnson, whose votes alone would have elected Stowell. The two groups, 3.5 percent of the electorate, had determined the result, demonstrating that politics as usual in New Bedford had ground to a halt.[28]

The Whigs redoubled their efforts, exacting economic retribution on voters who defied them. In the April 1842 town elections (with no Liberty candidates), they triumphed. Even though Democrats had tried "every means, honorable and dishonorable . . . to induce colored voters to cast the [Democratic] ticket yesterday. . . . A goodly number of them were not to be deceived by pretended friendship manufactured expressly for Election Days, and voted the Whig ticket." Judge Crapo won reelection handily, Congdon took back his seat as selectman, and H. G. O. Colby, who had defended Grinnell's railroad against Ruggles, narrowly won as moderator against a "Democratic Abolitionist," the Quaker lawyer Timothy G. Coffin. Complaints multiplied of employment denied and men fired from city jobs: "Where are the men who lighted the public lamps one year ago?," describing two who worked for the town "for 8 or 9 years" but were "turned out of employment because being abolitionists, they could not and would not go to the polls and vote the whig ticket!" Whig sanctions fell especially hard on colored men. The November 1842 legislative election was spoiled on the first trial, but carried by the Whigs on the second, with *The Emancipator* reporting how the "Whig aristocracy, who own most of the wealth of the place," had used their power. Liberty men "in the employ of the Whigs, or dependent on them . . . [were] either turned out of employ, or threatened, and one man will lose about $500 worth of employ the next year, on account of his integrity." To win, "they coaxed, threatened, overseerized, bullied, dismissed from employ, and used every other oppressive means . . . to either carry the Liberty men over to the Whigs, or prevent them from going to the polls." This pressure had limited results: "five Liberty men only were carried over or stayed away, while our vote increased from 40 to 44." The writer stressed "their contemptible meanness towards poor colored men." Seeing a black man about to cast a Liberty ballot, a "Whig tried to persuade and coax him to exchange it for a Whig vote." Failing in that endeavor, "he put on the airs of an overseer, and straitened up in great dignity, and with awful solemnity told him, 'if he voted THAT TICKET never to call at his house again for any more SWILL!!!'" *The Emancipator* explained "in large towns numbers of persons support themselves by feeding swine with the offal which they collect at the kitchen doors of the houses." It made a good story even a year later—"The swill case," wherein "a wealthy nabob withdrew his permission to a man of color to get the offal of the kitchen for his pigs."[29]

Developments in 1843 reinforced the effectiveness of antislavery for partisan purposes, and also its limits. When truly important matters were at stake, offices and patronage, New Bedford's Whigs and Democrats acted as conventional members of their parties. The first instance involved the "Democratic Abolitionist" Rodney French, bane of the Whigs and outspoken friend of black men. In fall 1843, French undercut any claims to radicalism when he accepted appointment from the arch slaveocrat, President John Tyler, to the extremely lucrative position of collector of customs for New Bedford. *The Emancipator* commented acidly that this demonstrated the "Tyler-Calhoun policy, to disarm the free spirit of the North . . . by a display of magnanimity in appointments. . . . Other things being equal, a profession of abolition, united with a willingness to support the party, is as good a recommendation for office among the Calhoun ranks, as in those of Clay." It underlined the partisan connotations: "Mr. French is a strong Garrisonian, and hates the Liberty party."[30]

French's office undermined his party's claims to abolitionist votes, but so did the Whigs nominating Joseph Grinnell in 1843's special election to fill Bristol County's seat in the U.S. House. In response, the Democrats ran state senator Sampson Perkins, charging Grinnell "stands at the head of a corporation, which has treated the colored population with more barbarity than any other in the whole Commonwealth," reminding black voters of his admission "that he would not ride in the same car with a colored man" and insisting, "No true abolitionist can vote for Mr. Grinnell." Perkins had voted "in favor of the repeal of the odious Intermarriage law" and for a bill guaranteeing "protection of the rights of colored citizens on the rail-roads," and the New Bedford Anti-Slavery Society endorsed him, noting "the assertion that Mr Grinnell is an abolitionist [was] ridiculous," since "the Abolitionists (the colored especially) know what treatment they have received" at Grinnell's hands, "and a man more obnoxious to them scarcely could be found." None of this mattered; Grinnell defeated Perkins easily in the town (1,181 to 907), carrying the district by similar margins. A clue to how the Whigs pulled this off came in early October. To blunt Grinnell's reputation as a Negrophobe, they claimed antislavery's moral prestige by welcoming John Quincy Adams at the Town Hall, where he delivered an impassioned address against Texas's annexation. The ex-president was conveyed to City Hall in Joseph Grinnell's carriage, where the unimpeachably abolitionist James B. Congdon read a welcome.[31]

In 1844, New Bedford embodied the crisis in abolitionist politicking, based on the tensions between a major party compromised by its southern links and a minor party paralyzed by sectarian "movement politics." Its black voters were pulled in every direction, their enmities exacerbated by outside agitators, including a young Frederick Douglass, a rising star of the Garrisonian lecture circuit. By September of that year, charges of perfidy circulated nationally around the race pitting Democrat James K. Polk, an ardent supporter of annexing Texas, against Whig Henry Clay, who avoided defining his position on this vital issue. The stakes were high. Many abolitionists believed only Clay would block Texas coming into the Union, which could lead to many new slave states. That Clay owned dozens of slaves, insisted black people were fundamentally inferior and alien, and spoke of abolitionists with contempt, was irrelevant. He acknowledged that slavery was morally wrong and did not wish its extension. New Bedford's selectman James B. Congdon represented the local Whigs' view. Visiting Nantucket, he was hailed as a "prominent and active abolitionist" who "has labored for many years on behalf of the downtrodden slave. . . . He was induced thus publicly to advocate the election of

HENRY CLAY, influenced mainly by the avowed hostility of that distinguished statesman to the annexation of Texas" (a patently untrue claim). From this perspective, Liberty nominee James Birney was a dangerous spoiler, and both Garrisonians and Whigs acted accordingly, without scruple. To Birney's partisans, conversely, the notion of electing the slaveholder Clay to restrict slavery was a violation of basic principle. They took Whig attacks on Birney as manifestly dishonest, especially when parroted by abolitionists like Garrison or Douglass. The Liberty men had a party-building strategy, which required attacking the Whigs and accepting the election of Democrats when that resulted. They maintained that, when matters came to a head, the Whigs were hopelessly compromised. Given that most abolitionists voted for Harrison in 1840 only to end up with a Virginian dedicated to slavery's expansion, John Tyler, as president, this argument had weight.[32]

The fight for New Bedford's antislavery voters had state and national implications, and in October, the Garrisonians sent in their big guns to attack Birney. The resulting fight featured masculine one-upmanship and competing assertions of corruption. Liberty men charged that the black Garrisonians touring the state (Douglass and Salem's acidulous Charles L. Remond) did the Whigs' bidding for pay, and Whigs did throng meetings where Birney was denounced as a mercenary scoundrel. Douglass's account in *The Liberator* captures the fury of black men on different sides in this grudge match (and his zest for slander). On Douglass's arrival, Milton Clarke, another ex-slave and a well-known Liberty lecturer, asked him "to fill a number of [speaking] appointments." While proclaiming "the deepest sympathy" for his "brother fugitive," Douglass put in the knife, announcing his "deep disgust" with the Liberty Party treating Clarke as "a mere tool," keeping him "in leading-strings" like a toddler. He described their dueling meetings, relishing his "exposing the corruption" of Birney's party, which led to "Mr. Ezra R. Johnson, a Liberty party man" (and "a ruffian and a bully") denouncing him "as a liar." These charges and countercharges aired in *The Liberator*, the *National Anti-Slavery Standard*, *The Emancipator*, and many local Liberty papers. The Liberty men fought back, and on election's eve, a biracial assemblage denounced the visitors as "ambitious, intriguing declaimers" in town "for the express purpose of supporting and encouraging pro-slavery Whigs and their abettors, and consoling the milk-and-water abolitionists' conscience in voting for Henry Clay."[33]

————

Polk's victory, followed by Texas's annexation in March 1845 and war with Mexico in 1846, stunned both Whigs and Liberty men, leaving the former even more disgusted with "third party" spoilers, denounced as "unprincipled tricksters" who had, by "throwing away their votes . . . *annexed Texas and caused this war.*" New Bedford's Whigs had to contrast Clay's overwhelming victory locally with his narrow defeat nationally (he beat Polk by more than 20 percent in the city, and almost 12 percent statewide). The town's Liberty Party gained the same tiny vote in 1844 as before, a mere forty-nine votes or 2.3 percent, far below their statewide 8.3 percent. Evidently, most of the town's antislavery voters went for Clay. There is no record of Liberty Party activism in New Bedford following that election, although county party meetings continued.[34]

Between 1841 and 1844, New Bedford had lived up to its reputation as an advanced laboratory for disruptions of normal electioneering: Democrats attacked Whigs as racist; Liberty men and Garrisonians "spoiled" to prevent New Bedford from sending representatives to the state legislature; Whigs blackmailed black and white men to keep them voting right. In one sense, it was a perfect arena, in that everything was tried, but in another sense, these experiments all failed, as the Whigs maintained control. It began on a high note, with David Ruggles unmasking Whig hypocrisy followed by a united front between abolitionists. Those gains soon evaporated because of the higher law of partisan loyalty driving Democrats and Whigs, and the priority abolitionists gave to their internal schisms. Racial solidarity went by the boards, as black men slandered each other in 1844. Finally, since the Liberty Party was the most disruptive factor in these years, theirs was the biggest failure. In 1841, that organization had perhaps four dozen voters; three contentious years later, that number was almost exactly the same. And then it disappeared.

Black Men in Leadership

Why devote attention to electoral politics in one very rich small city? New Bedford's overlapping rivalries between Whigs, Democrats, Liberty men, and Garrisonians had a special feature—they were emphatically biracial. In the 1840s, New Bedford was the only city of consequence where black men regularly appeared as party leaders. This breakthrough came at the beginning, because the brothers Johnson extended their practice of independent action by helping found the Liberty Party locally. Just before the presidential vote in 1840, the *Ballot Box*, a campaign paper backing James G. Birney, listed the "Freemen's Tickets" stitched together in a few states (the party did not yet have a name). Massachusetts was the best-organized, with full slates for both houses of the legislature, and one of the three senatorial nominations for Bristol County was Ezra Johnson.[35]

That high-profile nomination was not repeated, but over the next four years, the Johnson brothers were regularly elected to town and county party offices: in late 1842, the three-man resolutions committee for a local convention included Richard; a few months later, at the founding of a permanent Liberty Association, Ezra Johnson was elected secretary and treasurer, and his brother to its seven-man Board of Managers; in summer 1843, Ezra was elected to the County Committee of nine men; subsequently, Richard was one of five vice presidents at a county convention; in November 1843, Ezra was secretary of a congressional nominating meeting; finally, a year later, at the 1844 Congressional District convention, a Johnson was elected to a seven-man Executive Committee. These offices may seem minor, but they had no precedent.[36]

The defection of two men from the town's wealthiest black family defied the Whig oligarchs, but there is no evidence of their being ostracized. In these same years, however, a different Johnson practiced a transgressive politics exciting the special disgust of Garrisonians of both colors. The latter's antipathy to Liberty men derived from what they saw as opportunism. Garrison's followers constantly defamed Liberty Party leaders as "office seekers" out for boodle. This was ridiculous in New Bedford, where that party commanded few votes, but it had a racial edge—that certain black men sought the limelight at the expense of the slave, and did not know their place. The Johnson brothers were spared this open contempt. Anger focused on Henry Johnson, a skilled and obstreperous prankster. Beginning as a fugitive, notorious as a partisan disrupter, he ended up as a militia captain and lawyer before the war. His life traces the narrative of ordinary black politics, minus the moral authority of abolitionism.

Even by New Bedford's standards, Henry Johnson was not a man to be controlled. In 1843–44, he made himself a lightning rod for resentment of the Whigs. At the June 1843 county Anti-Slavery Convention controlled by Garrisonians, he defended the "Liberty party with a good deal of energy," casting the sole vote against the usual antiparty resolution. Later that summer, he visited Maine with David W. Ruggles (not the famous New Yorker, perhaps a relative). Ostensibly they went to lecture to whites who had never seen an escaped slave. Johnson reported his successes in *The Liberator* under the heading "Labors of New Bedford Boys." While in Augusta, however, he spoke out in ways deeply offensive to Garrison. To whites, Johnson endorsed the Liberty Party, saying he had supported both Democrats and Whigs, but was "turned out of employment in one of these parties" after he "trod upon the corns of your Whig editors." Denounced anonymously by a New Bedforder, Garrison cast him into darkness with ample condescension: "We have received a communication from New-Bedford, signed 'Henry Johnson.' . . . It is too incorrectly written, and too abusive, for a place in our columns. To suppress it is an act of kindness to the author."[37]

Johnson enjoyed his infamy. In April 1844, a mass meeting "irrespective of party" was convened "to take some measures against the threatened annexation of Texas to the Union." It featured Whig and Democratic abolitionists and leading black Garrisonians like the elder Richard Johnson. Henry Johnson denounced them all, with *The Liberator*'s correspondent reporting that someone who had tried "to divert the meeting from its object by introducing some political slang, in a manner at once characteristic, and offensive to every man present, was permitted to retire" (that is, he was thrown out). Shortly after, an all-black meeting voted "to rebuke the outrageous conduct of Henry Johnson," who had "placed us in a very unenviable position . . . by assuming to be the representative, and to speak the sentiments of the colored people." He was censured for "attempting to have the impression go out that we are committed in favor of the (falsely so called) 'Liberty Party.'" He could not be "our representative, because we profess to be honest men, and therefore cannot be represented by him," asserting he betrayed "the friends of the slave for a few coppers." Ruggles insisted on his inclusion with Johnson as a "modern Judas," suggesting both men remained unbowed.[38]

Free Soilers, 1847–1854

Whig hegemony in Massachusetts was wrecked by the crisis brought on by the Wilmot Proviso in late 1846, to bar slavery from territories acquired by war with Mexico. Locally, New Bedford's realignment began in 1847–48 with a personal grouping led by a wealthy outsider, the merchant Abraham Howland. In spring 1847, he united most of the Democrats, some of the Whigs, former Liberty supporters, and the black electorate, and was elected the city's first mayor, easily winning re-election through 1851. Meanwhile, a local branch of the Free Soil Party formed in late 1848 for the presidential election, and Bristol County Free Soilers rapidly became powerful enough to determine election results, with Ezra and Richard Johnson prominent in party leadership in the early 1850s. In both city and county, then, black New Bedforders anticipated the sudden coming of the Republican Party in the 1850s—a powerful antislavery electoral coalition in which black voters were accommodated but greatly outnumbered.[39]

Henry Johnson was the phoenix rising from the Liberty Party's ashes. Sometime before the Civil War he began practicing as an attorney; by 1846's First of August celebration, he had attached "Esq." to his name. He also moved deep into the partisan stew and reaped significant patronage. In 1847, the legislature made New Bedford a city, thus entitled to a mayor, and Howland staged his coup, with the help of men like Henry Johnson. Just before the vote, "members of the democratic and liberty parties" attended Whig caucuses to back Howland's candidacy, and in the resulting election he swamped two prominent Whigs, H. G. O. Colby and James Congdon, with 963 votes versus 564 for the two combined, and sixty-eight for the regular Democrat. Johnson evidently participated in this coalition with other Liberty men, as following Howland's overwhelming reelection in 1848 with 1,097 of 1,209 votes, he appointed Johnson as one of the city's two common criers. For the next three years, Howland dominated New Bedford's politics, stitching together a "Howland party." The Whigs' *Mercury* assailed this coalition as a band "marshaled by renegade Whigs, but having a rank and file derived from the Democratic party of New Bedford, (now disorganized,) to which it is entirely indebted for its success, and which in its division of spoils has been conspicuously remembered," while Howland ran essentially unopposed.[40]

Partisan affiliations disappeared in New Bedford's municipal politics during the Howland era, but continued in presidential, congressional, and state elections. Approaching 1848's presidential contest, the parties broke up and reformed at a dizzying pace. On June 7, the Whigs met for one day in Philadelphia and nominated the slaveholder Zachary Taylor for president, after which Massachusetts "Conscience" (meaning abolitionist) Whigs, led by Charles Sumner, Henry Wilson, and Charles Francis Adams, bolted their party to form the new Free Soil Party with Liberty men and a faction of "Barnburner" New York Democrats. The Free Soilers held a mass convention in Buffalo in early August and nominated Martin Van Buren for president, but by then, the majority of New Bedford Democrats had already repudiated their party's nominee, Lewis Cass, in favor of Van Buren.[41]

The ideological pulls on local Whigs showed in late August, when 153 in New Bedford signed a public letter supporting Joseph Grinnell's reelection. Many were longtime abolitionists, including William Rotch, Jr., George Howland, Jr., Joseph Ricketson the 2nd, Samuel Rodman, William G. Taber, and James B. Congdon. Most remained Whigs, but two weeks later, Congdon, long a Whig stalwart, chaired the meeting where thirty men drawn equally from Whig, Liberty, and Democratic ranks were elected delegates to the Massachusetts Free Soil Convention, which named Congdon to the party's State Central Committee. At this convention, Henry Johnson made his move, as New Bedford's delegation included no black men despite their electorate's importance. He showed up anyway, and it became his great coming-out. Immediately after speeches by *Emancipator* editor Joshua Leavitt and Charles Sumner, "a colored man in the gallery" stood up and began talking about "a meeting of colored people in New Bedford, on Saturday night last." His speech, quoted at this chapter's opening, was full of folksy asides about his "go-ahead-ism" and how Democrats and Whigs at home would be "somewhat alarmed." It elicited appreciative "laughter and cheers" followed by "great and repeated applause." Crucially, Johnson declared he came from "a large meeting of four or five hundred legal voters, colored citizens of that place," a number to catch any professional politician's eye. He "had the honor of acting as their scribe, and they unanimously agreed to support the nominees of the Buffalo Convention." Johnson had put New Bedford's black men on the state's electoral map.[42]

Clearly worried, New Bedford's Whigs repeatedly warned those "legal voters" about Van Buren's record; in early October, after Sumner extolled the former president in a local address, the *Mercury* pointed out, "He forgot to mention that in forming a Constitution for New York, Mr. Van Buren was opposed to a colored man's having a right to vote, without a property qualification." Two weeks later, after detailing the former president's opposition to abolitionist measures, it asked "the colored voters of this city, to examine well Mr. Van Buren's position on this subject, before they give him their votes. . . . Can you vote for such a man?" These attacks had little effect: Van Buren easily outstripped the Democrats' Lewis Cass, with 618 or 28.5 percent of the vote, more than ten times the Liberty Party's 1844 tally, Cass receiving a mere 438 or 20 percent. Taylor barely carried the city with 51 percent, suggesting a massive defection of black votes, and Douglass reported, "The colored voters in New Bedford almost to a man voted the Free Soil Ticket." The Whigs were also worried about their congressman, Joseph Grinnell, given his threadbare antislavery credentials, since Mayor Howland had mounted an "independent" candidacy against him. To foil this challenge, they imported the philanthropist Abbott Lawrence, one of the Boston Associates who founded New England's textile industry. Reportedly, Lawrence "told the colored citizens of New Bedford, the *Fugitives*, to vote for" his friend Grinnell, "and their interests would be well taken care of in Congress."[43]

After 1848, a new political dynamic operated in New Bedford and Bristol County. As elsewhere in Massachusetts, the Free Soilers (later renamed Free Democrats) became a major party in a tripartisan environment. Shorn of their "Conscience" wing, the Whigs were now the party of order, "Hunkers" in the slang of the time. Their leading man was the patrician lawyer John H. Clifford, "about the most aristocratic gentleman in Bristol County" according to Douglass, who once worked for him. Clifford served as attorney general of Massachusetts for most of 1849–58, and governor in 1853–54. Having also lost their antislavery wing, the town's Democrats receded considerably. The Free Soilers were now led by the former Democrat Rodney

French. His becoming the admired champion of the "colored citizens," and, with their help, the city's radical mayor, is a key part of New Bedford's unique legacy of black power.[44]

Black New Bedforders found new space inside electoral politics with the onset of Free Soilism. Following the December 1850 passage of the Fugitive Slave Act (FSA), New Bedford's "fugitive slaves and free negroes" earned a national reputation for political clout in alliance with the flamboyant French. The FSA's overturning of habeas corpus, treating all free persons of color as potential stolen property with financial incentives to law officers who certified recapture, radicalized northern politics. In New Bedford, tumultuous meetings approved plans for fight rather than flight. Moderate whites were overwhelmed; the wealthy Whig Charles W. Morgan chaired the first meeting on October 10, and wrote in his diary, "The coloured people behaved most injudiciously for their own interests—they advocated loudly and noisily the extremest measures." Following the second, he recorded, "The abolitionists & negroes had it all their own way." Most provocative was French's damning Joseph Grinnell, who had absented himself from this vital House vote to attend to an errand at the Treasury Department. French reminded his audience of Abbott Lawrence's assurances in 1848, "The people were then told to vote for Mr. Grinnell because he was right in regard to the interests of the colored people. But now what had they got for these promises? They have got this Bill—(holding a copy of the Fugitive Slave Law in his hand)." New Bedford's "colored citizens" had signaled their defiance in that fall's election to replace Grinnell, who stepped down to avoid defeat. In October, the Whig candidate Zeno Scudder publicly broke with President Fillmore, who had pushed through the Compromise of 1850, including the FSA. Writing Ezra and Richard C. Johnson, Scudder declared he would "advocate and act for the repeal of the 'Fugitive Slave Law,'" calling it "a most flagrant abuse of political power, and a burlesque on the genius of our free institutions." For this, he was censured by the administration organ in Washington and various Boston Whig papers.[45]

March 1851 saw a perfect storm of interracial solidarity, cementing the city's infamy in the South. Boston abolitionists sent word that a 100-strong posse was coming by sea to snatch fugitives, and at six on a Sunday morning, French rang the Liberty Hall bell to warn the town. Following on the "rescues" of William and Ellen Craft in November 1850 and Shadrach Minkins in February 1851, the threat was real. The boat never came, but 900 angry black men and women gathered to receive it. A leading southern paper ridiculed the "invasion of New Bedford Niggerdom by Uncle Sam's steamboat and posse" as "a grand fuss and a big scare" propagated by "white negrophilists," but the mobilization proclaimed New Bedford's militancy, entering local lore as "that memorable and never to be forgotten Sabbath morning," when the bell "'rang' a peal, that with the aid of electricity and steam, was heard in the twinkling of an eye, as it were, over both Continents." In short order, the merchants of New Bern, North Carolina, with whom French had traded, announced his vessels would be refused entrance, since he had "called on the fugitive Slaves and free negroes to arm themselves" on that Sunday. French replied he would give up all business with southerners, using the opportunity to proclaim that Massachusetts's chief justice, Lemuel Shaw, "at a public dinner table, soon after the passage of the Fugitive Slave Law . . . remarked . . . 'There is not a slave upon a Southern plantation who has not a perfect, God-given right to demand his immediate liberty of his master at any moment, and if it is denied him, to take it over all opposition, at any expense of blood or life.'" French further insisted that "The fugitive slaves and free negroes here, needed no word of mine, to excite them to resist," describing a local judge who refused money to help a fugitive flee, "but if you want a 'six barrel Pistol' to defend your liberty on Massachusetts soil, and will promise to use it if necessary, I will give it to you." As a longtime Democrat, French knew how to add insult, that his black constituents had armed themselves "with as fixed a determination as Jackson prepared to resist the British at New Orleans, and . . . in quite as commendable and praiseworthy a cause." Finally, were he a runaway "pursued by any one claiming me as a slave . . . the first man who approached me . . . I would shoot down if in my power, and as many of his posse as seemed necessary." It is not hard to see why African Americans loved his "spirited, racy, and caustic speech, in which he handled the slave hunters, their attornies [sic, meaning John H. Clifford], apologists and abettors, without gloves." French won mayoral elections in 1853 and 1854 with their backing, with one reporting in the latter year, "Never did colored freemen work more assiduously on the glorious temple of freedom than did the men of this city." The difference between Abraham Howland's 1851 shutout of a regular Whig, 866 to 168, and French's thirty-vote squeaker in 1853 over the incumbent Whig, William Rotch, Jr., 1,052 to 1,022, underlines the black vote's centrality.[46]

Despite their vigorous participation, black men were absent from the Free Soil Party's public leadership until 1851, although the patronage granted Henry Johnson under Mayor Howland in 1848 continued, and by 1852 he was "Chief of the Lamp-Lighting Department," in charge of much of the municipal budget. Edmund Anthony, editor of the party's *Standard*, did not recognize other black leaders by sight, as in this report on an anti-FSA meeting: "Mr. Henry Johnson, a fugitive slave, ascended the platform and made an eloquent speech. . . . During the evening speeches were made by two colored men, who spoke very well and to the point and were listened to with marked respect and attention." The first public recognition came in May 1851, at a "Congratulation Meeting" on Charles Sumner's election to the Senate, with French presiding and Richard C. Johnson and the Reverend Leonard Collins two of six vice presidents. After that black men were regularly included as delegates, officers, and speakers, and the Free Soilers' *Standard* also began referring to "Colored voters, Free Soilers, and liberal democrats" and "the free colored men of the North and the free democratic voters" as natural allies.[47]

In this context, rather than party regularity or deference, a distinctly black partisanship reemerged. In fall 1852, New Bedford's black Free Soilers, led by Ezra Johnson, challenged their party's gubernatorial candidate, Horace Mann, a Whig-turned-Free Soil congressman who had confronted preslavery members in the House with great eloquence. In January 1852, Mann wrote a Cincinnati black convention avowing that the races had different capacities: "As compared with the Caucasian race, I suppose the African to be inferior in intellect, while in sentiment and affection the whites are inferior to the blacks. May not independent nations of each race be greatly improved by the existence of independent nations of the others?" adding an implicitly procolonization sentiment, "I believe there is a band of territory around the earth, on each side of the Equator which belongs to the African race." Ezra Johnson wrote Mann to ask if those were still his sentiments, and Mann restated his belief in "certain physiological and psychological differences. . . . The Caucasian excels the other in intellect; while the African excels . . . in the affectional or emotional part of their nature," and would prosper in a different "climate" for which he was "made and adapted." A meeting of black Free Soilers (the Johnsons, William Henry Woods, Henry O. Remington, and Henry Johnson) censured their party's standard-bearer's racialism as "untenable, illiberal, unjust, and only sustained by that partial judgment, which measures men by their complexion." They had "not the remotest idea of leaving this country either for Liberia, Canada, or the West Indies. Our ancestors have endured severe hardship and privations for more than a century." Mocking Mann, they added that since they were "now told, that our race excel the Caucasian in the affectional part of our natures, it would be a strange incongruity and wide departure from this theoretical dogma, to abandon our homes and enslaved brethren."[48]

In 1853, after electing French as mayor, New Bedford's black men upped the ante. Henry Remington (later the city's premier colored Republican) organized a petition against the legislature appropriating $10,000 for a statue posthumously honoring Daniel Webster. The 'godlike Daniel' remained the Whigs' avatar, but to many others he had disgraced New England by engineering the Compromise of 1850. Remington's petition suggested placing his statue "in front of the Court House, surrounded with chains," and the *Standard* enthusiastically agreed, calling the statue's sponsors "imbecilic, contemptible, and inefficient," and asking what "obligations the colored citizens are under to Mr. Webster, or what reasons they may have for reverencing his memory. We can think of none." Going even further, in 1854, black New Bedforders petitioned "the Mayor and Aldermen to add the names of all colored citizens to the jury box," a right never publicly granted anywhere; although there is no record indicating the result, the *National Anti-Slavery Standard* opined, "The petition will probably be granted."[49]

A final breakthrough came in 1854. Following May passage of the Kansas-Nebraska Act, abrogating the Missouri Compromise and opening the entire West to slavery, the Bay State's politics exploded. The Whigs went into free fall and Democrats took a body blow. "Anti-Nebraska" coalitions emerged locally as did the "Know-Nothing" American Party as a way station for Whigs, its intense anti-Catholic nativism providing a temporary alternative to anti-slavery. Where black men would fit in these new alignments was an open question. In New Bedford, it was answered decisively at a "great gathering of the people in Liberty Hall . . . crowded to overflowing, in accordance with a call for a public meeting of all parties" to address "the Nebraska Bill, the repeal of the Fugitive Slave Bill, and the formation of a new party for freedom." Mayor French presided, and Henry Wilson, soon to be elected U.S. senator by a Know-Nothing legislature, spoke. Of the various resolutions, *The Liberator*'s correspondent singled out "the one offered by Ezra R. Johnson, Esq., of this city . . . supported by him in a speech of much power and ability." Consider this tableau: an outspoken black partisan standing on the same stage as Henry Wilson, later vice president of the United States. Nor did Johnson simply attack slavery or the Democrats who had passed "the Nebraska Bill"; he proposed all-out armed resistance, that each black man should "practice the art of using fire-arms, as the most efficient means of defence, and if the kidnappers pounce upon him . . . shoot them down." With a touch of black comedy, Johnson suggested that in such a case, if a jury did not "bring in a verdict of 'justifiable homicide,' but man-slaughter," the black gunman could be "further protected in the State Prison until this slave question is settled. . . . There he will be better fed, clothed and treated, than in the rice swamps and cotton fields of the South, and have a chance to obtain mental and spiritual culture." Following this speech, one of the nation's richest men, "Edward M. Robinson, Esq., the millionaire," called for a hand vote, as "people wanted to know how their neighbors voted. . . . When the question was put on the passage of the resolutions, Whigs, Democrats, Free Soilers and the entire audience rose in their favor."[50]

Thus was New Bedford's Republican Party founded, with black men active in its creation. In 1855, when the "great Republican State (mass and delegate) Conventions" were "held in Worcester," Henry Johnson spoke at the public meeting before thousands, along with the party's luminaries and other men of color like Boston's Dr. John S. Rock. African Americans would be recognized in the new party; their presence certified the party's abolitionist credentials and they might gain minor employment, but from that point on their visibility receded. In the 1856 presidential campaign, all factions in New Bedford other than the regular Democrats converged into the Republican coalition backing Frémont for president. Its "Grand Rallies" featured leading whites and Whigs, even Joseph Grinnell, alongside men like French, but none of the black leaders. Men of color instead played symbolic roles, as when, at the "largest political meeting ever held in this city" on Election Eve, French "called for John Butler [a well-known black New Bedforder], who had come all the way from California to vote. He was conducted to the platform amid great cheering. Mr. Butler subsequently made a few remarks." Black Republicans organized a separate meeting to urge "the propriety of voting at the ensuing Presidential election. Remarks were made on the subject by Messrs. H. O. Remington, Henry Johnson, Wm. H. Woods, and others."[51]

Republican Ascendance, 1856–1860

The emergence of a broad Republican front in 1855–56 out of the shambles of Know-Nothingism, the old Whig Party and the radicals in the Free Democracy (formerly Free Soilers) visibly diminished the importance of New Bedford's African American electorate. When Whigs controlled roughly half the electorate and Democrats and Free Soilers split the rest, black voters were courted by both Whigs and Free Soilers, since they could either push the former into the majority or help the Free Soilers edge out the Democrats. The Free Soil *Republican Standard* reported carefully on black men's participation in party leadership, and urged "Colored voters" to beware of Whig blandishments. Its editor, Edmund Anthony, noted acidly how "Fillmore and Webster slave catchers," meaning Whigs, who had formerly opposed "Coalition" with Free Soilers, now tried to use "Abolitionists" by "nominating coalition tickets for home consumption—making themselves busy in arranging with the Free Soilers for lecturers . . . insisting at the corners of the streets that 'coalition was perfectly right and proper,' and calling upon all men, no matter their complexion, to support this movement." After 1856, when Frémont carried two-thirds of New Bedford's vote and old-line Democrats and Know-Nothings divided the remainder, black votes mattered less, and their leaders disappeared from party platforms. Over the next four years, "mass meetings" and conventions met several times a year to advocate Republican victories and elect delegates to county, district, and state conventions, with hundreds of white men listed as vice presidents, secretaries, or speakers, but black leaders were left out. Black voters were still recognized, as in the *Standard*'s 1857 boast about how Republicans outwitted the "Gardnerites" (supporters of Know-Nothing governor Henry Gardner) who were trying to trick an illiterate black man. They brought him to the polls "and placed a Gardner ticket in his hands," until walking through the crowd, "he was asked for whom he wished to vote. He replied for [the Republican Nathaniel] Banks, and held up his ticket and asked if it was the right one. He was told it was not, and was supplied with a Banks ticket." As in Maine, Republicans celebrated black loyalism with jovial mockery; following an uneventful election, the *Standard* reported, "The most serious display of feeling was that of the ducking of an unfortunate colored man by his sable friends for changing his vote after he had once pledged it."[52]

In lieu of public recognition, Republicans offered tangible rewards. By 1856, several black men were city lamplighters. In 1856 and 1857, the Common Council and aldermen in joint session elected Henry Remington superintendent of street lamps by (the job formerly held by Henry Johnson), and, in the latter year, another black Republican, Lloyd H. Brooks, was made city messenger, both well-paid positions. In 1858, Remington was elected one of forty-nine delegates to the Republican state convention, and William H. Woods was put on the party's twelve-man City Committee. This pattern of party regularity and sporadic appointments continued through 1860 and well past the war.[53]

In retrospect, the multiparty environment of the early 1850s and French's 1853–54 mayoralty were the peak of black political influence in New Bedford. In those years, black men presented themselves as voters and party leaders at New Bedford's enormous First of August celebrations commemorating West Indian emancipation in 1834, with thousands arriving by train and boat from elsewhere. The "Firsts" have been studied as abolitionist "festivals of freedom," but their partisan purposes have attracted little notice: the white politicians who threw open their houses, coverage in party newspapers, and what black men themselves said. In New Bedford, the electoral show was at the center. This tradition took off in 1848, with the Howland Organization's politics of interracial fusion. That year, 3,000 people made "an honorary call upon his lordship, the Mayor," listened to the fiery Liberty man-turned-Free Soiler Henry Highland Garnet, and held "a large Free Soil meeting at City Hall." The committee was chaired by Henry Remington, the town's leading black politician in the 1850s; hitherto obscure, he had begun building his machine, establishing a tradition of mutual homage. In 1851, another vast crowd was "called to order by Henry O. Remington, Chief Marshal . . . ably seconded by Henry Johnson, George Marshall, Augustus W. Monroe, Mr. Wood and others."[54]

Rodney French's accession to power in 1853 brought this spectacle of black men's empowerment to a higher level. That year's First saw a rally of "from three to four thousand persons, young and old, male and female, arrayed in their best attire," with "large delegations from Boston, Providence, Taunton, and numerous other cities and towns in and out of the Old Bay state." Conducted like white party assemblies, it combined the parading of local biracial alliances with an assault on white leaders possessing insufficient "backbone." West Indian emancipation only came to the fore briefly, in Douglass's keynote. The goal was to arrange Massachusetts's black electorate before the seat of power, as "the grand City Hall of New Bedford, standing right in the center of the city, surrounded by the beauty, and fashion and wealth of that wealthy place, was thrown open to accommodate the colored citizens in celebrating the glorious First . . . gratifying proof of the progress of the Anti-Slavery cause. Ten years ago, that hall could not have been obtained for such a purpose.—Now it seemed to be regarded simply as a matter of course." After marching "through the principal streets," the crowd rallied again at "the house of the Mayor of the city. Hon. Rodney French, a gentleman whose many good works are in the mouths of all the colored citizens of New Bedford. Loved and honored by these latter, it is not surprising that he is an object of hate and dread to the cotton Whigs, and the fogy Democrats."[55]

This display of partisan force foregrounded both French and the black men who enabled his election. No New Bedforder would have failed to notice that Free Soil Party leaders managed the show, especially "The Marshal of our day, Mr. REMMINGTON [sic]," who "performed his duty to the admiration of all," a business requiring "much tact and some dignity. Mr. REMMINGTON possesses both—enough to lead an army." At the day's culmination, this political general took the stage with his lieutenants around him. Other than a few old Garrisonians like J. B. Sanderson and Solomon Peneton, all were Free Soil delegates, officers, and speakers (some of whom had city jobs), including Remington, Lloyd H. Brooks, John Goings, David W. Ruggles, John Briggs, Henry Johnson, Shadrach Howard, and John Freedom.[56]

Black politics in Massachusetts had reached its apogee, and its leaders were prepared to attack. To underline they were far from "captured," the day ended with an indictment of the state's white Free Soil Party leaders by the veteran organizer William J. Watkins, down from Boston for that purpose. During the early 1850s, Watkins led the campaign to force Massachusetts to nullify the whites-only proviso in the federal militia law and charter the black military companies springing up around the state. Like jurying, this was a final test of citizenship, but at the recent state constitutional convention, Free Soilers under the sway of Whig luminaries had failed that test. Watkins lit into the "omissions of duty on the part of Massachusetts Free Soilers," sneering that their backbones were rubbery ("gutta percha") and, worse, they were dissemblers, "a host of eloquent talkers in the cause of liberty" who ignored black people when it counted. At the convention, white Free Soilers had evoked Crispus Attucks to create "a 'sensation,' and there they left us. What man among them vindicated our rights as citizens of the United States? . . . Not one. [The conservative Whig] Rufus Choate laid down the law, and Charles Sumner, with all his 'backbone,' bowed acquiescence; and Henry Wilson said Amen, perhaps reluctantly." Watkins ended with a threat: "The colored people of Massachusetts have worked faithfully for their political friends. We have been threatened with starvation, with the loss of the means of subsistence," but "our votes have been written in the sand. We did not forget them; their base ingratitude shall be written in marble, for the benefit of our children's children."[57]

In 1856, Frémont swept Upper New England, with almost 54 percent in New Hampshire, over 60 percent in Maine and Massachusetts, and a remarkable 78 percent in Vermont. After that, the region as whole adopted the commonsense nonracialism represented by an 1851 anecdote attributed to "A wealthy Friend (Quaker) of New Bedford" who told someone enquiring "whether a fugitive slave would be safe in that city" that "if he is hungry we will feed him, if naked clothe him. He will be safe here. We have about 700 fugitives here in this city, and they are good citizens, and here we intend they shall stay." In the city itself, this became a matter of pride, with the formerly Whiggish *Mercury* in 1857 disparaging the white suffrage provision of Oregon's state constitution as "a truly savage idea," since disfranchising men "because they have a skin not absolutely white or absolutely black, is to perpetuate in modern times the relics of an old barbarism, founded in ignorance and superstition. . . . Our colored brethren are certainly citizens, precisely as much as those whose skins are white. They breathe the common air and must pay their taxes if they acquire property, and their lives must be protected under the law." Similarly, earlier that year, the Free Soil-turned-Republican *Standard* expressed its satisfaction that "a few years ago, the idea of electing a colored man to any office of honor or profit would have been considered preposterous," but black people had "progressed in self-respect and intelligence, under the blessings of freedom," and "many a 'black Republican' would now stand a better chance of being elected to office, and would assuredly fill it more ably and faithfully, than some of his white Democratic fellow citizens," noting that locally, "there are at least two municipal officers 'of African descent,' diligent, capable, and popular men."[58]

The limits of that common sense were clear: recognition and praise, with Senator Henry Wilson evoking the "colored sailors" of New Bedford in the Oregon debate, "as good sailors as their fathers were good soldiers in the days of the Revolution," but not more material gains. In 1857, one Common Council member argued for adding $500 to the $2,500 Fourth of July appropriation, to fund the First of August as "an act of justice," since "the colored people composed a large and respectable portion of the population and paid a share of the taxes" but could not "take part in the celebration of the Fourth on account of the laws of the country," meaning, presumably, the *Dred Scott* decision. His proposal was voted down 12–9. Certainly, there were "municipal officers 'of African descent,'" as well as black men holding minor party offices, but most of Republican New Bedford's government and civil society remained as monochromatic as before. In a typical year, the city employed about 350 firemen, organized into a dozen companies and paid $25 annually with stipends for officers, and every company's roster listed in the annual city directory. Other than in 1849, however, when a "Nathan T. Johnson" was listed as a member of the Hook & Ladder Fire Company, not a single black man of any prominence can be identified as a fireman over twenty years. Given that the firemen were a major constituency, their whiteness speaks to the separation maintained in this flagship of black political influence. That black men had more power there than anywhere else does not mean they had equal or proportionate political weight.[59]

The new Republican order settled into a familiar rhythm after 1856. The intense partisan strife of the decade's first half abated. Militant antislavery was now ingrained among the white majority, and colored citizens were welcome to join in ritualized expressions of the common feeling. New black men came to the fore, including Bela C. Perry, hailed in the *Mercury* for his miraculous hair restorer, and a recent fugitive from Virginia, Sam Nixon. Renaming himself Thomas Bayne, he made himself a doctor and dentist, listed in city directories in 1856 and after. Bayne provided the last fillip to the city's reputation as the nation's most "Negrophilic" polity.

The year 1860 was the year of revolution (or at least disunion) following John Brown's execution and continuing Republican ascendancy in the North, while the Democrats broke into sectional pieces. In New Bedford, a brief reemergence of independent black politics caused a stir. That April, the "millionaire" Edward Mott Robinson resigned his Fourth Ward Council seat and Bayne, "the well known colored dentist on Cheapside," made an "Independent" run for the seat "supported by the Republican and Temperance parties" against a Democrat, Morrill Robinson, Jr. The race was very close, but Robinson apparently prevailed in the initial count 122 to 115, although a Rhode Island newspaper reported "an informality in the votes cast for Mr. Robinson," and one of Bayne's black supporters, John W. Reams, crowed in the New York *Weekly Anglo-African* that "instead of being beaten by seven votes, Dr. Thomas Bayne is really elected a Councilman from Ward Four. . . .

I deeply sympathize with the Loco Focos and negro haters who may be forced to sit with him in council"; Bayne is not listed anywhere as a councilman following the election, so the final result remains unclear.[60]

Bayne's candidacy highlights how New Bedford's measure of black power combined episodic audacity and long-term incorporation into regular politics. Seen from New York or Boston, let alone Portland or Providence, his winning the seat (or coming close) was remarkable, marking New Bedford as the region's "Very Sebastopol of Niggerdom," in the words of the Catholic archdiocese's *Boston Pilot* just after Lincoln's election. Closer to home, it indicated the frame within which New Bedford's black voters and politicians operated. They were recognized; they voted freely; they might exert some weight, but they could not expect to gain regular nominations, and office was what was wanted, not just minor patronage and party roles. Third-party or independent politics from 1837 to 1854 had gained them temporary advantage, but that day was gone, for the moment.[61]

After this last demonstration of New Bedford's ultraism, it was business as usual, with the city's black electorate a subordinate constituency of its dominant party. After 1856, there was no reporting of their electoral mobilizing, although presumably the black Republicans got out their vote. That this was a deliberate policy of effacement was evident after Lincoln's sweep. The men on the platform at the big "Republican Demonstration" in mid-November 1860 were white, but a subsequent victory celebration broke the color line. The Democrat-turned-Free Soiler-turned-Republican Rodney French gave a historical valedictory of antislavery politics, going back to the Liberty Party. A longtime black Free Soiler and Republican, A. W. Munroe, sat on the stage as vice president, and at the close, "Mr. Ezra R. Johnson," who had led the local Liberty men, "also briefly addressed the meeting."[62]

That New Bedford's black Republicans saw themselves as regional leaders became clear in summer 1858, when they took the initiative to overcome the Garrisonian antipolitics limiting political action by black men elsewhere in New England. That year's state convention, which they organized and hosted, and follow-up regional meetings in 1859–60 confirmed the Afro-Yankees' self-respecting determination and their ambivalence regarding the Republican Party, as they imagined moving beyond mere political equality in the Yankee Republic.

Chapter 7

We Are True Whigs

Reconstruction in Rhode Island

> There is not so much scolding about letting the blacks vote as we expected.
> They pass it off this way, that they would rather have the negroes vote than
> the d___d Irish.
>
> —Elisha Potter, Jr., to John Brown Francis, July 1842

> As men, we are true Whigs, friends to social order, true to our fellow-man,
> to our God, and to our country.
>
> —A letter from the Colored Whigs of Providence, denouncing abolitionists,
>   January 1845

> We say to the colored people of Rhode Island . . . the only party of freedom
> is the Whig party, that the only way in which they can make their votes
> count for freedom in this election, is to vote for the Whig electors. . . . You
> know the party to which they belong and to which you belong, the
> party . . . which extended to you the right of suffrage, and gave you a voice,
> in the election of the rulers. Ingratitude is not a vice which belongs to the
> colored race. . . . SUPPORT THE PARTY WHICH HAS SUPPORTED YOU.
>
> —*Providence Journal*, November 9, 1848

The 1840–43 events in Rhode Island constitute the single most dramatic assertion of black political influence, as voters and armed men, prior to 1860.
They prefigure the dynamics of Radical Reconstruction, a grubby mix of racial assertion and ruling-class manipulation in which black men made their
own way in a fight between whites.

Rhode Island's black politics began in the early 1840s, and from the first
revolved around opportunistic clientelism. After disfranchising black men in
1822, the tiny state saw a complete reversal. For once, the bottom rail was put
on top. In the Dorr War of 1842, a coalition of whites sought to overturn the
state's extremely restricted suffrage, which empowered a state government
dominated by rural landholders. In response, conservative whites welcomed
the armed assistance and votes of black men against an insurrectionary movement named for its leader, the lawyer Thomas Wilson Dorr. As Robert Cottrol has documented, Providence's colored voters remained a permanent
reserve army for decades. Long past the Civil War, a freehold qualification

for naturalized citizens disfranchised nearly all Irishmen, by now the back-bone of the state's swelling industrial proletariat. In Rhode Island, birthright trumped race as the qualifier for full citizenship, with naturalized citizens only gaining "full political equality" in 1928.[1]

Rhode Island represents a road taken only once in the antebellum era. A cross-class biracial alliance openly contested a faction claiming to represent "poor white men." During the crisis of the early 1840s, black men leveraged citizenship by maneuvering between white power blocs, backing one side with weapons and ballots, but this was hardly a heroic tale. The Law and Order Party that recruited black voters in 1842 (later the state's Whig Party) consisted of practical men. Their representative figure was Henry Bowen Anthony, editor of the *Providence Journal*, governor in 1849–51, and senator in 1859–84. With "a record nearly unmatched in the annals of American nativism," the most that can be said for Anthony is that he evidently loathed "the damned Irish" more than "the negroes." In 1869, he singlehandedly held up the Fifteenth Amendment to ensure it would not force enfranchisement of the Irish "race." In this version of politics, black men gained representation but hardly power. Unlike in New Bedford, a mere thirty-five miles away, or Portland, Rhode Island's black Whigs won neither party offices nor meaningful patronage.[2]

Rhode Island inverted the triumph of Jacksonian Democracy. The Jacksonian nightmare imagined "aristocrats" joining with "negroes" or "Indians" to subjugate white men. In Rhode Island, that paranoid dream became a fixed reality, to the consternation of Democrats everywhere, as "naturalized citizens" were put down hard. An 1846 memorial from Irishmen to the state's General Assembly bemoaned "the stigma which is thus affixed to naturalized citizens," since "the colored population . . . are allowed to exercise the right of suffrage, as freely as it is accorded to any white native citizen . . . thereby degrading naturalized citizens below the colored population." The North's free black men refused to romanticize Rhode Island's reenfranchisement, however. As Frederick Douglass acidly observed after 1848's election, "if the Whigs should nominate Satan himself, they might calculate upon a large dark vote in Rhode Island."[3]

Little Rhody

The peculiar political success of black Rhode Islanders derived from the state's antique electoral system, with a freehold franchise based on Charles II's 1664 Royal Charter. After the Revolution, northern Rhode Island experienced a remarkable industrialization led by the entrepreneur (and abolitionist) Moses Brown, who pioneered the nation's first water-powered mill with Samuel Slater in 1793. The state "dominated . . . yarn and textile production" in the early republic, and was second in production of cotton goods, after Massachusetts. By 1860, it was "the most highly industrialized state" with the majority of its workforce in factories.[4]

In contrast to this economic take-off, democracy declined sharply in Rhode Island in 1775–1840. The freehold requirement was easy to meet in a dispersed agrarian society, and had endowed the colony with an exceptionally large electorate. But as the urban population ballooned, the electorate declined. By 1840, a mere one-third of white men voted in the highest turnout since 1800. Pretensions that this bipartisan system represented the yeomanry preserving their way of life were belied by constant manufacturing of "fagot votes." An 1829 pamphlet described a leading Democrat's electoral machine. Elisha Potter's constituents were derided as "his vassals, and *his* slaves," and his control over them spelled out in detail: "Mr. Potter . . . is a great landholder. He owns many farms. . . . Did he ever lease one without an agreement, made by the tenant, not only to pay the rent, but also to vote for his landlord on all occasions? He leases corners of land for life, to poor men, to build little houses upon, and thereby become freemen. . . . They are his *men*, bound by the most *solemn* promises, to vote for *him*." With no secret ballot, such requirements were easily enforced.[5]

Lacking the requisite lease deprived a man of more than suffrage. Only freeholders could serve on juries or act as plaintiffs in most civil suits; a non-freeholder could not even get a writ without a freeholder's pledge. Nor were voters represented in any proportionate fashion. The colonial allocation of legislative seats remained in place, and the dwindling "South County" towns dominated. In 1840, Providence contained 21 percent of the state's population but elected only four of the seventy-two assemblymen, each representing 5,793 residents, while tiny Jamestown sent two representing 182 inhabitants, and ten other towns' assemblymen represented fewer than 1,000. This "quasi-feudal" arrangement was hardly accidental; as a Dorrite wrote in 1842, the Landholders (as they were called) "considered the original charter of Charles 2d, as an act of incorporation giving to the freemen of the State, and their successors, a perpetual existence as a body corporate, with powers which could not be impaired without their own consent."[6]

Most Rhode Island Democrats were profoundly nonideological, having little truck with Jeffersonian populism or Jacksonian democracy. The arch-conservative Potter (and his son of the same name) were far more representative Democrats than the would-be revolutionary Thomas Dorr. For decades, an "incongruous alliance" between "remnants of the old Federalist aristocracy and old Jeffersonian yeomanry" blocked suffrage reform, representing a rump of country landholders. Dorr came late to this party—he was a classic bourgeois radical, chameleon-like in his partisanship. His father, Sullivan Dorr, son of a prominent Massachusetts merchant, had lived in China in 1799–1803, amassing a fortune, and married into a distinguished Providence family. Thomas, born in 1805, attended Exeter and Harvard, and learned law from New York's Chancellor Kent. He was admitted to the bar in 1827, but declined a legal career. A romantic enthusiast of many causes, including abolition, he was a Whig assemblyman in the 1830s, and ran for Congress as an antislavery Democrat in 1839. By September 1840, however, Dorr had severed his abolitionist ties, joined the newly formed Suffrage Association, and was elected head of the state Democratic committee. By mid-decade, following a few months as the extralegal "People's Governor," and then exile and a conviction for treason upon his return, he had become an orthodox Negrophobic Jacksonian.[7]

During the 1820s and 1830s, equal suffrage remained an issue, but for white men only. Rhode Island resembled the proverbial frog in a pot over a low fire—nothing changed until the frog was all boiled up. "Constitutionalists" demanded a republican document with expanded voting and proportional representation, not a monarchical charter, but their campaigning had little effect. The proposed reforms almost always stipulated suffrage should remain "white," as in a draft constitution in 1824, defeated by the voters, and an 1829 rally of "mechanics" demanding the vote for all white men who paid taxes or served in the militia. Even when the workingmen's leaders Seth Luther and William I. Tillinghast called for suffrage on Massachusetts's terms, "that American citizens should be allowed to vote on condition of a specific residence in the State, and the payment of taxes," they seemed unaware that Massachusetts enfranchised black men. Patrick Conley sums up the position of the Constitutionalists in the 1830s: "all white, male, native-born citizens twenty-one and older with one year's residence in the state" should vote if they paid a property tax, but "a freehold should still be required of naturalized citizens." Dorr's 1834 *Address to the People* denounced disfranchising the majority of *white* men, although he proposed all "native-born citizens" should vote for delegates to a proposed convention. Racial disfranchisement was so axiomatic that when black freeholders petitioned in 1831 for either voting rights or "exemption from taxation," they were refused because of "the difficulty suggested by the Hon. E. R. Potter, of deciding who was black and who was not. It was feared that many men, to escape the payment of taxes, would claim to be black when they had no title to the claim." There was considerable abolitionist agitation, with a state antislavery society organized in 1836, but its leadership was entirely white. Black people attended meetings, but were never asked to speak and by 1840, Rhode Island abolitionists admitted they were "somewhat dormant."[8]

The state's substantial community of color (3,238, or 3 percent of the state's population of 108,830 in 1840, versus 8,669, not quite 1.2 percent of Massachusetts's 737,699) lived in isolated subordination, the obverse of New Bedford. In 1839, a writer in *The Liberator* attempted optimism: "At Newport a larger number of colored people attend worship than of whites, in proportion to the population. . . . It is generally thought that of beggars, the proportion is larger among the whites than blacks." This young white man detailed multiple legal restrictions, dating from colonial times, to indicate that "the colored people of this State" were still "very much oppressed." An old law granted white men licenses "for a trifling sum . . . to keep taverns, ale-houses, victualling-houses, cook-shops, &c. &c. to retail wines and strong liquors; but the colored man is denied the privilege." "Disorderly houses, if kept by negroes and mulattoes," could lead to the owners being bound out as indentured servants, and no black woman "that may have a child by a white man, shall be permitted to charge it upon him." A black civil sphere surfaced only in the 1820s, although Providence became "a center of black temperance" in the 1830s. Men of color in Boston, Salem, and Portland marched in public and voted circa 1800, but there is little evidence for that in Rhode Island, nor did the state produce businessmen like John Remond, Richard and Nathan Johnson, or Reuben Ruby and Christopher C. Manuel, let alone the Boston cohort. Black Rhode Islanders were not treated as citizens, even in the basic sense of physical security. Their most notable memoirist remembered, "Colored people had little or no protection from the law at those times, unless they resided with some white gentleman that would take up their case for them." It was common "for colored people to be disturbed on the street, especially on the Sabbath." White men would lounge in "the doorways of the stores, looking at the people as they passed, insulting them, knocking off men's hats and pulling off ladies' shawls." Unlike in Massachusetts and Maine, white plebeians wreaked havoc in black neighborhoods with little hindrance. After the 1824 Hardscrabble riot, when "the town watch prudently refrained from interfering" while twenty houses were destroyed, a few men were indicted. Their lawyer declared they had defended "the morals of the community" against "the most corrupt part of the black population," producing an acquittal. In the 1831 Olney's Lane riot, the mob proceeded unchecked for four nights, ignoring the mayor and watch until the militia arrived and, pelted with stones, fired into the crowd.[9]

Somebody Else's Revolution

Decades of caste-like segregation framed black Rhode Islanders' actions during the Dorr War. The Suffrage Association instigating that putsch saw their struggle as white man's business, and scholars have taken them at their word, incorporating African American agency on a separate track. Until the 1970s, the histories ignored black men, but narratives since then include the Dorrites' drawing the color line. This scholarship acknowledges their pillorying by abolitionists and black men for insisting on white suffrage's "expediency," and by Landholder conservatives as "mobocrats" for assaulting abolitionists, but misses black men's centrality in how the Dorr War was perceived nationally, and how the state's politics were shaped subsequently.[10]

The Dorrites' rebellion had the following chronology. In March 1840, the Suffrage Association was founded by obscure "mechanics and workingmen" who "took every precaution to avoid an entanglement with the political parties of the day." Initially, membership stipulated "any American citizen, resident in Rhode Island, of the age of twenty-one years, may become a member of this Association, by signing the Constitution." It grew rapidly into a mass movement attracting both radical democrats like Dorr and regular Democrats out of power following Van Buren's defeat in 1840. In August 1841, the Suffragists held an extralegal election for delegates to a People's Convention, which met in October–November to promulgate a "People's Constitution" proposing near-universal white manhood suffrage. In early November, a legal Landholders convention authorized by the legislature framed their own new constitution, which awarded easy suffrage to native-born whites while maintaining the property requirement for naturalized citizens. Over December 27–29, 1841, voters approved the People's Constitution in another extralegal balloting, and in May 1842, two rival governments convened in Providence, with "Governor" Dorr appealing to national Democrats to sustain his regime while hoping for President Tyler's neutrality. To break an armed standoff, Dorr and a ragtag band attempted to seize the state arsenal on May 18, 1842, and when that coup failed, he fled the state and the People's Government collapsed. Dorr returned and on June 25–28 tried to reconvene his legislature at a village near the Connecticut border, but his armed supporters melted away as state troops approached. He again went into exile in friendly Democratic states until returning in May 1844 for a treason trial that led to imprisonment for life (he was amnestied the following year). That fall, Democrats across the Union rallied under banners reading "Polk, Dallas, and Dorr!," with their editorialists denouncing how "the existing constitution of Rhode Island . . . ALLOWS NEGROES TO VOTE," and its government had "organized and armed companies of negroes" and "PLACED GUARDS OF ARMED NEGROES OVER FREE WHITE SUFFRAGE MEN," all of which was true.[11]

Historians insert African Americans in this chronology as follows. In August 1841, the state's principal black leader, Alfred Niger, tried to exploit a loophole in the rules for electing delegates to the People's Convention, which did not specify that only whites could vote; regardless, he was turned away in Providence's Sixth Ward. Anti-Suffragists broadcast this exclusion to lambaste the Dorrites' "democratic" bad faith. In response, the Suffrage Association's Executive Committee nominated Niger for treasurer in late September, but this face-saving proposal was sharply rebuffed at a general meeting. A black "remonstrance" to the People's Convention a few weeks later warned that if they put whites-only suffrage into their new constitution, "the poisoned chalice may be returned to the lips of those who departed from their principles, and retributive justice place them under severe restrictions and endurable chains." Few Suffragists cared, and a motion to strike "white" was defeated, 46–18. White abolitionists rallied against the People's Constitution in late 1841, aided by outsiders like the young Douglass, stimulating the Dorrites to violence which further tainted their cause. Finally, in summer 1842, after hundreds of black men joined Providence's home guard, their loyalty was hailed in celebrations of Dorr's defeat. The constitution ratified on November 21, 1842 gave "all native male citizens of the United States (except Narragansett Indians, convicts, paupers, persons under guardianship and non compos mentis)" the vote; a separate ballot gave electors the opportunity to add the word "white," but the Dorrites boycotted, and a new constitution with black suffrage passed overwhelmingly.[12]

Instead of examining these chronologies side-by-side, however, we should consider how the Dorr War was seen then, as a struggle for power across divisions of class and race, "native" and "naturalized," in which a biracial alliance controlled by white elites suppressed an all-white popular movement. William J. Brown, the young black leader who received a lucrative contract to feed the state militia during the Dorr War, remembered how the losers explained their defeat. An entrepreneurial shoemaker, in the late 1840s he moved to a neighborhood with "many Suffrage people," who were "not overburdened with love for the colored people." Supposedly, if "not for the colored people, they would have whipped the Algerines [meaning Landholders; 'Algerine' was a popular trope for tyrant], for their fortifications were so strong that they never could have taken them. . . . Why then did you surrender your fort, I asked, if you had eleven hundred men to defend it. They said 'Who do you suppose was going to stay there when the Algerines were coming up with four hundred bull niggers?'"[13]

According to Brown, Providence's black leaders were excluded from the Suffrage Association on grounds of expediency, plus a specious promise that if black men supported white-only suffrage, they would be rewarded later. At some point, Providence's black leaders appointed a committee "to confer with the Suffrage party and tell them if they felt oppressed we were more so, and we would unite with them for free suffrage if we could share equally with them when they obtained it." They appeared at a meeting "and laid the case before the party. One of their leaders [probably Dorr] made a long speech in our behalf. Many opposed our immediate equal union with them, but wanted us to unite and help get their rights and then they would see about ours." When the committee "were instructed to tell them we could not agree to those terms . . . the man who made the long speech said to our committee 'Report to your people that we leave you just where we found you,' and we decided to have nothing to do with them." As a disillusioned Dorrite put it, "nine tenths" of his fellows "were bitterly opposed to the admission of colored people to the ballot boxes." Once regular Democrats came on board, exclusion by color was inevitable. They would go all out for "unconditional universal suffrage; and their wide spread sympathy, and extensive benevolence, could see no way by which a citizen of the United States, resident in Rhode Island, native or foreign born, except he wore a colored skin, could be rightfully excluded from the ballot box."[14]

Black men had planted the seed for their future alliance against the "Suffrage people" by petitioning the legislature in January 1841 for the "same rights of suffrage enjoyed by their more favored white fellow citizens" or exemption from taxes. They were rudely dismissed, with "the member of the house from Newport . . . saying: *Shall* a Nigger be allowed to go to the polls and tie my vote? No, Mr. Speaker, it can't be. The taxes don't amount to more than forty or fifty dollars; let them be taken off," and they were. The Suffragists then showed their true colors. Instead of suffrage for all freeholders regardless of complexion, or keeping a decent silence, they invoked the racial exemption to back white suffrage. A March 12, 1841 meeting resolved that "by freeing the colored population from taxation," the legislature had "recognized the great principle which our forefathers fought for in the Revolution, viz. that taxation without representation is unjust. . . . Resolved, That the white non-freeholders of this State should immediately take strong action, morally and physically to free themselves from the unjust burthens imposed upon them."[15]

In fact, the Suffragists never achieved a consensus on who should vote, especially whether to include only native-born white men or all whites, and formally barred debate on this core issue. A minority of sincere democrats wished to enfranchise all male citizens without exception, but the partisan Democrats had no interest in letting "a Nigger to go to the polls." In between these two, a large party of expediency sought "the greatest good for the greatest number," which meant that "minor questions" such as whether black men or foreigners should vote must be avoided. In April 1841, the Suffragists passed a binding resolution that "we as an Association have nothing do with the qualifications of an Elector." The association's president, Dr. John A.

Brown, a "Thompsonian botanical" physician, represented this group; caught between abolitionists and Negrophobes, he spoke at length "of the great difficulty which he had had in keeping the mouths of the suffrage people shut upon this subject" at the People's Convention in November 1841.[16]

Anti-Suffragists used this irresolution to hoist the self-proclaimed "democrats" on their own petard. Even in conservative Rhode Island, open Negrophobia was risky. Eight hundred seventy-five men had signed the 1836 call for a state antislavery society and 375 attended its first meeting, a powerful constituency in an electorate of a few thousand. The Landholders perceived this weakness even before the August 1841 elections for the People's Convention, and some Suffragists intimated that Alfred Niger was an agent provocateur in attempting to vote on that occasion. The furor when he appeared, and subsequent publicity, does suggest deliberate disruption. The principal Landholder newspaper, the *Providence Journal*, reported "a little difficulty . . . in the Sixth Ward, where a respectable colored man, named Alfred Niger, offered his vote," and was "challenged on the ground that colored men had no right to vote." Both Niger and some men who came with him to the poll argued, "The call of the Convention was to the male inhabitants of lawful age, and legally resident . . . which he and his friends declared included colored men. The vote was finally rejected, and the Clerk resigned and another was elected."[17]

The main anti-Suffrage polemicist, Dorr's brother-in-law Samuel Ames, writing as "Town Born" in the *Journal*, highlighted their inconsistency, announcing, "Much fault has been found with the Association by some cavillers, because upon their own principles they do not seem inclined to admit our colored brethren to an equal participation in suffrage." Evoking the Declaration of Independence, he asked why "the mere accident of color" authorized disfranchisement—why "exclude from this large liberty, intended by God for all, those whose skins are a little darker, any more than those whose skins may by chance be a little lighter in color than our own?" Describing Niger's attempt, he explained "the Association thought it might be too great a shock to public sentiment to allow colored men the privilege," but "to avoid giving offense to our abolition friends, the call was so worded as to include them," leading to "inconsistency and double-dealing." He reproduced the Suffragists' sophistry, telling black men "Rome was not built in a day, my friends, Wait—wait patiently upon *Providence*, and your time will yet come. . . . You cannot be helped now, but you have every thing to expect from this movement hereafter," exactly as William J. Brown remembered decades later.[18]

Town Born's mockery evidently resonated, as "Several Members" of the association replied, insisting Niger's exclusion was an unfortunate accident.

They also let the cat of expediency out of the bag in explaining why their draft Constitution restricted voting to whites. Suffragists were "unanimous in favor of a liberal extension of Suffrage" and "the general principle, that payers of taxes are entitled to a voice in the appropriation of those taxes." They differed only on "minor questions" including "whether colored people shall become voters and on what terms [and] under what cautionary restrictions natural foreigners [*sic*] shall vote." To avoid quarrels, "they early passed a Resolution, not to discuss these minor points . . . but to leave them to be settled by the Convention." Attempts were made to introduce distractions, but "Dr. J. A. Brown, the President . . . has always resisted their introduction. In this course, he has always been sustained by the Association, almost unanimously." Then came the oddest piece of their tortuous explanation—the Executive Committee's nomination of Niger as the Suffrage Association's treasurer. This letter clarifies their intent, how "for the honest purpose of benefitting the cause of Suffrage, by obtaining a decided expression of the Association *against having any concern with colored people* [italics added] a colored man living in this city [Niger], was nominated for the office of Treasurer . . . against the highly respected member who fills that office." Niger's nomination was apparently intended to draw out and then suppress the abolitionist minority, as "The member who made the nomination, frankly stated that he should vote against his own nomination, and hoped others would do the same. . . . [The Association] deeming the nomination inconsiderate, refused to consider it, by a vote nearly unanimous."[19]

This pathetic effort to keep "the mouths of the suffrage people shut upon this subject" failed, however, as neither white Landholders, nor black freemen, nor abolitionists were willing to keep quiet. Soon after, black men disrupted the opening of the People's Convention with their "remonstrance" demanding nonracial suffrage. The three camps among the Suffragists debated over the next two days. The few abolitionist delegates pleaded for democratic principles, warning that taking the white line would alienate those electors who expected consistency. White supremacists dismissed that claim, with a Major Mowry sneering, "If we let niggers vote they will be elected to office; and a nigger might occupy the chair where your honor [Dr. Brown] sits. A pretty look that would be." The next day, appeals for "human rights" were dismissed by another delegate insisting they must seek "the greatest good of the greatest number, to use those means which should best insure success. (Applause) Black [*sic*] had no right to vote in neighbouring states, and under the present constitution of society, there was no sympathy between the blacks and whites. It was endangering the whole project . . . endangering the rights of 15000 white men." President Brown brusquely delivered the majority verdict: "All the towns [outside Providence] had been called the night previous, and the delegates from all but one, expressed the honest conviction that their constituents were opposed to let in the blacks." Then came the most revealing speech. Dorr was the preeminent Suffragist, with a long antislavery record, and even in spring 1842, out-of-state Whigs labeled him "the most rabid and ultra abolitionist in all of New England." His talk, surreptitiously transcribed for the *Journal*, betrayed his real impulses, that he must accept "the assertions of members relative to the feelings of their constituents," even if "they had taken counsel of their fears" rather than their principles. The People's Constitution "was not democratic in the broadest sense of the word, but he would not take up time in showing it; it was a matter of expediency, and as such, its adoption must be considered." Having signaled his acquiescence, Dorr eulogized black Revolutionary soldiers, with more "eloquent remarks upon the great principles involved." The vote was 46–18 in favor of keeping "white," and no one walked out. Like the majority, Dorr was interested in power, whether for himself, the "fifteen thousand" white men he claimed to represent, or both.[20]

Dorr's realpolitik was underlined when the People's Convention reconvened in mid-November, as abolitionists mobilized to defeat the People's Constitution in the popular ratification vote set for the end of December. Dorr argued against allowing them to speak, saying time "would be taken up without any change of opinion . . . and would open the whole subject again." More than that, he baited them, saying the Suffragists "were fully able to take care of ourselves. If we could not do the business we were sent to do, others should be sent to do it—and he did not wish people, perhaps from other States, to dictate to us what to do." Disparaging abolitionists as foreign meddlers opened the door to mobbing, suggesting Dorr was more the demagogue contemporaries saw than a "people's martyr." These events, from Niger's rejection at the polls through Dorr's word-twisting, cast obloquy on the Suffragists, and Town Born again parodied their explanations to black men: "Divided from us at your birth, you must be separated from us even in the great change that we propose. . . . You must sit in *the gallery* here, as in our Meeting-houses and Theatres. You may ride along in the same train of revolution with us if you please, but alas! it *must be* in the James Crow car!!! . . . We must not avow at this time that 'all men are created free and equal,' but are obliged to restrict this unmeaning generality and act as if all white men only were created free and equal." This mockery was a prelude to how race undid the Suffrage cause.[21]

Mobocrats and Democrats

To stop the People's Constitution, radical Garrisonians and Rhode Island reactionaries briefly turned bedfellows. Town Born had already made the

Suffragists' racialism ridiculous, and the Rhode Island Anti-Slavery Society (RIASS) declared "a combined and vigorous effort" against "the gross inconsistency of this free suffrage movement." *The Liberator* announced "Stirring Meetings in Rhode Island" during December by a corps of agitators, including Stephen Foster, Abby Kelley, Parker Pillsbury, and the young Douglass: "Woonsocket, on the 2d and 3d inst.; and another at North Scituate, on the 7th and 8th. . . . At Fiskville and Phenix, on the 14th and 15th; at Kingston, on the 21st and 22d; at Newport, on the 24th and 25th; and at Providence, on the 27th and 28th."[22] These sorties demonstrated how effective the Garrisonians could be inside conventional politics. Moral radicals need a hard target—a visibly odious wrong. The Suffragists' pharisaical justifications for demanding popular democracy while denying black suffrage provided that. Abolitionists then deliberately delegitimized the Suffrage cause by inviting assaults, which angered many who cared little about black rights but were disgusted by the Dorrites' suppressing free speech.

Encouraged by their leaders, white Suffragists mobbed the abolitionists' meetings, attacking speakers. In Newport, "one of the strongest . . . holds of slavery, in New-England," Abby Kelley described how her "first meeting was disturbed by certain 'persons of standing' [including] D. J. Pearce, a former member of Congress. . . . Brother P. [Pillsbury] was stamped down, and Pierce [*sic*] made an inflammatory speech, appealing to the old pro-slavery prejudice." Pearce charged that these radicals "were employed by the landed aristocracy, to defeat the people's Constitution; as foreign intruders, and impudent intermeddlers." Her final meeting was "broken up by a mob of between 500 and 1000, which followed myself and friends to our lodgings . . . pelting us with decayed apples, eggs, &c." Kelley was quite satisfied with the effects: "Few can see a crowd following a defenceless woman through the streets, hurling missiles at her, and shouting like so many fiends, without inquiring 'why?'" In Providence, she met "a still more boisterous and malignant crowd, determined to drown every voice that was raised," after which she "went home, accompanied again by the howls and snow-balls of the suffrage party."[23]

These attacks clarified the Dorrites' real nature, and the Landholders' chief ideologist, Brown professor William G. Goddard, weighed in under various pseudonyms. In December 1841, he too mocked the Suffragists for contending "every white man" should vote. "Why," he asked, "upon their own principles, exclude black men?" After the mobbing began, Goddard pilloried the Dorrites as men who "violated . . . in the most shameful manner, the liberty of speech. The Anti-Slavery men found that they could discuss, without interruption, all subjects, save one. Whenever they assailed what they deemed to be an objectionable provision relative to suffrage . . . king mob kindled into fury." The Suffragists had stripped themselves bare, and Dorr was shown to be personally complicit. In August 1842, an RIASS leader described how "at one of these riotous meetings" in Providence, Dorr entered the hall "and stood some fifteen or twenty minutes a looker on. He saw and heard the hissing and the shuffling of feet, whenever a speaker referred to the Suffrage Constitution. Five words from him might have made all quiet—but, no! He walked silently out—plainly intimating to his party, Go on—stop the freedom of speech, lest our Constitution be disgraced in the eyes of the people." After describing the organized disruptions, he captured Dorr's reasoning from "expediency": "I know, says he, the word white is wrong, but a majority would have it in the Constitution," and if these abolitionists tried to show that inconsistency, then "drown their voices by hisses and yells, stamping the feet, stoning and snow-balling the windows; follow them home, and pelt them with snow-balls, until they enter their dwellings. And this they did, repeatedly, and Thomas W. Dorr never opened his mouth to stop it. I therefore put Thomas W. Dorr down as a mobocrat."[24]

The People's Constitution was approved handily, nonetheless, but in early 1842, the Landholders legislature drove a wedge into the Suffragist coalition by amending the Constitution to enfranchise all native-born whites, while keeping the freehold requirement for immigrants (on Christmas Eve, Goddard had painted a nativist dystopia, that "the political power of the State is to be wrested from the farmers, and confided to the hands of the foreign population . . . now rapidly accumulating in our cities and manufacturing villages. . . . These people, strangers to our interests—slaves to their own passions . . . the tools of crafty politicians, will govern the state"). An armed standoff steadily escalated from April to June, with two governors, two legislatures, and two state militias occupying Providence. In reality, however, their power was never really balanced. After passing a law criminalizing participation in Dorr's administration, the "Charter Government" began jailing prominent Suffragists, and the Dorrites' lack of nerve revealed itself, with many of their leaders recusing themselves; by that time, Boston's Catholic bishop had informed his priests in Providence that their flock was interdicted from participating in the People's Government.[25]

Neither side paid much attention to black men until June 1842. The first stage of the Dorr War had begun at 2 A.M. on May 18, when Dorr marched on the state armory with 200 men but failed to attack it, after which his force disintegrated and he fled. Men of color came into the narrative five weeks later when Dorr crossed the border, and rumors swept Providence he had amassed a force to loot and pillage. The Charter Government gathered 3,500 men to attack Dorr's encampment and the Afro-Yankees inserted themselves. On the same day the Charter forces drove armed Dorrites from Chepachet

Village near the Connecticut border, the *Providence Journal* reported, "The COLORED POPULATION of our city have come forward in the most honorable manner, and taken upon themselves the charge of the fire engines . . . to assist in the protection of property from fire and plunder, while the other inhabitants are engaged in the defense of the State." In an era when "incendiaries" burning towns was the trope of revolution, "taking charge of the fire engines" was urgent. Many, like Brown's president Francis Wayland, believed the Dorrites intended to fire the city. Black men did more than watch for arson. They also joined the Volunteer Police Corps, a thousand-man home guard to patrol a city full of disloyal Suffragists. An eyewitness reported they were mustered "in the ranks according to their height and I saw no manifestation of disrespect . . . all praised and honored them for their noble devotion to the interest of the great cause of regulated civil liberty." The implications of armed black men enforcing martial law were clear in a June 27 "Notice from Mayor Thomas M. Burgess" requiring "all persons, not on patrol or other duty . . . to retire to their homes by ten o'clock. . . . In case of alarm of fire, the Police Companies will immediately assemble at their alarm-posts under arms. . . . All persons are cautioned not to attack or insult any patrol or guard: such offenses will be severely punished. . . . The patrols and guards must be obeyed."[26]

That the Dorrites never laid siege to Providence did not diminish black men's service. In mid-July, the *Journal* noted, "We have several times spoken of the conduct of the colored population, during the difficulties which have beset this State. Not only did they volunteer to take charge of the fire department, but many of them attached themselves to the military companies and performed a great deal of fatiguing duty." It quoted the *New York Courier*, a leading conservative Whig paper: "The colored people of Rhode Island deserve the good opinion and kind feelings of every citizen of the State, for their conduct during the recent troublous times in Providence," adding the encomium, "The fathers of these people were distinguished for their patriotism and bravery in the war of the revolution." In mid-July, an abolitionist recorded, "Their services were generally applauded. . . . Colored servants were cordially welcomed to the parlors and front windows of their masters, to witness the military displays. They were no longer repulsed and treated as an infamous race, but the courteous bow, or welcome smile, greeted them at every corner of the street"; briefly, it was as if "the whole city had become abolitionists in one night." Embedded in this letter was the first record of a startling fact—the Charter government's offer of suffrage. "The Charterists" made themselves the "best friends" of black Rhode Islanders by proposing "to them the direct enjoyment of the elective franchise." On June 23, 1842, with Dorr still at Chepachet, the legislature called for elections to a September constitutional convention with voting open to all native-born men without distinction of color and no property requirement. This offer had brought out the black volunteers, since, while it gave the Charter government "credit more for their ingenuity, than for an open and manly defence of human rights," it was "successful in securing the confidence of the colored people, and about one hundred are said to have immediately volunteered to take up arms for the landholders."[27]

Providence's 1840 population was 23,171, and a disciplined biracial Police Corps incorporating 100 or more black men could hardly escape notice; in mid-July, the *Journal* reported, "The colored men were among the earliest on the ground" at an incident of "INCENDIARIANISM." Erik Chaput has assembled impressive evidence of hard-bitten "Law and Order" men, as they now styled themselves, swayed by the sight of black men in arms. On July 22, Elisha Potter, Jr. (son of the reactionary Democrat), wrote former governor John Brown Francis that "there is not so much scolding about letting the blacks vote as we expected. They pass it off this way, that they would rather have the negroes vote than the d___d Irish." Brown's president Wayland wrote Whig senator James Simmons, "To allow native born colored citizens to vote like other citizens" was reasonable, since "in our late troubles," they had "proved themselves worthy of the right of suffrage; they were to a man the friends of liberty and law and order." Their loyalism resonated nationally. One week after Dorr's flight, a Georgia Democratic newspaper railed, "The negroes of Rhode Island are being armed, and organized into companies for the purpose of assisting the *King* [Governor Samuel King] in putting down Gov. Dorr and the Suffrage Party," equating Whig opposition to Dorrism with Negrophilia: "Thus they go, 'cheek by jowl' against the rights of freemen; the negro with his musket and the whig editor with his quill." Conversely, Truman Smith, a Connecticut Whig congressman, defended the Navy's employing black sailors by evoking "the noble band of negroes in Providence who had volunteered to protect the city from the torch of the barn burning incendiaries." Adding insult to the Dorrites' humiliation, during Providence's July 5 victory parade, "a band of colored musicians" marched, "playing upon the instruments which were taken from Dorr's band at Chepachet"; the parade also featured each ward's integrated City Guards.[28]

After Dorr's ignominious flight, his supporters resembled the Rebels of 1865, seething in defeat. In mid-August, *The Liberator* interviewed a disillusioned Dorrite who described their easy descent into racialism, how Niger "was abused and driven away" in August 1841, and then, "at a caucus while their Convention was in session, it was declared from all quarters, that it would not do to leave out the word white in the qualification of voters." The Charterists' proffer of suffrage to black men was specified. They had "called a Convention, and nobly refused to make any distinction in the voters," so his fellow Dorrites derided them as "the milk and molasses party. Such epithets, and worse, he heard among the men . . . when preparing to leave for the camp at Chepachet. News of the call of the Convention had that day been received; and nigger party, 'checker-board party,' 'amalgamationists,' were the terms heaped upon them."[29]

Permanent voting rights were not guaranteed, however. Nonracial voting for a September constitutional convention and the November ratification election extended the tradition of the Revolutionary era, when "all men" participated in framing constitutions. At the convention, delegates wavered and black men petitioned. The franchise committee proposed "white" suffrage, but were opposed on various grounds. Suffrage was finally referred to another committee, which suggested enfranchising "every native white male citizen" who either paid "a tax of one dollar or perform[ed] Military or Engine duty." This too was refused, and they returned with an article specifying suffrage for "every white male native citizen," who had "paid a personal or registry tax of one dollar" and every other "male citizen" with a "freehold estate . . . of the value of one hundred and thirty-four dollars . . . or which shall rent for seven dollars per annum," putting black men and the foreign-born in the same second tier. This also was rejected, and finally a "Mr. Jackson offered a resolution for submitting the question of Blacks being allowed to vote, in a separate article to the People," which was agreed, with the entire suffrage motion passing, 53–12. November's election included a separate ballot, asking, "Shall the blank in the first line of Section second of Article second of said Constitution be filled by the word WHITE?" Law and Order leaders either hoped to assuage racialist feeling among their base or presumed black suffrage would pass, and men of color turned out in large numbers. The new constitution retaining the freehold qualification for naturalized citizens passed 7,024–51, and only 1,004 (24 percent) of the 4,161 who voted on black suffrage chose to add "white," the single instance of an antebellum electorate approving black men voting.[30]

The year 1842 was the heroic moment for Rhode Island's men of color. They had gotten all they would get, a recognized place in a state's electoral politics. In the next election, in April 1843, they again carried the day, with the *Providence Journal* affirming that "in five of the seven towns which the Dorrites have carried, the foreign and floating population . . . smothered the voice of the real, substantial, home-bred population," but fortunately elsewhere, "the colored voters have almost unanimously voted to maintain the laws [and] have given the most satisfactory proof of their fitness for the exercise of the franchise"; angry Dorrites reported that black voters had "marched like slaves to the townhouses [city halls] to vote" in Providence and Bristol.[31]

The victory of Rhode Island's "checkerboard" Law and Order Party, de facto Whigs, immediately entered the national debate. The Democrats' *Washington Globe* declared the party line that the Dorrites were "put down by the Algerines and negroes combined," and their Ohio organ charged, "The voting is exclusively among the Algerines, the enemies of a poor white man voting at all, and more especially if he happens to be a naturalized *foreigner*." Local Dorrites echoed this language, as William J. Brown remembered. He was in a store in 1842 when a wealthy man who "had loaned them [the Dorrites] twelve thousand dollars to carry out their object" announced, "I have concluded to fight; them Algerines have got the niggers to help them out, and I will not stand it. I think it the duty of every man to come up and help, when niggers are allowed to vote against us."[32]

Rhode Island Suffragists' advocacy of extralegal, plebiscitary mass democracy also provoked an open split between Northern and Southern Democrats. The latter never accepted the Suffragist claim that a simple majority of "the people" established sufficient sovereignty to replace the constitutional order, fearing that that logic might empower *all* "people," even slaves, to participate in government. The Democracy's contradictions were on display, and a bipartisan South condemned Dorrism as, in John C. Calhoun's words, the "death-blow of constitutional democracy." Northern Democrats responded with a widely disseminated report by New Hampshire congressman Edmund Burke, *Rhode Island in 1842*, commonly known as *Burke's Report*. It relied on John S. Harris, secretary of the People's Convention; hardly a workingman, he was "the owner of dwelling-houses and other real estate . . . owner of stock in several of the banks." Harris emphasized how their cause faced black and abolitionist opposition, and a sympathetic Burke reprinted the black "remonstrance" to the People's Convention, and Harris's declaration that "nearly the whole of the lectures and speeches made in opposition" to the People's Constitution "were made by the abolition society." To reassure southerners, Harris stressed that his colleagues knew "something about the different races of mankind" and "well understood . . . *the political meaning in civil government in this country of the word* PEOPLE. They have never contended, and they never will contend, that it means, or signifies ALIENS, INDIANS, OR SLAVES." Whether free persons of color were part of "the people" was left unclear.[33]

The Whiggery's Rise and Fall

There were several constants to Rhode Island's politics from 1844 to 1854, when the long-dominant Whigs finally fractured: first, black Whigs as a reliable balance of power; second, the sympathy felt by white Whigs for their colored allies versus the "foreign" danger; finally, how the Whig-Negro alliance was denounced outside the state.

Nativism drove Rhode Island's politics. Universal manhood suffrage would have redrawn the electoral map: in 1860, there were only 1,260 naturalized voters in a population of 17,368 foreign-born white males (two-thirds Irish) versus 66,723 native-born men; if all the former voted, the electorate would have expanded dramatically, destroying the old order. This population remained almost entirely disfranchised until 1885, as the "refusal to sell land to Catholic immigrants prevented them from acquiring political rights." Anti-foreign polemics, often just vulgar slurs on "papists," had been ubiquitous but took on a new urgency following the Dorr War. Charles Jackson, heading the Liberation ticket promising to free Dorr, won the governorship by a mere 149 votes in 1845. When he came up for reelection in 1846, Law and Order Party handbills quoted Democrats saying they would "OFFSET THE IRISHMEN AGAINST THE NIGGERS," by getting rid of the property requirement for naturalized citizens, and then asked: "Admit Irishmen to vote without restriction, and what influence is left to native citizens? Have we come to this, that a farmer in the county of Washington, who is possessed of his acres, and who has always lived there, is to have his vote *tied* by an Irishman who has just come over?" Those farmers would "become the slaves of *Roman Catholic tyrany* [sic]! The Pope of Rome has but to issue his mandate to the *priests*, and those priests will ever after control all your elections."[34]

Such charges heated up again in the early 1850s, when Democrats challenged Whig control, typified by the *Providence Journal*'s declaration that "Rhode Island is in the hands of the men of Rhode Island. We propose to keep it in such hands. Our opponents propose practically to annex it to Ireland." When the Democrats won in 1853, they proposed genuinely democratic reforms, including permitting the $1 "registry tax" to be paid up to three days before an election instead of by the prior December 31, reducing residency to six months, and permitting "any man who found his name *not* on the voting list" to vote "after swearing he was a qualified voter," a red flag to Whigs fearing the "scum and filth of New York" would be imported as voters. The Whigs defeated two referenda on calling a constitutional convention, and returned to power in 1854; in 1855, the Know-Nothings (essentially conservative Whigs) swept Rhode Island. The new General Assembly asked the state's congressional delegation "to urge . . . a law imposing severe penalties against the introduction or importation into this country of foreign paupers and foreign criminals," since they would "corrupt the public morals and endanger the public safety." Congress should amend naturalization "to require a previous continuous residence of twenty-one years in this country to enable an alien to become a citizen." These resolutions had no legal force, but that legislature also "unanimously passed an act forbidding all justices and judges in the State to take cognizance of petitions of aliens to become naturalized citizens of the United States," a policy underlining the relative status of the native-born, including black men, over immigrants.[35]

Outside the state, Democrats maintained their outrage. In 1852, a Lancaster, Pennsylvania, newspaper published "A Catechism for Adopted Citizens," asking, "Who were in favor of allowing negroes to vote in Rhode Island, but were against giving the same privileges to foreigners?" and the New Hampshire Democratic organ reminded readers that the 1842 Law and Order constitution "gives negroes rights and privileges which it denies to naturalized foreigners, for negroes can vote without property," while voting rights for immigrants were a "scare-crow, held up by the federal [i.e., Whig] leaders to deter the people from entrusting the government to Democrats." Such charges were accurate. The state's otherwise reactionary Whigs *did* describe slavery as "a great evil, moral, political, and social"; they *were* "in favor of its abolition" and would "do anything fairly within the Constitution to accomplish that object." The *Providence Journal* affirmed its respect for black people with "a candor which should put to blush some of its Whig contemporaries," reported Douglass, declaring, "We do not regard the colored population as an evil to be got rid of. We know that here they form a valuable part of the community; and if they are not so elsewhere, we think that part of the fault is to be found in the disabilities under which they are placed. . . . The colored race is capable of self-government and of high cultivation." We cannot presume bad faith in these declarations. In 1855, a white man wrote Douglass about his five-year sojourn in Providence. Outraged by a recent Horace Greeley polemic insisting free people of color were "indolent, improvident, and licentious," he reported white Rhode Islanders appreciated their "industry, providence and purity of morals," citing the "uniform sentiment" of employers that "they are a very industrious, well behaved class; I do not know how we should get along without them; I had much rather employ them than the Irish; they are more trustworthy."[36]

Rhode Island's black Whigs set themselves apart from other black politicos by displaying their strict party regularity. In December 1844, some of them went into the RIASS's annual meeting "to create a disturbance" by denouncing Frederick Douglass. In November, he had visited, and because "most of the colored voters in the State [had] voted for Clay," he "felt it his duty to rebuke them for their recreancy, and did so, in the most kind and considerate, but plain and uncompromising manner." Not surprisingly, "this gave great offence . . . and one of them came into the [December] meeting and presented a string of resolutions, rebuking Douglass for his interference, and complaining severely of his injustice." Whigs were evidently concerned about voter disaffection ("there was more or less disposition among certain politicians, to urge the disaffected portion of the colored men to get up a disturbance"). Subsequently, "the Whig colored population" publicly rebuked "the insulting remarks of Mr. Douglass towards the voters of this State who voted for Henry Clay," attacking with "bitter indignation" not only him (they would "treat the remarks with that contempt that the author justly deserves") but abolitionists in general, declaring "as freemen" and "true Whigs," they were "friends to social order, true to our fellow-man, to our God, and to our country."[37]

Rhode Island's black men remained Whigs for as long as the party existed. They played no role in the state's tiny Liberty Party or its Free Soil successor dominated by former Democrats. Birney got five votes in the state in 1844, and its Liberty Party only organized in 1846, gaining a mere 243 votes for their 1847 gubernatorial candidate. The only notable antislavery politician was Democrat Thomas Davis, a longtime RIASS leader, himself an Irish immigrant (albeit a Protestant), and the sole departure from black Whiggism came when he "seduced" black voters in his 1853 congressional race, a claim backed up by Henry Anthony's *Providence Journal*. Following a black anticolonization meeting that June, Bowen published a tirade insisting "the colored people of this city have acted very foolishly" since "the plan of colonization is one of the greatest and most beneficent ideas of modern times" and would "elevate the colored race by giving to them the mighty work of civilizing a continent." Certainly, "forced colonization" was "unrighteous" since "the negroes have a good place here, and a good right here. They fill useful stations in society, and the loss of many of them would be a misfortune to the rest of the community." His attack was clarified by the comment, "The greater part of them, at the last election, deserted the old friends who had always stood by them. . . . The colored men who sold their votes for money to the Democratic party at the last election turned this city against us. . . . The colored people have given the power in the State to the Democrats, and the consequence is, that we are to have a new constitution, which will extend the suffrage to everybody else, and will take it from the colored men," although the Democrats' failed constitutional revision did not racialize suffrage. Local Free Soilers (who had appealed for black votes in 1852) huffed that some backed the Democrats "because Mr. Davis, who had been known all over the State as an abolitionist, sanctioned that ticket by his name, and labored, personally, for its success.—They did not see that in voting for him, they were voting . . . for the deep slaveocracy which is now the very life blood of that party." Just as likely, black men ignored Free Soilism because that party gave equal priority to enacting prohibition and combating "the intrigues of Catholicism" as to antislavery, ignoring free black people. Like the Whigs, Rhode Island's Free Soilers insisted, "A Roman Catholic cannot be a republican, either in theory or practice."[38]

Whiggism ran deep. In 1847, when the local Liberty Party imported a prominent ex-slave, Henry Bibb, William J. Brown remembered with satisfaction how on Election Day, Bibb arrived at the polls and "taking up a Liberty ticket he said, 'I hope the colored people will sustain this ticket.' Several of our people being present and knowing that that ticket was nothing more than Democratic bait to draw off the colored voters, came down with vengeance on the tickets, much to the great surprise of Bibb. . . . We made him understand it was not all gold that glitters. He left our quarters and went about his business, and the Law and Order [Whig] party elected their candidates."[39]

Apparently, Whigs did more than argue. Weeks later, Bibb recorded how "perfectly disgusted" he was "at the professors of religion with *Deacon G. Williams* of Providence, at their head, leading them on to vote . . . for the so called *law* and *order* party . . . but another name for the pro-slavery *whig* party. The people are grossly deceived and misled by the leaders of this party. They went so far as to print Liberty with law and order over some of their tickets, and telling the colored people that they were the true Liberty Party." Bibb's evidently confused the name of one of the black Whigs: "Deacon G. Williams" was almost certainly the Baptist Deacon George Willis, a prominent man since the 1820s.[40]

In 1848, the Free Soil Party pulled black votes throughout New England, but not in Rhode Island. Van Buren got 6 percent in Providence and 6.6 percent statewide, but these were from white Democrats, and black men could have doubled his total in the city. Local Free Soilers hoped "the colored voters of this State would array themselves under the banner of Free Soil," but instead "they went over in a body to the enemy. . . . They deserted the ranks of that band who were their true friends . . . [and] voted for the man who holds hundreds of human beings in Slavery [Zachary Taylor]." The *Providence Journal* exulted, "The vote of this class of citizens last Tuesday was highly creditable. Notwithstanding the extraordinary exertions which were made to seduce them from their allegiance to the party with which they have always acted, only four of them so far as we can learn, voted for Van Buren." One week later, during the RIASS's annual meeting, "some persons about the door of the hall gave three cheers for Gen. Taylor, whereupon F. Douglass proposed three cheers for Liberty. . . . Three more were given about the door for 'Old Zack,' when F. D. proposed that the same persons give three cheers for 'Old Zack's' three hundred slaves, which, after some hesitation, were given." Given the prior ill-feeling, those hecklers were probably black. These antagonisms persisted. Two years later, "Old Zack's" successor, Millard

Fillmore, signed the Fugitive Slave Act and Samuel Ringgold Ward, a black Liberty Party leader, laid the blame on "the black men of Rhode Island who voted for this administration." They were "among the guiltiest of the men responsible for this bill. Let them face their own doings." If taken as runaways, "they will endure but the legitimate results of their abominably wicked treachery to the cause of freedom, in 1848. To say, hereafter, that the Whig party is better than the Democratic party, is to utter a falsehood, refutable by reference to this kidnapping, Whig bill."[41]

From the Bottom Up: A Wardheeler's Perspective

References to Providence's black Whiggery usually echo Ward's disdain, but from the inside, what mattered was not the "cause of freedom," but party regularity and respect. Providence contained 356 men of color in the 1850 census, a reliable balance of power. Statewide, Robert Cottrol estimated their 700 to 1,000 voters as 4 to 6 percent of the electorate. Black men often provided the victory margin; in 1843, Law and Order gubernatorial candidate James Fenner won Providence by 150 votes (2,632 to 2,482) over the Suffragist Thomas F. Carpenter, and would have lost the city minus black ballots. The Law and Order Whigs constantly proclaimed their agency in enfranchising blacks. In 1848, they urged a "vote for the Whig electors . . . you know the party to which they belong and to which you belong, the party . . . which extended to you the right of suffrage." This counterpoint of party appeals and abolitionist disapproval only begins this story, however. Fortunately, the principal black Whig left a record, *The Life of William J. Brown*. Apparently transcribed verbatim, since Brown was blind and in a nursing home, his tales of obscure political skirmishes appear out of sequence. What comes through is the voice of a party man who took care of himself first, much like a Tammany committeeman bringing out his ward's Irish voters. Through these anecdotes, we see the complexity of relationships among black people and between black men and white politicians.[42]

Brown was twenty-seven during the Dorr Rebellion, already a successful shoemaker in an era when "no colored men except barbers had trades, and that could hardly be called a trade. . . . To drive a carriage, carry a market basket after the boss, and brush his boots, or saw wood and run errands, was as high as a colored man could rise." He was a social entrepreneur, at thirteen forming the Young Men's Union Funds Society, the nucleus of his later machine, including Charles Cozzens, George Willis, Jr., and Charles Burrell. Three decades after the Dorr War, he described it entirely in terms of black men taking advantage of white men's troubles. The alliance with the Law and

Order Party came up only in passing, for its practical aspects; while other black men integrated into the Police Companies, he and another man "went to work cooking for the soldiers, and remained eleven weeks, during which time the soldiers took the fort at Chepachet."[43]

Brown's memory was specific regarding his recruitment as a party worker, mustering votes for the Law and Order constitution in late 1842. Suffragists "threatened to mob any colored person daring to vote that day." In a scene remarkably similar to election days during Radical Reconstruction, he and other leaders gathered several hundred men the night before, ready to go to the polls armed: "In order to keep them we must have something to eat, for if the Democrats got hold of them we could not get them to vote, for they would get them filled up with rum so that we could not do a thing with them; so in order to secure them we had to hunt them up, bring them to the armory, and keep men there to entertain them." After gathering "coffee, crackers, cheese . . . shaved beef" and "a lot of muskets," they were ready. "When the polls were opened, those in the first ward went to vote in a body, headed by two powerful men." A hostile contemporary account adds veracity to his memory, describing upper-class Whigs serving a repast of "boiled ham, tongues . . . with a sufficiency of the wherewithal to wash it down" to poor black men, "bustling about with assumed importance, endorsing the dark-ies' names on their tickets, and filling their plates with the most delicate vi-ands. After they were well filled, these waiting white men marshaled the colored corps, and marched them to the polls." For years, Democrats alleged that Providence's colored men voted for "crackers, cheese, and ham," and Brown remained indignant that in 1847, Douglass himself "said he had heard we were bought up on election day on crackers and cheese. . . . He received his information from an Abolitionist in the Democratic party."[44]

White leaders took black votes for granted until 1847, when a Democratic victory loomed (perhaps because they encouraged the Liberty Party to run a ticket, Brown alleged). A Whig named Henry L. Bowen, who had served as "a special commissioner" in 1842 "to examine all persons arrested under martial law, and to commit or discharge the same as the circumstances of the cases may require," offered Brown money to round up black voters. Bowen had formerly relied on James Hazard, whom Brown disparaged as "a man who liked to have people think he was worth twice as much as he really was." Hazard's men were ineffective and appealed to Brown to bring out his group. The reason for the decline is intriguing: "Many colored voters were not able to write their names, and disliked getting some one at the town house [city hall, controlled by Whigs] to write for them, and so refused on that account, the Law and Order party became weakened thereby." Brown made a deal with

Bowen: "Mr. Balch was there to do the writing, and I was there to see that my men voted right." The Whigs won, and Brown received $2, two days' wages.[45]

The year 1848 was Brown's hardest time. Briefly, Free Soilers imagined winning the North via a coalition of Liberty men, antislavery Whigs, and Barnburner Democrats who hated southerners more than Negroes. In Rhode Island, the Free Soilers were former Suffragists, presenting Brown with a quandary. The Whig candidate "was a slaveholder, Zachary Taylor. We did not like the idea of voting for a slaveholder and called a meeting on South Main street to see what we should do." He went reluctantly, "fearing it would prove injurious to my interest. I was in that part of the city working at shoe making, my custom was good, and I knew that if I attended that meeting and spoke in favor of the Whig candidate, I should lose [local whites'] custom and perhaps get hurt." That coda, "and perhaps get hurt," suggests Brown's difficult position: a neighborhood full of Suffragists resented his electoral clout but black electors might view his Taylorism as betrayal. The meeting was "packed with people, and about one hundred and fifty people filled out to the hall door." Fortunately for Brown, George Willis opened the discussion, saying, "We must be decided in favor of one party or the other, and his opinion was of the two evils, we must choose the least; and his choice was in favor of Zachary Taylor, the Whig candidate," as if the Free Soilers did not exist. Others "in harsh terms denounced the Democratic party." Finally, the crowd insisted on hearing from Brown. He declared, "We were not to decide upon the man, but the party. If we were to decide on the candidate, it would be not to cast a vote for Taylor, for he is a slaveholder; and this I presume is the feeling of every colored voter, but we are identified with the Whig party, and it is the duty of every colored person to cast his vote for the Whig party, shutting his eyes against the candidate; as he is nothing more than a servant for the party." Having demonstrated that a Louisiana slaveholder, the hero of the Mexican War, was no better than a black man, all equally servants of the party, he "sat down amid loud cheering."[46]

Brown repeatedly returned to how the 1848 election gave him leverage in the party. To Henry Bowen, he implied threats: "Now . . . we are called to act with the party whose candidate is a slave-holder," and "we cannot conscientiously vote for such a man [ignoring their 1844 votes for Henry Clay]. The Democrats are running a Liberty and Free Soil ticket, and calling on the colored voters as abolitionists to sustain them." Brown wanted to run his own campaign, with his own headquarters. Bowen told him, "Hire as many men as you want . . . and when the election is over make out a bill of all your expenses and I will settle it." Brown became a boss. The Whigs elected a governor in September, and in the presidential race, "I drummed up the colored voters. . . . We were successful and carried the election; Mr. Bowen was praised for his skillful management, and I beat the bush while he carried off the bird." Bowen's skill getting out the vote earned him Providence's postmastership. Brown's reward was a measure of white respect, and some actual birds. He had "stepped into Mr. Hall's grocery to get some groceries" and Hall addressed him respectfully, "'Here, Mr. Brown, is something left for you.' He went to the back part of his store and brought me a fine pair of chickens. I asked who sent them. He said 'Uncle Zach. Taylor.' I said, 'give my compliments to Uncle Zach, and tell him, with pleasure I receive them.'" Brown then visited his father "on Sunday afternoon, as I was accustomed to do," and "Father asked me what great speech I had been making." The father was "downtown with his wagon," and a white businessman "hallowed after him" and "came to the wagon with a large turkey in his hand, saying, 'Noah, I was at a meeting not long since, and heard William. . . . He made a first-rate speech; I couldn't have made a better one if I had tried myself, and I am going to give you this turkey for having such a son.'"[47]

Brown was assiduous. After the election, Bowen had him "go around and see if there were strangers that had been here long enough to vote, and see that their names were registered, and at the next election they would pay me. I collected quite a number," much as Democrats enrolled recent Irish immigrants. His capacity to move a large constituency drew notice. Eventually his landlord, a Democrat, pressured him to deliver votes and gain the landlord a patronage appointment. Brown replied with dignity, "We are identified with the Whig party, who . . . had given the colored people the power of elective franchise. I am thereby brought under deeper obligations to sustain that class of our community . . . in preference to all others."[48]

Brown's memoir mixed frankness and silence. He completely omitted the struggle for "equal school rights" before the war, led by the wealthy ex–New Yorker George T. Downing, and his overall elision of the 1850s suggests the Whigs' patronage system had run its course. In this context, Brown's relationships with "that class of our community," Providence's entrenched upper class, bears examination. Brown conveyed those ties in describing how his patron, Robert H. Ives, visiting him at an asylum for the blind near Boston after shoemaking ruined his eyes. Brown's fellow white inmates were shocked by Ives's solicitude, wanting "to know if that was the millionaire that sent me there. . . . They were surprised to see him sit down beside me and be so sociable. I told them the rich white people of Providence associate with all respectable colored people; and we associate with them, because from them comes our support," adding as an afterthought, "We also are in harmony with the poorer class of white people, and treat them well."[49]

In Brown's stories, eminent family names constantly recur as a network of clientage. "Mr. Ives" was a partner in Brown & Ives, the city's most important mercantile house (other than Moses, the Brown brothers were famous slave traders, and one owned William J. Brown's grandfather—thus his surname). Brown was born in a house owned by Dr. Pardon Bowen, whose half-brother Jabez Bowen, Sr., was the state's deputy governor in 1781–86. The latter's son was Henry Bowen, secretary of state in 1819–49, and *his* son, Henry L. Bowen, was Brown's party boss. In his own eyes, Brown's connections to these families marked him as superior to Irishmen and factory laborers, even if the latter did not agree. He also knew the politician Wingate Hayes, elected Speaker of Rhode Island's House in 1859. Brown boasted how Hayes had secured his Young Men's Friendly Union Society "the first charter ever granted to a colored society of Rhode Island" in 1844. During the school integration fight, Hayes led the opposition, which suggests why Brown kept silent.[50]

In the 1850s, leadership passed from Brown to the hotelier George T. Downing, proprietor of Newport's Sea-Girt House "on the Downing block." Downing extended the region's tradition of carriage-trade militancy dating from John Remond and Prince Hall, and white elites welcomed his New York–style "spacious and elegant hotel." He also challenged structures of subordination long accepted by black families. Brown labored in the interstices of party as a broker, playing off one white man against another. He could not have imagined himself sitting in the legislature's gallery trading quips with reporters while he was attacked on the floor, as Downing reported doing in 1859. Brown remembered his service to "rich white people," whereas Downing was never a servant, and grew up thinking of rich whites as his equal. His father, Thomas, was a restaurateur lauded as "the Delmonico of New York" by Governor Samuel Tilden, and on his death in 1903, the younger Downing's friendships with men like Charles Sumner were celebrated. Downing was simultaneously transgressive and authoritative. He brought New York's autonomous black political culture with him and had little time for the Rhode Island's parochialism, dismissing its black leaders in *Frederick Douglass' Paper* soon after arrival. Nonracial suffrage was a "happy incident" of the Dorr War, but "the party benefited by this incident, have fallen into an error. They have voted blindly for the party which claims to have extended to them the right to vote," as if the black Whiggery was merely "an error." He also eulogized Dorr—"It is because of him and his influence that we enjoy that right, rather than to any creditable intent on the part of those who prate annually, or just preceding every election day of the credit due themselves." Downing saw what men like Brown could not, that they had gained little more than minor party employment and Election Day rituals.[51]

Jim Crow in Providence

Rhode Island's school integration battle began in 1857 and only succeeded postbellum. The distinction between Upper and Lower New England remained in place. No Republican in Boston, Portland, or New Bedford would have publicly demeaned black men, but Rhode Island's Republicans repeatedly did, led by Henry Bowen Anthony's *Providence Journal*. His party contained no admixture of old Liberty men, maintaining an older Whig politics based on deference received and favors given. Abolitionists dominated Maine's Supreme Judicial Court and led Massachusetts's Republican organization, but most of Little Rhody's self-denominated "American-Republicans" (signifying their coalition with Know Nothings) remained conservative nativists. They accommodated black voters to keep out "foreigners," and beyond that men like Anthony would not go.

A series of events highlight the paradoxes of Rhode Island's black politics. In the same 1855 article where he derided Black Whiggism, Downing reported, "Our Legislature passed an act yesterday, granting unto a military company of this city, composed of colored men, the use of the States arms [*sic*], the most that it could do, and more than any other State has done." Rhode Island Whigs had indeed done "more than any other State," directly violating the 1792 Militia Act. This unprecedented instance of state recognition was noticed in North and South, but thereafter nothing more was heard— the black "military company" never paraded in public. Who composed it and arranged its chartering remain mysterious.[52]

What came next was simply perverse. Elsewhere in New England, black men gained office as a quid pro quo for votes. In Providence, it came "through a joke." In May 1857, a longtime black leader, Thomas Howland, won office in a Providence ward. The "regular Republican candidates were chosen viva voce," which was technically illegal, and some Democrats decided "to mortify Zachariah Tucker, Esq., of the same ward . . . formerly an influential Democrat . . . who had become obnoxious . . . by his conversion to Republicanism, by electing him Clerk . . . with Thomas Howland, a colored stevedore, as Warden." Howland "demanded to be sworn into office," but soon after decided to take his family to Liberia, and became a minor cause célèbre when the State Department refused him a passport.[53]

At the same time and unheralded, a black man gained office elsewhere in the state. A month after Howland's election, James L. Clarke was appointed to Newport's City Watch, presumably as a reward for electoral loyalty; an 1860 article noted black men fielded "one hundred and twenty voters," a substantial electorate in a town whose turnout in presidential years did not exceed 1,300, although poll books covering twelve elections from 1842 to 1848 record a more modest black turnout averaging not quite twenty-five voters or 3.1 percent of the electorate. A hint of their electoral role came in 1856, when a Democratic paper sneered that "seberal colored gemmen will have prominent positions on de platform as officers ob de meeting" for Frémont, the Republican presidential candidate. Clarke served as a special police constable or watchman for years without attracting notice, like other men of color in New England towns.[54]

The fragility of black rights in Rhode Island were underscored a month before Howland's election, however, in Glocester, a milltown near Providence. A Boston Republican newspaper reported, "The Democratic canvassers in the town of Gloucester [sic], R.I., struck the names of the colored voters in that town from the lists before the election on Wednesday, alleging that they were justified in this outrageous action by the decision in the case of Dred Scott. *The Providence Journal* intimates that legal proceedings will be commenced against them," another story reprinted nationally.[55]

Providence's "equal school rights" campaign began that same spring in 1857, and was emphatically modern—a determined interracial social movement, well organized along established modes, cannily employing the hegemonic language of Yankee republicanism—all to no avail. It was repeatedly frustrated by a political establishment claiming the name "Republican" but little interested in egalitarianism. The latter insisted there was no problem, only an outsider (George T. Downing) sowing trouble. Under pressure, these Republicans insisted it was fundamentally "inexpedient" to make any change. Finally, pushed harder, the state's elite co-opted the movement's constituency via gestures of incorporation (and outright bribery), although many black families rejected integration for their own reasons.

Downing's committee spent years ping-ponging between Providence's School Committee and the state's General Assembly. Both had solid Republican majorities, and in both they faced insults and repudiation. Equivocation by eminent allies was especially embarrassing. Throughout 1857, they claimed Brown's President Wayland as a supporter, but eventually had to admit that he "drew up the memorial . . . to the General Assembly, and then declined signing it, because he thought that, in the present state of public mind, it would be injurious to press the set in question!," listing other dignitaries who betrayed a "shilly-shally, give-and-take, hot-and-cold, yes-and-no manner."[56]

The struggle began at an April 1857 Providence City Council meeting where Rev. Samuel Wolcott was excluded from reelection to the School Committee because he "was objected to by Council-man Greene . . . on the ground that he was in favor of abolishing the colored schools." Wolcott got only eight of thirty-three votes, although the "Council are all Americans and

Republicans but three or four, and strongly condemn the late decision of the Supreme Court of the United States in not recognizing colored people as citizens. How much better men at heart are they than Chief Justice Taney?" These Jim Crow Republicans spared no effort in blunting support for integration. A delegation led by former governor William Hoppin and Providence mayor William Rodman visited a "colored school" and reported effusively in the *Journal* how they "were particularly struck with the proficiency of the pupils" and their competence in the "mental algebraic process, put to them by various members of the Committee," giving "abundant proof of the pupils' capacity and the teachers' success." A meeting chaired by Downing denounced the "fallacious arguments of inexpediency," resolving "as free men and women" they had their "own rights and interests in connection with our children's education," with the revealing addition that "the employer of this city . . . that would attempt to coerce an employee in expressing his wishes and feelings in regard to this school . . . [was] base; a specimen of shriveled humanity." They turned to the General Assembly with a petition from Ichabod Northup signed by 668 people, but got short shrift in that body's Education Committee. Only a single member's minority report recommended "no distinction of color, religion, or nativity . . . in the organization of public schools," to which the committee's chair replied, "A good school has been established for the colored people in Providence, and . . . it was best to let well alone, and let the city manage its schools as it saw fit." Several representatives called the petitioners "respectable citizens" who were "suffering a great hardship, and if their school is half as bad as represented by the Superintendent it ought to be abolished." Eventually a segregationist proposed, "It is not expedient that any action should be taken at this time . . . and that the whole subject should be left to the electors of the city of Providence," which passed on a voice vote. The Free Soiler Edward Harris observed, "The colored people here receive more genuine sympathy from the Democrats than from the Republicans. The latter promise the most, and perform the least."[57]

After this defeat, Downing's committee went to court. In August 1858, a veteran activist, John T. Waugh, sent his son to the neighborhood school, where he was refused entrance, and the committee convinced the father to sue. When they got to court, "Judge Shaw non-suited us, upon some petty technical point, without giving us a hearing." Waugh's temerity provoked the *Journal* into a vulgar outburst, that Reverend Wolcott wanted "our public schools quite broken up . . . rather than that one little nigger boy should be compelled to go to the school that has been assigned to him . . . instead of the one that the caprice and the misdirected discontent of his father prefer for him." Downing's committee repeated that phrase "one little nigger boy" (an allusion to a popular sentimental poem) with satisfaction.[58]

In early 1859, the establishment's counteroffensive peaked. First, they drew a color line by admitting a few lighter-skinned children into white schools; whites had long sanctioned racial passing to divide, with Downing's committee noting in 1857, "Some few colored persons that have their children in white schools, think it is in their interest to oppose the movement." Reverend Wolcott clarified the School Committee had been asked "to certify that the promising daughter of a well known colored man in the city was sufficiently bleached to exempt her from the proscriptive sweep of the ordinance." The teachers in the black schools and their husbands also mobilized against integration. One individual, George Head, even changed his racial identity ("now claims to be a white man") and was granted a license to sell liquor, historically reserved for whites. His child was admitted to the local school, and he "invited all colored people who would remonstrate against the bill to come into his place and drink free rum." The resulting petition to maintain separate schools gave nervous Republicans an excuse. Downing reported, "On a direct vote we would have carried this General Assembly" but for "the opposition had it arranged that some black slaves . . . sho'd place their name to a paper saying in substance that they did not desire to enjoy the same superior facilities for becoming educated which their white neighbors do." Downing insisted the signatures "were obtained by false representations—a number supposing that they were favoring the abolition of caste in schools. Some of the names were FORGED. . . . However . . . here was a piece of paper with forty-five names on it," adding for good measure, that "nearly every man who consented to have his name there . . . was a sot."[59]

Following the presentation of Head's petition, Assemblyman Flagg, chairman of the Education Committee, stood up to "abuse Mr. Downing," who was present, "attacking his motives, charging him with misrepresentation." Other Republicans professed "great personal regard for Mr. Downing," but given "a difference of opinion among the colored people," referred it to the next session. Downing's report also alluded to a black teacher, Elizabeth J. Smith, "whose school is reduced from eighty to sixteen" but who was "retained as a teacher notwithstanding . . . because of a hold which it is believed she has on some of the school committee, causing them to be afraid to remove her."[60]

Despite Downing's allegations of corruption, most of black Providence opted to preserve the few professional jobs they had. In 1857, Downing proclaimed integration was desired by "the intelligent, the wealthy and the respectable of the colored people," implicitly conceding the majority disagreed. His partisans insisted the resistance stemmed from how black folk became "timid, and perhaps seemingly passive, when some one may approach them in a domineering manner, saying 'What do your people want? Do we not give you schools? How much better things are than they were. You must not press this matter. We want to be your friends.' . . . Some colored persons will, when thus approached . . . wince" and retreat. Decades later a latecomer to the campaign, the prosperous former slave George Henry, admitted that "two-thirds of the colored population was against us." Henry himself initially opposed the campaign: "The first petition was to break up the colored schools, and let the children go into the different ward schools. Upon that I bolted, and declared I would never sign my name. . . . All said they would never agree to break up a school that their forefathers worked so hard to establish." Eventually Henry decided "that my child should go to school in my own ward, where I pay taxes and vote," but many never assented.[61]

Downing and his white allies fought back. In spring 1859, Reverend Wolcott was denied renomination to Providence's School Committee. In response, Democrats and Republicans in his Sixth Ward formed a "Citizens Ticket" including Wolcott and another minister, which their opponents labeled "nigger nominations."[62] There was no closure to this battle, and only in 1866 did the General Assembly legislate nonracial schools. The war made the difference, as in 1862, the different factions among Rhode Island's black men, including William J. Brown, enthusiastically answered the governor's call for black soldiery. They could again be useful.

Coda

The New England Impasse

When hostile editors and the Afro-Yankees both used terms like "Sebasto-pol" and "Gibraltar" to describe antebellum New England, they invoked the image of a fortress, a high ground from which an army rebuffed sieges and commanded land and sea. These allusions implied power, thus this part's ti-tle, "The New England Redoubt," defining it as the place where African Americans could claim political efficacy.

There is another meaning to these words. A redoubt can also mean the place where an armed body is penned in, at an impasse with its enemies. Af-rican Americans in Upper New England knew they had rights that white men must respect, they were told so by their political allies as early as Jef-ferson's time, and by the 1850s they were incorporated into the party exer-cising hegemony over the region. But only a day's train ride south exposed them to very different political regimes. In New York City or Philadelphia, let alone Cincinnati or Chicago, the Fugitive Slave Act was still enforced, and white mobs still operated. Outside of Yankeeland and its Greater New England of western New York, northern Ohio, Michigan, Wisconsin, Iowa, and parts of other states, white racial violence was a fact of life.

Not surprisingly, in the fluid political context of the late 1850s, few black Yankees perceived themselves as stymied. The limits on their political am-bition were not yet apparent. Many, like the Boston lawyer Robert Morris, were decidedly optimistic. Early in the decade, Free Soilers had nominated the Bostonians Lewis Hayden and William C. Nell for state representative, and in 1849 Governor George Briggs had made Morris the second black jus-tice of the peace in the state, while black men occupied significant party roles in places like New Bedford. Only in the decade's later half did the tension between symbolic representation and actual power show itself. Republican luminaries like Senator Henry Wilson continued to speak at black-organized events, showing respect. In 1861, Massachusetts's avowedly abolitionist governor John A. Andrew made his friend Lewis Hayden the official messenger for the secretary of state, a lifetime position and an unprecedented honor. As the preceding studies of Portland and New Bed-ford demonstrate, however, men like Hayden had limited influence within the Republican Party. Patronage and offices yes, power no, and thus an impasse.[1]

The resulting dilemma played out through three conventions held in 1858–61, seeking to address the question that confronts the formerly powerless who have fought their way into the electoral arena: what next? Understanding these meetings' failure to chart a clear path requires a brief review of black politics in Massachusetts as a whole, one of the three states (besides New York and Ohio) where black men were active statewide, in Boston, New Bedford, Salem, Nantucket, Worcester, and even hill towns in the west. Their elevation had peaked in 1855, when Massachusetts went beyond any other state in legislating equality; in the words of the vitriolic *New-York Herald*, "Now the niggers really are just as good as white folks. The North is to be Africanized." In 1854, uniting around a shared distaste for alcohol, "Romanism," and slavery—the three avatars of the Democracy—Whigs, Free Soilers, and African Americans had flocked into the American ("Know-Nothing") Party. Winning almost every seat in the legislature, the Americans enacted a radical program, including the compulsory integration of all public education.[2]

Massachusetts's American Party also sent Henry Wilson to the Senate; by then, he had made himself black men's favorite by declaring at the 1853 constitutional convention, "The Constitution of this Commonwealth knows no distinction of color or race. A colored man may fill any office in the gift of the people. A colored man may be the 'Supreme Executive Magistrate' of Massachusetts,' and 'Commander-in-chief of the army and navy.'" Wilson's election was hailed by John S. Rock, the brilliant black doctor and attorney (later, the first African American admitted to practice before the U.S. Supreme Court, in 1865) as "a bright and glorious triumph secured by this new party." Over 1855, Rock reported to *Frederick Douglass' Paper* on Massachusetts's progress. In early April, he foresaw the future Republican majority, once Know-Nothingism waned: "No permanent political organization can be started in Massachusetts, or in the United States, unless it is anti-slavery, and favors temperance and Protestantism." In May, he declared, "The agitation here has produced a marked and wonderful effect; a black man feels here that he is a man, 'to all intents and purposes.' No political disabilities stand in his way to prevent him, if he has friends enough to fill any office in the gift of the people." From there on, victories piled up, as the American Party democratized the state for native-born men while excluding Irish Catholics through literacy and residency requirements (proposing, although not passing, a twenty-one-year naturalization period). By September, Rock could crow, "The Anti-Catholic and Know Nothing movement have done a good work for the colored people. The colored man stands as much above an Irishman here as he does beneath him in Philadelphia; and as black as we are, we would not change positions with him if we had to take the brogue still hanging to his tongue, along with us." In comparison to white Know-Nothings, however, Rock was not a bigot. Like many black people, he disliked the Irish for specific political reasons, that "whenever you found a Catholic you found a noisy Fugitive Slave Law advocate—a volunteer bloodhound, eager to hunt—'the nagers.'"[3]

Two public clashes signaled how the black bottom rail had briefly come out on top. At a November 1854 Know-Nothing victory rally in Worcester, William J. Watkins was encouraged to humiliate an Irishman. Noting "the poor slave seemed to have been wholly forgotten" by the party speakers, he asked "whether or not I can, as a colored citizen, consistently dance to this Know Nothing music? I understand that the colored citizens of Massachusetts have, this day, almost unanimously voted the 'Know Nothing' Ticket. . . . Have we, as colored citizens, any thing to expect from your new party?" The chairman replied, "We know no man by the color of his skin. . . . We take our colored citizens by the hand as brethren, and will do all in our power for their elevation." At that, reported Watkins, the crowd went into a "perfect furore of excitement. Men gathered around us from every quarter, and thanked us for having put the question at *such* an hour," on Election Night. Then a man named Rafferty got up to ask why would they "give the colored population more privileges than do the Irish who are white people. Who builds your railroads and your telegraphic wires?" Watkins mocked his claims about "our inferiority, &ct." and was invited on stage. To "the question, '*who builds your railroads?*' we gave Mr. Rafferty to understand, we *thought* those who build our railroads, and those who fill our alms-houses, *are intimately related.*" Truly this was turnabout. "The meeting then assumed a decidedly anti-slavery tone, and everybody, save Mr. Rafferty, seemed delighted."[4]

The second occasion came inside Massachusetts's State House, catalyzed by Lewis Hayden, an escaped Kentucky slave whose mother had been driven insane by sexual abuse, by now an emblem of black resistance.[5] On February 13, 1855, the legislature's Joint Special Committee on Federal Relations held hearings on a Personal Liberty bill which would effectively nullify the Fugitive Slave Act. An Alabama slaveholder, John W. Githell, defended slavery by arguing only the "poorest specimens" ran away. Hayden responded by mocking "my brother Githell" to the spectators' satisfaction: "I have always said, Mr. Chairman, that you get here the poorest specimens of slaves. My brother Githell asserts it as a fact and thereby he and myself are agreed. Now, sir, you have all seen Frederick Douglass, Mr. [William Wells] Brown, and other fugitive slaves, and if they are among the worst specimens then you need have no fear of letting loose those now in bondage! (Sensation and applause.)" After more of this skewering, Hayden made "a direct appeal to Mr. Githell . . . how he could stand up in an enlightened community, and before God, and claim fifty human beings as his slaves, each of whom is as much entitled to his freedom as Mr. G." The *New York Evening Post* added further insult by describing Githell as "an inferior looking man, of dark complexion, long, straight, black hair, very much resembling an Indian. . . . His style was peculiarly that of the illiterate Southerner—He seemed to repudiate the grammar and the dictionary altogether." Imagine this man's returning home to tell his neighbors of being dressed down by a Negro slave in the presence of white legislators. Such experiences bred secession.[6]

How did the momentum of protest actually affect party politics? Following the all-out push for Frémont in 1856, the Yankee Republic fell into a lull, broken only by the shock of *Dred Scott*. Republicans were dominant at home but faced an entrenched Democratic administration that had won 59 percent of the Electoral College. How much more could black Yankees gain, given their small electorate? Republicans loved a rousing speech by a colored man confirming them as defenders of "Northern rights," and in a few places they needed black votes, but that did not require accepting them into party leadership. Real intraparty clout, let alone nominations for office, would not be on offer until a bloody war had further changed the terms.

To break the logjam, New Bedforders called a statewide convention. Until then, black Garrisonians, notably Boston's William Nell and Charles Lenox Remond in Salem, had blocked the organization of state conventions in New England, although they were the vehicle of black political life everywhere outside the Yankee Republic. Opposition to all-black meetings was deeply held. In 1843, as momentum grew for the first National Colored Convention since 1835, Boston's leadership first voted to boycott, and then sent Douglass and Remond with instructions to oppose anything contradicting Garrisonian strictures. At subsequent national conventions in 1847, 1848, 1853, and 1855 New Englanders usually played minor roles. The mid-1850s attempt to establish a permanent National Council of the Colored People foundered largely because Nell, as Massachusetts's representative, disrupted its functioning from a "conscientious doubt as to the legality of the action of this Convention."[7]

On June 16, 1858, disgusted by Chief Justice Taney's "palpably vain, arrogant assumption, unsustained by history, justice, reason or common sense," a New Bedford meeting issued "a call for a Mass [meaning open to all] State Convention to be held in this city, Aug. 2d, 1858," following the annual First of August attended by thousands. It immediately generated sneering coverage from Democratic newspapers, with the *New York Herald* jibing at the "Mass Convention of Niggers to Consider Their 'many Grievances'—the Fugitive Slave Bill is to be Destroyed, and the Dred Scott Decision Reversed by Colored Persons." It also proved a disappointment. The convention's leadership reflected a bargain between New Bedford and various other camps: New

Bedford's Republican stalwarts Henry O. Remington, Lloyd H. Brooks, and John Freedom among the former, and both old Garrisonians like Nell and Remond and Republican ward leaders in Boston like Lewis Hayden and Robert Morris among the latter. The eminent William Wells Brown opened the meeting, declaring as their objective "to influence the action of the Legislature of Massachusetts . . . to assume a defiant attitude towards the Dred Scott decision, and . . . pass a law that, if any man comes into Massachusetts claiming any of our citizens as slaves, he shall be tried, convicted, and sent to the State Prison." It then blew up over Remond's "ultra-ism." He was a Byronic figure hurling thunderbolts, calling for vengeance and the destruction of the Slaveholders' Republic. A striking appearance accented this theatricality: a bony, very dark face with an aquiline nose; a hard stare; a high ridge of hair pulled up on one side like a scalp lock. Unremitting defiance had served Remond well in two decades of preaching abolition to small-town whites, but his stance was now widely regarded as anachronistic. On August 2, 1858, he led off by insulting the thousands who had fled to Canada after the Fugitive Slave bill went into operation as "cowards, and time-servers, and apologists." He "referred to parties, and asked what either of them had done for freedom. The free soil and republican parties had, alike, been false. We must depend upon our own self-reliance. If we recommend to the slaves in South Carolina to rise in rebellion, it would work greater things than we imagine." He closed by suggesting that only a "black William Wallace with his claymore" would bring freedom, proposing that a committee "prepare an address suggesting to the slaves at the South to create an insurrection."[8]

Given that most of those present were active Republicans, hoping to pressure their party for greater access, Remond's performance was insulting and pointless. The gulf between Remond and the black Republican politicos was quickly apparent. Robert Morris declared, "Let us be bold, and they'll have to yield to us." If anyone tried to take a slave in New Bedford, Boston's black men would "come down three hundred strong." He then vehemently rebutted Remond's antipartyism, insisting on the "progress of the colored people in this State. Formerly they were all slaves; now they are free, and can vote. He believed in voting. He should stump his district, and thought he might be elected to the Legislature. He advised the colored people to stand together and to vote together. Let them demand a member of the school committee, and then a representative [to the legislature]."

This debate continued on the second day. After the convention approved a resolution censuring emigrationism, meaning Henry Highland Garnet's new African Civilization Society, Remond again moved that a committee "prepare an address suggesting to the slaves at the South to create an insurrection." The verbatim record here is instructive: he "didn't want to see people shake their heads . . . and turn pale. . . . He wanted to see the half-way fellows take themselves away, and leave the field to men who would encourage their brethren at the South to rise with bowie-knife and revolver and musket." Josiah Henson, leader of the Canadian expatriates, reputedly the model for Stowe's Uncle Tom, delivered a slashing rebuke, that "he never turned pale in his life" (the reporter noting "Father Henson is a very black man"), adding that "if the shooting time came, Remond would be found out of the question. As he didn't want to see three or four thousand men hung before their time, he should oppose any such action, head, neck and shoulders. . . . 'When I fight,' said Father H., 'I want to whip somebody.'" Others added scorn, but Remond gloried in his isolation, like a Patrick Henry or perhaps "The Toussaint of America," as an admiring white paper called him, declaring, "If he had one hundred relations at the South, he would rather see them die today than to live in bondage. He would rather stand over their graves, than feel that any pale-faced scoundrel might violate his mother or his sister at pleasure. He only regretted that he had not a spear with which he could transfix all the slaveholders at once. . . . Give him liberty, or give him death." *The Liberator*'s correspondent reported this was "by far the most spirited discussion of the Convention." All that was achieved at the meeting's conclusion was "to print the proceedings in pamphlet form," and the net effect of Remond's melodramatics was to distract, which may have been his intention.[9]

The Afro-Yankees were left unsettled. Many were Republicans, but there were still Garrisonians opposed to conventional politics, and others turned to emigration. This discord was publicized a year later, when a first-ever regional convention met in Boston on August 1, 1859, "to take action in reference to the Presidential campaign in 1860." The organizers were drawn from Portland, four cities in Massachusetts, Newport and Providence, and Connecticut. Their intent was to make demands as an organized faction by holding up Rhode Island's Jim Crow Republicans for execration. To this end, George T. Downing was elected president. After paeans to "learning and wealth," Downing got down to business: "The ballot is a power in this country, which should not be lost sight of by us. Were it more generally exercised by the colored people, the effect would be very perceptible." He proposed forging a bloc vote as leverage. Not only should black men vote where they could, there should be "a concert of action in doing so," in which case, "the effect would be irresistible." The hint was clear, given that most of the Republican presidential candidates were either silent or opposed to black suffrage: "Will the Republican party . . . put in nomination . . . a man for whom we can, with some degree of consistency, cast our ballots? . . . We cannot vote for a man who subscribes to the doctrine, that, in struggling for freedom in a Presidential or any other election, he ignores the rights of the colored man." Downing had laid down the marker. Whether the convention would act on it was another matter. Eventually the Garrisonian Nell, as secretary, brought in a lengthy list of resolutions from the Business Committee expressing wishes and hopes, although they did eventually echo Downing, that in "States of the Union where the Republican party is in the ascendant [and] the elective franchise of colored citizens is denied or its privileges abridged," they "would earnestly call upon the party to take a manly position upon this and co-relative questions."[10]

After more speeches, including Garrison's perennial claim that "nothing had gratified him so much as the reputation which he had gained of being a black man, and so long as slavery should exist on the face of the earth, he begged to be regarded as thoroughly one of their color," the convention adjourned. Its second day saw no more progress—another list of resolutions, insisting on "total abstinence" and "respectfully recommend[ing] an agricultural life . . . as calculated to develop the character, moral, mental and physical." A motion to appoint "a Central Committee of two persons from each State . . . outside of Massachusetts, to devise ways and means for executing the plans or suggestions contained in resolutions," became "the subject of considerable discussion," another indication of resistance to black political autonomy. After its adoption, the delegates again censured Garnet's African Civilization Society, a foregone conclusion in a convention of Republicans and Garrisonians, and turned to the business of denouncing Rhode Island's reactionary "American Republicans." One Rhode Islander, James Jefferson, declared he "went from Maryland, a slave State, to Rhode Island a free State [and] found Republican rule as oppressive in Rhode Island, as [what] he had experienced in Maryland." After more such execrations, Downing issued a declaration that "he hoped . . . would appear in all the Boston papers," asserting that "the Republican party in Rhode Island" was responsible for "the denial to the colored men of their rights in that State." Having sounded this futile note of warning, this convention adjourned; Downing himself was worn out, and in summer 1860 announced his retirement from politics.[11]

The problem for men like Morris (if not Downing) was that they already had won everything available. It was their proud boast regarding Massachusetts that "nor does a single law remain on her Statute Book, prejudicial to the rights or interests of any man, or class of men, on the ground of complexional differences," as stated in a petition requesting the legislature to nullify *Dred Scott*. That petition's referral to the Committee on Federal Relations for action by a 174–23 vote indicates the respect with which colored men's appeals were received. Throughout the region, the color lines mandated by federal law were now routinely circumvented, from the chartering of black militia companies to issuing state passports so African Americans could travel abroad. Black men were admitted as lawyers and doctors; a few served in low-level government positions, and they could anticipate elected offices opening up. They had made significant strides in overcoming legal segregation, and in 1860, the Aldermen of Worcester broke yet another barrier by empaneling two black men as jurors. Their votes were sought, pointing the way to the normal exercise of political influence, and Morris was proved right in 1866, when David Walker's son Edwin was elected to Massachusetts's legislature from Boston's Ward Six.[12]

The last meeting of Massachusetts's leaders underlined the fragility of their stronghold. "Colored citizens from the various portions of the Commonwealth" met on February 14, 1861 in Boston to consider not their advancement, but their survival. Accretions of local, state, or regional equality were always provisional, as *Dred Scott* had shown, and further attacks on black citizenship were now bruited. On February 8, the original seven states of the Confederacy declared their Provisional Constitution and a Peace Conference of Northern and Southern leaders met to avert war. By that time, the Crittenden Compromise, a last-ditch project to preserve the Union by amending the Constitution to protect slavery, had added an explicit pledge by the northern states to disenfranchise their black citizens via constitutional amendment. At the Boston meeting, former antagonists united in desperation. Dr. J. B. Smith of New Bedford, recently a emigrationist, declared, "They had nothing to live for if their liberties are further infringed. He would submit to no more oppression on the part of this barbaric nation." George T. Downing offered a resolution "that the colored people will never be driven from the United States by any compulsion; insisting on the retention of the Personal Liberty Law on our statute book, and proclaiming that they will continue to demand from the Legislature of Massachusetts the most absolute equality in every respect before the laws." He proposed an "APPEAL TO THE WHITE CITIZENS OF THE STATE," pointing out the essential fact about the Yankee Republic's history. The goal of these compromises was not "to strike at so small a political power as ourselves, but at the white citizens of the States of New England. They would humiliate the New England States because of their fidelity to that portion of the Declaration of Independence which declares 'That all governments derive their just powers from the consent of the governed,' in the understanding of which the New England States include the colored citizen."[13]

At the end, one man announced despondently that "everything looked dark. They could expect nothing from the free States," but Morris again sounded a hopeful note—he was "confident that, ere three years, colored men would be in the Legislature, so convinced was he that Massachusetts is advancing in aid of the colored people. He thought the colored people were the most to blame, that they do not help themselves as they ought." On this note, the war came, and after an agonizing delay New England sent forth a black vanguard, in the old sense of those who march into deadly fire, via the heroism of the Fifty-Fourth Massachusetts. "Massachusetts men" of both races illustrated the promise of New England by staining the parapets of Fort Wagner with their blood. The question remained, however: to what end?

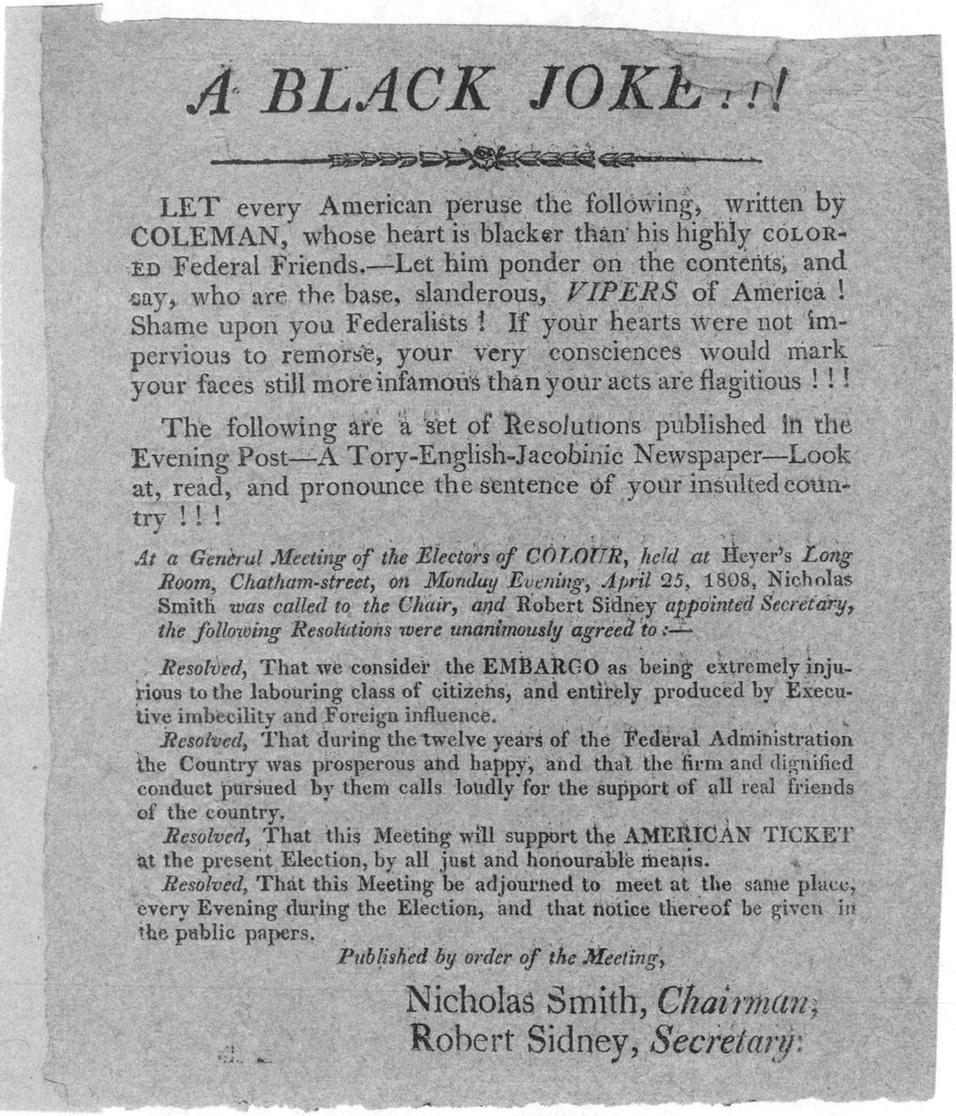

A BLACK JOKE!!!

LET every American peruse the following, written by COLEMAN, whose heart is blacker than his highly COLOR-ED Federal Friends.—Let him ponder on the contents, and say, who are the base, slanderous, *VIPERS* of America! Shame upon you Federalists! If your hearts were not impervious to remorse, your very consciences would mark your faces still more infamous than your acts are flagitious ! ! !

The following are a set of Resolutions published in the Evening Post—A Tory-English-Jacobinic Newspaper—Look at, read, and pronounce the sentence of your insulted country ! ! !

At a General Meeting of the Electors of COLOUR, held at Heyer's Long Room, Chatham-street, on Monday Evening, April 25, 1808, Nicholas Smith was called to the Chair, and Robert Sidney appointed Secretary, the following Resolutions were unanimously agreed to:—

Resolved, That we consider the EMBARGO as being extremely injurious to the labouring class of citizens, and entirely produced by Executive imbecility and Foreign influence.

Resolved, That during the twelve years of the Federal Administration the Country was prosperous and happy, and that the firm and dignified conduct pursued by them calls loudly for the support of all real friends of the country.

Resolved, That this Meeting will support the AMERICAN TICKET at the present Election, by all just and honourable means.

Resolved, That this Meeting be adjourned to meet at the same place, every Evening during the Election, and that notice thereof be given in the public papers.

Published by order of the Meeting,

Nicholas Smith, *Chairman,*
Robert Sidney, *Secretary:*

Figure 1 "A BLACK JOKE!!!," 1808.

A rare example of the street-level politics of race in the early republic—a broadside posted by Manhattan Republicans to denounce Federalists. The particular target is the *Evening Post*, edited by William Coleman, which cooperated closely with men of color like Robert Sidney. "A BLACK JOKE!!!: Let every American peruse the following, written by Coleman, . . ." 1808, 27 × 23 cm, broadside, call no. SY1808 no.46, New York Historical Society.

Figure 2 Lemuel Haynes.

Lemuel Haynes was born in Connecticut in 1753 and ordained
in 1785 after military service. He became an eminent Congregational
minister in Vermont, an outspoken Federalist in the Jeffersonian
era. From Carter G. Woodson, *The History of the Negro Church*
(Washington, DC: Associated Publishers, 1921).

Figure 3 Alexander Twilight, c. 1830s.

The "Iron-Willed Schoolmaster," Alexander Twilight (b. 1795)
was a Revolutionary veteran's son, and the first man of color to
graduate from college (Middlebury, 1823). He educated much of
Vermont's elite and was elected to the state legislature in 1836.
Courtesy of the Orleans County Historical Society and Old
Stone House Museum, Brownington, Vermont.

Figure 4 Robert Purvis, c. 1840s.

From a wealthy southern background, Robert Purvis (b. 1810 in Charleston) was the ultimate example of Philadelphia's "elite of our people," a Garrisonian resolute in his commitment to aid the fugitive. Courtesy of the Boston Public Library.

Figure 5 "The Results of Abolitionism!," 1835.

This woodcut alleges evil capitalists would put Irish immigrants under black men. A white owner orders his black labor boss to "hurry up the white laborers" while the skilled bricklayers (also black) insult them: "You bogtrotters, come along with them bricks." Courtesy of the Library Company of Philadelphia.

Figure 6 Charles Lenox Remond, c. 1850s.

Son of a politically connected caterer and merchant in Salem, Charles Lenox
Remond (b. 1810) gained transnational fame as an orator, maintaining his stance
of defiance through the 1850s. Courtesy of the Boston Public Library.

Figure 7 Robert Morris, c. 1850s.

Born in Salem in 1823, Robert Morris was the second African American to pass the bar, in 1847. He became a Free Soil Party leader in Massachusetts in the late 1840s and was appointed a justice of the peace in 1849. Courtesy of the Social Law Library in Boston, Massachusetts.

Figure 8 Henry Highland Garnet, 1881.

Born a slave in Maryland in 1815, Henry Highland Garnet was
the most prominent black Liberty man, later a Republican, and
then an emigrationist in the late 1850s. He was the first black
man to address Congress, in 1865, and was named minister to
Liberia in 1881. Courtesy of the National Portrait Gallery,
Smithsonian Institution.

Figure 9 Samuel Ringgold Ward, c. 1851.

Like his cousin Henry Highland Garnet, Samuel Ringgold Ward
was born a slave on the Eastern Shore in 1817. He escaped to
become a minister in New York, a Liberty Party stalwart, and
ultimately that party's vice presidential candidate in 1850–51
before decamping to Canada, the British Isles, and Jamaica.
From Samuel Ringgold Ward, *Autobiography of a Fugitive Negro:
His Antislavery Labours in the United States, Canada, and England*
(London: John Snow, 1855).

Figure 10 James McCune Smith.

Born in 1813, and educated like Henry Highland Garnet and Samuel Ringgold Ward at New York City's African Free School (AFS), James McCune Smith was the first accredited black physician and a longtime Whig until he moved left in the 1850s into the leadership of Gerrit Smith's Radical Abolitionist Party. This engraving was made by Patrick Reason, another of the brilliant alumni of the AFS. Courtesy of the New-York Historical Society.

Figure 11 Stephen Myers.

Stephen Myers was born a slave near Albany, around 1800. Little known in his own time and forgotten after, he worked for governors from DeWitt Clinton through William Seward and was the main black leader in Thurlow Weed's Whig and Republican organizations from the 1840s to his death in 1870. From I. Garland Penn, *The Afro-American Press and Its Editors* (Springfield, MA: Willey, 1891).

Figure 12 Gerrit Smith and Frederick Douglass.

At the August 1850 Cazenovia, New York Fugitive Slave Law Convention. Gerrit Smith stands to Frederick Douglass's right, gesturing. From the Collection of the Madison County Historical Society, Oneida, New York.

Figure 13 John Mercer Langston, c. 1868.

Born free in Virginia in 1829, John Mercer Langston was Ohio's leading black Republican and the nation's best-known black elected official. He was dean of Howard University's law school when this was taken, minister to Haiti in the 1870s, and won a seat in Congress from Virginia in 1888. Courtesy of the Library of Congress Prints and Photographs Division.

White Allies

African Americans worked in alliance with a group of Federalist, Whig, Liberty Party, Free Soil, and Republican leaders, several of whom are pictured here.

Figure 14 John Quincy Adams, 1843.

During his time in Congress (1831–48), the former president embodied Yankee Republicanism. He led a group of northern antislavery Whigs, inspiring William Seward and many others by denouncing not only slavery but racialism, asserting the equal citizenship of his "countrymen." Courtesy of the National Portrait Gallery, Smithsonian Institution.

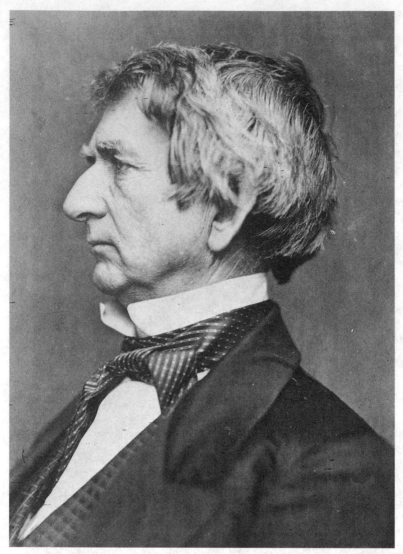

Figure 15 William Henry Seward, c. 1852.

Born in 1801, William Henry Seward grew up in a slaveholding household. As New York governor (1839–42) and senator (1849–61), he was the most popular Whig and Republican leader in the North's largest state and an outspoken ally of black people. Courtesy of the Library of Congress Prints and Photographs Division.

Figure 16 Thurlow Weed, c. 1855–1865.

Thurlow Weed (b. 1797) was William Seward's closest ally in the Antimasonic, Whig, and Republican Parties for over four decades. Famous as a partisan manager, Weed was firmly antislavery as long as that did not conflict with Seward's or his party's goals. Weed maintained a long relationship with black Whigs like Stephen Myers and Thomas Downing. Courtesy of Library of Congress Prints and Photographs Division.

Figure 17 Joshua Giddings.

Joshua Giddings (b. 1795) represented the Western Reserve in Congress from 1838 to 1859, inheriting John Quincy Adams's role as the foremost congressional opponent of the Slave Power. He was a loyal Whig until 1848, after which he led Ohio's Free Soil Party. Courtesy of Library of Congress Prints and Photographs Division.

Figure 18 Salmon P. Chase, c. 1861–1865.

Salmon Chase's life traces the arc of antislavery politics. Born in 1808, he was a conventional Whig in the 1830s, Ohio's principal Liberty Party leader 1841–47, architect of the Free Soil Party in 1848, an "Independent Democratic" senator in 1849–55, and Republican governor in 1855–60. Throughout he aggressively defended black people and their rights. Courtesy of the Mathew B. Brady National Photographic Art Gallery, Library of Congress Prints and Photographs Division.

Figure 19 Rodney French.

Rodney French is the outlier as both a fiercely partisan Democrat and an outspoken abolitionist in the 1840s. He became New Bedford's leading Free Soiler, elected mayor of the nation's richest city in 1853 via an all-out push by his black supporters. Courtesy of New Bedford Whaling Museum.

The New York Battleground

New York centers the antebellum quest for black citizenship, and that history revolves around two fundamental continuities. The first is an almost unbroken narrative of black political activism before and after most black Yorkers were disfranchised in 1821. Before that date, they exercised more influence than any other black constituency in the early republic. The creation in 1821 of a special "freehold" requirement for colored men foretold the future White Democracy of Martin Van Buren and Andrew Jackson. Their story does not end in 1821, however. A statewide campaign of resistance began in the 1830s and became a major factor in the state's politics during the 1840s. By the 1850s, thousands of black men had regained the franchise, and their maneuvering for advantage between numerous major and minor parties changed the electoral calculus in the Union's most important state.

The second continuity in this history is New York's ever-growing economic, political, and cultural dominance. Its self-designation as the "Empire State," saluting the conquest of the Iroquois Confederation and colonization of a vast hinterland, was no exaggeration. New England by itself could not lead the North, and Pennsylvania receded in influence after 1800. New York alone could link New England and the Mid-Atlantic to the Midwest to forge a "Northern party." Republicans chose Abraham Lincoln as their candidate in 1860 for practical reasons, but the model for a broad antislavery front was the Whig machine built by William Seward, Thurlow Weed, and Horace Greeley in 1837–54. Not for nothing did Charles B. Ray, editor of New York City's *Colored American*, exclaim in 1841 regarding the "New York Legislature," "The colored people of this country have more interests at stake, in the doings of this body, than in the doings of all the other legislative bodies in the country. For this is the Empire State. And as goes the State of New York, in other civil and political matters, so goes the nation."[1]

The year 1840 is a good benchmark for New York's importance. By then, the Empire State had assumed a commanding position demographically, containing more than one in six free Americans. Minus their "negro representation," the entire Deep South (then the states of Georgia, Alabama, Mississippi, Louisiana, and Arkansas; South Carolina's electors were still chosen by its

Clinton

Franklin

Essex

St Lawrence

Warren

Hamilton

Washington

Saratoga

Fulton

Montgomery

Rensselaer

Schenectady

TROY

ALBANY

Albany

Schoharie

Columbia

Greene

HUDSON

Ulster

Dutchess

Sullivan

Putnam

Orange

Westchester

Suffolk

Rockland

Queens

New York

WILLIAMSBURG

Kings

Richmond

Herkimer

Otsego

Delaware

Lewis

Oneida

PETERBORO

Madison

Chenango

Broome

Jefferson

Oswego

Onondaga

SYRACUSE

AUBURN

Cayuga

CORTLAND

Cortland

Tioga

Tompkins

Chemung

Wayne

Seneca

Ontario

Yates

Steuben

Monroe

ROCHESTER

Livingston

Allegany

Orleans

Genesee

Wyoming

Niagara

BUFFALO

Erie

Cattaraugus

Chautauqua

New York counties in 1850, those shaded are the "Smith Lands"

Map III.1 New York counties, 1850

legislature) had less than half as many actual voters (202,109) as New York's 441,543. Only with its 1,245,112 slaves adding the weight of 747,067 votes via the "federal ratio" of 3/5 representation could the Cotton Kingdom outweigh New York in Congress and the Electoral College. Economic and cultural power accentuated New York's predominance. The Erie Canal's link to the Midwest generated spectacular growth in cities like Syracuse, Buffalo, and Rochester; via the Hudson, New York City thus became the entrepôt for Ohio, Indiana, Michigan, Illinois, and eventually the whole Great West. By 1840, New York produced 17.6 percent of the nation's income, more than all of New England or the seaboard South, and Manhattan was the nation's unquestioned financial and commercial capital, exercising an "informational hegemony" through its banks, newspapers, and domination of foreign trade, and as the site of the nation's first stock exchange and main entry point for immigrants.[2]

Unsurprisingly, New York played a decisive role in choosing presidents; only twice before 1860 did a candidate win without it. In 1840, it controlled one-seventh of the Electoral College. Sheer size would have meant less, however, if a particular party predominated, as in Whiggish Massachusetts or Jeffersonian Pennsylvania. Instead, New York developed "the most sophisticated and efficient political organizations of any state," with competition always intense. In the 1820s, Van Buren built a national party on the basis of his disciplined Bucktail Republican organization, to overcome the sectional discord surfaced by the Missouri Crisis. At home, however, the Jacksonians never dominated, and by the mid-1840s, anger at the southern diktat in national party councils divided the Democrats into permanent "Hunker" and "Barnburner" factions. New York also earned a reputation as uniquely open to multiparty politics. The disruptions of the Second Party System all began there, from the Antimasonic crusade in the late 1820s through the Liberty and Native American parties of the 1840s and the Free Soilers in 1848. In the 1850s, voters in state elections regularly chose between four or five tickets.[3]

There is also a distinctly historiographical reason for New York's centrality in black political history. Until late in the twentieth century, the only substantial scholarship on antebellum black voting was Dixon Ryan Fox's 1917 article "The Negro Vote in Old New York." Because of its lasting influence, Fox's analysis requires consideration. In a peculiar way, rife with racialist condescension regarding "the Negro's" inherent docility, Fox underlined how there had always been some black politics, that it always involved cross-class alliances, and there had always been white party leaders prepared to put class above race. To explain why black voters in his day remained loyal to the Party of Lincoln, Fox cast their partisanship not as a result of the Civil War, but as a primordial affiliation, "an affection for the master that no shock of fortune could disturb." In this telling, their loyalty stretched from Federalists to

Whigs to Republicans—aristocrats all: "They were Whigs because their fathers had been Federalists. If there had never been a Negro south of the Potomac, still the Negro in New York never would have voted the Democratic ticket."[4]

Fox began with a series of interrelated assertions: first, that "the Federalist party was the party of the aristocracy"; second, that "since slaves in this colony were a luxury, rather than an investment in agriculture, we should expect to find them belonging largely to members of this party; the records show such to have been the case"; finally, that "Federalist masters preferred to see their Negroes free, and led the movement in New York state for their betterment." These had been popular Jeffersonian claims, repeated long after the Federalists were extinct, and Fox gave them the status of historical fact. However, with one exception, his facts are all belied by plentiful evidence. First, slaves in the Province of New-York were never "a luxury" of the wealthy. Most were laborers belonging to or hired by Dutch farmers. Second, New York's actual aristocrats, the "manor lords," included an entire faction (the Livingston family) embedded in Republican leadership from the party's founding. Beyond that, George Clinton, the party's acknowledged founder, may have disdained aristocratic airs, but he was hardly a horny-handed son of the soil, any more than the fabled dandy Aaron Burr, another key leader. Fox's account contained one vein of truth, however: some "Federalist masters" (meaning the Patroon Stephen Van Rensselaer and others like him) did "prefer to see their Negroes free," and did organize "the movement in New York for their betterment," meaning the New York Manumission Society founded in 1785 by future Federalists like Alexander Hamilton and John Jay. The latter led the battle for an emancipation law as governor in 1795–1800. Black men were well aware of these facts and rewarded their emancipators electorally.[5]

Fox kept reiterating this mix of truth and invention, including the claim that "the Negroes had been reared in Federalist households" next to the accurate statement that "their cause had been advocated by distinguished Federalists, and now under the auspices of that party, freedom was provided," leading to his summary that "when they reached the estate of citizens, their political attachment could be easily foretold. . . . As soon as any slave was freed, he became a voter, on the same terms as a white man. . . . The erstwhile slave became in politics a client of his former master," capped by an image of black men entering politics as tools of the gentry: "the Negro change[d] his butler's coat for cap and jeans." Fox's partisanship, as an Irish Catholic Democrat, was underlined by whom he chose to quote. At the 1821 convention, General Erastus Root, a "radical" Bucktail, authored the slur that Fox repeated ninety-six years later, about how "a few hundred Negroes of the city of New-York, following the train of those who ride in their coaches, and whose shoes and boots they had so often blacked, shall go to the polls of the election and change the political condition of the whole state. . . . Thus would the whole state be controlled by a few hundred of this species of population in the city of New York."[6]

Fox's depiction of black voters as docile tools of white men clearly drew upon the Dunning School of historians led by the Columbia historian William Archibald Dunning; Fox had taken his PhD at Columbia and joined its History Department in 1912. In their telling, Radical Reconstruction was an exercise in domination by white "carpetbaggers" and "scalawags" over other whites through manipulating the bossed vote of childlike freedmen. Looking northward, Fox treated the violent racialism of the antebellum New York Democrats as an understandable fact of life. In his account, one hears the voice of an old Tammanyite recounting how they fought off black voting in 1846 and 1860, until forced to tolerate it after 1870.

Fox's article is artful, he was a skilled historian of New York, and his sources are impressive. He insisted, for instance, that the "Negro Vote" did not cease its importance after 1821. In later scholarship, this fallacy reigns, bifurcating the state's history into pre- and postdisfranchisement even among those who pay attention to black political aspirations. It is more useful to posit a deep continuity. The intent to bar black men from the polls was less successful than heretofore presumed, for many reasons: because the $250 freehold became increasingly easy to acquire; because Whigs and Republicans took evidence of taxpaying as proof of a freehold; because in 1846–50 the philanthropist Gerrit Smith distributed deeds for land to thousands of black men.

Chapter 8

Negroes Have Votes as Good as Yours or Mine

Coming to Grips in New York, 1777–1821

The creation of an order of citizens who are to have no legislative or representative share in the government, necessarily lays the foundation of an aristocracy of the most dangerous and malignant kind, rendering power permanent and hereditary in the hands of those persons who deduce their origin through white ancestors only.

—Council of Revision of the State of New-York, March 21, 1785, vetoing a gradual emancipation bill disfranchising freedmen

A great majority of the coloured men of this city, probably nine out of ten, have always voted for the federal ticket, and those who dared not directly disfranchise them, have had recourse to the abominable artifice of throwing in their way, such numerous difficulties to be overcome, and such expenses to be incurred, as amounts nearly . . . to an insurmountable obstacle.

—*New-York Evening Post*, April 16, 1811

No man of colour, unless he shall have been for three years a citizen of this state, and for one year next preceding any election, shall be seized and possessed of a freehold estate of the value of two hundred and fifty dollars . . . and shall have been actually rated, and paid a tax thereon, shall be entitled to vote.

—*Constitution of New York, Section One*, 1821

Black politics in New York grew out of its extreme polarities. As a colony, New York had "the largest and harshest slave system north of the Chesapeake," renowned for its brutality, including mass executions by rope and faggot resembling the aftermath of Caribbean slave revolts. In large part because the Dutch majority counties surrounding Manhattan constituted a slave society, emancipation came very slowly, defeated in 1785, finally passed in 1799, completed only in 1827. Yet New York also developed the early republic's most dynamic biracial politics, reflecting Federalists' commitment to nonracial suffrage (although Republicans sometimes also recruited "Electors of Colour"). In the early 1810s, New York City's black electorate tilted the statewide balance of power, spurring the nation's first partisan campaign for racial disfranchisement by Republicans claiming slaves were illegally voting.

Crucially, as Paul Polgar has argued, this innovative effort at racialized voter suppression was "the contingent product of party politics" rather than "the inevitable corollary of a white racist exclusionary ethos." It culminated at the 1821 constitutional convention, where Martin Van Buren's Bucktail faction eliminated most black electors, although Federalists and Clintonian Republicans preserved suffrage for a handful of freeholders of color.[1]

A Polyglot Empire

The evolution of the Province of New-York resists any sorting into a black-white binary. It was "the least English of all Britain's North American colonies," a conquered territory peopled largely by immigrants from continental Europe. From 1623 to 1664, Dutch New Amsterdam had welcomed all Protestants, and as late as in the 1740s, the province had a non-English majority comprising Hollanders, Huguenots, Germans, Jews, and others. Strategic intermarriage produced a pan-ethnic ruling class lording over vast Hudson Valley manors, and the rivalries of this quasi-feudal elite dominated colonial politics, but their endogamy did not close the larger divide between Anglo-Americans and those whose first language was Dutch, German, or French. These "isolated ethnoreligious communities" engaged in politics only "through deference to the mediation of powerful landlord families," and included large numbers of slaveholders who resisted emancipation as long as they could: Van Buren was their ultimate representative. Defining these many peoples as white regardless of language or denomination thus had special importance, what Thelma Wills Foote has called "a reterritorialization of Englishness" to encompass German, Dutch, and even French Protestants.[2]

This patchwork of settler colonialism was further attenuated by the colony's geography. Rather than solid blocs of settlement, as in New England or southeastern Pennsylvania, New York developed in discrete, narrow bands from far out on the Atlantic to deep into its hinterland, connected only by axes at Manhattan and Albany. Each piece had its own character—the little New England of eastern Long Island; the Dutch counties around Manhattan and up the Hudson; new settlements along the Mohawk, although the military power of the Iroquois Confederation long blocked westward expansion. Because northern New York constituted a natural invasion plane from or to Canada and the continuing threat of a Franco-Indian alliance, the colony was also exceptionally warrish, with four major conflicts between 1689 and 1763, and Burgoyne's 1778 defeat near Saratoga the Revolution's decisive battle.[3]

The Revolution repeated an established pattern of military mobilization, invasion, and counterattack, but upended existing arrangements of class and race. Southern New York became the center for militant, biracial Loyalism.

Plebeian Tories of all races competed for power, with thousands of white ten-ants on the Hudson manors and thousands of enslaved people around New York City choosing the King. These black and white Loyalists made the lower Hudson, Long Island, Staten Island, and East Jersey into a "Neutral Zone" ravaged by guerrilla warfare. A desperate state government, exiled to Kings-ton, implemented sweeping repression, including a Committee on Intestine Enemies and a Confiscation Act listing seventy-nine landowners attainted for life, including entire dynasties like the DeLanceys and Philipses (after the Revolution, Federalists recruited former Loyalists and by 1787 had repealed these acts).[4]

The Revolution's civil war broke the power of the British-aligned Iroquois and much of the old patriciate, and its postwar reconstruction proved spec-tacularly successful. New York had grown from 18,000 to 168,000 between 1698 and 1771, but it was still sixth in population in the new nation. Fifty years later, New York was the most populous state, as the frontier west of Albany exploded from under 30,000 to 720,000 in 1790–1820. Economic expansion paralleled the demographic surge. The banishment of Loyalist landowners made millions of expropriated acres available for distribution to veterans and speculators. Entrepreneurs like William Cooper opened up the vast north-west, and along the Hudson and on Long Island the old semifeudal arrange-ments turned capitalist, with shorter leases and fewer pretensions to manorial control. Already a mercantile hub, New York City's takeoff led the nation. By 1810, it had surpassed Philadelphia as northern America's central port and a center for industrial innovation. Driving out the Iroquois and mapping the west to sell to Yankee immigrants laid the basis for the nineteenth century's greatest state-led project, DeWitt Clinton's "big ditch," the Erie Canal, which made lower Manhattan the nation's center for finance capital.[5]

Black Life in New Amsterdam and New York

Just as British New York was sui generis, so too were black Yorkers' lives in the two centuries from 1623 (when the first "European" settling Manhattan was a man of color) to 1827's final emancipation. There was no direct progres-sion from slavery to freedom; repeatedly, conditions worsened. Slavery under the Dutch was a conditional status rather than lifelong and hereditary. A free community germinated "based on personal freedom, landownership, religion, and local institutions," with black neighborhoods near today's Wash-ington Square and along the Bowery, but the dozens of black farmers who met the conquering British in 1664 lost their land or moved away, as British law cemented a more binding servitude. New York's elite continued import-ing Africans throughout the eighteenth century, who mixed with captured

"Spanish Negroes" to produce a population as cosmopolitan as their owners; at 1827's celebration, a teenage James McCune Smith saw many "with gay bandanna handkerchiefs, betraying their West Indian birth: neither was Africa itself unrepresented, hundreds who had survived the middle passage, and a youth in slavery joined in the joyful procession."[6]

In the 1700s, rather than a *society with slaves* like other northern colonies, the ubiquity of racially bound labor and the draconian methods used to control it made the Hudson and Long Island counties a *slave society* of a distinct ethnoreligious character. In Craig Wilder's characterization, the Dutch farmers of Kings, Richmond, and Dutchess Counties "chose mastery" by either buying or renting chattels, "a way of life premised upon the domination of other people, a fact that makes them peculiarly akin to the Southern planter class." Farther north in Columbia County, the father of the most famous Dutch American, Martin Van Buren, was a tavernkeeper who owned six slaves in 1790, the year that young Martin married into a family owning thirty-six; even in 1824, the future president possessed at least one. To further underline its distinctiveness, slavery in New York was punctuated by mass executions in 1712 and 1741 in response to insurrection. The chimerical "Negro Plot" of 1841, with thirteen black men burned at the stake and seventeen plus four whites hanged, long remained part of the city's folk memory, and as late as 1775, a black man was burned in Poughkeepsie for arson.[7]

New York's counterrevolution signified freedom for black people. Joined by thousands of southern freedpeople arriving on British ships, black Yorkers profited materially, politically, and psychologically during the 1776–83 British occupation. Guerrilla chiefs like "Colonel Tye" and Stephen Bleuke terrorized Patriot farmers across the Neutral Zone, and black-manned blockhouses dominated the Hudson; one received an official visit from the future William IV in September 1781. Three thousand people of color sailed for Canada in November 1783, and then the wheel turned back. By 1790, the slave regime was restored, with two-thirds of the city's black population still in bonds, and a larger percentage in the six river counties. While the state's free black population increased from 1,119 to 3,449 by 1800, the number of slaves in New York City expanded by one-quarter. Refuting later assumptions about Revolutionary freedom, Manhattan and its hinterland remained the North's major slaveholding site.[8]

Failed Disfranchisement and Delayed Emancipation

Most accounts assume New York's black politics began with 1785's failed emancipation, but their origin lay earlier. In 1777, during the rebel state's internal wars, elections were held at which "all adult men, regardless of property holdings, could vote" for a constitutional convention and, although the number of black electors was certainly small, there were already "black, mulatto, and mustee [another term denoting a person of mixed race] citizens . . . entitled to a vote," as noted below. At the convention, John Jay failed in an attempt to disfranchise Catholics, and the 1777 constitution authorized "every male inhabitant" possessing a modest "Freehold of the value of twenty pounds" ($50) or who "rented a tenement . . . of the value of forty shillings" ($5) and paid a tax, to vote for the Assembly, with a substantial one-hundred-pound ($250) freehold required to vote for state senators and the governor. By enacting nonracial suffrage, the 1777 constitution created either a long-term political problem or a great opportunity. Whoever emancipated and thus potentially enfranchised the thousands of male slaves and their sons could gain an electoral advantage. In Suffolk, Kings, Queens, Richmond, New York, Dutchess, Westchester, Ulster, Columbia, and Albany, black voters might be decisive; local politicians knew who owned slaves and how many, just as they could count the votes of tenants obliged to their "manor lords."[9]

The 1777 Constitution created two executive bodies that shaped future black politics. First, a Council of Revision (the governor, chancellor of the Court of Equity, chief justice, and several other supreme court justices) reviewed every law, with a two-thirds legislative vote required to overturn its veto, and this body periodically protected black voting rights in the thirty years from 1785 to 1815. Second, a Council of Appointment controlled almost all offices in the state, including mayors. By 1821, its patronage extended to 15,000 jobs, compared with a mere 3,000 federal appointments. The council consisted of four senators elected by the Assembly plus the governor, making control of the state assembly uniquely important and ultimately empowering black voters.[10]

After eight years of war and a few of peace, the threat of an enlarged black electorate suddenly arose in 1785, soon after the January 25 founding of the New-York Society for Promoting the Manumission of Slaves, and Protecting Such of Them as Have Been, or May be Liberated (generally referred to as the New York Manumission Society). Several Quakers (widely derided as Tories) petitioned the legislature to enact gradual emancipation, as in Pennsylvania, Connecticut, and Rhode Island. In March, New York's Assembly agreed to a slow emancipation, with barriers hedging freedom: no interracial marriage; no jurying or testifying against whites; above all, no voting or office-holding. Facing opposition to these restrictions from the Senate, the Assembly surrendered everything except the suffrage bar. To this the Senate concurred, but the Council of Revision vetoed any emancipation predicated on disfranchisement. Its impassioned defense of nonracial republicanism is discussed later in this chapter, but first we should consider why disfranchisement was attempted.[11]

Historians have presumed 1785's disfranchising impulse was based upon objections to black people as citizens, but a racialist impulse was not necessarily the driver. Writing in a prominent city newspaper, "American" emphasized it was not blackness impelling his opposition to their suffrage but disloyalty. It was "contrary to the principles of our Independence . . . to disfranchise citizens," but that had been done "not long since," meaning the legislature's May 1784 disfranchisement of Loyalists, with "Citizens" denied "a vote at an election" for a reasonable motive, "to preserve the liberty of the state." That same revolutionary necessity should be extended to Negroes: "On the same principle as above, it would be greatly injurious to this state if all the negroes should be allowed the privileges of white men, unless there could be devised some possible means consistent with liberty, to separate them from white people." After slurs about "their participating in government, seated in our Senate and Assembly, General Quacco here, Col. Mingo there" (allusions with some force when the name "Colonel Tye" evoked a shudder), the writer got down to business. A large black vote would lead to "a total subversion of our liberties," as, "in combination with their friends the Quakers," black men "would give every assistance to our enemies, as we have already experienced their fidelity in the late contest, when they fought against us by whole regiments, and the Quakers at the same time supported every measure of Great-Britain to enslave us." Emancipation was a plot by "pretended supporters of liberty" whose "motives are obvious; for the moment the period of the emancipation of negroes arrives, it will cause them, with others," meaning unrepentant Loyalists, "to have a greater influence in the government, which the Quakers as well as some others, fervently wish for." The writer concluded on an anxious note: "If they were free and on an equal footing with us, God knows what use they would make of their power; a very bad one I fear."[12]

"American" made a legitimate argument. Like their Quaker allies, black Yorkers were demonstrably pro-British. But the Council of Revision had no use for this "arguing from expediency." Their veto began by pointing out that, according to the state's constitution, freed slaves would perforce enter "in the rank of citizens . . . as such entitled to all the privileges of citizens, nor can they be deprived of these essential rights without shocking those principles of equal liberty which every page in that Constitution labors to enforce." It raised a future danger—that "this class of disfranchised and discontented citizens . . . at some future period may be both numerous and wealthy," and under "ambitious and factious leaders, become dangerous to the State and effect the ruin of a Constitution whose benefits they are not permitted to enjoy."

For a moment, the anonymous writer sounded like a theoretician of white-skin privilege, arguing complexional suffrage authorized a caste system, "an order of citizens" with "no legislative or representative share in the government" versus "an aristocracy of the most dangerous and malignant kind, rendering power permanent and hereditary in the hands of those persons who deduce their origin through white ancestors only." The final scenario, based on sexual realities, was practical. At some future date, totally white Americans would "not amount to a fiftieth part of the people" and "the desire of power will induce those who possess it to exclude competitors by extending" one-drop whiteness "to the seventeenth generation." At that point "every man will have the blood of many more than two hundred thousand ancestors running in his veins, and that if any of these should have been colored, his posterity will, by the operation of this law, be disfranchised." Coming back to the present, it added there were "black, mulatto, and mustee citizens who have heretofore been entitled to a vote," and the new law would disfranchise them, "under the idea of political expediency, without their having been charged with any offense," the worst possible violation of republicanism.[13]

Slavery and Freedom, 1786–1799

Emancipation's failure set New York apart from the rest of the North for the next forty years, other than New Jersey. Whereas Pennsylvania and the New England states legislated or judicially mandated emancipation during the Revolutionary era, freedom legislation only passed in 1799 in New York, with another generation to complete the process, producing a remarkable contrast between entrenched slavery in the rural Dutch counties and an empowered black citizenry in the state's cities, including New York, Albany, and Hudson. This combined and uneven process pointed toward the special character of New York politics, with black suffrage championed by the same Federalists who fervently opposed universal suffrage. John Jay, New York's Emancipator, wrote the English abolitionist William Wilberforce in 1810 that "those who own the country are the most fit persons to participate in the government of it." In 1821, Jay's son, Peter, fought to maintain the freehold qualification while insisting men of sufficient property should vote regardless of complexion. Even in the 1830s, the eminent Federalist jurist James Kent, who had worked to safeguard black suffrage, wrote, "All theories of government that propose the mass of the people virtuous, and able and willing to act virtuously, are plainly utopian" and "the admission of universal suffrage and a licentious press are incompatible with government and security to property."[14]

Future Federalists championed emancipation and black rights even before partisan identities cohered. The association dated from the 1777 convention, where the aristocratic Gouverneur Morris, son of the state's largest slaveholder, tried to mandate the legislature taking "the most effective measures . . . for abolishing domestic slavery." He lost, but the constitution's other authors are telling: Jay and Robert R. Livingston. One cannot overstate Jay's importance—he came just behind Washington and Hamilton in his party's firmament as the beau ideal of a republican gentleman embodying a "moral Federalism" regarding race. The Huguenot Jay stood out among the Revolutionary generation for his admonitions that their "prayers to heaven for liberty will be impious" minus emancipation. In early 1785, while New York debated disfranchisement, he told Benjamin Rush that he wanted to end "all unjust and unnecessary discriminations" so that "all our inhabitants of every colour and denomination shall be free and equal partakers of our political liberty." Crucially, the open national division between Federalists and Republicans emerged in 1795 because the Jay Treaty he negotiated with Britain accepted the latter's refusal to return thousands of slaves emancipated by their troops, which Jay defended as honorable.[15]

Emancipation had high stakes in New York. On the one hand, the state's leaders envisioned themselves as cosmopolitan republicans; on the other, much of the white yeomanry remained committed to their mastery over others. Although emancipationism did not follow strict party lines, Federalists usually led. New York's dominant politician for four decades, George Clinton, founder of its Republican Party and governor in 1777–95 and 1801–5, belonged to the New York Manumission Society but "it was only a gesture," as his core electorate lay in the slaveholding counties. When Clinton beat Jay for the governorship in 1792, his men attacked Jay's antislavery views, and after Jay finally won in 1795, his administration was closely linked to emancipation, although the final legislative votes showed no partisan divide.[16]

New York Federalism's interracialism extended well beyond legislation. When parties were still networks of county "interests" rather than well-developed organizations, personal repute mattered, and Jay excelled in this respect. It is difficult to imagine another governor to whom a man of color would have written in 1796, describing himself on the envelope as "William Hamilton a black man," and inside as "one of those whom the generality of men call Negroes," but also "a native of New York." Young Hamilton (long rumored to be Alexander Hamilton's natural son) assailed "the Americans" who dared call theirs "a land of liberty and equality, a christian country when almost every part of it abounds with slavery and oppression." He implied a Saint-Dominguan future: "These slaves were stolen from their own Country. . . . When their purchasers buy them they know they were stolen property therefore they were equal to thieves. . . . Has God appointed us their slaves? I answer No. His word says [him] that stealeth a man and selleth him shall surely be put to death." In closing, he urged Jay to lead an abolitionist crusade—"The intent of my writing to you was this: . . . Is it not high time that the scandal of this country should be taken away that it might be called a free nation? Indeed and in truth is it not time that negroes should be free?"[17]

Nonracial republicanism's institutional base was the New York Manumission Society (NYMS). Until recently, historians treated this society as a mechanism for elite social control, but a less-presentist analysis stresses it sought "a progressive enlightenment for black and white Americans together," in which gradual emancipation facilitated the former slaves' "transition into republican citizens." Certainly, these white men were paternalistic, but they were also thoroughly environmentalist and thus antiracialist, at least in contrast to Jefferson. The NYMS set up a registry where freedpeople could deposit their certificates of manumission, to prove their status in future contests over ownership. In 1787, it also founded the African Free School, which by 1814 had educated more than 2,300 black children at public expense.[18]

The Jays exemplified this ethnocultural milieu permeated by Anglophone and Anglican benevolence. Republicans scoffed at Federalists as "the English party" for good reason, a telling charge in republican America. Federalists welcomed ex-Loyalists into their ranks, and both their party and organized abolitionism were tied to the newly formed Protestant Episcopal denomination and Trinity Church, at pains to formally separate themselves from the Church of England. Trinity welcomed black people after the Revolution, marrying dozens every year, whether free or still enslaved, the most significant form of recognition possible. Together, this nexus of society, church, and school constituted an apparatus of "cultural Federalism" like what developed in Philadelphia, but in this case enabling a formidable bloc vote, and the long-lasting Republican slur about former slaves following former masters to the polls.[19]

Consider the NYMS versus the Pennsylvania Abolition Society (PAS). Rather than supervising the black community, like the PAS's zealous Friends, the New Yorkers tolerated their self-organization. An 1801 incident underlines the difference. Madame de Volunbrun, a wealthy Frenchwoman from Saint-Domingue, emigrated to Manhattan with her former slaves, freed by France's 1794 decree. Apparently, after she sought to ship them south for sale, hundreds of black men surrounded her house, threatening violence. The NYMS acted as a broker in securing freedom, explaining that when agents of the Frenchwoman "attempted to seize" the black refugees, they "were protected by certain black men of their acquaintance, who were countenanced by several very respectable citizens." New Yorkers should "decide who are the most dangerous men in society, the *black or white Frenchmen*," warning the latter "that the benevolent characters throughout the United States, composing the Manumission Societies, have long been sensible that the *Black People held slaves in our country, who were actually within the jurisdiction* of the *French Government* at the period of passing the *Decree manumitting the Slaves,* are entitled to all the *rights* and *privileges* of *Freemen*." These societies would *"grant all requisite protection to these Black People."* A hysterical reply by a "Friend of Order" alleged that "a mob of 200 negroes" had assembled "threatening to burn homes," noting, "A firm belief has taken root amongst the negroes, that every attempt at liberty, let it be in conformity or in opposition to the law, will be supported by the quakers and the Manumission Society." It is difficult to imagine any such scenario in Philadelphia involving either the PAS or black leaders.[20]

A Black Electorate Emerges, 1800–1807

Black Yorkers entered politics at an advantageous time, as a developing party system intersected with emancipation. Interest in mobilizing or suppressing black electors derived from two factors. The first was the furious partisan war of 1805–16, when New York Federalists waged a vigorous counteroffensive amid Republican factionalism. The second was the state's two-tiered electoral system, very different from Pennsylvania and Massachusetts's taxpayer suffrage. Even in 1821, only 38.7 percent of adult men qualified to vote for governor and state senators via possession of land worth $250; in New York City only 24 percent met that standard. This apparatus afforded inspectors at the polls many opportunities to exclude; in 1804, the young Van Buren was challenged in Kinderhook for owning insufficient property. In this context, New York's black electorate drew notice because of its weight as "Assembly Voters" in three major counties. Two remained Federalist in every election from 1804 to 1820: Albany and Columbia, controlling six and four Assembly seats, respectively, until 1809, when Schenectady was carved out of Albany, cutting its representation to four. The third was New York (Manhattan), with nine seats until 1808's reapportionment, when the Assembly increased from 100 to 112, and the city gained two. Although Republicans had controlled that delegation since 1800, from 1809 to 1816 the parties traded control by tiny margins, and the black vote became crucial.[21]

The partisan frame was paramount: New York Federalists were the best-organized in the nation. They created their party's first statewide organization in 1801, pioneering cohesive town, county, and district structures under a State Corresponding Committee. They also benefited from intra-Republican strife. At no point after 1800 were New York Republicans united. Their fissiparous tendencies birthed Vice President Aaron Burr's 1804 run for governor and DeWitt Clinton's 1812 presidential candidacy, challenging the incumbent Madison with Federalist backing, apostasy on a grand scale given that his uncle George was Madison's vice president until dying in office early that year. The younger Clinton carried the North other than Vermont and Pennsylvania, remaining a national figure into the 1820s while New York's Republicans split into pieces. His machinations were hardly unusual. Republicans endured constant schisms, including those led by Burrites, who persisted long after their idol's eclipse. Indeed, an early recognition of black voters came during Burr's 1804 gubernatorial run. A paper supporting the regular Republican, Morgan Lewis, reported that on "the day preceding the commencement of the election, Mr. Burr had assembled at his house . . . a considerable number of *gentlemen of colour*—upwards of twenty . . . headed by a celebrated perfumer in Broadway . . . to court the favour of the people of colour in aid of his election." Apparently these men were all freeholders and able to vote for governor.[22]

The underlying premise here bears repeating, that western Long Island (including today's Brooklyn and Queens) and the Hudson River counties were the North's largest slaveholding region. Emancipation and nonracial citizenship thus had immediate electoral consequences, generating a bloc of potential voters available for mobilization. The emancipation act of 1799 by its silence implied black citizenship and suffrage. New York County saw the most dramatic evidence of this emergence. In 1790, 10.5 percent of the city's population of 33,131 was black with two-thirds still enslaved. By 1810, the city had tripled to 96,373 and blacks still constituted over 10 percent of that population, but nearly all were free, and those men voted.[23]

Little scholarship exists on freedpeople in the larger hinterland, besides Graham Hodges's invaluable *Root & Branch: African Americans in New York & East Jersey, 1613–1863* and a few dissertations. The urban story is told with great subtlety in Shane White's *Somewhat More Independent: The End of Slavery in New York City, 1770–1810*, which paints a vivid picture of how the city's people of color "vigorously resisted slavery" after the Revolution, establishing "a tradition of opposition . . . that few, if any, states could equal." Black Manhattanites were exceptionally well organized, which Craig Wilder attributes to West African practices of forming secret societies and a folk culture of physical defiance and open rebellion, accelerated by the temporary sphere of freedom under the British in 1776–83. The newly freed participated aggressively in the city's raucous street mobilizations and Election Day fracases rather than organizing a separate "shadow" politics, in part because of their strong economic position. White shows that a larger proportion of the city's men of color acquired trades or small businesses than elsewhere. Early on, they took over much of the city's favorite trade in consumables, as oyster sellers. Excluded from the largest economic interest group, the licensed cartmen, they entered the remunerative night soil business, and many became hackney coachmen. Some prominent tradesmen were black, like the tobacconist Peter Williams, Sr., sexton of the John Street Methodist Church, and many owned groceries, where workingmen tippled cheaply, while Bancker Street's black-run dancing cellars, saloons, and brothels became a notorious vice zone. Most visibly, black men controlled the chimney-sweeping trade without which houses readily caught fire. Philadelphia had black sweepmasters, including Richard Allen, and John Remond monopolized that business in Salem, but nowhere else did they function as a guild and an organized voting bloc. In sum, White argues, the "vast majority . . . seem to have been incorporated successfully into the dominant culture," aided by clustering in self-sufficient groups around their well-appointed churches, which "fostered a strong sense of community among blacks . . . probably better off in some ways than their white neighbors."[24]

Prior to 1804, references to black voters were usually jibes. In 1794, an Otsego County Federalist reported that in Unadilla, Republicans brought "every man in the town . . . able to travel" to the polls, "both white and *black*." A 1798 report from Orange County alleged that when Federalists "permitted their negroes (or rather commanded them) to raise a pole" mocking Jeffersonian liberty poles, "these impudent fellows set about the rebellious employment, called '*thinking*,' the result of which was this striking motto— 'FREEDOM TO AFRICANS.'" In 1799, Manhattan Republicans charged that Federalists "grossly violated" the elections law in that even "Negroes were taken out of the streets, and encouraged to impose upon the Inspectors." Most intriguing was the 1801 charge that a judge called "nocturnal meetings" at his city mansion with "enormous supplies of home crackers and cheese" to pull black votes for the Patroon, Stephen Van Rensselaer, the Federalists' gubernatorial candidate, and "if they all would vote the ballots they received from you, after election unto each man you'd make some handsome present." This Republican attack alluded to the politics of emancipation, the judge's "effrontery" in telling "the deluded Africans that Stephen Van Rensselaer and yourself had gained them their liberty, and that if he became Governor all their race would be made free, and entitled to hold offices in the state. . . . It was, as you well know, when George Clinton was Governor, and when we had a Republican Senate and Assembly, that the first effective law was passed for the abolition of slavery," a blatant lie. Already, it was alleged black men preferred Federalists, as in the 1800 jibe about one of the Livingstons driving "an old negro" five miles to vote "for the *old Gubbernur*" but then "he turned off . . . and voted for the federal ticket."[25]

An 1806 article in the Federalist *Evening Post* underlined how "Africans" had long voted as they wished. In 1801, Republicans sought to unseat the incumbent Federalist mayor, Richard Varick, by electing a Republican legislature which would choose a new Council of Appointment and purge men like Varick. Supposedly, *"Vote for us, and we'll turn out the Mayor*, was the *hue and cry* raised round the city," which "the cartmen and grocers, and other licensed persons, regarded . . . as a sort of promise. . . . Many a poor soul was lugged up to the polls [and] gave in his vote for the democratic ticket. . . . All the negroes to a man, voted the same way, for they too were promised." Black men wanted access to the licenses required for the city's most privileged employment, the cartmen controlling street traffic, but the "democrats" betrayed them in favor of another despised group. Addressing the overwhelmingly native-born cartmen, the *Post*'s editor, William Coleman, gloated that the result was *"six or seven hundred licensed Irishmen.* Nay, was not there a beginning to extend the licenses, according to promise, to the negroes? . . . A negro regularly received his license one day, and had it taken away the next on discovering it would raise too much of a hubbub among the white cartmen."[26]

Here we see the early republic's "wages of whiteness," in David Roediger's phrase, albeit in 1800 whiteness and nativity were still mixed up, with the native-born cartmen fighting to keep out both "Irishmen" and "negroes." Partisan politics further strengthen Roediger's argument for how class and race segmented the working class, albeit that black men operated much like whites: both used the state to either break open or maintain control over labor markets, as a different example shows. In this period, black men dominated licensed chimney sweeping, based on the exploitation of boys sent up chimneys. An 1805 account documents how, like the cartmen, black sweepmasters deployed their bloc vote to reward friends and punish enemies. In 1804, the city's fire warden and engineers petitioned its Federalist-controlled government for regulations to prevent fires and protect the sweeps, "small black boys . . . mostly owned by free black men," who were "guilty of the most cruel and abominable practices." A law was made, a supervisor appointed, and offices opened, but "the owners of the boys, principally negroes" objected. The *Post*'s Coleman, later known for courting black electors, pointed out "negroes have votes as good as yours or mine, and probably better than either, for some of them have freehold votes." They constituted "a numerous and influential band at elections" and had "complained, and expostulated, and threatened" against this infringement on property rights. Without delay, a "new Board of friends of the people [Republicans] repealed it."[27]

Clearly, in the early 1800s black men backed whichever faction or candidate offered rewards. In 1803, during Republican efforts to expand the restrictive municipal suffrage, a Federalist editorial insisted "this alteration" would add "to our present flock of *Irish freemen*, an insult to our citizens, and an injury to our Country, the whole host of Africans that now deluge our City," who would then "be placed upon an equal with our citizens." Only in 1807 did black men's negotiations with Federalists emerge into the open. Clintonian Republicans expected Governor Morgan Lewis to step down in favor of Daniel D. Tompkins, but Lewis refused and split the party. In the city, Federalists and Burrites backed Lewis and black men joined their "Coalition." The ensuing fight led to the first published appeal "TO THE INDEPENDENT ELECTORS AMONG THE PEOPLE OF COLOUR," soliciting votes for Tompkins. The writer admitted, "Fellow Citizens, The appellation by which I address you, and to which I claim your particular attention, together with the supposed fewness of your number, may excite considerable observation." Nonetheless, "considering you as men, and as brethren, and having capacities accordingly to act, I do not feel that repugnancy in the acknowledgement, which too often forms the barrier of distinction between us," and promoted Tompkins's antislavery credentials. They should "aid the election of a man, by whom the *injured cause of your oppressed* brethren hath been strenuously advocated and defended," deriding Governor Lewis as a "bosom friend" of an unnamed slaveholder who held "*nine hundred of your African brethren in abject slavery!*" Black men should "avenge their wrongs, and by the assistance of your suffrages, evince to the world that the name of TOMPKINS is worthy of . . . your united support."[28]

This was no onetime effort. Two weeks later, another pro-Tompkins paper stressed that the Republican legislature had passed laws hindering slaveowners wishing to sell chattels out of state, "to shield these devoted sufferers from the severest bondage that the avarice of man can subject them to. . . . It originated with our city representation. . . . People of colour, to whom are you indebted for this amelioration of your condition?" The Federalists responded with "A Caution. The people of colour are cautioned against a set of wicked men, who are going about deceiving them, & telling them the federalists mean to reduce them again to slavery, & many other equally wicked falsehoods." In response, the Republican *Advertiser* derided how "a certain Federal character, once honoured with the Mayoralty of our city [Varick]," was "solicited by a respectable man of colour, for information respecting the propriety of driving a Horse and Carriage without having a license" and replied "I've no laws or information in my books for *Nagurs*."[29]

On May 2, having lost the city vote, the Clintonian *American Citizen* angrily declared, "The federalists so managed as to secure nineteen-twentieths of the black votes. In the Seventh Ward they brought up negro and negress two and two in federal coaches . . . labeled '*American ticket*'—filled with 'American' lads and lasses!," adding Federalists had also "naturalized about

400 Scotch royalists!" Local Clintonians' defeat was blamed on "The Coalition . . . all huddled" together at the polls: "federalists—Lewisites—Burrites, and negroes!" Two contemporary accounts describe that year's campaigning. In March, Clintonians reported acerbically on a Lewisite "general meeting" organized by prominent Livingstons ("Mat, and Bob, and Peter R.") and an unnamed man of color ("the yellow man") attended by a crowd of "men and boys, white and black." Later, Washington Irving wrote a woman friend about this "purgatory of an Election." He worked for Josiah Ogden Hoffman, a lawyer and Federalist assemblyman, and as a pollworker "shook hands with the mob." Under orders, he dove into the "holes & corners . . . sweep offices & oyster cellars" to pull black voters. While sneering at "Negroes," he acknowledged "they have all turned out for the federalists to a man!," especially in the Seventh Ward, where "we had them up in an enormous drove in the middle of the day waiting round the poll for the chance to vote," while Federalist scions named Hamilton and King milled around.[30]

Before the November 1807 city election, Republicans tried again. Reprinting the *Post*'s invite to "the Federal electors of Colour . . . to attend a general meeting at Deefy & Wilmot's Tavern," it asked, why would black men "suffer themselves to be wheedled into the support of federal men and measures? Who are really their friends?" given that "the "manumission society" was "very principally if not entirely composed of REPUBLICANS." It then charged that Federalists permitted visiting southerners to hold slaves in the city jail, but "when the republican party obtained a majority at the board, the federal ordinance was abolished." Back in power, "the *federal* Board has . . . revived the old ordinance," so how "can you vote for such men?"[31]

Accounts focused entirely on black men are deceptive, however. They were hardly the only suspect group of voters, and attempts to mobilize or control their votes fit within a larger struggle over who were legitimate voters, and whether particular groups should be forced to prove their citizenship at the polls.

Certificate Wars

At the 1821 convention, the most telling argument for disfranchisement was that "a few hundred Negroes of the city of New-York, following the train of those who ride in their coaches, and whose shoes and boots they had so often blacked, shall go to the polls of the election and change the political condition of the whole state. A change in the representation of that city may cause a change in your assembly, by giving a majority to a particular party, which would vary your council of appointment, who make the highest officers of your government. Thus would the whole state be controlled by a few hundred of this species of population in the city of New York." This was no random slur from an obscure Negrophobe. It came from a distinguished political figure, Delaware County's Erastus Root (lieutenant governor in 1823–24, Speaker of the Assembly in 1827–28 and 1830, a fixture into the 1840s as a state senator), and Root's claim remained the core Democratic charge, quoted in an 1842 report to the Democratic-controlled Assembly. It was also accurate in its assertion that Manhattan's men of color could "go to the polls of the election and change the political condition of the whole state," and understanding why is key to New York's black politics.[32]

Today, multimember legislative districts are standard practice in Europe and Latin America but virtually unknown in the United States. In the early nineteenth century, however, they were common. Until 1847, New York's Assembly was divided into county delegations. Every county (sometimes two grouped together) elected at least one member, and most sent several. County assembly delegations were not elected as blocs, however; instead, a voter cast as many ballots as the county had seats, and party organizations focused on holding their supporters together to avoid ticket-splitting. New York City had the largest delegation, nine of 108 seats until 1808, when the Assembly expanded to 112 and the city's share to eleven. City Republicans gained control in 1797, and elected their slate through 1809. Although a party could lose the city and carry the Assembly, as Federalists did in the latter year, winning this group was obviously desirable.

Why did one state's lower house matter so much? Here we encounter the peculiar character of New York's governance, in which an obscure assemblyman might exert more power than a member of Congress. Until 1821's constitutional revision, every office in the state was filled by the Council of Appointment, consisting of the governor and four senators elected by the Assembly. Control of the Assembly determined control of the council determined control of the early republic's major pork barrel. When the Assembly changed hands, thousands of office-holders were replaced, as in 1807, 1808, 1810, 1811, 1813, and 1815. Electing the Council of Assembly was hardly the Assembly's only plenary power. Until 1828, New York's presidential electors were chosen on a legislative joint ballot, meaning that particular year's Assembly majority might decide who was president. The combination of these two powers turned each spring's Assembly elections into a continual plebiscite, with decisive import in presidential years. Every seat was worth contesting, and Republicans viewed with alarm the collapse of their party's control in New York City in 1807–10. The former year had demonstrated the Federalists' capacity to link up with dissident Republicans, and, in addition, they had found a new constituency: black men. If the city went Federalist, the state was up for grabs, as General Root warned.

That 1821's disfranchisement ended a decade-long battle over black voting is well known. Beginning in 1811, Republicans passed laws requiring free men of color to prove their status by producing certificates of manumission. What is new is the discovery of ample precedent for this targeted voter suppression. New York had a long history of requiring legal documentation for a particular group to vote. Well before 1811, Federalists routinely demanded certificates from naturalized "foreigners," meaning Irishmen, who were presumptively Republican. That practice shaped popular awareness of the certificate war waged against presumptively Federalist black men.

In 1798, a Federalist Congress extended the period required for naturalization from five to fourteen years, mandating the filing of multiple certificates. On April 14, 1802, in time for spring elections, a Republican Congress reinstated the five-year residency rule, empowering any state "common law" court to naturalize, including issuance of the official forms that could be demanded at the polls. The first fight over certificates in New York came just days later, revolving around which body could issue them and who would accept them. After the first day's voting, a Federalist paper issued a "Caution To The Inspectors" from "A Natural-Born Citizen." Samuel Wortman, Republican clerk of the Mayor's Court, had "undertaken to naturalize the United Irishmen by the job, at Two Dollars per head," on top of which "the Mayor's Court is now holding a session" devoted to "the business of naturalization." Supposedly, Wortman was issuing "certificates of his own manufacture." Inspectors were instructed to "call for the certificates of all aliens born, and, if they are not on a proper FIVE *Dollar Stamp*," reject them. Republicans acknowledged, "A certified copy of the naturalization law was received from Washington on Monday last; the following day (the first day of the election) many patriotic aliens applied to the Mayor's court to be admitted citizens," with twenty-six naturalized, producing "great alarm among the federalists." A prominent Federalist lawyer challenged every Irishman with an improper certificate at one poll, after which Wortman tried sending his new voters to another ward, where they "very properly met with the same fate."[33]

Demands that self-denominated "Republican Aliens" be required to produce certificates remained a staple of partisan denunciations, as in this 1815 Republican editorial mocking a Federalist who had said "to a *black* man yesterday, 'how scandalously you are treated by the *democrats*,' in making you bring certificates or somebody to swear for you, before you can vote," at which an Irishman intervened to say "Not quite so badly . . . as we are by the *federalists*, who take a black man's word and refuse an Irishman's oath—a friendly *voucher* entitles a black man to vote—an Irishman must produce a certificate of naturalization—*black* men may *swear in*—*Irishmen* may swear till they are black in the face without being allowed to vote unless they produce a *certificate!*"[34]

The first salvo came after 1807's election, when Federalists charged that "out of eleven hundred votes, it is ascertained that upwards of five hundred have been given in by foreigners; who came with their certificates and who therefore could not be refused, altho' instances were not wanting where the alien was unable even to name the person by whose oath he had been proved to have resided five years in this country." In 1808, the *Evening Post* reported worse frauds, how "the inspectors of the First Ward committed an Irishman to prison for offering to vote upon another man's certificate of naturalization. . . . At the Eighth Ward three Irishmen voted on two certificates, nor was it till a fourth came up to vote on one of the same papers that the fraud was discovered." Editor Coleman added bitterly, "This is what is called freedom of election, and the voice of the people, and all that; this is the way our administration is supported, by a tribe just fresh from the bogs of Ireland." By comparison, the voters of African descent were notably peaceful; there was no equivalent of Coleman's charge that "after closing the poll, a mob of nearly 600 Irishman . . . *drove every American Federalist from the neighborhood.* They moved about in a mass, crying down with him! kill the federal scoundrel!"[35]

For the next two years, Republican factions battled for and against the Irish influence, with Tammany Hall fiercely Hibernophobic into the 1810s.[36] Finally, in 1810, Republican dissension aided the Federalists in breaking the party's lock on the city's Assembly delegation. This disaster impelled Republicans to unite in suppressing black Federalists while bringing the Irish into the fold. Even before Election Day, Clintonians attacked the Federalists as Negrophiles and nativists, describing how "An adopted citizen" who had long voted "was yesterday prohibited by the federal inspectors from voting on his *alleged* citizenship, and sent home after his certificate of naturalization. An *African* presented himself directly after—was challenged on his freedom, and his certificate of emancipation demanded—but he was *presumed* to be qualified, and suffered to vote on his own oath." A clear white line was drawn: "Thus are Irishmen and Scotchmen, (when they are republicans, God save the mark!) and Englishmen, Germans, &c. treated—thus are natives of *Europe* treated—and thus are natives of Africa preferred by these federal impostors. If 'all men are equal,' as we hold and believe, why are not Europeans entitled to equal rights with Africans?"[37]

Despite these occasional comparisons, most efforts to gain Irish or black votes operated separately. Both Federalists and Republicans continued trying to enlist black men. A spring 1808 Federalist "general meeting of the Electors of Colour" censured Jefferson's Embargo on Atlantic trade as "extremely injurious to the labouring class," an example of "Executive imbecility and foreign influence" following "the twelve years of the Federal Administration [when] the country was prosperous and happy." In response, angry Republicans charged, "A black trick—The federalists are buying the votes of the people of colour in various ways. Last Sunday evening they hired boys to break the windows of the African Church, and afterwards they very LIBERALLY came forward with a collection to pay for them." After Republicans lost, they returned to charging Federalists "*by some means*, secured the votes of the people of colour. The federal ticket was generally denominated the *African Ticket*. The lanes and alleys, the high ways and low ways, the cellars and brothels were scoured by the federalists."[38]

Surprisingly, the organized campaign to suppress black votes began not in the city, but up the river in Hudson, Columbia County's metropole, founded by Rhode Island Quakers in 1783. Its freedmen had long claimed their suffrages, until in 1808 local Republicans, likely led by a young Martin Van Buren, figured out how to block them: if a former slave had become a citizen, like a naturalized alien, why not make him produce the equivalent proof? This linkage was made plain by Hudson Federalists' denunciation in that year of how "the bare word" of one man was "accepted by the inspectors as a proof of his naturalization, (he being a foreigner) while free men of color who voted for years past, were required to produce positive proof of their manumission, before they could be admitted." One of them, "a *free-holder*, was compelled to ride four miles after his certificate of manumission, which he had held for several years." The war of certificates had commenced.[39]

Hudson Republicans' tactical innovation inspired their city colleagues to similar steps. In early 1809, to gin up black voters, Federalists invited one of their leaders into the public sphere. Joseph Sidney, the leading black Federalist ("Sambo Sidney" to Republicans) gave a venomous oration against "the mad democracy of the southern states." He championed Federalists as the true Founders with whom the "interests of the middle and eastern states are intimately connected," a party that "while in office, gave to commerce every possible encouragement," painting the "*Anti-Federal* or *Democratic party*" as "a set of ambitious, designing, and office-seeking men" venturing forth from a "native cave of filth and darkness." Finally, he mocked Jefferson, asking, "Is the great idol of democracy *our* friend?" Certainly not, "else he would respect the rights of our African brethren; several hundred of whom he keeps as *slaves* on his plantations." An orthodox Federalist, Sidney hailed George Washington: "This illustrious and humane man, feeling that slavery was incompatible with the principles for which he fought, most generously emancipated every slave that he owned, and gave to each a portion sufficiently large to answer his exigencies, until he could procure employment."[40]

Why did Federalists insert a black man into this charged electoral environment? Sidney was no political amateur (by 1817, he was rounding up votes for Republicans), and likely demanded a quid pro quo for delivering his constituents. He got that. The *Evening Post* hailed "Sidney's Oration," calling him "a man of sound principles and a good federalist," and urging "he ought at least to be indemnified by a liberal purchase of his pamphlet, which sells at only a shilling a piece. The hint I hope will not be lost on the respectable society of friends nor on federal gentlemen," who could pick it up at the paper or at Hutson's Intelligence Office, an employment agency operated by a prominent black man. The Federalists proceeded apace. On April 24, the "Electors of Color" met at "Hyer's Long Room" to hail "the exertions of the Federal Minority in Congress" and give "our utmost approbation" to the "nominations made at the General Meeting of the Federal Republicans." Two days later, on April 26 (the second of three Election Days), Manhattan Federalists reported a "*Shameful violation,*" that "the Republican Inspectors of the Fourth Ward yesterday rejected the vote of a free man of colour, on the ground that one of the Inspectors *deemed it convenient to suspect,* that he was born in slavery." Any black man might have to "produce legal evidence of his manumission," clearly a "systematic plot to disfranchise a large portion" of the electorate. "Men of Color!" were summoned to action. They must "resist, by every honorable effort, this insidious attempt to destroy the most invalulable [*sic*] principle of Freemen—*the elective franchise.*"[41]

In 1810, the battle over black men's votes went public in a flurry of legislative initiatives highlighting competing certificates. The Assembly's Republican minority proposed disfranchising nearly all freedmen via a reverse grandfathering, that "no black person or persons" who were "slaves at the adoption of the constitution of the United States, shall be admitted to vote at any election hereafter." Federalists countered with an amendment to the elections law "to allow their votes to people of colour, otherwise qualified, unless proof of slavery be made by the challenger." In the Republican-controlled Senate, the Federalists' gubernatorial candidate, Jonas Platt of Oneida, introduced a similar bill weeks before the election, and Republicans snorted Platt's bill "would compel inspectors of elections to admit" a slave to vote, since "evidence of his having been a slave sometime since would not be sufficient to exclude, or compel testimony of manumission." Federalists supposedly wished to put slaves "in a better situation than a naturalised citizen." The latter "must produce his certificate of naturalization:—whereas a slave might, according to Mr. Platt, vote of course, unless his slavery could be established at the time of his voting." Irishmen were queried: "Naturalised citizens, what think you of this attempt to put you in a worse situation than negroes?," and that fall Republicans published an address "To the Independent Irishmen of the city of New-York," purportedly from one of their own, asking, "Why then have we been proscribed? Why have *negroes* the high privilege of freemen, and not the descendants of Erin? . . . Countrymen, rouse from your slumbers! defend your rights!"[42]

The April 24–26, 1810 elections saw the usual partisan mobilization in New York City. An April 13 "meeting of citizens of colour" declared they would give "their suffrages to such candidates only as are known to be friendly to an amelioration of their unfortunate condition"; only the newspaper where this notice appeared suggested these candidates might be Republicans. A rival meeting approved candidates nominated by the "Federal committee" while denouncing Republican attempts to "to deprive us of voting." The claim that slaves were voting came to the fore. Before the balloting ended, Republicans insisted, "Very few of the Africans who have voted at this election are entitled to the privilege. Most of them labor under an embarrassment [slavery] which precludes them from that essential right, a right which appertains to freemen and citizens only." To explain their imminent loss, Republicans asserted that "the received doctrine of the federalists" permitted slaves voting, even if an Irishman had "a greater right to come forward to the poll, and upon being asked the question whether he is a citizen or not, to tell the inspectors they have no right to ask it." The same article damned Republican factionalism, which had produced Federalist control of city hall and the "appointment of Inspectors . . . who by adopting the rule of permitting the negroes to vote (without suffering the inquiry to be made as to their being slaves) has added an increase of at least 800 electors on the federal side," a number likely drawn from the 1805 city census recording 818 enslaved men. The editor then projected a dystopian scenario in which Federalists would use slaves as they had once mustered a tenant bloc vote in the river counties. It was falsely claimed that "the federalists . . . are the principal slave holders in this state," and soon, by "renting tenements and paying taxes for their slaves," they would "terminate every election in their favour." Resentment at Federalist victory and the accompanying lack of deference produced an account describing Manhattan's streets as teeming with "drunken impudent negroes and wenches" empowered by "our honest federal corporation." Much like the white nightmares of Reconstruction in James S. Pike's *The Prostrate State* and Thomas Dixon's *The Clansman*, it described how "the honest and *friendly* partizans of virtuous federalism have so emboldened the 'black federal gentlemen,' and in some instances the '*ladies*' of their family, that not only democratic men, but their wives, daughters, and sons, get twirled in an instant from the walk into dirt, filth, &c. when met by these emblems of darkness, if an immediate pass is not given."[43]

Before turning to Republican efforts to suppress or control black votes, there is an important proviso. Voting brought black men a measure of respect, and white politicians certainly encouraged it from sincere republicanism or partisan opportunism, but voting never entitled black men to full participation in the political economy or political society. They were barred from most licensed trades and the city's famous fire companies, visible markers of inequality. Black men's separate and unequal position within the city's laboring classes was underlined by displays of the all-white "mechanic interest," the parades of tradesmen with their tools and the celebrated Democratic-Republican societies of the 1790s. During election campaigns, plebeian whites thronged the constant rota of ward meetings, whereas black men did not attend, vote, or speak at meetings with whites or share in minor party offices, meeting only as citywide "electors of colour." Not a single identifiable black man appears on the voluminous 1810 membership roll of the city's Federalist-organized Washington Benevolent Society. Such forms of inclusion may have seemed impossible, but need not have been, given how many votes black men gave. Only a few years later, their New England counterparts fulfilled all those functions—caucusing with, speaking to, and sharing platforms and offices with white men.[44]

1811: The Party Line Holds

The decade-long legislative fight leading to a constitutional disfranchisement was the nation's first sustained campaign for white suffrage, and clearly originated in partisan imperatives. From 1811 to 1815, the push to exclude black voters united otherwise divided Republicans in the face of a Federalist resurgence. Even in 1812, when DeWitt Clinton's men allied with Federalists to back his presidential candidacy and the regulars stayed loyal to Madison, Republicans maintained their internal consensus on depriving Federalists of black votes. Led by Clinton, Republican legislators passed a "certificate law" in 1811 and backed versions of that law over the next four years, while Federalists, with Stephen Van Rensselaer in the fore, continued to support nonracial suffrage. This campaign differed in both form and intent from the explicitly racial provision enacted in 1821. Until 1816, Republicans hoped to take black men's votes; the latter were twice as useful, after all. In New York City, they encouraged "Colored Republicans" to identify with the Party of Jefferson, and if these men demonstrated their loyalty, Republican officials distributed the necessary certificates gratis, just as they had for their Irish supporters. It was only in the late 1810s that some Republicans began proposing whiteness as the criterion for citizenship.[45]

Throughout this period, the central impetus for disfranchisement was New York Federalists' recovery from electoral oblivion. In 1804, Jefferson crushed the South Carolinian Charles C. Pinckney everywhere, including New York, and the Federalists did not even field a gubernatorial candidate. By 1806, the state Senate was entirely Republican, and other than contingents from Albany and Columbia, the Federalists held almost no Assembly seats. The year 1808 began the Federalist comeback through attacks on Jefferson's disastrous Embargo on nearly all foreign commerce, and they surged to forty-five seats in the Assembly, followed by a triumph in 1809, electing seven senators (out of thirty-two) and winning a narrow Assembly majority (although the city delegation stayed Republican).

In 1810, the Republicans regained the Assembly, 65–37, and in March–April 1811, this legislature rammed through the bill requiring black men to produce certificates of manumission at the polls. In the city, however, Federalists took six of eleven seats. On April 30–May 2, 1811, Republicans retained the Senate (26–6) and Assembly (66–38) but lost all eleven city seats. In 1812, holding onto their Manhattan bloc, Federalists retook the assembly and in November, that body divided into three over which presidential electors to back: Federalists with fifty-eight versus Clintonians with twenty-nine and Madisonians with twenty-two; on a joint ballot with the Senate, Clinton won 74–45 (gaining almost all Federalist votes), with twenty-eight Republicans abstaining. This was the apex of Federalist power. In January 1813, the Columbia Federalist Jacob Rutsen Van Rensselaer was elected Assembly speaker, and Rufus King was elected senator. In 1813, amidst an unpopular war, the Federalists retained the Assembly but in 1814, the Republicans regained it, and in 1815, this legislature passed more stringent measures targeting Manhattan's black voters.[46]

As this précis suggests, control of New York City's eleven-member Assembly delegation was the proximate cause for suppressing African American voters. Counting ballots cast in city Assembly races demonstrates how black men's reported 500 to 1,000 votes had such weight. In 1809, only nineteen votes separated the least popular victor, a Republican, and the top loser, a Federalist (4,919 to 4,900), with Republicans averaging 4,993 votes versus the Federalists' 4,871, a margin of 122. In 1810, Republicans won statewide but lost six city seats by tiny margins—the top Federalist received 5,323 votes, only sixty-one more than the lowest-polling winner, a Republican. In 1811, despite passage of the "certificate bill" targeting black men, Republican support collapsed. Federalists took all eleven seats by huge margins, with 1,307 votes separating the bottom of their slate from the Republicans. Tellingly, the Federalists easily took the formerly Republican Fifth, Sixth, and Seventh Wards where most black men lived.[47]

The plan to suppress African Americans' votes was planned with considerable discretion. On March 9, 1811, Assemblyman Thomas S. Lester of Suffolk introduced a bill "to prevent fraud at elections" by banning fagot deeds and allowing voluntary highway labor to fulfill the taxpaying requirement. Two weeks later his committee added "that whenever any black person or person of color shall present himself to vote . . . he shall produce to the inspectors . . . a certificate of his freedom" from any county or town clerk, which passed on a party-line vote, 56–24. Anticipating the elections, Federalist Thomas P. Grosvenor of Columbia County moved to postpone the certificate requirement until May 10, and lost. On March 25, after a third reading, Stephen Van Rensselaer made the rhetorical gambit of trying to substitute a new title, *"An act to deprive a portion of citizens of the elective franchise,"* and the bill went to the Senate. There was little subtlety by this point. When Robert Bogardus, a newly elected city Federalist, spoke in favor of Van Rensselaer's motion, calling the Republican bill "an invasion of the rights secured by the constitution. . . . If a majority of the house persisted in passing the bill, they must be influenced by motives other than those they avowed, and by such they dare not avow on the floor," a Washington County Republican replied, "I might with equal truth retort upon him the charge of being influenced by the fear of losing his own election, unless it shall be again secured by the preponderance which his party may acquire by a union of their own strength with that of the *Negro Slaves* of New-York."[48]

The Senate's process underlines the Republicans' unity. On March 26, the Senate passed the Assembly's bill. On March 29, Senator DeWitt Clinton, the state's most powerful Republican, lately reappointed mayor of New York, brought in a revised version "to prevent fraud at elections," which passed again, but on March 30, the Council of Revision rejected the bill's provision enfranchising anyone who swore he was twenty years old, since it allowed "minors to vote." Amended and returned to the council, the bill was again vetoed, now because of its racial intent. As in 1785, the council's decision is worth quoting in depth. The majority found it wrong to burden men born free but of the wrong complexion, adding "the description of *person of colour* . . . is too vague and uncertain to afford a determinate test," given "all the gradations of the mixed races between the African black and the clear complexion of the white man and even beyond it" (the bill's final version substituted "mulatto" for "person of colour" to allay this objection). Allegations based on rumor, or vagaries of phenotype, would impose on those "whose ancestors have uninterruptedly enjoyed the elective franchise, under the colonial as well as this state government . . . the humiliating degradation of being challenged in consequence of a supposed taint." Respectable men could face "wanton insult and contumely, merely on account of their complexion, whether produced by the accidental circumstances of birth, climate or disease." The bill was plainly antirepublican—"a particular description of persons . . . under the constitution . . . entitled to the elective franchise, many of whom were born free" would lose "rights to which they are now entitled in common with other citizens." In particular, "no adequate means are afforded" to regain the suffrage, "as there is no provision for compelling the attendance of witnesses before the officers." Men of color were subjected "to the *will and pleasure* of others" who were "interested in withholding the requisite evidence of freedom." Finally, it was wrong to assert that "all black men, and men of color are presumed to be slaves until they prove that they are free," requiring "proof to other tribunals, and two several certificates." Many such men were "born free" and therefore did not possess manumission papers, and the freedmen were "scattered throughout the state." There was "no doubt . . . this act would not be known to many of those interested . . . in time" to vote.[49]

Republicans were disgusted. "The old system of making votes by special conveyance [fagot votes] will be continued; and the preference of blacks to whites [meaning naturalized Europeans] still kept up in New-York, where the former are admitted to vote on their own credit, while the latter are not accepted without certificates." On April 8, the Assembly added a "fourth enacting clause" with multiple fees required to gain a certificate. The Patroon moved to expunge but lost 53–38. On April 9, the council accepted a final version with no explanation; Federalists later charged Governor Tompkins had changed his vote. The amended bill did provide an enforcement mechanism, that any of the named officers "on application of a black or mulatto person" must "issue a summons, requiring any person" to testify regarding an individual's freedom, and if that person refused "he or she may be committed to the common gaol of the county." The law went into effect just twenty-one days before voting started.[50]

The Federalists responded angrily, with the *Evening Post* pointing out on April 16 that "this act is loaded with provisions upon provisions . . . as, not only will prevent *slaves*, but most of the coloured freemen from giving their votes." The reason was obvious: "a great majority of the coloured men of this city, probably nine out of ten, have always voted for the federal ticket." Republicans did not dare to "directly disfranchise them" and so "had recourse to the abominable artifice of throwing in their way" these difficulties. On the same day, the Albany *Balance* printed the speech of twenty-eight-year-old New York City assemblyman Thomas Mercein, a rare "mechanic" among Federalists (he was a prosperous baker and Huguenot-turned-Episcopalian, like the Jays). He had missed the final vote but returned to damn the Republicans, insisting that any man "black, or white, or yellow, if free, and possessed of the requisite qualifications . . . is equally entitled to the privileges of our constitution, with any member of this house; and we have no power vested in us, whereby we can *constitutionally* deprive him of those privileges." How could color constitute "evidence of his being a bondsman," since every voter had to meet the suffrage qualifications? "A person, whatever may be his complexion, having hired a tenement, been assessed and paid taxes, ought and must be considered as free."[51]

The final Federalist attack came six days before the election, in a precis of "the late amendment to the election law, commonly denominated the *Negro Bill*," laying the responsibility directly on "a *great fountain*," meaning Clinton: "It was an artful project of the *Candidate* to secure his own election. He well knew that six hundred federal votes were taken from respectable freeholders of colour in the city of New-York, many of whom were born free, or manumitted in other states; the near approach of the ensuing election would consequently preclude them from obtaining the necessary proof to enable them to vote," explaining how the Federalists tried to amend and the council's objections, and how Clinton ("a member of the Manumission Society") finally rammed it through by the dodge of first suspending "that rule of the Senate, which requires a bill to have its three readings on different days," and then giving it three readings "in three hours time," followed by a threat to force the council's approval by mooting a bill to add two judges to the supreme court.[52]

The Republicans tried, but they did not always succeed. As many Irishmen could attest, requiring a certificate was not the same as summary disfranchisement. If anything, the certificate law impelled black men to guarantee their votes by finding law officers to issue the necessary certificates so they could vote in the April 30–May 2, 1811 elections. In doing so, they registered the clearest evidence of their voting in every corner of the state. As Sarah Gronningsater's brilliant archival work demonstrates, within days of the "Negro Bill's" appearance as a paid notice in newspapers, men of color found the appropriate officials to issue certificates in Ulster, Richmond, Schenectady (a remarkable twenty-four men), Ontario, Albany, and Greene Counties. That Republicans would use the certificate requirement to cut into their opponent's margins was shown in Columbia County, in a long-running imbroglio involving a future president.[53]

Counting Black Men Out

Just south of Albany, straddling the Hudson's eastern bank and Massachusetts's border, Columbia County's distinctive "Revolutionary settlement" has been examined in depth by John L. Brooke. It was also the home ground of the master of electoral mechanics, Martin Van Buren, who played a significant role in its byzantine racial politics. In the early 1800s, Columbia was notorious for fagot voting organized by "the Federalist Columbia Junto of

Elisha Williams, William W. Ness, and Jacob Rutsen Van Rensselaer," who dominated the county via tenants' votes. Republicans repeatedly eked out victories in its biggest town, Hudson, however, in part by disfranchising reliably Federalist black voters. Embedded in this tale of elections turned by a few ballots is the fact that voting by formerly enslaved black men was largely unremarkable in the republic's early years. Nonracial constitutions like New York's were accepted on their own terms. A man showed up at the polls and if he met the requirements (or was known to the inspectors), no one excluded him on the basis of complexion or previous condition of servitude. It took time to discover that these characteristics were a means to suppress votes, because of the opportunities built into unregulated electoral systems—if there is a way to admit more of one's supporters or bar the opposition's, it will be discovered.[54]

Investigations of the significance of black voting in early America should rest on two calculations: the proportion of African Americans in the larger electorate and the degree of competitiveness. How many potential black voters resided in Hudson, and how many were needed to turn an election? The 1810 manuscript census lists householders by name, including women usually denominated as "Widow." It does not count all voting-age black men, however, simply enumerating the number of free people of color and slaves in each household. Still, the evidence suggests a substantial constituency: twenty-seven black male householders were named (among a free black population of 199 plus ninety-six slaves), versus 649 white men, so by that reckoning men of color constituted 4 percent of the city's electorate. That estimate may be low, however: the 1820 census did itemize free people of color by age and gender, and in that year, Hudson contained 951 white and seventy-two black men of voting age, 7 percent of the electorate.[55]

The capacity to mobilize, suppress, or convert 4–7 percent of the available voters was decisive given the closeness of Hudson's elections. Between 1808 and 1812, local offices routinely hinged on fewer than ten votes:

- In 1811, Republicans elected three of the four assessors with 358, 358, and 357 votes, followed by one Federalist with 353.
- In that same year, Federalists elected one constable with 357 votes, and the parties tied at 352 votes to elect the other two, while a Federalist was elected collector with 354 votes over a Republican with 345.
- In 1812, the tallies for constable were 359 (a Republican) followed by 358 and 356 (two Federalists), while Republicans elected three assessors with 362, 361, and 361 votes, followed by a three-way tie between a Republican and two Federalists, each with 360.

As we have seen, in 1808 Hudson Republicans began disfranchising by requiring proofs of freedom. This campaign escalated in 1809, when a purported observer described a Federalist "meeting, black and white," which "consisted of at least two hundred, federal computation." An orator told them, "Gentlemen and brethren—the last laws of Congress are unconstitutional laws. Squire Williams [Elisha Williams of the 'Junto,' one of the state's preeminent lawyers] says so—and more than that, you mus'nt speak to any democrat if you meet him in the street" (that the 1810 census listed Williams's owning four slaves did not undermine his influence). Black Federalists were supposedly peeved that after being "told Squire G___r [Assemblyman Thomas P. Grosvenor] would come up and make a speech," he reneged. Notably "our *black brethren*" wanted one of their own "as a candidate for alderman" and "like to have mutinied at not having a candidate." They had one black man in mind: "Robin was proposed as a candidate for alderman," but they were told "it could not take place; the list could not be altered—promised to take him up next year." Eventually the Federalists "put the gentlemen of color off by telling them massa Sandy would do as well—one of us next year." Sandy was likely Alexander Van Alstyne, a Federalist with many black relatives. Weeks later, "Robin South-Street" responded in the Federalist paper, calling the Republican editor Charles Holt "dat jacobin printer," and intimating sexual perfidy, "de said feller be vere thick with de gentlemen of colour—*and de ladies of colour too*." Embedded in the racial flummery was a threat: "De said printer . . . *has no right to meddle with such tings*. . . . Robin is bold to say, dat he can think better, speak better, act better and have de better character as de jacobin printer. And dat printer too did not give Robin's speech right up at de Windmill Hotel." Supposedly, this black man declared "de cunntry was in de hands of de Virginian junto—dat de Virginian junto makes slaves of de poor black man, and kick and thump dem like horses—and dat de plack man ought not support such set of tyrants, and ought to oppose every body who would support dem." Black men doubtless did not appreciate how their Dutch-inflected speech was caricatured by the white Federalist editor, but they likely agreed with the sentiment. Assertions that Federalists did not deliver for these voters were belied when another Junto member, Jacob Rutsen Van Rensselaer, pushed a law through the Assembly "allowing people of colour, after being manumitted, to hold real estate, and to enjoy all the privileges of freemen."[56]

Far from Hudson, city Republicans picked up the trope of "negro meetings." In 1810, the New York *Columbian* suggested it was "*A good joke*" when Federalists denounced "republicans making voters in *Hudson*, above all other places in the State!" as those "sweet tempered, mild and honorable gentlemen" went in for "negro meetings, with cash and rum to last them a fortnight!"

After the election, Hudson Republicans raged about how Federalist "villainy, bribery, corruption and intrigue" meant "Every thing that wore the shape of a human being, black or white, was worth *one hundred pounds*, long enough, at least, to vote [as a freeholder] for Jonas Platt. . . . Almost every negro in this city had the *honor* of voting for that gentleman." In 1811, the same local editor mocked Federalists pretending to be "Friends of the Poor": "If they were real friends to the poor," they would have run a joint ticket with Republicans, instead of winning through "sums wantonly expended . . . in the support of negro meetings to secure the black votes." As of 1810, however, Hudson Federalists began making their own claims of illegal voting, attacking "the corrupt and abandoned character of the democrats," superintended by "the *cozening* lawyer . . . that little fellow," clearly Van Buren (elsewhere derided as "the little surrogate"; he was appointed county Surrogate in 1808). Republicans supposedly connived to manumit a slave so he could vote and "Perl, a free negro, was permitted to swear that he was a freeholder" with his "oath . . . bottomed on a deed from Judge Van Ness's brother-in-law, for *four feet of land*." This "modern doctrine of establishing freeholds by oath" must be stopped or decent Federalists "must submit to be out voted by free negroes, and other vagabonds swarming around the country." Federalists simultaneously championed an "honest African" who had refused a bribe: "Console [the Republican operative] for the disdain and contempt with which both himself and bribe was treated by this." The black man gave an "indignant look at your republican autocrat," making him "shrink in disgrace . . . followed by this significant apostrophe . . . 'Ha, massa H. I shall remember you for this.'"[57]

In 1811, Federalists charged more dirty tricks, led by Republican mayor Robert Jenkins, who, in the latter year, allowed "an alien, a slave, a non resident, [and] a minor" to vote. He "assumed the right of presiding at the poll" and if a man "who belonged to what is called the democratic party, was challenged, he immediately presented the *printed* form of an oath to which his name was subscribed, and his ballot was received." A nineteen-year-old white boy, along with "John Ripley, a black boy," and a third minor, were allowed to swear "to the *naked fact,* that *Ripley was born free,*" so that a minor slave might vote, and other slaves were manumitted on Election Day to vote, including "Francis Thomas, a black man . . . the slave of Marshal Jenkins, deceased." Supposedly, on Election Day, he "was manumitted by Thomas Jenkins, the Executor of Marshal. . . . Who taxed this black man? When, and to whom, did he pay his tax? If taxed while he remained a slave, it was illegal." Another man, Matthew Potter, was challenged as a slave but "Cornelius Miller, Esq." (Van Buren's law partner) declared he had seen a will freeing Potter upon payment of $100. What really stuck in the Federalists' craw was "votes rejected," as in "the case of Robin, a black man" (presumably the same

"Robin" as earlier), who "had been sued as a freeman . . . had been taxed . . . had paid taxes, and . . . had voted in the city of Hudson for nine years past"; nonetheless the mayor and recorder disallowed him.[58]

Buried in this story was a small but significant event. The legislature's Republican majority had just passed its bill requiring certificates of manumission, and now that majority put it to use. In Hudson, ten men of color led by Jacob Waldron, a man of substance, went to the polls as accustomed. Republican inspectors demanded their certificates, which were duly produced. They were signed by a Federalist judge, Samuel Edmonds, just turned out of office by a newly appointed Republican Council of Appointment. Edmonds had not received notice of his disestablishment when he issued the certificates, but the inspectors still declared them invalid. Those men—the mayor's brother (Seth Jenkins, Jr.), Daniel Clark, and William Coventry—were also Republican candidates for assessor, and won their seats by margins smaller than the ten votes, defeating a Federalist ticket which included Edmonds. Federalists sued, leading to the state supreme court's 1814 decision, *Jenkins v. Waldron*, upholding the Republican inspectors, whose lawyer was Van Buren.[59]

The struggle over which black men should vote climaxed in 1812. Hudson Federalists assailed Republicans for multiple tricks, whether abusing the "certificate law" or bribing black voters with alcohol. The city saw a "partial triumph of democracy" through "the pretended non-qualification" of the same "ten black men, whose right to vote had never been questioned for ten years, previous to the last year." Since their suit was in court, Federalists presumed "the mayor would not attempt to call into question the legality of their qualifications," so new certificates were not obtained, but Jenkins barred them again. The Republicans knew how to recruit as well as exclude. Federalists claimed they "were swindled out of the election," first by rejecting "five black men, with federal tickets," and then "some of the democratic electioneering committee" conveying them to a tavern "where this committee was in perpetual session: here they so thoroughly plyed them with the *aqua Jamaica* . . . that they soon consented to take democratic tickets, and to try the poll once more." Van Buren appears again, as with "a wink or a nod, from the electioneering magician present," the inspectors let them vote. Just after the polls closed, "a scouring party of the Mayor's returned with a black man, a *pauper*, from the poor-house, where he has been supported at the expense of the city for these two years." The mayor found "some deficiency" in his documents but "then whispered to the Recorder, who immediately followed the *pauper* out," and the mayor kept the poll open, so the pauper had his opportunity. "This single vote—the vote of this pauper, secured to the democrats the election of two of their Assessors, and prevented the election of a federal candidate for Collector."[60]

Paupers, rum, faked documents—these were a small piece of Columbia County's notorious manufacturing of votes. Manumitting a slave to bring him to the poll was little different from temporarily conveying a deed to a long-time tenant, enabling him to vote. Usually it was Republican counties reporting tallies greatly exceeding the number of eligible voters; in 1814, turnout exceeded the legal electorate by 263 percent in Genesee, 197 percent in Allegany, and 185 percent in Niagara. In Hudson, the practice of offering inducements to some black men while blocking others continued. In 1813, the *Columbian* noted the Federalists carried the city by twenty-one votes, predicated on "the almost unanimous suffrage of the sable electors," and in 1813 it claimed that in Hudson a "*black federalist* [was] *better than a white republican*," as two men were in jail for misdemeanors, and the black man "had his sentence remitted by the federal justices and went to the poll and voted their ticket," while the white "was refused. . . . Verily, a federal vote hath wondrous power, to wash the blackamoor white, to cleanse the lepers, and set the prisoner free." Federalists acknowledged his release, but the insistence he "voted the federal ticket we believe to be unfounded; for Isaac Dayton, Esq. a leader of democracy says he knows that he voted the democratic ticket." Direct cash payments featured, as "Augustus Dickson . . . says he was promised Five Dollars to vote the democratic ticket," $1 immediately and $4 after, but the Republicans welshed, a "case of bribery united with the most depraved meanness." In addition, "Nicholas Van Hoesen, a black man . . . states that he received, as the price of his vote . . . a bank bill, which upon examination proves to be a Counterfeit bill!"[61]

Days after the 1814 election, Van Buren won his supreme court appeal on behalf of the inspectors who refused Jacob Waldron and nine others' ballots in 1811. The circuit court had awarded modest damages to Waldron et al., but the higher court's decision by the Republican Ambrose Spencer, cited for decades, insisted that only proof of an intention to disfranchise was punishable, if the inspectors upheld the law in good faith. The absence of publicity given this decision is inexplicable, given how fervently Federalists damned partisan legislation. It signaled the hardening consensus among Republicans that would play out in 1815–16.[62]

———

It must be stressed that Hudson was not a special or unique enclave of black electoral participation. Albany, then one of the nation's major urban centers, included a substantial electorate of black small businessmen primarily engaged in the river trade. As early as 1809, several of these men participated in Federalist election meetings (and were recognized as such, an honor never won in Manhattan). As late as 1821, they were derided by Van Buren's

Bucktails for electing that city's Federalist grandees as convention delegates, although Bucktails had attempted to recruit some of them.[63]

Stalemate

Little changed in the four years between the 1811 bill and the more stringent 1815 law. In 1812, Federalists in the Senate proposed voiding the "Negro Bill," knowing the Republican majorities in both houses would never agree. This process repeated in 1813, but now with a Federalist majority in the Assembly. On January 23, the Assembly discussed a "revised, engrossed Bill from the Senate, regulating elections" and "expunged those sections of the old law making it necessary for blacks to prove their freedom. This passed with a very great majority. . . . The Senate, it is understood, will not readily concur." On February 18, the Senate narrowly passed parts of the bill (13–12) but refused to delete the racial clause (18–6); six days later, the Assembly voted 48–29 "that the house should insist on their said amendments." Finally, on March 16, its Federalist majority "receded from their amendment, allowing people of colour . . . to vote, without producing certificates." A new elections bill was promulgated maintaining the required certificates.[64]

In New York City, the 1812, 1813, and 1814 elections saw a heightened competition for black votes. In 1812, Republicans fielded two competing Assembly tickets and ignored black voters, but in 1813, as the Federalist ascension peaked, Republicans worked to gain some. The context was a spirited campaign for governor by the Federalist Stephen Van Rensselaer, an aggressive defender of black voting rights, against the incumbent Daniel Tompkins (ultimately, Van Rensselaer fell short with 48 percent). On April 27, 1813, the *Evening Post* prominently displayed a notice, "*ATTENTION!* PEOPLE OF COLOUR" from "A FREE MAN OF COLOUR." He addressed his "Brothers" directly, "The leaders of the Democratic party . . . fearing that their nefarious efforts, to prolong their political existence, will be ineffectual, have in a paroxism [sic] of despair, turned their attention to the electors of color, for this purpose certain individuals are making the greatest exertions, to deceive and coax you to support their detestable system of administration." Although Tompkins had once supported black rights, when it came to "voting for the law respecting certificates of freedom, in the council of revision" in 1811, he reportedly declared, "*I admit I have heretofore been a friend to the rights of those people . . . but I find I have gone far enough, and if my vote shall be necessary to carry this law into operation, I shall vote for it.*"[65]

Black Republicans responded forcefully. John Teasman, former principal of the African Free School (overseen by the Manumission Society and funded by the Federalist Common Council), brokered this alliance after his Federalist patrons fired him in early 1809. Allying with Republicans brought rewards. In March 1810, Mayor DeWitt Clinton convinced the Federalist-controlled Assembly to charter the African Society for Mutual Relief. One year later, on March 25, 1811, the same day the Assembly passed Clinton's disfranchising "Negro Bill," Teasman gave a speech celebrating that anniversary, praising "the wise and honorable Legislature of this state," which, "when the way was properly prepared, took you into social citizenship, gave you a charter, placed you on a level with other civil societies of the state, and rendered you a body politic." He also singled out "his Excellency DeWitt Clinton, present mayor of this city," who twice brought their request and "His Excellency, Daniel D. Tompkins, the governor, and lieutenant governor Broome, and both houses" for warmest thanks.[66]

By election's eve in 1813, "the Tompkintonian people of color of the 5th ward" had set up a headquarters at Mrs. Mary Weaver's Academy on Walker Street. Republicans (whom Federalists mocked as "distinguished lovers of the human race") attended "every nightly meeting" to "squeeze hands and finish with a speech; after which a paper is handed around the room for signatures pledging themselves to vote for the war ticket." Most dramatically, a large painted flag hung outside the building with "a striking likeness of Governor Tompkins" and John Teasman "represented in the act of very cordially shaking hands together" (Federalists derided Teasman as "Jacob Barker's chairman"; Barker was Tammany's head). Two days later, however, the *Evening Post* reported sardonically that Teasman's "vote was twice rejected yesterday for want of a proper certificate of his freedom."[67]

Republicans outside the city remained uncomfortable with black voters. A few weeks later, their flagship *Albany Argus* derided the renewed Federalist Assembly majority as a "Black Representation," in that "the recent election in our state affords perhaps the first instance on record in this country, of the political complexion of a house of assembly being decidedly negro votes. It is a notorious fact that the votes of the people of color in the City of New-York, carried in the federal assembly ticket, and thereby secured a federal majority in the lower house! It is stated that the black votes exceeded five hundred, and were almost exclusively given to our opponents." Nationally, Jeffersonian editors repeated the claim that "five federal members in the city of New York in 1813 (which will take a majority in the State Legislature, if any majority they have) were chosen by negro votes." This railing was largely ineffectual, however, as attempts at barring "negro votes" remained a dead letter, given the willingness of officials to issue the necessary certificates.[68]

In response to Tammany's efforts, black Federalists ginned up their submachine in fall 1813 through meetings in the "Upper" and "Lower" parts of the city appointing ward delegates. In response, a smaller group of "Citizens of Colour" resolved "that Republican principles are favorable to the equal rights of mankind," asserting the spurious claim that "the right of suffrage" was "extended on account of the exertions of the Republican Party" in 1804. The black Republican leaders, Nicholas Aray, Cesar Nicholas, and John E. Moore, were obscure men, however, whereas many of the Federalist ward-heelers were leaders of benevolent societies or sweepmasters. At a subsequent meeting, Republicans of color charged that Federalists controlling the city allowed visiting southerners to lodge their slaves in the city prison. They would "remove from office the federal members of the corporation, and . . . promote the election of republicans in their stead." Partisan tensions rose, with the "harmony and peace" of the earlier Republican gathering disrupted by persons coming "from the federal meeting, held in Bancker-street . . . endeavoring to excite confusion and riot."[69]

The spring 1814 election passed off uneventfully. Republicans regained their Assembly majority and swept New York City's delegation. Before the election, their black supporters held a meeting at the Walker Street Academy avowing Republicans were "the genuine patriots and defenders of this country." A black Federalist was damned as "employed by the federal party to endeavor to cause confusion and riot" in their meeting. Postelection, a Federalist paper noted acerbically that a government employee had "offered an influential coloured man his rent free for the ensuing year, if he would join the democratic party, and electioneer for them. The coloured man, with honorable indignity, spurned the offer." In late summer, the rival party leaders, John Teasman and Joseph Sidney, led mobilizations of their partisans to work on the city's fortifications, anticipating a British attack. They succeeded handsomely, bringing as many as 1,000 to the works. A few months later, during a renewed Republican drive for disfranchisement, a Federalist paper commented, "that the patriotism displayed by the people of colour in this county, during the late exigencies of this country, in erecting the redoubts, &c was calculated to procure rather Legislative patronage than oppression," but that proved an idle hope.[70]

The Battle Joined, 1815–1816

The 1821 convention was a mopping-up rather than a climax. Racial exclusion was already in place in the city, part of Van Buren's consolidation of power around his Bucktail organization. The watershed came in 1815–16, when Federalists still contested for statewide control amid deep partisan rancor; in Harvey Strum's summation, "No other state entered the war more bitterly divided than New York and no state emerged from the war as politically split." New York's militia had fared badly in battle, and the Federalist counties largely abstained from military service. Elsewhere the war's end may have produced "good feelings," but a second war with the British settled nothing in the Empire State. Regarding Manhattan's black electors, Republicans in 1815 combined a new, tougher "Negro Bill" specific to the city with renewed efforts to recruit black voters. Federalists still in control of the city's Common Council, and thus appointment of election inspectors, refused to obey the bill, allowing black men to "swear in," backed by the elite of the New York bar. In the 1815 election, won by Federalists, and then in 1816, when Republicans swept the boards, black men's suffrage was contested more fiercely than any time before the Civil War.[71]

The period 1815–16 saw startling reversals in New York politics. In 1814, Republicans won the Assembly for the first time since 1810, but in spring 1815, Federalists rebounded, winning a one-vote majority in the Assembly meeting in 1816, with hopes of taking the governorship that fall. Their revival proved short-lived. Hope centered on Senator Rufus King, one of the few Founders still active and a patriotic War Federalist. In 1816, his party first nominated King for governor of New York and then for president. In each case, he lost badly, beaten soundly by Daniel Tompkins in the spring, carrying only Massachusetts, Connecticut, and Delaware in the fall; hereafter, King remained in the Senate via a personal arrangement with Van Buren. As in Pennsylvania, the elimination of the Federalist threat prompted Republican schisms, with Van Buren fashioning an early version of the Jacksonian Democracy out of his Bucktail Republicans (referring to emblems worn in Tammany parades) while DeWitt Clinton's supporters anticipated the Whigs' nationalist agenda, attracting Federalist support. Clintonians and Bucktails caucused together in the legislature, avoiding separate nominations until 1819, when "the Republican party in New York . . . ceased to exist." In the city, Tammany Hall, now the local Bucktail machine, recruited renegade Federalists, some of whom offered personal connections to black voters.[72]

In winter 1815, Federalists did not foresee another attempt to eliminate their black electors. Only on March 17 did Assembly Republicans announce legislation specifically targeting New York County's men of color. Individual voters, no matter how long they had voted and what certificates they possessed, were now required to obtain new certificates from the mayor, recorder, or register, all Republicans, requiring more fees plus detailed affidavits proving property holding, residence, where and when they paid taxes, place of birth, age, and even height. After a long debate, the first clause requiring new certificates passed 51–38. An Albany Federalist, James Emott, peeled off enough Republicans to add language stipulating that if the "mayor, recorder or register, shall refuse such certificate," ignoring "the evidence produced, or shall unduly delay the same" he would pay a fine "for each offence."[73]

The *Evening Post* arraigned the measure: "A more daring attempt to rob a certain portion of this community of their vested, constitutional rights, was never entertained by the most ferocious French Jacobin who raised the bawl of liberty and equality, while he was dragging his victim to the lamp post or the guillotine." The *Post* focused on Register William T. Slocum, the principal officer to take affidavits and do the measuring, noting black men would "hold their right to vote entirely at the mere will and pleasure of this Wm. T. Slocum. . . . And who is this William T. Slocum? Is it William T. Slocum of the Society of Friends?," hinting his fellow Quakers should apply pressure to this former officer of the Manumission Society. It instructed the bill's author, New York City assemblyman and Tammany Sachem Ogden Edwards (who had declared in debate that "a colored man [is] not one of us"), that "the God of nature has created a colored man as free as you are." Many "colored men" had already complied with the law and posted the certificates of freedom "which a democratic legislature . . . saw fit to proscribe," but "here comes another law, interposing other obstructions, and requiring qualifications more arbitrary, more expensive, more vexatious, and more unjustly odious." Then came the suggestion of impending tyranny: "If this is not sufficient to ensure success to democracy, they will next seize upon some other class of electors, and, under various pretences [*sic*], disfranchise them too." Coleman, the preeminent Federalist editor, then proposed a form of resistance at odds with his party's proclaimed conservatism: "I call upon the Inspectors of the several wards . . . to shew their respect for the rights of the colored people, by taking the Constitution and the Constitution only for their guide." Civil disobedience was now a matter of party and patriotic duty.[74]

On March 27, the act was again debated, and the Columbia Federalist, Elisha Williams, unsuccessfully moved postponing past the election. The majority then enacted a third clause requiring an affidavit unless a black man satisfied "the inspectors . . . that he is in all respects qualified to vote, by the oath of one or more credible witnesses" (perhaps intended to enable Republican inspectors to accept black voters if backed by "credible" Republicans). Jacob R. Van Rensselaer, also of the Columbia Junto, offered a lethal substitute, that in elections for governor and state senator requiring a $250 freehold, if "any person shall vote for either of the said officers, knowing himself not entitled," he could be penalized up to $1,000 and a year in jail, with the same penalty for "every inspector" who permitted this crime; moreover, county judicial officers would be required to "charge grand juries to enquire into all such offences." Van Rensselaer aimed at the thousands of Republicans in western counties who lacked final titles to their land and thus, at least formally, voted illegally. After these delaying actions, the third clause passed 52–32 and the whole bill was engrossed, including a onetime grandfathering of black men with existing certificates, required only to submit affidavits five days before the coming election.[75]

With an overwhelming Republican majority, the Senate's process was abbreviated. On April 6, the journal recorded an affidavit from a William Thorn, "stating . . . that a slave owned by him, by the name of Benjamin, voted at the last election in the city of New-York, notwithstanding his objection to the same, made at the poll." What a picture—a slave-owner futilely insisting to Federalist inspectors that a voter was his property! On April 7, the bill passed without debate. Four days later, Republicans on the Council of Revision approved it over opposition from Chancellor James Kent and Supreme Court Justice Jonas Platt; the former's dissent emphasized how those who "heretofore have given due proof of their freedom" were subjected "to a new mode of ascertaining their real and personal estates . . . rendering [that] provision unequal and partial" and "further unequal by subjecting those who reside in the city of New York to proofs and burdens, not required of those who reside elsewhere." All these "checks and regulations so multiplied, must tend greatly to impair the value" of voting and, passed just before the election, would "oblige the persons affected by it, either to abandon the right altogether, or to submit to excessive diligence and great and painful inconvenience . . . creating a precedent," which might "be extended on grounds equally just to other descriptions of citizens, and prove fatal to the liberties of our country." This opinion could be and was read as a justification for nullification.[76]

Federalist "electors of colour" met to hail "the dignified and energetic protest against the bill by his honor Chancellor Kent," and editor Coleman repeated his call to ignore the act as "unconstitutional, of no binding force whatever," to be "utterly disregarded by the Inspectors." His was a radical foundationalism: "The Constitution knows of no distinction between one class of freemen, and another, and in no instance, recognizes any shade of difference in complexion," and no temporary legislative majority could make one. He was sure "this attempt, to defeat the electors" will "meet the fate of all similar acts of persecution, and bring up a greater number of coloured federal voters than ever yet have been seen." Far upstate, in Washington and Warren Counties, Federalists damned "the democrats" for "forbidding" black men "to vote without the consent of the Register of that city." They noted "the federalists opposed it, because they hold, '*that all men are created equal*,'" and the legislature might as well "require all the *farmers* in this country to go to some officer and beg for *permission* to vote."[77]

Federalists then posed a black man against the Republicans, via a speech from a freedman blocked from testifying in court because he lacked a certificate. He "got a certificate afterwards from old master" and "was taxed, and I paid the tax; I hired a house—and I lived free man, more than ten years. And every year I voted too." In 1813, he got "a *new* certificate—pay six shillings for 'em," but in 1815, he "must get new certificate over again—pay twelve shillings for 'em. . . . And Missa *Slocum* says, coloured people can never be free, tell he measure 'em. . . . What you measure 'em for then, Missa Slocum. O, says he for fun—for to make negro mad—and plague him—and bother him—'cause he love to vote *fetheral*." Finally, the black man denounces Slocum, explaining why the "fetherals" was indeed his party:

> You pretend to be great publican and liberty man—two or three years
> you come round, every 'lection, smelling round 'mong coloured people,
> to try to make democrat of 'em—and when you find colored people
> know too much to be democrat, like ignorant fool, then you mean to
> bother 'em, eh! But colored people bother you yet, Mr. Slocum. . . .
> Colored people know very well Gen. Washington give his slaves all
> free—and John Jay he make 'em free here—& federals all gentlemen;
> no *hook'em sneevy*, like you—Pretend to be for liberty, and then take
> 'em away.[78]

The Republican response was to blame the British. Regulations to block "illegal votes" were "stigmatized by federalists as *disfranchising* acts," but slavery was the "consequence of the abominable trade in human flesh sanctioned by the British government," and therefore "*The original condition of American blacks is slavery.* More is the pity, but so it is." All that was required was "evidence of the just and happy exception from this rule," and then "our fellow-citizens unfortunately of that color" would be "on a perfect equality with their white neighbors." In any case, Federalists would "rather to enslave ten whites than liberate one black who would vote against them." "Republican Citizens of Colour" continued meeting and Republican papers appealed for black votes by lying: "The federal prints are making much noise," but the act's "only objects . . . are to *prevent those from voting at elections who are not housekeepers,*" followed by red herrings, that Federalist "friends of G. Britain are justifiers of those pilfering and manstealing generals who have carried into captivity and sold since the war many people of colour." Outside the city, however, the Republican state organ suggested the problem was simply black voting: "Many contend, that as the blacks do not participate in the burthens of militia duty, and of serving as jurors, they ought to be prohibited the privilege of voting," and the new bill merely blocked slaves "from participating in privileges which neither our constitution nor laws grant them."[79]

The Republican plan surfaced on Election Eve. A Federalist observed "a number of people of color" outside Register Slocum's door, and "asked them good naturedly what they were about." Supposedly, after "a good republican meeting," they filled out "affidavits, according to law, which they had just been putting under master's door, as he was gone to-bed." Informed it was "too late, the law required them to be taken five days before the election," they explained that Slocum had already filled in the date. Further trickery was soon evident. Former Federalists Josiah Hedden and Lewis Angevine, now "rank and bitter democrats," used their old associations to mislead the Sixth Ward's electors of color. Supposedly, Hedden, the Sixth Ward's alderman and justice of the peace, told a Republican conclave in Albany that he "held the 6th ward in his hand, and pledged himself, if he was retained in office, he would secure to the democratic ticket a majority of one hundred." There was a "negro committee" in the Sixth and Hedden declared he and Angevine, "being yet considered federal," could "procure two thirds of the colored people to vote as they desired them to, as certain arrangements had been made." Whether these "arrangements" were payoffs, a faked Federalist ballot substituting the Republican slate, or enrolling voters via Slocum's good offices, is unknown.[80]

All these Republican schemes availed little. As the election opened, an Albany editor warned that suppressing black Federalists had boomeranged: "REPUBLICANS! Remember that this and the two succeeding days, determine your political fate. . . . In New-York, the *Negro Bill*, so called, which owes its existence to the misguided exertions of the last delegates from that city . . . has offended the free blacks, and their friends the *Abolition Society*; in New-York . . . it is more than probable, that this bill will be the means of defeating the republican ticket; such at least is the opinion of the best informed of our friends in that city." By the last day, Clinton's *Columbian* could only throw darts at how the Federalists managed the city's constituencies.

> The Post, in all its affected anxiety for our "colored brethren," and disappointment that one of them is not on the republican ticket, has not told us the reason why they are not represented, or who they are represented by, among the federal candidates. It would have the Irish republicans refuse their votes because they have no candidate—and why not the blacks. The blacks and Irish are the two classes of voters put together by the federalists, as the allies upon which they depend for success. We don't know which party will thank them most for this compliment.

Federalists carried nine of the city's Assembly seats by margins averaging ninety-seven in a low-turnout election. They even carried Ward Six, 524–508. Going into 1816 the "Negro Bills" had signally failed.[81]

In the following year, stakes were high. The 1815 results showed that in a contest where "every individual voter held immense value," black votes were invaluable to one party. Winning nine city assemblymen restored a bare Federalist majority of 62–61. Federalists intended to run Rufus King for governor, with cross-party appeal and eminence. Would they hold the city delegation and Assembly and elect their first governor since 1801, based on the "esteem King enjoyed throughout the state," in the April 30–May 2 elections? The city's electorate might determine the nation's balance of power, since the legislature elected in spring 1816 would also elect New York's presidential electors in November.[82]

The month prior to Assembly elections saw constant infighting over the city's black vote. The Federalists led off in a new newspaper, *The Courier*. On March 25, it cited the Constitution's provision that "*every free male* citizen of the state shall, if possessed of certain other qualifications, be entitled to vote. . . . *Coloured* people, therefore, as well as *whites*, are entitled, *of right*, to a vote. . . . Their right to vote has never been questioned in this state, and it cannot be questioned." Republicans had imposed a $1.37½ poll tax plus Register Slocum's fee, and up to 600 black men might be disfranchised because they were poor, which should "shock and disgust every man . . . who is a real republican." Not one in ten men of color could "well afford" to pay. *The Courier* then issued a promise, that since "they are persecuted because they have uniformly voted with the federal party," that "party will not forsake them now. . . . It shall cost them nothing. The federal party is able and willing to pay the tax which democrats have put upon them."[83]

The *Evening Post* followed up with another brief for why inspectors must ignore the 1815 law. The Constitution declared "'every male inhabitant,' not every *white* male inhabitant; nor every *free* inhabitant" could vote, since "freedom is implied by the qualification he must be *rated*, and have paid taxes; a qualification not applicable to a slave, inasmuch as no slave is capable of possessing property." Suffrage was "a right indefeasible, unconditional and absolute. . . . He cannot alienate it; it is an absolute right." Before 1815, some "prudent" Federalists "who did not like the trouble of resisting . . . gentlemen consulting their own ease" had counseled getting the certificates. He cited one inspector, "a professional man too," who declared "with oracular solemnity, that the law must be constitutional, because no law . . . could ever be otherwise, being stamped with the sanction of the council of revision." As a consequence, "electors . . . with colored skins, but who had been taxed and had paid their money towards the support of the government, set about proving to the satisfaction of the inspectors that they were free." And what happened? "More colored votes were given against" the Republicans than ever before, so they passed yet another "Negro Bill." Coleman noted that if the city contained "1000 colored votes, it will nett Massa Slocum . . . about $500 dollars." Since it was an "*ex post facto* law," Congress might as well decide that immigrants who "had acquired the rights of citizenship, and obtained their certificates accordingly, should be divested . . . unless they again comply with certain new, vexatious, and arbitrary conditions." The new proviso allowing black men to vote based on "*the oath of one or more credible witnesses*," indicated the Republicans' "shuffling trepidation" and "consciousness of guilt." Coleman had his own trepidations. Would the necessary "spirit and firmness" motivate each inspector "to treat with the disregard which it merits, an act . . . in contempt of the constitution" and "receive the votes of colored people, precisely on the same conditions he receives those of other electors"?[84]

In the Assembly, Peter Augustus Jay, the Emancipator's son, proposed "a bill to repeal the unconstitutional law," losing 60–59 because of a single Federalist defection. Republican racialism showed itself more openly, with one city Republican suggesting Federalists customarily brought over black Jerseyans in "waggons" to vote, and another "democratic member" describing men of color as "like dogs, following their masters around." Meanwhile, Republicans were busy registering their own black partisans. The *Courier* indicted those responsible: Mayor Jacob Radcliff, a former Federalist; the Sixth Ward renegades (Josiah Hedden and Lewis Angevine); the onetime black Federalist, Joseph Sidney. Nightly meetings were held, hailing Tompkins's "eminent services rendered . . . during the period of the late war." Republicans even organized in rural Harlem and Manhattanville in the wealthy Ninth Ward. Alarmed, Federalists charged "the most extraordinary artifices" by Hedden as "justice of the police office" in the Sixth, including releasing a man from jail to vote Republican. Another Federalist paper announced that Radcliff "holds a levee, every afternoon at 4 o'clock, which is kept open till after dark, when people of color are measured in the most dignified manner; and then importuned for their votes." On Election Eve, Federalist orators denounced "Coody Tories and African Tories" ("Coodies" was slang for apostate Federalists).[85]

To further repel black voters, Federalists exposed Republican malfeasance. In early April, *The Courier* described a February 15, 1815 letter written by the current Republican district attorney, John Rodman, to a member of the Council of Appointment, lobbying for the position. Rodman competed with two established Republicans, but although "he had long been a decided bitter opponent of democracy," he got the appointment. Printed in the *Post* just before the election, the letter detailed how since 1812 he had "exerted my little talents in supporting the republican party." As "standing secretary of the republican general committee in New York" he had drawn up bills "to prevent abuses in voting by people of colour" and other reforms. Rodman emphasized the vital importance of this service, that "very much depends on their passing, to give us a majority next spring—The negro bill, particularly, we think of the highest importance." Here was proof that the intention to disfranchise stemmed not from concerns about slaves voting, but to provide "a majority."[86]

Republicans found ways to get black votes. On April 27, the *Post* published an affidavit by Squire Williams, that "crossing the Park, Joseph Sidney met him, and requested this deponent to go to the City Hall for the purpose of getting a new certificate," gratis. Williams "found at the door of the Mayor's office several coloured men," who inquired regarding his party. He replied, "I shall not inform you which party; I always intend voting for those I like best—To which they replied, you cannot get a new certificate unless you swear to vote for the republican ticket." At this point, Alderman Hedden promised "if he would swear to vote for the republican ticket, he could get a new certificate without any expense" but otherwise no "new certificate at all." It was one thing to assert bribery, another to file an affidavit naming a white politician. By then, the options were clear: a man could guarantee his suffrage by submitting to measurement, with the fee remitted for promising to vote Republican, or he could refuse and count on Federalist inspectors to "do their duty."[87]

The Federalists were ready. On May 1, the *Evening Post* crowed that, in the first day's voting, "the majority of inspectors of every ward, but one, decided in the affirmative," meaning black men could vote without new certificates, while the *National Advocate* carried a letter from the Sixth Ward's Republican inspector, denouncing its two Federalist inspectors, who "thought proper to pronounce" the April 11 law "unconstitutional and to disregard its provisions." The *Post* printed a statement from the city's most eminent legal figures declaring the bill "unconstitutional, and should not be enforced. The constitution of the state has made no distinction as to the colour of the inhabitants, entitled to vote at elections," adding, "The legislature had no authority to make a distinction in this respect," which echoed Chancellor Kent. The signers were of unquestionable probity: Richard Harison, whom Washington had appointed the first U.S. district attorney in 1789, serving to 1801; David B. Ogden, a former assemblyman; George Griffin, an eminent litigator and the model for Pickwick in the *Pickwick Papers*; Samuel Boyd, who helped Hamilton publish *The Federalist* and cofounded the *Evening Post*. Republicans called these pillars of the establishment "anarchists" preaching "*jacobinical* instruction," invoking Harison's supposed Loyalism and their failure to support the most recent war, while Federalists crowed, "The inspectors of every ward have vindicated the principles of the Constitution, by receiving, without distinction, the votes of all duly qualified freemen."[88]

The Federalists were routed, nonetheless. Tompkins crushed King statewide, 45,514 to 38,749, and the Republican Assembly ticket triumphed in New York County by an average margin of 1,103 votes in a turnout of 10,673. There were no specific references to black votes denied, but midway through, Alderman Hedden went to the Sixth Ward poll, where "he officiated as challenger of votes; for the purpose of intimidating some and influencing and controlling others of the electors." At Tammany Hall, with 5,000 in attendance, "the SIXTH WARD's report was received with the loudest burst of applause," as "the republican inspector of that ward exerted every nerve in the late struggle." The clue to Republican victory was the *Shamrock*'s description of how "the sixth ward, emphatically styled the 'Irish ward,' has come out with an overwhelming majority." Apparently, "the adopted citizens" knew that "'Refuse king (not Rufus King) was the watchword'" and he was "unmercifully pelted by the countrymen of Emmet, Sampson and McNeven" (three United Irishmen now prominent in New York politics). The motivator in this instance was King's supposed Hibernophobia rather than Federalists' Negrophilia.[89]

The Road Taken, 1817–1821

Black disfranchisement intersected with the struggle against property requirements for voting in the last northern state to maintain those restrictions. The contestants were impressive—future leaders of the Jacksonian Democracy versus historic representatives of classical Federalist republicanism, including a Founder's son, the major legal theorist of the American bar, and Stephen Van Rensselaer, the Patroon of Rensselaerswijck, the nation's wealthiest man. As at the 1837–38 Pennsylvania convention, this conflict pitted class against race, opening the suffrage for poor white men while closing it for men of color.[90]

Consider the implications if racial disfranchisement had failed in New York. In September 1821, Federalists briefly convinced enough delegates to strike "white" from the new constitution's suffrage clause. If they had prevailed, black Yorkers would have remained a concentrated voter bloc in the nation's largest state. The Age of Jackson would have included an experienced cohort of black partisans at its center. Instead, New York fit into a larger conjuncture in which the Lower North of New York, Connecticut, and Rhode Island racialized their polities. Here we see the outline for Martin Van Buren's union of "the planters of the South and the plain Republicans of the north" around the preservation of slavery, limited government, and states' rights. Black men as citizen-voters contradicted this vision of a white men's republic and had to be eliminated.

———

New York's disfranchisement was the product of a general realignment. After 1815, the Empire State's politics revolved around the battle between Van Buren and DeWitt Clinton. This fight formally opened in late March 1817, when Clinton humiliated the Dutchman at a convention to nominate a candidate to replace Governor Tompkins, inaugurated vice president on March 4. Clinton took the nomination and won 97 percent of the April 29–May 1 vote, with Federalist backing, sidelining Van Buren. The worm turned, and by 1820, the latter had so effectively counterorganized that Clinton barely won reelection against Tompkins, by now Van Buren's proxy. In 1822, Van Buren's Bucktails forced Clinton from office via a constitutional revision cutting short his term. Clinton staged a final comeback in 1825 as the victorious "People's Party" candidate for governor against a regular Republican, serving until his death in 1828. The Bucktail campaign to seize all levers of power from the Clintonians explains their disfranchising a small but concentrated group of black voters. The extra factor was the Missouri Crisis, which threatened Republican unity because of the persistent fear that Clinton would again position himself as the "Northern" candidate in 1820.[91]

After 1816, New York Federalists ceased functioning as a statewide party. Their river county bulwarks kept electing assemblymen, but most city Federalists backed Clinton's faction, with a bloc of so-called Highminded Federalists defecting to Tammany Hall. According to Tammany's *National Advocate*, after 1816 all factions desisted from mobilizing black voters. Formerly, "When parties ran very high in this city, both sides availed themselves of the legal rights of the people of colour, and their votes, in many instances, have given the ascendancy to one or the other party. By common consent, and the result of reason and prudence, the co-operation of blacks has for some years past been voluntarily relinquished." The Bucktails' new enemies were pro-Clinton Irishmen. In response to their exclusion from the Republican Assembly ticket, the Irish rioted inside Tammany Hall in 1817, provoking favorable comparisons between "peaceable and orderly Africans" and "FOREIGN DEMAGOGUES." For several years, Clintonian committees and tickets were almost entirely Irish, although Tammany consistently prevailed.[92]

Where were the black voters? In 1817, Joseph Sidney tried to call a "General Meeting" of "The Republican Citizens of Colour," but his move was repudiated as "premature and incorrect. . . . The general committee have not authorized such a notification." After that, the black electorate retreated until Clintonians mobilized them against Tammany, as events in state and national politics suggested African American men could again play a role. In 1818, General Erastus Root of Delaware County, an intractable Bucktail assemblyman, opened the debate on a new constitution. Its goal should be, he declared, "Abolishing the Council of Appointment, and vesting their power in the Governor with the concurrence of the Senate. Abolishing the Council of Revision, and placing their veto . . . in the hands of the Governor . . . equalizing the elective franchise in respect to senators and assemblymen, and extending it to all free white males." His proposed racializing received little attention, as the Missouri Crisis intervened and no politician could afford to appear pro-southern (as antiblack laws surely did), although Root kept up his invective about pro-British Federalists and how "many of the gentlemen *then high in office*, owed their elevation to a *black population*, to 6 or 700 votes of negroes in the city of New-York; aye, sir, gentlemen high in office owed their elevation to *Sambo* and *Quashe*."[93]

In February 1819, James Tallmadge, Jr., a lame duck Clintonian congressman from Dutchess County, instigated the Missouri Crisis with a fiery speech in the House denouncing the entry of a new state that would open the vast West to slavery. Clintonians immediately began recruiting black voters in the city for his state senate race, denouncing Tammany's racialism: "The *people of color*, are not be ridiculed out of their rights by the low and despicable wit of the [National] Advocate. They view JAMES TALLMADGE, jun. as the enlightened and humane advocate of their oppressed race and we presume will support him at the polls." This mobilization was rooted in internal Republican conflicts and led by the city's register, Garrit Gilbert, and Charles Christian, an Irish cabinetmaker who had replaced Josiah Hedden as the Sixth Ward's special justice; they received their offices when Governor Clinton gained control of the Council of Appointment in 1818. Once again, meetings were organized of "THE INDEPENDENT ELECTORS OF COLOUR," and again their opponents sneered at how they "were addressed by Garrit Gilbert; we do not know whether he lamented he was not born in Africa, as he did that he was not born in Ireland." Supposedly, Gilbert deplored "how ill they had been treated by the Corporation on the subject of hogs—called upon them to assert their rights like freemen, and support the Governor to the exclusion of the savages at Tammany Hall," noting that as register, he could take "their names, and qualify them to vote, provided they received their tickets from him." Privately, one of Tallmadge's associates wrote a relative of the candidate on Election Day, "There is a prospect of the General's success [like many politicians, he enjoyed a militia title]. He will get the Quaker Votes. The Manumission Society and the People of Color will generally support him—and he will get a number of federal votes."[94]

The certificate war had started up again, and for the next two years, Mordecai Noah, the *National Advocate*'s editor, waged war against Clintonians, who in turn derided him as "the hireling editor of the south, the advocate for slavery of the blacks and power of their masters over the free states by their black population!" Noah charged that Clintonians, in league with Federalist conspirators, undermined the Union, and that these same men thought black men should vote. He had a point. While the *Columbian* denounced "Bucktail hostility to blacks" and how Noah was "constantly ridiculing those of that unfortunate race who are entitled to votes," its partisan intent was clear: "And this because Governor Clinton is an enemy of slavery, and is condemned and opposed by the south on that account!"[95]

Although Clintonians kept trying, the effort to revive a black voting bloc in New York City was largely stillborn. Tammany controlled the polls, and its commitment to voter suppression was evident on June 21, 1821, in the special election for delegates to the constitutional convention. As in 1777, suffrage was open to all men who paid taxes, served in the militia, or worked on the roads. In New York City, however, "in eight wards out of ten, the Inspectors of the Election REFUSED to receive the votes of the people of colour, because they have not complied with a former vexatious law, wholly unknown to the law calling the Convention." One Federalist paper again urged confrontation. Black men should "present themselves . . . saying, I am a free man and I want to vote. If asked, Were you born free? they should answer, I am free, and I am ready to take the test oath, and an elector should then *require* the inspectors to administer it to him." If refused again, "let the vote be opened before witnesses, and the name of the voter offering it, be put upon the back of it, and let all such votes be carefully preserved" for some unspecified "ulterior measures." Black men kept voting in the Federalist counties, however, including Albany, and the election for convention delegates may have brought them out in larger numbers. In April 1821, two of Albany's black leaders publicly repudiated the use of their names in "Extras" printed by the Bucktail *Albany Argus*. Jacob Evertson, a longtime Federalist, had seen his name listed "as one of the committee to support the *bucktail faction*," and flatly averred, "I am no bucktail." Benjamin Lattimore, Jr., wrote a Federalist editor to declare he "was determined not to countenance a party, who are in favour of the EXTENSION OF SLAVERY," alluding to Missouri, and would he "be so good as to make known to the electors of this county, that it was done without my consent. I shall not mingle in the strife of the bucktail faction."[96]

Already, during the campaigning for a convention, demands began appearing to enfranchise all "free white males" but no one else via elimination of the "freehold" property qualification. In 1820, a notice was published in Ontario County suggesting that if Governor Clinton kept blocking a convention (as he had), "county conventions" should "nominate . . . candidates for delegates in a state Convention" and "instruct the town inspectors" to "poll all the white male inhabitants over twenty years of age." In the Assembly, a Tompkins County representative proposed "an amendment with respect to the qualification of voters" to the legislation calling the convention, declaring that if suffrage "is not to be extended to all free white male citizens," the constitution should specify "that none shall be excluded for the want of a certain amount of *property*; and that nothing shall be allowed to deprive a man of his elective franchise, except habitual intemperance." As with General Root earlier, the official report in the *Journal of the Assembly* did not include the word "white," for reasons unknown.[97]

Major Noah's Siege

A remarkable figure, Mordecai Manasseh Noah ("Major Noah" because of his militia rank) drove the demand for racial disfranchisement. After a career in Pennsylvania politics and a stint as consul in Tunis, he was hired in 1817 by his uncle Napthali Phillips, a prominent Tammanyite, to edit the *Advocate*. There he became one of the republic's earliest advocates of racial modernity, at a time when "the racialization of American politics was not yet fully in place" and "whiteness was . . . still being invented, in a way that left its contradictions visible." That a proud Jew orchestrated this campaign hinted at the stakes—an inclusive, pluralist whiteness traded for a complexional exclusion, a new, hard line of color.[98]

Throughout, Noah fashioned a carapace of benevolence over his racialism, promoting the New York Auxiliary of the American Colonization Society, regularly carrying the good news from Africa's coast. Regarding his adopted city, however, Noah's editorials were calculatedly paranoid. During the Missouri Crisis, he pinned all the blame on partisan machinations: "Marry what a fuss was made about slavery *all at once*; forty years had passed away without any attempt to gain a *political* point by agitating the question." Later that summer, he described how Federalists and antislavery Republicans in Congress had renewed "their fantastic tricks . . . shedding more crocodile tears, to get the reins of power in their hands." Regarding "what is meant by a republican form of government," as required by the Constitution for admission as a state, he insisted "representation, freedom of the press, and an equal participation of civil and religious liberty by all white males above the age of 21, is sufficiently republican." Always, he invoked the sanctity of "the Union," as in minding one's own business: "Let us correct our own faults before we interfere with the faults of our neighbors." Well after the crisis abated, Noah continued indicting "the wicked faction" which was still "using every effort to revive the power of the old federal party" and "create geographical distinctions, which eventually were to divide the union, and give a blow to the republic . . . beyond the power of recovery." He was happy to declare that he had "invariably blamed the north, and justly, for exciting those [sectional] feelings."[99]

Days after the June 1821 vote for delegates to the fall constitutional convention, Noah laid out his whole argument for abrogating black suffrage. He conceded that not even "one hundred blacks out of this city vote," nevertheless "their votes, if properly called out, would have no inconsiderable weight in deciding a closely contested canvass." Prejudices, laws, and red-herrings were jumbled together to reach those who reasoned by emotion—that the presumed impossibility of black men's election to office somehow rendered their voting illegitimate, plus the precedent of the 1792 Militia Act and their customary exclusion from juries. Above all was the threat of black power, that "the fictitious importance which they have acquired by the agitations of the Missouri Question" meant that if "emancipation proceeds," as many presumed, "we may have a vast addition to our present number in the northern states; hence the necessity of some permanent provision in the contemplated amendments to the constitution." Here he got down to it: "Can we place them on the bench as judges? Will the white people elect them as legislators or governors; give them seats in the jury boxes, and rank in the army and navy; invite them to their tables, and give them their daughters in marriage? *They will not.*" At the end, he returned to the old charge, that "at the late election . . . the domestics of several candidates on the federal ticket came up to vote for their masters. The number, it is true, was trivial, but when united for any object in a close contest, these blacks may decide upon a ticket."[100]

Anticipating counterarguments, in mid-July 2020 Noah dismissed any constitutional precedents or common law requirements. Black men should be disfranchised "on grounds of expediency, because no one will deny their natural rights, or will believe that the mere 'tincture of the skin' is to destroy claims which are inalienable." Natural rights were not the same as political rights, however, and his opponents would have to prove "the expediency of allowing people of color to vote." He threw in an attack on Federalist leaders, that "in Albany county . . . the gentlemen who 'sit in high places,' owe their election in the Convention to the votes of colored persons. In this city . . . federal gentlemen" with "a black vote in the family, were sure to bring it to the polls," which "tended very considerably to decrease the republican majorities."[101]

Noah's long siege against black citizenship was no individual foible. He was a party man through and through, and as editor of a principal Bucktail organ, he "followed Van Buren's directions," pledging "any service" in his correspondence with the leader. It is inconceivable that an outsider like him, with no personal base, would have gone his own way on a major issue; the responsibility for denaturalizing black Yorkers must properly belong not to outspoken "radicals" like Noah and Erastus Root, but to the "little magician" behind the scenes, since, if Van Buren thought Noah was going too far, he would have stopped him.[102]

Putting on a Show

The 1821 convention not only formalized New York City's de facto disfranchisement for the entire state, it marked the advent of racialism as a political principle. General Root and Major Noah had hinted at the potency of racial appeals, but overt white *ressentiment* was not yet commonplace. Republicans had invoked the danger of illegal "slave voting" since 1809, but even in 1821 many could not yet stomach the new racialism. The convention's debates document that resistance to whites-only suffrage cut across party alignments, leading to its temporary defeat. John Jay's son Peter mounted a last-ditch defense of nonracial citizenship, heading a conservative bloc opposed to both racialism *and* democracy ("universal suffrage") but, above all, a *racialized democracy*. Joining him were a slew of eminent figures: Supreme Court Justice Jonas Platt, who as a state senator and gubernatorial candidate in 1810 had proposed legislation guaranteeing black voting rights and, as a member of the Council of Revision, voted against the last "Negro Bill" in 1815; Chancellor James Kent, the august judicial authority, who wrote that 1815 veto; Stephen Van Rensselaer, lieutenant governor in 1795–1801 and gubernatorial candidate in 1801 and 1813, who championed black voting rights in the Assembly; finally, Senator Rufus King, principal author of the Northwest Ordinance and the Federalists' 1816 gubernatorial and presidential candidate, who had made a historic attack on slavery during the Missouri Crisis. For a few days, these men enforced respect for a moral economy in which a man's complexion was irrelevant, and many Republican "country members" deferred to them until Bucktail leaders used parliamentary maneuvers to produce a different result.[103]

Revisiting New York's 1821 convention requires upending certain myths about Martin Van Buren. The nineteenth-century historian George Bancroft (a Democrat whom Van Buren had appointed to office) promulgated a romantic narrative regarding this masterful political operative, repeating his self-description as a "plain republican" from "small freeholder" stock who had endured "a youth filled with the hardships of poverty, which the poor have learned to endure," as another biographer put it in 1929, out of which he climbed by sheer moxie. This rags-to-riches story is at odds with the facts. The Van Burens helped found the seventeenth-century Dutch patriciate, and young Martin's career began with patronage from elite family connections. His father, Abraham, may have only kept a tavern, but their household included six slaves, more than most wealthy city merchants. Conflating a substantial slaveholder with a sturdy yeoman suggests the worldview of Dutch settlers in southern Africa, so labeling this particular Hollander a "herrenvolk Democrat" is no metaphor. His long experience suppressing black votes in Hudson clarifies Van Buren's agency in driving men of color out of politics. At the convention, his famous subtlety was at work; he avoided the personal taint of racial animus, leaving it to other Bucktails like Colonel Samuel Young and Root. Behind the scenes, Van Buren simply ensured that Federalists were kept off the key committees.[104]

Negro disfranchisement was a cog in the Bucktails' commitment to universal suffrage for white men and their disciplined focus on long-term power: they wanted all of their supporters to be able to vote for all offices. Disempowering their enemies, whether Federalist, Clintonian, or black, was an added bonus. By 1821, this protoparty controlled the legislature and most state offices other than governor. Van Buren sought to further solidify this dominance by adding thousands of white men to the Bucktails' base while permanently suppressing the Federalist-Clintonian black electorate in the city and counties like Albany and Columbia. For good reason, they also worried about future black voters. In 1817, as a gesture of bipartisan benevolence, Governor Tompkins had spurred legislation requiring final emancipation in 1827, meaning a substantial expansion of black voters when the 10,000 enslaved people counted in the 1820 census were emancipated on July 4 of the latter year.[105]

Ironically, one of the most trenchant analyses of 1821's disfranchisement remains that of the politician-historian Jabez Delano Hammond, a Clintonian congressman in 1815–17 and a state senator in 1817–18. Writing two decades later, having known all the participants, he insisted that debates over white men's rights versus nonracial republicanism were little more than blather masking opportunism. The elimination, retention, or expansion of a constituency with a particular partisan leaning was what mattered. How else to explain why delegates "most anxious to abolish the property qualification and extend the right of suffrage to all white men, were equally zealous to exclude black citizens from the right to exercise the elective franchise?" Conversely, delegates "who most strenuously contended for retaining the freehold qualification as respected white citizens, were very solicitous to prevent an exclusion of the blacks from an equal participation." Noting that "the colored electors of New-York and Albany had generally voted the federal ticket," he commented with some irony that "it would perhaps, be uncharitable and unjust to charge gentlemen, on either side . . . with having been influenced in any considerable degree by party considerations." He also pointed to how the most vociferous racialists, Young and Root, had not long before championed black causes, in Young's case promoting the raising of black regiments in 1814, in Root's, urging legislation in 1820 "declaring that *slavery* could not exist in this state, being inconsistent with its constitution and laws."[106]

New York's white democrats feared the consequences of universal nonracial suffrage because they could count. All politicians had to reckon with the influx of "Assembly voters" into future races for governor and the state Senate. As previously noted, in 1820, only 38.7 percent of men qualified to vote for these offices via possession of a $250 freehold. Based on the 1820 census, unrestricted suffrage for all offices would bring in not just tens of thousands of new white voters but also 6,996 free men of color, constituting 2.4 percent of the state's electorate of 293,280. The 1820 census also counted 2,545 en-slaved black men of voting age who would become voters as of 1828, plus a large number, enslaved and free, who were not yet twenty-one, but would be both free and of voting age as of 1828. By that year, universal suffrage cou-pled to emancipation would have authorized a black electorate approximat-ing 11,488 men, more than 3 percent of the state's adult male population. Given that Clinton won re-election as governor in 1820 by a mere 1,457 votes over Daniel Tompkins, these future voters were certainly enough to matter, es-pecially where Clinton's margins were tiny, in the downstate counties where universal nonracial suffrage would create large numbers of black electors. He carried Dutchess by 158 out of 2,928 votes cast; Kings by 45 out of 661; Queens by 22 out of 1,328. Tompkins won New York County comfortably with 2,197 of the 3,279 ballots, but 2,500 new black voters would radically shift that coun-ty's electoral profile (as Jacob Radcliff would advert in debate). Table 8.1 shows the sixteen counties containing 38 percent of the state's white male population in 1821 but 84 percent of its free black men; these counties elected fifty-four of the 126 assemblymen. As table 8.2 indicates, by 1828 the black electorate would become a decisive balance of power in three of the boroughs that today make up New York City (increasing from 12.6 percent to 15 percent in Queens, from 7.7 percent to 15.5 percent in Kings, from 1.7 percent to 13.7 percent in Richmond) with substantial electorates in Manhattan, the counties lining the Hudson and farther afield in Suffolk, Schoharie, and Schenectady.

Still, Hammond may have been too quick to presume venal partisanship explained all. Bucktail references to "monkeys and baboons" suggested a more enduring antipathy, and the philosophical premises shared by the Fed-eralist old guard were equally rooted. Consider Chancellor James Kent. No one's opinion carried more weight in interpreting the relation of "political" to "natural" rights, and he had repeatedly avowed, as a member of the Coun-cil of Revision, that complexional distinctions were unnatural. Informed by the common law tradition, Kent believed the law's authority rested on its rad-ical absoluteness, that "the universality of the sense of a rule or obligation is pretty good evidence that it has its foundations in natural law." Creating an artificial category of citizens deprived of rights they already possessed because of an artificial distinction undermined the authority of the law.[107]

———

Black suffrage was hardly the chief topic in Albany that fall. Other disagree-ments took up weeks, especially who would control patronage once the Coun-cil of Appointment was abolished, and the apportionment of Senate seats. Neither involved race, and suffrage debates extended well beyond black

Table 8.1 New York's electorate in 1821

County	Adult white males	Free men of color/percentage of potential electorate	1820 turnout for governor
Albany	7,937	223/2.7	2,748
Columbia	7,740	270/3.4	2,961
Dutchess	10,019	391/3.8	2,928
Greene	4,723	126/2.6	1,774
Kings	2,503	209/7.7	661
New York	26,840	2,527/8.6	3,729
Orange	8,365	265/3.1	2,909
Queens	4,217	589/12.6	1,328
Rensselaer	8,369	160/1.9	3,302
Richmond	1,243	21/1.7	548
Rockland	1,979	83/4.0	833
Schenectady	2,608	87/3.2	931
Schoharie	4,623	74/1.6	1,967
Suffolk	5,103	293/5.4	2,107
Ulster	6,183	154/2.4	2,209
Westchester	6,923	391/5.3	2,209
Total	109,375	5,863/5.4	33,144

Table 8.2 New York's potential electorate in 1828

County	Adult white males	Free men of color as percentage of potential electorate
Albany	9,657	382/3.8
Columbia	9,529	568/5.6
Dutchess	12,330	676/5.2
Greene	5,857	220/3.6
Kings	3,020	555/15.5
New York	32,348	3,017/8.5
Orange	10,393	591/5.4
Queens	5,031	891/15.0
Rensselaer	10,364	314/2.9
Richmond	1,494	236/13.7
Rockland	2,346	175/6.9
Schenectady	3,191	148/4.4
Schoharie	5,696	200/3.4
Suffolk	6,129	428/6.5
Ulster	7,652	665/8.0
Westchester	8,405	592/6.6
Total	133,442	9,658/6.7

versus white. The convention opened on August 28 and completed its business on November 10, with the document ratified on January 15–17, 1822 by a margin of 74,732 to 41,402. Suffrage first came up on September 19, when former U.S. senator Nathan Sanford (a Clintonian who lost his seat to Van Buren in 1820), elected as a unity candidate from New York City, reported the Committee on the Suffrage's proposal "to abolish all existing distinctions, and make the right of voting uniform," on the grounds that "those who bear the burthens of the state, should choose those that rule it." Effectively, this was taxpayer's suffrage, via "a poll tax on every male citizen, of 21 years, of 62 1–2 cents per annum." He stressed that "this scheme will embrace almost the whole male population of the state." It was left to another committee member, John Z. Ross from Genesee, to add that, while "all men are free and equal," some men were "only in a state of nature," and "for them many rights . . . are necessarily abridged, with a view to produce the greatest amount of security and happiness to the whole community." Therefore, "the right of suffrage is extended to white men only," since black men did not "share in the common burthens or defence of the state," and were "a peculiar people, incapable . . . of exercising that privilege with any sort of discretion, prudence, or independence," as if black men had not voted for decades. He equated black men with aliens and minors, all "incapable of exercising" the suffrage correctly. After noting, "In nearly all the western and southern states . . . even in Connecticut, where steady habits and correct principles prevail, the blacks are excluded," he argued that "an extension to the blacks would serve to invite that kind of population to this state." A petition just received from New York City's black men was dismissed as "instigated by gentlemen of a different colour, who expect to control their votes."[108]

Stephen Van Rensselaer delivered the rebuttal, holding the line against universal suffrage while protecting black rights. He would allow all men "who contributed in money to the state, or county, or town, who have residence in the towns, or any legal settlement, to vote" but did not want to enfranchise "a wandering population, men who are nowhere to be found when the enemy, or the tax gatherer, comes." He proposed a taxpayer suffrage, as in Pennsylvania or Massachusetts, in which every man who "within the last two years shall have been assessed and paid a state, county, or town tax . . . shall be entitled to vote for" all offices, a break with Federalist orthodoxy. As in Pennsylvania sixteen years later, the goal was to exclude poor men who were easily bought. Peter Jay then insisted that the voters authorizing the convention believed "provisions would be made to extend the right of suffrage," and not "that this right was in any instance to be restricted." Black men had committed no collective crime and "were born as free as ourselves, natives of the same country, and deriving from nature and our political institutions, the same rights and privileges." He invoked the federal Constitution's "privileges and immunities" clause, asking how "can you deny [suffrage] to a citizen of Pennsylvania who comes here and complies with your laws, merely because he is not six feet high, or . . . of a dark complexion?" Notions "that the intellect of a black man, is naturally inferior to that of a white one" had been "so universally exploded, that I did not expect to have heard of it in an assembly so enlightened as this," a case of wishful thinking. His final shot was that New Yorkers had "taken high ground against slavery, and all its degrading consequences" during the Missouri Crisis. If they passed whites-only suffrage, "you will hear a shout of triumph and a hiss of scorn from the" South. Why then, to "gratify an unreasonable prejudice" would they "stain the constitution . . . with a provision equally odious and unjust?"[109]

Now the gloves came off, and General Root stepped in. He was an effective politician, in and out of New York's legislature and Congress since 1798. Having begun by suggesting that unnamed Federalists were traitors during the late war, he moved on to equating black men with aliens, since "in case of an invasion or insurrection, neither the alien nor black man is bound to defend your country. They are not called on, because it is supposed there is no reliance to be placed in them, they might desert the standard and join your enemy," an allusion to black men's tendency to sign up with the British given the chance. Finally, he uttered the sentences repeated many times after, that "a few hundred free negroes of the city of New-York, following the train of those who ride in their coaches, and whose shoes and boots they had so often blacked, shall go to the polls of the election, and change the political condition of the whole state."[110]

Unexpectedly, Robert Clarke, a fellow Bucktail from Root's Delaware County, spoke up against racialism, insisting "the word 'white'" was "repugnant to all the principles and notions of liberty . . . we have heretofore professed to adhere, and to our declaration of independence." He was emphatic: "The people of colour are capable of giving their consent, and ever since the formation of your government they have constituted a portion of the people, from whence your legislators have derived" their authority. In reply, Young offered more of the usual, that black men were especially likely "to sell their votes to the highest bidder," nor was suffrage "a natural right" since men under twenty-one were barred. He concluded with an impossible tableau, that "when the colours shall intermarry—when negroes shall be invited to your tables—to sit in your pew, or ride in your coach, it may then be proper to . . . remodel the constitution so as to conform to that state of society." Jay then moved to strike "white" and Chancellor Kent weighed in. If a black freeholder "entitled to vote in Vermont, removes to this state. Can we constitutionally exclude him from enjoying that privilege?" In reply, Young again derided these "metaphysical refinements," adding if voting was "natural, inherent . . . it ought to be further extended. In New-Jersey, females were formerly allowed to vote . . . on that principle, you must admit negresses as well as negroes." Rufus King reiterated that "every freeholder your laws entitle to vote. He comes here, he purchases property, he pays you taxes, conforms to your laws; how can you then, under the article of the constitution of the United States which has been read, exclude him?" Bucktails might assert "this provision . . . extends only to civil rights: such is not the text, it is to all rights."[111]

The next day, the Federalist Abraham Van Vechten, from one of the oldest Dutch clans, indicted "as numerous a class of white electors" who were also "depraved" and whose votes could also be bought, yet no one cared to disfranchise them. The Clintonian James Tallmadge, Jr., instigator of the Missouri Crisis, then made a strategic error, asking why "require the disfranchisement of this unfortunate race," given that "in a warmly contested election about two years ago" only "about one hundred blacks . . . voted at the polls in the city of New-York . . . and in the contested election last spring" (meaning his failed campaign for state Senate against Peter Livingston) "but one hundred and sixty-three," indicating that a registry of those with certificates was kept. The onetime Federalist mayor, Jacob Radcliff, now a leading Bucktail, pointed out that many states had constitutions with white-only suffrage approved by Congress without objection. The practical rationale was then explicated for rural delegates: "The principle of extension would give us 2,500 negro votes in the city of New-York." Just because "gentlemen from the country . . . felt no pressure from the evil," he hoped they would not "let loose upon that city a host of voters that might give law to the whites, and . . . affect the remotest corners of the state," adding that only 163 voted but more than 500 had applied to vote.[112]

Peter Jay then asserted a profound antiracialism. How could "free born natives of" New York with "all the qualifications required from others" be disfranchised "merely because their complexion displeases us?" He dismissed Young ("I have yet, sir, to notice the arguments of the gentleman from Saratoga . . . avowedly addressed, not to our reason, but to our prejudices"), asserting that nonracial suffrage represented republicanism's essence—"It has been always taught here that we should abhor privileged classes as they exist in Europe; but we are about to create, not a privileged class, not an order of nobility, but an order of degradation." To his less cosmopolitan colleagues, he insisted, "There is no such reluctance in Europe, nor in any country in which slavery is unknown. It arises from an association of ideas. Slavery, and a black skin, always present themselves together to our minds," expressing the hope prejudice would disappear with slavery's removal. Summoning better angels, he condemned Young's logic that "I despise you, not because you are vicious, hut merely because I have an insuperable prejudice against you." Whether Jay's passion convinced them, or Van Buren permitted a gesture of respect to men whose respect he dearly wanted, a sufficient number of Bucktails, including Van Buren himself, voted to strike "white," 63–59, on September 20.[113]

When the convention took up suffrage again on September 24, race mixed with other concerns. At one point, Van Buren avowed the sacred relation between "taxation and representation," as shown "by the triumph they effected, over the strongest aversions and prejudices . . . on the question of continuing the right of suffrage to the poor, degraded blacks." Federalists continued inveighing against "universal suffrage" as granting the vote to a "floating, ignorant, and mercenary class of voters." By then, however, some arrangement had been made regarding black suffrage. On September 29, the New York City Bucktail Ogden Edwards, attacked at home for what one of Rufus King's sons called his "Negro Vote" backing Jay's motion, moved that the entire suffrage question "be referred to a select committee consisting of thirteen members, and that the committee also report their opinion upon the expediency of excluding people of colour from the right of suffrage." Edwards had spoken out forthrightly days earlier that it was "no better than robbery to demand the contributions of coloured persons towards defraying the public burdens, and at the same time to disfranchise them." His motion passed on a voice vote without discussion, and its original intent remains unclear; a quarter-century later, an abolitionist newspaper referred to Edwards (then the gubernatorial candidate of the Native American Party), as "the member of the Constitutional Convention in 1821, who moved that the subject of suffrage be referred to a select committee, in order that coloured citizens might be included." The Federalists were either caught unawares or hoped for a good result; they offered no opposition. The convention's president, former vice president Daniel Tompkins (now a broken alcoholic), named a committee tilted sharply toward Bucktail radicals without a single Federalist. Nine of its thirteen members had voted against Jay's motion, so the elimination of black suffrage was a foregone conclusion.[114]

The convention moved on to hard-fought issues of power, such as whether justices of the peace should be elected or appointed from Albany. On October 6, the Committee of Thirteen returned with a "proviso" to open suffrage to nearly all white men and retain the $250 freehold requirement for men of color, now extended to all offices. To make black voting even more arduous, a three-year residency requirement was added. All could see the proviso's intent to disfranchise black men while mollifying those who would not vote for total exclusion. A fierce debate ensued, including Jay's last-ditch plea: "However we may scorn, and insult, and trample upon this unfortunate race now, the day was fast approaching when we must lie down with them in that narrow bed appointed for all the living. . . . There the prisoners rest together; they hear not the voice of the oppressor. The small and the great are there; and the servant is free from his master. In commingled and undistinguished dust we must all repose, and rise together at the last day. God has created us all equal; and why should we establish distinctions?" Olney Briggs, a Schoharie Bucktail, responded with scathing vulgarity. Would "the honorable gentleman from Westchester . . . consent to lie down, in life, in the same feather bed with a negro? . . . It was said that the right of suffrage would elevate them. He would ask whether it would elevate a monkey or a baboon to allow them to vote." Extraneous issues intruded, including Van Buren's opposition to enfranchising city proletarians, aligning himself with Federalists on an issue of class. Ezekiel Bacon, a dissenting member of the Committee of Thirteen, called the Proviso "an attempt to do a thing indirectly which we appeared . . . to be ashamed of doing." He spoke the truth, that "this freehold qualification is, as it applies to nearly all the blacks, a practical exclusion, and if this is right, it ought to be done directly," otherwise the convention would be guilty of "the most obvious inconsistency . . . that although property either real or personal, was no correct test of qualification in the case of a white man, it was a very good one in that of a black one." His frankness had no effect. Others tried to mitigate the exclusion. An Onondaga Bucktail who had voted against Jay's original motion proposed lowering the freehold requirement to $100, and another Bucktail, who had also voted against Jay and sat on the committee, tried inserting "or shall own and possess other taxable property of the value of five hundred dollars." Both failed without a recorded vote, and on October 8 the proviso passed overwhelmingly, 74–38, as the Bucktails had converted a sufficient number of the "country members" who formerly voted to strike "white."[115]

Adding insult, on October 12, the convention took up the basis of representation, a straight fight between city and country; Tammany disdained black men and disliked the Irish but wanted all inhabitants counted, while rural delegates sought to limit the city's weight. Tompkins championed his home county, insisting it was wrong that the city, "from a population of aliens and free blacks, should have a greater share in the representation of the state, than the county of Richmond would have for its whole number of white citizens." To solve the dispute, Radcliff proposed a representation "according to the number of free inhabitants, excluding aliens, persons of colour not taxed, paupers and convicts," which passed without a division. Given how few free people of color were taxed, "Free white inhabitants" thus became the denominator for representation and citizenship in New York. The final proviso text passed 76–32 on October 27. Herkimer Bucktail Sanders Lansing (another "no" voter on Jay's motion) proposed grandfathering "all persons . . . previous to the ratification of this constitution, entitled to vote according to the existing laws of this state," and lost.[116]

"It Is Probable the Question Will Be Re-considered"

Examining responses to Jay's temporary success clarifies why it was quickly overturned. A Reading, Pennsylvania, newspaper reported, "The whole of Wednesday last was taken up . . . debating . . . whether free persons of color, should or should not be excluded." After noting the margin for Jay's motion, it asserted, "It is probable the question will be re-considered." Unrestricted nonracial suffrage in the second-most-populous state resonated immediately among proslavery interests. The *Charleston Patriot*, a leading southern paper, published a report that perhaps emanated from Noah (his mother was from that city, and he had lived there). It disdained "the plea that they have certain 'inalienable rights' (the language of Mr. JAY and others . . .) whilst the right of sitting in the Legislature, or on a Jury, or of serving in the Militia, is denied them." A familiar baiting began—"Why then, Mr. JAY, do you disqualify them in fact, whilst you privilege them by law? Why do you not enable intelligent blacks to assist in making your laws, to act as Magistrates and Jurors?" The threat of black power was invoked, that "a class of persons . . . whose votes are for sale in the market to the highest bidder," after being "discharged periodically from the jails and penitentiaries, may turn the scale of a closely contested election, and place even the Chief Magistrate of the State in office."[117]

Closer to home, Noah had noted on September 22 that "a disposition prevails to permit the blacks to vote, without providing for their being represented in the legislature, and performing jury and militia duty. . . . They have no interest in our elections, and as their votes are bought and sold, the elective franchise is of no real benefit to them," remarkably similar language to the Charleston report. Two days later, following Jay's victory, Noah stacked up arguments—that "if the country members, in favor of the blacks, were to witness the use which their employers make of their votes in this city, we feel persuaded that their opinions would undergo serious alteration." After the usual endorsement of their "natural rights," he reiterated the claim that since blacks were excluded by custom from "the legislature . . . the bench, the bar, the jury box and the battalion, it is perfectly ridiculous to give them the right of suffrage—a right which they do not appreciate, which they cannot value, and which in this city, particularly in the federal wards, is a mere vendible article." Noah then reported on how the city's white and black people had taken the news, that "the people [meaning whites] generally condemn the vote given in their favor; it creates great sensation in this city." Conversely, the black minority "now assemble in groups; and since they have crept in favour with the convention, they are determined to . . . solicit a seat in the assembly or in the common council, which, if refused, let them look to the elections. They can out vote the whites, as they say. One black gentleman most respectfully insinuated, that he thought 'as how he mout be put on the grand jury!'" The following day, Noah, on behalf of Tammany, served notice to "that part of our delegation, who from the best of motives, voted in their behalf": they should "reconsider their votes." (A side issue arose when an indignant group of African American men demanded that Noah print their rejoinder to his insults regarding an all-black production of *Richard III*. He refused, adding that if "the vote of the Convention is not changed [they] will be too important to trifle with. They will chose [*sic*] the College of Cardinals, and other important officers.")[118]

These assertions led up to Noah's October 2 article headed "RECONSIDERATION." By then, the Tammanyite Ogden Edwards had already proposed the Committee of Thirteen, and Noah declared he had "the best reason to believe, and the best grounds to hope, that, on further reflection, the convention will be assured of the expediency of adopting the term '*white* citizen.'" Supposedly, "members . . . led astray by their good feelings" naively accepted that "it is robbery to make the blacks pay their portion of the public burdens, and yet deny them the right of suffrage." He made a quasi-constitutional argument: "Those that pay anything, pay it for personal protection and comforts; for lighting the city, for watchmen, firemen; for protection by the laws, for equal and exact justice, for freedom of thought, of speech and of religion. . . . The right of suffrage belongs to them who *bear arms in defense of their country; who do jury duty, and who are represented in the councils of the state*." Ignoring that black men did serve in wartime and had long enjoyed the suffrage, Noah repeated that awarding "people of color" the vote equaled delegating "the rights of white men" to an alien caste. They had never discharged "the duties of white men," so there could be "no justice . . . in affording them a privilege of no personal value . . . which has been, and will be, abused." Maintaining black suffrage was an attempt to foment "a division of the union," led by men "who would take delight in saying to the southern states—'*Look here; we will make you uneasy in your dwellings, and revenge your political influence, by shewing to your blacks that we can make them free, and given them the entire rights and privileges of their masters. BEWARE!*'"[119]

Tellingly, Federalists who had long supported black men's suffrage now deserted them. William Coleman, editor of the *Evening Post*, had joined the "Highminded" group and noted "the statement in the American that they can give 1500 votes, is not much out of the way; and when added to the number of transient blacks which will always get their votes into the ballot boxes" should "have weight with thinking men of all parties." This sent a signal. Black men over the next decades might quote Jay, Kent, and King, but Jay's victory had clearly been illusory.[120]

Rufus King's correspondence with his sons Charles and John A. King (later the state's first Republican governor, in 1857) illuminates the convention's internal processes. The elder King voted uniformly against both universal and whites-only suffrage, and his sons agreed with him on the former but not the latter; John A. King had served as a Bucktail assemblyman from Queens County (today's western Long Island) since 1819, and in March of that year, founded the anti-Clinton *New-York American*, which mocked agitation of slavery during the Missouri Crisis and came out for white suffrage in early September 1821.[121]

These father-and-son letters were genial and mutually respectful. The dominant concern of all three men was "universal suffrage," meaning mob rule. In this context, Rufus King noted in passing that "the Patroon [Stephen Van Rensselaer] has moved an amendment, which [is] nominally withdrawn, in order to try the question on striking out the word *white*, by which the coloured People wd be included. . . . Probably it will be struck out." He suggested the motion would contain "a clause . . . directing the legislature to [bar] all Persons of colour from settlement in the state, except Citz of any State, and also a Registry of such coloured Inhabitants are now residing"; clearly alarums about a deluge of escaped slaves had resonated, although no such motion was made. Later, when the Committee of Thirteen was authorized, King explained that Bucktail "radicals" had taken over the Convention, and Tompkins, who named the committee, was "thoroughly in this business radical," leading to a gloomy prediction, "We can expect nothing" except that a delay might slow the radicals' momentum toward universal suffrage. Van Buren hoped to restrain them (he "thinks all will yet go well").[122]

Most revealing are the sons' letters. John informed his father in early October that "New York," meaning the city, "is making common cause against [the?] Negroes—all seem to regret that the privilege of voting should have been continued to them—this feeling also extends to our county [Queens]. I understand that the country members in the Convention have been and will be [unwilling?] to retrace their steps upon this subject." Eight days later, Charles confessed his "satisfaction at the Exclusion of Negros unless freeholders," despite his father's voting otherwise, although he could "not understand how those who stood on the Constitutional objection" (that the "privileges and immunities" clause barred disfranchisement) "could vote for the proviso—Seeing that that objection applies [with] as much force, to partial as to entire restriction—If you cannot Constitutionally disfranchise them, neither can you require from *them* Exclusively, Extraordinary qualifications." The most revealing comment came in late October, after all had been settled. John King noted the heavy price that Ogden Edwards would pay for voting "yes" on Jay's motion: "Edwards' Negro Votes will I fear cost him his office of Counsellor to the Corporation [city government]." Vengeful Tammany leaders would "unite the two offices of Counsellor and Attorney." Michael Ulshoeffer, the Bucktail who stood to claim the single office, reported the "vindictive feeling" against Edwards, that "much excitement still prevails in the City upon that question. . . . Those of the delegation who voted for letting in the Blacks would not either be forgotten or forgiven."[123]

As the younger Kings' letters indicate, opposition to racialized suffrage was identified with location more than party: it was the "country members" who did not comprehend the danger of black votes. Who were these rural delegates? The votes for Jay's amendment were scattered across upstate, and nearly all were identified as Bucktails. No other pattern is visible; many counties sent divided delegations, as with Delaware's Clarke and Root. The absence of agreement among men otherwise united exposes the newfangled character of "radical" racialism. It had to be learned. Jay's assertions about how all people "must lie down" in death "in that narrow bed appointed for all the living," anachronistic today, were still powerful then. It was not yet self-evident that a freeborn native of the state was not a "freeman" like other men because of his complexion.[124]

If there was a turning point in the early republic's politics, it came in Albany in 1821, given the importance of the party-building process that Van Buren completed with Jackson's triumph in 1828. His task was to make a northern party face south in service of a nationalist ("unionist") mission, which required subordinating New York's large antislavery (or just antisouthern) constituencies. Van Buren, Samuel Young, and Erastus Root had to cajole their followers to turn black Yorkers into a separate caste. The proximate cause was what Noah insisted upon, that black voters could be decisive in the city and its environs, and their importance would be magnified by emancipation. And yet, the legacy of their electoral participation over many decades could not be erased. From 1777 to 1821, black men had entered into the state's political culture, building enduring ties with parts of its elite—the many judges and officials, including Republicans, who kept issuing certificates of freedom through June 1821 so black men could vote. Minus the pervasive, violent enforcement of caste in the South's postbellum Jim Crow regime, black New Yorkers continued to understand themselves as citizens, and acted on that understanding, with allies among the state's white political class, in part because men like Peter Jay and Robert Clarke had "put on record a series of powerful arguments in favor of constitutional equality."[125]

Consequences: Expected and Unintended

New York's new constitution did two things. First, it greatly expanded the electorate. The 1821 electoral census, prior to constitutional revision, counted 56,877 men who paid taxes or mustered in the militia but still could not vote at all; all but a handful of them could now vote like other men, as long as they were white. In addition, the $250 freehold requirement to vote for governor and state senators was now removed for the 202,510 "Assembly voters." The effect on elections for governor and state senators was enormous, given that only 93,437 men voted in 1820's gubernatorial election. The second consequence, ignored at the time, was to define a new category of "aliens, paupers, and people of color not taxed," enumerated in precise detail in decennial state censuses for decades to come, and excluded from the basis of representation. The results were stark. In 1825, Albany County, a stronghold of black voting, enfranchised 7,592 whites and only twelve blacks (in a grace note, the prominent black Federalist Jacob Evertson was made a public Notary in 1823). In that year, Dutchess recorded 8,957 white and twenty-eight black voters; Kings, 2,039 and ten; New York County, 8,283 and sixteen. Most towns had a single black voter—or none; statewide, they totaled 298, versus the 191,139 men who voted in 1824's gubernatorial race.[126]

There was a second, lasting consequence, however. In the long run, Martin Van Buren got a comeuppance for the "proviso" by which his men disfranchised thousands of black men while still offering ballot access to a few hundred. In the 1820s, he avoided the taint of gross racialism that would have alienated gentlemanly Federalists like Rufus King (in the Senate together in 1822–25, they shared a boardinghouse). In 1836, however, when Van Buren ran for president, opportunistic Whigs hung New York's remnant of "Negro Suffrage" around his neck in countless newspaper articles quoting the 1821 proceedings. His "Negro vote," in the words of a Delaware broadside, indicated his "agency at thus making a negro superior to the white man at the ballot box," a charge repeated in 1840 when he ran for reelection. Van Buren's supporters replied in kind with an 1844 biography, when he again hoped to be president: "The Negroes, with scarcely an exception, adhered to the Federalists. Their number in the city of New York was very great, and parties in that city were so evenly divided, that it was often sufficient to hold the balance between them, at times, too, when the vote of New York, in the legislature, not unfrequently decided the majority of that body." No matter how much he might prefer to forget them—his voluminous *Autobiography* never mentioned New York's black people, let alone their suffrages—Little Van could never quite leave New York's black voters behind.[127]

Chapter 9

We Think for Ourselves

Making the Battleground, 1822–1846

We are a Whig, and vote with the Whigs, and we wish to inform the Whigs, that the President of the American Colonization Society [Henry Clay] never can be President of the United States. One presidency at a time must suffice for him. . . . If he will but go to Liberia, that paradise of the whole earth, he may there exercise his office . . . but if he stays here, Martin Van Buren before Henry Clay.

—Samuel E. Cornish, in *The Colored American*, March 29, 1838

[We] have thought it important to inquire . . . whether, in your opinion, leading minds in the Liberty party would consent to vote for such men as delegates to the proposed convention without distinction to party, as may be in favor of an extension of the suffrage right to colored citizens. . . . The Liberty vote thrown in favor of the Whig candidates would elect them.

—Confidential letter from New York City's black leaders to Gerrit Smith,
    June 13, 1845

We propose but very slight modification of the laws in relation to Negro Suffrage. In Virginia, white men vote for the Negroes. In New York, we intend to allow the Negroes themselves to vote. . . . And who will say that our plan is not the best? If it be right, in the Slave States, to allow Masters to vote for their Slaves, (as is the case,) can it be wrong, in the Free States, to allow Free men to vote for themselves?

—Thurlow Weed's *Albany Evening Journal*, March 9, 1846

The above sampling of partisan engagements documents New York's stark difference from other states (excepting Ohio). In the four states of the Yankee Republic, black men retained the ballot without a struggle, eventually adding Rhode Island. In Pennsylvania, Philadelphia's black electorate abstained for decades until they were disfranchised in 1838 along with actual black voters in the rural counties. In New York, they voted in every corner of the state until 1821, and fought statewide for decades to overcome the property requirement imposed that year. That battle reinforced an "organizing tradition" capable of overcoming bitter defeats in the 1846 and 1860 referenda on nonracial suffrage.[1]

This chapter traces the first stage of this fight, the 1837–46 campaign demanding "equal suffrage for colored persons." In those years, black Yorkers built a statewide apparatus copied by African Americans throughout the North. Their emergence as a political class was premised on a working relationship with the "radical" wing of New York's Whigs, led by the former Antimasons William Henry Seward (governor in 1839–42), Thurlow Weed (principal party leader and editor of the *Albany Evening Journal*), and Horace Greeley (editor of the influential *New-York Tribune*). Beginning in 1840, however, a second electoral option presented itself, the Liberty Party led by Gerrit Smith. Throughout the first half of that pivotal decade, Whigs competed with the Liberty men. In this charged environment, both parties fought for black men's allegiance, no matter how few votes they commanded.[2]

A Fulcrum in Black and White

In *The Concept of Jacksonian Democracy: New York as a Test Case*, Lee Benson described New York as the North "in microcosm," and this observation rings especially true for how black politics fit into the larger whole. Between 1785 and 1821, it captured every variation of the First Reconstruction, remaining a "society with slaves" until 1827 while freed black men voted in increasing numbers until 1821. A new dialectic surged in the late 1830s and 1840s, as New York's Whigs built an antislavery current within their national party, and their most committed partisans deserted to found the Liberty Party. Simultaneously, masses of Irish immigrants cemented Tammany Hall as the nation's most powerful (and most intensely Negrophobic) party machine. Taken together, these factors made the state a fulcrum for the convergence of white electoral politics with a well-organized black political class.[3]

Two men illustrate the possibilities. For decades, the state's politics revolved around William Seward. As governor in the early 1840s and then U.S. senator in 1849–61, he commanded a personal network directed by Weed, the era's most astute political operator. Seward was "the archetypal 'modernizing' Whig who embraced the market revolution and sought to harness an activist government in the service of economic development." He had also grown up with slavery (his parents owned seven) and loathed it from personal experience; in Sarah Gronningsater's apt phrasing, he "lived through two American slave emancipations" and was "as much a politician from the 'Slave North' as from the 'Free North.'" New York businessmen needed his vote-catching appeal, and had to accept that he was the rarest of white leaders, a public friend to black people. As governor, he sent a series of studied insults to Virginia executives seeking the extradition of three black seamen who encouraged a Norfolk slave carpenter to stow away on their ship. After this man was recaptured and shipped home from New York, Virginia wanted the three sailors arrested for stealing property. The resulting "Virginia Controversy" played out over Seward's governorship, with national implications: in 1842 Virginia passed a Non-Intercourse Act mandating searches of all vessels traveling to and from New York, with a bond of $1,000 required from the master, and other southern states announced their solidarity. Seward never backed down, insisting that black Yorkers were entitled to "the protection of the State of which they are citizens," and that "the general principle of civilized communities is in harmony with that which prevails in this State, that men are not the subjects of property." To underline his sympathies, in 1842, he made the abolitionist Lewis Tappan the state's agent to rescue kidnapped black people, and wrote Thomas Clarkson, dean of British abolitionists, that he regarded "slavery as a great moral evil, as unjust in principle, a violation of inalienable human rights, inconsistent with the spirit of the Christian religion, and injurious to the prosperity and happiness of every people among whom it exists."[4]

Worst of all for conservatives, Seward courted and received the plaudits of New York's black men. On his exiting office in January 1843, tributes from these constituents poured in, and he replied with a public letter, avowing, "If I were sure during my administration of the government of this State, I had entitled myself to the gratitude of its disfranchised members, or those held in bondage beyond its borders, then should I be satisfied that happiness which no eminence affords awaits me in an unenvied repose." He acknowledged their disappointment: "It does not soothe the regret that I feel, when I remember how much less of good I have accomplished, than it now seems to me a magistrate clothed with so great power and influence ought to have done," concluding on a note of uplift: "I congratulate you on the prospect opening upon your race. The sympathies of civilized man throughout the world are excited in your behalf." Slavery was "a system of oppression condemned by the spirit of Christianity, and inconsistent with the fundamental principles of Republican Government," and their "practical exclusion from Suffrage, however plausibly excused, is only one of the forms of that institution still lingering in this State." In that same year, the Ohio Liberty Party leader Salmon Chase tried to recruit him as their party's 1844 presidential candidate, "premature Republicanism" indeed, involving two future stalwarts of Lincoln's cabinet.[5]

Seward's demonstrative solidarity continued out of office. In 1846, he defended a deranged black murderer, telling jurors, "The color of the prisoner's skin, and the form of his features" should not influence them, as "he is still your brother and mine, in form and color accepted and approved by his Father, and yours, and mine; and bears equally with us the proudest inheritance of our race—the image of our Maker." Throughout the 1840s and 1850s, he patronized black newspapers and wrote on senatorial letterhead supporting black suffrage. In 1851, having rocked the Senate by denouncing the Fugitive Slave Act, he rushed to sign bail bonds for the defendants following Syracuse's famous "Jerry Rescue," including four men of color, and his house in Auburn became a well-known stop on the Underground Railroad. Seward's opposition to slavery was not a singular idiosyncrasy, however. Rather, it was key to the worldview of the masses of northern Whigs for whom he spoke. He was a canny, ambitious man, who long aimed for the presidency. Explicit racial sympathies were strategies to build his party and career, based on an estimate that antislavery voters would eventually constitute a majority and his egalitarianism would stand him in good stead; he also backed Catholic rights in the 1840s, highly unusual for a Whig.[6]

Out in abolitionism's heartland of western New York, Seward had a rival: Gerrit Smith, one of America's wealthiest men and a principal founder of the Liberty Party. Smith's father, Peter, had been John Jacob Astor's partner, making the son the largest landholder in the state. He did not fritter his fortune, however, investing in prime commercial holdings along Lake Ontario while giving away Rockefelleresque sums. Few whites equaled Smith's abhorrence of "that monster, prejudice" and his pride at being called "a colored man." For a generation, black men relied on his financial aid, and their correspondence offers invaluable insights into interracial politicking. Smith believed in empowering others to achieve their own liberation, donating a vast acreage in the late 1840s to help 3,000 black men meet the freehold requirement to vote. He served one term in Congress in 1853–54, but thereafter, while Seward and Weed founded the state's Republican Party, he moved into quixotic third-partyism as the Radical Abolitionist Party's candidate for president in 1856 and 1860, and governor in 1858.[7]

Smith and Seward's respective milieus were the poles between which abolitionists maneuvered, and black men put themselves at the center. The state's black leadership cadre dwarfed other states in its size, geographic scope, ambition, and audacity. They boasted a dozen nationally known figures spread across Albany, Troy, Syracuse, Rochester, Buffalo, Brooklyn, and New York City, plus hundreds of prominent local men. Between 1837 and 1846, this leadership created modern black politics through a burgeoning infrastructure focused on protest, lobbying, strategic alliances, and partisan mobilization. Consider the innovations introduced during these years: annual state conventions; a state central committee and county committees; a constant schedule of county, town, and city ward-level conventions; finally, a series of effective newspapers, lifting black political discourse to a qualitatively higher level. New York's black men made themselves consequential despite a minimal electoral presence until the late 1840s. The decennial *New-York Census* recorded the exact number of "aliens, paupers and people of colour not taxed," the few who were "taxed," and finally those eligible to vote, in every town and urban ward. Where there were voters of color, it was a mere handful: in 1835, in an electorate of 422,634, a mere 578 were black (Albany had fifteen black and 10,941 white voters; New York County had 43,091 white but only 68 black). Even by 1845, after years of mobilization, no more than 2,000 black men voted, in James McCune Smith's assessment. The key number here, however, was those who might cast a future ballot, especially if party officials stretched the freehold requirement by accepting "fagot deeds" or Election Day oaths; as chapter 10 documents, the number of black electors increased dramatically in the 1850s.[8]

Yankees and Yorkers

Like Pennsylvania, the Empire State was split into distinct regions. Unlike in Pennsylvania, however, those regions cohered into a whole through the axis of the Erie Canal and the Hudson, connecting North America's interior with the Atlantic world, a political geography constituted by two successive great migrations, each of which gave one of the major parties a particular ethnic culture.

The postrevolutionary Yankee migration shaped upstate New York's ingrained ethos of passionate reform. Whitney Cross's classic *The Burned-Over District* traced this "case history in the westward transit of New England culture," describing them as "a people extraordinarily given to unusual religious beliefs, peculiarly devoted to crusades aimed at the perfection of mankind and the attainment of millennial happiness." Charles Finney's Second Great Awakening began in Rochester in 1830, followed by Mormonism, Fourierist phalanxes, the sexual communism of John Noyes's Oneida community, and more. Cross's history of "isms" had partisan implications, as these Yankees made northern and western New York the base of Antimasonry and then a Whiggism shaped by "the common party ideal of a prosperous, pious, literate society of free men, as opposed to the 'shame' and 'plague' of a slave society." They were followers of Seward and devoted readers of Horace Greeley's *New-York Tribune*, and measurably "more alert than most other Americans" in terms of literacy, the number of journals they published, and the number of college graduates. Not incidentally, the Liberty Party began in western New York and, with it, black men's first gaining significant party offices and statewide nominations.[9]

The second of these migrations was the Famine-driven exodus of Irish peasants a generation later. These desperate people, speaking heavily accented or no English, practicing an alien faith, met with intense hostility. In response, the Irish claimed their whiteness via a loathing of black people driven by resentment of "mean, heartless white-livered Yankees . . . steeped in Abolition schemes—seeking to exalt the Negro and debase the Irishman . . . seeking to give the vote to the negro and take it away from the Irishman." The Irish told each other that sympathy for the slaves was a sham; scratch an abolitionist and find just another "infidel . . . a bigoted Protestant always." When Yankees eulogized John Brown in December 1859, "Irish Friends of the South in Northern Cities" proposed a secret United Constitutional Irish Association to physically attack Republicans, "freesoil capitalists" who were "withholding the price of Irish labor, while trying to incite the negro of the South to rebellion."[10]

From the 1830s, the Irish cemented the Democracy's domination of New York City, which kept them competitive statewide. In the 1840s, it was routinely recorded that the Irish "come to the polls on election day shouting, 'Down with the Nagurs! Let them go back to Africa where they belong.'" Henry Highland Garnet's comment at an 1856 convention was the politest response: "I cannot be permitted to vote for even a pound-keeper" while "they extend civil rights to foreigners. . . . The oppressed Irishmen, once naturalized, are the loudest shouters and bitterest foes of the Negro." William J. Wilson, writing as "Ethiop" in *Frederick Douglass' Newspaper*, voiced a franker Hibernophobia. After watching a Brooklyn rally, he compared them to a "menagerie . . . with their long scraggly hair over low brows, and narrow faces, with huge projecting teeth and dull sluggish eyes . . . a collection, overmatching in apparent ferocity, any wild animals gathered in this country."[11]

The entry of vast numbers of Yankees followed by a mass Hibernian influx has long constituted the two poles of antebellum New York's social history. An unheralded, smaller migration from a different direction shaped New York's politics in subtler ways, prolonging its status as a "society with slaves." After the Revolution, groups of slaveholding southerners came north to New York's frontier, seeding its newly formed counties with enclaves of both enslaved and recently freedpeople in intimate contact with antislavery Yankees. This "Southern Entrance" resulted from the same land promotion schemes that brought in New Englanders. Hundreds of slaves arrived via "forced migrations from nearly exhausted plantation lands" organized by eminent Virginians like the Fitzhughs. As one ex-bondsman remembered, these Virginians believed "the more slaves a man possessed in that country the more he would be respected and the higher would be his position in society." By 1810, the band of counties from Lake Ontario to the Pennsylvania border (Ontario, Steuben, and Seneca) held so many enslaved black people that the legislature required masters to free those brought since 1800 if hired out for seven years. In towns like Bath and Sodus, the migrants formed new black communities, and counties outside "the Genesee Country" like Tompkins (containing Ithaca) also included bondspeople brought from the Chesapeake. As late as 1837, touring for the *Colored American*, Charles B. Ray wrote of a community in Geneva, abutting Seneca Lake, who "number about two hundred and fifty, nearly all of the elder of whom are from the south, brought here by their masters as slaves, and retained in slavery for some time afterwards."[12]

The slave narratives describing this emigration emphasize its political consequences—that both slaveholders and chattels found themselves surrounded by whites opposed to slavery. Peter Wheeler, brought from New Jersey, described local whites urging him to flee: "Peter, your master can't touch a hair of your head, and if you want to be free you can, for we've tried that experiment here lately; and we've got a good many slaves free in this way, and they're doing well." Austin Steward, imported from Virginia as one of Captain William Helm's slaves, recounted how more and more "took French leave" (ran off), with Helm sponsoring a "joyous reunion" so as to capture them and ship them south for sale. In 1814, Steward approached prominent whites as to his legal status. They referred him to members of the Manumission Society, who explained he was free under the 1810 law. He moved to Rochester and opened a butcher shop, fighting off Helms's attempts to claim it and him in court.[13]

These moves of people across terrain were conditioned by a more traditional political geography, the signs on roads marking different sovereignties. Upstate New York constituted a double borderland. To the east was the Yankee Republic, in particular Vermont, with its aggressive racial egalitarianism. To the north and west was the principal border with British territory, including Montreal, Quebec, Toronto, and the towns along Lakes Erie and Ontario. Rather like Chicanos since 1848, or the Native American peoples of the Northern Plains, Black Yorkers participated in a "distinct . . . community that crossed international boundaries." Most of the thousands of fugitives who entered Canada over several decades came via lake ports like Oswego or walked across near Niagara, with the experience of entering freedom "under the Lion's Paw" constantly remarked.[14]

Men of color routinely depicted the advantages in border-crossing. In 1859, the Reverend Jermain W. Loguen, stationmaster of Syracuse's Underground Railroad office, traced his remarkable life. Soon after fleeing Tennessee in 1834, he crossed into Canada. There he encountered the black militia that helped repress the 1837–38 Upper Canada Rebellion. Their martial attributes augured a future liberation struggle: "Should pro-slavery folly and persistence raise the spirit of the North, or any part of the country, to the point that admits the African element in a war for freedom, the blacks of Canada will be found overleaping national boundaries; and, gathering the sympathizing forces in the line of march, will imprint upon the soil of slavery as bloody a lesson as was ever written." He had been "urgently solicited by the Government of Canada to accept the captaincy of a company of black troops in the Provincial Army," but decided he would take up the fight at home. The Canadian option changed political calculations, one reason why enterprising black men like Douglass, Henry Highland Garnet, and Samuel R. Ward moved to western New York.[15]

Building a Political Class

There are no objective conditions that guarantee political insurgency, but factors such as heightened consciousness, durable institutions, money, and alliances all matter. Some African Americans took full advantage of their environment, and others did not. In Bucks, Lancaster, and Allegheny Counties in Pennsylvania, they acted, whereas the elite of Philadelphia perceived their options more pessimistically. After 1821, New Yorkers demonstrated a distinct historical awareness, and enjoyed many structural assets plus a grounding in the mechanics of ward-based electoralism. Minus disfranchisement, New York State would have centered black political power; as it was, they transcended disfranchisement to wage the largest political campaigns by black men before the Civil War. The impetus for this struggle came from a network of like-minded men in counties across the state who built a durable political apparatus. To other people of color, this was their victory: a political class extending into the Empire State's nooks and crannies, hundreds of men who met annually to mobilize on a common program.

Black Yorkers were empowered by their access to economic opportunities. New York State included hundreds of small traders and artisans of color and a surprising number of landowning farmers like the Essex County freeholder Mintus Northup, father of Solomon. As everywhere, black barbers were common, but New York's towns also featured black grocers, cleaners, tailors, and butchers; a significant number of boatmen and stewards on the lakes and rivers; and eventually dozens of teachers, plus small cadres of skilled professionals in Manhattan and Brooklyn. One individual reveals the extent of this economic opportunity. As Shane White has uncovered, all New Yorkers knew of "Wall Street's First Black Millionaire," Jeremiah G. Hamilton. This outrageous character fascinated Manhattan's penny press. His presence in New York's courts and counting houses underlined that there was no absolute limit on persons of color, even as Hamilton tried to prove in court he was not a "negro," while the *Colored American* mocked him as "a dark Mulatto boy, with very short and frizzly hair" who pretended to be a "SPANISH gentleman."[16]

A different kind of advantage came through the tradition of white philanthropists providing support for black education, not only Manhattan's African Free School, the premier educational institution for people of color, but the nation's first black-run high school in 1831, and later two integrated institutions of higher education, the Oneida Institute and New-York Central College, which trained many future leaders. This backing stemmed from the relationship between New York State's black folk and a fraction of the state's postrevolutionary elite, former Federalists, usually Anglicans, and surprisingly often Huguenots. This group included Rufus King's sons Charles and John (the former was editor of the *New York American*; the latter the state's first Republican governor in 1857), the merchants Arthur and Lewis Tappan, Stephen Van Rensselaer, and the tobacco magnate Jacob Lorillard. Above all there was the personal connection to the Jays. The founder's son Peter had championed their cause in 1821, and for the next four decades his brother, Judge William Jay, penned forceful attacks on racialism. Judge Jay's son, John Jay II, maintained this tradition of Anglo-Huguenot solidarity. In the late 1830s, father and son together took up cudgels for Alexander Crummell, one of New York's remarkable "young colored men," later a leading Black Atlantic intellectual eulogized in *The Souls of Black Folk*. Like his forebears, young Jay was a devout Episcopalian, despite that denomination's miserable record on slavery. Crummell was two years younger, and a parishioner at St. Philip's Church, the venerable black Episcopal congregation. In 1839, he applied to the city's General Theological Seminary, and Bishop Samuel Onkerdonk refused admission to avoid offending southern seminarians. The Jays went into action, anonymously attacking the bishop in King's *New York American*. Crummell finally received ordination in Boston, after which he studied at Cambridge in England, but by then the intradenominational contest was on. From 1844 to 1853, John Jay II fought at every Diocesan Convention for the admission of St. Philip's delegates, while serving so relentlessly as a lawyer for fugitives that he was assaulted in court. Finally, in 1853, the Episcopal hierarchy gave in, with George Templeton Strong reporting in his diary, "Another revolution. J J's annual motion carried at last, and the nigger delegation admitted." Jay continued his disruptions into the war years. It would be a grave mistake, however, to imagine the first Chief Justice's grandson was a mere gadfly, or his family were outliers. After the war, he was elected head of the Union League, and served as minister to Austria, president of the New York State Civil Service Commission, secretary of the

New-York Historical Society, president of the Huguenot Society, and finally president of the American Historical Association. The Jays and their associates practiced elite politics among the elite, and exercised their prerogative to insist on the inclusion of men of color in the elite's institutions.[17]

As elsewhere, analyses of New York's black leadership are skewed by how scholars focus on the metropole. We know much more about the city men, because of their physical concentration and visibility in major newspapers, as well as a Manhattan-centric historiography. By the 1830s, the city's vanguard encompassed two generations, fathers and sons both metaphorically and literally. The first generation featured two men born free on the Eastern Shore, Thomas Downing and Samuel E. Cornish, whose importance to black political advancement can hardly be exaggerated. Downing (b. 1791 in Chincoteague, Accomac County, Virginia) was a famous restaurateur, "our celebrated 'free colored American,' the great T. J. Downing himself," as James Gordon Bennett, notoriously racist editor of the *New York Herald*, described him. Commanding an establishment to which visitors like Dickens were taken, Downing had a nose for a unique ingredient (the freshest oysters on the Jersey shoreline), and the intelligence to present that dish in opulent surroundings at Broad and Wall Streets, epicenter of the new American capitalism. Like certain expatriates in Europe's great cities, he created a place simultaneously exotic and comfortable, and for forty years New York's men of power met daily at Downing's. Downing was also openly political, never shying away from a fight. In 1837, he personally conveyed to Albany a twenty-foot-long petition demanding equal suffrage, and in the 1850s he was a member of the Committee of Thirteen overseeing electoral strategy, while suing any whites who got in his way, including battles over his exclusion from street cars in 1841 and 1855. One of the least-noticed parts of his biography was his son George's recollection that "close was the friendship that existed between the family and the veteran editor, Thurlow Weed," indicating that Thomas Downing remained an active Whig as long as that party existed.[18]

The Reverend Samuel E. Cornish (b. 1795 in Sussex County, Delaware) was this generation's other emblematic figure. If any man was the progenitor of black politics, it was Cornish. Usually remembered as an editor, first of *Freedom's Journal*, the nation's first black newspaper in 1827, then its short-lived successor, the *Rights of All*, in 1829, and finally of the *Colored American*, beginning in 1837, Cornish was much more than that. He began a long line of openly partisan ministers, who followed his path in confronting white men to insist on black political autonomy. In Cornish's case, the heresy was doubled, in that he rejected both Garrisonian anti-politics and the abolitionist "one-idea" strategy that birthed the Liberty Party. Like Thomas Downing, Cornish remained committed to major-party politics, which could only mean the Whig Party until the crisis of the 1850s. In its own way, that stance proved to be as independent as any.

After Downing and Cornish, a second generation of "colored young men" asserted itself, all born in the 1810s and most graduates of the African Free School (AFS) at Mulberry and Grand Streets. This storied cohort included Thomas's son George T. Downing, Henry Highland Garnet, Samuel Ringgold Ward, Patrick and Charles L. Reason, James McCune Smith, Isaiah De Grasse, Thomas Sidney, Alexander Crummell, Philip A. Bell, John J. Zuille, and the famous Shakespearean Ira Aldridge, among others. A fair number were southern born and knew slavery firsthand, as in Cornish's casual comment in his *Rights of All* newspaper regarding the vicious "Cannon Gang" of kidnappers: "The Editor is a native of Sussex county Del. and once saw two men hung for a similar offence in the same county," and how Garnet and Ward (both fugitives, the former born in 1815 in New Market, Kent County, Maryland, "on the plantation of Colonel William Spencer"; the latter born 1817 somewhere on Maryland's Eastern Shore) referred to each other as cousins. Otherwise, what brought them together was a time and a place: New York at the outset of Jacksonian Democracy, the AFS, the early, stirring days of Garrisonian "immediatism," all refracted through their own lives.[19]

It is mistaken, however, to imply that these Manhattanites gradually extended their educated leadership beyond the city to create New York State's black politics. They were the most visible but not necessarily the most important, and in the 1840s leadership gravitated to the arc of cities stretching west from Albany and Troy along the great canal. Well before that, however, black communities in northern and western New York produced major figures. A different generational succession is personified by the barber Richard P. G. Wright, an immigrant from Madagascar who settled in Schenectady after the Revolution and its preeminent black leader for decades, and his son Theodore Sedgwick Wright (b. 1797), who studied at Princeton Theological Seminary and succeeded Cornish as pastor of the First Colored Presbyterian Church in Manhattan, in turn preparing Garnet for the ministry. The Wrights were not alone: the first impulse to conventioneering came not from the city, but from two Albany men, Stephen Myers and John A. Stewart, in 1831. Where the city did lead, however, was in the founding of a series of black-edited newspapers, in an era when newspapers were the principal instrument of political agitation and influence.[20]

From *Freedom's Journal* to the *Colored American*

Effective legislative and electoral action requires organs for publicity and mobilization. No white-edited newspaper could be that vehicle for African

Americans. Founding a paper under black control was a necessary condition for the emergence of a self-conscious black politics, and here New York State's centrality becomes evident. Between 1827 and 1847, all of the black newspapers were published in New York State. Of those the two most important were *Freedom's Journal* (1827–29) and the *Colored American* (1837–41), which together document the evolution from political caution to aggressive statewide campaigning.

Freedom's Journal is celebrated as a watershed, proof that men of color were "up and doing" like white men, but it was barely political, or rather, its politics were mainly cultural and mimetic, an exercise in respectable self-presentation. Its pages featured column after column of high-minded fluff of little relevance to black Americans, projecting an ethos of refinement and Atlantic culture. On occasion, it included polite debates on colonization and reports on relevant legislation, plus regular news from Haiti, but given the onslaught of Negrophobia in the later 1820s, the *Journal* was circumspect in documenting the limited freedom enjoyed by most free people of color, and the total absence of freedom for the vast majority.

Consider the January 18, 1828 issue. It led with a fanciful story set in France ("VER-VERT. OR, THE PARROT OF THE NUNS"), and then a brief reprint, "Blessings of Slavery," on South Carolina banning "the instruction of people of colour in reading and writing." Historical anecdotes ("Queen Elizabeth's Fanaticism," "Mahmound II, The Reigning Sultan of Turkey"), homilies, and tidbits filled the rest, other than "Theresa, a Haytien Tale," about a black mother protecting her daughters from the French Army, and another reprint on Philadelphia's High Constable returning from "an excursion through the States of Louisiana and Mississippi, in pursuit of the coloured children, who were stolen away from this city." Back page advertisements furnished the main evidence of community life, including many private schools for children and adults, James Gilbert's Clothes Dressing Establishment at 422 Broadway, F. Wiles's boardinghouse at 159 Church Street for "genteel persons of colour," and B. Mermier's "REFRESHMENT HOUSE," also at 422 Broadway, featuring "choicest Liquors and Refreshments." Cornish, now the paper's general agent, published two business propositions, offering 2,000 acres of land within seventy miles of the city at less than half price to "coloured farmers," and a notice for "G. & R. Draper, (Coloured Men.)" in Baltimore, manufacturers of "all kinds of Smoking and Chewing TOBACCO," who had sent him "a large box of their TOBACCO, for sale." Agents for the *Journal* were listed at bottom right, ranging from Maine well into the slave states (Yarmouth and Portland, Boston, Salem, Providence, New Haven, and Norwich, Newark, New Brunswick, Princeton, Trenton, Philadelphia, Columbia, Carlisle, Flushing, Brooklyn, Albany, Schenectady, Rochester, Buffalo, Wilmington, Baltimore, Washington, Alexandria, Fredericksburg, Richmond, and New Bern, Elizabethtown, and New Salem in North Carolina). This was an organizing cohort in embryo, with names that recur throughout this narrative: Reuben Ruby in Portland; John Remond in Salem; David Walker in Boston; Alfred Niger and George Willis in Providence; Austin Steward in Rochester; Richard and Theodore Wright in Schenectady and New York, respectively; Stephen Smith in Columbia; and John B. Vashon in Carlisle.

As this list suggests, *Freedom's Journal* was a collective effort at self-determination by black men across many states, to speak for themselves and to each other. Cornish and the *Journal's* backers assembled considerable resources: salaries for the editors, an office, printers, paper. Ultimately, it was a debacle, however, as the principal editor, Bowdoin graduate John Russwurm, converted the *Journal* to colonizationism in 1828 and then departed for a long career in Liberia. Cornish's short-lived second effort in 1829, the *Rights of All*, had a stronger voice, challenging many black men's refusal to engage in politics, but he could not make a go of it. That required a younger man, Philip Alexander Bell, born in 1808. Bell had attended the African Free School and was active throughout the prewar decades before moving to California, where he edited two papers. On January 7, 1837, Bell debuted the *Weekly Advocate*. The following month, Cornish came on board as editor at the suggestion of "a number of our leading men" who "have interested themselves to advise and assist us." The name change was presumably at his instigation. In Bell's words, "It is necessary to go on further and say, that it is 'for the people of color.' . . . 'THE COLORED AMERICAN' will be a better name. It is short, emphatic and distinctive. We are Americans—colored Americans, brethren,—and let it be our aim to make the title 'Colored American,' as honorable, and as much respected before the world, as 'white Americans,' or any other."[21]

Cornish brought high-level support from Arthur and Lewis Tappan, Gerrit Smith, and other leading abolitionists, but the race-specific name guaranteed his paper's disavowal by Philadelphians like James Forten, who had supplied three-quarters of *The Liberator's* early subscribers. Forten's circle drew the line at anything "complexional." For five years, the *Colored American* struggled under this boycott, at peak garnering only 300 subscribers in Philadelphia. At first, it did well enough, reaching 1,650 subscribers in its first year, 800 in New York City and "more than three-fourths . . . from our own people," but those numbers declined sharply by 1839 because of "hard times" and the paper's outspoken politics. Its subscription base, just enough to maintain publication, was built by going town-to-town to spread the word. The key agent and eventually the principal editor was Charles Bennett Ray. Ray was a transplanted Yankee (born in 1807 in Falmouth, Massachusetts), who came south after his expulsion from Wesleyan in 1832 because of southern students' objections. He crisscrossed the state with enormous energy, visiting Newburgh, Poughkeepsie, Troy, Albany, Syracuse, Geneva, Rochester, Buffalo, and Lockport in 1837 and Schenectady, Utica, Whitesboro, Oswego, Peterboro, Cazenovia, Waterville, Rome, Canandaigua, Le Roy, Niagara, Perry, Buffalo, Lockport, Rochester, and Utica in 1838, with excursions into Pennsylvania, Lower New England, and Ohio. These travels gave Ray a unique understanding of how black people actually lived in the free states, which he communicated in vigorous, anecdotal reports introducing black Americans to each other while building a political network.[22]

Although the *Colored American* reprinted topical anecdotes and human-interest stories in the style of *Freedom's Journal*, its focus was much more political. Under Cornish's direction (he relinquished the editorial chair in early 1839, moving to New Jersey, but continued to write editorials), those politics were Whiggish and worldly in equal measure. Its worldliness displayed itself in close attention to persons of color under the Union Jack, whether in Canada's black regiments, whose well-drilled presence excited admiration from visiting African Americans, candidacies for elected office by Jamaican free men of color, or emigration to Trinidad under the auspices of Nova Scotia's lieutenant governor. Cornish's Whiggism was less boosterish and quite practical. He repeatedly declared "We are a Whig" because at last a party had won power in his city and state that included leaders who declared their aversion to slavery and sympathy with the free people of color (although on occasion Cornish suggested he had nursed hopes for Van Buren as a fellow New Yorker, and turned to the Whigs from disgust with the new president's truckling to the South). By mid-1837, he was expressing satisfaction with New York City's newly elected Whig mayor, who, as noted in chapter 1, had used his inaugural speech to defend the city's "Several thousands of colored people" denied poor relief by the Democrats during that year's depression.[23]

How to measure the *Colored American*'s impact? Too often, we treat newspapers as if they were all equal other than the few with national significance—in those days, *Niles' Register*, later the statewide party organs and the "Administration" paper in Washington; today the *New York Times*, the *Wall Street Journal*, and a few others. In fact, some were much more influential than others, as indicated by how often they were reprinted, so how do we assess the reach of the *Colored American*? Certainly, it sharpened debate and political community among its intended audience of "colored Americans." Its effect within white print culture is harder to assess. Cornish and Bell participated in the "exchange" system authorized by Congress in the 1792 Post Office Act, but most editors refused to acknowledge the *Colored American*. In spring 1837, a few southern papers briefly noted "A Dark Business," a paper published in New York by "a *black* man," but that was all. Cornish's Whiggism drew more attention, with the state Democratic organ, the *Albany Argus*, reprinting a sarcastic piece titled "A Formidable Alliance" that quoted Cornish's declaration "We are a Whig and vote with the Whigs" to mock that party. That fall, the New Orleans *Daily Picayune* huffily announced, "We received yesterday a copy of 'The Colored American,' and would thank the editor not to permit his offspring to intrude on us again. We have no wish to be on familiar terms with his kindred, or with any others of the colored race." Otherwise the *Colored American* was ignored. Its one widely reprinted article came in December 1841, on "The Management of the President's House," noting John Tyler had hired the White House's first black butler at an impressive salary.[24]

From another angle, however, the *Colored American* was influential in ways that broke sharply with presumptions of black men's obligations to white people. Its other main audience was white abolitionists, among whom it became required reading, so much so that colonizationists tried to steal its readership via a dubious *Colored Man's Journal*. A particular instance stands out, underlining the authority that black men claimed on matters political thanks to Cornish. Even while disagreeing with him on everything related to partisan politics, Joshua Leavitt, editor of *The Emancipator* (soon to become the Liberty Party's national organ), approvingly cited Cornish's blackballing Henry Clay as a Whig presidential candidate. In late 1839, *The Emancipator* suggested that Cornish had defined the terms for the Whigs, then meeting in national convention in Harrisburg: "We do not suppose a single delegate will go to Harrisburgh [*sic*] with the belief that Henry Clay can be elected President of the United States. Our brother Cornish settled that question two years ago." One year later, defending his nascent party against claims of "utter insignificance," Leavitt asserted, "Be our 'insignificance' ever so 'utter,' we had influence enough to prevent the election of Henry Clay to the Presidency in 1840. . . . No intelligent Whig will deny that Mr. Clay was the first choice of the great body of the Whig party in 1839. . . . We renew the declaration, first issued by the Rev. Samuel E. Cornish, in the Colored American, that 'Henry Clay can never be President of the United States.' If he wishes to be President of anything more than the Colonization Society, let him go and be President of Liberia." The notion that a black editor had singlehandedly determined the fate of the Whigs' iconic leader was something new under the sun, why Cornish deserves to be remembered as the gray (or perhaps "colored") eminence of the new black politics.[25]

Reentering the Partisan World, 1837–1839

During Van Buren's presidency, amidst a terrible depression, New York State saw the beginnings of a three-sided battle over race and rights which would last through Lincoln's election. An invigorated black political class began a drive for voting rights, coinciding with the Whigs' ascent against the entrenched Democratic "Regency," which converted the Democrats' 94–34 Assembly majority in 1837 into a Whig majority of 100–28 in 1838, electing Seward governor. New York's Whigs became their party's premier state organization, marked by Seward's willingness to play the race card on behalf of his citizens of color. The statewide suffrage campaign surged in 1838–40, and a cadre of New York City's young black men proposed a state convention focused on enfranchisement, a seminal event when it transpired in 1840. In these same years, white abolitionists in western New York began the campaign for "political action," meaning independent antislavery nominations. This controversial move permanently split the national movement, in turn spurring unprecedented assertions of black political independence.

For more than a decade after the new constitution came into force in 1822, there was no effort to return voting to a nonracial basis, suggesting black men largely accepted it. In 1825, Governor DeWitt Clinton proposed an amendment to grant suffrage simply on the basis of "citizenship, full age, and competent residence." Committees were formed in both houses to act on his various recommendations. The Senate committee incorporated his proposal with fulsome arguments about "liberal republican" principles, but no mention of the property qualification for colored electors, and when it came to the full Senate for consideration, the motion was divided by general agreement. After unanimously passing the first section granting universal suffrage to "male citizens," there were two days of debate over the provision requiring a $250 freehold for black men, which was finally reaffirmed 27–6. The failed effort to reenact nonracial suffrage was led by the Clintonian John C. Spencer, who had authored the legislature's ringing defense of black citizenship during the Missouri Crisis, later a leading Antimason and Whig.[26]

To revise the constitution so as to reenfranchise black voters required mastering a complex process: an amendment had to be approved in two consecutive legislative sessions before submission to a popular vote. The legislative and electoral calendars thus dictated plans for action. The legislature usually met from January to May, followed by a fall election season, with annual elections for the entire state assembly, and one-third of the state Senate, and biannual elections for governor. Black Yorkers perfected a statewide apparatus to reach simply the first stage in this process, a positive vote by both houses of the legislature in sequential years.

Although petitions for equal suffrage were submitted in 1834 (and perhaps also in 1835), the statewide campaign began in earnest in 1837. Relying solely on the *Colored American* paints a false picture, however, by putting the city at the center. The original push came from a biracial coalition in upstate. When the Assembly opened on January 7, the Genesee Whig Charles O. Shepard submitted a petition from "Gerrit Smith and others . . . to extend the right of suffrage without regard to color" and "repeal the laws authorizing slavery in the state of New-York," meaning the "nine months' law" allowing a slave-owner temporary residence. The St. Lawrence County Democrat Preston King (who ten years later led "Barnburner" Democrats into the Free Soil Party, and in the 1850s helped found the Republican Party) proposed the petition "be denied and rejected," a highly unusual procedure. Whigs expressed confusion while Shepard "contended at great length for the abstract right of the colored man," citing the 934 black taxpayers who could not vote, until debate came to a head. King's intent was clear: to force the Whigs to go on the record on "whether the right of suffrage should be extended to the blacks. Every member ought to be prepared to meet that question at once. He was opposed to placing the black man on a par with the white in this respect." He then baited the Whigs, expressing his surprise that "gentlemen who were known to act politically with the 'native' party," meaning Whig collaboration with an anti-immigrant ticket in New York City, "which would wrest the right of voting from a man born in England, Ireland, Scotland, or on the continent of Europe . . . now [were] standing out with so much vehemence in favor of extending the right of suffrage to the African." King's proposal to reject the petition passed 76–44, but a surprising thirteen Democrats broke ranks.[27]

The next petition was presented on February 3 from "39 persons of color in Troy," one of the state's best-organized black communities. It excited a daylong "feverish excitement," Weed reported sardonically in his *Albany Evening Journal*. Democrats argued "that the Petition revived the Abolition excitement; that its object was agitation and turmoil; and that its consequences would be anarchy and disunion." After deriding this hysteria, Weed drily noted, "If there is any reason or soundness in their position, then it becomes of the duty of the Regency [the Democratic machine] to withdraw the right of suffrage from the $250 freehold blacks. For if it is proper to permit a colored man to vote who has a $250 free-hold, it cannot be *treasonable* to inquire into the propriety of enlarging the colored franchise of the state." This time the party line held, as Democrats voted as a bloc to deny a referral, 74–23 (three Whigs defecting). From here on, the campaign took off, with petitions bearing hundreds of signatures from black and white people in Rensselaer, New York, Kings, Genesee, Oneida, Albany, Madison, and Ontario Counties.

On the final May 13 vote to accept the judiciary committee's refusal to act on these petitions, however, twenty Whigs voted with the Democrats, for a lopsided 100–11 tally, including Luther Bradish, later celebrated for his pro-black stance. The eleven who voted for action in 1837 came from counties with high tallies for "equal suffrage" in the 1846 referendum: Essex and Washington along the Vermont border, and a block in the "burned over" west (Genesee, Ontario, Monroe, and Niagara; the latter two containing substantial black populations in Buffalo and Rochester), plus one outlier from the city.[28]

Given that the majority of Whig assemblymen had refused to vote for any action on black suffrage, the 1837 session offered little grounds for optimism minus a radical shift in the state's political equation. Such a change occurred that fall, stimulating renewed hopes. In November 1837, Samuel Cornish hailed the "WHIG TRIUMPH," declaring, "The politics of the whole state have been completely revolutionized," but then adding, with a certain wariness, "We have voted with the Whigs—their views in politics are measurably our views, yet while we rejoice with them, we rejoice with trembling. We know something of the corruption and the deceitfulness of the human heart" and "doings of political men, when in power." He made an urgent plea to his "Brother Whigs," asking them to "mete out righteousness to every citizen, whatever be his complexion . . . enfranchise, as one of your first acts, the forty thousand colored freemen, illegally robbed of their privileges, and of their rights," ending on a positive note: "We confess that we have more hope in your wisdom and righteousness, than we have ever had in any preceding body of men, exalted to the same responsibility and power."[29]

The year 1838 dawned as exceptionally promising, and a petition campaign generated 9,300 signatures from thirty counties "praying for the repeal of all laws which make a distinction amongst the people of the State on account of color." The standard text, printed in the *Colored American*, was hardly deferential. It reminded the assemblymen of the declension from their revolutionary fathers, when "by the former constitution of the State, all citizens, whatever might be their complexion, and from whatever ancestors descended, were placed upon the same footing. Its patriotic framers did not think it consistent . . . to divide freemen into castes." Not only had "the present Constitution . . . established color as a qualification for voting," even worse, it "actually took from many . . . the right of voting . . . which they had enjoyed since the first organization of the State Government." Black Yorkers asked for "the abolition of an odious distinction, which, while it acknowledges them as citizens, denies them the rights which all others possess as attached to that honorable appellation."[30]

This campaign must be placed within the larger frame. Every day, the *Journal of the Assembly* recorded numerous petitions: for and against creating new counties; to compensate a local contractor, erect a bridge, or improve a road; personal requests, like changing a name or legalizing a divorce. Petitions for black suffrage were in no way unusual, and even larger numbers from the same counties requested guarantees of jury trials for accused fugitives or opposed Texas's annexation. Although the 9,300 signers presumably included thousands of voters, the assemblymen surely knew there were many more who objected to deleting the property qualification, and how the Whigs controlling the judiciary committee and the Assembly disposed of suffrage petitions reveals this awareness. On April 18, a Kings County Whig, Benjamin Silliman, representing the committee's majority, asked that they "be discharged from the further consideration" of petitions "which ask for the repeal of all laws making a distinction between the people of this State on account of color." They were "laid on the table" with no debate and no roll call. The hopes invested in a "Whig Triumph" had proved illusory.[31]

Unwilling to accept defeat, in June the city's young men, led by Thomas Sidney and Philip Bell, formed the New York Association for the Political Elevation and Improvement of the People of Color, effectively an extraparty organization for men who insisted on participating in formal politics despite their disfranchisement. Although little noticed then, Patrick Reason proposed that "said Associations, when formed, be requested to send delegates to a General Political Convention of the Colored people, to be held at Albany, at such time as shall be appointed by the Executive Committee." The ascendancy of these youths (Sidney was barely twenty-one) did not go unchallenged. Alongside the formation of ward committees covering the city, a war of words stirred along generation lines. As early as December 1837, Cornish declared, "The young men of New York must talk less, and DO MORE, or the subject of their political rights will never be properly presented before our State Legislature." He wanted them to "give their money freely" for the campaign, stressing, "The practice of meeting and spending hours in idle speechifying, without contributing the necessary funds, must give place, and that immediately, to more efficient doings."[32]

This was comparatively mild, but in March 1838 Cornish cracked down hard. After hearing Sidney's "heart stirring and eloquent" oratory at a meeting ("undoubtedly, one of the most talented youth of the age"), Cornish went for the jugular. "Mr. Sidney is defective in judgment and prudence. His mind needs the rigors of mental discipline. Were he my son, his first lesson in the morning, and last in the evening, should be on PRUDENCE. His judgment is in great danger of being perverted, if not enfeebled, by the brilliancy and

fertility of his imagination." Which of Sidney's remarks "was extremely im-
prudent?" Apparently, he referred to "physical resort," meaning violent resistance, as "the means of bodily emancipation," a subject older colored men
avoided at all costs. "Civil agitation is the weapon—no other should be spoken of or countenanced," Cornish insisted. Sidney dismissed this "idle
wind . . . the wonted approbatory style in which self-assuming and self-
presuming age, condescends to notice the essays of 'young aspirancy,'" and
Cornish slapped back: "He should remember that he is a youth, and if he intends to be a public man, he is public property." The campaign went forward
nonetheless, with two committees working in parallel, and the younger men
increasingly in the lead.[33]

The suffrage drive stalled in 1839, with the *Colored American* ruing it had
"expected great things from the 'Political Association;' but the opposition
that laudable body met with, in a great measure paralyzed their exertions."
Its editor, Charles B. Ray, came around to the idea "that a general Convention of this great State should be held. . . . A central State committee should
be appointed to whom all the petitions should be sent. . . . We should also
have an agent in Albany." He called on the men he knew from his tours to
organize the convention, "Rich of Troy, Cross of Catskill, Payne of Newburgh,
Johnson of Albany, Wright of Schenectady, Duffin of Geneva, Grant of Oswego, Stewart of Rochester, Francis of Buffalo, Lee of Palmyra," the nucleus
of the emerging political class. At an August 1, 1839 meeting of the Political
Association, the decision was taken that "a Convention should be held at some
central point within the State to adopt such measures as may seem expedient in furtherance of the interests of our people and of the objects of this association." This call came amidst proposals to revive the national conventions,
which veterans like Ray knew would bring together men who agreed on little.
A statewide meeting to gain actual rights, gathering those who shared a common experience, was something else.[34]

In abolitionism's biracial arena, 1839 was decisive in establishing black
Yorkers' independence from white direction. Only a few Philadelphians ever
criticized the PAS's no-voting policy. Boston's black community remained
loyal to Garrison long after the 1840 schism between his group and the "political abolitionists." Unlike these others, black New Yorkers demonstrated
their autonomy in public, and their self-determination was personalized, pitting Cornish against the nation's wealthiest abolitionist, Gerrit Smith, president of the New-York Anti-Slavery Society (NYASS). Cornish fundamentally
disagreed with Smith about how to *do* politics. Smith and his allies saw the
electoral arena as an extension of their movement, leading them to create a
political party with no chance at office, versus Cornish (and others like James
McCune Smith), who backed a party that could win office and enact laws.

Cornish was a Whig because he favored an inside, "half-a-loaf" strategy, and the Whigs were the only option. This struggle predicted the longest-running debate among American radicals, given the United States' state-enforced two-party electoral system: should one operate inside or outside, or somehow keep a foot in both?

Cornish's dissent began with his opposition to the NYASS's stance in the 1838 state election. The society declared that sincere abolitionists could vote only for candidates who pledged support for abolitionist demands (jury trials for accused fugitives, nonracial suffrage, barring slaveholders bringing chattels into New York for nine months), a stance that the *Colored American* endorsed. Ironically, given his later record, the state society sought to punish William Seward, the Whig gubernatorial candidate, who refused to take a definite stance on these issues. Gerrit Smith and William Jay had submitted detailed questionnaires to the nominees for governor and lieutenant governor. The Democrats ignored them, Seward replied evasively, while Luther Bradish, his running mate, avowed his outright abolitionism, including his own question-and-answer regarding suffrage, asking, "In what part of the existing Constitution of the State" was possession of a freehold by "the white citizen made an indispensable condition?" and answering, "Nowhere. It is, in relation to the colored citizen, an exclusive distinction. And it is an odious one." The NYASS's intervention worried Whig leaders, especially after Smith and Jay urged their 10,000 members to vote for Bradish but cast blank ballots for governor, with the margin between Seward and his running mate intended to demonstrate the movement's clout.[35]

Following the election, Cornish attacked the spoiling strategy as ruinous, especially for black men barely hanging on to suffrage. People of color had a basic interest in supporting any party that might aid them, and should pressure both major parties simultaneously, repeating his anathema on Clay: "1500 abolition votes [were] given in this city for Seward, and more than 1800 for Bradish.—In the State, Bradish has received more than 20,000 votes from abolitionists, and Seward more than 15,000. Their election has been effected by abolition suffrage; and should the Whigs find no better candidate for the Presidency of the United States, in the fall of 1840, than the president of the 'American Colonization Society,' alias the 'Negro Shipping Company,' abolition votes will turn the victory the other way, by the re-election of Martin Van Buren." He then declared his dissent: "As an abolitionist we have felt bound . . . to abide by the views and decisions of the majority of our friends and brethren . . . while as a public sentinel we have felt bound to publish, freely, our dissent from those views." The NYASS's plan was "impolitic and derogatory," since "every abolitionist who is governed by principle, is bound by that principle to vote for the best men, irrespective of political creed or party . . . but he has no right to withhold his influence and sacrifice his weight in the creation of the 'powers that be,' because all the candidates do not come up to his standard. He has no more, moral right, to throw away his vote, than he has to prevent the vote of another." He pointed out the obvious: "The successful candidates, in this state, have succeeded, wholly, on the ground of abolition suffrage; the official abolition creed, notwithstanding.—Thousands upon thousands of abolitionists have voted the whole Whig ticket, in opposition to the general instructions of the body. This we should have done, had we voted at all."[36]

Cornish was not done battling for the right. In late summer 1839, as agitation for "political abolition" intensified, he authored a four-part series titled "Signs of the Times," attacking the strategy proposed by Gerrit Smith and other upstate leaders. There was a sharp edge to Cornish's critique. He invoked the Antimasons, who began as a righteous campaign for social and political reform but ended up the tools of "designing demagogues and selfish politicians, seeking power and place"; now the same "wolves in sheep's clothing . . . would soon corrupt, divide and desecrate our holy cause." Another foray in third-party politics would lead to abolitionists also being "deceived and corrupted" by "Satan and his legions." Beyond that, Cornish demonstrated how abolitionists would marginalize themselves from access to power, because the spoiling strategy, "with a refinement of charity bordering on self-righteousness, ties up their hands so that, in half the States, they cannot vote, and in the other half, not more than one in every ten, can do it."[37]

In response, Smith exercised his authority at the NYASS annual meeting to urge "no more money for the Colored American" because of its "publication . . . of articles in favor of voting for pro-slavery men," meaning Whigs. Cornish responded fierily: "We HURL AWAY the charge. . . . We are in favor of men who go for the abolition of slavery in the District of Columbia and the Territories, for universal suffrage and for the rejection of all applications made for admission into the Union by slaveholding Territories, though they go not the 'Albany resolution,'" meaning the independent nominations pursued by Smith's crowd. In *The Emancipator*, William Goodell baited "the Rev. Samuel E. Cornish," for approving "the course of those who went for 'a whole Whig ticket,' last autumn," citing Whig papers that quoted Cornish to recruit abolitionist voters. "Why not be honest at once, and say outright, that whiggism is to be considered of more importance than abolitionism?" Philip Bell and Charles Ray, by now publisher and editor of the *Colored American*, defended Cornish's right to speak, while disagreeing with him on independent nominations. Bell's October 1839 comment damning "Prescription" by whites like Smith suggested a deep suspicion: "We are not surprised—we always knew that such was the spirit with which the white man would act towards his 'colored brethren.'" He spoke directly to these brethren. "As long as we let them think and act for us; as long as we will bow to their opinions and acknowledge that their 'word is counsel and their will is law,' so long they will outwardly treat us as men, while in their hearts they still hold us as *slaves*." Weeks later, Ray issued his own challenge: "Our friends . . . must learn that as colored men, we are more competent to judge in some cases, in this cause than themselves. . . . Brother Cornish had a right to express his views in any form without incurring the influence of our worthy friends against our paper. . . . Our friends must hereafter remember that we think for ourselves."[38]

Onto the Main Stage

The years from 1840 to 1846 constitute a crucial crossover point in U.S. history. In 1840, the possibility of disunion and civil war was a bugaboo to frighten voters, a pipe dream for extremists. Six years later, after the United States annexed Texas and invaded Mexico, that possibility was measurably closer. In New York, national events were complicated by the battle between the Whig and Liberty Parties for antislavery voters and a suffrage campaign accurately described as "the most intensive and extensive black political effort of the country up to that time." That campaign crested in 1846, when its leaders attempted a subtle triangulation between the Whigs and Liberty men to produce a pro-suffrage majority at a state constitutional convention. They failed, and in the resulting referendum on "equal suffrage for colored persons," 72 percent of the electorate, including a majority of Whigs, voted no. This instance and others suggest that Whig leaders used "equal suffrage" as bait to draw white antislavery voters, but without the requisite parliamentary discipline, or support from their base, to implement that reform.[39]

The campaign for a constitutional amendment paralleled the Liberty Party's rise. As Lee Benson documented, the Democrats were never hegemonic in New York, and a modest 2 percent shift in the electorate decided most elections.[40] The Whigs controlled the state in 1838–41 by ever-slimmer margins, after which the Liberty men cut sufficiently into their electorate to make statewide victory difficult, since "Whig declines almost equaled the Liberty totals."[41] From the Liberty men's perspective, Whig antislavery was a response to their threat. Sensing power, they went all out to defeat the openly abolitionist Whig Luther Bradish for governor in 1842. The Liberty candidate, Alvan Stewart, got 7,263 votes, a third of Bradish's losing margin (186,091 to 208,872) versus the Democrat William Bouck. By 1843, the Liberty Party had reached their peak, with 15,000 loyal voters statewide, a hard bloc capable of crippling the Whigs. In that context, getting the small pool of black voters to back one's party mattered considerably, even driving party strategies. These dynamics climaxed in 1844, when New York's Liberty men supposedly deprived Clay of their state's electoral votes, and thus the presidency. Historians have documented how those votes were already lost to the Whigs, and Seward wrote Clay that his loss was due to New York City Whigs alienating immigrant voters by jumping on the nativist bandwagon, nonetheless long thereafter, 1844 was cited as a disastrous instance of a minor party spoiling an otherwise rational choice.[42]

For black men, their 1837–39 mobilizing was but a prelude to the next decade's systematic organizing. Consider the many "firsts" initiated in New York State in these years: the first statewide political convention leading to a permanent state organization of black men; the first national black convention devoted to politics (at Buffalo in 1843); the first black delegates to a state party convention (other than Reuben Ruby at Maine's 1834 Whig founding), followed by the first election of black men to state party offices; most significant, the first large-scale organized intervention by black men into white men's politics.

Two of Manhattan's "young men," James McCune Smith and Henry Highland Garnet, exemplified the competition for leadership. Between them, they stood for the new militancy, preparing the ground for Douglass, who had none of their advantages of education and patronage. Both were born in the 1810s, McCune Smith in 1813 and Garnet in 1815. Garnet was born enslaved in Kent County, Maryland, as noted. After his family fled to New York, he met Smith at the African Free School, after which both strove to gain the university education denied to black men. Before that, Garnet shipped twice to Cuba as a cabin boy before joining the inaugural class of the first black high school in 1831. Then, while serving an indenture on Long Island, he suffered a severe leg injury leading to amputation in 1841. All of these trials contributed to Garnet's legend, which began in 1835 when he was one of several black youths enrolled at the Noyes Academy in Canaan, New Hampshire. Local townspeople assaulted the school and Garnet, employing "a double-barreled shot-gun [and] blasting from his window soon drove the cowards away." He matriculated at Beriah Green's Oneida Institute in Whitesboro, graduating in 1840, and was hired to teach school and pastor a fledgling black Presbyterian church in Troy, which he made into a thriving center of activism. In that year, he also addressed the American Anti-Slavery Society's annual meeting, beginning a political career founded on sustained audacity, which culminated in his becoming the first African American to address Congress in 1865. In Garnet's day, speaking in public was the sine qua non of a political man, and national reputations were sustained via oratorical power—Daniel Webster's being the best-known. Garnet understood himself as that kind of man, and he astounded whites with his slashing brilliance; after the apocalyptic

"Address to the Slaves of the United States of America" speech at the 1843 convention, a local newspaper reported, "So powerful was the denunciation, that one of the first clergymen of the city, an anti-abolitionist, was heard, on going out, to declare, that were he to act from the impulse of the moment, he should shoulder his musket and march South."[43]

Although Smith was no orator and kept both his legs, his trajectory was equally dramatic. He was the son of an enslaved woman from Charleston, South Carolina, and the white merchant who brought her to New York; he was freed by the 1827 emancipation act. A remarkable scholar, he wanted to be a doctor, but that was impossible in the United States, so he earned three degrees at the University of Glasgow between 1834 and 1837, returning to New York as a credentialed physician. The *Colored American* published his diary and made him an editor, dinners were given in his honor, and he too addressed the AASS (in 1838, before Garnet), while setting up a successful practice on Lower Broadway. By the 1850s, Smith was writing for *Frederick Douglass' Paper* as "Communipaw," publishing learned lectures, and was a candidate for New York's secretary of state on the Radical Abolitionist ticket. Oddly, the burgeoning scholarship on him has ignored his long history as a sharp-tongued electoral partisan. In an 1847 article, Garnet, his one time antagonist, put it directly: "In politics, Dr. Smith is a whig," an understatement since Smith led the black Whigs who contested fiercely with Garnet's Liberty men. This contest had two axes. Smith and men like him believed the best opportunity to regain suffrage lay within the major party system. Given Democratic hostility, the Whigs were their only possible allies. Whiggish political action, they believed, required hostility to third parties as well as "exclusive" organizing by conventions of colored men. For Smith and his allies, such meetings risked nullifying their influence. As one asserted at a July 1840 "large public meeting of the colored citizens of New York" to discuss the pending state convention, "The colored population is but one fiftieth part of the population. . . . A vast majority of the whites are opposed (by prejudice) to the political elevation of the colored people. . . . It is contrary to reason . . . to say that any separate political movement on the part of the colored people (now shut out from political rights) can obtain for them the said political rights." The reporter observed that "Dr. Smith supported the resolutions . . . at great length,—and in his usual forcible manner," until the meeting ran out of time. Smith had a distinct propensity for working within the system so as to probe its limits: at the American Anti-Slavery Society's 1842 meeting, he proposed the organization appropriate $2,000 "for the purpose of testing, in the Supreme Court of the United States, whether the citizens of each State shall be allowed the privileges and immunities of citizens in the several States." His resolution was tabled, too daring even for Garrisonians.[44]

Garnet's move to Troy was not incidental. In the 1840s, leadership shifted north to Albany and Troy (eight miles apart) and west to Rochester, Buffalo, Geneva, and Syracuse (even in 1844, the latter two had more black voters than New York City). Urban intellectuals like Samuel R. Ward and Garnet took upstate pastorates, in Ward's case a white church in Wayne County, where he hailed his congregants as the "honest, straight-forward, God-fearing descendants of New England Puritans" who didn't care about the "mere accident of the colour of a preacher." Equally important was a black Yorker who never sought Ward's or Garnet's transatlantic fame—Albany's Stephen Myers, born a slave in Rensselaer County in 1800 (or perhaps 1790), and freed sometime in the 1810s, after which he served DeWitt Clinton and a long line of state political leaders. Long before the 1840s' annual conventions, he organized a regional black convention in Ithaca in 1831. Throughout the prewar decades, Myers headed a well-organized black political network centered on Albany (in 1820, the nation's eighth-largest city), working closely with Whigs like Weed. In 1839, he had performed a vital service for Governor Seward, during an acute political crisis. That July, the "Anti-Rent" or "Helderberg War" broke out in the upper Hudson River counties. Following the death of the Patroon Stephen Van Rensselaer, his heirs attempted to collect decades of unpaid rents from his 80,000 tenants. The result was armed insurgency. In December, a state posse was threatened by a much larger number of rebels, amid a full militia mobilization. Seward's autobiography, written with his son, described the scene: "The city was full of rumors of disasters to the expedition, that they were hemmed in, they were without food and shelter, etc. The Governor . . . dispatched Stephen Myers with two wagon-loads of bread and meat," and waited for good news. Other than a later reference to Myers as one of "the colored citizens of Albany" thanking the governor on his leaving office, there is no further reference to Myers. With McCune Smith's help, he also published the *Northern Star and Freeman's Advocate*, the state's only black paper between the *Colored American*'s demise in December 1841 and the founding of Douglass's *North Star* in 1847. By the 1850s, Myers was acknowledged as New York's premier black "wire puller," able to mobilize colored voters statewide, adept at lobbying lawmakers; Douglass called him "the colored Thurlow." As a longtime Whig, Myers pushed against the radical current in upstate. Garnet and his allies were more ideologically ambitious than Myers and McCune Smith, responding with contempt to behind-the-scenes operating. Garnet commanded allegiance for his forensic and literary skill and his proud blackness, as the reputed grandson of African nobility, but there were also practical reasons for his Libertyism. The third party afforded him a greater field of action than the Whigs ever would. Seward might proclaim his respect for black men, but he never invited them to speak at a Whig convention.[45]

Any discussion of these men—Smith, Garnet, Myers, Ward, and many others—is abstract unless they are placed in situ, operating collectively. The locations of their annual conventions in 1840 (Albany), 1841 (Troy), 1842 (Utica), 1843 (Buffalo), 1844 (Schenectady), and 1845 (Syracuse) document how upstate leaders drove the new phase of struggle. The original focus of these meetings was formally nonpartisan—to appeal to the public at large and legislators, whether Democrats or Whigs, to erase the odious stain created in 1821, and "return to the pure faith of [our] republican fathers," meaning nonracial suffrage. As each year went by, however, more and more black men were drawn to the Liberty Party's forthright radicalism and biracial fellowship. Key leaders of the suffrage campaign, notably Garnet as chairman of the State Central Committee, renounced nonpartisanship and worked to align their growing network with that party. This move angered other leaders, including McCune Smith in New York City and Myers in Albany, splitting the black suffrage movement in 1843–44 just as the Liberty Party reached the peak of its influence. To the surprise of Democrats, who barely carried the state for Polk in 1844, early in 1845 the Whigs began campaigning for a convention to revise the state's constitution, including ending the $250 freehold requirement for men of color. These maneuvers reached a peak in 1846, ending in disaster for the Liberty Party and the black suffrage movement. To unravel this complex political scenario, involving three parties plus an organized extraparty movement, requires breaking down the narrative year by year.

1840: The Year of Decisions

The year 1840 began auspiciously. In late April, an Albany Whig, Friend Humphrey, presented a petition in the state Senate, asking for equal suffrage. It was signed by Thurlow Weed, other prominent whites, and three of Albany's best-known black men, William H. Topp, Michael Douge, and the Reverend Benjamin Paul, with a Democratic paper alleging, "The politics of the signers as far as known are designated by the letter W, indicating the *Whigs*."[46] The year also saw two watersheds. For the first time, black men argued over which party to support on a statewide basis, and in the nation's largest electoral arena. In spring 1840, the Liberty Party formally announced itself at an upstate New York convention, and from the outset, black men were involved— while Whigs mounted a "log cabin and hard cider" campaign for William Henry Harrison, black Yorkers debated the merits of Harrison versus the slaveholder-turned-abolitionist James G. Birney, the Liberty nominee. Concurrently, in August of 1840, well over 100 black leaders gathered in Albany for an unprecedented state convention focused on regaining the franchise, a new model for political action very different from the national gatherings in 1830–35. The tension between nonpartisan campaigning by black men with any white allies they could find and a competition between black men over which party to support defined the next six years, leading up to 1845–46, when it briefly seemed black leaders would bring Whigs and Liberty men into coalition to regain equal suffrage.

Since the 1840 Convention of the Colored Inhabitants of the State of New York, to Consider Their Political Disabilities was the axis from which subsequent black political action pivoted, we begin there. It opened at Albany's Hamilton Street Baptist Church on August 18, 1840, as 134 "delegates poured in from all directions," with its deliberations "very harmonious and happy"; although planning began in August 1839, it had come together suddenly in late spring and summer 1840, perhaps because of the enthusiasm generated by that year's presidential campaign. Any notion that New York City men would dominate because of their numbers or sophistication was clearly off the table. Older men who had collaborated on *Freedom's Journal* and the first convention movement were joined by the city's "young men," with Rochester's Austin Steward as president, eminent vice presidents from Albany, Schenectady, and New York City (J. T. Raymond, R. P. G. Wright, and William P. Johnson, respectively), Garnet, the Albanite William Topp, and Charles Reason as secretaries, and a Business Committee of the Reverends Charles B. Ray and Theodore Wright plus Buffalo's Abner Francis. The politics were "pure republicanism," wedding that ideology's supple force to a newer nativism, as outlined in chapter 1. Patriotism was emphatically affirmed, that "this country is our country; its liberties and privileges were purchased by the exertions and blood of our fathers," the people's "hopes are our hopes; their God is our God; we were born among them; our lot is to live among them, and be of them; where they die, we will die; and where they are buried, there will we be buried also." Appealing to those in power, it ignored the schisms dividing abolitionists, whether "political action," women's rights, or the sins of the proslavery churches, and avoided possible distractions, such as temperance, the Liberty Party, and the presidential race. The most notable assertion was unequivocal independence from white control, that "while it is our duty to co-operate with all friends in the cause of human liberty, it is not less important to our peculiar condition that we should embody the unbiased opinions of our own people as occasions may require in public Conventions." Above all, a profound optimism suffused the convention's deliberations, epitomized by Alexander Crummell's "Address to the Colored Citizens," which declared their rights an irresistible fact: "The principle of rectitude is as universal among men as the light of the sun. . . . From our own human consciousness can we make our most earnest and effectual entreaties to our fellow men in power. Such an appeal cannot but be heard. It will receive deference from its very nature."[47]

Speeches, addresses, and proceedings were a form of public argumentation, published in newspapers and printed in bulk, but so was the opportunity to show black men could conduct themselves with decorum and forethought. Weed and other powerful Whigs attended the convention and paid close attention, as Ray noted the following year, presumably because they saw concrete planning. The convention's purpose, unlike any of those preceding it, was to initiate sustained political action via a statewide push for equal suffrage. It elected a seven-man State Central Committee from Albany and Troy, chaired by the twenty-four-year-old Garnet, to coordinate 33 five-man county committees covering most of the state, naming 101 individuals to these committees with the expectation they would recruit others.[48]

It would be a gross error, however, to examine this more political version of the "black convention movement" in isolation. Unlike the 1830s' meetings, New York's conventions were deeply embedded in the partisan matrix of state and nation. Every year through 1845, these ostensibly nonpartisan meetings operated in tandem with the Liberty Party's electoral mobilizing. Unlike in New England, New York's third party generated immediate interest among men of color. A cohort of Albany's black leaders were among the 122 delegates at the April 1, 1840 National Anti-Slavery Nominating Convention in that city, including Primus Robinson, John T. Raymond, Richard Thompson, George C. Harper, Michael Douge, and Rev. Benjamin Paul. Once that ticket was in the field, support rapidly grew. Within weeks, Paul and Douge convened meetings at the former's Hamilton Street Baptist Church to back the new party, resolving "that we most heartily concur in the recent Anti Slavery nominations of Honorable J. G. Birney for President, and Hon. Thomas Earle for Vice President, of the United States, and we respectfully call upon all our brethren entitled to vote to sustain them at the coming election." That Douge and Paul had just joined leading Whigs like Thurlow Weed in petitioning the legislature for equal suffrage suggests considerable political autonomy, if not temerity.[49]

Given that the report of the meeting at Paul's church appeared in the *Colored American*, read by black and white leaders around the North, it could hardly be ignored. From the first, New York's Liberty Party opened itself to black men, and they reciprocated. In the same week as their Albany convention in August 1840, Charles Ray made clear his paper's stance: "Abolitionists in the State, who have become sick at heart of the two political parties, on account of their succumbing to the slave power . . . have now before them a ticket for which they can vote in good conscience, without scattering their votes to the winds, or disfranchising themselves by staying at home." Stressing it was "certainly right to go the whole liberty ticket," he left room for ticket-splitting, given Seward's record—that if "there are men for any office . . . you are satisfied with, and would like to see them . . . continued in office, substitute them [write them in] upon the anti slavery ticket instead of some one already there."[50]

The August 1840 convention to nominate a state Liberty ticket demonstrated the party's biracialism. The young, eloquent, very black Reverend Samuel Ringgold Ward was elected a delegate from Gerrit Smith's town of Peterboro and opened two of its sessions with prayer, a position of honor, and following the convention, considerable attention was given to a debate in Cazenovia between Ward and an abolitionist editor who opposed "independent nominations" (Ray reported he also had been "appointed a delegate to attend, and should have been happy in so doing, but important duties" kept him away). A report by William P. Johnson, the *Colored American*'s agent, indicates the demonstration effect of even a single ballot cast for the third party. He was in Coxsackie, Greene County, where "there are a few legal [black] voters" but only "one colored American . . . who is going to vote right, not only now, but while there is a single slave setting upon the ballot box looking to see whether he cast his vote for freedom or slavery. The political parties he tells me have tried in vain to make him believe that it is of no use to vote for the Anti-Slavery nominations, because their candidates cannot be elected. He replies then let my vote be thrown away with the rest, and after many days I shall find it, and I shall have too, the consciousness to know, that I have not tasted, touched nor handled the unclean thing. (Slavery.)"[51]

To accommodate all positions, the *Colored American* opened its pages in late September. Immediately, "Liberty" attacked the Whigs. Many black voters "suppose by voting for Harrison and Tyler that they are voting for the slave" but "Tyler is a slaveholder. . . . I have heard it stated that the man is a slave breeder, as well as a trader . . . a man who sells children by the pound." In response, "Justice for All" suggested that "Liberty" was equally underhanded, seeking "political capital, de facto, for Martin Van Buren and Richard M. Johnson." Why withhold "the name of Richard M. Johnson, the Loco foco candidate for the same office who is also a slaveholder?" Liberty replied by charging Justice did "not write for the love of the slave, but [to] create capital for the whig party." A prominent black Garrisonian, Thomas Van Rensselaer, then took an openly pro-Whig position. Their petitions to the Whig-controlled legislature had been "received, referred, and reported upon, favorably, and laws past [sic] according to our prayers." How could "an Abolition Legislature . . . have done more?" The people of color would "expose ourselves to the charge of treachery, if we lend our influence to get up party merely because of a name." He then baited the Liberty men as racist, indicating rising expectations among men like him, that "the reason given to me for not putting colored men on the [Liberty] ticket was, that it would make the party odious in the eyes of other political parties . . . evidence that they had not carried out Abolition principles." Ray replied this was incorrect, the party had indeed tried to nominate a black man—him! "As to there being no men of color among the anti slavery nominations . . . ourself was asked if we would stand, as was also another in the same meeting" but "neither . . . could run on account of a constitutional provision in our case" (presumably not owning the requisite freehold). This sparring continued through Election Day, though all evidence suggests the black electorate stayed with the Whigs, as in 1844, when the slaveholder Clay was the candidate.[52]

1841: Hopes Dashed

The black conventioneers moved expeditiously. By January 1841, the *Colored American* was gathering petitions for a concerted push, and on January 15, Oswego's assemblyman William Duer moved a constitutional amendment with a nativist edge, that "every male citizen of the age of twenty-one years, who can read and write the English language, and who, for two years next preceding any election at which he may offer to vote, shall have been an inhabitant of this State, shall be entitled to vote for all officers elective by the people." On February 18, Garnet's Central Committee received "a candid and patient hearing" from the Assembly's Judiciary Committee and on March 10 "a favorable report . . . was accepted by the House" minus the English-literacy requirement, with Garnet reporting "the general sentiment about the capitol that the bill will pass the House by a great majority, and will go through the Senate almost unanimously," since Weed's powerful *Albany Journal* backed it. Optimism continued throughout the spring, while Whig leaders delayed any vote. Finally in June, the *Colored American* declared "a better state of feeling in regard to our rights, than ever before. . . . But, brethren, the Legislature has closed its session, and though we have seen much to encourage us in the doings of that body . . . they did not pass the bill as we believe they might have done."[53]

Despite this optimism, 1841 was the suffrage campaign's highest point, as the Whigs would not control the legislature again until 1847. Their overwhelming majorities had shrunk to a thin margin, likely why many wished to avoid voting on enfranchising black men given the thousands of downstate Whigs who evinced no sympathy for black voters, even as fellow Whigs.

Bearding the South with aggressive antislavery rhetoric and even action was one thing; authorizing "equal suffrage" was another. Already, when Weed's signature headed the 1840 suffrage petition, Democrats mocked this gesture as "a Morgan," meaning a trick to manipulate gullible voters.[54]

Sorting out why Duer's amendment never came to a vote is like wading into a swamp. Periodically, Whigs from abolition-friendly counties spoke passionately for it; Genesee's David Scott declared it "an exceedingly important subject" which "his constituents were anxious . . . should be acted upon and that speedily," adding later that "in his county . . . a large convention had recently been held" to back it with "more than 500 persons . . . present; and he could tell certain gentlemen that their constituents at home were looking at this subject with anxiety, and under the expectation that it would be agitated." Some Democrats suggested this passion was about corralling votes, but an Irish Democrat from the city, William McMurray, also sought "political capital" by demanding to chair a select committee on the amendment. As the *Colored American* reported with bemusement, "One party . . . ever inimical to our rights, takes up the matter, and recommends action upon it. The other party, astounded at such a move . . . accuses them of insincerity, and here ensues a debate, in which they forget the question . . . and bring in extraneous matter, and fire away at each other."[55]

In two key procedural votes, enough Whigs sided with Democrats to sideline any final decision. On April 19, the Washington County Whig Erastus D. Culver moved "further consideration of the report . . . to provide for the extension of the right of suffrage to colored persons." He lost 46–29, with twenty-six Whigs voting yes, and ten, including the Speaker, Peter Porter, voting no; if all Whigs voted in favor, the house would have had to consider black suffrage. On May 3, the Rensselaer County Whig William Van Schoonhoven again moved considering the report, and lost 50–37; crucially, "Mr. Worden, who presented the report from the judiciary committee, opposed the motion."[56]

Given these votes, the Democratic *Argus*'s cynical assessment rings true, that "the mere incipient step towards the proposed reform, was put to sleep on the table . . . the moment it was brought into the house," despite an "abundance of time . . . to pass a deliberate judgment on its merits." The amendment "was designed simply to make a show of regard for the interests and elevation of a down-trodden race, and to catch votes, if possible, in certain quarters," meaning upstate white voters defecting to the Liberty Party. Whig leaders waited "until the session was drawing to a close," with legislators "impatient of discussion" and adverse to "a protracted debate." Knowing they could "call it up in the early part of the session . . . they permitted it to lie, until the time for discussion had gone by, and then began the game of calling for it!" Despite many such gestures, "The proposition slept soundly among the things left on the Speaker's table," until Van Schoonhoven "made the last effort. . . . But the special orders [mandating the priority for consideration] interposed . . . and this question of extending the franchise" was put off like the "mass of other business in embryo."[57]

And yet, black men had got their hopes up for good reason. Seward's January message opening the legislature referred to "an unfortunate race, which, having been plunged by us into degradation and ignorance, is excluded from the franchise by an arbitrary property qualification incongruous with all our institutions." Had Whig legislators lied to Garnet when they assured him passage was assured? The support from prominent Whigs was real, indicated by a petition of 214 "White Citizens" from Schenectady, which Democrats noted was signed by "our mayor, A. C. Gibson, a *white conservative* lawyer, and our representative elect to the next congress, A. L. Linn, a *white whig* lawyer." Thurlow Weed editorialized in late March that the amendment was "in accordance with the spirit of the age and the genius of our Institutions. We have amongst us a numerous class of citizens differing only in complexion from ourselves. They are laboring to overcome the disabilities to which the laws and usages of a less enlightened age had subjected their race." Like Seward, he believed the freehold requirement was "an incongruous and odious test." If it was intended to verify with "what degree of intelligence and patriotism that class of electors would exercise their privilege," there was "a most satisfactory answer. There is not in our State a class of electors who estimate of their privilege more highly, who discharge their Elective responsibilities with more independence or who are imbued with a more faithful spirit of devotion to our Government and Institutions." Charles B. Ray knew this editorial's import—"Mr. Weed has got upon the right side of this question," and it was the convention that got him there. This endorsement was not "made either from motives of interest or policy, but are the settled principles of the editor's mind, arrived at from being better informed in regard to our people. Their rising and improving state . . . showed itself in the Albany Convention and its proceedings, with both of which Mr. Weed is familiar, having been present at several meetings of the Convention."[58]

Why then did the very influential Weed have so little influence? Why did it prove impossible to bring the proposed amendment to the Constitution to a vote? Democrats' insistence that the speeches, the committee report, and the promises to Garnet were maneuvers to drown out the siren call of the Liberty Party must be considered; after the last attempt to force a floor vote, Ray said essentially the same thing: "Perhaps they [the Whigs] are waiting to feel of the people, and perhaps they have not the disposition to do anything more, and perhaps, again, they have done as much as they have, to court the votes of abolitionists and the colored people. Doubtless they will receive some." Other political developments are relevant here, however. First, the early months of 1841 saw the climax of Seward's fight with Virginia; second, while sidestepping equal suffrage, Whig legislators acted decisively to restrict slavery's intrusion into their state.[59]

Democrats were outraged by their governor writing his Virginia counterpart that "it is absurd in this State to speak of property in immortal beings, and consequently of stealing them, as it would be to discourse of a division of property in the common atmosphere." The debate over his remarks brought on a shocking charge. On Friday, January 29, a city assemblyman, Paul Grout, gave a long speech alleging that "delay and hesitation on the part of the governor of New York, arose out of the circumstance that the latter preferred, before sending his final answer to the governor of Virginia, to submit it for the revision and advise of certain 'colored gentlemen' here at the north! Yes, sir, the 'colored gentlemen' of the city, whose views and wishes, rather than the obligations of the constitutional compact, the governor was desirous to consult and obey!" Subsequently, another Democrat quoted a letter from an anonymous Virginia Whig, aghast that Seward would "descend from the high and elevated station of chief executive . . . to such a low and degrading act, as to consult the free negroes of Albany, about his final decision of a constitutional obligation." Clearly, "he is and has been playing for the free-negro and abolition vote of your state." In this larger context, the *Colored American* took the Whig legislature's tabling of a vote on suffrage in stride. "GOVERNOR SEWARD'S LETTER" insulting the Virginians at "great length" provided manifold satisfactions: "It is higher ground than heretofore taken by the Governor in this controversy, and we should think by this time, that Virginia understood his position and would give up the chase. They have the right kind of material to deal with in Governor Seward. None could do better." On May 25, at the session's end, black Yorkers gained something more tangible, the repeal of the "nine months' law" which permitted slaveholders' keeping their chattels with them when visiting the Empire State. "NEW YORK A FREE STATE," the *Colored American* blared. This was a line in the sand, underlining Seward's stance that New York did not recognize property in human beings.[60]

In August 1841, black suffrage campaigners did what organizers must: claim a partial victory and soldier on, urging their supporters, "Brethren, be not discouraged; such disappointments should only act as a stimulus. . . . Our late Convention was successful, inasmuch as the attention of the Assembly was so far turned to the burden of our prayers, as to be disposed to give us a favorable Report. Should not this, then, be received as an encouraging inducement?" They met again in convention in almost equal numbers to 1840, repeating the demand that "as natives . . . the same political privileges may be extended to them as to foreigners," many of whom do "not understand the nature of our institutions, and . . . even may be a cast-off from the respectable society of the old world." They named thirty-nine county committees and elaborated more extensive lobbying strategies, including distributing minutes of both conventions to all legislators, holding county conventions, hiring an agent to tour the state, one-on-one lobbying, and getting "the Address we have adopted published in all the county papers," followed by county conventions in Poughkeepsie, Rensselaer, Jamaica, and Albany.[61]

Meanwhile, a Kings County Liberty Party convention to ratify James Birney's renomination for 1844 indicated that some black men were considering a different path. The town of Brooklyn sent nineteen delegates, including Arthur Tappan and three prominent black men (Peter Croger, Sylvanus Smith, and William J. Wilson), while Williamsburg, a center of black activism, sent forty-one, including William J. and Willis Hodges (brothers who left Southampton County, Virginia, after Nat Turner's rebellion), William Hamilton, Jr. (son of the eminent black leader), and Henry Garnet; Sylvanus Smith was elected to a five-man county committee with Tappan. The *Colored American*, on its last legs, gave a measured assessment of Whiggism. It noted, "We must give them great credit . . . for at least three acts effected by them while they held the reins of government . . . the act granting trial by jury in defence of personal liberty. The second authorizing the Governor to send, at the expense of the State, for any person who might be kidnapped from the State; and the third . . . the glorious act rescinding the shameful nine months law, and sweeping forever the last vestige of slavery from the statutes of the State. . . . These are acts for which the Whigs alone are responsible." Still, when it came to equal suffrage, "the Whigs, at the last Legislature handled this question as with gloves, and feared and quaked at every step." The significance of the black vote, however minimal, was highlighted that November, when the *Courier and Enquirer*, a heretofore Negrophobic Whig paper, announced, "Our colored population are a shrewd and discerning sort of people," upon discovering that in one upstate town not a single black man voted the Liberty ticket.[62]

1842: Into the Wilderness

The year 1842 was the suffrage campaign's nadir. The Whigs' delaying action in 1841, Democratic ascendance in that fall's election, and the *Colored American*'s closing shop in December dispelled any coherent strategy. Then everything worsened. The Democratic Senate censured Seward on Virginia, and passed a bill repealing jury trials for accused fugitives. In November 1842, the

Whigs lost the governorship. Since 1838, black suffragists had maintained internal unity against external pressures like Gerrit Smith's anathema on the *Colored American*. With their Whig allies out of office, these differences now became public and increasingly uncivil. As in New Bedford, an alliance of convenience between gradualist Whigs and black Garrisonians united against the Liberty Party.[63]

Hopes for incremental progress in 1842–44 were undercut by larger political dynamics. Seward's borrow-and-spend, pro-development policies plus growing Liberty Party strength upstate undermined the Whigs' electoral position. Seward eked out reelection in November 1840 but in 1841 his party lost the Assembly, 95–33, and the Senate, 17–15. Expectations of suffrage reform were dashed, and the Democrats responded to the 1842 petition drive with open hostility, with many Whigs going along. The Assembly's Judiciary Committee unanimously repudiated equal suffrage, and eighteen of thirty Whigs affirmed its report; the committee's chairman, John Cramer, Democrat of Saratoga and a delegate in 1821, dredged up all the old claims. He insisted that in 1777, "the number of free negroes was so small" that nonracial suffrage had no meaning. Emancipation had unintentionally "opened the ballot box to a large population of this kind." Suffrage was "not a natural right; it is a political privilege" meaning "restrictions are indispensable. . . . If negroes could justly complain of being deprived of natural rights by these restrictions, equally could minors, aliens, females and in short resident citizens." Britain had "introduced this unfortunate class into our country. This generation found them in a state of bondage. It was not our fault, neither was it theirs; we did them justice; we abolished servitude, bestowed upon them the protection of equal laws . . . while exempting them from some of the burthens." But "voluntary emancipation" had brought "vast hordes of negro voters . . . within the qualifications intended only, by the constitution of 1777, for the white population." It was all a matter of "expediency," and "not even a small portion of them" had bothered to meet "the property qualifications required." As always, Cramer evoked the "instinctive repugnance [which] exists in the white race," a feeling "organic, universal, and permanent." Then came the familiar charge that elites would use blacks to rule over whites, that "were the elective franchise granted to the extent demanded . . . an ignorant and degraded portion of the community would often control the whole result, and thus make laws for the whole state. . . . Measures, principles, and policy, deeply affecting the happiness and prosperity of the two millions of whites, might all depend on the suffrages of eight thousand negro voters. And, it is needless to add, that these suffrages would too often be under the control of the wealthy and aristocratic portion of the community." He concluded by quoting General Root's comment in 1821 denouncing the "few hundred negroes of the city of New-York, following the train of those who ride in their coaches, and whose shoes and boots they had so often blacked."[64]

Controversy over a new black newspaper demonstrated rising tensions. In early 1842, an Albany group of John G. Stewart, Charles Morton, and Stephen Myers began publishing *The Northern Star and Freeman's [later Freedman's] Advocate*, backed by that city's black businessmen, with an extensive network of agents in the Hudson Valley and Upper New England. While attending to political matters, it promoted itself as a temperance organ, with front pages given over to homilies, sermons, and reports on anti-alcohol meetings, linking moral reform inside the black community with skepticism regarding abolitionism and even immediate emancipation. In this discourse, the politics of uplift trumped any other activism: in a series of March 1842 editorials, the *Northern Star*'s editors declared that if "the colored people of these United States become a temperate people . . . they would gain more credit for themselves than all the abolitionist friends could do for us," reprinting with approval an editorial from Weed's *Albany Evening Journal*, which stated, "Whenever it can be said (and not gainsayed,) that the free blacks are a sober, industrious and intelligent people, capable of self-government, the only argument in favor of slavery falls to the ground. Let our colored citizens, then, engage heart and hand in this temperance movement, and they will do more for themselves and their enslaved brethren, than all the effort of abolition societies can accomplish in a century."[65]

There was nothing deferential about the *Northern Star*, however. Rather than encomia to white patrons, it picked fights. Noting the refusal to hire black youth as apprentices and black men as "mechanics," or even rent "tenements" to black people for fear of losing business, it denounced "the indifference manifested by abolitionists, in regard to the adoption of some effectual measures for advancing the welfare of the free people of color," and their "gross inconsistencies," insisting, "Until abolitionists eradicate prejudice from their own hearts, they can never receive the unwavering confidence of the people of color." In the same issue, the *Star*'s editors coupled an effusive championing of "St. Domingo" (its "well regulated government" brought into existence by "Toussaint, Christophe, and Petion," who "overcame some of the best generals of Europe, and destroyed 60,000 of as brave soldiers as any in the world") with a repudiation of immediate emancipation. They reasoned, "While we denounce slavery as the iniquity of iniquities, we cannot expect that nearly 3,000,000 of enslaved population can, with safety to themselves or to society, change their condition to that of independent freemen in a day, or a year." The editors wanted to know what exactly "the ultra," as in radical Garrisonian, "doctrine [had] performed for the benefit of our race," since "to fill the south with tracts, which merely excite the anger of the master, and are worse than useless, nay, cruel, to the slave," had led to "new restrictions to the little liberty they now enjoy." If a ban on family breakups could be "urged upon the south gradually," other ameliorations "will follow." There was no equivocation. Given the "ignorant and debased condition" of American slaves, "they cannot be considered as qualified to be drawn from their almost brutal state of existence, and be thrown upon (to them) a new world, the laws of which by mere instinct alone, can neither be appreciated or understood." At this point, the editors sounded little different from those genteel white Whigs who backed colonization, but then Haitian military power was evoked, and a not-at-all genteel threat declared. If "Southern men" did not act, and "if the reign of equal justice is not extended to us, the vengeance of an oppressed people will break forth, and proclaim to the oppressor that it were better to die honorably than to live condemned, disgraced and ill treated."[66]

Clearly, some black men remained orthodox Whigs in their commitment to measured reform. While proclaiming "We are neutral in politics," the *Star*'s editors boasted, "We would not be governed by a certain party," meaning the Liberty men, and printed Seward's address on the "Virginia Controversy," calling it an "able and fearless document, and worthy the Executive of an enlightened and FREE PEOPLE, irrespective of parties or conditions in life." They were "approving of Mr. Bradish" (Seward's lieutenant governor) as that year's gubernatorial candidate, while exhibiting disdain for everyone else, whether Liberty men or "Loco Focos" (although praising the election of a Democrat as Albany's mayor). Their paper gained endorsements from Whigs like Weed but also, more surprisingly, from Garrisonians.[67]

Retribution was swift. The Liberty Party's *Tocsin of Liberty* and the black-edited *People's Press* accused the *Northern Star* editors of "colonizationism," the worst sin imaginable. In response, the *Star* doubled down on its commitment to pressing the South toward gradual emancipation, since in Haiti, "the slaves were better prepared, in every respect, than in our southern states. A large proportion, consisting of household servants, were instructed by the French, (who were lenient masters,) and were permitted to visit the towns, and accumulate wealth for themselves. This class were distinguished by some of the noblest traits of character. . . . But turning aside from this class; what were not the horrors of St. Domingo?" The Haitian Revolution had unleashed "all the passions of ignorant beings displaying more than brutal impulses. Far and wide the imploring cries of mercy were unheeded, the soil was flooded with blood, from the sucking babe to the decrepit old age. Had these slaves been properly educated," as they hoped American slaves would be, "such scenes of inhuman butchery would have been unheard of, and liberty would have been proclaimed by the voice of humanity." New York's drawn-out emancipation was held up as exemplary. "Our own liberty in this state was gradual, and we urge for our southern brethren, education and laws to prevent the brutal severing of domestic ties, of husband, wife and children." Somehow, "liberty" would come, "and with liberty, the knowledge how to appreciate and enjoy it. Civil war is to be avoided if possible; for horrid would be the carnage. . . . Whatever may be the Tocsin's thoughts, we are not prepared to hail as blessings, arson, rapine, and murder." It insisted, "We have since very repeatedly been informed by our colored friends, that we had expressed sentiments which they had entertained for years," reporting that an Albany meeting scorned the Tocsin's assertion that the paper was "supported . . . mainly by anti-abolitionists and colonizationists. . . . Our paper is published by an association of colored persons, and the editorial has always been conducted by COLORED MEN. We are supported by persons of all parties, abolitionists, colonizationists, democrats and whigs." From that point, matters degenerated into a sectarian squabble. The Tocsin editor was denounced as "the scribbling hack and touchstone of a political junto," and a minister, very likely Garnet, called "a dribbling divine," while the People's Press was slammed as "Loco Foco." The Star's politics were practical rather than symbolic, focused on the needs of ordinary black folk rather than a few of the talented: "We do not consider political action and the 'abolishing of negro pews,' and a few other things of that kind, the most effectual measures for advancing our interests." Certainly, abolitionists had "opened seminaries" to colored men like Garnet, but "if the editor thinks that colored people believe that opening seminaries form the most effectual means for bettering their condition, we can assure him that he is very much mistaken. . . . Will he do us the favor to inform us how many colored young men from the multitude of seminaries which he informs us have been opened 'through abolition influence' are employed by abolition merchants and lawyers as clerks, and also what is the objection to employing colored persons who are sufficiently qualified for such purposes?"[68]

We should take seriously the Star's claims to represent black opinion. One of its editors was John G. Stewart, who had published the nation's third, short-lived black newspaper, the Monthly African Sentinel and Journal of Liberty in 1831–32, and its agent and publisher was Stephen Myers, with long antislavery credentials. Myers had aided fugitives since 1831, and was elected to the State Central Committee in 1840. His activism never waned, mostly inside a world of black men and women about which we know little; by late 1842, he had built a network of temperance organizations, many female-headed, all over the Hudson Valley and western Massachusetts, with adjuncts as far afield as Cincinnati and Cleveland, proof that "shadow politics" hardly required abstention from electoral politics. Through and past the Civil War he maintained close ties to Weed and Seward's machine. In 1843, James McCune Smith joined him as coeditor and they continued to publish for years to come, although since no issues survive after January of that year, we can only presume its politics remained moderate, soliciting "even Mr. Van Buren himself . . . [for] the list of patrons," as Gerrit Smith commented to Garnet, with disgust.[69]

We know little about the August 1842 state convention in Utica. Its call, presumably by Garnet, invited delegates "WITHOUT RESPECT TO COM-PLEXION OR PARTY," indicating tensions over all-black organizing and pro-Libertyism. It dispensed with optimism, admitting, "The cloud which for many years has hung over us, is still in its wonted position. If there has been any alteration in it, it has only been the augmentation of its size and the deepening of its darkness." Garnet attempted to rally his troops, proclaiming, "Shall we haul down our standards, and meanly retire from the field? . . . No—no, is the hearty response of every true-hearted New-Yorker." But his "firm and unanimous determination never to cease meeting . . . until the last vestige of legalized oppression shall be legislated from the Statute Book" rang flat.[70]

1843: Garnet Ascendant

As 1843 began, New York's Liberty Party surged, impressing black men disillusioned with the Whigs. In 1840, the *Colored American* backed Birney as a matter of principle; by 1842, the increasing Liberty vote proved the party's tenacity. Much of the black leadership, led by Garnet, Ray, and Samuel R. Ward, bet on the Liberty men. The years in which this venture played out marked Garnet's ascendancy as the first African American who was a recognized party leader. His audacity was like Danton's: he dared, dared again, and kept daring, and black people admired his bravado.

During the 1830s, a few black men were elected "managers" of the American and New England Anti-Slavery Societies, but party office was something else. In Portland and a few other places, they held minor positions, but none occupied state or national leadership positions. That barrier was broken at the Liberty Party's second National Nominating Convention on May 12, 1841 in New York. The 159 delegates elected, in standard fashion, "a committee of five . . . to present business to the Convention" including "Messrs. Alden, of Mass., Tracy, of New Hampshire, Goodell, of N.Y., Harned, of Penn., and Ray, of New York." Given that business committees effectively managed conventions, the import of putting the *Colored American*'s editor in leadership was clear—the Liberty men would compete with Whigs by granting black men recognition.[71]

In 1841–42, Massachusetts Liberty Party conventions repeatedly featured Garnet as a speaker, and by 1843, he was the most prominent black Liberty man, vaunting his status as "the first colored man that ever attached his name to that party." Garnet speaking out of state was one thing, but appearing on a Liberty platform in New York while chairing the State Central Committee would have undoubtedly alienated Whigs, and the 1840–42 conventions avoided any such partisanship. His dual role came into focus in August 1843, however, when he engineered a coup via back-to-back conventions in western New York: the first national black convention in eight years in Buffalo on August 15–19; the fourth New York state convention of black men, a one-day affair in Rochester three days later; a National Liberty Party Nominating Convention, again in Buffalo, on August 30–31.[72]

Garnet's role at the 1843 National Convention of Colored Citizens is now well known. During the 1960s, scholars rediscovered his insurrectionary "Address to the Slaves of the United States of America," which the delegates refused to endorse or even publish. Better known at the time, however, was Garnet's leading them to a resounding endorsement of the Liberty Party, overturning decades of Whiggism and Garrisonian anti-electoralism. Anticipating this result, Philadelphia's leadership boycotted, surrendering any national leadership, with Massachusetts's Remond and Douglass and Buffalo's William Wells Brown the isolated Garrisonians amid a much larger group, including five men from Michigan, eight from Ohio, and individual delegates from Georgia, North Carolina, Virginia, and Illinois.

Although its *Minutes* were deliberately opaque, the convention was evidently a battle. *The Liberator*'s correspondent was outraged: "It was evident there were those present who had come with the determination to carry certain measures," meaning endorsing the Liberty Party, while permitting "as little debate as possible, except by themselves." He reported days of infighting, as "the Massachusetts delegates, and a number of others, entered their protest against such a sectarian, anti-liberty, anti-abolition position." Shouted debates, attempts to control the floor, and repeated reconsiderations of Garnet's "Address to the Slaves" dragged out the proceedings. Many of Garnet's allies finally deserted him after considering the implications if a speech advocating violence by the enslaved was reported in Southern papers; Cincinnati's delegate A. M. Sumner pronounced its publication "fatal to the safety of the free people of color of the slave states."[73]

The convention's most consequential decision came early, when it approved Garnet's resolution stating, "It is the duty of every lover of liberty to vote the Liberty ticket so long as they are consistent with their principles." This was Garnet's trump card as a party leader, that he had carried a national black convention to outright endorsement. The state convention of colored men a few days later affirmed that decision, resolving that since the Democrats "positively refused" to give equal suffrage, and Whigs "neglected to go to the extent of their ability" to pass it, "we will in no case whatever vote with either of the proslavery parties of the land, since that would be, in our judgment, giving our suffrages against ourselves." On that basis, Garnet returned to the Liberty Party national convention in Buffalo, joined by Ray and Ward. A white delegate reported his arrival at "a sort of informal meeting in the Court House," where "that noble specimen of humanity, Henry H. Garnet . . . informed the friends present that the colored people had recently held a National Convention . . . that they then passed a resolution, adopting the principles of the Liberty party, which had but two opposing votes . . . [and] that the colored people of New York, held a state convention in Rochester, and that a similar resolution was passed."[74]

Garnet, Samuel Ward, and Charles Ray all played visible roles at the 1843 Liberty convention. Ward led prayer at one of the evening sessions, and spoke during debate; Ray served as New York's member on the committee taking the roll, and one of five secretaries; Garnet was named to the Nominating Committee with luminaries like Salmon P. Chase and gave a memorable speech. Although no version survives, McCune Smith regarded it later as his most important, and the Buffalo *Commercial Advertiser*'s reporter found it a revelation: "To see him stand up in all the native dignity of manhood, and listen to his thrilling eloquence, as he recounted the wrongs of his race, was enough to awaken in every right thinking mind, an indignant abhorrence of a system that would hold him, or such as him, in slavery." To seal the arrangement, the convention passed a resolution to "cordially welcome our colored fellow citizens to fraternity with us in the Liberty party," a step no party had ever taken. Both sides benefited from this alliance. A display of black leaders becoming Liberty men was a propaganda coup; in upstate counties with just a few black men, their depositing a Liberty ticket at the polls sent a strong message to wavering Whigs. For some of New York's free men of color, the benefits were equally self-evident: recognition by white men and authority among them; avowal of racial equality by a political party attracting a steadily increasing vote; the possibility of elevation. In an electoral environment dominated by Democrats, with Seward returned to private life and the Whigs quiescent, these were tangible gains.[75]

1844: Casting the Veto

The year 1843 was black Libertyism's high point. In 1844, New York's black leaders pursued divergent strategies, buffeted by the larger world. The 1844 election marked a decisive transition in national antislavery politics, the first time that "voting for the slave" turned a presidential election. Henry Clay gambled once more that his statesmanship would overcome doubts about his character. The Whigs were confident of victory, despite the growing Liberty vote in key states, and worked hard to convince northern voters that only Clay could block Texas's annexation, while libeling James G. Birney as a secret "Loco Foco." It was not enough. Although historians dispute this claim, in contemporary understanding, New York's Liberty vote was three times greater than Polk's margin of victory, and cost Clay the presidency.

In this context, Garnet's attempt to carry his constituency with him to the Liberty Party backfired, dividing New York's black political class into angry factions. Black and white Garrisonians tied his "Address to the Slaves" to his Libertyism, damning him as an opportunist and an impostor. He had gone farther than most black men could stomach, declaring the enslaved should confront their masters,

> and tell them plainly, that you *are determined to be free*. . . . Tell them in language which they cannot misunderstand, of the exceeding sinfulness of slavery, and of a future judgment, and of the righteous retributions of an indignant God. Inform them that all you desire is FREEDOM, and that nothing else will suffice. . . . If they then commence the work of death, they, and not you, will be responsible for the consequences. You had better all die—*die immediately*, than live slaves and entail your wretchedness upon your posterity. If you would be free in this genera-tion, here is your only hope. However much you and all of us may desire it there is not much hope of redemption without the shedding of blood. If you must bleed, let it all come at once—rather *die freemen than live to be slaves*.

In response, Maria Weston Chapman, *The Liberator*'s interim editor, up-braided him as foolish, jejune, a poor excuse for a Christian minister: "All colored men are not abolitionists. The same evil influences are at work to tempt the selfish heart beating beneath a colored bosom, that are potent to hold the fearful white man in thralldom." Her proof was the convention's en-dorsing the Liberty Party, which "is new organization, and new organ-ization is pro-slavery," the Garrisonian catechism. Having indicted the foremost black political leader as "pro-slavery," she then instructed him: "We entreat the Rev. H. H. Garnet to consider betimes the track at the entrance of which he stands. He is a professed minister of the gospel of Christ. Does he find that gospel in harmony with his address? . . . We fervently hope that Mr. Garnet had no other or further intentions, than merely to write what he thought a high-sounding address." Garnet's response was scathing, profess-ing that he was "Astonished . . . to think that you should desire to sink me again to the condition of a slave, by forcing me to think just as you do." He was clear: "I am a Liberty party man—you are opposed to that party—far be it from me to attempt to injure your character because you cannot pronounce my shibboleth. If . . . I must think and act as you do . . . then I do not hesitate to say that your abolitionism is abject slavery."[76]

Garnet could dismiss Chapman, but he faced a more serious challenge from inside New York's black community. Many veterans objected to the Liberty Party alliance; in June 1844, *The Liberator* gleefully reprinted an article from the *Northern Star,* now edited by James McCune Smith and the Reverend J. W. C. Pennington, stating, "We believe that the liberty men hate whiggery, more than they hate slavery, and that they love office more than they love anti-slavery. . . . 'We fear these office-seeking liberty men.' . . . And we speak . . . the views of a very large proportion of the free colored people in the free States." As described in chapter 5, Maine Whigs used this article to damn the Liberty Party as corrupt. Then, in September 1844, McCune Smith led the city's delegation to that year's convention in Schenectady to formally protest against the previous year's resolution. He argued that basing the acquisition of the franchise "upon the success of a *party* which must ever comprise but a portion of the people" put black New Yorkers "in the position of men asking from two political parties the power, to enable them to overthrow those parties." One upstate delegate, Albany's Richard Thompson, recounted that when 1843 convention delegates called on Democratic governor William Bouck "asking for favorable mention of the extension of the franchise," he had requested the convention's minutes, which Garnet avoided at all cost because "those very minutes denounced the party to which Governor Bouck belonged." New York City's protest was rejected 38–11, with the convention refusing to even record it, and Smith's delegation walked out. Particularly aggravating was being outvoted by thirty-three delegates from Schenectady and Troy, "with a joint total colored population of less than 1,000," versus "New-York, containing 20,000 free colored people." Back in Manhattan, Smith and his allies called a meeting to repudiate the state convention. To their surprise, Garnet appeared, and in Smith's recollection two decades later, won over the crowd. When Smith called for the vote, "in an instant Garnet was up. His tall form seemed to dilate as with uplifted arm and flashing eye he exclaimed 'The eagle screams of liberty, why may not I?'" The audience was carried away with "shouts and cheers," so that Smith and company were "dreadfully voted down."[77]

After that, the rawest charges were exchanged. Smith and his colleague Ulysses B. Vidal asserted in the *National Anti-Slavery Standard* that the Liberty Party alliance was "a *means* by which to help into power certain political aspirants who have made specious promises, thus confirming the charge which have been urged against the people of color, that their votes could be bought for a price." Elsewhere, Smith called the Liberty Party an "irreverent admixture of blasphemy and demagoguism." Reverend Theodore Wright responded in *The Emancipator*, ruing that "Whigism and worldly, wicked and blinding expediency, are the monsters we are called upon to resist. . . . There are men of color, men of learning and talents for which we delight to honor them, who, nevertheless, are at this late day wielding all their influence in efforts to dissuade their brethren from coming out openly and manly on the side of liberty principles! . . . Dr. Smith and his clan are making a desperate struggle."[78]

Garnet's fundamental problem was his inability to deliver votes. Observers agreed that most of New York's black voters backed Clay; six years later, a prominent activist, Joseph C. Holly, wrote Clay directly, remembering the "enthusiasm" with which "the majority of the colored voters, went for the anti-annexation candidates." Following the election, Garnet charged corruption, denouncing Smith and Myers by name as "the Sweet Cake Party" who, after "fawning around the feet of their oppressors," were used by these same white Whigs, "their masters," to "hunt down their own race to disgrace them." He painted an ugly picture, that these men "sometimes . . . receive a few dollars to support their worthless papers," and "just before elections . . . are taken into the back parlors of their oppressors—that is, when everybody else has gone abroad. Then they are stroked on the head, and while the polls are open, they are called 'the trustiest of their kind.' . . . They are as decidedly pro-slavery as any party this side of South Carolina." How could men as proud as Smith and Garnet reconcile after speaking of each other in these terms? They did, nonetheless, uniting in 1845 to craft a subtle inside/outside strategy of leveraging Whigs and Liberty men to win equal suffrage.[79]

"Sambo Goes Coon"

The scholarship on New York's 1846 constitutional convention runs on separate historiographical tracks. The first story traces the state's antebellum partisan wars in which 1846 concluded a generation-long conflict over the state's economic role. After several decades in which Clintonians and Whigs promoted intensive state-aided development, the debate was resolved in favor of the small-government model promoted by orthodox Jacksonians. In that history, the defeat of "Equal Suffrage for Colored Persons" in the November 1846 postconvention referendum is a footnote. Conversely, in the scholarship on black suffrage in New York, 1846 registers as a second great setback, between the 1821 convention and another referendum loss in 1860. This latter narrative focuses on black activists lobbying the Liberty Party for joint delegate nominations with the Whigs (what would later be called "fusion"), to control the convention and insert nonracial suffrage into the Constitution minus a "separate submission" to the electorate. That effort failed spectacularly. Gerrit Smith's adamant opposition blocked fusion outside of a few western counties. The Democrats won an overwhelming majority of the convention delegates and invited the state's white men to vote equal suffrage up or down, guaranteeing its defeat.[80]

Investigating the partisan motivations behind the renewed effort for nonracial suffrage demonstrates that these two histories were not separate but deeply intertwined. It was the Seward Whigs, not black or Liberty men, who originated the scheme to call a convention and insert "universal suffrage" into the state constitution, as part of a larger strategy to overturn a formidable Democratic majority: in 1843, Democrats controlled the Senate 22–10, and the Assembly 92–36, and in 1844 they maintained the same overwhelming Assembly margin, increasing their Senate majority to 26–6. Beginning in early 1844, the Sewardites sought to split the Democrats over the question of a convention. This opportunity arose because of the deepening rift in Democratic ranks between laissez-faire "Barnburners" and conservative "Hunkers." Then, following their defeat in the fall 1844 presidential race, the Whigs envisioned something truly new, a majority coalition of the "outs." In that election, the nativist American Party won all sixteen New York City Assembly seats, helping cut the Democratic majority in the lower house to only sixty-seven in 1845, and the Anti-Renters, tenants on the vast Hudson River estates engaged in low-level insurrection since 1839, awarded bipartisan legislative endorsements with considerable impact. Besides these two emerging blocs, the Sewardites hoped to use black suffrage to recoup the 15,000 Liberty men who refused to vote for Clay. Nor was this strategy hidden, as black suffrage became a rallying cry throughout 1845 for the upstate Whigs who got their instruction from Weed's *Albany Evening Journal* and Greeley's *New-York Tribune*, although the New York City Whig organ, James Watson Webb's *Courier and Enquirer*, publicly dissented.[81]

That this campaign ultimately failed does not make it less interesting. Rhode Island had shown northern Whigs how reenfranchising black men could shift the balance of power. Weed and Seward apparently envisioned a similar coup. Managing the complexities of recuperating various constituencies into the Whig Party was not simple. Liberty men did not accept that they were responsible for the disaster of Polk's election and the immediate annexation of Texas. Many Whigs found it difficult to associate with Liberty Party members, whose spoilage had foisted a slaveholder president committed to imperial conquest upon the nation.

We see the tensions in this two-front war in the correspondence of the central managers among the "radical" Whigs, Weed and Seward. Even before the election, Seward had proclaimed to abolitionists that "I am one of you," writing Weed privately that the question of Texas's annexation would "convert Clay into the Abolition candidate of the North," a hope ruined by Clay's equivocation on the matter. Seward's postelection letters to Gerrit Smith expressed his fundamental solidarity regarding emancipation, especially after "the peril to which the cause of freedom is exposed by the sad result of the recent election." They were fellow travelers who had chosen different paths: "It would be unmanly for you and me to dispute about the responsibility for that result. The same wide difference of opinion that has hitherto existed in regard to our respective courses remains," but also "a common devotion to the common cause." Two months later, after the legislature opened, Seward asserted his expectation that they would collaborate in practical ways: "In this state the obvious interests of the Whig Party (to do no violence to their sympathizers)" led "to efforts for a Convention to extend the Right of Suffrage. I doubt not that we shall have your aid."[82]

Whereas Seward proposed alliance to Smith on the basis of shared values, Weed cast it in opposite terms to their old colleague from the Antimasonic Party, Francis Granger, an eminent Whig. The latter was Weed's confidante for decades, but so disgusted by the notion of allying with Liberty men that he temporarily broke off relations. To his "old and cherished friend," Weed explained that he agreed regarding "the perverse and dishonest course of Political Abolitionists." His and Seward's overture was an effort to save the thousands misled by men like Smith:

> The "Liberty Party" demagogues have beguiled ten or twelve thousand honest men and true Whigs from their allegiance to the country. The [consequences] of their power over these Electors, last fall, has opened the eyes of many, and will open the eyes of many more. We cannot afford to loose [sic], and ought not to loose, honest but misguided friends. You and I and the Whigs with whom we act, are better friends to the Slave, and truer advocates for Emancipation, than the "Liberty Party" organs and leaders. Shall we, then, allow these Organs and Leaders to hold a power which they wield, year after year, with such fatal effect, against the Country?[83]

Seward and Weed could count. They knew most black men identified as Whigs, and there was no reason to think these men would change their coats, given the chance to vote for Seward's party. New York's electorate in 1844's gubernatorial election totaled 487,283 and the Whigs had lost by only 10,033, so the hoped-for gain was tantalizingly concrete—many commentators referred to a potential black electorate of 10,000, based on the 1845 state census. Moreover, Whigs expected that the opportunity to enfranchise black men would bring white Liberty men back to their allegiance as Whigs. Of course, they had more than one goal for a convention, including reorganizing the judiciary and dividing the state into single-member Assembly and Senate districts. All of these hopes required a broader coalition, which they assembled with considerable success, and ultimately black men's votes proved unnecessary. In August 1845, Democratic governor Silas Wright declared martial law and sent in the militia to put down the most militant Anti-Renters. In October 1846, the latter convened and endorsed his opponent, John Young, who became the first Whig governor since Seward.[84]

The Whigs' plan was revealed on January 8, 1845 when a newly elected Rochester assemblyman, William Bloss, proposed a constitutional amendment abrogating the complexional property qualification, specifying that "in future no other test, proof or qualification shall be required of or from persons of color in relation to the exercise of their right of suffrage, than is in this constitution required of or from white persons." Bloss exemplified the complexity of abolitionist politics. He was the local Underground Railroad conductor, editor of an abolitionist newspaper, and the sort of father who put his son's hand "in the deep whip-welts on the back of an escaped woman slave," and instructed him, "When there is another law like this in the land, do you disobey it." The Whigs appointed him door-keeper of the State Assembly in January 1838, but in 1840 he was a Liberty candidate for the Assembly, to which he finally won election in 1844 as a Whig. Bloss arrived in Albany poised to lead an assault on both racial caste and the Democrats, and Weed's *Evening Journal* foregrounded his demand for a convention without restrictions, rather than one mandated to address only the Democrats' economic concerns. That this was a coordinated campaign became evident over that winter and spring, as upstate Whigs met to demand "Constitutional Reform," including "the abrogation of all property qualifications for the exercise of the right of suffrage, placing all citizens upon an equality, without distinction of color."[85]

In this context, Whigs made a high-profile appeal to black men. With Weed's support, Bloss invited the "educated and intelligent colored physician of the city of New York" (and eminent Whig), James McCune Smith, to speak in the Assembly chamber on April 2, 1845. Smith's address made a comprehensive case: that the Empire State had been founded on the principle that "there shall be no *caste*, or difference of rank, among the free people of this commonwealth" and the 1777 constitution had "cheerfully admitted, that 'all men were equal' whatever may have been the color of their skin." Despite claims that people of color were free from "*personal tax*," the state "taxes their property; and if this property is worth less than $250, they are compelled to pay *taxes on it*, but cannot vote" with the city's 5,000 "colored householders" each levied $60 annually via their rent. Repeatedly, he evoked the Revolution, that "this may be called *indirect* taxation—so was the stamp act—so was the ship money—it is taxation; it takes away from these men, the lawful fruits of their labor." The freehold qualification was also an inducement to corruption: "It says, 'come, man of color! swear that you are worth $250 worth of real estate; your vote will then go as far, will be paid for as well as the vote of any white man. Perjure yourself that your [*sic*] may be enriched with a bribe.'" Smith acknowledged the concerns of the delegates in 1821. They knew "that the Act of Emancipation . . . would, in 1827, set free, many thousand colored men, who had been brought up to all the ignorance and degradation, which are essential to slavery." It would have been "fair that a mental test should be required for the candidates for citizenship," presumably literacy. But while "only twenty" of the colored men petitioning the 1821 convention could sign their names, it was "almost impossible" to find an illiterate colored person born since then. He concluded with a report on the schools, churches, temperance societies, libraries, and "a Temperance Newspaper . . . published by a colored man in this city, Mr. Stephen Myers," certainly familiar to many Whigs.[86]

For the moment, Weed and his allies had seized the day. Linking up with the American Republicans (the New York City nativists) and a few Barnburners, they pushed through a vote authorizing a convention on May 13. A downstate Whig paper reported, "The main object of the convention, as is generally understood, is to make all officers elected by the people except judicial and military, to revise the judiciary system and placed upon a new footing, and to abolish all property qualifications for voters," while the Democratic *Herald* bewailed "the bitter, discourteous, and savage manner in which the democratic members" had behaved, "approaching a state of complete disorganization." Hunkers reacted with disgust, outlining how Whigs would gather up the Anti-Renters and move on to "the *Abolitionists*, persevering and powerful. They wish the constitution placed at their disposal, that they may abolish all distinctions in color, and let the negroes vote as freely as the whites." These same men had been "the very aristocrats" at the 1821 convention. Then and now, "their object seems to be to bring down the poor white man to the level of the negro, that they might lord it over both." Finally, there were "the *Native Americans* [the American Republicans], and with them we know, a foreigner is worse than a negro. They would extend the privilege of the one, and curtail those of the other."[87]

The exemplary statement of the Hunker perspective was a May 3 Senate speech by G. D. Beers suggesting equal suffrage was another of Seward's plots, akin to his maneuvering for Catholic votes: "Every body understands why they want a convention; it's a grand time; a democratic Governor has been compelled to come down upon the anti-renters in his message, and by a call on the military. These men have been heretofore tickled by the same executive that undertook the tickle the Catholics in New-York city. The echo of that former executive has been heard on this floor, talking turkey to the abolitionists on the subject of negro suffrage." Fortunately, "The people have got a word to say about the bargain by which the negroes are to come into the bosom of the whig party to vote down the democrats; for it is generally understood that Sambo goes coon. (A laugh.)." ("Coon" was then an epithet for Whig, as Henry Clay was dubbed "the old coon" by admirers to signal his rural roots.) Beers pointed out how easily Liberty men could be seduced. "What is there in our present constitution at which an abolitionist would start, except the word 'white?' What would he care for restrictions on the debt-creating power in the new one, if under it the negro should be allowed to vote?" He concluded with the racial edge beloved of Democrats: "I don't want a mulatto constitution. (Laughter.) I'm free to say it. I want black and white put where the people can choose between them. The whigs being sure of the negro votes, the question is, would they try to get them in? . . . I don't believe they would stick at anything to secure a majority in the convention."[88]

None of these attacks did the Democrats much good. In August 1845, Governor Wright cracked down on the Anti-Renters, and Seward exulted to one of his confidantes, "I have seen satisfactory indications that the Barnburners will not deem it safe to deny suffrage to the Colored Race, nor to insist on submitting that question independently to the People. Of course the Hunkers will follow suit. Can you conceive any more splendid triumph for the sound and wise men of our Party than this!" Looking toward the spring, it seemed that equal suffrage might prevail, and with it a Whig victory. Seward maintained his "immense prestige" among Whigs and his weight was entirely behind the campaign. In October, he emphasized in a public letter to black leaders, "I look impatiently for the restoration of your right of suffrage," adding, "It is the duty of every friend of equal suffrage to vote for those delegates, in the Whig or Democratic parties, that are in favor of extending to the colored people of this state, equal suffrage." He envisioned not merely "the elevation of a large portion of my fellowmen, to higher social virtues and enjoyments . . . but also an influence which will strengthen public opinion, and direct it to the banishment of human Slavery from the face of the earth. Be assured, then, that the votes I shall cast for a Convention and a Constitution, which will be harbingers of such results, will be the most cheerful exercise of the elective franchise in my life." Privately, he wrote Weed that even Barnburners like the former president's son and conservative Whigs like Millard Fillmore felt the pressure; he had "found John Van Buren . . . making up his mind, slowly and reluctantly, to consent to answer the people of color favorably on their demand for the elective franchise," while Fillmore reported he "had a letter from the colored people, and wanted to answer it by saying he would dispose with the property qualification, and substitute one of capacity to read and write."[89]

Meanwhile, New York City's black leaders wrote Gerrit Smith "strictly confidential" letters, urging Whig-Liberty cooperation in nominating delegates. The first, on June 13, 1845, asked if "leading minds in the Liberty party would consent to vote for such men as delegates to the proposed convention without distinction to party." It was a hard-headed appeal, noting the Liberty men's "commanding vote" in seventeen counties, stressing that "the nomination of such men as the Liberty party will vote for can be secured and then these men can be elected," but only if "the Liberty vote [is] thrown in favor of the Whig candidates." A questionnaire followed on July 30 from the Whigs McCune Smith and Ulysses Vidal, asking Gerrit Smith whether he favored black suffrage and considered the convention an opportune time for the removal of the property qualification. In late August, the annual black state convention met in Syracuse. After the usual denunciation of enfranchising "naturalized foreigners" when "native born citizens are denied the same rights," it urged "the friends of equal suffrage of all parties, to vote for no delegates but those who are in favor." Charles B. Ray chaired, Garnet was a delegate, and Samuel R. Ward backed the resolution, suggesting a newfound unity. Here one intuits Thurlow Weed's hand. While black men pressured Gerrit Smith, his *Journal* reported approvingly on the "Colored Suffrage Convention," urging Liberty men to put principle above party: "Those of them, who are honest, cannot but see the necessity of uniting with the Whigs. . . . They possess not only the balance of power in the United States, but in several separate States and congressional districts," but to date the only result had been "to the detriment . . . of the oppressed race."[90]

Democrats scoffed at how the Whigs "profess to be the friends of human rights, and promise the abolitionists if they will vote for whig delegates to the Convention, and thereby secure a whig majority . . . they will extend the rights of suffrage." It was "merely a game they purpose to play upon the abolitionists to secure their votes, and when they are obtained, they will act on the subject of the negro suffrage as they please, and no one believes they will legislate as the friends they now pretend to be to the blacks." Then came the usual baiting, that Whigs should prove their sincerity by engaging in "free intercourse with negroes in all social and domestic circles. . . . The whigs should permit blacks to sit with them at table or in church, to enter into co-partnership with them in business, and to admit them to their dress circles and social parties. They should also approve of our legislative halls being filled with negro Senators and Congressmen, or pulpits with the negro clergymen, and our seats of justice with negro judges and expounders of the law." The

Brooklyn Eagle ramped up the familiar polarity of Irishmen versus Negroes to the detriment of the latter, calling Whigs "the faction" whose "great object was to restrict the right of suffrage in one direction, and extend it in another." By early 1846, Democratic papers outside New York took note of this latest Whig plot "to place the blacks on a par with the white voters," to which Weed replied tartly that if "the Slave States" allowed "Masters to vote for their Slaves," should not "the Free States . . . allow Free men to vote for themselves?"[91]

The campaign for the April 28, 1846 delegate elections was four-sided. Seward Whigs upstate and black leaders appealed to Liberty men for fusion (effectively, voting for Whigs), with the Whigs denouncing Gerrit Smith as a false prophet when he refused to budge. Smith fired back at the Whigs and their black allies as "pro-slavery." Democrats defined themselves as the defenders of white working men, repeating ad nauseam that Whigs were corrupt Negrophiles. The wild card was the downstate Whigs, who had no use for Weed's campaign or black voters. Like Senator Beer, they did not want "a mulatto constitution." In fall 1845, Greeley failed to push a pro-suffrage resolution through a convention of city Whigs, and after that conservative Whig papers like Webb's *Courier* openly disdained pro-suffrage efforts.[92]

When 1846 opened, the political momentum for fusion seemed strong. Greeley wrote the Indiana Whig Schuyler Colfax that "the Birneyites [Liberty men] will mostly vote with us unless the Locos make them believe that they too are for Black Suffrage which they threaten to do. . . . We are full of hope, however." From Syracuse, the Reverend Samuel May wrote Garrison that Gerrit Smith and his ally William Goodell "go for a strict party vote, which will certainly throw the Convention into the hands of the so called Democrats. . . . But most of the Syracuse members of the [Liberty] party think it their duty to vote for such men as will pledge themselves to go for the rights of the colored people." By late February, however, it was clear that most Liberty men would not cooperate, and, as Greeley feared, enough Democrats in upstate counties would publicly back equal suffrage to muddy the waters. Gerrit Smith convinced his fellow partisans to reject fusion, publishing addresses damning engagement with the major parties as morally odious, even deriding the importance of black men regaining the vote. On February 27, the Albany-based State Central Committee of black men sent an urgent letter "TO GERRIT SMITH, ESQ., And other Leaders of the Liberty Party," published in McCune Smith and Myers's *Northern Star* and reprinted in Weed's *Evening Journal*. It specified, "Some of the leaders of your party have given publicity to sentiments and intentions in relation to their choice of delegates . . . which we consider as antipodes to our moral and intellectual advancement, inimical to our prosperity, and directly opposed to our release from an unjust and odious distinction" regarding suffrage. Their demand was direct. "We consider this a matter of vast importance . . . a subject that appeals to your sense of right and wrong, of conscious responsibility and consistency, and divested of its fig-leaf covering, (that is of the color of the skin,) and based upon the immutable principles of justice. . . . We call upon you to meet in open, manly generous and Christian-like manner." They had had "an expectation arising almost to a certainty" of Smith's support for fusion, "but judge of our surprise, pain, and disappointment, when we found Gerrit Smith . . . the dauntless apostle of liberty . . . the black man's defender and friend . . . abandoning the poor and needy in an hour so propitious to their cause." They did not "ask the dissolution of your party, but that instead of making nominations which cannot possibly benefit either you or us, you will give your votes and use your influence to elect such men as pledge themselves, if elected, to use their influence against disfranchising us longer."[93]

Smith's "Reply to Colored Citizens of Albany" denied entirely that "suffrage is the issue," describing the Whigs as "men, who think slaveholders fit to administer Civil Government." He asked, "Would I not be a traitor to the slave, if I were to vote for them?—and would he not also be a traitor to the slave who should ask me to vote for them?" To him, black men's precarious foothold inside American politics was complicity with "treason." In New England, they voted for Whigs and therefore "on behalf of American slavery," and "if to-day, the right of suffrage were restored to the colored men of this State, tomorrow would see them enrolled in pro-slavery parties," since "more than three-fourths of the colored men who voted . . . in the Fall of 1844, voted for those, who belong to the class, that traffic in colored people, whip colored women, and steal colored babies," meaning Henry Clay. He concluded in biblical terms, as one Christian to another: "I rebuke you. It is meet, that they, who think you their inferiors [the Whigs], should show their contempt for you by flattering you," versus Liberty men who "think you their equals. . . . Shame on the black men, who, for gain, however great, can thus join with the crucifiers of the poor black slave!"[94]

In response, Whigs pilloried the philanthropist with his own words: "We were not a little surprised to hear Mr. S. speak so indifferently in regard to Negro Suffrage. Although he professed to be in favor . . . yet he considered them quite unfit to exercise it" since "those that possessed the requisite amount of property voted almost to a man with the whigs in 1844, and declared it his opinion, *that if the Convention should create them electors, it would only be adding 7,000 or 8,000 to the Whig ranks*!" Whigs in Madison, Smith's home county, went further, mocking him: "Gerrit Smith has "only 'one idea' . . . opposition to the Whig party" (the Liberty men's "one idea" was immediate emancipation). Did not his "gross inconsistencies" demonstrate to

Liberty voters "that Mr. Smith's great desire is, that locofocoism should control the Convention"? Whigs had grounds for their contempt. Into the fall, Smith continued to rail against them as the "most deceitful and, therefore, most dangerous, class of our enemies" given that "there is no more danger, that our sham Democrats will be mistaken for friends of our cause, than that naked wolves will pass for sheep." His moral hubris revealed itself when the *National Anti-Slavery Standard* published William Bloss's reply to a questionnaire from black Whigs regarding his candidacy as a delegate. Bloss repudiated "every species of artificial caste" as "death," insisting that the "principle of the political equality of every man should be guarded as the pivotal or central thought or idea of our government." He disparaged racial hierarchies as "a mere whim of the imagination. I firmly believe that 'God hath made of one blood all nations of men to dwell on all the face of the earth,'" extolling the genius of African men from Virgil to Toussaint ("the Washington of St. Domingo"), including a brace of colored Americans: "Smith, Purvis, Ward, Garnet, Remond, and Douglass." Bloss's political argument was equally emphatic. "Some of the Liberty party men regard this effort to restore the right of suffrage to the colored people of this State as a very insignificant affair," but antislavery Whigs like him believed that adding "some thousands of voters whose influence will necessarily be given to the cause of emancipation . . . might modify the politics of this State, and" then "the hand of New-York might mould the political form of the nation." He added, "Every vote that the Abolitionists shall cast for the Liberty party will greatly prejudice the rights of our colored citizens and jeopardize the interest of the slave."[95]

Where convenient, Democrats played me-too politics, with Greeley noting in early April that in the absence of "anti-slavery sentiment, there the locofocos are red-mouthed and vociferous against black suffrage at all hazards. Hostility to 'nigger' is their greeting card, by which they hope to carry the delegates in the city and all close river counties. But west of Albany, where . . . thorough anti-slavery men . . . hold the balance of power in several important counties, they endeavor to blank the suffrage question by going for 'separate submission.'" The dominant note in the city came from "A CARTMAN," writing the Democratic *Globe* to denounce "the secret enemies of republicanism, who are straining every nerve to degrade all poor laboring white men to a level with the negro." The class appeal was direct: "If the amendment be adopted, creating at once so many thousand negro voters in this city, it will be idle longer to think of preventing negroes from obtaining cartmen's licenses," and those merchants who "prefer servile cartmen instead of others of manly independence" will "employ negroes, thereby directly commanding as many votes as they have negroes employed." He mocked the bourgeois reformers "making such an ado about the votes of their dear friends, the negroes, who are they? Men whose delicate palms are often soiled by the touch of the huge paw of a cartman or any other laborer? No, most assuredly not! they compose that class who are taught from their earliest infancy to consider themselves as superior to, and born to rule over the toiling millions." They would force "the children of the poor into companionship [with black children], against which the soul of every pure minded man revolts, as his stomach would against a dish of carrion." The abolitionists' intent was diabolical: "The amendment proposed by these negrosouled philosophers, offers a premium to all shiftless black vagabonds in every State in the Union to come and settle down with us . . . creating an order of negro nobility; for in no other State, where there are any considerable number, is the elective franchise open to them." Downstate Whigs did not indulge in this invective, but were emphatic that "we must put down all the new coalitions the Albany Evening Journal is almost daily proposing, or else go down," as one editor put it, with another denouncing "the recent attempts of the Albany Evening Journal to identify the Whig party of this State with the Abolition party."[96]

Before the vote, Weed's *Journal* highlighted Liberty defections, but only in five central and western counties did Liberty men endorse sympathetic Whigs. The results of the election were devastating, with the Democrats winning a commanding majority of delegates, 78–44 (the remaining six were independents). The bitterness of the losers, whether blacks, Whigs, or Liberty men, was deep, with Greeley commenting sadly it was bad enough that "the great mass of the swindling pretenders to Democracy will vote to deprive Colored Men of all votes in framing the Laws they are required to obey," but even worse, "enough short-sighted, hollow-hearted, expediency-governed Whigs will unite with them to give them a triumph." Weed kept Gerrit Smith in his sights: "Mr. Smith is right in apprehending that *his* political association has been seriously damaged, first by helping Texas into the Union, and now by defeating Free Suffrage." These questions "were in the hands of Abolitionists. The Liberty Party in this State, could have given the country an Anti-Texas President, and Anti-Texas Senators in Congress, in 1844; and in 1846, they could have obtained the Right of Suffrage for the Colored Man." South of Albany, however, Whigs caviled, with one paper insisting Weed had propagated a "falsehood" in the spring, that "Whig candidates were in favor of granting to all negroes the right to vote," adding absurd stories about "the affection that the locofocos have for the Negroes."[97]

The convention opened on June 1, but by common consent put off debates on the franchise until late September, before adjourning on October 9. A Democratic-controlled committee proposed a suffrage clause stipulating only white men could vote, to which four amendments were offered: first, to remove the word "white," which was defeated 63–37; second, to reduce the property qualification for black men to $100, which lost 50–42; third, to remove all property requirements, defeated 75–29; finally, to affirm the $250 freehold requirement, and make "Equal Suffrage for Colored Persons?" a separate ballot question, allowing both parties to avoid the issue, which passed. These votes confirmed the divide between Democrats and Whigs: 80 percent of the former wanted to disfranchise black men or allow them only the existing suffrage, while 80 percent of the Whigs voted at some point for equal suffrage. Seeing the writing on the wall, Whigs ignored the suffrage question in the weeks before the November 3, 1846 vote. In October, an Anti-Renter convention endorsed the Whig John Young against the incumbent Democratic governor Wright. Young won by 10,000 votes, and the new constitution was easily ratified (221,528 to 92,436), but equal suffrage lost by an even more decisive margin, 224,366 to 85,406. No more than 40 percent of Whigs backed it, and the twelve downstate counties recorded only 9,911 pro-suffrage votes versus 49,509 for the Whig or Liberty Party gubernatorial candidates. The only part of the electorate that positively correlated with pro-suffrage voting were the Yankee towns backing antislavery Whigs and Liberty men, plus a few Democratic counties bordering Vermont, like Clinton.[98]

From then on, New York State's black men fought with increasing professionalism but a cold eye to the wall facing them: the 72 percent of the state's electorate that opposed their rights. McCune Smith, architect of the fusion strategy, underwent a profound change of heart. Just before New Year's Eve of 1846, he wrote his sometime nemesis, Gerrit Smith, "There is in that majority a hate deeper than I had imagined." He had thought they would win, and "now when looking *into* it, I am alarmed & humbled," adding "the direction in which our people must labour" was unclear. All he could think was, "The heart of the whites must be changed, thoroughly . . . permanently changed." That same month, Samuel R. Ward published a rebuke to black Whigs like Smith: "Last Spring, [the Whigs] were all for Suffrage. They needed votes then. But . . . the Anti-Suffrage vote was so large as to indicate very clearly, that Locos were not alone in this disposition to rob the poor. Let us hear no more of this distinction between Whigs and Locos, on Suffrage. . . . I hope the committee of colored gentlemen at Albany, who more than impliedly censured Gerrit Smith last Spring, will ponder this part of the matter well. What do they think of the Whigs by this time? . . . What says my good friend, Dr. J. M'Cune Smith . . . ?"[99]

Black men thus entered 1847 in a paradoxical position. On the one hand, their electoral participation had been rejected by more than seven out of ten white voters. On the other, they retained the support of a phalanx of the state's most powerful men, and almost three in ten whites did back them, in ten counties constituting a biracial majority. When a new party at last came to power whose base was in those counties and others like them, black men would have a chance at full political participation.

Smith's Land and Liberation

The year 1846 was simultaneously the end of one suffrage campaign and the beginning of something very different. At its center were Gerrit Smith and the same black leadership that fruitlessly appealed for fusion. In early 1846, while exchanging recriminations in public, they initiated a joint effort to colonize 3,000 black men into upstate counties as independent farmers able to meet the freehold requirement. Smith's hope was to enfranchise these men across eight counties from the Hudson Valley to the Canadian border (see map III.1). In January, he announced plans to sell off 750,000 acres at a series of public auctions, to pay off back taxes so he could make the planned grants free and clear. Although Smith tried to keep his scheme of land distribution private, by late summer it leaked, with a Massachusetts editor reporting, "I have just seen a copy of a deed of some forty acres of land in Hamilton county, New York, given by the celebrated landholder, Gerrit Smith, Esq., to a colored man, residing in that county."[100]

Like most antebellum reformers, Smith distrusted cities as havens for "rumsellers" and corrupt politicians; a November 14, 1846 letter expressed his hope that "thousands upon thousands of my colored brethren" will "quit their city life." By dedicating themselves "to the cultivation of a manly & independent character upon their own broad acres," they would gain real freedom. Smith gave control of the scheme to committees of black leaders, each charged with recruiting men for certain counties. Between mid-1846 and late 1847, he dispensed 140,000 acres in forty- to sixty-acre lots to any temperate man they recommended, sufficient to guarantee a $250 tax assessment if "improved," although by his own admission the bulk concentrated in the Adirondacks counties of Franklin and Essex was fit only for timbering. At no point did Smith pull back from the project. By decade's end, most of his land was gone, and arguments sputtered among black men over its administration.[101]

The "Smith Lands" project, as it was called, suggested a materialist understanding of republicanism based in the political independence commanded by free men on their own freeholds. As the purest exponent of Christian egalitarianism, Smith took the hard line, seeking to put a vanguard out in front of wavering white abolitionists and the masses of urban black folk. The project's demise underlines the obsolescence of this ideal; while educated men like Garnet and McCune Smith inveighed against city life, the settlements proved unforgiving terrain for laborers from Manhattan and Brooklyn minus community trading networks, friendly local governments and neighbors, or access to credit. Much greater resources were required; Smith himself estimated each settler needed $100 to start. Yet the hope of an independent black peasantry integrating into rural America remained compelling long after, in Reconstruction, the post-Reconstruction exoduses to Oklahoma and Kansas, and Booker T. Washington's Black Belt agricultural extension program. And as we shall see in chapter 10, accounts of the Smith Lands' failure may be overstated. Smith did not succeed in fostering a rural black electorate, but he apparently gained suffrage for numbers of black men anyway.

Chapter 10

Consult the Genius of Expediency

Approaching Power, 1847–1860

It is the colored aristocracy of this metropolis, dealers in shell-fish and whitewash . . . that has saved the whig party. . . . But for this vote of the highly respectable colored citizens of the city and State, the whigs would have been routed. . . . Downing and the colored voters have decided the day, and Downing and the colored voters ought to celebrate the triumph. . . . Oysters and whitewash hold the balance of power, and . . . the colored aristocracy—whigs to the backbone—have decided the election. Downing is master of the field.

—James Gordon Bennett in the *New York Herald*, November 10, 1849

Men and Brethren:—An unexpected blow has been levelled against us. WASHINGTON HUNT, Governor of our State, in his recent annual message, has descended from the high position he occupies. . . . We view his expressions and recommendations as an outrage to our feelings, an insult to the growing liberal sentiment of the people of this state, to which sentiment sustained by the votes of colored citizens, he owes his election.

—"To the Colored Citizens of the State of New York," January 1852

We regard the Republican party, all things considered, as more likely than any other to effect this desirable end [equal suffrage], and advise the eleven thousand colored voters of this State to concentrate their strength upon the Republican ticket. . . . We do not for a moment endorse all the tenets of that party; we are Radical Abolitionists, and shall ever remain so; but we regard [Gerrit Smith's] nomination [for Governor] . . . as calculated to give aid and comfort to the enemy, by electing the Democratic candidate.

—William J. Watkins, addressing the State Suffrage Association, September 1858

From late 1846 to November 1860, the Empire State's black politics tracked the old parties' breakdown, leading to the consolidation of New York's Republicans in 1855. Alongside Free Democrats, Know-Nothings, most Whigs, and some Barnburner Democrats, black men coalesced into this new party, which welcomed all while remaining fundamentally Whiggish, acknowledging William Seward's preeminence and under Thurlow Weed's practical direction.

In 1847, New York's Whigs were ascendant. They had returned to power in 1846, and the Wilmot Proviso, while disastrous for national party cohesion, benefited northern antislavery Whigs like the Sewardites, who enjoyed how it discombobulated Democrats. From 1847 to 1850, the Whigs won nearly all state-wide offices. Even the new Free Soil Party's 1848 nomination of Martin Van Buren on a platform opposing slavery's extension aided Weed's men, since it forced the Democrat Lewis Cass into a humiliating third-place finish in the Empire State. The Whig Zachary Taylor carried the state with 48 percent, helped by Weed declaring, "We have assurances . . . that Gen. TAYLOR, though a Southern man, is of the school of WASHINGTON, JEFFERSON, MADISON and MARSHALL, regarding Slavery as an evil, and opposed to its extension." They also took thirty-two of thirty-four congressional seats and large majorities in the legislature, sending Seward to the Senate in 1849.[1]

Soon discord visited the Whigs too, however. Seward's rival, Millard Fillmore, unexpectedly assumed the presidency in July 1850 after Taylor's death, and backed the Compromise of 1850, which would ultimately wreck his party. In retrospect, Whig unity was crippled the moment Seward gave his famous "Higher Law" speech in the Senate on March 11, 1850, turning New York's Whigs into the state's "the most vehement anti-extension party." From then on, the question became, how would the Sewardites engineer a realignment while maintaining themselves as a potential majority party? After 1850, a profusion of tickets filled ballots: three different Democratic factions (Barnburners, who only briefly joined the Free Soilers; "Soft Shells" willing to fuse with them; "Hard Shells" or Hunkers, who were not), Whigs, Free Democrats, Liberty men, soon slates of Know-Nothings and temperance men. The Know-Nothing American Party's rise in 1852–54, powered mainly by Whigs seeking to avoid the slavery question, merely delayed realignment. Throughout, Weed steered his apparatus through a long effort "to bring conscience politics into the traditional party system." Finally, in 1855, a half-new, half-old party came together around Seward's charisma and Weed's acumen, and open to black men.[2]

Most narratives of northern black life after 1850 focus on the desperation prompted by the Fugitive Slave Act, which abolished habeas corpus for free persons of color. However, while some upstate communities saw substantial emigration to Canada, black leaders evinced little despair: anger, disgust, uncertainty even, but no turning back. Their upward trajectory had two phases. The years 1847–54 constituted the crossover point when black Yorkers proved their ability to maneuver between the parties, largely because they finally gained sufficient votes with which to bargain. They responded vigorously to the Free Soil movement in 1848, and in 1849 delivered a bloc vote in New York City which both Whigs and Democrats admitted gave three out of four statewide and most city offices to the Whigs, allowing them to hold onto the state Senate, and tie the Assembly. The city's black leaders repeated this feat in 1850 by helping elect the Whig Washington Hunt governor by the narrowest margin in state history. When Hunt betrayed them by publicly supporting colonization, black leaders blasted him with such force that he recanted. These moves were initiated by the city's Committee of Thirteen, seasoned politicos allied with the upstate cadre based in Albany and Troy; both groups had deep ties to the Seward Whigs. From an electoral perspective, this leadership displayed great strategic flexibility. New York's chaotic partisanship gave them three options: the antislavery wing of the Whigs, elevated by Seward's prestige; the Free Soil (later Free Democratic) Party, originally tainted by the Barnburner Democrats' racism but congenial to black men after their departure; finally, Gerrit Smith's Liberty Party, which began nominating black men for local, state, and even national office.[3]

Before turning to this narrative, however, we will consider three distinctive features of antebellum New York's black politics: a leadership cohort ranging from political insiders to flamboyant agitators; a sophisticated patronage apparatus connecting them to white elites; a steadily growing base of voters.

Douglass and Other "Representative Men"

One cannot speak of black politics in New York after 1846 without addressing Frederick Douglass's outsized role. His 1847 move to Rochester shifted the axis of black leadership to the country's interior, even while he remained an outsider playing to national and international audiences. That Douglass chose Rochester was telling. He went into the original command post of "political abolitionism" to stake a claim, even if it took him several years to dispense with Garrisonian antielectoralism. Western New York was the home ground for antislavery Whiggery and the Liberty Party's remaining stronghold; thanks to the great Canal, the Burned-Over District was also the epicenter of the North's radical bourgeoisie (as outlined in chapter 9), where Douglass could expect more support than anywhere outside Old England.

The year 1847 was propitious for a new man. For a decade, black Yorkers had fought to regain their suffrage rights, and the November 1846 defeat exceeded their worst expectations. Douglass entered ground cleared for him by that loss. His outsize presence and transatlantic connections reenergized the state's political milieu. He restored to New York its national voice via the *North Star*, later *Frederick Douglass' Paper*, which became a principal medium of communication for abolitionists of all varieties. And for the next thirteen years, Douglass's perpetual ambivalence, as a halfway-Garrisonian until 1851, and after that a wanderer between the parties (Free Democratic, Liberty, Radical Abolitionist, Republican), made his paper a clearinghouse for black men's intramural debates.

Institutional and factional politics aside, the other factor is that this particular man was a star, in the modern sense. Rarely has any American equaled his international repute and celebrity-drawing power. Democrats gnashed their teeth at "that insolent and pestilent 'colored' demagogue," yet nothing could be done to him; he was safe in abolitionism's base and utterly unafraid, having given and received violence of all kinds. Strange things happened as a consequence of fame. Not only was "Fred. Douglass" evoked repeatedly as an avatar or demon in Congress, the uses made of his name sometimes descended to farce. How else to interpret Rochester's anti-Seward "Silver Gray" Whigs voting to nominate their neighbor Douglass for the State Assembly in 1851, only to receive his lordly dismissal?[4]

Douglass never sought to dominate New York State's black politics. Its political class was too established for such a coup. Consider those already sketched here: Thomas and George Downing, Samuel E. Cornish, James McCune Smith, Henry Highland Garnet, Stephen Myers, and finally, Douglass's great rival, the Reverend Samuel Ringgold Ward, the first person of African descent nominated for national office. The similarities and differences between Douglass, Ward, and Myers capture the range of the Empire State's leadership. Not only were all three editors, adepts at the patronage game required to maintain a newspaper, they were all partisans, albeit with very different approaches. The sophisticated polemics between Ward and Douglass over electoral politics in summer 1848, versus Myers's focus on doing rather than speaking, illuminates this set of players.[5]

As earlier with Garnet, the Liberty Party projected its biracialism via Ward. Born enslaved on the Eastern Shore in 1817, he attended Manhattan's African Free School, and pursued the ministry. Also like Garnet, he was a legendary orator; Seward reportedly declared "he never heard true eloquence until he heard Samuel R. Ward speak." In the mid-1840s, he achieved repute as a Liberty Party "big gun" who took a hard line against accommodation with Whigs or Free Soilers. At the August 1848 convention in Buffalo that founded the Free Soil Party, he astonished the vast crowd, according to Douglass.[6]

The focus here, however, is Ward's disagreement with Douglass, who, in 1848 and later, opted for what was then called "expediency." Ward's long, erudite "Address to the Four Thousand Colored Voters of the State of New York" in the September 1, 1848 *North Star* proposed a strategy of electoral purity, to demonstrate power by again spoiling, as the Liberty Party had done in 1844. He insisted they could "hold the balance of political power in the Empire State," since only "five thousand votes" had separated Polk and Clay. Ward's main target was "the artful and designing demagogues" who urged black men to vote for Van Buren, despite the Free Soilers' platform omitting any support for their "Equal and Inalienable Rights," and the state Free Soil Party's nominating well-known Democratic Negrophobes. Like Gerrit Smith, Ward damned black voters for "their criminal readiness to vote . . . according to the dictation . . . of those who are our most ruthless oppressors." The 1846 "rejection of the Equal Suffrage clause in the present Constitution" came naturally because "colored men" had shown they "either did not care about political equality, or if they possessed it, they would barter it away for the smallest price."[7]

In the same issue, Douglass demolished Ward with short, sharp explanations for why black men should back the Free Soilers. Certainly, the Buffalo Free Soil platform "does not include the Equal and Inalienable Rights of all men," but "the times create their own watch-words; and the watch-word of one generation may not always be appropriate to another. We would as willingly fight the battle of liberty and equality under the banner of 'Free Soil and Free Men,' as that of the Declaration of American Independence." Fighting over phrases was a distraction, what Douglass cared about was "what that party proposed to do, rather than the doctrines they proposed to teach," and if the party's program "involved no departure from moral principle . . . we should not hesitate to give our aid and vote to such a party." Douglass then hit Ward precisely on his illogic: "The address condemns the 'Free Soil Party,' because some of its leading men—such as Senator [John A.] Dix—entertain wrong views and prejudices against the colored people. . . . The views of Senator Dix, if we understand them, are quite similar to those of Senator Morris, of Ohio, who was Mr. Ward's [the Liberty Party's] candidate for the Vice-Presidency up to 1844." Douglass proposed a practical approach to such whites, asking, "Should we refuse to co-operate with them in securing a great good, because they may possess these prejudices? Certainly not. One of the most successful modes of removing prejudice, is to act with such men just so far as we can without a compromise of fundamental truths." He proved his point by painting a vivid picture of Ward's personal triumph at Buffalo: "The presence of such a man as Mr. Ward as a delegate . . . was one of the most powerful blows ever dealt upon the thick skull of American prejudice against colored persons. Thousands had an opportunity afforded them on that occasion of learning, for the first time in their lives, something of the manly energy of the black man's mind. We saw thousands listening to his eloquent words with astonishment, mingled with admiration, and all probably went home with a higher and more truthful estimate of our race than they ever entertained before."

Douglass's command of logic suggests why white men avoided facing him in debate. He easily disposed of Ward's "last objection . . . against voting for the Free Soil nominees," which was "the action of the Barnburner Democrats of this State with respect to the Right of Suffrage" in 1846. One can imagine Douglass's Cheshire grin: "To give this argument any force, it must be shown that the Free Soil party stand just now on this question where the Barnburners then stood, otherwise the logic is just about as good as this: Gerrit Smith, in 1830, was in favor of sending black men out of this country to Africa; therefore, black men cannot vote for Gerrit Smith, in 1848, without an abandonment of self-respect."

Finally, he hinted Ward was an unwitting dupe: "We know him too well to suspect him of any desire to play into the hands of the Cass and Taylor parties; but we know just as well that such will be the inevitable and almost only effect of his position. Indeed, such has already been the effect," quoting Weed's *Albany Journal* on Ward's return to his base in Cortlandville, where he declared "his hostility to the nomination of Martin Van Buren, and his determination to take the stump, and advise his abolition friends not to give the Ex-President their votes. . . . The meeting had a good effect. A few Whigs who had remained undecided whether to support General Taylor, came away from the meeting fully satisfied" that Van Buren had no claim "to the support of Northern men on the score of his anti-slavery opinions!" and they could "now give 'Old Zack' their hearty support." Then came Douglass's own disclaimer, absolving himself: "We shall vote for neither of the candidates. With our views of the pro-slavery character of the American Constitution . . . we could as soon run our hands into a fiery furnace, as into the American ballot-box, if thereby a man was to be elected who would swear to support that accursed bond of Union." Of course, others would ask, "If these be your views, are you not inconsistent in advising men to vote for Mr. Van Buren? We may be, but we think not. . . . We say to the multitude who are rushing to the ballot-box, see to it that you do not add to the sin of voting at all, the great sin of slave-rule, slavery-extension, and the perpetuity of slavery in the District of Columbia." Van Buren owed the former slave some thanks, since just as Samuel Cornish had damned Clay in 1838, ten years later, another black editor now gave a seal of approval.

Rites of Patronage

The second feature of this period underscores these leaders' partisan connections. Patronage is a highly variable concept, premodern in its origins. Some patronage of black people took place entirely between whites, as in Weed writing Horace Greeley in 1846, "If you don't know Frederick Douglass you ought to, for he is an uncommon man. If he finds you draw him out in conversation," or Walter Forward, the eminent Pittsburgh Whig and former treasury secretary, asking Gerrit Smith in 1847 to find a place in a New York law office for George Vashon, a recent Oberlin graduate and son of one of Pittsburgh's black leaders, John Vashon, since Pennsylvania's bar drew the color line. Smith in turn asked Seward to take the young Vashon into his office, expressing it would be "an important service to the anti-slavery cause" which would "greatly increase the love which tens of thousands of hearts, among both black and white men, bear to you." Upon investigation, Seward explained that "the introduction of the person you speak about would lead to the immediate withdrawal of all the force we have in the office," since none would "tolerate the candidate whose skin is tinged with a hue deriving from an African sun."[8]

Alternatively, patronage is sometimes organized from the bottom up. By the late 1840s, black Yorkers had built their own patronage apparatus extending into the conservative Whigs among the state's commercial bourgeoisie and some leading Democrats, all evidently wanting the reputation of "philanthropists"—how else to explain their sending money and endorsements to black enterprises, knowing their sponsorship would be publicized? A few examples illustrate this pattern. Millard Fillmore was hardly famous for antislavery sentiments, yet he wished his name associated with the annual celebration of black freedom in his hometown. In 1849, Buffalo's Committee of Arrangements for the First of August acknowledged "the receipt of sundry letters from different gentlemen, among whom they would mention the names of the Hon. Millard Fillmore, Vice President of United States." Similarly, in 1851, in his *Impartial Citizen*, the vehemently radical Samuel R. Ward thanked "Hon. H. S. Conger . . . for the present he sent us at Cortland," adding, "How we do like such Congressmen," notwithstanding Conger was a Whig and Ward, as a Liberty Party leader, routinely excoriated Whigs. A few months later, Ward expressed appreciation to Seward (among other prominent white men) "for their liberal donations." In 1857, another conservative Whig, former governor Myron Clark, personally endorsed *Twenty-Two Years a Slave and Forty Years a Freeman* by his former neighbor in Canandaigua, Austin Steward. Douglass, of course, constantly printed notices of the cash and other favors received from prominent whites, especially Seward.[9]

The recognized master of patronage was Stephen Myers. In early 1850, he held a "Fair" to benefit his new *Telegraph and Temperance Journal*, and Weed promoted it, hailing him as "that indefatigable man, Stephen Myers. . . . Yesterday was the first day it opened, and . . . the most sanguine anticipations of those by whom it was got up were more than fully realized," since among the "ladies and gentlemen" attending were "Lt. Gov. Patterson" (a Whig), "Gen. Dix" (the Democratic senator whom Seward had just replaced) "and a number of the Members of the Legislature." Myers kept it up—the following year he listed donations from nearly all state senators (most Whigs gave $10, and most Democrats $2). There was nothing exceptional about these gifts. Subsequent issues recorded $10 donations from the conservative Massachusetts Whig Edward Everett and New York's most powerful Democrat, "the Hon. Horatio Seymour, Governor." Myers would take anyone's money, but he could not be bought; in 1852, he sued the Albany School Commissioners "for having turned his three children out of the district school."[10]

Patronage, as sponsorship, beneficence, or protection, comes in many forms. Sometimes it implies the subordination of the patronized, but it can also empower them through association with those holding political and societal authority. In that sense, the Smith Lands project was the highest form of political patronage extended to New York's black men, amplified to the state's population through respectful press coverage; Gerrit Smith may have been a holy fool, but his wealth was fabulous. His power resonated, and he gifted thousands of persons of African descent with it. For the moment, whites' racial contempt was muted, since Smith was simply too rich to mock, at least at home in New York.

In 1848, under Myers's guidance, the state's Whig elite took up sponsorship of one part of the Smith Lands project. The vehicle for this move was the Florence Farming Association. Backed by others, including James McCune Smith, Myers set out to create a diversified business venture in Florence, an Oneida County town near Utica, including projected potash and lumber operations. Weed's *Journal* announced soon after the November 1848 election, "We understand that a number of enterprising colored men in this and other States . . . have contracted for one hundred village lots. . . . Several of our most worthy colored citizens are engaged in the enterprise, and, from the spirit which they evince, and their general intelligence, we cannot doubt that the experiment will prove successful." A New York City paper promoted the project as intended "to induce the colored citizens of Albany, New York, Boston, and Philadelphia, to follow farming or mechanical pursuits in the new settlement rather than be barbers, servants, etc etc, as they are in the cities. In Florence . . . there are water privileges for saw mills and grist mills, and indeed everything necessary to make a flourishing settlement," an article picked up nationwide. The association secured the Assembly chamber in January 1849 to have Samuel R. Ward "lecture upon Agriculture, and other subjects connected to the interests of the colored people," while Myers visited black communities like New Bedford to build a multistate enterprise, and deployed agents to sell lots while McCune Smith and Charles B. Ray gathered "subscriptions" from leading Whigs: Comptroller Millard Fillmore, soon to be vice president; Governor-Elect Hamilton Fish; Christopher Morgan, New

York's secretary of state; John C. Spencer, a pillar of the Clintonians, Anti-masons, and Whigs, former New York secretary of state, and former secretary of the treasury.[11]

Not all approved of this interracial enterprise. In early 1849, Henry Bibb, the black Liberty man, called the Florence Farming Association "a humbug" which would "do great injury to the anti-slavery cause if it is not exposed" as "the cunning trick of an unprincipled clique, whose chief object is to build themselves up on the benevolence of our anti-slavery friends." On arriving in Utica, Bibb had found the tale of black men "going out to Florence to build mills, open factories, etc . . . all false." Douglass also published a letter from Gerrit Smith, saying he had only "a few hundred acres left" in Florence, "of very moderate fertility" and "not favorably situated." Better "for the colored people to emigrate to lands which are given to them, even if they are of inferior quality, as are most of the lands" he had deeded. If they purchased tracts "at their full value . . . they should buy such as are fertile, easy of cultivation, and advantageously situated." This communication led to Douglass's public disavowal, writing Myers, "There is much doubt in this region, as well as elsewhere among our people, as to the desirableness of emigrating to the Florence Settlement" given "the wildness of the country, the infertility of the lands, the distance and the difficulties of the way to market, and the entire absence of water power."[12]

In response, New Bedford's Leven Tilman, a Florence Farming Association agent, explained its goals. Since "persons living in other States could not participate in [Gerrit Smith's] rich gift. . . . When the Florence enterprise was started by our friend, Stephen Myers, and others . . . many very respectable colored persons, living in the surrounding States, were induced to make purchases." Unlike the Adirondacks counties, Oneida had "superior" facilities, with "large and flourishing towns, such as Utica, Rome, Clinton, Whitesboro." After Myers and others consolidated their holdings, more "lands were purchased from Gerrit Smith's agent . . . to establish the settlement at Florence, for the purpose of farming, dealing in lumber, manufacturing potash, and practicing various trades." He ended on a classic note of frontier aspiration: "Our forefathers, have made this country, once a wilderness, a delightful home for their oppressors, the Anglo-Saxon race. We, their offspring, to this day are 'hewers of wood and drawers of water,' degraded, crushed beneath public sentiment and popular religion. Henry Clay and his coadjutors . . . the giants in this nation, are still using their power to keep us down, still determined to drive us out . . . to colonize us to Africa. But this is our country, the soil on which we were born. Here are our homes. Let us build ourselves up by all righteous means. Let us cherish no divisions among ourselves. United we stand, divided we fall." Over the next year, representatives traversed the northeast, collecting tools, clothing, and donations, with friendly encomia from Whig editors. Like most such gambits, the association dwindled away, leaving a handful of black men owning small properties. For a brief moment, however, it demonstrated that African Americans could go into business backed by eminent whites.[13]

A final version of patronage extended in both directions, as mutual regard across partisan, religious, or ethnic divides. In this case, the medium of exchange was personal ties between self-made men. Thomas Downing, the restaurateur, was on famously good terms with Wall Street, the metropolitan editors, and politicians like Seward (a hint of this is his sending to the governor in Albany "some oysters of a Superior quality from my own beds" after Seward publicly defied Virginia). The *New York Herald*'s James Gordon Bennett was an extremely powerful editor and an outright Negrophobe who delighted in mocking black people's accents, supposed odor, and pretensions. Yet over decades Bennett evinced his respect for "the great T. Downing . . . oysterman," transferring this esteem to the younger Downing through covering his success in Newport and activism in Rhode Island. The Downings' regard for Bennett was equally public. When Bennett wrote in 1860 that "our old friend, and sometime correspondent, George Downing, colored—oysters in every style—has met with some pecuniary disaster which will prevent him from shelling out to his numerous creditors," the latter stipulated, "I admit the force of the words 'your old friend' for I have always felt that you were a personal friend of the Downings," reporting he was solvent and "negotiating to go to Charleston in a steamer to cater to a party going to the Charleston Convention," meaning the Democrats' national convention. In Old New York, it seems, businessmen's ententes were sometimes so cordial they transcended lines of both party and complexion. These courtesies were extremely loaded in the atmosphere following John Brown's execution; Downing's letter produced a venomous comment from an Alabama editor, suggesting "the nigger George Downing, the oyster dealer" should take heed before he "goes to Charleston." Perhaps he should "send a letter of inquiry to Mr. Mayor Macbeth, or editor Carlisle, of the Charleston 'Courier,' asking about the laws in reference to locking up free *Nigs* who boldly go to Charleston on steamers or any other way. . . . If master George Downing goes to Charleston, he will be very likely retained there to improve and open the Cooper and Ashley rivers permanently."[14]

The Black Vote in New York

The final factor in the upward trajectory of the 1850s was the black electorate's rapid expansion, enough to count in close elections statewide or locally.

Black and white, friend and foe, cited this progress. In 1845, the state census counted a mere 1,001 voters out of 2,025 "People of Color–Taxed." On that basis, McCune Smith claimed an electorate of 2,000; apparently, he presumed all taxpayers would take the necessary oath. Just three years later, S. R. Ward addressed the "Four Thousand Colored Voters of the State of New York," and in 1849 Whigs and Democrats acknowledged they exceeded "one thousand" in Manhattan alone. By 1852, Myers was referring to "our 5,000 voters," and an address from that year's black state convention asserted that the "property qualification [was] so small in amount that every colored man who chooses may become a voter: four-fifths of the adult colored natives of this State are now entitled to vote under it." Given that the 1850 federal census counted almost 13,000 voting-age men of color, the potential electorate thus exceeded 10,000. The number kept going up. In 1854, white newspapers reported there were "about three thousand men entitled to vote in this city [New York] and Brooklyn" and Henry Highland Garnet told the 1856 state convention that they mustered "5,000 or 6,000 colored voters, about half of whom lived in New-York and Brooklyn." By the late 1850s, black leaders asserted, "We number 10,000 votes in this State alone, a force not to be despised, if equipped and put in order."[15]

In the three- and four-way races of the 1850s, with statewide offices won by tiny margins, 5,000 to 10,000 voters, roughly 1 to 2 percent of the electorate, mattered a great deal. In the early 1850s, black voters might choose between Whig, Free Soil, Liberty, or even Know-Nothing tickets, but in 1855 most anchored themselves to the Republicans. With the Democrats an impossibility, black electors could have been ignored as a "captured" constituency, and some Republican leaders preferred to ignore them. Fortunately, Gerrit Smith reorganized the remnants of the Liberty organization into a Radical Abolitionist Party. On that basis, he waged quixotic candidacies for president in 1856 and 1860 and governor in 1858. Smith retained just enough appeal among black Yorkers to keep open their possible defection, reminding white Republicans to court their vote.

How do we know these claims were more than speculative exaggerations which Democrats echoed to tar their opponents as negro-lovers? Unlike in 1825, 1835, and 1845, the 1855 state census no longer reported the statewide aggregate of black voters, with totals for each town or city ward. In early 1855, the Whigs controlling New York's legislature pushed through changes in the census. Appointment of marshals was vested in the Whig secretary of state, Elias Leavenworth of Syracuse, instead of locals. He promulgated new *Instructions for Taking the Census* that specified recording only "People of Color–Taxed" and "–Not Taxed." The final census simply counted 9,330 black taxpayers, alongside "Natural-Born Voters," "Naturalized Voters," and "Aliens." That number showed an almost fourfold increase since 1845, and on that basis, the historian of black suffrage Phyllis Field suggested that, as in the prior year, the voters should be estimated at half of the taxpayers, meaning an electorate of 4,600.[16]

There are multiple problems with using the state census in this way, however. The Hudson sample of the manuscript census described below shows that entire families were often listed as "People of Color–Taxed," since the rationale for counting black bodies was to establish the basis of representation: the 1821 Constitution specified that neither "People of Color–Not Taxed" nor aliens counted for that purpose. Is it possible to use the manuscript census of 1855 to determine an actual number? In principle, yes, since the marshals were required to indicate all voters, and those men can be cross-referenced with those indicated as "Black" or "Mulatto." A sample from Hudson, a historic site of black voting, documents a substantial increase in black voters in 1845–55 and how much larger their electorate would become minus the "freehold" requirement. In 1845, there were seven "People of Color–Taxed" in Hudson, only four of whom were voters, versus 317 not taxed, in an electorate of 1,122. Ten years later, at least twenty-three black men were listed as voters, an almost 600 percent increase, and eight more were not listed as either "taxed" or "not taxed," most of whom owned land and thus could claim the right to vote, with an additional thirty-three voting-age men listed as "People of Color–Not Taxed." Given that the census recorded 1,171 voters in Hudson in 1855, black men were at least 2 percent of the electorate (perhaps as much as 2.6 percent); if all sixty-four voted, however, they would have constituted a much larger bloc, 5.5 percent.

A single sample is hardly definitive. Putting aside the difficulty of hand-counting every black voter in 1855, equally important was how a voter's qualifications were asserted at the poll, if challenged. Until the late 1850s, New York had no prior registration of voters, after an abortive Whig attempt to impose a "Registry Law" on Tammany's Irish-born voters in 1840 (which Seward opposed). The 1834 election law spelled out the process applicable to all, and that language stayed the same despite major revisions in 1842 and 1847: "If the vote of any person offering it is challenged, and any vote may be challenged by any inspector, or any other person entitled to vote at the same poll, one of the inspectors shall declare to the person challenged, the qualifications which are set forth in the oath, and if after hearing this statement of the qualifications, the person offering to vote shall state himself to be duly qualified, and the challenge shall be persisted in, then the oath shall be administered." McCune Smith's reference during his April 1845 speech to the Assembly is here clarified, that the freehold qualification "says, 'come, man of color! swear that you are worth $250 worth of real estate; your vote will then go as far, will be paid for as well as the vote of any white man. Perjure yourself that your may [*sic*] may be enriched with a bribe.'" He made a similar assertion in 1855: "History will record it to our credit, that while under the property qualification clause, we could all vote with slight, if any impediment; yet our regard for the solemnity of our oaths restrained us, except where we could swear to the literal truth," although it seems unlikely most black men agreed with the physician regarding the binding "solemnity of their oaths." In that context, as the "Persons of Color–Taxed" mushroomed from 1845 to 1855, many may have decided, or were assured by friendly judges of election, that if they could swear to being a taxpayer, they should vote: the number recorded as "voters" in the state census was not determinative; what mattered was how many went to the polls, and one notes the absence of prosecutions for perjury, or elections contested because of "illegal" black voting.[17]

There is another reason why several thousand black men may have felt comfortable swearing to their ownership of a freehold. Gerrit Smith had given away 3,000 deeds in the late 1840s. Heretofore, scholars have presumed (as it was assumed then) that few of those men kept their land and became voters. Barring massive excavation of local records and family histories, we cannot say how many stayed for any length of time, but surely not many. Some were bilked on arrival, and many had their land sold for unpaid taxes; in 1852, someone in a position to know, Stephen Myers, stipulated that "a few have gone on their land and occupied it, and are doing very well, considering the disadvantages they had to contend with, that is for the want of money to obtain farming implements," and in 1853 he implored, "Colored land holders, you must pay your taxes, and not suffer your land to be sold for Taxes. The Hon. Gerrit Smith gave deeds to four thousand men [*sic*] in this State, those were given to us to better our condition as citizens. We should go to work and improve our lands forthwith." Finally, in October 1854 Charles B. Ray and Mc-Cune Smith issued a broadside to the "Grantees" urging them to "REDEEM YOUR LANDS!!," much of which had been "SOLD FOR TAXES in Dec. 1852, for the Tax due for the year 1849," but could be reclaimed if the taxes were paid within two months. Eight years later, Smith noted "the only men who yet remain there [as] successful cultivators of the soil went from Troy."[18]

Certainly, some hung on. In the eight counties (see map III.1) where deeds were awarded (Ulster, Delaware, Madison, Oneida, Fulton, Hamilton, Essex, Franklin), the 1855 census recorded a nearly sixfold increase since 1845 in the "People of Color–Taxed." Other fragments suggest some stayed. In the 1940s, a black woman in Ithaca remembered her grandfather and other men getting land from Smith "so they could vote." The 1852 black convention's "Address to the People of the State of New York" noted, "Colored men hold offices in the gift of the people in Essex county, in this State; have refused office in

Oneida, and have been nominated," both counties with large numbers of settlers. In 1849, John Brown moved to Essex County's Timbuktoo settlement to aid new farmers, and some remained when his body came home. In 1859, Thomas Wentworth Higginson visited Brown's family and remarked that, despite their being "grossly defrauded by a cheating surveyor . . . some of the best farms . . . in that region are still in the hands of colored men."[19]

From a strictly electoral perspective, however, it is irrelevant whether a man carved out a farm in the Adirondacks, as long as he held onto his deed. One unexplored possibility is that Smith's deeds enfranchised men where they actually lived. He gave away a vast number in New York City and Brooklyn, and, suddenly, the electorates in those counties became a noticeable force. Certainly, no contemporary made this claim, even when black Manhattanites asserted their thousand-plus votes had delivered the state to the Whigs in 1849 and again in 1850. But in an 1857 letter to the *New-York Tribune*, Smith guessed that "probably less than fifty" families remained on their land, while specifying that about half of the grantees still owned their land, meaning they had sufficient property to vote.[20]

A final consideration is the likelihood of systematic underenumeration and the deliberate refusal to list property in the federal censuses administered by the "assistant federal marshal for each ward," meaning in 1860 Democratic appointees committed to holding down Republican margins. Inspecting the manuscript census indicates this bias, since in some municipalities many pages record black heads of household and their occupations with no listing of personal or real property, including men who surely did hold property, such as Myers, who does not appear in any antebellum census. The scholar Robert Swan found consistent in how between black Brooklynites were listed in city directories and the federal census, with an average undercount of 23 percent in 1820–50, and there is similar evidence for Ontario County, a center of black activism, while contemporary black activists regularly asserted they were grossly undercounted.[21]

1848: The Year of "Free Soil"

In 1848, most antislavery men anticipated the arrival of a new electoral coalition able to contend for national power. What made that larger formation possible was a narrow focus on "Free Soil," meaning no more slave states. This was a suitably ambiguous premise entirely avoiding the questions of "free for whom?" and "free of what?" The new party brought together most Liberty men, Massachusetts's Conscience Whigs, and New York's Barnburner Democrats, and threatened the sectional balance, especially after it chose Martin

Van Buren as its presidential nominee with John Quincy Adams's son, Charles Francis Adams, as his running mate. Its founders, notably Ohio's Salmon P. Chase, hoped it would draw large numbers from both major parties. The consequences for black men were mixed. In Massachusetts and Ohio, African Americans quickly found a home as Free Soilers. In New York, however, few Sewardites left their party, and the Liberty Party's hard core stuck with Smith, so Barnburners dominated the Empire State's Free Soil organization. These ex-Democrats detested the Slave Power but had no use for black Yorkers. To them, "free soil" meant new territories free of black people, and their gubernatorial candidate, John A. Dix, had led opposition to black suffrage in 1846.[22]

The August 1848 Free Soil Convention in Buffalo demonstrates how the dynamics of race complicated alliance-building. It was a free-for-all, with 20,000 men, mostly former Whigs and Democrats, cheering speakers who vented their anti-Southernism. According to the *North Star*'s Martin R. Delany, a handful of black men attended as actual delegates, including Ward, the Clevelander John Malvin, and Michigan's Henry Bibb. At one point, "loud calls arose for Douglass," according to the official record. Barnburners surrounding the Whig in the chair insisted the "nigger" should not be recognized, but he spoke briefly nonetheless to "deafening cheers," claiming a bad throat but wishing them "God speed your noble undertaking. . . . The audience appeared to feel great disappointment when they learned that Mr. Douglass could not address them." The Liberty Party's Bibb told a sarcastic story about Democratic presidential candidate Louis Cass, whom he knew personally, and who refused to sign a suffrage petition because he was "not at liberty to make any political declarations." The politically agile Ward, a delegate from Cortland County, New York, gave a resounding speech and then ostentatiously walked out to signal his rejection of Van Buren. Those were brief appearances amid the hubbub surrounding thousands of white men reconciling across party lines. To conciliate the Barnburners, the new party's platform ignored the concerns of free black people—nothing regarding fugitive slave laws, Black Codes, or the rights to testify in court or to attend public schools, let alone suffrage. Post-1848, Free Soilers in some states addressed those issues and welcomed black men, but the New York party stayed all white until the early 1850s. Although this was a clear regression from the Liberty Party's inclusivity, black Yorkers debated ardently whether to back Van Buren, and many did.[23]

The Colored National Convention in Cleveland on September 6 displayed that debate. The delegates were mainly from western New York, Ohio, and Michigan. Its terse stenographic proceedings show strong support for the Free Soil option. Albany's William Topp, various Ohio leaders, and Martin R. Delany, then an editor of Douglass's *North Star*, all backed it. Without directly endorsing the party, the resolutions on electoral action suggested black men should vote Free Soil, which required some careful wording. At first, a resolution passed recommending "to our brethren throughout the several states, to support no person or party . . . that shall not have for their object the establishment of equal rights and privileges, without distinction of color, clime or condition." Clearly, this excluded the Free Soilers. After delegates like Topp declared they would back Van Buren anyway, it was overturned by the passage of a second resolution stating, "We heartily engage in recommending to our people the Free Soil movement, and the support of the Buffalo Convention." Delany then offered a third resolution, that black voters should "support such persons and parties alone as have a tendency to enhance the liberty of the colored people of the United States," which left the door open for backing antislavery men in any party. Overwhelming majorities favored both resolutions authorizing black men to do whatever they might find necessary, and they returned home to get out their vote.[24]

This ambiguity persisted through Election Day. Although Ward damned Van Buren, other black Yorkers hedged their bets. In late September, H. W. Johnson of Canandaigua wrote in the *North Star* that he would vote for Van Buren, since "he now stands upon the Buffalo platform" of restricting slavery, but not for John A. Dix, urging "Ward and Garnet, Smith and Crummell, and all others [to] speak out, and endeavor to save our countrymen from the everlasting infamy of having voted for Gen. Dix." Johnson acknowledged that some would oppose Van Buren because "the Free Soil party did not declare in favor of universal suffrage," adding, "I must differ from these gentlemen," drawing a distinction between slavery's "national character" and suffrage as a state issue. Even Gerrit Smith was ambivalent. The *Ram's Horn*, edited by the former Garrisonian Thomas Van Rensselaer, urged Smith to back the Free Soilers, and in New York City Van Rensselaer chaired a meeting where Myers, "editor of the *Northern Star and Colored Farmer* of Albany . . . insisted upon the support of the nominees of the Buffalo Convention by the colored voters," as well as backing "good men for members of the Legislature of the State, and Free Soil and Liberty party men." Smith responded that Van Buren's "position in respect to the extension of slavery is infinitely preferable to that of Gen. Cass or Gen. Taylor; and that they who pass by him to vote for them, give very poor evidence of being themselves opposed to the extension of slavery." Although he personally would not vote for Van Buren, many took this as a backhanded endorsement like that by Douglass. We cannot know for whom New York's black men voted, although after the election, Delany described how "the Whigs, seeing there was no alternative, at once assumed the position of the Free Soil party" and "a majority of those opposed to the slave power, supported the Whig nomination for the present." Whether black men joined that majority was unclear. In November 1849, Thurlow Weed celebrated the return of black voters to the Whigs by noting they supported the "'Free Soil' party, so long as that party maintained its integrity. But when it abandoned the distinctive feature of its organization, and sacrificed a great principle for 'the spoils,' these honest and intelligent Electors withdrew their allegiance."[25]

The partisan terrain shifted again in 1849–50, opening a renewed bid for black voters. In 1849, the Barnburners returned to the Democratic fold, forging a "Coalition" between the state's Free Soil organization, under their control, and the Hunker Democrats, including Tammany Hall. Seward kept the Whigs viable among antislavery voters, and the Liberty Party remained, even if it received only 2,545 votes in New York in 1848, one-sixth of its average a few years earlier. This rump, clustered around Smith's home base in Madison County, then took a leap toward political equality by nominating black candidates for local and statewide office. Samuel R. Ward was elected to its three-member state central committee and nominated for the State Assembly in September 1848; in 1849, he began publishing his *Impartial Citizen* as a party organ and accepted the nomination for secretary of state, while Jermain Loguen ran for state senator in Onondaga County, and William Derrick for coroner in Chenango County. In September 1850, however, the Liberty men did something remarkable. At their national convention, 140 of the 206 delegates backed Ward as their vice presidential candidate alongside Gerrit Smith for president; the runner-up was a Wisconsin Free Soil congressman, Charles Durkee, elected to the Senate as a Republican in 1855. Until June 1851, when Ward withdrew for obscure personal reasons, he was listed in Liberty newspapers as one of their two nominees for national office. What did these candidacies, and Ward's in particular, actually signify? Did anyone hear the tree fall? White abolitionists appear to have been perplexed or embarrassed, and paid them little notice. The organ of the Free Soil Party, Gamaliel Bailey's *The National Era*, never mentioned any of the Liberty Party's black candidates. In the regular press, however, Ward's nomination received considerable notice, and these articles, scandalized or respectful, proved its worth. Like the 1848 Seneca Falls convention's demand for women's suffrage, his candidacy briefly made the unimaginable a possibility. When a renegade Whig attacked Weed's editorial noting Ward's candidacy with "evident satisfaction and approbation," Weed retorted, "We know several very intelligent, worthy 'colored gentlemen' for whom we would vote cheerfully if they were candidates against some very *unworthy* white persons whom we also know."[26]

In Bed with a Governor

After 1848, black Whiggism persisted but with more electoral impact. Some upstaters like Ward, Loguen, and Buffalo's Abner Francis remained Liberty men, but the core Manhattan leadership, now dubbed the Committee of Thirteen, reasserted itself. In fall 1849, black leaders delivered their entire city electorate to the Whigs, attracting national notice and helping Whigs elect three of the four state officers on the ballot that year, maintain their state Senate majority, and take enough of Manhattan's Assembly delegation to tie that body. The Whigs also elected eleven of the city's eighteen aldermen and ten of their assistants, gaining a majority on the City Council. The official Democratic organ in Washington commented with disgust, "The negro vote, amounting to 1200 or 1500, has given the State to the Whigs . . . the most degraded classes of voters are enlisted under the banners of the money aristocracy," while the Whigs' *Boston Atlas* gloated, "The Whig party is the party of freedom, and always was."[27]

The Committee of Thirteen timed its intervention for just before the November 6 balloting. They convened two mass meetings in lower Manhattan, on Friday, November 2, and late in the evening of Monday, November 5. The impetus was "the coalition of the barnburners with Tammany Hall," which convinced the black electors, after much debate, that "it is the solemn duty of the ten or twelve hundred colored voters of the city and county of New York, to exercise the right which they possess," followed by a sober denunciation of the Democratic–Free Soil alliance and an endorsement of the Whigs. Bennett's *Herald*, anti-Whig and antiblack but partial to Thomas Downing, covered the meeting in detail, leading to his oddly triumphalist assertion postelection, quoted at this chapter's head, that "the colored aristocracy . . . has saved the whig party." For a moment, it seemed like 1813, with black men's votes controlling the state before fearful whites' eyes.[28]

Two anecdotes attendant to this election illuminate the barriers to black men voting, and the impact when they did, even far away in the deep South. First, throughout the nineteenth century, Manhattan elections saw violence at the polls controlled by different Tammany factions. Black men inserting themselves led to the following in the notorious "Irish Sixth" Ward, gleefully described in the *Herald*: "In this ward, the most amusing incident was a negro hunt. A colored voter in the forenoon, having made his appearance at one of the polls, some of the 'bhoys took it into their heads to give him a lickin. . . . He took to his heels in beautiful style, and never was there a rarer hunt. Through Centre street, and the streets adjoining, he ran for his life, amidst shouts and yells, while his pursuers chased him most vigorously, still keeping close on his track, till at length," he got away. Farther afield, a Mississippi paper extracted from the *Herald*'s verbatim report on the November 2 debate between black leaders, with racist interpolations:

> *Mr. Downing*—They have deceived us in the last presidential election [meaning the Barnburner Democrats-turned-Free Soilers]. This is the very test upon which the same party broke off from the old rotten locofocos in Tammany Hall. No party ever so degraded themselves as they did this fall, by uniting with such fellows as Sickles and Strahan, the lowest of the low. [Daniel Sickles was a Tammany leader, later a Civil War general.]
>
> *Mr. Zuille*—There is no use in denouncing Sickles and Strahan. They are too low. We have been always denouncing them. We are not saying what we mean in that resolution. The resolution says one thing, and the advocacy of it says another. It is the recreant free soilers that ought to be denounced.
>
> *Mr. Downing*—Sickles and Strahan are the lowest of God's creation, for they have no more principle than a beast, and nothing can be lower than that. (Ya! ya! ya!)
>
> *Mr. Townsend*—They are the men God says he does not know. (Renewed cachinnations.)
>
> *Mr. Percell*—Why, then, do you level your musket at what you cannot see? for what God does not know, you cannot know or see. (Great laughter.) . . .
>
> *Sambo*—Dat's de Coon!
>
> The fifth resolution was then offered. . . . This, which pledges the colored gemmen to whiggery, was also discussed at length, and adopted with three dissenting voices.[29]

The most trenchant analysis was in Weed's *Albany Evening Journal*, reporting "THE VOTE OF FREEHOLD ELECTORS." As always, Weed declared his respect for black men, that "if there be a class of Voters who, above all others, may be supposed to act firmly and honestly upon all the questions affecting Human Bondage, it is the men of color who are fortunate enough to reside in Free States. They are left to choose between the several political parties. And they are impelled by every consideration of duty, interest, sentiment and sympathy, to vote with the party that proves itself most truly and faithfully in favor of EMANCIPATION." He reproduced the "NOTICE" for the meeting in lower Manhattan, listing the entire committee (John J. Zuille, Thomas and George Downing, Daniel J. Elston, William A. Tyson, Francis

Myers, Lewis H. Putnam, Peter Guignon, J. H. Townsend, and Dr. John V. De Grasse) and their resolutions—remarkable, given the attitude expressed toward his party: "It is inexpedient for us, at the present time to identify ourselves with either of the great political parties. . . . It is the duty of every lover of his country and well wisher of his race, to support such men at the coming election as are pledged to the principles of free soil, free speech and free men. . . . The doctrine set forth in the creed of democracy, at Tammany Hall, on *the 29th of October,* is unworthy of the name of democracy, and meets our universal disapprobation. . . . The candidates nominated by the coalition of the democrats and free soilers are unworthy the confidence of a free people, and ought to be defeated at the coming election, and that we will use our utmost influence to effect the same. . . . The best front at present presented by the two great political parties, is that of the Whigs; which, whilst it is not all that we wish, yet we will assist, and cause our political strength to be felt."

The antebellum period produced no stronger proof for black men's electoral weight than this article: the nation's most powerful party manager seeking to influence white voters by showing them what black voters said. Weed added, "A personal acquaintance with several of the men who participated in the deliberations of that Meeting, enables us to say that there was as much good sense and intelligence there as characterize the meetings of those who enjoy higher advantages and claim superior knowledge." His political intent was clear: "The Colored Electors, in view of the principles and character of both parties, with no motive but to cast their votes with the party that is most truly devoted to the cause of 'Free Soil,' 'Free Speech,' 'Free Labor,' and 'Free Men,' decided in favor of the WHIGS. The cause of the *real* friends of Emancipation is a severe rebuke to the Abolitionists, Liberty Party Men and Free Soilers who was swallowed up in the Coalition. And it at the same time furnishes the highest evidence that the Whig Party, while faithful to the other great interests of Republicanism, is the party to which the injured and oppressed must look for all that can be done for their relief and protection."[30]

Weed's praise disgusted Samuel Ward, who reported, "The Whigs are now in ecstasies because ten sixteenths of their majority in New York City was given by colored men. . . . What such black men mean, we cannot divine. Surely they must regard self-respect as a useless commodity." Henry Highland Garnet joined in, in a published letter to Zuille "and other Colored Whigs of New York City," proclaiming, "Ye Have Sold Yourselves for Nought." In 1850, Ward went further, charging outright graft, that "with a golden bribe in his hand a New York City black man hired some and caused others to vote the Whig ticket . . . aided by some of the most influential of the same class in the Empire city; and what is still worse they found the most part of our people *sinable* and coaxable enough to do the dirty deed of meanness." Black Whigs fired back, with George Downing stating their case frankly. Not only was it "base slander . . . PERFECTLY AND ENTIRELY FALSE" that he or anyone else accepted bribes, but "as to any expediency evinced by the colored voters of New York . . . I think it justifiable, if voting at all . . . were justifiable . . . the best interest of the whole of the oppressed colored men of the land . . . was forwarded by the course they then pursued."[31]

In November 1850, the black leadership again exerted itself, this time on behalf of the Whigs' gubernatorial candidate, Washington Hunt, who won by 262 votes out of 432,382 cast. Subsequent events forced a reconsideration. In his first message as governor in January 1851, Hunt took stands likely to please abolitionists. While acquiescing to the Compromise of 1850 "as a final settlement of these territorial controversies," he suggested continuing ten sions stemmed from southerners' "sectional jealousy, or a supposed necessity for nurturing the spirit of disunion," and defended "free soil" politics. New Yorkers had always legitimately "objected to the extension of slavery over a country acquired by our common efforts," and would not "concede that it affords any ground of complaint . . . still less that it can justify secession, revolution, or any effort to overthrow the free Constitution established by our fathers." He referred to the Fugitive Slave Act as national law "of paramount authority" but noted it was "repugnant to the sentiments of many of our people," stipulating that "in enforcing the claims of one section . . . we should not trespass upon the rights of the other. While the claim of the southern slaveholder to recapture his slave is fully admitted, the right of the northern freeman [meaning his state's black citizens] to prove and defend his freedom is equally sacred. Both are alike under the protecting care of our common constitution," an equation certain to unsettle white southerners. Having hinted at state-sanctioned resistance, he concluded with a standard Whig bromide, that by "uniting . . . in a kind and dispassionate spirit" congressmen from both sections would fix "such clauses as may be found defective."[32]

In January 1852, Hunt sent a different message, defending the Union-as-it-must-remain combined with racial dystopianism. Since "the constitution . . . wisely left the states free to regulate their domestic affairs, the dissimilarity in their local institutions furnishes no just ground for mutual complaints." Slavery was "produced by causes over which the founders of the Constitution had no control, and for which we, their descendants, cannot be deemed responsible." He equated the South's "spirit of disunion" with abolitionist "fanaticism." Given the size of the slave population, any "amelioration must be . . . gradual" and "left to the voluntary action of the people most immediately concerned." In the North, "although the free people of color enjoy a certain degree of liberty, they are commonly treated as an inferior race, and deprived of the social and political rights without which freedom is but an empty name." He insisted that, even if "their condition amongst us is deplorable in the extreme," any progress was "morally impossible." The black population was supposedly declining, suggesting that "the African, like the Indian race, cannot permanently co-exist on the same soil with the whites, and that a separation is necessary to prevent their ultimate extinction." Hunt then hailed the American Colonization Society as "the only organized agency which has contributed to accelerate this separation or produce practical results beneficial to the African race . . . by placing them where they may enjoy the blessings of free government" and "spread civilization and religion" to Africa, while affording "owners . . . willing to liberate their slaves an asylum for their reception." Colonizationists were "spreading christianity and civilization over a portion of the earth . . . sunk for ages in heathen barbarism," followed by the remarkable falsehood that "a majority" of Africa's population "are in the most abject slavery." He hoped the ACS's plans would be "sustained by the liberal action of the national government," including "employment of government steamers to transport colored emigrants from this country." Any move toward emancipation in even the medium term was dismissed, and "African colonization must be regarded as the only effective auxiliary of voluntary emancipation." Hunt concluded by asking legislators for "a liberal appropriation" to the ACS. One of his allies subsequently proposed $20,000.[33]

In response, the Committee of Thirteen convened a convention in Albany on January 5, 1852, and published an address "To the Colored Citizens of the State of New York," denouncing Hunt's message as "an outrage to our feelings [and] an insult to the growing liberal sentiment of the people," underlining that Hunt had been "sustained by the votes of colored citizens" to whom "he owes his election." They lobbied the governor in person, producing an apology. As reported at New York's Abyssinian Baptist Church soon after, "The committee [George Downing, William Topp, and Stephen Myers, all longtime Whigs] was very respectfully and cordially received by his excellency. He introduced conversation by saying that he was not as great an enemy of the colored people as was supposed." When he attempted to justify his support for colonization, "the committee . . . remarked that the colored man certainly had sufficient to struggle against, without having the Governor of the State to thus rear himself against them . . . he replied that . . . 'he was the friend of the colored people; that he would do anything for their advancement and improvement; that he was in favor of the extension of the elective franchise; that he voted for the same,' for which he was thanked." They were in no mood to be mollified. At the city meeting, Downing proposed they "withdraw their support from the Whig party, to which it had been given for years past," and mobilize "the 5,000 colored voters of the State" for a nominee "who will be a friend to progress and freedom." Inside the city, arguments had already been made to deliver their bloc to the Liberty Party. In March 1851, Lewis H. Putnam and Robert Hamilton (son of the revered William Hamilton) issued a "Report on Political Relations" to a citywide meeting, insisting, "We must abandon our individual connection with the old parties, and establish an organization throughout the State. . . . The necessity of identifying ourselves with the liberty party has been before us for the last twelve years; but as we could not see how our interest could be promoted by that organization, we have acted on a different basis [e.g., backed the Whigs] . . . the colored people and the liberty party should unite upon a plan that will enable us to act in an effective manner, in all the counties."[34]

Hamilton and Putnam's proposal was too little, too late. Twelve years earlier, there were so few black voters that they exerted only a moral and indirect influence. Now, their electorate could tilt a close election, but the Liberty Party had become little more than irritant, although a famous mob action, Syracuse's "Jerry Rescue" on October 1, 1851, demonstrated its residual standing as a biracial front. On the same Saturday that U.S. marshals seized the fugitive William "Jerry" McHenry, the party's state convention had assembled nearby. Alerted to the capture, Gerrit Smith, Samuel R. Ward, and Jermain Loguen led a crowd of 2,500 which took McHenry from his cell and sent him to Canada. At a climactic moment, Ward mounted the jail steps to ask whether the Democrats and Whigs who passed the Fugitive Slave Act and "execute it before our faces, shall receive our votes, or shall by those votes be indignantly rebuked. Tell me, ye sturdy working men of Onondago [sic], shall your votes be consecrated to the latter, or prostituted to the former? Do you swear fealty to freedom this day? Do you promise, so help you God! so to vote, as that your sanction never more shall be given to laws which empower persons to hunt, chain, and cage, MEN, in our midst? (cries of 'yes, yes')." Smith and Ward then strolled through the crowd, arm in arm. Later, Smith defended the nineteen rescuers in court after Seward personally bailed them, and prosecuted a marshal for kidnapping. Smith's 1852 election to Congress was a final triumph for radicalism. He ran first in a three-way race, helped by his support for free trade. In Washington, Smith cut a strange figure, representing the nation's abolitionists, black and white. On May 3, 1854, he told the House's slaveholders that they would repent if they met free black men, wishing "that noble man, Frederick Douglass, could be allowed to stand up here, and pour out the feelings of his great heart, in his rich and mellow, and deep voice. . . . I regard him as the man of America."[35]

Stasis and Maneuver, 1852–1854

Entering another presidential election year, it seemed the old was dying but the new could not yet be born. Again, the Whigs united around a southern military hero with a vaguely antislavery reputation, General Winfield Scott, but the Democrats under New Hampshire's Franklin Pierce, a true "Northern Man with Southern Principles," won overwhelmingly. In New York, men like Douglass and Myers cast around distractedly, showing up everywhere but never making their commitments unequivocal.

Douglass had moved on from formal antielectoralism. By now, he was a will-o'-the-wisp, attaching himself to different antislavery parties, always keeping his options open. He attended the Liberty Party's national convention in September 1851 as a delegate, served on a committee, and gained election to its twelve-person National Committee, but the following August, he spoke at the Free Democratic Party's convention, and afterward announced, "We shall, perhaps, surprise some and grieve others when we declare now, our fixed purpose to support with whatever power we possess, JOHN P. HALE for President and GEORGE W. JULIAN for Vice-President . . . the candidates unanimously nominated by the 'Free Democratic' party at Pittsburgh." Having promised "to the free Democracy the aid of our pen, voice and vote," he added a characteristic disclaimer: "This pledge . . . is given with the distinct understanding, that, should these gentlemen in accepting their nomination write letters of a compromising character, we shall drop them and take up such as are already in the field, by the action of a small division of the Liberty Party."[36]

Douglass's double-game was modest in comparison to Myers's frank hedging of bets. In spring 1852, he announced his support for three possible candidates: "We say, if there is no chance for Gerrit Smith . . . or John P. Hale, we would like to see the best man selected as the nominee for president. We would like to see a man of liberal and independent views, in favor of the largest liberty selected from the two great political parties; that man we believe, will be Major General Winfield Scott," Seward and Weed's candidate. As late as August, Myers' Whiggism was on display, intimating that the general sentiment was to renominate Washington Hunt for governor, and reprinting "Henry Clay's Address to Young Men." In September, however, Myers displayed an impressive all-partyism. He began by saluting the Free Democrats' Pittsburgh convention, and reprinted Douglass's endorsement of Hale, saying, "We select this, because it is just what meets our views," putting Hale and Julian on his masthead. Just below, however, was a notice for the "Liberty Party Convention" followed by "Our Recent Movements. We left Albany, in company with William H. Topp, to attend the liberty party convention at

Peterboro. We arrived there on 1 September," noting the other black men present, and that he, Douglass, and Topp all spoke. Without blushing, these same three then went to Syracuse for "the Ratification Meeting of the Free Democracy" endorsing Hale and Julian, where Myers spoke, "expressing sympathy with its action, and offering for its use the columns of his paper, the *Telegraph and Temperance Journal.*" *Frederick Douglass' Paper* reported what Myers omitted, that the "Free Democracy of the First Assembly District at Hudson, Columbia Co., elected Stephen Myers, of Albany, editor of the *Telegraph and Temperance Journal*, their representative to the State Convention at Syracuse."[37]

Election Day 1852 in Brooklyn offers a snapshot of why the black vote counted enough that Democrats would try to steal it. Since 1841, the black sections of Kings County, in particular Williamsburg (first a village within the town of Bushwick, then its own town in 1840, then a city in 1852), had backed the Liberty Party. Apparently, that support continued into the 1850s. Local Democrats saw a way to get those several hundred votes by buying off Dr. Peter Ray, brother of Charles B. Ray, to deceive them with false printed tickets ("Liberty" at the top, listing Democrats' names below). Selling one's vote was an old tradition, but in this case, black voters were "led into evil, by the treachery of one of their number," although they had "the merit of intending to do right, and, unlike a large proportion of the whites of New York and its vicinity, are above selling their votes, and are indignant at having them sold for them."[38]

Leaving Dr. Ray's chicanery aside, Douglass's and Myers's multiple engagements were not simply opportunistic. They represented a sophisticated understanding of their role as arbiters of antislavery probity within an increasingly disaggregated party system. If a man like Myers could maintain his relationship with powerful Whigs like Weed while expressing his affiliation with more radical options, he signaled that neither he nor those like him could be captured: in a visible sense, more power to them.

There was a peculiar, static feeling to politics between Pierce's November 2, 1852 victory, confirming the Slave Power's control of the federal government, and the Kansas-Nebraska Act's passage on May 30, 1854, which threw the entire party system onto the rocks. Prior to that moment, all waited for some break, with Douglass writing Seward soon after Pierce's inauguration, "The political parties are much out of joint. The peace of the Democratic party is, evidently, but a patched up affair. It is, simply, a putting new wine into old bottles. The Whig party has failed, and fallen to pieces. *You*, my dear Sir, have the organizing power, and have the voice to command and give shape to the cause of your country, and to the cause of human liberty. For my part, I long to see the day when it shall be proclaimed, from one end of this Union, to the other, that *Wm. H. Seward* is no longer a member of the old Whig party, but is at the head of a great party of freedom, of justice, and truth," a prescient forecast.[39]

Outside of electoral politics, abolitionism's familiar "agitation" persisted, its annual cycles of local and regional conventions, bazaars, lectures, and memorials disconnected from Whig and Democratic infighting. In New York, the Democrats surged back to power, with Horatio Seymour easily winning the governorship in 1852, while the Whigs came under siege from Know-Nothings and temperance forces. Nativism, in particular, drew in the majority of downstate Whigs, horrified by the specter of New York City's immigrant majority, and dismayed by Sewardism's antislavery focus. Conservative Whigs operated in a party in which "a sizable majority . . . were, in fact, Seward enthusiasts," so most "flocked to the American party" in 1854–55, by their departure paving the way for a unified antislavery organization under the name "Republican."[40]

The 1854 gubernatorial race documents this partisan fracture, with five candidates competing on a larger number of tickets. An obscure western New York Whig, Myron Clark, represented the anti-liquor groundswell as the candidate of the Whigs plus the Anti-Nebraska, Anti-Rent, Free Democratic, and Temperance Parties, prevailing with 33.38 percent of the electorate, a 309 vote margin, over the Soft-Shell Democratic incumbent Seymour (33.32 percent), the American Daniel Ullmann (26.03 percent), and the Hard Shell Democrat, Greene Bronson (7.21 percent); the Liberty Party's William Goodell received a paltry 289 votes. An indication of the time's unsettled quality was the *New-York Tribune*'s spreading the rumor that Douglass might get the Whig nomination to fill Gerrit Smith's unexpired congressional term. It came to nothing, but the fact that an editor of Greeley's standing would float this notion suggests the break-up of conventional political understandings.[41]

Yet even within abolitionism's routine, progress was made. In New York City, citadel of anti-abolitionism, the rising black middle class won a signal civil rights victory, blocking the onset of legally sanctioned segregation in the North's metropolis. This triumph mixed up various identities, leading to the vindication of feminine respectability as a marker of class and gender over ethnicity and race. On Sunday, July 16, 1854, the schoolteacher Elizabeth Jennings, daughter of the respected Thomas Jennings, left home for the First Colored Congregational Church, where she played the organ. She tried to board the Third Avenue streetcar, although people of color were only guaranteed admission to specially marked omnibuses. What ensued was the usual ugly scene faced by black men and women who believed they had rights. The conductor, aided by a policeman, threw her off the car, beat her, and tore her dress. But Jennings, her father, and his associates, led by the Reverend J. W. C.

Pennington, would not tolerate such an assault. They took the company, the conductor, and the driver to court, and in spring 1855 won major damages, $225 plus costs. The company, fearing further lawsuits, desegregated its lines, and by the Civil War the other Manhattan lines had followed suit.[42]

Jennings is sometimes cast as Rosa Parks's forerunner, but that misses the subtext of what she said to the conductor, what New York's Whig newspapers said about her, and what black people around the nation heard. The key dialogue, savored by all, was Jennings putting the conductor in his place. She told him he was "a good for nothing impudent fellow," demanding to know where he was from, to which he replied, "I was born in Ireland." Her response suggested confidence in her class standing, "that he was none the worse or better for that, provided he behaved himself and did not insult genteel persons." This self-assurance was not misplaced, since she won the case outright, as an educated, Christian gentlewoman regardless of complexion. Greeley's *Tribune* commented that the decision confirmed the rights of "respectable colored people" versus "German or Irish women, with a quarter of mutton or a load of codfish," a pointed sally given the ubiquitous slander that black people smelled so horribly no white person could endure them. The case reverberated nationally, as Pennington and McCune Smith founded a Legal Rights Association and published a "NOTICE" in *Frederick Douglass' Paper*, announcing to black Americans "1. That all our public carrier-conveyances are now open to them on equal terms. 2. No policeman will now, as formerly, assist in assaulting you. 3. If any driver or conductor molests you, by laying the weight of his finger upon your person, have him arrested, or call upon Dr. Smith . . . Mr. T. L. Jennings . . . or myself . . . and we will enter your complaint at the Mayor's office. 4. You can take the conveyances at any of the Ferries or stopping places. Ask no questions, but get in and have your five cents ready to pay. Don't let them frighten you with words; the law is right, and so is the public sentiment." Pennington subsequently sent men to court arrest on other lines and bring suit, generating an angry denunciation by the Sixth Avenue line's secretary to Mayor Fernando Wood.[43]

Republican Convergence, 1855–1860

Beginning in early 1855, most of the Empire State's antislavery forces converged in the new Republican organization. The long-held hope for a "Northern party" capable of winning power was realized, and with it, full participation by the state's black men. Although equal suffrage was not achieved until the Fifteenth Amendment's passage in 1870, the years leading to Lincoln's victory document the maturation of New York's black politics, a realization of the political capital invested since 1837.

Across the North, the Republican Party emerged from the "Anti-Nebraska" coalitions formed for the 1854 elections. Each state party differed in the relative influence of Whigs, Know-Nothings, Free Democrats, and old Liberty men, and how many Democrats broke ranks to join their historic enemies. The various groupings calling themselves "Republican" unified at a June 1856 convention in Philadelphia to nominate a ticket of California's senator John C. Frémont and New Jersey's senator William Dayton. All of these organizations looked to New York because of its outsize weight in national politics, and Seward's prominence in the Senate. Since entering that chamber in 1850, he had become a principal figure defining the debate between American slavery and American freedom, while remaining a Whig powerbroker. In New York, the new party's coalescing was relatively simple: it was essentially Whig, as outside of Manhattan and Brooklyn "their entire party apparatus had moved into it virtually unchanged," including nearly all Whig papers and officeholders. Shorn of conservatives like Fillmore and Washington Hunt, joined by Free Democrats, ex–Liberty men, and some Barnburners, this was the party that entered the fray against slavery—and sometimes for black political rights.[44]

Phyllis Field's 1982 *The Politics of Race in New York* is still the definitive account of the black suffrage campaign's interaction with party politics, although recent attention has focused on Gerrit Smith's Radical Abolitionist Party (RAP), also founded in 1855, with some significant black participation. The RAP was the Liberty Party under a new name, and a useful goad to the Republicans, but focusing on this small group misses a more profound development: the public and private alliance between the state's black political class and the Republican machine commanded by Thurlow Weed, a relationship much deeper than black participation in the Whig, Liberty, and Free Soil Parties. As an openly antislavery party able to win state elections, the Republicans were genuinely new, and in power their legislators repeatedly voted as a bloc in favor of equal rights. In response, New York's black Republicans generated a statewide effort, the New York State Suffrage Association, "designed as a Negro political party for the state," with Douglass as its formal head, and the team of Stephen Myers and William J. Watkins as its operational center, with Watkins privately employed by Weed to gin up white abolitionists and black men to cast Republican ballots.[45]

The Republicans' ideological and geographic bases outline how 1855–60 differed from what came before. From 1847 to 1854, the Whigs, even with overwhelming legislative majorities, ignored black suffrage petitions. The 1846 referendum had exposed the absence of an internal consensus for black suffrage, and even Whigs like Weed, who claimed their devotion to "Emancipation," saw no point in losing again. Following the Whigs' dissolution, a new consensus emerged. Opposition to the Slave Power's octopus-like control over national politics made black men's rights a litmus test for the ideals of northern republicanism. Closer to home, anxiety over corruption of the body politic by foreigners pervaded political discourse via the rise of the Know-Nothings. Incoherent on other issues, these ex-Whigs proposed barring foreigners from office, a voter registry to curtail illegal voting by aliens, literacy tests, and greatly increasing the period of naturalization. Within this charged frame, Field explains, black suffrage stood for the first-class citizenship reserved to native-born Protestants, a way to defy the South while repudiating Tammany Hall Democrats.[46]

What did this new consensus mean in practice? Legislation to eliminate the constitution's $250 freehold requirement was introduced in the Senate and Assembly every year from 1855 to 1860, and passed three times by large majorities in both. If the amending process had not been "extremely difficult, requiring approval by a majority of elected members of both houses of the legislature, publication of the proposed change three months before the next general election of state senators (chosen biennially), the consent of a majority of the legislators chosen in *that* election, and finally ratification by at least half of the eligible electorate," it could easily have been legislated, since the Republican caucus in Albany, elected mainly from central and western New York, was well to the left of the party's electorate. Downstate Republicans, whom the party needed to win statewide, were unconvinced by appeals to republican principle. They liked black men as fellow voters no more in 1860 than they had in 1846. This tension translated into a bewildering inconstancy, since Republican leaders could not afford to alienate either their abolitionist or conservative wings.[47]

The Beachhead, 1855–1856

The impetus for a renewed suffrage campaign was the collapse of stable two-party competition after 1853; in Field's summary, "Until 1860 fragmentation of the electorate remained the rule." Had the Democrats remained united, they would have kept winning, as in 1852–53, but their internal divisions were too deep, and for several years they ran competing tickets as "Hards" and "Softs." At the peak of disorder, the 1855 Assembly included five party groupings—sixty-seven Whigs, elected in that party's last gasp; fourteen Hard Democrats and an equal number of Softs, plus four Democrats not explicitly aligned with either faction; twenty-one Americans (Know-Nothings); and seven Free Democrats.[48]

It was this Assembly, full of soon-to-be Republicans elected as Whigs, that first passed suffrage. At its January 1855 opening, a petition arrived from black

Long Islanders. Referred to the Judiciary Committee, it seemed set to die, but a freshman Whig from historically antislavery Oneida County, Levi Blakeslee, offered a floor resolution for equal suffrage. Shortly after, Ben Field, a Yankee Whig from Orleans County, introduced a similar resolution in the Senate. In the anti-southern fervor produced by an official censure of the Kansas-Nebraska act, Field's bill passed, but was referred back to committee along with various nativist amendments and died, with a majority of "National [conservative] Whigs and budding nativists, those most hostile or indifferent to the slavery issue," voting for the referral. The Assembly proceeded differently. Blakeslee's amendment came to a vote and passed 66–34, "the first time a branch of the New York legislature had endorsed the principle of equal suffrage," with nearly all the Whigs voting yes. If there was a beachhead, this was it, although it took a long time to move off that beach.[49]

These legislative developments galvanized black leaders. On September 4, 1855, longtime Whigs and old Liberty partisans met in Syracuse to form the State Suffrage Association, with leadership divided between the city's Committee of Thirteen and Myers's network in the Upper Hudson (Poughkeepsie, Catskill, Kingston, Hudson, Troy, Albany, and Schenectady). This convention avoided any taint of party and focused on reviving the suffrage campaign. It implemented the unfulfilled hope of the 1840s to hire traveling "lecturers," with five experienced men assigned to specific regions (Watkins, Loguen, Myers, G. F. Iverson, and Charles B. Ray). It further recommended "the formation of suffrage and political leagues in every city or town where colored persons reside," to direct votes to sympathetic legislative candidates, and requested black clergymen to "impress upon their congregations the duty of using every means in their power to secure their political rights." A proposal to "recommend to the colored voters . . . wherever there can be found a competent colored person to nominate them to any and all the different offices in the gift of the people" was rejected, and Myers's proposal that Douglass be nominated in the Twenty-Seventh Senatorial District never acted upon.[50]

The convention's most important action was appointing Myers as the association's permanent lobbyist in Albany. He was the driving force for black political activism over the next five years, fostering relationships with Republican legislators, pressuring them to introduce bills, overcoming the roadblocks erected by cautious party leaders. As demonstrated by his earlier entrepreneurialism in the Florence Farming Association and publishing ventures, Myers could tap a well of support among the state's Whiggish bourgeoisie; as early as 1842 he noted in the *Northern Star* that he raised funds from "gentlemen in the city, who were not abolitionists by name, but abolitionists in heart. . . . I can always get money in this city to help slaves off." His influence was visible in early 1855 when he secured the Assembly chamber for Douglass through his job as steward of Albany's leading temperance hotel, the Delavan House. Douglass explained that Myers's "position at the Delavan, and sharing, as he evidently does, the cordial esteem of many members of the Legislature, enabled him to obtain the Capital for the purpose of the lecture, without opposition or difficulty."[51]

Myers's feat was linking Weed's party apparatus to the State Suffrage Association, as the latter's official representative, while representing the Republicans to the growing black electorate. As early as October 1855, he spoke for the Republicans to the "colored electors of Catskill" in Greene County. Even the location of this meeting suggests a new empowerment, since the river counties had long been dominated by reactionary Anglo-Dutch Democrats. By 1855, however, the potential black electorate was 367 or 5.3 percent of the county's 6,952 voters. Underlining his dual role, only weeks before, Myers set up an affiliate of the State Suffrage Association in Dutchess County.[52]

What was the source of Myers's influence? How did he get state senators to introduce bills and chivy legislative committees to overcome their worries about electability? As the quotation above "money . . . to slaves off" help suggests, the key to Myers's relationship with white businessmen and politicians was his Underground Railroad (UGRR) work, combining illegal direct action with aboveground partisan politics, displaying fugitives in public to enhance his authority. Public documents bearing his name, private correspondence with party and business leaders, and hostile eyewitnesses all testify to Myers's backing from prominent whites. He mailed out fund-raising "Circulars" on letterhead listing the address of the Albany Anti-Slavery Office, signed "S. Myers, Conductor of the Underground Railroad." He wrote men like John Jay II as the "Superintendent" (a title the *New York Times* also granted him, without irony) requesting a renewal of his regular subvention, and his funders included Weed, Seward, Republican governors John A. King and Edwin Morgan, Horace Greeley, and Weed's backers in New York City's mercantile class, including Simeon Draper (president of the Bank of Commerce, chairman of the New York Republican State Committee in 1860–62, collector of the Port of New York in 1864–65), Moses Hicks Grinnell (president of the Chamber of Commerce and of the Merchants Clerks' Savings Bank, Lincoln's host on his 1860 campaign visit, also collector of the port in 1869–70), and Robert Bowne Minturn, a prominent shipper, all contributing $10 to $25 per year, in Weed's case $100, no small sum.[53]

Myers clearly enjoyed the pleasures of defiance. In February 1858, the Albany correspondent of the New York *Journal of Commerce* recorded his disgust at seeing "six runaway negroes marched through the streets under the protection of Stephen Myers, a black man, who claims to be the President of the 'Underground Railroad,' but who is really the agent of an Abolition organization which occupies itself in running off darkies from New York to Canada. . . . After visiting the office of a distinguished anti-slavery gentleman, who at present holds a political appointment of responsibility in New York," the fugitives "were conducted to the side door of a leading Free Soil journal," which could only be Weed's *Evening Journal*. This story was reproduced nationwide and in several prominent southern papers. Slaveholders had their outrage stoked, but Myers paraded his charges for local consumption, to remind white Republicans they had sworn to protect the fugitive, and this resolve was backed by their party's leaders. The UGRR was thus far more than a humanitarian project, or direct action against slavery. It was also an intensely politicized bridge into white homes, families, and wallets. Helping slaves to British soil while proclaiming that act in print and manifesting it on the state capital's thoroughfares documented how interracial solidarity undermined slaveholders' property rights. To publish a missive from Seward endorsing a meeting was a routine transaction, as were the enthusiastic reports on the UGRR in Weed's *Journal*. To send cold, frightened families to Auburn, expecting the senator to house them in his barn and feed them, however, was a demand cloaked in deference. Myers's feat, as with Robert Morris in Boston, or John Mercer Langston in Oberlin, was to translate these personal acts into partisanship and move them onto the electoral and legislative terrain. There, Myers excelled, "the industrious and almost ubiquitous Steve," a black reporter dubbed him in 1855, hailed as "the colored member of the Senate *and* Assembly!" by William J. Watkins after Myers arranged for him to address the legislature in 1859, extolled for his "ceaseless vigilance" by the Reverend J. Sella Martin, a black Garrisonian who otherwise viewed conventional politics with disgust.[54]

Myers's personal influence came through years of slogging. He began lobbying for a suffrage bill in 1856, which proved a holding action, since the November 1855 elections had stalled the Republican tide. The Americans won all statewide offices and a large share of the legislature. For the moment, there was no majority party in New York, as Republicans kept half of the Senate (sixteen seats) versus twelve Americans and just four Democrats, while the Assembly had forty-seven Democrats of various sorts, forty-four Americans, a mere thirty-five Republicans, and two Whigs. It took forty-nine ballots over sixteen days to elect a Democrat as speaker, and then only by exhausted agreement. No suffrage bill would pass this house, so attention shifted to the Senate, where Myers convinced Samuel Cuyler, a former Liberty man and devoted abolitionist representing Seward's home base in Cayuga County, to move a suffrage resolution despite it not having been reported out of committee. The debate on Cuyler's bill indicates how the ground had shifted, with even some Know-Nothings pro-suffrage. Erastus Brooks, a New York City American, moved to add "a good moral character" and the ability "to read any article of the Constitution, or any section of the statutes of the State," qualifications aimed at immigrant voters. Another American, James Ferdon, from Putnam, Rockland, and Westchester, attacked Cuyler for discovering "the greatest things in the world—Temperance, and the right of negroes to the elective franchise," but proposed permitting "every citizen . . . who can read and write" to vote. A downstate Democrat-turned-Republican, Edward Madden, acknowledged his change of heart. He would vote for expunging the property qualification after voting to keep it in 1846, since the black man is "with us and of us." Finally, the Tammanyite Dan Sickles spoke for the hard-core Democrats, "ridiculing the amendments and contending that there was no necessity for the resolutions, as the people, when voting for the Constitution of 1846 gave an emphatic approval to the 'Qualification clause' [the free-hold requirement for black men] and their sentiments had not changed."[55]

In prior years, a debate on black suffrage would have excited press attention, but it drew little in 1856, other than an upstate Republican editor's comment, "Colored persons in this State as a rule, are far better qualified to vote than a certain other class who are manufactured into Electors after (and generally before) a five years' residence in the Country, without being seized of a freehold of $250." The great dramas of spring 1856 were far removed from New York's legislative halls. In May, violence broke out in both Washington and Kansas. On May 21, a proslavery militia sacked Lawrence, capital of the Kansas "free staters," and guerrilla war broke out across the territory. The fighting spilled onto the national stage the next day, May 22, when South Carolina congressman Preston Brooks attacked Senator Charles Sumner, beating his head in with a gold-tipped cane to southern plaudits. A few nights later, in retaliation for Lawrence, John Brown led a group that massacred five proslavery men near Pottawatomie, Kansas. These shocks gave Republican radicals great momentum, as "Bleeding Kansas" and bloodied Sumner pulled in Democrats and Know-Nothings, propelling "a united outpouring of moral energy" for Frémont that was "almost frightening in its intensity."[56]

The 1856 campaign put black Yorkers in a difficult position, compelled to choose between their benefactor Gerrit Smith and Frémont, attractive to Republican kingmakers because of his military record. Smith's Radical Abolition Party formed in June 1855 declaring it alone would implement immediate emancipation using constitutional means, and did not "propose to sever the free from the slave States, and thus leave the slaves in hopeless bondage, or subject them to the necessity of achieving their emancipation by bloody insurrection." Like the Liberty Party, the RAP foregrounded black leadership, with McCune Smith signing the initial call and chairing its founding convention.

Douglass, Garnet, Watkins, and Loguen attended its National Nominating Convention in May 1856, and Douglass was briefly considered as a vice presidential nominee, but as a New Yorker he could not run alongside Smith. Also like the Liberty Party, however, most black participation was at the top, and its 1856 convention call, signed by hundreds from many states, included almost no men of color. In fall 1856, the Radical Abolitionists' appeal to black voters consisted largely of denunciations of how "the colored people, led on by Frederick Douglass" (who had defected to the Republicans along with Garnet and Watkins), were "preparing to run into *such* a party [the Republicans], as they never did into any other," remembering bitterly how the Liberty Party alone had advocated "the equal rights of free colored citizens," yet it never "received a tithe of the votes of colored voting citizens." In the final poll, Smith received a mere 165 votes in his own state.[57]

The State Suffrage Association went all-in for Frémont, helped by party funding, since they now had enough voters to matter. This was not a rerun of past Whig efforts, but a red-hot campaign. All of the state's black leaders other than McCune Smith and Loguen backed the Republicans, and grassroots meetings were ardently pro-Republican. Douglass dropped the Radical Abolitionists in mid-August, campaigning around the nation for Frémont, much noticed by Democrats. Garnet, who had always derided accommodation to majoritarian strategies, led the same move at a state convention in Rev. William J. Hodges's church in Williamsburg that month. While the Republican Party "was not all they desired . . . so far as it goes it was right." He was not always so restrained. "In the midst of his speech at Clifton" during a First of August celebration, he stopped and "called for three cheers for Frémont." After he got them, he added some truly Black Republicanism: "We believe—whites and blacks—that God has ordained to the colored race in this country, liberty; and liberty we intend to have. We intend to get it at the ballot-box, if we can. If we cannot get it there, we are resolved to use the SWORD, and THE SWORD TO THE HILT!" When it was over, Frémont carried New York and the Greater New England states with one-third of the national poll, and Watkins wrote Weed in exultant and exhausted tones, "The battle has been fought, the victory has been won. The Right has triumphed. . . . For God was with us in the struggle" but, still, "John C. Frémont is not to be the next President of the Republic." He had "worked hard to influence" his fellow black men, but "the establishment was still doing all they could to crush me," presumably meaning Gerrit Smith and his allies. It was clear for whom he labored: "Now, Mr. Weed, all that I have, to seek of those [on] whose behalf I have faithfully worked, day and night, is to help me in my present extremity. I spent of the money I received from you but $28 for my own personal wants. Will you please see Wm Johnson . . . in order that I may see a little 'material aid' in view of my labors, and also the position in which the stand that I have taken has involved me."[58]

The passions of 1856 were hardly abated by James Buchanan's decisive victory, and the assumption of his supporters plus the 21 percent of the electorate that backed the American Party's Millard Fillmore that this result reaffirmed sectional comity. What came next was more polarizing than anything heretofore—a newly made constitutional justification for slavery and white supremacy as organic to American nationhood. As an editorial in Weed's *Evening Journal* stated before Christmas 1856, the suit by the former slave Dred Scott could have momentous consequences. It had been converted into a "politically contrived plan, for acquiring the influence of the Supreme Court of the United States to these new Democratic claims for the benefit of Slavery—1st. That the owner of human beings can lawfully sojourn with them in a Free State, and maintain his claims to them as his 'chattels,' the laws of that State or the Law of Nations to the contrary notwithstanding. 2d. That men of color, though gifted as Fred. Douglass, Ward, McCune Smith, or Garnet, or as gifted as angels in virtue and intelligence, are *not* 'citizens' of the United States." The shock of Roger Taney's March 1857 decision would radicalize reluctant whites and bring them into the "party of freedom." In New York, Taney's abrogation of black citizenship was seen as an attack on men like those named by the *Journal*, good republicans with whom good Republicans should be proud to be associated.[59]

1857: The Year of Confusion

The year 1857 was either a comedy of errors played by feckless Republican leaders or a cruel joke played on New York's black political class, showing the limits of their influence. Driven by Frémont's victory with 46 percent in a three-way race, the Republicans swept 1856's election: a Senate majority of nineteen over nine Democrats and four Americans, and domination of the lower House with eighty one assemblymen, versus thirty-eight Democrats and eight Americans. The new Republican governor, John A. King, was Rufus King's son. Despite this solid Republican front, after the equal suffrage amendment passed through the legislature, it was then lost or sabotaged at the executive level, missing the deadline for publication three months before the November 3, 1857 election.

In mid-February, Senator Cuyler again introduced his amendment, denouncing the property qualification as "so manifestly unjust and oppressive; so perfectly at variance with the genius of our institutions and the doctrines of democratic equality." In a state where many white men had heard "Douglass, Ward, McCune Smith, or Garnet" speak, the freehold requirement fell "with redoubled force upon the refined, the intellectual and aspiring," since it was "based solely upon complexion, a circumstance *entirely* beyond [a man's] control." The appeal to class was direct, that such a man was "forced to see oft times the *vile*, the *drunken* and *abandoned*, assert and maintain his rights to vote . . . while *he* must receive in sorrow and in silence this deep disgrace, this high indignity." Finally, there was the sectional argument, that racial disfranchisement was "a relict of Slavery," passed "in obedience to the demands of Slavery, or in subserviency to a spirit engendered by that vile institution," and "if we mean to be honest *Democrats, Americans,* or *Republicans,* we will do all in our power to permit the colored man to stand up clad in all the rights of manhood," preserving "our institutions from the touch of the foul monster."[60]

Resolutions to amend the constitution passed on party-line votes, 21–5 in the Senate and 75–27 in the Assembly. The Republican press paid little attention, as equal suffrage was fodder for Democrats. The latter raised their usual war cries of a plot "to add ten thousand voters to the ranks of the Black Republicans of the State" via "a Black Regiment, which shall march through the breach in the State Constitution!," but the *Albany Evening Journal* and the *New York Evening Post* felt that George Downing's slashing rebuttal to Chief Justice Taney made for better press that spring.[61]

Then came the mysterious error, or betrayal. The suffrage resolution was forwarded to the governor, although it was the secretary of state's responsibility to publish it in time. The document languished unnoticed all summer in his secretary's desk—or so Republican editors and the governor claimed. Belatedly, the *Tribune* reported, "An awkward blunder has been made at Albany by somebody. . . . The publishing, it seems, has been neglected so far, and, as only two months remain before the election, it is now too late to comply with the technical requirement of the constitution." The case got murkier, however, after a Democratic paper reported that "the *Evening Journal,* in order to shift the responsibility of the suppression from the Republican managers, intimated that the Know Nothing Secretary of State, Mr. Headley," was responsible. To repel the charge, that official investigated and found "that the amendment resolution was never in the Secretary of State's office at all; that the Republican clerks of the Senate and Assembly instead of sending it to that office, according to custom and as required by duty, sent it to the Executive Department . . . where it was found yesterday. Gov. *King suppressed it*—or at least, by inaction annulled." Indeed, "the most charitable view that can be taken . . . is that the Governor and his party had their minds so concentrated on 'Bleeding Kansas' and New York plunder, that he forgot and overlooked everything else." Weed's *Evening Journal* continued to claim simple incompetence, that the resolution was "transmitted, by mistake, to the executive. . . . The private secretary, separating the resolutions from the bills . . . by inadvertence, laid the former aside," where it had "laid unobserved ever since." Pinning blame on a lowly "deputy clerk of the senate," it conceded only that "republican officials" were guilty of "an unconscious neglect of duty."[62]

These claims excited glee from Democrats inside and outside the state, who accused Governor King of "gross neglect of a plain official duty" with "few parallels in the history of the State. Whether it was culpable and unpardonable carelessness . . . or a dislike to be brought to the level of the negro, will be long the subject of some doubt." The *New York Herald*, leading Democratic paper in the nation, exhibited its schadenfreude at the "Seward-Weed clique" realizing that the "measures of the last Legislature in behalf of negro suffrage . . . were going a little too far for the good of the party," so they were "coolly suffocated. . . . The Governor, or . . . Weed and his staff" decided "it is not judicious to give niggers an equal right to vote with white men." A Buffalo paper noted Republicans would now "escape the odium of submitting to the people what could not fail to be a most unpopular measure," and it might be just "a trick, as many people shrewdly suspect."[63]

Since Myers had stopped publishing his weekly, *Frederick Douglass' Paper* was the state's only black editorial voice. At first, Douglass expressed a mix of disappointment, disbelief, and uncertainty as to Republicans' responsibility, calling the "blunder" evidence of "disgraceful inactivity" and stipulating that "the passage of the Amendment last winter amounts to nothing. . . . So important a measure ought to have been attended to, and it would not have been suffered to die for want of the necessary preliminaries, if its pseudo friends had been sincere." Even if a "lamentable and culpable defection," if Republicans "in the ascendant, shall fail to expunge the Property Qualification clause . . . then they, amid all their professions of sympathy for the slave, are as 'a sounding brass, and a tinkling cymbal,'" hypocrites just as Democrats alleged: "We have spoken thus plainly, because plainness of speech is demanded by the exigency in which the negligence or something worse of our Republican Governor or Secretary of State, and the cool silence of our Republican journals have involved us." Two weeks later, Douglass published the *Evening Journal*'s official explanation, commenting that "some things were *not* forgotten by the parties alluded to in the statement, of minor importance in comparison with this. If the *Journal* and other Republican organs wish to make amends for their acknowledged neglect, let them break the significant silence they have so long maintained on this question. . . . This, we hope, they will *not* forget. This, they must not suffer to be 'stuffed away in the *pigeon holes*' of forgetfulness," a sarcastic reference to the secretary's desk.[64]

Douglass had signaled his watchful waiting, and others agreed. At a late September meeting in Manhattan, William J. Watkins advised, "As a people it was settled that they could not rely upon either of the three political parties." The Democrats had endorsed *Dred Scott*, and "of the 130,000 Americans, not 10,000 would vote for enfranchising the colored man. . . . As to the Republicans, not over two-thirds would give their votes in favor of wiping out of the Constitution the unjust and odious clause requiring a property qualification. It followed that the colored citizens must unite for their own defence—'Who would be free themselves must strike the blow.'" There it laid. Republicans blamed Know-Nothings, Democrats blamed Republicans, black men blamed all of them. In his next annual message to the legislature, Governor King counterattacked along partisan lines, regretting that "in the hurry of business . . . these resolutions were inadvertently sent to the Executive Chamber, among many other bills, and not requiring . . . the signature of the Governor, they were laid aside, and, not being called for by the proper officer," meaning Headley, "they were overlooked, and so failed to be published" in time. "Concurring entirely in the policy of these resolutions, I invite your consideration to the propriety of reenacting them."[65]

1858: Radicalism's Last Hurrah

The year 1858 was not auspicious for the amendment. The Republicans lost considerable ground in fall 1857, barely hanging on to a plurality in the Senate with fifteen seats versus fourteen Democrats and three Americans, and declining to a minority of sixty-one in the Assembly. It took another three-week deadlock for the Democrats to elect a Speaker in the latter. The likelihood of passage was thus nil unless all of the Americans voted with the Republicans, and the former were split. The main action became the fall governor's race, seen as dictating Republican chances to carry the state in 1860. Rebounding from 1857, the black leadership's decisions brought their political empowerment to a head. The issue was straight-out: would New York's black voters help elect another Republican governor, Edwin D. Morgan (a prominent businessman, chairman of the Republican National Committee in 1856–64, Weed's choice), or return to Gerrit Smith, running as the abolitionist and temperance candidate on the "People's Ticket?" The consequences were considerable. Party veterans knew the Liberty Party's base vote in the 1840s was 15,000, virtually all white. If Smith pulled those votes and added a black electorate of 6,000 to 10,000, plus the thousands who had backed Myron Clark in 1854 as the Temperance Party candidate, the potential for spoiling was obvious; Democrats piled on, urging black men to show their support for Smith or face charges of "ingratitude."[66]

The prospect of Smith receiving the 50,000 votes he expected gave Republicans pause. As Greeley's *Tribune* put it, "We regard Mr. Smith as a good man engaged in a very bad business. Just as in 1844, he and a few like him, by drawing off 15,000 Anti-Slavery votes from Clay and Frelinghuysen, elected Polk and Dallas, and secured Texas to the Slave Power in our Union, at the cost . . . of a most needless and unjust war with Mexico." Now, he was "doing all in his power to throw New York once more under the wheels of the Juggernaut of Slavery Propagandism, elevating to power the most debauched and unprincipled faction that ever existed—to wit, the 'Soft' Democracy. . . . Every vote he receives over a thousand will be subtracted from the poll of the Republicans, as he and his backers must know."[67]

The appeal made on Smith's behalf to black voters was entirely personalistic. He was their "old tried friend, champion, and benefactor. . . . No man living has more completely identified himself with you, and your rights and interests. . . . In every respect he will claim the same rights for you that he claims for himself. To elect him would be as great a victory for you as to elect one of your own number." Simultaneously, however, as in 1844, 1846, 1848, and 1856, those who did not accept his leadership were rebuked as corrupt. The Liberty Party warhorse William Goodell, now editor of the *Radical Abolitionist*, bemoaned how Greeley's *Tribune* was "in extacies [*sic*] to find a few colored men foolish, or mercenary, or servile enough to be bought into their party. . . . Already your bitterest and most contemptuous enemies are chuckling over the fact that certain persons of your number have come out for Morgan. . . . Already, as formerly in old Whig times, they are quoting it in evidence that you are not Abolitionists . . . that you are not opposed to the Fugitive Slave bill; that you do not seek equality of suffrage with the whites."[68]

This rehashing ignored how much had changed since "old Whig times," whether the overwhelming Republican legislative majorities for "equality of suffrage," or the practical tenders Republicans made to black men. Smith did not hire black lecturers to promote his People's Ticket or issue broadsides aimed at voters of color, as he did with German-speakers. The *Radical Abolitionist* and his campaign newspaper, the *Gerrit Smith Banner*, rarely addressed the people of color directly. The latter printed "9 Reasons Why You Should Vote for Gerrit Smith," including "To put down the Rum Traffic," with no mention of black suffrage, and then belatedly added the next day what he would do for them: "He would TRY to protect them" from kidnappers, certainly "more than any Governor of the State has yet done," followed by a slander on the Reverend Hodges, suggesting he opposed Smith because of the latter's "advocacy of liquor prohibition." Hodges and his brother fired back via the Republican press. The *Evening Post* announced a "Colored Men's Ratification Meeting in Brooklyn . . . Gerrit Smith Repudiated," where Willis

Hodges declared their independence. "They must stir, and move, and work for [political rights] themselves. . . . He sometimes thought they would get along a great deal better if there were not any abolitionist white men. These men take all the meat and give shucks to the colored people. Gerrit Smith was a great abolitionist. He wants them all to vote for him, because he is a great friend of the colored race. But he knows it is all foolishness. If the eleven thousand colored people should vote for him, and so give the election to the Democrats, the slaveholders would all say that it was the voice of New York for slavery. . . . Mr. Morgan was a good friend to colored people. He will go for giving them their rights, for letting them vote, and be allowed to hold office." His brother "moved that they should have frequent meetings. . . . He meant to pull the lion's beard. If Gerrit Smith defeated Mr. Morgan, he would have no more to do with him."[69]

A final squib "TO COLORED VOTERS" captured the Radical Abolitionists' patronizing tone: "Will you betray your only reliable friend now, at the only time you can manifest your gratitude for the sincere interest he has always taken in your welfare? Which candidate for Governor would defend your rights and Liberties with his own blood, if necessary?" Smith's record made no difference: the black electorate went for the party not the man, helped by Seward's momentous October 25 speech in Rochester, "The Irrepressible Conflict," declaring that "the United States must and will, sooner or later, become either entirely a slave-holding nation or entirely a free-labor nation." The *National Era* crowed that this "stopped everything like a diversion of the Republican vote to Gerrit Smith, even if there was any serious movement that way before." Beyond arguments of practicality, many black men were not as "radical" as Smith, who added to his antislavery and anti-rum policies a pure Jacksonian laissez-faire regarding tariffs, trade, and immigration. Just before the election, the *Post* reported on a meeting of the Hodgeses' "Colored American Morgan Association" where William Hodges attacked Smith's free trade stance, "as it prevents laborers in this country from obtaining work, and gives it all to people in other countries that are opposed to ours. This country is ours as well as the white man's, and it is our duty to work and vote for its prosperity." Regarding Smith's opposing more stringent naturalization, he would also "take issue with him there. The doctrines of the American party on that subject were right. We ought to have such a law to protect our citizens from foreign influence, which operates against our free institutions, and foreign competition, which works badly against our laboring community."[70]

Versus Smith's noblesse oblige, Weed's Republicans made a systematic effort. In September 1858, black Republicans called a statewide meeting to make their constituency a solid phalanx. Facing opposition from Garnet and McCune Smith, Watkins pushed through a denunciation of Smith as a tool of the Democrats coupled with why the Republicans deserved support, since "securing the elective franchise" required "the defeat of the so-called Democratic party, our most inveterate enemy." He declared, "We regard the Republican party, all things considered, as more likely than any other to effect this desirable end, and advise the eleven thousand colored voters of this State to concentrate their strength upon the Republican ticket. . . . We do not for a moment endorse all the tenets of that party; we are Radical Abolitionists, and shall ever remain so; but we regard [Smith's] nomination . . . as calculated to give aid and comfort to the enemy, by electing the Democratic candidate." Garnet reported to Smith that the convention was "packed by Republican influences" and "Republicans showered their money upon" it to secure endorsement: "Watkins, poor Watkins, went over to the enemy, and is employed as their agent to stump the State for the Republicans." Watkins himself wrote Smith to insist, "I have no more changed my Radical Abolition Principles than did the majority of Radical Abolitionists who voted for Frémont. . . . It is with me a question of Policy, as well as of Principle; and I maintain that we may when a great end is sought to be attained, consult the genius of Expediency, without sacrificing one iota of moral Principle." He was firm: "I have not been 'sold' to the '*Prince of the State Regency*' [meaning Thurlow Weed], nor even hired by him, or any one else. . . . I wish you had been nominated by the Republican Party. As it is, I think my duty lies in the direction I have taken." This was fundamentally deceptive. Shortly after, Watkins boasted of meeting with Weed in an October 7 letter to the *Tribune*, attacking John Thomas, editor of another Smith paper, the *Hour and the Man*: "I have been '*closeted with the Prince of the State Regency!*' *Mirabile dictu!* Can it be that Mr. Watkins, '*a colored man*,' has had this greatness thrust upon him? It is even so. Now, what *will* become of the Union? . . . I wished before entering upon my duties, to converse with men whom I know to be truer friends to the black man than some who, though very loud in professing adherence to the principle, do not see fit to crystallize their professions into practical life." He had, indeed, been "hired by" Weed, but that relation remained behind the scenes.[71]

Publicly, Watkins (known as the "New York Thunderer") went after Smith in language few white men had ever heard from a black man. Writing Greeley at the *Tribune* ("your widespread and invaluable journal"), whose readership was then approximately 1.5 million, he stated that, while there was "no man living whom I more highly respect" than Smith, "his nomination . . . must operate disastrously upon the hopes of the disfranchised colored citizens," since the Democratic Party was "the black man's most determined and efficient enemy, a consolidated despotism which must be utterly overthrown." Watkins would not "join in any movement which, for any reason whatever, is welcomed . . . by the Buchanan Democracy." His authority came from black not white: "I was elected by the Troy Convention to canvass the State" for the Republicans, and he disdained "the imperative edicts of presumed superiority, or the vulgar insinuations of pampered insolence." Watkins repeated his insult at an Ohio meeting after Morgan's victory, insisting, "He held himself to be a free man, and as such he would not suffer the pampered insolence of any man . . . to dictate and control, and when Gerrit Smith said that all colored men who didn't vote for him, were wolves in sheeps clothing, he had simply to say that Mr. Smith had insulted his manhood." Attacks on eminent whites were Watkins's specialty, if one remembers his 1853 New Bedford speech damning Sumner and Wilson. His message was clear. What would later be called "solidarity" was welcome but conveyed no right of direction. Smith's day had passed. Black men still needed his money, but he could expect no more deference, certainly not from Watkins, who was invited to speak in the Assembly chamber soon after the Republicans' 1858 victory, with his lectures on "the Suffrage Question" promoted by Weed, the state's preeminent political manager.[72]

While Watkins toured the state promoting Morgan, Myers published the *Voice of the People*, taking the same hard line: "There is not the remotest chance of Mr. Smith's election. MORGAN WILL BE THE NEXT GOVERNOR. . . . We, the 11,000 colored voters of the State, must stand just where we can be of some service in the struggle. If we ever gain any political rights, we must look to the Republican party. . . . The Radical Abolitionists can do nothing for us now, and we have not time to wait till the millennium for the Right of Suffrage, or for Equal School Rights." Evidently, there was uncertainty among some black voters. The *Gerrit Smith Banner* reported a pro-Smith meeting at Brooklyn's Zion's Church which did not permit Watkins to speak, and Reverend Hodges defended himself in the *Tribune* after receiving letters "from my colored brethren in different parts of this State . . . inquiring of me the reason why I do not support the Hon. Gerrit Smith." He condemned Smith's radicalism, citing his stance "on calling out the State troops, in opposition to the enforcement of the Fugitive Slave Law, Woman's Rights, No Tariff, and no Naturalization laws. . . . If the colored people as a body should [back him] . . . our enemies would say that colored people were opposed to the Constitution and General Government. . . . They would say that we wanted our colored women to be legislatresses, and all parties would oppose our having the elective franchise on that ground." He then turned the charge of corruption around: "I therefore call upon our colored men not to embrace the pernicious doctrines of Gerrit Smith through the agents of the Democratic party or his colored Land Committee. These he has made his agents to try and deceive us, and induce us to sell our manhood as well as our birthright for a small quantity of land, money or favor."[73]

In 1858, black Yorkers occupied a momentarily privileged position, which internal disagreement only strengthened; no one could take for granted their "eleven thousand votes." Morgan's final margin over the Democrat Amasa Parker was 27,440 out of 555,073 votes, with the American Party candidate gaining 61,137, and large-scale defections by men of color would have placed the Republican at risk. Instead, Smith received a mere 5,470 votes, exactly 1 percent. Few abolitionists went for his forlorn hope after Seward's "Irrepressible Conflict" speech, which Smith conceded "did more than all things else to damage my prospects. It passed for an Abolition speech." The year 1858 was the last time abolitionists attempted to spoil an election, which had never appealed to most black voters, who preferred a party that could exercise actual power.[74]

Adding insult, one Louisana editor again got into the gutter about "Gerrit," the "chief among the niggers' friends," who had "given away scores of thousands of acres to the colored images of their Maker, dreaming fondly that his black brethren would settle upon the estates, thrive and raise up little darkies to worship Smith and vote the straight Abolition ticket," followed by minstrelish images of "the legs of some big runaway nigger thrust under his mahogany," and the "lazy nigger preachers [who] make a hotel of his mansion at Peterboro." Smith's betrayal by New York's black electors, the "nigger landholders" who "sold his bounty and spent the money in brass rings, red waistcoats, onions and whisky," was satisfying: the "sable ingrates refuse *en masse* to go for him! . . . Not a solitary nigger ballot can he get!" This southerner got one thing right: "the New-York darkies don't want to 'fro away' their votes." Like the Know-Nothings who had jumped to the Republicans, they too wished to "unite all the elements of opposition to the 'slave-driving Democracy.'"[75]

The Battle Joined, 1859–1860

The two years prior to Lincoln's election were chaotic but triumphal for New York's Republicans, black and white. The state was deeply identified with antislavery through Douglass and Seward, the South's twin bêtes noires, and both were linked to the October 1859 raid on Harpers Ferry. Papers found with John Brown exposed Douglass as his collaborator and he barely escaped southern justice. When "federal officers" arrived in Rochester, Lieutenant Governor Robert Campbell visited Douglass to warn him that Governor Morgan was obliged to honor an extradition request from Virginia. Douglass crossed the Canadian border forthwith, exciting the rage of Brown's executioner, Virginia governor Henry Wise. Seward, regarded by southerners as the raid's intellectual author, was attacked in lethal terms, with the *Richmond*

Whig running an advertisement offering $50,000 for his head. He added insult to injury by riposting to Representative William Smith after Harpers Ferry that "he was more than willing to accept free Negro voters from Virginia in exchange for the German and Irish voters in New York State who were such stubborn Democrats."[76]

In 1859, the Republicans finally achieved dominance in New York with Morgan's convincing victory in November 1858, gaining almost 46 percent of the vote for governor in a three-way race. Their 17–13 Senate majority (with two remaining Americans) increased to 23–9 in fall 1859, and they controlled the Assembly almost 3–1 with ninety-one seats in both years. It was in Republicans' power to pass equal suffrage, and they did, albeit with pushes from individual members rather than party leaders and constant pressure from their black constituents. Field's analysis here is to the point: the Republican hard base lay in western New York, including formerly Democratic counties along Pennsylvania, which shifted decisively in the 1850s. Many legislators from the west were open abolitionists like Cuyler, eager to denounce Democrats as the Slave Power's pimps. Typical was Allegany assemblyman Deacon E. Maxson, another UGRR conductor and former Liberty man. In early 1860, he slashed into Democratic "negro haters" on scientific grounds, asking "why a man with a large amount of coloring matter in the under layer of cuticle should not exercise the elective franchise on the same terms as those not distinguished by this cutaneous peculiarity." Equality of rights was "the genius of our government," and Democratic racialism was "in keeping with the dark spirit of the middle ages." The Maxsons and Cuylers pulled their party left, but Republican legislators from the downstate counties knew their voters were far from abolitionist. In this context of Republican uncertainty, only Myers's relentless lobbying, and his Suffrage Association publicly delivering thousands of votes to Morgan, produced legislative action.[77]

During these years, Watkins and Myers subdued any remaining third- or anti-partyism, insisting on a cold-eyed alliance with Republicans based on that party's access to power. Douglass repeatedly objected, but they did not back down, and the resulting polemics constitute the most sustained debate over black electoral politics before the Civil War. In early 1859, Douglass attacked the Republicans, tilting back to a purist radicalism, as was his wont. In reply, Watkins made the case for closing ranks, insisting, "Every word uttered, and every act performed by our leading men . . . should tend to the promotion of that harmony of action, and that continuity of effort, in our divided ranks, without which we have no right to expect success." Douglass needed to stop "berating, *ad nauseam*, those to whom we are constantly appealing for help. . . . We make ourselves supremely ridiculous, when, with a club as heavy as we can carry, we strike at the only men who have the power, politically, to place us . . . in a position which will give us influence, and command respect." Watkins spoke with personal authority: "No one sees more clearly than I do, the shortcomings of our 'Republican leaders.' . . . But knowing, as I have an opportunity to know, that those leaders of the party who have the Equal Suffrage movement committed to their legislative management and control, are right on the subject," it was unhelpful for men like Douglass to "denounce indiscriminately the leaders of the Republican party, thus throwing a stumbling block in the way of those of us who are still clinging to that party (unfaithful though it be)" so as to get a suffrage bill. He reminded Douglass of his 1856 arguments for Frémont: "Expediency does not always involve a compromise of moral principle, a dereliction of duty. If I mistake not, we were commanded in the good book to be as 'wise as serpents.'" Watkins concluded by describing how "during the past three weeks . . . I have addressed more than fifteen thousand of 'the people,' in behalf of the Equal Suffrage movement," and "Never before have I met with so cordial a reception," including his speech in the Assembly chamber, which was "densely crowded. Nearly every member of both houses was present," a reminder of his close relationship with party leaders like Weed.[78]

Douglass fired back, but Watkins was not having any of it. "My offense, in your eyes, seems to be in acting with the Republican party, in order to effect certain reforms. Well, what other practical thing can I do? How much have you done by voting for Garrett Smith [*sic*]? How much will you accomplish by voting for him in every election for a score of years to come? The only difference between us is, that one acts on the practical side of the question, and the other on the theoretic. . . . Every body knows that for the next generation, probably, either the Democrats or Republicans will rule the State and Union. . . . The only real question before a man seeking for the equal rights of all men is, shall I vote for the Republican party or for the Democratic party? All other talk is a waste of words—mere hair-splitting." He suggested Douglass was jealous, and turned "a cold shoulder upon" the suffrage campaign because "you are not very desirous that success should crown the special effort a few of us are now making." Watkins and Myers's disavowal of Smith in 1858 remained the sticking point: "The Republican party is not, Sir, what I desire it to be [but] I am not one of those who, calling themselves Radical Abolitionists, seem to fatten upon the inconsistencies of its leaders, and because of their want of moral stamina, consign them, along with 'Stephen, *the colored* Thurlow,' to '*utter darkness*.'" He charged that "the defeat of the *Colored Black Republican Equal Suffrage Movement* . . . is the consummation devoutly to be wished by you" since the "triumph of our movement" would justify "the course adopted by nearly all the colored voters" in 1858. Watkins added, "If what you say is correct," the Republican Party "is worse than modern Democracy," which was foolish. The Republicans had cohered around "the Idea of extending the area of Freedom," as "a political crystallization of that Anti-Slavery sentiment and feeling . . . smothered in the Whig and Democratic parties, and which at last, burst the cerements of corruption, and with God's sunlight flashing all around it, stood out like a promontory in the deep, blue sea, a monument of the second Revolution in our nation's history." He concluded with a nasty shaft, that Republicans had "accomplished *at least as much* practical good as those Radical Abolitionists who do little else but meet annually and quadrennially, to go through certain political motions as a compliment to the wealthy philanthropist from whom some of them are continually receiving evidences of '*distinguished consideration.*'"[79]

Douglass would usually bow to expediency, but Thomas Hamilton, editor of his new rival, the *Weekly Anglo-African*, maintained his distrust for the Republicans. In fall 1859, Watkins went at him too, insisting there were only "two parties . . . those who are . . . *opposed* to slavery [and] those who are *in favor of* this accursed evil." Admitting the Republicans were timorous, he insisted on electoralism's zero sum logic: "The Republican party is the only political party in the land in a position, numerically speaking, to strike a deathblow to American slavery. . . . It *must* do so in order to preserve its distinctiveness, its vitality. If it is not right, let Abolitionists strive to make it right . . . by going into the party and renovating and revolutionizing it." Hamilton remained unmoved. As late as March 1860, he suggested the Republican Party's "larger professions of humanity" made it "by far [the] more dangerous enemy. . . . Their opposition to slavery means opposition to the black man—nothing else," though he too would come around eventually.[80]

In early 1859, the proposed amendment passed through the legislature with little fanfare, although it took a personal intervention by Madison County senator John Foote, a friend of Gerrit Smith's, and a similar effort in the House, to force floor votes. It helped that Democrats had something more urgent to trouble them than an enlarged black electorate. The Republicans and Americans together backed a "Registry Bill" to challenge the thousands of illegal immigrant voters in New York City. An effective voter registration process had grave implications for Democratic standing, since Manhattan, with its seventeen seats, furnished between 30 percent and 41 percent of their Assembly delegation in 1856–60. Characteristically, Democrats (in this case James C. Rutherford, himself an immigrant) insisted that making men register was a plot by Know-Nothings and Republicans "in favor of placing a black nigger on a par with a white Irishman," with the latter concealing their intention because they "would not dare put themselves in opposition to the German Republicans of the State, however contemptuously they may be willing to treat the Irish."[81]

The Republican sweep in fall 1859 put equal suffrage on the table, as its second passage by the legislature mandated submission to the people. In March 1860, Myers used his powers of persuasion to slide suffrage through the legislature on a flash vote, with the *Anglo-African*'s correspondent noting that without his "efforts that morning with the committee," the suffrage bill "would have doubtless remained in their hands, not to be introduced this session." At that news, Hamilton reversed his position, noting that while some still "took occasion to upbraid" Myers and Watkins "with political chicanery in giving their support to the Republican Party," this deal-making made eminent sense. "We do not presume to say what understanding existed between these gentlemen and the Republican Party—we only know if it was the passage of the franchise resolutions, then the Republican Party is so far true to its pledges." Given the chance to convince the white majority to "declare whether they will make the State a pure democracy," the correct answer to "Men and brethren, shall we go in?" was emphatically *yes*. Readers should organize a "Franchise Club" anywhere with five black men, meet weekly, collect funds, and send their officers' names to the editor for forwarding to the State Suffrage Association.[82]

By then, black discourse had a harder edge, following Harpers Ferry and Brown's martyrdom, and they were not alone. Even the hardened politico Thurlow Weed wrote, regarding "Old Ossawattomie Brown," "Since the day when Paul spoke to Agrippa we have heard nothing more truly sublime than his response to the tribunal before which he stood to receive sentence of death." Politesse and caution were pushed aside. Black men declared their audacity in comments to packed meetings about "the beautiful Irish women with their black husbands and dazzling little babies" (the prevalence of such unions noted in an 1857 state report); the venerable Thomas Downing refusing a routine oath because Taney had declared him a noncitizen; Downing, when presented to Stephen A. Douglas visiting Newport, mocking the Democratic presidential candidate in his imperturbable fashion. On Election Day 1860, the always-Negrophobic *New York Herald* described how a streetcar conductor let a black man in from the rain, but "the darkey took advantage of the kind offer," saying "he had as much right there as anybody else, and he didn't want any of his impudence," and "after the 6th of November they'd show white folks how to treat colored people." Steven Hahn has documented rumors of insurrection running through the South around Lincoln's election, but this story suggests intimations of liberation were felt also in the North.[83]

More prosaically, in the months before 1860's election, the links between New York's black political apparatus and the Republican machine became increasingly public. Weed's *Journal* promoted Watkins's two-week upstate tour just before the election, and a Long Island Republican mass meeting included the Brooklyn leader (and former Liberty man) Sylvanus Smith and George Downing sitting on the dais as vice presidents. To keep pressure on the Republicans, a May 10, 1860 New York City convention staked out an independent position, that black men had "been depending on the Abolitionists of this State, and now upon the Republicans; but no men but ourselves can do our work for us." Watkins evoked John Brown to suggest that "one such movement as that in Virginia, is worth more than all our speaking," backing a resolution that they could only win "over the dead carcass" of the Democrats, but "there was also corruption" in the Republicans. This stance presumably reflected the requirements of unity, since Garnet and McCune Smith would never have participated in a strictly Republican convention. Smith maintained that line as president of the New York County and City Suffrage Association, writing Gerrit Smith for financial support and insisting, "Our organization steers entirely clear of party." In September, he demanded Myers desist from calling another statewide meeting, as "such a Convention may directly or indirectly identify the colored people with one of the leading political parties—which would be suicidal to the Suffrage cause" by attracting "the attention and hostility of the foreign vote and the Democrats . . . otherwise . . . busy enough with their own party quarrels." The suffrage campaign was obscured by the fervor for Lincoln, but it was the most aggressive operation African Americans organized before the war, including a grassroots network to get out the vote, massive literature distribution, and traveling lecturers. By the fall, there were forty-eight clubs in Manhattan alone, another eighteen in Brooklyn, and McCune Smith was mailing out tracts by the thousands.[84]

For black Yorkers, the final sprint to November 6, 1860 was paradoxical. There was little doubt Lincoln would carry the state. Running against a "Fusion" ticket uniting all the Republicans' opponents, Lincoln won New York 54–46 percent, a 50,000-vote victory. That certainty fueled black men's joy at helping defeat the Slave Power. Thomas Downing spent Election Eve reassuring his Democratic clients that, since Lincoln would win, they had nothing to lose, handing out pro-suffrage ballots along with specially curated oysters. Black leaders had no illusions, however, that all white Republicans would vote to end the property qualification; privately, McCune Smith told Gerrit Smith he had "heard from several other sources, that the vote against suffrage will be a diminished one," but "whatever the results, the movement is getting up a fine tone of thought and action especially among our young men." On Election Day, Greeley's *Tribune* printed a listing for where to obtain "Equal Suffrage Ballots" at black businesses in Manhattan and Brooklyn, along with dozens of articles promoting Republican candidates and assailing Democrats for importing felons, sailors, and those "lacking complete naturalization" to vote. The limits of Republican support for suffrage were evident in a letter from "OLD SUFFOLK" hailing the party's congressional candidate but noting that while "our County Committee has sent out only ballots *against* negro suffrage . . . we shall see that this Assembly District has the other sort also, in order that practical Christian voters may have a chance to uphold the Golden Rule."[85]

As always, Bennett's *Herald* campaigned hyperbolically, with a lengthy September disquisition on "THE NEGRO SUFFRAGE QUESTION. WILL THE PEOPLE SANCTION IT? Historical Account of the Subject from the Adoption of the Constitution of 1777. Opinions of Several of the Most Distinguished Men of New York, &c., &c., &c.," reproducing Erastus Root and Samuel Young's attacks from 1821 and insisting "the delegated representatives of the people, as well as the people themselves, have deliberately passed judgement," but "the abolitionists are not content, and will not submit to the voice of the people." It asserted there had never been any agitation against the property qualification, ignoring the flood of petitions since 1837. The referendum was merely a trick of the Republican Party, always ready to "embrace within its folds every faction and ism," including a manipulated "negro" vote, to get its hand on boodle ("Those fifty thousand negro votes are worth a mint of gold. With them, how comparatively easy it would be to fill the legislative halls at Albany with bodies of plundering scoundrels"). There was "not the least blame to be attached to the negroes themselves," since they were "sensible of their degradation, and consequent inferiority in a social position, and . . . perfectly content with their condition as assigned in the order of nature." Despite knowing the Downings, Bennett wrote that black people "desire no social equality, nor demand the right of voting, occupying public offices, enjoying political distinctions equal with the Anglo Saxon race. The thinking, reflecting portion of them are happy and content in their present position, as house servants, hotel waiters, ostlers, barbers, bootblacks, &c, &c." Sometimes the *Herald* dispensed with folderol, asserting simply that "the nigger votes are wanted again. . . . It remains to be seen whether a sufficient number of white men can be found . . . willing to consummate the act of self-degradation which will bring them down to . . . the same political status as the niggers of the Five Points."[86]

The Democratic assault on "niggerism" was unremitting. At their Manhattan "Monster Mass Meeting of Minute Men," the air was filled with songs like "they love the nigger, better than the red, white, and blue," and roaring speeches about how, for Republicans, it was "negro here, negro there, and negro everywhere." Azariah Flagg's *Plattsburgh Republican* ranted about "fantastic and wild Negro idolatry" as "the great dogma in the political faith of that party," now hoping to "attain by the votes of their black allies . . . the ascendancy that already trembles in their grasp." Why should "a foreign citizen, no matter how wealthy or intelligent," wait five years to vote, while "a negro fresh from the Everglades of Florida—or still more debased, a black denizen of the Five Points of N.Y. will, if this amendment be adopted be admitted at once to every immunity of citizenship"? Republicans would surely "attempt at some propitious period, to elevate a Negro to the seat of Washington and Jefferson!" since "if this amendment is adopted," the black electorate "may be counted hereafter by tens of thousands." White men in the Adirondacks should imagine an "array of Negro voters issuing in New York from their festering dens and the hiding places of crime and debauchery to pollute the ballot boxes and possibly to decide our State and National Elections!"[87]

The absence of Republican consensus was evident. In mid-September, the Republican *Commercial Advertiser* reproduced the *Herald*'s "Historical Account" of "THE NEGRO SUFFRAGE QUESTION" to support its insistence that "Mr. Lincoln's Views," including opposition to black suffrage, "were proof of his conservatism," guaranteeing "a peaceful, conservative and conciliatory administration." A few days later, even the *Tribune*, the epitome of "Black Republicanism," distanced itself from the suffrage referendum. Answering an Illinois correspondent asking, "Which of the States have granted to the Negro the Elective Franchise? When were these laws passed and which was the dominant party at the time?" Greeley responded it "would require a week's faithful, intelligent labor for their complete and satisfactory answer. We can use our time to better advantage." Republicans should not bother answering "the slang of their opponents and . . . their bugaboo stories." Stand on the Republican national platform, which ignored black suffrage, and if someone says "any thing outside of that Platform, it is his own affair, not that of the Republican party." This "Negro Suffrage bosh" put "the cart in place of the horse," as most of the original states had not disfranchised on racial grounds. "They usually imposed some small property qualification, or exacted the payment of a tax, which had the effect of excluding most negroes from the class of voters—not because they were Black, but because they were poor." Supposedly, it was Democrats who gave New York's black freeholders the vote, in 1821, an absurd proposition. "Massachusetts and Rhode Island allow Blacks to vote if they pay their taxes; Connecticut does not let them vote at all. But all this has nothing to do with the Republican party, having existed under all parties." The *New York Times* followed suit after the election, celebrating the referendum's defeat as proof "that the Republican Party, with its majority in the State of 50,000, has decidedly pronounced against admitting colored men to a political equality with the whites. The fact ought to enlighten the South somewhat as to the imputations habitual with them upon the motives and sympathies of the Republican Party. It ought to convince them how little of truth there is in the belief that it favors the doctrine of negro equality, and proposes to place in the h ands of the negroes any share of political power."[88]

In upstate's more congenial environment, Weed's *Journal* maintained its nonracial republicanism, that "the Property Qualification" was "a relict of the old British Colonial system. . . . The injustice of this was soon seen and acknowledged after Independence was attained, and white men were relieved from it. It is now proposed to remove it entirely. The idea of giving one man a political right because he has money, which is withheld from another because he has not, is so palpably unfair, that those who wish to defeat the Amendment, are obliged to misrepresent and distort the question." Race was pushed to the side. How could it be "just to make the right to vote depend upon having or not having $250. For if it is conceded to be right in the case of the black, it follows that it is right in the case of the white man also." One week before the election, it printed a letter "To the Voters of the State of New York. From James P. Johnson, President, Albany County Suffrage Club" insisting that Americans could hardly "boast of this as being a Democratic Government," and repeating the nativist appeal, that it was obviously wrong to "create grades in Society. The white man who has been scarcely long enough in this country to obtain the right of voting, is taught that he is superior to the colored man born on the soil." Finally, on November 1, the *Journal* spoke directly to party members. Democrats opposed equal suffrage because "it would add ten thousand votes to the Republican party, enabling it to carry close elections. . . . If this is conceded, and the only objection made is that it will strengthen the Republican party, we do not see what excuse any Republican can have for neglecting to vote for the Amendment."[89]

None of these appeals had any appreciable effect. Along the Hudson, in Manhattan and Brooklyn, and out on Long Island, Republican leaders ignored or opposed the amendment. Statewide, a bare majority of Republican voters supported equal suffrage, largely because some solidly Democratic anti-suffrage counties in 1846 were now as firmly Republican and pro-suffrage. The share of the electorate backing full political rights for black men increased from 27.6 percent to 36.3 percent. The city's environs again posted lopsided majorities against, in Brooklyn (29,399 to 5,341), Manhattan (37,471 to 1,640), Queens (5,763 to 481), and Richmond (2,530 to 145). The major difference was in black men's response. Defeat in 1846 left many disoriented and discouraged, but in 1860 there was no pessimism, in part because of the Republican victory. Fourteen years of hard experience had tuned their instincts, and they could hardly have expected an outright win. What mattered was that they carried their party, without significant support from its leaders, in the face of a virulent Democratic campaign linking Lincoln, black men voting, "nigger magistrates," and black sexuality into a web of threats.[90]

The tenacity of New York's political class echoed through one of McCune Smith's last polemics with Garnet, in January 1861. Retreating from politics, the outspoken minister (now pastoring the city's prestigious Shiloh Church) had been promoting his African Civilization Society, an emigrationist project with a friendly connection to the Colonization Society. Dismissing any idea that it was time to flee and sounding like Robert Morris at the 1859 New England convention, the doctor proclaimed his people's steady advance: "We are hourly approaching that affranchisement for which we are bound to struggle. Look at the advancement in wealth, intelligence, and esteem that our people have made within the last ten years. In one of the eastern states (Massachusetts) we have advanced from step to step until we stand on equal citizenship. In Philadelphia, there is a school taught exclusively by colored teachers, in which youth pursue studies as far and with greater thoroughness than was taught in colleges from which you and I were excluded on account of our complexion. In New York City, in that very neighborhood, through which we often fought our way to school and from school, an *Irish constituency* have erected on the old site a splendid new school house for colored children. In the recent election in our State, although opposed by the leaders of both political parties, for political reasons, we obtained seventy thousand more votes for the elective franchise than we obtained fourteen years ago; and we are assured by those who know, that if the vote shall be taken at an election not Presidential, we can carry the State!" New York's leaders, veterans of the nation's largest battleground, went into wartime bloodied but unbowed, their ranks unbroken despite recurring internal controversies, their connections to men of power functional, their appreciation of who they could and could not rely upon as precise as any group of political men in the republic.[91]

Coda

Losing and Winning in the Empire State

Self-evidently, the Civil War was a watershed in African American politics, but it is important to recognize the continuities from ante- to postbellum, in terms of policy, partisan alignments, and the ongoing activism of the men who had led black organizing before the war. Nowhere was this continuity stronger than in New York State. In some regards, the old battles—of upstate versus the city; Irish versus black; Tammany versus Whig—never went away.

First, the Empire State's Democracy was only temporarily humbled. It maintained a fierce "white man's" politics during and after the war under Governors Horatio Seymour (1863–64) and John T. Hoffman (1869–72). The strength of New York's racialist Democracy was made evident in the July 1863 Draft Riots, the worst episode of urban violence in U.S. history, when thousands of black people fled Manhattan in fear of their lives while Governor Seymour and Catholic archbishop John Hughes refused to denounce the primarily Irish rioters.

Second, in 1821, 1846, and 1860, the state had been roiled by conventions or referenda regarding black suffrage, and that battle did not cease. In 1869, the Republican Party led one more effort and again failed at the polls, albeit by much smaller margin, 53–47 percent, amid a Democratic sweep. Any account of black New Yorkers' politics must acknowledge that neither before nor after the great battle of freedom were the majority of white New Yorkers willing to accord them the political equality they enjoyed in 1777–1821. Nonracial male suffrage only came to New York with the Fifteenth Amendment's ratification on February 3, 1870, enforced that fall by federal marshals putting down Tammany's thugs.

However, one doubts that black Yorkers saw their history as a trajectory of failure. They had built an electorate big enough to count; they had earned the respect of white men whom everyone else respected; and this respect was displayed in public.

A Life in the Struggle

One individual, Stephen Myers, represented (and was seen to represent) the legacy of black politics in New York, and it seems appropriate to give him the last word. Rather than winning or losing, he persevered and advanced as much as he was able. Following Lincoln's triumph, Myers felt empowered to write "Govner Seward" before the inauguration, explaining that "a large number of my freinds have requested" that he ask Seward to "try to secure for me the stewardship of the White House." Although "confident that I could discharge that duty with sattisfaction to the president," he had "another situation" in mind, as "messenger to the Collector of the Port of New York." That collectorship was the nation's most lucrative patronage position, and serving as his messenger would guarantee impressive visibility, equivalent to Lewis Hayden's appointment later that year as messenger to Massachusetts's secretary of state. Myers knew that, as the state's senior senator, Seward controlled federal patronage under the new administration, and it would "be in your power to get that for me." He raised his long service to the party: "I hav work as faithfull for the party for the last fourteen years as any person could do I am satisfied that I have brought many hundreds antislavery votes in the republican party," and alluded to their personal history, that he had not held any appointment since 1839 when "you sir appointed me to act in the Helderburgh war," adding, "I should hav felt better if it had been" Seward "nominated and elected President of the United States." Amid the approach of war, there is no record of Seward's answering this appeal, surely one of many hundreds he received.[1]

During the war years, Myers made himself an Army recruiter, but his men were turned down as New York State volunteers, so he sent them to join the Fifty-Fourth Massachusetts. After the war, he maintained his standing as a regular Republican. He last featured in the state's byzantine politics as a symbol. In early 1869, as the final referendum on equal suffrage approached, a colorful Tammany figure, Col. Michael C. Murphy, sought to embarrass the Republicans by forcing them to vote on a resolution naming Myers the Assembly's assistant doorkeeper. After various gross jests (to make him superintendent of ventilation), Republicans voted to table the motion. The New York City *Commercial Advertiser* blasted "Ungrateful Republicans," adding a biography of the venerable Myers as "a more reputable man than many of the members of the Assembly; and quite as intelligent as the great body of them. Indeed, Stephen Myers's autobiography would make a very interesting political history. He commenced life as a house servant with Governor Tompkins. He was for many years a waiter on the tables of Governor Clinton, Yates, Van Buren, Throop, Marcy, Seward, and many more of the distinguished statesmen of the State, who have resided in and about Albany. Myers's recollections of politicians who have figured in the history of this State are very remarkable."[2]

At the end, Myers got a taste of the respect and money he had earned. In May 1869, the *New York Herald*, still ferociously Democratic, reported that the city had a new postmaster, General P. H. Jones, and Myers, "a famous colored engineer on the underground railroad in the dread days of abolitionism, has been appointed doorkeeper to the General's office. He has a remarkable recollection of faces, and in this respect at least will make an excellent man for the post." A few weeks later, Myers performed a final party duty, presiding over a State Convention of Colored Men in Binghamton, where he issued "an appeal to the colored men to trust in the Republican party and work together for its interests, for by doing so they were helping themselves." Early in the New Year, he expired, bringing forth tributes mixing nostalgia and real feeling from across the spectrum. The Democratic *Argus* spoke of him as

> An old man whose genial, dark face was very familiar to all the citizens of Albany. . . . To miss Stephen Myers' presence from the Capitol will seem almost as strange as it would to remove one of the grey pillars which support, rather than adorn, that venerable structure. . . . Like most old men whose lines of life have been cast in public places, Stephen Myers lived rather in the past than in the present. . . . In "days lang syne," when De Witt Clinton filled the Executive Chair, Mr. M. filled a confidential position beneath him, and it cannot be denied that he did much towards brightening the understandings of that great man. . . . John Van Buren, prince of good fellows . . . saw so many strangers that he was led to say, with semi-humorous pathos: "Ah, me! The old, familiar faces are passing away; Steve Myers is left, but with that exception the famous men of the last generation are gone—all gone!"[3]

Weed's *Evening Journal* took the death of this fellow Whig and Republican seriously, declaring, "He was, to a far greater extent than many men occupying a much more conspicuous social position, a man of note. He was born in the city at a time when the men and women and children of his race constituted a portion of almost every thrifty household," a circumspect admission that they all contained slaves. "The boys of the most aristocratic families then deemed it no disparagement to their dignity to be on familiar terms with the colored lads of their own age. With all such, Stephen was a great favorite. . . . Many of these youngsters, after their heads grown gray, often found pleasure in going over with him the 'larks' of their youth." It then got down to history: "Stephen was born a slave, and, until emancipated by the State law, belonged to Dr. Eights [Jonathan Eights was a prominent Albany physician]. He was afterwards a favorite servant in the families of Chancellor

Lansing, the Patroon, Governor Clinton and others, and at all parties and public receptions, he was the recognized and chosen master of ceremonies. He was, in this way, brought in contact with all the most distinguished officers of the war of 1812; and, later, with all the most noted politicians and statesmen who enjoyed the hospitality and intimate friendship of De Witt Clinton." One notes the slippage. If Myers was "emancipated by the State law," meaning in 1827, then his long connection with Clintonians, Whigs, and Republicans must have begun when he was not "a favorite servant" but a favored slave. The editor then detailed his history as a "conspicuous . . . ' agitator' for the rights which the laws withheld from his race," and as an editor ("His paper lived longer than many others . . . less, perhaps, because of its ability than because of the indomitable perseverance which he exhibited in securing for it . . . continuance," meaning money).

Consider what was omitted here. Myers's decades as a partisan mobilizer and the suffrage campaigns he helped lead were elided in favor of the safely historical labor of abolitionism, which Republicans loved to retrospectively eulogize. "It was as a bold and successful Agent of the 'underground railroad' that he acquired his most substantial fame. . . . He aided hundreds if not thousands of fugitive slaves to escape from their masters. During the existence of the Fugitive Slave law, he was particularly active, and had the sympathy and co-operation of our citizens to a greater extent than at any previous period. . . . His house was the ever-open hostelry of these fugitives; and when the blood-hounds were in too hot pursuit . . . Stephen could always find a sure place of refuge for them in the homes of any of our citizens." It concluded with a note of fond condescension: "Others of his race, far his superior in intellect and scholarship, survive him; but none possess a stronger hold upon the friend-ship and respect of our citizens. He had faults, of course; and sometimes his best friends had reason to complain that he was not always discreet in his actions; but he was earnest and honest, and all who knew him only wish now to remember the good he accomplished in the benevolent and philanthropic aspirations which rendered him a faithful friend of his race, and an earnest, hopeful and unwearied worker for their deliverance from personal and political bondage." This tribute completed the work of removing this devoted party man from the world of parties, elevating him into the role of a simple, sincere advocate for the downtrodden. Looking forward from 1870, past the short-lived epic of Radical Reconstruction, we see how black politics, hardly "benevolent and philanthropic," were already obscured by comforting myths about "the dread days of abolitionism."[4]

PART IV

A Salient on the West

On the Civil War's eve, Ohio became the most impressive site of black political power. Overcoming sweeping constitutional proscriptions, African Americans made it their banner state, achieving greater weight inside Ohio's electoral politics than anywhere else. From 1855 to 1860, charges that "negro votes" tipped Ohio's elections were fought out in its press and legislature, a state supreme court decision, and even the U.S. Congress. Given that state elections were decided by at most a few thousand ballots, and many fewer in local or congressional races, these charges should be taken seriously. Black voter mobilization reflected systematic partisan engagement with a specific character. Ohio had no history of Whig submachines as in Portland or Providence, or blocs of "colored electors" periodically mobilized, as in New York City and State. Instead, like the New Bedforders, black men sought incorporation into regular party structures, in this case the Free Soilers and then Republicans, not as auxiliaries but as delegates and campaigners. And while they occasionally contested for office elsewhere, the election of the Oberlin-educated lawyer John Mercer Langston to important local positions was a nationally recognized marker of advancement.

What set Ohio off from the rest of the original Northwest Territory was the northeastern counties known as the Western Reserve. Formally speaking, "the Reserve" designates the ten counties stretching 120 miles west from the Pennsylvania border along Lake Erie, including Ashtabula, Cuyahoga, Erie, Geauga, Huron, Lake, Lorain, Medina, Portage, and Trumbull, plus parts of Ashland, Mahoning, Ottawa and Summit. Known originally as "New Connecticut" because of the latter's colonial claim, they were incorporated into the federal territory in 1800, and filled up with Yankees after statehood in 1802. The Reserve's self-conscious New Englandism, equally anti-southern and antislavery, developed slowly, but by 1824, as Donald Ratcliffe has shown, Ohio had an internal version of the nation's sectional divide, aligning the Reserve with John Quincy Adams as the North's candidate after a generation of southern dominance. An influx of crude, irreligious Pennsylvanians into the state's middle region exacerbated a sense of Yankee superiority, making the Reserve the ultimate expression of "Greater New England" by the 1830s. Minus this bloc of prosperous counties, Ohio would have fit cleanly into the

Middle Border, the band of states on either side of the Ohio River sharing "a traditional western political culture," in which "slavery represented more than contradicted democratic ascendance," with "white supremacy . . . interwoven into the fabric" of the whole. Instead, northern Ohio became the alternative to that version of the Lower North, capable of bringing this politically central state with it on occasion.[1]

The Reserve mattered not only as a center of New Englandish culture and abolitionism, but in the partisan terms understood by white politicians. With 13 percent of the state's population in 1860, it could not be ignored by Republicans or their Whig predecessors; both counted on large majorities in the Reserve to overcome Democratic dominance elsewhere. Within the Reserve, the town of Oberlin had a unique role, as the embodiment of not just "free soil" but a genuinely free West; Democrats (who repeatedly tried to revoke its charter) called it "the great national manufactory of ultra-abolitionists." That small place, with only 1,133 residents in 1850 (one in five black), represented a truly purified republicanism, a biracial politics minus clientage. A "town of rare New England character," as John Mercer Langston fondly remembered it, its prosperous black artisanry participated at every level of politics, while black and white youths studied and ate together at Oberlin College, which had educated 100 men and women of color by 1865, thirty-two of whom gained degrees.[2]

In Oberlin, black men did not just vote, get elected to town office, serve as constables, and send their children to integrated schools. They also did not walk in fear of whites. Langston was repeatedly insulted when he began his legal practice there in 1854. His response was to publicly thrash a series of white men (including two lawyers, both Democrats), to general approval. Even more dramatically, after a deputy U.S. marshal (a Democratic appointee) wrote a Kentucky slaveowner in 1858 to discuss recapture of a man then living in the town for a reward, the fugitive in question chased him into a hotel and beat him with a cane. Oberlin's significance in state and national politics climaxed with the Oberlin-Wellington Rescue and trial in 1858–59, which epitomized Ohio's fusion of radicalism in the street, in party conclaves, and at the ballot box. One of the last mass actions challenging the Fugitive Slave Act, the Rescue and subsequent courtroom confrontation had partisan implications at the national level. A biracial mob took a fugitive away from U.S. officers, inflicting considerable damage on them in the process. Not only did thousands visit the jailed Rescuers, their trials pitted the state against James Buchanan's administration: the president ordered a Navy steamer to Cleveland to enforce the law, and Ohio's Republican attorney general, Christopher Wolcott, appealed the first two convictions on grounds of habeas corpus to the state's supreme court. Senator Benjamin Wade declared that if habeas was not granted by the court, "the People of the Western Reserve must grant it—*sword in hand if need be*," and Governor Salmon Chase spoke at a huge Cleveland rally on their behalf. Other than New Bedford, no other place in the antebellum United States matched this record of defiant egalitarianism, although Cleveland came a close second, as another "transplanted Yankee town of Ohio" where the Democrats repeatedly ranted that "Negro voters" controlled the elections, and school "authorities never observed the word 'white,' but admitted the colored children . . . on equal terms with whites."[3]

Black Ohio's vindication was all the more remarkable because, from the state's founding in 1803 until 1849, its notorious Black Laws designated African Americans as a separate caste, not even "citizens for protection." At its 1802 constitutional convention, Ohio had almost enfranchised its few black settlers, but the final document established white suffrage and otherwise ignored free persons of color. In 1804, the legislature barred black persons from testifying against whites, rendering them vulnerable to fraud or violence, and in 1807 it required free people of color to register with the state and post a $500 bond, capped by laws in 1829 and 1831 excluding them from public schools, asylums, and the poor-relief system. This juridically degraded status distinguished Ohio from the varieties of black citizenship along the seaboard from Maine to Pennsylvania, and, although by the 1830s black observers described the registration and bond requirement as "a dead letter on the Statute Book," the bans on courtroom testimony and attending public schools were rigorously enforced.[4]

Yet rather than retreating into "shadow politics," the subordinate status assigned to persons of color generated a solid united front. There is no record of black Ohioans fighting over Whig versus Liberty Party affiliations, as in New York, let alone whether to vote, as in Pennsylvania. When they did organize separate institutions, as in the School Fund Society set up in the 1830s to create a parallel state education system, those were outward-facing. This unity derived from the demands imposed by an openly hostile political environment. Ohio's partisan arena was fundamentally less friendly to black people than New York or New England. It had no equivalent to the dynamic tension between Seward, the master of party politics, and Gerrit Smith, the fabulously wealthy philanthropist, both allies to black people. What Ohio did feature was the foremost strategist of "political abolitionism," Salmon P. Chase. As the leader of the state's Liberty Party in the 1840s, then bringing that party into the Free Soil coalition in 1848–54, and finally at the head of the mighty Ohio Republican Party in 1855–60, he forged the nation's strongest antislavery electoral force. In the final prewar years, Ohio's Republicans were matched only by Upper New England in accommodating, and sometimes fostering, open displays of black political power.

Surprisingly, then, Chase has a negative scholarly reputation, versus his coworkers in white antislavery politics: John Quincy Adams, of course, but also Seward, Henry Wilson, Thaddeus Stevens, or Ohio's own Joshua Giddings. All of these men are treated with respect, whereas Chase is usually cast as a conniving, Machiavellian figure, crippled by ambition. Why persons with strong ideological convictions should not also be ambitious is a mystery, or an expression of bourgeois moralism. Chase earned his reputation as "the attorney general for fugitive slaves," and his many detractors were white; black people never found him a problem. Like Seward, he demonstrated how deep political convictions could harmonize with electoral self-interest. The difference between them was profound in partisan terms, however. Seward always moved inside a larger party machine, only sometimes carrying it with him. Chase began far out on the margins with the Liberty Party, and no other Liberty man moved as far into the center of power, first as a Free Soil or "Independent Democratic" senator, then a Republican governor, finally as Lincoln's secretary of the treasury. His career underlines Corey Brooks's argument that the Liberty Party was the nucleus for the Republicans. In Ohio, Chase lit that spark.[5]

Chapter 11

We Do Not Care How Black He Is

Ohio's Black Republicans

Let a man be Christian or infidel; let him be Turk, Jew, or Muslim; let him be of good character or bad; even let him be sunk to the lowest depths of degradation; he may be witness in our courts if he is not black.

—Judge Peter Hitchcock of the Ohio supreme court, commenting on the state's Black Laws, 1846

[The Republicans] got up in the morning savage and hungry, worked the wagons, sweat the negroes, and swept the county.

—*Cleveland Plain Dealer*, on Lorain County's overwhelming majority for Frémont, 1856

Up in the upper part of the state, on the Lake Shore and Reserve, we have gone so far as to say that anybody that will take the responsibility of swearing that he is more than half-white, shall vote. We do not care how black he is.

—John Mercer Langston, 1865

Ohio's history defines a black politics distinct from the seaboard states founded as colonies. As a territory governed under the Northwest Ordinance of 1787, it began as a society without slaves, a place for white Americans to start afresh. Ohioans were also physically closer to both slave societies and complete freedom than whites to the east. Their state bordered on Kentucky and Virginia, where most blacks remained slaves (unlike in Maryland and Delaware), and enjoyed a vigorous commercial relationship with the Deep South via the Ohio and Mississippi Rivers. The physical border between slave and free was also much more visible; whereas the Mason-Dixon Line was invisible on the Chesapeake's dusty tracks, the Ohio River was a powerful obstacle, protecting a vast region stretching down to the Gulf. Conversely, British Canada's ultimate free territory was also much closer, as it was only 200 miles from Cincinnati's docks to a wharf in Sandusky on Lake Erie. White Ohioans witnessed constant escapes, as slaves fled across the river ice in winter and stowed away on riverboats in summer, streaming north along dozens of hidden tracks. These stark polarities—whiteness versus blackness, freedom versus slavery—made Ohio the original "dark and bloody ground," a place of acute sectional and partisan divisions, where Yankee triumph led to a Radical Reconstruction of black citizenship before 1861.[1]

A particular moment suggests how one scholar's description of antebellum Cincinnati as embodying "a schizophrenic northern and southern personality occupying the same . . . body" applies to the state as a whole. In 1850, a constitutional convention met in Columbus. As in every state where black suffrage had been barred or made conditional, petitions were received asking for equal rights. In Ohio, however, they were countered by petitions inconceivable in the Mid-Atlantic and New England states. Significant numbers of Ohio whites demanded "the extradition of the black population" from the state, regardless of when they had arrived, with one representative avowing, "A majority of the people of the county I represent, without regard . . . to whether they are of the democratic party, or of the whig party, believe with the fathers of this State—the pioneers of 1802, when they drew up the constitution under which we are now assembled, that this should be a State for the white man, and the white man only." White politicians said things like this almost everywhere, but in Ohio, some meant it literally. Yet a Free Soil delegate presented to this same convention a petition for black suffrage, and when asked if it came "from colored people" (who had no right to petition, some thought) declared, "The memorialist is one of my constituents, and one of those who aided in my election. . . . He has the same right to be heard as the constituents of any gentleman on this floor." Further, the petitioner (William Howard Day, in fact) was "well educated, as much of a man, and quite as much of a gentleman as any of those who are opposed to the appropriate reference of this memorial. . . . If any one here wishes to discuss the propriety of granting the prayer of the memorial, the gentleman from whom it emanated will be ready to meet them any where, and I know he will be found abundantly able to sustain himself."[2]

White Soil and Black Laws

Regarding black citizenship, Ohio's founding represents a notable instance of the road-not-taken. Its few men of color had been enfranchised under federal legislation authorizing the vote for all "male citizens of the United States who reside within the said territory," and some apparently did vote in the October 12, 1801 elections for delegates to the statehood convention. At least some of the original white settlers envisioned a "constitution that will set the natural rights of the meanest African and the most abject beggar upon an equal footing with those citizens of the greatest wealth," as a manifesto from Newmarket Township in Ross County (settled by Virginians) declared. At that convention, moreover, a short-lived majority voted to enfranchise black men already resident and their descendants, a decision overturned only by the tie-breaking vote of its president, the Virginian Edward Tiffin.[3]

But for that vote, Ohio would have countered the disfranchisement creeping over the Lower North after 1800. Having banished that possibility, the convention "proceeded to form a constitution having no direct reference to the status of the negro," leaving them to "occupy the same relation to the government as Indians or unnaturalized foreigners," as an early historian put it, although the convention rejected explicit mentions of racial caste. That ambiguity vanished after statehood in 1803, perhaps because Ohio's new leaders were Virginians who opposed slavery but had voted against black suffrage. From 1804 to 1807, Ohio's legislature passed a series of Black Laws intended to "deprive African Americans of all but a little more than residency, assuming they could prove their free status," while discouraging immigration. An 1804 act "to regulate black and mulatto persons" permitted those who had arrived before June 1 of that year to stay if they paid a small fee, but from then on "all African-Americans . . . were expected to hold a county-issued certificate to prove their free status." Next, an 1806 law claimed to protect the state from a flood of runaways who would become public charges by requiring arrivals to post a $500 bond, backed up by two white men qualified to "guarantee their good behavior and welfare." Finally, an 1807 act banned any testimony in court by persons of color against whites, clarifying they truly had no rights that the latter should respect.[4]

For the next quarter-century, African Americans rarely elicited notice in Ohio's electoral battles. Its white men agreed on one thing: they did not want black people, enslaved or free, in their state. This consensus was amply illustrated by two developments in 1819: a 5–1 referendum vote against holding a constitutional convention because of rumors its secret purpose was to reintroduce slavery; a campaign of extralegal violence to drive out 300 manumitted slaves sent from Virginia by their deceased owner, an Englishman named Gist, who left money to buy them farmsteads in Brown County. The core issues of black politics, voting and citizenship rights, were irrelevant to a white settler society imprinting itself on the Indian lands secured by General Anthony Wayne's victory at Fallen Timbers in 1794. Ohio did not remain a raw frontier for long, however, experiencing the North's most sustained demographic and economic expansion prior to the Civil War (although even into the 1830s, large portions remained unbroken forest). With an extensive canal network by the late 1820s, access to New Orleans via the Ohio and the eastern and Canadian markets via Lake Erie, it was a crossroads for early capitalist development. From a mere 42,159 inhabitants in 1800, the state's population reached 230,760 by 1810 and 937,903 by 1830. This growth hardly slowed, and by 1850, Ohio's population of almost two million was the nation's third-largest, with Cincinnati sixth among the nation's cities; by 1860 it also boasted the nation's largest railroad network.[5]

Ohio's vertiginous progress was the product of "a fluctuating mass of highly mobile peoples who were overwhelmingly strangers to one another," the majority of whom owned their own land. A frontier environment, minus the great proprietors of colonial New England and New York or Virginia's county grandees, fostered a precocious popular electoralism. Donald Ratcliffe argues that Ohio was "thoroughly democratized" by the early 1800s, with functioning statewide party organizations, after the "internal revolution" of a statehood campaign which banished forever the "ancient regime of influence and deference" identified with Federalist control. Republicans predominated from the state's founding, but Ohio's Jeffersonians resembled Pennsylvanians in their ardent factionalism. Dissent over Jefferson's Embargo and the drift to war with England temporarily revived the Federalists, but the racial consensus held, with no party or faction advocating for either black citizenship or a revival of legal bondage. People of color kept arriving from southward, but were tolerated as the equivalent of "aborigines who could remain in the state," in the words of Ohio's most prominent Federalist, Jacob Burnet. Southern abolitionists (Quakers and others) also arrived, producing a surprisingly strong antislavery movement in the 1810s and 1820s. Garrison's mentor, Benjamin Lundy, founded Ohio's first antislavery society in St. Clairsville in 1815, and two years later *The Philanthropist*, a pioneering abolitionist journal, began publishing in Mount Pleasant, a Quaker town in Jefferson County. By that point, Ohio's political culture was beginning to divide along ethnocultural lines, all in some way related to race and slavery: a southern tier containing a large southern in-migration; self-conscious Yankees on the northeastern Reserve; the central "backbone" counties full of Scotch-Irish and Pennsylvania Dutch bringing the Keystone State's Negrophobia; a significant Quaker presence in eastern and southeastern counties; finally, after 1830, mainly Catholic Germans in Cincinnati.[6]

Black Settlers on White Soil

Throughout the antebellum period, Ohio contained the majority of black Midwesterners: 25,279 in 1850, versus 11,262 in Indiana, 5,436 in Illinois, 2,583 in Michigan, 635 in Wisconsin, 333 in Iowa, and a mere 39 in Minnesota. These people were hardly undifferentiated, however, and how they came to Ohio is key to the state's history. Each of this book's parts has delineated a particular version of northern black rural life. Upper New England saw the early settlement of extended family groups integrated into the communities around them. Southern Pennsylvania's larger-scale slavery generated a rural proletariat existing on the margins, with the constant arrival of migrants from the Chesapeake, all subject to legal and extralegal "Jim Crow." New York included both of these patterns and more. As in New England, landowning small farmers, artisans, and businessmen incorporated into the small-town life of the Burned-Over District in western New York, while the slaveholding Dutch counties along the Hudson resembled Pennsylvania, albeit with a more deeply rooted slave system. Ohio's black peoples differed from the eastern states in three distinct ways, as an entirely immigrant population who founded their own self-sufficient rural settlements and achieved a substantial level of economic security.

First, Ohio began with almost no black population, as only 337 people of color were listed in the 1800 federal census of the territory then including eastern Michigan. Virtually all black Ohioans emigrated post-statehood from the Upper South, mainly Virginia. Some accompanied their former masters like Thomas Worthington, who came to Ross County in 1796, serving as senator in 1803–7 and 1810–14, and governor in 1814–18. In other cases, large groups were freed and sent north, like the Gist slaves, a practice continuing into the pre-Civil War years. Many self-manumitted via purchase and came as families; in 1835, for instance, the majority of Cincinnati's people of color were ex-slaves, over 30 percent of whom had bought themselves.[7]

Second, these freedpeople organized a network of independent villages unique in its scope; in 1840, *The Philanthropist* catalogued eleven colonies in eight counties, some with a few dozen residents and others considerably larger; the most impressive, in Jackson County, was founded by Thomas Woodson, Sally Hemings's eldest son by Thomas Jefferson, father of Lewis Woodson, the Pittsburgh leader. Travelers commented on these settlements as examples of what black people could achieve if they left the cities.[8]

Third, both these rural communities and growing black urban populations in Cleveland, Columbus, Cincinnati, and Chillicothe achieved a notable degree of economic success. This was a classic immigrant story of self-conscious strivers. The majority of black Ohioans remained laborers and tenants, but their white neighbors throughout the state saw an emerging middle class embodying Protestant self-reliance, including a notable proportion of tradespeople (by 1850, Cincinnati alone contained 136 barbers), and the nation's highest percentage of black property owners, in Ross County. By the 1830s, a seasoned statewide leadership of twenty-plus men had gathered, primarily businessmen like John Malvin, a Cleveland carpenter and lumberman connected to the city's founders, and David Jenkins, a painter and plasterer who secured city and state building contracts in Columbus in the 1840s while beginning his career as the state's black lobbyist.[9]

Map 11.1 Ohio counties, 1850; percentage of free-colored men (age 21–100) out of total (age 21–100) male population per county

A stable network of all-black settlements in the southern counties had political implications. The state's proximity to slave territory stimulated a massive Underground Railroad apparatus, and produced many passionate tales recounted by whites to the Railroad's ethnographer, Wilbur Siebert. These were dismissed by later historians as apocryphal, and for a long time, Ohio's UGRR history was taken seriously only by black scholars. More recently, historians and geographers have documented that this history was no myth. For a narrative of partisan politics, what matters is how employing, hiding, transporting, and protecting runaways intruded into Ohio's conventional politics. By the 1830s, these local fights drew in prominent whites, including judges, lawyers, and sheriffs, forcing them to make choices; by the 1850s, they had national implications.[10]

Finally, emigration from the South into Ohio had a special aspect. Because of its southern flavor and proximity, Ohio, especially Cincinnati, became the preeminent destination for white men sending their "colored" families northward for safety and an education. By the 1830s, these mixed-race people were a visible group. Seen through the rose-colored glasses of John Mercer Langston, writing in old age, "If there has ever existed in any colored community of the United States, anything like an aristocratic class of such persons, it was found in Cincinnati." Langston himself, a "little Virginia gentleman," as admiring adults called him in his youth, was one of those boys whose fathers wanted their progeny to be something other than poor black bastards. He was born in 1829, the last child of a planter and Revolutionary veteran, Ralph Quarles, who entered into a lifelong relationship with his manumitted slave, Lucy Langston. Quarles's will provided for his youngest son John to be sent to white friends in Ohio, where he grew up as a member of the household, unaware of his racial status. As a young man he might have emigrated and lived as white, or taken up a New York law school's offer in 1850 if he would "consent to pass as a Frenchman or a Spaniard hailing from the West Indies Islands, Central America or South America." Langston chose a different road, resisting the advantages of paternity and complexion. His pursuit of fame as a tribune of black people began with the efforts of his older brothers William, Gideon, and Charles, all sent to Ohio by their father before him. The latter two were Oberlin's first black students, men of substance, economically successful and politically active. They took charge of their little brother at a young age, removing him from the white family and ensuring his exceptional training, leading to law and theological degrees from Oberlin.[11]

The Langston brothers were surrounded by others like them. John married Caroline Wall, daughter of a "Col. Stephen Wall, a very wealthy and influential citizen of Richmond County, North Carolina, [who] had brought his children to this liberal Quaker village [Harveysburg], and . . . settled them in easy, in fact affluent circumstances. . . . So influential were those to whom he committed their business and education, that they were treated everywhere, in church, school and the community, as if they were children of its very best and most prominent family." Her brother O. S. B. was a village marshal in Oberlin and then the first black Army captain during the Civil War. African Americans of this provenance brought distinct advantages to Ohio's black politics, including considerable wealth. John Mercer Langston bought land worth almost $5,000 on receiving his legacy, and his brother Charles owned an 1,100-acre farm near Columbus. They also deployed their biracial

Americanism effectively. During the 1859 Oberlin-Wellington trial, Charles told the jury, "I have been taught by my Revolutionary father . . . and by his honored associates, that the fundamental doctrine of this government was that *all* men have a right to life and liberty, and coming from the Old Dominion, I brought into Ohio these sentiments, deeply impressed upon my heart!" Above all, if they could convincingly claim one parent was white, and the other not-all-black, they could vote.[12]

"Nearer White Than Mulatto"

In most histories, 1829 was a pivotal year for black Ohioans. Their status was hardly noticed outside the state until Cincinnati's people of color increased from 2 to 10 percent of the city's population since 1820, fomenting a notable episode of Negrophobia. In memory, city authorities and white mobs attempted a mass expulsion, enforcing the Black Laws to make employment impossible, backing up those threats with violence. Long after, that mobbing symbolized black subordination in Ohio, and the urgency of a national black politics. It stimulated Bishop Richard Allen to organize the Negro Convention Movement, and David Walker to issue his famous *Appeal*. More than sixty years ago, however, Richard Wade exploded the notion that white rioters drove out hundreds of desperate people. A planned emigration to Canada began well before the riot, to pressure Cincinnati's authorities by depleting the city's labor supply, and during the melees, black Cincinnatians defended themselves effectively; afterward, eight white men were convicted and fined. The embarrassment produced by unchecked lawlessness wrought a sea-change in community attitudes, diminishing the standing of local colonizationists and bringing the Black Laws into disrepute, so much that the Englishman Edward Abdy described black Cincinnatians a few years later as "the victors" who "have been suffered to reside in the place unmolested" ever since.[13]

The 1829 riot was notorious, but a legal ruling two years later had greater long-term impact. In 1831, Ohio's supreme court decided that "black," "negro," and "mulatto" described only those persons with a preponderance of African descent. In 1829, a woman named Polly Gray had been convicted of robbery, based on the testimony of a black person. Her lawyer insisted this testimony should have been excluded because Gray was white under Ohio law, which defined a mulatto as "begotten between a white and a black," whereas Gray had one quadroon grandparent and was "of a shade of color between the mulatto and white." The court accepted this logic, overturning her conviction and asserting that persons "of a race nearer white than a mulatto . . . should partake in the privileges of whites." They added that their decision was partly because, "We are unwilling to extend the disabilities of the statute [of blackness] further than its letter requires, and partly from the difficulty of defining and ascertaining the degree of duskiness which renders a person liable to such disabilities." Nor was *Polly Gray v. Ohio* a quirk remaining in force through inertia and stare decisis. It was affirmed in a series of decisions in the 1830s and 1840s, and again in 1859, in the latter case overturning legislation by Democrats insisting that white meant "pure white."[14]

No scholar has probed the motives that led jurists from both major parties to violate their constitution's evident original intent by establishing a caste of people who could go to court against whites and vote, if male, although their "African blood" was legally recognized. These decisions did not employ the reasoning used in southern court cases of the 1840s and 1850s, in which a "performative whiteness" was conjured out of local reputation, social associations with whites, or phenotypical detail. Instead a nominal criterion of hypodescent made persons who were to some degree "colored" legally "white," even if they associated with black people and were known as such. One possible explanation is ethnocultural, since many of these judges were Yankees. Reuben Wood, who served on the court in 1833–47, and later a term as a Democratic governor, was born in Vermont. Peter Hitchcock, who served in 1817–33, 1835–42, and 1845–52 (and whose 1846 ruling included the acerbic comment that a "Turk, Jew, or Muslim" could vote in Ohio but not a native-born man of color), was born in Connecticut and attended Yale; he opposed slavery as early as 1826, and backed black rights as a Whig delegate at the 1850 constitutional convention. Ebenezer Lane, who served 1830–45, as chief justice after 1840, and wrote several of the decisions, was from Massachusetts, and attended Harvard.[15]

Ohio's color-caste jurisprudence could have negative consequences, allowing someone like Polly Gray to escape justice. As the 1857 State Convention of Colored Men noted angrily, when one man of color killed another in Cleveland in 1846, he avoided conviction because the witnesses were black and he was "nearer white." Such legal parsing led to surreal scenes, as when a judge admitted John Mercer Langston to the bar in 1854 only after Langston's white supporters asserted that technically "under the law of Ohio Mr. Langston was a 'white man'" and therefore could be licensed, with the chief justice inspecting him closely, since "it was material to know by actual sight what his color was. . . . He must be construed into a *white man*, as he was at once upon sight." As Langston remarked four decades later, this was "a beautiful hocus pocus arrangement."[16]

How early, how often, and where did black men vote in Ohio? The evidence suggests that in the late 1830s some men of color realized their opportunity, since when complaints first surfaced in 1840, the fact of "nearer white" men voting was recognized. Ohio's electoral practices were peculiarly conducive to permitting this latitude. As Kenneth Winkle has demonstrated, Ohio's constitution delegated "authority over two basic rights—suffrage and poor relief—to its local administrative units, townships." In practice, this left "extremely broad discretion to the voters of a township in interpreting both 'inhabitancy' and 'residence,'" and "each of Ohio's 2,000 townships reserved the right to define the boundaries of its own electorate," meaning the party controlling a township could grant suffrage to virtually any man, regardless of whether or not he was naturalized, resident, or completely white. This system of local control was extended by detailed election laws in 1831 and 1841; in Winkle's summation, "the complicity of local party officials could secure almost anyone legal suffrage, even in a divided township." Just as Democrats routinely allowed unnaturalized immigrants to vote, some black men voted anywhere that Whigs, Free Soilers, or Republicans controlled the polls, and some also voted as Democrats when the latter found their votes useful. How many votes could they cast? The 1850 census recorded 12,691 black males in Ohio, approximately 5,822 of whom were of voting age. The same census-takers categorized 56 percent of Ohio blacks as phenotypically "mulatto," so approximately 3,000 could claim they were white enough to vote; whether that claim would be accepted must have varied greatly, but we also know that on the Reserve, it was taken at face-value and, in Langston's boast from 1865, they did not "care how black he is." These were small numbers, but statewide victory margins were often razor-thin, with gubernatorial races decided by 1,872 of 242,810 votes cast in 1842, 971 of 299,993 in 1844, and a mere 324 of 297,208 in 1848.[17]

For how this process worked, see the depositions of three white men in the Democrat Clement L. Vallandigham's challenge to the Republican Lewis D. Campbell's election to Congress in 1856 (discussed in detail below). Thomas Millikin, a Democratic judge of elections in a Republican ward, was asked about four voters, three of whom he knew. He averred that "there was in each a visible admixture of African blood" but he could not "give any very satisfactory opinion upon" how much they had; what mattered was that "at the election the votes of these persons were admitted upon their own evidence as to color; no other evidence on that subject being offered." He was asked if "any of said colored persons [were] sworn in as to the proportion of white blood they contained," and answered that two had been sworn but "The others do not appear, from the poll books, to have been sworn in. [Alfred] Anderson had been sworn at a previous election, and was not sworn at this," and a fourth man's vote "was received upon the statement of Anderson, as they came to the polls together and voted." Finally, he admitted receiving "the votes of the four persons named as colored on the ground that if they had more than half white blood they were entitled to vote at said election," and "upon their own testimony only. That . . . was the test." A few days later, William J. Mollyneaux gave similar evidence for

Election Day in another township, naming a long list of African American voters, and said, "Those persons known as democrats bitterly opposed their voting. The opposition, the republicans, favored their voting," and, since two out of the three judges were for Campbell, they voted despite Democratic challenges. Joseph D. Ringwood, one of the "friends of Vallandigham" at that poll, agreed that "they were all challenged," and that Democrats "had made an arrangement to have Dr. Garver inside at the polls for the express purpose of challenging these identical men," presumably with medical testimony as to their predominantly "negro blood," but "the judges decided that these persons had a right to vote, because they were more than half white."[18]

Evidently, by the 1850s if not before, Ohio's black men used every ballot they could. Such a decision involved serious risks. Ohio's permitting lighter-skinned men of African descent to vote drew a clear line through the people of color, and outsiders like James McCune Smith and Martin Delany commented acerbically on "yellow" men making themselves a "privileged class by birth." Inside Ohio, however, there was little debate, although resentments against those claiming color-privilege for their children may have simply gone unrecorded. When the Garrisonian H. Ford Douglas proposed a resolution at the 1851 state convention that "no colored man can consistently vote under the United States Constitution," he was countered by Charles Langston declaring he "would vote under the United States Constitution on the same principle . . . that I would call on every slave, from Maryland to Texas, to arise and assert their *liberties*, and cut their masters' throats if they attempt again to reduce them to slavery." He hoped "that colored men will vote, or do anything else under the Constitution, that will aid in effecting our liberties." Douglas's resolution lost 28–2. Unlike in Latin America, where mixed-race people often aligned with white interests, Ohio's African Americans accepted that some could vote and others could not; if all men of African descent voted on the Reserve, as John Mercer Langston claimed, perhaps that mitigated complexional distinctions. Their leaders unified around the strategy of voting their maximum strength, while pressing to end all color barriers. They talked as little as possible about their own differences, other than "Charlie" reporting in New York's *Weekly Anglo-African* in 1860, "I am glad to see the quadroons and octoroons vote in Ohio; but I must say I hate the court, the State, the people, or the constitution that would be so mean."[19]

Gathering Forces, 1831–1847

The rise of antislavery politics in Ohio can be told either as "How Some Whigs Became Antislavery" or "How the Liberty Party Became the Balance of Power." It bears repeating, however, that Ohioans were not starting from the position of New England, New York, or Pennsylvania, all of which originally recognized black citizenship. In Ohio, people of color were born into, or acquired upon entrance, a minimal negative liberty as denizens rather than citizens. From that position they attempted to move into a political body that had explicitly rejected them. That the demand to make them citizens by repealing the Black Laws came up so powerfully testifies to the radicalization of some whites and the demands of a highly competitive partisan environment, wherein a bloc of white antislavery voters was often decisive.

Ohio was central to the rise of "political abolitionism" in the 1840s, but did not begin that way. Whigs were the base of antislavery politics in New England and New York, but antislavery Whigs were always a minority inside the Ohio party. The leading scholar of its Black Laws specifies that "Most Whigs in Ohio shared the philosophy of those who had initially codified" that legislation, and "were hostile to any efforts to reverse them." The state's first major antislavery politician was "a typical Administration Democrat," Senator Thomas Morris. In 1836, he denounced the congressional "gag" on antislavery petitions, coining the phrase "the Slave Power," and as a consequence, fellow Democrats denied him renomination to the Senate in December 1838. Morris went on to help found the state's Liberty Party and was that party's vice presidential candidate in 1844. Ohio's antislavery politics also differed in the absence of venerable precedents. There were no Jays or Otises, no legacy of "first emancipation" as in Pennsylvania, no myth of colorblindness as in New England; more practically, there was no equivalent to the Pennsylvania Abolition Society or the New York Manumission Society, elite interest groups protecting the recently emancipated and the fugitive.[20]

And yet, immediatist abolitionism exploded in Ohio as rapidly as in New England and upstate New York. By 1835, when the Ohio Anti-Slavery Society (OASS) was founded, the state boasted 100 local affiliates of the American Anti-Slavery Society, and by 1837, it was second only to New York, with 15,000 dues-paying abolitionists. In that context, sentiment grew that the Black Laws were unjust, in particular the ban on African Americans testifying against whites. After the state society's founding, the frequency and size of petitions for repeal steadily increased, with one from the Reserve in 1838 signed by 4,000 voters; in that year, the Ohio House passed a "gag" automatically referring petitions on the Black Laws "to a select committee where they would receive no further consideration." Given that "from 1832 to 1853 the state was almost evenly divided" between the two parties, however, Whigs could not afford to ignore these constituents, and several prominent Whigs were OASS leaders, including state senator Leicester King. The potential for spoiling was demonstrated in 1838, when abolitionists switched their votes to Democrats to reward Thomas Morris and punish Whig governor Joseph

Vance for extraditing John Mahan, a prominent abolitionist, to Kentucky on charges of aiding fugitives. A Whig paper acknowledged that "the defeat of the Whig candidate for Governor" and a "change in the General Assembly" were a direct result of abolitionist defection, since they "hold the balance of political power in a number of the counties of the State, sufficient to decide the party complexion of the Legislature." The reprisal from Whig antiabolitionists was fierce, even on the Reserve. In 1839, state senator Benjamin Wade (later a Radical Republican senator) was denied renomination from "two of the strongest Whig counties in the state" because of his antislavery stance. All parties felt the heat, with the Democrats' *Ohio Statesman* sneering that "abolitionism has become merely political and used to subserve the views of office-seekers who find Whiggery, unaided, too weak" to get them into office. Their railing at "Whig abolition judges" followed a courtroom melee in which a judge, prosecutor, sheriff, and local citizens in Marion County fought off a gang of Kentucky slavecatchers. Known long after as the "Black Bill rescue," it underlines the radicalization of some Whigs and why the Liberty Party took off so quickly after 1840.[21]

The careers of two pious Yankee lawyers, originally Whigs with conventional political ambitions, documents how some whites woke up to antislavery. Salmon Chase was born in New Hampshire in 1808 and moved to Cincinnati as a boy to be raised by his uncle, Ohio's Episcopal bishop. After attending Dartmouth, he passed the bar and began a successful practice in Cincinnati. In 1836, he witnessed mob attacks on the office and printing press of James Birney's newspaper *The Philanthropist*, and came to his defense against the city's elite, who endorsed the violence. Birney then asked him to represent a servant, Matilda, against the Kentuckian who claimed her. That trial and a subsequent series of cases made Chase famous as the "attorney general for fugitive slaves," as his well-argued briefs laid a strong basis for limiting slavery's reach. He functioned as a conventional Whig through 1840, when he was elected to Cincinnati's City Council, but then moved into the Liberty Party and built it into a formidable electoral formation. Joshua Giddings's conversion was less dramatic. Born poor in 1795 in Connecticut, he grew up on the Reserve, and became the protégé of one of its leading politicians, Elisha Whittlesey, who represented the "best characteristics of conservative New England Federalism." Like Chase, Giddings was a successful litigator, notable for his leadership in evangelical reform as president of the local Bible Society, a church elder, and a colonizationist. Whittlesey had been elected to Congress in 1822, and in the 1830s led "one of the strongest, most stable local Whig machines in the North" before moving into federal office as auditor and then first comptroller of the treasury. Giddings inherited his seat and his organization, winning his district three to one in 1838, but on arrival in

Washington, his witnessing the Slave Power's hold over Congress and slave coffles being marched through the capital's streets made him a relentless prosecutor of slaveholders.[22]

Here the contrast with New York's Whiggery is illustrative. At no point was any Ohio Whig comparable to Seward, as a charismatic governor who battled other states on behalf of his black constituents. Giddings's authority was restricted to one of Ohio's nineteen congressional districts as of 1840, although his reelection in 1842 by a vote of 7,469 to 393 following censure by the House for defending the enslaved men who had seized the *Creole* and taken it to the British Bahamas gave him great moral stature (even the vitriolic Virginian Henry A. Wise admitted it was "the greatest triumph ever achieved by a member"). The most commanding figure among Ohio Whigs was Thomas Corwin (U.S. House, 1831–40; governor, 1840–42; senator, 1845–50; secretary of the treasury, 1850–53), never consistently antislavery and in the later 1850s a leader of those conservative Republicans who sought to decouple their party from the "Negro" issue.[23]

As elsewhere, the character and fortunes of the Whig Party dictated the possibilities for black political engagement. From the mid-1830s to the early 1840s, Ohio Whigs hoped to dominate the state on the coattails of favorite son William Henry Harrison's presidential candidacies. As one of four Whig nominees in 1836, he carried the state with 52 percent against Van Buren, and in 1840, he beat Van Buren again with 54 percent. After that, however, Democrats narrowed the gap because of the Liberty Party's success at drawing off Whigs. In 1842, former state senator Leicester King, a "celebrated businessman" and "principal owner of the Pennsylvania and Ohio Canal," won 5,124 votes as the Liberty Party's gubernatorial candidate, versus the Democrat Wilson Shannon's winning margin of only 1,812. In 1844, the Whigs returned to power with Mordecai Bartley, although his margin was only 971 (0.3 percent), and he won by advocating repeal of the Black Laws, a litmus test for antislavery voters, while King got 8,898, underlining the Whigs' vulnerability. But even when Whigs controlled the state from 1845 on, with the Democrats "reduced to squabbling factions," there were always enough of them to join with Democrats in blocking repeal. In 1845, with Bartley's support, Senate Whigs modified the testimony law to permit black witnesses if certified by a white man, but could not get their bill through the House. In 1846, the successful Whig gubernatorial candidate William Bebb again made repeal part of his platform, but again Whigs in the legislature delayed action.[24]

———

Ohio's black political trajectory is briefer than in the east. Churches and associations formed in the 1820s, a generation after Boston, New York, and Philadelphia, but by 1833 there were twenty African Methodist Episcopal (AME) churches, with the nation's first black Baptist Association, founded in 1836. Cincinnati sent a delegate to the national conventions in 1830 and 1834, and vice presidents and corresponding secretaries were appointed for Ohio on three occasions. Given the two weeks required to travel from Cincinnati to Philadelphia, this contact between seaboard and interior is impressive. Organized black politics arrived as well, in response to the upsurge in colonizationism, "wildly popular" in Ohio in the late 1820s, and new Black Laws, passed in 1829 and strengthened in 1831, which barred children of African descent from the new system of common schools, and denied persons of color any legal settlement in the state, making them ineligible for poor relief. In Chillicothe, a Colored Anti-Slavery Society formed, led by Walter Claiborne Yancy, and in 1837, the Cleveland businessman John Malvin called a meeting to organize a network of private schools, backed by a School Fund Society; this was the first state meeting convened by black men, perhaps inspiring New York's better-known 1840 convention. Over the next decade, Ohio's black men practiced a version of New York's development, via regular conventions, a State Central Committee, and one newspaper, the *Palladium of Liberty* in 1843–44, minus the Empire State's close engagement with political parties.[25]

Black Ohioans played a role in the repeal campaign, although at least initially they were shut out of the OASS, which replicated Pennsylvania's defining "abolitionist" as "white." The School Fund Society worked with Leicester King in 1837 to introduce a motion in the senate overturning the law creating whites-only common schools. Their self-organization under adverse circumstances did not go unnoticed. Throughout its existence, the *Colored American* paid homage to Ohio's black settlements, with long reports on their schools, land and stock owning, crop production, and encomia from local whites on their temperance and good credit. Seen from New York City, Ohio exemplified how black people should leave the cities, give up demeaning service occupations, and become independent farmers. Ohio was not depicted as a model of separate development and withdrawal, however. The *Colored American* emphasized not just their rapid land accumulation and how much corn and grain they brought to market in a year, but how these farmers were integrated into the economic life of where they lived.[26]

To the east, black men participated since the Revolution as Federalists, Whigs, and Liberty men, but there is little such evidence for Ohio prior to the 1850s. What we know of black electoralism until then comes from court cases, hostile newspaper accounts, and a single contested election. Black Ohioans enjoyed a rich associational life, petitioning the legislature and holding local and state indignation meetings, but their connection to partisanship is visible mainly through coverage in the state's Democratic organ, the

Ohio Statesman, edited in Columbus by Samuel Medary, a powerful figure who tarred even conservative Whigs as "fanatic" abolitionists seeking "negro votes."

The possibility of black men exercising political rights in common with whites first surfaced during the tumultuous 1840 election, in two ways. The first was the *Statesman*'s scare campaign deploying the phrase "Negro Votes." Ohio's Democrats, as elsewhere, claimed that William Henry Harrison was the candidate of the "Bank-Abolition-English-Federal" party. In Ohio, Medary focused on demanding that Whig gubernatorial candidate Thomas Corwin explain his "Negro Votes," meaning his vote to discuss modifying the Black Laws in the Ohio House in 1822. This campaign came to a head in September with a blaring indictment: "PEOPLE OF OHIO, BEWARE! BEWARE!!—THE UNION OF THE OHIO ABOLITIONISTS AND OHIO WHIGGERY IS COMPLETE—THE BLACK SPIRITS OF FANATICISM ARE AT THEIR WORK—ABOLITIONISM, LIKE ANTI-MASONRY, HAS SUNK ITSELF INTO FEDERAL WHIGGERY, WORKINGMEN OF OHIO, & DEMOCRATS, LOOK OUT!" The threat was spelled out: "Let this party get the power, and our State will be overrun with negroes from Kentucky and other parts of the Union, and our laws of Ohio will be altered so as to give them ALL THE PRIVILEGES the abolitionists ask." Corwin supposedly wanted to "give the ignorant, depraved and degraded *nigger*, the power to *swear away* the lives of white men and women." He was a "Garrisonian abolitionist, dyed in the wool" and "would raise the naturally degraded blacks of the State to the same level with the whites." Clearly, the phrase "Negro Votes!" did not refer to black men voting, although Medary also alleged black men had participated as "delegates" from the Reserve at a mammoth Harrison rally.[27]

The fact of men of color voting came up when an eminent Whig, John C. Wright (U.S. House, 1823–29; state supreme court judge, 1831–35; lately the *Cincinnati Gazette*'s editor), contested his defeat in a Hamilton County Senate race. The Whigs claimed that large numbers had been imported from Kentucky and other Ohio counties to vote for the Democrat, and they took hundreds of depositions to prove those charges. The voluminous Senate report included a handful of accounts of black men voting or attempting to vote as "nearer white." Confusion about phenotype as a reliable marker of race was apparent. One white was asked whether a man he knew, Amos Hubbard, was a "mulatto" and answered, "Judging from his complexion, I should suppose he was half way between a white man and a mulatto. N. G. Pendleton, Thos. Corwin, and Daniel Vanmeter are about the same complexion. I have never seen them in company. Mr. Hubbard's hair is inclined to curl or twist—not as much as some white men I am acquainted with, of fair and light complexion" (besides "Black Tom" Corwin, whose complexion is addressed in chapter 1,

Pendleton was a Cincinnati Whig elected to Congress that year, and the other man may have been John Vanmeter, a Pike County Whig legislator). Whereas degrees of coloration or curliness were subject to interpretation, the authority of election judges was unequivocal. In one instance, a group of five black men went to vote in October's election, because they had formerly or believed they had that right. When the Democratic judges discovered that all but one intended to vote Whig, they ruled them all out, but at the November presidential election let one of two brothers vote because he declared he would vote Democratic. The Senate report confused matters further, since among the several hundred "illegal voters" it listed men who believed themselves to be sufficiently white to vote, whereas other black men were apparently accepted as "legal voters."[28]

After 1840, anecdotes accrued of black men trying to vote and the Whigs recruiting mixed-race voters, while black leaders inclined toward the Liberty Party. A short-lived newspaper, the *Palladium of Liberty*, edited by David Jenkins in Columbus from late 1843 into 1844, expressed disgust with the major parties, supporting James G. Birney for president. It also reported a meeting where a prominent Columbus man of color, W. L. McAfee, was formally shunned because on Election Day he labeled another man a fugitive from Kentucky, thus ineligible to vote. By then, Medary's *Statesman* was printing denunciations of black Whigs, like the report from Miami County on the 1844 governor's race, that the Whig "Bartley's majority at our annual election in this township, was 154, and Clay's majority at the election just passed, is 136, and two *niggers*, making, in all, 138." Medary mocked Whig attempts to repeal the Black Laws in early 1845, that "the Senate, last evening, passed a bill to encourage the settlement of blacks in our State.—They will now be ready to swear a white man into any place they desire." White laborers would "be thrown into competition with a horde of blacks brought into our State from the South. . . . For forty years we have lived in peace and comfort under our laws, but because a few half negroes voted the whig ticket, and the abolitionists are to be bought up, we have this extraordinary conduct of this Whig Legislature." A Cincinnati Whig was attacked for ardently recruiting "negroes" to offset the foreign-born vote, and two Columbus Democrats were prosecuted for dragging black men away from the polls. In late 1845, it was alleged that a Democrat had been "beaten by *one vote*, and that one vote given by a *negro*. . . . He was opposed by federalists, abolitionists, disaffected democrats, and negroes. Tipton, the federal candidate, pledged himself to vote for repeal of the negro laws, and this secured him the votes of the abolitionists and the negroes."[29]

The most authoritative assessment on Ohio's racial politics in the 1840s came from Salmon Chase. In spring 1845, Cincinnati's black community honored him for a decade's legal work on their behalf. In his reply to their presentation of an elaborate silver pitcher, Chase declared his "disapprobation of that clause in the constitution which denies to a portion of the colored people the right of suffrage. True Democracy makes no inquiry about the color of the skin, or the place of nativity, or any other similar circumstance of condition.—Wherever it sees a man, it recognizes a being endowed by his Creator with original inalienable rights." He would "propose no action against the constitution. But, whenever a convention shall be called to revise that instrument, I trust that this anti-suffrage restriction will be erased," since it was "already as ridiculous in practice as it is wrong in theory." Given that Ohio's supreme court had "established the rule that all persons nearer white than half, are white within the meaning of the constitution and laws . . . it becomes necessary, therefore, in every case, when a vote is tendered at the polls, to scrutinize the complexion and ascertain the exact shade," and there were "certainly voters in the State, distinguished too by personal worth and political position, who would have reason to fear an impartial application of such of a test." Chase's comments clarify that voting by men of color was a settled practice by then, with "scrutinizing and ascertaining" equally common. His reference to men "distinguished by . . . political position" likely meant "Black Tom" Corwin or perhaps other swarthy whites. As we shall see, a decade later, that silver pitcher would come back to haunt Chase and his as-yet-unfounded Republican Party.[30]

Gaining Rights, 1848–1855

After 1848, Ohio's black men benefited from extraordinary turmoil in the state's party system. As Stephen Maizlish has argued, Ohio "played "the critical, leading role in [the] . . . shift toward sectionalism and Civil War." In 1844, national tensions over slavery aided the Whigs, since Democrats could not support Texas's annexation and maintain the favor of a majority of Ohioans. The Whigs claimed the antislavery space by deploying their in-house radical, Joshua Giddings. Like his mentor, John Quincy Adams, Giddings demonstrated that one could be both firmly antislavery and a loyal Whig. After 1844, however, it became harder to maintain this fiction. Whigs twice won the governorship with candidates committed to repealing the Black Laws, only to have those pledges frustrated despite Whig legislative majorities. This failure tarnished their reputation with antislavery men, especially on the Reserve and with black Ohioans; David Jenkins commented in early 1848, "The law-making party in Ohio (the Whig) claim to be the true friends of our race, yet will not repeal the odious Black Laws, in themselves infamous enough to disgrace any nation." Once again, "notice was given of an intention to bring in a repeal bill; but little can be hoped in regard to its passage" for strictly partisan reasons: "Many of the influential members of both branches of the Legislature, say that it is out of their power until after the Presidential election."[31]

In 1848, this reasoning by expediency would no longer suffice. The national Whigs' nomination of the slaveholder Zachary Taylor, less appealing in Ohio than the Kentuckian Henry Clay, "gave a shock to the Whig antislavery men which they could not stand." As one observer put it, "The result was, instant rebellion; which proved too strong for all the efforts of the Whig leaders." Giddings jumped ship to the Free Soilers and campaigned fervently for Van Buren. He took his constituents with him, and Van Buren beat Taylor in the Reserve, winning 35,523 (10.8 percent) of the vote statewide, and delivering Ohio to the Democrats' Lewis Cass, who won by 16,176. From that point on, the Ohio Whig Party was "shattered. . . . Stripped of its antislavery wing, the party of Henry Clay would never again pose a serious threat in an Ohio election." This was third-party politics with a vengeance, and for the next decade, the "political antislavery organizations would . . . have a controlling influence over Ohio politics."[32]

The party battles before 1848 were but a prelude to the schisms and temporary alignments of the next seven years, until Ohio's Republican Party emerged in late 1855. In 1849, the state saw one of the period's most notorious partisan bargains, which redounded entirely to the benefit of black people. The 1848 elections sent a small group of Free Soilers to Columbus, and in early 1849 they cooperated with Democrats to take control of the legislature. In return, the Free Soilers gained repeal of key Black Laws (the ban on black testimony against whites; the requirement for immigrants to post a $500 bond; the exclusion of black children from public education) and sent Free Soil architect Salmon Chase to the U.S. Senate. These maneuvers generated permanent antipathy to Chase among Whigs, since he collaborated closely with Samuel Medary, the "undoubted leader of the Ohio Democratic Party," and an avowed racist who focused entirely on "the bidding for lucrative state offices and printing contracts." A recent Chase biographer argues he secured repeal because of Medary's "unquenchable thirst to rule the state for power and profit made him open to bargaining," but the former Free Soiler A. G. Riddle wrote in 1887 that Democrats had also moved in an antislavery direction, asserting, "The causes which changed the Reserve from Whig to Free-soil, were not without large influence on the old parties," quoting the January 1849 Democratic convention's declaration that "the people of Ohio look upon slavery everywhere as an evil" and will "use all power given by the terms of the national compact, to prevent its increase, to mitigate and finally eradicate the evil." He thought this "quite warranted the hope and expectation of Mr. Chase . . . that the party might be speedily and thoroughly evangelized on the subject, and excused [his] personal identification with the Democracy," versus "the groundless assertion that the Black laws were repealed only by conspiracy."[33]

In Washington, Chase sought to attach himself to the national Democratic Party, rather than acting as an independent Free Soiler. Since the early 1840s, he had cherished the hope of gathering all antislavery men into a major party so as to actually govern. For the moment, it seemed as if Ohio's Free Democratic Party (as the Free Soilers renamed themselves) might disappear. Almost none of its legislators were reelected in 1850, and Chase endorsed Democrat Reuben Wood for governor in 1851, rather than the Free Democrat Samuel Lewis. Instead, led by Giddings, the Free Democrats came back hard. In 1852, their presidential candidate, New Hampshire senator John P. Hale, won 8.8 percent in Ohio, far ahead of his national tally, and in 1853, Lewis, again their gubernatorial candidate, tripled his vote to a remarkable 17 percent as the Whigs imploded; the Free Democrats' renascence empowered black men's entrance into party politics, as described below. By 1854, meanwhile, Chase had been repudiated by the state's Democrats, and with no chance of reelection, he led the opposition to Stephen A. Douglas's Nebraska Bill. The national reverberations of his "Appeal of the Independent Democrats" and subsequent duel with Douglas on the Senate floor began the complicated process that birthed Ohio's Republican Party. That jerry-rigged coalition of Free Democrats, Whigs, Know-Nothings, and a few regular Democrats was the first Republican formation to win a state election, in 1855.[34]

Where did Ohio's black men fit into these years? Certainly, since 1840, an increasing number voted, as Democrats kept noting (the "one poor drunken negro whig" in Richland County in 1852, who invoked "the deepest curses upon the democracy, and particularly our democratic trustees, because the whig leaders had failed to get in his vote," and the "EIGHT NEGRO VOTES" tallied that same year in Columbus). In 1850 the anti-political Garrisonian Stephen Foster noted with pleasure that they voted easily in Oberlin and W. H. Day asserted they had become the balance of power in Cleveland. There is scattered evidence of black participation in the Liberty Party. In 1844, Walter C. Yancy, a Butler County leader, gave a rousing speech at the party's convention, and in 1846, the party put Joseph Mason on the road as a lecturer, and (to little fanfare) nominated the Cleveland barber John L. Watson for county sheriff. These years also document a familiar pattern of black leaders speaking as Liberty men while ordinary men of color preferred the Whigs. In 1840, Medary commented acerbically that Columbus's "negro row" was lit up to celebrate Harrison's victory, like other Whig neighborhoods, and reports regularly cited Whigs bringing them to the polls; Democrats certainly made these charges for effect, but a resolution at the 1849

State Convention of the Colored Citizens of Ohio demanded they stop voting for "men-stealers," meaning Whigs. In 1848, some prominent leaders, including Alfred J. Anderson in southwest Butler County and C. H. Langston in Columbus, were enthusiastic Free Soilers, but there is no evidence of participation in that party's campaign as speakers or attempts to mobilize black voters. Indeed, Whigs on the Reserve baited Free Soilers for their silence on black suffrage.[35]

The most concrete result of the Black Laws' repeal was the development of a black-controlled education system in Cincinnati, a singular instance of "shadow" politics moving into the public sphere. The fight for black schools in the Queen City was one of the most successful political campaigns by free people of color prior to the Civil War, producing an astonishing rise in student enrollments and a notable legal victory. After the General Assembly mandated schools for black children in 1849, Cincinnati's black male taxpayers quickly elected their own six-man School Board, as the law authorized. Hamilton County's treasurer then refused to release the substantial funds available to them, $2,177.67, claiming the Constitution's provision that only white men could vote invalidated the board's formation. In *State ex. Rel. Directors of the Eastern and Western School Districts* (1850) Ohio's supreme court overturned this decision, and the schools opened. Despite steps backward (in 1853, a Democratic legislature repealed the funding bill, which was restored by Republicans in 1856), black organizers, notably John Isom Gaines, created an entire network of public schools unlike anything in the North or South. By 1859, Cincinnati's people of color controlled five school buildings and significant funds.[36]

Cincinnati's black community managed this feat because of its prior self-organization. As of 1844, that city featured the nation's only secondary institution for black students, the Gilmore School, funded by a bequest from Hiram Gilmore, a New England Methodist, and the equal of elite white academies, including a "chapel, a playground, and gym equipment." This establishment educated some of the nineteenth century's most distinguished men of color, including P. B. S. Pinchback, lieutenant governor (and briefly governor) of Louisiana; John Mercer Langston; Peter H. Clark; and Monroe Trotter. It helped that Gaines and his cohort (including his nephew Clark, a principal black educator postbellum) associated with whites who would play central roles in Ohio's Republican Party, including Rutherford B. Hayes, George Hoadly, and Alphonso Taft. Nor were these gains restricted to Cincinnati. Statewide, almost 7,000 black children went to all-black schools by 1861, reaching parity with the education available to whites.[37]

From 1849 on, black politics moved to a new level. That year's state convention committed itself to independent action, vowing to "pursue their own course," while "thanking their white friends for all action put forth on our behalf." It met in the hall of Ohio's House of Representatives, presumably through Free Soil influence, and its deliberations were observed by many whites and commended in the press; legislators "invited negro delegates to call at their rooms," with the Garrisonian *Anti-Slavery Bugle* trumpeting, "The colored man has been allowed to come up, without insult and without reproach—to enter into a place hitherto deemed sacred to the white man alone." The convention voted to print 500 copies of John Brown's 1848 pamphlet containing *Walker's Appeal* from 1829 and Garnet's 1843 "Address to the Slaves": given that it was Cincinnati's A. M. Sumner who had warned in 1843 that Garnet's speech would expose free black people along the Middle Border to physical retribution, this was a major step. They maintained their optimism at the January 1850 convention in Columbus. The journalist William Howard Day declared that "the colored men" of Cleveland "were able to control the elections; that men now place 'Free Soil' over the heads of their papers, to secure patronage." They formed the Ohio Colored American League, appointing six lecturers to canvass the state for equal suffrage at the upcoming constitutional convention, as well as "one man in every county to take the number of voters" and "make arrangements for public meetings."[38]

This brief honeymoon was soon over. From the September 1850 passage of the Fugitive Slave Act until the Republican Party's founding, Ohio's politics polarized, with some white men announcing their intent to resist that act by violence, including Giddings's 1852 statement, "I would sooner see every slave holder of the nation hanged than to witness the subjugation of northern freemen to such a humiliating condition. If this law continues to be enforced, Civil War is inevitable. In my own district are many fugitives who have informed their masters where they can be found"; in many Whig-Republican counties, that intent was acted on, as R. J. M. Blackett has documented in considerable detail. In this frame, black men entered into mainstream politics and gained access to the state's leading politicians, even Democrats. A nine-man delegation from the 1851 convention pressed Governor Reuben Wood, an antislavery Democrat allied with Free Soilers, to endorse unrestricted suffrage at the upcoming constitutional convention. They quoted an 1850 letter from William Seward hailing New York's black voters, and asked pointedly, "Is not this due the colored men who, under the restrictive clause of the present Constitution, have cast their ballots for your Excellency, as the standard-bearer of their principles?" Their 1852 convention published letters from white leaders, including Senator Benjamin Wade (still a Whig, later a Republican), who announced, "I rejoice to see that the colored people have taken their own destiny into their own hands. . . . The color of the skin is nothing." In 1854, white Free Soil leaders invited John Mercer Langston to the State

House to present a "Memorial to the General Assembly of the State of Ohio" from that year's convention. Although Frederick Douglass had spoken in the Senate chamber in 1850, in 1854 the Democratic majority refused to hear Langston. In response, a Whig-dominated Select Committee on Petitions and Memorials from Colored Persons made his speech the main text of their report, declaring, "The various reasons for extending the right of suffrage to colored persons are so ably set forth in the memorial of J. Mercer Langston . . . that nothing further in the way of arguments seemed to be required."[39]

Gains in party recognition hardly balanced the furious desperation suffusing black Ohio in light of the Fugitive Slave Act. The 1850–51 constitutional convention rebuffed advances in black rights by overwhelming majorities, although none of the Black Laws were reinstated. As anti–"negro equality" petitions poured in, every delegate from outside the Reserve voted against nonracial suffrage, 66–12 (and then 75–13), against black men in the militia, 62–22, or integrated schools, 61–26. The anger that ran through Ohio's black conventions in those years stimulated a quixotic effort by a few young men, led by John Mercer Langston, to promote emigration. Although Martin Delany dominates the narrative of emigrationism in this decade because of his 1853 National Emigration Convention in Cleveland, its impact is overstated. No significant leaders attended, it was entirely Delany's show. Langston's campaign was more consequential, since if black Ohio had turned away from antislavery politics, the consequences would have resonated nationally. From 1850 to 1852, in a fervor of romantic nationalism inspired by Hungary's Louis Kossuth, Langston urged his colleagues to campaign for a territory on the United States' margins, to activate the dream of "an actual black nationality." He and his brother Charles wrote Senator Chase, asking Congress to grant land taken from Mexico where they could "peaceably settle and enjoy our own Political rights as do the inhabitants of other territories." Veterans like David Jenkins were not convinced. Despite Langston's eloquence, only one in five delegates to the 1852 convention endorsed his plan and he gave it up, taking the floor at Delany's 1853 convention to rebut any plan of leaving.[40]

Langston's subsequent path was central to black politics, as no other man of color achieved as much before the war. He had come under the wing of the prominent judge Philemon Bliss, which led to a political career. Giving up on emigration, he helped open the Free Democratic Party to black men, lecturing statewide for John P. Hale in 1852, including standing on the same platform with Hale and Chase in support of his friend Norton P. Townsend's election to the state Senate, and in 1853 the Free Democrats in Lorain County elected him one of four delegates to the 1853 state convention. By then, black leaders were active in the party, including W. H. Day unsuccessfully lobbying at its 1852 convention for a commitment to complete civil equality, including a threat to withhold their votes: "Under the construction of the Constitution by the Supreme Court, some of us vote. We mean to cast that vote only for our friends. Free Democracy is an alluring name, and we love it; but names should be, with us, of no regard, excepting so far as they are truly the exponents of principles." In 1854, Langston went into the Anti-Nebraska coalition that gathered together all antislavery men, the Republicans' precursor. His ambiguous racial identity and wit drew large crowds, and his ability to confound hecklers made converts on the spot. That September he passed the bar, and rather like Robert Morris in Boston, established a practice among liquor dealers and poor whites, especially the Irish, who assumed that he could gain them an equal chance in the Reserve. By 1855, his abilities, education, and forensic skill convinced white leaders that he deserved elevation, like other talented young men, via a sponsored nomination. Langston had bought a large farm in Brownhelm Township, a flourishing agricultural area of 1,200 residents. Three parties (Whigs, Democrats, and Independent or Free Democrats) competed. In March 1855, Langston rode to the latter's nominating caucus with Charles Fairchild, a member of a family "prominent in the church and controlling in social circles"; one brother was a professor and later president of Oberlin, and a second was president of Berea in Kentucky. Fairchild asked permission to nominate Langston for township clerk, the officer handling all legal affairs, including tax collection and disbursement, and on April 2, he won office by "a handsome majority, even though I am the only colored man who lives in this township," as he reported in *Frederick Douglass' Paper*.[41]

Contending for Power, 1855–1860

In the six years leading to secession and war, black men steadily increased their visibility in Ohio politics, aided by its African American population growing 45 percent between 1850 and 1860, from 25,279 to 36,673. Men like the Langstons joined the Republican Party to push it toward equality. Taking advantage of the state's peculiar racial order, they mounted a voting rights campaign to guarantee maximum leverage for men "nearer white than black," while pressing for full suffrage. When their right to vote was challenged in a famously contested House election, they took it to the state's supreme court, which overturned a law Democrats passed in 1859 barring men with "any visible admixture" of "African blood" from voting. Finally, in the Oberlin-Wellington Rescue of 1858–59, Charles Henry Langston led a mob to attack U.S. marshals and slavecatchers and turned the resulting prosecution into a show trial, radicalizing Ohio Republicans and propelling the Langstons to statewide prominence as truly "Black Republicans." In Blackett's words, southerners had learned by then that "the security of their property rested, in large part, on the whims of the Ohio electorate."[42]

Political scientists have long demonstrated that it is statistically impossible for a single group's votes to determine an election result, given how many constituencies (let alone individuals) simultaneously make decisions. Nonetheless, in Ohio in the late 1850s, everyone recognized the "negro vote" as one of the two blocs subject to judicial or legislative fiat, the other being "adopted citizens." Democrats fought at the polls and in the legislature, the courts, and even in Congress to exclude black voters, claiming that they alone gave the Republicans office. Despite this campaign, backed up by extensive documentation of where, when, and with what effect men of color voted, the Democrats repeatedly lost, culminating in fall 1860 with an effort to allege that Ohio's "14,000 negro voters" would give the state to the Republicans and the presidency to Lincoln.

Democrats Charge

We begin by examining when, and with what intended effect, these charges were made. Starting in 1855, during Salmon Chase's campaign for governor as candidate of the new Republican or "People's" Party, Democrats alerted white men to the danger of "Negroes Voting." In late summer, the *Plain Dealer* noted that "the fusionists [Republicans] of Lorain county at their meeting to appoint delegates to the late fusion convention" had voted "It is the sense of this Convention that the colored people are entitled to have the elective franchise given them," followed by the jibe common in any Democratic paper: "Down with the Germans and Irish—up with the Negro." Medary's *Statesman* brought Chase's 1845 "speech to the Negroes of Cincinnati" into the picture, to blare "Chase in favor of Negro voters!—The proof at hand!!," accurate enough, since he had declared his "disapprobation of that clause in the Constitution which denies to a portion of the *colored people the right of suffrage*. True democracy makes no inquiry about the *color of the skin*" (emphasis in original). He added for good measure, "CHASE IN FAVOR OF NIGGER CHILDREN ATTENDING THE SAME PUBLIC SCHOOLS WITH THE WHITES," equally true.[43]

When Chase won with 49 percent in a three-way race against the incumbent Democrat, William Medill, with 43 percent, and a Know-Nothing, former governor Allen Trimble, with 8 percent, the *Plain Dealer* denounced the "Great Chase Negro Celebration at Oberlin!" and at year's end detailed the new danger. Delaware newspapers had published conflicting reports regarding "Do Negroes Vote in Ohio?" and in response the Cleveland paper published a letter from E. F. Munson, the Oberlin postmaster (a Democratic appointment). He had been "at the polls" all day, and reported "More than twenty-five negroes voted for S. P. Chase." He had *"challenged the negroe votes*," but "most of 'colored brudders' would swear that they were more than half white, and the *Board* would receive their votes. Almost all who came up to vote were as *black* as 'Uncle Tom.'" The *Plain Dealer*'s editor added his own evidence: "Negroes, black as erebus, voted in Cleveland on that day, and voted for CHASE and the balance of the Know Nothing ticket.—The fact that the Constitution of the State denies them that right, is not a barrier to their vote. . . . If they swear they are more than half white, and the judges are Abolitionists, there is no negroometer [*sic*] yet invented to test the proportion of colored blood in an ardent colored man's veins, and he votes what he deems nearest to the Abolition ticket, which was the Know Nothing ticket last fall."[44]

Once in power, Republicans acted quickly to limit the "foreign vote," not surprising given how many Republicans had lately been Know-Nothings. In response, Ohio Democrats resurrected the familiar opposition between white men with accents and native men with dark complexions, attacking the Republican bill "compelling Foreigners throughout the State to go to the Cincinnati, or the Cleveland District Court to get their naturalization papers. This will effectually disfranchise thousands per year, who are too poor to pay the necessary expenses. A poor German or Irishman living in a remote part of the State has got to go from one hundred to two hundred miles, take along his witnesses, pay the expenses . . . instead of applying to his own County Court, as heretofore. This is a Know Nothing Black Republican trick. . . . Negroes are to be allowed to vote without naturalization papers."[45]

All-out black mobilization for Frémont in summer 1856 further stirred the pot. At first, the *Statesman* simply announced, "Colored Men in the Field for Frémont," followed by where Langston would be speaking. In the fall, however, restraint vanished, and Democrats characterized the presidential race as between "Frémont and Nigger Supremacy, or Buchanan and a government for white men!" with dark murmurings about "Oberlin darkies . . . stumping it with all their might for Frémont" and "a learned nigger, said to be a graduate of Oberlin," presumably Langston, on the stump. The potential for a large black vote produced an awkward mix of threats and purportedly friendly warnings. Typical was an early October declaration that Columbus "has been thrown into no little excitement under the rumors that the Frémont party were pulling the negroes in this city to get them to vote to kill the votes of white men. . . . We would advise the negroes to not suffer themselves to be used by mere demagogues who care nothing for them further than to use them. . . . The Constitution of Ohio uses the word *white* in regard to voters, and until that Constitution is changed let the negroes be content to live under it as it is."[46]

Democratic concerns became more practical once voting began in October (Ohio held its state and congressional elections a month before the presidential vote). In Cleveland, the *Plain Dealer* reported, "The fusion majority in this city proves to be just about the Negro vote. . . . The Democrats propose to hold the black man to the same observance of laws that they do the white man," meaning proof of residency and a certificate of naturalization if he was a foreigner. "Now if white men, natives and foreigners, are thus made subject to Law, why should not black men? But the latter are allowed to vote by Fusion Judges without asking them their age, where from, or whether naturalized or not. If they are only *black* they vote." Elsewhere it was reported that on the Reserve "the Republicans from Oberlin marched *arm in arm* with the negroes, and nearly all the 'kullered pussons' on the ground wore silk badges with Frémont and Dayton printed thereon," and "At a recent fusion meeting in Bucyrus, Ohio, Gov. Chase addressed a portion of his remarks to a large number of negroes who were present, assuring them that the time was not far distant when they could not only march in procession but *vote* also!" The big news in late October was not the upcoming presidential vote, but Clement L. Vallandigham's challenge in southwest Ohio's Third Congressional District, where the incumbent Lewis D. Campbell claimed victory by nineteen out of 18,657 votes cast (discussed in more detail below). Vallandigham immediately announced that Campbell's margin came via illegal votes, including those of "negroes," and the *Statesman* cheered him on, adding that "the Democrats, at every poll throughout the State on the 4th of November, should challenge these negro voters, and make a record of them, so that we can ascertain something like the number in the State, if they are permitted to vote." A new tactic was thus unveiled, accompanied by a new discourse asserting black alienage, anticipating the *Dred Scott* decision. Democrats now discovered that the *Polly Gray* decision and its subsequent affirmations referred to the original state constitution, which defined voters as "white male *inhabitants*." The 1851 constitution specified voting by "white male *citizens*," which made the Ohio supreme court's previous rulings irrelevant. "Citizenship of the United States" was now "a necessary qualification for an elector or voter" and it was "the well settled doctrine of the Federal Courts that none but pure white persons are, or can become citizens of United States. Different states may adopt different qualifications of citizenship for their own citizens, but citizenship of a State and citizenship of the United States are two distinct matters," an affront to states' rights and an indication of Democratic desperation.[47]

The 1856 presidential election, in which Frémont won Ohio with 48 percent to Buchanan's 44 percent (Fillmore received only 7 percent), provided more evidence that black men were voting in substantial numbers with active

Republican cooperation. In Cleveland, Democrats noted sardonically that in a Republican ward, the judges "were very willing to receive the votes of the African gentlemen" until "one of the latter went up to vote" and "somebody said something about 'good Democratic vote,' and Fusion Judges immediately looked on the dark side of the subject and concluded that he was too black. On opening the darkey's ticket, it was discovered that a Frémont vote had been lost, and everybody laughed except the very solemn judges." More seriously, in Xenia in southwestern Ohio, the local Democratic boss reported, "65 negroes voted in this township in the last election. I have the names of all the negroes and if you wish I can furnish them to you," adding, "At this rate, the Democrats have been beaten in Ohio by negro votes alone." Noting what Frémont's victory foretold for their party, Democrats repeated that the new constitution's reference to "citizens" meant that "every negro or mulatto [who had been] permitted to vote in Ohio since" its adoption was "an illegal voter, and should be so held," and "the Judges of elections receiving such votes should be dealt with under the law." Republicans "carry out this provision as regards the word 'citizen' in reference to foreign emigrants, to the utmost limit, and yet in the face of the very same provision, stuff the ballot boxes with negro votes, by permitting men to vote who are not *white*."[48]

The year 1857 marked a step backward. In the spring, Democrats and conservative Republicans in the legislature blocked the effort of Oberlin's newly elected representative, Professor James Monroe, to move an equal-suffrage amendment to the Constitution. Democrats came back hard in the fall elections, with Medary's *Ohio Statesman* promoting the supposed "Congo Creed" as the essence of Republicanism—that "a negro is human—he has a soul—he has an intellect as far as the right of suffrage or any other rights of citizenship is concerned, he should be placed on an equality with the rest of mankind." Cleveland's *Plain Dealer* printed a drawing of the silver pitcher given Chase in 1845, and next to it a caricature of a black man, with the headline "EYE ON THE PITCHER / NIGGER IN THE PITCHER," calling the Republicans "THE PITCHER PARTY" and assailing them with newfangled polygenetics:

The superiority of the Caucasian or white race over all other races of men has been an admitted fact ever since the world began. This race started in Asia, spread throughout Europe, and is now fast overrunning the American continent. It is first to carry with it civilization, christianization, the mechanic arts, the prowess of war, and the blessings of peace. Whenever it amalgamates with any of the inferior races, it deteriorates [*sic*] itself, but elevates that with which it mixes. Nothing can resist its onward march to Universal empire. This is its "manifest destiny."

Republicans sought to "make this a Republic of Congoes, Coolies, and all other kinds of colored men," and chief among them was "the present chief magistrate," who saw his position "as a mere stepping stone to that higher point of his ambition, the Presidency. The starting point in this, his Black Republican race for the Presidency, was duly signalized by the colored people of Cincinnati in the presentation of a 'SILVER PITCHER,'" pointing to the crude drawing, "showing his real sentiments on the subject of negro equalization with the whites and their consequent amalgamation." The end result would be "the deterioration of the whites, the partial elevation of the blacks, and the general corruption of American manners, society, and blood; producing a mongrel race of men, mulattoes, minks, and monkeys." Democrats advanced this charge so often that Republicans derisively referred to them as "Congos."[49]

Democrats pivoted to implementing the *Dred Scott* decision, since "the Supreme Court of the United States has recently decided that negroes, whether slave or free, that is, men of the African race, or of African descent, are not *citizens* of the United States." Ohio's supreme court ruling "that a person of more white than African blood is white, and therefore entitled to vote" was "completely overruled," and "the Judges at the coming city election" must now submit. This line was taken at every election hereafter. In the fall, the *Plain Dealer* issued grandiose threats: "The Democracy are determined to put an end tomorrow to negro and mongrel voting. . . . The plea of ignorance will avail them nothing in their defence as the *law* presumes everyone to have a knowledge of the plain provisions of the Constitution." Black men should ignore "the advice of Fusion Lawyers and Judges as they will be *utterly powerless* to defend in a *court of law* (and they know it)" any men of color who voted, and "The Vigilance Committees in the different Wards will take down the names of all negroes or mongrels whose vote any fusion judge may receive." Two days later, it crowed the "CITY OF CLEVELAND PERMANENTLY DEMOCRATIC. . . . Twice now in succession, and within a year, have our gallant Democracy carried this city by over *three hundred majority*. . . . The Negroes have done voting and the Black Republicans will soon be defunct!"[50]

The *Plain Dealer* tracked where men of color did vote: "The Negro Vote of Ohio . . . is variously estimated at 1,200 to 1,500. In this county they range from 150 to 200. In Lorain they count about 150. Over 100 voted in Oberlin whose names are regularly registered and challenged by the Democrats. In Lake, Geauga and Ashtabula, all vote without a why or wherefore. It is safe to put down the negro vote in the Reserve at from 500 to 800," but "the great body of them live in the Southern part of the State. . . . How many are allowed to vote in these regions remains to be known. There are between 15 and

20,000 free blacks in the State, all anxious to vote and who the Republicans declare have a right to vote and shall vote." Late that month, after Chase squeaked to reelection by a margin equal to the estimated black vote, the *Cincinnati Enquirer* blazoned "White Man Elected by Black Men's Votes," adding the latter had "saved his bacon," while a Massachusetts Democratic paper asserted that if Ohio's Democratic gubernatorial candidate lost, "it is by the negro vote." In November, the *Statesman* concluded bitterly that Chase's victory came through "twelve or thirteen hundred negro votes," with the *Plain Dealer* adding, "He will make a good nigger governor."[51]

Minus any state election, 1858 saw a relative hiatus in racial politicking. If Democrats did not charge "negro votes," Republicans would certainly not raise the issue. As 1859 opened, however, Democrats controlling the legislature moved to disfranchise men of any African descent and punish those permitting them to vote, with the *Plain Dealer* gloating over "A BLOW TO OBERLIN. One Hundred Votes Lost to Chase." The new law clarified "an Ohio voter to be one *without any African blood*. Had such a law been in force two years ago, Mr. Chase would have been defeated and Mr. Payne elected. The whole Democratic State ticket would have been elected. There is no doubt that colored votes decided the outcome of that election." The *Statesman* hailed "The White Bill," guaranteeing, "We shall have no more state officers elected by negro votes." The penalties were severe enough to repel voters of color and judges of elections, requiring the latter to "reject the vote of any person offering to vote at said election, and claiming to be a white male citizen of the United States, whenever it shall appear to such judge or judges that the person offering to vote has a distinct and visible admixture of African blood, with any Judge who violates this prescription fined from $100 to $500, and one to six months in jail." Democrats in and out of Ohio posed this "Good Law" against the nativists of Greater New England: "While Republican Massachusetts is amending its constitution to prevent adopted citizens voting for two years after they are naturalized, and Republican Connecticut passes a law that no person shall vote unless he can read and write the English language . . . to exclude German adopted citizens from voting—and Republican New York and Republican Michigan are proposing to amend their constitutions, so as to put negroes on a political equality with white citizens," Ohio Democrats were "legislating for white men—not against them; and assigning to the black man, and those in any way springing from him, their proper position in society."[52]

One state senator's expostulation in March 1859 suggests how harried Democrats felt. Cincinnati's A. S. Bagley alluded to the 1840 election when "a large number of them voted," and moved into why the "White Bill" was necessary. "It is by no means a rare occurrence, in many counties of this State, for this class of persons to vote, or to *offer* their votes. They do it at almost every election. In some cases where the Judges are of the right stripe, they are permitted to vote, in others, they are refused, and a prosecution is the result," egged on by some "malicious white person" to "harass and annoy [Democrats] with these vexatious suits." After invoking *Dred Scott* at length, Bagley appealed to his fellows by painting two pictures of where racial mixing might lead. In the Deep South, he warned, especially on the "Rice, Sugar, and Cotton plantations . . . where the white children are nursed by negro wenches, and where a large portion of their youthful days are spent in company with negro children, and you will see an assimilation in the habits and manners of the whites to those of the negroes. They talk, they laugh, they gesticulate like them," drawn into dissipation by the "twanging . . . of the banjo." This was "a violation of the laws of God. The two races can never live together upon terms of social and political equality." Slavery's proximity had ruined white southerners, *"vitiated* their mental energies, and *prostrated* their physical." To accompany this vision of racial decadence, Bagley offered his personal observation of tangible black power. In 1840, he was living in Massachusetts and "witnessed a sight at the polls that I hope I shall never see again. In a ward in the city of Boston live a large number of negroes. By the laws of that State these negroes are allowed to vote. They, not contented to go to the polls in a proper manner, as white men did must make a *display* of their ebony and their ivory, by forming a procession and marching to the polls and casting their votes in a body for 'Tippecanoe and Tyler too.'"[53]

Democrats' triumphalism over the "Visible Admixture" bill was brought to an abrupt end when, up in the Reserve, a judge of Lorain County's Court of Common Pleas declared "the State Law forbidding negro voting to be unconstitutional," instructing a Grand Jury to "disregard any complaint made" under it. Readers were reminded that "there are from seventy-five to one hundred fifty negroes in and about Oberlin . . . in the habit of voting at that precinct for years, encouraged to do so by the Professors and Preachers of that delectable Institution." Going into the fall 1859 election, Democratic editors warned voters that "in the northern part of the state, Republican judges of election, despite the law which declares that none but white citizens shall vote, allow hundreds and thousands of negroes to deposit their ballots!" In 1857, "a majority of the white people voted for Payne, but the negroes unconstitutionally stepped in and decided the contest for Chase." Apocalyptic threats were again issued via the drawing of a scale with black and white people evenly balanced, and a headline blaring, "THE BALANCE OF POWER. THE NEGROES BALANCE THE SCALE!"[54]

By now, the Oberlin-Wellington Rescue had further polarized the state. Chase had hinted he would order out the militia to protect the Rescuers if ordered to jail, producing the headline "CHASE ORDERS BALL-CARTRIDGES TO BE MADE TO FIRE UPON U.S. OFFICERS," followed by a quotation from his quarter-master general: "We had the cartridges already made." Giddings had supposedly declared, "I would slay anyone who should pollute my residence to recapture a fugitive," and as for the U.S. marshals, "THOSE PIRATES SHOULD HAVE BEEN DELIVERED OVER TO THE COLORED MEN AND CONSIGNED TO THE DOOM OF PIRATES, WHICH SHOULD HAVE BEEN SPEEDILY EXECUTED," reportedly adding in his *Ashtabula Sentinel*, "I look forward to the day when there shall be a servile insurrection in the South; when the black man, armed with British bayonets and led by British officers, shall assert his freedom and wage a war of extermination against his master, when the torch of the incendiary shall light up the towns and cities of the South and blot out the last vestige of slavery." In response, on Election Eve, the *Plain Dealer* urged,

> WHITE MEN, REMEMBER!
> The Negros [*sic*] with their illegal votes elected the present Governor. On the 11th we are bound to overcome this "Black Balance." Let every man be early at the polls and condemn by his vote
> NEGRO EQUALITY,
> and their conjugal associates. On that day you will be called upon to decide whether Federal officers shall be handed over unceremoniously to
> BLACK HANGMAN [*sic*]
> who are to be tried for such murder by a
> GIDDINGS JURY.[55]

The Republicans won anyway, and a Pennsylvania paper reported, "The negroes of Dayton," far from the Reserve, "publicly celebrated the success of the *Republican* ticket in the market house on Wednesday afternoon . . . and why shouldn't they? The *negro vote* of Ohio is as large as the Republican majority." Capping Democrats' defeat, early in 1860, Ohio's supreme court invalidated the "Visible Admixture" law in *Anderson v. Millikin*. Democrats in the legislature then tried to push through a referendum amending the Constitution to specify that "every person having a visible and distinct admixture of African blood shall not have the privilege of an elector, or to hold office, or sit on juries," making the argument that "a man is either white, or he is not; he is either of the Caucassian [*sic*] race, or he is not." The Republican majority in the legislature held, and putting "Negro suffrage" on the ballot was defeated 47–43. All that Democratic editors could offer following this defeat was a familiar epigraph: "REPUBLICAN DEFINITION. *Question*—What is a white man? *Answer*—One who has a visible admixture of African blood in his veins." After the spring 1860 election, the Cleveland Democrats returned to bewailing their fate: "The Republicans and Negroes carried the city yesterday, by about 600 majority, being a gain of some 150 over last year's vote for Mayor. The whole of the City, County, and State patronage in the hands of the Republicans brought to bear upon the election" turned the tide. By this time Democratic unity had frayed badly, with the *Plain Dealer* admitting their men had "no heart to organize. So long as the South are insisting upon a slave code and the administration is supporting an organ here to bully Democrats into the support of that odious doctrine, Democrats will have no courage to organize."[56]

In fall 1860, Democrats sought to purge Justice Jacob Brinkerhoff, a former Democrat, assigning to him the responsibility for *Anderson v. Millikin* since, under this decision, *"Fourteen thousand negros will vote the Black Republican ticket in Ohio,* notwithstanding the new Constitution. . . . When it becomes known throughout the South that in Ohio, negroes are allowed political equality with the whites, this State will be inundated with runaway slaves and free blacks from all the States, seeking social equality," leading to "amalgamation, a mongrel population and a mixed government." In the weeks before the October election, the *Statesman* hit the Republicans hard. On September 28, it asked, "Are the Republicans in Favor of Negro Suffrage?" listing every Republican legislator who had voted against their referendum. A week later it insisted "the Republican Supreme Court" would nullify *Dred Scott* by letting black men vote, so that "hundreds, if not thousands, of this class (chiefly on the Western Reserve), will vote the Republican tickets at our annual and Presidential elections." On October 5, it damned Brinkerhoff on all fronts. He, Chase, and Attorney General Christopher Wolcott had allowed the Oberlin-Wellington Rescuers to get off scot-free, suggesting that Brinkerhoff "is in favor of all runaway slaves of the South, and the 30,000 in Canada, coming to Ohio to remain safely, and take from our white people the labor that belongs to them . . . of seating in our schools negro children side by side upon perfect equality with our white children."[57]

Brinkerhoff was reelected, clear evidence that by 1860 the radical stance on "negro equality" could survive assault in Ohio. The *Statesman* commented that his 50,000-plus Reserve majority included "an addition of 5,000 or 6,000 fraudulent votes," as evidence accrued of black men voting throughout the state. In Cleveland, "full blooded negroes voted in several of the wards yesterday. At the Second ward negroes as black as coal peddled tickets. Negroes hired carriages and carried white men to the polls. Negroes were everywhere," leading one Pennsylvania Democratic paper to comment, "The startling, the humiliating fact appears that Ohio, a sovereign State of the Union, is UNDER NEGRO RULE. To such a disgrace would the Black Republican party reduce the whole country. This thing is too shameful, too sickening, too revolting, to contemplate." Nor was it just a matter of voting; earlier in 1860, a black man named Irvin Scott was elected supervisor of a road district in Logan County, and the *Cleveland Leader* noted that the city now had a black deputy constable.[58]

November 1860 saw the final Democratic assault. Under the headline "The Republican a Negro Party," the Democrats described Republican goals as "the abolition of negro slavery wherever it exists" and "the elevation of the negro to a perfect equality with white citizens"; the first claim was accurate enough for most Republicans, and if the second applied only to some, so much the worse for the rest. It pointed to a plain truth, that "when Republicanism speaks of the rights of the States, it does not mean to include the right to maintain negro slavery as one of them. On the contrary, it intends war upon the States upholding slavery, until it is abolished, or they are disserved from the Union." After that came the hysteria—the Republicans wanted to "not only free the negro wherever he might be held as a slave, but to give him the right to vote at all elections, to sit on juries, to be a justice of the peace, a constable, a county officer, a sheriff, a county commissioner, a senator or representative in the State Legislature, a judge of the Supreme Court, in place of Brinkerhoff, a Secretary of State, or a Governor."[59]

Then it was over. Given the opposition's disarray, Lincoln's victory was nearly certain in Ohio. He beat Stephen A. Douglas 51 percent to 43 percent with the other candidates, Southern Democrat John C. Breckinridge and Constitutional Unionist John Bell, each receiving 3 percent. On Election Day, all the *Plain Dealer* could do was report their party's humiliation, how "a gentleman called at our office for a ticket. He said he had been at the polls and was met by a big buck nigger, who thrust a Black Republican vote in his face and urged him to vote it. He cut short the argument in favor of equality by wheeling on his heel and taking time for reflection, concluded that was not his party, and that the government should remain in the hands of white men, so he called for a DOUGLAS ticket and voted." A Pennsylvania Democrat noted that Ohio Republicans might "strenuously and indignantly" deny "that 14,000 *negroes* voted at the State *election*," that it "was much less than this, and that they were *mulattoes*," but "we don't see what difference it makes whether 5,000 or 14,000 negroes voted in Ohio, when the principle of negro equality is admitted by allowing them to vote at all."[60]

Republicans Bob and Weave

Democrats' racialism had lost its efficacy by 1859. Republicans successfully fended them off, even while men of color became increasingly prominent in their party, and black voters a part of their majority. Prior to 1859, the standard Republican tactic was to ignore Democrats' race-baiting as not worthy of reply. In 1859–60, however, following passage of the "Visible Admixture" bill, Republicans counterattacked, insisting they were respecting settled law, and placing on Democrats the responsibility for men of African descent voting and the Black Laws' repeal. This strategy seems to have been effective, both because it is easier to defend an existing policy than to propose a new one and because individual Democrats were responsible for these constitutional precedents. As Republicans underlined, the supreme courts that affirmed *Polly Gray v. State* consisted mainly of Democrats, including Reuben Wood, who voted to maintain the "nearer white" distinction in key cases and then served as governor in 1850–53. Besides this durable charge, the 1849 deal with Free Soilers to repeal most Black Laws was a sharp knife in Democrats' ribs. Republicans could disclaim responsibility for black men's testifying against white men, including in the multiple suits after African Americans were not allowed to vote.[61]

There were variations within the Republican message. Sometimes black men's voting was defended, and other times it was disclaimed. An October 1859 editorial from Erie County, far west in the Reserve, denounced "A Campaign of Lies" by the "Slave Democracy," making a "terrific hue and cry about negro suffrage and negro equality, falsely charging the advocacy of these measures upon the Republican party," when the evidence would "convict them of the very 'congoism'" they imputed to Republicans. Democrats had voted as a bloc in 1849 "to allow *negroes to sit upon juries with white men*, and to give them the benefit of the poor laws," followed by a list of those Democrats now "vociferous on the subject of the Congo Creed and negro equality" who had "voted to allow negroes to sit on juries in Ohio!" No one "went further for *negro equality* than the Locofoco [Democratic] Supreme Court in the case of Thacker versus Hawk and others," citing the votes of Justices Wood and Matthew Birchard. Versus this dissimulation, a Cleveland Republican affirmed the court's definition of "white" to include "mulattoes" as "the just and the only legal rule still," enacted by "a Supreme Court, of which Gov. Wood, Judge Read and Judge Birchard, then Democrats, were members," adding it had been "satisfactory and followed in all parts of the State, until . . . would-be-Gov. Payne failed of an election by some 1200 votes [in 1857]. Then his organs took up the wail of 'negro voting,' and that he had been defeated, 'cheated out of an election by nigger votes!'" It defended this "class of voters, many of them born in Ohio, who had heretofore enjoyed the elective franchise under both constitutions," now under attack by Democrats. The latter had passed "an unconstitutional act at the last session, designed to strike down rights well established and long exercised; not because mulattos in Ohio, as a body, lack the qualifications of good citizenship and fealty to the constitution and laws, but simply because they do not, in the exercise of an intelligent judgment, *vote the Democratic ticket!*"[62]

Many Republicans stuck to the letter of the law by insisting that "no negro is a voter in Ohio," based on the Ohio supreme court's repeated rulings that a "negro" was a person of predominantly African descent, adding for good measure, "the law is just the same now that it has been for the last thirty years." The 1859 debate between gubernatorial candidates documents this finessing. The Democrat, Rufus Ranney, tried to pin his Republican opponent, William Dennison, asking, did he favor "the law passed by the last General Assembly, refusing to negroes and mulattoes the privilege of voting? He presumed Mr. Dennison was in favor of some shades of African voting. He wanted to know how black a man must be to be excluded. He wanted to know whether a man who was part African could be a whole citizen. If he excluded a race at all he would be in favor of excluding all grades of it. He would not offer a reward for amalgamation by giving the mulatto rights not granted to the pure blood." Dennison would not be drawn, replying that it was "not a question of color, but a question of admixture of blood. But away with all this trifling. I am opposed to the law. I am in favor of leaving the Constitution as it was before the passage of this law. I am opposed to any interpretation of the word white, except it be a judicial interpretation. I am in favor of the Constitution of the State of Ohio just as it is, without Legislative interpretation or amendment on this question."[63]

Comfortable in their "conservative" (a favorite word) defense of the "Constitution of the State of Ohio just as it is," Republicans added a battery of other charges to conciliate their base and break down the Democrats. One was to mock Democratic "fanaticism," their "barbarous" attitudes and "negro-plantation feeling." In this narrative, Democrats obsessed over race in a prurient and guilty fashion, whereas level-headed Republicans avoided this swamp of feeling. These insinuations became quite ripe when Republicans identified their opponents with slavery's most morally corrupting aspects. Who were Ohio's best-known voters of color, after all, but visibly mixed-race men, like the Langstons, who declared themselves to be the children of white fathers? Republicans could have it all ways, defending these men's "preponderant" whiteness while admitting their slight tinge of blackness and arraigning the Democrats as "debauched and demoralized" by their virulent racialism. Despite humane state supreme court rulings that "any person having a predominance of white blood" should be treated as a white person, "and not a negro or mulatto," now "the poor, innocent products of lust and passion are to have the sins of father or mother, *who was entirely white*, visited upon them in the shape of disfranchisement," like a "mark upon children born out of lawful wedlock." In the civilized world, "barbarism of that sort has been done away with, except in the Slave States and with slaves, where the child follows the condition of the mother, though the father might be the lord of 500 slaves." In a lopsided tribute to racial hierarchy, this editor declared, "If white blood predominate in a man, that blood and that status which attaches to that blood, should certainly clothe him with the prerogatives and rights of a white man. If it were not so, the white man himself were degraded, and not the black man."[64]

On occasion, speaking to the right kind of audience, some Republicans went further, into denunciations of racial hierarchy or racialism of any kind. Giddings was the state's best-known radical, but it was his longtime rival Ben Wade (now a U.S. senator) who declared in late 1859, "I loathe from the bottom of my soul any man who refuses to anything in human shape, all the rights and privileges he claims for himself. I know no high, no low, no black, no white—all are created by one God, and all are entitled to the same privileges." In this case, the quotation is taken from a Democratic paper, which printed it under the heading "The Republican Creed." In some of Ohio, some of the time, that was an accurate description.[65]

Who Voted and Where

Regardless of wordslinging, year-in and year-out Democrats alleged that black men were voting, while Republicans minimized their participation in facilitating those ballots. As before, the hard evidence comes from court cases and election challenges. In this arena, one figure stands out: a politico named Alfred J. Anderson, by his own account of one-eighth African descent. Anderson exemplified Ohio's black political class—southern born, of mixed race, emphatically bourgeois, in southwestern Butler County. Like other prominent Ohioans of color, he had no personal connection to slavery yet identified with his people, as a prominent Mason and AME layman, and a trustee of Wilberforce College. Also like many others, he was a successful barber. By 1860, he owned $1,200 in real estate and $550 in personal property. One can imagine this immaculately coiffed professional presenting himself on Election Day to wary Democratic election judges; ultimately, his insistence on participating as a citizen played out nationally.[66]

In October 1856, Representative Lewis D. Campbell, a former Whig who had led opposition to the Kansas-Nebraska Act and was an antislavery candidate for House Speaker in 1855, narrowly won reelection in Butler. For the third time, he defeated Clement Vallandigham, a Democrat known for prosouthern sympathies, later an infamous Copperhead during the Civil War. Campbell won by nineteen votes and Vallandigham challenged his victory on various grounds, including that thirty men of color (including Anderson) had voted, asserting that the 1851 Constitution invalidated state supreme court decisions allowing "nearer white" men to vote.[67]

Campbell had a record of supporting black rights. After passage of the Fugitive Slave Act, he wrote his constituents, "I condemn and denounce it on all occasions. I am against its iniquitous and unjust provisions and against all men who sustain it. It is the greatest outrage ever perpetrated upon liberty. I would trample it underfoot. . . . I will utterly disregard its obligations, and will never cease my opposition until it is wiped from the statute books." In 1856, however, he backed the Know-Nothing Fillmore, and appealed to southern-born whites in his district, reportedly declaring "the nigger business was an outside issue" having "no business in the American [Know Nothing] party, and, for his part, he wished to keep the gemmen ob [*sic*] color out." After Vallandigham issued his challenge, however, Campbell spoke out against racial baiting. Immediately after the election, Campbell told Republicans in Dayton, his hometown, that he "would sooner have" the vote of Anderson, who was his barber, "than that of certain 'white border ruffians' who had tried to drive him [Anderson] from the polls." In early December, he was interrupted in the House with derisive comments regarding his election by "negro votes." His response was convoluted but courageous. First, Campbell explained the Ohio rulings, issued by "Democratic judges," that "whenever white blood predominates" a man may vote, followed by the assertion that "there was one negro vote given in my own district; that is, a vote was cast by a man who, being more of the black than of the white blood, was not authorized to vote under the decision of our courts," and that "I am credibly informed he voted for my opponent," followed by "(Laughter.)" Baited further, he sent up to be read by the Clerk an affidavit from Anderson:

1. My mother, now a resident of this place, and the wife of R. G. H. Anderson, (whose name I do now and always have borne, from considerations of a private character,) is, under the decision of the supreme court of the State of Ohio, a white woman; she being, to the best of her knowledge, seventy-five one-hundredths white, the remainder made up of African and Indian.

2. My father, James Shannon, brother of ex-Governor Wilson Shannon, formerly a resident of St. Clairsville, Ohio, and afterwards a practicing lawyer in my native city, Wheeling, Virginia, was a white man.

3. I have been a bona fide resident of the State of Ohio for twenty-six years last past, and of that portion of the city of Hamilton, known as the second ward, for five years last past. I am a freeholder in said ward, pay taxes, work the public highways, and discharge the various duties required by law of other citizens.

I therefore claim that, under the decisions of the court, *I am a white male citizen of the State of Ohio, and entitled to the right of suffrage.* [emphasis added]

This was followed by a deposition from his mother, Mary T. Anderson:

I believe the foregoing statement of my son, Alfred J. Anderson, is true in every particular.

I am his mother. My father was a white man, and my mother was a mulatto; being an admixture of African and Indian. Alfred is the son of James Shannon, a white man, as he has stated, and acknowledged by Mr Shannon to be his son by testimonials which can be published when required.

Giddings then produced "Renewed merriment" with a "point of order. I call my colleague to order for attempting to bring one of his constituents into disrepute by showing his father to be a brother of Governor Shannon," a Democrat. But this interchange was not finished. Campbell replied to Giddings in this fashion: "My colleague will excuse me. I was driven to the necessity of referring to this fact by a number of questions propounded. Let the gentleman on the other side decide whether the Shannons are white men or not. (Laughter.)" LaFayette McMullen, a Virginia Democrat, challenged Campbell for his introducing "negroe testimony" into the House, a grave breach of decorum, and Campbell replied with a startling affirmation: "I know the character of this man Anderson, and with all respect to gentlemen, I would as soon take his word as that of (after a pause) any man on this floor."[68]

The fight over Campbell's seat resonated at every level—in Congress, in Ohio, and at Anderson's local poll in Hamilton, where he repeatedly tried to vote as accustomed and finally succeeded, with statewide implications. In Congress, a decision in Vallandigham's favor was likely since Democrats controlled the House. Campbell made little effort to defend his seat, other than delaying the process and hoping Know-Nothing friends among southern members would shield him. While Vallandigham's lawyers collected depositions to prove their case regarding "illegal" votes, Campbell lagged. After wrangling over competing reports from the investigating committee, Campbell finally lost his seat in May 1858. Almost all congressmen dealt with the contest on strictly procedural grounds, avoiding discussion of "negro votes," but Vallandigham, as a committed ideologue, would have none of it. In the final debate, he instructed the House that whatever Ohio's supreme court declared, the word "'white' needs no gloss; it has no synonym; it admits of no definition. It means white—pure white; and not any shade or any variety of shades between white and black. Such it is in philology and the arts. White and black are the two between which there is a large variety of colors. No artist ever confounds these terms; no man in ordinary conversation confounds them. He may speak of a dark blue, or a light brown, or of a bright yellow; but never of a dark white, or a light black." This mystical aesthetics, propounded to a chamber full of the pink, tan, beige, and mottled grey or red faces of European-American men, rested on an absolute hierarchy, that "the term 'white,' in constitutions" was "intended "to distinguish primarily between the African race and all others—between a servile race and races which are free." Vallandigham added a partisan edge. Alluding to rumors that New York Republicans wanted to run a particular "mulatto" for Congress, he baited them, that "if these sixteen mulattoes and persons of color [Campbell's voters] are white male citizens of the United States, because they are nearer white than black, then they are eligible to membership of this House. . . . You have already been threatened with Fred Douglass, whiter than the lightest of these sixteen; and in his person, in a little while longer, you may have to meet this question again." He concluded by comparing the North's free people of color to Europe's Red Republicans, denouncing them as a "spurious and mongrel race . . . [who] will be your highwaymen; your banditti; they will make up your mobs. With just enough of intelligence, derived from a white ancestry, to know, and enough of brutishness, inherited from the old African stock, to avenge . . . they are the sans culotte, who, led on by the worst of white men, will make your revolutions and overthrow your governments." Republicans did not bother to respond to Vallandigham's implied prediction of guillotines on the Capitol's steps, but they did not back down from the letter of the law. Ohio Republican Benjamin Stanton flatly affirmed that "persons having more than one half white blood, and less than one half African blood, are legal voters under the constitution and laws of Ohio."[69]

At the national level, Democrats charged like bulls frenzied in the ring, while Republicans maneuvered dexterously around the ambiguities of "negro equality," and which black men, where, and under what circumstances might vote. Nothing could be resolved, given the two parties' fundamentally different notions of what the republic had been and should become or remain. In Ohio, however, the question could be resolved, and in that sense, the Campbell-Vallandigham case had immediate results favoring the Republicans. It opened a window into how men of color actually came to the polls, as the depositions supporting Vallandigham's challenge showed that dozens like Alfred Anderson routinely voted in Butler County, just north of Cincinnati, with considerable uncertainty over who should be assigned any "color." A man named John M. Mitchell was described as a "mulatto," but Anderson specified, "In my opinion there is none [no African blood]. . . . In his business relations he passes as a white man, and in his domestic relations he associates with colored people." A white man named William J. Mollyneaux named sixteen "mulattoes" whom he knew and who had voted in October 1856. They "came up themselves [and] stuck their tickets in, and there was a delay about receiving them, but they were finally received." He presumed there were Democratic challenges, since that party was "bitterly opposed," but Republicans "favored their voting" and "two out of three" election judges were Republicans. Here we see why ordinary Democrats perceived a terrible fraud, watching their traditional opponents admit known men of color to the polls. Black voting augured both permanent minority status and racial humiliation in one's own town, a dystopia of the worst sort.[70]

Anderson pressed forward with his one-man campaign. After voting for Campbell in the October 1856 congressional elections, he returned in November to back Frémont. The same judge of elections, Thomas Millikin, refused him a ballot, and Anderson brought suit, taking his case to Ohio's supreme court. On February 14, 1860, in *Anderson v. Millikin et al.*, the Court overturned the Democrats' insistence that "visible admixture" alone disfranchised a man. Anderson reported in *The Liberator* that this decision "restores the election privilege to a large and influential body of colored men in this state," and how in 1856 "my ballot was rejected altho I had been a voter at the same poles [*sic*] for many years." Millikin's rebuff grew out of "rancor and bitterness," when "it was found that the colored votes for Mr. Campbell was precisely 19—showing clearly—that the locofocos lost the election by the votes of colored men alone." Anderson's satisfaction was visceral: "No wonder then that the Democracy felt like murdering all the 'niggers' in the district. Violence was threatened if I would attempt to vote again. I did attempt it [and] I have been fortunate enough to assist in the defeat of some of my Negro hating democratic opponents."[71]

Anderson's suit did not stand alone. Such cases obtruded throughout the later 1850s, demonstrating the increasing black voter presence throughout the state. In fall 1856, a black Cincinnatian, Jesse Buckley (or Beckly), "some few shades darker than alabaster, offered his vote at the Fourth Ward polls, and it was refused by the Judges, Rufus K. Paine, Wm. H. Glass and Michael Cleary, upon the ground that he was not 'a citizen of the United States' according to the meaning of the act of Congress." Buckley had brought witnesses, to test his standing in the courts. He sued for $1,000 in damages and the city solicitor defended the Democratic judges three times. In "each case the jury failed to agree," so Buckley's lawyer finally got the suit moved to nearby Warren County, and in 1858 a jury awarded the black man $500, a large amount by the standards of the day. A year later, Democrats used this decision to try to unseat the judge, since he had "charged the jury that the plaintiff was entitled to his vote, being over half white, and should be allowed damages."[72]

Not all of these cases involved men who were "nearer white." In 1858, William Whipper, son of the Pennsylvania leader, attempted to vote in Charlestown, Portage County. Perhaps because of its location on the Reserve, Whipper did not claim to be predominantly white, instead "feeling I had a right to vote notwithstanding my dark complexion, I went to the polls and offered my vote, which was rejected." A white man, Frederick Loomis, backed him up, insisting the law explicitly barred only minors and criminals, and Whipper should be allowed to vote. Loomis "insisted on my right to vote, until I obtained it." The case became a brawl, illustrating the larger stakes involved. A Democratic liquor dealer prosecuted Loomis, while Oliver P. Brown, the area's most prominent Republican, acted as his counsel. Suits multiplied elsewhere in 1860. A prosperous Cleveland tailor, Freeman H. Morris, "having about one-fourth negro blood in his veins, presented himself at the First Ward voting place" but was denied. "Action was brought against the judges of election . . . for illegally rejecting his vote. They pleaded in defense the recent action of the legislature, rejecting the *vote* of every person having *negro* blood in his veins. . . . Judge Foote [a prominent abolitionist] declared for the plaintiff, declaring the 'Black Law' to be unconstitutional." The most intriguing case came in Huron County, in the Reserve's west. Democratic trustees in Greenfield Township invoked the "visible admixture" law to block Stephen Robinson from voting, although he was an "old and highly respected citizen of Greenfield, and has voted there for over twenty years. He has repeatedly been elected to office and now holds . . . civil offices in the township. No one would suspect any such 'admixture' from his appearance." The mystery of why this wealthy farmer was barred from voting (he was listed as "white" and owned land worth $7,000 in the 1860 census) is perhaps clarified by his place of birth—Albany County, New York, in 1795—and his middle name: "Van Ranzler." One deduces he was manumitted by the Patroon and moved to Ohio to begin a new life, after serving in the War of 1812.[73]

The trouble Democrats faced in Ohio's courts clarifies Senator Bagley's anger about "malicious suits," and so they turned to challenging election results, with their Cleveland organ reporting in fall 1859 "that the HON. CHAS. WINSLOW, Democratic Senator in this county, contests the election of BRECK to the Senatorship, on the ground of Negro voting," plus plans to contest the election of Republican William P. Cutler to Congress in 1860 in Muskingum County, east of Columbus, on the grounds that "Mr. Cutler is elected by the votes of negroes." The *New York Herald*, hoping for a repeat of Vallandigham's success, reported Cutler had only a "sixty-four majority over H. J. Jewett, democrat" and "in a large number of precincts negroes voted the republican ticket . . . in consequence the democratic candidate was defeated."[74]

Black Republicans Enter

The escalating fight over voting rights was a logical consequence of Ohio's black men entering the Republican Party as a bloc, analogous to their going into Massachusetts's Free Soil Party in 1849–51, except that, in Ohio, Republicans were poised to become the dominant party. Black leaders had two goals: to take revenge and "destroy the Democratic Party," and to make the Republicans their own. Their mobilization began during the hard-fought 1855 gubernatorial election, when, even in Cincinnati, men of color came out to vote for Salmon Chase "for the first time in their lives." Up in the Reserve, J. M. Langston pushed through a resolution at the Lorain County Republican convention welcoming "all citizens, of whatever name, birthplace, color, or religion" and endorsing black suffrage. The state Republican convention ignored black rights, but Langston and others went all-out for Chase, leading a Democratic paper to brand the Republicans the party of "negro stump speakers! negro voters! negro jurors! negro office-holders!" The State Convention of Colored Men in early 1856 trumpeted their gains and rejoiced "in the death of the Whig Party . . . the waning influence of the Democratic Party . . . the inauguration of the Republican party," noting in their address to the people that because "of your Supreme Court, a large portion of our people are already in the possession of the elective franchise. These men are not above the average of colored men in intelligence and morals. . . . Yet, by an accident of color, they are enfranchised."[75]

While turning out their voters, Langston and his colleagues maintained their demand for full suffrage. In summer 1856, he toured the state, addressing large crowds for Frémont and provoking barely veiled threats from Democrats, and in 1857 he addressed the legislature to advocate it. That fall, Democrats won legislative majorities while Chase barely squeaked to reelection, confirming fears that overt "Negrophilism" cost votes. Conservative Republicans led by Corwin proposed a coalition with Democrats in 1858, and radicals from the Reserve (Joshua Giddings, Oliver Brown, and Philemon Bliss) were denied renomination, but these reverses did not deter the black leadership. At their November 1858 state convention, David Jenkins declared he "saw in the decline of the Democratic party, and the rise of the Republican, omens of hope for the colored people." Langston followed, saying, "He hated the Democratic party because it was pro-slavery," exhorting "his friends to oppose by every means in their power, that party. The people were killing it everywhere, through the North, and he was glad to know it. His motto was, 'The Democratic party must be destroyed.'" That meeting also founded the Ohio State Anti-Slavery Society (OSASS), with J. M. Langston as its president and his brother Charles the executive secretary, operating out of a Columbus office.

This organization was notably egalitarian regarding gender, with "black women . . . accorded full membership privileges," and the rising intellectual Frances Ellen Watkins "participated prominently." J. M. Langston's keynote address to the OSASS went beyond demanding equal rights to advocate "the right and duty of resistance by force of arms" where necessary. In 1859, the Democrats passed their "Visible Admixture" bill to ban voting by men of any color, which was overturned, and after the Republicans won that fall, Charles Langston memorialized the General Assembly, demanding it strike all references to the word "white," and that since "the next legislature will have a large Republican majority, and many of its members have been elected in part by the *labor* and votes of colored men . . . may we not confidently hope that this body of *freedom* will give to colored men their *civil* and *political* rights."[76]

The main event in the evolution of this truly "black" Republicanism was the September 1858 Oberlin-Wellington Rescue and trial, one of those confrontations edging the South toward disunion. Like the multiple Boston "rescues" in 1850–54, Pennsylvania's 1851 Christiana Riot, and Syracuse's "Jerry Rescue" that same year, it sent a message that officers enforcing the Fugitive Slave Act could be attacked by "negroes" who would then be defended by powerful whites. The Rescue must be viewed through a partisan filter, as it was then—biracial Republicanism versus Democratic white Unionism. In the Oberlin-Wellington case, after the Rescuers were indicted, Republican officials prosecuted the marshals and their associates as kidnappers, and rather than damaging these Republicans' political fortunes, this stance helped them consolidate power. This narrative operated locally, in the conflict between the Langston brothers and their Democratic opponents, and at a state and national level, in the confrontation between the Buchanan administration and Ohio's Republicans led by Chase, already nursing presidential ambitions.

From a black perspective, the party-ness of the Rescue was rooted in J. M. Langston's ascent to political authority in Russia Township, which included Oberlin, after first winning office in nearby Brownhelm. In April 1857, he won election as Oberlin's town clerk (the first of many offices he held). His opponent, Anson Dayton, was the town's only other lawyer. Dayton's response was to become a Democrat and secure a patronage job as deputy U.S. marshal, an ideal position to make money and exact revenge on black men. These activities placed Dayton in danger, however, and black men eventually drove him out under threat of death. In September 1858, he connived with a Kentucky slaveholder to seize the seventeen-year-old fugitive John Price. What followed resembled other slave rescues—a crowd surging around a barred-up room, purposeful black men threatening violence, negotiations with the posse and then a fight, with doors broken down and a fugitive rushed away, finally a grand celebration of northern men's triumph over southern principles. It was the legal battle that seized the nation's attention. Cleveland's U.S. attorney, directed by Washington to make an example, indicted thirty-seven men, including many prominent white Oberlinians. Twelve were black, and three of those were fugitives. Their move to the Cleveland jail made the trial into a partisan spectacular, as the judge and jurymen were chosen as loyal Democrats, while the defense featured eminent Republicans, including a former Assembly speaker and a former state supreme court judge.[77]

The climax was Charles Langston's widely reprinted speech, with its passionate invocation of the biblical call to aid the fugitive. He declared, "When I come to be claimed by some perjured wretch as his slave, I shall never be taken into slavery. And as in that trying hour I would have others do to me, as I would call upon my friends to help me; as I would call upon you, your Honor, to help me; as I would call upon you [*to the District-Attorney*], to help me; and upon you [*to Judge Bliss*], and upon you [*to his counsel*], so help me GOD! I stand here to say that I will do all I can, for any man thus seized and help, though the inevitable penalty of six months imprisonment and one thousand dollars fine for each offense hangs over me! We have a common humanity. You would do so; your manhood would require it; and no matter what the laws might be, you would honor yourself for doing it; your friends would honor you for doing it; your children to all generations would honor you for doing it; and every good and honest man would say, you had done right!" A photo of the prisoners was made into a line-cut engraving in *Frank Leslie's Weekly*, the nation's most popular magazine, and thousands visited the jail, including John Brown, recruiting men for Harpers Ferry. Joshua Giddings revived the Revolutionary-era Sons of Liberty as a paramilitary organization, with hundreds signing pledges to defend the prisoners at all costs. On May 24, 1859, immediately following Charles Langston's and another man's conviction, Cleveland saw an enormous rally in its main square, with thousands coming from all over Ohio, carrying banners invoking the Revolution: "1765. Down with the Stamp Act. 1859. Down with the Fugitive Act." Much of the crowd of 10,000 was black, and the *Plain Dealer* sneered that the organizers were "almost forced to light candles for the Orators to speak by." They marched to the jail, where Charles Langston climbed a fence to lead them shouting "No!" when asked if they would tolerate the Rescuers' imprisonment. This event made Ohio's biracial Republicanism visible in state and national politics. Twelve leading men were on the stage, including Giddings and Representative Edward Wade. At the last minute, Chase arrived to place his government's authority and Ohio's militia behind defying Buchanan; in so doing, Chase positioned himself for 1860 as the Midwest's radical leader, although he probably ruined any chance he had at the Republican nomination.

The most remarkable speaker was John Mercer Langston, taking his place as a Republican luminary fit to stand next to his governor. Nor was this all. A fight brewed days later at the Republican state convention. The Republican chief justice of Ohio's supreme court, Joseph Swan, had refused the attorney general's writ of habeas corpus for Charles Langston and Simeon Bushnell, the two men convicted in early May. Chase and other radicals wanted to deny Swan renomination, which risked alienating conservative Republicans. Roelof Brinkerhoff, brother of the justice, brokered an arrangement where Swan was dumped, and the Ohio party formally repudiated the Fugitive Slave Act. That fall, Republicans won a solid statewide majority, proving that in the swirling atmosphere of the moment, radicalism was no bar to victory.[78]

Ohio's black Republicans thus entered 1860 in a uniquely favorable position, following multiple victories: inside their state, in the vindication of the Oberlin-Wellington Rescuers; inside their party, in its clear move to the left, aligning them with its top leaders; in the courts, where *Anderson v. Millikin* confirmed that men of color would vote wherever Republicans controlled the polls. Their contribution to a Republican victory in this key state was recognized nationally when, just before Election Day, the *New York Herald*, assessing the "Influence of the Negro Vote on the Presidential Contest," declared that if black men provided Lincoln's winning margin in Ohio, he "could not constitutionally be sworn," since they were not legal voters under *Dred Scott*. "Union men" were advised to watch the polls and "ascertain the number," but Lincoln's winning margin was large enough to obviate that strategy. This backhanded tribute was the best recognition for how far Ohio's black men had traveled.[79]

Coda

Ohio, Flanked

The Radicals may have considered themselves in the saddle, but as war approached many of Ohio's voters and elected officials did not accept Republican hegemony, especially along the border. Ohio eventually became a prime site for the recruitment of colored troops, and its postbellum Republican Party welcomed black men, but the state's political divisions did not subside. Cincinnati elected an "ardently pro–Southern Democrat" as mayor on April 1, 1861. On April 4 he permitted the recapture of a slave and on April 5 the "unmolested transit of cannon for the Confederacy," less than a week before Fort Sumter was fired upon. Once fighting broke out, Cincinnati's black men were forced into labor on fortifications for the Union Army that was supposed to protect them as citizens of a Northern "free" state.[1]

The actions of Ohio's congressional delegation in 1861 epitomized the state's schizophrenic character. Ohio's Republicans played a central role in their national party, with Chase becoming secretary of the treasury in March 1861. At the end of January, Toledo's Republican congressman James Ashley reported an "Amendment to the Act for the Rendition of Fugitives from Service or Labor" which effectively mandated compensated emancipation. It stipulated that if a person was claimed as a fugitive, a legal officer in the state where that person resided should estimate the value of his or her labor. If that money was produced, the owner would be required to manumit, and if the slaveholder refused, the court should "cause to be made out and delivered to the party so depositing the money for his or her freedom, a certificate of discharge and the fugitive shall be free and released from all legal obligations to serve said claimant and this certificate shall be a bar to all proceedings of a like character in any court against said party." If this was an effort to stave off internal war, it was hardly conciliatory, since the compensation would be determined by a northern official, likely a Republican, effectively voiding the slaveholder's property rights.[2]

Ashley hardly represented his entire party, let alone his state. In late January 1861, a bloc of Democrats and conservative Republicans voted an antimiscegenation bill, the first in Ohio's history. The eminent Thomas Corwin had also returned to the House as a Republican in 1859, and in early 1861 he proposed giving the South an ironclad guarantee against any Republican revolution by revising the Constitution to stipulate that "no amendment shall be made . . . which will authorize or give to Congress the power to abolish or interfere, within any State, with the domestic institutions thereof, including that of persons held to labor or service by the laws of said State." It got enough Republican support to pass both House and Senate, and if the Confederates had not precipitated war, sufficient states might have ratified the "Corwin Amendment" to maintain the status quo antebellum. Meanwhile, an Ohio Democrat, Garret Davis, proposed that the Middle Border should preempt the abolitionists of Greater New England and the secessionists of the Deep South by forming "a great central confederation" of "Southern New York, New Jersey, Southern Pennsylvania, Delaware, Maryland and the whole area of country lyeing [sic] within the basin of the Mississippi." Neither of these schemes had anything to offer black people, free or enslaved. Their purpose was to keep white people from killing each other.[3]

Rather than a clear polarization between freedom and slavery, or nonracial equality versus white supremacy, Ohio in 1861 demonstrates the spectrum of opinion even in a Republican "banner state." The divisions cutting across villages, towns, and counties derived from traditional partisan affiliations which took on new force in wartime. They underline the challenges facing the small black political class in Ohio, and throughout the North. They were now part of a majority party positioned to exert state power, but their position within that coalition was provisional, as by no means all Republicans supported their rights, and outside of the Republican Party, no one did. In both wartime elections, the Democrats remained a vigorous force, led by War Democrats who fought for no other purpose than to preserve the Union— certainly not to free the slaves, let alone extend nonracial citizenship. War Democrats were hardly the worst problem. Clement Vallandigham's continued political viability demonstrates the precarity of black politics in the Midwest. He would have voted to expel every person of color in the state if he could, and end the war on Confederate terms, yet was elected to Congress from a district full of people of color like Alfred J. Anderson in 1858 and 1860, and openly avowed his southern sympathies right up to his arrest on May 5, 1863 for preaching disloyalty.

Into the twentieth century, "Bloody Shirt" politics allowed Ohio Republicans to maintain their support for black rights, led by otherwise conservative Republicans like Joseph Foraker, William McKinley, and Warren G. Harding. The Party of Lincoln proved a thin reed in other respects, though, and utterly unwilling to protect the millions of freedpeople south of the Ohio River. The Buckeye State remained in the later nineteenth century what it had become in the years before the war—an island of formal if fragile equality.

Conclusion

Going to War

This study leaves off after Lincoln's election on November 6, 1860, but before the shelling of Fort Sumter began on April 12, 1861. No one then would have imagined those in-between months as any kind of endpoint. For antislavery voters and politicians, this was a pause, before "the continuation of politics by other means." Certainly, the ascendance of the Republican Party to national power, winning almost 40 percent of the popular vote in a four-way competition, marked a historic break. Everyone, including many slaves, knew that a northern party now controlled the federal government on a platform of choking off the economies of those states built upon slave labor, while effectively inviting their slaves to flee.

In the mind of the white South, Republican rule meant that the statutory bans on the protection of slave property mandated in many northern states would be extended to the national level, meaning no more federal marshals helping recapture fugitives, no more territories opened to slave labor, and its expulsion from the vast New Mexico Territory. The Republicans, they feared, would ban the intrastate slave trade, the use of slave labor in federal employment, and federal appointments for those connected to slaveholding. Given the Whig antecedents of the majority of Republicans, massive tariffs would be enacted to protect northern business and labor while greatly increasing the costs of consumption in the South. The laws criminalizing slave-trading would be enforced, ending a lucrative business for American merchants and captains flying false flags and entrance of contrabands via Cuba. The "peculiar Institution" would wither away, and the absurdities of the Yankee Republic, visible in New Bedford, Boston, Portland, Providence, Albany, Syracuse, Brooklyn, and Cleveland, all the places where black men voted en masse, would be visited upon the rest of the nation. It is little wonder that the Deep Southern states led by South Carolina engaged in maximalist politics, declaring secession in December 1860 so as to force the issue—would northern men fight to carry out what a majority of them had just backed at the polls, or would a sufficient number of conservative Republicans join with Douglas Democrats and ex-Whig Constitutional Unionists to engineer a compromise? The latter seemed a real possibility, but Lincoln held his party together and waited the southerners out, putting the burden on them to dissolve the Union.

How did the North's men of color understand their position in early 1861? They did not know Lincoln, unlike Chase, Seward, Wilson, Sumner, and other leading Republicans, but they knew he had been chosen for his record in opposing not only slavery's extension but also its moral legitimacy with great forensic ability, while exhibiting no connections to the abolitionist milieu of the Liberty and Free Soil Parties, let alone the obstreperous politics of the free people of color. Although northern Illinois had its own slice of Greater New England, it was long ranked among the free states most friendly to slavery. Lincoln had never met any of the black leaders who feature in this narrative, let alone received testimonials from them; he had never written their conventions to manifest his solidarity, argued for them in court or on the floor of a state constitutional convention or legislature, or bailed them after a "rescue." Quite the contrary. During his famous debates with Stephen A. Douglas in 1858, he had perfectly articulated the distinction between opposing slavery as fundamentally un-republican, and supporting black citizenship. For Republicans seeking to rebut charges of Negrophilia, like the *New York Times*' Henry J. Raymond, Lincoln was a godsend.

We can presume black leaders understood the logic of the Republican Party's choice in May 1860, that none of the party leaders they trusted had as good a chance as Lincoln at winning election precisely because of their connections to "radicalism" and black people. Lincoln had proved himself an incisive debater, but he was otherwise a tabula rasa. He could not be attacked for promoting a "higher law" like Seward, receiving "negro votes" like Chase, or declaring, "A colored man may be the 'Supreme Executive Magistrate' of Massachusetts," like Henry Wilson, let alone defending them in court after attacking federal marshals, as Thaddeus Stevens and Charles Sumner had done. These are the things black men knew, and yet they came to no shared conclusion about how to proceed. For every Robert Morris or James McCune Smith proclaiming his optimism, equally astute figures like George T. Downing or Henry Highland Garnet remained deeply wary of the Republicans.

Before a final consideration of how wartime service extended African Americans' commitment to participating in the nation, we should assess their position in the aftermath of Lincoln's victory.

Taking Stock

There is a paradox regarding black men's political influence circa 1861: it was considerably less in the five states where their right to vote was unchallenged, from Rhode Island to the Canadian border, than in those where it was still fought over. There were large differences between Portland, Providence, and New Bedford on the eve of war, but in all of them, the Afro-Yankee vote was essentially "captured," in the parlance of political science. The region's Democrats were less Negrophobic than in the Lower North, but could hardly remain within their party and appeal for black votes. The Republican coalitions dominating New England after 1856 could accommodate black voters without conceding them more than minor patronage. If Radicals had sufficient weight, as in Massachusetts and Maine, they offered recognition to men of color. In Providence, where the Republicans were mainly former Know-Nothings, black voters remained a tool to be deployed against the Irish proletariat. Only where they had a sufficient number of votes, in New Bedford, Boston's Ward Six, and Portland, could they gain official party roles. Claims on elected office would wait until after the war.

In New York and Ohio, where only some black men voted, they had greater weight. The African American electorates in those states were both considerably larger and subject to Democratic suppression, and white Republicans could not afford to lose those votes. They had also organized statewide over two decades, in regular conventions with long-standing "central committees," as black Yankees attempted only late in the day. If all of New England, or even just all of Massachusetts, had been organized along the lines of New York or Ohio, black New Englanders could have exerted greater influence on their states' Republican parties. In Rhode Island, where their vote was proportionally much larger than elsewhere in the region, the black electorate remained largely subordinate.

Stating these regional differences points out a basic fact about antebellum black politics, the lack of a national strategy, and why this book pays scant attention to the Colored National Conventions of 1843, 1847, 1848, 1853, and 1855. Those were important sites for debate, but they played little role in setting any common direction. The one effort at national coordination, the National Council of the Colored People founded at the 1853 Rochester meeting, was stymied by the noncooperation of hardcore Garrisonians like William Nell. Does this lack of central organization and the tendency to act as adjuncts to white party organizations foretell the limited achievements of northern black politicians within the postbellum "Party of Lincoln?" Perhaps. For the moment, one can only point to their fundamentally unresolved position in 1865, in the midst of what would be called, in other contexts, a national revolution.

In Service to the National Revolution

On its face, the war's coming changed everything. The shape of politics altered so completely in 1861–65 that the entire prewar apparatus seemed suddenly anachronistic. The struggles for suffrage, "personal liberty" laws, an end to Black Codes, and access to public schools moved into the background, as did the enormous effort to get into the political parties. In their place was the story told in the narratives stimulated by the later twentieth-century black freedom movement, of military service and mass self-emancipation as enslaved people fled to the Union army. This emphasis on sudden wartime change conceals the deeper continuities of black political struggle, and the continuing saliency of the North's prewar political class. That constituency's central demand had been to gain entrance to, and recognition within, the state, in this case the "States" studied here, pushing the North toward an emancipationist politics that would liberate the South. Wartime changed the form but not the substance of that demand. Clearly, black men entered the state on a previously unimaginable scale. Two hundred thousand of them, the majority formerly enslaved, gained the standing and rights of soldiers, and the smaller number who were noncommissioned officers (and even, by war's end, a few commissioned officers) won a status above the mass of white enlisted men. Their incorporation into the state was justified by the nation's leaders on military grounds—that black men were needed and only a defeatist would refuse their services. From some perspectives, this type of recognition was the most desirable, since it involved an explicit grant of status in the state's hierarchy. Yet, as was also obvious, those black men served—they did not represent or bargain. They cast no votes and had no authority, except that which was deeded to them, to use their muskets as directed. They had no meaningful command of soldiers, and no influence on the war's course, or a voice within its councils.

Service, with all its nuances, was the leitmotif of black politics in the Civil War. Yet asking who served and where, and what kind of service they had formerly performed (and for whom), adds multiple layers of ambiguity. What was truly new about black politics in wartime was the agency that the South's former "servants" now exerted within a militarized polity, offering their bodies while demanding help and recognition of every kind. Before the war, the overwhelming majority remained in bondage's fetters, while some thousands of fugitives either sought freedom in the anonymity of the free states, or moved through them to Canada. Suddenly, amid war's chaos, the enslaved appeared as a whole people, the oft-cited four million now making themselves visible. Beginning in the war's earliest months, hundreds of thousands of hungry, ragged "contrabands" filled the roads and fields around the Union armies, shocking white Northerners accustomed to minstrel shows with happy "darkies" capering. Once that encounter took place, once Northern white men marched south, nothing would ever be the same.

The image of those armies on the march, eventually incorporating tens of thousands of black men into their ranks, demonstrates a larger continuity, and how the war squared a circle for African Americans, bringing them back to another time of emancipation. From the First to the Second American Revolutions, black people had understood their liberation and enfranchisement as necessarily in service to some form of white men's power. They were always too realistic to imagine an entirely self-generated emancipation—Turner and Vesey might be stirring martyrs, but it is unlikely any black American thought of himself as a Toussaint Louverture. In the first instance, in 1775–83, they had taken advantage of all sides, serving where they could, although the only truly liberating army had been Britain's. Between 1790 and 1860, they had sought allies to support, preferably as loyal partisans inside the mainstream. At last that stream bent toward them in the 1850s, producing a northern party prepared to repudiate the corrupted version of republicanism spreading weed-like since 1800. At the war's climax in 1863–65, the military necessity invoked by the Emancipation Proclamation again made their service necessary. As a consequence, most Northern black men also went south, recruited by their own leaders; 70 percent volunteered to fight, three times the average for white men. They could not know the result of this mobilization, but there was no recourse. Sitting out the war was no option for the enslaved; Southern victory or a negotiated settlement, returning to the "Union as it was" by sacrificing black rights, had to be avoided at all costs.

How should we evaluate the wartime conduct of the black leadership, the political class whose history this book tells? Even as they threw themselves into battle, the value of their sacrifice, and those they sacrificed, remains an open question. Did they save the republic, or were they used and used up by it?

Clearly the decision to incorporate into the revolutionary party-state forged by the Republicans was wholehearted. It consummated the hopes of several lifetimes. For leaders like Douglass, J. M. Langston, and William J. Brown, the honor of being asked to recruit soldiers—and present them with hand-sewn regimental colors, as Langston remembered with enormous pride—signaled political advancement beyond anything previous, since those regiments served the federal government, heretofore off-limits. It was only the obduracy and racial contempt of many white Republicans that kept black men from utterly fusing their national, racial, and partisan loyalties after January 1, 1863. Powerful episodes pointed in that direction: the martyrdom at Fort Wagner, where "our men went on and on" in the face of terrible fire, in Sergeant Lewis Douglass's grim recollection; the massacres at Fort Pillow and the other battlefields where Confederates butchered black prisoners; the pogrom carried out by New York City's Irish and German working people in July 1863; the growing identification with Lincoln felt by men like Douglass.

The war thus moved forward on two parallel tracks still difficult to reconcile. From 1860 through the final months outside Richmond, many black leaders remained skeptical of Republican intentions, since only expediency drove enough of them to enact revolutionary measures. Yet equally often these same leaders brought forth extraordinary epiphanies over the prospect of slavery's death, and black men helping to kill it. Emancipation itself was universally understood as an epochal moment of liberation.

The central problem was that no matter how incoherent and opportunistic, Lincoln's party was their only hope, and that assemblage of old Whigs, renegade Democrats, and former abolitionists was a minority in the nation and only intermittently a majority party in the North. Black men bemoaned Lincoln's censuring those generals who freed slaves or enlisted black troops in 1861–62, his delays in emancipation in 1862–63, his advocacy of colonization and willingness to conciliate the Confederacy, but the political logic of this strategy was inescapable. At no point could the Republicans risk rebellion in the Border States or provoke a Democratic victory in 1864.

Black men and women knew that their condition and future were the war's cause and the willingness of black men to fight for the Union was welcome, but that their own concerns would always be secondary to what Republicans found useful in winning the war. That party, from its Radicals to its most conservative bourgeois interests, was committed to a national revolution, a great state-making project akin to those carried out by postcolonial governments. Slavery and the Slave Power stood in their way, and given the chance they would destroy both.

The conduct, progress, and results of the war produced contradictory results for African Americans. Evidently, they gained in political status, since their battlefield sacrifices were fully recognized, and they had gained in their claim to citizenship, because those sacrifices, coupled to slavery's extinction via the Thirteenth Amendment, removed the largest barrier—a separate and unequal status guaranteed by law. Yet their progress in gaining actual rights and power was much less clear. One could hope that a soldier made a voter, but there was no certainty of that in April 1865, when not a single black man had yet been enfranchised as a result of the war, with only faint suggestions by Lincoln and others that "some" might vote. Slavery was extinguished, but ninety years after the American Revolution began, black politics constituted a possibility, an unresolved demand, as it would for the next century, through and long past the Second Reconstruction. Despite or because of the war's carnage, Americans still could not agree on who was an American.

Martial Men and "White Men!"

The titles of this book's parts and chapters employ military metaphors—of battlegrounds, redoubts, defaults, retreats, impasses, salients, and more. This choice of words reflects my understanding of politics as deeply conflictual: a practice in which one engages so as to succeed, conquer, or triumph, but even more so as *not* to lose, be vanquished, and obliterated. The politics of antebellum America could not have been farther from Louis Hartz's consensual "liberal tradition," in which white men long cooperated to keep conflict to a reasonable level until slavery somehow deranged them. This emphasis on combat is how black men saw it then. They understood themselves as warriors for the right—for themselves as individuals, for their people, and especially for their "brethren in chains." Think of Douglass's oft-quoted evisceration of the soft-hearted liberalism of his day: "If there is no struggle there is no progress. Those who profess to favor freedom and yet deprecate agitation are men who want crops without plowing up the ground; they want rain without thunder and lightning. They want the ocean without the awful roar of its many waters. This struggle may be a moral one, or it may be a physical one, and it may be both moral and physical, but it must be a struggle. Power concedes nothing without a demand. It never did and it never will."

What is lost in modern accounts is how much men like Douglass relished that storm, how they waded straight into it, taking the brickbats from the mob and turning them back again. They practiced politics from a desire for vindication, born of horrific personal experience, and this account honors their appetite for battle in all its forms by naming it in those terms. Douglass himself understood the nature of political struggle better than many today. He was not interested in exerting agency for its own sake, in developing autonomy, or even resistance. He did not seek mutual understanding or reconciliation with his enemies, the slaveholding class and their abettors; he sought to show them up, face them down, and make them writhe in ignominy. In short, he was interested in winning. And he was also very interested in his own victory and fame; in the mid-nineteenth century's first flush of entrepreneurial capitalism and the conquest of nature, it was presumed that men (and increasingly women) *should* seek to advance themselves, that ambition and public repute were part of their mission in life. Douglass had before him a series of great men, Clay, Webster, and others, who sought and, for a while, attained heroic status. He aimed for no less than them, and he was hardly alone. The men who populate this study, many of them quite famous in their day, including Garnet, Ward, McCune Smith, Delany, and Langston, all had that goal—to become "representative American men," as McCune Smith famously named Douglass.

At book's end, however, I return to an image evoked at its beginning, of Stephen A. Douglas whipping up the crowd during his 1858 debates with Lincoln to chant, "White Men! White Men!" as he declared the United States "a community of white men." On the platform with him, Lincoln backed and filled, denouncing slavery as a great wrong and defending the humanity of black people, including black women, while disavowing any support for black citizenship. It is easy to say that Lincoln was doing what he had to do to win in a state like Illinois, and that confronting the Slave Power was the central political demand of the time, requiring that black citizenship be deferred. We have heard claims like that ever since 1865. Black citizenship, full and absolute citizenship for *all* the people who do not fit into the category of "White Men!," has been and continues to be put on hold, and then actively suppressed and denied, despite our many Reconstructions. Lincoln's bargain helps clarify what black politics was and continues to be—the right to participate, to vote, with all the rights that attend voting, but even more the right to be treated as a citizen with rights equivalent to any other. It is painfully clear, as I complete this book, that those rights are not yet won. Black politics are now what they were in 1800, 1821, or 1858—the politics of equal citizenship, a reminder of the fundamental continuities in American history. If we believe in equal citizenship, we are still fighting for black politics.

Appendix

Black Leaders and Their Electorates

This appendix uses different manuscript censuses to assemble a prosopography of the black leadership class in some key sites discussed in this book. It focuses mainly on the Afro-Yankees in Portland's Ward One, New Bedford, and Providence, the subjects of part 2, but includes comparable groups in New York's Hudson River Valley and Butler County, Ohio.[1]

New England's black political class shows a clear pattern, albeit with some variations. First, this leadership group of 106 property-owners cannot in any meaningful way be called a petty bourgeoisie (meaning merchants, proprietors, shopkeepers, skilled tradesmen, professionals). At least three-quarters (seventy-nine) were working-men. By far the most common category was the thirty-five men who identified themselves as "laborers," a term with many possible meanings, followed by twenty-one who worked on the water (mariners or sailors, a fisherman and two cooks). To these add a set of occupations based on semiskilled physical labor, including six barbers and hairdressers, six waiters, three porters, three teamsters or draymen, two coachmen, a stevedore, an ostler (someone employed in a stable), and a carpenter. This was a preindustrial proletariat as well as a political leadership.

The second distinctive characteristic of this group was that sixty-two of them (58 percent) were immigrants from the Lower North/Upper South borderland: Maryland (twenty-one), Virginia (nine), Pennsylvania (six), New York (five), the District of Columbia (five), North Carolina (four), New Jersey (three), and Delaware (two), plus seven who did not give a place of birth, indicating likely fugitive status.

The typical New England political leader was thus a free man of color or self-manumitted runaway who moved north to find work and relative freedom, exactly like Douglass in 1838. On arrival, this man went hard to work, carting, carrying, serving, loading, building, or going to sea, jobs requiring a strong back and reliability, and by so doing acquired a modest competence. Two-thirds of these men owned between $100 and $1,000 in real or personal property, which made them better off than the mass of workingmen who were tenants, but hardly well off.

Turning to what makes each of these cities distinctive, in Portland two factors stand out: first, the predominance of maritime occupations (fifteen of thirty-one men), and second, the absence of wealthy proprietors or men of business (one proviso, however: we have no way of tracking how many Portlanders were away at sea when the census was taken, some of whom as ships' officers might have been quite well off). As elsewhere, the leadership of this furthest northern city came from the south, with nineteen of the thirty-one born in the Mid-Atlantic and Chesapeake (see table A.1).

New Bedford resembles Portland in many ways. Twenty-six (68 percent) of its leaders were immigrants from the Lower North/Upper South with another five listing their birthplace as "unknown," indicating fugitive status, and only five from New England.

Table A.1 Black propertyholders in Portland's first ward, 1850

Name	Age	Occupation	Value of real property ($)	Birthplace
Josiah Jones	31	Mariner	500	Maryland
Wm. H. Franklin	44	Mariner	300	Maryland
James Jackson	36	Fisherman	300	Connecticut
George Bush	41	Mariner	100	?
Ezekiel Sanford	n/a		300	Virginia
Charles Webb	47	Mariner	400	Virginia
Thomas Clark	54	Cook	1,800	Pennsylvania
John H. Anderson	30	Waiter	400	Maryland
Philip Manuel	38	Laborer	100	Cape de Verde
Thomas Sanford	57	Mariner	800	District of Columbia
John Gibson	50	Mariner	400	New York
George Potter	45	Laborer	750	North Carolina
Benjamin Joseph	60	Laborer	500	New Hampshire
Wm. Fortune	27	Mariner	250	New York
John Siggs	69	Laborer	300	?
Abraham Talbot	55	Laborer	500	Maine
Abraham W. Niles	42	Laborer	1,500	Maine
John Paris	47	Mariner	1,000	Maryland
Richard P. Bradley	33	Mariner	600	Rhode Island
Henry Daniels	34	Laborer	300	Virginia
Isaac Johnson	46	Laborer	500	Maryland
Peter Francis	50	Mariner	500	Maine
Randall White	38	Mariner	1,000	Virginia
Charles F. Eastman	28	Barber	950	Maine
Caleb Johnson	72	Mariner	500	Pennsylvania
James Ball	61	Laborer	800	Pennsylvania
Amos N. Freeman	40	Clergyman (Cong.)	2,000	New Jersey
Peter Pierre	89	Laborer	1,500	Martinique
Charles Pierre	25	Laborer	200	Maine
William Brown	39	Barber	800	Maryland
Elbridge P. Talbot	29	Mariner	1,200	Maine

Note: From the 1850 U.S. Manuscript Census.

Sixty percent were laborers, sailors, or stevedores, and all but one of the others worked with their hands, including two waiters, two hairdressers, a painter, a barber, a gardener, a coach driver, a blacksmith, and an ostler—semiskilled workers, but certainly not capitalists. Where it differs from Portland is in its leadership's relative wealth. The average holding among Portlanders was $679, whereas in New Bedford it was $2,229, led by quite rich men like Nathan and Richard Johnson, and even minus those two, the New Bedforders averaged $1,318 (see table A.2).

Table A.2 Black propertyholders in New Bedford, 1850

Name	Age	Occupation	Value of real property ($)	Birthplace
John Wardsworth	52	Painter	900	North Carolina
George Coleman	50	Gardener	9,110	Virginia
James B. Dyer	31	Soapmaker	3,500	Massachusetts
William H. Brown	26	Sailor	1,800	Massachusetts
Charles Allen	47	Laborer	1,100	West Indies
Archibald Clark	70	Laborer	1,500	Maryland
Solomon Carter	38	Mariner	400	Maryland
Thomas Smith	40	Sailor	1,000	North Carolina
David Luden	50	Laborer	150	North Carolina
William Piper	59	Ostler	2,600	Virginia
Henry H. Smith	40	Waiter	250	Massachusetts
Domingo Barrow	42	Sailor	500	Cape Verde
Richard Johnson	70	Merchant	19,000	Pennsylvania
Nathan Johnson	n/a	Waiter	15,500	Pennsylvania
William Berry	39	Hair Dresser	2,400	Unknown
Francis Jackson	35	Laborer	150	New Jersey
Henry Vincent	22	Hair Dresser	1,300	Massachusetts
James J. Bird	39		750	Unknown
Joseph R. Harrison	40	Laborer	1,100	Pennsylvania
Thomas Jones	38	Stevedore	1,100	Virginia
Robert Parker	27	Barber	600	Virginia
Robert Hatten	30		600	Virginia
Loyed H. Brooks	28	Laborer	600	District of Columbia
David Sulivan	n/a	Laborer	1,500	New Jersey
William Quene	34	Laborer	1,000	Maryland
Henry Quene	n/a	Blacksmith	500	Unknown
Solomon Peneton	38	Grocer	600	Unknown
George Thomas	55	Laborer	500	New York
John Moorfield	33	Laborer	600	Unknown
James Cook	37	Laborer	300	Maryland
Caleb Johnson	n/a	Laborer	600	New York
John Dixon	43	Laborer	500	Maryland
Josiah Stephenson	44	Laborer	900	District of Columbia
Alex Offley	46	Laborer	500	Maryland
William H. Harrison	36	Laborer	600	District of Columbia
William Brown	42	Coach Driver	1,000	Maryland
C. H. Williams	50	Butcher	100	Delaware
Littleton Charity	32	Laborer	165	Massachusetts

Note: From the 1850 U.S. Manuscript Census.

Providence offers a contrast to the prior two cities, with two-thirds of its men of property homegrown Yankees (twenty-seven), mainly Rhode Islanders, reflecting a localist culture (or that it was less attractive to immigrants). Most of the propertied men were born in Providence, like William J. Brown, but in other respects, they resembled their peers in Portland and New Bedford, in that the majority (twenty-three) worked with their hands, as laborers (seven), teamsters (four), porters (three), waiters (three), or coachmen (two), or as a drayman, mariner, cook, or barber. Providence also included a category of skilled labor that seems odd—five "farmers" or "gardeners," who amassed considerable wealth (an average of $3,100). It also had public proprietors (grocer and saloonkeeper), businesses rare among black men in this period, one of whom was the notorious George Head, worth $5,000. It is a mistake to associate greater wealth with skill or ownership, however, as eleven of the nineteen worth $1,000 or more were workingmen, including the political leaders Alfred Niger (a barber), John T. Waugh (a waiter), Ransom Parker (a laborer), and Ichabod Northup (a porter) (see table A.3).

A profile of the 745 black voters in these cities (from the 1850 census, for consistency) shows little difference between leaders and the broader constituency. Forty-seven percent had emigrated from the Lower North and Upper South, a proportion that would have been much higher but for the 185 (25 percent) born in Rhode Island. These men were overwhelmingly working class, with two-thirds listing themselves as laborers (206), mariners of some sort (156), waiters (45), or barbers and hairdressers (37), and smaller numbers in other manual occupations as porters, stevedores, blacksmiths, coachmen, draymen, teamsters, ostlers, and truckmen. Almost one-fifth (143) gave no occupation, leaving only 15 percent occupying skilled positions or in some kind of business; almost all of the latter were in miscellaneous traditional trades, as a boot or shoemaker, a carpenter, mason, tailor, well digger or whitewasher, owner of a fruit stand, clothing store or pawnshop, and the like.

What conclusions should we draw from this? First, that New England's black electorate was remarkably homogeneous with few class differences, which may have encouraged identifying and voting as a bloc. Second, that their relegation to a small set of occupational niches, and evident exclusion from many others, whether in manufacturing (then burgeoning in New England), the skilled trades, or the range of public-facing retail occupations and businesses, let alone the professions, would have further inculcated a distinctive consciousness and the need to operate as a political unit.

Table A.4 documents Hudson, New York's cohort of twenty-three black voters in 1855. It demonstrates both continuities and differences from New England. On the one hand, as in the states to the north and east, the overwhelming majority were workingmen: laborers, porters, and boatmen, with a few barbers and waiters doing indoor labor. Those occupying slightly higher occupations filled miscellaneous jobs (a clothier, a clerk, a wigmaker); there were no equivalents to the wealthy merchants found in New Bedford, for instance. These men's origins were very different, however: a majority were born in Columbia County, where Hudson was the county seat, and almost two-thirds were New Yorkers, with only three immigrants from southward (and three more listing their birthplaces as unknown). This localism, so at odds with the urban

Table A.3 Black propertyholders in Providence, 1860

Name	Age	Occupation	Value of real property ($)	Birthplace
John P. Hazard	56	Teamster	2,700/0	Rhode Island
Elijah Hall	64	Butcher	700/0	Massachusetts
John P. Shumbell	64	Farmer	2,200/0	Batavia, East Indies
William H. Brown	32	Porter	0/150	Maryland
Daniel P. Champion	29	Drayman	0/150	Rhode Island
Ichabod Northup	56	Porter	3,200/0	Rhode Island
Ransom Parker	55	Laborer	1,800/0	New Hampshire
Spencer Waters	50	Jobber	800/0	Maryland
Charles Monroe, Jr.	48	Gardener	2,000/0	Massachusetts
Jeremiah Monroe	47	Bar Maker	0/300	Rhode Island
Jacob Hall	40	Laborer	1,000/400	Maryland
Zadi Jones	56	Teamster	0/300	Massachusetts
John T. Waugh	40	Waiter	1,500/0	District of Columbia
George Henry	38	Gardener	3,500/200	Rhode Island
George Head	40	Grocer	3,000/2,000	Rhode Island
John N. Smith	39	Waiter	2,000/200	Maryland
William Babbitt	40	Cook	0/100	Rhode Island
Joseph Nahar	56	Mariner	2,500/600	Surinam
Lucius Hattan	46	Miller	4,000/500	Connecticut
John Mason	43	Pattern Maker	0/700	Rhode Island
Benjamin Pettis	39	Caterer	0/50	Massachusetts
Albert Straight	29	Teamster	0/50	Rhode Island
Nathaniel Perkins	56	Caterer	1,000/500	Rhode Island
Manuel Ferrer	56	Horse Farmer	5,000/500	Connecticut
Richard Sands	47	Coachman	0/100	Rhode Island
Samuel Rodman	40	Doctor	400/0	Rhode Island
Charles Brown	40	Coachman	0/30	Pennsylvania
George W. Hazzard	43	Teamster	0/75	Rhode Island
Henry Hallis	40	Laborer	300/100	Delaware
Samuel Williams	38	?	0/500	Maryland
Josiah Barron	32	Waiter	0/300	Rhode Island
James H. Collins	48	Laborer	400/0	Maryland
John C. Francis	53	Gardener	2,100/0	Maryland
Francis Talbot	50	Porter	1,100/0	Rhode Island
James C. Burke	58	Saloonkeeper	900/0	Rhode Island
Donald W. Gardner	55	Laborer	1,200/100	Rhode Island
Alfred Niger	63	Barber	1,900/0	Connecticut
Enoch Freeman	53	Laborer	250/0	Connecticut
Spencer C. Read	32	Carpenter	200/400	Rhode Island
Joseph Hicks	49	Preacher	300/0	New York
Walter Boothe	40	Laborer	1,500/0	Maryland

Note: From the 1850 U.S. Manuscript Census.

Table A.4 Hudson, New York's black electorate, 1855

Name	Age	Occupation	Birthplace
Hiram Van Alstyne	48	Carman	Columbia
George W. Welden	36	Porter	Dutchess
George H. Thurston	36	Porter	Unknown
Peter Brink	40	Porter	Unknown
Elias Johnson	45	Laborer	Columbia
Peter Buckuyk	39	Laborer	Columbia
Loyd Tillman	39	Laborer	Virginia
Frank P. Livingston	38	Boatman	Columbia
William Morris	36	Clerk	Columbia
Richard Burton	45	Clothier	Columbia
Chancy Van Huesen	42	Laborer	Massachusetts
William H. Green	51	Wigmaker	Pennsylvania
Garret Deyo	30	Barber	Ulster
William Cummings	65	no trade	Columbia
Jacob Thomas	34	Waiter	Columbia
Peter Gilbert	34	None	Columbia
Joseph Pell	52	Hostler	Unknown
John Williams	43	Laborer	New Jersey
Thomas C. Oliver	36	Methodist Preacher	Massachusetts
John Jackson	36	Boatman	Columbia
Benjamin F. Pell	25	Barber	Columbia
Anthony Jackson	33	Laborer	Columbia
John Deyoe	28	Barber	Dutchess

Note: From the 1850 U.S. Manuscript Census.

Afro-Yankees, is further reinforced by these men's names: seven appear to be the sons or grandsons of men who were black householders and thus voters in Hudson in 1810, given the surnames Van Alstyne, Van Huesen (recorded as Van Hoesen then), Thurston, Livingston, and Jackson.

Finally, table A.5 documents the twenty-six potential black voters in Oxford Town, Butler County, Ohio, some of whom had been named in congressional testimony as "illegally" voting for Rep. Lewis Campbell in 1856. These men were remarkably similar to the New England cohort, in that nearly all (twenty-two) were immigrants from the South, mainly Virginia; the average age of these southerners was thirty-six, with the oldest arriving in 1798, and the youngest during the 1830s, documenting that this was a continuous stream. Their occupations are also familiar: laborers, barbers, waiters, a few more skilled workers (gardener, blacksmith, plasterer, whitewasher), one minister, no proprietors or professionals. Although their average wealth was modest, only $478 in real and personal property, it is striking that all but a few men in their early twenties had some wealth, and fourteen owned their dwellings, suggesting the relative economic prosperity available to black families even in southwest Ohio, near the Kentucky border.

Table A.5 Potential black electorate in Oxford town, Butler county, Ohio

Name	Age	Occupation	Real/personal property ($)	Birthplace	Color
H. Jackson	35	Gardener	400/100	Virginia	M
*John Robins**	25	Barber	1,800/200	North Carolina	M
Preston Jackson	22	Farm Laborer	none	Virginia	M
William Proctor	40	Master Blacksmith	800/200	Virginia	B
John Handy	33	Laborer	600/75	South Carolina	B
Eli Williams	31	Master Plasterer	500/300	Kentucky	B
D. B. Clay	52	Laborer	600	Virginia	B
Thomas Clay	24	Cook	none	Ohio	B
John Myers	35	Laborer	500/50	Tennessee	D
Berry Jackson	41	Farm Laborer	300/200	Virginia	B
Paul Brooks	25	Barber	0/100	Georgia	B
Wm. Lawrence	30	Whitewasher	0/50	North Carolina	M
Simon Grimes	38	Master Barber	0/300	Virginia	B
Jeremiah Lewis	50	Methodist Minister	1,000/200	Virginia	B
Lawson Huffman	47	Carpenter	600/0	Virginia	M
Dan Brooks	28	Laborer	600/100	Virginia	B
Sam Childers	45	Hostler	0/150	Kentucky	M
Aaron Williamson	24	Waiter	none	Ohio	B
Wm. Yancy	25	Waiter	none	Ohio	M
Massie Bridges	58	Laborer	1,000/50	North Carolina	B
R. Bowser	22	Barber	none	North Carolina	M
Cyrus Cowen	50	Physician	450/0	Kentucky	B
John Roberts	22	Laborer	none	Kentucky	B
Charles Sawyer	26	Barber	0/200	Ohio	M
Beverly Tyler	33	Servant	500/250	Virginia	B
Wm. Cummings	39	Laborer	0/250	Virginia	B

Note: From the 1860 U.S. Manuscript Census. M = Mulatto; B = Black.
* Those men whose names are italicized were likely the same men deposed during the Campbell-Vallandigham contest in 1857.

Acknowledgments

This book began as something quite different from what you are reading now. In the mid-1990s, I decided to write a history of Black Power since Reconstruction. I believed then and I believe now that the question of Black Power (defined as "political power for black people," rather than as a movement or set of ideas) is a deep throughline for not only the history of African Americans, but all our history. Years of research followed, supported by generous fellowships from the American Council of Learned Societies and the Woodrow Wilson Center at the Smithsonian. By the time I began writing in 2004, however, I had come upon elements of a largely unknown story of black political and electoral participation stretching back to the Revolution. The first product was my article in the *American Historical Review* in 2008, "'As a Nation, the English Are Our Friends': The Emergence of African American Politics in the British Atlantic World, 1772–1861." By then, the necessity of writing a book about black American politics in what I call the First Republic was clear: there was so much that had gone unnoticed although in plain sight, and those discoveries changed my entire understanding of the period. After an unsuccessful draft was rejected by one publisher, I was fortunate enough to find Chuck Grench at UNC Press, and—ten years later—here is the result.

I would not have been able to write this book without the guidance of James B. Stewart, Gary B. Nash, and Eric Foner. Over many years, they have reads drafts, chapter by chapter, and pointed me in the directions I needed to go. I am in their debt. More recently, Steve Kantrowitz brought his expertise on New England to that section, and made it much better, and my colleague Louise Stevenson gave me excellent advice on the Pennsylvania chapters. Since 2013, David Waldstreicher has been a companion in arms in every sense, reading my work, bringing me much more deeply into a historiography in which I had not been trained, organizing a major conference together on "black politics in the long nineteenth century," and then editing a collection based on that meeting. Deep thanks to him. I also want to thank Robin D. G. Kelley for the backing he provided when I began the original project.

At Franklin and Marshall College, I have benefited from a supportive department. Ann Wagoner, our Academic Department Coordinator, went above and beyond, and I value her professionalism greatly. Our library staff was invaluable to this project, as I placed great demands on those handling interlibrary loans. I have had many student researchers, a few of whom deserve special mention: Jahanzaib Choudhry, Marie Frazer, Josh Panter, and Stephanie Yu; over several years, Christina McSherry showed remarkable assiduity in ferreting out sources. Marie produced my Ohio map, and Emily Mansfield did excellent work on the others. I also thank the Provosts and Deans of the College, who have provided leaves and generous research funding at key points.

Two fellowships were crucial to the process, a Fulbright at University College Cork in 2005–6, when I was getting started, a very happy memory, and a National Endowment for the Humanities fellowship during a sabbatical in 2014–15, which allowed me to write all of Part II.

The archivists at various repositories greatly facilitated my research over the years, including the Historical Society of Pennsylvania, the New-York Historical Society, the Library Company of Philadelphia, the Boston Public Library, and the Rare Books and Manuscript Library at the Columbia University Libraries, where Robb K. Haberman and his colleagues were helpful in digging items out of the Jay Family Papers. I also want to thank Georg Mauerhoff at Readex for providing me with years of free access to the full series of *America's Historical Newspapers*, without which I would not have found much of the evidence needed for this book.

I express my appreciation to the directors and staff at the following, for giving me a chance to present my work for critique: the McNeil Center for Early American Studies at the University of Pennsylvania (and especially Dan Richter); the Gilder Lehrman Center for the Study of Slavery, Resistance, and Abolition at Yale (thanks to David Blight); the Harriet Tubman Institute for Research on Africa and Its Diasporas, York University (with appreciation to Marc Stein); The Fire Every Time: Reframing Black Power across the Twentieth Century and Beyond conference at the College of Charleston's Avery Research Center (thanks to Rob Chase); the History Workshop series at the University of Delaware; the Institute for Critical United States Studies at Duke University. In October 2018, James Oakes and David Waldstreicher organized a workshop reading of the manuscript at the Graduate Center of the City University of New York, where I got very useful feedback from them and others, including Sarah Gronningsater, Matthew Karp, and John Blanton—special thanks to everyone who participated.

I have too many good friends and colleagues to name here, other than a few. Roy Rosenzweig was a steadfast guide, and I miss him. Jim Miller hired me at Trinity in 1994 and asked me to write an article on Harold Cruse, which led to interviewing him; the insights I gained from reading and talking with Professor Cruse regarding the ethnoracial structure of American politics undergird this study. Beyond that, Jim was a lovely, funny human being and I miss him too. Philip Ruhl is my oldest and dearest friend, and has stuck with me through difficult times, and I thank him for that, and the hikes. Doug Anthony has been my pal since I got to Franklin and Marshall in 2001, always a person whose advice I take. Matt Butterfield and Monica Cable have given me a home-away-from-home in Lancaster, deeply appreciated. Mark Davis and Jim Howe are the finest men I know, and always bring joy. Margaret Power is the best kind of historian-comrade, and we will continue to struggle together inside and outside the profession. Last are two people who have shown me what it means to be a long-distance runner in political struggle, Bill Fletcher, Jr., and Max Elbaum. Since my commitments to history and politics are inseparable, I thank them too.

My parents, Dey Erben Gosse and Anthony Gosse, died before I could finish this book, and I wish they could have seen it. My intellectual capacities, such as they are, are largely due to their efforts and examples. I am very lucky to have three fine siblings, Tony and Charley Gosse and Caroline Elmendorf—I hope they like it. I wish Monica Bychowski Holmes, my mother-in-law, who took a keen interest in my progress, had a chance to read this book, but she was taken from us in an untimely way.

My daughter, Johanna O'Mahony Gosse, a scholar in her own right, is a great light in my life; I look forward to all her good things. Her mother, Eliza Reilly, talked with me about my research in black politics over many years, and I thank her. Watching my "illegal" stepsons, Sam and Jonah Frere-Holmes, grow up has been a privilege and pleasure (to borrow Rick Bragg's immortal metaphor about step-parenting, I'm the dog who caught a fine car). Finally, there is Deborah K. Holmes, my sweetheart, who makes life fine, and has backed this book in many ways, reading chapters and listening to my inchoate ideas, above all by urging me to write a book that people who are not professional historians will want to read. Cara mia!

Van Gosse
July 2020

Notes

Abbreviations in the Notes

AANYLH	*Afro-Americans in New York Life and History*
AEJ	*Albany Evening Journal*
CA	*Colored American*
FDP	*Frederick Douglass' Paper*
FJ	*Freedom's Journal*
GSP	Gerrit Smith Papers
GUE	*Genius of Universal Emancipation*
HSP	Historical Society of Pennsylvania
IC	*Impartial Citizen*
JAH	*Journal of American History*
JER	*Journal of the Early Republic*
JNH	*Journal of Negro History*
NASS	*National Anti-Slavery Standard*
NE	*National Era*
NS	*North Star*
NYHS	New-York Historical Society
OS	*Ohio Statesman*
OSJ	*Ohio State Journal*
PD	*Plain Dealer*
PF	*Pennsylvania Freeman*
TWP	Thurlow Weed Papers, University of Rochester
WAA	*Weekly Anglo-African*
WHSP	William Henry Seward Papers, University of Rochester
WMQ	*William and Mary Quarterly*

Introduction

1. Steven Hahn, *The Political Worlds of Slavery and Freedom* (Cambridge, MA: Harvard University Press, 2009), 6, 52–53.

2. See Winthrop Jordan, *White Over Black: American Attitudes toward the Negro, 1550–1812* (Baltimore: Penguin Books, 1969), 450–52, quoting from Smith's pamphlet, *The Pretensions of Thomas Jefferson to the Presidency Examined*; Paul Finkelman, "The Problem of Slavery in the Age of Federalism," in *Federalists Reconsidered*, ed. Duron S. Ben-Atar and Barbara B. Oberg (Charlottesville: University of Virginia Press, 1999), 148 (I avoid the term "Democratic Republicans" to describe Jefferson's party, since party members rarely used it themselves); Johnson quoted in Philip F. Detweiler,

"Congressional Debate on Slavery and the Declaration of Independence, 1819–1821," *American Historical Review* 63, no. 3 (April 1958): 609.

3. Richard H. Sewell, *Ballots for Freedom: Antislavery Politics in the United States, 1837–1860* (New York: W. W. Norton, 1976), 327; *Liberator*, November 2, 1860.

4. "Debate on the Constitution of Missouri, Speech of Mr. Morrill, of New Hampshire," *City of Washington Gazette*, December 18, 1820.

5. See Leon F. Litwack, *North of Slavery: The Negro in the Free States, 1790–1860* (Chicago: University of Chicago Press, 1961), 75 (the 1860 census recorded 5,752 black males in those states, some number of whom were of voting age); William Cheek and Aimee Lee Cheek, *John Mercer Langston and the Fight for Black Freedom, 1829–1865* (Urbana: University of Illinois, 1989); Phyllis F. Field, *The Politics of Race in New York: The Struggle for Black Suffrage in the Civil War Era* (Ithaca, NY: Cornell University Press, 1982); Robert J. Cottrol, *The Afro-Yankees: Providence's Black Community in the Antebellum Era* (Westport, CT: Greenwood, 1982); Kathryn Grover, *The Fugitive's Gibraltar: Escaping Slaves and Abolitionism in New Bedford, Massachusetts* (Amherst: University of Massachusetts Press, 2001); Stephen Kantrowitz, *More Than Freedom: Fighting for Black Citizenship in a White Republic, 1829–1889* (New York: Penguin, 2012). See also the *Black Abolitionist Papers* documentary series, including six printed volumes, and the even more comprehensive microfilm collection at www. http://bap .chadwyck.com. It is telling that a thesis completed well over a century ago (Emil Olbrich, *The Development of Sentiment on Negro Suffrage to 1860* [Freeport, NY: Books for Libraries Press, 1971, originally published 1912]) remains invaluable.

6. Ward's reference to Wisconsin remains mysterious, although Sewell, *Ballots for Freedom*, 334, traces that state's campaign for black suffrage, including how in 1855, "in response to petitions circulated by Milwaukee Negroes," former Whigs who became Republicans revived the effort and "by 1857 . . . had made it a party issue."

7. James Oakes, *The Radical and the Republican: Frederick Douglass, Abraham Lincoln, and the Triumph of Antislavery Politics* (New York: W. W. Norton, 2008); Eric Foner, *The Fiery Trial: Abraham Lincoln and American Slavery* (New York: W. W. Norton, 2011); Oakes, *The Scorpion's Sting: Antislavery and the Coming of the Civil War* (New York: W. W. Norton, 2014). That there were and are other kinds of political agency besides electoral and party politics is a given. As this book was finalized, several books came out that address those types of politics, including R. J. M. Blackett, *The Captive's Quest for Freedom: Fugitive Slaves, the 1850 Fugitive Slave Law, and the Politics of Slavery* (New York: Cambridge University Press, 2018); Andrew Delbanco, *The War Before the War: Fugitive Slaves and the Struggle for America's Soul from the Revolution to the Civil War* (New York: Penguin, 2018); Kellie Carter Jackson, *Force and Freedom: Black Abolitionists and the Politics of Violence* (Philadelphia: University of Pennsylvania Press, 2019); and John L. Brooke, *"There Is a North": Fugitive Slaves, Political Crisis, and Cultural Transformation in the Coming of the Civil War* (Amherst: University of Massachusetts Press, 2019). All of these books focus on the centrality of fugitivity (the condition of being a fugitive) in Northern political life and its constant disruption of the normal flow of business, especially after passage of the Fugitive Slave Act of 1850. Anyone wanting to grasp the totality of black politics will want to consult those, as well as Manisha Sinha's commanding revision of abolitionist historiography, *The Slave's Cause: A History of Abolition* (New Haven, CT: Yale University Press, 2016)

and David Blight's epic biography of the most important abolitionist, *Frederick Douglass: Prophet of Freedom* (New York: Simon and Schuster, 2018).

8. Don E. Fehrenbacher, *The Dred Scott Case: Its Significance in American Law and Politics* (New York: Oxford University Press, 1978), 352, points out that ruling's essential legal flaw, that Taney repeatedly "revealed . . . his determination to treat emancipation as legally meaningless and to mix free Negroes with slaves in one legal category based on race" in the face of plain evidence, including the treaties annexing Florida, Louisiana, and half of Mexico to the United States which granted citizenship to *all* free inhabitants with no mention of race or color (405); for nullification in Maine, see 432, noting its legislature put "the legal services of county attorneys at the disposal of accused fugitive slaves" and decreed the immediate "emancipation of any slave carried into the state"; for New Hampshire, see Eric Foner, *Free Soil, Free Labor, Free Men: The Ideology of the Republican Party before the Civil War* (New York: Oxford University Press, 1995), 285; for Vermont, Elise A. Guyette, *Discovering Black Vermont: African American Farmers in Hinesburgh, 1790–1890* (Burlington: University of Vermont Press, 2010), 101.

9. Frederick Douglass, *My Bondage and My Freedom* (New York: Miller, Orton & Mulligan, 1855), 347.

10. A note on Douglass, since he looms large. The historiography of antebellum black activism poses two opposing traditions, of abolitionism at home versus emigrationism abroad, with Martin R. Delany as Douglass's polar opposite, pulling figures like Henry Highland Garnet toward a politics retrospectively named "black nationalism." I think this is a false dichotomy. Emigrationism did surface periodically but never became a lasting program. The deeper division was between versions of radicalism, either Garrisonian or third party, versus what I call the "Black Whig tradition," focused on developing ties with white politicians and parties to carve out more space for black people's freedom. Douglass recurs throughout this book, but he does not center it because he chose to maintain his independence as an agitator, lecturer, editor, and author, avoiding the tedium of organizational politics, its compromises, and basetending. U.S. history abounds in prominent radicals like him who disdain the party system because of its rigidities. In Europe and elsewhere, such men and women have been more likely to enter into or form electoral formations. After 1865, however, Douglass embraced the Black Whig tradition, becoming the archetypal Black Republican, an orthodox party man. In doing so, he moved, with greater fanfare, into the position occupied by black men predating him in places like Portland and New York City.

11. Sean Wilentz, *The Rise of American Democracy: Jefferson to Lincoln* (New York: W. W. Norton, 2005), 138, xviii (also 27, asking "How successful, overall, was the democratic impulse that arose during the Revolution? Narrowly defined, the results, as inscribed in the state constitutions, can appear modest. As of 1790, fewer than half of the original thirteen states provided an approximation of white manhood suffrage by replacing freehold qualifications with minimal taxpaying requirements"). Race and slavery do not figure at all in Wood's canonical *The Creation of the American Republic, 1776–1787* (Chapel Hill: University of North Carolina Press, 1969), while in *The Radicalism of the American Revolution* (New York: Knopf, 1992), Wood briefly alludes to slavery as either a version of the "patriarchal dependence" to which many whites were also subject or the economic institution permitting a uniquely republican plantocracy

(see pp. 42, 50–55, 115, 172–73, 179, 277). In two paragraphs on p. 51 he acknowledges the incommensurability of chattel slavery with a revolution that made "the interests and prosperity of ordinary people—their pursuits of happiness—the goal of society and government" (8). Finally, on pp. 186–87, he asserts slavery's demise was the natural result of the Revolution making it "excruciatingly conspicuous," thus setting "in motion ideological and social forces that doomed the institution of slavery in the North and led inexorably to the Civil War." For his final summing up of the Revolution's triumph, see pp. 6–7; the other reference is to Gary B. Nash, *The Forgotten Fifth: African Americans in the Age of Revolution* (Cambridge, MA: Harvard University Press, 2006).

12. Alexander Saxton, *The Rise and Fall of the White Republic: Class Politics and Mass Culture in Nineteenth-Century America* (London: Verso, 1990); David Roediger, *The Wages of Whiteness: Race and the Making of the American Working Class* (London: Verso, 1991); Don E. Fehrenbacher, *The Slaveholding Republic: An Account of the United States Government's Relations to Slavery* (New York: Oxford University Press, 2001). These books deploy a more nuanced understanding of antebellum racialism than implied by my summary here, but the net effect has been as indicated—totalizing rather than dialectical; see Robert Pierce Forbes, *The Missouri Compromise and Its Aftermath* (Chapel Hill: University of North Carolina, 2007), 1; also David Brion Davis's insight that instead of acknowledging "Racial slavery" as "an intrinsic and indispensable part of New World settlement from Chile to French Canada—not an accidental or unfortunate shortcoming on the margins of the American experience," it "became the dark underside of the American Dream—the great exception to our pretensions of perfection, the single barrier blocking our way to the millennium, the single manifestation of national sin" (Davis, *Challenging the Boundaries of Slavery* [Cambridge, MA: Harvard University Press, 2003], 32).

13. Daniel Walker Howe, *The Political Culture of the American Whigs* (Chicago: University of Chicago Press, 1979), 9; Howe, *What Hath God Wrought: The Transformation of America, 1815–1848* (New York: Oxford University Press, 2007), 653, 4.

14. James Brewer Stewart, "Modernizing 'Difference': The Political Meanings of Color in the Free States, 1776–1840," *JER* 19, no. 4 (Winter 1999): 692–93.

15. Rogers M. Smith, *Civic Ideals: Conflicting Visions of Citizenship in U.S. History* (New Haven, CT: Yale University Press, 1997).

16. Howe, *What Hath God Wrought*, 578; Hahn, *Political Worlds*, 13.

17. Michael F. Holt, "Winding Roads to Discovery: The Whig Party from 1844 to 1848," in *Essays on American Antebellum Politics, 1840–1860*, ed. Stephen E. Maizlish and John J. Kushma (College Station: Texas A&M University Press, 1982), 129.

18. Jerrold G. Rusk, *A Statistical History of the American Electorate* (Washington, DC: CQ Press 2001), 178: 28.9 percent in Vermont, 28.6 percent in Massachusetts, 26.6 percent in Wisconsin, 26.4 percent in New York, 16 percent in Michigan, 15.1 percent in New Hampshire, 13.9 percent in Maine, 12.7 percent in Illinois, 10.8 percent in Ohio, and farthest behind in Connecticut (8 percent), Rhode Island (6.6 percent), Iowa (4.9 percent), and Pennsylvania (only 3 percent); as often the case, New Jersey came last with 1 percent.

19. See Van Gosse, "In the Woodpile: Negro Electors in the First Reconstruction" in *Revolutions and Reconstructions: Black Politics in the Long 19th Century*, ed. Van Gosse

and David Waldstreicher (Philadelphia: University of Pennsylvania Press, 2020) for these other states; and Gosse, "'As a Nation, the English Are Our Friends': The Emergence of African American Politics in the British Atlantic World, 1772–1861," *American Historical Review* (October 2008): 1003–28 for their transnational engagements.

20. Elsewhere, I have proposed structuring U.S. politics through 1860 via an evolving set of "racial political orders"; see Van Gosse, "Patchwork Nation: Racial Order and Dis-Order in the Antebellum United States," *JER* 40, no. 1 (Spring 2020): 45–81; Donald Robinson, *Slavery in the Structure of American Politics, 1765–1820* (New York: Harcourt Brace Jovanovich, 1971), 438; Ronald P. Formisano, "The Edge of Caste: Colored Suffrage in Michigan, 1827–1861," *Michigan History* 55, no. 1 (Spring 1972): 20.

21. Regarding King, David Brion Davis notes that "up to that time no statesman or political leader in the world had publicly made such a radical declaration of slavery's illegality"; see Davis, *Challenging the Boundaries of Slavery*, 42; Donald J. Ratcliffe, *The Politics of Long Division: The Birth of the Second Party System in Ohio, 1818–1828* (Columbus: Ohio State University Press, 2000), xii, an acute narrative of this otherwise neglected period.

22. Quoted in Anthony Gronowicz, *Race and Class in New York City before the Civil War* (Boston: Northeastern University Press, 1997), 42.

23. Foner, *Free Soil, Free Labor, Free Men*, 9.

24. Blackett, *The Captive's Quest for Freedom*.

25. As Martha S. Jones puts it, "The struggle proceeded in large part without any engagement with the problem that gender posed for understanding and arbitrating rights. The early debate about citizenship largely assumed it to be a problem between and about men." See Jones, *Birthright Citizens: A History of Race and Rights in Antebellum America* (New York: Cambridge University Press, 2018), 152.

26. Barbara Clark Smith, *The Freedoms We Lost: Consent and Resistance in Revolutionary America* (New York: New Press, 2010), xi–xii, traces how "the 'common ground' of colonial political life" fostered "a surprising range of occasions on which ordinary men's status was sufficient and ordinary men's knowledge was enough to establish significant political agency. Recovering those occasions involves recovering types of freedom that many British subjects of the eighteenth century assumed themselves to possess. That project takes us beyond the vote, that act of consent which later generations put would put at the center of political life." Later she notes, "Men of low status . . . and even colonial women occasionally acted as a group to intrude their own moral sensibilities onto the public stage. Yet, for the most part, when African-Americans, European-American boys, or women took part, their participation depended on their indistinguishability, a capacity to blur into the midst of their betters" (43), adding, "The most common popular disorder of the era was the food riot," reinstating a moral economy in which everyone shared (53).

27. Foner, *Free Soil, Free Labor, Free Men*, xxviii, notes black men's "rapid decline in economic status" in the prewar decades made "the goal of economic independence . . . almost unimaginably remote" for most; Bruce Levine, *Half Slave and Half Free: The Roots of the Civil War* (New York: Hill and Wang, 1992), 49, documents that well into the nineteenth century, up to 70 percent of the North's white farm population were landowners; W. E. B. Du Bois's recollection of his western Massachusetts relatives captures this precarious existence: "The family were small farmers on Egremont

Plain, between Great Barrington and Sheffield. . . . The bits of land were too small to support the great families born on them and we were always poor," so that by his birth, "economic pressure was transmuting the family generally from farmers to 'hired' help"; see Du Bois, *Darkwater: Voices from within the Veil* (New York: Harcourt & Brace, 1920), 6.

28. Dorothy Sterling, ed., *We Are Your Sisters: Black Women in the Nineteenth Century* (New York: W. W. Norton, 1984), 96, 100; Cheryl A. Smith, *Market Women: Black Women Entrepreneurs, Past, Present, and Future* (Westport, CT: Praeger, 2005), 37; Suzanne Lebsock, *The Free Women of Petersburg: Status and Culture in a Southern Town, 1784–1860* (New York: W. W. Norton, 1984), 90.

29. Quoted in *A Memorial Discourse by the Rev. Henry Highland Garnet, Delivered in the Hall of the House of Representatives, Washington City, D.C., on Sabbath, February 12, 1865. With an Introduction by James McCune Smith, M.D.* (Philadelphia: Joseph M. Wilson, 1865), 35.

30. Jeffrey L. Pasley, *"The Tyranny of Printers": Newspaper Politics in the Early American Republic* (Charlottesville: University of Virginia Press, 2001), 3; Richard R. John, *Spreading the News: The American Postal System from Franklin to Morse* (Cambridge, MA: Harvard University Press, 1995), 41, 56. John traces how the Postal Act created an unprecedented system of free exchange of newspapers, guaranteeing reciprocity of information across a vast territory: "By the 1840s every newspaper published in the United States received free of charge an average of 4,300 different exchange newspapers every year"; the federal government had "established a national market for information" unlike any other in the world, and "sixty years before a comparable national market would emerge for goods. . . . By 1800, the postal system transmitted 1.9 million newspapers" annually, and by 1820 that figure was six million, by 1830, sixteen million, and by 1840, thirty-nine million (37–38).

31. "Letters from Negro Leaders to Gerrit Smith," *JNH* 27, no. 4 (October 1942): 432–53.

32. A word about my use of the census is in order. I relied on the Historical Census Browser maintained by the University of Virginia to aggregate detailed data by state and county, and I mourn its closure; the century-old publication, US Bureau of the Census, *Negro Population, 1790–1815* (Washington, DC, 1918), continues to prove its utility.

33. James Oakes, "Conflict vs. Racial Consensus in the History of Antislavery Politics" in *Contesting Slavery: The Politics of Bondage and Freedom in the New American Nation*, ed. John Craig Hammond and Matthew Mason (Charlottesville: University of Virginia Press, 2011), 292.

Chapter One

1. The "Address" was signed by the convention's president, Austin Steward (a formerly enslaved prosperous butcher in Buffalo), Garnet, and a fellow "young colored man" from New York City, Charles L. Reason (later a professor), as its secretaries, and the Albany merchant tailor William H. Topp. Its style, plus Garnet's leadership in state conventions through 1845, suggest he was the author. Earlier that year, in his first pub-

lic appearance at the American Anti-Slavery Society's annual meeting, he spoke as a "true American patriot" hailing "the moral sublimity of the spirit of the pilgrims" because they had "laid the broad foundation of republican institutions." In a similar appropriation, Garnet declared "*our* fathers pressed forward with holy and patriotic zeal in the road to that national independence which the revolution of seventy-six opened to them." His filiopiety toward the "fathers of the revolution" was the ideal platform for denouncing "the base conduct of their degenerate sons" who countenanced slavery (see the *PF*, May 21, 1840, repr. from *Emancipator*). It bears remembering that, long before anyone else, Sterling Stuckey paid close attention to the political thinking of men like Garnet, see his *Ideological Origins of Black Nationalism* (Boston: Beacon Press, 1972).

2. A major exception to the occlusion of Black Americanism is Mia Bay, "'See Your Declaration, Americans!': Abolitionism, Americanism, and the Revolutionary Tradition in Free Black Politics," in *Americanism: New Perspectives on the History of an Idea*, ed. Michael Kazin and Joseph A. McCartin (Chapel Hill: University of North Carolina Press, 2006), 25–52, including the insight, "Hindsight has sometimes fostered a view of the early nineteenth-century free black community as a powerless and poorly-organized group buffeted by an increasingly large web of racial restrictions, who had little claim on American citizenship. But it is far from clear that African Americans ever viewed themselves in such terms. Northern black opposition to colonization was fueled by decades of active pursuit of American rights and freedoms on the part of free blacks" (35). Leslie M. Alexander, *African or American? Black Identity and Political Activism in New York City, 1784–1861* (Urbana: University of Illinois Press, 2008) examines New York City's leadership, and places those men's focus on republican citizenship within "a nascent Black Nationalism in nineteenth century America," in which "shared African heritage served as a basis for collective identity." She argues that after engaging with "Pan-Africanism" and Haitian emigration in the 1810s and 1820s, the city men, fearing "they would be involuntarily removed from the United States . . . assumed a defensive posture. They decided to publicly denounce their African heritage and assert an American identity, a tactical move that had a lasting impact on the black community . . . [but] their choice to remain in the United States did not reflect an abandonment of African liberation; rather, it indicated a significant shift in political strategy" (xiv, xvi, xix). Her chapter 4, "'Our Own Native Land,' 1830–1839," documents how this discursive strategy played out through culture and identity rather than this book's focus on politics. In addition, in a book published after I had finished this study, Christopher James Bonner, *Remaking the Republic: Black Politics and the Creation of American Citizenship* (Philadelphia: University of Pennsylvania Press, 2020) makes a powerful argument regarding black citizenship politics, that "By claiming rights as citizens, black people therefore helped make citizenship more important, pushing the status toward the center of lawmaking discussions, arguing that it should be a cornerstone for individuals' rights and their relationship to American governments. Through their political work, black people built a new republic, one that rested on a legal order in which citizen status connected individuals to the federal government through a web of rights and obligations . . . a radical political project working within the rhetorical pathways that the uncertain terms of citizenship provided" (4–5, 8). I emphatically agree.

3. *FDP*, July 15, 1853. The reference to "the same Bible" alluded to those without access to Scripture except through their "Romish" priests.

4. Daniel Walker Howe, "The Evangelical Movement and Political Culture in the North during the Second Party System," *JAH* 77 (March 1991): 1234; Rita Roberts, *Evangelicalism and the Politics of Reform in Northern Black Thought, 1776–1863* (Baton Rouge: Louisiana State University Press, 2010), 2–3, argues that, following "conversion to Christianity, a significant and influential population of northern blacks viewed the developing American republic and their place in the new nation through the lens of evangelicalism." After the Revolution, "American Protestantism had combined evangelicalism, republican political ideology, and common sense moral reasoning to produce a Christianity distinct from that of the rest of the western world" and therefore "when blacks converted, they embraced a religion more open to innovation, more democratic, and more experiential," providing "a foundation upon which to envision the new nation as one of promise and inclusivity" (33–34). Other scholars, notably Martha S. Jones, emphasize a citizenship politics based in the rights to own and convey property, to sue and be sued, to gain official recognition and protection (as in permits to travel or own weapons), all of which were gained and defended by free people of color even in slave states; see Jones, *Birthright Citizens: A History of Race and Rights in Antebellum America* (New York: Cambridge University Press, 2018), for a comprehensive examination of citizenship politics in Baltimore.

5. See Roberts, *Evangelicalism and the Politics of Reform*, 8, "Racial identity came later, in the post-Reconstruction era," whereas earlier, they claimed "an identity that is more definitive of an ethnic identity than a racial identity."

6. William Blackstone, *Commentaries on the Laws of England: A Facsimile of the First Edition of 1765–1769* (Chicago: University of Chicago Press, 1979), 357, 127.

7. William J. Novak, "The Legal Transformation of Citizenship in Nineteenth-Century America," in *The Democratic Experiment: New Directions in American Political History*, ed. Meg Jacobs, William J. Novak, Julian E. Zelizer (Princeton, NJ: Princeton University Press, 2003), 85–107, argues for citizenship's relative insignificance in the early republic, suggesting a "modern understanding of citizenship and statecraft" has been "read back into reluctant historical material" (86), and that before 1865 it "simply did not figure as a particularly significant part of that eminent discussion of American public law" (88). Certainly, there was no "coherent conception of national citizenship rights" that pertained to "public law" (92), but emphasizing that absence elides the constant evocations of *republican* citizenship in ordinary conversation.

8. James H. Kettner, *The Development of American Citizenship, 1608–1870* (Chapel Hill: University of North Carolina Press, 1978), 54, quotes Blackstone, that "allegiance is such as is due from all men born within the king's dominions immediately upon their birth," just as "immediately upon their birth, they are under the king's protection." Kettner adds that "no subject could ever lose his natural allegiance. He might abjure the kingdom and leave the country, but he could not break the tie that bound him," which "resembled the natural family, where a common paternity made sons and daughters into brothers and sisters" (19, 23). As is evident, I rely on Kettner's insights; see 5, 29 for the later quotations.

9. Douglas Bradburn, *The Citizenship Revolution: Politics & the Creation of the American Union, 1774–1804* (Charlottesville: University of Virginia Press, 2009), 246, notes the Articles of Confederation "provided U.S. citizenship to free blacks in numerous states. In the midst of war, free black Americans who pledged allegiance to the cause were more fully citizens of the United States than they would be by 1800."

10. Kettner, *Development of American Citizenship*, 9, 74–75, 106.

11. Quoted in Kettner, *Development of American Citizenship*, 179, 220.

12. *NE*, March 3, 1859.

13. William Jay, *An Inquiry Into the Character and Tendency of the American Colonization and American Anti-Slavery Societies*, 3rd ed. (New York: Leavitt, Lord, 1835), 42; William Yates, *Rights of Colored Men to Suffrage, Citizenship, and Trial by Jury, Being a Book of Facts, Arguments and Authorities, Historical Notices and Sketches of Debates—with Notes* (Philadelphia: Merrihew and Gunn, 1838), 58; *NASS*, October 30, 1845, for that convention's "ADDRESS TO THE PEOPLE OF THE STATE OF NEW-YORK"; Lecture 25, "Of Aliens and Natives," in James Kent, *Commentaries on American Law*, 4th ed. (1840), 2:258. For further evidence of Kent's influence, see *NE*, December 25, 1856, deriding Senator Reverdy Johnson's claim as "counsel for the defendant" in *Dred Scott* that the Constitution "never intended 'to consider black men as citizens'" by quoting Kent (Kent was also cited in the Maine Supreme Judicial Court's nullification of *Dred Scott* ["Rights of Free Negroes in Maine: Can They Vote? Opinion of the Supreme Judicial Court," *NE*, August 25, 1857]); J. Herman Schauinger, *William Gaston: Carolinian* (Milwaukee, WI: Bruce, 1949), 170. Don E. Fehrenbacher suggests that the 1778 vote's importance lies mainly in how it was remembered, asserting South Carolina's amendment was defeated because "Congress, hoping to avoid the necessity of resubmitting the Articles to the states, rejected *all* proposed amendments, including one that would have removed the word 'white' from the apportionment of militia quotas" (Don E. Fehrenbacher, *The Dred Scott Case: Its Significance in American Law and Politics* [New York: Oxford University Press, 1978], 66).

14. [Frederick Watts], *Report of Cases Argued and Determined in the Supreme Court of Pennsylvania*, vol. 6, *May to September 1837*, 3rd ed., *Revised and Corrected by W. Wynne Wister* (Philadelphia: Kay & Brother, 1880), 558; see Rogers M. Smith, *Civic Ideals: Conflicting Visions of Citizenship in U.S. History* (New Haven, CT: Yale University Press, 1997) for a catalog of this judicial record, in particular "Blacks and Jacksonian Law," 253 on.

15. David Waldstreicher, *Slavery's Constitution: From Revolution to Ratification* (New York: Hill & Wang, 2009); Kettner, *Development of American Citizenship*, 230; also Bradburn, *Citizenship Revolution*, 17–18, "Nowhere does the Constitution define who or what a citizen might be; nowhere does it explicitly assign the privileges and duties of a citizen; nowhere does it clearly delineate the relationship of state citizenship to national citizenship; nowhere does it clarify who should settle fights between the states and the nation"; Supreme Court Justice Bushrod Washington, the president's nephew, repeatedly affirmed that "the citizen of one state is to be considered as a citizen of each, and every other state in the union," in the language of an 1821 Circuit Court case, and Chief Justice Taney himself ruled in the 1849 *Passenger Cases* that "every citizen of a State is also a citizen of the United States. . . . We are one people, with one common

country. We are all citizens of the United States"; Kettner, *Development of American Citizenship*, 254–56, 312, 324.

16. Bradburn, *Citizenship Revolution*, 81, quoting Jay's decision in *Chisholm v. Georgia*, which Congress overturned via the Eleventh Amendment barring the Supreme Court from reviewing suits brought in state courts, 288. As Bradburn points out, "The limited nature of the central government assured the persistence of slavery in Virginia, just as it guaranteed free blacks the right to vote in Vermont" (290).

17. Many sources state incorrectly that the society was founded at the meeting on December 21, 1816 referred to below, but the "Memorial" sent to Congress on January 14, 1816, signed by B. Washington and describing the earlier meeting in the Capitol, demonstrates otherwise; see Philadelphia *Weekly Aurora*, January 21, 1816; Claude Clegg, *The Price of Liberty: African Americans and the Making of Liberia* (Chapel Hill: University of North Carolina Press, 2004).

18. Quoted in Gary B. Nash, *The Forgotten Fifth: African Americans in the Age of Revolution* (Cambridge, MA: Harvard University Press, 2006), 147–48; *Constitution of the American Society of Free Persons of Colour, For Improving Their Condition in the United States; for Purchasing Lands; and for the Establishment of a Settlement in Upper Canada, also The Proceedings of the Convention, with their Address to the Free Persons of Colour in the United States* (Philadelphia: J. W. Allen, 1831), 10, in *Minutes of the Proceedings of the National Negro Conventions,1830–1864*, ed. Howard Holman Bell (New York: Arno, 1969).

19. This figure is from the 1820 census, counting free persons of color in the New England and Mid-Atlantic states (Maine, Vermont, New Hampshire, Massachusetts, Rhode Island, Connecticut, New York, Pennsylvania, and New Jersey) which recognized them as citizens, if not always as voters, excluding states carved out of the Northwest Territory where their status was less clear; Hemphill quoted in Nash, *Forgotten Fifth*, 153.

20. Nathaniel H. Carter and William L. Stone, Reporters, *Reports of the Proceedings and Debates of the Convention of 1821, Assembled for the Purpose of Amending the Constitution of the State of New-York* (Albany, NY: E. & F. Hosford, 1821), 200, 192, 186.

21. The most lasting conflict involved the thousands of black seamen circumnavigating the Atlantic as citizens of the northern states or Great Britain. Black mariners were the most visible group of free black workers, a fifth or more of the American merchant marine (see W. Jeffrey Bolster, *Black Jacks: African American Seamen in the Age of Sail* [Cambridge, MA: Harvard University Press, 1997], 2). Early on, their status as Americans was accepted even by politicians loyal to slavery. The crisis leading to the second war with Britain began in 1807 when a Royal Navy ship impressed four American seamen. That two were black scarcely bothered the Jeffersonian "war hawks" denouncing the invasion of America's rights, or Jefferson himself. Half a century later, Republican newspapers mocked Taney by quoting Jefferson's proclamation that "this enormity . . . was committed with the avowed purpose of taking by force from a ship of war of the United States a part of her crew," it having "been previously ascertained that the seamen demanded were *native citizens of the United States*" (*NE*, April 2, 1857). Tolerance for black mariners ended after the supposed "Negro Plot" to seize Charleston, South Carolina, in 1822, led by Denmark Vesey, a former sailor. Vigilant to conspiracies, South Carolina, Georgia, North Carolina, Alabama, and Louisiana passed

laws requiring the jailing of black sailors on entering port, regardless of whose citizens they were. The British protested, and Secretary of State John Quincy Adams tried resolve their concerns, but South Carolina's legislature voted to ignore the federal judge who ordered the sailors' release (see Philip M. Hamer, "Great Britain, the United States, and the Negro Seamen Acts, 1822–1848," *Journal of Southern History* 1 [January 1935]: 3–28). Over many decades, neither Britain nor the northern states could enforce their citizens' rights in southern ports (see George Levesque, *Black Boston: African American Life and Culture in Urban America, 1750–1860* [New York: Garland, 1994], 238, on how this fight pushed Massachusetts to "dramatize . . . its acknowledgement of the citizenship rights of its black population").

22. Quoted in William C. Nell, *The Colored Patriots of the American Revolution, with Sketches of Several Distinguished Colored Persons, to Which is Added a Brief Survey of the Condition and Prospects of Colored Americans* (Boston: Robert F. Wallcut, 1855), 331–32. See Jones, *Birthright Citizens*, 30–33, for a detailed explication of this case. A Westchester meeting resolved that New York must "protect its citizens in the enjoyment of this constitutional right, without regard to their complexion," following which Clinton wrote President Adams, calling the District of Columbia law "void and unconstitutional in its application to a citizen"; Horton was released forthwith (32).

23. For these quotations, see Andrew K. Diemer, *The Politics of Black Citizenship: Free African Americans in the Mid-Atlantic Borderland, 1817–1863* (Athens: University of Georgia Press, 2016), 45, 75; Roberts, *Evangelicalism and the Politics of Reform*, 105; Paul Goodman, *Of One Blood: Abolitionism and the Origins of Racial Equality* (Berkeley: University of California, 1998), 41; Richard H. Newman, *The Transformation of American Abolitionism: Fighting Slavery in the Early Republic* (Chapel Hill: University of North Carolina Press, 2002), 114, 130; William Lee Miller, *Arguing over Slavery: John Quincy Adams and the Great Battle over Slavery in the United States Congress* (New York: Vintage, 1998), 110. In 1830, the Reverend Peter Williams, Jr., pastor of New York's St. Philip's Church, declaimed in an address "for the benefit of the colored community in Wilberforce, in Upper Canada" that "we are NATIVES of this country; we ask only to be treated as well as FOREIGNERS," adding, "Not a few of our fathers suffered and bled to purchase its independence; we ask only to be treated as well as well as those who fought against it"; his address was included in the "Sentiments of the People of Color," in Garrison's *Thoughts on African Colonization* (New York: Arno, 1969, orig. pub. 1832), 66–67.

24. Quoted in William Jerry MacLean, "Othello Scorned: The Racial Thought of John Quincy Adams," *JER* (Summer 1984): 154.

25. Jay, *An Inquiry Into the Character and Tendency of the American Colonization and American Anti-Slavery Societies*, 42, 43, 45, 148.

26. *NS*, February 8, 1850.

27. Speech in Philadelphia, October 23, 1854, in C. Peter Ripley, ed., *The Black Abolitionist Papers*, vol. 4, *The United States, 1847–1858* (Chapel Hill: University of North Carolina Press, 1991), 248.

28. For Irish Negrophobia, see Carl Wittke, *The Irish in America* (Baton Rouge: Louisiana State University Press, 1970). John Wertheimer, "The Green and the Black: Irish Nationalism and the Dilemmas of Abolitionism," *New York Irish History* 3 (1990–91): 5–15,

stresses that the Irish saw abolitionism as "a spurious pretext through which intolerant Yankee reformers hoped to use to gain national power in order to stamp out the rights of the foreign-born" (5). Their "bitter attitudes towards England" generated anger at "the zealot, the fanatic, the morose and gloomy Puritan" who was "seeking to exalt the Negro and debase the Irishman . . . seeking to give the vote to the negro and take it away from the Irishman" (9–10, quoting different sources). David J. Hellwig's "Black Attitudes toward Irish Immigrants," *Mid-America* 59 (January 1977): 39–49, and "Strangers in Their Own Land: Patterns of Black Nativism, 1830–1930," *American Studies* 23, no. 1 (Spring 1982): 85–98, underscore that "black Americans reacted differently to immigrants than did white natives," seeing them from the perspectives of both "insiders and outsiders . . . strangers in their own country," wherein "the presence of immigrants and the preference they received over black citizens fostered the feeling of apartness" (86).

29. *CA*, June 17, 1837.

30. Quotations drawn from Phyllis F. Field, *The Politics of Race in New York: The Struggle for Black Suffrage in the Civil War Era* (Ithaca, NY: Cornell University Press, 1982), 60, 59, 71, 123, 135; also *FDP*, December 1860.

31. James Oliver Horton and Lois E. Horton, *In Hope of Liberty: Culture, Community, and Protest among Northern Free Blacks, 1700–1860* (New York: Oxford University Press, 1997) synthesizes this social history; *William Lloyd Garrison, 1805–1879, the Story of His Life, Told by His Children*, vol. 1, *1805–1835* (New York: Century & Co., 1885), 374.

32. See Marc M. Arkin, "The Federalist Trope: Power and Passion in Abolitionist Rhetoric," *JAH* 88 (June 2001): 75–98, on "a continuity of New England culture" linking Federalist anti-Southernism to radical abolitionism.

33. *Daily Picayune*, January 22, 1840; "Rory O'Rourke's Last Serenade" in *Northern Standard* (Clarksville, Texas), August 4, 1849, repr. from *Delta*; an especially grotesque version had the handyman Mulrooney misunderstanding an order to feed warm mash to the "black filly." When Phillis, the black cook, responds to his demand with "Taint no such a thing. Go way, our poor white Irisher! I tell 'ee I won't. Who ebba heard ob a coloured 'ooman taking a bran mash afore?," he force feeds her, head in a vise, to the master's great amusement (see "An Irish Story" in *New-Hampshire Patriot*, August, 2, 1854; *Times Picayune*, October 14, 1855; and *Macon Telegraph*, July 20, 1858); *National Era*, September 23, 1852, for the Cromwell reference; *Trenton State Gazette*, July 3, 1851, for a story featuring the line "I was forced to borrow money from that tame *negur*, the exciseman"; *Daily Ohio Statesman*, July 17, 1858, also repr. in the Columbus, Georgia, *Ledger-Enquirer*, February 18, 1858, and other papers. In "Horace Greeley a White Man," a Wisconsin newspaper correspondent overheard three Irish servants discussing the famous editor, the punch line being "Sure an' he's a *white man*!" "Av coorse he's a white man," says another "in a patronizing tone," to which the third responds, "Wall, be my sowl, I've been deceived in the old fellow entirely, I thought he was a *naygur*" (*Weekly Wisconsin Patriot*, December 29, 1855).

34. Dale T. Knobel, *Paddy and the Republic: Ethnicity and Nationality in Antebellum America* (Middletown, CT: Wesleyan University Press, 1986) ably analyzes the "love and theft" at work among the Hibernophobes, for whom "American character was ethnic character, *Anglo*-American character" (96). In his analysis, black Ameri-

canism clung to a fragile perch, since by the prewar decades "ethnicity was no longer treated as a matter of 'character,' culture, and environment but of blood, and nationality was no longer understood as attainable by any who met certain standards of intelligence and morality" (99), whereas I see the cacophony of images as an arena in which black men positioned themselves within the nation; for faction fighting, see Kerby A. Miller, *Emigrants and Exiles: Ireland and the Irish Exodus to North America* (New York: Oxford University Press, 1985), 60–61. The Reverend Samuel E. Cornish's campaign against "Prejudice in the Churches" did suggest that the spiritual corruption of Jim Crow churches meant that soon "Infidelity, and Popery will fill the land, and over spread the ruins of the church" (*CA*, March 18, 1837, also May 6 and November 18, 1837), and Andrew Diemer notes that the AME Church's *Christian Recorder* "frequently printed strikingly anti-Catholic rhetoric" (*Politics of Black Citizenship*, 180). Antipopery certainly informed black Anglophilia; see Wells Brown, after visiting Oxford in the 1850s, reporting on how "at one time popery, sent protestants to the stake and faggot; at another, a papist King found no favor with the people. A noble monument now stands where Cranmer, Ridley, and Latimer [three Anglican martyrs], proclaimed their sentiments and faith, and sealed it with their blood" (*FDP*, October 2, 1851).

35. *Liberator*, May 18, 1860.

36. *Weekly Advocate*, February 4, 1837. Hailing papers like *The Liberator*, the editors stressed, "We have, however, peculiar difficulties to encounter, and we act with a fearful weight of responsibility resting upon us. We stand ALONE in the field! Hitherto the native-born Colored AMERICAN has been without an ADVOCATE," shortly renaming their paper the *Colored American* (for black American nationalism more generally, see Patrick Rael, *Black Identity and Black Protest in the Antebellum North* [Chapel Hill: University of North Carolina Press, 2002], 46–47, 83–84, 90). For some of the last public manifestations of African cultural heritage in the North, see William J. Brown, *The Life of William J. Brown of Providence, R.I., With Personal Recollections of Incidents in Rhode Island* (Freeport, NY: Books for Libraries Press, 1971; orig. pub. 1883), 83–84, describing the 1822 founding of Providence's first black church, when "a military company (called the African Greys)" escorted "the African societies to their new house of worship" as the latter "wore their regalias. The president of the societies, who was their commander, was dressed to represent an African chief, having on a red pointed cap, and carried an elephant's tusk in his hand; each end was tipped with gilt"; Stewart, "Modernizing 'Difference': The Political Meanings of Color in the Free States, 1776–1840," *JER* 19, no. 4 (Winter 1999): 694, 696.

37. This was a "Dr. Harris of Franoestown, N.H.," quoted in "an Address to the Citizens of Rhode Island, on the Right of Suffrage, by the Executive Committee of the Rhode Island State Anti-Slavery Society," published in *The Liberator*, December 10, 1841; Richard Allen and Absalom Jones, *A Narrative of the Proceedings of the Black People, During the Late Awful Calamity in Philadelphia in the Year 1793: and a Refutation of Some Censures Thrown Upon Them in Some Late Publications* (Philadelphia: William A. Woodward, 1794); on building fortifications during 1814, see Gary B. Nash, *Forging Freedom: The Formation of Philadelphia's Black Community, 1720–1840* (Cambridge, MA: Harvard University Press, 1988), 212–13, also Robert J. Swan, "John Teasman: African-American Educator and the Emergence of Community in Early

Black New York City, 1787–1815," *JER* (Autumn 1992): 353–54; on Jackson, see *Pamphlets of Protest: An Anthology of Early African-American Protest Literature, 1790–1860,* ed. Richard Newman, Patrick Rael, and Philip Lapsansky (New York: Routledge, 2001), 24; Donald E. Everett, "Emigres and Militiamen: Free Persons of Color in New Orleans, 1803–1815," *JNH* 38 (October 1953): 377–402; and Adam Rothman, *Slave Country: American Expansion and the Origins of the Deep South* (Cambridge, MA: Harvard University Press, 2005), 112, 155.

38. Certainly, the First Rhode Island Regiment (the Continental Line's one official black unit, organized in 1778) served well in several battles, and Salem Poore probably did shoot the British major Pitcairn in the eye at Bunker Hill. But any serious history of the Revolution documents that the Deep South states blocked recruitment of black men, and considerably larger numbers fought for Britain in New York's environs, the Chesapeake's Eastern Shore, and the South Carolina Low Country. Douglas R. Egerton, *Death or Liberty: African Americans and Revolutionary America* (New York: Oxford University Press, 2009) is an excellent synthesis.

39. A search of Readex's *America's Historical Newspapers* scanning thousands of newspapers through 1860 found very few references to Britain's arming American slaves, mostly in the run-up to the Civil War; in late 1859, debating how to respond to John Brown's raid, the *Mobile Register* insisted most slaves had been loyal, and "few sought refuge on Lord Dunmore's ships" (repr. in *National Era*, November 24, 1859); Merton L. Dillon, *Slavery Attacked: Southern Slaves and Their Allies, 1619–1865* (Baton Rouge: Louisiana State University Press, 1990) details this great fear recurring in southern political culture, from the Quasi War with France in 1798 through coastal scares early in the new century regarding "French negro incendiary prisoners" off Savannah, British ships containing black troops in Charleston Harbor, and a supposed Virginia plot, with an informer, "Poor Black Sam," reporting English emissaries were "disrupting the niggres," telling them "the Inglish will land and then they will be free" (76). In 1831, slaves hearing of Turner's rebellion presumed the British had landed, with one saying, "If they really were in the County killing white people . . . it was nothing and ought to have been done long ago" (153).

40. Erica Armstrong Dunbar, *A Fragile Freedom: African American Women and Emancipation in the Antebellum City* (New Haven, CT: Yale University Press, 2008), 6, documents women's agency in Philadelphia's associational milieu, how "as African American women organized mutual aid societies and built their churches, they policed themselves and the larger free black community through disciplinary tribunals within the black church. Black women used the church to protect the sanctity of marriage, protect women from abusive husbands, and maintain order and stability within the free black community"; Martha S. Jones, *All Bound Up Together: The Woman Question in African American Public Culture, 1830–1900* (Chapel Hill: University of North Carolina Press, 2007), 10, 60.

41. In his *The Negro Christianized: An Essay to Excite and Assist that Good Work, the Instruction of Negro-Servants in Christianity* (1706), Mather declared, "Their *Complexion* is sometimes made an Argument why nothing should be done for them. A *Gay* sort of argument! As if the great God went by the Complexion of Men, in His Favours to them! As if none but *Whites* might hope to be favoured and Accepted with God! . . . Away with such Trifles! The God who *looks on the Heart,* is not moved by the colour of

the *Skin*; is not more propitious to one *Colour* than another"; quoted in Winthrop D. Jordan, *White over Black: American Attitudes toward the Negro, 1550–1812* (Baltimore: Penguin Books, 1969), 258. Similarly, in *The Selling of Joseph* (1700), Sewall insisted, "It is most certain that all Men, as they are the Sons of *Adam*, are Coheirs; and have equal Right unto Liberty, and all other outward comforts of Life. *GOD hath given the Earth* [with all its Commodities] *unto the Sons of* Adam, *Psal* 115.16. *And hath made of One Blood, all Nations of Men, for to dwell on all the face of the Earth, and hath determined the Times before appointed, and the bound of their habitation: That they should seek the Lord"*; see Samuel Sewall, *The Selling of Joseph: A Memorial*, ed., with notes and commentary, by Sidney Kaplan (Amherst: University of Massachusetts Press, 1969), 7. This sentence, "And hath made of One Blood . . ." became the touchstone of the Christian egalitarianism grounding abolitionism, on some level unanswerable for any believing Protestant. John Wood Sweet, *Bodies Politic: Negotiating Race in the American North, 1730–1830* (Philadelphia: University of Pennsylvania Press, 2006), 60, points out that Sewall's pamphlet was sharply rebutted in public, and that "for more than half a century, public challenges to slavery virtually stopped."

42. Wood's *Radicalism of the American Revolution* is masterful on this demolition of existing hierarchies, while barely acknowledging its effect on those at the bottom, Americans of the wrong complexion. Padraig Riley, *Slavery and the Democratic Conscience: Political Life in Jeffersonian America* (Philadelphia: University of Pennsylvania Press, 2016), 35, explains how the Federalist commitment to class as a basis for social order made them "less inclined toward racism than Republicans, as they believed in an organically ordered society in which 'respectable' African Americans could find a legitimate place, and in which deference, rather than race, governed social difference." Reading debates at twenty-four state constitutional conventions in 1821–70, Rowland Berthoff documents that ordinary white men rarely invoked scientific racialism, as "their concept of politics and society lagged well behind that of the leading theorists," motivated rather by "an old-fashioned logic to their prejudices . . . a literally classical republicanism." Revolutionary unity had required according "the privileges of citizenship to tenants, employees, and others of small property or none." Having admitted this lower tier of "dependents" into their republic of equal liberty, the question became, "Who would be less than a full citizen? Hitherto neither women and blacks, as such, had necessarily been subordinate," but that premise came under fire, leading to the exchange of a premodern class system for a modern racial-gender hierarchy; Berthoff, "Conventional Mentalities: Free Blacks, Women, and Business Corporations as Unequal Persons, 1820–1870," *JAH* 76 (December 1989): 756, 758, 759.

43. Quoted in David N. Gellman and David Quigley, eds., *Jim Crow New York: A Documentary History of Race and Citizenship, 1777–1877* (New York: New York University Press, 2003), 120, 125.

44. Jordan's *White over Black* includes twenty-six instances where "complexion" was used by authors from Shakespeare (*The Merchant of Venice* and *Othello*) to Franklin, usually to mark what we would now call "race," although Franklin used it to distinguish white Englishmen from "swarthy" Germans (see pp. 13, 15, 37, 60, 94, 97, 102, 119, 143, 165, 173, 248, 253, 254, 255, 259, 277, 278, 305, 369, 407, 416, 497, 524, 525); Abolition Act quoted at http://www.slavenorth.com/penna.htm; quoted in Laura F. Edwards, *The People and Their Peace: Legal Culture and the Transformation of*

Inequality in the Post-Revolutionary South (Chapel Hill: University of North Carolina Press, 2009), 233.

45. Nicholas Hudson, "From 'Nation' to 'Race': The Origin of Racial Classification in Eighteenth-Century Thought," *Eighteenth-Century Studies* 29 (Spring, 1996): 247–64, traces how the science of separate biological groups encompassing national stocks "began to emerge at some point in the eighteenth century" (248) leading to "a *continental* division of humanity" (255), so by the mid-nineteenth century, race and nation fused in a "formidable and grotesquely fruitful remarriage" (258), permitting the grading of each people in a vast hierarchy; on "complexion" authorizing antiracialism, see Princeton University president Samuel Stanhope Smith's 1810 *Essay on the Causes of Variety of Complexion and Figure in the Human Species*, long definitive for those seeking to refute the new racial science (Sweet, *Bodies Politic*, 279, gives the context for Smith's essay, originally a 1787 oration); Jay, *Inquiry*, 40, 373, 374.

46. William Jay, *On the Condition of the Free People of Color* (New York: Arno, 1969; orig. pub. 1839), 373, 374, 381, 395; Jay to Dr. Henry Bowditch, March 19, 1845, as quoted in Robert A. Trendel, Jr., "William Jay: Churchman, Public Servant and Reformer" (PhD diss., Southern Illinois University, 1972, New York: Arno, 1982; Dissertations in American Biography Series), 390; Stephen Myers to John Jay II, December 14, 1858, in Jay Family Collection, box 46, Columbia University, "I will just give a statement of the number of fugitives that your father has sent here within the last eight years before his death 3 from Norfolk Virginia 2 from Alexandria 2 from New Orleans last tow he sent me from North Carolina"; William Jay to Francis Lieber, March 9, 1858, quoted in Trendel, "William Jay," 214.

47. Quoted in Miller, *Arguing over Slavery*, 349.

48. "Remarks of Charles Lenox Remond, Before the Legislative Committee in the [Massachusetts] House of Representatives, respecting the rights of colored citizens in travelling, &c.," *Liberator*, February 25, 1842.

49. Quoted in C. Peter Ripley, ed., *The Black Abolitionist Papers*, vol. 1, *The British Isles, 1830–1865* (Chapel Hill: University of North Carolina Press, 1985), 469–71.

50. Quoted in George E. Baker, ed., *The Life of William H. Seward, with Selections From His Works* (New York: Redfield, 1855), 125.

51. *NE*, April 26, 1849, reporting a speech given on February 23, also May 17, 1849, reprinting the *Cincinnati Chronicle* on how the "dark and swarthy hue which overshadows the features of Senator Corwin . . . which entitles him to the soubriquet of '*Black Tom*,' was strikingly illustrated by an incident at the Navy Department, where a visiting office-seeker mistook him for the 'negro' messenger, but fortunately 'Mr. C., who enjoyed the joke, told him to give himself no uneasiness; that such mistakes were of frequent occurrence, and his only astonishment was, that he had not been apprehended before this as a fugitive slave'" (this self-deprecating humor continued; see *Bellefonte Central Press*, January 21, 1859, "Tom Corwin, of Ohio, is much in the habit of cracking jokes at the expense of his complexion, which is none of the lightest" and charged with favoring black suffrage, he reportedly said, "Certainly, gentlemen," passing his hand over his face, "certainly I favored it. You would not expect me to deprive *myself* of a vote!"); for the Buffalo representative, a "Mr. Miller," see *FDP*, February 17, 1860.

52. *Liberator*, April 5, 1850.

53. *NS*, December 8, 1848, repr. from Columbia *Spy*. Their petition to the legislature declared, "As Americans and Pennsylvanians, we feel as deep an interest in the reputation, prosperity and progressive improvement of our common country as any other class of citizens who can claim nativity by the accident of birth"; *FDP*, June 29, 1855.

Chapter Two

1. Richard S. Newman, *Freedom's Prophet: Bishop Richard Allen, the AME Church, and the Black Founding Fathers* (New York: New York University Press, 2008), 209; Gary B. Nash, *Forging Freedom: The Formation of Philadelphia's Black Community, 1720–1840* (Cambridge, MA: Harvard University Press, 1988), 191. See Newman, "Faith in the Ballot," *Common-Place* 9, no. 1 (October 2008): 1, for a definition of shadow politics as "an alternative universe of political activity (a liminal space in which powerless people act in place of and in conscious opposition to prevailing political practices and norms)," premised on "antebellum disfranchisement in virtually every northern state." He describes how black men "created a vibrant universe of political activities that existed just below the more formal stratum of mainstream civic politics," with "localized voting, electioneering, and constitution making . . . a constant part of African Americans' autonomous political culture." His largest claim is that "the beginnings of a modern black politics occurred in autonomous (and quasi-autonomous) northern churches" wherein "the practice of politics—holding elections and referenda, establishing polling places, and running for office—occurred unimpeded" (3). His argument is challenged by this book's evidence that disfranchisement was much less successful than usually asserted. Recent scholarship, specifically Andrew Diemer's *The Politics of Black Citizenship: Free African Americans in the Mid-Atlantic Borderland, 1817–1863* (Athens: University of Georgia Press, 2016), examining Philadelphia and Baltimore, and Martha Jones's *Birthright Citizenship: A History of Race and Rights in Antebellum America* (New York: Cambridge University Press, 2018), also on Baltimore, have rebutted older definitions of "shadow politics" as inward-facing. Jones stresses that "the incorporation of a church, the purchase of a land and a building, and arranging for the emancipation of an enslaved minister were tasks that offered lessons in law" (18) and that "when they entered the courthouse . . . Black petitioners looked more like rights-bearing people than the degraded subjects they were intended to be. They took part in courthouse culture. They secured the support of leading white men. They navigated the clerk's office and the courtroom. They assembled the endorsements of lawyers and judges into an authority that ensured they would live, in small but important ways, unmolested," all of which made them "more and more like persons with rights" (70). Diemer sees the Philadelphia-Baltimore borderland as "the center of the politics of black citizenship" in that "African Americans advocated on behalf of specific, limited citizenship rights. While almost every African American believed that free blacks were entitled to broad equality, for practical purposes many black activists focused on specific citizenship rights, especially those necessary for the defense of free blacks from kidnapping or reenslavement" (6–7), "a kind of practical antislavery uniquely suited to their region" (143–44). In his view, "the independent institutions of free black life that flourished in this period must be seen not as a means of withdrawal from public life but rather as assertions of

black citizenship—as a part of black engagement with a broader, public world" (50), a thesis that holds true for Baltimore, but not, I argue, for Philadelphia, given the larger state context.

2. James T. Lemon, *The Best Poor Man's Country: Early Southeastern Pennsylvania* (New York: W. W. Norton, 1976) is the classic account; http://www.slavenorth.com /penna.htm.

3. Newman, *Freedom's Prophet*, 43; Gary B. Nash and Jean R. Soderlund, *Freedom by Degrees: Emancipation in Pennsylvania and Its Aftermath* (New York: Oxford University Press, 1991), 75 and passim argues that "the rapid contraction of slavery" arose from an "interlocking set of phenomena," including the 1763 imposition of a confiscatory head tax on slave imports, mortality among the existing population, wartime desertions, selling slaves south, and manumission; for demographics, see pp. 36, 18 (based on Chester's population before 1789, when Delaware County was created, the 1820 figure representing both counties).

4. See Nash, *Forging Freedom*, 148 on black Philadelphia's class structure (in 1816, about one in five men were other than day laborers, carters, ordinary seamen, or stevedores; 11.6 percent were proprietors of some sort, and 6.8 percent were artisans, plus a few professionals, 0.6 percent); Julie Winch, *Philadelphia's Black Elite: Activism, Accommodation, and the Struggle for Autonomy, 1787–1848* (Philadelphia: Temple University Press, 1988), 2; John Davies, "Saint-Dominguan Refugees of African Descent and the Forging of Ethnic Identity in Early National Philadelphia," *Pennsylvania Magazine of History and Biography* 134, no. 2 (April 2010): 109–26; and Gary B. Nash, "Reverberations of Haiti in the American North: Black Saint Dominguans in Philadelphia," *Pennsylvania History* 65 (1998): 44–73.

5. Julie Winch, "'A Person of Good Character and Considerable Property': James Forten and the Issue of Race in Philadelphia's Antebellum Business Community," *Business History Review* 75, no. 2 (Summer 2001): 261–96, 272–73.

6. For this general immiseration, see Carl Douglas Oblinger, "New Freedoms, Old Miseries: The Emergence and Disruption of Black Communities in Southeastern Pennsylvania, 1780–1860" (PhD diss., Lehigh University, 1988), esp. 166 on, and Theodore Hershberg, "Free Blacks in Antebellum Philadelphia: A Study of Ex-Slaves, Freeborn, and Socioeconomic Decline," *Journal of Social History* 5, no. 2 (Winter, 1971–72): 183–209; for the white proletariat, see David R. Roediger, *The Wages of Whiteness: Race and the Making of the American Working Class* (New York: Verso, 1991); *Proceedings of the Colored National Convention, Held in Franklin Hall, Sixth Street, Below Arch, Philadelphia, October 16th, 17th and 18th, 1855* (Salem, NJ: National Standard Office, 1856), 22, documenting that 912 (32 percent) of 2,856 were unable to work at their "Trades and Professions" in Maine, Vermont, Massachusetts, Connecticut, New York, New Jersey, Pennsylvania, Ohio, Illinois, Michigan, California, and Oregon.

7. The Rev. Wm. Douglass, *Annals of the First African Church, in the United States of America, Now Styled, The African Episcopal Church of St. Thomas, Philadelphia, In Its Connection with the Early Struggles of the Colored People to Improve Their Condition, With the Co-Operation of the Friends, and Other Philanthropies; Partly Derived from the Minutes of a Beneficial Society, Established by Absalom Jones, Richard Allen and Others, in 1787, and Partly From the Minutes of the Aforesaid Church* (Philadelphia: King & Baird, 1862), 13, 15; Newman, *Freedom's Prophet*, 64–65, on when Bethel was founded;

Richard Allen, *The Life Experience and Gospel Labors of the Rt. Rev. Richard Allen, To Which Is Annexed The Rise and Progress of the African Methodist Episcopal Church in the United States of America, Containing a Narrative of the Yellow Fever in the Year of Our Lord 1793, With an Address to the People of Color in the United States, Written by Himself and Published by His Request* (New York: Abingdon, 1960, repr. of 1831 ed.), 25; Julie Winch, *A Gentleman of Color: The Life of James Forten* (New York: Oxford University Press, 2002), 142–43; Richard Allen and Absalom Jones, *A Narrative of the Proceedings of the Black People, During the Late Awful Calamity in Philadelphia in the Year 1793: and a Refutation of Some Censures Thrown Upon Them in Some Late Publications* (Philadelphia: William A. Woodward, 1794).

8. *Annals of Congress*, January 30, 1797, 4th Cong., 2nd Sess., 2018–19.

9. *Annals of Congress*, Thursday, January 2, 1800, 6th Cong., 1st Sess., 229–30.

10. See the *Independent Chronicle and the Universal Advertiser* (Boston), June 12–16, 1800; *The Oriental Trumpet* (Portland), June 18, 1800; *Columbian Courier* (New Bedford), June 20, 1800; *Eastern Herald* (Portland), June 23, 1800; *Salem Gazette* (Salem), May 26, 1801; *The Republican, or, Anti-Democrat* (Baltimore), January 5, 1802.

11. Winch, *Gentleman of Color*, 156; Nash and Soderlund, *Freedom by Degrees*, 131–34. Those counties each held over 100 slaves, totaling 774, which was 45 percent of the total. In 1801, the PAS described the bill as "ostensibly providing for the total abolition of slavery, but containing provisions highly injurious and oppressive to the blacks," asking, with some justification, "Why is the fund for the redemption of slaves to be created by a heavy and exclusive tax on the people of color, when many of them have pined away their best days in a cruel bondage, and from the weight of declining years are now barely able by their industry to supply the common wants of nature, and are not permitted the full rights of citizenship?" In 1802, the High Court of Errors and Appeals unanimously denied a suit that sought freedom for a woman on the grounds that slavery was unconstitutional in Pennsylvania; see Edward Needles, *An Historical Memoir of the Pennsylvania Society for Promoting the Abolition of Slavery; The Relief of Free Negroes Unlawfully Held in Bondage, and For Improving the Condition of the African Race. Compiled From the Minutes of the Society and Other Official Documents, by Edward Needles, and Published By Authority of the Society* (New York: Arno, 1969, repr. of 1848 ed.), 48, 49, 42; Loring Dewey of the American Colonization Society, quoted in Winch, *Gentleman of Color*, 215.

12. Needles, *Historical Memoir*, 55, 56–57, the latter statement from 1809; *Aurora General Advertiser*, July 27, 1804; *Poulson's*, February 6, 1807; January 1, 1808; August 3, 1810; *Otsego Herald*, April 23, 1808; *New-York Evening Post*, July 12, 1804 from the *Philadelphia Freeman's Journal*; see also Nash, "Reverberations of Haiti," 73n99, for the arrests of two men.

13. J. Thomas Scharf and Thompson Westcott, *History of Philadelphia, 1609–1884* (Philadelphia: L. H. Everts, 1884), 1:567; Needles, *Historical Memoir*, 61; Winch, *Gentleman of Color*, 169–74; *Poulson's*, January 17, 20, 27; February 11, 17, 1814.

14. Winch, *Philadelphia's Black Elite*, 21; Winch, *Gentleman of Color*, 174; *Poulson's*, September 19, 1814; Scharf and Westcott, *History of Philadelphia*, 1:575: the committee reasoned it "improper . . . to have the proposed legion organized . . . when there is so short a supply of arms and accoutrements for our white citizens. . . . Under a proper

regulation these people of color might be employed as fatigue parties on the work . . . detached from the white citizens who may be so employed."

15. Since the late 1600s, dissident Friends had confronted their slave-owning coreligionists, and in the 1750s, the Huguenot refugee and Quaker convert Anthony Benezet organized a transatlantic movement for emancipation, circulating pamphlets, agitating inside the Philadelphia Yearly Meeting, and instigating lobbying of Parliament and colonial governments to end the slave trade; see the superb biography by Maurice Jackson, *Let This Voice Be Heard: Anthony Benezet, Father of Atlantic Abolitionism* (Philadelphia: University of Pennsylvania Press, 2009), and Betty Fladeland, *Men and Brothers: Anglo-American Anti-Slavery Cooperation* (Urbana: University of Illinois Press, 1972). Recently, Kirsten Sword has argued that the PAS founders, radical Quakers like Benezet and the artisan Thomas Harrison, "staged a disappearing act" by recruiting "talented non-Quaker gentlemen to provide a public face for emergent antislavery institutions," part of "a wider pattern of deceptive self-representation designed to make antislavery appear to be a popular, nonsectarian, national cause well before it actually became one," as a "a genteel and benevolent concern for distant victims." After the Revolution, this "politically palatable politics based on racial distance" came to the fore, "based on appeals to the benevolent sensibility of gentlemen of feeling and education and an emphasis on their ability to act on behalf of those who putatively could not"; see Sword, "Remembering Dinah Nevil: Strategic Deceptions in Eighteenth-Century Antislavery," *JAH* 97, no. 2 (September 2010): 318, 333, 340; for the definitive account of the PAS's "distinctly conservative style of activism" based on "elite patronage, refined legal and political strategy, and careful tactics," see Richard S. Newman, *The Transformation of American Abolitionism: Fighting Slavery in the Early Republic* (Chapel Hill: University of North Carolina Press, 2002), 16, 28, 62, 61.

16. Robert Duane Sayre, "The Evolution of Early American Abolitionism: The American Convention for Promoting the Abolition of Slavery and Improving the Condition of the African Race, 1794–1837" (PhD diss., Ohio State University, 1987), 161–62 describes how the convention hoped to "awe blacks into better behavior," with its 1801 address read to "659 families with 2,313 members" in Philadelphia; quotations are from the *Address from the Committee for Improving the Condition of the Free Blacks, to the Members of the Pennsylvania Abolition Society, and to the Public in General* (Philadelphia: Printed by John Ormrod, 1800); similarly, *An Address from the Pennsylvania Abolition Society to the Free Black People of the City of Philadelphia, and its Vicinity* (Philadelphia: Printed by John Ormrod, 1800) railed against "idleness, dissipation, frolicking, drunkenness, theft, cheating or any other vice" and "those disgraceful scenes of folly and intemperance, which we have had too frequent occasion to observe, on the First day of the week," stressing the importance of inculcating "submission, obedience, and an obliging disposition" among "those of your colour, who are slaves"; see Needles, *Historical Memoir*, 72, on visiting black churches in 1822 to lecture on "virtue, sobriety and industry; so that . . . they might become good and useful citizens."

17. Beverly C. Tomek, *Colonization and Its Discontents: Emancipation, Emigration, and Antislavery in Antebellum Pennsylvania* (New York: New York University Press, 2011), 29–30; *The Tickler*, February 14, 1810; intriguingly its editor, George Helmbold, was a fierce Federalist; see Padraig Riley, *Slavery and the Democratic Conscience: Po-*

litical Life in Jeffersonian America (Philadelphia: University of Pennsylvania Press, 2016), 74.

18. Winch, "Person of Good Character," 267, quoting a letter from that year; *Liberator*, June 29, 1832; *NS*, March 10, 1848.

19. Richard S. Newman first unearthed this crucial text; see Newman, "'We Participate in Common': Richard Allen's Eulogy of Washington and the Challenge of Interracial Appeals," *WMQ* 64, no. 1 (January 2007): 117–28, which he elsewhere called "the first document by an African American commenting on national politics in the early republic" (see Newman, "Liberation Technology: Black Printed Protest in the Age of Franklin," *Early American Studies* 8, no. 1 [Winter 2010]: 195); "Eulogy of Washington," *Philadelphia Gazette and Universal Advertiser*, December 31, 1799, repr. in *New York Spectator*, January 2, 1800, and *Baltimore Federal Gazette*, January 3, 1800; also *American Mercury* (Hartford) and *J. Russell's Gazette* (Boston), both January 16, 1800, emphasizing it showed "that the African race participate in the common events of our country."

20. Amid a voluminous scholarship, see J. G. A. Pocock, "The Classical Theory of Deference," *American Historical Review* 81, no. 3 (June 1976): 516–23, with its oft-quoted explanation that traditional practices of deference presumed that "the nonelite regard the elite, without too much resentment, as being of a superior status and culture to their own, and consider elite leadership in political matters to be something normal and natural. . . . Deference is expected to be spontaneously exhibited rather than enforced," with "the deferential man . . . frequently depicted as displaying deference as part of his otherwise free political behavior" (516); on Washington's candidacy, see Richard R. Beeman, "Deference, Republicanism, and the Emergence of Popular Politics in Eighteenth-Century America," *WMQ* 49, no. 3 (July 1992): 402; in July 1800, the black leader Cyrus Bustill was called "Citizen Sambo" in the Federalist *Gazette of the United States* because he attended a Democratic Society meeting with men like Benjamin Rush (see Edwin Wolf and Maxwell Whiteman, *The History of the Jews of Philadelphia from Colonial Times to the Age of Jackson* [Philadelphia: Jewish Publication Society of America, 1956], 209); in 1807, the Republican Frederick Wolbert's candidacy for Sheriff was mocked because, during the prior year's election, "The most infamous arts was practised to obtain his election; Paupers, boys of eighteen years of age, and even NEGROES* were suffered to vote," with the asterisked note reporting, "Before the Commissioners which sat at the State House 'Maugo' a Negro was produced, who had voted for Mr. Wolbert in the Northern Liberties" (see *Tickler*, October 12, 1807; also Scharf and Westcott, *History of Philadelphia*, 1:526).

21. See G. S. Rowe, "Black Offenders, Criminal Courts, and Philadelphia Society in the Late Eighteenth-Century," *Journal of Social History* 22, no. 4 (Summer 1989): 685, acknowledging that "black defendants" never gained "equality and justice before the law," since by every measure "blacks fared more poorly in Pennsylvania courts than did whites. Even so, reformers in Philadelphia, in conjunction with court personnel, achieved a legal system sensitive to black rights, and certainly more fair and just in its practices than society outside the courts"; the PAS's connections to Federalism were evident in the person of the preeminent lawyer William Rawle, a Quaker Loyalist during the Revolution, the city's first U.S. federal attorney in 1791–99, and a longtime PAS officer.

22. Oblinger, "New Freedoms, Old Miseries," 137 and passim, has breakdowns of the class and occupational structure in West Chester, Columbia, Lancaster, York, and Gettysburg, showing how the upper one-quarter to one-third were linked to Quaker benefactors. In West Chester, for instance, "four ex-slave clans from the two surrounding townships" dominated the black community "through their economic and social ties with elite Quaker families," and "over half of the town's black population was engaged in semi-skilled, and skilled occupations directly related to the sale of goods and services to the rich . . . a relatively cohesive Quaker elite which retained political, social, and economic hegemony" (82,102), while in Gettysburg, "two-thirds were descended directly from prominent white families" (82).

23. Gary B. Nash, *The Forgotten Fifth: African Americans in the Age of Revolution* (Cambridge, MA: Harvard University Press, 2006), 48, 51, lists a cohort of mostly itinerant Methodists or Baptists, including Harry Hosier, Peter Spence, Thomas Paul, Daniel Coker, Allen, John Gloucester, Nero Prince, David George, Lemuel Haynes, John Marrant, and John Chavis; my account of Allen's fight relies on Newman, *Freedom's Prophet*; see 135, 167, 168 (for Binney, see Allen to Daniel Coker, February 18, 1816, in Dorothy Sterling, ed., *Speak Out in Thunder Tones: Letters and Other Writings of Black Northerners, 1787–1865* [Garden City, NY: Doubleday, 1973], 32–33). Methodism was then the United States' largest denomination, in part because it "enticed believers with a vision of social and individual perfection," including good works; see Rita Roberts, *Evangelicalism and the Politics of Reform in Northern Black Thought, 1776–1863* (Baton Rouge: Louisiana State University Press, 2010), 107.

24. Newman, *Freedom's Prophet*, 170; Newman, *Transformation of American Abolitionism*, 97; the scholarship on the ACS is considerable, and especially relevant are Douglas R. Egerton, "'Its Origin Is not a Little Curious': A New Look at the American Colonization Society," *JER* 5 (1985): 463–80; Eric Burin, "Rethinking Northern White Support for the African Colonization Movement: The Pennsylvania Colonization Society as an Agent of Emancipation," *Pennsylvania Magazine of History and Biography* 127, no. 2 (April 2003): 197–229; Tomek, *Colonization and Its Discontents*.

25. Claude Clegg, *The Price of Liberty: African Americans and the Making of Liberia* (Chapel Hill: University of North Carolina Press, 2004), 34. The reference to their opposition is from R. J. M. Blackett, *The Captive's Quest for Freedom: Fugitive Slaves, the 1850 Fugitive Slave Law, and the Politics of Slavery* (New York: Cambridge University Press, 2018), 131.

26. Sheldon Harris, *Paul Cuffe: Black America and the African Return* (New York: Simon and Schuster, 1972); Lamont D. Thomas, *Paul Cuffe: Black Entrepreneur and Pan-Africanist* (Urbana: University of Illinois Press, 1988). See Winch's *Philadelphia's Black Elite*, 29–34, and *Gentleman of Color*, 179–86, on Forten and Cuffe's private discussions; Purvis quoted in Nell, *Colored Patriots*, 177.

27. *National Intelligencer*, December 21, 1816, repr. in *Albany Register*, January 10, 1817 (John Randolph stressed deporting free people of color would maintain slavery, since they suborned the slaves into rebellion and thievery); *National Intelligencer*, December 30, 1816; Forten to Cuffe, quoted in Winch, *Gentleman of Color*, 190. Another article from the *Intelligencer* described how "in Philadelphia, the people of color were in great agitation on the subject of being colonized. Some person in Washington, had sent a printed circular addressed to the ministers of religion among the people of color, and

to some others who were respectable among them. The circular contained an inflammatory address on the subject of the proposed colony, urging the free blacks to sign petitions against the execution of the intended plan. A printed petition was also sent to them ready for signing. They had called a meeting of their people at one of their churches in the city, at which they reckoned three thousand to be present"; see the *Ulster Plebeian* (New York), May 24, 1817, "Colonization of Free Blacks, from the National Intelligencer."

28. "A Voice from Philadelphia," repr. in William Lloyd Garrison, *Thoughts on African Colonization: or an impartial exhibition of the doctrines, principles and purposes of the American colonization society. Together with the resolutions, addresses and remonstrances of the free people of color* (Boston: Garrison & Knapp, 1832), 9; *Liberator*, August 1, 1835; Forten to Cuffe quoted in Winch, *Gentleman of Color*, 191.

29. By the 1830s, references to Philadelphia's indomitability were ubiquitous; see "From a distinguished Philanthropist, in the State of New York [Lewis Tappan], to a highly respected colored gentleman, in Philadelphia [Forten]," *National Enquirer*, February 22, 1838, ruing Pennsylvania's disfranchisement by evoking "the noble sentiment of the meeting in Philadelphia, convened in 1817, for the purpose of protesting against the scheme of African Colonization, the proceedings of which were signed by thyself as Chair" (later examples include *NS*, June 29, 1848 on "the faithful band of Philadelphia, Pa., in 1817, with James Forten, Richard Allen, and other noble patriots at their head, [who] faithfully stood their ground" and H. Ford Douglass in Canada's *Provincial Freeman*, August 15, 1857, "We are disappointed in Pennsylvania, sadly disappointed with respect to its Anti-Slavery character," remembering how Forten early on "gave earnest of his hatred of Slavery and love of liberty," and *Christian Recorder*, February 27, 1869, remembering the "public meeting in this city in the month of January 1817," quoting its resolutions); see Winch, *Gentleman of Color*, 202, on a white New Englander told by Forten that "the 250,000,000 who had for centuries been the oppressors of the remaining 600,000,000 of the human race would find the tables turned upon them and would expiate by their own sufferings those which they had inflicted on others"; on colonization in the Keystone State, see Tomek, *Colonization and Its Discontents*, esp. chaps. 6–8; "A Voice from Philadelphia" in Garrison, *Thoughts on African Colonization*, 9.

30. *Poulson's*, August 12, 1817, on an August 10 assemblage; also an August 11 letter from "The Friends of the unfortunate Africans," insisting that "THE IDEA OF COMPELLING A SINGLE AFRICAN TO LEAVE THE UNITED STATES . . . NEVER HAS BEEN ENTERTAINED," noting "the opposition of the free Blacks at Georgetown [meaning the District of Columbia]" and how "the same error was infused into the minds of the free Africans in this city"; for the *Resolutions and Remonstrance*, see *Poulson's*, November 18, 1819; on the American Convention, see Tomek, *Colonization and Its Discontents*, 39–41, and the letter "To the Public" from "a Virginian and a member of the Colonization Society . . . [but] NO SLAVE HOLDER," in *Poulson's*, May 6, 1819, noting how the American Convention was using "the weight of their character and influence against" the ACS, because of "the unwillingness of the people of colour to go there"; *Franklin Gazette*, June 24, July 20 and 21, August 11 and 12, 1818.

31. See Ric N. Caric, "From Ordered Buckets to Honored Felons: Fire Companies and Cultural Transformation in Philadelphia, 1785–1850," *Pennsylvania History* 72,

no. 2 (Spring 2005): 117–58, esp. 133: "Firefighting was an extremely important civic function; young apprentices and journeymen eagerly embraced the opportunity to show themselves as independent men ready and willing to serve the community even though they did not own houses, were not independently employed in businesses, and did not have any of the other traditional signs of personal independence," and 122, 153, on firemen's habits: "Buy large amounts of alcohol, consume other refreshments, and engage in boasting, witticisms, practical jokes, and story-telling in the effort to gain recognition from the gathered crowds," and his observation on 137, "What most firemen apparently did was drink."

32. *Franklin Gazette*, July 9 and 11, 1818; *Poulson's*, July 14, 1818.

33. *Franklin Gazette*, July 22, 1818.

34. *Franklin Gazette*, July 22, 1818.

35. Scharf and Westcott, *History of Philadelphia*, 3:1907; as late as 1832, William Whipper and Robert Purvis published a blistering denunciation of local colonizationists; see their *A Remonstrance against the proceedings of a meeting, held November 23, 1831, at Upton's, in Dock Street* (Philadelphia, n.p., 1832), quoted in Diemer, *Politics of Black Citizenship*, 69.

36. Nash, *Forging Freedom*, 260, 273; Julie Winch, ed., *The Elite of Our People: Joseph Willson's Sketches of Black Upper-Class Life in Antebellum Philadelphia* (University Park: Pennsylvania State University Press, 2000), 106.

37. Entry for October 22, 1822, in "The Diary of Samuel Breck, 1814–1822," *Pennsylvania Magazine of History and Biography* 102, no. 4 (October 1978): 505; Winch, *Gentleman of Color*, 293.

38. Entry for October 24, 1833, in "The Diary of Samuel Breck, 1827–1833," *Pennsylvania Magazine of History and Biography* 103, no. 2 (April 1979): 249–50: "I continued my walk south, and saw Paul Beck's improvements, and visited Mr. Forten's (a colored man) sail loft. . . . He is a very respectable man and fought at sea during the Revolution" (the Samuel Breck Papers at HSP include a July 22, 1828 letter from Forten, giving a Mr. Marckley more time to repay a loan if Breck guaranteed it); Winch, *Philadelphia's Black Elite*, 22–23; Winch, *Gentleman of Color*, 230.

39. Matthew Mason, *Slavery and Politics in the Early American Republic* (Chapel Hill: University of North Carolina Press, 2006), 121, 138–45; Julie Winch, "Philadelphia and the Other Underground Railroad," *Pennsylvania Magazine of History and Biography* (January 1987), 3–22.

40. William R. Leslie, "The Pennsylvania Fugitive Slave Act of 1826," *Journal of Southern History* 18, no. 4 (November 1952): 429–45; Diemer, *Politics of Black Citizenship*, 57, notes that this episode featured "the most direct political action by free blacks that Pennsylvania had yet witnessed," including Bishop Allen visiting Harrisburg to lobby, and corresponding with the city assemblyman, William Meredith, who led the effort to block the bill.

41. Quoted in Winch, "Philadelphia and the Other Underground Railroad," 15; Jesse Torrey, *A Portraiture of Domestic Slavery in the United States: With Reflections on the Practicability of Restoring the Moral Rights of the Slave, Without Impairing the Legal Privileges of the Possessor; and A Project of a Colonial Asylum for Free Persons of Colour: Including Memoirs of Facts on the Interior Traffic in Slaves; and on Kidnapping*

(Philadelphia: Published by the Author, 1817), 45–59; Oblinger, "New Freedoms, Old Miseries," 57–58, 119; on Lancaster, see the African American Records Collection, 1780–1984, Lancaster County Historical Society, ser. 2, folders 1–3, and folder 8 for an 1823 certificate.

42. Winch, *Gentleman of Color*, 215; *Information for the Free People of Colour Who Are Inclined to Emigrate to Hayti* (Philadelphia: J. H. Cunningham, 1825), 4, rose-colored propaganda on the island's population, rivers, exports, and cities, stressing that "all religious professions are tolerated" (emigrants were divided into a "First Class," consisting of "small communities . . . for the purpose of improving uncultivated or neglected lands," the only ones provided up to fifteen acres per "sober, industrious farmer" plus four months of subsistence [7]; the two other classes had to sign contracts to rent land or sharecrop "to repay in six months the expenses of their passage" [9]); for the collapse, see Winch, *Gentleman of Color*, 211–18; and Winch, *Philadelphia's Black Elite*, 51–55; *Minutes and Proceedings of the Second Annual Convention of the Free People of Color in the United States, Held by Adjournments, in the City of Philadelphia, From the 4th to the 13th of June inclusive, 1832* (Philadelphia: Published by Order of the Convention, 1832), 8, repr. in *Minutes of the Proceedings of the National Negro Conventions, 1830–1864*, ed. Howard Holman Bell (New York: Arno, 1969).

43. Paul N. D. Thornell, "The Absent Ones and the Providers: A Biography of the Vashons," *JNH* 83, no. 4 (Autumn 1998): 284–301.

44. *FJ*, February 8, 1828.

45. See *Ariel*, vol. 2, no. 4, June 14, 1828; *FJ*, July 18, 1828, a "Philadelphia Report," concluding in the July 25 issue; *FJ*, June 20, 1828, reporting a March 28 meeting of "Coloured Gentlemen, Citizens of the Commonwealth of Pennsylvania," with Whipper as secretary; also June 6, 1828, on Whipper's nomination to speak at Bethel; December 26, 1828, for an "Extract" from his address, appealing to young men to avoid the "public houses," lest the "cup of intemperance will overtake many, do they not resist those baneful attractions."

46. *FJ*, July 11, 1828.

47. John Gloucester, Jr., *A Sermon, Delivered in the First African Presbyterian Church in Philadelphia, on the 1st of January, 1830, before the Different Coloured Societies of Philadelphia*, quoted in Winch, *Elite of Our People*, 46.

48. Newman, *Freedom's Prophet*, 62 (the quotation is from Douglass, *Annals of the First African Church, in the United States of America, Now Styled, The African Episcopal Church of St. Thomas, Philadelphia*, 24); Reverend William D. Catto, *A Semi-Centenary Discourse, Delivered in the First African Presbyterian Church, Philadelphia, on the Fourth Sabbath of May, 1857: With a History of the Church from Its First Organization: Including a Brief Notice of Rev. John Gloucester, Its First Pastor* (Philadelphia: Joseph M. Wilson, 1857), 27. After noting how Jones's "one Episcopal church" was "ever the firm and abiding friend" of Gloucester (46), Catto described how "an offer was made, and a very strong inducement held out to Mr. Gloucester to relinquish his efforts and give the weight of his influence, the energies of his mind in another direction, and ample provision, &c., should be afforded him" (47–48). See Winch, *Gentleman of Color*, 166–68 on St. Thomas, and 224–25 on fighting in 1821–22; Douglass, *Annals of the First African Church*, 115, 125, describes the "angry tumult" in 1810 and another in

1825; Newman, *Freedom's Prophet*, 210–20, traces the violent 1820 split at Bethel and founding of the Wesley Church, "the black underclass's most sustained response to Allen's brand of leadership"; Catto, *A Semi-Centenary Discourse*, 68–74, describes the schism at First Presbyterian.

49. *Minutes of the Fourth Annual Convention for the Improvement of the Free People of Colour in the United States, held by adjournments in the Asbury Church, New-York, from the 2d to the 12th of June inclusive, 1834* (New York: Published by Order of the Convention, 1834), 7, repr. in Bell, *Minutes of the Proceedings*.

50. "The First Colored Convention," *The Anglo-African Magazine*, October 1859, repr. in Bell, *Minutes of the Proceedings* (see the *Genius of Universal Emancipation*, August and October 1830, for reports of Grice printing a 25-cent map of Canada's new black settlement); delegates from Rhode Island, Connecticut, New York, New Jersey, Ohio, Maryland, Delaware, and Virginia attended; see *Constitution of the American Society of Free Persons of Colour, For Improving Their Condition in the United States; for Purchasing Lands; and for the Establishment of a Settlement in Upper Canada, also The Proceedings of the Convention, with their Address to the Free Persons of Colour in the United States* (Philadelphia: J. W. Allen, 1831), iii, 5, 9, repr. in Bell, *Minutes of the Proceedings*; James Brewer Stewart, "The New Haven Negro College and the Meanings of Race in New England, 1776–1870," *New England Quarterly* 76, no. 3 (September 2003): 323–55; *Minutes and Proceedings of the Second Annual Convention*, 35.

51. A fine critique is Frederick Cooper, "Elevating the Race: The Social Thought of Black Leaders, 1827–50," *American Quarterly* 24, no. 5 (December 1972): 605, discussing how "present-day historians" have gone looking for "traditions which anticipate today's concerns with revolutionary politics or black nationalism. . . . However useful this approach may be to current political movements, it suggests that the ideas of blacks in the past are not worth examining in their own right"; see Alexis de Tocqueville, *Democracy in America* (New York: D. Appleton, 1899), 593, analyzing how "Americans of all ages, all conditions, and all dispositions constantly form associations. They have not only commercial and manufacturing companies, in which all take part, but associations of a thousand other kinds, religious, moral, serious, futile, general or restricted, enormous or diminutive"; the May 1833 *GUE* reprinted from *Poulson's* an article by a black man that "refutes the slanders" against the "designs and objects" of that year's meeting and the June 1833 issue editorialized against inaccurate coverage in the *New-York Commercial Advertiser*, a leading Whig paper, which had been reprinted in the *Norwich Courier* (Norwich, CT), May 1, 1833 (repr. from *Boston Centinel*), the *New Hampshire Sentinel* (Keene), May 3, 1833 (repr. from *Cincinnati Journal*), the *New-Bedford Mercury*, May 3, 1833, and the *Southern Patriot* (Charleston, SC), May 4, 1833. See *Richmond Enquirer*, July 4, 1833, for a more accurate report, repr. from the *Pennsylvanian*. The *CA*, June 30, 1838, has Pennington's remembrance of the 1833 convention allowing the ACS's secretary, R. R. Gurley, to speak to the delegates and "a large portion of the enlightened people of the city of Philadelphia," after which he was rebutted ("JUNIUS C. MORELL, alone, pocketed Gurley with exceeding ease").

52. *CA*, June 9, 1838; *Minutes and Proceedings of the Third Annual Convention for the Improvement of the Free People of Colour in these United States, held by adjournments in the City of Philadelphia, from the 3rd to the 13th of June inclusive, 1833* (New York: Pub-

lished by Order of the Convention, 1833), 31, repr. in Bell, *Minutes of the Proceedings*; *Minutes and Proceedings of the Second Annual Convention*, 13.

53. *Minutes and Proceedings of the Third Annual Convention*, 32. For an excellent analysis of the New York delegates' role in producing this clear anti-emigrationist consensus in 1832–33, see Leslie M. Alexander, *African or American? Black Identity and Political Activism in New York City, 1784–1861* (Urbana: University of Illinois Press, 2008), 81. The 1831 convention noted "the many oppressive, unjust and unconstitutional laws" to which they were subject, and thus "the propriety of memorializing the proper authorities," since the Constitution "guarantees in letter and spirit to every freeman born in this country, all the rights and immunities of citizenship" but also noted that "Education, Temperance and Economy" were "best calculated to promote the elevation of [colored] mankind to a proper rank and standing among men"; see *Minutes and Proceedings of the First Annual Convention of the People of Colour, Held by Adjournments in the City of Philadelphia, from the Sixth to the Eleventh of June, Inclusive, 1831* (Philadelphia: By Order of the Committee of Arrangements, 1831), 5, repr. in Bell, *Minutes of the Proceedings*, followed by a suggestion in the "Conventional Address" to "investigate the political standing of our brethren wherever dispersed" (12); in 1834, two Connecticut delegates proposed, "Whereas, there are certain grievances connected with the elective franchise, as now enjoyed by a portion of the *free people of colour* in our country, which demand prompt and efficient action," a committee should report back at the next convention, which did not happen; see *Minutes of the Fourth Annual Convention*, 18; *Minutes and Proceedings of the Second Annual Convention*, 35–36; *Minutes and Proceedings of the Third Annual Convention*, 33. Cooper, "Elevating the Race," 617, explains the perspective that "prejudice was a black problem—caused by their own deficiencies—rather than a white problem—the result of deeply ingrained biases and an oppressive social system. . . . Self-improvement would *in itself* raise blacks from degradation."

54. William A. Alcott, "Moral Reform," in *American Quarterly Observer* (Boston: Perkins, Marvin, 1834), 3:172–83, clarifies it meant the extension of temperance principles to all forms of "licentiousness," defined as "abuses of the animal appetites" (173); *Minutes of the Fifth Annual Convention for the Improvement of the Free People of Colour in the United States, held by adjournments in the Wesley Church, Philadelphia, from the First to the Fifth of June inclusive, 1835* (Philadelphia: Printed by William D. Gibbons, 1835), 23, repr. in Bell, *Minutes of the Proceedings*, identical to what passed in 1834 (oddly, in 1835, they had approved a resolution that "this convention recommend to the free people of color throughout the U. States [*sic*], the propriety of petitioning congress and their respective state legislatures to be admitted to the rights and privileges of American citizens, and that we be protected in the same"); the classic study is Leonard L. Richards, *"Gentlemen of Property and Standing": Anti-Abolition Mobs in Jacksonian America* (New York: Oxford University Press, 1970); *Minutes of the Fifth Annual Convention*, 6, repr. in Bell, *Minutes of the Proceedings*.

55. *Minutes and Proceedings of the First Annual Convention*, 4, repr. in Bell, *Minutes of the Proceedings*; Tunde Adeleke, "Afro-Americans and Moral Suasion: The Debate in the 1830s," *JNH* 83, no. 2 (Spring 1998): 128–30. In his biography of Garrison, James Brewer Stewart describes how immediatism in the mid-1830s "projected the opening

of a totally new era of Christian prosperity, equality, and harmony throughout the entire nation, a competitive society unparalleled in its inclusiveness where biblical morality, unimpeded social mobility, and personal autonomy would benefit and uplift all Americans, whether white or black" (*William Lloyd Garrison and the Challenge of Emancipation* [Arlington Heights, IL: Harlan Davidson, 1992], 74).

56. See Winch, *Philadelphia's Black Elite*, 102–28, and Howard H. Bell, "The American Moral Reform Society, 1836–1841," *Journal of Negro Education* 27, no. 1 (Winter 1958): 34–40; *National Enquirer*, August 24, 1836; *National Reformer*, September 1839. The society did denounce the white Protestants who Jim Crowed people of color; see *National Reformer*, October 1838. For "social control" by benevolent elites, the classic study is David J. Rothman, *The Discovery of the Asylum: Social Order and Disorder in the New Republic* (Boston: Little, Brown, 1971).

57. *The Minutes and Proceedings of the First Annual Meeting of the American Moral Reform Society, Held at Philadelphia, in the Presbyterian Church on Seventh Street, below Shippen, from the 14th to the 19th of August, 1837* (Philadelphia: Merrihew and Gunn, 1837), 30, 34, 35, 37, 42, 46, 47.

58. See the *CA*, June 24, 1837, for this association's constitution and by-laws; *CA*, August 26, 1837.

59. *CA*, September 9, 1837.

60. *CA*, September 2, November 25, November 18, December 2, 1837.

61. *CA*, December 9, 1837.

62. *National Reformer*, December 1839.

Chapter Three

1. In 1816, Assemblyman Thomas Morgan named Dauphin, Bucks, Lancaster, and Allegheny as permitting black voting, and John M'Cahen, a Democratic delegate to the 1837–38 convention, added Cumberland, York, Juniata, and Westmoreland, as well as "many other counties." See *Journal of the Convention of the Commonwealth of Pennsylvania, to Propose Amendments to the Constitution, Commenced and Held at Harrisburg, on the Second of May, 1837, Reported by John Agg* (Packer, Barrett, and Parke: Harrisburg, 1837–38), 9:380. At points Adams, Washington, and Franklin were also cited, and in the 1850s, the Reverend Samuel Miller of Johnstown in Cambria County noted he had voted until 1838. See R. J. M. Blackett, *The Captive's Quest for Freedom: Fugitive Slaves, the 1850 Fugitive Slave Law, and the Politics of Slavery* (New York: Cambridge University Press, 2018), 112.

2. In 1808, a total of 111,482 men voted, many more than 1805. For the House's basis of representation and 1816 turnout, see Philip Shriver Klein, *Pennsylvania Politics, 1817–1832: A Game without Rules* (Philadelphia: Historical Society of Pennsylvania, 1940), 26, 406.

3. Kenneth W. Keller, "Rural Politics and the Collapse of Pennsylvania Federalism," *Transactions of the American Philosophical Society* 72, no. 6 (1982): 57; Charles McCool Snyder, *The Jacksonian Heritage: Pennsylvania Politics, 1833–1848* (Harrisburg: Pennsylvania Historical and Museum Commission, 1958), 3–4 and passim; James A. Kehl, *Ill Feeling in the Era of Good Feeling: Western Pennsylvania Political Battles, 1815–1825* (Pittsburgh: University of Pittsburgh Press, 1956), 18–19.

4. I rely here on Klein's classic work, *Pennsylvania Politics, 1817–1832*, 3–5, 26–29 (cataloguing that nearly half of state legislators were Scots-Irish and most of the rest Germans, while the former monopolized the state supreme court and the president judgeships of the county courts), 40, 24, 12. See also Patrick Griffin, *The People with No Name: Ireland's Ulster Scots, America's Scots Irish, and the Creation of a British Atlantic World, 1689–1764* (Princeton, NJ: Princeton University Press, 2001). Irish voters became controversial as early as the 1790s. The state's most influential editors, William Duane and John Binns, were Anglophobe Irish exiles, representing a community whose potential power greatly concerned nativist Federalists.

5. Sanford W. Higginbotham, *The Keystone in the Democratic Arch: Pennsylvania Politics, 1800–1816* (Harrisburg: Pennsylvania Historical and Museum Commission, 1952), 13, 77, 100.

6. Kim T. Phillips, "William Duane, Philadelphia's Democratic Republicans, and the Origins of Modern Politics," *Pennsylvania Magazine of History and Biography* 101, no. 3 (July 1977): 365–87; *Spirit of the Times* (Mercersburg), October 31, 1817.

7. Higginbotham, *Keystone*, 7–8, noting that the "ratable male population" was "only five per cent less than the entire male population."

8. Kehl, *Ill Feeling*, 147; *Washington Reporter*, September 23, 1816; *Doylestown Democrat*, December 27, 1837.

9. *Washington Reporter*, September 23, 1816.

10. *Pennsylvania Journal*, May 7, 1785; Harry Marlin Tinkcom, *The Republicans and Federalists in Pennsylvania, 1790–1801: A Study in National Stimulus and Local Response* (Harrisburg: Pennsylvania Historical and Museum Commission, 1950), 210; *Herald of Liberty* (Washington), October 26, 1801, repr. from the *Lancaster Journal*.

11. See Sean Wilentz, *The Rise of American Democracy: Jefferson to Lincoln* (New York: W. W. Norton, 2005), 225–28, on the "bloc of between forty and fifty Northern Republicans" cohering around "an antislavery Jeffersonian reading of politics and the Constitution."

12. Emil Olbrich, *The Development of Sentiment on Negro Suffrage to 1860* (Freeport, NY: Books for Libraries Press, 1971, orig. pub. 1912), 56–69; Edward J. Price, Jr., "The Black Voting Rights Issue in Pennsylvania, 1780–1900," *Pennsylvania Magazine of History and Biography* 100, no. 3 (July 1976): 356–73; Robert Mittrick, "A History of Negro Voting in Pennsylvania During the Nineteenth Century" (PhD diss., Rutgers University, 1985); Julie Winch, *Philadelphia's Black Elite: Activism, Accommodation, and the Struggle for Autonomy, 1787–1848* (Philadelphia: Temple University Press, 1988), 135–36; Eric Ledell Smith, "The End of Black Voting Rights in Pennsylvania: African Americans and the Pennsylvania Constitutional Convention of 1837–1838," *Pennsylvania History* 65, no. 3 (Summer 1996): 279–99; Christopher Malone, "Rethinking the End of Black Voting Rights in Antebellum Pennsylvania: Racial Ascriptivism, Partisanship and Political Development in the Keystone State," *Pennsylvania History* 72, no. 4 (Autumn 2005): 466–504; two exceptions are Fawn M. Brodie, *Thaddeus Stevens: Scourge of the South* (New York: W. W. Norton, 1959), 66, describing how "in the larger cities such Negroes were simply kept off the tax rolls," and, more recently, Nicholas Wood, "'A Sacrifice on the Altar of Slavery': Doughface Politics and Black Disfranchisement in Pennsylvania, 1837–1838," *JER* 31 (Spring 2011): 75–106; Alexis de Tocqueville, *Democracy in America* (New York: Library of America, 2003), 233; the

city and county of Philadelphia were separate until 1854, with the county containing twenty-eight other districts, townships, or boroughs. In 1810, 45 percent of 23,287 Pennsylvanians of color lived in the county, with its share stabilizing at 39 percent in 1820 (of 30,413) and 41 percent in 1830 (of 38,333).

13. Quoted in Edward Needles, *An Historical Memoir of the Pennsylvania Society for Promoting the Abolition of Slavery; The Relief of Free Negroes Unlawfully Held in Bondage, and For Improving the Condition of the African Race. Compiled From the Minutes of the Society and Other Official Documents, by Edward Needles, and Published By Authority of the Society* (New York: Arno, 1969, repr. of 1848 ed.), 25; for the extensive debate over suffrage in 1790, see *The Proceedings Relative to Calling the Conventions of 1776 and 1790 That Formed the Present Constitution of Pennsylvania, Together with the Charter to William Penn, the Constitutions of 1776 and 1790, and a View of the Proceedings of the Convention of 1776, and the Council of Censors* (Harrisburg, PA: Printed by John S. Wiestling, 1825), 153, 158, 171, 198–200, 223, 231, 253, 300, 346–47, 374. In 1838, delegate William Darlington prefaced his reading of a December 21, 1837 letter from Gallatin to Joseph Parrish by saying that "a gentleman of high respectability, the father of a member of this body . . . informed me that he recollects the fact being publicly talked of the next day . . . that an effort was made to introduce the word 'white,' and that it was struck out on the motion of Mr. Gallatin"; see *Proceedings and Debates of the Convention of the Commonwealth of Pennsylvania, to Propose Amendments to the Constitution, Commenced and Held at Harrisburg, on the Second of May, 1837, Reported by John Agg* (Harrisburg: Packer, Barrett, and Parke, 1837–38), 10:45. Another delegate recollected Gallatin ("his complexion sallow") stating "that if the word were so introduced, he did not know but he himself might be excluded from voting" (*Proceedings and Debates of the Convention*, 10:123).

14. Quoted in Julie Winch, *A Gentleman of Color: The Life of James Forten* (New York: Oxford University Press, 2002), 294; *Proceedings and Debates of the Convention*, 2:478 (Benjamin Martin of Philadelphia), 9:328 (John Sturdevant of Luzerne), 350 (William Meredith of Philadelphia County); *Proceedings and Debates of the Convention*, 10:23 (Woodward).

15. *CA*, March 3, 1838; *PF*, December 13, 1849.

16. A recent example is Julie Winch, "Free Men and 'Freemen': Black Voting Rights in Pennsylvania, 1790–1870," *Pennsylvania Legacies* 8, no. 2 (November 2008), asserting that only black male "property holders and thus taxpayers" could vote (16), and that this requirement kept "hundreds of thousands of less affluent white men across the state from voting" (17); see Lee Soltow and Kenneth W. Keller, "Rural Pennsylvania in 1800: A Portrait from the Septennial Census," *Pennsylvania History* 49, no. 1 (January 1982): 25–47 for how taxables were surveyed by county to ascertain the basis of representation in the General Assembly (a taxable was "an adult tax-paying person who resided in the township surveyed," and in 1799 the legislature specified what could be taxed, including "land, houses, livestock, slaves, mills, furnaces, and ferries"; crucially, "single free men 21 and over without occupations and without property were also taxed," with the authors estimating that only 6–11 percent of men were excluded [27–28]); *Proceedings and Debates of the Convention*, 2:496.

17. *Liberator*, March 19, 1831 (Garrison titled the letter "Lost Rights").

18. Needles, *Historical Memoir*, 86–87; *Friend* repr. in *Liberator*, April 18, 1835; *Proceedings and Debates of the Convention*, 1:149; *Proceedings and Debates of the Convention*, 3:83; *Enumeration of the Taxable Inhabitants of the City of Philadelphia, 1800*, Pennsylvania State Archives. The 243 names were compiled from those signing the many notices and appeals published in Philadelphia newspapers in 1790–1810, plus the membership of St. Thomas's Episcopal, the most prestigious church; see Rev. Wm. Douglass, *Annals of the First African Church, in the United States of America, Now Styled, The African Episcopal Church of St. Thomas, Philadelphia, In Its Connection with the Early Struggles of the Colored People to Improve Their Condition, With the Co-Operation of the Friends, and Other Philanthropies; Partly Derived from the Minutes of a Beneficial Society, Established by Absalom Jones, Richard Allen and Others, in 1787, and Partly From the Minutes of the Aforesaid Church* (Philadelphia: King & Baird, 1862). The twenty-eight assessed were not the most prominent. Eight were denoted not by occupations like white men (e.g., "John Adams, President") but as "Negro," presumably a synonym for "free servant." Most black men had common Anglo-Saxon names, so one of the four "William Grays" (a revenue officer, grocer, brewer, and shoemaker) may have been the black William Gray; that possibility adds fourteen possible "taxables." All that is certain are those men listed as "Negro," including some of the elite (Arthur Donaldson, the schoolteacher; Richard Allen, listed as a shoemaker; "Absolom Jones, Doctor of Divinity"; Joseph Watson, "sailmaker," James Forten's foreman, although Forten himself was not listed). A search of these names in Philadelphia County's 1798 federal tax assessment shows a similar pattern of not assessing black men, although a federal assessment would not have allowed them to vote in Pennsylvania. It is difficult to determine if a particular "James Dexter" or "William Brown" was the man of color of that name. None of the best-known (such as Forten or Absalom Jones) shows up in the 1798 records, although perhaps one of the six "Richard Allens" listed was the black minister. Very few of the twenty-eight men listed in the 1800 city assessment appear in the 1798 federal lists; one who does is Donaldson (accessed via Ancestry.com. *Pennsylvania, U.S. Direct Tax Lists, 1798* [database on-line]. Provo, UT: Ancestry.com Operations, 2012).

19. *Proceedings and Debates of the Convention*, 9:381, 388.

20. See *Poulson's*, January 20, 1814, for this quotation from the second letter; *To the Honourable the Senate and House of Representatives of the Commonwealth of Pennsylvania, In General Assembly Met: The Memorial of the Subscribers, free people of colour, residing in the City of Philadelphia* (Philadelphia, 1833), 2, "On behalf of a large and respectable meeting of the people of colour, convened in the City of Philadelphia, January 15, 1833," signed by John Bowers, chairman, and John B. Depee, secretary. The act itself, dated March 28, 1832, is reproduced on pages 11–12.

21. *CA*, January 27 and May 3, 1838; the March 29, 1838 *American* noted that it had received the *Appeal*, which appeared on April 19. Prior to that, the only evidence of action against disfranchisement in Philadelphia was a June 1837 meeting at Bethel church, which agreed to lobby for suffrage. Only on January 6, 1838 did Frederick Hinton and Charles Gardner go to Harrisburg to present that meeting's memorial to the Philadelphia Whig James A. Biddle (see Andrew K. Diemer, *The Politics of Black Citizenship: Free African Americans in the Mid-Atlantic Borderland, 1817–1863* [Athens: University of Georgia Press, 2016], 97–98).

22. *Democratic Press*, March 5, 1816.

23. *The Investigator* (Charleston, SC), September 18, 1812, reported the September 5 meeting to plan this drive, with subscribers including former congressman Robert Waln, longtime PAS directors Rawle, John Pemberton, and William Lewis, John Sergeant, Condy Raguet, Joseph Hopkinson, C. J. Ingersoll, Nicholas Biddle, Tench Coxe, Stephen Girard, Horace Binney, Zachariah Poulson, and Mathew Carey (see also the "Miscellaneous Subscriptions" file, box 5-C, at HSP; most were Federalists, although a few were prominent Republicans like Coxe and Girard); on the WBS, see Albrecht Koschnik, *"Let a Common Interest Bind Us Together": Associations, Partisanship, and Culture in Philadelphia, 1775–1840* (Charlottesville: University of Virginia Press, 2007), 79–80, and more generally for "cultural Federalism"; Washington Benevolent Society Correspondence, HSP, *Plan of a Loan*, with "Property of W. Rawle" handwritten, dated May 23, 1814 (the original 159 subscribers in 1815 did not include men of color but a later list totaling 200 included Forten and Cassey); Higginbotham, *Keystone*, 298–99, 312.

24. Wharton was elected to fifteen one-year terms between 1798 and 1824 by joint votes of the common council and aldermen; Philadelphia did not elect its mayor directly until 1839; *Democratic Press*, February 13, 1816.

25. *Vermont Republican*, March 18, 1816, reprinting the *Democratic Press*, February 23, 1816; *Shamrock*, March 2, 1816 (New York); *American Mercury*, March 5, 1816 (Hartford, CT); *Ulster Plebeian*, March 19, 1816 (Kingston, NY), *American Watchman*, March 5 and April 24, 1816 (Wilmington, DE); in 1808, 12,592 men voted for governor in Philadelphia City and County; see *A New Nation Votes* at https://elections.lib.tufts .edu/catalog/6d56zw822; the 1820 census counted 1,746 men of color at the ages of twenty-six through forty-four plus 628 at the age of forty-five and over, and calculating by the usual method (x .42) for the 1,030 at the ages of fourteen through twenty-five produces an estimated 433 at the ages of twenty-one through twenty-five, for a total potential electorate in Philadelphia County of 2,807); Edward C. Carter II, "A 'Wild Irishman' under Every Federalist's Bed: Naturalization in Philadelphia, 1789–1806," *Pennsylvania Magazine of History and Biography* 94, no. 3 (July 1970); *Tickler*, October 8, 1808; *Democratic Press*, March 11, 1816.

26. *Democratic Press*, March 8, March 25, and October 14, 1816 (the first has an imagined dialogue between "White" and "Black" societies, with the former gloating over "our designs for the benefit of our mother country, and in due time, for ourselves . . . to the consolation of our British friends").

27. For 1816's very low turnout, see Higginbotham, *Keystone*, 322. Estimating 50 percent of the white men at the ages of sixteen through twenty-five in the 1820 census were voters leads to a potential electorate of 212,867; the actual turnout was 134,483 or 63 percent. Morgan's amendment would have empowered an additional 4,533 likely voters statewide or 2.1 percent of the white electorate in a state where elections frequently hinged on a few thousand votes. (In 1820, the census grouped "Free Colored Males" in age ranges of fourteen through twenty-five [3,348], 26–44 [3,890], and forty-five and over [1,900]. Estimating 42 percent in the first group were twenty-one and over produced a potential electorate of 7,196, which, multiplied by 63 percent, produced 4,533. All turnout figures calculated using Philip Lampi's "A New Nation Votes" website, http://elections.lib.tufts.edu.)

28. *Democratic Press*, April 14, 1814; *Journal of the Twenty Sixth House of Representatives of the Commonwealth of Pennsylvania, Commenced at Harrisburg, Tuesday the Fifth of December, in the Year of Our Lord One Thousand Eight Hundred and Fifteen, and of the Commonwealth the Fortieth* (Harrisburg, PA: James Peacock, 1816), 20.

29. *Journal of the Twenty Sixth House of Representatives*, 223; *Niles' Weekly Register*, February 17, 1816; *West Chester Federalist*, quoted in *Democratic Press*, February 23, 1816; *Democratic Press*, February 10, 1816; *Journal of the Twenty Sixth House of Representatives*, 457; *Democratic Press*, February 29, 1816; *Niles' Register*, March 16, 1816; *Democratic Press*, March 11, 1816; *Journal of the Twenty Sixth House of Representatives*, 457–58, 546–47, 565–72, 578; *Journal of the Senate of the Commonwealth of Pennsylvania, Which Commenced at Harrisburg the Fifth Day of December, in the Year of Our Lord One Thousand Eight Hundred and Fifteen, and of the Independence of the United States of America the Fortieth, Volume XXVI* (Harrisburg, PA: James Peacock, 1815), 364–65.

30. *Washington Reporter*, January 29, August 5, September 16, 1816.

31. *Washington Reporter*, September 23, 1816; Dee E. Andrews, "Reconsidering the First Emancipation: Evidence from the Pennsylvania Abolition Society Correspondence, 1785–1810," *Pennsylvania History* 64 (Summer 1997): 237.

32. *Spirit of the Times*, January 5, 1818. An article titled "Blending" suggested the governor-elect "appears to have practiced this art in all his several relations of life. First with his brother John and the king of the Ethiopians,* in Franklin County," then later, he "blended the democrats and federalists of Franklin so as to secure his election for three years to the assembly." The asterisk is to "Judge Bard"; G. M. S., "The High Court of Errors and Appeals and Negro Suffrage," *American Law Register* 6, no. 4 (February 1858): 250, 249.

33. One of the few scholarly accounts of this phenomenon is David Waldstreicher and Stephen R. Grossbart, "Abraham Bishop's Vocation; or, the Mediation of Jeffersonian Politics," *JER* 18, no. 4 (Winter 1998): 649n44, detailing how handfuls of black men were "sworn in" as voters in particular towns from 1790 on.

34. G. O. Seilhamer, *The Bard Family: A History and Genealogy of the Bards of "Carroll's Delight" Together with a Chronicle of the Bards and Genealogies of The Bard Kinship* (Chambersburg, PA: Kittochtinny, 1908), 204, quoting *Aurora*, May 28, 1817. The Bards were from Antrim near Belfast. Archibald's father, Richard, bought 5,000 acres on land claimed by Maryland in 1741, and fought Indians for years, leading to his and his wife's harrowing captivity in 1758–60. In 1798, he gave his son (born in 1765) 226 acres on the "northern part of the old Bard plantation" on which he "built the fine stone mansion in which he lived until his death" (157, 193, 201). Similarly, the Findlays, also Ulstermen, went out to Mercersburg before the Revolution, when it was "an entrepot, where goods to be sent west of the mountains were brought in wagons . . . at the base of the Blue Ridge," and married into a prominent family, the Irwins (see William C. Armor, *Lives of the Governors of Pennsylvania, With the Incidental History of the State, from 1609 to 1872* [Philadelphia: James K. Simon, 1872], 323–25. On the black folk attached to the Bard-Findlay network, see pp. 15–17 of the manuscript census for Peters and Montgomery townships, accessed via www.archives.com, July 15, 2013 via a search for "Archd Bard." These include John Findlay (3 FPOC), his brother William (5 FPOC, 1 slave), Thomas Bard (5 FPOC, 1 slave), Archibald Irwin, the future governor's father-in-law

(5 FPOC, 2 slaves), James Irwin (2 FPOC), Archibald Bard (7 FPOC, 1 slave) and Joseph Irwin (4 FPOC).

35. October 27 and 31, 1817.

36. *Spirit of the Times*, October 31, 1817.

37. See *Star of Freedom*, February 25 and March 4, 1818, for the Senate committee report. The petitions came from Cumberland, Lancaster, and Montgomery, but no facts were provided and no witnesses appeared; *Spirit of the Times*, July 13, 1818. David G. Smith, *On the Edge of Freedom: The Fugitive Slave Issue in South Central Pennsylvania, 1820–1870* (New York: Fordham University Press, 2013) traces the history of Franklin, Cumberland, and Adams County in subsequent decades.

38. *Carlisle Republican*, July 4, 1820, also *Washington Review and Examiner* on August 7, quoting Findlay's response to Hannah's husband's 1801 writ of habeas corpus (later that month, the Carlisle paper published an account of a local "African Celebration" at a white man's farm, full of toasts like "Our broders in de Soudern tates. Why he no all run off an come to Pennsillvania, where dey hab a vote and mos hold an office?," mocking "De Kongressmen ob dese tates who voted fur de slabery question" regarding Missouri's admission, and singling out "Billy Findlay" as one of "de Bunch of men eaters," see *Carlisle Republican*, July 18, 1820); pro-Findlay papers included the *Lancaster Free Press*, July 6, 1820, "Hiester and Slavery" from the *Pennsylvania Gazette*, also in the *Washington Reporter*, July 17, and the *Franklin Gazette*, July 19, 1820 (the next day the latter printed the 1807 "MANUMISSION OF NEGRO GEORGE," with Findlay's language quoted above, and affidavits from local officials attesting to it; the September 8 *Franklin Gazette* reproduced the court record from Berks, Hiester's home county, showing various slaves registered over a quarter-century); *Franklin Gazette*, July 20, 1820 (from the *Harrisburg Republican*), August 15, 1820 (from the *Bucks Messenger*, a report on a "Democratic Republican Meeting" against Missouri's admission), August 4, 18, 12, 28 (from the *Chambersburg Republican*, an affidavit sworn August 17), and 26, 1820; *Village Record, or Chester and Delaware Federalist*, December 6, 1820.

39. In early 1819, a prominent journal published a long article describing how "one eighth part of the population of Philadelphia enjoys this singular and impolitic privilege" of not being taxed (and thus not voting), "not from the express provision of the constitution or laws, but by a kind of tacit permission from the rest of their fellow citizens. The real estate of which they may happen to be owners, is, we believe, assessed like that of others, but from the payment of personal taxes, they are altogether privileged." It pointed to the danger of black Pennsylvanians realizing their power, and urged immediate disfranchisement; see *Analectic Magazine*, March 1819, 282–83. This argument anticipated those made in New York, leading to disfranchisement, and would be resurrected in Pennsylvania in 1837–38.

40. *Pennsylvania Archives* (Harrisburg, PA: Secretary of the Commonwealth, 1874–1919), Fourth Series, 5:392–93 (December 5, 1822). In a subsequent message (453, December 4, 1823), Hiester noted "some persons possessing all other requisite qualifications have been deprived of their votes, by their names being, either accidentally, or through design, omitted in the assessment of taxes," an allusion to Philadelphia's refusal to assess black men. For Shulze's message, see *Pennsylvania Archives* 4th ser., 5:663–64 (December 6, 1826).

41. See William G. Shade, "'The Most Delicate and Exciting Topics': Martin Van Buren, Slavery, and the Election of 1836," *JER* 18, no. 3 (Autumn 1998): 459–84, on Northern Democrats' turn toward Negrophobic politics to guarantee Van Buren's nomination in the face of attacks by Calhounites and southern Whigs.

42. A fine local account, also by Shade, is "Pennsylvania Politics in the Jacksonian Period: A Case Study, Northampton County, 1824–1844," *Pennsylvania History* 39 (1972): 313–33; Hans Trefousse, *Thaddeus Stevens: Nineteenth-Century Egalitarian* (Chapel Hill: University of North Carolina Press, 1997) on Pennsylvania Antimasonry; for Stevens's formation, see Bradley R. Hoch, *Thaddeus Stevens at Gettysburg: The Making of an Abolitionist* (Gettysburg, PA: Adams County Historical Society, 2005); see Brodie, *Thaddeus Stevens*, 64, for the assumption "that Thaddeus Stevens had written the message"; *National Enquirer*, January 14, 1837, lists "T. Stevens" as one of seventy-one Adams County signers to the call, and the February 11 issue lists "Henry A. Ritner" as a Washington County delegate, while *The Liberator*, June 16, 1837, noted "$15, contributed by that distinguished champion of equal rights, THADDEUS STEVENS of *Pennsylvania*" to the AASS; *Philadelphia Inquirer*, October 11, 1836, quoting "Extracts from the Registry Law"; *National Gazette*, May 18, 1839, repr. in *Philadelphia Inquirer*, December 15, 1837.

43. Hoch, *Thaddeus Stevens*, 126, 128; Smith, "End of Black Voting Rights," 284; *Easton Sentinel*, September 7, 1838.

44. Scholars list six men (the Pennsylvanians Robert Purvis, James McCrummill, John Vashon, and Abraham Shadd, plus Boston's John Barbadoes and New York's Peter Williams) as members of the first AASS board, but Buffalo's William Allen and Pittsburgh's Samuel Williams were almost certainly men of color (only McCrummill, sometimes spelled McCrummell, Purvis, and Barbadoes were delegates); see *Proceedings of the Anti-Slavery Convention, Assembled at Philadelphia. December 4, 5, and 6, 1833* (New York: Dorr & Butterfield, 1833), 7, 14; Daisy Newman, *A Procession of Friends: Quakers in America* (Richmond, IN: Friends United Press, 2007), 89. The Hicksite-Orthodox schism stemmed from the Philadelphia Yearly Meeting barring the venerable Elias Hicks in 1819 because of his antislavery preaching; for Ward's comment, see *Impartial Citizen*, June 28, 1851; John L. Myers, "The Early Antislavery Agency System in Pennsylvania," *Pennsylvania History* 31 (1964): 62, describes Pennsylvania as "one of the last of the free states to establish a militant antislavery auxiliary affiliated with the American Anti-Slavery Society," meaning the Pennsylvania Anti-Slavery Society (PASS), whose *National Enquirer*, later the *Pennsylvania Freeman*, routinely employed Friends' dating ("ninth day of twelfth month"). The Pennsylvania Abolition Society Papers at HSP include other societies' records. None of the ninety persons signing the *Constitution and Preamble of the Junior Anti-Slavery Society of Philadelphia* (1836) are identifiable as black, nor are any of its officers listed in minutes covering several years. *The Constitution of the Philadelphia City Anti-Slavery Society* (1839) was signed by ninety-two men; only two were men of color (F. A. Hinton and James Needham). Finally, the *Constitution, Bylaws, and List of Officers of the Young Men's Anti-Slavery Society of the City and County of Philadelphia* (1835) lists eighteen officers, only one of whom was black (Robert B. Forten); nine were among its 102 founders.

45. *National Enquirer,* August 10, 1837 (the reporter, "R.," asked, with asperity, "Upon what ground, can any person who subscribes to the fundamental principle of anti-slavery doctrine, question the expediency of any *individual* (who is an abolitionist) joining an anti-slavery society? Is not the objection, which is made *against colored persons only,* grounded altogether upon prejudice?"; *Liberator,* February 11, 1837; *Proceedings of the Pennsylvania Convention Assembled to Organize a State Anti-Slavery Society, at Harrisburg, On the 31st and 1st, 2nd, and 3rd of February, 1837* (Philadelphia: Merrihew and Gunn, 1837), 5, 3, 28, 52–53, 79–81. Black delegates were part of the large Philadelphia group (Robert Purvis, James McCrummill, John C. Bowers, Charles W. Gardner, and James Forten), plus Morel from Dauphin, John C. Peck from Carlisle, and Stephen Smith from Lancaster. For Morel's speech, see the *PF,* February 11, 1837.

46. *PF,* January 3, 1850. Convention reports (sometimes as "Eastern Pennsylvania, Delaware and New Jersey") document the same Quakers meeting year-in and year-out. See *PF,* May 14, 1840, on the eastern society's annual meeting, where blacks were perhaps ten of 233 delegates, all from Philadelphia. Participation then dropped precipitously. At a December 1841 special meeting, they were three of 104 (*PF,* December 29, 1841). In 1846, Purvis was elected president, but no other person of color was recorded (*PF,* August 13, 1846). At the Eleventh Annual Meeting in 1848, Purvis was again president, but the only other persons of color present were W. W. Brown and William Powell of New York (*PF,* August 17, 1848). For later meetings where Purvis stood alone, see *PF,* January 2, 1851, December 25, 1851, December 23, 1852. Van Rensselaer could have saved his breath; at the December 1848 meeting, Dr. J. J. G. Bias had voiced similar disillusionment, that "the colored man encountered prejudice every where, among all classes, not excepting abolitionists. Where among them do you find colored boys taken into printing offices, counting rooms, or stores? . . . Until they practice their own theories, they cannot expect the confidence of the colored people. We care not under what name the party comes which gives us our rights,—Whigs, Democrats, Free Soilers, or Abolitionists," only to be reproved by another black delegate, Mrs. Mary Grew (*PF,* December 28, 1848).

47. Carl Douglas Oblinger, "New Freedoms, Old Miseries: The Emergence and Disruption of Black Communities in Southeastern Pennsylvania, 1780–1860" (PhD diss., Lehigh University, 1988), 83; Willis L. Shirk, Jr., "Testing the Limits of Tolerance: Blacks and the Social Order in Columbia, Pennsylvania, 1800–1851," *Pennsylvania History* 60 (1993): 35–36; Dr. Leroy T. Hopkins, "Black Eldorado on the Susquehanna: The Emergence of Black Columbia, 1726–1861," *Journal of the Lancaster County Historical Society* 89, no. 4 (1985): 117–18 describes how in 1819 the Wrights brought a community of fifty-six freed by Captain Izard Bacon in Henrico County, Virginia, and another 100 freed by Sally Bell in Hanover County. The 1830 census showed that 430 free people of color were 21 percent of the town.

48. Shirk, "Testing the Limits of Tolerance," 37; *Lancaster Journal,* September 19, 1823: "Stephen Smith, of Columbia, respectfully informs his friends and the public, that he has on hand, a great stock of LUMBER, particularly SHINGLES, which he will sell low for cash.—ALSO Horses and Gigs to hire"; Hopkins, "Black Eldorado," 118–19; William Frederic Worner, "The Columbia Race Riots," *Lancaster County Historical*

Society Papers (1922): 26:175, 187, 185; *PF*, December 29, 1841, on Smith's donating $50 at a PASS meeting; most gifts were $1–5; Worner, "Columbia Race Riots," 177.

49. *Lancaster Journal*, August 24, 1824; Oblinger, "New Freedoms, Old Miseries," 90, 101, Table of "Black Occupational Structure, Columbia, 1834," lists 181 laborers, twenty-four skilled workers, thirty in services, and nine professionals and proprietors.

50. Oblinger, "New Freedoms, Old Miseries," 126–28, describes the mob's leaders as "relative newcomers . . . nearly all members of a new Democratic local political establishment"; see also 130–31 on Smith's real estate empire rising in tandem with "the rapid growth of unassimiliable fugitives . . . the creation, beginning in the 1820s, of a larger *visible* black indigent class"; on the Philadelphia riots, see Smith, "End of Black Voting Rights," 283, and for local coverage, *Lancaster Journal*, August 15 and 19, 1834.

51. Quoted in Worner, "Columbia Race Riots," 179.

52. Worner, "Columbia Race Riots," 180, 182, drawing on the *Columbia Spy*; Thomas P. Slaughter, *Bloody Dawn: The Christiana Riot and Racial Violence in the Antebellum North* (New York: Oxford University Press, 1991), 176–79.

53. Quoted in Worner, "Columbia Race Riots," 181–82; *Columbia Spy*, March 7, 1835; *Lancaster Journal*, April 19, 1835.

54. Of 130 black Columbians identified as heads of households in the 1840 census (which does not include other men in those households), thirty-seven were assessed as "Freeholders" in the town's 1835 tax rolls (accessed at the Lancaster County Historical Society). Most had a house and lot worth $150–300, but eight possessed property worth $500 or more. In the two other categories of taxpayers, "Inmates" (tenants) and unpropertied "Freemen," only five can be identified as men of color using the 1840 and 1850 federal censuses, leaving at least eighty-eight not assessed and thus kept off the voter rolls; *Columbia Spy*, December 12, 1868.

55. *Lancaster Journal*, April 6, 1832, June 13, 1834, October 3, 1834.

56. *Weekly Notes of Cases Argued and Determined in the Supreme Court of Pennsylvania, the County Courts of Philadelphia, and the United States District and Circuit Courts for the Eastern District of Pennsylvania. By Members of the Bar*, vol. 2, *Including Cases Argued and Determined During the Year Ending September 30, 1876* (Philadelphia: Kay & Brother, 1876). *Hobbs et al. against Fogg* is on 553–60, with the section quoted on 553.

57. *Weekly Notes of Cases Argued and Determined in the Supreme Court of Pennsylvania*, 709, records a January 1876 case in Luzerne County's Court of Common Pleas. Betsey (or Elizabeth) Allen was listed as a woman of color in the 1830 census; the 1876 case described her as dying in 1848. The family of Anson (or Henson) Allen, Fogg's half-brother, recurs in various censuses; for instance, in 1850, a mulatto family consisting of Anson Allen, 42, butcher, born in Connecticut; Mary Allen, 37, born in Pennsylvania; Elizabeth Allen, 60, born in Connecticut (a sister of Fogg's?); and Watson Allen, 16, born in Pennsylvania, also a butcher, resided in Providence Township. Regarding Fogg's age, in the 1870 census, on June 28, he listed himself as sixty-seven, indicating birth in 1802 or 1803, but he was apparently nine years older, as a *FamilySearch International* listing via www.archive.com (January 11, 2013) produced a "William Fog," son of "Betsey Fog," born August 14, 1793 in New London, Connecticut; in late July 1860, he told the census taker he was fifty-five, making his birth year 1805. In the 1820 census, he was listed as a white man, suggested biracial parentage. In 1880, Fogg acknowledged

his age as eighty-five. The assessment of Fogg's wealth is based on compiling a list of property holders from the 1850 manuscript census for Scott Township; the number of families is confirmed by the assessor's handwritten totals.

58. Stewart Pearce, *Annals of Luzerne County; A Record of Interesting Events, Traditions, and Anecdotes. From the First Settlement in Wyoming Valley to 1866*, 2nd ed. (Philadelphia: J. B. Lippincott, 1866), 198, noting that Greenfield was formed in 1816, and its "original settlers came from Connecticut and Rhode Island in 1797, but since then many Germans have purchased lands." It was utterly rural even in the later 1860s, with one village of fifteen dwellings, and a grand total of six mills, one store, one church, and one tavern. Perhaps this setting made it easier for a few people of color to pass unnoticed; Higginbotham, *Keystone*, 26, 28, 48, 65, 174, 175, 195, 204, 26, on its fealty to the minority party; see also Pearce, *Annals of Luzerne County*, 516: "The great majority of the people of Luzerne were Federalists."

59. [Frederick Watts], *Report of Cases Argued and Determined in the Supreme Court of Pennsylvania*, vol. 6, *May to September 1837*, 3rd ed., *Revised and Corrected by W. Wynne Wister* (Kay & Brother, 1880), 554.

60. The *Wyoming Herald*'s report was reprinted in the *New York Commercial Advertiser*, January 26, 1837, the *New York Spectator*, January 31, 1837, and the *Baltimore Gazette and Daily Advertiser*, January 28, 1837 (from Philadelphia *United States Gazette*).

61. See Higginbotham, *Keystone*, 26, 174, 268, on the statewide elections of 1799, 1808, and 1812, when Bucks was a notable outlier from Republicanism. Fox was closely allied with longtime state senator William T. Rogers, who succeeded him as major general of the Bucks and Montgomery militia when Fox was appointed judge in 1830.

62. The best account is Lyle L. Rosenberger, "Black Suffrage in Bucks County: The Election of 1837," *Bucks County Historical Society Journal* (Spring 1975): 28–35.

63. See *National Enquirer*, January 14, 1837, for a list by county; Bucks was behind Philadelphia, Chester, Allegheny, Washington, and Westmoreland, and tied with Adams, well ahead of others; *Proceedings and Debates of the Convention*, 2:476.

64. Snyder, *Jacksonian Heritage*, 86, 222–23 (appendices with votes by county).

65. Nick Salvatore, *We All Got History: The Memory Books of Amos Webber* (Urbana: University of Illinois, 2006), 9, examines this "small, well-organized and relatively young" community, comprising 264 people in 1820, the majority under age 24, 12 percent of the larger township, and 18 percent of the county's free black people (Richard Allen helped form a Colored Methodist Society there in 1809, one of five founding AME congregations in 1816, and in 1817, the Bethlehem Colored Methodist Church was built, sponsoring "new churches in Bensalem in 1820 and in Buckingham in 1837" [10]); Malone, "Rethinking the End of Black Voting Rights in Pennsylvania," stresses the "transformation in the dominant racial belief system" (470–71), with Pennsylvania Democrats becoming the "party of the white man's republic only after party competition was reintroduced in the state. . . . Race and the question of black suffrage became significant when and only when blacks were loyally voting for the Whig Party" (490–91); Marvin Meyers, *The Jacksonian Persuasion: Politics and Belief* (Stanford, CA: Stanford University Press, 1957) is invaluable on the Jacksonians' "half-formulated moral perspective . . . always more a decalogue of moral prohibitions than an articulate set of social ends and means" (10, 254)—they yearned for "a laissez-faire society" which

"would re-establish continuity with that golden age in which liberty and progress were joined inseparably with simple yeoman virtues" (12); *Doylestown Democrat*, September 27, 1837.

66. *Bucks County Intelligencer*, August 2, November 1, 8, 1837; *Doylestown Democrat*, October 4, 1837; *Bucks County Intelligencer*, July 26, 1837; Margaret Hope Bacon, *But One Race: The Life of Robert Purvis* (Albany: SUNY Press, 2007), 76–78; R. C. Smedley, *History of the Underground Railroad in Chester and the Neighboring Counties of Pennsylvania* (Mechanicsburg, PA: Stackpole Books, 2005; repr. of 1883 edition), 355–61; *Bucks County Intelligencer*, August 16, 1837; *National Enquirer*, January 14, 1837.

67. *Doylestown Democrat*, repr. in *Liberator*, September 1, 1837; *Doylestown Democrat*, September 6, October 4, 1837; *National Enquirer*, November 15, 1837.

68. *Doylestown Democrat*, October 25, 1837 (the estimate of the black electorate was made via the 1840 manuscript census in those townships); Keller, "Rural Politics," 59, lists Falls, Lower Makefield, Bristol, Bensalem, and Middletown as historically pacifist and thus Federalist; W. W. H. Davis, *History of Bucks County, Pennsylvania, From the Discovery of the Delaware to the Present Time* (Doylestown, PA: Democrat Book and Job Office, 1876), 811; *Doylestown Democrat*, December 27, 1837; *Wisconsin Territorial Gazette and Burlington Advertiser* (Iowa), November 11, 1837; *Opinion of the Honorable John Fox, President Judge of the Judicial District Composed of the Counties of Bucks and Montgomery, Against the Exercise of Negro Suffrage in Pennsylvania. Also: The Vote of the Members of the Pennsylvania Convention, on the Motion of Mr. Martin, To Insert the Word "White," as One of the Proposed Amendments to the Constitution* (Harrisburg, PA: Packer, Barrett and Parke, 1838), 3. The Democrats did not challenge the narrow victories by Whigs' three state House nominees, who received 3,292, 3,320, and 3,278 votes, respectively, with a Democrat gaining 3,314 to win and two others losing by very close margins, with 3,233 and 3,263 votes, respectively.

69. See *Doylestown Democrat*, October 18 and 25, 1837, the latter featuring a notice of the October 28 meeting signed "Hundreds of German Voters," and November 1 for reports on all three meetings; *Bucks County Intelligencer*, November 8, 1837 (regarding Cummings, a search of Bucks County tax rolls for Plumstead shows him listed first in 1804, and then every year for 1806 to 1837, so his voting "for forty years" is substantially accurate); on Rev. Irvin, see Davis, *History of Bucks County*, 806.

70. *Doylestown Democrat*, November 22, 1837 (the 1840 census recorded 456 black men of color ages twenty-four and older; adding thirty-five in the group of 242 at the ages of ten through twenty-three totals 491). The claim that the Whigs hoped to gain 5,000 new votes statewide actually underplayed the potential black electorate.

71. *Bucks County Intelligencer*, November 15, 1837.

72. *Doylestown Democrat*, December 6, 1837.

73. *Doylestown Democrat*, December 20, 1837.

74. *Doylestown Democrat*, January 17, February 7, 1838.

75. *Doylestown Democrat*, January 31, 1838 (for coverage of Fox's decision, see *Southern Patriot* [Charleston], January 16, 1838; *Connecticut Herald* [New Haven], January 23, 1838; *Richmond Enquirer*, January 23, 1838; *New Hampshire Patriot and State Gazette*, February 12, 1838); *Harrisburg Keystone*, repr. in *Doylestown Democrat*, February 28, 1838.

76. *Bucks County Intelligencer,* October 4, November 1, November 8, December 20, 1837, and January 17, 1838.

77. *Bucks County Intelligencer,* February 7, 1838.

78. *Proceedings and Debates of the Convention,* 3:91; *National Gazette,* June 7, 1838.

79. Wood, "'Sacrifice on the Altar of Slavery.'"

80. *Proceedings and Debates of the Convention,* 10:69; 2:487, 493.

81. Brodie, *Thaddeus Stevens,* 116. These votes were all in May 1837. The notorious "cravat in a mud hole" speech is in *Proceedings and Debates of the Convention,* 3:167.

82. Repr. in *Liberator,* November 10, 1837; *Philadelphia Inquirer,* January 20, 1838; *Proceedings and Debates of the Convention,* 2:531. Most Irish immigrants in this period came from the Irish-speaking parts of the island.

83. *Proceedings and Debates of the Convention,* 5:449–50.

84. *Proceedings and Debates of the Convention,* 3:167–68.

85. *Proceedings and Debates of the Convention,* 3:85 and 5:418; *Keystone* repr. in *Liberator,* October 13, 1837.

86. *Proceedings and Debates of the Convention,* 10:64–65.

87. This count of who was present and who switched sides relies on A. David Bateman's expert tabulation, which he kindly shared (there were other anomalies, such as delegates opposing their parties but present for only one vote, but a core of thirty-nine Negrophobe Democrats versus twenty-eight nonracial Antimasons and five nonracial Whigs anchored both the June 1837 and January 1838 votes); *Telegraph* repr. in *PF,* February 8, 1838. Only one delegate transcended the binary of nonracial suffrage anchored to class versus limitless white manhood suffrage. Thomas Earle, Philadelphia lawyer, radical Democrat, and Liberty Party vice presidential candidate in 1840, denounced residency and taxpaying requirements while declaring "every man" regardless of race or complexion "born on the soil of Pennsylvania had a right to vote" (*Proceedings and Debates of the Convention,* 10:38). His last-ditch filibuster evoked historical, scientific, and legal precedents from the Articles of Confederation through the Missouri Crisis, holding up documents including the passport granted the Reverend Peter Williams (an eminent black New Yorker), and Governor Dewitt Clinton's 1826 letter demanding Gilbert Horton's freedom as a citizen of New York.

88. For coverage of the decision, see *Southern Patriot* (Charleston, SC), January 16, 1838; *Connecticut Herald* (New Haven), January 23, 1838; *Richmond Enquirer,* January 23, 1838; *New Hampshire Patriot and State Gazette,* February 12, 1838. The Charleston, Richmond, and New Hampshire papers were state Democratic organs.

89. [Watts], *Report of Cases Argued and Determined in the Supreme Court of Pennsylvania,* 6:558, quoting *Fogg v. Hobbs.*

90. *Proceedings and Debates of the Convention,* 10:56–57.

91. See *Proceedings and Debates of the Convention,* 10:12, for Forward describing James McCune Smith's gaining degrees in Scotland. Everyone knew of Forten, whom Democrats singled out as an exception proving nothing (Banks of Mifflin called him "the yellow man—Fortune—who, by-the-by, had the *mis*-fortune to possess the wrong colour," since he "owned large real estate, and had money in abundance, at command" [10:112] and, earlier, Benjamin Martin painted assailed black degradation with "one solitary instance of a good result . . . a black gentleman in Philadelphia County, James Fortune, a sail maker, who is an exception. . . . He has accumulated property, obtained

a respectable standing, and, in consequence of his color, is noticed more than a white man would be in the same situation" [3:83]); *Poulson's*, repr. in *Pittsburgh Gazette*, January 25, 1838, also *National Enquirer*, January 25, 1838, naming three of the four.

92. *Proceedings and Debates of the Convention*, 10:106–31, on these amendments losing by greater margins than the main vote; *Doylestown Democrat*, January 31, 1838.

93. *National Enquirer*, February 8 and March 1, 1838; quoted in G. M. S., "High Court of Errors and Appeals and Negro Suffrage," 240, and 241–48 for a meticulous examination of the court's entire seventeen-year docket showing no such ruling.

94. *PF*, September 26, 1839; Bacon, *But One Race*, 72; *National Enquirer*, August 30, 1838; *PF*, May 23, 1840, repr. from the *Christian Witness* (eventually, the committee reported that "under the existing state of things, it would be inexpedient"); Diemer, *Politics of Black Citizenship*, 104, notes that in the fall 1838 ratification election, black voting "emerged as one of the most visible and contentious elements of the proposed constitution," with some Whigs and Antimasons defending the old constitution, and *The Pennsylvanian*, a Democratic paper highlighting on Election Day: "All who are opposed to NEGROES voting—All who are opposed to LIFE OFFICES—All who desire an extension of the Right of Suffrage—WILL VOTE FOR THE AMENDMENTS."

Coda

1. Julie Winch, *A Gentleman of Color: The Life of James Forten* (New York: Oxford University Press, 2002), 328, cites J. Miller McKim in the *National Anti-Slavery Standard* describing the presence of all classes and colors, including "our wealthiest and most influential citizens."

2. Donald Yacovone, "The Transformation of the Black Temperance Movement, 1827–1854: An Interpretation," *JER* 8, no. 3 (Autumn 1988): 295.

3. Julie Winch, *Philadelphia's Black Elite: Activism, Accommodation, and the Struggle for Autonomy, 1787–1848* (Philadelphia: Temple University Press, 1988), 148–50; Margaret Hope Bacon, *But One Race: The Life of Robert Purvis* (Albany: SUNY Press, 2007), 99.

4. *Liberator*, September 9, 1842; *National Reformer*, January 1839 (another article specified that the vestry allowed the Philadelphia Library Company of Colored Persons to use of St. Thomas's on November 19, 1838, with the proviso "that the speaker does not involve the question of *Abolition* or *Colonization*"; Whipper closed with an invocation: "Spirit of 1817, we invoke thy presence among these thy degenerate sons"); *Liberator*, September 1, 1848; Winch, *Philadelphia's Black Elite*, 152.

5. Mifflin Wistar Gibbs, *Shadow and Light: An Autobiography, with Reminiscences of the Last and Present Century, with an Introduction by Booker T. Washington* (Washington, DC, 1902), 25; *CA*, August 3 and 17, 1839. Ten years later, Martin R. Delany found Lancaster's black community much the same, "generally well to do" and "intelligent" but marked by a profound "indifference," with their social life focused entirely on their church (*NS*, February 16, 1849).

6. Julie Winch, ed., *The Elite of Our People: Joseph Willson's Sketches of Black Upper-Class Life in Antebellum Philadelphia* (University Park: Pennsylvania State University Press, 2000). Willson, like Purvis, was the son of a prosperous white southerner who sent him north.

7. Joseph A. Borome, "The Vigilant Committee of Philadelphia," *Pennsylvania Magazine of History and Biography* 92, no. 3 (July 1968): 320–51, traces this history, with the committee formed in 1837 becoming dormant, then reorganized in 1839 and reactivated in 1843 but ineffective because of factionalism until it "disintegrated" as of 1852 (328); *Proceedings of the Colored National Convention, Held in Franklin Hall, Sixth Street, Below Arch, Philadelphia, October 16th, 17th and 18th, 1855* (Salem, NJ: National Standard Office, 1856), 10–12.

8. See Ira V. Brown, "An Antislavery Journey: Garrison and Douglass in Pennsylvania, 1847," *Pennsylvania History* 67, no. 4 (Autumn 2000): 533–51, for the rigors of crossing the state; *NS*, January 28, 1848; Eric Ledell Smith, "The Pittsburgh Memorial: A Forgotten Document of Pittsburgh History," *Pittsburgh History* (Fall 1997), 107–8, 109, 110–11 (voters in the city's 1835 election totaled 1,621, making black electors a substantial bloc; see Leonard P. Curry, *The Corporate City: The American City as a Political Entity, 1800–1850* [Westport, CT: Greenwood, 1997], 98).

9. *CA*, July 3, 1841, a letter dated June 18; *Proceedings of the State Convention of the Colored Freemen of Pennsylvania, Held in Pittsburgh, on the 23rd, 24th and 25th of August, 1841, for the Purpose of Considering Their Condition, and the Means of Its Improvement*, in Philip S. Foner and George E. Walker, eds., *Proceedings of the Black State Conventions, 1840–1865*, vol. 1, *New York, Pennsylvania, Indiana, Ohio, Michigan* (Philadelphia: Temple University Press, 1980), 111.

10. See *NASS*, February 26, 1852, "Memorial of the People of Color" to the General Assembly, reporting on their property and propriety, signed by James McCrummill, John C. Bowers, Stephen Smith, and several others, "in behalf of a large and overwhelming meeting of the Colored Citizens"; *FDP*, April 29, 1852, a "Great Anti-Colonization Meeting" with forty-four sponsors little different from those calling meetings twenty years earlier; *NASS*, February 14, 1857, "Mass Meeting of Colored Citizens in Philadelphia," to denounce David Paul Brown, Jr., for accepting appointment as a commissioner under the Fugitive Slave Act; *Anti-Slavery Bugle*, April 11, 1857, "The Voice of the Colored People of Philadelphia," to denounce the *Dred Scott* ruling; *FDP*, February 17, 1860, "Meeting of Colored Citizens of Philadelphia," to denounce another group which had asked Virginia Governor Henry A. Wise for the bodies of the Harpers Ferry attackers Shields Green and John Copeland. R. J. M. Blackett, *The Captive's Quest for Freedom: Fugitive Slaves, the 1850 Fugitive Slave Law, and the Politics of Slavery* (New York: Cambridge University Press, 2018), 337, points out that in the 1850s "the black community never failed to appear" when fugitives had been seized, "filling hearing rooms and gathering in the streets outside," but then describes an 1860 case when ten men were arrested after rushing the marshals, and "whatever unity there was soon after the arrest of the ten evaporated in the weeks before their trial" with two feuding defense committees (352–53).

11. *Provincial Freeman*, February 5, 1855.

12. *NS*, January 5 and June 22, 1849. Remond detailed how "Church members and ministers would not enlist, because some prominent men and advocates of the cause, were opposed to pro-slavery churches and ministers; others because, some of the speakers were opposed to Oddfellow Societies; their Tomfooleries and extravagances; thirdly, and lastly, another portion were so morally fastidious, that they could not co-

operate in obtaining their political rights, because some of the officers of the Convention were in their opinion of doubtful moral character."

13. Gerald S. Eggert, "The Impact of the Fugitive Slave Law on Harrisburg: A Case Study," *Pennsylvania Magazine of History and Biography* 109, no. 4 (October 1985): 538.

14. R. J. M. Blackett, "'... Freedom, or the Martyr's Grave': Black Pittsburgh's Aid to the Fugitive Slave," *Western Pennsylvania Historical Magazine* 61 (April 1978): 133–34, quoting *Pittsburg Gazette*, July 11, 1850; *FDP*, February 9, 1855.

Part II

1. Douglas Bradburn, *The Citizenship Revolution: Politics & the Creation of the American Union, 1774–1804* (Charlottesville: University of Virginia Press, 2009), 237–38, argues correctly that "the vast majority of non-enslaved blacks across the United States lived within the bounds of the law, but not as accepted citizens of the United States of America. At best, they could obtain an approximation of citizenship within a particular state, as specified by the individual state legislature," with "their status ... liable to change with the whims of politics; they had no sacred rights." He suggests that the "most comparable status in eighteenth-century British law is that of 'denizen,'" an assigned role, while noting, "In a few states, free blacks possessed nearly all the rights of white citizens." I do not disagree but note that those "few states" constituted a substantial regional bloc, and their position within the confederal nation acted as a standing challenge.

2. Massachusetts Anti-Slavery Society, "To the Abolitionists of Massachusetts," *Liberator*, August 10, 1838, repr. in Aileen S. Kraditor, "The Liberty and Free Soil Parties," in *History of U.S. Political Parties*, vol. 1, *1789–1860, From Factions to Parties*, ed. Arthur M. Schlesinger, Jr. (New York: Chelsea House, 1973), 771–74; Kraditor, *Means and Ends in American Abolitionism: Garrison and His Critics on Strategy and Tactics, 1834–1850* (New York: Ivan R. Dee, 1989), 156, the "vast majority of abolitionists who were Whigs"; *Liberator*, September 6, 1844.

3. "To the Democratic Republican Party of Alabama," in *The American Party Battle: Election Campaign Pamphlets*, ed. Joel H. Silbey, vol. 1, *1828–1854* (Cambridge, MA: Harvard University Press, 1999), 173–74; *Richmond Enquirer*, July 7 and September 25, 1840.

4. Edward S. Abdy, *Journal of a Residence and Tour in the United States of North America, from April 1833 to October 1834* (London: John Murray, 1835), 2:9.

5. Mary Hershberger, "Mobilizing Women, Anticipating Abolition: The Struggle against Indian Removal in the 1830s," *JAH* 86, no. 1 (June 1999): 15–40; my debt to Daniel Walker Howe, *The Political Culture of the American Whigs* (Chicago: University of Chicago Press, 1979) is evident.

6. Kevin Phillips, *The Cousins' Wars: Religion, Politics, & the Triumph of Anglo-America* (New York: Basic Books, 1999), 361, for a chart, "New England as the Center of Splinter Party Support in U.S. Presidential Elections," capturing the Liberty Party's spectacular growth, 1840–44: from 1.3 percent to 8.2 percent in Massachusetts; 1.5 percent to 8.5 percent in New Hampshire; 0.6 percent to 8.1 percent in Vermont; from a few dozen to 5.7 percent in Maine.

7. During 1841–42 the Massachusetts party featured Garnet (*Emancipator*, September 23, 1841, February 24, 1842, March 4, 1842), and he later traveled regionwide (*Berkshire County Whig* (Massachusetts), November 2, 1843, *Emancipator*, November 9, 1843, March 21, 1844, reprinting the Vermont *Voice of Freedom*, November 12, 1845, on Garnet in Connecticut, January 12, 1846, "laboring for a season" in Vermont, *Portland Advertiser*, November 13, 1844); *Liberty Standard* (Hallowell, ME), October 19, 1842.

8. John L. Brooke, *The Heart of the Commonwealth: Society and Political Culture in Worcester County, Massachusetts, 1713–1861* (Cambridge: Cambridge University Press, 1989), 369, defined "men of moral Whig origin" as "within the same intersection of Antimasonry, Whiggery, and temperance that characterized . . . the antislavery coalition of the late 1830s."

9. Leonard L. Richards, *The Life and Times of Congressman John Quincy Adams* (New York: Oxford University Press, 1986); William Lee Miller, *Arguing over Slavery: John Quincy Adams and the Great Battle over Slavery in the United States Congress* (New York: Vintage, 1998); Frederick W. Seward, *William H. Seward: An Autobiography, From 1801 to 1834. With a Memoir of His Life, and Selections From His Letters, 1831–1846* (New York: Derby and Miller, 1891), 292–93.

10. Josiah Quincy, *Memoir of the Life of John Quincy Adams* (Boston: Phillips, Sampson and Company, 1856), 411 (on slavery), Richards, *Life and Times*, 125 (Calhoun), 159 (to Polk); Jackson to General Armstrong, October 22, 1844, in Samuel Flagg Bemis, *John Quincy Adams and the Union* (New York: Knopf, 1956), 474–75: "Who but a traitor to his country can appeal as Mr. Adams does to the youth of Boston?"; Richards, *Life and Times*, 99, "He spoke out when the Washington police singled out black prisoners for abuse. During his Presidency he set an example by always receiving blacks and Indians, stating that he much preferred hearing their grievances than dealing with the endless line of white office-seekers" (privately, Adams may have expressed as much contempt for African Americans as he did for others, but the public stance is what matters); Boston *Daily Atlas*, August 5, 1843, reprinting the *Utica Gazette* on Adams telling a group that acting otherwise would have made him "wholly unworthy of the confidence or suffrages of his fellow citizens of any color," also Middletown, Connecticut, *Constitution*, November 29, 1843, on a Cincinnati neighborhood with "a plain white banner . . . stretched across the street with the inscription 'John Quincy Adams, the Able Defender of the Rights of Man'" and *Liberator*, December 8, 1843, reprinting *Cincinnati Philanthropist* on his telling colored leaders his regret that any "Fellow-Citizens" were excluded from the official reception, abjuring any "distinctions arising from color between citizens of the United States"; *Emancipator*, June 16, 1842.

11. Quincy, *Memoir of the Life*, 400, 411; Miller, *Arguing against Slavery*, 469 (other versions simply have Adams replying "Five hundred millions. Yes, let it come"); Giddings's memoir, *History of the Rebellion*, is quoted in Miller, *Arguing against Slavery*, 538–39. The reference to Pittsburgh's black community is absent from most contemporary coverage, other than one reference to his "Pittsburgh speech"; see *Philadelphia Inquirer*, February 28, 1844, *North American and Daily Advertiser* (Philadelphia), reprinting the *Baltimore American*, February 28, 1844, *Richmond Whig*, February 27, 1844 and Washington *Globe*, February 22, 1844.

12. See Christian G. Samito, *Becoming American under Fire: Irish Americans, African Americans, and the Politics of Citizenship during the Civil War Era* (Ithaca, NY: Cornell

University Press, 2009), 18: "Know Nothings also acted to curtail the political power of recent immigrants. Massachusetts, Connecticut, Rhode Island, and Maine forbade state courts from participating in naturalization procedures in any way, and New Hampshire restricted its state judges, so that naturalization could take place only in the more limited number of federal courts in those states."

13. Bruce Laurie, *Beyond Garrison: Antislavery and Social Reform* (Cambridge: Cambridge University Press, 2005); Stephen Kantrowitz, *More Than Freedom: Fighting for Black Citizenship in a White Republic, 1829–1889* (New York: Penguin, 2012). *More Than Freedom* documents how that process played out in Republican electioneering in Boston's Ward Six during the 1850s. There is one minor addition to his and Laurie's accounts. As far back as 1834, some black Bostonians were active Whigs. For an example of this sub rosa practice, see the imbroglio in April 1841, when they were excluded from the Whigs' memorial procession honoring the late President Harrison. A Democratic paper acidly reported they were not allowed to march "unless they would go behind all the rest. They had a meeting . . . and proposed, as an organized body, to attach themselves to Ward 6, which had given the greatest number of *colored* votes to General Harrison. Their marshal waited on the Chief Marshal, JOSIAH QUINCY, JR., and informed him of their intention of complying with the invitation of the city authorities. The Mayor was present at the interview, and he united with the Chief Marshal in endeavoring to dissuade the colored people from joining the procession altogether, on the ground that there would be a mob! . . . It was of no use for Mr. Alexander to plead that the colored voters, almost to a man, had voted for the dominant whig party, and on the occasion of the election had been treated with the utmost civility and respect by all parties, distinguished white citizens, without a taint of abolitionism about them, walking arm in arm with black men to the polls, descending and condescending to all sorts of equality with them; and were these same colored voters to be mobbed out of the funeral procession of him whom their so eagerly solicited votes had helped to make President! It was of no use" (*Norfolk Democrat* [Dedham, MA], May 7, 1841). Characteristically, *The Liberator* on April 23 and May 7, 1841 also reported how "the colored citizens of Boston were not allowed to walk in the procession!" but omitted the partisan context.

Chapter Four

1. Joanne Pope Melish, *Disowning Slavery: Gradual Emancipation and "Race" in New England, 1780–1860* (Ithaca, NY: Cornell University Press, 1998), xiii–xiv.

2. James Brewer Stewart with George R. Price, "The Roberts Case, the Easton Family, and the Dynamics of the Abolitionist Movement in Massachusetts, 1776–1870," in Stewart, *Abolitionist Politics and the Coming of the Civil War* (Amherst: University of Massachusetts Press, 2000), 67.

3. Melish, *Disowning Slavery*, 3.

4. See Rosalind Cobb Wiggins, ed., *Captain Paul Cuffe's Logs and Letters, 1808–1817: A Black Quaker's "Voice From Within the Veil"* (Washington, DC: Howard University Press, 1996), 131–48, on his two-month visit to England, including petitioning the Privy Council for a trading license, and dining with the Duke of Gloucester and the young Lord John Russell, later prime minister (his negotiations in Washington are quoted in 212–13, 211); *New-England Palladium*, January 14, 1814, quoting *Baltimore Whig*.

5. See Wendy Warren, *New England Bound: Slavery and Colonization in Early America* (New York: W. W. Norton, 2016), on "the popular story" of how "New England became an exceptional land of hard work and bountiful crops and thrift and curtness and fervent religiosity. Puritans, we call these fabled people, a sort of shorthand used to describe a motley array of Protestants interested in reforming a Church of England they considered too encumbered by vestiges of Roman Catholicism." In this mytho-history, slavery and race constitute "an exceptional absence," even though all the famous Puritans "owned slaves, sold slaves, [and] had daily interactions with them" and "the region in many ways depended on plantation slavery—those plantations were simply offshore" (3, 9, 12); see also John Wood Sweet, *Bodies Politic: Negotiating Race in the American North, 1730–1830* (Philadelphia: University of Pennsylvania Press, 2006), 1, describing the popular consensus that "New England's colonial past—distinguished by family values, religious liberty, and social equality—not only set New England apart from the rest of the country but also blazed the path the rest of the new nation was destined to follow"; Perry Miller, *The New England Mind: From Colony to Province* (Cambridge, MA: Harvard University Press, 1953) and Miller, *The New England Mind: The Seventeenth Century* (Cambridge, MA: Harvard University Press, 1954); Kelly Olds, "Privatizing the Church: Disestablishment in Connecticut and Massachusetts," *Journal of Political Economy* 102, no. 2 (April 1994): 277–97; and David M. Ludlum, *Social Ferment in Vermont, 1791–1850* (New York: AMS, 1966; Columbia University Press, 1939), 46 (Vermont never had a formal Standing Order, but 1783 legislation privileged whichever church organized first, usually the Congregationalist).

6. Daniel J. McInerney, *The Fortunate Heirs of Freedom: Abolition and Republican Thought* (Lincoln: University of Nebraska, 1994), 36; Kevin Phillips, *The Cousins' Wars: Religion, Politics, & the Triumph of Anglo-America* (New York: Basic Books, 1999), xv; William H. Seward, *Life of John Quincy Adams, Sixth President of the United States* (Philadelphia: Henry T. Coates, 1855), 18.

7. David Hackett Fischer, *The Revolution of American Conservatism: The Federalist Party in the Era of Jeffersonian Democracy* (New York: Harper & Row, 1965) examines the ruling cliques in each colony; Richard D. Brown and Jack Tager, *Massachusetts: A Concise History* (Amherst: University of Massachusetts Press, 2000), 92: "Towns were highly responsive if not always effective. . . . State government was remote. Every town seemed to have its own constitution, written in the minds of its inhabitants and preserved in the multitude of precedents contained in the town records. Maintaining order was the routine achievement of *people* in the nearly three hundred communities around the state"; even after Massachusetts's 1780 constitution rationalized representation, the minimum number of taxable "polls" (adult men other than paupers) required to elect a representative was a mere 150, or about 700 residents overall (Brown and Tager, *Massachusetts*, 96); Stephen Kantrowitz, *More Than Freedom: Fighting for Black Citizenship in a White Republic, 1829–1889* (New York: Penguin, 2012), 102, describes how Massachusetts election laws "gave small blocs of voters and third parties unusual power. . . . Even black voters, might be able to exert some political power, and third parties could be small without being marginal."

8. Brown and Tager, *Massachusetts*, 148: "Nearly everyone was taught at an early age to make personal moral judgments and was pressed to develop an active conscience, no matter what his or her denomination, social class, or community."

9. Harlow W. Sheidley, *Sectional Nationalism: Massachusetts Conservative Leaders and the Transformation of America, 1815–1836* (Boston: Northeastern University Press, 1998), 89 passim; Michael Sherman, Gene Sessions, and P. Jeffrey Potash, *Freedom and Unity: A History of Vermont* (Barre: Vermont Historical Society, 2004), 131, on Vermont's annual population increase averaging 8 percent in 1791–1810, from 85,000 to just under 218,000 inhabitants.

10. David Waldstreicher, *In the Midst of Perpetual Fetes: The Making of American Nationalism, 1776–1820* (Chapel Hill: University of North Carolina Press, 1997), 251, 252, 254, on "three distinct nationalist regionalisms" in the early republic (251).

11. Mary Stoughton Locke, *Anti-Slavery in America, from the Introduction of African Slaves to the Prohibition of the Slave Trade (1619–1808)* (Gloucester, MA: Peter Smith, 1965, orig. pub. in Radcliffe College Monographs, No. 11, 1901), 93; Margaret C. S. Christman, *The First Federal Congress, 1789–1791* (Washington, DC: Smithsonian Institute Press, 1989), 50, quoting William A. Duer that he was "eccentric, witty, downright and sarcastic; and seemed to take pleasure in worrying his more sensitive colleagues." An example of his visceral antislavery is a March 21, 1790 letter quoted on page 157: "The house . . . have suspended all business, merely to attend to the Ravings of the South Carolina & Georgia Delegates, in attempting to prove the Lawfullness and good policy of Slavery. . . . A stranger would be led to imagine that Slavery is the only sacred thing in the United States—whilst Religion, Law & Liberty are only of consequence as they are made subservient to the establishment of the most odious Slavery & despotism."

12. For an early example of Thatcher's style, see *The Negro in the Congressional Record*, vol. 1, *1789–1801*, Peter M. Bergman and Jean McCarroll, comps. (New York: Bergman, 1969), 215–16 for an April 1789 debate on "Duties on Imports." When a southerner proposed taxing molasses, one of his region's major imports, used in distilling, Thatcher countered on behalf of "the people of New England. . . . Suppose a member from Massachusetts was to propose an impost on negroes, what would you hear from the Southern gentlemen, if fifty dollars was the sum to be laid? . . . If the pernicious effects of New England rum have been justly lamented, what can be urged for negro slavery?" Thatcher was not the only Yankee Federalist who enjoyed baiting slaveholders. In debating the 1795 Naturalization Bill, the Virginia Republican William Branch Giles tried to add antiaristocratic, implicitly anti-Federalist language requiring would-be citizens to "renounce all pretensions" to ranks and titles. Supported by Thatcher, the Massachusetts Federalist Samuel Dexter "attacked the pretensions of slaveholders to be such zealous democrats" by proposing requiring the immigrant to renounce slavery and swear that he "holds all men free and equal." Giles called this "a hint against Southern members" by making slavery "a jest," with Madison adding it would have "a very bad effect" upon slaves. After another southerner evoked the "immense scene of slaughter" in Saint-Domingue, denouncing such "extremely improper and dangerous" ideas, Giles's motion passed (Douglas Bradburn, *The Citizenship Revolution: Politics & the Creation of the American Union, 1774–1804* [Charlottesville: University of Virginia Press, 2009], 134–36, and Rachel Hope Cleves, "'Hurtful to the State': The Political Morality of Federalist Antislavery," in *Contesting Slavery: The Politics of Bondage and Freedom in the New American Nation*, ed. John Hammond and Matthew Mason [Charlottesville: University of Virginia Press, 2011], 209–10, noting that Dexter got twenty-eight Federalist votes,

eighteen from New England, plus two Massachusetts Republicans, and how "the voting pattern, both sectional and partisan, suggests the inextricable connections between regional morality and political imperatives in Federalist antislavery initiatives," a republicanism that "concatenated partisanship with righteousness" so men like Thatcher and Dexter could act "simultaneously from moral and party imperatives that cannot be separated"); after Dexter proposed renouncing slavery, Thatcher added "and that he never will possess them" (*Philadelphia Gazette*, January 2, 1795); *Annals of Congress*, 5th Cong., 2nd Sess., 1306–11 (March 23, 1798); Hammond, "'Uncontrollable Necessity': The Local Politics, Geopolitics, and Sectional Politics of Slavery Expansion," in Hammond and Mason, *Contesting Slavery*, 145; *Annals of Congress*, 6th Cong., 1st Sess., 244 (January 3, 1800).

13. *Annals of Congress*, 5th Cong., 1st Sess., 658 (November 30, 1797); Peter S. Field, *The Crisis of the Standing Order: Clerical Intellectuals and Cultural Authority in Massachusetts, 1780–1833* (Amherst: University of Massachusetts Press, 1998), 1, on how men like these "dominated their society as much as any other social class before American independence"; Locke, *Anti-Slavery in America*, 126; Merton L. Dillon, *Slavery Attacked: Southern Slaves and Their Allies, 1619–1865* (Baton Rouge: Louisiana State University Press, 1991), 48; Dwight quoted in John Saillant, *Black Puritan, Black Republican: The Life and Thought of Lemuel Haynes, 1753–1833* (New York: Oxford University Press, 2003), 136, 141; the best treatment is Peter Hinks, "Timothy Dwight, Congregationalism, and Early Antislavery," in Steven Mintz and John Stauffer, *The Problem of Evil: Slavery, Freedom, and the Ambiguities of American Reform* (Amherst: University of Massachusetts Press, 2007), 148–61, emphasizing his commitment to "black inclusion and interracial fellowship" (155).

14. After helping settle Cape Cod in 1635, Thatcher's family produced generations of powerful men. Besides slaveholders, Thatcher was contemptuous of the poor, foreigners, and illiterate Westerners. The longest-serving member in Congress's first decade and a strict party-liner, he enthusiastically supported the Alien and Sedition Acts. As a Massachusetts supreme court justice after 1801, he ordered out the militia to enforce Maine's Great Proprietors' rights. Thatcher's contempt for racial difference gave him no trouble at home; his only real heresy was to mock the Standing Order, with opponents accusing him of "impiety and irreligion," because of his friendship with the English Unitarian Joseph Priestley (see William C. diGiacomantonio, "A Congressional Wife at Home: The Case of Sarah Thatcher, 1787–1792," in *Neither Separate nor Equal: Congress in the 1790s*, ed. Kenneth R. Bowling and Donald R. Kennon [Athens: Ohio University Press, 2000], 156, 177–78; Manning J. Dauer, *The Adams Federalists* [Baltimore: Johns Hopkins University Press, 1953], 227 [December 28, 1798] on Thatcher's attitude toward Westerners, and roll calls on 290, 294, 300, 307, 312, 318, 323; Linda K. Kerber, "The Paradox of Women's Citizenship in the Early Republic: The Case of Martin vs. Massachusetts, 1805," *American Historical Review* 97, no. 2 [April 1992]: 362; Alan Taylor, *Liberty Men and Great Proprietors: The Revolutionary Settlement on the Maine Frontier, 1760–1820* [Chapel Hill: University of North Carolina Press, 1990], 129–31, 227; Jenny Graham, "Revolutionary in Exile: The Emigration of Joseph Priestley to America, 1794–1804," *Transactions of the American Philosophical Society* 85, pt. 2 [1995]: i–xii, 1–213); Elaine MacEacheren, "Emancipation of Slavery in Massachusetts: A Reexamination, 1770–1790," *JNH* 55, no. 4 (October 1970): 290.

15. Christopher Leslie Brown, *Moral Capital: Foundations of British Abolitionism* (Chapel Hill: University of North Carolina Press, 2006), 46–47; Padraig Riley captures how after 1800, the "Federalists . . . forced New England Republicans to confront the contradiction at the heart of their political coalition, which fought simultaneously to expand democracy in the North and protect the power of slavery in the South." He emphasizes a shift among this region's Jeffersonians, since they began as fully antiracialist as the Federalists. The foremost proto-Republican ideologue of the 1790s was Connecticut's Abraham Bishop, who in 1791 published "The Rights of Black Men" to hail Saint-Domingue's revolt. As late as 1803, the Massachusetts Republican congressman John Bacon, who championed black citizenship in the 1780s, spoke up against legislation to bar mariners of color from entry, even if U.S. citizens. Increasingly after 1800, however, "democracy and nationalism bound whites to a slave society, as northern Republicans looked to southern masters like Jefferson to lead them to political freedom," with figures like Bishop describing themselves as "white slaves" subordinated by Federalist masters (Riley, *Slavery and the Democratic Conscience: Political Life in Jeffersonian America* [Philadelphia: University of Pennsylvania Press, 2016], 16, 2, 46).

16. Lorenzo Johnston Greene, *The Negro in Colonial New England* (New York: Columbia University Press, 1942; republished by Atheneum, 1969), 167, followed by considerable detail, that a slave had "the same right to life as had the apprentice. . . . If a master killed his slave he was answerable as if he had killed a freeman," and that "slaves, as persons, might also acquire, receive, hold, and transfer property" (177), with "virtually the same rights in the New England courts as did freemen. Slaves could offer testimony either for or against white persons even in cases not involving Negroes" (179), and could contract, with "the master . . . as firmly bound as if he had contracted with a freeman," plus "the right to trial by jury, and before trial they must be regularly indicted for crimes in the same manner as free white malefactors" (184–85); Sweet, *Bodies Politic*, 4, complicates this narrative by including the region's Native American communities, pointing out that "by the time of the Revolution, almost one third of all New England households included at least one black member. In such a setting, the lives of conquered Indians, enslaved Africans, and English settlers grew densely entwined" (he further notes that British settlers would not "give up the notion that their polity was for whites only" but also that "slavery in New England was never simply private, rarely absolute, and not always permanent" [63]); William D. Piersen, *Black Yankees: The Development of an Afro-American Subculture in Eighteenth-Century New England* (Amherst: University of Massachusetts Press, 1988), 26, "Puritan precepts of patriarchal control led Massachusetts leaders to organize groups of unattached white male servants into artificial family units and to place stray bachelors and maids under the family discipline of local households. . . . Slavery . . . continued to follow this biblical model of the patriarchal family."

17. Harvey Amani Whitfield, *Blacks on the Border: The Black Refugees in British North America, 1815–1860* (Burlington: University of Vermont Press, 2006), 3, focuses on the "similar work patterns, community life, external pressures, and demography" of the free people on both sides of the border, noting that Nova Scotia's black population in the nineteenth century was close to 5,000.

18. Daniel R. Mandell, "Shifting Boundaries of Race and Ethnicity: Indian-Black Intermarriage in Southern New England, 1760–1880," *JAH* 85, no. 2 (September 1998): 466–501.

19. Quoted in Douglas R. Egerton, *Death or Liberty: African Americans and Revolutionary America* (New York: Oxford University Press, 2009), 46, 59; Locke, *Anti-Slavery in America*, 85, describes a petition from Connecticut slaves on a confiscated Loyalist estate asking legislators not to "sell good honest Whigs and friends of the freedom and independence of America"; see also Sidney and Emma Nogrady Kaplan, *The Black Presence in the Era of the American Revolution* (Amherst: University of Massachusetts Press, 1989), 27–30 on various petitions; Roy E. Finkenbine, "Belinda's Petition: Reparations for Slavery in Revolutionary Massachusetts," *WMQ* 64, no. 1 (January 2007): 101, summarizing this escalation of protest; James Swan, *A Dissuasion to Great-Britain and the Colonies, From the Slave-Trade to Africa, Shewing the Injustice thereof, &c., Revised and Abridged* (Boston: J. Greenleaf, 1773), ix, "This edition appears in the world, at the earnest desire of the Negroes in Boston, in order to answer the purpose of sending a copy to each town"; the tradition of "Negro Elections," whereby slaves gathered annually in many towns to celebrate at their masters' expense and elect leaders, undergirded this organizational capacity, and in New Hampshire, five "Negro officers" were among twenty men petitioning the legislature in 1779; MacEacheren, "Emancipation of Slavery in Massachusetts," 301; as Timothy Breen points out, "At a critical moment in the development of Western liberal political thought, the slaves of Massachusetts brought the testimony of their own lives before a public increasingly unwilling to defend social and economic categories of unfreedom" (T. H. Breen, "Making History: The Force of Public Opinion and the Last Years of Slavery in Revolutionary Massachusetts," in *Through a Glass Darkly: Reflections on Personal Identity in Early America*, ed. Ronald Hoffman, Mechal Sobel, and Fredrika J. Teute [Chapel Hill: University of North Carolina Press, 1997], 73).

20. See Oscar and Mary Handlin, eds., *The Popular Sources of Political Authority: Documents on the Massachusetts Constitution of 1780* (Cambridge, MA: Harvard University Press, 1966), 20–21; *Continental Journal*, March 19, 1778; *Independent Chronicle* and *Continental Journal*, January 8, 1778.

21. *Continental Journal*, April 9, 1778 (he also alleged, "It hath been argued, that were Negroes admitted to vote, the Southern States would be offended, and we should be soon crowded with them from thence," and the Reverend John Barry later published his dissent as a delegate during convention debates, attacking the claim that "by erasing this clause out of the constitution, we shall greatly offend and alarm the southern States," *Independent Chronicle*, September 23, 1779); resolutions quoted in Handlin and Handlin, *Popular Sources of Political Authority*, 231, 248–49, 263, 277, 282, 302, 312, including the four other towns that dissented from racial suffrage (Sutton, Blanford, Georgetown, and Hardwick). The year 1778 was also the year that Massachusetts opened its militia to men of color; see Sweet, *Bodies Politic*, 202, on how a new law "explicitly sanctioned the enlistment of Negroes and removed color restrictions for draft substitutes," although in that year and the next additional bills also passed "explicitly prohibiting the enrollment of Negroes and Indians in units intended to serve specific assignments in defense of the state."

22. J. R. Pole, "Suffrage and Representation in Massachusetts: A Statistical Note," *WMQ* 14, no. 14 (October 1957): 569; Jeremy Belknap to Ebenezer Hazard, January 25, 1788, quoted in Robert J. Dinkin, *Voting in Revolutionary America: A Study of Elections in the Original Thirteen States, 1776–1789* (Westport, CT: Greenwood, 1977), 42;

Charles H. Wesley, *Prince Hall: Life and Legacy* (Washington, DC: United Supreme Council, Southern Jurisdiction, Prince Hall Affiliation, 1977), 72, 42; Sidney Kaplan, "Blacks in Massachusetts and the Shays' Rebellion," *Contributions in Black Studies* 8, no. 2 (2008): 5–14, points out that Hall and other Masons petitioned the General Court one month later, requesting funding for emigration to Africa, and their offer to aid against Shays may have been a feint; Rita Roberts, *Evangelicalism and the Politics of Reform in Northern Black Thought, 1776–1863* (Baton Rouge: Louisiana State University Press, 2010), 62; Locke, *Anti-Slavery in America*, 134n4.

23. *American Mercury*, January 21, 1793, and New York *Diary or Loudon's Register*, January 29, 1793; Belknap writing the Virginia jurist St. George Tucker, quoted in Wesley, *Prince Hall*, 51.

24. Brown and Tager, *Massachusetts*, 173; Kunal M. Parker, "Making Blacks Foreigners: The Legal Construction of Former Slaves in Post-Revolutionary Massachusetts," *Utah Law Review* 75 (2001): 75–124.

25. Dixon Ryan Fox, "The Negro Vote in Old New York," *Political Science Quarterly* 32, no. 2 (June 1917): 254; *Constitutional Telegraph* (Boston), September 20, 1800; Saillant, *Black Puritan, Black Republican*, for a powerful explication of why black men inclined to Federalism; Fischer, *Revolution of American Conservatism*, 10; W. Jeffrey Bolster, *Black Jacks: African American Seamen in the Age of Sail* (Cambridge, MA: Harvard University Press, 1997), 153, 75–76, adding that 1,174 of 6,560 American sailors held prisoner by the British in 1815 were men of color.

26. *Independent Chronicle*, October 30, 1800; *New York Gazette*, November 16, 1798; *Independent Chronicle*, September 8, 1800; *Constitutional Telegraphe*, December 17, 1800 (three years later, the Republican *Chronicle* admitted that in 1798 "great numbers white and black, little school boys and negroes, were parading the streets with great and small cockades" [*Independent Chronicle*, January 2, 1804]); *Massachusetts Mercury*, September 16, 1800, listed 163 "Blacks" and 74 "Mulattoes and Indians," describing how "the Officers of Police having made return to the Subscriber of the names of the following persons, who are Africans or Negroes, not subjects of the Emperor of Morocco nor citizens of any of the United States, the same are hereby warned and directed to depart out of this Commonwealth before the tenth day of October next, as they would avoid the pains and penalties of the law in that case provided, which was passed by the Legislature March 16, 1788"; *Independent Chronicle*, September 25 and October 2, 1800.

27. *Constitutional Telegraphe* (Boston), September 20, 1800, referring to two 1794 races, when Republican governor Samuel Adams defeated the Federalist William Cushing, Associate Justice of the U.S. Supreme Court, and Fisher Ames gained reelection to Congress over Doctor Charles Jarvis.

28. *Salem Gazette*, March 7, 1800 (Oliver Wolcott, Jr., was secretary of the treasury, and Timothy Pickering secretary of state); see *Massachusetts Mercury*, January 16, 1798, for an advertisement for Hawkins as "A Cook" and *Columbian Centinel*, January 4, 1800, for his death at 48; *Independent Chronicle*, January 29, 1801.

29. Quoted in James H. Robbins, "Voting Behavior in Massachusetts, 1800–1820: A Case Study" (PhD diss., Northwestern University, 1970), 11; even outside the state, its "Negro voters" were derided, as in a July 4, 1807 toast by Army officers in Rhode Island, "Our sister state of Massachusetts—may her Negro Voters take care of the rights of their Southern brethren"; *Providence Phenix*, July 7, 1807; *Independent Chronicle*,

June 4, 1812, *Rhode-Island Republican*, January 21, 1813, and *New-Hampshire Patriot*, June 15, 1813; *New-York Herald*, January 16, 1813, quoting the Boston *Columbian*; *Essex Register*, January 20, 1813, quoting *Independent Chronicle*; *Rhode-Island Republican*, January 21, 1813.

30. Pole, "Suffrage and Representation in Massachusetts," 588; *The First Book of the "Washington Benevolents"; Otherwise Called, the Book of Knaves* (Boston: Nathaniel Coverly, 1813), 13–14. That same year, under the heading "BLACK and WHITE ROSES!," the Republican *Boston Patriot*, July 17, 1813, satirized black Federalists during their annual parade (the white rose was a Federalist symbol): "Some of their Marshals were mistaken, by many, for officers of the Washington Benevolents; and this small mistake was occasioned by their wearing the WHITE ROSE," adding that their "corps of guards . . . [is] to be trained like the other independent companies; and that they mean to apply for a Charter, under the name and title of '*The Washington Benevolent Federal Black-Guards!—Vive la Republique!*'"

31. *The Diary of William Bentley, Pastor of the East Church, Salem, Massachusetts* (Salem, MA: Essex Institute, 1914), 2:429 (May 3, 1802) although the prior year Bentley met Prince Hall catering a "Turtle Feast of the Marine Society" and was impressed: "The Clergy were introduced to him, & the principal gentlemen took notice of him. Brother Freeman of Boston pronounced him a very useful man, & that the Masonic Negroes are evidently many grades above the common blacks of Boston" (379, July 11, 1801); Bentley's diary traces the accretion of respect accorded people of color—in 1793 he recorded approvingly how a neighborhood of "Negro huts had been erected," but "by the exertions of the neighbours had been cleared of their disagreable [*sic*] inhabitants" (2:38, August 8, 1793), but in 1809, he noted "the funeral procession of young Rose, wife of Saib [Derby], both lately servants of E. H. Derby deceased. It was an honour to Salem to see such a length of procession of decently clad & orderly blacks. 80 Blacks capable of dressing themselves in good fashion & of conducting with great solemnity, without the ignorant state & the awkward manner of a new situation, is favourable to the hopes of civil society" (3:437, June 1, 1809), and the following year, Bentley mentioned the visit of "the African minister Paul of Boston. . . . Many admire him" (3:490, January 11, 1810) ("Saib" or Sabe Derby was captain general of the Sons of the African Society, founded in 1805 "for the mutual benefit of each other, believing ourselves all times as true and faithful citizens of the Commonwealth in which we live"; see *Salem Gazette*, March 18, 1806); in 1817, Bentley recorded his respect for various black Salemites, referring to Schuyler Lawrence, whom he married to the teacher Chloe Minns, as "a man of good person & of good manners, attending on the best families in Marblehead & these are the first grade of Africans in all our New England towns" (4:435–36, February 6, 1817); on Bentley's partisan role, see Jeffrey L. Pasley, *"The Tyranny of Printers": Newspaper Politics in the Early American Republic* (Charlottesville: University of Virginia Press, 2001), 210; *Herald of Liberty* (Augusta), April 17, 1810; *Essex Register*, April 18, 1810; 16 (April 14, 1811).

32. *Diary of William Bentley*, 4:90 (March 17, 1812); *Essex Register*, March 17, 1813; *Independent Chronicle*, April 23, 1813; *Democratic Republican*, May 31, 1813 (Walpole, NH), repr. from *National Aegis* of Worcester; *American Mercury*, January 13, 1813; *Diary of William Bentley*, 4:376 (March 11, 1816), also *Columbian*, April 12, 1816, reprinting from *Salem Register*, "It ought never to be forgotten, that among the flock of Black

Merinoes impressed into the federal service at the election of 1812, was a *Black Ewe*, attired in men's clothes. The fact is well known, as honestly confessed by the woman herself some months after the election."

33. Henry M. Brooks, "Some Localities about Salem," *Essex Institute Historical Collections* (Salem, MA: Printed for the Institute, 1894–95), 31:115. For the concept of the submachine, see Harold F. Gosnell, *Negro Politicians: The Rise of Negro Politics in Chicago* (Chicago: University of Chicago Press, 1935).

34. Dorothy Burnett Porter, "The Remonds of Salem, Massachusetts: A Nineteenth-Century Family Revisited," *Proceedings of the American Antiquarian Society* 95, pt. 2 (October, 1985): 263, 265, 268, 273; *Essex Register*, April 30, 1808; *Salem Gazette*, November 24, 1813 and a January 30, 1811 notice specifying "All persons who wish to have their Chimnies swept, will please leave their names, and where their chimnies are to be found, with JOHN REMOND," with set prices; *Salem Gazette*, November 1, 1822 ("a supper at Hamilton Hall, served up in a style of elegance and good taste seldom equaled at any public entertainment in this town, and highly creditable to Mr. Remond"); *Salem Gazette*, October 14, 1823; *Salem Observer*, October 15, 1825 (President Adams and the state's elite parading from the hall); *Essex Register*, February 27 and June 29, 1826. In 1815, Remond added a restaurant or "Restorator" (*Salem Gazette*, October 24, 1815), and then an oyster house, at "his *little Winter Retreat*, in Washington Street" (*Salem Gazette*, November 15, 1816). By 1818, he was a wholesaler, with "1500 pots of pickled Oysters and Lobsters . . . warranted to keep in any climate," as well as "Cyder, Albany ale, Philadelphia porter," and pickles and sauerkraut for "masters of sailing vessels" (*Essex Register*, November 4, 1818). In 1825, he had on hand five tons of ham, one of pork shoulders, two of smoked beef, and two and one-half of "new milk cheese" (Porter, "Remonds of Salem," 269). His obituary in the *Boston Daily Advertiser*, March 7, 1874, noted he also dealt "in wines and liquor, a rare old stock of which" he kept in the hall. The Remond Family Papers at the Peabody Essex Museum include handwritten payment lists from the town's elite, and printed bills of fare for his lavish collations of the 1820s and 1830s; *FJ*, November 9, 1827.

35. See the advertisement in the *Salem Gazette*, May 5, 1815 and his death notice in the same, October 10, 1834 (the Remond Family Papers contain an 1824 invoice for $9.50 to Morris, a princely sum when $1 was a common daily wage, and the museum also holds Morris's Seamen's Protection Paper); as early as 1803, Bentley noted that "Mumford's negro whom I lately married" had been arrested for breaking into "the store of Capt. G. Crowninshield"; see *Diary of William Bentley*, 3:66–67 (December 28, 1803); Mumford's death at 70 was noted in the *Salem Register*, January 11, 1841; Oliver Thayer, "Early Recollections of the Upper Portion of Essex Street," *Essex Institute Historical Collections* 21 (1885): 211; *Diary of William Bentley*, 4:382–83 (April 22, 1816); *Newburyport Herald*, November 18, 1825; *Salem Gazette*, September 21, 1827.

36. *Salem Register*, July 12, 1847. Like Remond, he also dealt in wholesale food; see *Salem Register*, January 30, 1851, for his advertisement of "2500 Oysters at Boston prices." He died the following year, at the age of sixty-eight (*Salem Observer*, May 15, 1852).

37. Using the 1820 census to estimate the percentage of black men at the ages of fourteen through twenty-five who were of voting age as 42 percent produces a potential electorate of 216, versus 52,721 white men. Even Rockingham County, with the largest

black population, had only 109 possible voters, just under 1 percent of its white male electorate of 12,570; *City of Washington Gazette*, December 18, 1820.

38. The invaluable source is Erik R. Tuveson, "'A People of Color': A Study of Race and Racial Identification in New Hampshire, 1750–1825" (master's thesis, University of New Hampshire, 1995), although I disagree that "light skin color, wealth, education, and familiarity within his community" led to Cheswell being considered white (v); his first recorded presence was in the *New-Hampshire Gazette*, February 2, 1770, announcing the "Vendue" of fifty acres and house, and from then on, Cheswell appeared regularly, as an executor (May 18, 1770; January 4, 1771; March 31 and April 14, 1775; much later, in the *Sun*, October 7, 1810); selling land (January 10, 1772); and administering a public lottery (June 25, 1773); for his losing Senate race, see *New-Hampshire Gazette*, March 18, 1806. He came in third with 169 of 950, mostly from Newmarket.

39. David T. Dixon, "Freedom Earned, Equality Denied: Evolving Race Relations in Exeter and Vicinity, 1776–1876" in "Too Long in the Shadows: The Black Presence in New Hampshire," *Historical New Hampshire* 61, no. 1 (Spring 2007): 29–47, documents Exeter as the "focus of free black society in the state," retaining that position into the antebellum period, "largely as a result of an influx of black Revolutionary War veterans" who received land (29); Lynn Clark and Rebecca Courser, "Rural Free Black Settlement in Post-Revolutionary New Hampshire: A Study of Five Towns" in this same issue, 48–62, examines inland New Hampshire's "independent, land-owning farmers" (54), many of whom paid poll taxes early on; see also Reginald H. Pitts, "George and Timothy Blanchard, Surviving and Thriving in Nineteenth-Century Milford," in *Harriet Wilson's New England: Race, Writing, and Region*, ed. JerriAnne Boggis, Eve Allegra Raimon, and Barbara A. White (Durham: University of New Hampshire Press, 2007), 41–66, examining another prosperous veteran's family; Timothy Blanchard became his town's veterinarian. See also Pole, "Suffrage and Representation in Massachusetts," 583 on how, in 1792, New Hampshire allowed "persons excused at their own request from paying taxes" to be barred from voting, along with paupers, which may explain the divergence between men of color counted as "polls" and those not.

40. David M. Ludlum, *Social Ferment in Vermont, 1791–1850* (New York: AMS, 1966; Columbia University Press, 1939), 3; see also Sherman, Sessions, and Potash, *Freedom and Unity*, 132–34, on its youthful population and "rich farmlands" boasting "astounding productivity," a yeoman economy with no town larger than 3,000 well into the 1800s; Charles E. Tuttle, Jr., "Vermont and the Slavery Question," *Proceedings of the Vermont Historical Society* 6, no. 1 (March 1938): 4; *NS*, December 21, 1849.

41. Randolph A. Roth, *The Democratic Dilemma: Religion, Reform, and the Social Order in the Connecticut River Valley of Vermont, 1791–1850* (Cambridge: Cambridge University Press, 1987), 5, 12; Wilbur H. Siebert, *Vermont's Anti-Slavery and Underground Railroad Record* (New York: Negro Universities Press, 1969, orig. pub. 1937), 46; Tuttle, "Vermont and the Slavery Question," 7, also 4 (it fined "any person one hundred pounds who carried a Negro into the state to sell," with "the fine . . . paid not to the state but to the injured Negro"); Birney quoted in Reinhard O. Johnson, "The Liberty Party in Vermont, 1840–1848: The Forgotten Abolitionists," *Vermont History* 47, no. 4 (Fall 1979): 258.

42. *Vermont Republican*, September 18, 1815 (Windsor).

43. In 1820, the potential black electorate was 220, a mere 0.4 percent of the white electorate of 50,293; Elise A. Guyette, *Discovering Black Vermont: African American Farmers in Hinesburgh, 1790–1890* (Burlington: University of Vermont Press, 2010), 5, cites African Americans as 7 percent of Vergennes' population and 2.5 percent of Ferrisburgh's in 1790, while in 1800 they made up 3.8 percent of Braintree; in 1810, 3.6 percent of Windsor; and in 1820, 3.4 percent of Burlington and 2 percent of Hinesburgh; also Guyette, "The Working Lives of African Vermonters in Census and Literature, 1790–1870," *Vermont History* 61 (1993): 70, documenting how 2.5 percent of Rutland in 1840 and 1.9 percent of St. Albans in 1850 were black, when Hinesburgh was 2.9 percent and Bristol 2.4 percent; Jane Williamson, "African Americans in Addison County, Charlotte, and Hinesburgh, Vermont, 1790–1860," *Vermont History* 78, no. 1 (Winter/Spring 2010): 35, 37.

44. Timothy Mather Cooley, D. D., *Sketches of the Life and Character of the Rev. Lemuel Haynes, A.M., For Many Years Pastor of a Church in Rutland, Vt., and Late in Granville, New-York* (New York: John S. Taylor, 1839), 287, "About twenty young men at different times were under the instruction of Mr. Haynes," plus 315, 347, for letters from some (he was "one of the most esteemed and venerated counselors of my youth in the ministry. . . . He was a deep, original thinker, a learned man, and a very sound divine"); *CA*, March 11, 1837; David Sherman, *Sketches of New England Divines* (New York: Carlton & Porter, 1860); W. H. Morse, "Lemuel Haynes," *JNH* 4, no. 1 (January 1919): 32; Richard Newman, *Lemuel Haynes: A Bio-Bibliography* (New York: Lambeth, 1984) lists dozens of citations from every decade through the 1940s.

45. Cooley, *Sketches*, 59; "Introductory Remarks by William B. Sprague, D. D., Pastor of the Second Presbyterian Church in Albany" in Cooley, *Sketches*, xix; *Rutland Herald*, December 1, 1813 ("Deacon Chatterton's Complaint"). *Weekly Wanderer*, December 8, 1806 and *Vermont Republican*, October 29, 1810 list Chatterton as a justice of the peace.

46. Field, *Crisis of the Standing Order*, 2, stresses how their authority derived from the "formal and abstract manipulation of cultural symbols," using "biblical exegesis to reveal the 'deep structural' meaning of the sacred texts"; Cooley, *Sketches*, xxi, xxiv; Kaplans, *Black Presence in the Era of the American Revolution*, 125; Richard Newman, ed., *Black Preacher to White America: The Collected Writings of Lemuel Haynes*, 1774–1833 (Brooklyn, NY: Carlson, 1990), xiv, xxxi.

47. Saillant, *Black Puritan, Black Republican*, 117, 118, 119, 129, 123–24, 127–28; Lemuel Haynes, *The Nature and Importance of True Republicanism: With a Few Suggestions, Favorable to Independence: A Discourse, Delivered at Rutland, (Vermont,) the Fourth of July 1801.—It Being The 25th Anniversary Of American Independence* (Rutland, VT: William Fay, 1801), 5, 13.

48. Cooley, *Sketches*, 169–70, 142–44, 137.

49. John W. Lewis, *The Life, Labors, and Travels of Elder Charles Bowles, of the Free Will Baptist Denomination, Together with an Essay On the Character and Condition of the African Race by the Same, Also, An Essay on the Fugitive Law of the U.S. Congress of 1850, by Rev. Arthur Dearing* (Watertown, NY, Ingalls & Stowell's Steam Press, 1852), 71, 148; *Proceedings of the Orleans County Historical Society* (Newport, VT: The Society, 1918), 17–19 (untitled, F. W. Baldwin, biographical sketch of Twilight); Florence E. Waters, "The Old Stone House," *Vermonter* (June 1929), 83–87; William R. Cole, "Pioneer,"

Middlebury College Newsletter (March 1936), 4–5; George Colpitts, "With These Hands," *Vermont History* 25 (1957): 315–20; Gregor Hillman, "The Iron-Willed Black Schoolmaster and His Granite Academy," *Middlebury College Newsletter* (1974), 6–14; James Hayford, ed., *The Old Stone House Museum* (Brownington, VT: Orleans County Historical Society, 1986); Philip M. Bowler, Sr., "The Twilight Mystery Solved?" (unpublished ms., 1996); Michael T. Hahn, *Alexander Twilight: Vermont's African-American Pioneer* (Shelburne, VT: New England Press, 1998); *Woodstock Observer*, August 26, 1823, listing Twilight as one of seventeen graduates. Hillman's 1974 article asserted he was known locally as "colored," referring to a Corinth town history naming the Twilights as its first black settlers and how in 1948, when Vermont elected a black Republican legislator, supposedly a "first," "a lady in Newport" wrote "Not so!," plus that a Middlebury dean remembered an older dean (class of 1871), informing him of Twilight's race.

50. The exception was Donald Robinson, *Slavery in the Structure of American Politics, 1765–1820* (New York: Harcourt Brace Jovanovich, 1971), a resounding corrective; Hammond, "'Uncontrollable Necessity'" in Hammond and Mason, *Contesting Slavery*, 138; earlier, Robert Pierce Forbes argued that the sectional divide revealed by Missouri portended "a crack in the master narrative," followed by a decade of conflict with slavery at the center (Forbes, *The Missouri Compromise and Its Aftermath* [Chapel Hill: University of North Carolina, 2007], 3; Riley, *Slavery and the Democratic Conscience*, 134, 242).

51. In 1820, there were approximately 1,892 black men at the age of twenty-one and over in Connecticut, or 3.1 percent of the white electorate of 60,362. In Rhode Island, the 785 possible black voters would have constituted 4.5 percent of the white electorate of 17,304; see Robert P. Forbes, David Richardson, and Chandler B. Saint, "Trust and Violence in Atlantic History: The Economic Worlds of Venture Smith," in *Venture Smith and the Business of Slavery and Freedom*, ed. James Brewer Stewart (Amherst: University of Massachusetts Press, 2010), 64. The divergence between the Lower New England states is also evident. "Little Rhody" had only 83,059 inhabitants in 1820 versus Connecticut's 275,248. They had very different religious and political cultures, with a Standing Order and Federalist dominance fiercely maintained in Connecticut, while Rhode Island bred an "authentic folk religion" in its rural Baptist counties with "a highly decentralized form of government" where the "town, not the colony, was the principal seat of political authority" (Daniel P. Jones, *The Economic & Social Transformation of Rural Rhode Island, 1780–1850* [Boston: Northeastern University Press, 1992], 22, 28).

52. See Sean Wilentz, *The Rise of American Democracy: Jefferson to Lincoln* (New York: W. W. Norton, 2005), 119 on Connecticut as "the most conservative northeastern state," in which "a virtual oligarchy of Federalist notables and prominent Congregational clergymen . . . ran local affairs"; Chilton Williamson, *American Suffrage from Property to Democracy, 1760–1860* (Princeton, NJ: Princeton University Press, 1960), 165–66; David Waldstreicher and Stephen R. Grossbart, "Abraham Bishop's Vocation; or, the Mediation of Jeffersonian Politics," *JER* 18, no. 4 (Winter 1998): 649n44, documented that "few African Americans possessed the property to qualify for voting" by examining New Haven's freemen's admission records. In 1784, only one of approximately twenty-three qualified, and "he was never sworn in. . . . Prince Briant Hall

was sworn in in 1790, as was William Lamson in 1807, but . . . no others. . . . In nearby Wallingford, only one of the town's seven adult free male African Americans, Jack John, gained voting rights," in 1799.

53. *Windham Herald*, May 19, 1803; "A WHITE FREEMAN," wrote another Federalist paper asking, since Wallingford admitted "two citizens of colour, both democrats . . . to be free of this State," if those men should "obtain a clear majority of votes to represent said town, whether they would be returned as duly elected? . . . [and] admitted to seats in the house of the Representatives?" (*Connecticut Courant*, September 7, 1803); *Connecticut Journal*, April 23, 1816.

54. *Connecticut Courant*, July 5, 1814; *American Mercury*, September 8, 1818, on its sixth article stipulating that "All persons who have been, or shall hereafter previous to the ratification of this Constitution, be admitted Freemen according to the existing laws of this State, shall be or remain Freemen or Electors," immediately before the article restricting suffrage to "Every white male citizen of the United States"; *Connecticut Journal*, May 26, 1818; *Connecticut Mirror*, June 8, 1818; *American Mercury*, June 9, 1818.

55. Later developments underscored racial reaction in Connecticut versus states to its north, including the violent rejection of the proposal for a black Manual Labor College in New Haven in 1831 noted in chap. 3, and the Prudence Crandall case in 1833–34. After Crandall, a white Quaker, opened an academy to educate young women of color, she and they suffered intense local harassment, and the legislature passed a black law forbidding any such establishment. In *Crandall v. State* (1834), Judge David Daggett told the jury that African Americans were not citizens, and thus their rights had not been violated.

56. In addition to Melish, *Disowning Slavery*, see Irving H. Bartlett, *From Slave to Citizen: The Story of the Negro in Rhode Island* (Providence, RI: Urban League of Greater Providence, 1954), and Elaine Forman Crane, *A Dependent People: Newport, Rhode Island in the Revolutionary Era* (New York: Fordham University Press, 1985); Benjamin Franklin Wilbour, *Little Compton Families* (Little Compton, RI: Little Compton Historical Society, 1974), 519–20; Sweet, *Bodies Politic*, 330.

57. Robert J. Cottrol, *The Afro-Yankees: Providence's Black Community in the Antebellum Era* (Westport, CT: Greenwood, 1982), 43; Bartlett, *From Slave to Citizen*, 25; Sweet, *Bodies Politic*, 373; Patrick T. Conley, *Democracy in Decline: Rhode Island's Constitutional Development, 1776–1841* (Providence: Rhode Island Historical Society, 1977), 179–81; *Rhode-Island Republican*, May 8, 1811; *Columbian Phenix, or Providence Patriot*, March 16, 1811; *Providence Patriot*, June 20, 1818 (a similar bill was proposed in 1820; see Conley, *Democracy in Decline*, 190; for more evidence of Republican non-racialism, see *Providence Patriot*, September 19, 1818 and *Rhode-Island Republican*, October 17, 1818 ("no one can deny that every man, born in a land of freedom, and breathing the air of freedom, ought to enjoy the inestimable right of suffrage"); *Providence Patriot*, July 1, 1820; *Rhode-Island Republican*, September 19, 1821; *Rhode-Island American* (Providence), January 18, 1822.

58. James S. Leamon, "Maine in the American Revolution, 1763–1787" in *Maine: The Pine Tree State from Prehistory to the Present*, ed. Richard W. Judd, Edwin A. Churchill, and Joel W. Eastman (Orono: University of Maine Press, 1995), 143–44, describing the state as "a colony of a colony . . . an undeveloped region carved up for exploitation by

Massachusetts proprietors and merchants"; James S. Leamon, Richard S. Wescott, and Edward O. Schriver, "Separation and Statehood, 1783–1820" in Judd, Churchill, and Eastman, *Maine*, 170; Stephen A. Marini, "Religious Revolution in the District of Maine," in Judd, Churchill, and Eastman, *Maine*, 118, describing "new sectarian movements . . . a religious articulation of the emerging rural localist culture simultaneous and fully congruent with its political expression in Jeffersonianism"; Taylor, *Liberty Men and Great Proprietors* brilliantly describes this political, social, and economic environment; James S. Leamon, "Revolution and Separation: Maine's First Efforts at Statehood," in *Maine in the Early Republic: From Revolution to Statehood*, ed. Charles E. Clark, James S. Leamon, and Karen Bowden (Hanover, NH: University Press of New England, 1988), 88–117.

59. Randolph Stakeman, "The Black Population of Main, 1764–1900," *New England Journal of Black Studies* 8 (1989): 25, points out that in 1800, 818 free people of color lived in 92 towns, and by 1840, there were 1,355 across 113 towns; H. H. Price and Gerald E. Talbot, *Maine's Visible Black History: The First Chronicle of Its People* (Gardiner, ME: Tilbury House, 2006), 12–37, covers the black settlements, in one case long predating the Revolution; Randolph P. Dominic, Jr., *Down from the Balcony: The Abyssinian Congregational Church of Portland, Maine* (Portland: Collections of the Maine Historical Society, n.d.), 1, on how they were deemed "industrious even by [local] standards" and "viewed . . . with attitudes which ranged from benign neglect to paternalistic approval," in large part because "black labor was essential. . . . Negro stevedores all but ran the waterfront"; William Preble to John Holmes in Ronald F. Banks, *Maine Becomes a State: The Movement to Separate Maine from Massachusetts, 1785–1820* (Portland, ME: Maine Historical Society, 1973), 153; *The Debates, Resolutions and Other Proceedings of the Convention of Delegates, Assembled at Portland on the 11th, and Continued Until the 19th Day of October, 1819, for the Purpose of Forming a Constitution for the State of Maine, to Which Is Prefixed the Constitution* (Portland, ME: A. Stanley, 1820), 95.

60. *Debates, Resolutions and Other Proceedings of the Convention of Delegates, Assembled at Portland on the 11th, and Continued Until the 19th Day of October, 1819*, 63–64.

61. Josiah Quincy, *Memoir of the Life of John Quincy Adams* (Boston: Phillips, Sampson and Company, 1856), 112–14, an indication of how Adams's musings justified a later Yankee radicalism; Glover Moore, *The Missouri Controversy, 1819–1821* (Gloucester, MA: Peter Smith, orig. pub. 1953) was long the standard, meticulously researched but bristling with contempt for northern "philanthropists" hostile to their "white proletarian brothers" but with "a kind spot in their hearts for minority groups such as Indians and Negroes" (76). Moore argued the crisis was fomented by opportunists and Federalists in a bid for power, but passes over the second stage of the crisis, noting merely that "only on the free Negro and mulatto issue was it reasonable to suppose that Northern opinion would be sufficiently unanimous to enable the restrictionists to achieve their immediate goal—the rejection of Missouri's constitution" (142–43). Sean Wilentz, "Jeffersonian Democracy and the Origins of Political Antislavery in the United States: The Missouri Crisis Revisited," *Journal of the Historical Society* 4, no. 3 (Fall 2004): 375–401, overturned Moore, demonstrating the leading role of antislavery northern Republicans, but devoted a single paragraph to the second stage as "another

round of sectional brawling in the House" (382); his *Rise of American Democracy* described the debates over black citizenship as "punch-drunk brawlers" throwing "rhetorical haymakers at each other for weeks to come, in one wild round after another, each side standing its ground" (235), with no reference to what they said. Robert Pierce Forbes, *The Missouri Compromise and Its Aftermath* (Chapel Hill: University of North Carolina, 2007) offered a profoundly original reinterpretation but also elides the second crisis, noting only it spurred "an unlikely full-dress congressional debate over the question of black citizenship" (10). Riley, *Slavery and the Democratic Conscience*, 243–46, specifies that "Northerners, Republican and Federalist alike, mounted a clear and consistent defense of African American citizenship" (245), pointing out what was then obvious, "that free African Americans born in the United States had some claim to citizenship was hard to deny based on existing common law, which acknowledged the principle of birthright citizenship," so "Southerners, in response, began to invert the common law notion that being born free in a particular political community established political belonging and thus the protection of certain rights. Instead, they contended, one's status in a given community determined one's eligibility for citizenship" (246).

62. *Annals of Congress*, 16th Cong., 2nd Sess., 616 (December 12, 1820). This was Louis McLane of Delaware, elected as a Federalist but already developing the relationships that led to a career as a Jacksonian (senator from Delaware, then secretary of the treasury and secretary of state, finally minister to the Court of St. James; see John A. Munroe, *Louis McLane: Federalist and Jacksonian* [New Brunswick, NJ: Rutgers University Press, 1973]).

63. *Annals of Congress*, 16th Cong., 2nd Session, 47–48 (December 7, 1820).

64. *Annals of Congress*, 16th Cong., 2nd Sess., 596 (December 11, 1820); Otis's speech appeared in widely read national journals, including the *Daily National Intelligencer* on January 1, 1821. See *Concord Observer*, January 1, 1821 for Morril's speech, also *Daily National Intelligencer*, same date; for Mallary, see *Vermont Republican*, February 19, 1821. Eustis's speech was excerpted approvingly in the *Baltimore Patriot*, January 16, 1821, and *Columbian Centinel*, January 20, 1821, noting Eustis and Otis had together "vindicated the principles, and expressed the sentiments of their constituents"; also *Albany Gazette*, February 2, 1821.

65. *Annals of Congress*, 16th Cong., 2nd Sess., 80 (December 9, 1820), 83, 84, 86, 89. See also Matthew Mason, "The Maine and Missouri Crisis: Competing Priorities and Northern Slavery Politics in the Early Republic," *JER* 33 (Winter 2013): 675–700, on Holmes's stance, including Rufus King's suggestion he "fought under a black flag." For the local reception of his speech, see *Maine Gazette* (Bath), January 26, 1821, on members of Congress wasting the people's time and money: "Some of them indeed have amused themselves . . . in talking their two and *four* hours to convince us that 'colored freemen' are not 'freemen,' because they *are 'colored'*—Rather an anti-republican doctrine, to be sure."

66. *Annals of Congress*, 16th Cong., 2nd Sess., 92, 93, 97, 98 (December 9, 1820); *William Lloyd Garrison, 1805–1879, The Story of His Life, Told By His Children*, vol. 2, *1835–1840* (New York: Century Company, 1885), 80n1, quotes it from the *Columbian Centinel*, January 24, 1821.

67. *Annals of Congress*, 16th Cong., 2nd Sess., 105, 114 (December 9, 1820). In the first stage of the Crisis, Morril was among the few Yankees backing Clay's compromise,

following "the wishes of [Isaac] Hill's Concord Republican machine" and ignoring the instructions of New Hampshire's legislature (Forbes, *Missouri Compromise*, 82). Perhaps this speech was an effort at expiation.

68. *Annals of Congress*, 16th Cong., 2nd Sess., 618, 619, 620, 623 (December 12, 1820).

69. *Annals of Congress*, 16th Cong., 2nd Sess., 629, 630, 632, 633, 635 (December 12, 1820).

70. *Annals of Congress*, 16th Cong., 2nd Sess., 636–38 (December 12, 1820).

71. Riley, *Slavery and the Democratic Conscience*, 251, 253.

72. *Pittsfield Sun*, July 4, 1821, text of a "Report . . . to the House of Representatives"; *Free Negroes and Mulattoes, House of Representatives, January 16, 1822* (Boston, 1822), 2, 3, also reported in *Columbian Centinel*, January 16, 1822, and *Hampden Patriot*, January 23, 1822. For Upper New England's pauper disfranchisement, see Donald Ratcliffe, "The Right to Vote and the Rise of Democracy," *JER* 33, no. 2 (Summer 2013): 246. New Hampshire led the way in 1792, and Maine and Massachusetts added this category to their constitutions in 1819 and 1821, respectively. Kunal M. Parker, "State, Citizenship, and Territory: The Legal Construction of Immigrants in Antebellum Massachusetts," *Law and History Review* 19, no. 3 (Autumn 2001): 583–643, explicates how Massachusetts defined citizenship "as a barrier to the individual's right to enter, and remain within, territory." In the 1830s, as "the Commonwealth developed official discourses of citizenship, foreignness, and cultural difference . . . citizenship came to be endowed with a certain valence as the marker of the legitimacy of the individual's claims upon the community," although the point was "specifically to deny moral responsibility for resident immigrant paupers rather than to recognize moral responsibility for native paupers." Here he distinguishes between "popular" and "official nativism." The former "had empowering dimensions that sought to vindicate the average citizen's sense of entitlement to meaningful participation in the polity," which correlates to how Afro-Yankees saw themselves, versus the official version, never interested in "affirm[ing] natives' claims" (586, 591, 607).

73. *Journal of the Convention of Delegates, Chosen to Revise the Constitution of Massachusetts, Begun and Holden at Boston, November 15, 1820, and Continued by Adjournment to January 9, 1821* (Boston: Office of the Daily Advertiser, 1853; repr. by Da Capo, 1971); Matthew H. Crocker, *The Magic of the Many: Josiah Quincy and the Rise of Mass Politics in Boston, 1800–1830* (Amherst: University of Massachusetts Press, 1999); *William Lloyd Garrison, 1805–1879, The Story of His Life*, 277n1, citing Lewis Tappan.

74. Carl Patrick Burrowes, "A Child of the Atlantic: The Maine Years of John Brown Russwurm," *Maine History* 47, no. 2 (July 2013): 181, lists the Portland *Eastern Argus*, September 12, 1826 reprinted in eight other papers.

75. See *FJ*, December 19, 1828, for a speech by Walker explaining its "primary object . . . to unite the colored population, so far, throughout the United States of America, as may be practicable and expedient; forming societies, opening, extending, and keeping up correspondences, and not withholding any thing which may have the least tendency to meliorate *our* miserable condition"; as early as 1810, when the respected minister Thomas Paul spoke in Salem, "the wags of the town put a paper of dogrel rhymes in print & distributed them," suggesting that black men's rise was the reason for tearing them down (*Diary of William Bentley*, 3:490 [January 14, 1810]); Waldstreicher, *In the Midst of Perpetual Fetes*, 336 passim offers a subtle analysis of how these

toasts "explicitly comment on . . . variously divisive and unifying matters, but in a way that discredits blacks themselves, rather than any other class or partisan group," while noting that "despite their racist intent," the Bobalition parodies portrayed "blacks as remarkably aware of contemporary news and passionately committed to the particular meanings that public culture might have for them" (338); *Grand and Splendid BO-BALITION of Slavery, And "Great Annibersary Fussible," by de Africum Shocietee of Bosson* [dated "Uly 15, 1822"]; *Splendid Celebration of the "Bobalition" of Slavery, by the African Society* (dated "Bosson, Uly 14, 1823").

76. Lewis Bunker Rohrbach, ed., *Boston Taxpayers in 1821* (Camden, ME: Picton, 1988, orig. pub. 1822), lists seven of these men as taxpayers and thus voters: L. M. Blancard (190); Domingo Williams (192); Porter Tidd (179, 185); Thomas Dalton (56); Thomas Cole (42, 49); John G. Barbadoes (20); and George B. Holmes (90); and others presumably came later, like Walker; *Salem Gazette*, October 21, 1823, for Randamie's marriage, referring to his birthplace, and *Boston Patriot and Mercantile Advertiser*, February 20, 1828 for the bear grease; for Blancard, see the *Boston Gazette*, August 19, 1824, on his new shop, advertising for a journeyman and "a col'd Boy, as an apprentice"; similarly, Thomas Dalton opened a shop "to Polish Gentlemen's BOOTS & SHOES," hoping "to merit the custom of the enlightened gentlemen of this metropolis" (*Boston Intelligencer*, July 25, 1818), and James Gould sold "Soap, Candles, Palm Oil," and much more at his store in Charlestown (*Boston Patriot*, March 5, 1830); *Boston Gazette*, July 2, 1825, advertisement for G. B. Holmes's "Conabar," a "Fashionable Hair Cutting Establishment," and *Boston Intelligencer*, November 19, 1825; *Columbian Centinel*, November 12, 1828, depicts a young aristocrat, accompanied by razor and scissors, and Holmes's expertise in the "True Delineation of the present prevailing mode of cutting the hair in France and England, altogether different from the style here," following "the rules of physiognomy," with a separate ladies' salon; *Columbian Centinel*, October 3, 1830, on the "Bower of Fashion," run by "Hilton, Perfumer & Decorator, and successor to the late George B. Holmes," who "has taken that elegant and spacious establishment" and begs "the attention of the young gentlemen of Harvard University, whose patronage has already been so liberally extended." Tidd worked the region; see *Essex Register*, November 18, 1824, informing "the Ladies and Gentlemen of Salem and its vicinity, that he can furnish them with Music for Cotillion Parties, Balls or Assemblies," with "Orders left at John Remond's Oyster Shop, Front street"; the *New-Hampshire Gazette*, December 3, 1833, reprinted Tidd's *Boston Gazette* obituary, as a man "extensively known among the votaries of pleasure in this vicinity, where he had officiated as the leader of a cotillion band for twenty years or more"; *Boston Traveler*, January 13, 1832; *Columbian Centinel*, January 14, 1832. A window into these men's expertise is Robert Roberts, *The House-Servant's Directory, or a Monitor for Private Families Comprising Hints on the Arrangement and Performance of Servants' Work, with an Introduction by Graham Russell Hodges* (Armonk, NY: M. E. Sharpe, 1998), orig. pub. in 1827. Roberts was born in Charleston circa 1780, and worked for the wealthy merchant Nathan Appleton for many years, until moving to former governor Christopher Gore in 1825. He died a wealthy man in 1860, worth more than $7,500. His "monitor" was published in three editions. New Bedford will be examined in chap. 7. Nantucket will not be addressed, but had a substantial black petit bourgeoisie; see Lorin Lee Cary and Francine C. Cary, "Absalom F. Boston, His Family, and Nantucket's Black Community,"

Historic Nantucket (Summer 1977): 15–22, for a black sea captain and merchant, and his family network.

77. *Salem Gazette*, August 26, 1825, from Boston *Centinel*, repr. in at least one southern newspaper, *Pensacola Gazette*, October 1, 1825 (this linkage was not unique, as when black Baltimoreans gathered to celebrate France's belated recognition of the Black Republic, their final toast saluted "President Adams, Boyer and Bolivar"; Andrew K. Diemer, *The Politics of Black Citizenship: Free African Americans in the Mid-Atlantic Borderland, 1817–1863* [Athens: University of Georgia Press, 2016], 41); *Columbian Centinel*, January 27, 1827; *Boston Gazette*, February 5, 1827.

78. *New-England Galaxy*, July 14, 1820; see *New-England Palladium*, July 16, 1819, "The Committee of Arrangements of the Africans and their Descendants, present their grateful thanks to the Honourable Selectmen and Gentlemen of Boston, for the protection and countenance received from them on the celebration of 14th instant"; *National Aegis* (Worcester), February 13, 1828; for Walker's scrupulousness, see *Boston Traveler*, September 26, 1826, describing how "a man came into the shop of the Subscriber and offered for sale a pair of Horseman's Pistols and a Portmanteau," leaving the pistols but Walker averred that "circumstances induce me to believe they were stolen, and the owner can have them by paying for advertisement"; three years later, subsequent to his trial, Walker was still placing such ads. See *Columbian Centinel*, June 3, 1829, describing how a "William Die," claiming to be from Providence, had tried to sell a "Surtout Coat and Vests," and when Walker called for a police officer, he "ran off, leaving the things in my possession."

79. *Maine Cultivator and Hallowell Gazette*, January 3, 1846; by 1813, Manuel was informing "his old customers and the public" of a new location (*Portland Gazette and Maine Advertizer*, May 24, 1813). H. H. Price and Gerald E. Talbot, *Maine's Visible Black History: The First Chronicle of Its People* (Gardiner, ME: Tilbury House, 2006), 43, quoting *Portland Daily Press*, May 30, 1891; *Eastern Argus*, September 19, 1826, signed by Ruby, C. C. Manuel, Job L. Wentworth, John Siggs, Caleb Jonson, and Clemant Tomson.

80. *Portland Gazette and Maine Advertiser*, April 25, 1814 and November 12, 1822; *Gazette of Maine*, July 5, 1825; *Portland Advertiser*, August 19, 1825; *American Patriot*, November 11, 1825; *Eastern Argus*, April 11, May 9, and June 13, 1826.

81. He was not the first "royal slave" repatriated home; see Richard S. Newman, "Liberation Technology: Black Printed Protest in the Age of Franklin," *Early American Studies* 8, no. 1 (Winter 2010): 181 on Job Ben Solomon, taken in 1730, who ended up in Maryland, from where he wrote a letter in Arabic that led to his return via London; Terry Alford, *Prince among Slaves: The True Story of an African Prince Sold into Slavery in the American South* (New York: Oxford University Press, 2007, 30th Anniversary Edition), 129; *Boston Traveler*, August 26, 1828.

82. Natchez *Statesman and Gazette*, October 16, 1828; Alford, *Prince among Slaves*, 147–52.

83. Peter P. Hinks, *To Awaken My Afflicted Brethren: David Walker and the Problem of Antebellum Slave Resistance* (University Park: Pennsylvania State University Press, 1997) is definitive. Otis to the mayor of Savannah, February 10, 1830, quoted in Hinks, ed., *David Walker's Appeal to the Coloured Citizens of the World* (University Park: Pennsylvania State University Press, 2000), 98–99; Hasan Crockett, "The In-

cendiary Pamphlet: David Walker's Appeal in Georgia," *JNH* 86, no. 3 (Summer 2001): 305–18, adds considerable detail; *Journal of Commerce* repr. in the *Philadelphia Inquirer*, April 3, 1830; Floyd quoted in Henry Irving Tragle, *The Southampton Slave Revolt of 1831: A Compilation of Source Material* (Amherst: University of Massachusetts Press, 1971), 276.

84. Anne-Marie Taylor, *Young Charles Sumner and the Legacy of the American Enlightenment, 1811–1851* (Amherst: University of Massachusetts Press, 2001), 74.

85. *CA*, September 11, 1841; *Proceedings of the Colored National Convention, Held in Franklin Hall, Sixth Street, Below Arch, Philadelphia, October 16th, 17th and 18th, 1855* (Salem, NJ: Printed at the National Standard Office, 1856), 30, repr. in Bell, *Minutes of the Proceedings*. White men also evoked the New England trope of equality, like the Whig delegate at the 1846 New York constitutional convention arguing for "equal suffrage" by pointing out that "it adopted, [it] would place us upon the same boring as Vermont, Massachusetts and Rhode Island. He thought we might with safety assume the position which they occupy" (*AEJ*, October 2, 1846). After the defeat of "equal suffrage" in New York's referendum one month later, a Vermont editor remarked, "Were we citizens of such a State, we should blush at its name. As it is, we have no occasion for blushing in this respect. Vermont, from the commencement of her existence as a State, has ever placed the white and the colored man on the same footing; and we have cause of gratitude to the framers of our government that it is so"; *Vermont Chronicle*, repr. in *Boston Recorder*, December 31, 1846; William C. Nell, *The Colored Patriots of the American Revolution, with Sketches of Several Distinguished Colored Persons, to Which is Added a Brief Survey of the Condition and Prospects of Colored Americans* (Boston: Robert F. Wallcut, 1855), 111.

Chapter Five

1. See the Appendix for a prosopography based on the 1850 federal census.

2. *Eastern Argus*, April 7, 1870.

3. Louis C. Hatch, *Maine: A History* (New York: American Historical Society, 1919), 1:72, on how "opposition to the war [of 1812] and the Government found one of its most radical leaders in Samuel Fessenden," and Robert J. Cook, *Civil War Senator: William Pitt Fessenden and the Fight to Save the American Republic* (Baton Rouge: Louisiana State University Press, 2011), 11, describing the older Fessenden as "one of the district's most combative Federalists" and a lawyer for the Great Proprietors. He served in the Massachusetts legislature, 1814–19, represented Portland in Maine's legislature in the late 1820s, and was a major general of the state militia from 1818 to 1832.

4. Harry Gratwick, *Hidden History of Maine* (Charleston, SC: History Press, 2010), 77, for Ruby's 1834 advertisement in the *Portland Directory*, and *Lowell Daily Citizen and News*, November 24, 1874, from the *Portland Transcript*: "He drove the first hack on the streets of Portland; many of our older citizens can remember when he and Alex. Stevenson were about the only hack drivers in town"; *William Lloyd Garrison, 1805–1879, The Story of His Life, Told By His Children*, vol. 1, *1805–1835* (New York: Century and Co., 1885), 289; *Portland Advertiser*, October 29, 1832, and April 8, 1833 (on Ruby's appointment); *Eastern Argus*, March 16, 1821, reporting a new "Act providing for the due observation of the Lord's Day."

5. *Weekly Eastern Argus*, November 13, 1832 (earlier in *Tri-Weekly Argus*, November 7); repr. in the Whigs' *Portland Advertiser*, November 26, 1832.

6. *American Advocate*, July 30, 1834 (Hallowell); *Delaware Gazette*, repr. in *New-Hampshire Gazette*, October 7, 1834, and December 1, 1834, adding that at a convention earlier that year, a black man "was appointed and sat on the Select Committee of that body to nominate Mr. [Peleg] Sprague for Governor."

7. *Portland Advertiser*, April 6, 1825, April 28, 1826, and April 2, 1830 (in the latter year, John Robinson was named one of forty-one fire wardens; the one Portlander with that name was a black man in the 1820 census; none of these positions was salaried, as almost no one in Portland's government was paid a full-time wage—in 1828, the chairman of the selectmen received $120, the Town Clerk $30, and the Police Inspector $200, with only the treasurer and collector paid $750); *Eastern Argus*, November 11, 1828 and July 2, 8, and August 26, 1834; *American Advocate* (Hallowell), July 30, 1834 (James Bowes is on the separate list of Portland's black heads of households in the 1820 and 1830 manuscript censuses, as James Boaz in the latter case, with neither the census nor a search of newspapers finding any other man with this name in Portland; an indication of how these men functioned as a cohort in business as well as politics is that ten years earlier, C. C. Manuel had formed Maine's first brass band, with himself on flute, Bowes [or Boas] on bass drum, Skillings on bassoon, and three other men on clarinet, cymbals, and French horn); H. H. Price and Gerald E. Talbot, *Maine's Visible Black History: The First Chronicle of Its People* (Gardiner, ME: Tilbury House, 2006), 43; *American Advocate* (Hallowell), October 29, 1834; for Ruby's listing as a city officer, see *Portland Advertiser*, April 12, 1836, April 4, 1837, and April 10, 1838; the 1834–35 appointments cannot be found, although the Whigs dominated Portland throughout and it is likely Ruby maintained his position.

8. Hatch, *Maine*, 1:289 on how a meeting of the Maine Anti-Slavery Society was almost mobbed in Portland that year, with the Whigs quite hostile; *Washington Globe* quoted in *Vermont Gazette*, August 30, 1836; *Richmond Enquirer*, September 30, 1836.

9. *CA*, January 9, 1841; *Richmond Enquirer*, October 9, 1840 (Smith wrote the Van Buren administration's *Washington Globe*, so his allegations were reprinted nationwide; see *Portland Advertiser*, October 20, 1840, referring to "the Alabama Loco Foco paper received here" with "false statements regarding Mr. Fessenden," that his father had turned out black voters with a placard "containing the words 'No Slavery in the District'"); *Portland Advertiser*, October 13, 1840; *Ohio Statesman*, November 3, 1840; *CA*, November 7, 1840.

10. *Emancipator*, October 22, 1840.

11. Reinhard Johnson, "The Liberty Party in Maine, 1840–1848: The Politics of Anti-Slavery Reform," *Maine Historical Society Quarterly* 19, no. 3 (Winter 1980): 137–38, notes that the "greatest strength" of Maine abolitionists "was their unity," in that they never divided, with Garrison "almost unanimously disliked"; see Fessenden's obituary in the *New-Bedford Mercury*, April 2, 1869: "He received colored persons into his house, he took them with him to church, he visited them in their families, and encouraged them in every way to give them self-respect and a place in society" (Garrison's bitterness toward the Liberty men did not extend to the general, who was reelected a vice president of the Garrisonian American Anti-Slavery Society in 1842; see *Libera-*

tor, May 27, 1842); *Emancipator*, June 3, 1841, includes an advertisement for "Reuben Ruby's Oyster and Eating Room" in lower Manhattan.

12. Hatch, *Maine*, 2:313, 2:318.

13. *CA*, July 3, 1841, on a meeting convened by Freeman, Lewis, and Niles that resolved "to hold a Convention of the people of color in this State . . . for mutual consultation and general benefit of our people"; *CA*, September 4, 1841, for the call, proposing "an immediate effort for our moral and intellectual elevation," a convention to consider education, the plight of the slaves, intemperance, and "the future occupations of our offspring"; *Liberty Standard*, October 19, 1842. Black Portlanders continued collaborating with General Fessenden in antislavery work, like the annual "First of August" celebrations; see *Portland Advertiser*, August 8, 1843. As elsewhere in New England, the Liberty Party brought in black speakers, including the ex-slaves, Lewis and Milton Clarke; see *Liberty Standard*, June 13, July 4, 11, and 18, 1844, on their speaking during and after the state convention. A sampling of dozens of meetings in the Maine Party's *Liberty Standard*, listing hundreds of men, shows no prominent black Mainers participating, and the Free Soil State Convention on September 27, 1848 included no black delegates (*Liberty Standard*, August 10, 1848; *Free Soil Republican*, October 5, 1848); *Portland Advertiser*, March 26, 1844, listed Niles as a member of his ward's Vigilant Committee, and April 16, 1844, reported his appointment by the Common Council; see also March 18, 1845, listing him on the Vigilant Committee and as a vote distributor. He was reappointed a tythingman annually; see *Advertiser*, March 18, 1845, April 21, 1846, April 20, 1847, April 24, 1849, April 19, 1850.

14. A good example is the 1842 governor's race, when the party more than doubled its 1841 statewide total, from 1,662 to 3,700. In Portland, however, they polled only 3 percent (61 votes), while in Bangor, they racked up 14 percent (161); see *Liberty Standard*, September 28, 1842; July 1, 1844 (*The Liberator* had reprinted this article on June 28, one notes).

15. *Portland Advertiser*, August 17 and November 13, 1844.

16. F. Mark Terison, "Macon Bolling Allen: A Milestone for Maine," *Maine Bar Journal* (October 2000): 234–38; the original story from the *Portland American* appeared in the *North American and Daily Advertiser* (Philadelphia), July 11, 1844, *Maine Cultivator and Hallowell Gazette, Boston Evening Transcript*, and *Cape Ann Light* (MA), July 13, 1844, *New York Commercial Advertiser*, July 16, 1844, *Boston Weekly Messenger*, July 17, 1844, *Vermont Phoenix* (Brattleboro), and *Times-Picayune* (New Orleans, repr. from *Providence Journal*), July 19, 1844, *Hallowell Cultivator*, July 20, 1844, quoting *Belfast Republican, Portsmouth Journal of Literature and Politics, Niles' Register*, and *Poughkeepsie Journal*, July 27, 1844, *Auburn Journal and Advertiser* (NY), August 7, 1844.

17. Price and Talbot, *Maine's Visible Black History*, 158; *Maine Cultivator and Hallowell Gazette*, October 16, 1841, April 22, 1843, and September 18, 1847 ("Robert Benjamin Lewis of this town, has an invention . . . pronounced by good judges to be much superior"); Gratwick, *Hidden History*, 74–75.

18. *Free Soil Republican* (the just-renamed *Liberty Standard*), September 21, 1848; *Eastern Argus*, quoted in *Portland Advertiser*, November 14, 1848.

19. *Portland Advertiser*, November 14, 1848; *Liberator*, November 16, 1849.

20. Perhaps not incidentally, in the 1850s, Portland centered trade with Cuba, as "one of the main entrepots of sugar and molasses" (David Carey, Jr., "Latin American Influences in Nineteenth- and Twentieth-Century Portland," in *Creating Portland: History and Place in Northern New England*, ed. Joseph A. Conforti [Durham: University of New Hampshire Press, 2005], 95); *NE*, September 20, 1855, quoting *National Intelligencer*; Samuel Wells in 1856 was Maine's last Democratic governor until 1911.

21. *Portland Inquirer*, September 19, 1850, indicating nearly all votes for Free Soil legislative candidates came from Ward One (40 to 49 ballots for the three seats, with the leading Whig getting 214 and 173 for the leading Democrat); *Eastern Argus*, September 4, 1856 and September 7, 1860; *Portland Advertiser*, March 8, 1859, quoting the *Argus*; *Liberator*, November 1, 1850 for meeting; *Portland Daily Advertiser*, November 27, 1849, from *Bangor Whig*, on how Ruby "has shown us a specimen of gold dug by him, in California, weighing ten and a half ounces. . . . Mr. Ruby . . . remained in the mines about four months, during which time, he collected about three thousand dollars of gold"; Kent quoted in Don E. Fehrenbacher, *The Dred Scott Case: Its Significance in American Law and Politics* (New York: Oxford University Press, 1978), 354; *FDP*, February 2, 1855. The state's reputation as exceptionally friendly was well established. In 1851, the Reverend Samuel R. Ward noted in his newspaper, "The State of Maine offers better advantages, in our judgment, to emigrants, than any other State in the Union" (*IC*, August 23, 1851).

22. *Boston Courier*, March 9, 1854; *Schenectady Reflector*, March 10, 1854; *Times-Picayune*, attributing *Boston Post*, March 16, 1854; *Portland Advertiser*, March 15, 1854; *Philadelphia Press*, July 22, 1858, from *St. Louis Democrat*.

23. *Portland Advertiser*, September 23, 1856; *Liberator*, October 19, 1860; see S. B. Becket, *The Portland Directory and Reference Book for 1856–7* (Portland, ME: Brown Thurston, 1856), 243, and *Daily Eastern Argus*, April 14, 1863, for listings of Groves as a tythingman (as late as March 7, 1872, the Republican *Portland Daily Press* noted with satisfaction that Groves, "the oldest colored man in town, came out to vote yesterday. The weight of his 104 years was too much for the Democrats. It flatted them out," and his obituary later that year described a paradigmatic life: born in Maryland before the Revolution, hero of a shipboard fight against a French privateer in 1809, a favorite cook" who "could choose his vessel and employer. . . . When unfitted by age for going to seas . . . [he] collected 'old junk' about the wharves, which he picked into oakum and sold to the calkers" [*Portland Daily Press*, August 5, 1872]); *Eastern Argus*, September 16, 1867, an advertisement for "Mechanics and Laboring Men!" promoting injury insurance, endorsed by thirteen men, including Ruby, "Porter in Custom House"; *Eastern Argus*, September 11, 1868, "The Office Holder's Army," listing dozens of lucrative jobs at the Custom House.

24. *Liberator*, August 28, 1857; W. Jeffrey Bolster, *Black Jacks: African American Seamen in the Age of Sail* (Cambridge, MA: Harvard University Press, 1997), 172–74, describes how U.S. attorney general William Wirt had ruled in 1821 that "free persons of color" were not citizens and thus could not "be qualified to command vessels," leading to a black captain losing his license in Norfolk, but that Wirt's dictum was largely "ignored in the North"; *National Era*, August 27, 1857, reproduces the Maine decision; John Appleton, *The Rules of Evidence: Stated and Discussed* (Philadelphia: T. & J. W. Johnson, 1860), 271–72; David M. Gold, "Chief Justice John Appleton," *Maine*

Historical Quarterly 18, no. 4 (Spring 1979): 193–207; and Gold, "Constitutional Problems in Maine During the Civil War Era, 1857–1872," *Maine Historical Quarterly* 22, no. 3 (Winter, 1983): 128.

25. See *Portland Daily Press*, October 8, 1870, "Reception of Hon. G. T. Ruby . . . accompanied by Mayor Kingsbury, Rev. Doct. Shailer, Capt. E. P. Talbot, Mr. Reuben Ruby and wife." The mayor announced "the pleasure it gave him to see the prejudice against the colored people so far done away here as well at the South, when a Portland boy can be received in such a manner and come home honored with . . . so high an office"; Gratwick, *Hidden History,* 77.

Chapter Six

1. Ruggles's aid to fugitives in a Democratic-dominated city was one of the most impressive forms of nonelectoral politics, making him nationally famous; see Leslie M. Harris, *In the Shadow of Slavery: African Americans in New York City, 1626–1863* (Chicago: University of Chicago Press, 2004), 206–11, on this "mass movement" involving 10 percent of the city's black population, and Graham Russell Gao Hodges, *David Ruggles: A Radical Black Abolitionist and the Underground Railroad in New York City* (Chapel Hill: University of North Carolina Press, 2010); *New Bedford Mercury,* June 12, 1829 and July 26, 1833; Frederick Douglass, *My Bondage and My Freedom* (1855; repr., New York, 2003), 255.

2. *Philadelphia Press,* January 2, 1858, letter from a New Bedford Democrat, correcting a claim: "The whole number of *negro votes* would not exceed two hundred, instead of eight hundred and sixty"; Kathryn Grover, *The Fugitive's Gibraltar: Escaping Slaves and Abolitionism in New Bedford, Massachusetts* (Amherst: University of Massachusetts Press, 2001), 56 and 8–9, on the record of the city's overseers of the poor and a local church's rolls documenting hundreds not named elsewhere. Like anyone writing about New Bedford, I rely on Grover's deeply researched account.

3. Paul Frymer, *Uneasy Alliances: Race and Party Competition in America* (Princeton, NJ: Princeton University Press, 1999), 8, describes "electoral capture" as "those circumstances when the group has no choice but to remain in the party. The opposing party does not want the group's vote, so the group cannot threaten its own party's leaders with defection. The party leadership, then, can take the group for granted because it recognizes that, short of abstention or an independent (and usually electorally suicidal) third party, the group has nowhere else to go."

4. Grover, *Fugitive's Gibraltar,* 22–23 and 26: in 1855, per capita wealth per taxpayer was an astounding $5,979.84; per individual, $1,265.83; *Republican Standard,* August 21, 1851.

5. Zephaniah Pease, George A. Hough, and William L. Sayer, *New Bedford, Massachusetts: Its History, Institutions, and Attractions* (New Bedford, MA: Board of Trade, 1889), 40–41; Grover, *Fugitive's Gibraltar,* 20–22, on the founding families (Coffins, Ricketsons, Rotches, Tabers, and Howlands) intermarrying with later arrivals like the Rodmans, Congdons, Grinnells, and Anthonys.

6. Camillus Griffith quoting Sylvanus Macy in Grover, *Fugitive's Gibraltar,* 95; F. N. Boney, Richard L. Hume, and Rafia Zakar, *God Made Man, Man Made the Slave: The Autobiography of George Teamoh* (Macon, GA: Mercer University Press,

1990), 105; *Narrative of the Life of Frederick Douglass, An American Slave* (1845), in *Frederick Douglass: Autobiographies* (New York: Library of America, 1994), 92.

7. Grover, *Fugitive's Gibraltar*, 186 (Congdon) and 218, on a meeting where many attacked Grinnell for avoiding the vote on the Fugitive Slave Act of 1850, and earlier failure to support abolition in the District of Columbia. The links between two such men are evident in the diary of a third, Samuel Rodman (Zephaniah W. Pease, *The Diary of Samuel Rodman: A New Bedford Chronicle of Thirty-Seven Years, 1821–1859* [New Bedford: Reynolds Printing Company, 1927], hereafter *Rodman Diary*). Remembered as a friend of "Temperance, peace freedom [*sic*], the equal rights of all classes and colors" (9), Rodman was a leading merchant, industrialist, philanthropist, Whig, and abolitionist. Over three decades, he attended antislavery meetings, circulated petitions, and engaged with movement leaders like Garrison, while often recording his private conviction that Clay and Webster were right that "the agitation of the matter by Northern men . . . ought to be suspended and left to the calm reflection of the people most deeply and immediately interested" (190, February 18, 1839). He consistently supported Grinnell as "a very loving old Friend and an esteemed minister" (325, June 22, 1855). His abolitionism peaked in 1856, in horror at "the late outrage at Washington [Sumner's caning] and the enormities . . . now performed in Kansas under the sanction of our vile administration . . . which go far to fasten [the] conclusion in the minds of this section that Garrison's motto is right 'No Union with slaveholders'" (328, May 25–June 1, 1856), chairing the committee to aid Kansas Free Soilers (331, October 15, 1856). Yet five years earlier, Rodman and his brother sought to expand their textile operations via "the cooperation of Southern capital to remove our mill to Georgia . . . on such very favorable terms" (305, November 20, 1851).

8. See *Rodman Diary*, 238 (August 9, 1842), on a meeting of the Bristol County Anti-Slavery Society where "a disorderly rabble" drowned out the speakers, leading finally to "a melee," in which one black man was "brutally attacked in making his way to the door and rec'd and gave some hard blows"; Grover, *Fugitive's Gibraltar*, 19–21; *New Bedford Register*, May 3, 1842.

9. Local immediatism stirred in October 1831, when Benjamin Lundy visited. Soon Samuel Rodman began circulating petitions urging emancipation in the District of Columbia (*Rodman Diary*, 90, October 23, 1831, and 95 January 11–16, 1832), gathering hundreds of signatures including town leaders; *Whaleman's Shipping List and Merchants' Transcript*, August 28, 1855, "Tax-payers in New Bedford," records Ricketson as worth $46,000, Robeson $83,500, and Congdon $14,500; Frederick B. Tolles, "The New-Light Quakers of Lynn and New Bedford," *New England Quarterly* 32, no. 3 (September 1959): 291–319; *New Bedford Gazette*, April 27, 1835. Rodman's diary underlines temperance's importance to abolitionist Whigs. He campaigned continually to suppress illegal liquor sales among the town's sailors.

10. Daniel Ricketson, *The History of New Bedford, Bristol County, Massachusetts, Including a History of the Old Township of Dartmouth and the Present Townships of Westport, Dartmouth, and Fairhaven, from Their Settlement to the Present Time* (New Bedford, MA: Published by the author, 1858), 256 (the Cuffes and others did send a petition, but, as explained in chap. 5, the right had already been granted); *NE*, August 27, 1857, reprinting the *Fall River News* in light of *Dred Scott*, that "although the Collector believed black men had no rights that white men were bound to respect, yet he was

bound in this instance to respect the right of Capt. Cuffe. . . . President Madison regarded Captain Cuffe as a citizen of the United States."

11. *Liberator*, September 22, 1832; *CA*, July 22, 1837 (the senior Rotch was not, in fact, the town's founder); an 1831 attempt by the School Committee to establish "a separate Public School for the colored children" was rebuffed (*Rodman Diary*, 83, April 24, 1831).

12. See W. Jeffrey Bolster, *Black Jacks: African American Seamen in the Age of Sail* (Cambridge, MA: Harvard University Press, 1997), 177, on 700 black men serving as officers and harpooners in the 1840s and 1850s, albeit this labor was "dirtier, more dangerous, more estranging and worse paying than merchant or coastal shipping"; Richard Johnson's advertisement in the *New-Bedford Mercury*, February 25, 1814, reported he had "at his shop, in Water-Street . . . a good assortment of W. I. Goods, Groceries, etc.," followed by a list of teas, spices, tobaccos, crockery, paper, shoes, and more; Sidney Kaplan, "Lewis Temple and the Hunting of the Whale," *New England Quarterly* 26, no. 1 (March 1953): 78–88; *Liberator*, September 22, 1832, naming William Irvins "the best cooper in New-Bedford," Alexander Howard as a "first rate workman," Temple and William P. Powell as "first rate blacksmiths," William Cook, "a first rate rigger and navigator," who "can carry a ship to any part of the world. There are twenty of this class," and a "first rate house carpenter and one ship carpenter."

13. Grover, *Fugitive's Gibraltar*, 88, 121, 135; *CA*, July 22, 1837; *Alexandria Gazette*, August 14, 1837 (from *New Bedford Gazette*) on how "The Brig Rising States owned, by a company of colored men in this town" had put to sea very impressively; Grover, *Fugitive's Gibraltar*, 39. On E. R. Johnson's fortune, see *New York Commercial Advertiser*, August 28, 1874, reprinting the *Boston Globe*.

14. *Liberator*, April 16, 1831, reprinting an "amusing account of a scene at the late election . . . from *New-Bedford Mercury*."

15. *New-Bedford Mercury*, November 13, 1835, reprinting a Democratic circular in *New Bedford Gazette* "on the morning of the election," urging "Antimasons and Jacksonmen" to unite to protect themselves from "WHIG MOBS"; *New-Bedford Mercury*, November 11, 1836.

16. *New-Bedford Mercury*, November 15, 1833; *New Bedford Gazette*, October 23, 1837. Everett beat Morton 789–610 that year in New Bedford, and 817–663 in the following; see *Boston Courier*, November 15, 1838.

17. *New-Bedford Mercury*, October 27 and November 3, 1837. In 1837, they also manifested "an organic sense of their own rights" by petitioning Massachusetts's legislature against southern laws restricting the rights of visiting free people; see Grover, *Fugitive's Gibraltar*, 133.

18. For further evidence of their influence, see the story from 1841 regarding a Democratic editor in Nashville, J. G. Harris, who was critically wounded after reproving two Whigs who insulted Jackson; see *Emancipator*, February 4, 1841, on how "while in Massachusetts," Harris was "considered an abolitionist, and was once nominated by his party for the legislature, with particular reference to the wishes of a large and respectable number of citizens of color in New Bedford."

19. Lee V. Chambers, *The Weston Sisters: An American Abolitionist Family* (Chapel Hill: University of North Carolina Press, 2015).

20. See Earl F. Mulderink III, "The Whole Town Is Ringing with It," *New England Quarterly* 61, no. 3 (September 1988): 341–57, a thorough account omitting the partisan

subtext; *New-Bedford Mercury*, January 29 and February 23, 1840; *Liberator*, March 6 and 13, 1840.

21. Deborah Weston to Maria Weston Chapman, November 8, 1839, and to Anne Warren Weston, November 25, 1839, Weston Sisters Papers, Boston Public Library.

22. *Nantucket Inquirer*, November 13, 1839; *New-Bedford Mercury*, November 28, 1839 (earlier, Lindsey had published their endorsement: "That we most heartily concur in the nomination of Hon NATHANIEL B. BORDEN, SETH WHITMARSH and FOSTER HOOPER, Esqrs. For SENATORS from this County, as they are our *tried friends*, and we recommend them to the support of all genuine abolitionists," *New-Bedford Mercury*, November 11, 1839); *New-Bedford Mercury*, November 28, 1839.

23. *Emancipator*, November 5, 1840 and December 11, 1842.

24. Bruce Laurie, *Beyond Garrison: Antislavery and Social Reform* (Cambridge: Cambridge University Press, 2005), 43 passim is the best account of the "scattering" policy. Corey M. Brooks, *Liberty Power: Antislavery Third Parties and the Transformation of American Politics* (Chicago: University of Chicago Press, 2016), 92–93, details the remarkable results in state and region: in 1841, more than eighty towns in Massachusetts went unrepresented in the General Court, and in the 1842 congressional elections, they "delayed choices in eleven New England districts (four in Maine, six in Massachusetts, and one in Vermont)." As a result, plurality rules were eventually adopted for state legislative elections in Maine in 1847, and for Congress in Vermont in 1848 (268n3).

25. *New-Hampshire Patriot*, October 19, 1840; the *Mercury* never mentioned Grinnell (July 23, 1841), but a detailed account appeared in the Democrats' *New Bedford Register*, July 28, 1841. The story was picked up by the *Philadelphia Inquirer*, July 26, 1841, *National Aegis* (Worcester), July 28, 1841, and *Connecticut Courant*, July 31, 1841.

26. Laurie, *Beyond Garrison*, 114; Grover, *Fugitive's Gibraltar*, 172; Louis Ruchames, "Jim Crow Railroads in Massachusetts," *American Quarterly* 8, no. 1 (Spring 1956): 61–75; Ruggles in *Liberator*, August 6, 1841 on "JUSTICE HENRY A. CRAPO AND LYNCH LAW," noting Crapo was "a stockholder in said company, and therefore lawfully rendered incapable of occupying the bench of justice under such circumstances"; *Liberator*, July 21, 1841, on a meeting regarding the "outrage recently committed upon the person of David Ruggles," featuring the Democrat John Bailey in the chair with French as a speaker; *New Bedford Register*, August 4, 1841; *Boston Daily Atlas*, July 23, 1841; *Pennsylvania Inquirer*, July 26, 1841; *American Traveller* (Boston), July 27, 1841; *National Aegis* (Worcester), July 28, 1841; *Georgetown Advocate* (Washington, DC), July 29, 1841; *Newburyport Herald*, July 30, 1841; *North American and Daily Advertiser* (Philadelphia), July 30, 1841; *Schenectady Reflector*, July 30, 1841; *Connecticut Courant* (Hartford), July 31, 1841; *Floridian* (Tallahassee), August 7, 1841; *Alexandria Gazette*, December 3, 1841. See "The Autobiography of Rev. Thomas James," *Rochester History* 37, no. 4 (October 1975): 18 for another case in which Crapo "ruled that custom was law, and by custom colored people were not allowed to ride in cars in the company of white people. Furthermore railway corporations had the right to make their own regulations on such a subject, and consequently we had no cause of action."

27. *Liberator*, November 19, 1841; *Emancipator*, November 25, 1841.

28. *New-Bedford Mercury*, November 25, 1841 and *New Bedford Register*, November 24, 1841 (*The Emancipator* commented, "Mr. Stowell received ten votes above the

highest of his colleagues, and 24 more than the lowest; while four of the Liberty candidates together lack just ten votes of the highest on their ticket. As to the letter itself, we should think the experience of the last year will satisfy all real abolitionists of the value of such professions from those who continue to support pro-slavery parties," December 10, 1841).

29. *New-Bedford Mercury*, April 7, 1842; *New Bedford Register*, April 6, 1842; *New-Bedford Mercury*, November 23, 1842 (it is unclear if the lost city employment included black men; the annual lists of town officers did not include the lamplighters, although the black mariner Sylvanus Allen was a fireward in neighboring Fairhaven; see *New Bedford Mercury*, April 5, 1838); for election results, see *New Bedford Register*, November 16, 1842; *Boston Daily Atlas*, December 5, 1842; *Emancipator*, December 8, 1842 (the reference to losing "about $500 worth of employ" may refer to John Bailey, forced out of town by the Whigs; see *Liberator*, August 11, 1848, on a testimonial meeting); *Emancipator*, October 12, 1843.

30. *Emancipator*, September 14, 1843. After an 1844 "anti-Texas" meeting, Rodman commented, "Our collector, Rodney French, began one of his windy and forceless speeches [to run out the clock] . . . to keep in favor with the appointing power, the President, slave holder as he is and abolitionist as French has heretofore professed to be, but on which subject he is now careful to be very quiet" (*Rodman Diary*, 259, March 26, 1844).

31. *New Bedford Register*, November 1, 8, and 15, 1843 (the Liberty and "Abolitionist" slates received the same modest vote as before); *Emancipator*, October 5, 1843; William W. Crapo, "Extracts from the Diaries of John Quincy Adams and Charles Francis Adams, Relating to Visits to Nantucket and New Bedford," *The Old Dartmouth Historical Sketches* 47 (1919): 21, "We alighted from the cars and stepped into Mr. Grinnell's carriage."

32. *New Bedford Register*, October 22, 1844, reprinting *Nantucket Inquirer*; in September 1844, the Garrisonian *National Anti-Slavery Standard* (*NASS*) printed thousands of "Standard Extras" accusing Birney of embezzlement, calling him "the most objectionable candidate" and a "traitor in the camp" of abolitionism. Liberty men charged that Whigs exploited this implicit endorsement of Clay; see *NASS*, November 21, 1844, reprinting charges that "'Extras,' have been sent out by thousands, and sold to Whigs and Clay clubs to put down the Liberty party."

33. *Liberator*, November 1, 1844, describes Douglass and Remond disrupting "a Liberty Convention . . . with the story of financial misdeeds," and calling their own meeting, and since "the Whigs were holding a meeting at the Town Hall, at the same time . . . the major part of them came to our meeting"; *Liberator*, November 22, 1844, reprinting reports of Whig-Garrisonian collusion, for example, the Hartford *Christian Freeman* suggesting, "Douglass and Remond are in the pay of the Whigs" and *The Emancipator* insisting, "They must know they are being used as mere tools by men who would sell them at auction to the highest bidder," asking what could "induce a colored abolitionist" to back "the party which lauds and idolizes such a leader [as Clay]"; *Emancipator*, November 6, 1844, reporting an October 30 meeting.

34. *New-Bedford Mercury*, November 20 and June 5, 1846; *Boston Weekly Messenger*, November 13, 1844, reporting New Bedford's vote for Clay (1,251), Polk (813), and Birney (49). In 1843, the Whig, George A. Briggs, had defeated the Democrat, Marcus

Morton, 1,197 to 856, with Samuel Sewall, the Liberty candidate, receiving 52 votes (2.5 percent).

35. *Ballot Box*, October 31, 1840.

36. See *Emancipator*, October 27, 1842; March 9, 1843; August 24, 1843; October 12, 1843; November 3, 1843; November 6, 1844. The Johnsons did not carry all with them. At a meeting called by black Garrisonians in 1843, N. A. Borden proposed resolutions describing the upcoming National Convention of Colored Citizens as "exclusive in character . . . a useless waste of time and money," since "many of the prominent movers . . . in a time of trial, basely deserted the true friends of the slave . . . and went over to the ranks of new organization" (Liberty Party), which passed with only two dissenting votes; see *Liberator*, August 25, 1843.

37. *New Bedford Register*, June 28, 1843; Grover, *Fugitive's Gibraltar*, 314n27, on this Ruggles; *Liberator*, October 13, 1843; letter from Johnson in the Maine *Liberty Standard*, August 31, 1843, describing a lecture at Augusta's Baptist Church, quoted in C. Peter Ripley, ed., *The Black Abolitionist Papers*, vol. 3, *The United States, 1830–1846* (Chapel Hill: University of North Carolina Press, 1991), 413; *Liberator*, November 17, 1843.

38. *Liberator*, April 5 (the meeting included Sampson Perkins, Democratic selectman alongside well-known Whigs) and April 12, 1844.

39. See the Free Soilers' *Republican Standard*, September 12, 1850, listing residents paying an annual tax of $100, showing Howland's worth as $108,850.

40. *New-Bedford Mercury*, July 10, 1846; Grover, *Fugitive's Gibraltar*, 134, repeats Johnson's claim he was admitted to the bar in 1842, and the *Republican Standard*, October 6, 1859, reported on a Rhode Island case: "Henry rather astonished the Rhode Island people. Here his eloquence has been so long known, that his pleas at the bar excite no particular interest, not more than other distinguished advocates," quoting a Providence newspaper that "William Henry Johnson, (colored), Attorney at Law from the city of New Bedford, defended a case of divorce" and "all who heard his defense, say that it was one of the best ever made in the Supreme Court of Rhode Island on divorce cases," although a later town history reported that he "began to study law in the office of Francis L. Porter in 1860. He was admitted to the bar in 1864 and has continued to practice" (Leonard Bolles Ellis, *History of New Bedford and Its Vicinity, 1602–1892* [Syracuse, NY: D. Mason, 1892], 662); *New-Bedford Mercury*, April 16, 1847 on the coup in the ward meetings, and April 23, 1847 on the resulting election; *New-Bedford Mercury*, March 9, 1848; also May 19, 1848 on Johnson's appointment, apparently not the first black man to hold this post, as Douglass in 1853 called Johnson "the successor to 'Uncle Tom' Williams" (*FDP*, August 12, 1853); *New-Bedford Mercury*, October 12, 1849 on the "Howland Party"; *Republican Standard*, March 7, 1850, on the "Independent" Howland defeating a token Whig, 866 to 168, and March 6, 1851, on Howland getting 822 votes and "All others, 76."

41. *Emancipator*, July 26, 1848, on "Prospects of Cass in Bristol County."

42. *New-Bedford Mercury*, August 25 and September 8, 1848; *Massachusetts Spy*, September 13, 1848; *Emancipator*, September 20, 1848. One week earlier, it described how he "made a very eloquent speech, which was received with great applause."

43. *New-Bedford Mercury*, October 6, 20, and November 10, 1848; *NS*, November 18, 1848; *Republican Standard*, July 8, 1852.

44. Douglass, *My Bondage and My Freedom*, in *Frederick Douglass: Autobiographies*, 397.

45. Quoted in Grover, *Fugitive's Gibraltar*, 218–21; *Republican Standard*, October 10, 1850; for the administration's denouncing Scudder as agitator of the negro question," see *Emancipator*, December 19, 1850, and the *Mercury*'s angry reply that he was "not a South Carolina whig, a Mississippi whig, or even a Washington whig—but he is a Massachusetts whig and whig all over." The conservative *Boston Weekly Messenger*, December 25, 1850, noted "the correspondence . . . previous to the election, between Mr Scudder and a committee of the colored citizens of New Bedford," and on January 3, 1851, the *Mercury* quoted his letter, committing him to act "to prevent the admission of any new Slave State, or the organization of any new Slave Territorial Government."

46. *Republican Standard*, March 20, 1851; *Times-Picayune*, March 28, 1851, "The New Bedford Panic," and *Daily Union* (District of Columbia), March 21, 1851, from *Boston Courier*, "Tricks of the Agitators" mocking the "crazy abolitionists of this city" for circulating the story; *Republican Standard*, April 29, 1852; see Grover, *Fugitive's Gibraltar*, 263, on the replica bells French gave out, and how a "fugitive slave named James Williams is said to have rung another one, owned by French himself, from the rebuilt Liberty Hall" as John Brown was hanged; *Republican Standard*, October 2 and 30, 1851; *Daily Evening Standard*, April 1, 1851 (Rodman's diary often referred to French's ability to take over a meeting, as when a united temperance ticket was blocked by French's insistence on "equal distribution of town appointments among the different political parties," *Rodman Diary*, 217, March 20, 1841); *FDP*, March 17, 1854, a letter from T. Meyers Ward reporting on the reelection of "Rodney French, the champion of liberty, banner bearer of the free"; *Republican Standard*, March 7, 1850, on Howland's "Independent Ticket" including many Whigs; *Republican Standard*, March 10, 1853, on French's "Union" or "People's Ticket," broader than the Free Soil Party, which continued polling a minority vote in county elections; *Republican Standard*, November 17, 1853, lists the town's votes for governor: in 1852, Clifford received a majority of 1,184 versus Mann, the Free Soiler, with 791, and a Democrat, Bishop, with 346; the following year, the Whig gubernatorial candidate, Emory Washburn, got 1,263 votes versus 666 for Free Soiler Henry Wilson, and 507 for the Democrat, Bishop.

47. *New-Bedford Mercury*, January 23, 1852, "Mr. Henry Johnson, chief of the lamplighting department, yesterday exhibited to us some of the oil furnished for the street lamps, perfectly congealed by the cold"; *Republican Standard*, October 10, 1850; also November 6, 1851, on an abolitionist lecture where "a knot of gentlemen in a particular place in the hall . . . took occasion to hiss whenever the whigs were alluded to, but who seemed much pleased when allusions were made to other parties. After Mr Foster had concluded, a colored man got up and exhorted his brethren not to be led astray . . . but rather to attend the polls upon the 10th day of November, and vote the free soil ticket"; *Republican Standard*, May 8, 1851; also September 4, 1851 (a meeting to select fifteen state convention delegates, including Leonard W. Collins), and October 16, 1851 (a county convention with speeches including "Messrs. Church, Lapham, and Johnson," presumably Ezra Johnson, as "the latter gentlemen gave some interesting accounts in regard to the anti-slavery cause in California"), September 16, 1852 (fifteen delegates elected to the state convention, including two black men, John Goings and Ezra Johnson, with David W. Ruggles and John Briggs among the thirty substitutes),

October 15, 1852 (the First District Free Democratic Convention with Ezra Johnson as one of three secretaries), October 27, 1853 (another county convention, where Henry Remington was one of five vice presidents, with John Goings on the three-man committee to choose a County Committee); for black voters, see *Republican Standard*, September 16 and October 7, 1852.

48. *FDP*, October 22, 1852, reprinting the October 2 and October 5 correspondence between Mann and Johnson, and minutes of the October 11 meeting, from the *Standard*.

49. *Boston Daily Bee*, May 24, 1853; *Republican Standard*, May 26, 1853; *Newport Mercury*, May 6, 1854; also *NASS*, May 20, 1854.

50. *Liberator*, June 23, 1854.

51. See *FDP*, September 28, 1855. The lack of published delegate lists leaves it unclear whether the New Bedford or Bristol County delegations included black men; *Republican Standard*, November 6, 1856 (by then, French was long out of office, crushed by the former-Whig-turned-Know-Nothing George Howland in 1855, 1,836 to 715); *Republican Standard*, March 8, 1855 (as elsewhere, the "American Party" was largely a Whig effort to hang on to power); *NASS*, October 4, 1856, reprinting the *Standard* on an "An Anti-Slavery Convention . . . held at Liberty Hall."

52. In the first ballot for the county's congressional seat in November 1850, the Whig Scudder received 47 percent, the Democrat Charles B. Fessenden 25.5 percent, Free Soiler Simpson Hart 18 percent, and a fourth candidate 8.5 percent (*Republican Standard*, November 28, 1850); in 1851's gubernatorial race, it was Whig, 54 percent; Free Soiler, 24 percent; Democrat, 23 percent (*Republican Standard*, November 13, 1851); in 1852, in the county vote for governor, it was Whig, 44 percent; Free Soil, 29 percent; and Democrat, 27 percent; while in the city, the Free Soilers won 34 percent to the Whigs 51 percent, and the Democrats 15 percent, indicating the black vote's weight, a result duplicated the following year (*Republican Standard*, November 11, 1852 and November 17, 1853); *Republican Standard*, September 16, 1852 and April 29, 1852; *Republican Standard*, October 23, 1856 (the vote was Frémont, 1,800; Buchanan, 445; Fillmore, 423); *Republican Standard*, November 5, 1857); *Republican Standard*, December 10, 1857. Following a September 1855 "Fusion Meeting" joining Whigs like Henry Crapo and James B. Congdon with Free Soilers like Rodney French, black men no longer appear; see *Republican Standard*, September 20, 1855 (for their exclusion, see "Great Gathering of the People," October 18, 1855; "Second Grand Rally," October 25, 1855; "Republican District Convention," listing ninety men, October 16, 1856; a Frémont rally, October 23, 1856; "Republican Meeting," electing delegates for a Senatorial Convention, October 15, 1857; "Grand Rally of the Republicans," October 29, 1857; both "Citizens" and Republican meetings to nominate municipal officers, November 26, 1857; "Republican County Convention," December 3, 1857; "Senatorial Convention," October 21, 1858; "Seventh District Councillor Convention," plus city caucuses, October 28, 1858; "Republican Meeting," November 18, 1858; Republican Nominating Committee and "Citizens' Meeting," November 25, 1858; "Republican Meeting," September 15, 1859; "Republican County Convention," October 13, 1859; "Republican Meeting," October 27, 1859; Citizens Meeting "irrespective of party," November 24, 1859; "Republican Meeting," August 23, 1860; "Republican Caucus," September 27, 1860).

53. *FDP*, January 27, 1854, on a "correspondent of the New York Tribune writing from New Bedford" who passed "an intelligent looking Negro, trimming the street lamps," a recent fugitive; Grover, *Fugitive's Gibraltar*, 325, cites Henry Foster's and Thompson Hill's listing as lamplighters in the 1856 city directory; also Thomas Clark in the 1859 directory (328); *Republican Standard*, April 24, 1856 and *New-Bedford Mercury*, April 10, 1857; in 1856, black voters evidently supported the local "Citizens" ticket against the Know-Nothings, and Remington's replacing the incumbent superintendent was their reward. In 1855, the superintendent was paid $300 annually, the same amount as the city solicitor, and the messenger $350 (the mayor's salary was $800); see *Republican Standard*, April 26, 1855, September 11 and June 26, 1857.

54. See Mitch Kachun, *Festivals of Freedom: Memory and Meaning in African American Emancipation Celebrations, 1808–1915* (Amherst: University of Massachusetts Press, 2003); Jeffrey R. Kerr-Ritchie, *Rites of August First: Emancipation Day in the Black Atlantic World* (Baton Rouge: Louisiana State University Press, 2011); *Emancipator*, August 16, 1848; *Liberator*, August 15, 1851.

55. This account synthesizes reports in *FDP*, August 12, 1853 (by the editor), and *Liberator*, August 19 and 26, 1853 (the latter by William C. Nell).

56. This cadre overlapped little with the city's black property-holders, who resembled the Portlanders; see table A.2.

57. Hal Goldman, "Black Citizenship and Military Self-Presentation in Antebellum Massachusetts," *Historical Journal of Massachusetts* (Summer 1997): 157–83; William J. Watkins, *Our Rights as Men. An Address Delivered in Boston, Before the Legislative Committee on the Militia, February 24, 1853, by William J. Watkins, in Behalf of Sixty-Five Colored Petitioners, Praying for a Charter to Form an Independent Military Company* (Boston: Benjamin F. Roberts, 1853).

58. *Republican Standard*, November 1, 1850, reprinting the Boston *Chronotype*; *New-Bedford Mercury*, November 27 and June 25, 1857.

59. *Liberator*, May 28, 1858; *Republican Standard*, May 14, 1857, clearly a long-running effort; see request from Henry Johnson and others for $200, also denied, *Republican Standard*, July 22, 1852; *The New-Bedford Directory, Containing the City Register, a General Directory of Its Citizens, and a Special Directory of Trades, Professions, &c.* (New Bedford, MA: C. & A. Taber, 1849), 11. See also *New Bedford Directory*, 12–13 on the firemen's appointments and pay, noting, "The number connected to each company, and the annual compensation, are determined by the City Council." The 1839, 1841, 1845, 1852, and 1856 directories were also consulted. It seems unlikely that more obscure black men would have been enrolled but not their leaders.

60. *Republican Standard*, April 19, 1860; *Newport Mercury*, April 28, 1860; *Weekly Anglo-African*, April 28, 1860. The Negrophobic *Constitution* in Washington, DC, reported on May 2, 1860, "The negro-worshippers of New Bedford, Mass., have elected a black man named Thomas Bayne a member of the city council" but followed up on May 10 with a letter from New Brunswick saying, "Not quite so bad as that. . . . That a negro named Thomas Bayne received 107 votes for the office of councilman is sufficiently disgraceful. *He* was not elected, but a sound national democrat *was*."

61. *Boston Pilot*, November 18, 1860.

62. *Republican Standard*, November 15, 1860.

1. Patrick T. Conley, "No Landless Irish Need Apply: Rhode Island's Role in the Framing and Fate of the Fifteenth Amendment," *Rhode Island History* 68, no. 2 (Summer/Fall 2010): 79, "Only one in twelve or thirteen of the foreign-born of adult age was a voter," as of 1865; William G. McLoughlin, *Rhode Island: A History* (New York: W. W. Norton, 1986), 136. Robert J. Cottrol, *The Afro-Yankees: Providence's Black Community in the Antebellum Era* (Westport, CT: Greenwood, 1982) remains an outstanding study of black politics within the larger frame.

2. Patrick T. Conley and Matthew J. Smith, *Catholicism in Rhode Island: The Formative Era* (Providence, RI: Diocese of Providence, 1976), 42.

3. Petition from Irish leader Henry J. Duff in Conley and Smith, *Catholicism in Rhode Island*, 49, adding they did not "envy the colored population; on the contrary, they believe they have received nothing but what they are in justice entitled to; but, as the impression is abroad, that the colored race is inferior to the white and shaded population, the insult is more piercing"; *NS*, November 24, 1848.

4. McLoughlin, *Rhode Island*, 115, 120, 124.

5. Patrick J. Conley and Robert G. Flanders, Jr., *The Rhode Island State Constitution: A Reference Guide* (Westport, CT: Praeger, 2007), 11, suggests 75 percent of white men voted circa 1775; Patrick T. Conley, *Democracy in Decline: Rhode Island's Constitutional Development, 1776–1841* (Providence, RI: Rhode Island Historical Society, 1977), 219, reports 18 percent turnout in 1828, 22.4 percent in 1832, 24.1 percent in 1836, and 33.2 percent in 1840, when the national figure was 78 percent; *What a Ploughman Said About the "Hints to Farmers," Made Last April, by Men of "Trade"* (Kingston, RI: May 1829), 4. A few years later, Potter was derided as the "Duke of Kingston" controlling "about 100 freemen . . . by means of mortgages" (242).

6. Conley, *Democracy in Decline*, 222; McLoughlin, *Rhode Island*, 126; Edmund Burke, *Rhode Island in 1842. Majority Report of a Committee of Congress Appointed to Inquire into the Interference of the President in the Affairs of Rhode Island* (Washington, DC, 1844), 470; Sean Wilentz, *The Rise of American Democracy: Jefferson to Lincoln* (New York: W. W. Norton, 2005), 183; Jacob Frieze, *A Concise History, of the Efforts to Obtain an Extension of Suffrage in Rhode Island from the Year 1811 to 1842* (Providence, RI: B. F. Moore, 1842), 21–22.

7. Conley, *Democracy in Decline*, 227; this biographical summary is based on Erik J. Chaput, *The People's Martyr: Thomas Wilson Dorr and His 1842 Rhode Island Rebellion* (Lawrence: University Press of Kansas, 2013), 16–22, 47.

8. An 1833 address quoted in Frieze, *Concise History*, 24; Conley, *Democracy in Decline*, 205, 221, 253, 257, 262; *Liberator*, March 4, 1831, quoting *Providence Patriot*, and *Pawtucket Chronicle*, January 14 and 21, 1831, on the "Petition from Alfred Niger, et. al.," and how a committee "reported a bill exempting colored persons from taxation" but Potter moved its "indefinite postponement," because "if the bill should pass, there would arise much controversy in the state between the different degrees of color, as there was in the Circuit Court, about half and whole blood"; *Liberator*, November 27, 1840.

9. *Liberator*, October 18, 1839; Cottrol, *Afro-Yankees*, 20; *The Life of William J. Brown of Providence, R.I., With Personal Recollections of Incidents in Rhode Island* (Durham:

University of New Hampshire Press, 2006, orig. pub. 1883), 73–74 (an example of white protection was after Brown and another boy bested several such toughs, they cried murder: "One tall well-dressed man said . . . take these niggers to jail, for I have seen enough of their actions today. Without further information we were seized, and would have been dragged off to prison," but "Mr. Joseph Balch . . . came out of his apothe-cary shop. . . . 'No you won't, I know both of them, they are nice boys. . . . Go on, and nobody shall trouble you'"); John S. Gilkeson, Jr., *Middle-Class Providence, 1820–1940* (Princeton, NJ: Princeton University Press, 1986), 20, 22; Cottrol, *Afro-Yankees*, 54.

10. Marvin Gettleman, *The Dorr Rebellion: A Study in American Radicalism, 1833–1849* (New York: Random House, 1973); Conley, *Democracy in Decline*; Chaput, *People's Martyr* is the most comprehensive account.

11. Frieze, *Concise History*, 29 and 30–31: "After the fate of certain men had been de-cided by the election of 1840 . . . they came to the conclusion that the suffrage cause would afford them a very convenient hobby, ready saddled and bridled"; *Preamble and Constitution of the Rhode-Island Suffrage Association, Adopted Friday Evening, March 27, 1840* (Providence, RI: B. T. Albro, 1840); *Macon Weekly Telegraph*, March 26, 1844, and the *Illinois State Register*, May 10, 1844, on how the Dorrites were defeated by "a force of four thousand men in the field" consisting "of whites and negroes . . . to override and trample down the authorities of the people."

12. Ichabod Northup, Samuel Rodman, James Hazard, George J. Smith, and Ran-som Parker's memorial reproduced in Burke, *Rhode Island in 1842*, 113, also noting "were there no complexional hindrance . . . a more than proportionate number of our people . . . might immediately, according to the freeholder's qualification, become vot-ers" (111); Erik J. Chaput and Russell J. DeSimone, "Strange Bedfellows: The Politics of Race in Antebellum Rhode Island," *Common-Place* 10, no. 2 (January 2010): 3, cites the 1842 *Providence Directory* listing 287 black householders, a significant constituency.

13. *Life of William J. Brown*, 96.

14. *Life of William J. Brown*, 101; Frieze, *Concise History*, 30, 31. It is impossible to tell, from the sequence of events in Brown's recollection decades later, when this meet-ing took place, although it may be the session of the People's Convention at which the "remonstrance" noted above was presented.

15. Frieze, *Concise History*, 56; *Life of William J. Brown*, 49–50; *New Age and Con-stitutional Advocate*, March 19, 1841 (the Suffrage Association's official newspaper).

16. *Providence Journal*, September 14, 1841 (a letter from F. L. Beckford, secretary of the Suffrage Association) and October 9, 1841.

17. Gilkeson, *Middle-Class Providence*, 43; *Providence Journal*, August 30, 1841.

18. *Providence Journal*, September 15, 1841.

19. *Providence Journal*, October 2, 1841.

20. *Providence Journal*, October 9, 1841; *Providence Journal*, June 10, 1842, reprint-ing the conservative *New York Courier and Enquirer* (a little earlier, the Tyler admin-istration's organ insisted Dorrism would "convert the numberless blacks of the South into voters, who would vote down the southern state governments at their pleasures" [*Madisonian*, May 21, 1842, quoted in Chaput, *People's Martyr*, 146]; *Providence Jour-nal*, October 11, 1841).

21. *Providence Journal*, October 11, 1841.

22. *Liberator*, October 29, November 19, and December 10, 1841 (the last is quoted above); Chaput, *People's Martyr*, 63.

23. *Liberator*, January 21, 1842.

24. *Providence Journal*, October 29 and November 10, 1841 (in a series "To the People of Rhode Island") and December 18, 1841 (another series, "To the Farmers of Rhode Island, #2," now signed "Country Born"), collected in Francis W. Goddard, *The Political and Miscellaneous Writings of William G. Goddard* (Providence, RI: Sidney S. Rider and Brother, 1870), 2:55, 66, 76; [Goddard] in *Providence Journal*, January 11, 1842, in *Political and Miscellaneous Writings*, 119–20; *Liberator*, August 19, 1842.

25. [Goddard] in *Providence Journal*, December 24, 1841, in *Political and Miscellaneous Writings*, 90; Chaput, *People's Martyr*, 122.

26. *Providence Journal*, June 28, 1842; *Emancipator*, August 11, 1842.

27. *Providence Journal*, July 12, 1842; *Liberator*, July 22, 1842; Chaput, *People's Martyr*, 151.

28. *Providence Journal*, July 14, 1842; Potter, Jr., to Francis, July 22, 1842 in Francis Papers, quoted in William M. Wiecek, "Popular Sovereignty in the Dorr War—Conservative Counterblast," *Rhode Island History* 32 (1973): 48; Wayland to Simmons, September 21, 1842, quoted in Chaput, *People's Martyr*, 165 (Wayland was a key theologian of postmillennialism, which Howe describes as providing "the capstone to an intellectual structure integrating political liberalism and economic development with Protestant Christianity," and his eminence as both a Law and Order "conservative" and an antislavery man suggests that the space opened for nonracial politics was not entirely opportunistic; see Daniel Walker Howe, *What Hath God Wrought: The Transformation of America, 1815–1848* [New York: Oxford University Press, 2007], 287–88); *Macon Weekly Telegraph*, July 5, 1842; *Emancipator*, August 18, 1842, reprinting *New-York Express*; *Providence Journal*, July 6, 1842.

29. *Liberator*, August 19, 1842.

30. Chaput, *People's Martyr*, 165, quoting petitions submitted on September 19 and 20; *Newport Mercury*, September 17 and 24, 1842 (opposition to black suffrage can be seen in Potter, Jr. to John Brown Francis, November 14, 1842, quoted in Chaput, *People's Martyr*, 166, which accurately predicted Dorrites would call the new charter "the negro constitution," noting "some of our side very foolishly argue in favor of the Negroes because they are conservative and go with the wealthy part of the community . . . no argument could be more unpopular with the middling and poorer classes of the white people"); see Chaput and DeSimone, "Strange Bedfellows," 11, for the actual ballot.

31. *Vermont Phoenix* (Brattleboro), April 14, 1843, quoting the *Journal*; Catherine R. Williams, quoted in Chaput and DeSimone, "Strange Bedfellows," 12.

32. *Washington Globe*, December 8, 1842; *Ohio Statesman*, December 6, 1842, adding that Columbus Whigs ranked foreigners, especially Welshmen, on "a lower scale of human existence than the negro"; *Life of William J. Brown*, 102.

33. Calhoun quoted in Conley, *Democracy in Decline*, 333; Burke, *Rhode Island in 1842*, 107, 114, 117. Dorr had assured Burke by letter that a "slave was not actually a man," and that he never said slaves were "part of the sovereign power in the states to which they belong" (quoted in Chaput, *People's Martyr*, 177).

34. Peter J. Coleman, *The Transformation of Rhode Island, 1790–1860* (Providence, RI: Brown University Press, 1969), 244; the 1860 census does not break down the

foreign-born population by age, so their voting-age population cannot be ascertained, and while the figures for country of nativity are not broken down by gender, the percentage of immigrants born in Ireland was 67.6 percent; Chaput, *People's Martyr*, 77.

35. *Providence Journal*, April 1, March 30, April 3, 1851, quoted in Laurence Bruce Raber, "The Formation and Early Development of the Republican Party in Rhode Island, 1850–1865" (master's thesis, University of Rhode Island, 1965), 24, 46–47, 30, 32 (quote from the *Daily News*, February 20, 1852); *NE*, April 12, 1855 and March 5, 1857, citing *Providence Journal*.

36. *Lancaster Intelligencer*, October 26, 1852; *New Hampshire Patriot and State Gazette*, October 27, 1852; *Providence Journal*, January 14, 1850; *FDP*, February 25, 1853 and November 9, 1855.

37. *Liberator*, December 6, 1844, reporting on a November 27 meeting; *Providence Journal*, repr. in *NASS*, January 9, 1845.

38. *FDP*, December 31, 1852; for 1847, see *Newport Mercury*, April 10, 1847 (that year's "scattering" vote by Garrisonians was considerably larger—509); no black men participated in Liberty Party meetings in 1846–48 (see *Emancipator*, February 4, 1846 and *NE*, February 18, 1847 and April 6, 1848); *Providence Journal*, June 2, 1853; *FDP*, April 22, 1853, reprinting the state Free Soil paper, *Rhode Island Freeman*; for that party's appeal to black voters, see *Providence Journal*, October 28 and November 1, 1852; *Rhode Island Freeman*, June 30 and August 18, 1854, and February 17, 1854, defining its readers as "lovers of social order, Temperance, Freedom, Justice, Right" adding that as Free Soilers "deemed it inexpedient to nominate a ticket," readers should vote for whomever "will best sustain the prohibitory liquor law."

39. *Life of William J. Brown*, 93–94. Like many others, he routinely conflated Liberty and Free Soil.

40. *Emancipator*, April 21, 1847; *Life of William J. Brown*, 87–88, on a new Baptist church, with Willis one of three deacons.

41. *Emancipator*, November 9, 1848, on Van Buren's 397 city votes; *NE*, November 23, 1848, from *Providence Transcript*; *Providence Journal*, November 9, 1848; *NS*, December 8, 1848; *Impartial Citizen*, October 5, 1850.

42. Cottrol, *Afro-Yankees*, 79, 81–83 for tables measuring the likely black vote across seven elections; quoted in *NS*, November 24, 1848.

43. *Life of William J. Brown*, 60, 103.

44. *Life of William J. Brown*, 94; *Ohio Statesman*, September 13, 1842, quoting *Providence Herald*; *Life of William J. Brown*, 92–93.

45. *Providence Journal*, June 28, 1842 and *Newport Mercury*, October 22, 1842, describing how the commander of the Dorrites' artillery "was arrested last evening at Woonsocket . . . on a warrant for treason issued by Henry L. Bowen, Esq."; *Life of William J. Brown*, 92–93. For Brown and Hazard's rivalry, see the 1845 "Statement of the Committee for the Celebration of the First of August," signed by Hazard, disparaging Brown's Young Men's Union Fund society (*Manufacturers' and Farmers' Journal*, August 21, 1845). One presumes the "Mr. Balch" was the apothecary who had protected a young Brown from white thugs.

46. *Life of William J. Brown*, 94–95.

47. *Life of William J. Brown*, 100–101, 97–98. For his postmastership, see Bowen's obituary in *Providence Evening Press*, January 30, 1865.

48. *Life of William J. Brown*, 94, 98–99.

49. *Life of William J. Brown*, 106.

50. *Life of William J. Brown*, 1, 75; *Biographical Cyclopedia of Rhode Island* (Providence, RI: National Biographical Publishing Company, 1881), 133.

51. *Newport News* repr. in *FDP*, July 27, 1855; Tilden quoted in Lawrence Grossman, "George T. Downing and the Desegregation of Rhode Island's Public Schools, 1855–1866," *Rhode Island History* 36, no. 4 (November 1977): 99; S. A. M. Washington, *George Thomas Downing: Sketch of His Life and Times* (Newport: Milne Printery, 1910); *FDP*, March 9, 1855.

52. *FDP*, March 9, 1855; *American Citizen* (Jackson, MI), July 11, 1855; *Boston Recorder*, July 12, 1855; *Charleston Courier*, July 14, 1855; *Public Ledger* (Philadelphia), July 14, 1855; *Flag of Our Union* (Boston), July 28, 1855; *Weekly Advocate* (Baton Rouge), August 2, 1855.

53. *NE*, May 21 and 28, 1857, repr. in *Baltimore Sun*, May 19, 1857; *Newark Daily Advertiser*, May 20, 1857; *Annapolis Gazette* and *New-London Weekly Chronicle*, May 21, 1857; *Georgia Telegraph* (Macon), May 26, 1857; *Arkansas Intelligencer* (Van Buren, AR), June 7, 1857; *Sacramento Daily Union*, July 2, 1857. Howland was refused since "passports are not issued to persons of African extraction. Such persons are not deemed citizens of the United States. See the case of Dred Scott recently decided" (*Republican Standard*, October 22, 1857).

54. *Evening Post* (New York), August 28, 1860; *Newport Mercury*, November 10, 1860; see Richard C. Rohrs, "Exercising Their Right: African American Voter Turnout in Antebellum Newport, Rhode Island," *New England Quarterly* 84, no. 3 (September 2011): 402–21 and 418 (quoting *Newport Daily News*, August 26, 1856); *Newport Mercury*, June 6, 1857; June 12, 1858; June 23, 1860; September 8, 1860; December 8, 1860.

55. *Boston Daily Atlas*, April 2, 1857; *Baltimore Sun*, April 4; *Daily National Intelligencer*, April 6; *Alexandria Gazette* and *Portland Advertiser*, April 7; *Milwaukee Sentinel*, April 11; *National Era*, *St. Albans Messenger* (VT), and *Georgia Telegraph*, April 16.

56. *NE*, May 28, 1857, for a report that "a petition to the Legislature . . . bore the signature of the Rev. Dr. Wayland and Bishop Clark," and *Liberator*, December 25, 1857, for Downing's committee referring to "President Wayland, the author of our memorial," and January 29, 1858, for his recusal.

57. *Liberator*, April 24, 1857; *Providence Journal*, November 21, 1857, repr. in *Liberator*, December 11, 1857; *Liberator*, December 25, 1857; *FDP*, February 12, 1858, reprinting the *Providence Transcript*; *Liberator*, April 2, 1858.

58. *Newport Mercury*, August 28, 1858; *Life of George Henry: Together with a Brief History of the Colored People in America* (Providence, RI: H. I. Gould, 1894), 69; *Providence Journal* repr. in *To the Friends of Equal Rights in Rhode Island* (Providence, RI: n.p., 1859), 4; see the *Litchfield* [Connecticut] *Republican*, January 5, 1846, for a verse in dialect, "The Little Nigger Boy," about a mother mourning her son gone to sea.

59. *Will the General Assembly Put Down Caste Schools?* (Providence, RI: n.p., 1857), 6; *To the Friends of Equal Rights in Rhode Island*, 3 (Wolcott's statement appeared as an advertisement in the *Journal*, reproduced in this pamphlet with the *Journal*'s sneering reply); see *Douglass' Monthly*, April 1859 for Downing naming "John N. Smith, Chas. B. Burrill, the husbands of the school teachers whom the school committee employed to teach these caste schools; also, Geo. Waterman and others" (Burrill had been

a founding member of Brown's Young Men's Society and Waterman was a Baptist deacon [see *Life of William J. Brown*, 30, 88]); for George Head, see *Life of George Henry*, 68 and *FDP*, March 25, 1859; *Douglass' Monthly*, April 1859. Decades later, George Henry remembered, "I followed him [George Head] . . . out of the Court House, down the hill, and if he had opened his head I would have killed him dead on the spot" (*Life of George Henry*, 68).

60. *Douglass' Monthly*, April 1859.

61. Cottrol, *Afro-Yankees*, 91, cites the 1854 Providence School Committee report, when one black teacher received $500 and two others split $425, while whites got an average of $966.67 in the grammar school, but only $50 more in the primary school; *Will the General Assembly Put Down Caste Schools?*, 6; *Life of George Henry*, 67–68.

62. *Evening Press*, April 2, 1859, a moderate Republican paper; *To the Friends of Equal Rights*, 3, for the racial slur.

Coda

1. For the nominations, see Stephen Kantrowitz, *More Than Freedom: Fighting for Black Citizenship in a White Republic, 1829–1889* (New York: Penguin, 2012), 162–64, noting "a party that was part of a governing majority both took notice of black men's claims and included them on its slate"; *NE*, May 16, 1850, for Morris's appointment; Kantrowitz, *More Than Freedom*, 233 on Hayden's appointment and 231, describing the situation in Boston's Ward Six, where the city's colored voters constituted 15 percent of the electorate: "There were strict limits to what black activists could expect. . . . Powerful state and national Republican figures addressed meetings of 'colored voters' . . . and one black Republican was among the ward delegates who selected the party's nominee for state senate in 1859. . . . But many other convention delegations and ward meetings were entirely composed of white men."

2. For Salem, see chap. 5; for Nantucket, see Lorin Lee Cary and Francine C. Cary, "Absalom F. Boston, His Family, and Nantucket's Black Community," *Historic Nantucket* (Summer 1977): 15–22; for Pittsfield, see *Life of James Mars, A Slave Born and Sold in Connecticut. Written by Himself* (Hartford: Case, Lockwood, 1864); for Worcester, see its participation in the Massachusetts conventions described here; for Franklin County, see Elizabeth A. Congdon, "Calvin T. Swan, African-American Carpenter in Rural Massachusetts," in *Slavery/Antislavery in New England: The Dublin Seminar for New England Folklife, Annual Proceedings, 2003*, ed. Peter Benes (Boston: Boston University Press, 2003), 115–27, describing a rural yeoman of considerable means. Born in 1799, Swan was a large landowner, and "the extent to which his family was integrated among the otherwise white residents . . . was remarkable" (118), including serving as clerk of his school district in 1831–32 and 1835–36, on its School Committee at least twice, and activism in the Methodist Church and the county antislavery society; *Herald* quoted in Kantrowitz, *More Than Freedom*, 167.

3. Wilson is quoted in William C. Nell, *Colored Patriots of the American Revolution* (Boston: Robert F. Wallcut, 1855), 103–4; *FDP*, March 2, 1855, April 6, 1855, May 4, 1855 (see also George A. Levesque, "Boston's Black Brahmin: Dr. John S. Rock," *Civil War History* 26, no. 4 [December 1980]: 326–46); after many compromises, the Republican legislature, made up in part of former Know-Nothings, submitted to a popular vote in

1859 an additional two-year waiting period before naturalized citizens could vote, which passed with a very small turnout; *FDP*, September 14, 1855; *NE*, November 23, 1854.

4. *FDP*, December 1, 1854.

5. Stanley J. and Anita W. Robboy, "Lewis Hayden: From Fugitive Slave to Statesman," *New England Quarterly* (December 1973): 591–613.

6. *FDP*, March 2, 1855; also C. Peter Ripley, ed., *The Black Abolitionist Papers*, vol. 4, *The United States, 1847–1858* (Chapel Hill: University of North Carolina Press, 1991), 266–68.

7. See Philip S. Foner and George E. Walker, eds., *Proceedings of the Black State Conventions, 1840–1865*, vol. 1, *New York, Pennsylvania, Indiana, Michigan, Ohio* (Philadelphia: Temple University Press, 1979) and *Proceedings of the Black State Conventions, 1840–1865*, vol. 2, *New Jersey, Connecticut, Maryland, Illinois, Massachusetts, California, New England, Kansas, Louisiana, Virginia, Missouri, South Carolina* (Philadelphia: Temple University Press, 1980). The 1842 Maine and New Hampshire meeting described in chap. 5 was the exception; other than two from Connecticut, Douglass and Remond were the only New Englanders in 1843; *FDP*, May 18, 1855, reprinting the *New-York Tribune* on a National Council meeting. An earlier attempt turned into "an entirely discreditable affair," Douglass wrote, because Nell and William Howard Day, secretary-elect from Ohio, collaborated "to prevent any affirmation of the proceedings of the Council adopted in New York" (*FDP*, July 28, 1854).

8. *Liberator*, July 9, 1858; see *Charleston Courier*, July 21, 1858, on "A 'State Convention of Colored Citizens' is to be held at New Bedford," from *Boston Post* and the latter, August 2, 1858; *New York Herald*, August 2 and 4, 1858 (the *Boston Weekly Messenger*, August 4, 1858, noted how "the oligarchy who have grown fat upon spermaceti in this city of grease and whalebone, are as proud as any people in this land, and they do not relish the juxtaposition of ladies and gentlemen of color with them. But there is no help for it, especially as the negroes and their abolition allies have a majority of votes at the polls"); the account of the convention and quotations are all from *Liberator*, August 13, 1858. Remond had long made a specialty of baiting his audiences; consider him on May 29, 1844 at the New England Anti-Slavery Convention, where he heroized "Turner of Southampton, than whom a nobler soul has never risen upon the human race. . . . Sir, I will never contemptuously call him Nat Turner, for had he been a white man, Massachusetts and Virginia would have united to glorify his name and to build his monument. . . . Men say to me, 'Remond! You're wild! Remond! You're mad! Remond! You're a revolutionist!'" (quoted in Ripley, *Black Abolitionist Papers*, 3:442).

9. The admiring reference to Remond as a thwarted liberator who "at the South . . . would be an exceedingly dangerous man" is from the *New Bedford Standard*, repr. in *Liberator*, August 27, 1858.

10. *NE*, May 12, 1859; *Liberator*, August 19, 1859. The Committee on Permanent Organization included the old Liberty man John W. Lewis of Maine, the stalwart Republicans Hayden and Mark R. De Mortie of Boston, Henry O. Remington of New Bedford, and James Jefferson of Providence. Its list of officers was studded with veteran party activists, like Ezra R. Johnson, A. G. Jourdain, Jr., and Henry Johnson. William Wells Brown's address expressed vestigial Garrisonianism: "I confess that I am unfa-

vorable to any gathering that shall seem like taking separate action from our white fellow-citizens; but it appears to me that just at the present time, such a meeting as this is needed."

11. *Liberator*, August 26, 1859; *Evening Post*, August 28, 1860, "he has very seriously concluded that the best thing for him to do is to give up politics and speechmaking, and mind his own business. Negro orators and negro politicians are as plenty as negro minstrels. What is wanting, according to Downing's idea, is a few *practical* examples of the colored man's thrift and capacity for something higher than a subordinate and menial employment—of his ability, in short, to conduct a large business like white men, on his own account," quoting his reply to an invitation to speak at a First of August celebration, "I find the interest manifested on the part of our people in solid matters tending to secure the means of influence in the community so limited . . . [that] I do not feel called upon to make the sacrifices I would have to make in being any longer engaged in public matters. I feel that I am working for the people with whom I am identified in oppression, in securing a business name; I shall strive for my and their elevation, but it will be by a strict and undivided attention to business."

12. *Liberator*, January 21, 1859; Levesque, "Boston's Black Brahmin: Dr. John S. Rock," 330–31, on how Rock could not get a passport to go to France in 1857 from Secretary of State Lewis Cass so Massachusetts issued him one; Worcester's action was broadcast nationally by the Democrats, see *Ohio Statesman*, April 28, 1860 on more "Negro Equality," with "Massachusetts . . . taking another step forward, and placing the negro in the jury box."

13. *Liberator*, February 22, 1861.

Part III

1. *CA*, March 20, 1841.

2. The free population of the United States in 1840 was 14,195,805, and 2,428,921 (17 percent) lived in New York; Paul E. Johnson, *A Shopkeeper's Millenium: Society and Revivals in Rochester, New York, 1815–1837* (New York: Hill & Wang, 1978), 18, captures an isolated hinterland's transformation by the canal, as "the Genesee Valley became one of the great grain-growing regions of the world, and Rochester . . . America's first inland boom town"; for estimates of national, regional, and state incomes in 1840, see Richard A. Easterlin, "Interregional Differences in Per Capita Income, Population, and Total Income, 1840–1950," *Trends in the American Economy in the Nineteenth Century* (Princeton, NJ: Princeton University Press, 1959), 97–98; data on the city's economy are gleaned from Edwin G. Burroughs and Mike Wallace, *Gotham: A History of New York City to 1898* (New York: Oxford University Press, 1999), 434–46; the emphasis on information derives from L. Ray Gunn, "New York Modernizes: Economic Growth and Transformation," in *The Empire State: A History of New York*, ed. Milton M. Klein (Ithaca, NY: Cornell University Press, 2001), 346.

3. Hendrik Booraem V., *The Formation of the Republican Party in New York: Politics and Conscience in the Antebellum North* (New York: New York University Press, 1983), 3; see also Phyllis F. Field, *The Politics of Race in New York: The Struggle for Black Suffrage in the Civil War Era* (Ithaca, NY: Cornell University Press, 1982), 9: "Party politics in New York was played at a highly sophisticated level, the result of a long,

varied, and rich tradition of conflict and competition dating back to the colonial period. Politicians elsewhere paid attention to what went on in New York."

4. Dixon Ryan Fox, "The Negro Vote in Old New York," *Political Science Quarterly* 32, no. 2 (June 1917): 252, 275. One suspects that in 1917 Fox had in mind a particular "Old New Yorker," the Republican aristocrat Theodore Roosevelt, who had just rekindled his ties with black Americans by denouncing the East St. Louis race riot as "an appalling outbreak of savagery" by whites.

5. Fox, "Negro Vote in Old New York," 253.

6. Fox, 254–55, followed by this specific reference to Federalist leaders: "The freedmen who came into Albany from Rensselaerwyck where had they had been so kindly treated, or those who came from the great house of General Schuyler where so many had been granted freedom" would hardly "vote against 'the lord.'" It would have been more accurate to say, "The Negro left the Dutchman's farm, moved to the city, learned English, and struggled to find a trade."

Chapter Eight

1. Graham Russell Hodges, "Black Revolt in New York City and the Neutral Zone: 1775–83," in *New York in the Age of the Constitution, 1775–1800*, ed. Paul A. Gilje and William Pencak (Rutherford, NJ: Fairleigh Dickinson University Press, 1992), 25; Paul J. Polgar, "'Whenever They Judge It Expedient': The Politics of Partisanship and Free Black Voting Rights in Early National New York," *American Nineteenth Century History* 12, no. 1 (March 2011): 1, stressing that "historians have used the lens of a racially exclusive Jacksonian Democracy to read back into the historical record a sense of inevitability" (17). David N. Gellman, *Emancipating New York: The Politics of Slavery and Freedom, 1777–1827* (Baton Rouge: Louisiana State University Press, 2006), 202, also sees the campaign leading up to 1821 as motivated by "opportunism, political self-interest, and racially tinged partisan vindictiveness" rather than ideological commitments.

2. Daniel J. Hulsebosch, *Constituting Empire: New York and the Transformation of Constitutionalism in the Atlantic World, 1664–1830* (Chapel Hill: University of North Carolina Press, 2005), 218, and Ronald W. Howard, "From Proprietary Colony to Royal Province," in *The Empire State: A History of New York*, ed. Milton M. Klein (Ithaca, NY: Cornell University Press, 2001), 113; Thelma Wills Foote, *Black and White Manhattan: The History of Racial Formation in Colonial New York City* (New York: Oxford University Press, 2004), 60 (even in 1775, the twenty-six Anglican parishes were swamped by seventy-six Dutch Reform, fifty Presbyterian, twenty-six Lutheran, twelve Congregational, ten German Reform, and ten Baptist churches, plus twenty-two Quaker meetings; see Ronald W. Howard, "Advancing English Culture," in Klein, *Empire State*, 135, 153); Ronald W. Howard, "Provincial and Imperial Politics," in Klein, *Empire State*, 193; John L. Brooke, *Columbia Rising: Civil Life on the Upper Hudson From the Revolution to the Age of Jackson* (Chapel Hill: University of North Carolina Press, 2010), 54; Foote, *Black and White Manhattan*, 92. To understand the elite's connections, consider the Patroon Stephen Van Rensselaer, eighth lord of the vast Manor of Rensselaerswijck and a steadfast defender of black suffrage (under the Dutch system, every manorial head was a patroon, but the greatest among them was accorded

the honorific title of "the Patroon"). The Van Rensselaers "married and intermarried in a fashion similar to that of royalty" (William Bertrand Fink, "Stephen Van Rensselaer: The Last Patroon" [PhD diss., Columbia University, 1950], 5). His father, Stephen II, wed Catherine Livingston, daughter of Philip, a signer of the Declaration of Independence; his brother Philip married a Van Cortlandt, and his sister Elizabeth, a Schuyler.

3. Edward Countryman, "Never a More Total Revolution," in Klein, *Empire State*, 257, describes it as "three long, thin strips"; and Peter J. Galie, *Ordered Liberty: A Constitutional History of New York* (New York: Fordham University Press, 1996), 10, on New York as not "a single, geographically compact area" but "a series of trading posts"; see also Hulsebosch, *Constituting Empire*, 217, on how "the relationship with the Iroquois was central to New York's political culture" until the 1780s; Howard, "Provincial and Imperial Politics," 184.

4. Countryman, "Never a More Total Revolution," 245; Sidney I. Pomerantz, *New York: An American City, 1783–1803* (New York: Columbia University Press, 1938), 81.

5. Gilje, "Introduction," in Gilje and Pencak, *New York in the Age of the Constitution*, 13; Howard, "Advancing English Culture," 149; James W. Darlington, "Peopling the Post-Revolutionary New York Frontier," *New York History* 74, no. 4 (October 1993): 347; Evan Cornog, *The Birth of Empire: DeWitt Clinton and the American Experience, 1769–1828* (New York: Oxford University Press, 1998), 265–66. On New York as "the vanguard state of the developing nation," see Alan Taylor, *William Cooper's Town: Power and Persuasion on the Frontier of the Early American Republic* (New York: Vintage, 1995), 4.

6. Graham Russell Hodges, *Root & Branch: African Americans in New York & East Jersey, 1613–1863* (Chapel Hill: University of North Carolina Press, 1999), 6, 7, 9, 12; *A Memorial Discourse by the Rev. Henry Highland Garnet, Delivered in the Hall of the House of Representatives, Washington City, D.C., on Sabbath, February 12, 1865. With an Introduction by James McCune Smith, M.D.* (Philadelphia: Joseph M. Wilson, 1865), 24.

7. Hodges, *Root & Branch*, 31, asks, "Did the English then capture a slave society?" acknowledging that formally, the answer was no, because slavery was "not the sole form of labor," but arguing that "Dutch farmers and their bondspeople" produced "a slave-owning culture within a larger society"; Craig Steven Wilder, *A Covenant with Color: Race and Social Power in Brooklyn* (New York: Columbia University Press, 2000), 27 and 35–36, describes how the leading Dutch families all owned dozens, even in 1790, including the Cowenhovens (sixty), the Lefferts (fifty-eight), the Suydams (forty-nine), the Wyckoffs (forty-seven), and the Remsens (forty-four); for Van Buren, see Jerome Mushkat and Joseph G. Rayback, *Martin Van Buren: Law, Politics, and the Shaping of Republican Ideology* (DeKalb: Northern Illinois Press, 1997), 4, 7n21, and Brooke, *Columbia Rising*, 118; Jill Lepore, *New York Burning: Liberty, Slavery, and Conspiracy in Eighteenth-Century Manhattan* (New York: Knopf, 2005), 2, describes a mapmaker listing city landmarks in 1813, including "Plot Negro's burnt here," remembering them "chained to a stake, and there burned to death," and the black leader William Hamilton in 1827 referred to "the time of the Negro plot, when a kind of fanaticism seized the people of New-York" akin to the Salem witch trials (quoted in Paul A. Gilje and Howard B. Rock, *Keepers of the Revolution: New Yorkers at Work in the Early Republic* [Ithaca, NY: Cornell University Press, 1992], 243); Brooke, *Columbia Rising*, 138.

8. Hodges, *Root & Branch*, 153; Edwin G. Burroughs and Mike Wallace, *Gotham: A History of New York City to 1898* (New York: Oxford University Press, 1999), 286; Shane White, *Somewhat More Independent: The End of Slavery in New York City, 1770–1810* (Athens: University of Georgia Press, 1991), 16, on how 39.5 percent of whites in the counties around the city owned a slave, a higher percentage than in Maryland and the Carolinas.

9. Hulsebosch, *Constituting Empire*, 219, 347; see also Stefan Bielinski, "The Jacksons, Lattimores, and Schuylers: First African-American Families of Early Albany," *New York History* 77, no. 4 (October 1996): 389, for a black man named Jack Johnson listed on Albany's 1779 tax rolls, and even earlier, the 1767 roll including "Tom Corte, the neger" (379); Albert Edward McKinley, *The Suffrage Franchise in the Thirteen English Colonies in America* (Philadelphia: Publications of the University of Pennsylvania Series in History, 1905), 222–23, specifies that in Albany voters were natural-born or naturalized subjects of the king who paid a fee as freemen, and that a disputed 1773 election led to rules that "no alien could vote. . . . British subjects having resided six weeks in the city had the right to vote in the wards they inhabited" albeit "no bond servant could vote during the time of his service."

10. Cornog, *Birth of Empire*, 25.

11. Gellman, *Emancipating New York*, 46–53, is the most complete account, noting that the disfranchisers were rooted in slaveholding counties like Ulster, Kings, and Richmond.

12. *Loudon's New-York Packet*, April 4, 1785.

13. See Alfred Billings Street, *The Council of Revision* (Albany, NY: W. Gould, 1859), 268–69, "City of New York, March 21, 1785. . . . A bill entitled 'An act for the gradual abolition of slavery within this State,' was before the Council, which adopted the following objections, reported by Chancellor Livingston," suggesting this conservative aristocrat may have been their author; the best account is in Leslie M. Harris, *In the Shadow of Slavery: African Americans in New York City, 1626–1863* (Chicago: University of Chicago Press, 2004), 60, noting that "the council displayed a strong vision of the possibility of black activism in pursuit of equality and freedom."

14. Quoted in Dixon Ryan Fox, *The Decline of Aristocracy in the Politics of New York, 1801–1840* (New York: Harper Torchbooks, 1965 ed.), 9; Kent to Daniel Webster, January 31, 1830, and Kent to Moss Kent, April 3, 1835, quoted in William Kent, *Memoirs and Letters of James Kent* (New York: Da Capo, 1970, repr. of 1898 ed.), 207, 218.

15. Gellman, *Emancipating New York*, 33, 58; Edgar J. McManus, "Antislavery Legislation in New York," *JNH* 46, no. 4 (October 1961): 208, Jay quoted on 7; James Oakes, *The Scorpion's Sting: Antislavery and the Coming of the Civil War* (New York: W. W. Norton, 2014), 114, quotes Jay on why British repatriation of formerly enslaved people would be odious, comparing them to the Americans held captive in Algiers: "What would Congress, and indeed the world, think and say of France, if, on making peace with Algiers, [they] would give up those American Slaves to their former Algerine Masters? Is there any other difference between these two cases [other than] that the American Slaves in Algiers are *white* people, whereas the African Slaves at New York were *Black* people?" For nuanced insights into the contradictions between Jay's public professions and his participation in slaveholding, see Daniel Littlefield, "John Jay,

the Revolutionary Generation, and Slavery," *New York History* 81, no. 1 (January 2000): 91–132.

16. Gellman, *Emancipating New York*, 2, also 68–70 on failed attempts in 1788 and 1790 and 166–67 on defeat in 1796, by which time Federalists were using antislavery against Republicans; a 1798 amendment to tax free people of color to support the "free black poor" lost in the assembly, 59–25, setting up 1799's bipartisan approval of emancipation 68–23 (171, 176–79); Countryman, "Never a More Total Revolution," 247; on 1792, see Gellman, *Emancipating New York*, 131–34, also James Fairlie to Stephen Van Rensselaer, February 13, 1792, "The Great objection to Mr. Jay among the Dutch in Columbia Ulster & Albany is his public sentiments respecting Manumitting the Negroes, among many this is no objection but the Generality of the people think so" (quoted in Fink, "Stephen Van Rensselaer: The Last Patroon," 55). For Clinton, see Taylor, *William Cooper's Town*, 157, on how he "persuasively posed as the principled, egalitarian, and uncompromising patriot zealously defending the liberties of the common farmers and artisans."

17. Alan Taylor, "'The Art of Hook & Snivey': Political Culture in Upstate New York during the 1790s," *JAH* 79, no. 4 (March 1993): 1379, on how parties were "names that candidates claimed rather than organizations," and "both parties were loose and shifting alliances"; Hamilton quoted in "The Anti-Slavery Papers of John Jay, Collected by Frank Monaghan," *JNH* 17, no. 4 (October 1932): 491–93. For the original envelope, see John Jay Papers, Columbia University, box 10, file 122.

18. Paul J. Polgar, "'To Raise them to an Equal Participation': Early National Abolitionism, Gradual Emancipation, and the Promise of African American Citizenship," *JER* 31, no. 2 (Summer 2011): 2; Hodges, *Root & Branch*, 166, 181, 217.

19. Fox, *Decline of Aristocracy*, 25, 29; Hodges, "Black Revolt," 39.

20. *New-York Gazette*, August 6 and September 1, 1801.

21. Chilton Williamson, *American Suffrage from Property to Democracy, 1760–1860* (Princeton, NJ: Princeton University Press, 1960), 197; Brooke, *Columbia Rising*, 119.

22. David Hackett Fischer, *The Revolution of American Conservatism: The Federalist Party in the Era of Jeffersonian Democracy* (New York: Harper & Row, 1965), 52, 60, 80–83; Nancy Isenberg, "The 'Little Emperor': Aaron Burr, Dandyism, and the Sexual Politics of Treason," in *Beyond the Founders: New Approaches to the Political History of the Early American Republic*, ed. Jeffrey L. Pasley, Andrew W. Robertson, and David Waldstreicher (Chapel Hill: University of North Carolina Press, 2004), 129–58; *American Citizen*, April 28, 1804.

23. White, *Somewhat More Independent*, 26.

24. White, *Somewhat More Independent*, 148, 158–66, 186, 175, and 179–81 on the dynamic "black criminal infrastructure," framing his conclusion that the city "in the immediate postslavery period afforded a black male a much greater chance to work at a skilled trade"; Craig Steven Wilder, *In the Company of Black Men: The African Influence on African American Culture in New York City* (New York: New York University Press, 2001). Prominent men of color in the 1812 city directory included Joseph Sidney, cooper; Cesar Carr, oysterman; Adam Marshall and James Morris, sweepmasters; Caesar Francis, waiter; Cuffee Francis, smith; Thomas Miller, oysterman; Peter Williams, tobacconist; John Teasman, teacher; William Hamilton, carpenter; Thomas Sipkins,

grainer; Isaac Fortune, fruitshop; Richard Garrison, sweep; Daniel Berry, slop shop (used clothes dealer); Thomas Sanders, sawyer; Robert F. Williams, oyster house; Thomas L. Jennings, tailor; James Barclay, waiter (see *Longworth's American Almanac, New York Register, and City Directory, For The Thirty-Seventh Year Of American Independence* [New York: Longworth's, 1812], 282, 53, 206, 221, 112, 159, 246, 346, 214, 307, 135, 283, 111, 118, 24, 271, 346, 162, 16).

25. Jacob Morris to Colonel William Cooper, quoted in Alfred F. Young, *The Democratic Republicans of New York: The Origins, 1763–1797* (Chapel Hill: University of North Carolina Press, 1967), 508; *Albany Register*, November 5, 1798; *Argus or Greenleaf's Advertiser*, May 3, 1799; *Republican Watch-Tower*, April 29, 1801 (Van Rensselaer lost to Clinton, 28,408 to 20,843 or 54–46 percent, and the Federalists did not run another candidate until 1810); *Spectator*, May 3, 1800.

26. *Evening Post*, May 15, 1806; for Varick's fights with the cartmen, see Graham R. Hodges, "Legal Bonds of Attachment: The Freemanship Law of New York City, 1648–1801," in *Authority and Resistance in Early New York*, ed. William Pencak and Conrad Edick Wright (New York: New-York Historical Society, 1988), 237–40; Graham Russell Hodges, *New York City Cartmen, 1667–1850* (New York: New York University Press, 1986) traces the cartmen's role in the city's byzantine politics. The council appointed Edward Livingston as mayor, replaced by DeWitt Clinton in 1803.

27. Hodges, "Legal Bonds," 241, on black men's exclusion from licensed professions encouraged their move "into entrepreneurial callings such as catering," including challenges to "the monopolies of grocers and tavern keepers"; *Evening Post*, July 8, 1805; Paul A. Gilje and Howard B. Rock, "'Sweep O! Sweep O!': African-American Chimney Sweeps and Citizenship in the New Nation," *WMQ* 51, no. 3 (July 1994): 507–38. Their fight continued, successfully petitioning the city council in 1818, "fully persuaded, that Your Honorable Body will treat every man, whether white or black, according to his deserts" (527). The authors list more than fifty masters, at least three of whom (Richard Garrison, Adam Marshall, and John V. Henry) were Federalist activists.

28. *New-York Gazette*, January 3, 1803; *Public Advertiser*, April 9, 1807. Ray W. Irwin, *Daniel D. Tompkins: Governor of New York and Vice President of the United States* (New York: New-York Historical Society, 1968), 108, quotes the Quaker John Murray of the NYMS hailing Tompkins in 1809 as "uniformly an advocate for the cause of the oppressed Africans" (he was its counsel).

29. *American Citizen*, April 24, 1807; *Evening Post*, April 25, 1807; *Public Advertiser*, April 27, 1807.

30. *American Citizen*, May 2, 1807; *Albany Register*, March 19, 1807, repr. from *American Citizen*; Ralph M. Aderman, Herbert L. Kleinfeld, and Jenifer S. Banks, eds., *The Complete Works of Washington Irving: Letters, Volume I, 1802–1823* (Boston: Twayne, 1978), 231–32.

31. *American Citizen*, November 16 and 17, 1807.

32. Nathaniel H. Carter and William L. Stone, Reporters, *Reports of the Proceedings and Debates of the Convention of 1821, Assembled for the Purpose of Amending the Constitution of the State of New-York* (Albany, NY: E. & F. Hosford, 1821), 186; *Albany Argus*, May 6, 1842, quoting the March 29 report by Assemblyman John Cramer for the Judiciary Committee.

33. *New-York Gazette*, April 29, 1802; *Republican Watch-Tower*, May 5, 1802; *Evening Post*, May 5, 1802.

34. *Columbian*, April 24, 1815. On meetings of "Republican Aliens," see *American Citizen*, May 1 and 3, 1804.

35. *Balance* (Hudson) May 12, 1807, reprinting *Evening Post*; *Evening Post*, April 29, 1808.

36. In the longer view, nativism was never the property of one party or faction. As a British province, "Anti-Popery" united its divided settler class fractions, and well into the eighteenth century Catholics could not have their own priests and "knew better than to worship as openly as their Jewish neighbors" (Ronald W. Howard, "Colonial Culture: The Sacred and the Secular," in Klein, *Empire State*, 171). Unity-by-exclusion along religious lines found its strongest partisan in John Jay. In 1777, he tried to insert a bar on Catholic voting and office-holding into New York's constitution, requiring "professors of the religion of the church of Rome" who wanted to own land to swear before the supreme court that they abjured any "pope, priest or foreign authority on earth." He lost but succeeded in adding to its naturalization clause an oath disavowing loyalty to any "foreign king, prince potentate and state, in all matters ecclesiastical as well as civil," clearly including the Bishop of Rome. In his October 1774 "Address to the People of Great Britain," responding to the British declaring religious toleration in French Canada, Jay described Catholicism as a religion "that has deluged your island in blood, and dispensed impiety, bigotry, persecution, murder and rebellion through every part of the world" (Paul Finkelman, "The Soul and the State: Religious Freedom in New York and the Origin of the First Amendment," in *New York and the Union*, ed. Stephen L. Schechter and Richard B. Bernstein [Albany, NY: New York State Commission on the Bicentennial of the United States Constitution, 1990], 99); Elizabeth M. Nuxoll, ed., *The Selected Papers of John Jay*, vol. 1, *1760–1779* (Charlottesville: University of Virginia Press, 2010), 374, 105. In the 1780s, however, it was George Clinton's Whig faction that attempted to legislate Catholic exclusion, and Alexander Hamilton, Jay's closest ally, who fought it; at that time most prominent American Catholics were Federalists (Jason K. Duncan, *Citizens or Papists? The Politics of Anti-Catholicism in New York, 1685–1821* [New York: Fordham University Press, 2005], 69–72, 79).

37. *Columbian*, April 25, 1810.

38. *Evening Post*, April 26, 1808; *American Citizen*, April 28 and 30, 1808 (see Paul A. Gilje, *The Road to Mobocracy: Popular Disorder in New York City, 1763–1834* [Chapel Hill: University of North Carolina Press, 1987], 154, on the Common Council trying to protect black churches); *Public Advertiser*, April 29, 1808.

39. *Commercial Advertiser*, May 6, 1808, reprinting the Hudson *Balance*. Elsewhere, black electors were one more group, as when Herkimer County Federalists alleged Republicans "raked the cradle, and almost the grave; black, white, and tawny colored were all, in one common mass, drove (like a herd of swine) up to the polls" (*Albany Register*, May 26, 1809).

40. *Evening Post*, February 2, 1809. See *Columbian*, May 11, 1810, for a parodic letter from "Mingo Burnhaunch," complaining about "fun-loving boys" who threw brickbats at his house, attacking "the votes of Sambo Sidney, of Cesar Jackson, of myself, and all the host of colored gentlemen [who] have contributed to the support of the

federal ticket." Both the name and a reference to his "scraper" imply Mingo was a sweepmaster.

41. After the election, another Federalist paper "very cheerfully" republished Sidney's oration, calling it "filled with correct principles" appropriate to a "Gentleman of talents and of a liberal education" (*New-York Spectator*, April 29, 1809; also the *New York Herald*, repr. in the *Middlebury Mercury* [Vermont], May 17, 1809, *Farmer's Weekly Museum* [Walpole, New Hampshire], May 8, 1809); *Spirit of '76*, April 25, 1809; *Commercial Advertiser*, April 26, 1809; *Spirit of '76*, April 27; *New-York Spectator*, April 29.

42. *Albany Gazette*, March 14, 1810 (I am unable to find any record of this proposal in the *Journal of the Assembly* for this session); *Mercantile Advertiser*, March 19, 1810, repr. from the *Evening Post*; *Albany Register*, April 10, 1810; *Columbian*, November 20, 1810.

43. *Columbian*, April 13, 1810; *Commercial Advertiser*, April 24, 1810; *New-York Journal*, April 28, 1810 (see also *Columbian*, May 9, 1810, that "in this city under our own eyes, negroes well known to be slaves were suffered to vote without a question as to their freedom"); Fox, *Decline of Aristocracy*, 141 describes how in 1801 "over-zealous friends of the Patroon" suggested the "tenantry of Rensselaerswyck who owed for rent, of which there were probably thousands, would be prosecuted if they failed to cast their ballot for the manor-lord" in that year's election; *Columbian*, June 9, 1810.

44. Young, *Democratic Republicans of New York*, is the classic account; Washington Benevolent Society, "List of Members of the, With Addresses and Trades, 1810," a handwritten register at the New-York Historical Society, Miscellaneous Microfilm reel 21, cross-referenced with black householders in that year's federal census, plus searches for black Federalists like Joseph G. and Robert Y. Sidney. A hint at its whiteness comes from a Republican jibe that "a few of the poorer class are admitted as silent members. . . . They are graciously allowed to run errands, bring up voters at elections, hunt cellars for tattered negroes" (*Public Advertiser*, April 24, 1809).

45. Polgar, "'Whenever They Judge It Expedient,'" is the best account, although occasionally mistaken, for example, that the Council of Revision successfully vetoed the 1811 bill and that Republicans passed "a revised certificate bill in 1814 . . . tacking on amendments in 1815 and 1816."

46. Legislative data are drawn from the invaluable: https://en.wikipedia.org/wiki/New_York_State_Legislature. Federalists took nineteen of twenty-seven House seats in 1812's congressional elections, up from only five of seventeen in 1810; *Albany Argus*, March 9, 1813.

47. Electoral calculations were made using *A New Nation Votes: American Election Returns, 1787–1825*, at http://elections.lib.tufts.edu. In 1810, the leading Federalist, John Vanderbilt, received 1,497 in the Fifth, Sixth, and Seventh Wards; one year later, the lowest-polling Federalist, James Smith, garnered 1,965, with the nearest Republican getting 1,617; Polgar, "'Whenever They Judge It Expedient,'" 4, has a table showing that 65 percent of the 946 black male householders resided in these three wards: 271 in the Fifth Ward, 225 in the Sixth, and 121 in the Seventh.

48. *Northern Whig*, March 29, 1811; *Albany Register*, March 29, 1811. All citations to the legislature's deliberations are in note 50.

49. *New-York Evening Post*, April 22, 1811.

50. *Columbian*, April 8, 1811; see the *Journal of the Assembly of the state of New-York at their thirty-fourth session, begun and held at the city of Albany, the twenty-ninth day of January, 1811* (Albany, NY: S. Southwick, 1811), 231, 310, 311, 315, 316, 351, 358, 359, 360, 401, 404, 405, 406, 412. The Council's April 9 concurrence, not noticed by prior historians, is on 412. The Senate process matched that of the Assembly. On April 6, after the council's second veto, Jonas Platt tried blocking further consideration on procedural grounds and lost. With overwhelming votes in favor, it went back to the Assembly, and was then returned for a final vote. Federalist Daniel Paris moved to expunge the phrase "or mulatto," to protect freeborn men of mixed race or block charges of uncertain parentage, failing 20–8. Read the third time on April 8, it passed 17–7; *Journal of the Senate of the state of New-York: at their thirty-fourth session, begun and held at the city of Albany, the twenty-ninth day of January, 1811* (Albany, NY: S. Southwick, 1811), 143, 144, 163, 164, 196, 197, 199, 200, 201, 202; see *The Balance, and State Journal* (Albany), April 16, 1811 for the enforcement stipulation.

51. *New-York Evening Post*, April 16, 1811; *The Balance, and State Journal*, April 16 (also in the *Columbian* and the *Columbian Gazette* of Utica); Edmund P. Willis, "Social Origins of Political Leadership in New York City from the Revolution to 1815" (PhD diss., University of California, Berkeley, 1967), 346, listed Mercein's assessed worth as $2,600 in 1808 and $11,000 in 1815 (in 1813, the one year when Federalists controlled the Council of Appointment, he was appointed sheriff of New York County).

52. *Evening Post*, April 24, 1811. That the *Post* referred to black "freeholders" is intriguing, since that suggests ownership of real estate, and a considerably larger number of "Assembly voters."

53. Sarah L. H. Gronningsater, "'Expressly Recognized by Our Election Laws': Certificates of Freedom and the Multiple Fates of Black Citizenship in the Early Republic," *WMQ* 75, no. 3 (July 2018): 465, 480, 481, 484, 485, 489.

54. See Brooke, *Columbia Rising*, chap. 7, "Party and Corruption: The Columbia Junto and the Rise of Martin Van Buren, 1799–1812," 287.

55. John L. Brooke, "'King George Has Issued Too Many Pattents for Us': Property and Democracy in Jeffersonian New York," *JER* 33, no. 2 (Summer 2013): 187–217, describes New York as composing "several very different political universes," including the "Seemingly sleepy and apathetic low-turnout counties" in the east, which "provided the consistent base for the New York Jeffersonians," but Columbia was an exception, with turnout that "consistently topped 90 percent" (199, 202, 203, 212). Evidence that black voting had a history can be seen in the 1800 manuscript census. Hudson's population of 3,694 included 751 households; thirteen of those were headed by persons of color, with "(Free Black)" handwritten in, containing 196 persons. Another sixty-one households contained a total of 173 slaves. Among the thirteen black householders, a few names recur in 1810, including Tower Smith, Toby Wall, Joseph Ripley, and Charles Thurston. Presumably these were among the longtime voters whom Republicans attempted to disfranchise in 1808 and after.

56. *Hudson Bee*, March 14, 1809 (in 1820, when Williams gave fiery speeches against the Missouri constitution's racial exclusion, he owned two slaves, one a male between fifteen and twenty-six years old, and the other a girl under the age of fourteen, therefore born after 1799's emancipation, so these must have been indentures, which does not mitigate the implications); *Northern Whig*, April 18, 1809; see the Federalist *Balance*,

March 31, 1807, for Van Alstyne's party service and *Northern Whig*, April 13, 1813 on his election as an assessor, plus the 1810, 1820, and 1830 manuscript censuses for the numerous black Van Alstynes, including six out of forty-five householders of color in 1820; for Van Rensselaer's bill, see *The Balance*, January 28, 1809.

57. *Columbian*, May 9, 1810; earlier the *Hudson Bee*, March 14, 1809, reported Federalists "obtained a majority of 22" in the April 11 city election "by *all and any* means whatsoever" (100 more votes were cast than in 1808, when Republicans won, and "of these, 30 or 40 are always to be had by either party, and a sufficient number might have been obtained by the republicans without the least difficulty; but the *means* they despise and voluntarily left them to their opponents who with *corruption, bribery,* and *rum, rum, rum,* have gained the victory"); *Hudson Bee* repr. in *Albany Register*, May 11, 1810; *Hudson Bee*, March 29, 1811; *Northern Whig*, April 19, 1810 (another article alleged "a certain little gentleman . . . brought with him from Hudson, a package of printed blank Deeds to Kinderhook, to be used upon the spur of the occasion to multiply voters, and that one of those Deeds was filled up for Black Perl and some others"; for the "surrogate" reference and the bribe, see *Northern Whig*, April 26, 1810).

58. *Northern Whig*, April 12, 1811 (in 1810, Federalists charged "a slave, belonging to Jeremiah H. Strong" who, a few days before, had been "offered for sale," was "brought up and suffered to vote," and "was even escorted by his master" [*Northern Whig*, April 12, 1810]). The power of clan is evident here—Robert's brother was Elisha Jenkins, an ex-Federalist-turned-leading-Republican (secretary of state over many terms, eventually mayor of Albany). They were sons of Seth Jenkins, Sr. (who founded the town with Thomas Jenkins, mayor before Robert), as was Seth, Jr., who barred Jacob Waldron in 1811 (for this family, see Denis Tilden Lynch, *An Epoch and a Man: Martin Van Buren and His Times* [New York: Horace Liveright, 1929], 86). In the 1810 census, five of Hudson's seventeen white male householders named Jenkins owned slaves; there was also a black Peter Jenkins. Regarding the supposed slave who voted, Republicans responded, "The case of poor black '*Francis Thomas,*' (as the junto have the name) . . . will bear the test of the severest federal scrutiny. . . . The person to whom they allude, has been free and enjoyed the rights of a freeman for at least six or eight years—and . . . he was never the slave of the late Marshal Jenkins" (*Hudson Bee*, April 19, 1811).

59. The 1810 census listed Waldron as a householder in Hudson, and a man of that name earlier made "an application to the Commissioner of the Land Office for a grant of the ground under water in front of his farm and landing . . . in the township of Haverstraw and county of Rockland" (*New-York Gazette*, August 24, 1798); as late as 1840, Waldron was an Albany delegate to the Convention of the Colored Inhabitants of the State of New York, to Consider Their Political Disabilities (*CA*, September 12, 1840); *Hudson Bee*, March 29, 1811, has the Republican ticket; *Northern Whig*, April 5, 1811, lists Jenkins and Coventry with 358 votes, Clark with 357, Federalist, Jonathan Race, Jr. with 353, and Edmonds 352.

60. *Commercial Advertiser*, April 15, 1812.

61. See Harvey Strum, "Property Qualifications and Voting Behavior in New York, 1807–1816," *JER* 1, no. 4 (Winter 1981): 362; *Columbian*, April 9, 1813 and April 16, 1814; *Northern Whig*, April 19, 1814.

62. Jenkins and Others v. Waldron in 11 *Johnson's Reports* (1814), 114–17. Waldron asserted they "wickedly and designedly . . . refused his vote." The decision noted, "The

plaintiff is a black or coloured man; and . . . tendered a certified copy of a certificate" from Edmonds, dated April 9, 1811, adding he had "offered . . . to make any other proof of his qualification to vote that the inspectors might require, and to take the oaths required by law." The Republicans "rejected the plaintiff's vote, solely on the ground that Samuel Edmonds, at the time of giving the certificate of freedom, was not a judge according to law"; on April 10, Edmonds had received a notice from Marshall Jenkins, the county clerk, dated April 9, informing him of his replacement. All that was required was "a different certificate, or such a one as they should deem legal and valid." The court noted, "The plaintiff had, for 8 or 10 years previous to the election in 1811, voted for members of assembly, and at some of the elections during that period, some of the defendants were inspectors of the poll and received the plaintiff's vote." The local justice had found "no evidence whatever . . . to show that the defendants . . . were actuated by any corrupt or malicious motives towards the plaintiff, or by any other wish or desire than to discharge their duties." Van Buren tried to have the case dismissed, but Waldron was awarded three dollars and costs, which the supreme court overturned on the basis that "this action will not lie without alleging and proving that the defendants acted wilfully and maliciously, &c. The plaintiff must prove corruption, and a design to injure the plaintiff. The action does not lie for a mere error of judgment."

63. See Bielinski, "Jacksons, Lattimores, and Schuylers" on these African American tradesmen; the *Balance*, April 11, 1809, reported a meeting in support of Federalist candidates and listed several hundred men including Jacob Evertson, Isaac Hawkins, S. P. Schuyler (the first two are certainly men of color); *The Balance, & New-York State Journal*, April 6, 1810, reports another meeting attended by several likely men of color, including Peter Bane, Benjamin Juba, and John Johnson.

64. *Evening Post*, February 24, 1812; *Commercial Advertiser*, January 26, 1813; *Journal of the Assembly of the State of New-York at Their Thirty-Sixth Session: Begun and Held at the City of Albany, the Third Day of November, 1812* (Albany, NY: S. Southwick, 1813), 106. The vote was 61–22. *Albany Register*, March 16, 1813.

65. Harvey Strum, "New York Federalists and Opposition to the War of 1812," *World Affairs* 142, no. 3 (Winter 1980): 176, on Tompkins's margin dropping "from 6,610 to 3,234"; *Evening Post*, April 27, 1813.

66. Robert J. Swan, "John Teasman: African-American Educator and the Emergence of Community in Early Black New York City, 1787–1815," *JER* 12, no. 3 (Autumn 1992): 331–56; John Teasman, *An Address, Delivered in the African Episcopal Church, on the 25th March, 1811. Before the New York African Society, for Mutual Relief; Being the First Anniversary of Its Incorporation* (New-York: J. Low, 1811), 6, 7, 8. Sarah Levine-Gronningsater, "Delivering Freedom: Gradual Emancipation, Black Legal Culture, and the Origins of Sectional Crisis in New York, 1759–1870" (PhD diss., University of Chicago, 2014), 256, 258, points out that Tompkins's record on matters other than voting was quite credible. During the War of 1812, he supported the recruitment of black troops, writing Secretary of State James Monroe to that effect, and he had begun calling for total emancipation as early as 1812; it was "Republicans, in the end, who passed the first general emancipation act in United States history" under Tompkins's leadership.

67. *New-York Herald*, April 24, 1813. See also *Columbian*, April 26, 1813, alerting the public that "we will meet at this room on Monday, Tuesday, Wednesday and Thursday, for the purpose of distributing tickets"; *Evening Post*, April 28, 1813.

68. *Otsego Herald*, May 29, 1813, repr. from *Albany Argus*; *New-Hampshire Patriot*, June 15, 1813.

69. *Commercial Advertiser*, November 9, 1813: "A general meeting of the Electors of Colour, friendly to the cause of Liberty, Peace and Commerce" (the Federalist slogan) chaired by Richard Garrison with Robert Y. Sidney as secretary, announced "delegates from the following Wards to the committee of grievance, viz—Tenth Ward, William Blue; Eighth Ward, Thos. Lykins; Seventh Ward, John J. Johnson; Sixth Ward, Thomas Miller, Senr."; it called a meeting for the "lower part of the city" (*Evening Post*, November 11, 1813 and *Commercial Advertiser*, November 12, 1813 for the latter, with Adam Marshall, chair, and Thomas Sanders, secretary, approving "the proceedings of our brethren in the upper wards," and lamenting "the division in politics, among the electors of colour," establishing "a committee of grievances . . . distinct from anything of a political nature, calculated solely to promote habits of industry, honesty and sobriety," with delegates from the Fifth Ward, Robert F. Williams; Fourth Ward, Thomas L. Jennings; Third Ward, Samuel Claus; Second Ward, James Barclay; First Ward, Richard Chace); *Mercantile Advertiser*, November 10, 1813; *Columbian*, November 17, 1813; also *National Advocate*. About these men, consider that Robert Sidney and Thomas Miller were on the Committee of Twelve organizing celebrations of slave trade abolition in 1807 (*Evening Post*, December 16, 1807) and were active thereafter; Adam Marshall and Richard Garrison were sweepmasters, with the former heading the United Society of Chimney Sweeps (Gilje and Rock, "Sweep O!," 521, 528); Thomas Jennings (or Jinnings) remained a leading activist for decades; Claus (or Clause) was one of fourteen founders of the African Society for Mutual Relief on June 6, 1808, the preeminent benevolent institution, and he and Miller were among its eighty-five original incorporators in 1810, with Williams and Jinnings invited to join later (John J. Zuille, *Historical Sketch of the New York African Society for Mutual Relief, Organized in the City of New York 1808, Chartered by the Legislature of the State of New York, 1810, The Oldest Society of Its Kind in the United States* [n.p., c. 1892], 5, 27–28). Finally, Sidney, Miller, and Claus sat on the board of the Wilberforce Philanthropic Association (*Evening Post*, July 22, 1811).

70. *Columbian*, April 25 and 26, 1814; *New-York Gazette*, April 25, 1814; see a notice by the African Society, *Columbian*, August 19, 1814, organizing "a day's work at Brooklyn Heights," also a call to "the citizens of colour" to "make arrangements for a voluntary tour of duty on Harlem Heights," *Evening Post*, August 30, 1814, and a similar call in the *Columbian*, October 29, 1814. For the partisan element, see Baltimore *American and Commercial Daily Advertiser*, August 17, 1814, printing the Committee of Defense report, including "Journeymen Printers, 200, Patriotic Sons of Erin, 1000, Men employed by Ward & Tallman, 182, Joseph Sidney, with 150 coloured men, Asbury African, about 70, under Alexander Lattin"; *New-York Gazette*, April 19, 1815.

71. Strum, "New York Federalists and Opposition to the War of 1812," 183; besides Cornog, *Birth of Empire*, biographies of Van Buren describe New York's political labyrinth in the 1810s: Donald B. Cole, *Martin Van Buren and the American Political System* (Princeton, NJ: Princeton University Press, 1984); John Niven, *Martin Van Buren: The Romantic Age in American Politics* (New York: Oxford University Press, 1983); Denis Tilden Lynch, *An Epoch and a Man: Martin Van Buren and His Times* (New York: Horace Liveright, 1929).

72. Niven, *Martin Van Buren*, 72.

73. *Columbian*, March 22, 1815; see *Journal of the Assembly of the State of New-York, at their Thirty-Eighth Session (Second Meeting,) Begun and Held at the City of Albany, the Thirty-First Day of January, 1815* (Albany, NY: J. Buel, Printer to the State, 1815), 420–22. Emott's amendment passed 42–32, the only one of twelve roll-calls where significant numbers crossed party lines.

74. *Evening Post*, March 25, 1815; *New-York Gazette*, March 15, 1806, on the Council of Appointment naming him "Inspector of the State-Prison"; *American Citizen*, January 15, 1807, on his election as chairman of the NYMS's Standing Committee; *Commercial Advertiser*, May 4, 1807, listing Slocum as one of thirteen trustees with DeWitt Clinton of a free-school society for poor children.

75. *Journal of the Assembly of the State of New-York: at Their Thirty-Eighth Session,* 469–72, 477–78; Strum, "Property Qualifications and Voting Behavior in New York."

76. *Journal of the Senate of the State of New-York: at Their Thirty-Eighth Session, (second meeting,) Begun and Held at the City of Albany, the Thirty-First day of January, 1815* (Albany, NY: J. Buel, Printer to the State, 1815), 305–6, 326–28. In the 1810 census, a William Thorne in the city's Tenth Ward owned two slaves; *Spectator*, April 19, 2015.

77. *Evening Post*, April 18, 1815; *Northern Post* (Salem, NY), April 20, 1815.

78. *New-York Herald*, April 19, 1815. The April 22 *Post* charged that Slocum was "in needy circumstances" and black men were being taxed "to provide for his maintenance."

79. *Columbian*, April 4, 1815; *National Advocate*, April 22 and 24, 1815; *Albany Argus*, April 11, 1815.

80. *Evening Post*, April 24, 1815 (the *Post* added a Swiftian tale of Slocum struggling with a four-hundred-pound black man who "lives in Church-street and sells oysters. . . . Mr. Best protested he was too fat and pursy a man to stand long enough" to be measured, and, following "a scuffle . . . Best accidentally trod upon him, and smashed him" [*Evening Post*, April 26, 1815]); *New-York Herald*, April 26, 1815. Hedden's claims were credible; he had been a ward justice since 1810 (*Commercial Advertiser*, March 3, 1810) and was elected alderman as a Federalist in 1812 by a large majority.

81. *Albany Register*, April 25, 1815; *Columbian*, April 27, 1815 and May 1, 1815, noting the average city assembly vote dropped from 10,476 in 1814 to 9,333 in 1815, with a much larger Republican decrease.

82. Polgar, "'Whenever They Judge It Expedient,'" 9; Niven, *Martin Van Buren*, 52.

83. *Courier*, March 25, 1816. On April 10, it added, "Many a white man . . . would not vote, if it should cost him eleven and sixpence to do it."

84. *New-York Herald*, April 3, 1816, reprinting *Evening Post*; April 2, 1816.

85. *Evening Post*, April 9, 1816; *Journal of the Assembly of the State of New-York: At Their Thirty-Ninth Session, Begun and Held at the City of Albany, the Thirtieth Day of January, 1816* (Albany, NY: J. Buel, 1816), 357; *Courier*, April 14, 1816; *Columbian*, April 10, 11, 12, and 15, 1816; *National Advocate*, April 18, 22, and 26, 1816; *Columbian*, April 29, 1816, on them hailing Governor Tompkins for his "steady, humane and uniform conduct towards many of us, while a member of the Manumission Society," and claiming Republicans were "the guardians of equal rights and freedom, and the true friends of injured Africans"; *Evening Post*, April 23, 1816; *New-York Herald*, April 24, 1816; *Evening Post*, April 25, 1816.

86. *Courier*, April 4 and 5, 1816; *Evening Post*, April 29, 1816. Well past the election, the *Courier* mocked Rodman's "famous letter" in verse—"'Twas I sir who drew up a bill / (I humbly think with wondrous skill,) / Against the Blacks. They're quite too free, / To suit our purpose now you see" (May 22, 1816).

87. *Evening Post*, April 27, 1816. Gronningsater, "'Expressly Recognized by Our Election Laws,'" 495, notes that Radcliff issued eighteen certificates in 1816.

88. *National Advocate* and *Evening Post*, May 1, 1816 (also *Columbian*); *New-York Herald*, May 4, 1816; *Columbian*, *National Advocate*, and *Courier*, May 2, 1816.

89. *New-York Herald*, May 4, 1816; *Columbian*, May 4, 1816; *Shamrock*, May 4, 1816.

90. On Van Rensselaer's reputation, see Charles W. McCurdy, *The Anti-Rent Era in New York Law and Politics, 1839–1865* (Chapel Hill: University of North Carolina Press, 2001), 12: "Contemporaries took it for granted" that he "was the richest man in America," and various present-day websites list him as one of the wealthiest Americans of all time.

91. Cornog, *Birth of Empire*, 131.

92. *National Advocate*, April 23, 1819 and May 10, 1817. In 1817, the average assembly vote for the nine contested seats was 3,998 Bucktail versus 2,139 Clintonian, with similar margins in subsequent years. For the Irish-Clintonian alliance, see *Mercantile Advertiser*, April 2, 1819, for a Sixth Ward meeting backing "the PEOPLE'S consolidated ticket" of Federalist-backed Clintonians, with Charles Christian as chair, and a slate of Dougherty, Kelley, Mooney, Davey, McKesson, and McCarthy. The Federalists retained most Assembly seats in Queens, Dutchess, Columbia, Albany, and Rensselaer Counties through the Forty-Fourth legislature elected in spring 1820, a bloc of 19–21 votes. In 1819, they were shut out of the Senate, although their Assembly delegation expanded to thirty-two because of Republican fissures, but 1821 saw only motley "Clintonian-Federalist" nominations, and in 1822, New York became a one-party state.

93. *National Advocate*, March 22, 25, 26, 27, 1817; *Columbian*, April 1, 1818 (Root's motion as recorded in the official *Journal* omitted "white," simply directing that equal suffrage "ought to be extended to all free male citizens above the age of twenty-one years, and who may have resided in any county for one year, and actually been assessed and paid taxes"; see *Journal of the Assembly of the State of New-York: at their forty-first session, begun and held at the Capitol, in the city of Albany, the twenty-seventh day of January, 1818* (Albany, NY: J. Buel, 1818), 600 (March 27, 1818); *Watch-Tower*, March 8, 1819.

94. *Columbian*, April 22, 1819 (it informed an out-of-state editor "it is no '*novelty*' in this state for people of color to assemble to express their sentiments on the subject of candidates for office. In this city that class of people are *numerous and respectable*— they are voters, and many of them are *well educated*," *Columbian*, April 26, 1819); for Gilbert and Christian, see *New-York Daily Advertiser*, April 27, 1818 (Howard Rock, *Artisans of the New Republic: The Tradesmen of New York City in the Age of Jefferson* [New York: New York University Press, 1984], 157, gives Christian's occupation); *Columbian*, April 20, 1819; *National Advocate*, April 23, 1819, and April 20, 1819, that Gilbert "was bountiful in his complimentary salutations. . . . And yet, for all, said an intelligent person of colour, Mr. Clinton did not offer to put one of us on his ticket for the assembly"; Theodorus Bailey to Matthias B. Tallmadge, April 27, 1819, in Tallmadge Family Papers, NYHS.

95. *Columbian*, April 28 and 20, 1820. Cole, *Martin Van Buren*, 58–59, describes widespread concern among Bucktails and their southern allies that Clintonians and Federalists would create a northern antislavery party: "He [Clinton] had split with southern Republicans in 1812, and had united with Federalists to control the legislature in 1819. Many of Clinton's friends, including the Spencers, Solomon Van Rensselaer, William W. Van Ness, and Charles G. Haines, were well-known opponents of slavery."

96. In 1820, Noah again mocked Gilbert for visiting "the cellars in Bancker-street, and houses of bad character in the Collect, to register them and see that they vote for Dewitt Clinton," although the next day he charged, *De Witt Clinton has been in the constant habit of holding slaves!* and earlier he simply reported, "Col. Christian has called a meeting of the electors of *colour*" (*National Advocate*, April 21, 22, and 11, 1820); *Spectator*, June 22, 1821; Gronningsater, "'Expressly Recognized by Our Election Laws,'" 502–3, has evidence of an "uptick" in requests for certificates with seven filed in Ontario County in April 1821 versus two in 1819 and only one in 1820, while Albany saw nine more filed in time for the June election; *Evening Post*, April 19, 1821, "From the New York Statesmen."

97. *Rochester Telegraph*, February 22, 1820, reprinting from the *Ontario Messenger*; *American Journal* (Ithaca), March 15, 1820.

98. Jonathan D. Sarna, *Jacksonian Jew: The Two Worlds of Mordecai Noah* (New York: Holmes & Meier, 1981), 15, on Noah's consulship reflecting "a long tradition in the history of diplomacy: the appointment of Jews as intermediaries between Christian and Moslem countries"; Michael Warner, Natasha Hurley, Luis Iglesias, and Sonia Di Loreto, "A Soliloquy 'Lately Spoken at the African Theatre': Race and the Public Sphere in New York City, 1821," *American Literature* 73, no. 1 (March 2001): 28, 30.

99. *National Advocate*, November 1, June 2, August 26, December 27, 1820; March 3 and June 25, 1821.

100. *National Advocate*, June 29, 1821.

101. *National Advocate*, July 14, 1821.

102. Sarna, *Jacksonian Jew*, 39.

103. Joseph L. Arbena, "Politics or Principle? Rufus King and the Opposition to Slavery, 1785–1825," *Essex Institute Historical Collections* 101 (1965): 72; David Brion Davis, *Challenging the Boundaries of Slavery* (Cambridge, MA: Harvard University Press, 2003), 42: "Up to that time no statesman or political leader in the world had publicly made such a radical declaration of slavery's illegality."

104. George Bancroft, *Martin Van Buren to the End of His Public Career* (New York: Harper & Brothers, 1889) quoted in Donald B. Cole, *Martin Van Buren and the American Political System* (Princeton, NJ: Princeton University Press, 1984), 10; Denis Tilden Lynch, *An Epoch and a Man: Martin Van Buren and His Times* (New York: Horace Liveright, 1929), 38; Young remained an important Democrat for decades, in June 1848 chairing the convention of Barnburners that broke party unity to nominate Van Buren for the presidency in advance of the Free Soil Convention.

105. See Polgar, "'Whenever They Judge It Expedient,'" 13, that "if the Bucktails did not exclude free blacks from suffrage expansion, they risked enfranchising thousands of voters affiliated with their political adversaries."

106. Jabez D. Hammond, *The History of Political Parties in the State of New York, From the Ratification of the Federal Constitution to December, 1840, Fourth Edition,*

Corrected and Enlarged (Syracuse, NY: Hall, Mills, 1852), 2:21; 1:380–81, "Could it have been anticipated that Col. Young, who ably and zealously advocated this bill, would have been found in the convention of 1821, supporting, and probably by his influence, procuring to be inserted in the amended constitution, a clause which was intended forever further to degrade this down trodden race of men, to whose aid he now, in this time of imminent peril, resorted?"

107. Carl F. Stychin, "The Commentaries of Chancellor James Kent and the Development of an American Common Law," *American Journal of Legal History* 37 (October 1993): 445, 448. Kent's example is telling: "Homicide is justifiable in every case in which it is rendered necessary in self-defense. . . . The right of self-defense in these cases is founded on the law of nature, and is not, and cannot be superseded by the law of society" (449), a doctrine North Carolina's Chief Justice William Gaston invoked in 1838 to justify a slave killing his master.

108. Nathaniel H. Carter and William L. Stone, Reporters, *Reports of the Proceedings and Debates of the Convention of 1821, Assembled for the Purpose of Amending the Constitution of the State of New-York* (Albany, NY: E. & F. Hosford, 1821), 178–81.

109. Carter and Stone, *Reports of the Proceedings and Debates of the Convention*, 182–84.

110. Carter and Stone, 185–86.

111. Carter and Stone, 186, 190, 191–92.

112. Carter and Stone, 193, 197, 198, 199.

113. Carter and Stone, 200–201. Jay's slap at Young and reference to "privileged classes as they exist in Europe" are not in the *Proceedings*; see the *New-York American*, September 26, 1821.

114. Carter and Stone, *Reports of the Proceedings and Debates of the Convention*, 257, 281, 288; *New-York Daily Advertiser*, October 3, 1821; *NASS*, December 17, 1846.

115. Carter and Stone, *Reports of the Proceedings and Debates of the Convention*, 365, 369, 378. Chancellor Kent repelled attempts to substitute simple "white" suffrage by adverting he was "in favour of the proviso reported by the committee. . . . It was true, that the blacks were in some respects a degraded portion of the community, but he was unwilling to see them disfranchised, and the door eternally barred against them. The proviso would not cut them off from all hope, and might in some degree alleviate the wrongs we had done them. It would have a tendency to make them industrious and frugal, with the prospect of participating in the right of suffrage" (Carter and Stone, *Reports of the Proceedings and Debates of the Convention*, 364).

116. Carter and Stone, *Reports of the Proceedings and Debates of the Convention*, 407, 409, 558.

117. *Berks and Schuylkill Journal*, September 29, 1821; *Richmond Enquirer*, October 12, 1821, reprinting *Patriot*, October 3. For Noah's Charleston connections, see Sarna, *Jacksonian Jew*, 2, 13.

118. *National Advocate*, September 22, 24, 25 and 29, 1821.

119. *National Advocate*, October 2, 1821.

120. *Evening Post*, September 26, 1821.

121. See, as an example, *New-York American*, August 29, 1820, describing emancipation as an injustice equal to slavery, since it meant "liberating a population which can never participate in the privileges of the community," adding that the "greater por-

tion are worse off than if they had remained in a state of slavery." On September 6, 1821, it emphasized "the practical benefits . . . from the exclusion of blacks from the exercise of a privilege which they have always abused . . . whatever diversity of opinion may exist as to the abstract justice of giving a political distinction to colour."

122. Rufus King to John A. King, "Thursday morning" in late September; King to Charles King, September 30, 1821, both in box 19, folder 4, King Papers, NYHS. On universal suffrage, see his September 27 letter to Charles, "We have been engaged in debating the Right of Suffrage—there is too much disposition to make it in effect tho not in name universal," with militia service "as a qualification" passing "by a great majority, plus working on the roads. . . . We may as well in words admit all to vote, who are Citizens above 21 years, and who have visited a short Time among us."

123. John A. King to Rufus King, October 3, 1821; Charles King to Rufus King, October 11, 1821; John A. King to Rufus King, October 26, 1821, all in box 19, folder 5, King Papers, NYHS.

124. Jefferson, Washington, Oneida, Saratoga, Montgomery, Herkimer, Madison, Onondaga, Ontario, Genesee, Otsego, Albany, Rensselaer, Dutchess, Orange, Suffolk, and New York Counties all split over this vote.

125. Levine-Gronningsater, "Delivering Freedom," 270–71. See also Gronningsater, "'Expressly Recognized by Our Election Laws,'" 505–6, that "for a substantial number of New York politicians, completely destroying black suffrage had proved a bridge too far. As a result, the state's constitution continued to recognize black residents as 'citizens' with suffrage rights, albeit on a dramatically unequal basis. Black voters and their local allies had played vital roles in inspiring white antislavery powerbrokers to hold the line, both during the Missouri Crisis and at the 1821 constitutional convention. Certificates of freedom, and the discussion and paperwork around them, provided compelling evidence of black men's citizenship. Black suffrage was not a legal abstraction or something that happened only in one place; it was a visible practice throughout the state." An intriguing example of its long-term impact was Myron Holley, who issued certificates of freedom as Ontario County's clerk in 1813, and later helped found its Liberty Party.

126. Franklin B. Hough, *Statistics of Population of the City and County of New York, As Shown by the State Census of 1865, With the Comparative Results of This and Previous Enumerations, and Other Statistics Given by the State and Federal Census, From the Earliest Period, Document No. 13, Board of Supervisors, August 15, 1866* (New York: New York Printing Company, 1866), 19; Cornog, *Birth of Empire*, 142; Williamson, *American Suffrage*, 201; *Albany Argus*, April 25, 1823, listing "Appointments: City and County of Albany"; Hough, *Statistics of Population*, 60.

127. *Mr. Van Buren's Opinions* (Georgetown, DE: Sipple & Cannon, 1836); *Life of Martin Van Buren* (1844), quoted in Fox, "Negro Vote in Old New York," 263.

Chapter Nine

1. Charles M. Payne, *I've Got the Light of Freedom: The Organizing Tradition and the Mississippi Freedom Struggle*, 2nd ed. (Berkeley: University of California Press, 2007).

2. See Jabez D. Hammond, *Political History of the State of New York, from Jan. 1, 1841, to Jan. 1, 1847*, vol. 3, *Including the Life of Silas Wright* (Syracuse, NY: Hall & Dickson,

1848), 248, 290–91 on the division between what he termed "conservative whigs" and "radical whigs," and 536, where he notes that the "Radical whigs . . . constituted a large majority of the Whig party."

3. Lee Benson, *The Concept of Jacksonian Democracy: New York as a Test Case* (Princeton, NJ: Princeton University Press, 1961), 3, and 119 for how Tammany "operated a permanent efficient bureau which quickly converted aliens into naturalized citizens" and "steadfast Democrats."

4. L. Ray Gunn, "Society, Religion, and Reform," in Milton M. Klein, ed., *The Empire State: A History of New York* (Ithaca, NY: Cornell University Press, 2001), 384; Benson, *Concept of Jacksonian Democracy*, 13–14, describes how "from the time that Seward appeared on the political scene in 1824, the reciprocal relationships among internal improvements, social equality (broadly conceived), and free public education formed the dominant theme in his speeches, writings, and actions," quoting an 1839 speech, "It is the object of republican institutions to encourage and stimulate improvement of the physical condition of the country, and to promote the moral and intellectual advancement of its citizens; to discourage military ambition, and shun the causes which produce stagnation of enterprise and promote personal faction, that engross the passions of the people, and arrest the progress of improvement. If the theory of our constitution was fully expounded by its founders, its most complete security is to be effected by the highest attainable equality in the social conditions of our citizens"; Sarah Levine-Gronningsater, "Delivering Freedom: Gradual Emancipation, Black Legal Culture, and the Origins of Sectional Crisis in New York, 1759–1870" (PhD diss., University of Chicago, 2014), 369; Frederick W. Seward, *William H. Seward: An Autobiography, From 1801 to 1834; With a Memoir of His Life, and Selections from His Letters, 1831–1846* (New York: Derby and Miller, 1891, orig. pub. by D. Appleton, 1877), 490, 600, 636.

5. See *Hudson River Chronicle*, January 24, 1843, for Seward's letter to black men in Buffalo, dated December 26, 1842, and *NASS*, January 26, 1843, reporting a letter to Seward from New York City leaders, including Ulysses B. Vidal and James McCune Smith, expressing "the high admiration with which your conduct during the last four years has inspired them," and *Albany Weekly Patriot*, January 26, 1843, on a meeting resolving that his action regarding Virginia "deserves unqualifiedly the respect, esteem and gratitude not only of the colored citizens of this State and the United States, but of every lover of liberty throughout the world," with a committee of ten elected to present the address to him, and Seward's replies to various; Chase to James Birney, January 21, 1842, suggesting they substitute Seward (or John Quincy Adams) for Birney as their presidential candidate, in *Letters of James Gillespie Birney, 1831–1857*, ed. Dwight L. Dumond (New York: D. Appleton-Century, 1938), 2:661–62.

6. Seward, *William H. Seward*, 810; Glyndon G. Van Deusen, *William Henry Seward* (New York: Oxford University Press, 1967), 94–97 on the 1846 case, and 137 on the Jerry Rescue; *NS*, April 26, May 10 and 30, 1850, and April 17, 1851, thanking Seward for his support. The most recent biography is Walter Stahr, *Seward: Lincoln's Indispensable Man* (New York: Simon & Schuster, 2012).

7. See Octavius Frothingham, *Gerrit Smith: A Biography* (New York: G. P. Putnam's Sons, 1878); Ralph Volney Harlow, *Gerrit Smith: Philanthropist and Reformer* (New York: Russell & Russell, 1939); John Stauffer, *The Black Hearts of Men: Radical Aboli-*

tionists and the Transformation of Race (Cambridge, MA: Harvard University Press, 2002); NS, October 20, 1848, a letter from Smith to a black editor who had declared "Gerrit Smith is a *colored* man!," replying that if he were to vote for anyone who would "take part in the . . . crushing of your race [e.g., a Whig], I should forfeit the honorable and welcome name which you accorded to me; and . . . give proof that, after all, I am but a *white* man."

8. See *Census of the State of New-York For the Year 1825* in *Journal of the Senate of the State of New-York; at the Forty-Ninth Session* (Albany, NY: E. Croswell, Printer to the State, 1826) and *Census of the State of New-York For the Year 1835* (Albany, NY: Croswell, Van Bentritsen de Burt, 1836); *Christian Freeman*, May 22, 1845, reporting on a Convention of Colored Citizens, where Smith noted that "the 2000 colored voters in the State, now possessing $250 worth of real estate, could, by energetic efforts, extend the number to 10,000."

9. Whitney R. Cross, *The Burned-Over District: The Social and Intellectual History of Enthusiastic Religion in Western New York, 1800–1850* (Ithaca, NY: Cornell University Press, 1950), vii, 3, 103; Hendrik Booraem V, *The Formation of the Republican Party in New York: Politics and Conscience in the Antebellum North* (New York: New York University Press, 1983), 106.

10. Kevin Kenny, *The American Irish: A History* (Routledge: New York, 2000), 126, points out that "more than half" of the emigrants left from the "most-impoverished, often Gaelic-speaking, regions along the Atlantic seaboard" of western Ireland; a poem titled "Abolition Puritans," quoted in John Wertheimer, "The Green and the Black: Irish Nationalism and the Dilemmas of Abolitionism," *New York Irish History* 5 (1990–91): 10n63; *The Pilot* from 1851, quoted in Carl Wittke, *The Irish in America* (Baton Rouge: Louisiana State University Press, 1970), 129; Florence E. Gibson, *The Attitudes of the New York Irish toward State and National Affairs* (New York: Columbia University Press, 1951), 104–5, quoting a letter in the *Irish American* on December 10, 1859.

11. *New York Times*, May 11, 1850, quoted in Wittke, *Irish in America*, 125; *New-York Tribune*, September 24, 1856; *FDP*, January 4, 1855.

12. Helen I. Cowan, "Charles Williamson and the Southern Entrance to the Genesee Country," *New York History* 23, no. 3 (July 1942): 260–75; Kathryn Grover, *Make a Way Somehow: African-American Community Life in a Northern Community, 1790–1865* (Syracuse, NY: Syracuse University Press, 1994), 13, 19; Austin Steward, *Twenty-Two Years a Slave and Forty Years a Freeman*, with an Introduction by Graham Russell Hodges (Syracuse, NY: Syracuse University Press, 2002), 18; Tendai Mutunhu, "Tompkins County: An Underground Railroad Transit in Central New York," *AANYLH* 3 (1979): 17; *CA*, October 14, 1837.

13. Peter Wheeler, *Chains and Freedom, or, The Life and Adventures of Peter Wheeler, A Colored Man Yet Living, A Slave in Chains, A Sailor on the Deep, and A Sinner on the Cross*, with an Introduction by Graham Russell Gao Hodges (Tuscaloosa: University of Alabama Press, 2009), 46; Steward, *Twenty-Two Years a Slave*, 49, 57.

14. John R. McKivigan and Jason H. Silverman, "Monarchial Liberty and Republican Slavery: West Indies Emancipation Celebrations in Upstate New York and Canada West," *AANYLH* (January 1986): 7; Van Gosse, "'As a Nation, the English Are Our Friends': The Emergence of African American Politics in the British Atlantic World, 1772–1861," *American Historical Review* (October 2008): 1003–28.

15. *The Rev. J. W. Loguen, As a Slave and as a Freeman, a Narrative of Real Life* (Syracuse, NY: J. G. K. Truair, 1859, repr. 1968 by Negro Universities Press), 344. The shock of seeing black troops wearing the Queen's uniform was widely shared; see *Narratives of the Sufferings of Lewis and Milton Clarke, Sons of a Soldier of the Revolution, During a Captivity of More Than Twenty Years Among the Slaveholders of Kentucky, One of the So Called Christian States of North America, Dictated By Themselves* (Boston: Bela Marsh, 1846), describing how Lewis Clarke, born in 1815 in Madison County, Kentucky, "upon the plantation of my grandfather, Samuel Campbell" (7), finally reached Canada, where "Just before I got to Chatham, I met two colored soldiers, with a white man, bound, and driving him along before them. This was something quite new. I thought then, sure enough, this is the land for me" (42).

16. Most of the younger intellectuals, even the ordained ministers, pursued a moneymaking trade: Philip A. Bell sold coal, Samuel E. Cornish and Charles B. Ray were shoemakers, David Ruggles opened a grocery (in which he employed a teenaged Samuel R. Ward) and later a bookstore, Henry Garnet was a seafarer, and Thomas Van Rensselaer kept a "Temperance House" restaurant (Rhoda Golden Freeman, *The Free Negro in New York City in the Era before the Civil War* [New York: Garland, 1994], 207–10); Shane White, *Prince of Darkness: The Untold Story of Jeremiah G. Hamilton, Wall Street's First Black Millionaire* (New York: St. Martin's, 2015); *CA*, July 29, 1837.

17. David W. Blight, Anna Mae Duane, James O. Horton, and Thomas Thurston, *"Hope Is the First Great Blessing": Leaves from the African Free School Presentation Book* (New York: New-York Historical Society, 2008); *A Memorial Discourse by the Rev. Henry Highland Garnet, Delivered in the Hall of the House of Representatives, Washington City, D.C., on Sabbath, February 12, 1865. With an Introduction by James McCune Smith, M.D.* (Philadelphia: Joseph M. Wilson, 1865), 27–28, for McCune Smith on how a classical high school, meaning the "study of Greek and Latin languages," was disapproved even by "colored men, of admitted force of character" who were "opposed to this innovation" as useless, whereas figures like the Reverends Peter Williams, Theodore Wright, and Samuel Cornish "reasonably held that the vaunted superiority of the whites depended on their superior education"; Milton C. Sernett, "First Honor: Oneida Institute's Role in the Fight against American Racism and Slavery," *New York History* 66, no. 2 (April 1985): 101–22; another Huguenot Episcopalian, Lorillard of the famous tobacco company, was especially beloved, because he consistently employed black men in responsible positions and patronized St. Philip's, and his brother George gave the land for its first building (B. F. De Costa, *Three Score and Ten: The Story of St. Philips' [sic] Church, New York City* [New York: Printed for the Parish, 1889], 18); Robert Trendel, "John Jay II: Antislavery Conscience of the Episcopal Church," *Historical Magazine of the Protestant Episcopal Church* 3 (1976): 238, 241–42; Robert A. Trendel, Jr., "William Jay: Churchman, Public Servant and Reformer" (PhD diss., Southern Illinois University, 1972, New York: Arno, Dissertations in American Biography Series, 1982), ii.

18. See Carla L. Peterson, *Black Gotham: A Family History of African Americans in Nineteenth-Century New York City* (New Haven, CT: Yale University Press, 2011) on these two generations and their postbellum successors; *New York Herald*, October 14, 1856; John Hewitt, "Mr. Downing and His Oyster House: The Life and Good Works of an African-American Entrepreneur," *New York History* 74, no. 3 (July 1993): 229–52,

is the best account, relying on his son George T. Downing's "A Sketch of the Life and Times of Thomas Downing," *AME Church Review* (1888), which portrayed a prerevolutionary Eastern Shore where "slavery was not so strongly entrenched . . . the slaves were few in number and were more in the condition of subordinates in a patriarchal seclusion" (403), and stressed his trans-Atlantic and commercial connections, for example, Queen Victoria sending him a gold chronometer after sampling oysters shipped to London, his investments in banks and railroads, and that he and Virginia governor Henry A. Wise were "playmates in their boyhood days" (404) and Wise visited him in the city; for Downing's politics, see White, *Prince of Darkness*, 42, 43, 74, 114–16, 290, 293; the reference to Weed is in Downing, "Sketch of the Life and Times of Thomas Downing," 409.

19. *Rights of All*, May 1, 1829; James McCune Smith, "Sketch of the Life and Labors of Rev. Henry Highland Garnet," *Memorial Discourse by the Rev. Henry Highland Garnet*, 23; Alexander Crummell, *Eulogy on Henry Highland Garnet, D. D., Presbyterian Minister, Late Minister Resident of the U. S. to the Republic Of Liberia, Delivered Under the Auspices of the Union Bethel Literary and Historical Association in the Nineteenth Street Baptist Church, May 4, 1882* (Washington, DC, 1882), 8, describing their meeting at 137 Leonard Street where "as little boys, Garnet and myself became school-mates and life-long friends."

20. Gerald Sorin, *The New York Abolitionists: A Case Study of Political Radicalism* (Westport, CT: Greenwood, 1970), 90.

21. See Peter P. Hinks, *To Awaken My Afflicted Brethren: David Walker and the Problem of Antebellum Slave Resistance* (University Park: Pennsylvania State University Press, 1997), 102–3, on its provenance; Jacqueline Bacon, *Freedom's Journal: The First African-American Newspaper* (Lanham, MD: Lexington Books, 2007); *Weekly Advocate*, February 25, 1837.

22. *Weekly Advocate*, March 18, 1837, for public pledges by these eminent white men; for Philadelphia, see *CA*, November 25, 1837, and for overall circulation, December 23, 1837; the December 7, 1839, issue, announcing the likely "LAST NUMBER OF THE COLORED AMERICAN," referenced "very limited patronage . . . from the cities of New York, Philadelphia, and Boston. . . . In New York we have now about 600 subscribers, nearly one half of whom owe their subscription. Since June 1838, we have sent to Philadelphia at one time 300 copies, but we now send only 100"; for Ray's travels, see *CA*, September 2, 1837; October 14, 1837; November 4, 1837; September 8, 1838; September 15, 1838; September 22, 1838; September 29, 1838; October 20, 1838; November 3, 1838; November 10, 1838; David E. Swift, *Black Prophets of Justice: Activist Clergy before the Civil War* (Baton Rouge: Louisiana State University Press, 1989), 78, describes Ray's work as "something new for Afro-Americans—the systematic spreading of knowledge among blacks across the North," based on his "insatiable interest in people of all sorts," which gave Ray "a broad network of acquaintances and friends that would keep the *Colored American* afloat for nearly five years" and led to "the staging of successful black state conventions."

23. *CA*, September 14, 1839, a letter from Jehu Jones in Toronto; January 27, 1838 on elections in Jamaica and Antigua; October 5, 1839 for the Proclamation by His Excellency Lieutenant-General Sir Colin Campbell, K. C. B. Lieutenant Governor and Commander in Chief in and over Her Majesty's Province of Nova Scotia; *CA*, September 2,

1837, declaring, "We have always felt favorable to the politics of the present administration, but our preference has been for principles, not for men," proceeding to damn Van Buren as "a political demagogue" because of his anti-abolitionist stance, also November 18, 1837, "A year ago, we elected Mr. Van Buren by a very respectable majority indeed, and PRIDED OURSELVES in giving A PRESIDENT to the Nation. But alas! how soon was our honest pride, and our joy changed to sorrow. Our Idol deceived us, and sold himself to the south"; *CA*, June 17, 1837.

24. *Macon Weekly Telegraph*, May 16, 1837; *Southern Churchman*, Richmond, June 9, 1837; *Albany Argus*, May 29, 1838; *Daily Picayune*, September 4, 1838; *Portland Weekly Advertiser*, December 7, 1841; *Salem Gazette*, December 7, 1841; *Massachusetts Spy*, December 8, 1841; *Hampshire Gazette*, December 14, 1841; *Newport Mercury*, December 18, 1841; *Connecticut Courant*, January 1, 1842.

25. See *CA*, March 3, 1838, reprinting the *Colored Man's Journal* with contempt: "There is not a colored man north of the Potomac, who possesses talent enough to write a newspaper article, who entertains any such views as characterize the leading article, in that Paper. Nor is there one so base, and so destitute of principle, as to be willing to compromise all the interests of his brethren away in such a manner"; *Emancipator*, November 21, 1839 and December 17, 1840.

26. *Journal of the Senate of the State of New-York, At Their Forty-Eighth Session, Begun and Held at the Capitol, in the City of Albany, the third day of January, 1826* (Albany, NY: E. Croswell, 1825), 58–63, 136, 147. In 1827, at a ceremony celebrating emancipation, Austin Steward, later a leader in suffrage conventions, openly disdained any such effort. Since they already "held many of the dearest rights of freemen," in terms of "lives and personal liberties . . . rights of property," therefore "so long as we live under a free and happy government which denies us not the protection of its laws, why should we fret and vex ourselves because we have had no part in framing them, not anything to do with their administration." They should "enjoy without repining, the freedom, privileges, and immunities which wise and equal laws have awarded us," and, after all, "are we alone shut out and excluded from any share in the administration of government? Are not the clergy, a class of men equally ineligible to office? . . . And are we alone excluded from what the world chooses to denominate polite society? And are not the vast majority of the polar race excluded?" (an obscure reference). He concluded with a paean worthy of Booker T. Washington: "Look around you, my friends: what rational enjoyment is not within your reach? Your homes are in the noblest country in the world, and all of that country which your real happiness requires, may at any time be yours" (Steward, *Twenty-Two Years a Slave*, 75).

27. *CA*, August 19, 1837; *Jamestown Journal*, January 28, 1835, reprinted from the *New York American* a commentary noting, "According to the Constitution of New York a man with a dark skin, however intelligent and exemplary, shall not be a voter, except upon conditions burdensome and degrading, while the vilest of white men after taking a drunken oath of citizenship, are free to vote without any condition. . . . The colored population of this city are now about to proposition the Legislature to take the necessary measures for an amendment to the constitution, abolishing this unjust and odious distinction"; *Albany Argus*, January 10, 1837.

28. *Cabinet* (Schenectady), February 8, 1837, reprinting the *Albany Journal*; *Commercial Advertiser*, February 6, 1837; *Journal of the Assembly of the State of New-York at Their Sixtieth Session, Begun and Held at the Capitol, in the City of Albany, on the Third Day of January, 1837* (Albany, NY: E. Croswell, Printer to the State, 1837), 210, 414, 415, 416, 481, 560, 1232–33.

29. *CA*, November 18, 1837.

30. *Journal of the Assembly of the State of New-York at Their Sixty-First Session, Begun and Held at the Capitol, in the City of Albany, on the Second Day of January, 1838* (Albany, NY: E. Croswell, Printer to the State, 1838), 134, 139, 140, 143, 144, 208, 228, 252, 280, 292, 298, 305, 312, 313, 317, 326, 348, 370, 382, 387, 392–93, 399, 399–400, 405, 414, 430, 443, 444, 469, 503, 516–17, 647, 672, 681, 699, 723–24, 759, 760, 807, 885, 905, 971. Some were specific, as in "twenty-nine persons of color of the county of Albany" (759–60). The numbers ranged from forty-nine "Welch [*sic*] citizens" in Oneida County (503) to "three thousand seven hundred and thirty-seven ladies of the city of New-York" (443); *CA*, December 16, 1837.

31. *Journal of the Assembly of the State of New-York at Their Sixty-First Session*, 1101, describing the summary disposition of the suffrage petitions also refers to petitions from "about seventeen thousand" New Yorkers regarding legislation to guarantee jury trials.

32. *CA*, June 16, 1838, describing a June 7 meeting where Sidney moved to form the association (although they named older men like Samuel Hardenburgh and Thomas Downing as vice presidents, the key officers and executive committee were all young men); *CA*, June 23, 1838 for its constitution, submitted by Sidney, stating the goal of gaining "for the colored citizens of the state, equal political rights and privileges, as enjoyed and exercised by other citizens"; *CA*, December 30, 1837, the first listing of ward leaders followed by a larger list of forty-nine men on October 20, 1838, describing the association's "first Regular Quarterly Meeting"; *CA*, December 16, 1837.

33. *CA*, March 3, 1838 and April 12, 1838; for their progress, see the call signed "Shade of Teasman," *CA*, August 25, 1838, "Colored young men, awake! . . . Your grey haired seniors, worn out in the public service, expect it of you."

34. *CA*, July 27 and August 17, 1839.

35. *CA*, November 3, 1838 and September 15, 1838, both repr. from *Emancipator*, including a pledge form for "legal voters" to refuse to vote for candidates who would not endorse abolitionist proposals. Ray added a specific message "TO THE COLORED FREE-HOLDERS OF THE STATE OF NEW YORK, ESPECIALLY OF THE CITY," urging a vote for "the men who go for Universal Suffrage. Without distinction, for such men, let us vote—whatever may be their politics—and let us vote for none else but those." He added, "With regard to the Governors in nomination, neither is favorable to our rights, then we ought to vote for neither." For Whig consternation, see Bradish's correspondence, from the eminent and always antislavery John C. Spencer on October 8 ("There can be little doubt that at least 10,000 votes at the coming elections, depend in some" degree on abolitionists and they "in all probability will decide the coming election"), the Negrophobic editor James Watson Webb on October 10, outraged at "the Abolitionists, one fourth of whom are *fanatics* and three fourths *knaves*," insisting any agreement with them "will be certain death to our entire Party. In this City two-thirds

of our Whigs would prefer Van Buren and Marcy to Abolition," followed by Gerrit Smith on October 19, that by not responding, Seward "will lose more than ten thousand votes," finally Thurlow Weed on October 28, averring that, after Seward's equivocal answers, "the Ultras of both sides kick. Whigs, however, with few exceptions, will vote the ticket. But I am in great doubt about the Abolitionists. Some of their leaders have their own reasons for desiring to defeat, and thus disorganize the Whig Party. They may, and I fear will, endeavor to accomplish this by accepting your Answer and rejecting Seward's. They ought to be satisfied with both, but I fear me that some of the moving spirits will not," noting that "Seward resisted the earnest importunities of many influential friends here and in New-York, to make his Answer far more obnoxious to the Abolitionists"; all in "July–October 1838" folder, box 1, Luther Bradish Papers, NYHS.

36. *CA*, November 10, 1838.

37. *CA*, September 7 and August 17, 1839, also August 10 and 31.

38. *CA*, October 19, October 5 (quoting *Emancipator*), November 9, 1839.

39. Swift, *Black Prophets*, 125.

40. Benson, *Concept of Jacksonian Democracy*, 133.

41. John R. Hendricks, "The Liberty Party in New York State, 1838–1848" (PhD diss., Fordham University, 1959), 134; Hammond, *Political History of the State of New York, From Jan. 1, 1841, to Jan. 1, 1847*, 3:182, notes that William Henry Harrison won the state in 1840 by 13,302 but Seward retained the governorship by "only 5,203."

42. Vernon L. Volpe, "The Liberty Party and Polk's Election, 1844," *The Historian* 53, no. 4 (June 1991): 697, "Those 15,814 Liberty party votes in New York were simply no longer Clay's to lose; most had defected before the 1844 canvass"; Seward to Clay, November 7, 1844, WHSP, reel 29, "The Whig party in the state of New York gave 13,000 majority for General Harrison in 1840, and 2700 Abolition votes. During the three years thereafter the Abolition Party gained 13,000 chiefly from the Whig Party." After the proposed annexation of Texas, "I allowed myself the hope that Whig Abolitionists would return in part, and that we should either obtain some aid from the Loco Foco Party or that many would pass from them to the Abolition Party. . . . I think that we should have saved the state of New York in that manner, but for the entrance of another and very ruinous element into the canvass. The jealousy of the Whig Party or of a portion of it, against foreigners and Catholics has been a serious evil which I have endeavored to correct and was quite successful" until the city's Whigs "thought they could strengthen themselves by coalition with the Native Americans. A change of the Naturalization laws to affect future immigrants was proposed and too readily approved by the Whig Press," presumably "preliminary to a general attempt to disenfranchise the citizens already naturalized." In the end, "The Native Americans gave us one vote only for two of which they deprived us, and the result is our defeat in the state."

43. *Memorial Discourse by the Rev. Henry Highland Garnet*, 30 (from Smith's "Introduction"). See also Joel Schor, *Henry Highland Garnet: A Voice of Black Radicalism in the Nineteenth Century* (Westport, CT: Greenwood Press, 1977); Swift, *Black Prophets*, 114, captures his Byronic character as "a man of unblinking courage, intense emotions, forceful mind, flashing eloquence, and not infrequently, apparent arrogance . . . deeply restless [with] a volatile temper"; *Emancipator*, October 12, 1843, reprinting the *Buffalo Commercial Advertiser*.

44. Stauffer, *Black Hearts of Men*; Stauffer, ed., *The Works of James McCune Smith: Black Intellectual and Abolitionist* (New York: Oxford University Press, 2007); see *Emancipator*, September 15, 1847, reprinting Garnet's encomium to Smith from *The National Watchman*; another indication of his Whiggism is in Stauffer, *Works of James McCune Smith*, 97, quoting his "sad, weary, and disappointed heart" regarding Daniel Webster's apostasy over the Fugitive Slave Act in 1850; and Samuel Ringgold Ward's *Impartial Citizen*, April 6, 1853, commenting, "Communipaw is somewhat of a politician, although changeable in political matters, some years ago he was a Whig, he then fired his small artillery against the Liberty Party, in 1848 a Free Soiler, in 1852 after the organization of the Pittsburgh Platform bolted and united with the Liberty party"; *CA*, August 8, 1840; *Liberator*, May 27, 1842.

45. *Memorial Discourse by the Rev. Henry Highland Garnet*, 37–38, quoting minutes of the 1844 convention, that "in the towns of Syracuse and Geneva, among a colored population of some eight hundred, there are more voters according to the odious $250 qualification, than there are in New York city, which has eighteen or twenty thousand colored inhabitants"; Ward quoted in Ronald K. Burke, "The Antislavery Activities of Samuel Ringgold Ward in New York State," *AANYLH* 2, no. 1 (January 1978): 23; *Autobiography of Dr. William Henry Johnson, Respectfully Dedicated to His Adopted Home, the Capital City of the Empire State* (New York: Haskell House, 1970, repr. of 1900 edition), 45, referring to him as "Meyers"; *Liberator*, September 17, 1831, describing "a meeting of the people of color" on September 2, 1831 in Ithaca, where Myers was chosen president, resolving "that a Convention be held in Albany on the 1st of Nov. 1831"; Seward, *William H. Seward: An Autobiography*, 451. Seward's wife, Fanny, described the crisis in a letter to her sister: "It has been all war-war-war here. . . . The military company went out in wagons towards night the rain increased. . . . Numerous rumours were afloat—some said they were completely hemmed in by the tenantry who were prepared to resist them with arms—that they had encamped in the open air and were subjected to the fury of the elements—in want of food &c &c. . . . Henry [the governor] stayed until 12 oclock—(after having dispatched Stephen Myers (who keeps a provision store) with a wagon load of bread and meat—)," at 2 A.M. news came that "the company of soldiers had been met by upwards of 1000 of the tenantry armed with cudgels," and the following night, at 1 A.M., amid warnings of martial law, "Stephen was again dispatched with provisions" (letter from Frances Miller Seward to Lazette Miller Worden, December 10, 1839, https://sewardproject.org/18391210FMS_LMW1).

46. For the original "petition of Thurlow Weed and others, for the extension of the right of suffrage to people of color," see *Albany Argus*, May 11, 1840. Late in that presidential election year, the *Washington Globe*, September 25, 1840 (Van Buren's "Administration" paper), and the *Macon Weekly Telegraph*, October 13, 1840, reprinted an article from the *New York Standard* citing the petition as evidence of the "IDENTITY OF THE WHIGS WITH ABOLITIONISM," indicating how northern Whigs' sympathies made their national party vulnerable.

47. *CA*, August 17, August 22, and September 12, 1840, and January 9, 1841.

48. It attracted little notice in the white press, however. One major southern paper sneered at a "CONVENTION OF NIGGERS," noting inaccurately, "At present only colored citizens possessing real estate to the amount of $500 have a right to vote. Poor

fellows!—Can't their white brethren do something for them" (*Times-Picayune*, August 28, 1840).

49. *Emancipator*, April 9, 1840 (all belonged to the 49-man Albany County contingent); *CA*, May 23, 1840.

50. *CA*, August 22 and October 3, 1840.

51. *Emancipator*, August 20; *CA*, August 1 and September 19, 1840.

52. *CA*, September 26, October 3, 10, and 31, 1840. Oddly, Cornish and another man had called upon Vice President Johnson when he visited New York "and were treated with all the courtesies due from one gentleman to another" (*CA*, June 29, 1839).

53. *Journal of the Assembly of the State of New-York, At Their Sixty-Fourth Session, Begun and Held at the Capitol, in the City of Albany, on the Fifth Day of January, 1841* (Albany, NY: Thurlow Weed, Printer to the State, 1841), 117, 541; *CA*, March 13 and 20, June 12, 1841.

54. In 1826, William Morgan, then living in Batavia, New York, announced he would publish an expose of Freemasonry, and was then kidnapped and allegedly murdered by Masons. Outrage at the fraternity's covert networks among the elite led to the formation of the Antimasonic Party, part of the coalition that became the Whigs.

55. *Commercial Advertiser*, February 1, 1841, from the *AEJ*; *Albany Argus*, February 2, 1841; *CA*, February 6, 1841.

56. *Journal of the Assembly of the State of New-York, At Their Sixty-Fourth Session*, 877, 1051; *CA*, May 8, 1841.

57. *Albany Argus*, June 4, 1841.

58. *Journal of the Assembly of the State of New-York, At Their Sixty-Fourth Session*, 30; *CA*, February 14, 1841; *Albany Argus*, February 5, 1841; *Jamestown Journal*, March 24, 1841, reprinting *AEJ*; *CA*, March 27, 1841.

59. *CA*, May 8, 1841.

60. *CA*, May 15, 1841, reprinting Seward's letter to Virginia authorities; *Albany Argus*, March 19, 1841; *Albany Argus*, February 9 and March 19, 1841; *CA*, May 15 and 29, 1841.

61. *CA*, June 19, October 16, September 11 and 25, October 2 and 9, November 20, December 4, 1841.

62. *Emancipator*, September 16 and October 14, 1841 (Smith was a prosperous hog drover and a founder of the black village of Weeksville; for more on him, see Judith Wellman, *Brooklyn's Promised Land: The Free Black Community of Weeksville, New York* [New York: New York University Press, 2014]); see also *Emancipator*, July 29, 1841 for a notice that "the abolitionists of Williamsburg" were "requested to meet at the house of J. H. Warner" to endorse Birney and Morris for 1844, listing "William J. Hodges, Samuel Shapter, P. Shapter, Willies [*sic*] Hodges, T. C. Warner, Jas. Warner, J. H. Warner, John Bedient, John H. Fenton, Lewis H. Nelson, P. Shapter Jr., Wm. H. Pillow, Jacob Fields, Samuel Ricks," all black men; *CA*, November 20, 1841.

63. Seward, *William H. Seward: An Autobiography*, 596.

64. See *Journal of the Assembly of the State of New-York, At Their Sixty-Fifth Session, Begun and Held at the Capitol, in the City of Albany, on the Fourth Day of January, 1842* (Albany, NY: Thurlow Weed, Printer to the State, 1841), 1032; *Albany Argus*, May 6, 1842. The Democratic assemblymen John L. Sullivan of New York City, later famous

for asserting America's Manifest Destiny, and Abram Van Alstyne of Hudson, with a host of black relatives, were among the handful voting no.

65. The *Northern Star*'s third issue, February 3, 1842, included advertisements for "Primus Robinson's Recess," where "Persons can be accommodated with oysters, fruit and other refreshments," various tailors and upholstery furnishers, one of whom was also "Superintendent of the Albany Cemetery," Benjamin Lattimore's "Cheap Temperance Grocery and Provision Stores," and many more recesses, including both Thomas and Richard Thompson's, as well as William Johnson, who "keeps fresh poultry constantly on hand" and "TOPP AND VAN VRANKEN'S FASHIONABLE HAIR CUTTING," the last referring to the venerable leader, William Topp. For its agents, see the February 10, 1842 issue: Job Wentworth in Portsmouth; Abraham F. Boston in Nantucket; A. W. Niles in Portland; John Robinson in Boston (not one of the Garrisonians); H. Chandler in Bath; Henry Huston and Robert Garrison in Brunswick, Maine; Rev. John Lewis in Concord; W. Willy in Hallowell; John T. Carter in Augusta; James Cook in Belfast, New Hampshire; Eben Ruby in Durham. Myers's men in upstate included Martin Cross in Catskill, Francis Dana in Schenectady, and William Green in Hudson; *Northern Star*, February 17, 1842.

66. The quotation regarding abolitionists' prejudices is from the *Northern Star*, March 3 and all the rest are from March 17, 1842.

67. *Northern Star*, April 14, 1842, "The election, on Tuesday last, terminated the political conflict between the Whigs, the Democrats, and the Liberty party. We are neutral in politics; and therefore, like all other quiet and good citizens, shall content ourselves with the gentleman elected. By the way, speaking on the subject, we know of no man that would fill with more dignity or honor, the head of our municipal government, than [the Democrat] Dr. Staats"; *AEJ*, June 27, 1842, "The Northern Star And Freeman's Advocate . . . published weekly in this city by an association of colored persons, is devoted especially to the cause of Temperance and Education among the colored people. It well deserves encouragement and support from our citizens," also the Garrisonian *NASS*, October 6, 1842, "We always hail this neat little weekly journal with pleasure . . . intended to elevate the proscribed class to which they belong, to social and political equality, through the agency of Temperance, Education, and Morality."

68. *Northern Star*, March 31, April 7, April 14, December 8, 1842; unfortunately, the relevant issues of the *Tocsin* and the *People's Press* have not survived. Myers had a long relationship with the younger man. When a nineteen-year-old Garnet and comrades fled New Canaan, New Hampshire, in 1835, after their school was attacked by a mob, they sheltered in Albany with Myers's mother-in-law, and when Garnet relocated to Troy, he spoke at mass meetings organized by Myers (see McCune Smith's "Introduction" to the *Memorial Discourse by the Rev. Henry Highland Garnet*, 30, 33).

69. *Northern Star*, January 2, 1843, noting that "we intend, when any slave is sent to us, to do as we always have done since 1831, pass fugitives to Canada, where they can breathe the air of freedom," followed by a list of colored temperance societies, including the Edwin Jackson Society in Kinderhook (Jane B. Jackson, president, with ninety-seven members); the Hudson Female Gerritt Smith Society (Mrs. M. Jackson, president); the Hudson Washingtonian society (L. Tillmen, president, C. Van Husen, secretary, with 120 members), the Catskill Total Abstinence Society (B. Foot, president, M. Cross,

secretary, with sixty-two members), the Pittsfield Total Abstinence Society (A. Potter, president, forty-two members), the Lenox Female E. C. Delavan Society (Miss J. Hulbert, president, Miss M. Hall, vice president, Miss J. Schermerhorn, secretary, with twenty-two members), the Lenox Male C. S. Morton Society (J. Schermerhorn, president, with thirty-nine members), the Lee Stephen Myers Society (Samuel Smith, president, thirty-six members), the Buffalo Union Society (215 members), two societies in Cincinnati with 330 members, and the Cleveland Temperance Society with 142; Smith to Garnet, June 10, 1843, in GSP, box 41, adding it had "a character which the most famous Whigs and Democrats of our State approve of." As late as March 25, 1846, Greeley's *Tribune* reprinted a letter to constitutional convention candidates from the *Northern Star*.

70. *Emancipator*, July 7, 1842.

71. *CA*, May 29, 1841; Ray had a close relationship with party founders James Birney and Henry B. Stanton, corresponding with them while they attended the 1840 World Anti-Slavery Conference in London. Ray, Garnet, John J. Zuille, and Reverend Theodore Wright blocked attempts by Garrison's black supporters in the city to pass resolutions repudiating Birney and Stanton; see Dwight L. Dumond, ed., *Letters of James Gillespie Birney, 1831–1857* (New York: D. Appleton-Century, 1938), 1:575–78.

72. See *Emancipator*, September 23, 1841, February 24 and March 4, 1842 on his various addresses; *Liberator*, December 8, 1843.

73. *Liberator*, August 24, 1843; *Minutes of the National Convention of Colored Citizens: Held at Buffalo, On the 15th, 16th, 17th, 18th and 19th of August, 1843. For the Purpose of Considering Their Moral and Political Condition as American Citizens* (New-York: Piercy & Reed, 1843), 18, https://omeka.coloredconventions.org/items /show/278.

74. *Minutes of the National Convention*, 16; *Albany Weekly Patriot*, October 3, 1843; *Emancipator*, September 7, 1843.

75. *Emancipator*, September 14, 1843; repr. in *Cincinnati Daily Chronicle*, September 7, 1843.

76. Numerous newspaper accounts circulated, but a print version did not appear until 1848, when Garnet himself published it as *Walker's Appeal, with a Brief Sketch of His Life. And also Garnet's Address to the Slaves of the United States of America* (New York: J. H. Tobitt, 1848); *Liberator*, September 22 and November 17, 1843.

77. *Liberator*, June 28, 1844; in addition to the *Portland Advertiser*, July 2, 1844; see also *Salem Register*, June 17, 1844; the *Christian Watchman* (Boston), June 28, 1844; *Vermont Watchman and State Journal*, June 28, 1844; *NASS*, October 24, 1844; *Memorial Discourse by the Rev. Henry Highland Garnet*, 43.

78. *NASS*, October 24 and November 14, 1844, quoting Smith in *Northern Star*; *Emancipator*, October 30, 1844.

79. *NS*, February 1, 1850; *NASS*, November 14, 1844.

80. James Henretta, "The Strange Birth of Liberal America: Michael Hoffman and the New York Constitution of 1846," *New York History* 77, no. 2 (April 1996): 152, describes the Jacksonians' "new theory of state government—a populist vision of democratic control, fiscal responsibility, and judicial review," sharply limiting the ability "to incur debts, raise taxes, or lend the credit of the state," replacing the "expansive republican 'commonwealth'" associated with Clinton and Seward with "the limited

classical-liberal state"; Phyllis F. Field, *The Politics of Race in New York: The Struggle for Black Suffrage in the Civil War Era* (Ithaca, NY: Cornell University Press, 1982), 49–77; John L. Stanley, "Majority Tyranny in Tocqueville's America: The Failure of Negro Suffrage in 1846," *Political Science Quarterly* 84, no. 3 (September 1969): 412–35; Benson, *Concept of Jacksonian Democracy*, 318–20; Alan M. Kraut and Phyllis F. Field, "Politics versus Principles: The Partisan Response to 'Bible Politics' in New York State," *Civil War History* 25, no. 2 (June 1979): 101–18.

81. Jabez Hammond explains that the convention agitation began in 1843 when Michael Hoffman, the preeminent Democratic "radical," called an Albany meeting in Albany; see Hammond, *Political History of the State of New York, From Jan. 1, 1841, to Jan. 1, 1847,* 3:422, 424–28. Whigs saw an opportunity to split the majority, since Hunkers like Horatio Seymour were deeply opposed. In early 1844, Cayuga's Whig assemblyman Benjamin Hall proposed a convention bill, which the Hunkers barely held off, with Seymour inveighing against a Whig plot "to disorganize the democratic party in this state, and to which [he] feared it was the intention of a branch of their own party to ally itself." Seward made his views known, with Hammond quoting a Whig correspondent saying the former governor "deemed the judiciary system . . . the most defective part of" the constitution and "also was dissatisfied with the restrictions it contained on the elective franchise. He was consulted, and fully concurred in the policy of introducing a convention bill into the legislature of 1844." When the legislative session ended, forty-two of the forty-six Whig members published a lengthy manifesto demanding a convention, including a brief mention that "the spirit of the age condemns the narrow policy which, by a property qualification, disfranchises a small portion of the people" (*AEJ*, May 13, 1844). See also Charles W. McCurdy, *The Anti-Rent Era in New York Law and Politics, 1839–1865* (Chapel Hill: University of North Carolina Press, 2001), 120–24 on the Barnburners pushing a convention in 1843–44.

82. McCurdy, *Anti-Rent Era*, 146, covers events in 1844; WHS to GS, November 25, 1844 and January 21, 1845, in WHSP, reel 29.

83. Weed to Francis Granger, June 19, 1845, in TWP.

84. The ramifications of the 1845 and 1855 censuses are discussed below; Stanley, "Majority Tyranny in Tocqueville's America," 415, argues that "full suffrage would have meant about 10,000 Negro voters"; Wisconsin Whigs adopted a similar strategy; see Michael J. McManus, *Political Abolitionism in Wisconsin, 1840–1861* (Kent, OH: Kent State University Press, 1998), 23–25, on how Rufus King, grandson of the Federalist, led a Whig pro-suffrage campaign in 1845 46, soon after King replaced Weed as editor of the *AEJ* while the latter vacationed (see McCurdy, *Anti-Rent Era*, 167); Richard H. Sewell, *Ballots for Freedom: Antislavery Politics in the United States, 1837–1860* (New York: W. W. Norton, 1976), 114, also suggests that after Clay's defeat, some Whigs in and out of New York "hatched a scheme to recoup their fortunes by persuading disgruntled Democrats and frustrated Liberty men to join them."

85. *Spectator* (New York City), January 11, 1845, repr. from *Albany Argus* (in spring 1844, a Whig senator, Gideon Hard, had proposed a similar amendment, and a surprising four of the eight votes it received came from Democrats; see *AEJ*, April 1, 1844); Bloss's son quoted in Amy Hanmer-Croughton, "Anti-Slavery Days in Rochester," *The Rochester Historical Society, Publication Fund Series* (Rochester, NY: Published by the Society, 1936), 14:133; *Hudson River Chronicle*, January 9, 1838; *AEJ*, February 25, for

Bloss lambasting the Democrats by hailing "the revolution of 1837 and 1838" when "a ruined and abused people appealed to the Whigs to save them from their corrupt and false friends," concluding with a salute to the "40,000 persons disfranchised on account of their color," after which he asked, "Is then your Democracy cutaneous? Do you hold the doctrine that your Democracy is in your skin? and that there is so much virtue in a white skin, that, as a matter of course, it holds all other virtues in?"; *Washington Journal*, February 27, 1845, "The Whig Meeting at Argyle"; *AEJ*, February 21, 1845, reprinting the *Herkimer Journal* on "abolishing all property qualifications for office, and for extending the elective franchise"; *Auburn Journal*, June 11, 1845, listing the five "Objects of a Convention," including "The Abolition of All Property Qualifications for the Right of Suffrage," as part of "The advancing spirit of the age. . . . A man is not responsible for his complexion. Beneath a black skin may rest an honest heart, true independence, and an intelligent and inquiring mind." Bloss's life traces the arc of radicalization. Born in Massachusetts in 1795, he taught school in the south, opened a tavern in Rochester in 1823, and became a fierce temperance advocate and Antimason. By the 1830s he was an active abolitionist, working with black leaders, and founded the *Rights of Man* newspaper. After his legislative career ended, he joined Douglass in the campaign to end school segregation in Rochester, also supporting women's suffrage and later the Free Soilers in Kansas (https://rrlc.org/winningvote/biographies/william-bloss/, accessed October 14, 2016).

86. *Emancipator*, April 9, 1845, reprinting from the *AEJ*; *AEJ*, April 19, 1845.

87. *Poughkeepsie Journal*, April 26, 1845; *New York Herald*, April 26, 1845; see Hammond, *Political History of the State of New York, From Jan. 1, 1841, to Jan. 1, 1847*, 3:546–49 on how the future Whig governor John Young managed this maneuver, denounced by another future governor, the Democrat Horatio Seymour, as "throw[ing] open the tenures of property, the elective franchise, religious liberty, every thing settled by our constitution" in "attempts to galvanize the late whig party into existence, to suck up all the ill-humors of the body politic, in the hope of organizing a party that might cope with the great democratic party of the state . . . to combine all the elements of faction in one common bond of opposition to democratic principles"; *Albany Argus*, April 29, 1845, reprinting from the *Mayville Sentinel*; some Democrats reminded abolitionists that "these same whigs so singularly lost sight of [black suffrage] during the three years in which they had control of our state legislature" (*Ithaca Journal and Advertiser*, May 28, 1845).

88. *Albany Argus*, May 30, 1845. Although he represented a different senatorial district, Beers was from Erastus Root's Delaware County.

89. WHS to James Bowen, August 30, 1845, WHSP, reel 29; Booraem, *Formation of the Republican Party in New York*, 64, a reference to the 1850s; *NASS*, October 3, 1845 (the collusion between black leaders, white Garrisonians, and Whigs was on display when the *NASS* reprinted an article from Greeley's *Tribune* insisting black suffrage should be on the "conscience of every genuine Republican," given the "indiscriminate liberality with which the right of suffrage is conferred on all those who have white skins" (*NASS*, January 29, 1846); Seward to Weed, August 20, 1845, in Seward, *William H. Seward: An Autobiography*, 759.

90. John J. Zuille, Ransom Wake, John Peterson, Alexander Crummell, Henry Williams, George Montgomery, Benjamin Stanley to Gerrit Smith, June 13, 1845 in GSP, box 40, and Vidal and McCune Smith to Gerrit Smith, July 30, 1845, in GSP, box 34;

NASS, September 11, 1845; *AEJ*, August 9 and September 1, 1845, the *Auburn Journal*, Seward's hometown paper, October 29, 1845, reporting approvingly, "THEY KNOW THEIR FRIENDS": "A convention of colored persons was recently held at Geneva. They passed a resolution dissevering themselves from the 'Liberty Party,' and avowed their intention to vote for liberal minded men, irrespective of their politics, as representatives in the coming State Convention." Smith was not the only white man to whom black men appealed; see Stephen Myers to John Jay II, February 28, 1846 in box 46, Jay Family Collection, Columbia University Manuscripts Collection, seeking funds for his paper. In time-honored fashion, he evoked the legacy of 1821 when "the lamented Thomkins and Jay and Abraham Van Vechten Clark and many more patriots was in favor of giving to their injured colored citizens the free suffrage," and then got down to business: "we care nothing for the name of party it's the principle that we look at we would wish you Mr Jay get as many young gentlemen with your self to aid us in our publication up to the first Monday in June we send now at every number to every town and village gratuitously twelve cops we have called a convention at Albany in june of colored citizens whilst the convention is in session if we obtain the elective franchise our people will sustain a paper of their own . . . we are poor have not the means to go on without asking the aid of our white friends nessty compels us call on them at present our printing bills are heavy at present we desire to see you a member of this convention and also your father and gentlemen whose services we appreciate."

91. *Rome Sentinel*, September 30, 1845; *Albany Argus*, October 21, 1845, reprinting the *Eagle*; *AEJ*, March 9, 1846.

92. Field, *Politics of Race*, 416, and 418 for a table showing how many votes Whigs would have gained with equal suffrage, much larger than Polk's 1844 margin in the downstate counties: in Queens, where 10.9 percent of the population was black, 750 versus 204; in Dutchess, 430 versus 37; in New York County, 3,040 versus 1,917; in Richmond, 160 versus 14; in Ulster, 310 versus 152; in Westchester, 550 versus 154; Hammond, *Political History of the State of New York, From Jan. 1, 1841, to Jan. 1, 1847*, 3:565, describes how in late 1845, "serious divisions began to appear in [the Whigs'] ranks. The Courier and Enquirer came out openly against the convention, and more than insinuated that Mr. Young, Mr. Weed, and others, were too radical in their principles, and that they advocated wild and revolutionary theories, calculated eventually to unsettle the rights of property, and destroy social order. Gov. Seward was charged, if not in the public papers, in private circles, with abolition propensities, and a design to enlist the Irish Catholics in his favor personally."

93. Greeley to Colfax, January 22, 1846, quoted in Field, *Politics of Race*, 49; the *Auburn Journal*, edited by Benjamin Hall, part of Seward's personal network, was optimistic, on February 11 reporting that "The locofocos . . . still defend the old property qualification, but the tide is strongly against them," on March 11, however, reprinting a warning that "Southern Slave holders are watching with eagle eye, the stand that New York shall take in the Convention upon Negro Suffrage. . . . Should New York prove to be more pro-Slavery in this respect than Virginia (and we entertain fears that she will) slave holders will chuckle over the apostacy [*sic*] with infinite delight"; *Liberator*, February 13, 1846; *AEJ*, March 14, 1846.

94. *Albany Patriot*, April 1, 1846. The printed broadside, published by Smith, was dated March 13, 1846, addressed to "Messrs. William Rich, James Henderson, Francis

Lippins, John Wendall, Chas. S. Morton, Richard Thompson, William H. Topp," as "members of a State Central committee, whose object is to restore the right of suffrage to the colored people of the State."

95. *Auburn Journal*, March 11, 1846, reprinting *Syracuse Daily Journal*; *Madison County Whig*, March 25, 1846; Gerrit Smith, *To the Liberty Party of the County of Madison*, September 15, 1846; *NASS*, April 9, 1846 (Bloss acknowledged that he had helped found the Liberty Party "but a short experience . . . convinced me I was in error"). In Madison, Smith endured the mortification of his comrades' desertion. In early April he published a letter to county leaders declaring "the Liberty Party of Madison County is in ruins" since "a grave proposition" was "made in our nominating County Convention, to choose for our candidates proslavery, instead of anti-slavery, men" (Smith, *Peterboro, April 10, 1846.: Messrs. E.S. Bailey of Brookfield, A. Raymond of Eaton, and F. Rice at Cazenovia*). Smith's idiosyncratic fervor, alternately appalling and impressing the public, can be seen in another letter before the referendum describing how "a deep and cruel wrong has been devised against the fifty thousand colored people of this State. . . . First, That a man, for having a colored skin, shall be unrepresented in the Legislature. . . . Second, That a man, for having a colored skin, shall be denied his right to cast a vote," adding these were "persons born upon our soil, and of parents, many of whom shed their blood in its defence." The "most insulting and withering" aspect of "the New Constitution" was that it "prefers the white pauper, who subsists on the public charity, to the colored man, who earns his own bread," followed by an encomium to how black Yorkers, "in the midst of those temptations to low vice and utter abandonment, which, in such mighty hosts, assail extreme poverty," had shown "indomitable courage and unbending integrity" (Smith, *To the Voters of the State of New York*, October 10, 1846).

96. See Field, *Politics of Race*, 50–52, citing Clinton, Cortland, Madison, Onondaga, Chautaqua, and Tompkins; *Weekly Tribune*, April 8, 1846; *New-York Globe* quoted in *NASS*, March 19, 1846; *NASS*, March 19, 1846, reprinting the *New-York Express* and the *Newburgh Gazette*.

97. *AEJ*, April 23, 1846; *PF*, May 7, 1846, quoting Greeley's *Tribune*; *AEJ*, June 14, 1846; *Hudson River Chronicle* (Ossining), July 28 and August 4, 1846.

98. Here I rely on Field, *Politics of Race*, 49–66, and her assessment that "a bipartisan vote at the convention's close to submit the property qualification directly to the state's voters" allowed both parties to avoid any final "responsibility for its fate. Politicians simply put politics first; they treated the race issue cautiously as befitted its explosive nature" (57), also that the "Whig journals that had played hard for Liberty support in the spring could afford to drop the subject in the fall" (61) although Greeley's *Tribune* and Weed's *AEJ* continued their public support; Stanley, "Majority Tyranny in Tocqueville's America," 420, 423, 426 analyzes the suffrage vote by county: the twelve downstate were Queens (70 for versus 3,218 against), Suffolk, Dutchess, New York, Kings, Rockland (48 versus 1,286), Richmond (55 versus 1,161), Westchester, Orange, Ulster, Greene, and Columbia.

99. James McCune Smith to Gerrit Smith, December 28, 1846, GSP, box 34; *Albany Patriot*, December 16, 1848, repr. of Ward's letter to *Herkimer Freeman*.

100. *Newburyport Morning Herald*, February 27, 1846, "Gerrit Smith, the Abolitionist, advertises for sale something like three-fourths of million acres of land, all lying in

New York State, a good portion of it is to be sold at auction"; also *Boston Daily Bee*, March 3, 1846, "'Gerrit Smith of Peterboro', offers to sell his immense landed property at auction, in the months of June, July, and August next. The lands lie in 45 of the 59 counties of New York, and comprise about 750,000 acres. The auction will be held at fifteen different places, on as many different days"; *Massachusetts Ploughman and New England Journal of Agriculture* (Boston), September 12, 1846.

101. See Gerrit Smith to Charles B. Ray, Theodore Wright, and McCune Smith, September 10, 1846, in GSP, box 41, indicating he hoped news of the project "might have a somewhat good effect on the Convention now sitting in Albany"; an October 3, 1846 letter to these men, also in GSP, box 41, approved "the businesslike way in which you distribute the deeds," noting he had sent 576 to New York City with 288 remaining.

Chapter Ten

1. *AEJ*, August 10, 1848; also Corey M. Brooks, *Liberty Power: Antislavery Third Parties and the Transformation of American Politics* (Chicago: University of Chicago Press, 2016), 173. In 1847, Hamilton Fish won a special election for lieutenant governor with 52.63 percent over a Democrat and the longtime Liberty candidate, Charles O. Shepard, who received a surprising 4.16 percent; in 1848, Fish won the governorship with 47.56 percent against the Free Soiler John A. Dix (26.7 percent), and a Hunker (25.39 percent); in 1850, Washington Hunt defeated the Democrat Horatio Seymour with 49.64 percent to Seymour's 49.57 percent (the Liberty candidate received 3,416 or 0.079 percent).

2. Frederick J. Blue, *The Free Soilers: Third Party Politics, 1848–54* (Urbana: University of Illinois, 1973), 180; Hendrik Booraem V, *The Formation of the Republican Party in New York: Politics and Conscience in the Antebellum North* (New York: New York University Press, 1983), 77.

3. Leslie Alexander is hardly alone in asserting that "the Fugitive Slave Act of 1850 was just the first in a series of devastating setbacks that plagued Black New Yorkers during the decade before the Civil War," but this analysis is tenable only if one steps around the electoral arena; see Leslie M. Alexander, *African or American? Black Identity and Political Activism in New York City, 1784–1861* (Urbana: University of Illinois Press, 2008), 122.

4. *IC*, February 15, 1851, quoting *Albany Argus*; *FDP*, October 30, 1851, reprinting *Buffalo Commercial Advertiser*, including Douglass's letter asserting he had "always held . . . opinions diametrically opposed to those held by that part of the Whig party which you are supposed to represent. . . . I do not believe that the slavery question is settled, and settled forever. I do not believe that slave-catching is either a christian duty, or an innocent amusement. I do not believe that he who breaks the arm of the kidnapper, or wrests the trembling captive from his grasp is 'a traitor.'" He was, therefore, "wholly unfit to receive the suffrages of gentlemen holding the opinion and favoring the policy of that wing of the Whig party, denominated 'the Silver Grays.'"

5. This period marked Garnet's temporary eclipse, feuding publicly with Douglass and ready to depart for warmer climes. Myers continued publishing his renamed *Northern Star and Colored Farmer*, but no issues survive past January 1843; see *NS*, January 5, 1849, on Ward's taking it over.

6. *NS*, June 27, 1850, for this ubiquitous reference, and Martin R. Delany quoting an awestruck white journalist for whom Ward as an "animated statue of black marble, of the old Egyptian sort, out of which our white civilization was hewn. Every degrading association dropped away from his color, and it was as rich in blackness as the velvet pall on the bier of an Emperor"; *NASS*, March 11, 1847, quoting a Whig editor that the Liberty Party sent "their *big gun*, S. R. Ward, to defend the party" at an upstate convention against the Garrisonians Charles Remond and William Wells Brown.

7. *NS*, September 1, 1848.

8. Weed to Greeley, June 19, 1846, in TWP; GS to WHS, February 18, 1847, including letter from Forward to Smith, dated February 9, and WHS to GS, March 20, 1847, in WHSP, reel 29.

9. *NS*, August 24, 1849; *IC*, January 4 and August 23, 1851; Austin Steward, *Twenty-Two Years a Slave and Forty Years a Freeman*, with an Introduction by Graham Russell Hodges (Syracuse, NY: Syracuse University Press, 2002), xxvii; *FDP*, January 29, April 8, May 20, August 16, 1852, thanking Seward for sending copies of speeches, and November 19, 1852, listing a $5 contribution.

10. *AEJ*, February 5, 1850; *Telegraph and Temperance Journal*, May 1, 1851, lists thirteen senators, and that "monies received from the Members of Assembly will appear in our next"; also May 17, 1852 and April 6 and March 10, 1853 ("Senator Seward is one of those who always pays up, he does not forget our little paper. He has our thanks"); *AEJ*, June 14, 1852.

11. *AEJ*, November 24, 1848; *Baltimore Sun*, November 23, 1848, reprinting *New York Express*; *Sandusky Register*, November 2, 1848; *Philadelphia North American*, November 23, 1848; *Alexandria Gazette*, January 2, 1849; *Commercial Advertiser* (New York), January 9, 1849; *Farmer's Cabinet* (Amherst, NY), January 11, 1849; *New London Democrat*, January 13, 1849; *NS*, January 19, 1849, a letter from William H. Topp explaining how their proposal to have Ward speak passed "by a strong vote"; *NS*, February 16, 1849, on a New Bedford meeting where Myers described how black urbanites were "surrounded by unjust laws and prejudiced public sentiment. Everywhere great obstacles oppose our improvement and elevation. Law, public sentiment and popular religion unite to crush the colored man.—We see it and feel it in our souls. We are determined to have a change; ourselves only can bring about that change; ourselves must strike the blow"; *NS*, February 23, on a similar event in Pittsford, Massachusetts, and March 2, 1849, on the association denouncing Henry Bibb, and that "we recommend the Potash and Lumber Company to commence that business as early as possible"; *NE*, January 4, 1849, informing readers, "A building to hold seventy families will be finished by the 1st of January. The property has plenty of water power and grist and saw mills have been projected. . . . Messrs. Fillmore, Fish, Morgan, Spencer, and other prominent men of New York, have contributed to promote the object. Subscriptions will be received by Dr. McCune Smith, 105 West Broadway, New York"; *NS*, February 2, 1849, with more information on the $3,000 to be raised to support settlers "until the first crop can be raised," naming Ray, McCune Smith, "Rev. W. J. Logan of Syracuse" (Loguen), Ward, and Douglass as inspectors "to price the public property of the settlement after the public works are completed."

12. *NS*, February 16, March 2, March 16, and March 30, 1849 for Myers's detailed response, outlining the resources and opportunities in the town, on which Douglass

commented, "He is a deeply interested party. . . . It now appears that this land is owned by a company of persons, who, wishing to raise the price of their lands, and to increase their own wealth, use Mr. Myers to attract colored people," so his claims are "what a man may be expected to say while acting as the agent of a company of land speculators."

13. *NS*, March 30, 1849; *Providence Journal*, April 26, 1849 ("Farming utensils, money or wearing apparel will be thankfully received for use of the Company, as many of its members have just come from under oppression"); *AEJ*, May 5, 1849, announcing Myers lecturing to raise $3,000 to meet their contracts, noting "the want of provisions"; *Pittsfield Sun*, July 5, 1849; *Christian Watchman and Christian Reflector* (Boston), July 19, 1849; *Portsmouth Journal* (Portsmouth, NH), November 10, 1849, both reporting that Rev. Daniel Peterson, who had "good testimonials," was "soliciting aid for establishing a colony of colored men, at Florence, N.Y. on a tract of land granted for that purpose by Gerrit Smith"; the last reference is *NS*, November 2, 1849, on the "Settlers on Smith's Lands in Oneida Co." meeting in Florence, where Reverend Peterson reported on funds, books, and tools donated, and the settlers thanked local whites. In the 1850 federal census, black men headed twelve of the town's 471 households. Seven were born outside the state, including James Lax, who listed his age as 115 and his birthplace as Africa. All owned real property, ranging from the six who owned the minimum $50, all "laborers," to several more prosperous farmers, including Joseph Brown, worth $900.

14. Thomas Downing to WHS, March 29, 1841, WHSP, reel 126; typical is the *Weekly Herald* for November 10, 1849, on how "the distinguished colored leader and caterer, Mr. Downing, F.R.S., (fried, roasted and stewed,) 690 Broadway and 5 Broad street, has shown up superbly in the oratory and oyster line"; *Weekly Herald*, March 21, 1860. Some black people noted this friendship with disfavor; see *FDP*, July 8, 1859, for an attack on George Downing by William Herries following a contentious meeting to discuss Garnet's African Civilization Society. Herries cited the *Herald*'s report, "a sheet to which friend Downing can, I am sure, take no exception," and how later his "pale faced friends" from other newspapers had repeated Garnet's charge that Downing barred persons of color from his Newport establishment, which delegitimized his campaign to desegregate Rhode Island's schools, since "who . . . that values the institution of freedom, would allow their loved children to associate with those of the man who, making loud pretensions of his claims to human and social equality, is afraid to act out his principle, or sustain his sentiments, where he is able to do so without danger of any description?"; *Mobile Register*, March 29, 1860.

15. Franklin B. Hough, *Statistics of Population of the City and County of New York, As Shown by the State Census of 1865, With the Comparative Results of This and Previous Enumerations, and Other Statistics Given by the State and Federal Census, From the Earliest Period, Document No. 13, Board of Supervisors, August 15, 1866* (New York: New York Printing Company, 1866), 67; *AEJ*, November 19, 1849; for Smith's 1845 claim, see *Christian Freeman*, May 22, 1845; *Telegraph and Temperance Journal*, June 1, 1852; *FDP*, February 5, 1852; the 1850 federal census counted 23,452 males of color, and after subtracting 10 percent of the 4,556 from the ages of twenty through twenty-nine, one arrives at an estimated 12,976 men at the age of twenty-one and over; *Baltimore Sun*, November 8, 1854; also the *Cabinet* (Schenectady), November 28, 1854, that "about

3000 colored persons voted at the recent election"; for Garnet, *New-York Tribune*, September 24, 1856; for the larger number, see *WAA*, July 30, 1859; also *NASS*, October 9, 1858: "The number of colored men in the State of New York who possess the amount of property necessary to entitle them, under the Constitution, to the right of suffrage is supposed to be more than 10,000; a body sufficiently numerous, perhaps, in the present nicely balanced state of parties, to determine the result of the next election."

16. *Instructions for Taking the Census of the State of New-York, in the Year 1855; Issued by the Secretary of State, to the Officers Charged with the Duty of Taking It. Together With the Constitutional and Statutory Provisions Concerning the Same* (Albany, NY: Weed, Parsons & Co. Printers, 1855); Phyllis F. Field, *The Politics of Race in New York: The Struggle for Black Suffrage in the Civil War Era* (Ithaca, NY: Cornell University Press, 1982), 96.

17. Walter Stahr, *Seward: Lincoln's Indispensable Man* (New York: Simon & Schuster, 2012), 68–69; *Commercial Advertiser*, April 8, 1834; this language was repeated verbatim in the law as amended in later years; see *Journal of the Assembly of the State of New-York; at their Seventieth Session, Begun and Held at the Capitol, in the City of Albany, on the Fifth Day of January, 1847* (Albany, NY: Charles Van Benthuysen, Printer to the Legislature, 1847), 1:748; McCune Smith made a similar assertion years later; see "Communipaw" in *FDP*, April 8, 1859.

18. *Telegraph and Temperance Journal*, June 1, 1852 and April 6, 1853; "TO GERRIT SMITH GRANTEES!" [broadside], October 4, 1854, in GSP, box 145; James McCune Smith, "Introduction," in *A Memorial Discourse by the Rev. Henry Highland Garnet, Delivered in the Hall of the House of Representatives, Washington City, D.C., on Sabbath, February 12, 1865. With an Introduction by James McCune Smith, M.D.* (Philadelphia: Joseph M. Wilson, 1865), 53.

19. The "Recapitulation" in the *Census of the State of New-York, for 1845. Containing An Enumeration of the Inhabitants of the State, with other Statistical Information, in pursuance of Chapter Third of the First Part of the Revised Statutes, and of the act amending the same, passed on the 7th day of May, 1845* (Albany, NY: Carroll & Cook, 1846, unpaginated), listed 141 taxpayers and sixty-five voters in those counties and the *Census of the State of New-York, for 1855; In Pursuance of Article Third of the Constitution of the State, and of Chapter 64 of the Laws of 1855. Prepared from the Original Returns, Under the Direction Of Hon. Joel T. Headley, Secretary Of State, by Franklin B. Hough, Superintendent of the Census* (Albany, NY: Charles Van Benthuysen, 1856), 1–16, counted 820 taxpayers, although nearly all of this increase came in the three counties outside the Adirondacks—Ulster, Madison, and Oneida—which together included only 106 taxpayers and 51 voters in 1845, but ten years later had increased to 630 taxpayers; Milton C. Sernett, *North Star Country: Upstate New York and the Crusade for African American Freedom* (Syracuse, NY: Syracuse University Press, 2002), 199; *FDP*, February 5, 1852; Thomas Wentworth Higginson, "A Visit to John Brown's Household," *Atlantic Monthly* (December 1859), repr. in *Meteor of War: The John Brown Story*, ed. Zoe Trodd and John Stauffer (Maplecrest, NY: Brandywine, 2004), 188. Regarding the reference to holding office, see Christopher James Bonner, *Remaking the Republic: Black Politics and the Creation of American Citizenship* (Philadelphia: University of Pennsylvania Press, 2020), 35, on Willis Hodges reporting at the 1868 Virginia Constitutional Convention that he had been elected a town tax collector in Franklin County.

20. *New-York Tribune*, August 10, 1857, repr. in *New York Herald*, August 12, 1857, with Smith acknowledging he had "sold the best and gave away the poorest of my land," adding, "Of the three thousand colored men to whom I gave land, probably less than fifty have taken and continue to hold possession of their grants. What is worse, half of the three thousand, as I judge, have either sold their land or been so careless to allow it to be sold for taxes."

21. James D. Bilotta, "A Quantitative Approach to Buffalo's Black Population of 1860," *AANYLH* 12, no. 2 (July 1991): 33; Robert J. Swan, "An Estimate of Black Underenumeration in Federal Antebellum Censuses, A Test Case: Brooklyn, New York, 1790–1850," *Journal of the African-American Historical and Genealogical Society* 9, no. 4 (1988): 147–66; see also Kathryn Grover, *Make a Way Somehow: African-American Community Life in a Northern Community, 1790–1865* (Syracuse, NY: Syracuse University Press, 1994), 27, for James Duffin surveying its black population in 1847 for men who should receive freeholds by Gerrit Smith—of twenty-eight he named in Geneva, twelve were not listed in the 1850 census; Rhoda Golden Freeman, *The Free Negro in New York City in the Era Before the Civil War* (New York: Garland, 1994), 94, on the *Weekly Anglo-African*'s charges in 1860.

22. Blue, *Free Soilers*, 119.

23. *NS*, August 11, 1848 (the forty-three delegates named as from Aurora in Cayuga County included at least eight black men, according to the federal census—see the *Buffalo Weekly Republic*, August 8, 1848); *Oliver Dyer's Phonographic Report of the Proceedings of the National Free Soil Convention at Buffalo, N.Y., August 9th and 10th, 1848* (Buffalo: G. H. Derby, 1848), 21, 24; see also Brooks, *Liberty Power*, 148 on the response to Douglass and Eric Foner, "Racial Attitudes of New York Free Soilers," *Politics and Ideology in the Age of the Civil War* (New York: Oxford University Press, 1980), 86, on Barnburner attempts to block Douglass speaking; *NS*, September 1, 1848. The Whiggish *Buffalo Commercial Advertiser* reported with satisfaction on Ward as "a delegate from Cortland county . . . a very intelligent and respectable person" who "will not allow his claims to a seat to be set aside with impunity. This S. R. Ward is one of the finest specimens, intellectually and physically, of the African race we have ever seen. Intensley [*sic*] black, tall, erect and muscular, and moving with the easy grace of a panther, he has the manners and cultivation of a polished man of the world, and would command attention and respect in any assemblage. As the conferees were about coming into the convention to announce their nomination of Van Buren, Ward went out, not being willing, as we heard him say, to remain and ratify the nomination that he considered an abandonment of the Abolition organization and principles, and the result of improper influences. There are thousands who think like him and will refuse to recognize the bargain by which their leaders have attempted to transfer them to the support of the 'Northern man with Southern principles'" (repr. in the *Sandusky Register* [Sandusky, OH], August 18, 1848). The *Maine Cultivator and Hallowell Gazette*, August 26, 1848 also pointed out, "Is it not singular, that the only delegate to the Buffalo Convention, who had sufficient self-respect to refuse to countenance the juggle, by which Van Buren was put forth as an Anti-Slavery candidate, was a colored man?"

24. *Report of the Proceedings of the Colored National Convention, Held at Cleveland, Ohio, on Wednesday, September 6, 1848* (Rochester, NY: John Dick, at the North Star Office, 1848), 13, 9, 14.

25. *NS*, September 22, 1848; *Evening Post*, September 23, October 20 (reprinting Smith's letter published in the *Model Worker*), December 1, 1848; *AEJ*, November 22, 1848, quoting the *Auburn Daily Advertiser*: "Every colored voter, here, five in number, voted for General Taylor. They preferred to trust him and the Whig party, than Van Buren with all his mighty professions for the principles of 'free soil' and 'free men'"; *AEJ*, November 23, 1849.

26. Alan Morton Kraut, "The Liberty Men of New York: Political Abolitionism in New York State, 1840–1848" (PhD diss., Cornell University, 1975), 148; see C. Peter Ripley, ed., *The Black Abolitionist Papers*, vol. 4, *The United States, 1847–1858* (Chapel Hill: University of North Carolina Press, 1991), 27–29, for Ward's 1848 letter of acceptance as a nominee for the assembly; for Loguen, see Carol M. Hunter, *To Set the Captives Free: Reverend Jermain Wesley Loguen and the Struggle for Freedom in Central New York, 1835–1879* (New York: Garland, 1993), 182; for Derrick, see *IC*, October 10, 1849. Even these gestures got some national attention; see *Augusta Chronicle*, September 28, 1849, reprinting *Albany Argus*, "The Abolition party proper in the State of New York, being the Simon Pures who voted for Gerrit Smith for President last fall, are in the field with a State ticket, made out at Cortlandville last week. There is nothing new in the phase of the ticket, unless it consists in the fact that these partisans, as if to exhibit their unadulterated principles in stronger relief than ever, have placed on it Mr. S. R. Ward, the colored Divine, as Secretary of State," and a similar article in the *Mississippi Free Trader* (Natchez), October 17, 1849. The *National Aegis* (Worcester), October 10, 1849, was more approving, noting, "The Abolition party proper in New York have eschewed the coalition and nominated a colored man, Rev. S. R. Ward, for Secretary of State. We believe that all men of reflection will concede to these persons a higher degree of consistent regard to their principles, than if they had surrendered, like the Free Soilers, to the lust for office, the greed for plunder." The *Impartial Citizen* listed Ward as the party's vice presidential nominee from January 4 to May 17, 1851 (many prior issues are missing). The June 21, 1851 issue includes his decision not to run: "It was a mistake, we think, that nominations were made last fall. Mr. Smith will not run, and Mr. Ward still resides in New York State; that is, *Mrs. W.* resides there. Then there are abundant reasons, as numerous as need be, why the latter will not be a candidate." See also *AEJ*, October 4, 1850, *New London Daily Chronicle*, October 10, 1850, *Hartford Times*, October 12, 1850 ("so extravagant and absurd that they excited the contempt of sensible people of all parties. . . . The negro, Ward, beat all his white rivals in the race"), *Norwich Aurora* (Norwich, CT), October 16, 1850, *National Aegis* (Worcester), October 23, 1850; *Wisconsin Free Democrat* (Milwaukee), October 23, 1850 ("Samuel R. Ward, a colored man, and one of the noblest specimens of his race, was nominated for Vice President"), *Weekly Alta California* (San Francisco), December 7, 1850 ("Of all the ridiculous farces ever played for . . . the groundlings of the political theater, nothing has equal the grotesquences of the doings at Oswego. There the abolitionists of all colors, various as the spirits spoken of by the bard of Avon, assembled and cogitated"); *AEJ*, October 14, 1850.

27. For the background, see Richard H. Sewell, *Ballots for Freedom: Antislavery Politics in the United States, 1837–1860* (New York: W. W. Norton, 1976), 224, "Within weeks of the election Van Burenite spokesmen had made it clear that while they were not yet willing to dismantle their own organization or to abandon the Buffalo platform,

they craved reconciliation with their Hunker rivals." By June 1849 they had backed off "no more slave states and territory" and in August and September the two Democratic factions ("Free Soil" Barnburners and Hunkers) held a series of conventions, culminating in a September 14 joint meeting which nominated a coalition ticket. He adds, "Beyond doubt the hunger for spoils was basic" to the Barnburners, whose "leaders found intolerable the prospect of extended Whig domination" (227). For the election results, see *Daily Union*, November 8, 1849. Before the election, however, the Democratic–Free Soil "Coalition" fell apart publicly in Manhattan; see the *New York Herald*, November 10, 1849, "How the Democracy Came to Lose the Election—The Roaring Meeting in Tammany Hall on the Night of the Election," which notes that angry "regulars" registered their disgust by shouting, "What have John Van Buren (white man) and Fred Douglass (black man) done for the democracy?" For national coverage, see *Liberator*, November 23, 1849, reprinting *Herald* and *Atlas*; also *Portland Daily Advertiser*, November 15, 1849, describing how the *Herald* attributed Whig victory "principally to the fact that the colored voters, and old Anti Slavery men, generally voted with the Whigs," quoting it on "the decided stand taken in their favor by the whole mass of colored voters, from black to dirty white, numbering 1,200 to 1,500 in the city, and as many in the State." The result was that the Whig secretary of state Christopher Morgan won reelection 203,875 to 201,189 over a Democrat, Whig comptroller Washington Hunt won reelection by 205,034 to 199,134, and Whig treasurer Alvah Hunt won 204,137 to 199,134. All of these Whigs received the Anti-Rent endorsement, as did Democrat Levi S. Chatfield, elected attorney general. The Whigs held the Senate 17–15, and tied the Assembly 64–64 by electing twelve of sixteen assemblymen from New York County. Of course, Southern Democrats made much of this "late coalition of the Whig party with the Cuffy party of New York" to bash Georgia Whigs; see *Macon Weekly Telegraph*, December 4, 1849.

28. *Weekly Herald*, November 3, 1849, describes the first meeting, which went past midnight at Putnam's Hall in Church Street, also *FDP*, November 16, 1849. See *NASS*, November 8, 1849, for the most complete description of the two meetings, which the partisan press treated as one. Defeat had many fathers, with the national party's organ, the *Daily Union*, November 8, 1849, quoting a preelection Tammany address attacking the Barnburners for applying an "anti-slavery" test to candidates, repudiating "a coalition with traitors" who tried to apply "a sectional and fanatical brand."

29. *Weekly Herald*, November 10, 1849; *Mississippi Free Trader*, December 26, 1849.

30. *AEJ*, November 19, 1849.

31. *IC*, November 28, December 5, 1849, also June 12, 1850, a letter from Downing quoting Ward's earlier attack on him. The bribery charge also surfaced in William Powell to *NASS*, August 22, 1850, damning Greeley, the "modern Philosopher and wily Politician," noting that "for the love of *Power* and *Wealth* . . . this cowardly-sapient-once-poverty-stricken-Editor, at the last November election, did, directly and collaterally, deceive a *few* misguided *colored voters* in this city. It is said Greeley gave fifty dollars to electioneer for colored votes, to secure a Whig victory, by which 'the city was saved from Loco-foco misrule.'"

32. *Journal of the Assembly of the State of New-York; at their Seventy-Fourth Session, Begun and Held at the Capitol, in the City of Albany, on the Seventh Day of January, 1851* (Albany, NY: Charles Van Benthuysen, Printer to the Legislature, 1851), 1:26–30.

33. *Journal of the Assembly of the State of New-York; at their Seventy-Fifth Session, Begun and Held at the Capitol, in the City of Albany, on the Sixth Day of January, 1852* (Albany, NY: Charles Van Benthuysen, Printer to the Legislature, 1852), 29–30; for Hunt's colonizationism, see *New York Spectator*, April 17, 1851, reprinting the *Commercial Advertiser* on a meeting of the State Colonization Society in the Capitol "at which Gov. Hunt had consented to preside," although he canceled; also *AEJ*, January 15, 1852, reporting on that society's annual meeting voting "unanimous thanks" to Hunt for his message. In 1855, the society elected him one of three delegates to the ACS's national meeting, along with former governor Fish (*Daily National Intelligencer*, December 21, 1855). In the early 1850s, colonization was enjoying a major resurgence, with President Fillmore bringing most of his cabinet to the ACS's 1851 national meeting (see R. J. M. Blackett, *The Captive's Quest for Freedom: Fugitive Slaves, the 1850 Fugitive Slave Law, and the Politics of Slavery* [New York: Cambridge University Press, 2018], 94).

34. *FDP*, January 15, February 12, 1852; *NE*, February 5, 1852. Versions of this report had already appeared in the *Baltimore Sun* and the *Cecil Whig* (Elkton, MD), January 31, 1852, and the Democratic *Washington Examiner* (Washington, PA), February 7, 1852: "Let the Whigs lose 5000 votes in the Empire State, and where will they be?" For Hamilton and Putnam, see *NASS*, March 27, 1851, accompanied by a "Report on the Social Condition of the People of Color around New York City, and on the best means of ameliorating the same" from McCune Smith.

35. Samuel R. Ward, *Autobiography of a Fugitive Negro: His Anti-Slavery Labours in the United States, Canada, & England* (London: John Snow, 1855), 124–25; *National Era*, May 18, 1854.

36. *FDP*, September 25, 1851 and September 10, 1852.

37. *Telegraph and Temperance Journal*, May 17, August 17, September 1 and 25, 1852; *FDP*, October 1, 1852.

38. *Daily National Intelligencer*, November 15, 1852, reprinting *Journal of Commerce*, reporting "quite a stir among the colored voters in Williamsburg, about two hundred in number" because "the votes which they intended to give for JOHN P. HALE . . . were in fact given for the regular Democratic ticket," although the report was mistaken about their party; *NASS*, December 2, 1852, reprinting "a morning paper" on "a meeting last week" in Williamsburg, convened by William J. Hodges, which approved his brother Willis's resolution that "no person had a right to pledge or sell the coloured votes of this city, to either of the great political parties," detailing how Ray deceived various people, including Henry Dias and Jacob Fields, at "a meeting of the Liberty Party (which Party the coloured people of this city have been identified with for the last twelve years), on Monday evening, November 1," and taken "a large number of the Liberty Party tickets," promising to bring them to the polls but substituting "the Locofoco ticket." Ray brazenly "confessed that he did enter into a covenant" with the "Locofoco candidate for Congress . . . for a certain consideration of money," with "carriages . . . placed at his command [to] convey to the polls all coloured persons whom he could induce to vote" with substitute tickets, boasting "that he did cause 250 votes to be cast for the Locofoco party" as "he felt it his privilege to make a business of speculating with the coloured voters." Not surprisingly, the meeting censured him as "the darkest Ray that ever came over Williamsburg," hoping "the spirit of truth and justice

will drive him to his own company." Dr. Ray's obloquy did not last: a few years later he was secretary of the Colored Political Association of the City of Brooklyn and Kings County (Willis Hodges was president) and then an army surgeon during the war; see Craig Steven Wilder, *A Covenant with Color: Race and Social Power in Brooklyn* (New York: Columbia University Press, 2000), 77, 103. Repeated references to 200 black voters are backed up by a hand count of Kings County in the 1855 state census (via www .familysearch.org), showing exactly 222 voters. However, this cannot be taken as a precise record because, first, some leaders like Sylvanus (or Silvanus) Smith were not recorded as voters (he was among those listed as owning land but not as a voter); second, in some instances the "voter" box was checked for a man's wife rather than him; third, in many instances certain boxes (whether a man was a native-born or naturalized voter or an alien; his color, "white," "black," or "mulatto") were checked and then smudged out. The general impression is of the marshals exercising discretion combined with several hundred black men's determination to be recorded as electors.

39. Eric Foner, *Free Soil, Free Labor, Free Men: The Ideology of the Republican Party before the Civil War* (New York: Oxford University Press, 1995), 193, describes how until 1854, "northern Whigs believed that the slavery question had truly been driven from national politics. And despite the disastrous defeat of their presidential candidate Winfield Scott and the deaths of Clay and Webster, they clung to the hope that their party could once again become the broadly based national coalition" it was formerly; Douglass to Seward, April 23, 1853, in WHSP, reel 46. Douglass wrote to thank Seward for sending a copy of his collected speeches immediately upon publication; see George Ellis Baker to WHS, April 16, 1853, WHSP, reel 46 ("Fred Douglass shall have a copy some hour"). Douglass remained a Sewardite, telling a British audience in early 1860 that soon antislavery voters "would cast of three millions for their candidate, and carry Mr. Seward, the anti-slavery man, triumphantly up to the White House (cheers.) It was true that Seward was not altogether an abolitionist; but he believed that slavery should not be extended one inch beyond its present limits (hear;) held that there should be no slavery in the District of Columbia; and that in all parts of the Union there should be the right of freedom of opinion and free speech with regard to the question"; *FDP*, February 17, 1860.

40. Booraem, *Formation of the Republican Party*, 109, also 33, that "nativism in New York was almost necessarily an anti-Seward movement." Seymour beat Hunt 50 percent to 46 percent, with the Free Democratic candidate Minthorne Tompkins gaining most of the remainder.

41. *Macon Weekly Telegraph*, June 20, 1854, reprinting *Savannah Republican*, itself reprinting *Syracuse Standard*: "The day the Fred Douglass makes his appearance in the Capitol to take his seat as a member of the American Congress will be, the 'beginning of the end' of this Union. Mark that, ye furious, foolish fanatics"; *The Floridian and Journal* (Tallahassee) and *Philadelphia Inquirer*, June 24, 1854; *Charleston Courier*, August 19, 1854; *Massachusetts Spy*, August 23, 1854; *Vermont Mercury*, August 31, 1854, all reprinting the *Tribune*. Douglass himself copied the *Rochester Democrat*, June 30, 1854, reporting "the Silver Gray papers are discussing the propriety" of his nomination; see *FDP*, June 30, 1854.

42. John H. Hewitt, "The Search for Elizabeth Jennings, Heroine of a Sunday Afternoon in New York City," *New York History* 71, no. 4 (October 1990): 386–415.

43. See two important New England voices, the *Boston Atlas*, February 24, 1855 ("The Third Avenue Railroad Company of Brooklyn, have been mulcted in $250 and the costs of prosecution, for putting a colored woman off their cars by force. The jury agreed upon $225, but the Court added 10 per cent") and the *Congregationalist*, March 2, 1855 ("Elizabeth Jennings, a respectable colored woman, a teacher in one of the public schools, and organist . . . was very nicely dressed, and she is, moreover, a tidy looking person, far preferable as a companion in a railroad car to any of the tobacco-chewing, rum-drinking white rowdies who throng these vehicles," further describing her as a "woman of spirit"); for Jennings to the conductor, see Ripley, *Black Abolitionist Papers*, 4:231; also Leslie M. Harris, *In the Shadow of Slavery: African Americans in New York City, 1626–1863* (Chicago: University of Chicago Press, 2004), 270; *Tribune* quoted in *Provincial Freeman*, March 10, 1855; *FDP*, May 11, 1855; Pennington's court action in *Provincial Freeman*, June 16, 1855, see also Alexander, *African or American?*, 128–29, on Pennington losing a subsequent suit, until a February 1858 state supreme court decision finally banned racial discrimination in public transportation.

44. Booraem, *Formation of the Republican Party*, 82. See Harry J. Carman and Reinhard H. Luthin, "The Seward-Fillmore Feud and the Crisis of 1850," *New York History* 24, no. 2 (April 1943): 163–84, describing the Sewardites achieving control in 1850, quoting a letter to Fillmore from Jerome Fuller that "unless these slavery issues are disposed of, the danger is that a sectional party will arise. Weed and Seward would like to convert the Whig party into one. We must stay the progress of abolitionism or we are gone" (175).

45. John Stauffer, *The Black Hearts of Men: Radical Abolitionists and the Transformation of Race* (Cambridge, MA: Harvard University Press, 2002), has an extended discussion of the RAP; Joel Schor, *Henry Highland Garnet: A Voice of Black Radicalism in the Nineteenth Century* (Westport, CT: Greenwood Press, 1977), 139.

46. Field, *Politics of Race*, 85–86, 97–103 (even with a five-to-one majority in 1849, Whigs rejected suffrage petitions on a voice vote).

47. Field, *Politics of Race*, 80–81 ("only one other made it to the balloting stage" in 1846–60), 112–13.

48. Field, 81.

49. Field, 90–91.

50. See *FDP*, July 20, 1855 for the "Call for a State Convention of the Colored People of the State of New York," in Philip S. Foner and George E. Walker, eds., *Proceedings of the Black State Conventions, 1840–1865*, vol. 1, *New York, Pennsylvania, Indiana, Michigan, Ohio* (Philadelphia: Temple University Press, 1979), 88; *FDP*, July 27 and September 24, 1855.

51. *Northern Star and Freemen's Advocate*, December 8, 1842; *FDP*, February 23, 1855.

52. *FDP*, December 14, 1855, noting the meeting unanimously agreed that "the Republican Ticket was entitled to their support"; *Census for the State of New-York for 1855*, 76; *FDP*, October 19, 1855, reporting on a September 30 meeting in Poughkeepsie which Myers addressed as "agent for the County."

53. Stephen Myers, *Circular to the Friends of Freedom, May 22, 1858* (Albany: 1858); Myers to John Jay II, December 17, 1858, in Ripley, *Black Abolitionist Papers*, 4:407–11; also *Cincinnati Commercial Tribune*, March 4, 1858, reprinting the *Times* on the "Underground Railroad in New York," which cited Myers's favorable report as its su-

perintendent, that in the month's first twenty-three days, there had been thirty-six "through passengers, besides the usual amount of way travel." He even survived an interracial sexual scandal, the charge he had seduced "a very fair appearing white girl of about twenty years," Mary Brennan, who also worked at the Delevan Hotel, setting her up in a house and offering her $200. She sued him as "the father of her babe—yet unborn"; see *Daily Missouri Republican*, June 2, 1855, reprinting *Albany Atlas*, referring to him as "a celebrated character in Albany . . . a great favorite with the anti-slavery leaders" and "as black as the ace of spades."

54. Versions in *Daily Evening Traveller* (Boston), February 6, 1858, *Daily Citizen and News* (Lowell, MA) February 8, 1858, *The States* (Washington, DC), February 9, 1858, *Massachusetts Spy* (Worcester) and *Philadelphia Inquirer*, February 10, 1858, *Charleston Mercury* and *Charleston Courier*, February 12, 1858, *New England Farmer* (Boston), February 13, 1858, *Portland Advertiser*, February 16, 1858, *Daily True Delta* (New Orleans), February 21, 1858, *Columbus Enquirer* (Georgia), February 25, 1858; see also Ripley, *Black Abolitionist Papers*, 4:407, for a note that from November 1857 to May 1858, Myers sent 188 fugitives to Canada; for Weed's coverage of the UGRR, see *AEJ*, September 4, 1854, reprinting *Owego Times*, how a fugitive "father with his child 2 ½ years old, passed through this village on Sunday last, for Canada," after threats to sell the child and mutilation by "a brutal overseer," adding that the "only guide through his weary night wandering was the north star—to the slave the Star of Bethlehem," also January 29, 1856, a long report by William Still, headed "Pursuit of Freedom under Difficulties—Underground Railroad News," full of dramatic stories, repr. from Mary Ann Shadd Cary's *Provincial Freeman*, January 19, and January 4, 1858, "The *Syracuse Standard* says that Rev. Mr. Loguen performed the marriage ceremony on the 31st. inst. for a couple of fugitives from Delaware. . . . The party immediately started on a wedding tour by the Underground R. R. to Canada, where they expect to spend the honeymoon"; Frederick W. Seward, *Seward at Washington, as Senator and Secretary of State: A Memoir of His Life, and Selections from His Letters, 1846–1861* (New York: Derby and Miller, 1891), 258, for an 1855 letter where the senator noted, "The 'underground railroad' works wonderfully. Two passengers came here last night"; *FDP*, September 14, 1855, for "Cosmopolite" reporting on the state suffrage association meeting, February 11, 1859, for Watkins's speech in the assembly chamber, March 11, 1859, for Martin describing how "the legislative sharks" were "sporting with the helpless form of the disfranchised colored man," but noting Myers's efforts deserved "respect and commendation; for though I do not agree with him in political opinion, I think he is doing what no other man could do for us, and when we get our rights in this State, the efforts of Mr. Myers shall not be forgotten."

55. See Myers to Gerrit Smith, March 22, 1856, in Ripley, *Black Abolitionist Papers*, 4:326–27, "Sir I have been striving hard this winter with members of the senate and assembly to recommend an amendment to the constitution of this state so as to strike off the property qualification and let us vote on the same footing as the white mail citizens so as to have it once more handed down to the people I have got Senator Cuyler some weeks ago to get up a resolution in the Senat which is now under discusin and will com up again monday or tuesday I shall have one up in the assembly in a few days," adding he had also "gotten about sixty members pledged to go against" a bill to give $5,000 to the ACS; on Cuyler, see the National Park Service's Network to Freedom

mapping the UGRR, according to which the Cuylers "kept the most important Underground Railroad station on Lake Ontario's shore between Oswego and Rochester," from which they "sent freedom seekers to Canada on steamboats operated by a relative, Captain Horatio Nelson Throop" (and that Cuyler had been a Liberty man, and then a Free Soiler), see https://www.nps.gov/subjects/ugrr/ntf_member/ntf_member_details.htm?SPFID=4074857&SPFTerritory=NULL&SPFType=NULL&SPFKeywords=NULL; *New-York Tribue*, March 19, 1856.

56. *Jamestown Journal*, March 28, 1856; Booraem, *Formation of the Republican Party*, 220.

57. *FDP*, November 9, 1855; Stauffer, *Black Hearts of Men*, 20 (at the September 1855 state Liberty Party convention, Douglass had been nominated for secretary of state, with George B. Vashon for attorney general, see *FDP*, September 21, 1855); *Radical Abolitionist*, April 1856 (only four black men are identifiable), see the "Extra" of June 2, 1856, containing "Minutes of the National Nominating Convention," where Ohio's Peter H. Clark, William J. Watkins, and Douglass spoke, with Amos Beman named as Connecticut's National Committee representative; *Radical Abolitionist*, November 1856, quoting Douglass on why black people should support Frémont; the estimate of Smith's vote is in Ripley, *Black Abolitionist Papers*, 4:401n3.

58. See John Stauffer, ed., *The Works of James McCune Smith: Black Intellectual and Abolitionist* (New York: Oxford University Press, 2007), 154, quoting the latter as "Communipaw" in *FDP* on Brooklyn meetings. Early on, there was resistance; see *New-York Tribune*, July 30, 1856 on a "COLORED POLITICAL MEETING IN BROOKLYN" soon after the Republican convention, "for the purpose of organizing themselves into a Club," where a resolution hailing Frémont's nomination as "the embodiment of Northern sentiment" and "pledging, as far as we are permitted . . . to exercise the right of American citizens in the use of the ballot box, to remember him . . . in the coming election" caused objections and was "indefinitely postponed," followed by "a resolution declaring the meeting a 'Frémont League' . . . which caused great confusion, several speaking at the same time" so they adjourned; see *Illinois State Register*, August 22, 1856 and *Ohio Statesman*, August 29, 1856, quoting Douglass to prove Frémont was leagued with abolitionists, with the former adding, "Here we have the real negro himself, the black Douglass, throwing up his cap for the woolly horse; Massa John Charles is kinky enough for Fred Douglass," and *Mining Register, and Pottsville Emporium* (Pottsville, PA), August 23, 1856 counterposing two lists of leaders (one set backing Buchanan; another, including Seward, Greeley, Henry Ward Beecher, Stevens, and Douglass, backing Frémont) and *Daily Pennsylvanian*, September 19, 1856, "Let all who follow negro dictation and morals under the leadership of a negro editor mark well his reasons for this course," and *Columbian Register* (New Haven), November 1, 1856, reporting, "Fred. Douglass (black) made a speech on Saturday evening last, at a Frémont meeting in Milwaukee. Douglass is one of the most active soldiers in the Republican camp"; for Garnet, see *New-York Tribune*, September 24, 1856 and *Jeffersonian Democrat* (Monroe, WI), September 18, 1856, drawing on Bennett's *Herald*; W. J. Watkins to Weed, November 4, 1856, in TWP.

59. *AEJ*, December 19, 1856. Holding up exemplary men of color as superior to vulgar Democrats was a favorite trope for the *Journal*; see its 1858 comment when the ex-mayor of New York and Tammanyite Fernando Wood was "formally invited to a seat

on the floor of the Assembly" and "someone jocosely proffered a like compliment to FRED. DOUGLASS." When the Democratic *Argus* claimed the *Journal* was "hysterical" over "Negro Douglass" being refused, the Republican editor replied, "We certainly deem 'Negro Douglass' vastly Wood's mental and moral superior; but we would not, for that reason, tender him the empty honor of a seat within the bar of the Assembly Chamber. Unlike the Ex-Mayor, he has too much sense to relish any such silly ostentation"; *AEJ*, February 3, 1858.

60. *AEJ*, February 18, 1857.

61. Field, *Politics of Race*, 99; *Albany Argus*, March 27 and 31, 1857; *Evening Post*, March 20, 1857 ("Judge Taney admits the position that all persons who were citizens of the several states at the time the constitution was adopted became citizens of the United States. . . . This gives Downing an opportunity to floor the judge on the deadlock" by citing Massachusetts's enfranchisement of black men in 1780) and *AEJ*, March 25, 1857 ("This black man teaching law to the Democratic Chief Justice of the United States, shows him that the power of Congress to establish a uniform rule of naturalization, is to be exercised among aliens, and does not refer to and did not contemplate, native-born Americans," with more of Downing's examples).

62. *Tribune*, September 4, 1857; *Plattsburgh Republican*, September 5, 1857 from *Troy Budget* (this newspaper, founded by Azariah Flagg, a close ally of Van Buren, was the "party's leading organ in northeastern New York," see Lee Benson, *The Concept of Jacksonian Democracy: New York as a Test Case* [Princeton, NJ: Princeton University Press, 1961], 68); *AEJ* quoted in *Daily Union*, September 8, 1857.

63. *AEJ* quoted in *Daily Union*, September 8, 1857; *New York Herald*, September 6 and 7, 1857; *Daily Pioneer and Democrat* (St. Paul, MN), September 18, 1857, quoting *Buffalo Commercial Advertiser*.

64. *FDP*, September 4 and 18, 1857. Next to the latter, Douglass printed a white man named "B.," acknowledging "the disappointment and mortification you feel and express at the miserable blunder by which the suffrage question is delayed." Still, he was "inclined to accept the account of the matter as given in the *Journal*. No man who knows the Governor . . . will for a moment suspect him of countenancing any trick or evasions," and his secretary should not "be suspected of anything but a carelessness or forgetfulness." It was all somebody else's fault, "a clerk of the Senate" or the secretary of state, and even he had not "intentionally withheld them."

65. *New York Times*, September 30, 1857; *NASS*, January 9, 1858.

66. *Troy Times*, October 16, 1858: "Democrats are very busy in denouncing the colored men who intend to vote for Mr. Morgan on the score of ingratitude. If it is ungrateful for them to abandon Gerrit Smith because he gave them land, Irishmen should vote for him because he gave them food and money," a reference to Smith's ample contributions to Irish famine relief.

67. Quoted in *NE*, October 14, 1858. Gamaliel Bailey, editor of the *Era*, added that in the 1840s, "both the Parties were controlled by their Slaveholding wings." By their intransigence, the Liberty men "paved the way for the Free Soil movement of 1848, and the Republican Party of 1856, whose policy is precisely that which they urged with so much importunity." If New York's "Anti-Slavery voters" had any reason to think "the Republican Party occupies just the same position" as the Whigs, that perception would "multiply Mr. Smith's supporters by the score." This prospect was unlikely, however,

as most former Liberty men were now Republicans. Smith's supporters should recognize that "by uniting with the Republicans, they might prostrate the Administration Party in New York, give the finishing blow to Pro-Slavery Know Nothingism, and prepare the way for the inauguration in 1860 of the Free Power of the Country in the Capital of the Nation."

68. *Radical Abolitionist*, August 1858, "A Word to the Colored People," one of the few appeals. McCune Smith had written Smith in late summer indicating that Thomas Hamilton, who would shortly found the *Weekly Anglo-African*, wanted to start a campaign paper aimed at black voters, and needed $500 to begin, stressing that it "would do much good for the cause hereabouts and that it would gain many votes," to which the doctor added a caution, that "if I may venture a word of advice, do not write another letter on politics between now and 20th November," JMS to GS, August 23, 1858, GSP, box 34.

69. *Gerrit Smith Banner*, October 28 and 29, 1858; *Evening Post*, October 8, 1858.

70. *Gerrit Smith Banner*, November 1, 1858; *NE*, November 11, 1858, hailing the "GREAT REPUBLICAN TRIUMPH"; see also *AEJ*, January 5, 1859, for the official tally showing 54 percent of Smith's votes concentrated in eleven upstate counties: Allegany, Cattaraugus, Cortland, Jefferson, Oswego, Oneida, Onondaga, St. Lawrence, Wayne, Chautauqua and Madison—in the last, his home county, he received 636 votes or 12 percent of his statewide tally versus a mere fifty-eight in New York County and seventy-two in Kings, with their large numbers of black voters; *Evening Post*, October 26, 1858.

71. *NASS*, October 9, 1858; Garnet to Smith, September 16, 1858 in Ripley, *Black Abolitionist Papers*, 4:398; Watkins to Smith, September 27, 1858, in Ripley, *Black Abolitionist Papers*, 4:398–400 (Watkins was responding to the following in the *NASS*, October 2, 1858, "William J. Watkins, who has for several years occupied the place of associate editor of Frederick Douglass' Paper, is said to have dissolved his connection therewith. The reason for this step has not been authoritatively announced, but it is currently reported to have been a difference of opinion and feeling between Mr. Watkins and Mr. Douglass. *The Hour and the Man*, Gerrit Smith's new organ at Albany, says: 'We understand that Mr. Watkins, a colored man, lately divorced from Frederick Douglass' Paper, has been closeted in our city with the Prince of the State Regency, and has taken the stump to induce colored people to vote against Gerrit Smith and in favor of Morgan—beware of him!'"); *New-York Tribune*, October 7, 1858.

72. *New-York Tribune*, October 5, 1858, as "Gerrit Smith and the Colored Vote," repr. in the *AEJ*, October 7, 1858; *Anti-Slavery Bugle*, December 4, 1858; *AEJ*, January 15, 1859, "The Assembly Chamber was well filled last evening to hear Wm. J. Watkins speak on the Suffrage Question. He is a fluent speaker. His argument was logical, clear and convincing against the injustice of the property qualification, and his suggestions for action in reference to it sensible and practical. We observed a considerable number of the members of the Legislature, as well as citizens, among the audience. Mr. W. speaks on Monday evening at the Third-st. Church on Arbor Hill . . . at Schenectady on Tuesday, and at Hudson on Wednesday."

73. Quoted in *NASS*, October 9, 1858; *Gerrit Smith Banner*, November 1 (repr. the *Tribune*), and October 29, 1858.

74. *Radical Abolitionist*, December 1858.

75. *Louisiana Courier* repr. in *New-York Tribune*, November 17, 1858 as "SOUTHERN SYMPATHY FOR GERRIT SMITH."

76. Amy Hanmer-Croughton, "Anti-Slavery Days in Rochester," *The Rochester Historical Society, Publication Fund Series* (Rochester, NY: Published by the Society, 1936), 143–44; Seward, *Seward at Washington*, 440; Glyndon G. Van Deusen, *William Henry Seward* (New York: Oxford University Press, 1967), 215.

77. Field, *Politics of Race*, 137; John S. Minard, Esq., County Historian, *Allegany County and its People, A Centennial Memorial History of Allegany County, New York* (Alfred, NY: W. A. Fergusson, 1896), 651, on Maxson as a farmer's son and devout Baptist, ordained in 1853 and a professor of church polity and pastoral theology at Alfred University in the 1850s ("Mr. Maxson belonged to the old time 'Liberty' party in politics. . . . His Alfred home was ever a 'station' of the 'underground railroad' when that was in operation"); *AEJ*, February 20, 1860.

78. *FDP*, February 11, 1859.

79. *FDP*, March 4, 1859. One notes that Douglass published all these polemics against him, apparently unbothered.

80. *WAA*, September 24, 1859 and March 17, 1860.

81. Field, *Politics of Race*, 108–9; in 1856, fifteen of forty-seven; in 1857, fourteen of thirty-eight; in 1858, seventeen of fifty-seven; in 1859, twelve of twenty-nine; in 1860, thirteen of thirty-seven. Adding Kings County only accentuates the concentration of the state's Democratic vote. For trenchant analyses of why white plebeians were so deeply Democratic, see Anthony Gronowicz, *Race and Class in New York City before the Civil War* (Boston: Northeastern University Press, 1997), and, in particular, Wilder, *Covenant with Color*, 61, specifying Brooklyn's centrality in the transatlantic textile and sugar economies built on slave labor: "The ability to enslave African Americans was sustained because distinct interest groups came together under the banner of race. . . . The incorporation of the industrial working class into the Democratic party . . . offered the Irish and German population a party that defended their interests as workers and citizens, and redrew the lines of social division to include immigrants but exclude people of color"; *AEJ*, February 11, 1859.

82. *WAA*, March 24 and 31, 1860, also April 21, when Republican failure to file the resolutions required a revote, speedily accomplished; *WAA*, March 31, 1860. Hamilton claimed to be unimpressed by symbolism, but informed his readers that the black minister T. Doughty Miller had been invited to "open the session of the Assembly with prayer" (*WAA*, March 10, 1860).

83. Thurlow Weed Barnes, *Memoir of Thurlow Weed* (Boston: Houghton, Mifflin, 1884), 258, although clearly an editorial, but I cannot locate its original; on Irish women and black men, see *WAA*, January 28, 1860, describing an "Anti-O'Conor Meeting" after the leading Irish Democratic lawyer Charles O'Conor, representing a master in the famous *Lemmon v. The People* case, asserted that slavery was upheld by "essential justice and morality in all courts and places before men and nations," after which Garnet declared that in Ireland, the men "would have stoned him, and the daughters of the Emerald Isle would have whipped him within an inch of his life," and Jeremiah Powers baited O'Conor on his countrywomen's marital preferences; see also Freeman, *Free Negro in New York City*, 167, quoting an Assembly committee's report on tenements which found that "by ocular demonstration, it was ascertained that nearly all the

inhabitants were practical amalgamationists—black husbands and white (generally Irish) wives," plus the *Tribune*, January 26, 1861, reporting, "In all cases of intermarriage" in the city's 1860 census "the wife is white—none being returned of a white man marrying a black woman. Of the thirty-two white women whose husbands are black, eighteen were born in Ireland"; on Downing, see *Newark Daily Advertiser*, March 19, 1860, "Downing, the famous oyster man of N.Y., on Saturday refused to take an oath, on the ground that being colored, he was only a chattel under the Dred Scott decision," and *Evening Post*, August 13, 1860, on how "Mr. Downing, senior" was present when Douglas visited his son's restaurant, "and was presented to the Judge, who humorously inquired about his politics. To this the old gentleman responded, with that bland gravity so familiar to the oyster-eaters" of Wall Street, "declaring that his birth at the South and his friendship with the many southern gentlemen whose patronage had so liberally been bestowed on him, would . . . preclude him from sympathizing with Judge Douglas in his recent difficulties with them," meaning the Charleston convention which ruined Douglas's chances for the presidency; *New York Herald*, November 6, 1860.

84. *AEJ*, September 29, 1860, "William J. Watkins of Rochester will address the people on the political issues of the day," tracking his tour of fourteen cities and towns, October 1–17; *Commercial Advertiser*, August 13, 1860; *WAA*, May 19, 1860 (the main issue was whether the ballot should read "Property Qualification or No Property Qualification?" with militants like Garnet wanting a "yes or no" vote on "negro suffrage"); JMS to GS, June 2 and September 22, 1860, GSP, box 34, latter including letter to Myers, September 21, 1860; the September 22 letter included McCune Smith's proposal to distribute 400,000 tracts, each with a ballot, followed by an October 20, 1860 letter to Smith, citing a recent delivery of 25,000 to Douglass, 8,000 printed in German for the city, and their hope "to print Some in French could we afford it."

85. *Evening Post*, November 9, 1860. Reportedly Downing received them "with a smile of unusual politeness. . . . 'Nothing,' said he, 'opens a man's heart, or puts him in a mood to exercise the virtue of generosity, better than good feeding. I have therefore got a splendid oyster expressly for this occasion. . . .' Accordingly, when the well-fed voter came up to pay his shot, a circular, signed by James McCune Smith, was placed in his hands by Downing, and enclosed in this with three tickets . . . inscribed, 'for the proposed amendment to the right of suffrage.' 'What do you want me to do?' inquired one; 'I am a democrat, and can't vote for Lincoln.' 'As to that, sir,' would be the reply, 'Lincoln is safe enough; he is sure to be in. All I want is for you to give the poor colored man a chance. Let him now have a voice in choosing who is to govern him'"; JMS to GS, October 20, 1860 in GSP, box 34; *New-York Tribune*, November 6, 1860.

86. *New York Herald*, September 8, 1860.

87. *New York Herald*, October 9, 1860; *Plattsburgh Republican*, October 13, 1860.

88. *Commercial Advertiser*, September 13, 1860, "Negro Suffrage in this State. ITS HISTORY. Views of Mr. Lincoln"; *New-York Tribune*, September 15, 1860; *New York Times*, November 22, 1860.

89. *AEJ*, October 26, 1860, see articles using nearly identical language on August 2 and 27, September 5, October 1, and November 5. Weed first sounded the anti-aristocratic call on February 13, 1860, insisting "Property Qualifications are relics of a past age. If feudal times in Europe, freedom and freeholding were synonymous," and

"to this day property qualifications regulate the right of suffrage in Great Britain." Until the Revolution, "qualifications were required of *white* men. . . . They are only retained now in some of the Slaveholding States, which cling naturally to whatever concentrates power in the hands of the few at the expense of the many"; *AEJ*, October 31 and November 1, 1860.

90. Field, *Politics of Race*, 130, for the estimate that "only a little over half (54.5%) of the Lincoln voters could have favored increased black voting"; Kenneth L. Roff, "Brooklyn's Reaction to Black Suffrage in 1860," *AANYLH* 2, no. 1 (January 1978): 36, for county totals.

91. *WAA*, January 5, 1861.

Coda

1. Myers to WHS, February 20, 1861, reel 61, WHSP.

2. *Autobiography of Dr. William Henry Johnson, Respectfully Dedicated to His Adopted Home, the Capital City of the Empire State* (New York: Haskell House, 1970, repr. of 1900 edition), 61; *Commercial Advertiser*, January 23, 1869; *AEJ*, January 22, 1869 (a final motion to make him "Superintendent of the cloak room" was defeated in February by a tie, 45 to 45, with eleven Republicans voting no); *Commercial Advertiser*, February 10 and January 27, 1869.

3. *New York Herald*, May 19, 1869; *Troy Weekly Times*, June 12, 1869; *Albany Argus*, February 15, 1870.

4. *AEJ*, February 16, 1870.

Part IV

1. Donald J. Ratcliffe, *The Politics of Long Division: The Birth of the Second Party System in Ohio, 1818–1828* (Columbus: Ohio State University Press, 2000); Eric Foner, *Free Soil, Free Labor, Free Men: The Ideology of the Republican Party Before the Civil War* (New York: Oxford University Press, 1995), 106–7, defines Oberlin as one of the "centers of pure New England culture" spread across the Old Northwest, noting the electoral implications, that "these little New Englands, with their small towns and independent farmers, were not only centers of literacy, religion, and economic progress, but of Republican radicalism—and heavy Republican electoral majorities—as well"; Christopher Phillips, *The Rivers Ran Backward: The Civil War and the Remaking of the American Middle Border* (New York: Oxford University Press, 2016), 9–10. See Daniel Walker Howe, *What Hath God Wrought: The Transformation of America, 1815–1848* (New York: Oxford University Press, 2007), 139, on southern Ohio, Indiana, and Illinois as "Extended Virginia," but also "a diverse intermediate zone settled by people from the Middle Atlantic states."

2. A Democratic state senator quoted in Steven Lubet, *The "Colored Hero" of Harper's Ferry: John Anthony Copeland and the War Against Slavery* (Cambridge: Cambridge University Press, 2015), 47; John Mercer Langston, *From the Virginia Plantation to the National Capitol: Or the First and Only Negro Representative in Congress from the Old Dominion* (Hartford, CT: American Publishing Company, 1894), 97; Ellen N. Lawson and Marlene Merrill, "The Antebellum 'Talented Thousandth': Black College

Students at Oberlin Before the Civil War," *Journal of Negro Education* 52, no. 2 (Spring 1983): 142.

3. Langston, *From the Virginia Plantation*, 164–68; Nat Brandt, *The Town That Started the Civil War* (Syracuse, NY: Syracuse University Press, 1990), 113; William Cheek and Aimee Lee Cheek, *John Mercer Langston and the Fight for Black Freedom, 1829–1865* (Urbana: University of Illinois, 1989), 333–34; Frank U. Quillin, *The Color Line in Ohio: A History of Race Prejudice in a Typical Northern State* (Ann Arbor, MI: George Wahr, 1913), 33; the definitive work on antebellum black Cleveland is still Allan Peskin, ed., *North into Freedom: The Autobiography of John Malvin, Free Negro, 1795–1880* (Cleveland: Press of Western Reserve University, 1966), where he notes that "in 1843 . . . the Cleveland City Council began to subsidize the Negro schools out of the general revenue. . . . By the 1850s Cleveland had abolished segregated schools entirely [and] even had a Negro school teacher" (64).

4. *CA*, August 31, 1839, Pittsburgh's Lewis Woodson writing as "Augustine"; see also Ellen Eslinger, "The Evolution of Racial Politics in Early Ohio," in *The Center of a Great Empire: The Ohio Country in the Early American Republic*, ed. Andrew R. L. Cayton and Stuart D. Hobbs (Athens: Ohio University Press, 2005), 87, "enforcement proved almost universally lax."

5. John Niven, *Salmon P. Chase: A Biography* (New York: Oxford University Press, 1995) is the latest version of this narrative, referring often to "the driving ambition that lay concealed behind this dignified, cultivated man who seemed so open and passionate for the cause" (113), while conceding that at his career's climax, approaching the Republican presidential nomination in 1860, Chase "would not defer to conservative opinion when it came to principle even if it weakened his candidacy" (211); the great exception is the chapter titled "Salmon P. Chase: The Constitution and the Slave Power" in Foner, *Free Soil, Free Labor, Free Men*, presenting him as the key articulator of what became "the ideology of the Republican Party before the Civil War"; the most careful contemporary evaluation comes from Chase's onetime ally, Albert G. Riddle, "Recollections of the Forty-Seventh General Assembly of Ohio," *Magazine of Western History* 6 (1887): 351, describing him as "a man of large, exalted views, if ambitious above most men, it arose from conscious power to serve. . . . He never belonged to any political party in the ordinary sense of the term, and never betrayed a party. He had certain great purposes to accomplish, and the men or party who would advance them he unhesitantly employed. This explains his seeming changes"; Corey M. Brooks, *Liberty Power: Antislavery Third Parties and the Transformation of American Politics* (Chicago: University of Chicago Press, 2016), 2, arguing that "from the mid-1830s through the mid-1850s, a small, radical third-party challenge established the foundation for the most dramatic political upheaval in American history," with Ohio front and center.

Chapter Eleven

1. On Sandusky, see Charles Thomas Hickok, *The Negro in Ohio, 1802–1870* (New York: AMS, 1975, repr. of 1896 ed., published by Williams Publishing and Electric Company of Cleveland), 159.

2. "Introduction" in *Race and the City: Work, Community, and Protest in Cincinnati, 1820–1970*, ed. Henry Louis Taylor (Urbana: University of Illinois Press, 1993), xiv;

J. V. Smith, *Report of the Debates and Proceedings of the Convention for the Revision of the Constitution of the State of Ohio, 1850–51* (Columbus: S. Medary, Printer to the Convention, 1851), 28–29; also 458 for another asking for "the removal of the black and mulatto population from this State, and to prevent their further emigration into it," plus one asking that "henceforth none of the African race be permitted to settle" and "negroes at present among us be removed as soon as possible," and a final memorial requesting to deport all those with even "part negro blood" from the state (459); *OSJ*, June 25, 1850.

3. Stephen Middleton, *The Black Laws: Race and the Legal Process in Early Ohio* (Athens: Ohio University Press, 2005), 32, quotes an 1837 state senate report that they had "exercised the right of suffrage, in common with all other citizens, down to the adoption of our Constitution." The address "To the Citizens of Ohio" from an 1849 black convention asserted they voted for delegates to the original convention; see *Minutes and Address of the State Convention of the Colored Citizens of Ohio, Convened at Columbus, January 10th, 11th, 12th, and 13th, 1849*, Philip S. Foner and George E. Walker, eds., *Proceedings of the Black State Conventions, 1840–1865*, vol. 1, *New York, Pennsylvania, Indiana, Michigan, Ohio* (Philadelphia: Temple University Press, 1979), 231; Donald J. Ratcliffe, *Party Spirit in a Frontier Republic: Democratic Politics in Ohio, 1793–1821* (Columbus: Ohio State University Press, 1998), 70.

4. Frank U. Quillin, *The Color Line in Ohio: A History of Race Prejudice in a Typical Northern State* (Ann Arbor, MI: George Wahr, 1913), 14–15, 21; Middleton, *Black Laws*, 44, 48, 49, 51. As one scholar puts it, Ohio had evolved "a particular type of unfreedom . . . distinct from slavery but even more distinct from citizenship" (Michael Mangin, "Freemen in Theory: Race, Society, and Politics in Ross County, Ohio, 1796–1850" [PhD diss., University of California, San Diego, 2002], 35). The 1804 act also required black emigrants to produce manumissions "bearing the seal of the state from whence they came," and penalized anyone who illegally employed them $10–$50, with half to any informer (Betty M. Culpepper, "The Negro and the Black Laws of Ohio, 1803–1860" [master's thesis, Kent State University, 1965], 6–7).

5. See Donald J. Ratcliffe, *The Politics of Long Division: The Birth of the Second Party System in Ohio, 1818–1828* (Columbus: Ohio State University Press, 2000), 52–53, on how Methodists, Quakers, and Yankees successfully derailed the convention while the Gist slaves, so-called, faced "physical intimidation and even the kidnapping and sale of their children"; Kenneth J. Winkle, *The Politics of Community: Migration and Politics in Antebellum Ohio* (Cambridge: Cambridge University Press, 1988), 26. Harlan Hatcher, *The Western Reserve: The Story of New Connecticut in Ohio* (Indianapolis: Bobbs-Merrill, 1949), 207, notes that the area west of Cuyahoga was not settled until after 1815 and Lorain County (where Oberlin was "hacked out of a dense, unbroken wilderness" in 1832–33), was only founded in 1822.

6. Jeffrey P. Brown and Andrew R. L. Cayton, eds., *The Pursuit of Public Power: Political Culture in Ohio, 1787–1861* (Kent, OH: Kent State University Press, 1994), viii (by 1810, half of white men over the of age twenty-six owned their own fields minus mortgages or encumbrances, largely because of the Land Act that William Henry Harrison had pushed through Congress in 1800 as Ohio's territorial delegate); Ratcliffe, *Party Spirit*, 12, 44–45; Burnet quoted in Middleton, *Black Laws*, 45; James Rodabaugh, "The Negro in Ohio," *JNH* 31, no. 1 (January 1946): 16, notes, "After about 1815 Ohio

became the great battleground for abolitionists and conservatives [starting with] Quakers who settled in central and southeastern Ohio, supported by New Englanders"; Ratcliffe, *Politics of Long Division*, 85–90 has a precise mapping by county, correlating support for Adams in 1824 to antislavery and sectional feeling. He notes the ethnic basis of partisanship in 1828, in which support for Jackson affirmed "the political virtue of Americans who were not of English stock," the Scotch Irish and Pennsylvania Dutch (121), versus the Yankees and Quakers who backed the National Republican and Whig Parties.

7. The "French Negro" slaves grandfathered by territorial governor Arthur St. Clair resided in present-day Indiana and Illinois; see Paul Finkelman, "Evading the Ordinance: The Persistence of Bondage of Indiana and Illinois," *JER* 9, no. 1 (Spring 1989): 21–51; Mangin, "Freemen in Theory," 30–35; Edgar F. Love, "Registration of Free Blacks in Ohio: The Slaves of George C. Mendenhall," *JNH* 69, no. 1 (Winter 1984): 38–47, describes a group freed in North Carolina in 1855; Nikki M. Taylor, *Frontiers of Freedom: Cincinnati's Black Community, 1802–1868* (Athens: Ohio University Press, 2005), 82.

8. Repr. in the *CA*, October 31, 1840; on the Woodsons, see Byron W. Woodson, Sr., *A President in the Family: Thomas Jefferson, Sally Hemings, and Thomas Woodson* (Westport, CT: Praeger, 2001)."

9. Middleton, *Black Laws*, 88, notes that Cleveland's black population of 224 in 1850 nearly quadrupled to 800 by 1860, while Columbus had grown from a mere sixty-three in 1820 to approximately 1,300 by 1850, and Cincinnati's had tripled, from 1,090 in 1830 to 3,172 in 1850; Mangin, "Freemen in Theory," 160–61, emphasizes the "uniquely favorable economic conditions" for black development; on Cincinnati, see Taylor, *Frontiers of Freedom*, especially 103, 134–35; on Cleveland, see *North into Freedom: The Autobiography of John Malvin, Free Negro, 1795–1880; Edited and With an Introduction by Allan Peskin* (Cleveland: Press of Western Reserve University, 1966), 11–13, describing how local blacks had "earned the respect of the white community" through the presence of "successful Negro artisans, tradesmen, and small entrepreneurs who gave their colored community a middle-class flavor unmatched anywhere else," quoting the Whiggish *Cleveland Herald* in 1839 describing them as "industrious, peaceable, intelligent and ambitious of improvement"; on Oberlin, see William Cheek and Aimee Lee Cheek, *John Mercer Langston and the Fight for Black Freedom, 1829–1865* (Urbana: University of Illinois, 1989), 285–86; on Ross County, see Mangin, "Freemen in Theory," 133, 143, 160–61, 170–71, 177. In 1849, Martin Delany noted that the state's free people of color "are generally well to do—being industrious; they are mostly property holders, many of whom are farmers and mechanics, and consequently, men and women of means and money" (*NS*, October 5, 1849); Cheek and Cheek, *John Mercer Langston*, 138–43, has tables examining the leadership cohort that included Malvin and Jenkins, including their slave or freeborn status, phenotype, birthplace, profession, and education (half were barbers; see also page 56 for a profile of Cincinnati's elite in the late 1830s, twenty-two men, three-quarters of whom were Virginians, including six barbers, four carpenters, three hucksters, two whitewashers, the rest in the house and building trades); for Malvin's links to eminent whites including a town founder, Leonard Case, and the Democratic politician Samuel L. Starkweather (three times elected mayor), see *North into Freedom*, 50, 56.

10. Wilbur H. Siebert, *The Underground Railroad from Slavery to Freedom* (New York: Macmillan, 1898) based on surveys circulated to hundreds of veterans or their children; he supplemented his account in *The Mysteries of Ohio's Underground Railroads* (Columbus: Long's College Book Company, 1951); E. Delorus Preston, Jr., "The Underground Railroad in Northwest Ohio," *JNH* 17, no. 4 (October 1932): 409–36; Emmett D. Preston, "The Fugitive Slave Acts in Ohio," *JNH* 28, no. 4 (October 1943): 422–77; James Rodabaugh, "The Negro in Ohio," *JNH* 31, no. 1 (January 1946): 9–29; Keith P. Griffler, *Front Line of Freedom: African Americans and the Forging of the Underground Railroad in the Ohio Valley* (Lexington: University Press of Kentucky, 2004); Cheryl Janifer LaRoche, *Free Black Communities and the Underground Railroad: The Geography of Resistance* (Urbana: University of Illinois Press, 2014), in particular chap. 4; R. J. M. Blackett, *The Captive's Quest for Freedom: Fugitive Slaves, the 1850 Fugitive Slave Law, and the Politics of Slavery* (New York: Cambridge University Press, 2018), 224, referring to "Poke Patch, north of Ironton" for the route through Lawrence and Gallia, and the "Gist settlements in Sardinia, north of Ripley."

11. John Mercer Langston, *From the Virginia Plantation to the National Capitol: Or the First and Only Negro Representative in Congress from the Old Dominion* (Hartford, CT: American Publishing Company, 1894), 61, 73, 106–8; Taylor, *Frontiers of Freedom*, 134–35 notes that "single black women were the wealthiest group" of Cincinnati's elite, with four worth more than $10,000. This synopsis of Langston's early life is based on the Cheeks's exemplary biography and his own memoir.

12. Langston, *From the Virginia Plantation*, 142; Cheek and Cheek, *John Mercer Langston*, 179; Nat Brandt, *The Town That Started the Civil War* (Syracuse, NY: Syracuse University Press, 1990), 186–88.

13. Richard C. Wade, "The Negro in Cincinnati, 1800–1830," *JNH* 39, no. 1 (January 1954): 43–57; Griffler, *Front Line of Freedom*, 32.

14. *Polly Gray v. Ohio* in *Cases Decided in the Supreme Court of Ohio: Upon the Circuit at the Special Sessions in Columbus, Volumes 3–4* (Cincinnati: Robert Clarke, 1887), 353–54; although little noticed, the court had already made this ruling ten years earlier; see Middleton, *Black Laws*, 57: "The Ohio Supreme Court evolved a definition of whiteness in law when it reviewed *State v. George* (1821). Elizabeth George, a quadroon, was indicted for murdering her own infant child. The only witness to the crime was Mary Copper, an African-American. The defense objected to her testimony," suggesting George was legally white, and the court agreed, ruling, "A mixed-race individual with more than 50 percent Caucasian blood . . . was white and entitled to the privileges belonging to that race." The later cases are *Williamson v. Directors of School District*, 1834; *Thacker v. Hawk*, 1842; *Jeffries v. Ankeny*, 1842; *Chalmers v. Stewart*, 1842; *Jordan v. Smith*, 1846; *Alfred J. Anderson v. Thomas Milliken et al.*, 1860.

15. See Ariela J. Gross, "Litigating Whiteness: Trials of Racial Determination in the Nineteenth-Century South," *Yale Law Journal* 108, no. 1 (October 1998): 109–88, and Gross, *What Blood Won't Tell: A History of Race on Trial in America* (Cambridge, MA: Harvard University Press, 2008). The folk-logic of Ohio's jurists found echoes elsewhere. In *Gordon v. Farrar* (1844), a Detroit jury ruled a man of color could vote since "Saxon blood in him greatly predominates over the African." This was overturned by Michigan's supreme court in 1847, but they directed local election inspectors to decide on an elector's whiteness, and there is evidence that some adopted the Ohio standard

(Ronald P. Formisano, "The Edge of Caste: Colored Suffrage in Michigan, 1827–1861," *Michigan History* 55, no. 1 [Spring 1972]: 28).

16. *Proceedings of the State Convention of Colored Men of the State of Ohio, Held in the City of Columbus, January 21st, 22d & 23d, 1857*, in Foner and Walker, *Proceedings of the Black State Conventions*, 1:325; Langston, *From the Virginia Plantation*, 125; Cheek and Cheek, *John Mercer Langston*, 234.

17. Winkle, *Politics of Community*, 49, 51, 170, 164. The 1831 election law created a "board of election judges" who "alone accepted or rejected any voter's ballot." Since those judges were "the incumbent executives of the township and therefore the leaders of the local party in power . . . the permission of the party in power" was needed to vote (63–64, 76); *Emancipator*, November 9, 1843, noted several places where men of color had "been permitted to vote the Democratic ticket," although in one instance that individual "was excluded from the polls . . . because he had resolved to support the Liberty ticket."

18. U.S. House of Representatives, 35th Cong., 1st Sess., *Mis. Doc. No. 20, Ohio Contested Election.—Vallandigham vs. Campbell*, 104–6, 125–27. See table A.5 for census evidence on some of those men. Mollyneaux, named a "postmaster" in that year, lived in his mother's house next to one of them, John Robbins or Robins. In 1860, of the five who correspond to Mollyneaux's deposition, three were classed as "mulatto" and two as "black."

19. See C. Peter Ripley, ed., *The Black Abolitionist Papers*, vol. 4, *The United States, 1847–1858* (Chapel Hill: University of North Carolina Press, 1991), 220, for Smith's letter referring to William Howard Day and J. M. Langston as "our yellow friends" who voted in Ohio, and Martin Delany, "Political Destiny of the Colored Race, on the American Continent" in *Proceedings of the National Emigration Convention of Colored People, held at Cleveland, Ohio, August 24, 1854* (Pittsburg, PA: A. A. Anderson, Printer, 1854), 233; *Minutes of the State Convention, of the Colored Citizens of Ohio, Convened at Columbus, Jan. 15th, 16th, 17th and 18th, 1851* in Foner and Walker, *Proceedings of the Black State Conventions*, 1:261, 263; *WAA*, March 10, 1860. For a rare indication of tension, see the editor David Jenkins in his *Palladium of Liberty*, April 3, 1844, on how:

> our people are dissatisfied with almost every progic [*sic*] that has for its object our elevation. One class will raise the war cry against the other, and say it is wrong to let this, that, or the other exist; and will commence disunion; and say all manner of evil about one another. . . . On last Thursday a school commenced under the arrangement of the School Trustees according to the late decision of the Supreme Court this state [*sic*]; according to that decision all children of more white than black blood had a right to participate in the benefit of the common Schools, justly due to all; but because we are too dark and do not come with in the law, must we who are deprived of this blessing create disaffection amongst ourselves? No God forbid. . . . The money is in the treasury for that purpose; and if these children do not get it, the State will use it in some other way. By the report of last winter there was after all the expenses of schooling were paid, a surplus of $53000, left; why not let those that come within this law, come in for their share.

At a state convention that September, Rev. A. M. Sumner of Cincinnati motioned that while "the highest motives have led the Judges of the Supreme Court of Ohio to certain decisions relative to the enfranchisement and school privileges of persons of certain grades of color," nonetheless "the indiscriminate exercise of such privileges on the part of our people [is] dangerous to the peace, harmony, good order and cooperation of society in our respective communities." He accepted an amendment from C. M. Langston "that this Convention recommend the colored people of this State to fully embrace all the privileges not taken from them by the Legislature of the State" (*Palladium of Liberty*, October 2, 1844).

20. Middleton, *Black Laws*, 80; Jonathan Halperin Earle, *Jacksonian Antislavery & the Politics of Free Soil, 1824–1854* (Chapel Hill: University of North Carolina Press, 2004), 37, the best account of Morris's renegade career.

21. Middleton, *Black Laws*, 100–102; Culpepper, "Negro and the Black Laws of Ohio," 55; Winkle, *Politics of Community*, 176; Middleton, *Black Laws*, 122; Corey M. Brooks, *Liberty Power: Antislavery Third Parties and the Transformation of American Politics* (Chicago: University of Chicago Press, 2016), on Ohio abolitionists shifting votes to the Democrats; *CA*, November 10, 1838, reprinting the *Ohio Political Journal and Register*, "an able Whig paper, published at Columbus"; Vernon L. Volpe, "The Ohio Election of 1838: A Study in the Historical Method?," *Ohio History Journal* 95 (Summer–Autumn 1986): 85–100, argues that Whigs fabricated the perception of spoiling to justify their defeat, supported by abolitionists eager to exaggerate their weight, although he acknowledges that "many contemporaries convinced themselves that abolitionism had indeed played a critical role in the Whig defeat and it is in these misperceptions that the real significance of the election lies," driving Whigs to conciliate Reserve abolitionists (99); Vernon L. Volpe, "Benjamin Wade's Strange Defeat," *Ohio History* 97 (Summer–Autumn 1988): 122; *OS*, November 12, 1839; on Black Bill, see Preston, Jr., "Underground Railroad in Northwest Ohio," and James H. Anderson, *Life and Letters of Judge Thomas J. Anderson And Wife: Including a Few Letters From Children and Others: Mostly Written During the Civil War: A History* (n.l.: F. J. Heer, 1904), and Preston, "Fugitive Slave Acts in Ohio," 433, for the judge, a Virginian, describing himself as "Whig by inheritance."

22. John Niven, *Salmon P. Chase: A Biography* (New York: Oxford University Press, 1995), 44, 57–59 on Chase's Whig ties throughout the 1830s, including his seeking a state senate nomination in 1837 and backing Harrison in 1836, and 48–50 passim for his defense of Birney and the Matilda case; James Brewer Stewart, *Joshua R. Giddings and the Tactics of Radical Politics* (Cleveland: Case Western Reserve University Press, 1970), 6, 14–15.

23. Stewart, *Joshua R. Giddings*, 76, although in 1858, Corwin was the lawyer for a white man, William Connelly, accused of harboring fugitives in Cincinnati, winning a dramatic courtroom victory; see Blackett, *Captive's Quest for Freedom*, 253.

24. In Niven, *Salmon P. Chase*, 68; Ratcliffe, *Politics of Long Division*, 325; in 1845, Bartley threatened to send in the militia when Mercer County whites tried to drive out black settlers (Culpepper, "Negro and the Black Laws of Ohio," 21).

25. Culpepper, "Negro and the Black Laws of Ohio," 42; J. Brent Morris, *Oberlin, Hotbed of Abolitionism: College, Community, and the Fight for Freedom and Equality in Antebellum America* (Chapel Hill: University of North Carolina Press, 2014), 29 describes the rise of colonizationism, from the 1827 creation of a legislative committee to deal with the "serious political and moral evil" of free black people through 1834,

when Governor Robert Lucas was elected president of the ACS's Ohio auxiliary; as early as 1827, Lewis Woodson founded the African Education and Benevolent Society, followed by a meeting in Chillicothe which petitioned the legislature for "full privileges of citizenship" (Cheek and Cheek, *John Mercer Langston*, 32–33); *Scioto Gazette* (Chillicothe), September 7, 1837, on the "Convention of colored Delegates . . . in the city of Columbus . . . in pursuance to a call published in the Cleveland Herald, January, 1837," to form "a State School Fund Institution" with a scheme to raise $20,000 from "colored persons who may contribute to it, legacies, benevolent associations, religious institutions, from white persons, and from this State government, if such can be obtained" to shortly "commence building school-houses throughout the State," and *CA*, October 19, 1839, on the "second anniversary of the School Fund Institution of the colored people of Ohio . . . held in Columbus," with twenty delegates from ten counties (its report described several hundred students taught in nine different schools, with fourteen more not yet reporting).

26. The *Proceedings of the Ohio Anti-Slavery Convention, Held at Putnam, on the Twenty-Second, Twenty-Third, and Twenty-Fourth of April, 1835* (n.l.: Beaumont and Wallace, 1835) and *Report of the Third Anniversary of the Ohio Anti-Slavery Society, Held in Granville, Licking County, Ohio, On the 30th of May, 1838* (Cincinnati, OH: Samuel A. Alley, 1838) have no record of black participation as delegates or speakers; Middleton, *Black Laws*, 86.

27. *OS*, July 3, 1840, "Tell the people, Mr. Corwin, about those *negro votes*! That is what they want to hear," and July 24, 1840, "Tom Corwin and Negro Swearing"; August 21, 1840 (Corwin "had much better EXPLAIN his *negro votes*!"; Culpepper, "Negro and the Black Laws of Ohio," 50–51, clarifies that the 1822 proposal would have permitted "Negroes to testify in all cases involving Negroes, and another bill" would have admitted "Negro testimony when two whites attested that the character of the witness was at least as good as that of the average white's"; *OS*, September 16 and August 5, 1840, reprinting a long report from the *Sandusky Democrat* on "THE NEGROES AT FORT MEIGS. A MOST PALPABLE EVIDENCE OF THE COALITION BETWEEN HARRISON WHIGGERY AND ABOLITIONISM," with affidavits that a particular individual saw "SIX NEGROES, who wore on their hats papers, on which were printed in large letters 'LAKE,' and a large number of white persons who wore the same kind of badge, as he supposes, to designate themselves as delegates from Lake county."

28. *Appendix to Senate Journal. No. 1. Report of the Majority of the Standing Committee on Privileges and Elections, in the Matter of the Contested Seat of George W. Holmes, Esq., From the County of Hamilton, Presented by Mr. Taylor. In Senate of Ohio.—March 4, 1841*, 243, "Deposition of John S. Power" in *Journal of the Senate of Ohio, at the First Session of the Thirty-Ninth General Assembly, Held in the City of Columbus, and Commencing Monday, December 7, 1840, and in the Thirty-Ninth Year of Said State* (Columbus, OH: Samuel Medary, Printer to the State, 1840), and 383, "Deposition of James West":

> I am some part black blood. My father is supposed to be one quarter black, and my mother is a white woman. I am acquainted with John Patterson and Abraham Patterson, of Crosby township. They are reputed half blood; one half black, and one half white: they told me that on the 13th ultimo, in said Crosby township, they

voted the Van Buren ticket. . . . On the 13th ultimo, I went to the polls in Whitewater township, in Hamilton County, Ohio, where I reside, to vote. I went in company *with Jacob Malson, William Williams, John Holland, and Joseph Malson.* They are about the same blood as myself. Joseph Malson presented his ticket to vote: the judges refused to take it, saying that if one voted all would vote, and they should not take either. Myself, Jacob Malson, William Williams, and John Holland, wanted to vote the whig ticket, and Joseph Malson wanted to vote the Van Buren ticket. One of the judges, Mr. Glass, knew how we would vote in case we were allowed to vote. He was in favor of taking our votes, but the other two judges refused. At the presidential election, 30th ultimo, in the same township, the same judges took Joseph Malson's, the Van Buren man's vote, but refused me the right to vote, Mr. Glass being willing to let me vote, but the other two judges, Thomas Payne and Ashby Rittenhouse, refused me.

To confuse matters more, whereas depositions were taken from 298 men (listed by name), 266 of whom were entered in the "illegal" column, the report stated "the whole number of illegal votes cast for Holmes, amounts to 42 in number, and for Wright to 67" (12). Amos Hubbard and the Pattersons were listed as illegal voters, Joseph Malson was not listed at all. Another man of color, Elijah James, was listed as "Doubtful."

29. *Ohio Observer* (Hudson), November 23, 1843, reprinting a *Canton Repository* story about "a man named West": "In Columbiana county, a man named West, made application to vote at the polls of Green tp., in 1842 and was refused on the ground that he was a colored man. He sued the Judges of the election. On the trial, he proved that his father was a white man, and his mother a mulatto. The jury decided that there was no cause for action"; *Palladium of Liberty*, May 1, 1844, mocking Whigs who tried to convince black people to vote for Clay ("we acknowledge that we people of color are pretty *dum*, but we say the men who try to make us believe that the God who made of one blood all nations to dwell on the earth, and who is no respector of persons, we say they waste paper when they say God inspires Henry Clay"), and May 22, 1844 ("we have our party with universal Liberty as our motto, and that plain and honest man, JAMES G. BERNEY [*sic*], at our head"), August 28, 1844, reporting on a Liberty convention in the Tenth Congressional District, September 10, 1844 ("Well we think that we will go for Burny [*sic*], as he is the uncompromising candidate, and is opposed to slavery in any shape"), October 9, 1844 (following a Whig "Torch-Light Parade," "We wish the whole humbug was over, as we intend to bring out Birney's name as the next President"), October 16, 1844 (reprinting *Emancipator*'s endorsement of Birney); on McAfee, *Palladium of Liberty*, October 23, 1844 and November 13, 1844 for a subsequent meeting declaring the charge false; *OS*, November 13, 1844, February 14, 1845, November 27, 1844 ("a whig of this city, holding Native American doctrines . . . took such an interest in getting negro votes on the day of our election. The negroes being *natives*—it entitled them to more consideration than whites who happened to be born out of the country, perhaps in Canada"), April 11, 1845 (two Democrats tried for "interfering with and preventing negroes from voting in the north ward of this city," with a Whig city councilman the principal witness), October 20, 1845.

30. *The Address and Reply on the Presentation of a Testimonial to S. P. Chase, By the Colored People Of Cincinnati* (Cincinnati, OH: Henry W. Derby, 1845), 22.

31. Stephen Maizlish, "Ohio and the Rise of Sectional Politics," in *Pursuit of Public Power*, ed. Brown and Cayton, 117; *NS*, January 21, 1848.

32. *NE*, May 3, 1849; Maizlish, "Ohio and the Rise of Sectional Politics," *Pursuit of Public Power*, 131–32.

33. Little noticed, the Whigs had already passed a similar school law in 1848; see Culpepper, "Negro and the Black Laws of Ohio," 15; Niven, *Salmon P. Chase*, 115; Albert G. Riddle, "Recollections of the Forty-Seventh General Assembly of Ohio," *Magazine of Western History* 6 (1887): 350.

34. See Niven, *Salmon P. Chase*, 157–77, on the machinations of 1854–55. Chase's principal task was to pull enough of the Know-Nothings (mainly former Whigs) into the new party, while holding onto the Free Soilers.

35. *Palladium of Liberty*, February 14, 1844, also May 29, 1844 on a "meeting of the Moral and Social Reform Society of the colored citizens of Butler county. . . . W. C. Yancy, President"; *PF*, February 12, 1846, on how "Joseph Mason, a colored man, and said to be the son of Ex-Governor Mason, of Virginia, has been delivering anti-slavery lectures with great effect, at recent Liberty party meetings in Ohio"; for Watson, see *PD*, February 26, 1846, on a "County Convention at the Court House" and the ticket; *OS*, November 30, 1848, quoting the *Geauga Whig*, "Amongst all the advocates of free soil, we have heard none of them raise their voices in favor of freedom and free suffrage in Ohio" versus Reserve Whigs, who supported it, and "the repeal of the black laws *immediately*."

36. Cheek and Cheek, *John Mercer Langston*, 184: in 1852–53, 22 schools with 939 students, out of 6,862 possible attendees; by the next year, 48 schools with 2,439 enrolled of 9,756 possible students; by 1859–60, 159 schools, enrolling half of a possible 14,247; *NS*, March 9, 1849, for "an act to authorize the establishment of separate Schools for the education of colored children" which authorized the "trustees of each incorporated township" to either "admit the colored children resident . . . into the regular common schools" or "create one or more school district or districts" for them; they should then advertise "to the adult male colored tax payers residing in such district, to meet at a time and place specified in the notice, and choose their school directors," with "the powers, rights, and duties of the directors so chosen, and of their successors, shall be the same in respect to the school officers of their several districts" followed by instructions to make lists of the male taxpayers and youths from the ages of four through twenty-one, and deposit said with the county auditor to ensure no taxes paid by those families supported white schools, and vice versa, but specifying that in all other regards the black and white schools would "be governed by and have the benefit of all the provisions of said act of March 7 [1838], and the amendatory acts"; Charles W. Wadelington, "Ohio's Visible Admixture Principle" (master's thesis, Miami University, 1977), 49; Wendell P. Dabney, *Cincinnati's Colored Citizens: Historical, Sociological and Biographical* (New York: Negro Universities Press, 1970, orig. pub. 1926), 6.

37. Cheek and Cheek, *John Mercer Langston*, 180–84; Paul Finkelman, "Prelude to the Fourteenth Amendment: Black Legal Rights in the Antebellum North," *Rutgers Law Journal* 17 (Spring–Summer 1986): 470, noting that Ohio had "more black children attending school . . . than in all fifteen of the slave states combined."

38. *Anti-Slavery Bugle*, January 26, 1849 (One divines a partisan intention in the Whigs' *Ohio State Journal* commending the delegates' "ability, order, and decorum,"

including how Day and John L. Watson's speeches in the State House "exhibited much thought and patriotic devotion to their country and race, and were listened to with perfect attention," followed by an optimistic assertion that "the attention of the audience, and their perfect good behaviour, show a most cheering state of progress in the public mind," repr. in the *NE*, February 8, 1849); *Minutes of the State Convention, of the Colored Citizens of Ohio, Convened at Columbus, January 9th, 10th, 11th, and 12th, 1850*, in Foner and Walker, *Proceedings of the Black State Conventions*, 1:246, 252.

39. Preston, "Fugitive Slave Acts in Ohio," 458 (quoting Giddings on June 23, 1852), 463 (for his paper, the *Ashtabula Sentinel*, October 6, 1850, urging fugitives to either "flee to British soil" or "arm themselves at once. If the slave catcher comes, receive him with powder and ball, or dirk or bowie knife or whatever weapon may be most convenient. Do not hesitate. Slay the miscreant") and 468 (the *Ohio Republican*, November 8, 1850, on a meeting in Toledo, with Senator Benjamin Wade present, that passed a resolution "that come life or imprisonment, come fine or come death—we will neither aid nor assist in the return of any fugitive slave, but, on the contrary we will *harbor and secrete* and by all just means protect and defend him, and thus give him a practical godspeed to liberty"); *Anti-Slavery Bugle*, February 22, 1851, repr. from the *True Democrat* (Wood wavered, saying "his mind was not fully made up"); Cheek and Cheek, *John Mercer Langston*, 176; *Proceedings of the Convention, of the Colored Freemen of Ohio, Held in Cincinnati, January 14, 15, 16, 17 and 19, 1852*, in Foner and Walker, *Proceedings of the Black State Conventions*, 1:291, plus 297 for Langston's 1854 memorial. Blackett's *Captive's Quest for Freedom*, 255–65, records numerous instances where white elected officials actively resisted the Fugitive Slave Act, including the Addison White case in Champaign County in 1857, a Greene County sheriff leading a posse of hundreds to attack a deputy marshal backed by a Cincinnati judge (which brought in the Buchanan administration), and the Sara Bagby case in Cleveland in early 1861: she worked for congressman-elect A. G. Riddle and was defended unsuccessfully by leading Republicans.

40. Quillin, *Color Line in Ohio*, 81, 86; Cheek and Cheek, *John Mercer Langston*, 114, 170.

41. Cheek and Cheek, *John Mercer Langston*, 208 (other black Ohioans were also active; for instance, a young O. S. B. Wall was an elected delegate to its 1853 convention from Harveysburg; see Cheek and Cheek, *John Mercer Langston*, 252); *FDP*, October 15, 1852, reprinted Day's letter "To the Democracy of Ohio" in the Whigs' *Cleveland Herald*; also the Whiggish *Sandusky Register*, September 27, 1852, "Who are the True Friends of the Colored Man?," waxing sarcastic on how Free Democrats "forget, in the heighth of their zeal, that they have a duty to perform towards the colored man in their own State. At the recent Free Soil Convention, held in this place, the following resolution was placed in the hands of the business committee, by an intelligent, worthy man, who is so unfortunate as to be tinged with African blood. . . . He repeatedly called for it, and was from time to time reassured that it should come up, yet the Convention was closed, and the resolution smothered: 'by the organic law of Ohio, color is made a bar to exercising the election franchise. . . . Certain persons are prohibited the privilege of setting in the jury box, and that many worthy, poor, and unfortunate, are, on account of color, deprived of the benefits of the poor house, and the State Asylum, while at the same, colored people are taxed for their support. Resolved, that it is the duty of

the Free Democracy, to use all proper means, so as to change the existing law in these respects, as to give equal privileges to all'"; Cheek and Cheek, *John Mercer Langston*, 230–35; Langston, *From the Virginia Plantation*, 136; Langston in *FDP* quoted in Cheek and Cheek, *John Mercer Langston*, 259.

42. Blackett, *Captive's Quest for Freedom*, 265.

43. *PD*, August 28, 1855; *OS*, September 28, 1855. For that matter, early in 1855, not long after Cincinnati's black men formed their first militia company, the Attucks Blues, they were "congratulated personally" by Chase, a gesture worthy of Sumner, but risky for someone seeking the governorship within sight of Kentucky (Cheek and Cheek, *John Mercer Langston*, 194).

44. Cited in Maizlish, "Ohio and the Rise of Sectional Politics," 165; *PD*, December 28, 1855.

45. *PD*, March 17, 1856. In April 1857, the Republican legislature made it illegal to use any state or local prison to hold persons charged as fugitive slaves, with thirty to ninety days in jail and a $500 fine for "any violation of this Act by an officer of the State," and the next day passed an Anti-Kidnapping Act, with three to seven years in the penitentiary for anyone removing a person "without authority" (Preston, "Fugitive Slave Acts in Ohio," 472–73).

46. *OS*, July 27, 1856; Vernon L. Volpe, "Ohio of Republican Dominance: John C. Frémont's 1856 Victory in Ohio," in Brown and Cayton, *Pursuit of Public Power*, 165; *Newark Advocate*, August 15 and 20, 1856, quoted in Morris, *Oberlin*, 182; *OS*, October 7, 1856. On September 27, the *Statesman* claimed "Great Trouble in the 'Colored' Republican Ranks!" because Republican city authorities promised a black man a "Meat Stall in the Market House" but the white butchers objected, so the city made him leave. Supposedly, "the colored people" also demanded that "they be permitted to bury their dead in the GREEN LAWN CEMETERY." They had been duped into thinking "the Frémont party was a negro party," but now "very naturally thought it was time to *test* what *reality* there was in the movement, and hence these demands for *equality* now, and not trust them till after election."

47. *PD*, October 21, 1856; *Huntington Globe*, October 29, 1856, reprinting stories from various other papers; *OS*, October 25, 1856. At this point, however, Medary swerved off course, justifying some black voting with an exegesis of the Ohio's court's decisions, insisting that none "goes farther than that a quadroon is a white person" and "none but persons three-fourths white should claim the benefits of those decisions."

48. *PD*, November 5, 1856; *OS*, November 7 and 11, 1856.

49. Cheek and Cheek, *John Mercer Langston*, 323–24 *PD*, September 18, 1857; *OS*, August 30, 1857. For later uses of this peculiar trope, see *OS*, June 30 and July 24, 1858.

50. *PD*, March 30, October 12, and October 14, 1857.

51. *PD*, October 19, 1857; Harrisburg *Weekly Patriot*, quoting *Cincinnati Enquirer*, October 29, 1857; *Pittsfield Sun*, October 29, 1857; *OS*, November 10, 1857; *PD*, November 11, 1857. The actual evidence for a black balance of power was entirely anecdotal, however; as the *Ohio State Journal* pointed out, the *Statesman* offered merely a single conversation with the "leading locofoco of Athens county," who insisted "that in that county, upward of one hundred and fifty illegal votes were cast for Governor Chase by negroes," with the local Republicans countering that "the census tables of 1850 show

that there were only 106 colored persons in the whole county of all ages, sexes and conditions" (*OSJ*, November 18, 1857).

52. *PD*, February 9, 1859; *OS*, April 8 and 22, 1859; *PD*, April 8, 1859, reprinting the *Cincinnati Enquirer*; *OS*, May 4, 1859, "in the leading State and headquarters of the Republicans [Massachusetts], that party will be voting with their allies the Negroes to make white adopted citizens of these United States wait two years after naturalization before they vote" and May 11, 1859, on how "the Massachusetts Amendment" shows the "illiberal, proscriptive and persecuting" spirit of this party "which hates the foreign born citizen and has a corresponding love for the negro," since "white citizens of the United States are denied the exercise of the elective franchise by the fundamental law, while the negro is placed among the superior and law making caste."

53. *OS*, March 31, 1859.

54. *PD*, May 19, September 12, October 1, 1859.

55. These quotations from many sources, quite likely corrupted, were lined up in the *PD* of September 27, 1859; also *PD*, October 10, 1859.

56. *Erie Observer*, November 5, 1859; *OS*, March 21 and 22, 1860; *PD*, April 4, 1860; the *OS*, April 5, 1860, had its usual comments about black voting, for example, "37 negro votes in Xenia."

57. *PD*, October 1, 1860; *OS*, September 28, October 4 and 5, 1860.

58. *OS*, October 7 and 14, 1860; *Patriot and Union* (Harrisburg, PA), October 22, 1860, reprinting the *PD*; *Republican Compiler* (Gettysburg), October 29, 1860; Cheek and Cheek, *John Mercer Langston*, 365. On black voting far from the Reserve, see *PD*, October 22, 1860, quoting the Brown County *Georgetown Argus* on a black man, "fearing that public sentiment would not allow him to vote at the polls there, started off for Ripley on the morning of the election, where he knew his Abolition friends would allow him to vote, and he returned in the evening, boasting that he had voted, together with twenty-one other mulattoes!" For another use of Ohio as a negative example, see the Brooklyn *City News* asking its mainly immigrant electorate, "Do you want niggers to rule New York, as they do in Ohio?" quoted in Roff, "Brooklyn's Reaction to Black Suffrage," 33.

59. *OS*, October 19, 1860. Eric Foner, *Free Soil, Free Labor, Free Men: The Ideology of the Republican Party before the Civil War* (New York: Oxford University Press, 1995), 290–91 describes "the mainstream of Republican opinion" as "asserting that free Negroes were human beings and citizens of the United States, entitled to the natural rights of humanity and to such civil rights as would protect the natural rights of life, liberty, and property. . . . But most differentiated among natural rights, to which all men were entitled, civil rights—legal enactments which protected natural rights—and political rights, which could be regulated at the discretion of the majority."

60. *PD*, November 6, 1860; *Patriot and Union* (Harrisburg, PA), November 7, 1860.

61. For early versions, see the *OSJ*, October 10, 1855 ("Political Reminiscences—*Negro Testifying—Negro Voting—Negro Schools, Amalgamation, etc.* LOOK AT THE RECORD!," on how in 1849 Democrats voted "EITHER TO ADMIT THE BLACK AND MULATTO CHILDREN INTO THE REGULAR SCHOOLS, OR PROVIDE SEPARATE SCHOOLS FOR THEM! . . . They have led the way themselves, and the work so thoroughly, that little remains for anybody else to do") and *OS*, October 8, 1856, quoting the *OSJ*, that

"Republicans seek no man's vote who is not legally entitled to vote. . . . In the strong Democratic county of Hamilton mulattoes, or persons having a preponderance of white blood in their veins, do vote for we have seen them vote. The Supreme Court . . . has decided that such persons as we have named are legal voters under the Constitution. The Court which made that decision was a Democratic Court."

62. *Sandusky Register,* October 5, 1859; *Cleveland Leader,* October 17, 1859.

63. *Sandusky Register,* October 17, 1860; *Cleveland Leader,* September 12, 1859. For more examples of this strategy, see *Highland Weekly News* (Hillsboro), June 28, 1860, asserting the Democrats were "responsible for allowing people of color to testify in the courts, and to exercise the right of suffrage in cases where there is a preponderance of white blood," and *Sandusky Register* again on August 27, 1860, insisting, "We are in favor of 'white' men voting according to the Constitution and the laws of Ohio. There is no movement any where to enlarge the vote of the State by extending the right of suffrage to negroes. The Republican party has no where, in any State or National organization, taken position in favor of thus extending the right of suffrage," finally the *OSJ,* September 25, 1860, defending Judge Brinkerhoff for following precedents set by "Democratic Judges of the Supreme Court of Ohio."

64. *Wooster Republican,* April 14, 1859, reprinting the *Stark County Republican* that "the bill is exceedingly barbarous in its details, and its passage indicates the intense negro-plantation feeling that pervades the prostituted Democracy of Ohio," adding that were "this modern Stamp Act executed in some of our States, hosts of Democratic voters would be turned from the polls, and more than one Democratic statesman would be excluded from the United States Congress. It is a public fact, that the white population of our slave States are being corrupted with Africanism. The dark, sallow complexion we see in many Southerners, some of them men of distinction, is not all owing to the effects of climate"; *Wooster Republican,* March 22, 1860; *Cleveland Leader,* March 31, 1859, suggesting "no citizen of Ohio need longer marvel at the unjust and inhumane black laws of Slave States, even to the selling of free colored persons into life bondage. The same spirit exists in the Democratic leaders here. . . . The Constitution and the Supreme Court will prove the shield of the voters Democratic fanaticism would so heartlessly disfranchise and cruelly imprison."

65. *PD,* September 27, 1859.

66. David M. Fahey, "'Slavery is a Sin Against God and a Crime Against Man': Alfred J. Anderson and Oxford's Black Convention of January 7, 1853," *Old Northwest* 5 (Spring-Summer 1990): 3–17.

67. The main account is Robert J. Zalimas, Jr., "'Contest MY seat sir!': Lewis D. Campbell, Clement L. Vallandigham, and the Election of 1856," *Ohio History* 106 (Winter–Spring 1997): 5–30. Vallandigham alleged nineteen different instances of "electors" who should not have voted on the basis of age, nonresidency, not being naturalized, or "idiot and insane," and more, including "16. That Alfred J. Anderson, John M. Mitchell, James Robins, Reuben Redman, Thomas Tester, John D. Robbins, Alexander Proctor, Cyrus H. Cowan, Robert Goings, W. Griffith, and twenty-two others, mulattos and persons of color, not qualified electors under the constitution and laws of Ohio, were permitted to vote." In reply, Campbell made twenty-three countercharges, including "7. That persons half negro, or more, voted for you. 8. That persons not half white, and part negro, voted for you. 9. That persons half white and more,

entitled under the laws and decisions of the courts of Ohio to the right of suffrage, who would have voted for me, were refused the exercise of that right by the judges of the elections"; see U.S. House of Representatives, 35th Cong., 1st Sess., *Mis. Doc. No. 20, Ohio Contested Election.—Vallandigham vs. Campbell*, 2–3 and 6–8. The resulting depositions of dozens of men focused largely on charges of illegal voting on some basis other than race.

68. *Western Reserve Chronicle*, December 4, 1850, quoted in Preston, "Fugitive Slave Acts in Ohio," 465; see also *Proceedings of the Convention, of the Colored Freemen of Ohio, Held in Cincinnati, January 14, 15, 16, 17 and 19, 1852*, in Foner and Walker, *Proceedings of the Black State Conventions*, 1:276, with letters from "distinguished citizens" including Cassius Clay, Horace Mann, Charles Durkee, Benjamin Wade, Townshend, and the Hon. L. D. Campbell; Zalimas, "'Contest MY seat sir!,'" 11, 18; *Star* (Gettysburg, PA), December 12, 1856; *Cleveland Leader*, December 15, 1856.

69. *Congressional Globe*, May 22, 1858, 2320–21, 2327; Frank L. Klement, *The Limits of Dissent: Clement L. Vallandigham & the Civil War* (New York: Fordham University Press, 1998), 16, cites southerners who were "close personal friends of Campbell," such as John Gilmer of North Carolina.

70. *Congressional Globe*, May 22, 1858, 2323–24.

71. *Liberator*, February 22, 1860.

72. *AEJ*, June 26, 1858, reprinting the *Cincinnati Gazette*; *OS*, October 8, 1859.

73. *Anti-Slavery Bugle*, April 23, 1859, in C. Peter Ripley, ed., *The Black Abolitionist Papers*, vol. 5, *The United States, 1859–1865* (Chapel Hill: University of North Carolina Press, 1992), 15–17; *Agitator* (Wellsboro, PA), September 1, 1859, reprinting the *Cleveland Herald*; *Cleveland Leader*, October 17, 1859, reprinting the *Toledo Blade*. Robinson claimed damages of $1,000, with the article noting, "Another suit has been commenced in the same court, by a colored citizen of Norwalk . . . for the same cause. $500."

74. *PD*, October 12, 1859; *Sandusky Register*, October 22, 1860, quoting the *OS*; *New York Herald*, November 3, 1860.

75. See Cheek and Cheek, *John Mercer Langston*, 270, citing *FDP*, June 20, 1855 and the *Cincinnati Gazette*, August 2, 1855; even before that, Douglass's Queen City correspondent reported, "At the last election, many colored men voted. Our Constitution only forbids *blacks and mulattoes*, and we have many shades between these colors, and their votes cannot be legally refused"; *FDP*, August 3, 1855.

76. This paragraph relies on Cheek and Cheek, *John Mercer Langston*, 321–28; *Proceedings of the State Convention of Colored Men, Held in the City of Columbus, Ohio, Jan. 16th, 17th, & 18th, 1856*, in Foner and Walker, *Proceedings of the Black State Conventions*, 1:308, 311; *OS*, August 23, 1856: "We learn that Jenkins and Langston, (two colored individuals of this city,) are stumping the State for Frémont. Whether, upon their return home, they will be met at the depot by an escort, we refer to other sources for an answer"; *Proceedings of a Convention of the Colored Men of Ohio. Held in the City of Cincinnati, on the 23d, 24th and 26th Days of November 1858*, in Foner and Walker, *Proceedings of the Black State Conventions*, 1:308, 318, 332–34, 327, and 367–68 noting that the OSASS's first annual meeting in January 1860 appointed "134 men and women to lead auxiliaries in 31 counties," with many women present as delegates and on committees; *Anti-Slavery Bugle*, October 29, 1859.

77. Cheek and Cheek, *John Mercer Langston*, 296, 52 (as clerk he had overall financial responsibility for the township, including roads and poor taxes, as well as serving on the town council, and on April 20, 1857, he was made acting manager of the school system, serving in that and similar roles for another fourteen years). The following account draws upon Cheek and Cheek and Brandt, *Town That Started the Civil War*.

78. Quoted in Brandt, *Town That Started the Civil War*, 204; the Republican gubernatorial candidate, William Dennison, won with 52 percent in the first two-man race in the state since 1848.

79. *New York Herald*, November 1, 1860.

Coda

1. Edgar A. Toppin, "Humbly They Served: The Black Brigade in the Defense of Cincinnati," *JNH* 48, no. 2 (April 1963): 77.

2. Emmett D. Preston, "The Fugitive Slave Acts in Ohio," *JNH* 28, no. 4 (October 1943): 476. Ashley had no monopoly on demonstrations of radicalism. In March 1860, another Ohio Republican, Harrison Blake, had submitted legislation instructing the Judiciary Committee "to inquire into the expediency of reporting a bill giving freedom to every human being and interdicting slavery wherever Congress has the constitutional power to legislate on the subject," which fifty-nine of the seventy-three Republicans present supported; see Richard H. Sewell, *Ballots for Freedom: Antislavery Politics in the United States, 1837–1860* (New York: W. W. Norton, 1976), 358–59.

3. Charles Thomas Hickok, *The Negro in Ohio, 1802–1870* (New York: AMS, 1975, repr. of 1896 ed.), 70; Christopher Phillips, *The Rivers Ran Backward: The Civil War and the Remaking of the American Middle Border* (New York: Oxford University Press, 2016), 110.

Appendix

1. For Portland and New Bedford, the 1850 federal census was used; for Providence, I had to rely on the 1860 census, because the marshals chose not to record black people's wealth in 1850.

Index

Page numbers appearing in italics refer to figures. Page numbers followed by "m" refer to maps. Page numbers followed by "t" refer to tables.

African identity, 46, 76

African Independence celebrations, 199

African Methodist Episcopal (AME)
Church, 38, 72–73, 74, 509, 575n34,
600n65

African Society for Mutual Relief, 347,
656n69

Africanus, 40, 174

"African Washington Benevolent
Society," 107–8, 110

Afro-Indian communities of New
England, 168

Afro-New England diaspora, 168, 611n17

agency, black political, 9, 49, 567n26

Age of Jackson, 13, 20–21, 41

Age of Jackson, The (Schlesinger), 10

Albany Argus, 347, 360, 391, 408, 489

Albany County, New York, 324, 376

Albany Evening Journal: birthright and,
43; constitutional convention and, 422,
424, 428–29, 431; Douglass and, 471,
689n59; Dred Scott case and, 469, 470,
689n61; Duer amendment and, 407;
election of 1860 and, 482; on Myers,
489–90; Smith Lands project and,
442; suffrage and, 377, 393, 470, 485;
temperance and, 413; Underground
Railroad and, 466; on Ward, 440; on
Whigs, 212, 453–54

Albany polity, 345–46, 655n63

Aldridge, Ira, 387

Alexander, Leslie M., 569n2, 589n53,
677n3

Algiers, American slaves in, 65, 648n15

Allen, Anson, 599n57

Allen, Betsey, 124–25, 599n57

Allen, James, 79

Allen, Macon B., 213

Allen, Paddy, 125

Allen, Richard: about, 38, 62, 148; AME
church and, 72; Bethel church and,
64–65, 72–74; colonization and, 75;
Colored Methodist Society and,
600n65; conventions and, 86, 87, 502;
deference politics and, 70, 71;
expatriation to Haiti and, 82–83;

factionalism and, 86; kidnapping and,
586n40; schools and, 67

Allen, Sylvanus, 633n29

Allen, William, 597nn44

Allen family, 124–25, 599n57

"Amendment to the Act for the Rendition of Fugitives from Service or
Labor" in Ohio, 541

American and Foreign Anti-Slavery
Society, 119, 232

American Anti-Slavery Society (AASS):
Chapman and, 227; colonization and,
41; Fessenden and, 626n11; Garnet and,
400, 568–69n1; immigrant citizenship
and, 45–46; New Bedford and, 232;
Ohio and, 506; racial exclusion of,
117, 597n44; Smith and, 401; Stevens
and, 116

"American Attitudes towards the Negro,
1550–1812" (Jordan), 50

American Citizen, 328–29

American Colonization Society (ACS):
AASS and, 117; Abdulrahman and, 201;
about, 37–38, 40, 73, 572n17; black
conventions and, 88; Federalist Party
and, 96; Haiti emigration and, 83,
588n51; Hunt and, 456, 684n33; Noah
and, 361; in Ohio, 700n25; in Philadelphia, 74–76, 77, 79

American Convention for Promoting the
Abolition of Slavery and Improving the
Condition of the African Race, 69,
582n16

American Convention of Abolition
Societies, 77

Americanism of blacks, 44–45, 46–47,
48, 574–75n35, 576n38

American Moral Reform Society
(AMRS), 87, 91–93, 590n56. *See also*
National Moral Reform Society

American Party: Kansas-Nebraska Act
and, 244; in New England, 283; in New
York, 422, 436, 460, 469, 474, 477;
Republican Party and, 22. *See also*
Know-Nothing Party

American Republicans, 277, 288, 425

Cornish, Samuel E.: about, 87, 386–87, 537, 664n16; AMRS and, 92; black churches and, 86, 575n34; on Clay, 377; *Colored American* and, 27, 389, 390–91; *Freedom's Journal* and, 85, 386, 388–89; *Rights for All* and, 389; shadow politics and, 85, 86; Smith and, 396; suffrage campaign and, 395–99; on voting, 102; Whigs and, 394, 396–97

Corwin, Thomas: abolitionism and, 508, 699n23; about, 537; "complexion" and, 54, 578n51; constitutional amendment of, 541–42; suffrage and, 510

Costin, William, 156

Cottrol, Robert, 5, 188, 251, 272, 643n61

Council of Appointment of New York, 319, 327, 330, 358–59

Council of Revision of New York, 315, 319–21, 338–39, 358, 648n13

Courier and Enquirer, 411, 422, 428, 675n92

Coventry, William, 344, 654n59

Cozzens, Charles, 272

Craft, Ellen, 241

Cramer, John, 412–13

Crapo, Henry A., 230–31, 232, 632n26, 636n52

Crawford, George William, 19

Creole, 508

Crittenden Compromise, 289

Croger, Peter, 411

Cross, Martin, 671n65, 671n69

Cross, Whitney, 381

Crummell, Alexander, 385, 387, 404–5

Cuffe, Jonathan, 168

Cuffe, Paul: about, 160–61, 168, 223–24, 630–31n10; colonization and, 38, 63, 75–76

Cuffee, George, 114–15

Culver, Erastus D., 408

Cummings, Zachariah, 130

Cummins, John, 136

Cushing, William, 174, 613n27

Custom House employment, Portland, 209, 216, 217, 628n23

Cutler, William P., 536

Cuyler, Samuel, 466–67, 469–70, 478, 687–88n55

Dagget, David, 619n55

Daily Picayune, 391

Dallas, George Mifflin, 53–54, 256, 473

Dalton, Thomas, 198, 623n76

Daniels, Henry, 216

Darlington, William, 592n13

Davis, David Brion, 566n12, 567n21, 659n103

Davis, Garret, 542

Davis, Thomas, 270

Davis, Woodbury, 216

Day, William Howard, 496, 514, 516, 517–18, 644n7, 698n19, 703n38

Dayton, Anson, 538

Dayton, Isaac, 345

Dayton, William, 462

deference politics: about, 58, 61–62, 69–72, 583n20; black conventions and, 90; defiance of, 72–79, 223–24; *Freedom Journal* and, 83–85; kidnapping and, 81, 586n40; moral reform and, 90–93

De Grasse, Isaiah, 387

Delany, Martin R.: about, 145, 603n5; black vote and, 505; emigration and, 146, 517, 565n10; Free Soil party and, 449, 450–51; on Ohio, 696n9; on Ward, 678n6; women's rights and, 49

Dellet, James, 157

"democracy," views on, 4, 10–11, 44

Democratic Press, 107–8, 109–10, 594n26

Democratic Watchman, 2

Democrats: abolitionism and, 166; background and overview of, 11, 17, 18, 22; in Maine and, 208, 211, 626n6; Missouri Compromise and, 7; naturalization and, 269; in New Bedford, 225, 230–31, 232–34, 236, 245, 636n52; in New York 1837 to 1839, 311, 330, 392; in New York 1859 to 1860, 480–81, 691n81; New York constitutional convention and, 422, 425–26, 427–28, 430; New York gubernatorial

Eli, John, 198

emancipation: Civil War and, 548; in Massachusetts, 169–70, 612n19; in New York, 315, 316, 319–20, 321–24, 325, 364, 649n16; in Ohio, 541–42, 708n2; in Pennsylvania, 51, 57, 62, 65–67, 580n3, 581n11; in Vermont, 182; West Indian, 143, 246, 247. *See also specific organizations of emancipation*

Emancipation Act of 1780 of Pennsylvania, 51, 57

emancipation bill of 1800 in Pennsylvania, 66–67, 581n11

Emancipation Proclamation, 547

Emancipator, The: on Cornish, 391; on Harrison, 153; New Bedford politics and, 229, 232, 233, 632–33n28, 633n30, 633n33; Portland polity and, 210–11; suffrage campaign and, 398, 420

Emerson, John F., 223, 227, 228, 229

emigration, 565n10; AMMI and, 92; to Canada, 87, 88–89; to Haiti, 82–83. *See also* colonization of free blacks; immigration

Emigration Convention in Pittsburgh, 146

Emott, James, 349, 657n73

employment loss due to elections, 233, 633n29

England. *See* Britain

Episcopal church: African Methodist Episcopal (AME) Church, 38, 72–73, 74, 509, 575n34, 600n65; in Philadelphia, 64; seminary admission and, 385

Erie Canal, 14, 311, 317, 381

ethnoreligious communities of New York, 316, 646n2

Eustis, William, 195, 621n64

evangelicalism, 31, 154, 570n4

Everett, Edward, 226, 442, 631n16

Evertson, Jacob, 360, 376, 655n63

executions of blacks in New York, 318

Exeter, New Hampshire, 180–81, 616n39

expatriating free blacks, 37–38, 82–83

fagot voting, 175, 253, 339, 340–41

Fairchild, Charles, 518

Fairfield, John, 210–11

Farmer, Prince, 178, 179, 615n36

farmers, 25–26, 567–68n27

FAS (Free African Society), 64, 86

Federalists: background and overview of, 3, 17, 18, 19; Catholics as, 651n36; citizenship and, 37, 39; in Connecticut, 186–87; Haynes and, 183–84; in Hudson, New York, 342–45, 654n57; in Maine, 206; in Massachusetts, 172–78, 614n30; in New England, 150–51, 163; New York black electoral emergence and, 324–25, 326–29; New York certificate wars and, 331–35, 339–40, 349–52, 651n39; New York demise of, 358; New York disfranchisement and, 336, 337, 346–47, 348–49, 352–56, 652nn46–47; New York emancipation and, 312, 322–23; in Pennsylvania, 71–72, 96, 98, 100, 106–9, 583n21; in Rhode Island, 188

Fehrenbacher, Don E., 10–11, 565n8, 566n12, 571n13

Fenner, James, 188, 272

Ferdon, James, 467

Fessenden, Charles B., 636n52

Fessenden, Samuel, 205, 208, 209–12, 213, 215, 625n3, 626n9, 627n13

Fessenden, William Pitt, 206, 207, 210, 215, 626n9

Field, Ben, 464

Field, Peter S., 617n46

Field, Phyllis. *See Politics of Race in New York, The* (Field)

Fields, Jacob, 684n38

Fifteenth Amendment, 206, 252, 461, 487

Fifth Annual Convention for the Improvement of the Free People of Colour, 200

Fifty-Fourth Massachusetts, 290, 488

Fillmore, Millard: about, 22; colonization and, 684n33; Fugitive Slave Act and, 271–72; Ohio and, 521; patronage and, 441, 442, 678n11; as president, 241, 436;

as presidential candidate, 469, 521, 636n52; voter qualification and, 426–27

Findlay, William, 81, 99, 111–14, 595n32, 596n38

Findlay family, 112, 595n34

Finley, Robert, 77

fire-eaters, 18

firemen, black: in New Bedford, 249, 637n59; in Philadelphia, 77–79, 585–86n31; in Rhode Island, 264

First African Presbyterian Church, 86

First Colored Presbyterian Church, 387

First of August celebrations, 246–47, 249, 468, 627n13, 645n11

First Party System, 17

Fish, Hamilton, 442, 677n1, 678n11, 684n33

Flagg, Azariah, 483–84, 689n62

Florence Farming Association, 442, 443, 464

Floyd, John, 204

Fogg, William, 124–26, 599–600n57

Foner, Eric, 7, 567n27, 681n23, 685n39, 691n1, 694n5, 705n59, 707n76

Foote, John, 480

Foote, Thelma Wills, 316, 646n2

Foraker, Joseph, 542

Forbes, Robert Pierce, 11, 618n50, 621n61

foreigners: citizenship and, 33, 34, 41–46, 574n28; Dutch, 315, 316, 317, 318, 647n7; Native Americans and, 168; suffrage and, 135–36, 172, 175, 269; Washington Benevolent Society and, 107. *See also* Germans; Irish

Formisano, Ronald, 17

Forten, James: about, 38, 63, 148, 160; AFA and, 79; AMRS and, 91; citizenship and, 66; colonization and, 75–76; *Colored American* and, 389; death of, 142; deference politics and, 70–71, 72–73, 77, 585n29; engagement with whites of, 80, 586n38; expatriation to Haiti and, 82–83; as a Federalist, 106–7; Garrison and, 117; *Letters From a Man of Colour*, 61, 68, 105; nationalism

and, 77; Pittsburgh convention and, 145

Forten, James, Jr., 91–92, 119, 139, 143, 602–3n91

Forten, Robert B., 597n44

Fort Pillow massacre, 547

Fortune, Isaac, 650n24

Fortune, James, 602–3n91

Fort Wagner, battle at, 547

Forward, Walter, 139, 145, 441

Foster, Henry, 637n53

Foster, Stephen, 262, 514

Fox, Dixon Ryan, 172, 311–13, 646n4, 646n6, 652n43

Fox, John, 126, 127, 128–29, 131–33, 138–39, 600n61

Foy, William E., 213

Francis, Abner, 404, 452

Francis, Caesar, 649n24

Francis, Cuffee, 649n24

Francis, John Brown, 265

Frank Leslie's Weekly, 539

Franklin County, Pennsylvania, 111–14, 595n32

Franklin Gazette, 77, 114, 596n38

Frederick Douglass' Paper: bigotry and, 45; Douglass and, 437; Downing and, 276; gubernatorial race of 1858 and, 690n71; Irish and, 382; Langston and, 518; Legal Rights Association and, 461; presidential election of 1852 and, 459; Smith and, 401; suffrage resolution debacle and, 471–72, 689n64

Free African Society (FAS), 64, 86

Free Democratic Party: in New York, 435, 436, 437, 458, 462; in Ohio, 514, 517–18, 703–4n41

Freedom, John, 247, 286

Freedom's Journal, 83–85, 86, 200, 386, 388–89

freedom suits, 169

freeholder requirements: in New York (*See* freeholder requirements in New York); in Rhode Island, 251–53, 254, 258, 263, 266; taxpaying requirement replacement of, 565n11 freeholder requirements in New York: in 1850s, 446–47, 463, 467, 469–70; background and overview of, 15, 29, 309, 313, 315, 324; Clinton constitutional amendment and, 392; constitutional conventions and, 319, 360, 364, 370–71, 376, 425, 432, 674n87; Negro Bill and, 340, 343; petition on, 393; Smith land donation and, 380, 433; suffrage campaign and, 392, 393

Freeman, Amos N., 211–12

Free Soil Party: about, 7, 14, 21, 448–49; Douglas-Ward Dispute and, 438–40; in Maine, 207, 213–15, 627n13, 628n21; in New Bedford, 219, 220, 239–43, 245–48, 635–36nn46–47, 636n52; in New England, 150, 155, 157, 158, 282; in New York, 436–37, 438–40, 448–51, 453–54, 683n27, 689n67; in Ohio, 493, 513–14, 515, 516–17, 702nn34–35, 703n41; in Rhode Island, 270–71, 274

free versus slave political framing, 13

Frémont, John C., 22; New Bedford and, 245, 248; New York and, 462, 467, 468, 688n58; Ohio and, 520, 521–22; Portland and, 216

French, Rodney, 250, 308; in 1830s to 1844 politics, 228, 229, 230, 231, 233, 633n30; in 1847 to 1854 politics, 220, 240–42, 244, 245, 247, 635n46

Fretz, Abraham, 129, 133

Friend, The, 104

Frymer, Paul, 629n3

Fugitive Slave Act: about, 21, 22; Campbell and, 532; Massachusetts and, 284, 285–86; New Bedford and, 241–42, 635n46; New England and, 157, 215, 284–85–286; New York and, 411, 436, 455–56, 490, 677n3; Ohio and, 492, 516–17, 538, 540, 703n39; Pennsylvania and, 81–82, 146–47, 586n40; Rhode Island and, 272; Ward and, 55

Fugitive Slave Law Convention of 1850, 301

fugitive slaves: interstate battles on, 39, 81–82, 573n22; in New Bedford, 241–42, 248, 635n48; in New York, 383, 411, 465–66, 687n54; in Ohio, 525–26, 538–39, 541; in Pennsylvania, 62, 72, 81–82, 118, 121, 128, 144, 146–47. *See also* Fugitive Slave Act; Underground Railroad

Fuller, Thomas J., 201

"gag" on antislavery petitions, 5, 21, 40, 155, 210, 506

Gaines, John Isom, 515

Gallatin, Albert, 102, 161, 165, 592n13

Gardner, Charles, 593n21

Gardner, Henry, 246

Garnet, Henry Highland: about, *298,* 387, 400–403, 664n16, 665n19, 668n43, 669n45; "Address to the Slaves of the United States of America," 401, 417, 419–20, 516, 672n76; African Civilization Society and, 286; Americanism of blacks and, 46–47; ascendancy of, 416–18, 672n71; birthright and, 29–30, 568–69n1; Douglass and, 438, 565n10, 677n5; Frémont support of, 468; gubernatorial race of 1858 and, 474–75; Irish and, 382, 691n83; Liberty Party and, 155, 411, 419–20, 606n7; Myers and, 671n68; New Bedford and, 246; New York black conventions and, 404, 405, 427; New York electorate and, 445; Radical Abolition Party and, 468; suffrage campaign and, 403, 407, 420–21; Whigs and, 454

Garrison, Richard, 650n24, 650n27, 656n69

Garrison, William Lloyd: abolitionism and, 117; about, 152–53, 396; ACS and, 75; Americanism of blacks and, 44, 71; birthright and, 40, 573n23; conventions and, 90, 288; Fessenden and, 626n11; Henry Johnson and, 237–38; Whigs and, 225

Garrisonianism: about, 40, 152–53, 154; in Maine, 207, 211; in New Bedford, 219, 222, 230, 231, 235, 236, 237, 633n33; in New England, 285; in New York,

Howland, George, Jr., 222, 229, 239, 240, 636n51
Howland, Thomas, 277, 642n53
Hubbard, Amos, 510, 701n28
Hudson, New York, polity, 333, 341–45, 446, 554–56, 556t
Hudson, Nicholas, 578n45
Hughes, John, 42, 487
Humphrey, Friend, 403
Hunkers, 240, 311, 422, 425–26, 436, 451, 673n81, 682n27
Hunt, Alvah, 683n27
Hunt, Washington, 437, 455–57, 458, 677n1, 683n27, 684n33, 685n40
Hutchinson, Thomas, 169

identity of blacks from "African" to "American," 46, 76
immediatist abolitionism, 89, 149, 207, 506
immigrants and citizenship, 41–46, 574n28
immigration: to Canada, 383–84, 502, 664n15; to Massachusetts, 195–96, 222; to New York, 381–83; to Ohio, 498, 499, 501; to Philadelphia, 57, 67–68, 105, 119–20
Impartial Citizen, The, 1, 441, 451, 669n44
Independent, The, 43
Inquiry Into the Character and Tendency of the American Colonization and American Anti-Slavery Societies (Jay), 35, 41, 52
integration of New York public transportation, 460–61, 686n43
intermarriage, 168–69, 481, 541, 691n83
Irish: in Massachusetts, 283–84; in New England, 157, 607n12; in New York (*See* Irish in New York); in Ohio, 518, 520; in Pennsylvania, 98, 135–36, 591n4, 602n82; in Rhode Island, 252, 268, 640–41n34
Irish Friends of the South in Northern Cities, 382
Irish in New York: blacks as foe to, 382; as Clintonians, 358; Democrat Party and, 481, 691n81; draft riots and, 487; famine driven immigration of, 381–82, 663n10; Federalists and, 353; intermarriage and, 481, 691–92n83; naturalization and, 331–32, 334–35; Republicans and, 353, 357; suffrage and, 327–28; Tammany Hall and, 371, 378
Iroquois Confederation, 309, 316, 317, 647n3
"Irrepressible Conflict" speech (Seward), 474, 477
Irvin, Nathaniel, 130
Irving, Washington, 329
Irvins, William, 631n12
Iverson, G. F., 464
Ives, Robert H., 275–76
Ivins, Aaron, 94, 128

Jackson, Andrew, 4, 14, 20–21, 48
Jackson, Charles, 268
Jackson, Peter, 130, 131
Jacksonian Democrats: about, 10, 11–12, 18, 21, 50; birthright and, 35; in Maine, 206–8; in New York, 311, 421, 672–73n80; in Pennsylvania, 96, 121, 134, 147, 600–601n65; political slang and, 2; in Rhode Island, 252, 253
James, Elijah, 701n28
Jay, John: Catholics and, 651n36; citizenship and, 35, 37; disfranchisement and, 319; emancipation and, 312, 321–22, 648nn15–16; treaty with Britain and, 19
Jay, John, II, 385, 465
Jay, Peter Augustus: constitutional convention and, 363, 367–68, 369–71, 372, 375; nativism and, 39; Negro Bill and, 355; suffrage and, 321
Jay, William, 35, 39, 41, 51–52, 385, 578n46
Jay Treaty, 322
Jefferson, James, 288, 644n10
Jefferson, Thomas: Democracy party and, 4; New England and, 164; *Notes on the State of Virginia*, 51; as president, 337; presidential candidacy of, 3, 336; rumors about, 131; on Sidney, 333

Paine, Rufus K., 535

Palladium of Liberty, 509, 511, 698–99n19, 701n29, 702n35

Paris, Daniel, 653n50

Parker, Amasa, 477

Parker, Kunal M., 622n72

Parker, Ransom, 554

parodies: of abolitionism, *295*; of blacks, 197, 622–23n75; of Irish, 44–45, 574n33

Parrish, Joseph, 141

Parrott, Russell, 68–69, 77, 79

parties and party systems: background and overview of, 17–23; racial influences on, 3–4, 6–7. *See also specific parties and party systems*

Pasley, Jeffrey, 26

PAS (Pennsylvania Abolition Society). *See* Pennsylvania Abolition Society (PAS)

PASS (Pennsylvania Anti-Slavery Society), 117–19, 597–98nn44–46

patriarchalism: of Puritans, 167–68, 611n16; of Quakers, 70, 73, 77, 584n22; slavery and, 565n11, 665n18

patronage: deference politics and, 69; Haynes and, 183–84; in Maine, 216, 217; in New Bedford, 219, 224–25, 233–34, 242; in New England, 149, 157–58, 196–97; in New York, 319, 440–44, 488, 678nn10–11; in Ohio, 527; in Pennsylvania, 70, 112, 119–20; in Rhode Island, 275

Paul, Benjamin, 403, 405

Paul, Caesar, 181

Paul, Thomas, 181, 584n23, 622n75

pauper voting, 172, 196, 344–45, 622n72

Payne, Thomas, 525, 529–30, 701n28

Pearce, D. J., 262

Pearce, Stewart, 600n58

Pendleton, N. G., 510–11

Peneton, Solomon, 247

Pennington, James W. C., 42, 88, 420, 460–61, 588n51

Pennsylvania Abolition Society (PAS): about, 62; apathy of, 66–67, 581n11; compared to NYMS, 323–24;

deference politics and, 69–72, 81–82, 582n15, 583n21; Garrisonianism and, 117; tax paying requirement to vote and, 104

Pennsylvania Anti-Slavery Society (PASS), 117–19, 597–98nn44–46

Pennsylvania Colonization Society, 140

Pennsylvania Hall, 140

Pennsylvania polity: abolitionism antipolitics and, 117–19, 597nn44–46; background and overview of, 14–15, 57–59, 94–96, 95m, 98, 590n1; black voter disfranchisement in (*See* disfranchisement in Pennsylvania); Bucks County black voting and, 126–33, 600n61, 600nn68–70; Columbia race riots and, 119–24, 599n49, 599n54; conclusions on, 142–48; counties of, 95m; election law application in, 99–100, 109–11, 115; explication of, 96–101; Federalism and, 106–9; Fogg case and, 124–26; Franklin County gubernatorial elections and, 111–15, 596n32, 596nn37–39; free black community in, 62–65; Morgan and, 109–11, 594n27; Pittsburgh and, 94, 98, 110, 144–47, 604n10; power confrontations and, 115–17; restrictions on blacks in, 82, 83; social mobility in, 64; suffrage clause in, 102, 127–28, 133–34. *See also* Philadelphia polity

Pennsylvania Telegraph, 137

People's Convention and Constitution, 256–57, 259, 260, 261, 263, 267

People's Press, 414, 415, 671n68

periods of early republic, 18–23; 1790 to 1815, 19; 1816 to 1828, 19–20; 1829 to 1847, 20–21; 1848 to 1860, 21–23

Perkins, Sampson, 234, 634n38

Perry, Bela C., 249

personal liberty laws, 8, 157, 284, 289

Peters, John T., 186–87

Peterson, Daniel, 679n13

petitioning: of 1797 and 1800, 65–67; "gag" on antislavery, 5, 21, 40, 155, 210,

sectional nationalism, 44, 150, 164, 191, 204

segregation: in church, 64; railroad, 53, 230–31, 460–61, 632nn25–26, 686n43; of schools, 224, 493, 509, 513, 631n11, 694n3; on streetcars, 460–61, 486n43

Seilhamer, G. O., 595n34

self-emancipation, 546

self-purchase of slaves, 62, 499

separatist nationalism, 77

Sergeant, John, 107, 192, 594n23

service and black politics, 546–47

settlers in Ohio, black, 498–502, 696n9, 697n11

Sewall, Samuel, 50, 577n41, 634n34

Seward, Fanny, 669n45

Seward, William Henry: about, 5, 304, 309, 378–80, 412, 662nn4–5; Adams and, 162; ascendance of, 435–36; Clay and, 400, 668n42; "complexion" and, 54; constitutional convention and, 422–23, 673n81; Douglass and, 459–60, 685n39; Harpers Ferry and, 478; on Helderberg War, 402; "Irrepressible Conflict," 474, 477; Myers and, 488; patronage and, 444, 678n10; as a senator, 462; slavery and, 685n39; suffrage and, 7, 397, 409, 426, 668n35; Underground Railroad and, 465; Virginia controversy and, 410, 411; on Ward, 438; Whigs and, 155–56, 392, 403, 451

Sewardite Republicans, 16, 422, 436

Sewell, Richard H., 564n6, 673n84, 682–83n27

Seymour, Horatio, 442, 460, 487, 673n81, 674n87, 677n1, 685n40

Shadd, Abraham, 146, 597n44

shadow politics of Ohio, 515

shadow politics of Philadelphia: background and overview of, 61–64, 579–80n1; black apathy and, 67–69; black elite engagement with whites and, 79–81; black factionalism and, 85–86; black self-organization and, 64–65; conventioning and, 86–91; deference politics and (*See* deference

politics); defiance of, 72–77; petitioning, 65–67

Shannon, James, 532–33

Shannon, Wilson, 508

Shaw, Lemuel, 242

Shepard, Charles O., 393, 677n1

Shulze, Andrew, 115

Sickles, Daniel, 453, 467

Sidney, Joseph, 333–34, 348, 355, 356, 358, 649n24, 651–52nn40–41

Sidney, Robert Y., 652n44, 656n69

Sidney, Thomas, 387, 395–96, 667n32

Siebert, Wilbur, 500, 697n10

"Signs of the Times" (Cornish), 398

Silliman, Benjamin, 395

Silver Gray Whigs, 438, 677n4

Sipkins, Thomas, 649–50n24

Sketches of the Higher Classes of Colored Society in Philadelphia, 144

Skillings, Titus, 209, 626n7

Skinner, Richard, 183

Slater, Samuel, 253

Slaveholding Republic, The (Fehren-bacher), 10–11, 566n12

slavery: impact of 1860 Republican rule on, 543–44; in New England, 167–68, 611n16; in New York, 315, 317–18, 321–23, 382–83, 393, 647–48nn7–8; in Ohio, 495; party system and, 21; race relations and, 17; spread of, 19

slave trade, 67, 181, 227, 543, 582n15

Slocum, Freelove, 25

Slocum, Kofi, 168

Slocum, William T., 350, 352–53, 657n74, 657n78

Smith, Albert C., 210–11, 626n9

Smith, Barbara Clark, 24, 567n26

Smith, D. L., 147

Smith, Elizabeth J., 280

Smith, Gerrit: about, 27, 301, 380, 663n7; constitutional convention fusion plan and, 422, 423, 427, 428–30, 431, 675–76nn94–95; Free Soil party and, 450, 682n25; Fugitive Slave Act and, 457; as governor candidate, 472–77, 689–90n67, 690n70; land distribution

Smith (cont.)
 of (*See* Smith Lands project); Liberty
   Party and, 16; patronage and, 441;
   Radical Abolitionist Party and, 445;
   suffrage campaign and, 396, 397, 398,
   668n35
Smith, James, 122
Smith, J. B., 289
Smith, James McCune: about, *300*, 387,
   400, 401, 402, 403, 662n5, 669n44;
   Assembly speech of, 424–25; on black
   rights, 204; constitutional convention
   fusion plan and, 420–21, 427; on
   Douglass, 549; freehold qualification
   and, 446–47; gubernatorial race and,
   690; Legal Rights Association and,
   461; Liberty Party and, 418; New York
   and, 318, 381, 445, 663n8; *Northern
   Star* and, 416; presidential election of
   1860 and, 482, 692n85; Radical
   Abolition Party and, 467–68; Smith
   Lands project and, 442–44, 447,
   678n11, 679n13; suffrage and, 403, 486
Smith, John Jay, 101
Smith, John N., 642n59
Smith, Matthew J., 638n3
Smith, Peter, 380
Smith, Rogers M., 12
Smith, Stephen, 119, 120–21, 122–23, 146,
   389, 598n48
Smith, Sylvanus, 411, 482, 670n62, 685n38
Smith, Tower, 653n55
Smith, Truman, 265
Smith, William Loughton, 3, 192, 478
Smith Lands project: about, 433–34,
   676–77nn100–101; census of 1855 and,
   447, 681n10, 681n21; gubernatorial race
   of 1858 and, 476–77; patronage and,
   442–44, 678–79nn11–13
Snyder, Simon, 109
Society for the Colonization of Free
   People of Color of America. *See*
   American Colonization Society (ACS)
Soderlund, Jean R., 580n3, 581n11
soldiers, black, 47–49, 185, 546–48.
   See also veteran blacks

Solomon, Ben Job, 624n81
Somewhat More Independent (White),
   325–26, 648n8, 649n24
Sons of Liberty, 539
Sons of the African Society, 614n31
Souls of Black Folk, The, 385
sources for this study, 26–28
South-Street, Robin, 342, 343–44
Spaulding, Reverend, 177
Spencer, Ambrose, 345
Spencer, John C., 392, 443, 667n35, 678n11
spoiling strategy: in New Bedford,
   230–36, 239; in New York, 397, 398, 400,
   438, 477, 683n27; in Ohio, 506, 699n21
St. Clair, Arthur, 696n7
St. George's Methodist Church, 64
St. Philip's Church, 385, 573n23, 664n17
St. Thomas's Episcopal church, 64, 86,
   143, 593n18, 603n4
"Stand Up Law," 186
Stanton, Benjamin, 534
Stanton, Henry B., 672n71
State Central Committee of New York's
   black convention, 403, 405, 415, 428
State Convention of the Colored
   Freeman of Pennsylvania, 145–456
State Conventions of the Colored Men,
   Ohio, 503, 514–16, 517, 537, 702–2n38
*State ex. Rel. Directors of the Easter and
   Western School Districts*, 515
States' rights, 13, 191, 194
State v. George, 697n13
Stephens, Alexander, 36, 571–72n15
Stevens, Thaddeus, 5, 35, 103, 116, 135,
   136, 597n42, 602n81
Steward, Austin: about, 389, 568n1;
   manumission of, 383; New York black
   convention and, 404; patronage and,
   441; suffrage and, 666n26
Stewart, Alvan, 399
Stewart, James Brewer, 12, 46,
   589–90n55
Stewart, John A., 387
Stewart, John G., 413, 415
Still, William, 144, 146, 687n54
Stone, William L. 660n115

510–12, 530–34, 697nn14–15, 698–99nn17–19, 700–701nn28–29; power of, 9

Whitmarsh, Seth, 227, 229, 632n22

Whittlesey, Elisha, 507

Wide Awake march, 216

Wilbour, Isaac, 188

Wilder, Craig Steven, 318, 325, 647n7, 691n81

Wilentz, Sean, 10, 565n11, 591n11, 618n52, 620–21n61

Williams, Deacon G., 271

Williams, Domingo, 197, 198, 202, 623n76

Williams, E. J., 119

Williams, Elisha, 341, 342, 350, 356, 653n56

Williams, James, 635n46

Williams, Peter, 573n23, 597nn44, 602n87, 649n24, 664n17

Williams, Peter, Sr., 326

Williams, Robert F., 649n24, 650n24, 656n69

Williams, Samuel, 597n44

Williams, William, 701n28

Williamsburg, New York, 459, 684–85n38

Willing, Thomas, 63, 106, 107

Willis, Edmund P., 653n51

Willis, George, 271, 274, 389

Willis, George, Jr., 272

Wilmot Proviso, 13, 238, 436

Wilson, Henry, 5, 7, 239, 244, 248–49, 282, 283, 634n45

Wilson, William J., 382, 411

Winch, Julie, 585n29, 587n42, 592n16, 603n1

Winkle, Kenneth, 504, 698n17

Winslow, Charles, 536

Wirt, William, 628n24

Wise, Henry A., 478, 508, 665n18

Wolbert, Fredrick, 583n20

Wolcott, Christopher, 492, 527

Wolcott, Oliver, Jr., 175, 613n28

Wolcott, Samuel, 278–80, 281, 642n59

Wolf, Eric, 9

women, black: dressing as men to vote, 177, 614–15n32; labor and, 24–26; OSASS and, 538, 707n76; political exclusion of, 23, 567n25; roles of, 49–50, 576n40; women's rights and, 49

women's rights, 23, 49, 567n25

Wood, Fernando, 461, 688–89n59

Wood, Gordon, 10, 11, 565–66n11

Wood, Nicholas, 134

Wood, Reuben, 503, 514, 516, 529, 703n39

Woods, William Henry, 243, 245, 246

Woodson, Lewis, 93, 145, 499, 700n25

Woodson, Thomas, 499

Woodward, George, 102, 104, 136

Worthington, Thomas, 499

Wortman, Samuel, 331

Wright, H. B., 126

Wright, John C., 510

Wright, John L., 122, 123

Wright, Richard P. G., 387, 389, 404

Wright, Silas, 424, 426, 432

Wright, Theodore Sedgwick, 387, 389, 404, 421, 664n17, 672n71

Wright family, 119–20, 122, 123–24, 598n47

Yancy, Walter Claiborne, 509, 514, 702n35

Yankee republicanism, 170, 185–86, 205, 206, 217

Yates, William, 35

yellow fever epidemics, 47, 64–65

Young, John, 424, 432, 674n87

Young, Samuel, 363, 364, 368–69, 375, 659n104, 660n106

Young Men's Anti-Slavery Society, 228

Young Men's Union Funds Society, 272, 276

Zuille, John J., 387, 453–54, 672n71